CRIME IN THE UNITED STATES

CRIME IN THE UNITED STATES

2021

FIFTEENTH EDITION

EDITED BY SHANA HERTZ HATTIS

Lanham • Boulder • New York • London

Published by Bernan Press

An imprint of The Rowman & Littlefield Publishing Group, Inc.

4501 Forbes Boulevard, Suite 200, Lanham, Maryland 20706

www.rowman.com

800-462-6420

6 Tinworth Street, London SE11 5AL, United Kingdom

ISBN: 978-1-64143-487-4

E-ISBN: 978-1-64143-488-1

CONTENTS

LIST OF FIGURES

SECTION I

SUMMARY OF THE UNIFORM CRIME REPORTING (UCR) PROGRAM

SUMMARY OF THE UNIFORM CRIME REPORTING (UCR) PROGRAM

Bernan Press is proud to present its 15th edition of *Crime in the United States*. This title was formerly published by the Federal Bureau of Investigation (FBI), but is no longer available in printed form from the government. This edition contains final data from 2019, the most current year for which data is available.

This section describes the history of the UCR program, which collects the data used in *Crime in the United States* It also examines the best way to use the data in this publication.

Currently, the UCR program includes four data collections:

- National Incident-Based Reporting System (NIBRS) — Provides detailed incident information on 52 offenses including the victims, offenders, and property stolen, recovered, or damaged. In addition, NIBRS collects arrest data for those offenses plus 10 others. In 2018, approximately 44 percent of the law enforcement agencies that participated in the UCR Program submitted their data via NIBRS. The populations of these agencies represented approximately 37 percent of the population covered by agencies that submitted data to the UCR Program. Of the 38 states that the FBI has certified to report via NIBRS, 17 states submitted 100 percent of their data via NIBRS; the other NIBRS-certified states submitted data through both NIBRS and the Summary Reporting System. Among states still working toward NIBRS-certification, a few agencies submitted NIBRS data through direct contributions to the FBI.

- Summary Reporting System (SRS) — Furnishes aggregate offense counts for 10 Part I offenses and arrest data for an additional 20 offenses. The historic data collection will give way to make UCR a NIBRS-only data collection by January 1, 2021.

- Law Enforcement Officers Killed and Assaulted (LEOKA) Program — Offers information about officers who were killed or assaulted while performing their duties. The information is published and used to help agencies develop polices to improve officer safety. More information about LEOKA and the accompanying data is available in Bernan Press's *Justice Statistics: An Extended Look at Crime in the United States*.

- Hate Crime Statistics Program — Provides information on crimes motivated by offenders' bias against race, gender, gender identity, religion, disability, sexual orientation, and ethnicity. These data are also collected via NIBRS.

About the UCR Program

The UCR program's primary objective is to generate reliable information for use in law enforcement administration, operation, and management; however, over the course of the program, its data has stood out as one of the country's leading social indicators.

The UCR program is a nationwide, cooperative statistical effort of more than 18,000 city, university and college, county, state, tribal, and federal law enforcement agencies voluntarily reporting data on crimes brought to their attention. Since 1930, the FBI has administered the UCR program and continued to assess and monitor the nature and type of crime in the nation. Criminologists, sociologists, legislators, municipal planners, the media, and other students of criminal justice use the data for varied research and planning purposes.

Note for Users

It is important for UCR data users to remember that the FBI's primary objective is to generate a reliable set of crime statistics for use in law enforcement administration, operation, and management. The FBI does not provide a ranking of agencies; instead, it provides alphabetical tabulations of states, metropolitan statistical areas, cities with over 10,000 inhabitants, suburban and rural counties, and selected colleges and universities. Law enforcement officials use these data for their designed purposes. Additionally, the public relies on these data for information about the fluctuations in levels of crime from year to year, while criminologists, sociologists, legislators, city planners, media outlets, and other students of criminal justice use them for a variety of research and planning purposes. Since crime is a sociological phenomenon influenced by a variety of factors, the FBI discourages data users from ranking agencies and using the data as a measurement of the effectiveness of law enforcement.

To ensure that data are uniformly reported, the FBI provides contributing law enforcement agencies with a handbook that explains how to classify and score offenses and provides uniform crime offense definitions. Acknowledging that offense definitions may vary from state to state, the FBI cautions agencies to report offenses according to the guidelines provided in the handbook, rather than by local or state statutes. Most agencies make a good faith effort to comply with established guidelines.

The UCR program publishes the statistics most commonly requested by data users. More information regarding the availability of UCR program data is available by telephone at (304) 625-4830, or by e-mail at ucr@fbi.gov.

Data requests via e-mail cannot be processed without the requester's full name, mailing address, and contact telephone number.

Variables Affecting Crime: Caution Against Ranking

Until data users examine all the variables that affect crime in a town, city, county, state, region, or college or university, they can make no meaningful comparisons. In each edition of *Crime in the United States*, many entities—including news media, tourism agencies, and other organizations with an interest in crime in the nation—use reported figures to compile rankings of cities and counties. However, these rankings are merely a quick choice made by that data user; they provide no insight into the many variables that mold the crime in a particular town, city, county, state, or region. Consequently, these rankings may lead to simplistic and/or incomplete analyses, which can create misleading perceptions and thus adversely affect cities, counties, and their residents.

Considering Other Characteristics of a Jurisdiction

To assess criminality and law enforcement's response from jurisdiction to jurisdiction, data users must consider many variables, some of which (despite having significant impact on crime) are not readily measurable or applicable among all locales. Geographic and demographic factors specific to each jurisdiction must be considered and applied in order to make an accurate and complete assessment of crime in that jurisdiction. Several sources of information are available to help the researcher explore the variables that affect crime in a particular locale. The U.S. Census Bureau data, for example, can help the user better understand the makeup of a locale's population. The transience of the population, its racial and ethnic makeup, and its composition by age and gender, educational levels, and prevalent family structures are all key factors in assessing and understanding crime.

Local chambers of commerce, planning offices, and similar entities provide information regarding the economic and cultural makeup of cities and counties. Understanding a jurisdiction's industrial/economic base, its dependence upon neighboring jurisdictions, its transportation system, its economic dependence on nonresidents (such as tourists and convention attendees), and its proximity to military installations, correctional institutions, and other types of facilities all contribute to accurately gauging and interpreting the crime known to and reported by law enforcement.

The strength (including personnel and other resources) and aggressiveness of a jurisdiction's law enforcement agency are also key factors in understanding the nature and extent of crime occurring in that area. Although information pertaining to the number of sworn and civilian employees can be found in this publication, it cannot be used alone as an assessment of the emphasis that a community places on enforcing the law. For example, one city may report more crime than another comparable city because its law enforcement agency identifies more offenses. Attitudes of citizens toward crime and their crime reporting practices—especially for minor offenses—also have an impact on the volume of crimes known to police.

Making Valid Crime Assessments

It is essential for all data users to become as well educated as possible about understanding and quantifying the nature and extent of crime in the United States and in the jurisdictions represented by law enforcement contributors to the UCR program. Valid assessments are possible only with careful study and analysis of the various unique conditions that affect each local law enforcement jurisdiction.

Some factors that are known to affect the volume and type of crime occurring from place to place are:

- Population density and degree of urbanization

- Variations in composition of population, particularly in the concentration of youth

- Stability of the population with respect to residents' mobility, commuting patterns, and transient factors

- Modes of transportation and highway systems

- Economic conditions, including median income, poverty level, and job availability

- Cultural factors and educational, recreational, and religious characteristics

- Family conditions, with respect to divorce and family cohesiveness

- Climate

- Effective strength of law enforcement agencies

- Administrative and investigative emphases of law enforcement

- Policies of other components of the criminal justice system (that is, prosecutorial, judicial, correctional, and probational policies)

- Residents' attitudes toward crime

- Crime reporting practices of residents

Although many of the listed factors equally affect the crime of a particular area, the UCR program makes no attempt to relate them to the data presented. **The data user is therefore cautioned against comparing statistical data of individual reporting units from cities, counties, metropolitan areas, states, or colleges or universities solely on the basis on their population coverage or student enrollment.** Until data users examine all the variables that affect crime in a town, city, county, state, region, or college or university, they can make no meaningful comparisons.

Historical Background

Since 1930, the FBI has administered the UCR program; the agency continues to assess and monitor the nature and type of crime in the nation. Data users look to the UCR program for various research and planning purposes.

Recognizing a need for national crime statistics, the International Association of Chiefs of Police (IACP) formed the Committee on Uniform Crime Records in the 1920s to develop a system of uniform crime statistics. After studying state criminal codes and making an evaluation of the recordkeeping practices in use, the committee completed a plan for crime reporting that became the foundation of the UCR program in 1929. The plan included standardized offense definitions for seven main offense classifications known as Part I crimes to gauge fluctuations in the overall volume and rate of crime. Developers also instituted the Hierarchy Rule as the main reporting procedure for what is now known as the Summary Reporting System of the UCR program.

Seven main offense classifications, known as Part I crimes, were chosen to gauge the state of crime in the nation. These seven offense classifications included the violent crimes of murder and nonnegligent manslaughter, rape, robbery, and aggravated assault; also included were the property crimes of burglary, larceny-theft, and motor vehicle theft. By congressional mandate, arson was added as the eighth Part I offense category. Data collection for arson began in 1979.

During the early planning of the program, it was recognized that the differences among criminal codes precluded a mere aggregation of state statistics to arrive at a national total. Also, because of the variances in punishment for the same offenses in different states, no distinction between felony and misdemeanor crimes was possible. To avoid these problems and provide nationwide uniformity in crime reporting, standardized offense definitions were developed. Law enforcement agencies use these to submit data without regard for local statutes. UCR program offense definitions can be found in Appendix I.

In January 1930, 400 cities (representing 20 million inhabitants in 43 states) began participating in the UCR program. Congress enacted Title 28, Section 534, of the *United States Code* that same year, which authorized the attorney general to gather crime information. The attorney general, in turn, designated the FBI to serve as the national clearinghouse for the collected crime data. Since then, data based on uniform classifications and procedures for reporting have been obtained annually from the nation's law enforcement agencies.

Advisory Groups

Providing vital links between local law enforcement and the FBI for the UCR program are the Criminal Justice Information Systems Committees of the IACP and the National Sheriffs' Association (NSA). The IACP represents the thousands of police departments nationwide, as it has since the program began. The NSA encourages sheriffs throughout the country to participate fully in the program. Both committees serve the program in advisory capacities.

In 1988, a Data Providers' Advisory Policy Board was established. This board operated until 1993, when it combined with the National Crime Information Center Advisory Policy Board to form a single Advisory Policy Board (APB) to address all FBI criminal justice information services. The current APB works to ensure continuing emphasis on UCR-related issues. The Association of State Uniform Crime Reporting Programs (ASUCRP) focuses on UCR issues within individual state law enforcement associations and also promotes interest in the UCR program. These organizations foster widespread and responsible use of uniform crime statistics and lend assistance to data contributors.

Redesign of UCR

Although UCR data collection was originally conceived as a tool for law enforcement administration, the data were widely used by other entities involved in various forms of social planning by the 1980s. Recognizing the need for more detailed crime statistics, law enforcement called for a thorough evaluative study to modernize the UCR program. The FBI formulated a comprehensive three-phase redesign effort. The Bureau of Justice Statistics (BJS) agency in the Department of Justice responsible for funding criminal justice information projects, agreed to underwrite the first two phases. These phases were conducted by an independent contractor and structured to determine what, if any, changes should be made to the current program. The third phase would involve implementation of the changes identified.

The final report, the *Blueprint for the Future of the Uniform Crime Reporting Program,* was released in the summer of 1985. It specifically outlined recommendations for an expanded, improved UCR program to meet future informational needs. There were three recommended areas of enhancement to the UCR program:

- Offenses and arrests would be reported using an incident-based system

- Data would be collected on two levels. Agencies in level one would report important details about those offenses comprising the Part I crimes, their victims, and arrestees. Level two would consist of law enforcement agencies covering populations of more than 100,000 and a sampling of smaller agencies that would collect expanded detail on all significant offenses

- A quality assurance program would be introduced

In January 1986, Phase III of the redesign effort began, guided by the general recommendations set forth in the *Blueprint*. The FBI selected an experimental site to implement the redesigned program, while contractors developed new data guidelines and system specifications. Upon selecting the South Carolina Law Enforcement Division (SLED), which enlisted the cooperation of nine local law enforcement agencies, the FBI developed automated data capture specifications to adapt the SLED's state system to the national UCR program's standards, and the BJS funded the revisions. The pilot demonstration ran from March 1 through September 30, 1987, and resulted in further refinement of the guidelines and specifications.

From March 1 through March 3, 1988, the FBI held a national UCR conference to present the new system to law enforcement and to obtain feedback on its acceptability. Attendees of the conference passed three overall recommendations without dissent: first, that there be established a new, incident-based national crime reporting system; second, that the FBI manage this program, and third, that an Advisory Policy Board composed of law enforcement executives be formed to assist in directing and implementing the new program. Furthermore, attendees recommended that the implementation of national incident-based reporting proceed at a pace commensurate with the resources and limitations of contributing law enforcement agencies.

Establishing the NIBRS

From March 1988 through January 1989, the FBI developed and assumed management of the UCR program's National Incident-Based Reporting System (NIBRS), and by April 1989, the first test of NIBRS data was submitted to the national UCR program. Over the next few years, the national IUCR program published information about the redesigned program in five documents:

- *Uniform Crime Reporting Handbook*, NIBRS Edition (1992) provides a nontechnical program overview focusing on definitions, policies, and procedures of the IBRS

- *Data Submission Specifications* (May 1992) is used by local and state systems personnel, who are responsible for preparing magnetic media for submission to the FBI

- *Approaches to Implementing an Incident-Based System* (July 1992) is a guide for system designers

- *Error Message Manual* (revised December 1999) contains designations of mandatory and optional data elements, data element edits, and error messages

- *Data Collection Guidelines* (revised August 2000) contains a system overview and descriptions of the offense codes, reports, data elements, and data values used in the system

As more agencies inquired about the NIBRS, the FBI, in May 2002, made the *Handbook for Acquiring a Records Management System (RMS) That Is Compatible with the NIBRS* available to agencies considering or developing automated incident-based records management systems. The *Handbook*, developed under the sponsorship of the FBI and the BJS, provides instructions for planning and conducting a system acquisition and offers guidelines on preparing an agency for conversion to the new system and to the NIBRS.

Originally designed with 52 data elements, the redesigned NIBRS captures up to 57 data elements via 6 types of data segments: administrative, offense, victim property, offender, and arrestee. Although, in the late 1980s, the FBI committed to hold all changes to the NIBRS in abeyance until a substantial amount of contributors implemented the system, modifications have been necessary. The system's flexibility has allowed the collection of four additional pieces of information to be captured within an incident: bias-motivated offenses (1990), the presence of gang activity (1997), data for law enforcement officers killed and assaulted (2003), and data on cargo theft (2005). The system has also allowed the addition of new codes to further specify location types and property types (2010).

The FBI began accepting NIBRS data from a handful of agencies in January 1989. As more contributing law enforcement agencies become educated about the rich data available through incident-based reporting and as resources permit, more agencies are implementing the NIBRS. Based on the 2012 data submissions, 15 states submit all their data via the NIBRS and 32 state UCR Programs are certified for NIBRS participation.

Suspension of the *Crime Index* and the *Modified Crime Index*

In June 2004, the CJIS APB approved discontinuing the use of the *Crime Index* in the UCR program and its publications and directed the FBI to publish a violent crime total and a property crime total. The *Crime Index*, first published in *Crime in the United States* in 1960, was the title used for a simple aggregation of the seven main offense classifications (Part I offenses) in the Summary Reporting System. The Modified Crime Index was the number of Crime Index offenses plus arson.

For several years, the CJIS Division studied the appropriateness and usefulness of these indices and brought the matter before many advisory groups including the UCR Subcommittee of the CJIS APB, the ASUCRP, and a meeting of leading criminologists and sociologists hosted by the BJS. In short, the *Crime Index* and the *Modified Crime Index* were not true indicators of the degrees of criminality because they were always driven upward by the offense with the highest number, typically larceny-theft. The sheer volume of those offenses overshadowed more serious but less frequently committed offenses, creating a bias against a jurisdiction with a high number of larceny-thefts but a low number of other serious crimes such as murder and rape.

Recent Developments in UCR Program

In the fall of 2011, the APB recommended, and FBI Director Robert Mueller III approved, changing the definition of rape. Since 1929, in the SRS, rape had been defined as "the carnal knowledge of a female forcibly and against her will," (*UCR Handbook*, 2004, p.19). Beginning with the 2013 data collection, the SRS definition for the violent crime of rape will be: "Penetration, no matter how slight, of the vagina or anus with any body part or object, or oral penetration by a sex organ of another person, without the consent of the victim." This definition can be found in the *Summary Reporting System [SRS] User Manual*, Version 1.0, dated June 20, 2013. The FBI is developing reporting options for law enforcement agencies to meet this requirement, which will be built into the redeveloped data collection system.

In addition to approving the new definition of rape for the SRS, the APB and Director Mueller approved removing the word "forcible" from the name of the offense and also replacing the phrase "against the person's will" with "without the consent of the victim" in other sex-related offenses in the SRS, the NIBRS, the Hate Crime Statistics Program, and Cargo Theft.

In response to a directive by the U.S. Government's Office of Management and Budget, the national UCR Program has expanded its data collection categories for race from four (White, Black, American Indian or Alaska Native, and Asian or Other Pacific Islander) to five (White, Black or African American, American Indian or Alaska Native, Asian, and Native Hawaiian or Other Pacific Islander). Also, the ethnicity categories have changed from "Hispanic" to "Hispanic or Latino" and from "Non-Hispanic" to "Not Hispanic or Latino." These changes are reflected in data presented from 2012.

The national UCR Program staff continues to develop data collection methods to comply with both the William Wilberforce Trafficking Victims Protection Reauthorization Act of 2008 and the Matthew Shepard and James Byrd, Jr. Hate Crime Prevention Act of 2009. As a result, the FBI began accepting data on human trafficking as well as data on crimes motivated by "gender and gender identity" bias and "crimes committed by, and crimes directed against, juveniles" from contributors in January 2013.

UCR Redevelopment Project Update

To streamline the program's database management and quality control activities, the FBI created the UCR Redevelopment Project (UCRRP). The UCRRP's goal is to improve the efficiency, usability, and maintainability of the UCR Program's submission processes, databases, and quality control activities. Through the UCRRP, the UCR Program will improve customer service by decreasing the time it takes to analyze data and by decreasing the time needed to release and publish crime data. The program will also enhance its external data query tool so that the public can view and analyze more published UCR data from the Internet.

Another major goal of the UCRRP is to reduce, to the point of elimination, the exchange of printed materials between submitting agencies and the FBI. Beginning with the 2013 data collections, all data was to be submitted electronically, and after July 2013, the UCR Program no longer accepted paper submissions or the electronic submission of documents (for example, Portable Document Format files). The UCRRP has begun working with agencies to help them adopt electronic submissions via the NIBRS, electronic SRS, or Extensible Markup Language.

Due to a system upgrade in 2019, the FBI now calculates rates for each offense based on the individual offenses and population that were published for each agency in tables 8-11 in Section II. (Previous to 2019, when agencies were published in tables 8-11, but they had one or two offenses removed from publication due to not meeting

UCR publication guidelines, the agency's data was not used to calculate rates for this table.) This table provides the rate per 100,000 inhabitants and the number of offenses known to law enforcement for violent crimes (murder and nonnegligent manslaughter, rape, robbery, and aggravated assault) and property crimes (burglary, larceny-theft, and motor vehicle theft) nationally and by city and county groupings for law enforcement agencies submitting 12 months of publishable data for 2019. For the 2019 population estimates used in this table, the FBI computed individual rates of growth from one year to the next for every city/town and county using 2010 decennial population counts and 2011 through 2018 population estimates from the U.S. Census Bureau. Each agency's rates of growth were averaged; that average was then applied and added to its 2018 Census population estimate to derive the agency's 2019 population estimate.

Uniform Crime Reporting Program Changes Definition of Rape

For the first time in the more than 80-year history of the Uniform Crime Reporting (UCR) Program, the FBI has changed the definition of a Part 1 offense. In December 2011, then FBI Director Robert S. Mueller, III, approved revisions to the UCR Program's definition of rape as recommended by the FBI's Criminal Justice Information Services (CJIS) Division Advisory Policy Board (APB), which is made up of representatives from all facets of law enforcement.

Beginning in 2013, rape is defined for Summary UCR purposes as, "Penetration, no matter how slight, of the vagina or anus with any body part or object, or oral penetration by a sex organ of another person, without the consent of the victim." The new definition updated the 80-year-old historical definition of rape which was "carnal knowledge of a female forcibly and against her will." Effectively, the revised definition expands rape to include both male and female victims and offenders, and reflects the various forms of sexual penetration understood to be rape, especially nonconsenting acts of sodomy, and sexual assaults with objects. Beginning in 2017, only this revised definition of rape was used.

"This new, more inclusive definition will provide us with a more accurate understanding of the scope and volume of these crimes," said Attorney General Eric Holder. Proponents of the new definition and of the omission of the term "forcible" say that the changes broaden the scope of the previously narrow definitions by capturing (1) data without regard to gender, (2) the penetration of any

bodily orifice, penetration by any object or body part, and (3) offenses in which physical force is not involved. Now, for example, instances in which offenders use drugs or alcohol or incidents in which offenders sodomize victims of the same gender will be counted as rape for statistical purposes.

It has long been the UCR Program's mission to collect and publish data regarding the scope and nature of crime in the nation, including those for rape. Since the FBI began collecting data using the revised definition of rape in January 2013, program officials expected that the number of reported rapes would rise. According to David Cuthbertson, former FBI Assistant Director of the CJIS Division, "As we implement this change, the FBI is confident that the number of victims of this heinous crime will be more accurately reflected in national crime statistics."

Expanded Offense Tables

Expanded offense data are the details of the various offenses that the Uniform Crime Reporting Program collects beyond the count of how many crimes law enforcement agencies report. These details may include the type of weapon used in a crime, the type or value of items stolen, and so forth. Expanded homicide data provide supplemental details about murders such as the age, sex, and race of both the victim and the offender, the weapon used in the homicide, the circumstances surrounding the offense, and the relationship of the victim to the offender. In addition, expanded data includes trends (for example, 2-year comparisons) and rates per 100,000 inhabitants.

Expanded offense data, including expanded homicide data, are information collected in addition to the reports of the number of crimes known. As a result, law enforcement agencies can report an offense without providing the supplemental data about that offense. These additional tables can be found at https://ucr.fbi.gov/crime-in-the-u.s/2019/crime-in-the-u.s.-2019/topic-pages/expanded-offense.

About the Editor

Shana Hertz Hattis is a consulting writer-editor for Bernan Press. She holds a master of science in education degree in from Northwestern University and a bachelor's degree in journalism from the same university. She has previously edited *Vital Statistics of the United States: Births, Life Expectancy, Deaths, and Selected Health Data* and several volumes of *Crime in the United States* for Bernan.

SECTION II

OFFENSES KNOWN TO POLICE

VIOLENT CRIME

- MURDER

- RAPE

- ROBBERY

- AGGRAVATED ASSAULT

PROPERTY CRIME

- BURGLARY

- LARCENY-THEFT

- MOTOR VEHICLE THEFT

- ARSON

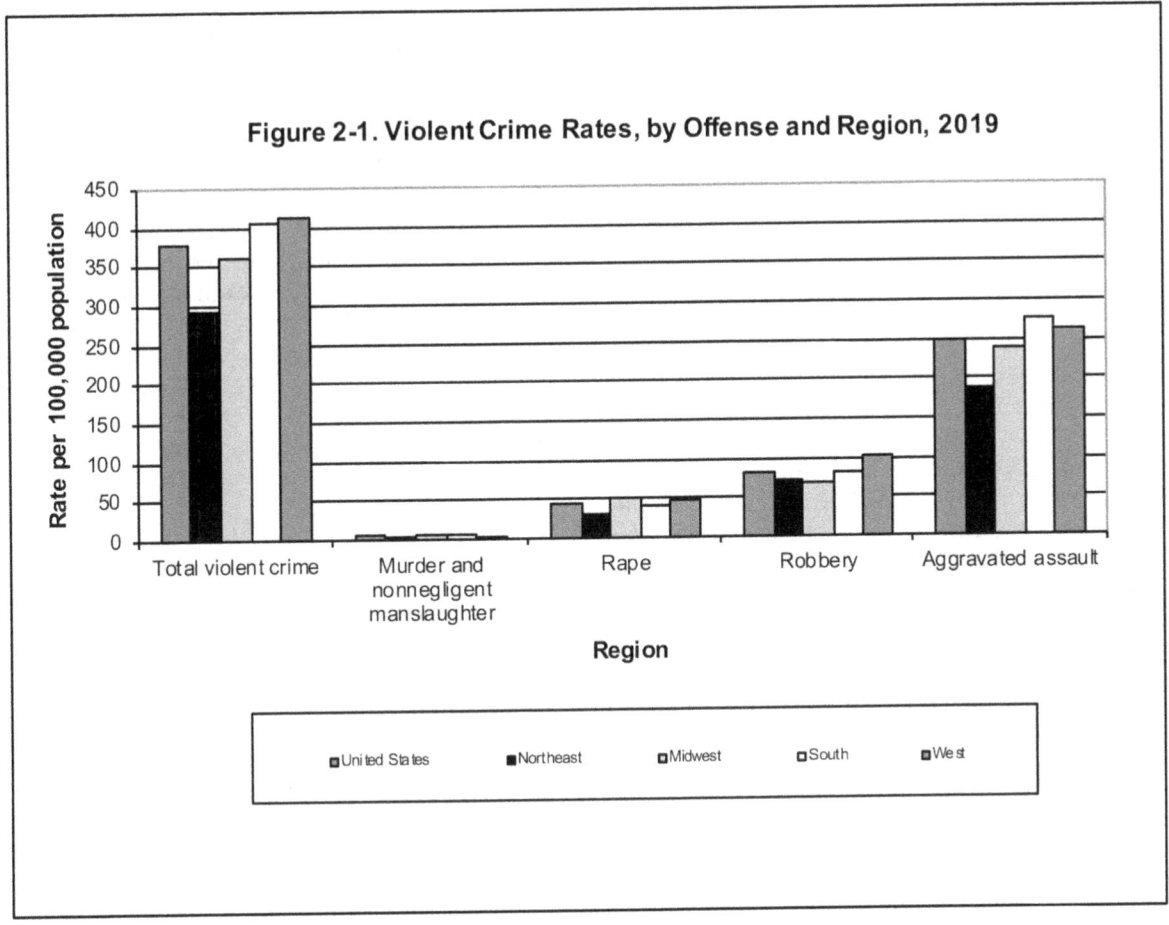

Figure 2-1. Violent Crime Rates, by Offense and Region, 2019

Definition

Violent crime consists of four offenses: murder and non-negligent manslaughter, rape, robbery, and aggravated assault. According to the Uniform Crime Reporting (UCR) program, run by the Federal Bureau of Investigation (FBI), violent crimes involve either the use of force or the threat of force.

Data Collection

The data presented in *Crime in the United States* reflect the Hierarchy Rule, which counts only the most serious offense in a multiple-offense criminal incident. In descending order of severity, the violent crimes are murder and nonnegligent manslaughter, rape, robbery, and aggravated assault; these are followed by the property crimes of burglary, larceny-theft, and motor vehicle theft. Arson is also considered a property crime, but the Hierarchy Rule does not apply to the arson offense. In cases in which arson occurs in conjunction with another violent or property crime, the arson and the additional crime are reported. More information on the expanded violent crime tables (which are available online but not included in this publication) can be found in Section I.

Important Note: Rape Data

In 2013, the FBI UCR Program began collecting rape data under a revised definition within the Summary Reporting System. Previously, offense data for forcible rape were collected under the legacy UCR definition: the carnal knowledge of a female forcibly and against her will. Beginning with the 2013 data year, the term "forcible" was removed from the offense title, and the definition was changed. The revised UCR definition of rape is: penetration, no matter how slight, of the vagina or anus with any body part or object, or oral penetration by a sex organ of another person, without the consent of the victim. Attempts or assaults to commit rape are also included in the statistics presented here; however, statutory rape and incest are excluded.

In 2017, the FBI Director approved the recommendation to discontinue the reporting of rape data using the UCR legacy definition beginning in 2018. However, to maintain the 20-year trend in Table 1, national estimates for rape under the legacy definition are provided along with estimates under the revised definition.

National Volume, Trends, and Rate

In 2019, an estimated 1,203,808 violent crimes occurred in the United States, a decrease of 0.5 percent from the 2018 estimate. An estimated 366.7 violent crimes were committed per 100,000 inhabitants in 2019, a decline of 1.0 percent since 2018. Aggravated assaults accounted for 68.2 percent of violent crimes, the highest percentage of violent crimes reported to law enforcement. Robbery accounted for 22.3 percent of violent crimes, rape accounted for 8.2 percent, and murder accounted for 1.4 percent of violent crimes. (Tables 1 and 1A)

Occurrences of rape (revised definition) and robbery incidents decreased from 2018 to 2019, with rape decreasing by 2.7 percent and robbery by 4.7 percent. Murdered and nonnegligent manslaughter increased 0.3 percent and aggravated assault increased 1.3 percent. (Tables 1 and 1A)

In longer-term trends, the 2019 estimated violent crime total was 0.4 percent above the 2015 level and 3.8 percent below the 2010 level. The 5-year and 10-year trend data showed that the violent crime rate decreased 1.9 percent between 2015 and 2019 and decreased 9.3 percent between 2010 and 2019. (Tables 1 and 1A)

In 2019, offenders used firearms in 73.7 percent of the nation's murders, 36.4 percent of robberies, and 27.6 percent of aggravated assaults. Although the largest percentage of murders were committed with firearms, weapons such as clubs and blunt objects accounted for more aggravated assaults (29.8 percent) than any other type of weapon. (Weapons data are not collected for rape offenses.) (Expanded Homicide Table 7, Expanded Offense Robbery Table 3, and Expanded Aggravated Assault Table; see <https://ucr.fbi.gov/crime-in-the-u.s/2019/crime-in-the-u.s.-2019/topic-pages/expanded-offense >for more information)

Many violent crimes are committed by people in known relationships. Figure 2 shows the number of murder victims who knew their offender. In the figure, the relationship categories of husband and wife include common-law spouses and ex-spouses. The categories of mother, father, sister, brother, son, and daughter include stepparents, stepchildren, and stepsiblings. The category of "acquaintance" includes homosexual relationships and the composite category of other known-to-victim offenders.

Regional Offense Trends and Rate

The UCR program divides the United States into four regions: the Northeast, the South, the Midwest, and the West. (More details concerning geographic regions are provided in Appendix IV.) The population distribution of the regions can be found in Table 3, and the estimated volume and rate of violent crime by region are provided in Table 4.

THE NORTHEAST

The Northeast accounted for an estimated 17.1 percent of the nation's population in 2019 and an estimated 13.1 percent of its violent crimes. The estimated number of violent crimes decreased 0.4 percent from 2018 to 2019. Murders decreased 4.8 percent in the Northeast. Rapes decreased 2.0 percent. Robberies declined 4.0 percent. Aggravated assaults, however, rose 1.4 percent from 2018. In 2019, there were an estimated 292.4 violent crimes per 100,000 inhabitants, a 0.3 percent decrease from 2018. (Tables 3 and 4)

THE MIDWEST

With an estimated 20.8 percent of the total population of the United States, the Midwest accounted for 19.8 percent of the nation's estimated number of violent crimes in 2019. The region had a 1.1 percent decrease in violent crime from 2018 to 2019. The estimated number of aggravated assaults increased 1.7 percent, while the estimated number of robberies fell 7.9 percent and the estimated number of murders fell 5.6 percent. The estimated number of rapes increased 1.0 percent. The rate of violent crime per 100,000 inhabitants in the Midwest was 361.7, a decrease of 1.2 percent from 2018 to 2019. (Tables 3 and 4)

THE SOUTH

The South, the nation's most populous region, accounted for 38.3 percent of the nation's population in 2019. Approximately 41.0 percent of violent crimes in 2019 occurred in the South. Violent crime increased 0.7 percent from 2018 to 2019, while the estimated number of murders rose 5.6 percent and the estimated number of aggravated assaults rose 2.1 percent. Robberies dropped 3.5 percent, while rapes decreased by 0.9 percent. The estimated rate of violent crime in the South was 406.6 incidents per 100,000 inhabitants in 2019, a 0.2 decrease from 2018. (Tables 3 and 4)

THE WEST

With 23.9 percent of the nation's population in 2018, the West also accounted for an estimated 23.9 percent of the nation's violent crime. Violent crime in the West decreased 2.1 percent from 2018 to 2019. Murders fell 2.3 percent, rapes dropped by 5.2 percent, robberies decreased 4.7 percent, and aggravated assault decreased 0.5 percent. The region's violent crime rate in 2019 was 413.5 per 100,000 inhabitants, a 2.7 percent drop from 2018. (Tables 3 and 4)

Community Types

The UCR program aggregates crime data into three community types: metropolitan statistical areas (MSAs), cities outside MSAs, and nonmetropolitan counties outside MSAs. Appendix IV provides additional information regarding community types. In 2019, approximately 86.0 percent of the nation's population lived in MSAs. Residents of cities outside MSAs accounted for 5.7 percent of the country's population, and residents living in nonmetropolitan counties accounted for 8.3 percent of the population. (Table 2)

In the areas reporting violent crimes to the UCR Program, approximately 89.6 percent of these crimes occurred in MSAs, while 5.9 percent occurred in cities outside MSAs and 4.1 percent occurred in nonmetropolitan counties. By community type, the violent crime rates were estimated at 395.2 incidents per 100,000 inhabitants in MSAs, 390.8 incidents per 100,000 inhabitants in cities outside MSAs, and 207.5 incidents per 100,000 inhabitants in nonmetropolitan counties. (Table 2)

Population Groups: Trends and Rates

In the UCR program, data are also aggregated into population groups; these groups are described in more detail in Appendix IV. The nation's cities had an overall decrease of 0.6 percent in the estimated number of violent crimes from 2018 to 2019. By city population group, cities with 10,000 to 24,999 inhabitants had the largest percentage decrease in the estimated number of violent crimes (2.6 percent). Metropolitan counties and suburban areas both experienced a 1.6 percent decrease in violent crimes from

2018 to 2019, while nonmetropolitan counties saw a 0.4 percent increase. (Table 12)

The law enforcement agencies in the nation's cities collectively reported a rate of 449.2 violent crimes per 100,000 inhabitants in 2019. Law enforcement agencies in the subset of cities with 500,000 to 999,999 inhabitants reported the highest violent crime rate, 796.3 violent crimes per 100,000 inhabitants; the violent crime rate for all cities with 250,000 or more inhabitants was 715.8 per 100,000 inhabitants. Agencies in cities with 10,000 to 24,999 inhabitants reported the lowest violent crime rate (254.8 incidents per 100,000 inhabitants). Law enforcement agencies in the nation's metropolitan counties reported a collective violent crime rate of 255.7 per 100,000 inhabitants, while agencies in nonmetropolitan counties reported a collective rate of 208.4 violent crimes per 100,000 inhabitants and suburban areas reported a violent crime rate of 243.3 violent crimes per 100,000 inhabitants. (Table 16)

Due to a system upgrade in 2019, the FBI now calculates rates for each offense based on the individual offenses and population published for each agency in tables 8-11. (Previous to 2019, when agencies were published in tables 8-11, but they had one or two offenses removed from publication due to not meeting UCR publication guidelines, the agency's data was not used to calculate rates for this table.) The FBI derived the offense rates by dividing the individual offense counts by the individual populations covered by contributing agencies for which 12 months of publishable data were supplied and then multiplying the resulting figure by 100,000. See Appendix V for the agency and population counts. (Table 16)

MURDER AND NONNEGLIGENT MANSLAUGHTER

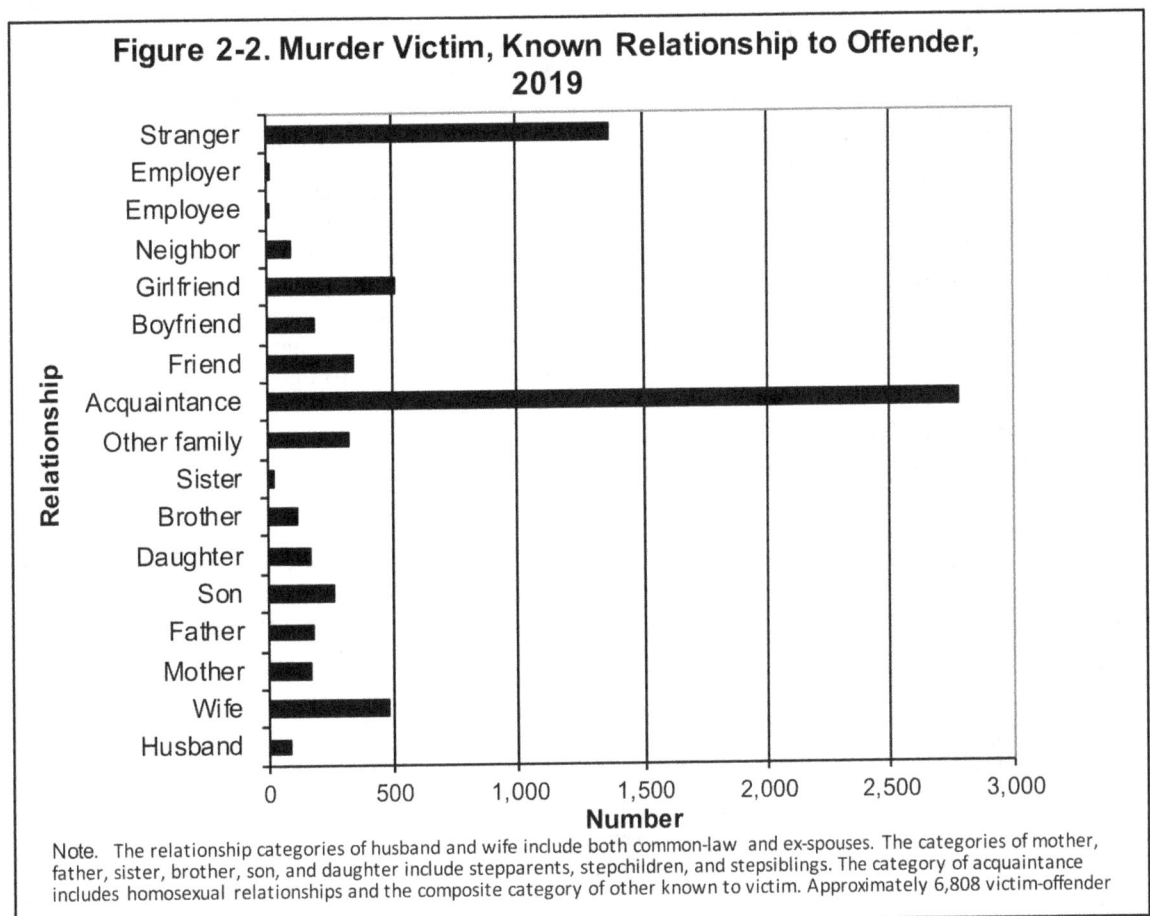

Figure 2-2. Murder Victim, Known Relationship to Offender, 2019

Note. The relationship categories of husband and wife include both common-law and ex-spouses. The categories of mother, father, sister, brother, son, and daughter include stepparents, stepchildren, and stepsiblings. The category of acquaintance includes homosexual relationships and the composite category of other known to victim. Approximately 6,808 victim-offender

Definition

The UCR program defines murder and non-negligent manslaughter as the willful (non-negligent) killing of one human being by another. The classification of this offense is based solely on police investigation, rather than on the determination of a court, medical examiner, coroner, jury, or other judicial body. The UCR program does not include the following situations under this offense classification: deaths caused by negligence, suicide, or accident; justifiable homicides; and attempts to murder or assaults to murder, which are considered aggravated assaults.

Data Collection/Supplementary Homicide Reports (SHR)

The UCR program's *Supplementary Homicide Report* (SHR) provides information about murder victims and offenders by age, sex, and race; the types of weapons used in the murders; the relationships of the victims to the offenders; and the circumstances surrounding the incident. Law enforcement agencies are asked to complete an SHR for each murder reported to the UCR program. Data from SHRs can be viewed in the Expanded Homicide Data section, found on the FBI Web site: https://ucr.fbi.gov/crime-in-the-u.s/2019/crime-in-the-u.s.-2019/topic-pages/expanded-homicide. More information on these reports and the expanded homicide tables can be found in Section I. Highlights from these tables have been included below.

National Volume, Trends, and Rates

An estimated 16,425 persons were murdered nationwide in 2019. This number was a 0.3 percent increase from the 2018 estimate, a 3.4 percent increase from the 2015 figure, and an 11.6 percent increase from the 2010 estimate. The 2019 murder rate, 5.0 offenses per 100,000 inhabitants, was a 0.2 percent decrease from the 2018 rate. However, this rate represented a 1.1 percent increase from the 2015 rate and a 5.1 percent increase from the 2010 rate. Murder accounted for 1.4 percent of the overall estimated number of violent crimes in 2019. (Tables 1 and 1A)

Regional Offense Trends and Rates

The UCR program divides the United States into four regions: the Northeast, the South, the Midwest, and the West. (More details concerning geographic regions are provided in Appendix IV.) In 2019, 48.7 percent of murders were reported in the South, the country's most populous region. The Midwest reported 20.8 percent of all murders, while the West reported 19.3 percent and the Northeast reported 11.2 percent. (Table 3)

THE NORTHEAST

In 2018, the Northeast accounted for an estimated 17.1 percent of the nation's population and 11.2 percent of its estimated number of murders. With an estimated 1,834 murders, the Northeast saw a 4.8 percent decrease from its 2018 figure. The offense rate for the Northeast was 3.3 murders per 100,000 inhabitants in 2019, a 4.7 percent drop from 2018. (Tables 3 and 4)

THE MIDWEST

The Midwest accounted for an estimated 20.8 percent of the nation's total population and 20.8 percent of the country's estimated number of murders in 2019. The Midwest reported an estimated 3,414 murders in 2019, down 5.6 percent from 2018. The region experienced a rate of 5.0 murders per 100,000 inhabitants in 2019, below its 2018 rate of 5.2. (Tables 3 and 4)

THE SOUTH

The South accounted for an estimated 38.3 percent of the nation's population in 2019 and 48.7 percent of the nation's murders, the highest proportion among the four regions. The estimated 8,002 murders represented a 5.6 percent increase from the 2018 figure. The region's estimated rate of 6.4 murders per 100,000 inhabitants represented an increase of 4.7 percent from the estimated rate for 2018. (Tables 3 and 4)

THE WEST

The West accounted for an estimated 23.9 percent of the nation's population and 19.3 percent of the estimated number of murders in 2019. The West experienced an estimated 3,175 murders, a 2.3 percent decrease from the 2018 estimate. The region's murder rate was 4.1 per 100,000 inhabitants, down 2.9 percent from 2018. (Tables 3 and 4)

Community Types

The UCR program aggregates data for three community types: metropolitan statistical areas (MSAs), cities outside MSAs, and nonmetropolitan counties outside MSAs. (See Appendix IV for definitions.) In 2019, MSAs accounted for 86.0 percent of the nation's population and 88.5 percent of the estimated total number of murders. MSAs experienced a rate of 5.1 murders per 100,000 inhabitants in 2019. Cities outside MSAs accounted for 5.7 percent of the U.S. population and (with an estimated 839 murders) accounted for 5.1 percent of the estimated murders in the nation. The murder rate for cities outside MSAs was 4.5 per 100,000 inhabitants. In 2019, approximately 8.3 percent of the nation's population lived in nonmetropolitan counties outside MSAs. An estimated 1,047 murders took place in these counties, accounting for 6.4 percent of the nation's estimated total. The murder rate in nonmetropolitan counties was 3.9 per 100,000 inhabitants. (Table 2)

Population Groups: Trends and Rates

The UCR program uses the following population group designations in its data presentations: cities (grouped according to population size) and counties (classified as either metropolitan or nonmetropolitan). A breakdown of these classifications is provided in Appendix IV.

From 2018 to 2019, the nation's cities experienced a 1.0 percent increase in homicides. Cities with under 10,000 residents experienced the greatest decrease, 3.5 percent, while cities with 10,000 to 24,999 residents experienced the biggest increase, 3.6 percent. Metropolitan counties experienced a decrease in homicides of 0.6 percent from 2018 to 2019, while nonmetropolitan counties experienced an increase of 0.5 percent. Suburban areas experienced a decrease of 1.4 percent. (Table 12)

In 2019, cities collectively had a rate of 5.7 murders per 100,000 inhabitants. Cities with 500,000 to 999,999 inhabitants had the highest murder rate (12.5 murders per 100,000 inhabitants). Cities with 10,000 to 24,999 inhabitants and cities with under 10,000 inhabitants had the lowest murder rate, each with 3.0 murders per 100,000 inhabitants. The homicide rate for metropolitan counties was 3.4 murders per 100,000 inhabitants, while the rate for nonmetropolitan counties was 3.8 murders per 100,000 inhabitants. Suburban areas had a homicide rate of 3.0 per 100,000 inhabitants. (Table 16)

Due to a system upgrade in 2019, the FBI now calculates rates for each offense based on the individual offenses and population published for each agency in tables 8-11. (Previous to 2019, when agencies were published in tables 8-11, but they had one or two offenses removed from publication due to not meeting UCR publication guidelines, the agency's data was not used to calculate rates for this table.) The FBI derived the offense rates by dividing the individual offense counts by the individual populations covered by contributing agencies for which 12 months of publishable data were supplied and then multiplying the resulting figure by 100,000. See Appendix V for the agency and population counts. (Table 16)

Supplementary Homicide Reports Data

VICTIMS/OFFENDERS

Based on 2019 supplemental homicide data (where the ages, sexes, or races of the murder victims were identified), 95.4 percent of victims were over 18 years of age, 20.5 percent were under 22 years of age, 8.2 percent were under 18 years of age, and the age of 0.6 percent of the victims was unknown. Of the 13,927 murder victims represented in the 2019 expanded tables whose gender was identified, 78.3 percent were male. Concerning race, 42.3 percent of victims were White, 54.7 percent were Black or African American, and 3.1 percent were of other races. Race was unknown for 234 victims. For murders in which the gender of the offender was identified, 63.6 percent were males; the sex of offenders for 27.7 percent of homicides was unknown. For the offenders for whom race was identified, 39.6 percent were Black or African American, 29.1 percent were White, and 2.1 percent were other races; 4,752 offenders (29.3 percent) were of unknown race. (Expanded Homicide Data Tables 1, 2, and 3)

VICTIM-OFFENDER RELATIONSHIPS

For incidents in which the victim-offender relationship was specified (including the designation of "unknown"), 13.0 percent of victims were slain by family members, 9.9 percent were murdered by strangers, and 28.3 percent were killed by someone they knew other than family members (acquaintances, neighbors, friends, employers, romantic partners, employees, etc.). The victim-offender relationship was unknown in 48.9 percent of incidents. (Expanded Homicide Data Table 10)

CIRCUMSTANCES/WEAPONS

Concerning the known circumstances surrounding murders, and including murders with unknown circumstances, 43.2 percent of victims were murdered during arguments (including romantic triangles) and brawls in 2019. Felony circumstances (rape, robbery, burglary, etc.) accounted for 24.6 percent of murders. Circumstances were unknown for 40.2 percent of reported homicides. Of the homicides for which the type of weapon was specified, 73.7 percent involved the use of firearms. Of the identified firearms used, handguns comprised 62.1 percent of the total. (Expanded Homicide Data Tables 8 and 11)

Justifiable Homicide

Certain willful killings must be reported as justifiable, or excusable, homicide. In the UCR program, justifiable homicide is defined as, and is limited to, the following:

- The killing of a felon by a peace officer in the line of duty

- The killing of a felon, during the commission of a felony, by a private citizen

Because these killings are determined by law enforcement investigation to be justifiable, they are tabulated separately from murder and nonnegligent manslaughter. Law enforcement reported 726 justifiable homicides in 2019. Of those, law enforcement officers justifiably killed 340 felons, and private citizens justifiably killed 386 offenders. (Expanded Homicide Data Tables 14 and 15)

RAPE

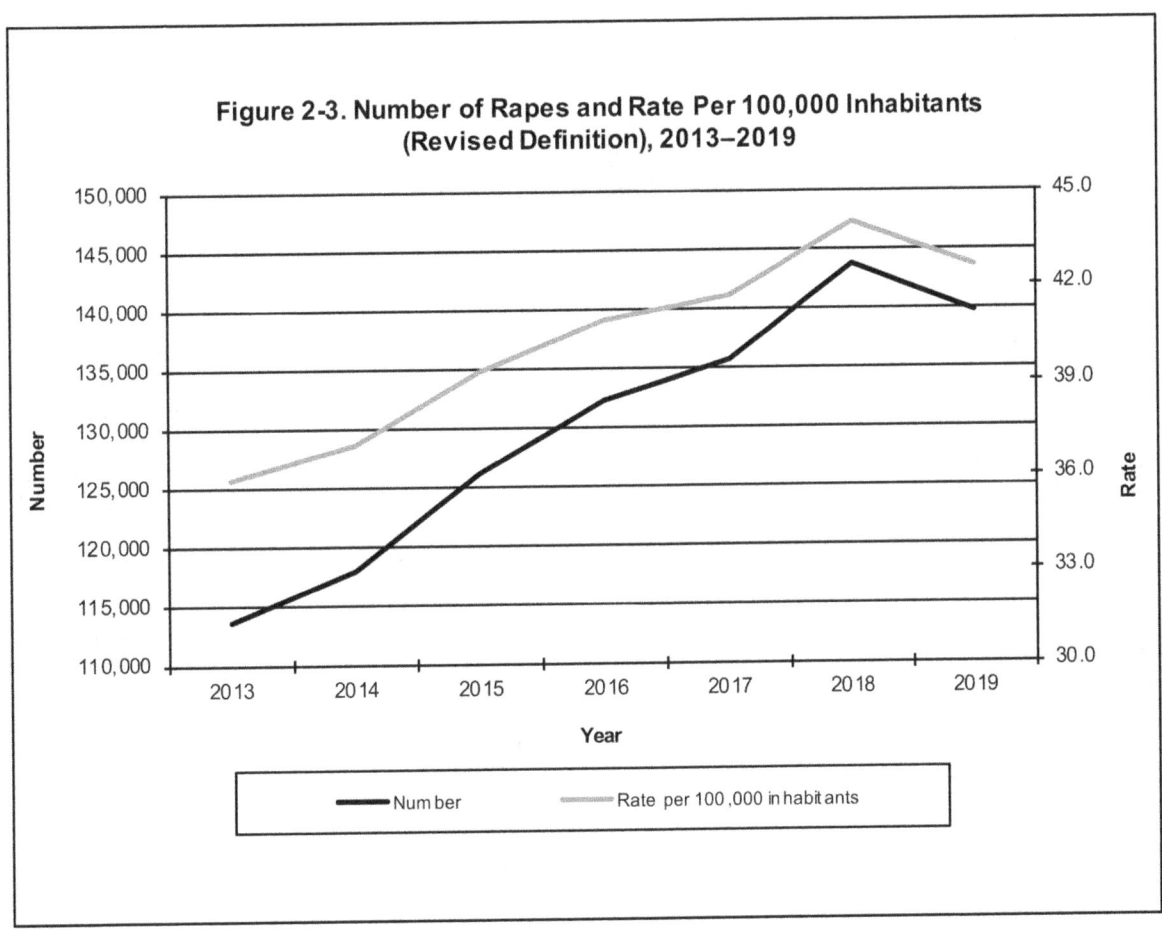

Figure 2-3. Number of Rapes and Rate Per 100,000 Inhabitants (Revised Definition), 2013–2019

Definition

In 2013, the FBI UCR Program began collecting rape data under a revised definition within the Summary Reporting System. Previously, offense data for forcible rape were collected under the legacy UCR definition: the carnal knowledge of a female forcibly and against her will. Beginning with the 2013 data year, the term "forcible" was removed from the offense title, and the definition was changed. The revised UCR definition of rape is: penetration, no matter how slight, of the vagina or anus with any body part or object, or oral penetration by a sex organ of another person, without the consent of the victim. Attempts or assaults to commit rape are also included in the statistics presented here; however, statutory rape and incest are excluded.

In 2016, the FBI Director approved the recommendation to discontinue the reporting of rape data using the UCR legacy definition beginning in 2017. However, to maintain the 20-year trend in Table 1, national estimates for rape under the legacy definition are provided along with estimates under the revised definition.

The UCR Program counts one offense for each victim of a rape, attempted rape, or assault with intent to rape, regardless of the victim's age. Non-consensual sexual relations involving a familial member is considered rape, not incest. All other crimes of a sexual nature are considered to be Part II offenses; as such, the UCR Program collects only arrest data for those crimes. The offense of statutory rape, in which no force is used but the female victim is under the age of consent, is included in the arrest total for the sex offenses category.

National Volume, Trends, and Rates

In 2019, the estimated number of rapes (revised definition), 139,815, decreased 2.7 percent from the 2018 estimate. The estimated volume of rapes in 2019 was 10.8 percent higher than in the 2015 estimate. (Tables 1 and 1A)

Regional Offense Trends and Rates

The UCR program divides the United States into four regions: the Northeast, the South, the Midwest, and the West. (More details concerning geographic regions are provided in Appendix IV) Regional analysis offers estimates of the volume of female rapes, the percent change from the previous year's estimate, and the rate of rape per 100,000 female inhabitants in each region.

NORTHEAST

The Northeast made up 17.1 percent of the U.S. population in 2019. An estimated 17,315 rapes—12.4 percent of the national total—occurred in the Northeast. This was an decrease of 2.0 percent from the 2018 estimated figure. The region's rate of rape occurrences – 30.9 per 100,000 inhabitants – was a 1.9 percent drop from 2018. (Tables 3 and 4)

MIDWEST

The Midwest accounted for 20.8 percent of the U.S. population in 2019. Of all the rapes in the nation, 24.4 percent occurred in the Midwest in 2019. The 2019 estimate (34.057 rapes) represented a decrease of 3.2 percent from the 2018 estimate. The region's rate of rape occurrences – 49.8 per 100,000 inhabitants – was a 3.4 percent drop from 2018. (Tables 3 and 4)

SOUTH

The South, the nation's most populous region, accounted for an estimated 38.3 percent of the nation's population in 2019; the region also accounted for an estimated 37.3 percent of the nation's estimated number of rapes. An estimated 52,119 victims reported rape in the South in 2019, down 0.9 percent from 2018. The region's rate of rape occurrences – 41.5 per 100,000 inhabitants – was a 1.7 percent drop from 2018. (Tables 3 and 4)

WEST

The West accounted for 23.9 percent of the nation's population in 2019. The region also accounted for 26.0 percent of the nation's total number of estimated rapes with an estimated 36,324 offenses. The West saw a 5.2 percent decrease in rapes from 2018 to 2019. The region's rate of rape occurrences – 46.4 per 100,000 inhabitants – was a 5.8 percent drop from 2018. (Tables 3 and 4)

Community Types

Using the U.S. Office of Management and Budget's designations, the UCR program aggregates crime data by type of community in which the offenses occur: metropolitan statistical areas (MSAs), cities outside MSAs, and nonmetropolitan counties outside MSAs. (Appendix IV provides more detailed information about community types.)

MSAS

In 2019, MSAs accounted for 86.0 percent of the nation's population and 84.8 percent of the nation's estimated number of rapes (revised definition). An estimated 118,572 victims were forcibly raped in metropolitan areas. MSAs had a rape rate of 42.0 per 100,000 inhabitants. (Table 2)

CITIES OUTSIDE MSAS

Cities outside MSAs are mostly incorporated areas that are served by city law enforcement agencies. Although accounting for only 5.8 percent of the U.S. population in 2019, cities outside MSAs accounted for 7.8 percent of the nation's estimated rapes (10,851 estimated offenses). Cities outside MSAs had a rate of 57.9 rapes per 100,000 inhabitants. (Table 2)

NONMETROPOLITAN COUNTIES

In 2019, approximately 8.3 percent of the nation's population lived in nonmetropolitan counties outside MSAs (counties made up of mostly non-incorporated areas that are served by noncity law enforcement agencies). Collectively, these areas had an estimated 10,392 rapes, representing 7.4 percent of the nation's estimated total. Nonmetropolitan counties had a rate of 38.3 rapes per 100,000 inhabitants. (Table 2)

Population Groups: Trends and Rates

The UCR program uses the following population group designations in its data presentations: cities (grouped according to population size) and counties (classified as either metropolitan or nonmetropolitan). A breakdown of these classifications is provided in Appendix IV.

From 2018 to 2019, the nation's cities experienced a 4.1 percent decrease in rapes. Cities with 500,000 to 999,999 inhabitants experienced the greatest decrease (7.9 percent). Metropolitan counties experienced a 3.6 percent decrease from 2018 to 2019, while nonmetropolitan counties experienced a 1.3 percent decrease and suburban areas experienced a 3.7 percent decrease. (Table 12)

In 2019, cities collectively had a rate of 47.6 rapes per 100,000 inhabitants. Cities with 250,000 to 499,999 inhabitants had the highest rate of rape (65.4 rapes per 100,000 inhabitants). Cities with 25,000 to 49,999 inhabitants had the lowest rate, with 38.4 rapes per 100,000 inhabitants. The rape rate for metropolitan counties was 34.2 per 100,000 inhabitants, and for nonmetropolitan counties, it was 41.1 per 100,000 inhabitants. Suburban areas had a rape rate of 33.9 per 100,000 inhabitants. (Table 16)

Due to a system upgrade in 2019, the FBI now calculates rates for each offense based on the individual offenses and population published for each agency in tables 8-11. (Previous to 2019, when agencies were published in tables 8-11, but they had one or two offenses removed from publication due to not meeting UCR publication guidelines, the agency's data was not used to calculate rates for this table.) The FBI derived the offense rates by dividing the individual offense counts by the individual populations covered by contributing agencies for which 12 months of publishable data were supplied and then multiplying the resulting figure by 100,000. See Appendix V for the agency and population counts. (Table 16)

ROBBERY

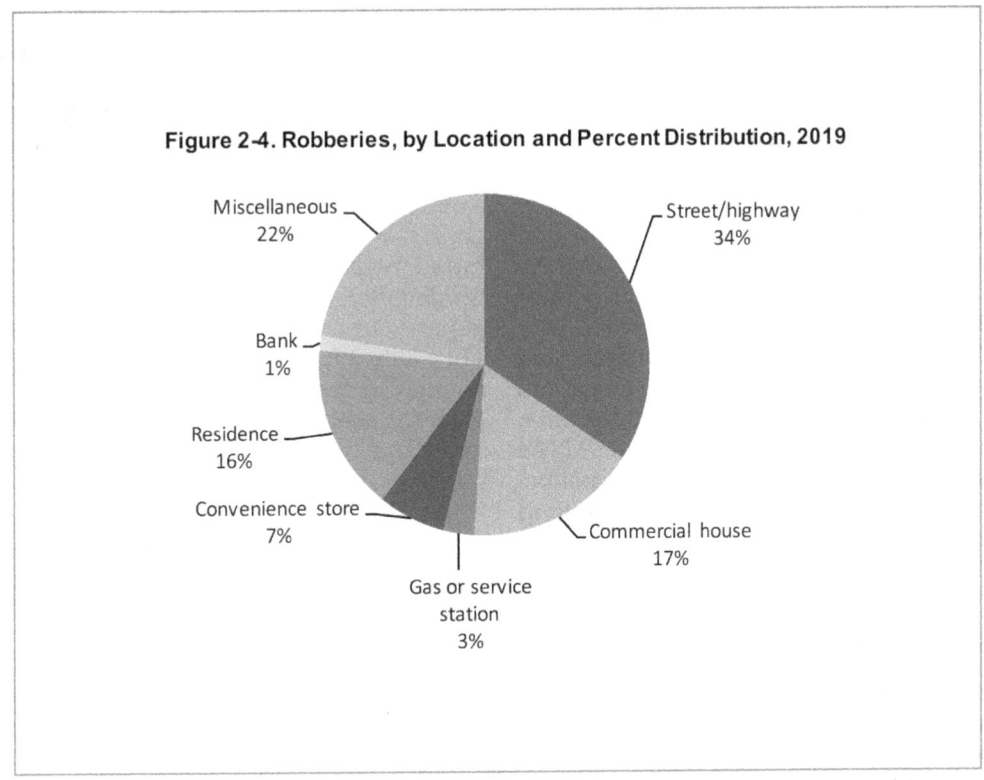

Figure 2-4. Robberies, by Location and Percent Distribution, 2019

Miscellaneous 22%
Street/highway 34%
Bank 1%
Residence 16%
Convenience store 7%
Gas or service station 3%
Commercial house 17%

Definition

The UCR program defines robbery as the taking or attempt to take anything of value from the care, custody, or control of a person or persons by force or threat of force or violence and/or by putting the victim in fear.

National Volume, Trends, and Rates

In 2019, the estimated robbery total (267,988) decreased 4.7 percent from the 2018 estimate. The 5-year robbery trend (2015 data compared with 2019 data) showed a decrease of 18.3 percent. The 2019 estimated robbery rate (81.6 per 100,000 inhabitants) showed a decrease of 5.2 percent when compared with the 2018 rate. (Tables 1 and 1A)

Regional Offense Trends and Rates

The UCR program divides the United States into four regions: the Northeast, the South, the Midwest, and the West. (More details concerning geographic regions are provided in Appendix IV.)

NORTHEAST

The Northeast, with an estimated 17.1 percent of the nation's population in 2019, accounted for 15.0 percent of the nation's estimated number of robberies. The estimated number of robberies decreased 4.12 percent from 2018. The rate for this region was 71.6 robberies per 100,000 inhabitants, down from 74.6 robberies per 100,000 inhabitants in 2018. (Tables 3 and 4)

MIDWEST

The Midwest accounted for 20.8 percent of the total population of the United States and 17.3 percent of its estimated number of robberies in 2019. An estimated 46,412 robberies occurred in the Midwest in 2019, a 7.9 percent decrease from the estimated figure from 2018. The region's robbery rate was 67.9 robberies per 100,000 inhabitants in 2019, down 8.0 percent from 2018. (Tables 3 and 4)

SOUTH

The South, the nation's most highly populated region, accounted for an estimated 38.3 percent of the nation's population and 38.3 percent of the nation's estimated number of robberies in 2019. Robberies accounted for an estimated 102,570 violent crimes in this region in 2019, representing a 3.5 percent decrease from the 2018 figure. The 2019 robbery rate in the South was 81.7 per 100,000 inhabitants, down 4.2 percent from 2018. (Tables 3 and 4)

WEST

The West was home to an estimated 23.9 percent of the nation's population and accounted for 29.5 percent of the nation's estimated number of robberies in 2019. The estimated number of robberies (78,933) in the region in 2019 represented a 4.7 percent decrease from the 2018 figure. The rate of robberies per 100,000 inhabitants in the West was 100.7, a 5.3 percent decrease from the 2018 rate. (Tables 3 and 4)

Community Types

The UCR program aggregates data for three community types: metropolitan statistical areas (MSAs), cities outside MSAs, and nonmetropolitan counties outside MSAs. MSAs include a central city or urbanized area with at least 50,000 inhabitants, as well as the county that contains the principal city and other adjacent counties that have, as defined by the U.S. Office of Management and Budget, a high degree of social and economic integration as measured through commuting. Cities outside MSAs are mostly incorporated areas, and nonmetropolitan counties are made up of mostly unincorporated areas served by non-city law enforcement.

In 2019, MSAs were home to an estimated 86.0 percent of the nation's population, and 96.4 percent of the nation's estimated number of robberies took place in these areas. Robberies in MSAs occurred at a rate of 91.5 per 100,000 inhabitants. Cities outside MSAs accounted for 5.7 percent of the U.S. population and 2.4 percent of the estimated number of robberies in the nation. The robbery rate for cities outside MSAs was 35.0 per 100,000 inhabitants. Nonmetropolitan counties made up 8.3 percent of the nation's estimated population and 1.1 percent of the nation's estimated robberies, with a rate of 11.2 robberies per 100,000 inhabitants. (Table 2)

Population Groups: Trends and Rates

The national UCR program aggregates data by various population groups, which include cities, metropolitan counties, and nonmetropolitan counties. A definition of these groups can be found in Appendix IV. The number of robberies in cities as a whole decreased by 4.9 percent between 2018 and 2019. Among the population groups and subsets labeled *city*, those cities with 10,000 to 24,999 inhabitants had the greatest decrease in the number of robberies (7.6 percent). Metropolitan counties had a 4.2 percent decrease in the estimated number of robberies, and nonmetropolitan counties showed a 3.1 percent decrease. The number of robberies in suburban areas fell 4.8 percent. (Table 12)

Among the population groups, the nation's cities collectively had a rate of 108.4 robberies per 100,000 inhabitants. Of the population groups and subsets designated *city*, those with 500,000 to 999,999 inhabitants had the highest rate (217.6 per 100,000 inhabitants), while those with fewer than 10,000 inhabitants had the lowest rate (34.4 per 100,000 inhabitants) of robberies. Of the two county groups, metropolitan counties had a rate of 38.7 robberies per 100,000 inhabitants, while nonmetropolitan counties had a rate of 9.6 robberies per 100,000

inhabitants. Suburban areas had a robbery rate of 40.6 per 100,000 inhabitants. (Table 16)

Due to a system upgrade in 2019, the FBI now calculates rates for each offense based on the individual offenses and population published for each agency in tables 8-11. (Previous to 2019, when agencies were published in tables 8-11, but they had one or two offenses removed from publication due to not meeting UCR publication guidelines, the agency's data was not used to calculate rates for this table.) The FBI derived the offense rates by dividing the individual offense counts by the individual populations covered by contributing agencies for which 12 months of publishable data were supplied and then multiplying the resulting figure by 100,000. See Appendix V for the agency and population counts. (Table 16)

Offense Analysis

The UCR program collects supplemental data about robberies to document the use of weapons, the dollar loss associated with the offense, and the location types.

ROBBERY BY WEAPON

Firearms were used in 36.4 percent of robberies in 2019. Offenders used knives or cutting instruments in 8.5 percent of these crimes, strong-arm tactics in 44.8 percent of offenses, and other dangerous weapons in 10.3 percent of offenses. (Table 19)

LOSS BY DOLLAR VALUE

Based on the supplemental reports from law enforcement agencies, the average loss per robbery was $1,797. Average dollar losses were the highest for banks, which suffered an average loss of $4,213 per offense. Residences lost an average of $2,560 per offense, and gas and service stations lost an average of $1,248 per offense. Commercial houses, which include supermarkets, department stores, and restaurants, had average losses of $1,772 per offense. An average of $1,529 was taken during robberies on streets and highways. An average of $1,006 was lost in each offense against convenience stores. (Table 23)

ROBBERY TRENDS BY LOCATION

Among the location types, bank robberies had the greatest percentage decrease from 2018 to 2019, declining 15.2 percent. Robberies that occurred at convenience stores decreased 6.9 percent. (Table 23)

By location type, the greatest proportion of robberies in 2019 occurred on streets and highways (35.1 percent). Robbers targeted commercial houses in 16.5 percent of offenses and also struck residences in 16.0 percent of offenses. Convenience stores accounted for 6.8 percent of robberies, followed by gas and service stations (3.2 percent) and banks (1.4 percent). (Table 23)

AGGRAVATED ASSAULT

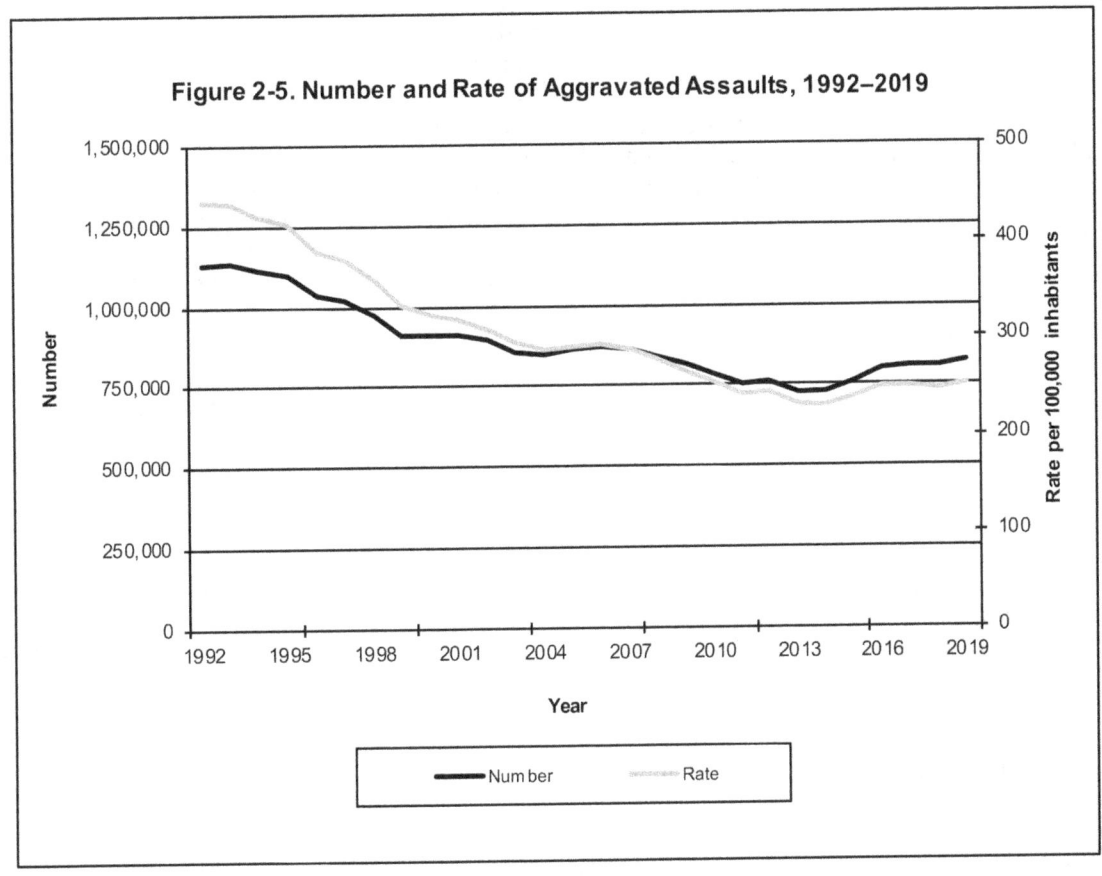

Figure 2-5. Number and Rate of Aggravated Assaults, 1992–2019

Definition

The UCR program defines aggravated assault as an unlawful attack by one person upon another for the purpose of inflicting severe or aggravated bodily injury. This type of assault is usually accompanied by the use of a weapon or by other means likely to produce death or great bodily harm. Attempted aggravated assaults that involve the display or threat of a gun, knife, or other weapon are included in this crime category because serious personal injury would likely result if these assaults were completed. When aggravated assault and larceny-theft occur together, the offense falls under the category of robbery.

National Volume, Trends, and Rates

In 2019, estimated occurrences of aggravated assaults totaled 821,182, a 1.3 percent increase from the 2018 figure and a 5.0 percent increase when compared with the estimate for 2009. The estimated rate of aggravated assault in 2019 was 250.2 per 100,000 inhabitants, a 1.0 percent decrease from 2010. (Tables 1 and 1A)

Among the four types of violent crime offenses (murder, rape, robbery, and aggravated assault), aggravated assault typically has the highest rate of occurrence. This trend continued in 2019. (Table 1)

Regional Offense Trends and Rates

The UCR program divides the United States into four regions: the Northeast, the South, the Midwest, and the West. (More details concerning geographic regions are provided in Appendix IV.)

NORTHEAST

The region with the smallest proportion of the nation's population (an estimated 17.1 percent in 2019) also accounted for the smallest proportion of the nation's estimated number of aggravated assaults (12.7 percent). Occurrences of aggravated assault increased 1.4 percent from 2018 to 2019, rising to an estimated 104,495 incidents. The region continued to have the lowest aggravated assault rate in the nation, at 186.7 incidents per 100,000 inhabitants, although this represented a 1.5 percent increase from the rate in 2018. (Tables 3 and 4)

MIDWEST

With 20.8 percent of the nation's total population in 2019, the Midwest accounted for approximately 19.9 percent of the nation's estimated number of aggravated assaults. Occurrences of this offense rose 1.7 percent from the estimated total for 2018, increasing to an estimated 163.279 incidents. The region's aggravated assault rate, at 239.0

incidents per 100,000 inhabitants, represented a 1.5 percent increase from the 2018 rate. (Tables 3 and 4)

SOUTH

The South, the nation's most highly populated region, accounted for an estimated 38.3 percent of the nation's population in 2019 and the largest amount of the nation's estimated number of aggravated assaults (42.4 percent). From 2018 to 2019, the estimated number of aggravated assaults increased 2.1 percent to a total of 347,874 incidents. The rate of aggravated assaults rose 1.2 percent to 277.0 incidents per 100,000 inhabitants. (Tables 3 and 4)

WEST

In 2019, the West was home to an estimated 23.9 percent of the nation's population. The region accounted for 25.0 percent of the nation's estimated number of aggravated assaults. From 2018 to 2019, the estimated number of offenses decreased 0.5 percent to a total of 205,534 incidents. The rate of aggravated assaults decreased 1.1 percent to 262.3 incidents per 100,000 inhabitants. (Tables 3 and 4)

Community Types

The UCR program aggregates data for three community types: metropolitan statistical areas (MSAs), cities outside MSAs, and nonmetropolitan counties outside MSAs. MSAs include a central city or urbanized area with at least 50,000 inhabitants, as well as the county that contains the principal city and other adjacent counties that have a high degree of social and economic integration as measured through commuting. Cities outside MSAs are mostly incorporated areas, and nonmetropolitan counties are made up of mostly unincorporated areas. (For additional information about community types, see Appendix IV.)

In 2019, 86.0 percent of the nation's population lived in MSAs, where the rate of aggravated assault was an estimated 256.5 per 100,000 inhabitants. Approximately 88.2 percent of all aggravated assaults occurred in MSAs. Cities outside MSAs (with 5.7 percent of the U.S. population and 6.7 percent of aggravated assaults) had the highest rate of aggravated assault at 293.4 offenses per 100,000 inhabitants. Nonmetropolitan counties accounted for 8.3 percent of the U.S. population and 5.1 percent of aggravated assaults. Nonmetropolitan counties had an offense rate of 154.1 aggravated assaults per 100,000 inhabitants. (Table 2)

Population Groups: Trends and Rates

Cities with 100,000 to 249,999 inhabitants experienced the greatest increase in aggravated assaults from 2018 to 2019 (4.4 percent). Cities with 10,000 to 24,999 inhabitants experienced the only decrease, 1.6 percent. The collective increase for all cities was 1.7 percent. In metropolitan counties, the number of aggravated assaults declined 0.6 percent; in nonmetropolitan counties, this number increased 1.0 percent. Aggravated assaults in suburban areas decreased 0.4 percent from 2018 to 2019. (Table 12)

Aggravated assault occurred at an estimated rate of 253.0 offenses per 100,000 inhabitants nationwide. The collective rate for cities was 287.7 aggravated assaults per 100,000 inhabitants. Among city population groups and subsets, rates ranged from a high of 505.8 offenses per 100,000 inhabitants (in cities with 500,000 to 999,999 inhabitants) to a low of 173.6 offenses per 100,000 inhabitants (in cities with 25,000 to 49,999 inhabitants). The aggravated assault rate was 179.5 in metropolitan counties and 154.0 in nonmetropolitan counties. It was 165.9 in suburban areas. (Table 16)

Due to a system upgrade in 2019, the FBI now calculates rates for each offense based on the individual offenses and population published for each agency in tables 8-11. (Previous to 2019, when agencies were published in tables 8-11, but they had one or two offenses removed from publication due to not meeting UCR publication guidelines, the agency's data was not used to calculate rates for this table.) The FBI derived the offense rates by dividing the individual offense counts by the individual populations covered by contributing agencies for which 12 months of publishable data were supplied and then multiplying the resulting figure by 100,000. See Appendix V for the agency and population counts. (Table 16)

Offense Analysis

AGGRAVATED ASSAULT BY WEAPON

Of the aggravated assault offenses for which law enforcement agencies provided expanded data in 2019, 27.6 percent involved personal weapons (such as hands, feet, and fists); 25.2 percent were committed with firearms; 17.5 percent involved knives or other cutting instruments; and 29.8 percent involved other weapons. (Table 19)

PROPERTY CRIME

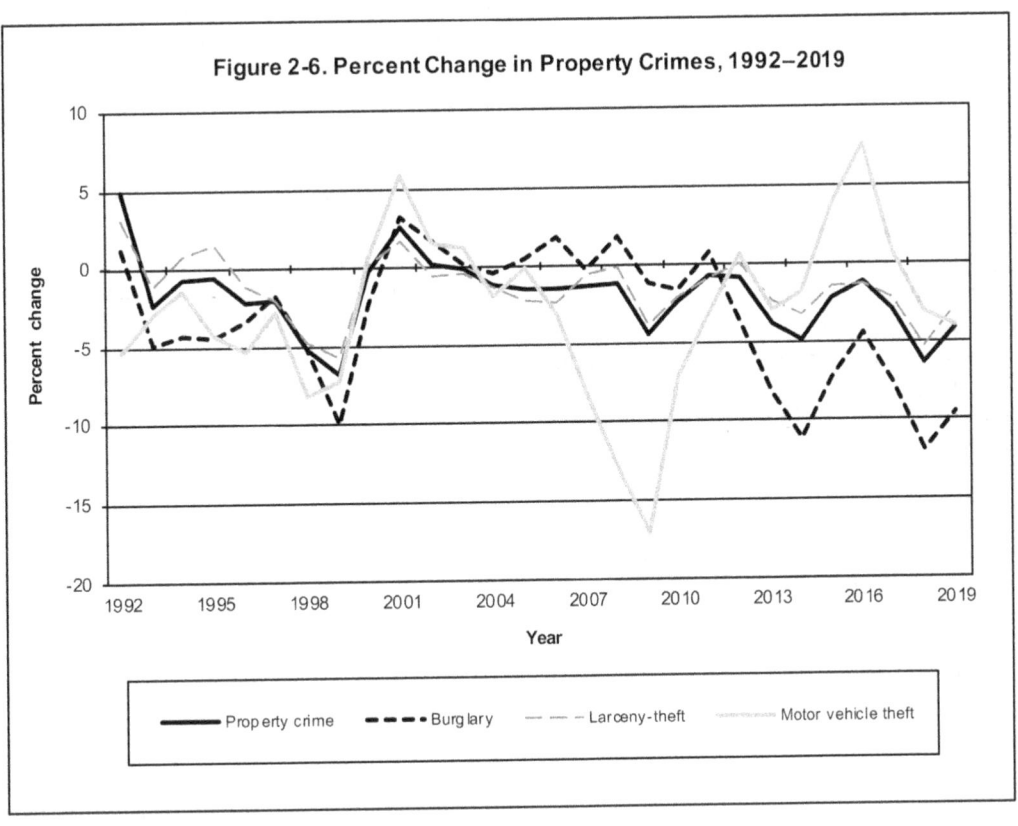

Figure 2-6. Percent Change in Property Crimes, 1992–2019

Definition

The UCR program's definition of property crime includes the offenses of burglary, larceny-theft, motor vehicle theft, and arson. The object of theft-type offenses is the taking of money or property without the use of force or threat of force against the victims. Property crime includes arson because the offense involves the destruction of property; however, arson victims may be subjected to force. Because of limited participation and the varying collection procedures conducted by local law enforcement agencies, only limited data are available for arson. Arson statistics are included in the trend, clearance, and arrest tables in *Crime in the United States*, but they are not included in any estimated volume data. More information on the expanded arson tables (which are available online but not included in this publication) can be found in Section I.

Data Collection

The data presented in *Crime in the United States* reflect the Hierarchy Rule, which counts only the most serious offense in a multiple-offense criminal incident. In descending order of severity, the violent crimes are murder and nonnegligent manslaughter, rape, robbery, and aggravated assault; these are followed by the property crimes of burglary, larceny-theft, and motor vehicle theft. The Hierarchy Rule does not apply to the offense of arson.

National Volume, Trends, and Rates

An estimated 6,925,677 property crimes were committed in the United States in 2019, representing a 4.1 percent decrease from the 2018 (2-year trend) estimate, a 13.7 percent decrease from the 2015 (5-year trend) estimate, and a 24.0 percent decrease from the 2010 (10-year trend) estimate. (Tables 1 and 1A)

From 2018 to 2019, motor vehicle theft decreased 4.0 percent; from 2015 to 2019, it increased 1.2 percent, and from 2010 to 2019, it decreased 2.4 percent. Larceny-theft decreased 18.0 percent from 2010 to 2019, 11.1 percent from 2015 to 2019, and 2.8 percent from 2018 to 2019. Burglary in 2019 declined 48.5 percent from 2010, 29.6 percent from 2015, and 9.5 percent from 2018. (Tables 1 and 1A)

The estimated property crime rate per 100,000 inhabitants in 2019 was 2,109.9 incidents per 100,000 people, a 4.5 percent decrease from the 2018 rate, a 15.6 percent decrease from the 2015 rate, and a 28.4 percent decrease from the 2010 rate. The rate of burglaries per 100,000 residents fell 51.4 percent from 2010 to 2019. The motor vehicle theft rates per 100,000 residents fell 8.0 percent from 2010 to 2019, and the larceny-theft rate declined 22.7 percent in that same timeframe. (Tables 1 and 1A)

Regional Offense Trends and Rates

The UCR program separates the United States into four regions: the Northeast, the Midwest, the South, and the West. (Geographic breakdowns can be found in Appendix IV.) Property crime data collected by the UCR program and aggregated by region reflected the following results.

NORTHEAST

The Northeast region accounted for 17.1 percent of the nation's population in 2019. The region also accounted for 10.9 percent of the nation's estimated number of property crimes in 2019. Law enforcement in the Northeast saw a 6.2 percent decrease in the estimated number of property crimes from 2018 to 2019. The property crime rate for the Northeast, estimated at 1,350.4 incidents per 100,000 inhabitants, was 6.1 percent less than the 2018 rate. (Tables 3 and 4)

MIDWEST

The Midwest, with 20.8 percent of the U.S. population in 2019, accounted for 19.1 percent of the nation's estimated number of property crimes. Law enforcement in the Midwest saw the number of property crimes decrease 4.8 percent from 2018 to 2019. The rate of property crime in the Midwest in 2019, estimated at 1,935.4 incidents per 100,000 inhabitants, represented a 4.9 percent decrease from the 2018 rate. (Tables 3 and 4)

SOUTH

The South, the nation's most populous region, accounted for 38.3 percent of the U.S. population in 2019. The region also accounted for an estimated 42.7 percent of the nation's property crimes. The South experienced a 2.7 percent decrease in its estimated number of property crimes from 2018 to 2019. The 2019 property crime rate, an estimated 2,355.3 incidents per 100,000 inhabitants, dropped 3.5 percent from the 2018 rate. (Tables 3 and 4)

WEST

In 2019, the West accounted for 23.9 percent of the nation's population. The West also accounted for 27.3 percent of the nation's estimated number of property crimes. From 2018 to 2019, the estimated number of property crimes in this region decreased 4.7 percent. The estimated property crime rate in the West in 2019, 2,411.7 incidents per 100,000 inhabitants, was a 5.4 percent decrease from the 2018 rate. (Tables 3 and 4)

Community Types

The UCR program aggregates data by three community types: metropolitan statistical areas (MSAs), cities outside metropolitan areas, and nonmetropolitan counties. (Additional in-depth information regarding community types can be found in Appendix IV.) In 2019, 86.0 percent of the U.S. population lived in MSAs and had 89.2 percent of all property crimes. The property crime rate for MSAs was 2,187.5 per 100,000 inhabitants. Cities outside metropolitan areas, which accounted for 5.7 percent of the total population in 2019 and 6.8 percent of property crimes, had a property crime rate of 2,500.3 per 100,000 inhabitants. Nonmetropolitan counties, with 8.3 percent of the nation's population in 2019 and 4.1 percent of property crimes, had a property crime rate of 1,034.1 per 100,000 inhabitants. (Table 2)

Population Groups: Trends and Rates

The UCR program organizes the agencies that contribute data into population groups, which include cities, metropolitan counties, and nonmetropolitan counties. (Appendix IV provides further details about these groups.) From 2018 to 2019, law enforcement in the nation's cities collectively reported a 3.5 percent decrease in the number of property crimes. All city groups experienced decreases in the number of property crimes; cities with 10,000 to 24,999 residents had the greatest decline, 5.8 percent. Metropolitan counties also experienced a decrease of 5.5 percent from 2018 to 2019, while property crime in nonmetropolitan counties and suburban areas dropped 7.0 and 5.0 percent, respectively. (Table 12)

The nation's cities collectively had a property crime rate of 2,492.2 incidents per 100,000 inhabitants in 2019, ranging from a high of 3,701.9 per 100,000 inhabitants in cities with 500,000 to 999,999 residents to a low of 1,947.6 per 100,000 inhabitants in cities with 10,000 to 24,999 residents. Metropolitan counties had a rate of 1,396.9 incidents per 100,000 inhabitants, and nonmetropolitan counties had a rate of 991.6 incidents per 100,000 inhabitants. The rate was 1,593.5 in suburban areas. (Table 16)

Due to a system upgrade in 2019, the FBI now calculates rates for each offense based on the individual offenses and population published for each agency in tables 8-11. (Previous to 2019, when agencies were published in tables 8-11, but they had one or two offenses removed from publication due to not meeting UCR publication guidelines, the agency's data was not used to calculate rates for this table.) The FBI derived the offense rates by dividing the individual offense counts by the individual populations covered by contributing agencies for which 12 months of publishable data were supplied and then multiplying the resulting figure by 100,000. See Appendix V for the agency and population counts. (Table 16)

Offense Analysis

The estimated dollar loss attributing to property crimes in 2019 was $15.8 billion. In 2019, the average dollar value per motor vehicle stolen in the United States was $8,886. The average dollar value of property taken during burglaries was $2,611, and during larceny-thefts, $1,162. Arson had an average dollar loss of $16,371. Arsons of industrial/manufacturing structures had the highest average dollar loss ($190,336). (Tables 1 and 23; Expanded Arson Table 2)

BURGLARY

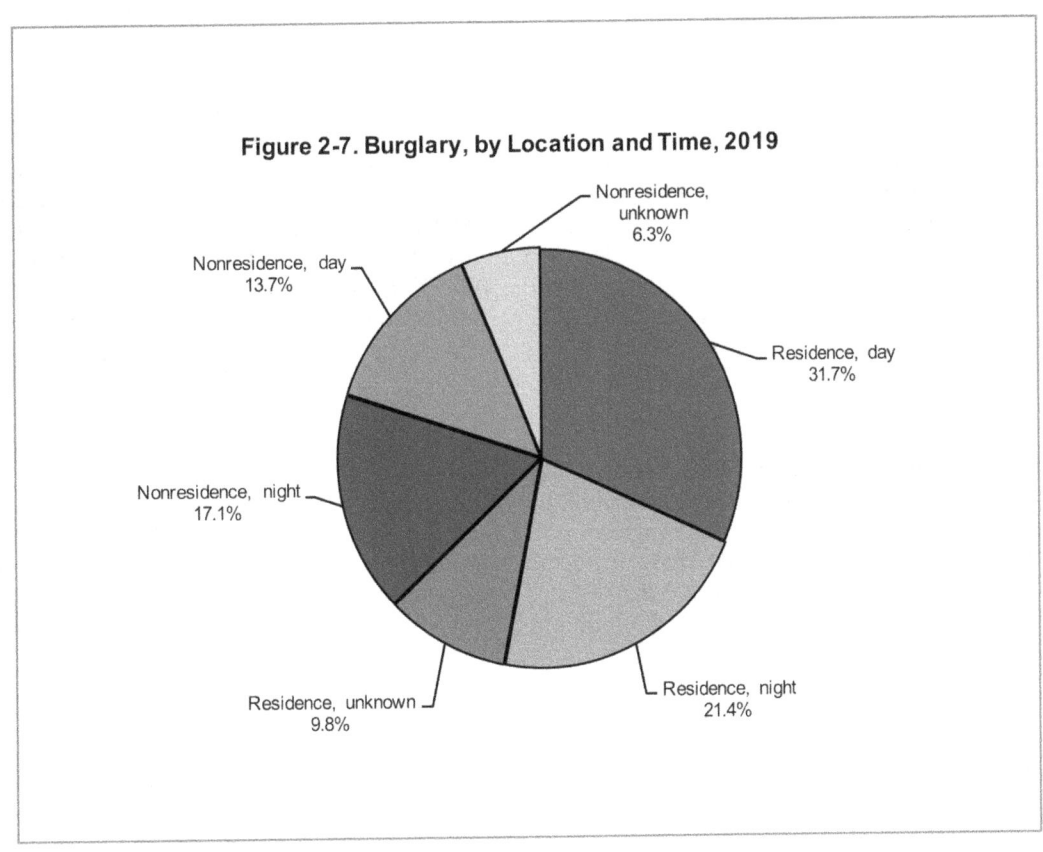

Figure 2-7. Burglary, by Location and Time, 2019

- Nonresidence, unknown 6.3%
- Residence, day 31.7%
- Nonresidence, day 13.7%
- Nonresidence, night 17.1%
- Residence, unknown 9.8%
- Residence, night 21.4%

Definition

The UCR program defines burglary as the unlawful entry of a structure to commit a felony or theft. To classify an offense as a burglary, the use of force to gain entry need not have occurred. The program has three subclassifications for burglary: forcible entry, unlawful entry where no force is used, and attempted forcible entry. The UCR definition of "structure" includes, but is not limited to, apartments, barns, house trailers or houseboats (when used as permanent dwellings), offices, railroad cars (but not automobiles), stables, and vessels (such as ships).

National Volume, Trends, and Rate

In 2019, there were an estimated 1,117,696 burglaries—a decrease of 9.5 percent when compared with 2018 data. There was a decrease of 31.2 percent in the number of burglaries in 2019 when compared with the 2015 estimate, and a decrease of 51.4 percent when compared with the 2010 estimate. Burglary accounted for 16.1 percent of the estimated number of property crimes committed in 2019. The burglary rate for the United States in 2019 was 340.5 incidents per 100,000 inhabitants, a 9.9 percent decrease from the 2018 rate. (Tables 1 and 1A)

Regional Offense Trends and Rates

The UCR program divides the United States into four regions: the Northeast, the Midwest, the South, and the West. (Details regarding these regions can be found in Appendix IV.) An analysis of burglary data by region showed the following details.

NORTHEAST

In 2019, 17.1 percent of the nation's population lived in the Northeast. This region accounted for 8.4 percent of the estimated total number of burglary offenses in the nation in 2019. The region's burglary rate, an estimated 167.5 offenses per 100,000 inhabitants, represented a decrease of 13.4 percent from the 2018 rate. The number of incidents declined 13.5 percent from 2018 to 2019. (Tables 3 and 4)

MIDWEST

The Midwest accounted for 20.8 percent of the nation's population in 2019. This region accounted for 19.3 percent of the nation's estimated number of burglaries. In this region, the estimated number of burglaries dropped 10.3 percent from 2018 to 2019. The Midwest had a burglary rate of 315.2 offenses per 100,000 inhabitants, a 10.4 percent decrease from the 2018 rate. (Tables 3 and 4)

SOUTH

The South, the nation's most highly populated region (38.3 percent of all inhabitants), had the most burglaries in 2019 (an estimated 501,817 incidents); however, this represented an 8.4 percent drop from its estimate in 2018. This region accounted for 44.9 percent of all burglaries in the United States. The estimated rate of burglary in the South was 399.6 incidents per 100,000 inhabitants, a 9.2 percent decrease from the 2018 rate. (Tables 3 and 4)

WEST

The West accounted for 23.9 percent of the nation's population in 2019. This region accounted for an estimated 27.4 percent of the nation's burglaries. The region's burglary rate was 391.4, a 10.0 percent decrease from the 2018 rate. The total number of burglaries (306,686) represented a 9.4 percent decrease from the 2018 estimate. (Tables 3 and 4)

Community Types

The UCR program aggregates data by three community types: metropolitan statistical areas (MSAs), cities outside MSAs, and nonmetropolitan counties. (See Appendix IV for more information regarding community types.) In 2019, 86.0 percent of the U.S. population lived in MSAs, and an estimated 85.2 percent of all burglaries occurred in this type of community. Inhabitants of cities outside MSAs accounted for 5.7 percent of the total population in 2019 and 7.4 percent of the estimated number of burglaries; nonmetropolitan counties, with 8.3 percent of the U.S. population, accounted for the remaining 7.4 percent of all burglaries. The burglary rates per 100,000 inhabitants were 337.2 in MSAs, 442.2 in cities outside MSAs, and 304.9 in nonmetropolitan counties. (Table 2)

Population Groups: Trends and Rates

In addition to analyzing data by region and community type, the UCR program aggregates crime statistics by population groups. Cities are categorized into six groups based on the number of inhabitants; counties are categorized into two groups, metropolitan and nonmetropolitan. (Appendix IV offers further details regarding these population groups.)

An examination of data from law enforcement agencies showed that the nation's cities experienced a collective 9.4 percent decrease in burglaries from 2018 to 2019. Burglaries decreased in all city groups and subsets, with cities with 10,000 to 24,999 inhabitants posting the greatest decrease (11.9 percent). The volume of burglaries decreased 10.7 percent in metropolitan counties, 8.9 percent in nonmetropolitan counties, and 10.6 percent in suburban areas. (Table 12)

The UCR program calculates burglary rates for population groups from the information provided by participating agencies that submitted all 12 months of offense data for the year. In 2019, the nation's cities had 368.1 offenses per 100,000 inhabitants. Cities with 500,000 to 999,999 inhabitants had the highest burglary rate at 577.9 incidents per 100,000 inhabitants. Cities with 25,000 to 49,999 inhabitants had the lowest burglary rate—284.1 incidents per 100,000 inhabitants. Metropolitan counties had a rate of 257.1 per 100,000 inhabitants, and nonmetropolitan counties had a rate of 290.3 per 100,000 inhabitants. The rate in suburban areas was 251.0 per 100,000 inhabitants. (Table 16)

Due to a system upgrade in 2019, the FBI now calculates rates for each offense based on the individual offenses and population published for each agency in tables 8-11. (Previous to 2019, when agencies were published in tables 8-11, but they had one or two offenses removed from publication due to not meeting UCR publication guidelines, the agency's data was not used to calculate rates for this table.) The FBI derived the offense rates by dividing the individual offense counts by the individual populations covered by contributing agencies for which 12 months of publishable data were supplied and then multiplying the resulting figure by 100,000. See Appendix V for the agency and population counts. (Table 16)

Offense Analysis

The UCR program requests that participating law enforcement agencies provide details regarding the nature of burglaries in their jurisdictions, such as type of entry, type of structure, time of day, and dollar loss associated with each offense.

Of all burglaries in 2019, 55.7 percent involved forcible entry, 37.8 percent were unlawful entries (without force), and 6.5 percent comprised forcible entry attempts. (Table 19)

Victims of burglary offenses suffered an estimated $3.0 billion in lost property in 2019; overall, the average dollar loss per burglary offense was $2,661. (Tables 1 and 23)

As in the past, burglars targeted residences more often than nonresidential structures. In 2019, burglaries of residential properties accounted for 62.8 percent of all burglary offenses. Of the burglaries for which time of day could be established, most burglaries of residences (33.7 percent of all reported burglaries) occurred during the day, while most burglaries of nonresidential structures (17.1 percent of all reported burglaries) occurred at night. (Table 23)

LARCENY-THEFT

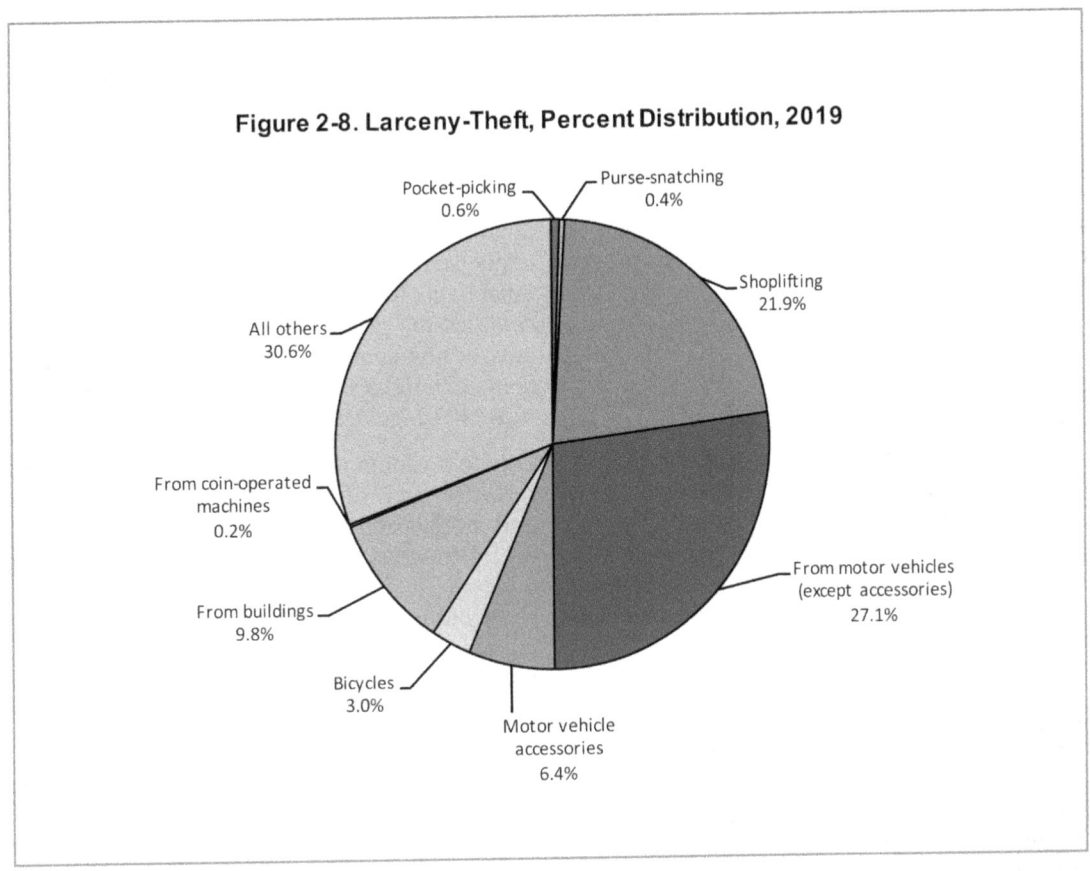

Figure 2-8. Larceny-Theft, Percent Distribution, 2019

Pocket-picking 0.6%

Purse-snatching 0.4%

Shoplifting 21.9%

All others 30.6%

From motor vehicles (except accessories) 27.1%

From coin-operated machines 0.2%

From buildings 9.8%

Bicycles 3.0%

Motor vehicle accessories 6.4%

Definition

The UCR program defines larceny-theft as the unlawful taking, carrying, leading, or riding away of property from the possession or constructive possession of another. Examples are thefts of bicycles, motor vehicle parts and accessories, shoplifting, pocket picking, or the stealing of any property or article not taken by force and violence or by fraud. Attempted larcenies are included. Embezzlement, confidence games, forgery, check fraud, and so on, are excluded from this category.

National Volume, Trends, and Rates

Larceny-thefts accounted for an estimated 73.4 percent of property crimes in 2019—an estimated 5,086,096 larceny-thefts nationwide. The estimated number of larceny-thefts declined 2.8 percent from 2018 to 2019. The 2019 estimate showed an 11.1 percent decline from the 2015 data and an 18.0 percent decrease from the 2010 estimate. The trend data also showed decreases in the larceny-theft rates per 100,000 inhabitants during these periods. The rate of larceny-thefts (1,549.5 per 100,000 inhabitants in 2019) declined 3.3 percent from 2018 to 2019 and 22.7 percent from 2010 to 2019. (Tables 1 and 1A)

Regional Offense Trends and Rates

The UCR program defines four regions within the United States: the Northeast, the Midwest, the South, and the West. (See Appendix IV for a geographical description of each region.)

NORTHEAST

The Northeast was the region with the smallest proportion (17.1 percent) of the U.S. population in 2019. The region also experienced the fewest larceny-thefts in the country, accounting for only 12.0 percent of all larceny-thefts. The estimated number of offenses in 2019 (611,369) represented a 4.9 percent decline from 2018, and the estimated rate—1,092.1 incidents per 100,000 inhabitants—represented a 4.7 percent decline. (Tables 3 and 4)

MIDWEST

With 20.8 percent of the U.S. population in 2019, the Midwest accounted for an estimated 19.2 percent of the nation's larceny-thefts (the same proportion as in 2018). The estimated number of offenses (977,491) declined 3.9 percent from the 2018 total, and the estimated rate of occurrence (1,732.4 incidents per 100,000 inhabitants) declined 4.0 percent. (Tables 3 and 4)

South

With nearly two-fifths of the U.S. population in 2019 (38.3 percent), the South had the nation's highest proportion of larceny-theft offenses: an estimated 42.8 percent. Estimated offenses in this region in 2019 totaled 2,175,494, a 1.7 percent decrease from the 2018 estimate. The South's larceny-theft rate—estimated at 1,732.4 offenses per 100,000 inhabitants—decreased 2.5 percent from the 2018 estimate. (Tables 3 and 4)

WEST

In 2019, an estimated 23.9 percent of the U.S. population lived in the West. This region was also where 26.0 percent of the nation's estimated number of larceny-thefts took place. Occurrences of larceny-theft decreased 2.7 percent from 2018 to 2019 to an estimated total of 1,321,742 offenses. The region's larceny-theft rate, estimated at 1,687.0 offenses per 100,000 inhabitants, represented a decrease of 3.4 percent from the 2018 rate. (Tables 3 and 4)

Community Types

The UCR program aggregates data for three community types: metropolitan statistical areas (MSAs), cities outside MSAs, and nonmetropolitan counties outside MSAs. MSAs include a central city or urbanized area with at least 50,000 inhabitants, as well as the county that contains the principal city and other adjacent counties that share a high degree of social and economic integration as measured through commuting. Cities outside MSAs are mostly incorporated areas, and nonmetropolitan counties are composed of unincorporated areas. (See Appendix IV for more information regarding community types.)

In 2019, MSAs were home to an estimated 86.0 percent of the nation's population and experienced 89.7 percent of the nation's larceny-theft incidents. Cities outside MSAs accounted for 5.7 percent of the U.S. population and 7.0 percent of larceny-theft offenses. Nonmetropolitan counties, which were home to 8.3 percent of the nation's population, accounted for 3.3 percent of the estimated number of larceny-theft offenses. The larceny-theft rates per 100,000 inhabitants were 1,615.8 in MSAs, 1,899.2 in cities outside MSAs, and 618.6 in nonmetropolitan counties. (Table 2)

Population Groups: Trends and Rates

In cities, collectively, occurrences of larceny-theft decreased 2.2 percent between 2018 and 2019. Cities with 10,000 to 24,999 inhabitants experienced the greatest decrease (4.7 percent). Larceny-theft increased by 0.1 percent in cities with 250,000 or more inhabitants, and this crime showed increases in all related subsets except for cities with 500,000 to 999,999 inhabitants, where a 2.1 percent decrease was registered. Larceny-theft continued to show decline in counties and suburban areas—nonmetropolitan counties experienced the greatest drop in larceny thefts, decreasing 7.4 percent, followed by metropolitan counties and suburban areas, with larceny-theft decreasing 4.2 and 3.9 percent, respectively. (Table 12)

Based on reports of larceny-theft offenses from U.S. law enforcement agencies that submitted 12 months of complete data for 2019, this offense occurred at a rate of 1,569.2 offenses per 100,000 inhabitants. The collective rate for cities was 1,862.7 offenses per 100,000 inhabitants. Among city population groups and subsets, cities with 500,000 to 999,000 inhabitants had the highest larceny-theft rate, 2,668.2 incidents per 100,000 inhabitants. Cities with 10,000 to 24,999 inhabitants had the lowest rate, at 1,525.0. In metropolitan counties, the rate was 990.8 incidents per 100,000 inhabitants; in nonmetropolitan counties, the rate was 593.4 incidents per 100,000 inhabitants. The rate in suburban areas was 1,197.3 incidents per 100,000 inhabitants. (Table 16)

Due to a system upgrade in 2019, the FBI now calculates rates for each offense based on the individual offenses and population published for each agency in tables 8-11. (Previous to 2019, when agencies were published in tables 8-11, but they had one or two offenses removed from publication due to not meeting UCR publication guidelines, the agency's data was not used to calculate rates for this table.) The FBI derived the offense rates by dividing the individual offense counts by the individual populations covered by contributing agencies for which 12 months of publishable data were supplied and then multiplying the resulting figure by 100,000. See Appendix V for the agency and population counts. (Table 16)

Offense Analysis

DISTRIBUTION

Table 23 provides a further breakdown of larceny-theft offenses, including shoplifting, thefts from buildings, thefts of motor vehicle accessories, thefts of bicycles, thefts from coin-operated machines, purse snatching, and pocket picking. The "all other" category, which includes the less-defined types of larceny-theft, accounted for 30.6 percent of all offenses in 2019.

LOSS BY DOLLAR VALUE

Larceny-theft offenses cost victims an estimated $5.9 billion dollars in 2019. The average value of property stolen was $1,162 per offense, $9 more than in 2018. Larceny-theft from buildings had the highest average dollar loss per offense at $1,663. Pocket picking had an average dollar loss of $1,235 per offense; thefts from motor vehicles (except accessories), $1,012; thefts of motor vehicle accessories, $690; purse snatching, $651; thefts from coin-operated machines, $829; thefts of bicycles, $569; and shoplifting, $338. (Tables 1 and 23)

Offenses in which the stolen property was valued at more than $200 accounted for 47.3 percent of all larceny-thefts in 2019. Table 23 provides further analysis, including the average dollar value per offense of all offenses in the overall category of property crime. (Table 23)

MOTOR VEHICLE THEFT

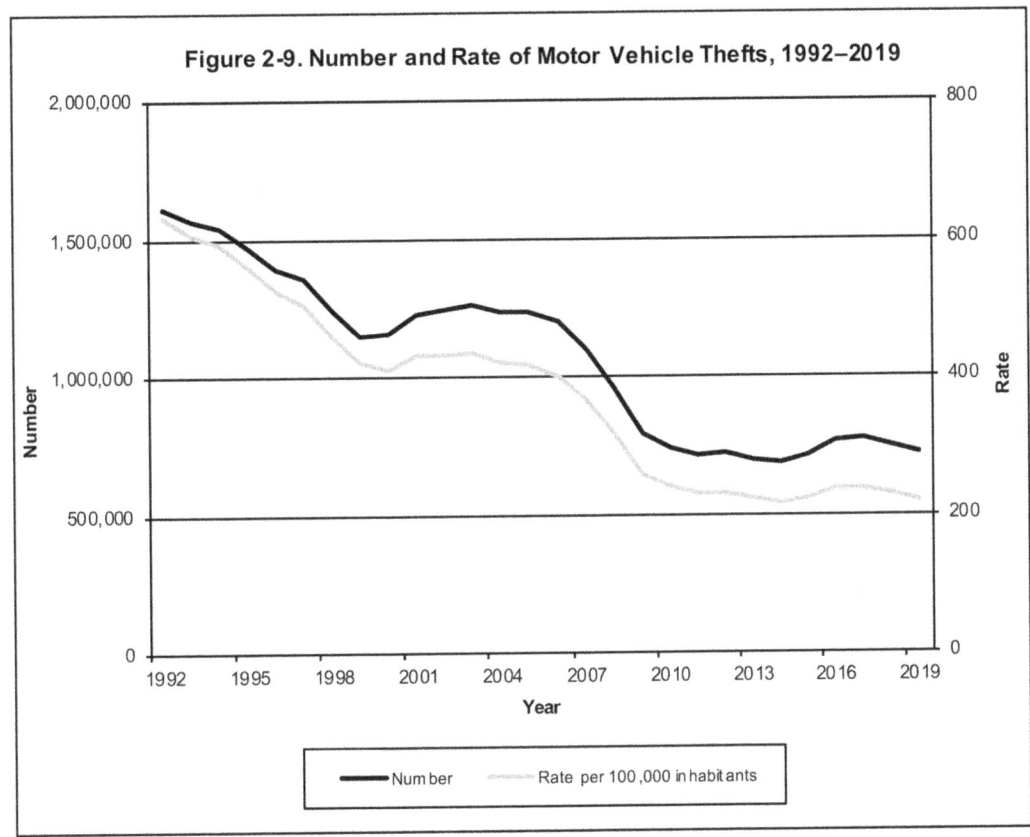

Figure 2-9. Number and Rate of Motor Vehicle Thefts, 1992–2019

Definition

The UCR program defines motor vehicle theft as the theft or attempted theft of a motor vehicle. The offense includes the stealing of automobiles, trucks, buses, motorcycles, snowmobiles, etc. The taking of a motor vehicle for temporary use by a person or persons with lawful access is excluded.

National Volume, Trends, and Rates

In 2019, an estimated 721,885 motor vehicle thefts took place in the United States. The estimated number of motor vehicle thefts decreased 4.0 percent when compared with data from 2018 but increased 1.2 percent when compared with 2015 figures. Occurrences decreased 2.4 percent when compared with 2010 figures. (Tables1 and 1A)

The estimated rate of motor vehicle theft in 2019 was 219.9 incidents per 100,000 inhabitants. The 2019 rate was 4.4 percent less than the 2018 rate, 1.0 percent less than the 2015 rate, and 8.0 percent lower than the 2010 rate. (Tables 1 and 1A)

Regional Offense Trends and Rates

In order to analyze crime by geographic area, the UCR program divides the United States into four regions:

the Northeast, the Midwest, the South, and the West. (Appendix IV provides a map delineating the regions.) This section provides a regional overview of motor vehicle theft.

NORTHEAST

The Northeast accounted for an estimated 17.1 percent of the nation's population in 2019. The region also accounted for an estimated 7.0 percent of its motor vehicle thefts. An estimated 50,801 motor vehicle thefts occurred in the Northeast in 2019, a 6.9 percent drop in occurrences from 2018. The estimated rate of 90.7 motor vehicle thefts per 100,000 inhabitants in the Northeast in 2019 represented a 6.8 percent decline from the 2018 rate. (Tables 3 and 4)

MIDWEST

An estimated 20.8 percent of the country's population resided in the Midwest in 2019. The region accounted for 17.9 percent of the nation's motor vehicle thefts. The Midwest had an estimated 129,542 motor vehicle thefts in 2019, a decrease of 2.1 percent from the previous year's total. The motor vehicle theft rate was estimated at 189.6 motor vehicles stolen per 100,000 inhabitants, a decrease of 2.2 percent from the 2018 rate. (Tables 3 and 4)

SOUTH

The South, the nation's most populous region, was home to an estimated 38.3 percent of the U.S. population in 2018 and accounted for 38.8 percent of the nation's motor vehicle thefts. The estimated 280,447 motor vehicle thefts in the South represented a 0.5 percent increase from the 2018 estimate. Motor vehicles in the South were stolen at an estimated rate of 223.3 offenses per 100,000 inhabitants in 2019, a rate that was down 0.3 percent from the 2018 rate. (Tables 3 and 4)

WEST

With approximately 23.9 percent of the U.S. population in 2019, the West accounted for 36.2 percent of all motor vehicle thefts in the nation. An estimated 261,095 motor vehicle thefts occurred in this region. This number represented an 8.7 percent decrease from the previous year's estimate. The region's 2019 rate of 333.3 motor vehicles stolen per 100,000 inhabitants was 9.3 percent lower than the 2018 rate. (Tables 3 and 4)

COMMUNITY TYPES

The UCR program aggregates data by three community types: metropolitan statistical areas (MSAs), cities outside MSAs, and nonmetropolitan counties. MSAs are areas that include a principal city or urbanized area with at least 50,000 inhabitants and the county that contains the principal city and other adjacent counties that have, as defined by the U.S. Office of Management and Budget, a high degree of economic and social integration.

In 2019, the vast majority (86.0 percent) of the U.S. population resided in MSAs, where approximately 91.7 percent of motor vehicle thefts occurred. For 2019, the UCR program estimated an overall rate of 234.5 motor vehicles stolen per 100,000 MSA inhabitants. Cities outside MSAs, with 5.7 percent of the U.S. population, accounted for 4.1 percent of motor vehicle thefts, and nonmetropolitan counties, with 8.3 percent of the population, accounted for 4.2 percent of motor vehicle thefts. The UCR program estimated a 2019 rate of 158.9 motor vehicles stolen for every 100,000 inhabitants in cities outside MSAs and a rate of 110.5 motor vehicles stolen per 100,000 inhabitants in nonmetropolitan counties. (Table 2)

POPULATION GROUPS: TRENDS AND RATES

The UCR program aggregates data by various population groups, which include cities, metropolitan counties, and nonmetropolitan counties. (A definition of these groups can be found in Appendix IV.)

In cities, collectively, the number of motor vehicle thefts decreased 4.3 percent from 2018 to 2019. Occurrences dropped in all groups and. subsets. Cities with 100,000 to 249,999 residents experienced the greatest decline at 7.0 percent. Nonmetropolitan counties experienced an increase of 0.4 percent, suburban areas experienced a decrease of 3.8 percent, and metropolitan counties experienced a decrease of 4.1 percent. (Table 12)

In 2019, cities had a collective motor vehicle theft rate of 265.5 per 100,000 inhabitants. Among the population groups and subsets, cities with 500,000 to 999,999 inhabitants experienced the highest rate of motor vehicle thefts with 494.2 motor vehicle thefts per 100,000 inhabitants. Cities with populations of 10,000 to 24,999 residents had the lowest rate of motor vehicle theft with 140.7 incidents per 100,000 in population. Within the county groups, metropolitan counties had a rate of 151.1 motor vehicles stolen per 100,000 inhabitants, while nonmetropolitan counties had a rate of 108.4 incidents per 100,000 inhabitants. Suburban areas had a rate of 147.3 per 100,000 inhabitants. (Table 16)

Due to a system upgrade in 2019, the FBI now calculates rates for each offense based on the individual offenses and population published for each agency in tables 8-11. (Previous to 2019, when agencies were published in tables 8-11, but they had one or two offenses removed from publication due to not meeting UCR publication guidelines, the agency's data was not used to calculate rates for this table.) The FBI derived the offense rates by dividing the individual offense counts by the individual populations covered by contributing agencies for which 12 months of publishable data were supplied and then multiplying the resulting figure by 100,000. See Appendix V for the agency and population counts. (Table 16)

Offense Analysis

Based on the reports of law enforcement agencies, the UCR program estimated the combined value of motor vehicles stolen nationwide in 2019 at $6.4 billion. In 2019, the average dollar value per motor vehicle stolen in the United States was $8,886. Automobiles were, by far, the most frequently stolen vehicles, accounting for 74.5 percent of all vehicles stolen. Trucks and buses accounted for 16.2 percent of stolen vehicles, and other vehicles accounted for 9.3 percent of stolen vehicles. (Tables 1 and 23; Expanded Motor Vehicle Theft Table)

By type of vehicle, automobiles were stolen at a rate of 171.9 cars per 100,000 inhabitants in 2019. Trucks and buses were stolen at a rate of 37.5 vehicles per 100,000 inhabitants, and other types of vehicles were stolen at a rate of 21.4 vehicles per 100,000 inhabitants. (Table 19)

ARSON

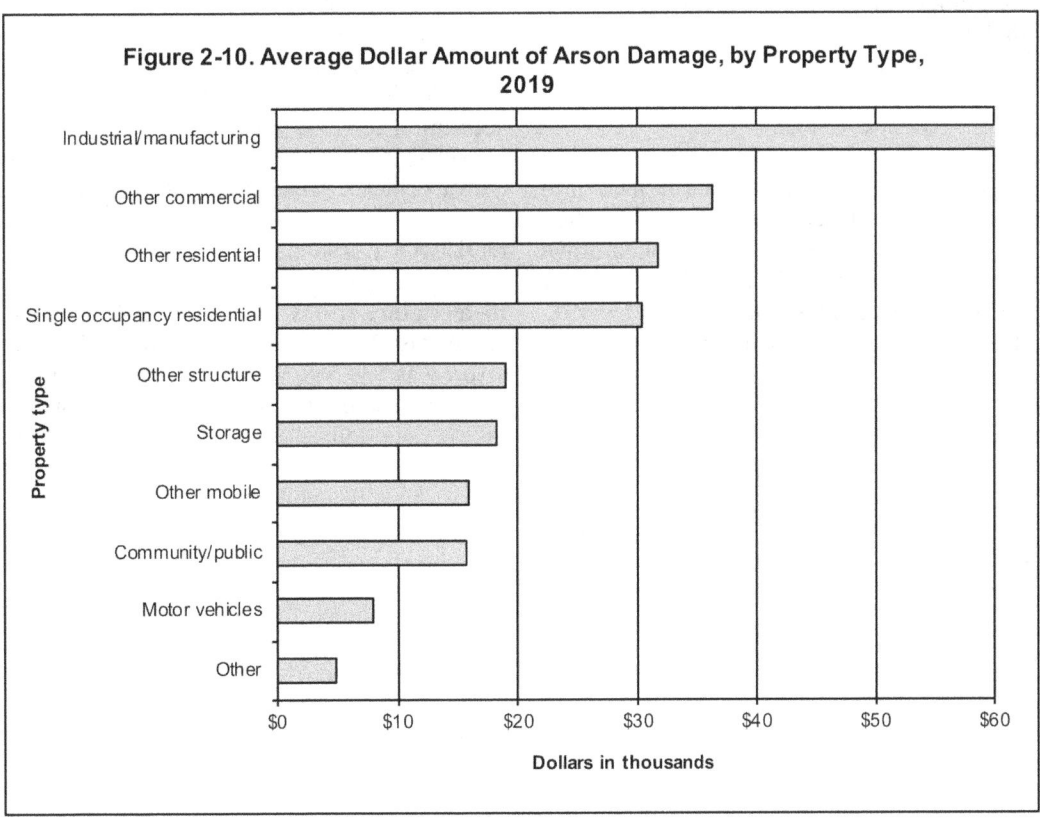

Figure 2-10. Average Dollar Amount of Arson Damage, by Property Type, 2019

Definition

The UCR program defines arson as any willful or malicious burning or attempt to burn (with or without intent to defraud) a dwelling house, public building, motor vehicle, aircraft, or personal property of another, etc.

Data Collection

Only fires that investigators determined were willfully set (not fires labeled as "suspicious" or "of unknown origin") are included in this arson data collection. Points to consider regarding arson statistics include:

National offense rates per 100,000 inhabitants (found in Tables 1, 2, and 4) do not include arson data; the FBI presents rates for arson separately. Arson rates are calculated based upon data received from all law enforcement agencies that provide the UCR program with data for 12 complete months.

Arson data collection does not include estimates for arson, because the degree of reporting arson offenses varies from agency to agency. Because of this unevenness of reporting, arson offenses are excluded from Tables 1 through 7, all of which contain offense estimations.

The number of arsons reported by individual law enforcement agencies is available in Tables 8 through 11. Arson trend data (which indicate year-to-year changes) can be found in Tables 12 through 15.

Population Groups: Trends and Rates

The number of arsons reported in cities 2019 was 3.2 percent lower than the number reported in 2018. Among the population groups labeled *city,* the group with 50,000 to 99,999 inhabitants reported the largest decrease (6.9 percent). Cities with 250,000 to 499,999 inhabitants showed the only increase (2.6 percent). Agencies in the nation's metropolitan counties reported an 11.5 percent decrease in the number of arsons, while those in nonmetropolitan counties reported a 7.5 percent decrease from 2017 to 2018. Those in suburban areas reported an 8.5 percent decline. (Table 12)

Arson rates in this paragraph were based on information received from 12,375 agencies that provided 12 months of complete arson data to the UCR program. An examination of data indicated that in 2019, the highest rate among city groups and subsets—23.4 arsons per 100,000 inhabitants—was reported in cities with 250,000 to 499,999 inhabitants. Cities with 10,000 to 24,999 inhabitants had the lowest rate of arson at 8.8 offenses per 100,000 inhabitants. Metropolitan counties had 7.7 arsons per 100,000 inhabitants, and nonmetropolitan counties had 8.9 arsons per 100,000 inhabitants. The rate in suburban areas was 8.0 arsons per 100,000 inhabitants. (Expanded Arson Table 1)

Offense Analysis

The UCR program breaks down arson offenses into three property categories: structural, mobile, and other. In addition, the structural property type is broken down into seven types of structures, and the mobile property type consists of two subgroupings. The program also collects information on the estimated dollar value of the damaged property.

Property Type

Arsons for the structural property type comprised 42.2 percent of arsons, while arsons for the mobile property type comprised 22.6 percent of arsons and 35.2 percent of arsons involved other types of property (such as crops, timber, fences, etc.). Of the arsons involving structures, 61.9 percent involved residential properties. Of the residential arsons, 72.3 percent were single-occupancy residences. Approximately 12.7 percent of structures were not in use when the arson occurred. Mobile arsons accounted for 22.6 percent of all arsons. Within this category, 94.0 percent of offenses involved the burning of motor vehicles. (Table 15 and Expanded Arson Table 2)

DOLLAR LOSS

In monetary terms, the average dollar loss in 2019 for arson was $16,371. The average dollar loss for a structural arson was $29,568. Within the structural arson category, the industrial/manufacturing subcategory had the highest average dollar loss at $190,336. Within that same category, single-occupancy dwellings had an average dollar loss of $30,308. Mobile property had an average dollar loss of $8,526. Other property types had an average dollar loss of $4,836. (Expanded Arson Table 2)

Table 1. Crime in the United States, by Volume and Rate Per 100,000 Inhabitants, 2000–2019

(Number, rate per 100,000 population.)

Year	Population[1]	Violent crime[2]		Murder and nonnegligent manslaughter		Rape (revised definition)[3]		Rape (legacy definition)[4]		Robbery		Aggravated assault	
		Number	Rate	Number	Rate	Number	Rate	Number	Rate	Number	Rate	Number	Rate
2000	281,421,906	1,425,486	506.5	15,586	5.5	X	X	90,178	32.0	408,016	145.0	911,706	324.0
2001[5]	285,317,559	1,439,480	504.5	16,037	5.6	X	X	90,863	31.8	423,557	148.5	909,023	318.6
2002	287,973,924	1,423,677	494.4	16,229	5.6	X	X	95,235	33.1	420,806	146.1	891,407	309.5
2003	290,788,976	1,383,676	475.8	16,528	5.7	X	X	93,883	32.3	414,235	142.5	859,030	295.4
2004	293,656,842	1,360,088	463.2	16,148	5.5	X	X	95,089	32.4	401,470	136.7	847,381	288.6
2005	296,507,061	1,390,745	469.0	16,740	5.6	X	X	94,347	31.8	417,438	140.8	862,220	290.8
2006	299,398,484	1,435,123	479.3	17,309	5.8	X	X	94,472	31.6	449,246	150.0	874,096	292.0
2007	301,621,157	1,422,970	471.8	17,128	5.7	X	X	92,160	30.6	447,324	148.3	866,358	287.2
2008	304,059,724	1,394,461	458.6	16,465	5.4	X	X	90,750	29.8	443,563	145.9	843,683	277.5
2009	307,006,550	1,325,896	431.9	15,399	5.0	X	X	89,241	29.1	408,742	133.1	812,514	264.7
2010	309,330,219	1,251,248	404.5	14,722	4.8	X	X	85,593	27.7	369,089	119.3	781,844	252.8
2011	311,587,816	1,206,005	387.1	14,661	4.7	X	X	84,175	27.0	354,746	113.9	752,423	241.5
2012	313,873,685	1,217,057	387.8	14,856	4.7	X	X	85,141	27.1	355,051	113.1	762,009	242.8
2013	316,497,531	1,168,298	369.1	14,319	4.5	113,695	35.9	82,109	25.9	345,093	109.0	726,777	229.6
2014	318,907,401	1,153,022	361.6	14,164	4.4	118,027	37.0	84,864	26.6	322,905	101.3	731,089	229.2
2015	320,896,618	1,199,310	373.7	15,883	4.9	126,134	39.3	91,261	28.4	328,109	102.2	764,057	238.1
2016	323,405,935	1,250,162	386.6	17,413	5.4	132,414	40.9	96,970	30.0	332,797	102.9	802,982	248.3
2017	325,147,121	1,247,917	383.8	17,294	5.3	135,666	41.7	99,708	30.7	320,596	98.6	810,319	249.2
2018[6]	326,687,501	1,209,997	370.4	16,374	5.0	143,765	44.0	101,363	31.0	281,278	86.1	810,982	248.2
2019	328,239,523	1,203,808	366.7	16,425	5.0	139,815	42.6	98,213	29.9	267,988	81.6	821,182	250.2

Table 1. Crime in the United States, by Volume and Rate Per 100,000 Inhabitants, 2000–2019—Continued

(Number, rate per 100,000 population.)

Year	Property crime		Burglary		Larceny-theft		Motor vehicle theft	
	Number	Rate	Number	Rate	Number	Rate	Number	Rate
2000	10,182,584	3,618.3	2,050,992	728.8	6,971,590	2,477.3	1,160,002	412.2
2001⁵	10,437,189	3,658.1	2,116,531	741.8	7,092,267	2,485.7	1,228,391	430.5
2002	10,455,277	3,630.6	2,151,252	747.0	7,057,379	2,450.7	1,246,646	432.9
2003	10,442,862	3,591.2	2,154,834	741.0	7,026,802	2,416.5	1,261,226	433.7
2004	10,319,386	3,514.1	2,144,446	730.3	6,937,089	2,362.3	1,237,851	421.5
2005	10,174,754	3,431.5	2,155,448	726.9	6,783,447	2,287.8	1,235,859	416.8
2006	10,019,601	3,346.6	2,194,993	733.1	6,626,363	2,213.2	1,198,245	400.2
2007	9,882,212	3,276.4	2,190,198	726.1	6,591,542	2,185.4	1,100,472	364.9
2008	9,774,152	3,214.6	2,228,887	733.0	6,586,206	2,166.1	959,059	315.4
2009	9,337,060	3,041.3	2,203,313	717.7	6,338,095	2,064.5	795,652	259.2
2010	9,112,625	2,945.9	2,168,459	701.0	6,204,601	2,005.8	739,565	239.1
2011	9,052,743	2,905.4	2,185,140	701.3	6,151,095	1,974.1	716,508	230.0
2012	9,001,992	2,868.0	2,109,932	672.2	6,168,874	1,965.4	723,186	230.4
2013	8,651,892	2,733.6	1,932,139	610.5	6,019,465	1,901.9	700,288	221.3
2014	8,209,010	2,574.1	1,713,153	537.2	5,809,054	1,821.5	686,803	215.4
2015	8,024,115	2,500.5	1,587,564	494.7	5,723,488	1,783.6	713,063	222.2
2016	7,928,530	2,451.6	1,516,405	468.9	5,644,835	1,745.4	767,290	237.3
2017	7,682,988	2,362.9	1,397,045	429.7	5,513,000	1,695.5	772,943	237.7
2018⁶	7,219,084	2,209.8	1,235,013	378.0	5,232,167	1,601.6	751,904	230.2
2019	6,925,677	2,109.9	1,117,696	340.5	5,086,096	1,549.5	721,885	219.9

Note: Although arson data are included in the trend and clearance tables, sufficient data are not available to estimate totals for this offense. Therefore, no arson data are published in this table.

X = Not applicable.

1 Populations are U.S. Census Bureau provisional estimates as of July 1 for each year except 2000 and 2010, which are decennial census counts.   2 The violent crime figures include the offenses of murder, rape (legacy definition), robbery, and aggravated assault.   3 The figures shown in this column for the offense of rape were estimated using the revised UCR definition of rape.   4 The figures shown in this column for the offense of rape were estimated using the legacy UCR definition of rape.   5 The murder and nonnegligent homicides that occurred as a result of the events of September 11, 2001, are not included in this table.   6 The crime figures have been adjusted.

Table 1A. Crime in the United States, Percent Change in Volume and Rate Per 100,000 Inhabitants for 2 Years, 5 Years, and 10 Years, 2010–2019

(Percent change.)

Year	Violent crime[1]		Murder and nonnegligent manslaughter		Rape (revised definition)[2]		Rape (legacy definition)[3]		Robbery		Aggravated assault		Property crime		Burglary		Larceny-theft		Motor vehicle theft	
	Number	Rate	Number	Rate	Number	Rate	Number	Rate	Number	Rate	Number	Rate	Number	Rate	Number	Rate	Number	Rate	Number	Rate
2010–2019	-3.8	-9.3	+11.6	+5.1	X	X	+14.7	+8.1	-27.4	-31.6	+5.0	-1.0	-24.0	-28.4	-48.5	-51.4	-18.0	-22.7	-2.4	-8.0
2015–2019	+0.4	-1.9	+3.4	+1.1	+10.8	+8.4	+7.6	+5.2	-18.3	-20.2	+7.5	+5.1	-13.7	-15.6	-29.6	-31.2	-11.1	-13.1	+1.2	-1.0
2018–2019	-0.5	-1.0	+0.3	-0.2	-2.7	-3.2	-3.1	-3.6	-4.7	-5.2	+1.3	+0.8	-4.1	-4.5	-9.5	-9.9	-2.8	-3.3	-4.0	-4.4

X = Not applicable.   1 The violent crime figures include the offenses of murder, rape (legacy definition), robbery, and aggravated assault.   2 The figures shown in this column for the offense of rape were estimated using the revised UCR definition of rape.   3 The figures shown in this column for the offense of rape were estimated using the legacy UCR definition of rape.

Table 2. Crime, by Community Type, 2018–2019

(Number, rate per 100,000 population, percent.)

Area	Population[1]	Violent crime[2]	Murder and nonnegligent manslaughter	Rape[3]	Robbery	Aggravated assault	Property crime	Burglary	Larceny-theft	Motor vehicle theft
United States	328,239,523	1,245,410	16,425	139,815	267,988	821,182	6,925,677	1,117,696	5,086,096	721,885
Rate per 100,000 inhabitants		379.4	5.0	42.6	81.6	250.2	2,109.9	340.5	1,549.5	219.9
Metropolitan Statistical Area	282,364,364									
Area actually reporting[4]	97.0%	1,090,149	14,227	116,181	254,202	705,539	6,017,626	921,725	4,447,364	648,537
Estimated total	100.0%	1,115,887	14,539	118,572	258,402	724,374	6,176,585	952,096	4,562,368	662,121
Rate per 100,000 inhabitants		395.2	5.1	42.0	91.5	256.5	2,187.5	337.2	1,615.8	234.5
Cities Outside Metropolitan Areas	18,735,723									
Area actually reporting[4]	89.5%	66,606	736	10,156	5,648	50,066	418,207	72,063	318,917	27,227
Estimated total	100.0%	73,219	839	10,851	6,556	54,973	468,446	82,852	355,832	29,762
Rate per 100,000 inhabitants		390.8	4.5	57.9	35.0	293.4	2,500.3	442.2	1,899.2	158.9
Nonmetropolitan counties	27,139,436									
Area actually reporting[4]	87.8%	50,778	918	9,763	2,421	37,676	247,858	71,394	149,495	26,969
Estimated total	100.0%	56,304	1,047	10,392	3,030	41,835	280,646	82,748	167,896	30,002
Rate per 100,000 inhabitants		207.5	3.9	38.3	11.2	154.1	1,034.1	304.9	618.6	110.5

Note: Although arson data are included in the trend and clearance tables, sufficient data are not available to estimate totals for this offense. Therefore, no arson data are published in this table.
1 Population figures are U.S. Census Bureau provisional estimates as of July 1, 2019.   2 The violent crime figures include the offenses of murder, rape (revised definition), robbery, and aggravated assault.   3 The figures shown in this column for the offense of rape were estimated using the revised Uniform Crime Reporting definition of rape.   4 The percentage reported under "Area actually reporting" is based upon the population covered by agencies providing 3 months or more of crime reports to the FBI.

Table 3. Crime in the United States, Population and Offense Distribution, by Region, 2019

(Percent distribution.)

Region	Population	Violent crime	Murder and nonnegligent manslaughter	Rape (revised definition)[1]	Robbery	Aggravated assault	Property crime	Burglary	Larceny-theft	Motor vehicle theft
United States[2]	100.0	100.0	100.0	100.0	100.0	100.0	100.0	100.0	100.0	100.0
Northeast	17.1	13.1	11.2	12.4	15.0	12.7	10.9	8.4	12.0	7.0
Midwest	20.8	19.8	20.8	24.4	17.3	19.9	19.1	19.3	19.2	17.9
South	38.3	41.0	48.7	37.3	38.3	42.4	42.7	44.9	42.8	38.8
West	23.9	26.0	19.3	26.0	29.5	25.0	27.3	27.4	26.0	36.2

Note: Although arson data are included in the trend and clearance tables, sufficient data are not available to estimate totals for this offense. Therefore, no arson data are published in this table.
1 The figures shown in the rape column were calculated using the revised Uniform Crime Reporting (UCR) definition of rape.   2 Because of rounding, percentages may not sum to 100.0.

Table 4. Crime in the United States,[1] by Region, Geographic Division, and State, 2018–2019

(Number, rate per 100,000 population, percent.)

Area	Population[2]	Violent crime[3] Number	Violent crime[3] Rate	Murder and nonnegligent manslaughter Number	Murder and nonnegligent manslaughter Rate	Rape[4] Number	Rape[4] Rate	Robbery Number	Robbery Rate
UNITED STATES[5,6,7]									
2018	326,687,501	1,252,399	383.4	16,374	5.0	143,765	44.0	281,278	86.1
2019	328,239,523	1,245,410	379.4	16,425	5.0	139,815	42.6	267,988	81.6
Percent change		-0.6	-1.0	+0.3	-0.2	-2.7	-3.2	-4.7	-5.2
NORTHEAST									
2018	56,046,620	164,441	293.4	1,926	3.4	17,674	31.5	41,794	74.6
2019	55,982,803	163,717	292.4	1,834	3.3	17,315	30.9	40,073	71.6
Percent change		-0.4	-0.3	-4.8	-4.7	-2.0	-1.9	-4.1	-4.0
New England									
2018	14,802,967	40,316	272.4	351	2.4	4,846	32.7	8,951	60.5
2019	14,853,290	37,992	255.8	290	2.0	4,998	33.6	7,448	50.1
Percent change		-5.8	-6.1	-17.4	-17.7	+3.1	+2.8	-16.8	-17.1
Connecticut									
2018	3,571,520	7,485	209.6	86	2.4	873	24.4	2,205	61.7
2019	3,565,287	6,546	183.6	104	2.9	771	21.6	1,929	54.1
Percent change		-12.5	-12.4	+20.9	+21.1	-11.7	-11.5	-12.5	-12.4
Maine									
2018	1,339,057	1,500	112.0	23	1.7	447	33.4	228	17.0
2019	1,344,212	1,548	115.2	20	1.5	516	38.4	188	14.0
Percent change		+3.2	+2.8	-13.0	-13.4	+15.4	+15.0	-17.5	-17.9
Massachusetts									
2018	6,882,635	23,424	340.3	138	2.0	2,465	35.8	4,084	59.3
2019	6,892,503	22,578	327.6	152	2.2	2,204	32.0	3,613	52.4
Percent change		-3.6	-3.7	+10.1	+10.0	-10.6	-10.7	-11.5	-11.7
New Hampshire									
2018	1,353,465	2,404	177.6	21	1.6	578	42.7	342	25.3
2019	1,359,711	2,074	152.5	33	2.4	590	43.4	313	23.0
Percent change		-13.7	-14.1	+57.1	+56.4	+2.1	+1.6	-8.5	-8.9
Rhode Island									
2018	1,058,287	2,326	219.8	16	1.5	494	46.7	453	42.8
2019	1,059,361	2,342	221.1	25	2.4	491	46.3	418	39.5
Percent change		+0.7	+0.6	+56.3	+56.1	-0.6	-0.7	-7.7	-7.8
Vermont									
2018	624,358	1,155	185.0	11	1.8	326	52.2	73	11.7
2019	623,989	1,262	202.2	11	1.8	278	44.6	71	11.4
Percent change		+9.3	+9.3	0.0	+0.1	-14.7	-14.7	-2.7	-2.7
Middle Atlantic									
2018	41,217,298	126,147	306.1	1,631	4.0	12,491	30.3	34,409	83.5
2019	41,137,740	127,367	309.6	1,489	3.6	12,465	30.3	33,541	81.5
Percent change		+1.0	+1.2	-8.7	-8.5	-0.2	*	-2.5	-2.3
New Jersey									
2018	8,886,025	18,536	208.6	285	3.2	1,424	16.0	6,364	71.6
2019	8,882,190	18,375	206.9	262	2.9	1,531	17.2	5,730	64.5
Percent change		-0.9	-0.8	-8.1	-8.0	+7.5	+7.6	-10.0	-9.9
New York									
2018	19,530,351	68,512	350.8	562	2.9	6,577	33.7	18,191	93.1
2019	19,453,561	69,764	358.6	558	2.9	6,583	33.8	18,068	92.9
Percent change		+1.8	+2.2	-0.7	-0.3	+0.1	+0.5	-0.7	-0.3
Pennsylvania									
2018	12,800,922	39,099	305.4	784	6.1	4,490	35.1	9,854	77.0
2019	12,801,989	39,228	306.4	669	5.2	4,351	34.0	9,743	76.1
Percent change		+0.3	+0.3	-14.7	-14.7	-3.1	-3.1	-1.1	-1.1
MIDWEST[5]									
2018	68,236,628	249,802	366.1	3,618	5.3	35,194	51.6	50,404	73.9
2019	68,329,004	247,162	361.7	3,414	5.0	34,057	49.8	46,412	67.9
Percent change		-1.1	-1.2	-5.6	-5.8	-3.2	-3.4	-7.9	-8.0
East North Central									
2018	46,886,387	174,319	371.8	2,646	5.6	24,678	52.6	38,727	82.6
2019	46,902,431	171,552	365.8	2,478	5.3	23,780	50.7	34,982	74.6
Percent change		-1.6	-1.6	-6.3	-6.4	-3.6	-3.7	-9.7	-9.7
Illinois									
2018	12,723,071	52,343	411.4	902	7.1	6,106	48.0	14,251	112.0
2019	12,671,821	51,561	406.9	832	6.6	6,078	48.0	12,464	98.4
Percent change		-1.5	-1.1	-7.8	-7.4	-0.5	-0.1	-12.5	-12.2
Indiana									
2018	6,695,497	25,009	373.5	418	6.2	2,486	37.1	5,737	85.7
2019	6,732,219	24,966	370.8	377	5.6	2,475	36.8	5,331	79.2
Percent change		-0.2	-0.7	-9.8	-10.3	-0.4	-1.0	-7.1	-7.6
Michigan									
2018	9,984,072	45,176	452.5	555	5.6	7,901	79.1	5,638	56.5
2019	9,986,857	43,686	437.4	556	5.6	7,235	72.4	5,350	53.6
Percent change		-3.3	-3.3	+0.2	+0.2	-8.4	-8.5	-5.1	-5.1
Ohio									
2018	11,676,341	34,426	294.8	596	5.1	5,852	50.1	9,608	82.3
2019	11,689,100	34,269	293.2	538	4.6	5,731	49.0	8,846	75.7
Percent change		-0.5	-0.6	-9.7	-9.8	-2.1	-2.2	-7.9	-8.0

Table 4. Crime in the United States,[1] by Region, Geographic Division, and State, 2018–2019—Continued

(Number, rate per 100,000 population, percent.)

Area	Aggravated assault Number	Aggravated assault Rate	Property crime Number	Property crime Rate	Burglary Number	Burglary Rate	Larceny-theft Number	Larceny-theft Rate	Motor vehicle theft Number	Motor vehicle theft Rate
UNITED STATES[5,6,7]										
2018	810,982	248.2	7,219,084	2,209.8	1,235,013	378.0	5,232,167	1,601.6	751,904	230.2
2019	821,182	250.2	6,925,677	2,109.9	1,117,696	340.5	5,086,096	1,549.5	721,885	219.9
Percent change	+1.3	+0.8	-4.1	-4.5	-9.5	-9.9	-2.8	-3.3	-4.0	-4.4
NORTHEAST										
2018	103,047	183.9	805,583	1,437.3	108,455	193.5	642,548	1,146.5	54,580	97.4
2019	104,495	186.7	755,968	1,350.4	93,798	167.5	611,369	1,092.1	50,801	90.7
Percent change	+1.4	+1.5	-6.2	-6.1	-13.5	-13.4	-4.9	-4.7	-6.9	-6.8
New England										
2018	26,168	176.8	228,239	1,541.8	36,877	249.1	173,141	1,169.6	18,221	123.1
2019	25,256	170.0	207,956	1,400.1	30,647	206.3	159,890	1,076.5	17,419	117.3
Percent change	-3.5	-3.8	-8.9	-9.2	-16.9	-17.2	-7.7	-8.0	-4.4	-4.7
Connecticut										
2018	4,321	121.0	59,356	1,661.9	7,983	223.5	44,181	1,237.0	7,192	201.4
2019	3,742	105.0	50,862	1,426.6	6,441	180.7	38,457	1,078.7	5,964	167.3
Percent change	-13.4	-13.2	-14.3	-14.2	-19.3	-19.2	-13.0	-12.8	-17.1	-16.9
Maine										
2018	802	59.9	18,201	1,359.2	2,712	202.5	14,712	1,098.7	777	58.0
2019	824	61.3	16,743	1,245.6	2,350	174.8	13,667	1,016.7	726	54.0
Percent change	+2.7	+2.3	-8.0	-8.4	-13.3	-13.7	-7.1	-7.5	-6.6	-6.9
Massachusetts										
2018	16,737	243.2	87,658	1,273.6	14,095	204.8	66,968	973.0	6,595	95.8
2019	16,609	241.0	81,317	1,179.8	12,341	179.0	62,844	911.8	6,132	89.0
Percent change	-0.8	-0.9	-7.2	-7.4	-12.4	-12.6	-6.2	-6.3	-7.0	-7.2
New Hampshire										
2018	1,463	108.1	17,201	1,270.9	1,908	141.0	14,396	1,063.6	897	66.3
2019	1,138	83.7	16,442	1,209.2	1,717	126.3	13,832	1,017.3	893	65.7
Percent change	-22.2	-22.6	-4.4	-4.9	-10.0	-10.4	-3.9	-4.4	-0.4	-0.9
Rhode Island										
2018	1,363	128.8	17,625	1,665.4	2,817	266.2	13,270	1,253.9	1,538	145.3
2019	1,408	132.9	16,259	1,534.8	2,321	219.1	12,580	1,187.5	1,358	128.2
Percent change	+3.3	+3.2	-7.8	-7.8	-17.6	-17.7	-5.2	-5.3	-11.7	-11.8
Vermont										
2018	745	119.3	8,211	1,315.1	1,496	239.6	6,451	1,033.2	264	42.3
2019	902	144.6	8,888	1,424.4	1,275	204.3	7,315	1,172.3	298	47.8
Percent change	+21.1	+21.1	+8.2	+8.3	-14.8	-14.7	+13.4	+13.5	+12.9	+12.9
Middle Atlantic										
2018	77,616	188.3	597,331	1,449.2	77,444	187.9	482,570	1,170.8	37,317	90.5
2019	79,872	194.2	565,457	1,374.5	67,353	163.7	462,674	1,124.7	35,430	86.1
Percent change	+2.9	+3.1	-5.3	-5.2	-13.0	-12.9	-4.1	-3.9	-5.1	-4.9
New Jersey										
2018	10,463	117.7	125,155	1,408.4	19,232	216.4	94,886	1,067.8	11,037	124.2
2019	10,852	122.2	118,637	1,335.7	16,399	184.6	91,902	1,034.7	10,336	116.4
Percent change	+3.7	+3.8	-5.2	-5.2	-14.7	-14.7	-3.1	-3.1	-6.4	-6.3
New York										
2018	43,182	221.1	281,543	1,441.6	31,158	159.5	237,243	1,214.7	13,142	67.3
2019	44,555	229.0	267,155	1,373.3	27,600	141.9	226,851	1,166.1	12,704	65.3
Percent change	+3.2	+3.6	-5.1	-4.7	-11.4	-11.1	-4.4	-4.0	-3.3	-3.0
Pennsylvania										
2018	23,971	187.3	190,633	1,489.2	27,054	211.3	150,441	1,175.2	13,138	102.6
2019	24,465	191.1	179,665	1,403.4	23,354	182.4	143,921	1,124.2	12,390	96.8
Percent change	+2.1	+2.1	-5.8	-5.8	-13.7	-13.7	-4.3	-4.3	-5.7	-5.7
MIDWEST[8]										
2018	160,586	235.3	1,389,261	2,035.9	240,009	351.7	1,016,958	1,490.3	132,294	193.9
2019	163,279	239.0	1,322,428	1,935.4	215,395	315.2	977,491	1,430.6	129,542	189.6
Percent change	+1.7	+1.5	-4.8	-4.9	-10.3	-10.4	-3.9	-4.0	-2.1	-2.2
East North Central										
2018	108,268	230.9	908,899	1,938.5	160,681	342.7	667,067	1,422.7	81,151	173.1
2019	110,312	235.2	850,937	1,814.3	141,361	301.4	633,277	1,350.2	76,299	162.7
Percent change	+1.9	+1.9	-6.4	-6.4	-12.0	-12.1	-5.1	-5.1	-6.0	-6.0
Illinois										
2018	31,084	244.3	246,679	1,938.8	39,317	309.0	187,517	1,473.8	19,845	156.0
2019	32,187	254.0	233,984	1,846.5	34,433	271.7	180,776	1,426.6	18,775	148.2
Percent change	+3.5	+4.0	-5.1	-4.8	-12.4	-12.1	-3.6	-3.2	-5.4	-5.0
Indiana										
2018	16,368	244.5	146,948	2,194.7	25,894	386.7	105,861	1,581.1	15,193	226.9
2019	16,783	249.3	132,694	1,971.0	21,795	323.7	97,176	1,443.4	13,723	203.8
Percent change	+2.5	+2.0	-9.7	-10.2	-15.8	-16.3	-8.2	-8.7	-9.7	-10.2
Michigan										
2018	31,082	311.3	166,186	1,664.5	31,834	318.8	116,876	1,170.6	17,476	175.0
2019	30,545	305.9	158,296	1,585.0	28,572	286.1	111,980	1,121.3	17,744	177.7
Percent change	-1.7	-1.8	-4.7	-4.8	-10.2	-10.3	-4.2	-4.2	+1.5	+1.5
Ohio										
2018	18,370	157.3	257,848	2,208.3	49,456	423.6	188,433	1,613.8	19,959	170.9
2019	19,154	163.9	240,291	2,055.7	43,894	375.5	177,725	1,520.4	18,672	159.7
Percent change	+4.3	+4.2	-6.8	-6.9	-11.2	-11.3	-5.7	-5.8	-6.4	-6.6

Table 4. Crime in the United States,[1] by Region, Geographic Division, and State, 2018–2019—Continued

(Number, rate per 100,000 population, percent.)

Area	Population[2]	Violent crime[3]		Murder and nonnegligent manslaughter		Rape[4]		Robbery	
		Number	Rate	Number	Rate	Number	Rate	Number	Rate
Wisconsin									
2018	5,807,406	17,365	299.0	175	3.0	2,333	40.2	3,493	60.1
2019	5,822,434	17,070	293.2	175	3.0	2,261	38.8	2,991	51.4
Percent change		-1.7	-2.0	0.0	-0.3	-3.1	-3.3	-14.4	-14.6
West North Central[5]									
2018	21,350,241	75,483	353.5	972	4.6	10,516	49.3	11,677	54.7
2019	21,426,573	75,610	352.9	936	4.4	10,277	48.0	11,430	53.3
Percent change		+0.2	-0.2	-3.7	-4.0	-2.3	-2.6	-2.1	-2.5
Iowa[5]									
2018	3,148,618	8,303	263.7	70	2.2	1,126	35.8	989	31.4
2019	3,155,070	8,410	266.6	60	1.9	1,164	36.9	863	27.4
Percent change		+1.3	+1.1	-14.3	-14.5	+3.4	+3.2	-12.7	-12.9
Kansas									
2018	2,911,359	12,861	441.8	122	4.2	1,664	57.2	1,420	48.8
2019	2,913,314	11,968	410.8	105	3.6	1,416	48.6	1,293	44.4
Percent change		-6.9	-7.0	-13.9	-14.0	-14.9	-15.0	-8.9	-9.0
Minnesota									
2018	5,606,249	12,403	221.2	107	1.9	2,475	44.1	2,946	52.5
2019	5,639,632	13,332	236.4	117	2.1	2,448	43.4	3,149	55.8
Percent change		+7.5	+6.9	+9.3	+8.7	-1.1	-1.7	+6.9	+6.3
Missouri									
2018	6,121,623	30,696	501.4	599	9.8	2,935	47.9	5,206	85.0
2019	6,137,428	30,380	495.0	568	9.3	2,917	47.5	4,959	80.8
Percent change		-1.0	-1.3	-5.2	-5.4	-0.6	-0.9	-4.7	-5.0
Nebraska									
2018	1,925,614	5,583	289.9	44	2.3	1,290	67.0	736	38.2
2019	1,934,408	5,821	300.9	45	2.3	1,253	64.8	792	40.9
Percent change		+4.3	+3.8	+2.3	+1.8	-2.9	-3.3	+7.6	+7.1
North Dakota									
2018	758,080	2,154	284.1	18	2.4	409	54.0	158	20.8
2019	762,062	2,169	284.6	24	3.1	437	57.3	179	23.5
Percent change		+0.7	+0.2	+33.3	+32.6	+6.8	+6.3	+13.3	+12.7
South Dakota									
2018	878,698	3,483	396.4	12	1.4	617	70.2	222	25.3
2019	884,659	3,530	399.0	17	1.9	642	72.6	195	22.0
Percent change		+1.3	+0.7	+41.7	+40.7	+4.1	+3.4	-12.2	-12.8
SOUTH[6,7]									
2018	124,569,433	507,232	407.2	7,581	6.1	52,571	42.2	106,258	85.3
2019	125,580,448	510,565	406.6	8,002	6.4	52,119	41.5	102,570	81.7
Percent change		+0.7	-0.2	+5.6	+4.7	-0.9	-1.7	-3.5	-4.2
South Atlantic[6,7]									
2018	65,229,624	242,214	371.3	3,929	6.0	23,082	35.4	53,483	82.0
2019	65,784,817	245,159	372.7	4,132	6.3	23,223	35.3	51,679	78.6
Percent change		+1.2	+0.4	+5.2	+4.3	+0.6	-0.2	-3.4	-4.2
Delaware									
2018	965,479	4,079	422.5	46	4.8	334	34.6	861	89.2
2019	973,764	4,115	422.6	48	4.9	310	31.8	790	81.1
Percent change		+0.9	*	+4.3	+3.5	-7.2	-8.0	-8.2	-9.0
District of Columbia[6]									
2018	701,547	6,995	997.1	160	22.8	450	64.1	2,415	344.2
2019	705,749	7,403	1,049.0	166	23.5	345	48.9	2,713	384.4
Percent change		+5.8	+5.2	+3.8	+3.1	-23.3	-23.8	+12.3	+11.7
Florida									
2018	21,244,317	81,980	385.9	1,107	5.2	8,438	39.7	16,884	79.5
2019	21,477,737	81,270	378.4	1,122	5.2	8,456	39.4	16,217	75.5
Percent change		-0.9	-1.9	+1.4	+0.3	+0.2	-0.9	-4.0	-5.0
Georgia									
2018	10,511,131	35,619	338.9	647	6.2	2,798	26.6	8,499	80.9
2019	10,617,423	36,170	340.7	654	6.2	2,922	27.5	7,961	75.0
Percent change		+1.5	+0.5	+1.1	+0.1	+4.4	+3.4	-6.3	-7.3
Maryland									
2018	6,035,802	28,330	469.4	491	8.1	1,991	33.0	9,716	161.0
2019	6,045,680	27,456	454.1	542	9.0	1,913	31.6	9,203	152.2
Percent change		-3.1	-3.2	+10.4	+10.2	-3.9	-4.1	-5.3	-5.4
North Carolina[7]									
2018	10,381,615	36,980	356.2	574	5.5	2,633	25.4	7,573	72.9
2019	10,488,084	38,995	371.8	632	6.0	3,247	31.0	7,599	72.5
Percent change		+5.4	+4.4	+10.1	+9.0	+23.3	+22.1	+0.3	-0.7
South Carolina									
2018	5,084,156	25,463	500.8	411	8.1	2,650	52.1	3,592	70.7
2019	5,148,714	26,323	511.3	464	9.0	2,460	47.8	3,294	64.0
Percent change		+3.4	+2.1	+12.9	+11.5	-7.2	-8.3	-8.3	-9.4
Virginia									
2018	8,501,286	17,357	204.2	417	4.9	3,072	36.1	3,610	42.5
2019	8,535,519	17,753	208.0	426	5.0	2,816	33.0	3,524	41.3
Percent change		+2.3	+1.9	+2.2	+1.7	-8.3	-8.7	-2.4	-2.8
West Virginia									
2018	1,804,291	5,411	299.9	76	4.2	716	39.7	333	18.5
2019	1,792,147	5,674	316.6	78	4.4	754	42.1	378	21.1
Percent change		+4.9	+5.6	+2.6	+3.3	+5.3	+6.0	+13.5	+14.3

Table 4. Crime in the United States,[1] by Region, Geographic Division, and State, 2018–2019—Continued

(Number, rate per 100,000 population, percent.)

Area	Aggravated assault		Property crime		Burglary		Larceny-theft		Motor vehicle theft	
	Number	Rate	Number	Rate	Number	Rate	Number	Rate	Number	Rate
Wisconsin										
2018	11,364	195.7	91,238	1,571.1	14,180	244.2	68,380	1,177.5	8,678	149.4
2019	11,643	200.0	85,672	1,471.4	12,667	217.6	65,620	1,127.0	7,385	126.8
Percent change	+2.5	+2.2	-6.1	-6.3	-10.7	-10.9	-4.0	-4.3	-14.9	-15.1
West North Central[5]										
2018	52,318	245.0	480,362	2,249.9	79,328	371.6	349,891	1,638.8	51,143	239.5
2019	52,967	247.2	471,491	2,200.5	74,034	345.5	344,214	1,606.5	53,243	248.5
Percent change	+1.2	+0.9	-1.8	-2.2	-6.7	-7.0	-1.6	-2.0	+4.1	+3.7
Iowa[5]										
2018	6,118	194.3	57,024	1,811.1	12,433	394.9	39,498	1,254.5	5,093	161.8
2019	6,323	200.4	54,699	1,733.7	11,710	371.1	37,847	1,199.6	5,142	163.0
Percent change	+3.4	+3.1	-4.1	-4.3	-5.8	-6.0	-4.2	-4.4	+1.0	+0.8
Kansas										
2018	9,655	331.6	77,449	2,660.2	12,792	439.4	56,726	1,948.4	7,931	272.4
2019	9,154	314.2	67,428	2,314.5	9,984	342.7	50,165	1,721.9	7,279	249.9
Percent change	-5.2	-5.3	-12.9	-13.0	-22.0	-22.0	-11.6	-11.6	-8.2	-8.3
Minnesota										
2018	6,875	122.6	112,186	2,001.1	16,206	289.1	85,849	1,531.3	10,131	180.7
2019	7,618	135.1	117,236	2,078.8	15,927	282.4	90,092	1,597.5	11,217	198.9
Percent change	+10.8	+10.2	+4.5	+3.9	-1.7	-2.3	+4.9	+4.3	+10.7	+10.1
Missouri										
2018	21,956	358.7	162,698	2,657.8	27,345	446.7	115,506	1,886.9	19,847	324.2
2019	21,936	357.4	161,946	2,638.7	26,414	430.4	114,460	1,865.0	21,072	343.3
Percent change	-0.1	-0.3	-0.5	-0.7	-3.4	-3.7	-0.9	-1.2	+6.2	+5.9
Nebraska										
2018	3,513	182.4	40,193	2,087.3	5,308	275.7	29,987	1,557.3	4,898	254.4
2019	3,731	192.9	39,449	2,039.3	4,745	245.3	29,719	1,536.3	4,985	257.7
Percent change	+6.2	+5.7	-1.9	-2.3	-10.6	-11.0	-0.9	-1.3	+1.8	+1.3
North Dakota										
2018	1,569	207.0	15,621	2,060.6	2,742	361.7	11,088	1,462.6	1,791	236.3
2019	1,529	200.6	15,066	1,977.0	2,608	342.2	10,666	1,399.6	1,792	235.2
Percent change	-2.5	-3.1	-3.6	-4.1	-4.9	-5.4	-3.8	-4.3	+0.1	-0.5
South Dakota										
2018	2,632	299.5	15,191	1,728.8	2,502	284.7	11,237	1,278.8	1,452	165.2
2019	2,676	302.5	15,667	1,771.0	2,646	299.1	11,265	1,273.4	1,756	198.5
Percent change	+1.7	+1.0	+3.1	+2.4	+5.8	+5.0	+0.2	-0.4	+20.9	+20.1
SOUTH[6,7]										
2018	340,822	273.6	3,040,614	2,440.9	547,925	439.9	2,213,649	1,777.0	279,040	224.0
2019	347,874	277.0	2,957,758	2,355.3	501,817	399.6	2,175,494	1,732.4	280,447	223.3
Percent change	+2.1	+1.2	-2.7	-3.5	-8.4	-9.2	-1.7	-2.5	+0.5	-0.3
South Atlantic[6,7]										
2018	161,720	247.9	1,510,368	2,315.5	251,583	385.7	1,131,644	1,734.9	127,141	194.9
2019	166,125	252.5	1,450,962	2,205.6	226,274	344.0	1,100,944	1,673.6	123,744	188.1
Percent change	+2.7	+1.9	-3.9	-4.7	-10.1	-10.8	-2.7	-3.5	-2.7	-3.5
Delaware										
2018	2,838	293.9	22,405	2,320.6	3,154	326.7	17,780	1,841.6	1,471	152.4
2019	2,967	304.7	21,931	2,252.2	2,968	304.8	17,359	1,782.7	1,604	164.7
Percent change	+4.5	+3.7	-2.1	-2.9	-5.9	-6.7	-2.4	-3.2	+9.0	+8.1
District of Columbia[6]										
2018	3,970	565.9	30,726	4,379.7	1,788	254.9	26,345	3,755.3	2,593	369.6
2019	4,179	592.1	30,821	4,367.1	1,843	261.1	26,645	3,775.4	2,333	330.6
Percent change	+5.3	+4.6	+0.3	-0.3	+3.1	+2.5	+1.1	+0.5	-10.0	-10.6
Florida										
2018	55,551	261.5	486,017	2,287.8	71,933	338.6	372,919	1,755.4	41,165	193.8
2019	55,475	258.3	460,846	2,145.7	63,396	295.2	358,402	1,668.7	39,048	181.8
Percent change	-0.1	-1.2	-5.2	-6.2	-11.9	-12.8	-3.9	-4.9	-5.1	-6.2
Georgia										
2018	23,675	225.2	277,803	2,642.9	46,816	445.4	205,631	1,956.3	25,356	241.2
2019	24,633	232.0	252,249	2,375.8	39,506	372.1	188,967	1,779.8	23,776	223.9
Percent change	+4.0	+3.0	-9.2	-10.1	-15.6	-16.5	-8.1	-9.0	-6.2	-7.2
Maryland										
2018	16,132	267.3	122,945	2,036.9	18,910	313.3	91,887	1,522.4	12,148	201.3
2019	15,798	261.3	117,901	1,950.2	16,862	278.9	89,780	1,485.0	11,259	186.2
Percent change	-2.1	-2.2	-4.1	-4.3	-10.8	-11.0	-2.3	-2.5	-7.3	-7.5
North Carolina[7]										
2018	26,200	252.4	243,323	2,343.8	57,450	553.4	169,376	1,631.5	16,497	158.9
2019	27,517	262.4	247,236	2,357.3	54,447	519.1	174,728	1,666.0	18,061	172.2
Percent change	+5.0	+4.0	+1.6	+0.6	-5.2	-6.2	+3.2	+2.1	+9.5	+8.4
South Carolina										
2018	18,810	370.0	156,330	3,074.8	29,957	589.2	111,427	2,191.7	14,946	294.0
2019	20,105	390.5	151,389	2,940.3	27,461	533.4	108,953	2,116.1	14,975	290.8
Percent change	+6.9	+5.5	-3.2	-4.4	-8.3	-9.5	-2.2	-3.4	+0.2	-1.1
Virginia										
2018	10,258	120.7	142,931	1,681.3	15,659	184.2	116,496	1,370.3	10,776	126.8
2019	10,987	128.7	140,213	1,642.7	13,900	162.8	116,044	1,359.5	10,269	120.3
Percent change	+7.1	+6.7	-1.9	-2.3	-11.2	-11.6	-0.4	-0.8	-4.7	-5.1
West Virginia										
2018	4,286	237.5	27,888	1,545.6	5,916	327.9	19,783	1,096.4	2,189	121.3
2019	4,464	249.1	28,376	1,583.4	5,891	328.7	20,066	1,119.7	2,419	135.0
Percent change	+4.2	+4.9	+1.7	+2.4	-0.4	+0.3	+1.4	+2.1	+10.5	+11.3

Table 4. Crime in the United States,[1] by Region, Geographic Division, and State, 2018–2019—Continued

(Number, rate per 100,000 population, percent.)

Area	Population[2]	Violent crime[3] Number	Violent crime[3] Rate	Murder and nonnegligent manslaughter Number	Murder and nonnegligent manslaughter Rate	Rape[4] Number	Rape[4] Rate	Robbery Number	Robbery Rate
East South Central									
2018	19,101,485	85,902	449.7	1,355	7.1	7,514	39.3	15,438	80.8
2019	19,176,181	83,666	436.3	1,409	7.3	7,200	37.5	13,952	72.8
Percent change		-2.6	-3.0	+4.0	+3.6	-4.2	-4.6	-9.6	-10.0
Alabama									
2018	4,887,681	25,567	523.1	383	7.8	2,032	41.6	4,047	82.8
2019	4,903,185	25,046	510.8	358	7.3	2,068	42.2	3,941	80.4
Percent change		-2.0	-2.3	-6.5	-6.8	+1.8	+1.4	-2.6	-2.9
Kentucky									
2018	4,461,153	9,719	217.9	250	5.6	1,875	42.0	2,469	55.3
2019	4,467,673	9,701	217.1	221	4.9	1,572	35.2	2,161	48.4
Percent change		-0.2	-0.3	-11.6	-11.7	-16.2	-16.3	-12.5	-12.6
Mississippi									
2018	2,981,020	7,929	266.0	214	7.2	596	20.0	1,700	57.0
2019	2,976,149	8,272	277.9	332	11.2	747	25.1	1,700	57.1
Percent change		+4.3	+4.5	+55.1	+55.4	+25.3	+25.5	0.0	+0.2
Tennessee									
2018	6,771,631	42,687	630.4	508	7.5	3,011	44.5	7,222	106.7
2019	6,829,174	40,647	595.2	498	7.3	2,813	41.2	6,150	90.1
Percent change		-4.8	-5.6	-2.0	-2.8	-6.6	-7.4	-14.8	-15.6
West South Central									
2018	40,238,324	179,116	445.1	2,297	5.7	21,975	54.6	37,337	92.8
2019	40,619,450	181,740	447.4	2,461	6.1	21,696	53.4	36,939	90.9
Percent change		+1.5	+0.5	+7.1	+6.1	-1.3	-2.2	-1.1	-2.0
Arkansas									
2018	3,009,733	16,904	561.6	222	7.4	2,341	77.8	1,593	52.9
2019	3,017,804	17,643	584.6	242	8.0	2,331	77.2	1,557	51.6
Percent change		+4.4	+4.1	+9.0	+8.7	-0.4	-0.7	-2.3	-2.5
Louisiana									
2018	4,659,690	25,314	543.3	533	11.4	2,105	45.2	4,600	98.7
2019	4,648,794	25,537	549.3	544	11.7	2,273	48.9	4,025	86.6
Percent change		+0.9	+1.1	+2.1	+2.3	+8.0	+8.2	-12.5	-12.3
Oklahoma									
2018	3,940,235	18,701	474.6	215	5.5	2,431	61.7	2,805	71.2
2019	3,956,971	17,086	431.8	266	6.7	2,268	57.3	2,369	59.9
Percent change		-8.6	-9.0	+23.7	+23.2	-6.7	-7.1	-15.5	-15.9
Texas									
2018	28,628,666	118,197	412.9	1,327	4.6	15,098	52.7	28,339	99.0
2019	28,995,881	121,474	418.9	1,409	4.9	14,824	51.1	28,988	100.0
Percent change		+2.8	+1.5	+6.2	+4.8	-1.8	-3.1	+2.3	+1.0
WEST									
2018	77,834,820	330,924	425.2	3,249	4.2	38,326	49.2	82,822	106.4
2019	78,347,268	323,966	413.5	3,175	4.1	36,324	46.4	78,933	100.7
Percent change		-2.1	-2.7	-2.3	-2.9	-5.2	-5.8	-4.7	-5.3
Mountain									
2018	24,511,745	108,278	441.7	1,101	4.5	15,175	61.9	18,575	75.8
2019	24,854,998	104,878	422.0	1,054	4.2	14,562	58.6	17,252	69.4
Percent change		-3.1	-4.5	-4.3	-5.6	-4.0	-5.4	-7.1	-8.4
Arizona									
2018	7,158,024	34,053	475.7	383	5.4	3,605	50.4	6,509	90.9
2019	7,278,717	33,141	455.3	365	5.0	3,662	50.3	6,410	88.1
Percent change		-2.7	-4.3	-4.7	-6.3	+1.6	-0.1	-1.5	-3.2
Colorado									
2018	5,691,287	22,851	401.5	215	3.8	4,328	76.0	3,781	66.4
2019	5,758,736	21,938	381.0	218	3.8	3,872	67.2	3,663	63.6
Percent change		-4.0	-5.1	+1.4	+0.2	-10.5	-11.6	-3.1	-4.3
Idaho									
2018	1,750,536	4,196	239.7	34	1.9	927	53.0	195	11.1
2019	1,787,065	4,000	223.8	35	2.0	809	45.3	155	8.7
Percent change		-4.7	-6.6	+2.9	+0.8	-12.7	-14.5	-20.5	-22.1
Montana									
2018	1,060,665	4,040	380.9	37	3.5	569	53.6	270	25.5
2019	1,068,778	4,328	404.9	27	2.5	624	58.4	205	19.2
Percent change		+7.1	+6.3	-27.0	-27.6	+9.7	+8.8	-24.1	-24.7
Nevada									
2018	3,027,341	16,715	552.1	202	6.7	2,329	76.9	3,862	127.6
2019	3,080,156	15,210	493.8	143	4.6	2,161	70.2	3,286	106.7
Percent change		-9.0	-10.6	-29.2	-30.4	-7.2	-8.8	-14.9	-16.4
New Mexico									
2018	2,092,741	17,637	842.8	153	7.3	1,302	62.2	2,646	126.4
2019	2,096,829	17,450	832.2	181	8.6	1,288	61.4	2,341	111.6
Percent change		-1.1	-1.3	+18.3	+18.1	-1.1	-1.3	-11.5	-11.7
Utah									
2018	3,153,550	7,551	239.4	63	2.0	1,854	58.8	1,237	39.2
2019	3,205,958	7,553	235.6	72	2.2	1,822	56.8	1,125	35.1
Percent change		*	-1.6	+14.3	+12.4	-1.7	-3.3	-9.1	-10.5
Wyoming									
2018	577,601	1,235	213.8	14	2.4	261	45.2	75	13.0
2019	578,759	1,258	217.4	13	2.2	324	56.0	67	11.6
Percent change		+1.9	+1.7	-7.1	-7.3	+24.1	+23.9	-10.7	-10.8

Table 4. Crime in the United States,[1] by Region, Geographic Division, and State, 2018–2019—Continued

(Number, rate per 100,000 population, percent.)

Area	Aggravated assault		Property crime		Burglary		Larceny-theft		Motor vehicle theft	
	Number	Rate	Number	Rate	Number	Rate	Number	Rate	Number	Rate
East South Central										
2018	61,595	322.5	492,535	2,578.5	100,456	525.9	342,552	1,793.3	49,527	259.3
2019	61,105	318.7	467,762	2,439.3	90,051	469.6	330,011	1,720.9	47,700	248.7
Percent change	-0.8	-1.2	-5.0	-5.4	-10.4	-10.7	-3.7	-4.0	-3.7	-4.1
Alabama										
2018	19,105	390.9	138,702	2,837.8	29,101	595.4	96,328	1,970.8	13,273	271.6
2019	18,679	381.0	131,133	2,674.4	26,079	531.9	92,477	1,886.1	12,577	256.5
Percent change	-2.2	-2.5	-5.5	-5.8	-10.4	-10.7	-4.0	-4.3	-5.2	-5.5
Kentucky										
2018	5,125	114.9	89,235	2,000.3	17,462	391.4	61,313	1,374.4	10,460	234.5
2019	5,747	128.6	84,769	1,897.4	15,443	345.7	59,130	1,323.5	10,196	228.2
Percent change	+12.1	+12.0	-5.0	-5.1	-11.6	-11.7	-3.6	-3.7	-2.5	-2.7
Mississippi										
2018	5,419	181.8	71,701	2,405.3	20,355	682.8	46,201	1,549.8	5,145	172.6
2019	5,493	184.6	70,707	2,375.8	18,660	627.0	46,300	1,555.7	5,747	193.1
Percent change	+1.4	+1.5	-1.4	-1.2	-8.3	-8.2	+0.2	+0.4	+11.7	+11.9
Tennessee										
2018	31,946	471.8	192,897	2,848.6	33,538	495.3	138,710	2,048.4	20,649	304.9
2019	31,186	456.7	181,153	2,652.6	29,869	437.4	132,104	1,934.4	19,180	280.9
Percent change	-2.4	-3.2	-6.1	-6.9	-10.9	-11.7	-4.8	-5.6	-7.1	-7.9
West South Central										
2018	117,507	292.0	1,037,711	2,578.9	195,886	486.8	739,453	1,837.7	102,372	254.4
2019	120,644	297.0	1,039,034	2,558.0	185,492	456.7	744,539	1,833.0	109,003	268.4
Percent change	+2.7	+1.7	+0.1	-0.8	-5.3	-6.2	+0.7	-0.3	+6.5	+5.5
Arkansas										
2018	12,748	423.6	89,177	2,963.0	19,520	648.6	62,350	2,071.6	7,307	242.8
2019	13,513	447.8	86,250	2,858.0	18,095	599.6	60,735	2,012.6	7,420	245.9
Percent change	+6.0	+5.7	-3.3	-3.5	-7.3	-7.5	-2.6	-2.9	+1.5	+1.3
Louisiana										
2018	18,076	387.9	152,996	3,283.4	31,291	671.5	110,066	2,362.1	11,639	249.8
2019	18,695	402.1	146,993	3,162.0	26,918	579.0	109,359	2,352.4	10,716	230.5
Percent change	+3.4	+3.7	-3.9	-3.7	-14.0	-13.8	-0.6	-0.4	-7.9	-7.7
Oklahoma										
2018	13,250	336.3	114,395	2,903.3	27,178	689.8	73,799	1,873.0	13,418	340.5
2019	12,183	307.9	112,587	2,845.3	26,577	671.7	72,632	1,835.5	13,378	338.1
Percent change	-8.1	-8.4	-1.6	-2.0	-2.2	-2.6	-1.6	-2.0	-0.3	-0.7
Texas										
2018	73,433	256.5	681,143	2,379.2	117,897	411.8	493,238	1,722.9	70,008	244.5
2019	76,253	263.0	693,204	2,390.7	113,902	392.8	501,813	1,730.6	77,489	267.2
Percent change	+3.8	+2.5	+1.8	+0.5	-3.4	-4.6	+1.7	+0.5	+10.7	+9.3
WEST										
2018	206,527	265.3	1,983,626	2,548.5	338,624	435.1	1,359,012	1,746.0	285,990	367.4
2019	205,534	262.3	1,889,523	2,411.7	306,686	391.4	1,321,742	1,687.0	261,095	333.3
Percent change	-0.5	-1.1	-4.7	-5.4	-9.4	-10.0	-2.7	-3.4	-8.7	-9.3
Mountain										
2018	73,427	299.6	630,953	2,574.1	107,336	437.9	447,137	1,824.2	76,480	312.0
2019	72,010	289.7	587,493	2,363.7	95,964	386.1	419,649	1,688.4	71,880	289.2
Percent change	-1.9	-3.3	-6.9	-8.2	-10.6	-11.8	-6.1	-7.4	-6.0	-7.3
Arizona										
2018	23,556	329.1	192,730	2,692.5	31,787	444.1	141,789	1,980.8	19,154	267.6
2019	22,704	311.9	177,638	2,440.5	28,699	394.3	130,788	1,796.9	18,151	249.4
Percent change	-3.6	-5.2	-7.8	-9.4	-9.7	-11.2	-7.8	-9.3	-5.2	-6.8
Colorado										
2018	14,527	255.2	154,292	2,711.0	21,757	382.3	110,518	1,941.9	22,017	386.9
2019	14,185	246.3	149,189	2,590.7	20,064	348.4	107,012	1,858.3	22,113	384.0
Percent change	-2.4	-3.5	-3.3	-4.4	-7.8	-8.9	-3.2	-4.3	+0.4	-0.7
Idaho										
2018	3,040	173.7	25,822	1,475.1	4,990	285.1	18,876	1,078.3	1,956	111.7
2019	3,001	167.9	21,793	1,219.5	3,927	219.7	16,295	911.8	1,571	87.9
Percent change	-1.3	-3.3	-15.6	-17.3	-21.3	-22.9	-13.7	-15.4	-19.7	-21.3
Montana										
2018	3,164	298.3	26,787	2,525.5	3,329	313.9	20,641	1,946.0	2,817	265.6
2019	3,472	324.9	23,440	2,193.2	2,887	270.1	18,176	1,700.6	2,377	222.4
Percent change	+9.7	+8.9	-12.5	-13.2	-13.3	-13.9	-11.9	-12.6	-15.6	-16.3
Nevada										
2018	10,322	341.0	73,998	2,444.3	17,741	586.0	44,341	1,464.7	11,916	393.6
2019	9,620	312.3	71,525	2,322.1	15,510	503.5	44,755	1,453.0	11,260	365.6
Percent change	-6.8	-8.4	-3.3	-5.0	-12.6	-14.1	+0.9	-0.8	-5.5	-7.1
New Mexico										
2018	13,536	646.8	70,722	3,379.4	16,102	769.4	44,592	2,130.8	10,028	479.2
2019	13,640	650.5	65,269	3,112.7	14,610	696.8	41,702	1,988.8	8,957	427.2
Percent change	+0.8	+0.6	-7.7	-7.9	-9.3	-9.4	-6.5	-6.7	-10.7	-10.9
Utah										
2018	4,397	139.4	76,294	2,419.3	10,079	319.6	58,406	1,852.1	7,809	247.6
2019	4,534	141.4	69,546	2,169.3	8,871	276.7	53,937	1,682.4	6,738	210.2
Percent change	+3.1	+1.4	-8.8	-10.3	-12.0	-13.4	-7.7	-9.2	-13.7	-15.1
Wyoming										
2018	885	153.2	10,308	1,784.6	1,551	268.5	7,974	1,380.5	783	135.6
2019	854	147.6	9,093	1,571.1	1,396	241.2	6,984	1,206.7	713	123.2
Percent change	-3.5	-3.7	-11.8	-12.0	-10.0	-10.2	-12.4	-12.6	-8.9	-9.1

Table 4. Crime in the United States,[1] by Region, Geographic Division, and State, 2018–2019—Continued

(Number, rate per 100,000 population, percent.)

Area	Population[2]	Violent crime[3]		Murder and nonnegligent manslaughter		Rape[4]		Robbery	
		Number	Rate	Number	Rate	Number	Rate	Number	Rate
Pacific									
2018	53,323,075	222,646	417.5	2,148	4.0	23,151	43.4	64,247	120.5
2019	53,492,270	219,088	409.6	2,121	4.0	21,762	40.7	61,681	115.3
Percent change		-1.6	-1.9	-1.3	-1.6	-6.0	-6.3	-4.0	-4.3
Alaska									
2018	735,139	6,555	891.7	47	6.4	1,212	164.9	896	121.9
2019	731,545	6,343	867.1	69	9.4	1,088	148.7	826	112.9
Percent change		-3.2	-2.8	+46.8	+47.5	-10.2	-9.8	-7.8	-7.4
California									
2018	39,461,588	176,604	447.5	1,739	4.4	15,506	39.3	54,328	137.7
2019	39,512,223	174,331	441.2	1,690	4.3	14,799	37.5	52,301	132.4
Percent change		-1.3	-1.4	-2.8	-2.9	-4.6	-4.7	-3.7	-3.9
Hawaii									
2018	1,420,593	3,622	255.0	40	2.8	709	49.9	951	66.9
2019	1,415,872	4,042	285.5	48	3.4	765	54.0	1,131	79.9
Percent change		+11.6	+12.0	+20.0	+20.4	+7.9	+8.3	+18.9	+19.3
Oregon									
2018	4,181,886	12,146	290.4	86	2.1	2,114	50.6	2,515	60.1
2019	4,217,737	11,995	284.4	116	2.8	1,778	42.2	2,276	54.0
Percent change		-1.2	-2.1	+34.9	+33.7	-15.9	-16.6	-9.5	-10.3
Washington									
2018	7,523,869	23,719	315.3	236	3.1	3,610	48.0	5,557	73.9
2019	7,614,893	22,377	293.9	198	2.6	3,332	43.8	5,147	67.6
Percent change		-5.7	-6.8	-16.1	-17.1	-7.7	-8.8	-7.4	-8.5
Puerto Rico									
2018	3,193,354	6,417	200.9	639	20.0	198	6.2	2,271	71.1
2019	3,193,694	6,479	202.9	606	19.0	215	6.7	2,121	66.4
Percent change		+1.0	+1.0	-5.2	-5.2	+8.6	+8.6	-6.6	-6.6

Table 4. Crime in the United States,[1] by Region, Geographic Division, and State, 2018–2019—Continued

(Number, rate per 100,000 population, percent.)

Area	Aggravated assault		Property crime		Burglary		Larceny-theft		Motor vehicle theft	
	Number	Rate	Number	Rate	Number	Rate	Number	Rate	Number	Rate
Pacific										
2018	133,100	249.6	1,352,673	2,536.7	231,288	433.7	911,875	1,710.1	209,510	392.9
2019	133,524	249.6	1,302,030	2,434.1	210,722	393.9	902,093	1,686.4	189,215	353.7
Percent change	+0.3	*	-3.7	-4.0	-8.9	-9.2	-1.1	-1.4	-9.7	-10.0
Alaska										
2018	4,400	598.5	24,345	3,311.6	3,985	542.1	16,364	2,226.0	3,996	543.6
2019	4,360	596.0	21,294	2,910.8	3,563	487.1	15,114	2,066.0	2,617	357.7
Percent change	-0.9	-0.4	-12.5	-12.1	-10.6	-10.2	-7.6	-7.2	-34.5	-34.2
California										
2018	105,031	266.2	941,644	2,386.2	164,645	417.2	621,779	1,575.7	155,220	393.3
2019	105,541	267.1	921,114	2,331.2	152,555	386.1	626,802	1,586.3	141,757	358.8
Percent change	+0.5	+0.4	-2.2	-2.3	-7.3	-7.5	+0.8	+0.7	-8.7	-8.8
Hawaii										
2018	1,922	135.3	41,027	2,888.0	5,709	401.9	29,600	2,083.6	5,718	402.5
2019	2,098	148.2	40,228	2,841.2	5,340	377.2	29,634	2,093.0	5,254	371.1
Percent change	+9.2	+9.5	-1.9	-1.6	-6.5	-6.2	+0.1	+0.4	-8.1	-7.8
Oregon										
2018	7,431	177.7	122,401	2,926.9	16,515	394.9	89,191	2,132.8	16,695	399.2
2019	7,825	185.5	115,170	2,730.6	14,724	349.1	85,261	2,021.5	15,185	360.0
Percent change	+5.3	+4.4	-5.9	-6.7	-10.8	-11.6	-4.4	-5.2	-9.0	-9.8
Washington										
2018	14,316	190.3	223,256	2,967.3	40,434	537.4	154,941	2,059.3	27,881	370.6
2019	13,700	179.9	204,224	2,681.9	34,540	453.6	145,282	1,907.9	24,402	320.5
Percent change	-4.3	-5.4	-8.5	-9.6	-14.6	-15.6	-6.2	-7.4	-12.5	-13.5
Puerto Rico										
2018	3,309	103.6	24,851	778.2	5,486	171.8	15,658	490.3	3,707	116.1
2019	3,537	110.7	22,441	702.7	4,291	134.4	14,483	453.5	3,667	114.8
Percent change	+6.9	+6.9	-9.7	-9.7	-21.8	-21.8	-7.5	-7.5	-1.1	-1.1

Note: Although arson data are included in the trend and clearance tables, sufficient data are not available to estimate totals for this offense. Therefore, no arson data are published in this table.
* = Less than one-tenth of 1 percent.
1 The previous year's crime figures have been adjusted.   2 Population figures are U.S. Census Bureau provisional estimates as of July 1, 2019.   3 The violent crime figures include the offenses of murder, rape (revised definition), robbery, and aggravated assault.   4 The figures shown in this column for the offense of rape were estimated using the revised Uniform Crime Reporting (UCR) definition of rape. See chapter notes for more detail.   5 Limited data for 2018 were available for Iowa.   6 Includes offenses reported by the Metro Transit Police and the District of Columbia Fire and Emergency Medical Services: Arson Investigation Unit.   7 This state's agencies submitted rape data according to the legacy UCR definition of rape.

Table 5. Crime in the United States, by State and Area, 2019

(Number, percent, rate per 100,000 population.)

Area	Population	Violent crime[1]	Murder and nonnegligent manslaughter	Rape[2]	Robbery	Aggravated assault	Property crime	Burglary	Larceny-theft	Motor vehicle theft
Alabama										
Metropolitan statistical area	3,728,978									
Area actually reporting	76.6%	12,880	182	1,141	1,706	9,851	65,789	12,388	47,299	6,102
Estimated total	100.0%	19,951	300	1,542	3,432	14,677	104,658	20,728	73,857	10,073
Cities outside metropolitan areas	528,518									
Area actually reporting	89.3%	3,327	36	297	266	2,728	17,915	3,140	13,382	1,393
Estimated total	100.0%	3,541	37	310	301	2,893	19,177	3,364	14,305	1,508
Nonmetropolitan counties	645,689									
Area actually reporting	72.4%	874	13	148	55	658	4,927	1,387	2,887	653
Estimated total	100.0%	1,554	21	216	208	1,109	7,298	1,987	4,315	996
State total	4,903,185	25,046	358	2,068	3,941	18,679	131,133	26,079	92,477	12,577
Rate per 100,000 inhabitants		510.8	7.3	42.2	80.4	381.0	2,674.4	531.9	1,886.1	256.5
Alaska										
Metropolitan statistical area	339,740									
Area actually reporting	100.0%	3,924	37	585	690	2,612	14,713	2,015	10,883	1,815
Cities outside metropolitan areas	127,436									
Area actually reporting	97.1%	1,032	9	225	71	727	3,555	467	2,760	328
Estimated total	100.0%	1,050	9	225	71	745	3,596	475	2,785	336
Nonmetropolitan counties	264,369									
Area actually reporting	100.0%	1,369	23	278	65	1,003	2,985	1,073	1,446	466
State total	731,545	6,343	69	1,088	826	4,360	21,294	3,563	15,114	2,617
Rate per 100,000 inhabitants		867.1	9.4	148.7	112.9	596.0	2,910.8	487.1	2,066.0	357.7
Arizona										
Metropolitan statistical area	6,926,575									
Area actually reporting	93.6%	26,975	314	3,203	6,171	17,287	163,728	25,572	121,711	16,445
Estimated total	100.0%	28,465	332	3,360	6,316	18,457	169,802	26,720	125,905	17,177
Cities outside metropolitan areas	126,113									
Area actually reporting	93.3%	4,280	26	294	75	3,885	6,061	1,419	3,868	774
Estimated total	100.0%	4,341	26	296	80	3,939	6,385	1,477	4,115	793
Nonmetropolitan counties	226,029									
Area actually reporting	100.0%	335	7	6	14	308	1,451	502	768	181
State total	7,278,717	33,141	365	3,662	6,410	22,704	177,638	28,699	130,788	18,151
Rate per 100,000 inhabitants		455.3	5.0	50.3	88.1	311.9	2,440.5	394.3	1,796.9	249.4
Arkansas										
Metropolitan statistical area	1,912,942									
Area actually reporting	95.3%	11,787	166	1,373	1,214	9,034	58,348	11,579	41,508	5,261
Estimated total	100.0%	12,317	172	1,444	1,277	9,424	61,525	12,103	43,905	5,517
Cities outside metropolitan areas	500,348									
Area actually reporting	93.8%	3,107	51	472	221	2,363	15,641	3,554	11,193	894
Estimated total	100.0%	3,268	53	497	233	2,485	16,457	3,748	11,767	942
Nonmetropolitan counties	604,514									
Area actually reporting	81.5%	1,703	15	334	37	1,317	6,709	1,825	4,081	803
Estimated total	100.0%	2,058	17	390	47	1,604	8,268	2,244	5,063	961
State total	3,017,804	17,643	242	2,331	1,557	13,513	86,250	18,095	60,735	7,420
Rate per 100,000 inhabitants		584.6	8.0	77.2	51.6	447.8	2,858.0	599.6	2,012.6	245.9
California										
Metropolitan statistical area	38,682,717									
Area actually reporting	99.9%	170,767	1,652	14,334	51,859	102,922	904,772	148,097	616,986	139,689
Estimated total	100.0%	170,793	1,652	14,336	51,862	102,943	904,915	148,134	617,075	139,706
Cities outside metropolitan areas	267,543									
Area actually reporting	100.0%	1,542	12	192	254	1,084	7,837	1,649	5,254	934
Nonmetropolitan counties	561,963									
Area actually reporting	100.0%	1,996	26	271	185	1,514	8,362	2,772	4,473	1,117
State total	39,512,223	174,331	1,690	14,799	52,301	105,541	921,114	152,555	626,802	141,757
Rate per 100,000 inhabitants		441.2	4.3	37.5	132.4	267.1	2,331.2	386.1	1,586.3	358.8
Colorado										
Metropolitan statistical area	5,045,741									
Area actually reporting	97.5%	19,666	187	3,326	3,505	12,648	133,050	17,395	95,114	20,541
Estimated total	100.0%	20,284	193	3,456	3,579	13,056	137,155	17,937	97,993	21,225
Cities outside metropolitan areas	343,675									
Area actually reporting	95.1%	1,000	8	258	69	665	8,475	1,152	6,813	510
Estimated total	100.0%	1,037	8	262	70	697	8,772	1,202	7,040	530
Nonmetropolitan counties	369,320									
Area actually reporting	95.1%	582	14	149	14	405	3,024	849	1,844	331
Estimated total	100.0%	617	17	154	14	432	3,262	925	1,979	358
State total	5,758,736	21,938	218	3,872	3,663	14,185	149,189	20,064	107,012	22,113
Rate per 100,000 inhabitants		381.0	3.8	67.2	63.6	246.3	2,590.7	348.4	1,858.3	384.0
Connecticut										
Metropolitan statistical area	2,964,813									
Area actually reporting	100.0%	6,227	92	675	1,883	3,577	48,028	5,955	36,501	5,572
Cities outside metropolitan areas	112,020									
Area actually reporting	100.0%	82	3	29	12	38	1,117	121	896	100
Nonmetropolitan counties	488,454									
Area actually reporting	100.0%	237	9	67	34	127	1,717	365	1,060	292
State total	3,565,287	6,546	104	771	1,929	3,742	50,862	6,441	38,457	5,964
Rate per 100,000 inhabitants		183.6	2.9	21.6	54.1	105.0	1,426.6	180.7	1,078.7	167.3

Table 5. Crime in the United States, by State and Area, 2019—Continued

(Number, percent, rate per 100,000 population.)

Area	Population	Violent crime[1]	Murder and nonnegligent manslaughter	Rape[2]	Robbery	Aggravated assault	Property crime	Burglary	Larceny-theft	Motor vehicle theft
Delaware										
Metropolitan statistical area	973,764									
Area actually reporting	100.0%	4,115	48	310	790	2,967	21,931	2,968	17,359	1,604
Cities outside metropolitan areas	None									
Nonmetropolitan counties	None									
State total	973,764	4,115	48	310	790	2,967	21,931	2,968	17,359	1,604
Rate per 100,000 inhabitants		422.6	4.9	31.8	81.1	304.7	2,252.2	304.8	1,782.7	164.7
District of Columbia[3]										
Metropolitan statistical area	705,749									
Area actually reporting	100.0%	7,403	166	345	2,713	4,179	30,821	1,843	26,645	2,333
Cities outside metropolitan areas	None									
Nonmetropolitan counties	None									
District total	705,749	7,403	166	345	2,713	4,179	30,821	1,843	26,645	2,333
Rate per 100,000 inhabitants		1,049.0	23.5	48.9	384.4	592.1	4,367.1	261.1	3,775.4	330.6
Florida										
Metropolitan statistical area	20,789,824									
Area actually reporting	99.9%	78,493	1,088	8,189	15,976	53,240	448,932	60,219	350,521	38,192
Estimated total	100.0%	78,513	1,088	8,191	15,979	53,255	449,076	60,247	350,626	38,203
Cities outside metropolitan areas	141,342									
Area actually reporting	92.9%	763	8	37	98	620	3,994	818	2,933	243
Estimated total	100.0%	804	8	37	102	657	4,169	876	3,035	258
Nonmetropolitan counties	546,571									
Area actually reporting	93.4%	1,839	24	217	125	1,473	7,040	2,112	4,381	547
Estimated total	100.0%	1,953	26	228	136	1,563	7,601	2,273	4,741	587
State total	21,477,737	81,270	1,122	8,456	16,217	55,475	460,846	63,396	358,402	39,048
Rate per 100,000 inhabitants		378.4	5.2	39.4	75.5	258.3	2,145.7	295.2	1,668.7	181.8
Georgia										
Metropolitan statistical area	8,820,462									
Area actually reporting	93.8%	28,497	542	2,310	6,964	18,681	200,844	30,111	150,187	20,546
Estimated total	100.0%	30,614	558	2,478	7,336	20,242	214,626	32,162	160,880	21,584
Cities outside metropolitan areas	638,977									
Area actually reporting	81.2%	2,485	51	175	420	1,839	18,897	2,988	15,125	784
Estimated total	100.0%	2,861	54	197	472	2,138	21,735	3,504	17,334	897
Nonmetropolitan counties	1,157,984									
Area actually reporting	90.3%	2,405	40	213	144	2,008	14,622	3,465	9,986	1,171
Estimated total	100.0%	2,695	42	247	153	2,253	15,888	3,840	10,753	1,295
State total	10,617,423	36,170	654	2,922	7,961	24,633	252,249	39,506	188,967	23,776
Rate per 100,000 inhabitants		340.7	6.2	27.5	75.0	232.0	2,375.8	372.1	1,779.8	223.9
Hawaii										
Metropolitan statistical area	1,142,377									
Area actually reporting	100.0%	3,087	28	450	1,021	1,588	34,247	4,441	25,308	4,498
Cities outside metropolitan areas	None									
Nonmetropolitan counties	273,495									
Area actually reporting	73.6%	680	16	288	48	328	4,444	656	3,196	592
State total	100.0%	955	20	315	110	510	5,981	899	4,326	756
Rate per 100,000 inhabitants	1,415,872	4,042	48	765	1,131	2,098	40,228	5,340	29,634	5,254
		285.5	3.4	54.0	79.9	148.2	2,841.2	377.2	2,093.0	371.1
Idaho										
Metropolitan statistical area	1,328,563									
Area actually reporting	99.8%	3,217	18	685	140	2,374	17,685	3,077	13,378	1,230
Cities outside metropolitan areas	100.0%	3,223	18	686	140	2,379	17,720	3,083	13,404	1,233
Area actually reporting	184,404									
Estimated total	97.5%	352	1	59	11	281	2,204	397	1,667	140
Nonmetropolitan counties	100.0%	362	1	61	11	289	2,274	410	1,719	145
Area actually reporting	274,098									
Estimated total	100.0%	415	16	62	4	333	1,799	434	1,172	193
State total	1,787,065	4,000	35	809	155	3,001	21,793	3,927	16,295	1,571
Rate per 100,000 inhabitants		223.8	2.0	45.3	8.7	167.9	1,219.5	219.7	911.8	87.9
Illinois										
Metropolitan statistical area	11,250,485									
Area actually reporting	97.4%	47,147	772	5,159	12,142	29,074	209,020	29,308	162,231	17,481
Estimated total	100.0%	47,898	777	5,288	12,266	29,567	214,444	30,102	166,463	17,879
Cities outside metropolitan areas	806,403									
Area actually reporting	84.3%	2,349	26	506	164	1,653	13,515	2,498	10,534	483
Estimated total	100.0%	2,571	26	533	172	1,840	15,028	2,834	11,639	555
Nonmetropolitan counties	614,933									
Area actually reporting	90.0%	1,016	29	244	26	717	4,108	1,360	2,436	312
Estimated total	100.0%	1,092	29	257	26	780	4,512	1,497	2,674	341
State total	12,671,821	51,561	832	6,078	12,464	32,187	233,984	34,433	180,776	18,775
Rate per 100,000 inhabitants		406.9	6.6	48.0	98.4	254.0	1,846.5	271.7	1,426.6	148.2
Indiana										
Metropolitan statistical area	5,267,529									
Area actually reporting	83.6%	20,739	314	1,922	4,908	13,595	102,535	16,775	74,430	11,330
Estimated total	100.0%	22,290	329	2,083	5,126	14,752	113,852	18,419	83,178	12,255
Cities outside metropolitan areas	550,564									
Area actually reporting	63.9%	939	9	110	92	728	7,715	902	6,315	498
Estimated total	100.0%	1,562	19	227	145	1,171	11,471	1,348	9,377	746

Table 5. Crime in the United States, by State and Area, 2019—Continued

(Number, percent, rate per 100,000 population.)

Area	Population	Violent crime[1]	Murder and nonnegligent manslaughter	Rape[2]	Robbery	Aggravated assault	Property crime	Burglary	Larceny-theft	Motor vehicle theft
Nonmetropolitan counties	914,126									
Area actually reporting	54.1%	672	15	99	41	517	3,938	1,062	2,427	449
Estimated total	100.0%	1,114	29	165	60	860	7,371	2,028	4,621	722
State total	6,732,219	24,966	377	2,475	5,331	16,783	132,694	21,795	97,176	13,723
Rate per 100,000 inhabitants		370.8	5.6	36.8	79.2	249.3	1,971.0	323.7	1,443.4	203.8
Iowa										
Metropolitan statistical area	1,936,796									
Area actually reporting	99.7%	5,897	47	767	785	4,298	40,335	8,397	27,930	4,008
Estimated total	100.0%	5,916	47	769	788	4,312	40,467	8,424	28,021	4,022
Cities outside metropolitan areas	571,915									
Area actually reporting	92.5%	1,680	8	250	67	1,355	10,388	2,050	7,640	698
Estimated total	100.0%	1,781	8	269	69	1,435	11,120	2,181	8,199	740
Nonmetropolitan counties	646,359									
Area actually reporting	97.7%	690	5	123	6	556	3,004	1,068	1,569	367
Estimated total	100.0%	713	5	126	6	576	3,112	1,105	1,627	380
State total	3,155,070	8,410	60	1,164	863	6,323	54,699	11,710	37,847	5,142
Rate per 100,000 inhabitants		266.6	1.9	36.9	27.4	200.4	1,733.7	371.1	1,199.6	163.0
Kansas										
Metropolitan statistical area	2,025,373									
Area actually reporting	95.0%	8,394	72	931	969	6,422	45,635	6,174	34,260	5,201
Estimated total	100.0%	9,339	83	1,033	1,151	7,072	51,894	6,979	38,847	6,068
Cities outside metropolitan areas	565,513									
Area actually reporting	96.5%	1,818	12	287	124	1,395	12,031	1,972	9,259	800
Estimated total	100.0%	1,865	12	297	124	1,432	12,329	2,050	9,457	822
Nonmetropolitan counties	322,428									
Area actually reporting	97.1%	743	10	83	18	632	3,103	926	1,800	377
Estimated total	100.0%	764	10	86	18	650	3,205	955	1,861	389
State total	2,913,314	11,968	105	1,416	1,293	9,154	67,428	9,984	50,165	7,279
Rate per 100,000 inhabitants		410.8	3.6	48.6	44.4	314.2	2,314.5	342.7	1,721.9	249.9
Kentucky										
Metropolitan statistical area	2,664,226									
Area actually reporting	99.9%	7,572	164	879	1,892	4,637	64,472	10,604	46,165	7,703
Estimated total	100.0%	7,572	164	879	1,892	4,637	64,511	10,610	46,193	7,708
Cities outside metropolitan areas	529,864									
Area actually reporting	98.0%	829	13	207	170	439	11,654	2,015	8,709	930
Estimated total	100.0%	833	13	207	172	441	11,784	2,041	8,804	939
Nonmetropolitan counties	1,273,583									
Area actually reporting	100.0%	1,296	44	486	97	669	8,474	2,792	4,133	1,549
State total	4,467,673	9,701	221	1,572	2,161	5,747	84,769	15,443	59,130	10,196
Rate per 100,000 inhabitants		217.1	4.9	35.2	48.4	128.6	1,897.4	345.7	1,323.5	228.2
Louisiana										
Metropolitan statistical area	3,915,216									
Area actually reporting	94.7%	21,056	475	1,939	3,632	15,010	125,043	21,718	93,822	9,503
Estimated total	100.0%	22,165	493	1,992	3,746	15,934	131,212	23,018	98,327	9,867
Cities outside metropolitan areas	267,576									
Area actually reporting	75.2%	1,588	23	117	174	1,274	8,226	2,008	5,939	279
Estimated total	100.0%	1,817	23	131	199	1,464	9,500	2,254	6,906	340
Nonmetropolitan counties	466,002									
Area actually reporting	96.7%	1,508	27	145	77	1,259	6,084	1,600	3,990	494
Estimated total	100.0%	1,555	28	150	80	1,297	6,281	1,646	4,126	509
State total	4,648,794	25,537	544	2,273	4,025	18,695	146,993	26,918	109,359	10,716
Rate per 100,000 inhabitants		549.3	11.7	48.9	86.6	402.1	3,162.0	579.0	2,352.4	230.5
Maine										
Metropolitan statistical area	799,195									
Area actually reporting	100.0%	872	8	247	138	479	10,593	1,277	8,929	387
Cities outside metropolitan areas	258,428									
Area actually reporting	100.0%	356	5	132	33	186	3,950	528	3,259	163
Nonmetropolitan counties	286,589									
Area actually reporting	100.0%	320	7	137	17	159	2,200	545	1,479	176
State total	1,344,212	1,548	20	516	188	824	16,743	2,350	13,667	726
Rate per 100,000 inhabitants		115.2	1.5	38.4	14.0	61.3	1,245.6	174.8	1,016.7	54.0
Maryland										
Metropolitan statistical area	5,895,999									
Area actually reporting	100.0%	27,100	538	1,861	9,150	15,551	115,527	16,382	87,952	11,193
Cities outside metropolitan areas	51,212									
Area actually reporting	100.0%	225	4	23	45	153	1,596	249	1,310	37
Nonmetropolitan counties	98,469									
Area actually reporting	100.0%	131	0	29	8	94	778	231	518	29
State total	6,045,680	27,456	542	1,913	9,203	15,798	117,901	16,862	89,780	11,259
Rate per 100,000 inhabitants		454.1	9.0	31.6	152.2	261.3	1,950.2	278.9	1,485.0	186.2
Massachusetts										
Metropolitan statistical area	6,863,792									
Area actually reporting	98.2%	22,199	152	2,159	3,588	16,300	79,955	12,124	61,784	6,047
Estimated total	100.0%	22,463	152	2,194	3,611	16,506	80,985	12,296	62,575	6,114
Cities outside metropolitan areas	28,711									
Area actually reporting	100.0%	115	0	10	2	103	332	45	269	18

Table 5. Crime in the United States, by State and Area, 2019—Continued

(Number, percent, rate per 100,000 population.)

Area	Population	Violent crime[1]	Murder and nonnegligent manslaughter	Rape[2]	Robbery	Aggravated assault	Property crime	Burglary	Larceny-theft	Motor vehicle theft
Nonmetropolitan counties										
Area actually reporting	100.0%	0	0	0	0	0	0	0	0	0
State total	6,892,503	22,578	152	2,204	3,613	16,609	81,317	12,341	62,844	6,132
Rate per 100,000 inhabitants		327.6	2.2	32.0	52.4	241.0	1,179.8	179.0	911.8	89.0
Michigan										
Metropolitan statistical area	8,189,617									
Area actually reporting	99.3%	38,719	510	5,465	5,247	27,497	138,960	24,755	97,615	16,590
Estimated total	100.0%	38,826	510	5,490	5,253	27,573	139,444	24,835	97,990	16,619
Cities outside metropolitan areas	578,810									
Area actually reporting	97.6%	1,684	12	541	67	1,064	9,096	1,025	7,676	395
Estimated total	100.0%	1,704	12	546	67	1,079	9,205	1,039	7,766	400
Nonmetropolitan counties	1,218,430									
Area actually reporting	96.2%	3,097	34	1,180	30	1,853	9,378	2,626	6,039	713
Estimated total	100.0%	3,156	34	1,199	30	1,893	9,647	2,698	6,224	725
State total	9,986,857	43,686	556	7,235	5,350	30,545	158,296	28,572	111,980	17,744
Rate per 100,000 inhabitants		437.4	5.6	72.4	53.6	305.9	1,585.0	286.1	1,121.3	177.7
Minnesota										
Metropolitan statistical area	4,394,131									
Area actually reporting	100.0%	11,396	105	1,973	3,047	6,271	100,569	13,139	77,450	9,980
Estimated total	568,835									
Cities outside metropolitan areas	95.7%	1,232	5	281	84	862	11,729	1,461	9,542	726
Area actually reporting	100.0%	1,233	5	281	84	863	11,754	1,464	9,563	727
Estimated total	676,666									
Nonmetropolitan counties	98.6%	695	7	192	18	478	4,862	1,310	3,048	504
Area actually reporting	100.0%	703	7	194	18	484	4,913	1,324	3,079	510
State total	5,639,632	13,332	117	2,448	3,149	7,618	117,236	15,927	90,092	11,217
Rate per 100,000 inhabitants		236.4	2.1	43.4	55.8	135.1	2,078.8	282.4	1,597.5	198.9
Mississippi[4]										
Metropolitan statistical area	1,439,666									
Area actually reporting	78.4%	3,235	141	432	883	1,779	30,660	5,668	22,012	2,980
Estimated total	100.0%	4,273	158	452	960	2,703	37,017	6,985	26,536	3,496
Cities outside metropolitan areas	554,808									
Area actually reporting	31.9%	931	38	112	144	637	7,037	1,698	4,967	372
Estimated total	100.0%	2,394	107	162	481	1,644	21,069	5,969	13,941	1,159
Nonmetropolitan counties	981,675									
Area actually reporting	28.2%	516	13	95	84	324	3,410	1,448	1,649	313
Estimated total	100.0%	1,605	67	133	259	1,146	12,621	5,706	5,823	1,092
State total	2,976,149	8,272	332	747	1,700	5,493	70,707	18,660	46,300	5,747
Rate per 100,000 inhabitants		277.9	11.2	25.1	57.1	184.6	2,375.8	627.0	1,555.7	193.1
Missouri										
Metropolitan statistical area	4,606,823									
Area actually reporting	99.5%	25,504	519	2,375	4,733	17,877	129,712	19,711	91,741	18,260
Estimated total	100.0%	25,679	520	2,381	4,740	18,038	130,293	19,864	92,117	18,312
Cities outside metropolitan areas	649,460									
Area actually reporting	96.4%	2,295	20	337	158	1,780	20,987	3,251	16,399	1,337
Estimated total	100.0%	2,394	20	338	159	1,877	21,518	3,317	16,845	1,356
Nonmetropolitan counties	881,145									
Area actually reporting	96.9%	2,245	28	193	59	1,965	9,852	3,139	5,351	1,362
Estimated total	100.0%	2,307	28	198	60	2,021	10,135	3,233	5,498	1,404
State total	6,137,428	30,380	568	2,917	4,959	21,936	161,946	26,414	114,460	21,072
Rate per 100,000 inhabitants		495.0	9.3	47.5	80.8	357.4	2,638.7	430.4	1,865.0	343.3
Montana										
Metropolitan statistical area	382,587									
Area actually reporting	100.0%	1,689	8	234	155	1,292	12,476	1,506	9,731	1,239
Cities outside metropolitan areas	230,654									
Area actually reporting	98.0%	1,500	9	226	30	1,235	5,995	625	4,838	532
Nonmetropolitan counties	100.0%	1,522	9	227	30	1,256	6,063	632	4,892	539
	455,537									
Area actually reporting	97.7%	1,087	10	159	20	898	4,796	731	3,481	584
Estimated total	100.0%	1,117	10	163	20	924	4,901	749	3,553	599
State total	1,068,778	4,328	27	624	205	3,472	23,440	2,887	18,176	2,377
Rate per 100,000 inhabitants		404.9	2.5	58.4	19.2	324.9	2,193.2	270.1	1,700.6	222.4
Nebraska										
Metropolitan statistical area	1,264,647									
Area actually reporting	99.6%	4,720	33	919	748	3,020	31,084	3,433	23,355	4,296
Estimated total	100.0%	4,766	33	950	748	3,035	31,147	3,433	23,418	4,296
Cities outside metropolitan areas	342,937									
Area actually reporting	94.1%	716	5	222	37	452	6,295	888	4,957	450
Estimated total	100.0%	727	5	226	37	459	6,523	918	5,142	463
Nonmetropolitan counties	326,824									
Area actually reporting	87.4%	289	7	69	7	206	1,512	334	985	193
Estimated total	100.0%	328	7	77	7	237	1,779	394	1,159	226
State total	1,934,408	5,821	45	1,253	792	3,731	39,449	4,745	29,719	4,985
Rate per 100,000 inhabitants		300.9	2.3	64.8	40.9	192.9	2,039.3	245.3	1,536.3	257.7
Nevada										
Metropolitan statistical area	2,801,329									
Area actually reporting	100.0%	14,359	127	2,008	3,232	8,992	67,801	14,711	42,280	10,810

Table 5. Crime in the United States, by State and Area, 2019—Continued

(Number, percent, rate per 100,000 population.)

Area	Population	Violent crime[1]	Murder and nonnegligent manslaughter	Rape[2]	Robbery	Aggravated assault	Property crime	Burglary	Larceny-theft	Motor vehicle theft
Cities outside metropolitan areas	48,376									
Area actually reporting	100.0%	211	5	40	16	150	1,179	237	825	117
Nonmetropolitan counties	230,451									
Area actually reporting	95.9%	593	10	102	37	444	2,456	529	1,604	323
Estimated total	100.0%	640	11	113	38	478	2,545	562	1,650	333
State total	3,080,156	15,210	143	2,161	3,286	9,620	71,525	15,510	44,755	11,260
Rate per 100,000 inhabitants		493.8	4.6	70.2	106.7	312.3	2,322.1	503.5	1,453.0	365.6
New Hampshire										
Metropolitan statistical area	857,832									
Area actually reporting	99.2%	1,376	16	329	221	810	9,917	1,019	8,389	509
Estimated total	100.0%	1,391	16	333	223	819	10,205	1,028	8,666	511
Cities outside metropolitan areas	465,800									
Area actually reporting	92.2%	581	17	214	79	271	5,373	562	4,488	323
Estimated total	100.0%	632	17	236	84	295	5,903	631	4,923	349
Nonmetropolitan counties	36,079									
Area actually reporting	92.3%	35	0	14	4	17	243	46	171	26
Estimated total	100.0%	51	0	21	6	24	334	58	243	33
State total	1,359,711	2,074	33	590	313	1,138	16,442	1,717	13,832	893
Rate per 100,000 inhabitants		152.5	2.4	43.4	23.0	83.7	1,209.2	126.3	1,017.3	65.7
New Jersey										
Metropolitan statistical area	8,882,190									
Area actually reporting	100.0%	18,375	262	1,531	5,730	10,852	118,637	16,399	91,902	10,336
Cities outside metropolitan areas	None									
Nonmetropolitan counties	None									
State total	8,882,190	18,375	262	1,531	5,730	10,852	118,637	16,399	91,902	10,336
Rate per 100,000 inhabitants		206.9	2.9	17.2	64.5	122.2	1,335.7	184.6	1,034.7	116.4
New Mexico										
Metropolitan statistical area	1,411,105									
Area actually reporting	91.4%	12,163	115	878	1,994	9,176	47,641	10,066	30,689	6,886
Estimated total	100.0%	12,859	117	903	2,022	9,817	49,041	10,693	31,294	7,054
Cities outside metropolitan areas	395,686									
Area actually reporting	94.4%	2,674	40	248	249	2,137	12,074	2,467	8,413	1,194
Estimated total	100.0%	2,963	41	251	280	2,391	12,630	2,688	8,716	1,226
Nonmetropolitan counties	290,038									
Area actually reporting	97.4%	1,598	23	133	38	1,404	3,503	1,191	1,645	667
Estimated total	100.0%	1,628	23	134	39	1,432	3,598	1,229	1,692	677
State total	2,096,829	17,450	181	1,288	2,341	13,640	65,269	14,610	41,702	8,957
Rate per 100,000 inhabitants		832.2	8.6	61.4	111.6	650.5	3,112.7	696.8	1,988.8	427.2
New York										
Metropolitan statistical area	18,100,822									
Area actually reporting	99.1%	67,175	546	5,653	17,891	43,085	250,291	24,744	213,411	12,136
Estimated total	100.0%	67,287	546	5,661	17,918	43,162	251,205	24,854	214,182	12,169
Cities outside metropolitan areas	499,079									
Area actually reporting	95.1%	1,113	4	287	110	712	8,359	1,255	6,895	209
Estimated total	100.0%	1,132	4	290	111	727	8,553	1,283	7,058	212
Nonmetropolitan counties	853,660									
Area actually reporting	94.6%	1,326	8	627	38	653	7,234	1,429	5,488	317
Estimated total	100.0%	1,345	8	632	39	666	7,397	1,463	5,611	323
State total	19,453,561	69,764	558	6,583	18,068	44,555	267,155	27,600	226,851	12,704
Rate per 100,000 inhabitants		358.6	2.9	33.8	92.9	229.0	1,373.3	141.9	1,166.1	65.3
North Carolina										
Metropolitan statistical area	8,503,759									
Area actually reporting	82.6%	27,331	421	2,093	5,952	18,865	171,283	32,606	125,793	12,884
Estimated total	100.0%	31,802	483	2,497	6,622	22,200	200,678	39,627	146,034	15,017
Cities outside metropolitan areas	588,106									
Area actually reporting	63.1%	2,256	37	203	382	1,634	15,667	3,686	11,181	800
Estimated total	100.0%	3,513	50	297	611	2,555	24,323	5,855	17,281	1,187
Nonmetropolitan counties	1,396,219									
Area actually reporting	73.5%	2,632	70	335	260	1,967	16,227	6,532	8,313	1,382
Estimated total	100.0%	3,680	99	453	366	2,762	22,235	8,965	11,413	1,857
State total	10,488,084	38,995	632	3,247	7,599	27,517	247,236	54,447	174,728	18,061
Rate per 100,000 inhabitants		371.8	6.0	31.0	72.5	262.4	2,357.3	519.1	1,666.0	172.2
North Dakota										
Metropolitan statistical area	382,454									
Area actually reporting	100.0%	1,230	10	261	151	808	9,400	1,585	6,873	942
Cities outside metropolitan areas	190,013									
Area actually reporting	99.9%	747	10	124	26	587	4,138	630	2,910	598
Estimated total	100.0%	747	10	124	26	587	4,139	630	2,911	598
Nonmetropolitan counties	189,595									
Area actually reporting	100.0%	192	4	52	2	134	1,527	393	882	252
State total	762,062	2,169	24	437	179	1,529	15,066	2,608	10,666	1,792
Rate per 100,000 inhabitants		284.6	3.1	57.3	23.5	200.6	1,977.0	342.2	1,399.6	235.2
Ohio[4]										
Metropolitan statistical area	9,386,086									
Area actually reporting	91.0%	29,614	489	4,445	8,287	16,393	189,426	35,722	137,623	16,081
Estimated total	100.0%	30,840	495	4,736	8,520	17,089	203,961	37,714	149,512	16,735

Table 5. Crime in the United States, by State and Area, 2019—Continued

(Number, percent, rate per 100,000 population.)

Area	Population	Violent crime[1]	Murder and nonnegligent manslaughter	Rape[2]	Robbery	Aggravated assault	Property crime	Burglary	Larceny-theft	Motor vehicle theft
Cities outside metropolitan areas	1,016,283									
Area actually reporting	78.2%	1,499	8	459	191	841	18,427	2,481	15,210	736
Estimated total	100.0%	2,001	8	611	263	1,119	24,942	3,337	20,641	964
Nonmetropolitan counties	1,286,731									
Area actually reporting	84.2%	1,225	29	325	52	819	9,442	2,349	6,280	813
Estimated total	100.0%	1,428	35	384	63	946	11,388	2,843	7,572	973
State total	11,689,100	34,269	538	5,731	8,846	19,154	240,291	43,894	177,725	18,672
Rate per 100,000 inhabitants		293.2	4.6	49.0	75.7	163.9	2,055.7	375.5	1,520.4	159.7
Oklahoma										
Metropolitan statistical area	2,636,166									
Area actually reporting	100.0%	13,071	209	1,637	2,070	9,155	81,441	18,566	52,513	10,362
Cities outside metropolitan areas	734,808									
Area actually reporting	96.9%	2,924	35	427	262	2,200	23,565	5,284	16,352	1,929
Estimated total	100.0%	2,925	35	427	262	2,201	23,572	5,286	16,356	1,930
Nonmetropolitan counties	585,997									
Area actually reporting	98.1%	1,070	22	200	36	812	7,415	2,666	3,685	1,064
Estimated total	100.0%	1,090	22	204	37	827	7,574	2,725	3,763	1,086
State total	3,956,971	17,086	266	2,268	2,369	12,183	112,587	26,577	72,632	13,378
Rate per 100,000 inhabitants		431.8	6.7	57.3	59.9	307.9	2,845.3	671.7	1,835.5	338.1
Oregon[4]										
Metropolitan statistical area	3,542,422									
Area actually reporting	99.4%	10,120	93	1,484	2,096	6,447	99,327	11,989	73,638	13,700
Estimated total	100.0%	10,176	93	1,494	2,098	6,491	99,681	12,034	73,924	13,723
Cities outside metropolitan areas	312,995									
Area actually reporting	97.2%	1,046	15	178	150	703	10,316	1,384	8,144	788
Estimated total	100.0%	1,064	15	182	151	716	10,490	1,411	8,279	800
Nonmetropolitan counties	362,320									
Area actually reporting	79.1%	618	7	82	21	508	3,965	1,009	2,438	518
Estimated total	100.0%	755	8	102	27	618	4,999	1,279	3,058	662
State total	4,217,737	11,995	116	1,778	2,276	7,825	115,170	14,724	85,261	15,185
Rate per 100,000 inhabitants		284.4	2.8	42.2	54.0	185.5	2,730.6	349.1	2,021.5	360.0
Pennsylvania										
Metropolitan statistical area	11,356,999									
Area actually reporting	99.2%	36,227	631	3,656	9,536	22,404	164,977	20,488	132,755	11,734
Estimated total	100.0%	36,357	631	3,662	9,548	22,516	165,748	20,577	133,398	11,773
Cities outside metropolitan areas	641,738									
Area actually reporting	94.8%	1,415	7	135	108	1,165	6,410	879	5,353	178
Estimated total	100.0%	1,439	7	136	108	1,188	6,554	898	5,476	180
Nonmetropolitan counties	803,252									
Area actually reporting	100.0%	1,432	31	553	87	761	7,363	1,879	5,047	437
State total	12,801,989	39,228	669	4,351	9,743	24,465	179,665	23,354	143,921	12,390
Rate per 100,000 inhabitants		306.4	5.2	34.0	76.1	191.1	1,403.4	182.4	1,124.2	96.8
Puerto Rico										
Metropolitan statistical area	3,193,694									
Area actually reporting	100.0%	6,180	572	205	2,086	3,317	21,967	4,115	14,227	3,625
Cities outside metropolitan areas										
Area actually reporting	100.0%	299	34	10	35	220	474	176	256	42
Total	3,193,694	6,479	606	215	2,121	3,537	22,441	4,291	14,483	3,667
Rate per 100,000 inhabitants		202.9	19.0	6.7	66.4	110.7	702.7	134.4	453.5	114.8
Rhode Island										
Metropolitan statistical area	1,059,361									
Area actually reporting	100.0%	2,342	25	491	418	1,408	16,259	2,321	12,580	1,358
Cities outside metropolitan areas	None									
Nonmetropolitan counties	None									
State total	1,059,361	2,342	25	491	418	1,408	16,259	2,321	12,580	1,358
Rate per 100,000 inhabitants		221.1	2.4	46.3	39.5	132.9	1,534.8	219.1	1,187.5	128.2
South Carolina										
Metropolitan statistical area	4,412,435									
Area actually reporting	99.0%	21,045	340	2,111	2,816	15,778	126,047	21,448	91,850	12,749
Estimated total	100.0%	21,415	345	2,140	2,844	16,086	127,857	21,830	93,137	12,890
Cities outside metropolitan areas	202,637									
Area actually reporting	97.2%	2,045	43	111	239	1,652	10,095	1,976	7,458	661
Estimated total	100.0%	2,114	46	113	246	1,709	10,430	2,055	7,696	679
Nonmetropolitan counties	533,642									
Area actually reporting	97.0%	2,717	72	201	197	2,247	12,737	3,462	7,904	1,371
Estimated total	100.0%	2,794	73	207	204	2,310	13,102	3,576	8,120	1,406
State total	5,148,714	26,323	464	2,460	3,294	20,105	151,389	27,461	108,953	14,975
Rate per 100,000 inhabitants		511.3	9.0	47.8	64.0	390.5	2,940.3	533.4	2,116.1	290.8
South Dakota										
Metropolitan statistical area	425,108									
Area actually reporting	99.5%	1,806	10	335	140	1,321	10,022	1,707	7,141	1,174
Estimated total	100.0%	1,809	10	335	140	1,324	10,031	1,711	7,144	1,176
Cities outside metropolitan areas	222,043									
Area actually reporting	97.1%	1,459	4	270	26	1,159	4,457	586	3,430	441
Estimated total	100.0%	1,481	4	273	26	1,178	4,553	604	3,501	448

Table 5. Crime in the United States, by State and Area, 2019—Continued

(Number, percent, rate per 100,000 population.)

Area	Population	Violent crime[1]	Murder and nonnegligent manslaughter	Rape[2]	Robbery	Aggravated assault	Property crime	Burglary	Larceny-theft	Motor vehicle theft
Nonmetropolitan counties	237,508									
Area actually reporting	85.8%	176	2	28	0	146	887	271	500	116
Estimated total	100.0%	240	3	34	29	174	1,083	331	620	132
State total	884,659	3,530	17	642	195	2,676	15,667	2,646	11,265	1,756
Rate per 100,000 inhabitants		399.0	1.9	72.6	22.0	302.5	1,771.0	299.1	1,273.4	198.5
Tennessee										
Metropolitan statistical area	5,346,297									
Area actually reporting	100.0%	35,287	449	2,360	5,894	26,584	152,843	23,900	112,931	16,012
Cities outside metropolitan areas	484,538									
Area actually reporting	100.0%	2,668	21	232	177	2,238	15,786	2,393	12,153	1,240
Nonmetropolitan counties	998,339									
Area actually reporting	100.0%	2,692	28	221	79	2,364	12,524	3,576	7,020	1,928
State total	6,829,174	40,647	498	2,813	6,150	31,186	181,153	29,869	132,104	19,180
Rate per 100,000 inhabitants		595.2	7.3	41.2	90.1	456.7	2,652.6	437.4	1,934.4	280.9
Texas										
Metropolitan statistical area	25,893,314									
Area actually reporting	99.6%	112,832	1,308	13,380	28,389	69,755	644,773	101,161	470,229	73,383
Estimated total	100.0%	113,040	1,309	13,400	28,406	69,925	646,291	101,452	471,296	73,543
Cities outside metropolitan areas	1,451,495									
Area actually reporting	96.5%	5,283	45	765	444	4,029	30,263	6,749	21,413	2,101
Estimated total	100.0%	5,400	45	787	446	4,122	30,904	6,940	21,807	2,157
Nonmetropolitan counties	1,651,072									
Area actually reporting	96.8%	3,010	55	633	136	2,186	15,847	5,458	8,618	1,771
Estimated total	100.0%	3,034	55	637	136	2,206	16,009	5,510	8,710	1,789
State total	28,995,881	121,474	1,409	14,824	28,988	76,253	693,204	113,902	501,813	77,489
Rate per 100,000 inhabitants		418.9	4.9	51.1	100.0	263.0	2,390.7	392.8	1,730.6	267.2
Utah										
Metropolitan statistical area	2,871,718									
Area actually reporting	99.8%	6,730	60	1,593	1,099	3,978	64,459	8,117	49,983	6,359
Estimated total	100.0%	6,755	60	1,601	1,102	3,992	64,792	8,162	50,248	6,382
Cities outside metropolitan areas	153,031									
Area actually reporting	86.2%	349	0	113	11	225	2,455	304	2,014	137
Estimated total	100.0%	414	0	134	11	269	2,797	360	2,281	156
Nonmetropolitan counties	181,209									
Area actually reporting	91.0%	338	12	77	11	238	1,768	307	1,279	182
Estimated total	100.0%	384	12	87	12	273	1,957	349	1,408	200
State total	3,205,958	7,553	72	1,822	1,125	4,534	69,546	8,871	53,937	6,738
Rate per 100,000 inhabitants		235.6	2.2	56.8	35.1	141.4	2,169.3	276.7	1,682.4	210.2
Vermont										
Metropolitan statistical area	221,448									
Area actually reporting	100.0%	444	5	114	32	293	3,786	406	3,284	96
Cities outside metropolitan areas	190,677									
Area actually reporting	100.0%	505	0	108	32	365	3,646	446	3,101	99
Nonmetropolitan counties	211,864									
Area actually reporting	100.0%	313	6	56	7	244	1,456	423	930	103
State total	623,989	1,262	11	278	71	902	8,888	1,275	7,315	298
Rate per 100,000 inhabitants		202.2	1.8	44.6	11.4	144.6	1,424.4	204.3	1,172.3	47.8
Virginia										
Metropolitan statistical area	7,489,609									
Area actually reporting	99.9%	15,713	344	2,340	3,338	9,691	126,904	11,783	105,821	9,300
Estimated total	100.0%	15,713	344	2,340	3,338	9,691	126,941	11,786	105,851	9,304
Cities outside metropolitan areas	243,163									
Area actually reporting	98.5%	572	15	114	75	368	5,840	655	4,903	282
Estimated total	100.0%	575	15	114	75	371	5,867	659	4,925	283
Nonmetropolitan counties	802,747									
Area actually reporting	100.0%	1,465	67	362	111	925	7,405	1,455	5,268	682
State total	8,535,519	17,753	426	2,816	3,524	10,987	140,213	13,900	116,044	10,269
Rate per 100,000 inhabitants		208.0	5.0	33.0	41.3	128.7	1,642.7	162.8	1,359.5	120.3
Washington	6,838,838									
Metropolitan statistical area	99.8%	20,734	182	2,937	5,002	12,613	189,481	31,171	135,283	23,027
Area actually reporting	100.0%	20,805	183	2,961	5,008	12,653	190,177	31,342	135,759	23,076
Estimated total	313,850									
Cities outside metropolitan areas	94.7%	924	7	224	108	585	8,892	1,633	6,427	832
Area actually reporting	100.0%	961	7	232	110	612	9,360	1,729	6,767	864
Estimated total	462,205									
Nonmetropolitan counties	100.0%	611	8	139	29	435	4,687	1,469	2,756	462
Area actually reporting	7,614,893	22,377	198	3,332	5,147	13,700	204,224	34,540	145,282	24,402
State total		293.9	2.6	43.8	67.6	179.9	2,681.9	453.6	1,907.9	320.5
Rate per 100,000 inhabitants										
West Virginia	1,156,599									
Metropolitan statistical area	84.7%	3,621	51	514	299	2,757	20,104	4,344	13,957	1,803
Area actually reporting	100.0%	3,939	55	547	324	3,013	21,838	4,730	15,162	1,946
Estimated total	174,190									
Cities outside metropolitan areas	82.7%	391	7	50	13	321	1,652	209	1,370	73
Area actually reporting	100.0%	708	8	82	33	585	3,754	303	3,332	119
Estimated total	461,358									

Table 5. Crime in the United States, by State and Area, 2019—Continued

(Number, percent, rate per 100,000 population.)

Area	Population	Violent crime[1]	Murder and nonnegligent manslaughter	Rape[2]	Robbery	Aggravated assault	Property crime	Burglary	Larceny-theft	Motor vehicle theft
Nonmetropolitan counties	83.1%	908	15	119	21	753	2,628	792	1,495	341
Area actually reporting	100.0%	1,027	15	125	21	866	2,784	858	1,572	354
Estimated total	1,792,147	5,674	78	754	378	4,464	28,376	5,891	20,066	2,419
State total		316.6	4.4	42.1	21.1	249.1	1,583.4	328.7	1,119.7	135.0
Rate per 100,000 inhabitants										
Wisconsin	4,350,936									
Metropolitan statistical area	98.8%	14,828	149	1,731	2,913	10,035	69,373	10,258	52,575	6,540
Area actually reporting	100.0%	14,878	149	1,748	2,915	10,066	70,020	10,365	53,091	6,564
Estimated total	642,215									
Cities outside metropolitan areas	93.7%	1,249	16	309	53	871	9,875	849	8,589	437
Area actually reporting	100.0%	1,287	16	313	54	904	10,579	902	9,220	457
Estimated total	829,283									
Nonmetropolitan counties	98.6%	893	10	198	22	663	4,992	1,376	3,257	359
Area actually reporting	100.0%	905	10	200	22	673	5,073	1,400	3,309	364
State total	5,822,434	17,070	175	2,261	2,991	11,643	85,672	12,667	65,620	7,385
Rate per 100,000 inhabitants		293.2	3.0	38.8	51.4	200.0	1,471.4	217.6	1,127.0	126.8
Wyoming										
Metropolitan statistical area	179,210									
Area actually reporting	81.0%	449	7	112	53	277	3,970	583	3,057	330
Estimated total	100.0%	553	7	128	58	360	4,304	698	3,239	367
Cities outside metropolitan areas	238,934									
Area actually reporting	91.9%	468	6	146	9	307	3,496	478	2,784	234
Estimated total	100.0%	492	6	154	9	323	3,724	510	2,964	250
Nonmetropolitan counties	160,615									
Area actually reporting	92.1%	194	0	39	0	155	973	170	716	87
Estimated total	100.0%	213	0	42	0	171	1,065	188	781	96
State total	578,759	1,258	13	324	67	854	9,093	1,396	6,984	713
Rate per 100,000 inhabitants		217.4	2.2	56.0	11.6	147.6	1,571.1	241.2	1,206.7	123.2

Note: Although arson data are included in the trend and clearance tables, sufficient data are not available to estimate totals for this offense. Therefore, no arson data are published in this table.
1 The violent crime figures include the offenses of murder, rape (revised definition), robbery, and aggravated assault.   2 The figures shown in this column for the offense of rape were estimated using the revised Uniform Crime Reporting (UCR) definition of rape. See chapter notes for further explanation.   3 Includes offenses reported by the Metro Transit Police and the Arson Investigation Unit of the District of Columbia Fire and Emergency Medical Services.   4 Agencies within this state submitted rape data according to the legacy UCR definition of rape.

Table 6. Crime in the United States, by Selected Metropolitan Statistical Area, 2019

(Number, percent, rate per 100,000 population.)

Area	Population	Violent crime	Murder and nonnegligent manslaughter	Rape[1]	Robbery	Aggravated assault	Property crime	Burglary	Larceny-theft	Motor vehicle theft
Abilene, TX M.S.A.	171,125									
Includes Callahan, Jones, and Taylor Counties										
City of Abilene	123,665	458	6	87	68	297	3,112	576	2,330	206
Total area actually reporting	100.0%	543	6	105	72	360	3,603	765	2,596	242
Rate per 100,000 inhabitants		317.3	3.5	61.4	42.1	210.4	2,105.5	447.0	1,517.0	141.4
Akron, OH M.S.A.[2]	703,784									
Includes Portage[2] and Summit Counties										
City of Akron	197,882	1,782	27	181	328	1,246	6,568	1,686	4,305	577
Total area actually reporting	94.5%	2,540	33	285	443	1,779	13,746	2,687	10,196	863
Estimated total	100.0%	2,616	33	318	455	1,810	14,445	2,770	10,781	894
Rate per 100,000 inhabitants		371.7	4.7	45.2	64.7	257.2	2,052.5	393.6	1,531.9	127.0
Albany, GA M.S.A.[3]	149,257									
Includes Dougherty, Lee, Terrell, and Worth Counties[3]										
City of Albany[3]	74,989	790	12	32	165	581	3,452	729	2,489	234
Total area actually reporting	97.4%	1,057	12	65	199	781	4,951	1,062	3,565	324
Estimated total	100.0%	1,071	12	66	202	791	5,057	1,074	3,650	333
Rate per 100,000 inhabitants		717.6	8.0	44.2	135.3	530.0	3,388.1	719.6	2,445.4	223.1
Albany-Lebanon, OR M.S.A.	128,105									
Includes Linn County										
City of Albany	54,993	70	1	10	16	43	1,467	128	1,242	97
City of Lebanon	17,304	29	0	11	0	18	372	22	323	27
Total area actually reporting	100.0%	175	6	35	24	110	2,743	342	2,162	239
Rate per 100,000 inhabitants		136.6	4.7	27.3	18.7	85.9	2,141.2	267.0	1,687.7	186.6
Albany-Schenectady-Troy, NY M.S.A.	879,862									
Includes Albany, Rensselaer, Saratoga, Schenectady, and Schoharie Counties										
City of Albany	97,221	736	4	60	189	483	2,919	445	2,315	159
City of Schenectady	65,504	528	3	56	133	336	1,770	248	1,392	130
City of Troy	49,286	296	3	25	73	195	1,365	225	1,035	105
Total area actually reporting	100.0%	2,266	14	350	483	1,419	15,367	1,743	12,988	636
Rate per 100,000 inhabitants		257.5	1.6	39.8	54.9	161.3	1,746.5	198.1	1,476.1	72.3
Albuquerque, NM M.S.A.[4]	918,114									
Includes Bernalillo, Sandoval, Torrance, and Valencia Counties										
City of Albuquerque[4]	561,920	7,596	84	486	1,699	5,327			20,634	5,425
Total area actually reporting	87.2%	9,004	91	564	1,768	6,581			23,626	6,025
Estimated total	100.0%	9,580	93	588	1,781	7,118			24,180	6,188
Rate per 100,000 inhabitants		1,043.4	10.1	64.0	194.0	775.3			2,633.7	674.0
Alexandria, LA M.S.A.	152,025									
Includes Grant and Rapides Parishes										
City of Alexandria	46,630	732	9	16	132	575	4,180	892	3,056	232
Total area actually reporting	82.5%	1,172	14	67	159	932	6,428	1,584	4,460	384
Estimated total	100.0%	1,291	16	71	165	1,039	6,900	1,682	4,805	413
Rate per 100,000 inhabitants		849.2	10.5	46.7	108.5	683.4	4,538.7	1,106.4	3,160.7	271.7
Altoona, PA M.S.A.	121,762									
Includes Blair County										
City of Altoona	43,429	264	0	83	22	159	675	142	481	52
Total area actually reporting	100.0%	406	1	111	33	261	1,510	271	1,163	76
Rate per 100,000 inhabitants		333.4	0.8	91.2	27.1	214.4	1,240.1	222.6	955.1	62.4
Amarillo, TX M.S.A.	266,054									
Includes Armstrong, Carson, Oldham, Potter, and Randall Counties										
City of Amarillo	201,036	1,447	15	161	246	1,025	7,835	1,439	5,425	971
Total area actually reporting	99.9%	1,584	16	194	257	1,117	8,578	1,650	5,862	1,066
Estimated total	100.0%	1,584	16	194	257	1,117	8,579	1,650	5,863	1,066
Rate per 100,000 inhabitants		595.4	6.0	72.9	96.6	419.8	3,224.5	620.2	2,203.7	400.7
Ames, IA M.S.A.	124,947									
Includes Boone and Story Counties										
City of Ames	68,237	135	1	44	21	69	1,171	138	975	58
Total area actually reporting	100.0%	249	2	64	22	161	1,745	256	1,381	108
Rate per 100,000 inhabitants		199.3	1.6	51.2	17.6	128.9	1,396.6	204.9	1,105.3	86.4
Anchorage, AK M.S.A.	306,136									
Includes Anchorage Municipality and Matanuska-Susitna Borough										
City of Anchorage	287,731	3,581	32	540	621	2,388	12,261	1,692	9,038	1,531
Total area actually reporting	100.0%	3,657	34	546	638	2,439	13,222	1,837	9,766	1,619
Rate per 100,000 inhabitants		1,194.6	11.1	178.4	208.4	796.7	4,319.0	600.1	3,190.1	528.8
Ann Arbor, MI M.S.A.	373,308									
Includes Washtenaw County										
City of Ann Arbor	122,893	309	2	77	46	184	2,124	197	1,789	138
Total area actually reporting	100.0%	1,327	8	250	143	926	6,159	743	4,940	476
Rate per 100,000 inhabitants		355.5	2.1	67.0	38.3	248.1	1,649.8	199.0	1,323.3	127.5

Table 6. Crime in the United States, by Selected Metropolitan Statistical Area, 2019—Continued

(Number, percent, rate per 100,000 population.)

Area	Population	Violent crime	Murder and nonnegligent manslaughter	Rape[1]	Robbery	Aggravated assault	Property crime	Burglary	Larceny-theft	Motor vehicle theft
Appleton, WI M.S.A.[3]	238,721									
Includes Calumet and Outagamie Counties										
City of Appleton	74,757	206	2	32	23	149	1,073	107	910	56
Total area actually reporting	97.4%	384	4	80	26	274	2,497	259	2,104	134
Estimated total	100.0%	392	4	82	27	279	2,599	266	2,195	138
Rate per 100,000 inhabitants		164.2	1.7	34.3	11.3	116.9	1,088.7	111.4	919.5	57.8
Asheville, NC M.S.A.[3]	463,796									
Includes Buncombe, Haywood, Henderson, and Madison Counties[3]										
City of Asheville[3]	93,641	695	6	59	163	467	5,923	833	4,552	538
Total area actually reporting	76.8%	1,221	12	116	215	878	11,093	2,373	7,709	1,011
Estimated total	100.0%	1,466	15	144	241	1,066	12,815	2,898	8,760	1,157
Rate per 100,000 inhabitants		316.1	3.2	31.0	52.0	229.8	2,763.1	624.8	1,888.8	249.5
Atlantic City-Hammonton, NJ M.S.A.	263,100									
Includes Atlantic County										
City of Atlantic City	37,593	323	11	29	182	101	1,738	130	1,519	89
City of Hammonton	14,003	25	0	1	4	20	115	25	78	12
Total area actually reporting	100.0%	672	13	49	272	338	6,314	857	5,174	283
Rate per 100,000 inhabitants		255.4	4.9	18.6	103.4	128.5	2,399.8	325.7	1,966.6	107.6
Augusta-Richmond County, GA-SC M.S.A.[3]	609,036									
Includes Burke, Columbia, Lincoln, McDuffie, and Richmond Counties, GA[3] and Aiken and Edgefield Counties, SC										
Total area actually reporting	96.5%	2,085	47	177	404	1,457	14,629	2,456	10,994	1,179
Estimated total	100.0%	2,199	49	186	411	1,553	15,097	2,580	11,292	1,225
Rate per 100,000 inhabitants		361.1	8.0	30.5	67.5	255.0	2,478.8	423.6	1,854.1	201.1
Austin-Round Rock-Georgetown, TX M.S.A.[3]	2,217,312									
Includes Bastrop, Caldwell,[3] Hays, Travis,3 and Williamson Counties										
City of Austin[3]	986,062	3,953	32	534	971	2,416	36,588	4,344	29,216	3,028
City of Round Rock	132,747	165	3	21	51	90	2,235	165	2,017	53
City of Georgetown	78,332	81	0	25	8	48	730	103	586	41
City of San Marcos	66,279	241	8	78	26	129	1,530	228	1,176	126
Total area actually reporting	99.9%	6,359	56	1,071	1,261	3,971	53,424	6,954	42,248	4,222
Estimated total	100.0%	6,361	56	1,071	1,261	3,973	53,442	6,958	42,260	4,224
Rate per 100,000 inhabitants		286.9	2.5	48.3	56.9	179.2	2,410.2	313.8	1,905.9	190.5
Bakersfield, CA M.S.A.	896,356									
Includes Kern County										
City of Bakersfield	388,080	1,766	34	116	701	915	16,074	3,888	9,277	2,909
Total area actually reporting	100.0%	5,567	84	455	1,238	3,790	29,604	7,595	16,126	5,883
Rate per 100,000 inhabitants		621.1	9.4	50.8	138.1	422.8	3,302.7	847.3	1,799.1	656.3
Baltimore-Columbia-Towson, MD M.S.A.	2,800,231									
Includes Anne Arundel, Baltimore, Carroll, Harford, Howard, and Queen Anne's Counties and Baltimore City										
City of Baltimore	597,239	11,101	348	324	4,856	5,573	25,748	5,414	16,395	3,939
Total area actually reporting	100.0%	19,564	434	1,025	6,797	11,308	66,044	10,213	49,114	6,717
Rate per 100,000 inhabitants		698.7	15.5	36.6	242.7	403.8	2,358.5	364.7	1,753.9	239.9
Bangor, ME M.S.A.	151,245									
Includes Penobscot County										
City of Bangor	31,872	35	1	1	15	18	1,168	64	1,076	28
Total area actually reporting	100.0%	67	1	7	20	39	2,355	221	2,060	74
Rate per 100,000 inhabitants		44.3	0.7	4.6	13.2	25.8	1,557.1	146.1	1,362.0	48.9
Barnstable Town, MA M.S.A.	211,470									
Includes Barnstable County										
City of Barnstable	44,032	178	2	22	14	140	425	61	350	14
Total area actually reporting	100.0%	691	2	113	29	547	2,017	401	1,542	74
Rate per 100,000 inhabitants		326.8	0.9	53.4	13.7	258.7	953.8	189.6	729.2	35.0
Baton Rouge, LA M.S.A.	852,152									
Includes Ascension, Assumption, East Baton Rouge, East Feliciana, Iberville, Livingston, Pointe Coupee, St. Helena, West Baton Rouge, and West Feliciana Parishes										
City of Baton Rouge	220,648	2,066	70	52	645	1,299	11,673	2,258	8,616	799
Total area actually reporting	98.8%	4,679	120	240	912	3,407	27,976	4,599	21,713	1,664
Estimated total	100.0%	4,721	120	241	915	3,445	28,266	4,661	21,926	1,679
Rate per 100,000 inhabitants		554.0	14.1	28.3	107.4	404.3	3,317.0	547.0	2,573.0	197.0
Battle Creek, MI M.S.A.[4]	133,965									
Includes Calhoun County										
City of Battle Creek	60,607	568	5	60	67	436	1,969	460	1,377	132
Total area actually reporting	99.9%	836	6	108	91	631			2,733	227
Estimated total	100.0%	836	6	108	91	631			2,733	227
Rate per 100,000 inhabitants		624.0	4.5	80.6	67.9	471.0			2,040.1	169.4

Table 6. Crime in the United States, by Selected Metropolitan Statistical Area, 2019—Continued

(Number, percent, rate per 100,000 population.)

Area	Population	Violent crime	Murder and nonnegligent manslaughter	Rape[1]	Robbery	Aggravated assault	Property crime	Burglary	Larceny-theft	Motor vehicle theft
Bay City, MI M.S.A.	103,201									
Includes Bay County										
City of Bay City	32,793	271	2	35	20	214	654	135	476	43
Total area actually reporting	100.0%	396	3	78	29	286	1,295	266	944	85
Rate per 100,000 inhabitants		383.7	2.9	75.6	28.1	277.1	1,254.8	257.7	914.7	82.4
Beaumont-Port Arthur, TX M.S.A.[3]	394,118									
Includes Hardin, Jefferson, and Orange Counties										
City of Beaumont	118,562	1,241	19	97	323	802	4,287	950	2,999	338
City of Port Arthur[3]	55,084	344	9	29	84	222	1,203	326	757	120
Total area actually reporting	99.9%	2,132	34	186	465	1,447	8,637	2,006	5,794	837
Estimated total	100.0%	2,133	34	186	465	1,448	8,644	2,007	5,799	838
Rate per 100,000 inhabitants		541.2	8.6	47.2	118.0	367.4	2,193.3	509.2	1,471.4	212.6
Bellingham, WA M.S.A	228,098									
Includes Whatcom County										
City of Bellingham	91,906	251	4	28	61	158	2,689	323	2,251	115
Total area actually reporting	100.0%	502	9	100	78	315	4,792	821	3,744	227
Rate per 100,000 inhabitants		220.1	3.9	43.8	34.2	138.1	2,100.9	359.9	1,641.4	99.5
Bend, OR M.S.A.	195,856									
Includes Deschutes County										
City of Bend	100,588	154	0	30	21	103	1,919	135	1,678	106
Total area actually reporting	100.0%	324	1	57	31	235	3,763	341	3,169	253
Rate per 100,000 inhabitants		165.4	0.5	29.1	15.8	120.0	1,921.3	174.1	1,618.0	129.2
Billings, MT M.S.A.[4]	181,514									
Includes Carbon, Stillwater, and Yellowstone Counties										
City of Billings[4]	110,198			75	98	499	4,499	608	3,266	625
Total area actually reporting	100.0%			103	106	679	5,468	721	4,008	739
Rate per 100,000 inhabitants				56.7	58.4	374.1	3,012.4	397.2	2,208.1	407.1
Binghamton, NY M.S.A.	237,535									
Includes Broome and Tioga Counties										
City of Binghamton	44,475	355	2	42	66	245	1,907	417	1,429	61
Total area actually reporting	99.4%	678	6	171	108	393	4,762	801	3,809	152
Estimated total	100.0%	678	6	171	108	393	4,773	802	3,819	152
Rate per 100,000 inhabitants		285.4	2.5	72.0	45.5	165.4	2,009.4	337.6	1,607.8	64.0
Bismarck, ND M.S.A.	128,869									
Includes Burleigh, Morton, and Oliver Counties										
City of Bismarck	74,705	228	1	64	36	127	2,079	225	1,647	207
Total area actually reporting	100.0%	394	5	104	44	241	2,983	340	2,295	348
Rate per 100,000 inhabitants		305.7	3.9	80.7	34.1	187.0	2,314.8	263.8	1,780.9	270.0
Blacksburg-Christiansburg, VA M.S.A.	167,936									
Includes Giles, Montgomery, and Pulaski Counties and Radford City										
City of Blacksburg	44,948	50	0	26	1	23	275	38	228	9
City of Christiansburg	22,700	31	0	7	4	20	466	28	424	14
Total area actually reporting	100.0%	323	2	106	20	195	2,781	332	2,311	138
Rate per 100,000 inhabitants		192.3	1.2	63.1	11.9	116.1	1,656.0	197.7	1,376.1	82.2
Bloomington, IL M.S.A.	172,429									
Includes McLean County										
City of Bloomington	78,107	387	1	49	57	280	1,096	171	851	74
Total area actually reporting	97.1%	601	3	115	82	401	2,312	324	1,851	137
Estimated total	100.0%	610	3	117	83	407	2,385	334	1,909	142
Rate per 100,000 inhabitants		353.8	1.7	67.9	48.1	236.0	1,383.2	193.7	1,107.1	82.4
Boise City, ID M.S.A.	749,238									
Includes Ada, Boise, Canyon, Gem, and Owyhee Counties										
City of Boise	231,314	649	4	164	44	437	3,653	470	2,952	231
Total area actually reporting	99.6%	1,874	10	436	83	1,345	9,275	1,507	7,063	705
Estimated total	100.0%	1,880	10	437	83	1,350	9,310	1,513	7,089	708
Rate per 100,000 inhabitants		250.9	1.3	58.3	11.1	180.2	1,242.6	201.9	946.2	94.5
Boston-Cambridge-Newton, MA-NH M.S.A.[3,5]	4,880,689									
Includes the Metropolitan Divisions of Boston, MA; Cambridge-Newton-Framingham, MA; and Rockingham County-Strafford County, NH										
City of Boston, MA[3,5]	698,941	4,244	42	231	1,039	2,932		1,703	10,590	
City of Cambridge, MA	119,908	334	1	26	67	240	1,983	161	1,724	98
City of Newton, MA	88,658	49	0	4	10	35	510	75	424	11
City of Framingham, MA	73,127	297	1	20	29	247	800	158	609	33
City of Waltham, MA	62,737	102	0	13	7	82	512	70	420	22
Total area actually reporting	98.8%	13,450	93	1,253	2,328	9,776		6,767	43,000	
Estimated total	100.0%	13,556	93	1,270	2,333	9,860		6,840	43,333	
Rate per 100,000 inhabitants		277.7	1.9	26.0	47.8	202.0		140.1	887.8	

Table 6. Crime in the United States, by Selected Metropolitan Statistical Area, 2019—Continued

(Number, percent, rate per 100,000 population.)

Area	Population	Violent crime	Murder and nonnegligent manslaughter	Rape[1]	Robbery	Aggravated assault	Property crime	Burglary	Larceny-theft	Motor vehicle theft
Boston, MA M.D.[3, 5]	2,032,861									
Includes Norfolk, Plymouth, and Suffolk Counties										
Total area actually reporting	98.7%	8,008	61	625	1,595	5,727		3,351	21,175	
Estimated total	100.0%	8,057	61	633	1,598	5,765		3,384	21,322	
Rate per 100,000 inhabitants		396.3	3.0	31.1	78.6	283.6		166.5	1,048.9	
Cambridge-Newton-Framingham, MA M.D.[3]	2,406,489									
Includes Essex and Middlesex Counties										
Total area actually reporting	98.6%	5,008	27	485	680	3,816	22,303	2,934	17,780	1,589
Estimated total	100.0%	5,065	27	494	682	3,862	22,543	2,974	17,966	1,603
Rate per 100,000 inhabitants		210.5	1.1	20.5	28.3	160.5	936.8	123.6	746.6	66.6
Rockingham County-Strafford County, NH M.D.	441,339									
Includes Rockingham and Strafford Counties										
Total area actually reporting	100.0%	434	5	143	53	233	4,770	482	4,045	243
Rate per 100,000 inhabitants		98.3	1.1	32.4	12.0	52.8	1,080.8	109.2	916.5	55.1
Boulder, CO M.S.A.	328,673									
Includes Boulder County										
City of Boulder	108,519	278	1	41	37	199	3,284	405	2,628	251
Total area actually reporting	100.0%	895	3	224	83	585	8,038	999	6,341	698
Rate per 100,000 inhabitants		272.3	0.9	68.2	25.3	178.0	2,445.6	303.9	1,929.3	212.4
Bowling Green, KY M.S.A.	179,183									
Includes Allen, Butler, Edmonson, and Warren Counties										
City of Bowling Green	69,627	203	4	63	55	81	3,250	386	2,610	254
Total area actually reporting	100.0%	275	6	85	62	122	4,188	645	3,184	359
Rate per 100,000 inhabitants		153.5	3.3	47.4	34.6	68.1	2,337.3	360.0	1,777.0	200.4
Bremerton-Silverdale-Port Orchard, WA M.S.A.	271,215									
Includes Kitsap County										
City of Bremerton	41,675	168	1	26	34	107	1,358	234	984	140
City of Port Orchard	14,684	66	0	7	14	45	492	74	376	42
Total area actually reporting	100.0%	709	4	157	81	467	5,392	989	3,944	459
Rate per 100,000 inhabitants		261.4	1.5	57.9	29.9	172.2	1,988.1	364.7	1,454.2	169.2
Bridgeport-Stamford-Norwalk, CT M.S.A.	929,479									
Includes Fairfield County										
City of Bridgeport	144,908	843	17	71	392	363	2,465	555	1,292	618
City of Stamford	130,678	264	5	27	87	145	1,803	196	1,446	161
City of Norwalk	89,440	183	1	8	29	145	1,247	133	989	125
City of Danbury	85,167	97	1	15	28	53	1,045	132	827	86
City of Stratford	52,034	71	1	13	25	32	859	97	654	108
Total area actually reporting	100.0%	1,619	28	162	609	820	11,232	1,542	8,325	1,365
Rate per 100,000 inhabitants		174.2	3.0	17.4	65.5	88.2	1,208.4	165.9	895.7	146.9
Brownsville-Harlingen, TX M.S.A.[3]	423,309									
Includes Cameron County										
City of Brownsville	184,418	776	0	82	143	551	4,553	631	3,801	121
City of Harlingen	65,481	273	0	54	54	165	3,152	443	2,613	96
Total area actually reporting	100.0%	1,588	4	233	236	1,115	10,705	1,670	8,682	353
Rate per 100,000 inhabitants		375.1	0.9	55.0	55.8	263.4	2,528.9	394.5	2,051.0	83.4
Buffalo-Cheektowaga, NY M.S.A.	1,123,277									
Includes Erie and Niagara Counties										
City of Buffalo	255,686	2,533	47	121	802	1,563	8,298	1,610	6,009	679
City of Cheektowaga Town	76,821	187	2	15	57	113	2,153	208	1,856	89
Total area actually reporting	98.2%	3,962	60	329	1,130	2,443	20,762	3,051	16,504	1,207
Estimated total	100.0%	3,980	60	332	1,133	2,455	20,987	3,073	16,699	1,215
Rate per 100,000 inhabitants		354.3	5.3	29.6	100.9	218.6	1,868.4	273.6	1,486.6	108.2
Burlington, NC M.S.A.[3]	168,317									
Includes Alamance County[3]										
City of Burlington[3]	54,108	460	10	42	66	342	2,490	534	1,815	141
Total area actually reporting	91.0%	631	13	60	88	470	3,926	895	2,804	227
Estimated total	100.0%	686	14	66	98	508	4,443	993	3,196	254
Rate per 100,000 inhabitants		407.6	8.3	39.2	58.2	301.8	2,639.7	590.0	1,898.8	150.9
Burlington-South Burlington, VT M.S.A.	221,448									
Includes Chittenden, Franklin, and Grand Isle Counties										
City of Burlington	42,958	174	2	41	13	118	1,110	109	976	25
City of South Burlington	19,687	22	0	6	4	12	687	32	647	8
Total area actually reporting	100.0%	444	5	114	32	293	3,786	406	3,284	96
Rate per 100,000 inhabitants		200.5	2.3	51.5	14.5	132.3	1,709.7	183.3	1,483.0	43.4
California-Lexington Park, MD M.S.A.	112,993									
Includes St. Mary's County										
Total area actually reporting	100.0%	231	1	29	46	155	1,880	333	1,476	71
Rate per 100,000 inhabitants		204.4	0.9	25.7	40.7	137.2	1,663.8	294.7	1,306.3	62.8

Table 6. Crime in the United States, by Selected Metropolitan Statistical Area, 2019—Continued

(Number, percent, rate per 100,000 population.)

Area	Population	Violent crime	Murder and nonnegligent manslaughter	Rape[1]	Robbery	Aggravated assault	Property crime	Burglary	Larceny-theft	Motor vehicle theft
Canton-Massillon, OH M.S.A. Includes Carroll and Stark Counties	397,244									
City of Canton	70,139	981	6	135	188	652	3,712	962	2,429	321
City of Massillon	32,433	72	1	26	14	31	743	116	610	17
Total area actually reporting	96.9%	1,328	9	239	236	844	8,608	1,918	6,128	562
Estimated total	100.0%	1,345	9	242	239	855	8,832	1,946	6,313	573
Rate per 100,000 inhabitants		338.6	2.3	60.9	60.2	215.2	2,223.3	489.9	1,589.2	144.2
Cape Coral-Fort Myers, FL M.S.A. Includes Lee County	767,771									
City of Cape Coral	194,183	226	5	16	36	169	2,176	274	1,739	163
City of Fort Myers	85,127	486	9	34	94	349	1,952	245	1,553	154
Total area actually reporting	100.0%	1,979	23	246	386	1,324	8,890	1,343	6,792	755
Rate per 100,000 inhabitants		257.8	3.0	32.0	50.3	172.4	1,157.9	174.9	884.6	98.3
Cape Girardeau, MO-IL M.S.A. Includes Alexander County, IL and Bollinger and Cape Girardeau Counties, MO	96,976									
City of Cape Girardeau, MO	40,077	233	6	24	46	157	1,432	215	1,145	72
Total area actually reporting	97.8%	370	7	32	46	285	2,027	378	1,540	109
Estimated total	100.0%	373	7	33	46	287	2,060	383	1,566	111
Rate per 100,000 inhabitants		384.6	7.2	34.0	47.4	295.9	2,124.2	394.9	1,614.8	114.5
Carson City, NV M.S.A. Includes Carson City	55,491									
Total area actually reporting	100.0%	193	0	47	11	135	711	152	487	72
Rate per 100,000 inhabitants		347.8	0.0	84.7	19.8	243.3	1,281.3	273.9	877.6	129.8
Casper, WY M.S.A. Includes Natrona County	79,489									
City of Casper	57,752	169	2	58	18	91	1,677	285	1,271	121
Total area actually reporting	100.0%	227	2	68	25	132	1,966	370	1,441	155
Rate per 100,000 inhabitants		285.6	2.5	85.5	31.5	166.1	2,473.3	465.5	1,812.8	195.0
Cedar Rapids, IA M.S.A. Includes Benton, Jones, and Linn Counties	272,728									
City of Cedar Rapids	134,007	345	2	27	83	233	4,470	837	3,268	365
Total area actually reporting	99.1%	505	2	56	89	358	5,498	1,077	3,947	474
Estimated total	100.0%	514	2	57	90	365	5,566	1,091	3,994	481
Rate per 100,000 inhabitants		188.5	0.7	20.9	33.0	133.8	2,040.9	400.0	1,464.5	176.4
Champaign-Urbana, IL M.S.A. Includes Champaign and Piatt Counties	226,393									
City of Champaign	88,891	827	2	73	94	658	2,203	300	1,777	126
City of Urbana	42,080	124	1	30	36	57	1,090	161	890	39
Total area actually reporting	99.2%	1,098	3	158	156	781	4,482	735	3,533	214
Estimated total	100.0%	1,099	3	158	156	782	4,507	739	3,553	215
Rate per 100,000 inhabitants		485.4	1.3	69.8	68.9	345.4	1,990.8	326.4	1,569.4	95.0
Charleston-North Charleston, SC M.S.A. Includes Berkeley, Charleston, and Dorchester Counties	804,618									
City of Charleston	138,254	516	8	51	95	362	3,124	292	2,335	497
City of North Charleston	115,312	1,114	26	103	229	756	6,941	853	5,123	965
Total area actually reporting	99.0%	3,148	72	328	497	2,251	21,218	3,031	15,573	2,614
Estimated total	100.0%	3,202	72	333	502	2,295	21,554	3,084	15,835	2,635
Rate per 100,000 inhabitants		398.0	8.9	41.4	62.4	285.2	2,678.8	383.3	1,968.0	327.5
Charlottesville, VA M.S.A. Includes Albemarle, Buckingham, Fluvanna, Greene, and Nelson Counties and Charlottesville City	219,120									
City of Charlottesville	48,453	157	0	32	22	103	1,124	122	924	78
Total area actually reporting	100.0%	385	5	102	38	240	3,104	314	2,617	173
Rate per 100,000 inhabitants		175.7	2.3	46.5	17.3	109.5	1,416.6	143.3	1,194.3	79.0
Chattanooga, TN-GA M.S.A.[3] Includes Catoosa, Dade, and Walker Counties, GA3 and Hamilton, Marion, and Sequatchie Counties, TN	564,924									
City of Chattanooga, TN	181,848	1,946	33	161	196	1,556	10,106	1,098	7,694	1,314
Total area actually reporting	97.1%	2,914	36	237	250	2,391	16,071	2,098	12,059	1,914
Estimated total	100.0%	2,969	36	242	255	2,436	16,332	2,150	12,244	1,938
Rate per 100,000 inhabitants		525.6	6.4	42.8	45.1	431.2	2,891.0	380.6	2,167.4	343.1
Chico, CA M.S.A. Includes Butte County	230,749									
City of Chico	95,826	557	0	100	104	353	2,406	272	1,753	381
Total area actually reporting	100.0%	1,024	7	180	167	670	5,322	1,111	3,343	868
Rate per 100,000 inhabitants		443.8	3.0	78.0	72.4	290.4	2,306.4	481.5	1,448.8	376.2
Cincinnati, OH-KY-IN M.S.A. Includes Dearborn, Franklin, Ohio, and Union Counties, IN; Boone, Bracken, Campbell, Gallatin, Grant, Kenton, and Pendleton Counties, KY; and Brown, Butler, Clermont, Hamilton, and Warren Counties, OH	2,217,647									

Table 6. Crime in the United States, by Selected Metropolitan Statistical Area, 2019—Continued

(Number, percent, rate per 100,000 population.)

Area	Population	Violent crime	Murder and nonnegligent manslaughter	Rape[1]	Robbery	Aggravated assault	Property crime	Burglary	Larceny-theft	Motor vehicle theft
City of Cincinnati, OH	303,335	2,562	64	280	872	1,346	13,051	2,765	8,935	1,351
Total area actually reporting	89.8%	4,923	90	872	1,438	2,523	40,924	6,551	31,014	3,359
Estimated total	100.0%	5,264	92	931	1,486	2,755	43,841	7,067	33,240	3,534
Rate per 100,000 inhabitants		237.4	4.1	42.0	67.0	124.2	1,976.9	318.7	1,498.9	159.4
Clarksville, TN-KY M.S.A.	309,897									
Includes Christian and Trigg Counties, KY and Montgomery and Stewart Counties, TN										
City of Clarksville, TN	159,996	926	14	103	116	693	4,467	543	3,457	467
Total area actually reporting	100.0%	1,201	21	150	151	879	7,005	1,145	5,176	684
Rate per 100,000 inhabitants		387.5	6.8	48.4	48.7	283.6	2,260.4	369.5	1,670.2	220.7
Cleveland, TN M.S.A.	124,685									
Includes Bradley and Polk Counties										
City of Cleveland	45,453	464	2	35	42	385	2,403	371	1,845	187
Total area actually reporting	100.0%	698	3	52	57	586	3,564	626	2,577	361
Rate per 100,000 inhabitants		559.8	2.4	41.7	45.7	470.0	2,858.4	502.1	2,066.8	289.5
Cleveland-Elyria, OH M.S.A.[2, 3]	2,051,044									
Includes Cuyahoga, Geauga, Lake, Lorain, and Medina Counties										
City of Cleveland	381,829	5,791	92	479	1,895	3,325	17,057	4,311	9,968	2,778
City of Elyria	53,806	137	4	35	37	61	921	207	665	49
Total area actually reporting	86.8%	7,897	119	748	2,387	4,643	33,474	6,909	22,694	3,871
Estimated total	100.0%	8,271	122	841	2,472	4,836	37,974	7,473	26,422	4,079
Rate per 100,000 inhabitants		403.3	5.9	41.0	120.5	235.8	1,851.4	364.4	1,288.2	198.9
Coeur d'Alene, ID M.S.A.	165,319									
Includes Kootenai County										
City of Coeur d'Alene	52,256	132	0	38	8	86	712	83	579	50
Total area actually reporting	100.0%	362	1	68	16	277	2,099	338	1,627	134
Rate per 100,000 inhabitants		219.0	0.6	41.1	9.7	167.6	1,269.7	204.5	984.2	81.1
College Station-Bryan, TX M.S.A.[3]	265,223									
Includes Brazos, Burleson, and Robertson Counties										
City of College Station[3]	119,246	225	1	48	43	133	2,098	391	1,529	178
City of Bryan	86,632	370	2	90	57	221	1,928	336	1,444	148
Total area actually reporting	99.4%	693	5	164	111	413	5,204	999	3,798	407
Estimated total	100.0%	696	5	164	111	416	5,228	1,004	3,814	410
Rate per 100,000 inhabitants		262.4	1.9	61.8	41.9	156.8	1,971.2	378.5	1,438.0	154.6
Colorado Springs, CO M.S.A.	747,633									
Includes El Paso and Teller Counties										
City of Colorado Springs	479,648	2,806	23	431	485	1,867	17,587	2,400	12,095	3,092
Total area actually reporting	98.5%	3,464	33	579	550	2,302	20,970	2,945	14,380	3,645
Estimated total	100.0%	3,482	33	582	554	2,313	21,290	2,972	14,645	3,673
Rate per 100,000 inhabitants		465.7	4.4	77.8	74.1	309.4	2,847.7	397.5	1,958.8	491.3
Columbia, MO M.S.A.[3]	209,738									
Includes Boone, Cooper, and Howard3 Counties										
City of Columbia[3]	125,017	401	11	69	74	247	3,243	499	2,431	313
Total area actually reporting	99.2%	566	14	100	85	367	4,552	708	3,390	454
Estimated total	100.0%	570	14	101	85	370	4,577	714	3,406	457
Rate per 100,000 inhabitants		271.8	6.7	48.2	40.5	176.4	2,182.2	340.4	1,623.9	217.9
Columbia, SC M.S.A.	841,451									
Includes Calhoun, Fairfield, Kershaw, Lexington, Richland, and Saluda Counties										
City of Columbia	133,790	1,037	29	88	220	700	7,027	916	5,216	895
Total area actually reporting	100.0%	4,909	71	412	696	3,730	28,376	4,480	20,448	3,448
Rate per 100,000 inhabitants		583.4	8.4	49.0	82.7	443.3	3,372.3	532.4	2,430.1	409.8
Columbus, IN M.S.A.[3]	83,691									
Includes Bartholomew County										
City of Columbus	47,991	67	0	40	17	10	1,439	130	1,254	55
Total area actually reporting	100.0%	122	0	58	19	45	1,864	208	1,559	97
Rate per 100,000 inhabitants		145.8	0.0	69.3	22.7	53.8	2,227.2	248.5	1,862.8	115.9
Columbus, OH M.S.A.	2,129,346									
Includes Delaware, Fairfield, Franklin, Hocking, Licking, Madison, Morrow, Perry, Pickaway, and Union Counties										
City of Columbus	906,120	4,561	81	882	1,810	1,788	29,974	5,809	20,606	3,559
Total area actually reporting	93.5%	5,889	112	1,284	2,088	2,405	48,501	8,551	35,380	4,570
Estimated total	100.0%	6,100	113	1,327	2,127	2,533	50,897	8,890	37,326	4,681
Rate per 100,000 inhabitants		286.5	5.3	62.3	99.9	119.0	2,390.3	417.5	1,752.9	219.8
Corpus Christi, TX M.S.A.[3]	429,610									
Includes Nueces and San Patricio Counties										
City of Corpus Christi[3]	329,320	2,616	31	266	496	1,823	11,347	1,961	8,494	892
Total area actually reporting	99.9%	3,165	35	313	536	2,281	13,605	2,443	10,112	1,050
Estimated total	100.0%	3,166	35	313	536	2,282	13,613	2,445	10,117	1,051
Rate per 100,000 inhabitants		736.9	8.1	72.9	124.8	531.2	3,168.7	569.1	2,354.9	244.6

Table 6. Crime in the United States, by Selected Metropolitan Statistical Area, 2019—Continued

(Number, percent, rate per 100,000 population.)

Area	Population	Violent crime	Murder and nonnegligent manslaughter	Rape[1]	Robbery	Aggravated assault	Property crime	Burglary	Larceny-theft	Motor vehicle theft
Crestview-Fort Walton Beach-Destin, FL M.S.A.	282,526									
Includes Okaloosa and Walton Counties										
City of Crestview	25,152	96	3	11	20	62	644	107	478	59
City of Fort Walton Beach	22,645	68	2	18	1	47	475	59	372	44
Total area actually reporting	99.7%	882	13	131	64	674	4,699	631	3,680	388
Estimated total	100.0%	885	13	131	65	676	4,718	635	3,694	389
Rate per 100,000 inhabitants		313.2	4.6	46.4	23.0	239.3	1,669.9	224.8	1,307.5	137.7
Cumberland, MD-WV M.S.A.	96,806									
Includes Allegany County, MD and Mineral County, WV										
City of Cumberland, MD	19,321	151	0	9	33	109	869	216	627	26
Total area actually reporting	98.5%	262	0	27	44	191	1,729	374	1,284	71
Estimated total	100.0%	266	0	27	44	195	1,762	381	1,307	74
Rate per 100,000 inhabitants		274.8	0.0	27.9	45.5	201.4	1,820.1	393.6	1,350.1	76.4
Danville, IL M.S.A.	75,878									
Includes Vermilion County										
City of Danville	30,642	536	7	50	65	414	1,370	341	957	72
Total area actually reporting	100.0%	710	7	92	74	537	2,161	602	1,453	106
Rate per 100,000 inhabitants		935.7	9.2	121.2	97.5	707.7	2,848.0	793.4	1,914.9	139.7
Davenport-Moline-Rock Island, IA-IL M.S.A.	379,899									
Includes Henry, Mercer, and Rock Island Counties, IL and Scott County, IA										
City of Davenport, IA	102,392	609	2	84	124	399	3,918	745	2,830	343
City of Moline, IL	41,701	219	1	36	26	156	978	190	727	61
City of Rock Island, IL	37,517	139	1	14	29	95	878	166	599	113
Total area actually reporting	96.7%	1,367	8	208	208	943	8,152	1,566	5,919	667
Estimated total	100.0%	1,392	8	212	211	961	8,353	1,596	6,074	683
Rate per 100,000 inhabitants		366.4	2.1	55.8	55.5	253.0	2,198.7	420.1	1,598.8	179.8
Dayton-Kettering, OH M.S.A.[3]	805,963									
Includes Greene, Miami, and Montgomery Counties										
City of Dayton	140,427	1,351	48	200	347	756	5,673	1,533	3,393	747
City of Kettering	54,974	56	1	27	13	15	794	139	604	51
Total area actually reporting	93.7%	2,551	60	487	623	1,381	16,890	3,287	12,128	1,475
Estimated total	100.0%	2,647	60	530	641	1,416	18,206	3,477	13,211	1,518
Rate per 100,000 inhabitants		328.4	7.4	65.8	79.5	175.7	2,258.9	431.4	1,639.2	188.3
Decatur, IL M.S.A.	103,506									
Includes Macon County										
City of Decatur	70,710	375	11	52	65	247	1,954	442	1,339	173
Total area actually reporting	100.0%	434	11	64	71	288	2,382	520	1,671	191
Rate per 100,000 inhabitants		419.3	10.6	61.8	68.6	278.2	2,301.3	502.4	1,614.4	184.5
Deltona-Daytona Beach-Ormond Beach, FL M.S.A.	664,033									
Includes Flagler and Volusia Counties										
City of Daytona Beach	69,834	794	13	18	109	654	2,833	380	2,213	240
City of Ormond Beach	44,005	133	1	13	15	104	1,119	158	894	67
City of DeLand	34,468	198	4	1	26	167	1,126	182	873	71
Total area actually reporting	100.0%	2,120	28	136	289	1,667	11,988	1,879	9,180	929
Rate per 100,000 inhabitants		319.3	4.2	20.5	43.5	251.0	1,805.3	283.0	1,382.5	139.9
Detroit-Warren-Dearborn, MI M.S.A.	4,320,314									
Includes the Metropolitan Divisions of Detroit-Dearborn-Livonia and Warren-Troy-Farmington Hills										
City of Detroit	663,502	13,040	275	952	2,346	9,467	28,550	6,820	14,844	6,886
City of Warren	134,653	648	8	89	83	468	2,465	569	1,540	356
City of Dearborn	93,902	305	4	36	56	209	2,104	201	1,637	266
City of Livonia	93,644	167	0	22	18	127	1,411	126	1,173	112
City of Troy	84,688	67	2	10	8	47	1,042	70	918	54
City of Farmington Hills	81,262	87	0	17	7	63	759	145	547	67
City of Southfield	73,335	200	1	33	45	121	1,508	358	898	252
City of Taylor	60,923	378	1	35	41	301	1,386	242	998	146
City of Pontiac	59,791	769	10	66	108	585	1,300	315	875	110
City of Novi	61,699	48	1	8	2	37	514	21	466	27
Total area actually reporting	100.0%	22,332	363	2,443	3,481	16,045	72,684	13,451	47,916	11,317
Rate per 100,000 inhabitants		516.9	8.4	56.5	80.6	371.4	1,682.4	311.3	1,109.1	261.9
Detroit-Dearborn-Livonia, MI M.D.	1,741,965									
Includes Wayne County										
Total area actually reporting	100.0%	17,147	313	1,499	2,891	12,444	46,878	9,438	28,410	9,030
Rate per 100,000 inhabitants		984.3	18.0	86.1	166.0	714.4	2,691.1	541.8	1,630.9	518.4
Warren-Troy-Farmington Hills, MI M.D.	2,578,349									
Includes Lapeer, Livingston, Macomb, Oakland, and St. Clair Counties										
Total area actually reporting	100.0%	5,185	50	944	590	3,601	25,806	4,013	19,506	2,287
Rate per 100,000 inhabitants		201.1	1.9	36.6	22.9	139.7	1,000.9	155.6	756.5	88.7

Table 6. Crime in the United States, by Selected Metropolitan Statistical Area, 2019—Continued

(Number, percent, rate per 100,000 population.)

Area	Population	Violent crime	Murder and nonnegligent manslaughter	Rape[1]	Robbery	Aggravated assault	Property crime	Burglary	Larceny-theft	Motor vehicle theft
Dover, DE M.S.A.	180,168									
Includes Kent County										
City of Dover	38,361	334	4	13	49	268	2,057	82	1,886	89
Total area actually reporting	100.0%	770	6	71	97	596	4,019	430	3,380	209
Rate per 100,000 inhabitants		427.4	3.3	39.4	53.8	330.8	2,230.7	238.7	1,876.0	116.0
Dubuque, IA M.S.A.	96,742									
Includes Dubuque County										
City of Dubuque	57,973	110	0	34	9	67	949	138	747	64
Total area actually reporting	100.0%	130	1	42	9	78	1,103	180	842	81
Rate per 100,000 inhabitants		134.4	1.0	43.4	9.3	80.6	1,140.1	186.1	870.4	83.7
Duluth, MN-WI M.S.A.[3]	288,792									
Includes Carlton, Lake, and St. Louis[3] Counties, MN and Douglas County, WI										
City of Duluth, MN	85,846	292	2	37	69	184	3,670	481	2,977	212
Total area actually reporting	100.0%	604	4	126	80	394	7,697	1,100	6,131	466
Rate per 100,000 inhabitants		209.1	1.4	43.6	27.7	136.4	2,665.2	380.9	2,123.0	161.4
Durham-Chapel Hill, NC M.S.A.[3]	644,500									
Includes Chatham, Durham, Granville, Orange and Person Counties[3]										
City of Durham[3]	280,282	2,046	37	121	626	1,262	10,672	1,972	7,942	758
City of Chapel Hill[3]	61,457	58	0	10	17	31	926	184	706	36
Total area actually reporting	96.7%	2,752	46	194	730	1,782	15,906	3,044	11,836	1,026
Estimated total	100.0%	2,830	47	203	744	1,836	16,639	3,183	12,392	1,064
Rate per 100,000 inhabitants		439.1	7.3	31.5	115.4	284.9	2,581.7	493.9	1,922.7	165.1
East Stroudsburg, PA M.S.A.	169,228									
Includes Monroe County										
Total area actually reporting	100.0%	400	4	64	28	304	2,551	379	2,089	83
Rate per 100,000 inhabitants		236.4	2.4	37.8	16.5	179.6	1,507.4	224.0	1,234.4	49.0
Eau Claire, WI M.S.A.[3]	169,360									
Includes Chippewa and Eau Claire Counties										
City of Eau Claire	69,195	191	0	58	22	111	1,634	252	1,317	65
Total area actually reporting	100.0%	363	5	118	26	214	2,600	423	2,046	131
Rate per 100,000 inhabitants		214.3	3.0	69.7	15.4	126.4	1,535.2	249.8	1,208.1	77.4
El Centro, CA M.S.A.	181,194									
Includes Imperial County										
City of El Centro	44,303	143	3	9	41	90	1,184	228	861	95
Total area actually reporting	94.7%	589	7	28	80	474	3,476	769	2,236	471
Estimated total	100.0%	615	7	30	83	495	3,619	806	2,325	488
Rate per 100,000 inhabitants		339.4	3.9	16.6	45.8	273.2	1,997.3	444.8	1,283.2	269.3
Elizabethtown-Fort Knox, KY M.S.A.	153,255									
Includes Hardin, Larue, and Meade Counties										
City of Elizabethtown	30,383	49	3	13	15	18	452	140	239	73
Total area actually reporting	100.0%	153	6	33	39	75	1,738	472	1,045	221
Rate per 100,000 inhabitants		99.8	3.9	21.5	25.4	48.9	1,134.1	308.0	681.9	144.2
Elmira, NY M.S.A.	83,232									
Includes Chemung County										
City of Elmira	26,958	83	1	0	40	42	831	172	643	16
Total area actually reporting	100.0%	178	1	19	45	113	1,445	238	1,174	33
Rate per 100,000 inhabitants		213.9	1.2	22.8	54.1	135.8	1,736.1	285.9	1,410.5	39.6
El Paso, TX M.S.A.[3]	845,194									
Includes El Paso3 and Hudspeth Counties										
City of El Paso[3]	686,793	2,422	40	310	338	1,734	10,378	1,048	8,479	851
Total area actually reporting	100.0%	2,816	41	369	363	2,043	11,967	1,296	9,661	1,010
Rate per 100,000 inhabitants		333.2	4.9	43.7	42.9	241.7	1,415.9	153.3	1,143.1	119.5
Enid, OK M.S.A.	60,773									
Includes Garfield County										
City of Enid	49,598	204	1	44	9	150	1,625	364	1,148	113
Total area actually reporting	100.0%	225	1	47	9	168	1,812	411	1,275	126
Rate per 100,000 inhabitants		370.2	1.6	77.3	14.8	276.4	2,981.6	676.3	2,098.0	207.3
Erie, PA M.S.A.	270,606									
Includes Erie County										
City of Erie	95,834	476	9	54	93	320	1,817	342	1,379	96
Total area actually reporting	99.5%	807	9	118	115	565	4,311	644	3,518	149
Estimated total	100.0%	809	9	118	115	567	4,322	645	3,527	150
Rate per 100,000 inhabitants		299.0	3.3	43.6	42.5	209.5	1,597.2	238.4	1,303.4	55.4
Eugene-Springfield, OR M.S.A.[4]	381,434									
Includes Lane County										
City of Eugene	173,183	675	2	123	180	370	6,184	964	4,614	606
City of Springfield	63,438	190	1	34	32	123	1,978	169	1,640	169
Total area actually reporting	99.1%			180	225	773	10,372	1,493	7,880	999
Estimated total	100.0%			181	225	777	10,440	1,499	7,938	1,003
Rate per 100,000 inhabitants				47.5	59.0	203.7	2,737.0	393.0	2,081.1	263.0

Table 6. Crime in the United States, by Selected Metropolitan Statistical Area, 2019—Continued

(Number, percent, rate per 100,000 population.)

Area	Population	Violent crime	Murder and nonnegligent manslaughter	Rape[1]	Robbery	Aggravated assault	Property crime	Burglary	Larceny-theft	Motor vehicle theft
Evansville, IN-KY M.S.A.	315,399									
Includes Posey, Vanderburgh, and Warrick Counties, IN and Henderson County, KY										
City of Evansville	117,700	721	11	90	153	467	4,917	588	3,926	403
Total area actually reporting	91.9%	990	17	130	172	671	6,954	912	5,455	587
Estimated total	100.0%	1,032	17	133	176	706	7,199	953	5,639	607
Rate per 100,000 inhabitants		327.2	5.4	42.2	55.8	223.8	2,282.5	302.2	1,787.9	192.5
Fairbanks, AK M.S.A.	33,604									
Includes Fairbanks North Star Borough										
City of Fairbanks	31,493	247	3	33	52	159	1,353	163	1,006	184
Total area actually reporting	100.0%	267	3	39	52	173	1,491	178	1,117	196
Rate per 100,000 inhabitants		794.5	8.9	116.1	154.7	514.8	4,437.0	529.7	3,324.0	583.3
Fargo, ND-MN M.S.A.	247,762									
Includes Clay County, MN and Cass County, ND										
City of Fargo, ND	127,423	574	5	111	78	380	3,978	830	2,757	391
Total area actually reporting	100.0%	735	5	153	105	472	5,794	1,164	4,066	564
Rate per 100,000 inhabitants		296.7	2.0	61.8	42.4	190.5	2,338.5	469.8	1,641.1	227.6
Flagstaff, AZ M.S.A.	144,001									
Includes Coconino County										
City of Flagstaff	75,013	367	1	42	43	281	2,371	140	2,169	62
Total area actually reporting	100.0%	664	8	78	55	523	3,527	284	3,118	125
Rate per 100,000 inhabitants		461.1	5.6	54.2	38.2	363.2	2,449.3	197.2	2,165.3	86.8
Flint, MI M.S.A.[4]	403,666									
Includes Genesee County[4]										
City of Flint	95,212	1,284	23	64	78	1,119	1,986	559	1,220	207
Total area actually reporting	100.0%	2,340	30	259	177	1,874			4,624	600
Rate per 100,000 inhabitants		579.7	7.4	64.2	43.8	464.2			1,145.5	148.6
Florence, SC M.S.A.	204,992									
Includes Darlington and Florence Counties										
City of Florence	37,640	447	7	29	58	353	2,496	388	1,909	199
Total area actually reporting	98.8%	1,678	34	140	220	1,284	8,235	1,927	5,665	643
Estimated total	100.0%	1,688	34	141	221	1,292	8,321	1,945	5,728	648
Rate per 100,000 inhabitants		823.4	16.6	68.8	107.8	630.3	4,059.2	948.8	2,794.3	316.1
Fond du Lac, WI M.S.A.	103,125									
Includes Fond du Lac County										
City of Fond du Lac	42,954	134	0	28	14	92	797	59	697	41
Total area actually reporting	100.0%	182	0	50	15	117	1,131	178	898	55
Rate per 100,000 inhabitants		176.5	0.0	48.5	14.5	113.5	1,096.7	172.6	870.8	53.3
Fort Collins, CO M.S.A.	355,815									
Includes Larimer County										
City of Fort Collins	170,889	371	1	41	36	293	3,713	350	3,135	228
Total area actually reporting	100.0%	833	3	124	63	643	6,683	691	5,533	459
Rate per 100,000 inhabitants		234.1	0.8	34.8	17.7	180.7	1,878.2	194.2	1,555.0	129.0
Fort Smith, AR-OK M.S.A.	249,623									
Includes Crawford, Franklin, and Sebastian Counties, AR and Sequoyah County, OK										
City of Fort Smith, AR	88,041	863	4	97	90	672	5,127	812	3,929	386
Total area actually reporting	99.6%	1,457	8	206	106	1,137	7,925	1,501	5,815	609
Estimated total	100.0%	1,462	8	207	106	1,141	7,944	1,506	5,828	610
Rate per 100,000 inhabitants		585.7	3.2	82.9	42.5	457.1	3,182.4	603.3	2,334.7	244.4
Fort Wayne, IN M.S.A.	412,827									
Includes Allen and Whitley Counties										
City of Fort Wayne	269,366	974	26	145	357	446	7,437	990	5,879	568
Total area actually reporting	94.4%	1,227	30	195	401	601	8,580	1,167	6,714	699
Estimated total	100.0%	1,259	30	196	403	630	8,726	1,200	6,811	715
Rate per 100,000 inhabitants		305.0	7.3	47.5	97.6	152.6	2,113.7	290.7	1,649.8	173.2
Gainesville, FL M.S.A.	329,709									
Includes Alachua, Gilchrist, and Levy Counties										
City of Gainesville	135,085	928	2	153	185	588	4,712	501	3,803	408
Total area actually reporting	100.0%	2,282	7	309	297	1,669	8,091	1,345	6,054	692
Rate per 100,000 inhabitants		692.1	2.1	93.7	90.1	506.2	2,454.0	407.9	1,836.2	209.9
Glens Falls, NY M.S.A.	124,339									
Includes Warren and Washington Counties										
City of Glens Falls	14,306	28	0	8	1	19	100	18	80	2
Total area actually reporting	98.0%	156	0	94	6	56	885	123	728	34
Estimated total	100.0%	158	0	94	6	58	906	126	745	35
Rate per 100,000 inhabitants		127.1	0.0	75.6	4.8	46.6	728.7	101.3	599.2	28.1
Goldsboro, NC M.S.A.[3]	123,222									
Includes Wayne County[3]										
City of Goldsboro[3]	34,085	267	2	7	50	208	1,985	380	1,506	99
Total area actually reporting	97.7%	501	4	10	82	405	3,298	865	2,180	253

Table 6. Crime in the United States, by Selected Metropolitan Statistical Area, 2019—Continued

(Number, percent, rate per 100,000 population.)

Area	Population	Violent crime	Murder and nonnegligent manslaughter	Rape[1]	Robbery	Aggravated assault	Property crime	Burglary	Larceny-theft	Motor vehicle theft
Estimated total	100.0%	511	4	11	82	414	3,376	887	2,229	260
Rate per 100,000 inhabitants		414.7	3.2	8.9	66.5	336.0	2,739.8	719.8	1,808.9	211.0
Grand Forks, ND-MN M.S.A.[3]	101,736									
Includes Polk County,[3] MN and Grand Forks County, ND										
City of Grand Forks, ND	57,459	166	0	25	23	118	1,422	218	1,101	103
Total area actually reporting	100.0%	255	1	42	24	188	2,080	336	1,594	150
Rate per 100,000 inhabitants		250.6	1.0	41.3	23.6	184.8	2,044.5	330.3	1,566.8	147.4
Grand Island, NE M.S.A.	75,855									
Includes Hall, Howard, and Merrick Counties										
City of Grand Island	51,821	236	1	55	14	166	1,323	189	1,034	100
Total area actually reporting	100.0%	285	1	60	15	209	1,456	224	1,118	114
Rate per 100,000 inhabitants		375.7	1.3	79.1	19.8	275.5	1,919.5	295.3	1,473.9	150.3
Grand Junction, CO M.S.A.	153,429									
Includes Mesa County										
City of Grand Junction	63,949	235	3	43	30	159	2,463	278	2,034	151
Total area actually reporting	99.2%	427	9	85	49	284	3,764	555	2,932	277
Estimated total	100.0%	435	9	85	50	291	3,893	562	3,049	282
Rate per 100,000 inhabitants		283.5	5.9	55.4	32.6	189.7	2,537.3	366.3	1,987.2	183.8
Grand Rapids-Kentwood, MI M.S.A.[4]	1,079,969									
Includes Ionia, Kent, Montcalm, and Ottawa Counties										
City of Grand Rapids	201,799	1,286	8	144	274	860	3,850	595	2,754	501
City of Kentwood	52,274	162	0	23	20	119	1,111	170	850	91
Total area actually reporting	99.9%	3,469	24	857	446	2,142			10,937	1,248
Estimated total	100.0%	3,472	24	857	446	2,145			10,952	1,249
Rate per 100,000 inhabitants		321.5	2.2	79.4	41.3	198.6			1,014.1	115.7
Grants Pass, OR M.S.A.	87,564									
Includes Josephine County										
City of Grants Pass	38,475	121	0	24	21	76	1,235	151	958	126
Total area actually reporting	100.0%	209	0	37	24	148	1,643	229	1,114	300
Rate per 100,000 inhabitants		238.7	0.0	42.3	27.4	169.0	1,876.3	261.5	1,272.2	342.6
Great Falls, MT M.S.A.[4]	81,418									
Includes Cascade County[4]										
City of Great Falls	58,637	302	0	39	18	245	3,405	318	2,826	261
Total area actually reporting	100.0%			43	21	314	3,653	375	2,983	295
Rate per 100,000 inhabitants				52.8	25.8	385.7	4,486.7	460.6	3,663.8	362.3
Greeley, CO M.S.A.[3]	321,385									
Includes Weld County										
City of Greeley	109,255	386	2	71	67	246	2,542	338	1,898	306
Total area actually reporting	94.7%	660	5	154	87	414	4,767	654	3,509	604
Estimated total	100.0%	694	5	158	93	438	5,246	701	3,894	651
Rate per 100,000 inhabitants		215.9	1.6	49.2	28.9	136.3	1,632.3	218.1	1,211.6	202.6
Green Bay, WI M.S.A.	323,107									
Includes Brown, Kewaunee, and Oconto Counties										
City of Green Bay	104,992	529	3	78	49	399	1,724	245	1,355	124
Total area actually reporting	100.0%	730	5	135	56	534	3,549	423	2,938	188
Rate per 100,000 inhabitants		225.9	1.5	41.8	17.3	165.3	1,098.4	130.9	909.3	58.2
Greensboro-High Point, NC M.S.A.[3]	772,854									
Includes Guilford, Randolph, and Rockingham Counties[3]										
City of Greensboro[3]	298,025	2,440	43	113	621	1,663	10,994	2,215	7,792	987
City of High Point[3]	113,307	828	19	44	133	632	3,726	621	2,705	400
Total area actually reporting	81.4%	3,738	69	216	825	2,628	18,073	3,793	12,660	1,620
Estimated total	100.0%	4,098	75	255	876	2,892	20,835	4,473	14,540	1,822
Rate per 100,000 inhabitants		530.2	9.7	33.0	113.3	374.2	2,695.9	578.8	1,881.3	235.7
Greenville, NC M.S.A.[3]	181,242									
Includes Pitt County[3]										
City of Greenville[3]	94,193	437	5	17	94	321	2,837	415	2,308	114
Total area actually reporting	96.3%	630	8	34	131	457	4,165	806	3,176	183
Estimated total	100.0%	657	8	37	135	477	4,383	852	3,335	196
Rate per 100,000 inhabitants		362.5	4.4	20.4	74.5	263.2	2,418.3	470.1	1,840.1	108.1
Gulfport-Biloxi, MS M.S.A.[3]	417,585									
Includes Hancock, Harrison, Jackson, and Stone Counties										
City of Gulfport	72,383	236	12	25	65	134	3,492	419	2,805	268
City of Biloxi	46,185	188	3	35	65	85	2,663	619	1,877	167
Total area actually reporting	95.3%	888	26	152	220	490	13,273	2,225	9,887	1,161
Estimated total	100.0%	924	27	158	228	511	13,849	2,300	10,356	1,193
Rate per 100,000 inhabitants		221.3	6.5	37.8	54.6	122.4	3,316.5	550.8	2,480.0	285.7
Hanford-Corcoran, CA M.S.A.	149,966									
Includes Kings County										

Table 6. Crime in the United States, by Selected Metropolitan Statistical Area, 2019—Continued

(Number, percent, rate per 100,000 population.)

Area	Population	Violent crime	Murder and nonnegligent manslaughter	Rape[1]	Robbery	Aggravated assault	Property crime	Burglary	Larceny-theft	Motor vehicle theft
City of Hanford	57,232	257	0	18	40	199	1,242	131	900	211
City of Corcoran	21,353	118	1	8	12	97	272	65	157	50
Total area actually reporting	100.0%	757	4	71	88	594	2,466	410	1,662	394
Rate per 100,000 inhabitants		504.8	2.7	47.3	58.7	396.1	1,644.4	273.4	1,108.3	262.7
Harrisonburg, VA M.S.A.	135,787									
Includes Rockingham County and Harrisonburg City										
City of Harrisonburg	54,387	112	0	32	17	63	924	68	813	43
Total area actually reporting	100.0%	172	0	62	19	91	1,583	208	1,296	79
Rate per 100,000 inhabitants		126.7	0.0	45.7	14.0	67.0	1,165.8	153.2	954.4	58.2
Hartford-East Hartford-Middletown, CT M.S.A.[3,5]	1,015,769									
Includes Hartford, Middlesex, and Tolland Counties										
City of Hartford	122,245	1,049	21	31	271	726	3,424	427	2,464	533
City of East Hartford	49,842	76	1	18	31	26	775	109	525	141
City of Middletown	45,963	38	0	5	10	23	613	62	474	77
Total area actually reporting	100.0%	2,021	32	197	565	1,227		1,999	13,411	
Rate per 100,000 inhabitants		199.0	3.2	19.4	55.6	120.8		196.8	1,320.3	
Hilton Head Island-Bluffton, SC M.S.A.	221,873									
Includes Beaufort and Jasper Counties										
City of Bluffton	24,812	46	1	9	10	26	220	35	175	10
Total area actually reporting	91.6%	784	11	69	138	566	3,085	499	2,374	212
Estimated total	100.0%	882	13	77	143	649	3,476	610	2,615	251
Rate per 100,000 inhabitants		397.5	5.9	34.7	64.5	292.5	1,566.7	274.9	1,178.6	113.1
Homosassa Springs, FL M.S.A.	147,739									
Includes Citrus County										
Total area actually reporting	100.0%	373	4	29	40	300	2,055	394	1,466	195
Rate per 100,000 inhabitants		252.5	2.7	19.6	27.1	203.1	1,391.0	266.7	992.3	132.0
Hot Springs, AR M.S.A.[4]	99,238									
Includes Garland County[4]										
City of Hot Springs	37,263	241	10	38	42	151	2,674	755	1,710	209
Total area actually reporting	100.0%	520	10	63	50	397			2,385	354
Rate per 100,000 inhabitants		524.0	10.1	63.5	50.4	400.0			2,403.3	356.7
Houma-Thibodaux, LA M.S.A.	208,034									
Includes Lafourche and Terrebonne Parishes										
City of Houma	32,771	209	4	17	22	166	1,489	169	1,260	60
City of Thibodaux	14,587	81	4	5	0	72	515	63	432	20
Total area actually reporting	97.9%	761	20	70	38	633	6,005	874	4,866	265
Estimated total	100.0%	779	20	70	38	651	6,097	899	4,928	270
Rate per 100,000 inhabitants		374.5	9.6	33.6	18.3	312.9	2,930.8	432.1	2,368.8	129.8
Huntington-Ashland, WV-KY-OH M.S.A.	356,404									
Includes Boyd, Carter, and Greenup Counties, KY; Lawrence County OH; and Cabell, Putnam, and Wayne Counties, WV										
City of Huntington, WV	45,675	330	4	56	59	211	1,792	456	1,147	189
City of Ashland, KY	20,222	59	3	11	14	31	740	96	608	36
Total area actually reporting	86.7%	826	12	145	91	578	5,254	1,164	3,588	502
Estimated total	100.0%	945	14	158	101	672	5,969	1,317	4,094	558
Rate per 100,000 inhabitants		265.1	3.9	44.3	28.3	188.6	1,674.8	369.5	1,148.7	156.6
Idaho Falls, ID M.S.A.	151,591									
Includes Bonneville, Butte, and Jefferson Counties										
City of Idaho Falls	62,088	172	1	37	11	123	940	264	608	68
Total area actually reporting	100.0%	310	2	54	14	240	1,651	443	1,092	116
Rate per 100,000 inhabitants		204.5	1.3	35.6	9.2	158.3	1,089.1	292.2	720.4	76.5
Iowa City, IA M.S.A.	175,274									
Includes Johnson and Washington Counties										
City of Iowa City	77,390	167	1	40	25	101	1,252	314	867	71
Total area actually reporting	99.4%	480	4	95	43	338	2,629	505	1,985	139
Estimated total	100.0%	485	4	96	44	341	2,658	511	2,005	142
Rate per 100,000 inhabitants		276.7	2.3	54.8	25.1	194.6	1,516.5	291.5	1,143.9	81.0
Ithaca, NY M.S.A	102,363									
Includes Tompkins County										
City of Ithaca	31,122	41	1	5	9	26	840	56	768	16
Total area actually reporting	100.0%	127	1	53	19	54	1,707	197	1,478	32
Rate per 100,000 inhabitants		124.1	1.0	51.8	18.6	52.8	1,667.6	192.5	1,443.9	31.3
Jackson, MI M.S.A.	158,260									
Includes Jackson County										
City of Jackson	32,503	360	4	51	37	268	1,344	206	1,025	113
Total area actually reporting	100.0%	814	5	162	50	597	3,173	420	2,528	225
Rate per 100,000 inhabitants		514.3	3.2	102.4	31.6	377.2	2,004.9	265.4	1,597.4	142.2
Jackson, TN M.S.A.	178,143									
Includes Chester, Crockett, Gibson, and Madison Counties										

Table 6. Crime in the United States, by Selected Metropolitan Statistical Area, 2019—Continued

(Number, percent, rate per 100,000 population.)

Area	Population	Violent crime	Murder and nonnegligent manslaughter	Rape[1]	Robbery	Aggravated assault	Property crime	Burglary	Larceny-theft	Motor vehicle theft
City of Jackson	66,915	650	17	30	97	506	2,473	374	1,904	195
Total area actually reporting	100.0%	1,093	21	66	129	877	4,179	751	3,062	366
Rate per 100,000 inhabitants		613.6	11.8	37.0	72.4	492.3	2,345.9	421.6	1,718.8	205.5
Jacksonville, FL M.S.A.	1,549,030									
Includes Baker, Clay, Duval, Nassau, and St. Johns Counties										
City of Jacksonville	909,142	5,886	129	554	1,294	3,909	30,088	4,906	22,373	2,809
Total area actually reporting	100.0%	7,353	143	779	1,456	4,975	38,810	6,410	28,976	3,424
Rate per 100,000 inhabitants		474.7	9.2	50.3	94.0	321.2	2,505.4	413.8	1,870.6	221.0
Janesville-Beloit, WI M.S.A.[3]	163,288									
Includes Rock County										
City of Janesville	64,687	148	1	38	28	81	1,577	137	1,397	43
City of Beloit[3]	37,025	154	4	19	31	100	1,114	122	921	71
Total area actually reporting	100.0%	380	5	75	69	231	3,247	356	2,738	153
Rate per 100,000 inhabitants		232.7	3.1	45.9	42.3	141.5	1,988.5	218.0	1,676.8	93.7
Jefferson City, MO M.S.A.	151,555									
Includes Callaway, Cole, Moniteau, and Osage Counties										
City of Jefferson City	42,793	119	2	30	23	64	1,101	125	910	66
Total area actually reporting	100.0%	334	7	58	29	240	2,826	490	2,127	209
Rate per 100,000 inhabitants		220.4	4.6	38.3	19.1	158.4	1,864.7	323.3	1,403.5	137.9
Johnson City, TN M.S.A.	203,289									
Includes Carter, Unicoi, and Washington Counties										
City of Johnson City	67,197	286	1	28	38	219	2,390	301	1,904	185
Total area actually reporting	100.0%	668	3	59	47	559	4,498	712	3,330	456
Rate per 100,000 inhabitants		328.6	1.5	29.0	23.1	275.0	2,212.6	350.2	1,638.1	224.3
Jonesboro, AR M.S.A.	133,624									
Includes Craighead and Poinsett Counties										
City of Jonesboro	78,261	537	13	74	58	392	2,982	1,092	1,758	132
Total area actually reporting	98.7%	733	15	131	65	522	4,077	1,405	2,440	232
Estimated total	100.0%	743	15	133	66	529	4,116	1,414	2,467	235
Rate per 100,000 inhabitants		556.0	11.2	99.5	49.4	395.9	3,080.3	1,058.2	1,846.2	175.9
Joplin, MO M.S.A.	179,103									
Includes Jasper and Newton Counties										
City of Joplin	50,635	307	2	63	63	179	3,677	521	2,815	341
Total area actually reporting	100.0%	593	3	107	83	400	6,555	1,028	4,863	664
Rate per 100,000 inhabitants		331.1	1.7	59.7	46.3	223.3	3,659.9	574.0	2,715.2	370.7
Kahului-Wailuku-Lahaina, HI M.S.A.	167,475									
Includes Maui County										
Total area actually reporting	100.0%	449	1	110	67	271	4,984	577	3,746	661
Rate per 100,000 inhabitants		268.1	0.6	65.7	40.0	161.8	2,976.0	344.5	2,236.8	394.7
Kalamazoo-Portage, MI M.S.A.	266,016									
Includes Kalamazoo County										
City of Kalamazoo	76,827	949	9	110	182	648	3,578	703	2,546	329
City of Portage	49,583	136	0	30	14	92	1,549	204	1,279	66
Total area actually reporting	99.2%	1,518	12	225	259	1,022	8,555	1,556	6,288	711
Estimated total	100.0%	1,523	12	226	259	1,026	8,583	1,560	6,311	712
Rate per 100,000 inhabitants		572.5	4.5	85.0	97.4	385.7	3,226.5	586.4	2,372.4	267.7
Kankakee, IL M.S.A.	109,111									
Includes Kankakee County										
City of Kankakee	25,872	236	4	29	53	150	873	156	675	42
Total area actually reporting	98.6%	423	5	58	90	270	2,072	297	1,690	85
Estimated total	100.0%	424	5	58	90	271	2,096	301	1,709	86
Rate per 100,000 inhabitants		388.6	4.6	53.2	82.5	248.4	1,921.0	275.9	1,566.3	78.8
Kennewick-Richland, WA M.S.A.	300,701									
Includes Benton and Franklin Counties										
City of Kennewick	84,072	253	2	54	49	148	2,487	378	1,907	202
City of Richland	58,514	100	2	24	9	65	1,199	195	949	55
Total area actually reporting	100.0%	660	8	136	111	405	5,851	945	4,391	515
Rate per 100,000 inhabitants		219.5	2.7	45.2	36.9	134.7	1,945.8	314.3	1,460.3	171.3
Killeen-Temple, TX M.S.A.[3]	454,647									
Includes Bell, Coryell, and Lampasas3 Counties										
City of Killeen	151,832	583	14	105	124	340	3,432	818	2,296	318
City of Temple	77,558	217	4	61	39	113	1,718	244	1,276	198
Total area actually reporting	99.3%	1,196	19	259	201	717	8,187	1,615	5,916	656
Estimated total	100.0%	1,202	19	259	201	723	8,231	1,624	5,946	661
Rate per 100,000 inhabitants		264.4	4.2	57.0	44.2	159.0	1,810.4	357.2	1,307.8	145.4
Kingsport-Bristol, TN-VA M.S.A.	305,838									
Includes Hawkins and Sullivan Counties, TN and Scott and Washington Counties and Bristol City, VA										

Table 6. Crime in the United States, by Selected Metropolitan Statistical Area, 2019—Continued

(Number, percent, rate per 100,000 population.)

Area	Population	Violent crime	Murder and nonnegligent manslaughter	Rape[1]	Robbery	Aggravated assault	Property crime	Burglary	Larceny-theft	Motor vehicle theft
City of Kingsport, TN	54,218	332	3	22	35	272	2,829	324	2,232	273
City of Bristol, TN	26,900	135	1	15	12	107	813	138	604	71
Total area actually reporting	100.0%	920	14	107	74	725	7,019	1,097	5,154	768
Rate per 100,000 inhabitants		300.8	4.6	35.0	24.2	237.1	2,295.0	358.7	1,685.2	251.1
Kingston, NY M.S.A.	177,151									
Includes Ulster County										
City of Kingston	22,844	68	2	13	10	43	498	59	419	20
Total area actually reporting	89.6%	249	4	72	19	154	1,740	234	1,439	67
Estimated total	100.0%	266	4	75	22	165	1,932	253	1,604	75
Rate per 100,000 inhabitants		150.2	2.3	42.3	12.4	93.1	1,090.6	142.8	905.4	42.3
Knoxville, TN M.S.A.	866,295									
Includes Anderson, Blount, Campbell, Knox, Loudon, Morgan, Roane, and Union Counties										
City of Knoxville	188,666	1,259	22	146	232	859	8,207	1,157	6,067	983
Total area actually reporting	100.0%	3,064	35	370	322	2,337	18,423	3,036	13,115	2,272
Rate per 100,000 inhabitants		353.7	4.0	42.7	37.2	269.8	2,126.6	350.5	1,513.9	262.3
Kokomo, IN M.S.A.	82,480									
Includes Howard County										
City of Kokomo	57,845	392	5	25	48	314	1,493	312	1,081	100
Total area actually reporting	98.7%	455	5	31	53	366	1,625	342	1,172	111
Estimated total	100.0%	458	5	31	54	368	1,651	345	1,193	113
Rate per 100,000 inhabitants		555.3	6.1	37.6	65.5	446.2	2,001.7	418.3	1,446.4	137.0
La Crosse-Onalaska, WI-MN M.S.A.[3]	136,997									
Includes Houston County,[3] MN and La Crosse County, WI										
City of La Crosse, WI	51,591	122	2	27	26	67	1,850	226	1,561	63
City of Onalaska, WI	18,825	10	0	2	2	6	522	24	491	7
Total area actually reporting	100.0%	169	2	31	28	108	2,820	337	2,391	92
Rate per 100,000 inhabitants		123.4	1.5	22.6	20.4	78.8	2,058.4	246.0	1,745.3	67.2
Lafayette, LA M.S.A.	489,368									
Includes Acadia, Iberia, Lafayette, St. Martin, and Vermilion Parishes										
City of Lafayette	126,694	664	14	16	148	486	5,454	1,032	4,101	321
Total area actually reporting	83.3%	1,726	31	98	257	1,340	11,013	2,399	7,963	651
Estimated total	100.0%	2,283	38	124	335	1,786	14,108	3,031	10,246	831
Rate per 100,000 inhabitants		466.5	7.8	25.3	68.5	365.0	2,882.9	619.4	2,093.7	169.8
Lafayette-West Lafayette, IN M.S.A.	233,135									
Includes Benton, Carroll, Tippecanoe, and Warren Counties										
City of Lafayette	72,585	352	5	38	55	254	2,388	387	1,844	157
City of West Lafayette	49,154	32	0	5	3	24	357	42	304	11
Total area actually reporting	83.1%	451	8	67	69	307	3,573	580	2,778	215
Estimated total	100.0%	520	8	73	78	361	3,960	649	3,059	252
Rate per 100,000 inhabitants		223.0	3.4	31.3	33.5	154.8	1,698.6	278.4	1,312.1	108.1
Lake Charles, LA M.S.A.	210,155									
Includes Calcasieu and Cameron Parishes										
City of Lake Charles	78,733	413	11	52	83	267	2,907	1,212	1,467	228
Total area actually reporting	95.2%	1,099	15	144	128	812	7,991	2,311	5,073	607
Estimated total	100.0%	1,151	19	145	130	857	8,189	2,349	5,222	618
Rate per 100,000 inhabitants		547.7	9.0	69.0	61.9	407.8	3,896.6	1,117.7	2,484.8	294.1
Lake Havasu City-Kingman, AZ M.S.A.	210,855									
Includes Mohave County										
City of Lake Havasu City	55,413	87	1	29	3	54	670	108	519	43
City of Kingman	30,600	100	0	9	12	79	1,342	208	1,039	95
Total area actually reporting	97.7%	452	6	67	59	320	5,347	1,124	3,736	487
Estimated total	100.0%	485	6	69	63	347	5,564	1,171	3,887	506
Rate per 100,000 inhabitants		230.0	2.8	32.7	29.9	164.6	2,638.8	555.4	1,843.4	240.0
Lakeland-Winter Haven, FL M.S.A.	717,190									
Includes Polk County										
City of Lakeland	112,237	350	7	63	97	183	3,230	438	2,589	203
City of Winter Haven	44,211	187	3	22	25	137	1,126	181	884	61
Total area actually reporting	100.0%	1,990	23	166	300	1,501	11,797	1,947	8,914	936
Rate per 100,000 inhabitants		277.5	3.2	23.1	41.8	209.3	1,644.9	271.5	1,242.9	130.5
Lansing-East Lansing, MI M.S.A.[4]	550,643									
Includes Clinton, Eaton, Ingham, and Shiawassee Counties										
City of Lansing	118,953	1,313	12	140	178	983	3,355	763	2,225	367
City of East Lansing	47,913	88	0	40	11	37	840	113	563	164
Total area actually reporting	100.0%	2,367	19	489	268	1,591			6,637	864
Rate per 100,000 inhabitants		429.9	3.5	88.8	48.7	288.9			1,205.3	156.9
Laredo, TX M.S.A.[3]	277,386									
Includes Webb County										
City of Laredo[3]	264,916	836	4	104	164	564	4,692	708	3,726	258

Table 6. Crime in the United States, by Selected Metropolitan Statistical Area, 2019—Continued

(Number, percent, rate per 100,000 population.)

Area	Population	Violent crime	Murder and nonnegligent manslaughter	Rape[1]	Robbery	Aggravated assault	Property crime	Burglary	Larceny-theft	Motor vehicle theft
Total area actually reporting	98.3%	882	6	108	167	601	4,944	767	3,862	315
Estimated total	100.0%	893	6	110	168	609	5,037	782	3,932	323
Rate per 100,000 inhabitants		321.9	2.2	39.7	60.6	219.5	1,815.9	281.9	1,417.5	116.4
Las Cruces, NM M.S.A.	218,180									
Includes Dona Ana County										
City of Las Cruces	103,520	514	10	64	57	383	3,707	654	2,746	307
Estimated total	100.0%	1,215	12	124	69	1,010	5,049	1,070	3,548	431
Rate per 100,000 inhabitants		556.9	5.5	56.8	31.6	462.9	2,314.1	490.4	1,626.2	197.5
Las Vegas-Henderson-Paradise, NV M.S.A.	2,270,103									
Includes Clark County										
City of Las Vegas Metropolitan Police Department	1,666,803	8,854	84	1,439	2,118	5,213	46,197	10,646	28,240	7,311
City of Henderson	317,732	543	9	75	191	268	5,554	907	4,093	554
Total area actually reporting	100.0%	11,935	112	1,661	2,808	7,354	58,207	13,003	36,145	9,059
Rate per 100,000 inhabitants		525.7	4.9	73.2	123.7	324.0	2,564.1	572.8	1,592.2	399.1
Lawton, OK M.S.A.[3]	125,205									
Includes Comanche and Cotton Counties										
City of Lawton	92,256	854	15	97	91	651	2,972	877	1,836	259
Total area actually reporting	100.0%	897	16	105	96	680	3,338	1,010	2,016	312
Rate per 100,000 inhabitants		716.4	12.8	83.9	76.7	543.1	2,666.0	806.7	1,610.2	249.2
Lebanon, PA M.S.A.	142,102									
Includes Lebanon County										
City of Lebanon	25,959	65	1	5	21	38	528	77	430	21
Total area actually reporting	97.9%	233	1	35	22	175	1,653	189	1,420	44
Estimated total	100.0%	237	1	35	22	179	1,683	192	1,445	46
Rate per 100,000 inhabitants		166.8	0.7	24.6	15.5	126.0	1,184.4	135.1	1,016.9	32.4
Lewiston, ID-WA M.S.A.	63,370									
Includes Nez Perce County, ID and Asotin County, WA										
City of Lewiston, ID	32,931	42	0	15	2	25	955	145	755	55
Total area actually reporting	100.0%	88	1	30	6	51	1,525	239	1,207	79
Rate per 100,000 inhabitants		138.9	1.6	47.3	9.5	80.5	2,406.5	377.2	1,904.7	124.7
Lewiston-Auburn, ME M.S.A.	108,026									
Includes Androscoggin County										
City of Lewiston	35,865	107	0	31	18	58	716	122	555	39
City of Auburn	23,214	34	1	13	5	15	511	56	445	10
Total area actually reporting	100.0%	186	1	65	25	95	1,454	219	1,170	65
Rate per 100,000 inhabitants		172.2	0.9	60.2	23.1	87.9	1,346.0	202.7	1,083.1	60.2
Lexington-Fayette, KY M.S.A.	520,442									
Includes Bourbon, Clark, Fayette, Jessamine, Scott, and Woodford Counties										
City of Lexington	326,070	967	26	175	362	404	9,776	1,537	7,333	906
Total area actually reporting	100.0%	1,200	27	235	417	521	14,148	2,156	10,732	1,260
Rate per 100,000 inhabitants		230.6	5.2	45.2	80.1	100.1	2,718.5	414.3	2,062.1	242.1
Lima, OH M.S.A.[2]	102,023									
Includes Allen County										
City of Lima	36,653	259	4	59	64	132	1,493	392	1,037	64
Total area actually reporting	93.8%	311	5	76	80	150	2,374	543	1,724	107
Estimated total	100.0%	322	5	79	82	156	2,480	558	1,810	112
Rate per 100,000 inhabitants		315.6	4.9	77.4	80.4	152.9	2,430.8	546.9	1,774.1	109.8
Lincoln, NE M.S.A.	337,340									
Includes Lancaster and Seward Counties										
City of Lincoln	291,128	1,115	5	323	166	621	8,008	988	6,566	454
Total area actually reporting	99.4%	1,149	5	345	166	633	8,394	1,043	6,863	488
Estimated total	100.0%	1,170	5	359	166	640	8,423	1,043	6,892	488
Rate per 100,000 inhabitants		346.8	1.5	106.4	49.2	189.7	2,496.9	309.2	2,043.0	144.7
Little Rock-North Little Rock-Conway, AR M.S.A.[4]	743,875									
Includes Faulkner, Grant, Lonoke, Perry, Pulaski, and Saline4 Counties										
City of Little Rock	198,382	3,009	38	209	391	2,371	12,145	1,760	9,316	1,069
City of North Little Rock	66,604	562	12	23	106	421	2,479	380	1,723	376
City of Conway	67,336	324	2	49	51	222	1,842	177	1,567	98
Total area actually reporting	99.9%	5,815	75	539	689	4,512				2,586
Estimated total	100.0%	5,819	75	540	689	4,515				2,587
Rate per 100,000 inhabitants		782.3	10.1	72.6	92.6	607.0				347.8
Logan, UT-ID M.S.A.	142,499									
Includes Franklin County, ID and Cache County, UT										
City of Logan, UT	52,029	113	3	35	5	70	691	105	549	37
Total area actually reporting	91.5%	169	6	70	6	87	1,163	173	899	91
Estimated total	100.0%	183	6	75	7	95	1,313	195	1,014	104
Rate per 100,000 inhabitants		128.4	4.2	52.6	4.9	66.7	921.4	136.8	711.6	73.0
Longview, TX M.S.A.[3, 4]	285,060									
Includes Gregg, Harrison, Rusk, and Upshur Counties										

Table 6. Crime in the United States, by Selected Metropolitan Statistical Area, 2019—Continued

(Number, percent, rate per 100,000 population.)

Area	Population	Violent crime	Murder and nonnegligent manslaughter	Rape[1]	Robbery	Aggravated assault	Property crime	Burglary	Larceny-theft	Motor vehicle theft
City of Longview	81,783	374	4	62	63	245	2,410	411	1,809	190
Total area actually reporting	99.7%	922	20	128	113	661		1,362		529
Estimated total	100.0%	924	20	128	113	663		1,365		530
Rate per 100,000 inhabitants		324.1	7.0	44.9	39.6	232.6		478.8		185.9
Longview, WA M.S.A.	109,465									
Includes Cowlitz County										
City of Longview	38,282	101	1	30	19	51	1,102	159	841	102
Total area actually reporting	100.0%	213	5	71	26	111	2,054	343	1,521	190
Rate per 100,000 inhabitants		194.6	4.6	64.9	23.8	101.4	1,876.4	313.3	1,389.5	173.6
Los Angeles-Long Beach-Anaheim, CA M.S.A.	13,236,726									
Includes the Metropolitan Divisions of Anaheim-Santa Ana-Irvine and Los Angeles-Long Beach-Glendale										
City of Los Angeles	4,015,546	29,400	258	2,274	9,652	17,216	95,704	13,809	66,253	15,642
City of Long Beach	467,974	2,369	34	249	958	1,128	11,297	2,185	6,754	2,358
City of Anaheim	353,915	1,120	8	141	396	575	8,258	1,123	5,904	1,231
City of Santa Ana	333,664	1,453	13	207	472	761	6,808	854	4,611	1,343
City of Irvine	292,673	188	1	52	66	69	3,823	574	3,086	163
City of Glendale	202,601	231	5	16	93	117	3,305	480	2,562	263
City of Torrance	145,183	280	3	26	114	137	2,853	399	2,161	293
City of Pasadena	141,913	613	4	46	147	416	2,866	570	2,036	260
City of Orange	139,830	180	3	18	76	83	2,184	387	1,546	251
City of Costa Mesa	114,047	312	0	52	104	156	3,739	450	2,934	355
City of Burbank	103,738	189	1	11	54	123	2,617	299	2,107	211
City of Carson	91,947	444	5	31	122	286	2,004	328	1,277	399
City of Santa Monica	91,621	664	3	40	247	374	3,964	577	3,143	244
City of Newport Beach	85,325	135	5	29	32	69	1,764	273	1,344	147
City of Tustin	80,356	141	1	16	61	63	2,118	241	1,694	183
City of Gardena	59,833	324	3	20	131	170	1,202	236	658	308
City of Arcadia	58,899	84	1	10	35	38	1,348	301	973	74
City of Fountain Valley	55,858	53	0	5	23	25	1,163	163	914	86
Total area actually reporting	100.0%	63,201	565	5,063	20,816	36,757	283,364	46,511	192,723	44,130
Rate per 100,000 inhabitants		477.5	4.3	38.2	157.3	277.7	2,140.7	351.4	1,456.0	333.4
Anaheim-Santa Ana-Irvine, CA M.D.	3,180,759									
Includes Orange County										
Total area actually reporting	100.0%	6,797	57	894	2,209	3,637	59,186	8,529	43,956	6,701
Rate per 100,000 inhabitants		213.7	1.8	28.1	69.4	114.3	1,860.8	268.1	1,381.9	210.7
Los Angeles-Long Beach-Glendale, CA M.D.	10,055,967									
Includes Los Angeles County										
Total area actually reporting	100.0%	56,404	508	4,169	18,607	33,120	224,178	37,982	148,767	37,429
Rate per 100,000 inhabitants		560.9	5.1	41.5	185.0	329.4	2,229.3	377.7	1,479.4	372.2
Louisville/Jefferson County, KY-IN M.S.A.	1,269,402									
Includes Clark, Floyd, Harrison, and Washington Counties, IN and Bullitt, Henry, Jefferson, Oldham, Shelby, and Spencer Counties, KY										
City of Louisville Metro, KY	675,501	4,640	94	201	1,008	3,337	26,287	4,316	18,037	3,934
Total area actually reporting	90.7%	5,345	103	306	1,159	3,777	34,835	5,482	24,355	4,998
Estimated total	100.0%	5,545	105	330	1,191	3,919	36,356	5,686	25,538	5,132
Rate per 100,000 inhabitants		436.8	8.3	26.0	93.8	308.7	2,864.0	447.9	2,011.8	404.3
Lubbock, TX M.S.A.[3]	320,574									
Includes Crosby, Lubbock, and Lynn[3] Counties										
City of Lubbock	259,208	2,613	10	268	468	1,867	11,940	2,391	8,324	1,225
Total area actually reporting	99.0%	2,682	11	285	472	1,914	12,898	2,601	8,971	1,326
Estimated total	100.0%	2,688	11	285	472	1,920	12,941	2,609	9,001	1,331
Rate per 100,000 inhabitants		838.5	3.4	88.9	147.2	598.9	4,036.8	813.9	2,807.8	415.2
Lynchburg, VA M.S.A.	263,190									
Includes Amherst, Appomattox, Bedford, and Campbell Counties and Lynchburg City										
City of Lynchburg	82,512	316	2	35	60	219	1,802	261	1,382	159
Total area actually reporting	100.0%	607	10	80	80	437	3,832	541	3,010	281
Rate per 100,000 inhabitants		230.6	3.8	30.4	30.4	166.0	1,456.0	205.6	1,143.7	106.8
Macon-Bibb County, GA M.S.A.[3]	229,193									
Includes Bibb, Crawford, Jones, Monroe, and Twiggs Counties[3]										
Total area actually reporting	100.0%	1,042	21	56	298	667	7,931	1,645	5,589	697
Rate per 100,000 inhabitants		454.6	9.2	24.4	130.0	291.0	3,460.4	717.7	2,438.6	304.1
Madera, CA M.S.A.	157,191									
Includes Madera County										
City of Madera	66,250	334	2	32	77	223	1,301	235	824	242
Total area actually reporting	100.0%	830	3	68	94	665	2,693	682	1,595	416
Rate per 100,000 inhabitants		528.0	1.9	43.3	59.8	423.1	1,713.2	433.9	1,014.7	264.6
Madison, WI M.S.A.[3]	666,719									
Includes Columbia, Dane, Green,[3] and Iowa Counties										
City of Madison	261,270	940	4	107	217	612	6,464	1,046	4,873	545

Table 6. Crime in the United States, by Selected Metropolitan Statistical Area, 2019—Continued

(Number, percent, rate per 100,000 population.)

Area	Population	Violent crime	Murder and nonnegligent manslaughter	Rape[1]	Robbery	Aggravated assault	Property crime	Burglary	Larceny-theft	Motor vehicle theft
Total area actually reporting	99.9%	1,445	8	201	291	945	11,164	1,686	8,594	884
Estimated total	100.0%	1,452	8	207	291	946	11,432	1,733	8,811	888
Rate per 100,000 inhabitants		217.8	1.2	31.0	43.6	141.9	1,714.7	259.9	1,321.5	133.2
Manchester-Nashua, NH M.S.A.	416,493									
Includes Hillsborough County										
City of Manchester	112,895	678	6	62	133	477	2,678	299	2,225	154
City of Nashua	89,586	129	1	69	20	39	1,151	81	1,016	54
Total area actually reporting	98.3%	942	11	186	168	577	5,147	537	4,344	266
Estimated total	100.0%	957	11	190	170	586	5,435	546	4,621	268
Rate per 100,000 inhabitants		229.8	2.6	45.6	40.8	140.7	1,304.9	131.1	1,109.5	64.3
Manhattan, KS M.S.A.[4]	130,661									
Includes Geary, Pottawatomie, and Riley4 Counties										
Total area actually reporting	100.0%	563	4	67	41	451			1,701	170
Rate per 100,000 inhabitants		430.9	3.1	51.3	31.4	345.2			1,301.8	130.1
Mankato, MN M.S.A.[3]	102,065									
Includes Blue Earth and Nicollet Counties										
City of Mankato	42,955	110	0	29	12	69	1,462	186	1,217	59
Total area actually reporting	100.0%	182	0	58	15	109	1,938	267	1,579	92
Rate per 100,000 inhabitants		178.3	0.0	56.8	14.7	106.8	1,898.8	261.6	1,547.1	90.1
Mansfield, OH M.S.A.	120,502									
Includes Richland County										
City of Mansfield	46,418	187	3	48	38	98	1,996	396	1,523	77
Total area actually reporting	98.5%	272	4	90	46	132	3,250	618	2,514	118
Estimated total	100.0%	276	4	91	47	134	3,309	622	2,567	120
Rate per 100,000 inhabitants		229.0	3.3	75.5	39.0	111.2	2,746.0	516.2	2,130.3	99.6
McAllen-Edinburg-Mission, TX M.S.A.[3]	871,926									
Includes Hidalgo County[3]										
City of McAllen	144,915	140	1	33	39	67	3,595	152	3,415	28
City of Edinburg	100,896	281	6	53	40	182	2,959	335	2,577	47
City of Mission	85,705	105	1	37	23	44	1,618	161	1,387	70
Total area actually reporting	99.0%	2,324	19	433	334	1,538	19,108	2,505	15,830	773
Estimated total	100.0%	2,345	19	436	337	1,553	19,284	2,533	15,963	788
Rate per 100,000 inhabitants		268.9	2.2	50.0	38.7	178.1	2,211.7	290.5	1,830.8	90.4
Memphis, TN-MS-AR M.S.A.[2,3]	1,344,796									
Includes Crittenden County, AR; DeSoto, Marshall, Tate, and Tunica2 Counties, MS; and Fayette, Shelby, and Tipton Counties, TN										
City of Memphis, TN	650,410	12,367	190	468	2,432	9,277	39,860	7,833	27,981	4,046
Total area actually reporting	95.8%	14,888	235	668	2,777	11,208	53,652	10,136	37,935	5,581
Estimated total	100.0%	15,068	237	706	2,785	11,340	54,510	10,341	38,501	5,668
Rate per 100,000 inhabitants		1,120.5	17.6	52.5	207.1	843.3	4,053.4	769.0	2,863.0	421.5
Merced, CA M.S.A.	274,771									
Includes Merced County										
City of Merced	83,854	540	5	34	103	398	2,342	396	1,439	507
Total area actually reporting	100.0%	1,520	12	82	202	1,224	6,898	1,418	4,089	1,391
Rate per 100,000 inhabitants		553.2	4.4	29.8	73.5	445.5	2,510.5	516.1	1,488.1	506.2
Miami-Fort Lauderdale-Pompano Beach, FL M.S.A.	6,235,390									
Includes the Metropolitan Divisions of Fort Lauderdale-Pompano Beach-Sunrise, Miami-Miami Beach-Kendall, and West Palm Beach-Boca Raton-Boynton Beach										
City of Miami	480,505	2,850	43	152	769	1,886	17,624	1,771	14,219	1,634
City of Fort Lauderdale	184,765	1,098	21	93	408	576	9,082	1,275	6,945	862
City of Pompano Beach	113,536	900	8	73	317	502	4,277	661	3,058	558
City of West Palm Beach	112,798	859	17	79	304	459	4,231	464	3,314	453
City of Boca Raton	101,163	186	3	36	63	84	2,183	244	1,769	170
City of Sunrise	96,919	191	4	17	63	107	2,014	157	1,673	184
City of Miami Beach	92,185	852	6	92	284	470	6,977	717	5,894	366
City of Deerfield Beach	81,602	351	6	31	99	215	2,161	211	1,703	247
City of Boynton Beach	79,360	566	4	30	120	412	2,618	254	2,147	217
City of Delray Beach	70,509	336	5	33	87	211	2,418	299	1,914	205
City of Jupiter	66,906	118	2	17	22	77	1,035	79	895	61
City of Doral	64,168	62	1	9	13	39	1,475	66	1,287	122
City of Palm Beach Gardens	57,236	78	1	9	22	46	1,295	71	1,173	51
City of Coral Gables	51,530	50	0	4	17	29	1,343	157	1,103	83
Total area actually reporting	100.0%	26,314	399	2,208	7,107	16,600	167,498	16,910	135,086	15,502
Rate per 100,000 inhabitants		422.0	6.4	35.4	114.0	266.2	2,686.2	271.2	2,166.4	248.6
Fort Lauderdale-Pompano Beach-Deerfield Beach, FL M.D.	1,963,433									
Includes Broward County										
Total area actually reporting	100.0%	7,332	110	692	2,134	4,396	50,026	5,481	39,400	5,145
Rate per 100,000 inhabitants		373.4	5.6	35.2	108.7	223.9	2,547.9	279.2	2,006.7	262.0

Table 6. Crime in the United States, by Selected Metropolitan Statistical Area, 2019—Continued

(Number, percent, rate per 100,000 population.)

Area	Population	Violent crime	Murder and nonnegligent manslaughter	Rape[1]	Robbery	Aggravated assault	Property crime	Burglary	Larceny-theft	Motor vehicle theft
Miami-Miami Beach-Kendall, FL M.D.	2,775,173									
Includes Miami-Dade County										
Total area actually reporting	100.0%	13,339	202	955	3,649	8,533	85,544	7,936	69,952	7,656
Rate per 100,000 inhabitants		480.7	7.3	34.4	131.5	307.5	3,082.5	286.0	2,520.6	275.9
West Palm Beach-Boca Raton-Boynton Beach, FL M.D.	1,496,784									
Includes Palm Beach County										
Total area actually reporting	100.0%	5,643	87	561	1,324	3,671	31,928	3,493	25,734	2,701
Rate per 100,000 inhabitants		377.0	5.8	37.5	88.5	245.3	2,133.1	233.4	1,719.3	180.5
Midland, MI M.S.A.	82,943									
Includes Midland County										
City of Midland	41,791	56	1	21	4	30	392	36	344	12
Total area actually reporting	100.0%	118	1	58	4	55	660	92	545	23
Rate per 100,000 inhabitants		142.3	1.2	69.9	4.8	66.3	795.7	110.9	657.1	27.7
Milwaukee-Waukesha, WI M.S.A.[3]	1,576,634									
Includes Milwaukee, Ozaukee, Washington, and Waukesha Counties										
City of Milwaukee	590,923	7,874	97	427	1,911	5,439	15,097	3,594	8,053	3,450
City of Waukesha	72,718	67	1	25	8	33	690	77	575	38
Total area actually reporting	100.0%	9,111	111	631	2,151	6,218	30,333	4,820	21,346	4,167
Rate per 100,000 inhabitants		577.9	7.0	40.0	136.4	394.4	1,923.9	305.7	1,353.9	264.3
Minneapolis-St. Paul-Bloomington, MN-WI M.S.A.[3]	3,643,083									
Includes Anoka,[3] Carver, Chisago, Dakota, Hennepin, Isanti, Le Sueur, Mille Lacs, Ramsey, Scott, Sherburne, Washington, and Wright Counties, MN and Pierce and St. Croix Counties, WI										
City of Minneapolis, MN[3]	431,016	3,990	46	459	1,289	2,196	19,469	3,397	13,172	2,900
City of St. Paul, MN	310,263	1,752	28	236	542	946	11,208	2,038	6,751	2,419
City of Bloomington, MN	85,902	203	3	54	61	85	3,079	183	2,731	165
City of Plymouth, MN	80,616	37	0	8	5	24	938	152	742	44
City of Eagan, MN	66,824	39	0	12	12	15	1,294	93	1,129	72
City of Eden Prairie, MN	64,777	52	0	13	14	25	700	68	610	22
City of Minnetonka, MN	54,497	30	0	8	7	15	772	91	643	38
City of Edina, MN	53,076	47	0	15	15	17	983	140	794	49
Total area actually reporting	99.9%	9,923	97	1,626	2,851	5,349	84,941	11,059	64,891	8,991
Estimated total	100.0%	9,926	97	1,627	2,851	5,351	84,987	11,062	64,932	8,993
Rate per 100,000 inhabitants		272.5	2.7	44.7	78.3	146.9	2,332.8	303.6	1,782.3	246.9
Missoula, MT M.S.A.	119,655									
Includes Missoula County										
City of Missoula	75,422	310	3	75	27	205	3,082	342	2,565	175
Total area actually reporting	100.0%	418	3	88	28	299	3,355	410	2,740	205
Rate per 100,000 inhabitants		349.3	2.5	73.5	23.4	249.9	2,803.9	342.7	2,289.9	171.3
Modesto, CA M.S.A.	549,632									
Includes Stanislaus County										
City of Modesto	216,542	1,758	13	94	399	1,252	7,183	1,149	4,849	1,185
Total area actually reporting	100.0%	2,908	25	170	724	1,989	14,274	2,628	9,155	2,491
Rate per 100,000 inhabitants		529.1	4.5	30.9	131.7	361.9	2,597.0	478.1	1,665.7	453.2
Monroe, LA M.S.A.	200,739									
Includes Morehouse, Ouachita, and Union Parishes										
City of Monroe	47,746	843	9	37	171	626	3,141	623	2,339	179
Total area actually reporting	96.5%	1,606	23	102	251	1,230	8,142	1,862	5,788	492
Estimated total	100.0%	1,631	23	102	253	1,253	8,353	1,903	5,948	502
Rate per 100,000 inhabitants		812.5	11.5	50.8	126.0	624.2	4,161.1	948.0	2,963.1	250.1
Morgantown, WV M.S.A.	140,923									
Includes Monongalia and Preston Counties										
City of Morgantown	31,281	67	0	9	5	53	489	71	383	35
Total area actually reporting	88.8%	244	1	41	11	191	1,515	309	1,098	108
Estimated total	100.0%	288	1	46	16	225	1,862	370	1,363	129
Rate per 100,000 inhabitants		204.4	0.7	32.6	11.4	159.7	1,321.3	262.6	967.2	91.5
Morristown, TN M.S.A.	142,399									
Includes Grainger, Hamblen, and Jefferson Counties										
City of Morristown	30,044	255	2	16	18	219	1,423	169	1,140	114
Total area actually reporting	100.0%	552	4	47	29	472	2,919	506	2,114	299
Rate per 100,000 inhabitants		387.6	2.8	33.0	20.4	331.5	2,049.9	355.3	1,484.6	210.0
Mount Vernon-Anacortes, WA M.S.A.	129,233									
Includes Skagit County										
City of Mount Vernon	36,274	55	0	13	17	25	1,140	126	899	115
City of Anacortes	17,483	20	1	2	6	11	387	67	306	14
Total area actually reporting	100.0%	201	2	40	42	117	3,178	506	2,433	239
Rate per 100,000 inhabitants		155.5	1.5	31.0	32.5	90.5	2,459.1	391.5	1,882.6	184.9

Table 6. Crime in the United States, by Selected Metropolitan Statistical Area, 2019—Continued

(Number, percent, rate per 100,000 population.)

Area	Population	Violent crime	Murder and nonnegligent manslaughter	Rape[1]	Robbery	Aggravated assault	Property crime	Burglary	Larceny-theft	Motor vehicle theft
Muskegon, MI M.S.A.[4]	173,362									
Includes Muskegon County										
City of Muskegon	37,178	308	8	27	46	227	1,293	252	911	130
Total area actually reporting	100.0%	786	17	127	103	539			3,434	264
Rate per 100,000 inhabitants		453.4	9.8	73.3	59.4	310.9			1,980.8	152.3
Myrtle Beach-Conway-North Myrtle Beach, SC-NC M.S.A.[3]	495,661									
Includes Brunswick County, NC3 and Horry County, SC										
City of Myrtle Beach, SC	34,860	415	3	52	98	262	3,916	304	3,384	228
City of Conway, SC	26,127	111	1	14	11	85	884	90	739	55
City of North Myrtle Beach, SC	16,942	71	1	15	10	45	1,115	108	910	97
Total area actually reporting	82.0%	1,586	19	253	223	1,091	13,645	1,862	10,789	994
Estimated total	100.0%	1,772	22	274	241	1,235	14,926	2,275	11,542	1,109
Rate per 100,000 inhabitants		357.5	4.4	55.3	48.6	249.2	3,011.3	459.0	2,328.6	223.7
Napa, CA M.S.A.	138,570									
Includes Napa County										
City of Napa	79,526	280	1	66	55	158	1,232	248	847	137
Total area actually reporting	100.0%	753	1	90	70	592	2,162	395	1,578	189
Rate per 100,000 inhabitants		543.4	0.7	64.9	50.5	427.2	1,560.2	285.1	1,138.8	136.4
Naples-Marco Island, FL M.S.A.	383,360									
Includes Collier County										
City of Naples	22,369	11	1	2	1	7	323	29	275	19
City of Marco Island	18,124	7	0	1	2	4	83	7	74	2
Total area actually reporting	100.0%	896	9	127	147	613	4,308	469	3,530	309
Rate per 100,000 inhabitants		233.7	2.3	33.1	38.3	159.9	1,123.7	122.3	920.8	80.6
Nashville-Davidson–Murfreesboro–Franklin, TN M.S.A.	1,941,822									
Includes Cannon, Cheatham, Davidson, Dickson, Macon, Maury, Robertson, Rutherford, Smith, Sumner, Trousdale, Williamson, and Wilson Counties										
City of Metropolitan Nashville Police Department	687,361	7,376	83	438	1,978	4,877	27,777	3,374	21,655	2,748
City of Murfreesboro	145,929	611	4	96	106	405	4,228	510	3,454	264
City of Franklin	83,517	138	0	15	10	113	926	58	814	54
Total area actually reporting	100.0%	11,078	118	804	2,313	7,843	47,565	5,896	37,196	4,473
Rate per 100,000 inhabitants		570.5	6.1	41.4	119.1	403.9	2,449.5	303.6	1,915.5	230.4
New Bern, NC M.S.A.[3]	124,876									
Includes Craven, Jones, and Pamlico Counties[3]										
City of New Bern[3]	30,187	125	0	5	21	99	999	195	787	17
Total area actually reporting	88.9%	321	4	29	38	250	2,683	810	1,738	135
Estimated total	100.0%	355	4	32	42	277	2,954	881	1,919	154
Rate per 100,000 inhabitants		284.3	3.2	25.6	33.6	221.8	2,365.5	705.5	1,536.7	123.3
New Haven-Milford, CT M.S.A.	802,507									
Includes New Haven County										
City of New Haven	130,494	1,168	13	45	321	789	4,958	659	3,580	719
City of Milford	54,898	29	1	0	16	12	1,028	95	853	80
Total area actually reporting	100.0%	2,189	28	208	643	1,310	16,938	2,046	12,729	2,163
Rate per 100,000 inhabitants		272.8	3.5	25.9	80.1	163.2	2,110.6	255.0	1,586.2	269.5
New Orleans-Metairie, LA M.S.A.	1,273,092									
Includes Jefferson, Orleans, Plaquemines, St. Bernard, St. Charles, St. James, St. John the Baptist, and St. Tammany Parishes										
City of New Orleans	394,498	4,516	121	774	1,013	2,608	20,879	2,143	15,785	2,951
Total area actually reporting	95.4%	6,765	198	955	1,377	4,235	38,541	4,351	30,206	3,984
Estimated total	100.0%	7,021	203	975	1,398	4,445	40,101	4,699	31,317	4,085
Rate per 100,000 inhabitants		551.5	15.9	76.6	109.8	349.1	3,149.9	369.1	2,459.9	320.9
Niles, MI M.S.A.	153,430									
Includes Berrien County										
City of Niles	11,106	86	0	20	17	49	366	49	274	43
Total area actually reporting	100.0%	845	5	168	79	593	3,340	503	2,540	297
Rate per 100,000 inhabitants		550.7	3.3	109.5	51.5	386.5	2,176.9	327.8	1,655.5	193.6
North Port-Sarasota-Bradenton, FL M.S.A.	831,795									
Includes Manatee and Sarasota Counties										
City of North Port	70,181	95	1	22	8	64	967	89	847	31
City of Sarasota	58,470	319	4	28	66	221	1,857	264	1,462	131
City of Bradenton	58,782	360	6	22	57	275	1,474	204	1,191	79
City of Venice	23,726	20	1	1	3	15	283	30	242	11
Total area actually reporting	100.0%	2,732	26	286	380	2,040	13,924	1,872	11,213	839
Rate per 100,000 inhabitants		328.4	3.1	34.4	45.7	245.3	1,674.0	225.1	1,348.0	100.9
Norwich-New London, CT M.S.A.	174,879									
Includes New London County										
City of Norwich	38,964	149	0	26	22	101	533	112	368	53

Table 6. Crime in the United States, by Selected Metropolitan Statistical Area, 2019—Continued

(Number, percent, rate per 100,000 population.)

Area	Population	Violent crime	Murder and nonnegligent manslaughter	Rape[1]	Robbery	Aggravated assault	Property crime	Burglary	Larceny-theft	Motor vehicle theft
City of New London	26,856	79	0	19	32	28	461	90	329	42
Total area actually reporting	100.0%	339	3	82	59	195	2,322	338	1,835	149
Rate per 100,000 inhabitants		193.8	1.7	46.9	33.7	111.5	1,327.8	193.3	1,049.3	85.2
Ocala, FL M.S.A.	361,126									
Includes Marion County										
City of Ocala	60,932	493	7	52	108	326	2,548	252	2,131	165
Total area actually reporting	100.0%	1,556	31	227	211	1,087	6,841	1,198	4,947	696
Rate per 100,000 inhabitants		430.9	8.6	62.9	58.4	301.0	1,894.4	331.7	1,369.9	192.7
Ocean City, NJ M.S.A.	91,575									
Includes Cape May County										
City of Ocean City	10,962	6	0	0	2	4	323	37	285	1
Total area actually reporting	100.0%	161	0	24	23	114	1,909	291	1,573	45
Rate per 100,000 inhabitants		175.8	0.0	26.2	25.1	124.5	2,084.6	317.8	1,717.7	49.1
Odessa, TX M.S.A.	164,546									
Includes Ector County										
City of Odessa	123,468	1,282	13	141	128	1,000	3,624	469	2,656	499
Total area actually reporting	100.0%	1,451	17	152	147	1,135	5,205	707	3,641	857
Rate per 100,000 inhabitants		881.8	10.3	92.4	89.3	689.8	3,163.2	429.7	2,212.8	520.8
Ogden-Clearfield, UT M.S.A.[3,4]	683,537									
Includes Box Elder,[3] Davis, Morgan,[4] and Weber Counties										
City of Ogden	87,875	384	6	84	63	231	3,211	484	2,382	345
City of Clearfield	32,217	56	0	12	5	39	369	38	292	39
Total area actually reporting	99.5%	1,162	9	360	121	672			8,619	978
Estimated total	100.0%	1,167	9	361	122	675			8,703	984
Rate per 100,000 inhabitants		170.7	1.3	52.8	17.8	98.8			1,273.2	144.0
Oklahoma City, OK M.S.A.[3]	1,411,162									
Includes Canadian, Cleveland, Grady, Lincoln, Logan, McClain, and Oklahoma Counties										
City of Oklahoma City[3]	657,819	4,751	75	539	888	3,249	26,918	6,206	16,922	3,790
Total area actually reporting	100.0%	6,506	108	886	1,133	4,379	43,321	9,577	28,189	5,555
Rate per 100,000 inhabitants		461.0	7.7	62.8	80.3	310.3	3,069.9	678.7	1,997.6	393.6
Olympia-Lacey-Tumwater, WA M.S.A.	289,877									
Includes Thurston County										
City of Olympia	53,286	254	2	25	70	157	1,854	244	1,409	201
City of Lacey	51,816	105	0	29	17	59	1,436	180	1,136	120
City of Tumwater	24,167	73	0	14	18	41	648	99	483	66
Total area actually reporting	100.0%	715	5	99	129	482	6,005	1,108	4,274	623
Rate per 100,000 inhabitants		246.7	1.7	34.2	44.5	166.3	2,071.6	382.2	1,474.4	214.9
Omaha-Council Bluffs, NE-IA M.S.A.	947,962									
Includes Harrison, Mills, and Pottawattamie Counties, IA and Cass, Douglas, Sarpy, Saunders, and Washington Counties, NE										
City of Omaha, NE	470,481	2,883	23	379	519	1,962	17,144	1,684	12,307	3,153
City of Council Bluffs, IA	62,427	493	6	39	57	391	3,649	529	2,629	491
Total area actually reporting	99.7%	3,891	34	571	629	2,657	25,055	2,792	18,061	4,202
Estimated total	100.0%	3,916	34	588	629	2,665	25,089	2,792	18,095	4,202
Rate per 100,000 inhabitants		413.1	3.6	62.0	66.4	281.1	2,646.6	294.5	1,908.8	443.3
Orlando-Kissimmee-Sanford, FL M.S.A.	2,614,835									
Includes Lake, Orange, Osceola, and Seminole Counties										
City of Orlando	292,120	2,157	25	204	536	1,392	14,100	1,464	11,362	1,274
City of Kissimmee	75,544	368	3	42	54	269	1,899	257	1,504	138
City of Sanford	60,844	497	2	62	116	317	2,127	315	1,689	123
Total area actually reporting	100.0%	11,242	120	1,179	2,298	7,645	62,756	9,389	47,901	5,466
Rate per 100,000 inhabitants		429.9	4.6	45.1	87.9	292.4	2,400.0	359.1	1,831.9	209.0
Oshkosh-Neenah, WI M.S.A.[3]	171,309									
Includes Winnebago County										
City of Oshkosh[3]	66,797	190	0	50	16	124	1,067	213	794	60
City of Neenah[3]	26,133	45	1	10	0	34	330	28	288	14
Total area actually reporting	100.0%	338	1	86	21	230	2,008	339	1,563	106
Rate per 100,000 inhabitants		197.3	0.6	50.2	12.3	134.3	1,172.2	197.9	912.4	61.9
Owensboro, KY M.S.A.	119,217									
Includes Daviess, Hancock, and McLean Counties										
City of Owensboro	60,107	135	6	30	33	66	2,432	358	1,874	200
Total area actually reporting	100.0%	159	8	41	34	76	2,896	490	2,152	254
Rate per 100,000 inhabitants		133.4	6.7	34.4	28.5	63.7	2,429.2	411.0	1,805.1	213.1
Oxnard-Thousand Oaks-Ventura, CA M.S.A.	847,049									
Includes Ventura County										
City of Oxnard	211,349	724	13	62	275	374	4,242	670	2,987	585
City of Thousand Oaks	127,811	88	0	27	23	38	1,392	244	1,084	64
City of Ventura	111,596	458	3	56	106	293	2,969	353	2,362	254

Table 6. Crime in the United States, by Selected Metropolitan Statistical Area, 2019—Continued

(Number, percent, rate per 100,000 population.)

Area	Population	Violent crime	Murder and nonnegligent manslaughter	Rape[1]	Robbery	Aggravated assault	Property crime	Burglary	Larceny-theft	Motor vehicle theft
City of Camarillo	69,628	58	0	22	16	20	817	100	676	41
Total area actually reporting	100.0%	1,830	24	232	527	1,047	12,634	1,946	9,454	1,234
Rate per 100,000 inhabitants		216.0	2.8	27.4	62.2	123.6	1,491.5	229.7	1,116.1	145.7
Palm Bay-Melbourne-Titusville, FL M.S.A.	599,498									
Includes Brevard County										
City of Palm Bay	115,520	396	8	71	59	258	1,981	334	1,499	148
City of Melbourne	83,668	579	1	80	87	411	2,802	439	2,219	144
City of Titusville	46,866	377	2	37	52	286	1,492	289	1,031	172
Total area actually reporting	100.0%	2,224	23	262	332	1,607	12,269	2,019	9,322	928
Rate per 100,000 inhabitants		371.0	3.8	43.7	55.4	268.1	2,046.5	336.8	1,555.0	154.8
Panama City, FL M.S.A.	186,063									
Includes Bay County										
City of Panama City	37,199	228	2	5	42	179	1,914	384	1,308	222
Total area actually reporting	100.0%	826	8	91	103	624	5,707	1,097	4,139	471
Rate per 100,000 inhabitants		443.9	4.3	48.9	55.4	335.4	3,067.2	589.6	2,224.5	253.1
Pensacola-Ferry Pass-Brent, FL M.S.A.	497,168									
Includes Escambia and Santa Rosa Counties										
City of Pensacola	52,801	312	3	35	38	236	1,888	287	1,508	93
Total area actually reporting	100.0%	2,037	32	247	355	1,403	10,827	2,189	7,862	776
Rate per 100,000 inhabitants		409.7	6.4	49.7	71.4	282.2	2,177.7	440.3	1,581.4	156.1
Peoria, IL M.S.A.	399,839									
Includes Fulton, Marshall, Peoria, Stark, Tazewell, and Woodford Counties										
City of Peoria	110,955	1,158	25	65	268	800	4,160	758	2,959	443
Total area actually reporting	94.9%	1,775	30	193	309	1,243	7,432	1,481	5,290	661
Estimated total	100.0%	1,807	30	198	312	1,267	7,735	1,524	5,530	681
Rate per 100,000 inhabitants		451.9	7.5	49.5	78.0	316.9	1,934.5	381.2	1,383.1	170.3
Phoenix-Mesa-Chandler, AZ M.S.A.[3, 4]	4,949,304									
Includes Maricopa and Pinal Counties										
City of Phoenix	1,688,722	11,803	131	1,139	3,197	7,336	55,974	9,471	39,427	7,076
City of Mesa	518,160	1,953	11	286	390	1,266	9,683	1,518	7,326	839
City of Chandler	259,881	593	4	134	102	353	5,382	547	4,458	377
City of Scottsdale	260,464	415	3	136	110	166	5,099	662	4,173	264
City of Tempe	196,499	889	8	141	209	531	7,420	922	5,891	607
City of Casa Grande[3]	58,366	274	2	27	33	212	1,336	149	1,071	116
Total area actually reporting	91.3%	19,721	208	2,313	4,672	12,528			85,599	11,791
Estimated total	100.0%	21,110	226	2,464	4,805	13,615			89,332	12,465
Rate per 100,000 inhabitants		426.5	4.6	49.8	97.1	275.1			1,804.9	251.9
Pine Bluff, AR M.S.A.[4]	88,005									
Includes Cleveland, Jefferson, and Lincoln Counties										
City of Pine Bluff[4]	41,505	644	23	23	96	502			1,448	271
Total area actually reporting	98.6%	782	28	50	102	602			1,906	366
Estimated total	100.0%	788	28	51	102	607			1,924	368
Rate per 100,000 inhabitants		895.4	31.8	58.0	115.9	689.7			2,186.2	418.2
Pittsfield, MA M.S.A.[3]	124,775									
Includes Berkshire County										
City of Pittsfield	42,268	300	2	36	31	231	796	263	490	43
Total area actually reporting	90.2%	446	2	73	43	328	1,617	431	1,119	67
Estimated total	100.0%	475	2	76	46	351	1,730	450	1,205	75
Rate per 100,000 inhabitants		380.7	1.6	60.9	36.9	281.3	1,386.5	360.6	965.7	60.1
Pocatello, ID M.S.A.	95,848									
Includes Bannock and Power Counties										
City of Pocatello	56,514	233	1	30	9	193	1,326	226	1,012	88
Total area actually reporting	100.0%	287	1	42	15	229	2,018	288	1,614	116
Rate per 100,000 inhabitants		299.4	1.0	43.8	15.6	238.9	2,105.4	300.5	1,683.9	121.0
Portland-South Portland, ME M.S.A.[3]	539,924									
Includes Cumberland, Sagadahoc,[3] and York Counties										
City of Portland	66,458	161	3	29	43	86	1,715	181	1,460	74
City of South Portland	25,686	48	0	17	8	23	563	39	505	19
Total area actually reporting	100.0%	619	6	175	93	345	6,784	837	5,699	248
Rate per 100,000 inhabitants		114.6	1.1	32.4	17.2	63.9	1,256.5	155.0	1,055.5	45.9
Portland-Vancouver-Hillsboro, OR-WA M.S.A.	2,500,376									
Includes Clackamas, Columbia, Multnomah, Washington, and Yamhill Counties, OR and Clark and Skamania Counties, WA										
City of Portland, OR	662,114	3,606	29	368	979	2,230	34,452	4,200	23,820	6,432
City of Vancouver, WA	185,034	889	3	206	185	495	5,998	888	4,302	808
City of Hillsboro, OR	110,549	274	0	77	56	141	2,164	175	1,779	210
City of Beaverton, OR	100,130	217	1	53	49	114	1,988	185	1,601	202
City of Tigard, OR	55,621	119	0	13	29	77	1,410	137	1,158	115
Total area actually reporting	98.5%	7,514	59	1,246	1,666	4,543	68,398	8,444	48,993	10,961
Estimated total	100.0%	7,565	59	1,255	1,668	4,583	68,684	8,483	49,221	10,980
Rate per 100,000 inhabitants		302.6	2.4	50.2	66.7	183.3	2,746.9	339.3	1,968.5	439.1

Table 6. Crime in the United States, by Selected Metropolitan Statistical Area, 2019—Continued

(Number, percent, rate per 100,000 population.)

Area	Population	Violent crime	Murder and nonnegligent manslaughter	Rape[1]	Robbery	Aggravated assault	Property crime	Burglary	Larceny-theft	Motor vehicle theft
Port St. Lucie, FL M.S.A.	486,186									
Includes Martin and St. Lucie Counties										
City of Port St. Lucie	199,433	293	7	43	47	196	1,696	177	1,438	81
Total area actually reporting	100.0%	1,161	24	200	194	743	6,184	764	4,991	429
Rate per 100,000 inhabitants		238.8	4.9	41.1	39.9	152.8	1,271.9	157.1	1,026.6	88.2
Poughkeepsie-Newburg-Middletown, NY M.S.A.	672,535									
Includes Dutchess and Orange Counties										
City of Poughkeepsie	30,422	235	3	26	63	143	513	73	402	38
City of Newburgh	28,070	317	3	19	82	213	640	137	484	19
City of Middletown	27,801	87	3	16	16	52	308	45	249	14
City of Woodbury Town	11,006	3	0	0	1	2	460	5	450	5
Total area actually reporting	89.7%	1,263	16	245	234	768	7,372	690	6,449	233
Estimated total	100.0%	1,286	16	246	235	789	7,443	696	6,512	235
Rate per 100,000 inhabitants		191.2	2.4	36.6	34.9	117.3	1,106.7	103.5	968.3	34.9
Prescott Valley-Prescott, AZ M.S.A.	234,899									
Includes Yavapai County										
City of Prescott Valley	46,700	93	3	11	6	73	474	51	404	19
City of Prescott	43,781	214	1	20	11	182	684	134	518	32
Total area actually reporting	100.0%	651	9	35	28	579	3,143	520	2,413	210
Rate per 100,000 inhabitants		277.1	3.8	14.9	11.9	246.5	1,338.0	221.4	1,027.3	89.4
Providence-Warwick, RI-MA M.S.A.	1,620,927									
Includes Bristol County, MA and Bristol, Kent, Newport, Providence, and Washington Counties, RI										
City of Providence, RI	179,762	892	13	106	241	532	5,413	715	4,224	474
City of Warwick, RI	80,749	76	2	29	8	37	1,239	108	1,073	58
Total area actually reporting	99.5%	4,566	38	724	779	3,025	22,801	3,637	17,335	1,829
Estimated total	100.0%	4,580	38	726	780	3,036	22,854	3,647	17,375	1,832
Rate per 100,000 inhabitants		282.6	2.3	44.8	48.1	187.3	1,409.9	225.0	1,071.9	113.0
Provo-Orem, UT M.S.A.[3]	646,530									
Includes Juab and Utah Counties										
City of Provo	117,189	135	1	44	13	77	1,767	163	1,476	128
City of Orem	98,686	89	2	37	11	39	1,970	156	1,673	141
Total area actually reporting	100.0%	583	7	204	51	321	8,264	859	6,865	540
Rate per 100,000 inhabitants		90.2	1.1	31.6	7.9	49.6	1,278.2	132.9	1,061.8	83.5
Pueblo, CO M.S.A.[5]	167,847									
Includes Pueblo County										
City of Pueblo[5]	112,381		5	110		481	4,801	894	3,208	699
Total area actually reporting	100.0%		7	110		519	5,859	1,077	3,928	854
Rate per 100,000 inhabitants			4.2	65.5		309.2	3,490.7	641.7	2,340.2	508.8
Punta Gorda, FL M.S.A.	187,062									
Includes Charlotte County										
City of Punta Gorda	20,458	18	0	0	4	14	278	11	260	7
Total area actually reporting	100.0%	367	2	41	20	304	2,114	273	1,708	133
Rate per 100,000 inhabitants		196.2	1.1	21.9	10.7	162.5	1,130.1	145.9	913.1	71.1
Racine, WI M.S.A.[3]	196,488									
Includes Racine County										
City of Racine	77,269	291	4	45	53	189	990	212	682	96
Total area actually reporting	79.1%	364	4	53	61	246	1,798	291	1,366	141
Estimated total	100.0%	625	1	77	131	416	2,801	546	2,067	188
Rate per 100,000 inhabitants		318.1	0.5	39.2	66.7	211.7	1,425.5	277.9	1,052.0	95.7
Raleigh-Cary, NC M.S.A.[3]	1,392,882									
Includes Franklin, Johnston, and Wake Counties[3]										
City of Raleigh[3]	477,828	1,222	5	164	322	731	8,520	1,200	6,572	748
City of Cary[3]	172,525	114	1	12	34	67	1,560	185	1,298	77
Total area actually reporting	99.3%	2,366	24	295	516	1,531	19,161	3,046	14,705	1,410
Estimated total	100.0%	2,404	24	299	521	1,560	19,469	3,117	14,921	1,431
Rate per 100,000 inhabitants		172.6	1.7	21.5	37.4	112.0	1,397.7	223.8	1,071.2	102.7
Rapid City, SD M.S.A.	140,743									
Includes Meade and Pennington Counties										
City of Rapid City	76,343	540	4	114	64	358	2,454	488	1,646	320
Total area actually reporting	100.0%	749	5	182	69	493	3,382	693	2,282	407
Rate per 100,000 inhabitants		532.2	3.6	129.3	49.0	350.3	2,403.0	492.4	1,621.4	289.2
Reno, NV M.S.A.[3]	475,735									
Includes Storey and Washoe3 Counties										
City of Reno[3]	254,349	1,419	12	178	308	921	5,344	822	3,343	1,179
Total area actually reporting	100.0%	2,231	15	300	413	1,503	8,883	1,556	5,648	1,679
Rate per 100,000 inhabitants		469.0	3.2	63.1	86.8	315.9	1,867.2	327.1	1,187.2	352.9
Richmond, VA M.S.A.	1,287,449									
Includes Amelia, Charles City, Chesterfield, Dinwiddie, Goochland, Hanover, Henrico, King and Queen, King William, New Kent, Powhatan, Prince George, and Sussex Counties and Colonial Heights, Hopewell, Petersburg, and Richmond Cities										

Table 6. Crime in the United States, by Selected Metropolitan Statistical Area, 2019—Continued

(Number, percent, rate per 100,000 population.)

Area	Population	Violent crime	Murder and nonnegligent manslaughter	Rape[1]	Robbery	Aggravated assault	Property crime	Burglary	Larceny-theft	Motor vehicle theft
City of Richmond	230,721	1,068	55	45	385	583	8,074	986	6,234	854
Total area actually reporting	100.0%	2,932	107	344	776	1,705	27,824	2,788	22,939	2,097
Rate per 100,000 inhabitants		227.7	8.3	26.7	60.3	132.4	2,161.2	216.6	1,781.7	162.9
Riverside-San Bernardino-Ontario, CA M.S.A.	4,632,925									
Includes Riverside and San Bernardino Counties										
City of Riverside	333,260	1,686	17	139	476	1,054	9,790	1,302	6,997	1,491
City of San Bernardino	216,715	2,858	46	140	906	1,766	9,081	2,029	4,974	2,078
City of Ontario	183,322	659	10	85	223	341	4,290	710	2,652	928
City of Corona	170,875	291	4	43	103	141	3,482	646	2,251	585
City of Temecula	116,630	166	1	8	72	85	2,626	318	2,018	290
City of Chino	93,348	329	3	35	96	195	2,224	376	1,649	199
City of Redlands	71,941	257	1	40	70	146	2,108	330	1,534	244
City of Palm Desert	53,776	136	3	7	24	102	1,848	338	1,382	128
Total area actually reporting	100.0%	19,730	265	1,386	5,252	12,827	105,402	20,268	65,805	19,329
Rate per 100,000 inhabitants		425.9	5.7	29.9	113.4	276.9	2,275.1	437.5	1,420.4	417.2
Roanoke, VA M.S.A.	313,075									
Includes Botetourt, Craig, Franklin, and Roanoke Counties and Roanoke and Salem Cities										
City of Roanoke	99,752	386	13	41	106	226	4,402	519	3,585	298
Total area actually reporting	100.0%	748	18	101	144	485	7,487	887	6,051	549
Rate per 100,000 inhabitants		238.9	5.7	32.3	46.0	154.9	2,391.4	283.3	1,932.8	175.4
Rochester, MN M.S.A.[3]	221,013									
Includes Dodge,[3] Fillmore, Olmsted,[3] and Wabasha Counties										
City of Rochester[3]	118,267	254	1	62	34	157	2,225	282	1,816	127
Total area actually reporting	100.0%	337	2	72	37	226	2,813	408	2,235	170
Rate per 100,000 inhabitants		152.5	0.9	32.6	16.7	102.3	1,272.8	184.6	1,011.3	76.9
Rochester, NY M.S.A.	1,064,123									
Includes Livingston, Monroe, Ontario, Orleans, Wayne, and Yates Counties										
City of Rochester	205,769	1,540	33	102	429	976	7,142	1,269	5,222	651
Total area actually reporting	99.2%	2,642	38	465	607	1,532	17,751	2,625	14,060	1,066
Estimated total	100.0%	2,647	38	465	607	1,537	17,819	2,633	14,118	1,068
Rate per 100,000 inhabitants		248.7	3.6	43.7	57.0	144.4	1,674.5	247.4	1,326.7	100.4
Rockford, IL M.S.A.	334,726									
Includes Boone and Winnebago Counties										
City of Rockford	145,717	1,711	14	125	282	1,290	4,848	1,001	3,458	389
Total area actually reporting	99.4%	2,121	20	224	315	1,562	7,201	1,419	5,237	545
Estimated total	100.0%	2,124	20	225	315	1,564	7,233	1,424	5,262	547
Rate per 100,000 inhabitants		634.5	6.0	67.2	94.1	467.2	2,160.9	425.4	1,572.0	163.4
Sacramento-Roseville-Folsom, CA M.S.A.	2,350,381									
Includes El Dorado, Placer, Sacramento, and Yolo Counties										
City of Sacramento	513,934	3,223	34	127	1,039	2,023	16,354	2,993	10,644	2,717
City of Roseville	141,744	259	4	32	96	127	3,154	389	2,518	247
City of Folsom	79,927	82	0	12	29	41	1,484	278	1,127	79
City of Rancho Cordova	75,869	225	5	12	56	152	1,422	233	1,004	185
City of West Sacramento	54,372	212	1	34	79	98	1,603	236	1,158	209
Total area actually reporting	100.0%	8,322	96	647	2,397	5,182	51,565	9,157	35,737	6,671
Rate per 100,000 inhabitants		354.1	4.1	27.5	102.0	220.5	2,193.9	389.6	1,520.5	283.8
Saginaw, MI M.S.A.	189,217									
Includes Saginaw County										
City of Saginaw	47,954	707	9	34	51	613	743	245	421	77
Total area actually reporting	100.0%	1,180	17	127	86	950	2,731	578	1,990	163
Rate per 100,000 inhabitants		623.6	9.0	67.1	45.5	502.1	1,443.3	305.5	1,051.7	86.1
Salem, OR M.S.A.[2]	435,428									
Includes Marion[2] and Polk Counties										
City of Salem	175,867	670	0	35	152	483	6,488	680	4,966	842
Total area actually reporting	99.9%	1,152	6	90	232	824	12,057	1,454	9,017	1,586
Estimated total	100.0%	1,176	6	114	232	824	12,057	1,454	9,017	1,586
Rate per 100,000 inhabitants		270.1	1.4	26.2	53.3	189.2	2,769.0	333.9	2,070.8	364.2
Salinas, CA M.S.A.	434,363									
Includes Monterey County										
City of Salinas	156,943	782	8	66	241	467	3,532	742	1,709	1,081
Total area actually reporting	100.0%	1,433	15	139	368	911	7,735	1,524	4,562	1,649
Rate per 100,000 inhabitants		329.9	3.5	32.0	84.7	209.7	1,780.8	350.9	1,050.3	379.6
Salisbury, MD-DE M.S.A.	413,262									
Includes Sussex County, DE and Somerset, Wicomico, and Worcester Counties, MD										
City of Salisbury, MD	33,132	294	0	19	58	217	1,422	207	1,170	45
Total area actually reporting	100.0%	1,370	5	124	193	1,048	8,572	1,491	6,817	264
Rate per 100,000 inhabitants		331.5	1.2	30.0	46.7	253.6	2,074.2	360.8	1,649.6	63.9
Salt Lake City, UT M.S.A.[3]	1,237,086									
Includes Salt Lake and Tooele Counties										

Table 6. Crime in the United States, by Selected Metropolitan Statistical Area, 2019—Continued

(Number, percent, rate per 100,000 population.)

Area	Population	Violent crime	Murder and nonnegligent manslaughter	Rape[1]	Robbery	Aggravated assault	Property crime	Burglary	Larceny-theft	Motor vehicle theft
City of Salt Lake City	202,426	1,442	13	234	403	792	11,452	1,290	8,902	1,260
Total area actually reporting	100.0%	4,536	37	882	901	2,716	41,240	4,904	31,788	4,548
Rate per 100,000 inhabitants		366.7	3.0	71.3	72.8	219.5	3,333.6	396.4	2,569.6	367.6
San Angelo, TX M.S.A.	121,245									
Includes Irion, Sterling, and Tom Green Counties										
City of San Angelo	101,072	357	5	56	32	264	3,173	512	2,437	224
Total area actually reporting	100.0%	398	6	82	34	276	3,491	607	2,632	252
Rate per 100,000 inhabitants		328.3	4.9	67.6	28.0	227.6	2,879.3	500.6	2,170.8	207.8
San Antonio-New Braunfels, TX M.S.A.[3]	2,552,063									
Includes Atascosa, Bandera, Bexar, Comal, Guadalupe, Kendall, Medina, and Wilson Counties										
City of San Antonio	1,559,166	11,046	105	1,630	1,965	7,346	67,422	8,172	51,469	7,781
City of New Braunfels	88,706	219	2	21	25	171	1,120	209	805	106
Total area actually reporting	99.8%	13,155	130	2,003	2,213	8,809	83,646	11,079	63,323	9,244
Estimated total	100.0%	13,166	130	2,004	2,213	8,819	83,725	11,096	63,376	9,253
Rate per 100,000 inhabitants		515.9	5.1	78.5	86.7	345.6	3,280.7	434.8	2,483.3	362.6
San Diego-Chula Vista-Carlsbad, CA M.S.A.	3,346,196									
Includes San Diego County										
City of San Diego	1,441,737	5,215	50	561	1,346	3,258	27,141	3,543	18,426	5,172
City of Chula Vista	275,230	904	3	61	265	575	3,816	486	2,503	827
City of Carlsbad	117,220	240	3	40	39	158	2,135	297	1,671	167
City of Poway	49,928	51	2	2	12	35	490	91	354	45
Total area actually reporting	100.0%	11,417	86	1,106	2,892	7,333	55,242	7,696	37,865	9,681
Rate per 100,000 inhabitants		341.2	2.6	33.1	86.4	219.1	1,650.9	230.0	1,131.6	289.3
San Francisco-Oakland-Berkeley, CA M.S.A.	4,739,872									
Includes the Metropolitan Divisions of Oakland-Berkeley-Livermore, San Francisco-San Mateo-Redwood City, and San Rafael										
City of San Francisco	886,007	5,933	40	324	3,055	2,514	48,780	4,644	39,887	4,249
City of Oakland	434,036	5,520	78	372	2,859	2,211	27,868	2,599	20,228	5,041
City of Berkeley	122,788	618	0	74	369	175	6,256	771	4,993	492
City of San Mateo	106,020	266	2	45	68	151	2,217	516	1,523	178
City of Livermore	91,418	193	2	30	39	122	1,554	139	1,279	136
City of Redwood City	87,427	189	0	32	70	87	1,343	165	1,014	164
City of Pleasanton	84,017	112	0	12	56	44	1,632	149	1,386	97
City of San Ramon	76,387	58	0	4	21	33	1,099	179	869	51
City of Walnut Creek	70,546	120	0	6	40	74	2,496	307	2,034	155
City of South San Francisco	68,251	166	2	19	64	81	1,484	230	1,074	180
City of San Rafael	58,819	230	0	23	87	120	1,686	299	1,173	214
Total area actually reporting	100.0%	22,317	201	1,718	10,305	10,093	167,013	18,004	127,917	21,092
Rate per 100,000 inhabitants		470.8	4.2	36.2	217.4	212.9	3,523.6	379.8	2,698.7	445.0
Oakland-Berkeley-Livermore, CA M.D.	2,826,061									
Includes Alameda and Contra Costa Counties										
Total area actually reporting	100.0%	13,872	150	1,022	6,435	6,265	95,286	10,096	70,324	14,866
Rate per 100,000 inhabitants		490.9	5.3	36.2	227.7	221.7	3,371.7	357.2	2,488.4	526.0
San Francisco-San Mateo-Redwood City, CA M.D.	1,655,482									
Includes San Francisco and San Mateo Counties										
Total area actually reporting	100.0%	7,929	50	652	3,725	3,502	66,284	6,907	53,571	5,806
Rate per 100,000 inhabitants		479.0	3.0	39.4	225.0	211.5	4,003.9	417.2	3,236.0	350.7
San Rafael, CA M.D.	258,329									
Includes Marin County										
Total area actually reporting	100.0%	516	1	44	145	326	5,443	1,001	4,022	420
Rate per 100,000 inhabitants		199.7	0.4	17.0	56.1	126.2	2,107.0	387.5	1,556.9	162.6
San Jose-Sunnyvale-Santa Clara, CA M.S.A.	2,002,715									
Includes San Benito and Santa Clara Counties										
City of San Jose	1,040,008	4,559	32	671	1,339	2,517	25,164	4,114	14,924	6,126
City of Sunnyvale	154,859	259	0	37	84	138	3,380	458	2,598	324
City of Santa Clara	131,173	214	0	35	73	106	4,748	363	4,013	372
City of Mountain View	84,599	165	0	20	49	96	2,463	321	2,030	112
City of Milpitas	82,344	102	2	15	48	37	2,193	201	1,791	201
City of Palo Alto	66,938	86	1	10	46	29	1,983	179	1,722	82
City of Cupertino	60,357	55	1	6	14	34	1,018	175	803	40
Total area actually reporting	100.0%	6,508	46	940	1,865	3,657	48,078	6,923	32,978	8,177
Rate per 100,000 inhabitants		325.0	2.3	46.9	93.1	182.6	2,400.6	345.7	1,646.7	408.3
San Luis Obispo-Paso Robles, CA M.S.A.	283,427									
Includes San Luis Obispo County										
City of San Luis Obispo	47,735	192	0	44	34	114	1,738	277	1,387	74
City of Paso Robles	32,528	53	0	9	13	31	646	78	523	45
Total area actually reporting	100.0%	630	5	95	77	453	5,119	995	3,800	324
Rate per 100,000 inhabitants		222.3	1.8	33.5	27.2	159.8	1,806.1	351.1	1,340.7	114.3
Santa Cruz-Watsonville, CA M.S.A.	273,351									
Includes Santa Cruz County										

Table 6. Crime in the United States, by Selected Metropolitan Statistical Area, 2019—Continued

(Number, percent, rate per 100,000 population.)

Area	Population	Violent crime	Murder and nonnegligent manslaughter	Rape[1]	Robbery	Aggravated assault	Property crime	Burglary	Larceny-theft	Motor vehicle theft
City of Santa Cruz	65,263	389	0	29	88	272	2,932	348	2,363	221
City of Watsonville	54,261	328	1	37	53	237	971	148	589	234
Total area actually reporting	100.0%	1,106	6	137	182	781	7,005	1,039	5,138	828
Rate per 100,000 inhabitants		404.6	2.2	50.1	66.6	285.7	2,562.6	380.1	1,879.6	302.9
Santa Rosa-Petaluma, CA M.S.A.	497,643									
Includes Sonoma County										
City of Santa Rosa	177,884	857	3	146	126	582	2,874	486	2,077	311
City of Petaluma	62,425	190	3	22	28	137	789	109	626	54
Total area actually reporting	100.0%	2,016	9	277	243	1,487	6,760	1,228	4,966	566
Rate per 100,000 inhabitants		405.1	1.8	55.7	48.8	298.8	1,358.4	246.8	997.9	113.7
Scranton–Wilkes-Barre, PA M.S.A.	553,678									
Includes Lackawanna, Luzerne, and Wyoming Counties										
City of Scranton	77,323	1,199	0	45	66	1,088	1,347	239	1,026	82
City of Wilkes-Barre	40,722	242	3	24	68	147	852	194	616	42
Total area actually reporting	95.4%	2,180	7	157	207	1,809	6,729	1,104	5,283	342
Estimated total	100.0%	2,220	7	160	210	1,843	6,974	1,133	5,488	353
Rate per 100,000 inhabitants		401.0	1.3	28.9	37.9	332.9	1,259.6	204.6	991.2	63.8
Sebastian-Vero Beach, FL M.S.A.	158,842									
Includes Indian River County										
City of Sebastian	26,232	19	0	6	4	9	297	20	262	15
City of Vero Beach	17,503	54	0	6	8	40	343	46	275	22
Total area actually reporting	100.0%	352	6	36	31	279	2,095	248	1,708	139
Rate per 100,000 inhabitants		221.6	3.8	22.7	19.5	175.6	1,318.9	156.1	1,075.3	87.5
Sebring-Avon Park, FL M.S.A.	105,547									
Includes Highlands County										
City of Sebring	11,008	57	6	9	13	29	481	131	339	11
Total area actually reporting	100.0%	280	11	30	58	181	2,341	546	1,709	86
Rate per 100,000 inhabitants		265.3	10.4	28.4	55.0	171.5	2,218.0	517.3	1,619.2	81.5
Sheboygan, WI M.S.A.[3]	115,305									
Includes Sheboygan County										
City of Sheboygan	48,035	172	0	48	10	114	783	88	676	19
Total area actually reporting	100.0%	207	0	59	11	137	1,272	125	1,103	44
Rate per 100,000 inhabitants		179.5	0.0	51.2	9.5	118.8	1,103.2	108.4	956.6	38.2
Sherman-Denison, TX M.S.A.[3]	134,857									
Includes Grayson County										
City of Sherman[3]	43,002	179	3	32	27	117	1,122	241	790	91
City of Denison[3]	25,432	106	1	22	5	78	464	103	304	57
Total area actually reporting	98.4%	338	5	71	40	222	2,162	494	1,454	214
Estimated total	100.0%	342	5	71	40	226	2,194	500	1,476	218
Rate per 100,000 inhabitants		253.6	3.7	52.6	29.7	167.6	1,626.9	370.8	1,094.5	161.7
Shreveport-Bossier City, LA M.S.A.	395,040									
Includes Bossier, Caddo, and De Soto Parishes										
City of Shreveport	187,556	1,462	35	133	294	1,000	9,189	1,626	6,915	648
City of Bossier City	69,044	546	2	52	72	420	3,225	461	2,382	382
Total area actually reporting	100.0%	2,225	41	201	371	1,612	13,978	2,403	10,451	1,124
Rate per 100,000 inhabitants		563.2	10.4	50.9	93.9	408.1	3,538.4	608.3	2,645.6	284.5
Sierra Vista-Douglas, AZ M.S.A.	126,231									
Includes Cochise County										
City of Sierra Vista	44,310	116	2	7	16	91	987	124	800	63
City of Douglas	15,786	10	0	0	0	10	594	88	486	20
Total area actually reporting	92.1%	207	3	11	19	174	2,283	448	1,678	157
Estimated total	100.0%	275	3	15	27	230	2,729	545	1,988	196
Rate per 100,000 inhabitants		217.9	2.4	11.9	21.4	182.2	2,161.9	431.7	1,574.9	155.3
Sioux City, IA-NE-SD M.S.A.	143,233									
Includes Woodbury County, IA; Dakota and Dixon Counties, NE; and Union County, SD										
City of Sioux City, IA	82,333	366	2	50	57	257	3,203	645	2,310	248
Total area actually reporting	100.0%	452	2	58	61	331	4,013	816	2,871	326
Rate per 100,000 inhabitants		315.6	1.4	40.5	42.6	231.1	2,801.7	569.7	2,004.4	227.6
Sioux Falls, SD M.S.A.	268,714									
Includes Lincoln, McCook, Minnehaha, and Turner Counties										
City of Sioux Falls	185,628	897	4	116	68	709	5,653	695	4,300	658
Total area actually reporting	99.3%	1,040	5	151	71	813	6,513	989	4,769	755
Estimated total	100.0%	1,043	5	151	71	816	6,522	993	4,772	757
Rate per 100,000 inhabitants		388.1	1.9	56.2	26.4	303.7	2,427.1	369.5	1,775.9	281.7
Spartanburg, SC M.S.A.	317,919									
Includes Spartanburg and Union Counties										
City of Spartanburg	37,754	448	6	24	77	341	2,450	440	1,839	171
Total area actually reporting	99.8%	1,597	23	104	175	1,295	8,708	1,937	5,949	822
Estimated total	100.0%	1,599	23	104	175	1,297	8,729	1,941	5,965	823
Rate per 100,000 inhabitants		503.0	7.2	32.7	55.0	408.0	2,745.7	610.5	1,876.3	258.9

Table 6. Crime in the United States, by Selected Metropolitan Statistical Area, 2019—Continued

(Number, percent, rate per 100,000 population.)

Area	Population	Violent crime	Murder and nonnegligent manslaughter	Rape[1]	Robbery	Aggravated assault	Property crime	Burglary	Larceny-theft	Motor vehicle theft
Spokane-Spokane Valley, WA M.S.A.	563,721									
Includes Spokane and Stevens Counties										
City of Spokane	220,432	1,520	6	230	311	973	13,048	1,743	10,026	1,279
City of Spokane Valley	100,983	311	1	38	82	190	4,465	483	3,626	356
Total area actually reporting	99.1%	2,140	13	351	428	1,348	21,565	3,048	16,540	1,977
Estimated total	100.0%	2,148	13	352	429	1,354	21,682	3,066	16,628	1,988
Rate per 100,000 inhabitants		381.0	2.3	62.4	76.1	240.2	3,846.2	543.9	2,949.7	352.7
Springfield, IL M.S.A.	206,349									
Includes Menard and Sangamon Counties										
City of Springfield	114,393	889	9	108	208	564	5,080	1,039	3,776	265
Total area actually reporting	97.9%	1,200	10	145	238	807	5,979	1,341	4,281	357
Estimated total	100.0%	1,205	10	145	238	812	6,047	1,352	4,333	362
Rate per 100,000 inhabitants		584.0	4.8	70.3	115.3	393.5	2,930.5	655.2	2,099.8	175.4
Springfield, MA M.S.A.	698,309									
Includes Franklin, Hampden and Hampshire Counties										
City of Springfield	154,306	1,397	20	81	358	938	4,005	746	2,766	493
Total area actually reporting	96.6%	3,222	31	354	551	2,286	11,950	2,131	8,836	983
Estimated total	100.0%	3,294	31	361	562	2,340	12,211	2,171	9,037	1,003
Rate per 100,000 inhabitants		471.7	4.4	51.7	80.5	335.1	1,748.7	310.9	1,294.1	143.6
Springfield, MO M.S.A.[3]	470,347									
Includes Christian, Dallas, Greene, Polk, and Webster Counties										
City of Springfield	169,235	2,571	11	356	319	1,885	13,188	2,068	9,436	1,684
Total area actually reporting	99.8%	2,974	17	435	348	2,174	17,244	2,885	12,285	2,074
Estimated total	100.0%	2,976	17	435	348	2,176	17,261	2,889	12,296	2,076
Rate per 100,000 inhabitants		632.7	3.6	92.5	74.0	462.6	3,669.8	614.2	2,614.2	441.4
Springfield, OH M.S.A.	133,886									
Includes Clark County										
City of Springfield	59,128	292	3	14	124	151	2,992	763	1,978	251
Total area actually reporting	92.6%	315	3	14	124	174	3,341	847	2,231	263
Estimated total	100.0%	330	3	17	127	183	3,554	871	2,413	270
Rate per 100,000 inhabitants		246.5	2.2	12.7	94.9	136.7	2,654.5	650.6	1,802.3	201.7
State College, PA M.S.A.	163,681									
Includes Centre County										
City of State College	58,633	54	3	11	8	32	548	36	497	15
Total area actually reporting	100.0%	200	3	99	20	78	1,466	177	1,255	34
Rate per 100,000 inhabitants		122.2	1.8	60.5	12.2	47.7	895.6	108.1	766.7	20.8
Staunton, VA M.S.A.	122,903									
Includes Augusta County and Staunton and Waynesboro Cities										
City of Staunton	24,931	51	0	18	5	28	473	35	419	19
Total area actually reporting	100.0%	210	2	46	13	149	1,756	255	1,360	141
Rate per 100,000 inhabitants		170.9	1.6	37.4	10.6	121.2	1,428.8	207.5	1,106.6	114.7
St. Cloud, MN M.S.A.[3]	200,776									
Includes Benton and Stearns Counties										
City of St. Cloud	68,311	298	0	73	50	175	2,443	225	2,044	174
Total area actually reporting	100.0%	371	1	88	57	225	4,102	393	3,444	265
Rate per 100,000 inhabitants		184.8	0.5	43.8	28.4	112.1	2,043.1	195.7	1,715.3	132.0
St. George, UT M.S.A.	175,978									
Includes Washington County										
City of St. George	89,160	181	2	48	13	118	1,397	229	1,023	145
Total area actually reporting	98.3%	293	3	81	20	189	2,455	397	1,856	202
Estimated total	100.0%	299	3	83	21	192	2,536	408	1,922	206
Rate per 100,000 inhabitants		169.9	1.7	47.2	11.9	109.1	1,441.1	231.8	1,092.2	117.1
St. Joseph, MO-KS M.S.A.	126,250									
Includes Doniphan County, KS and Andrew, Buchanan, and DeKalb Counties, MO										
City of St. Joseph, MO	75,872	431	2	124	54	251	4,355	584	3,132	639
Total area actually reporting	99.0%	505	3	146	56	300	4,868	680	3,453	735
Estimated total	100.0%	511	3	146	57	305	4,889	685	3,468	736
Rate per 100,000 inhabitants		404.8	2.4	115.6	45.1	241.6	3,872.5	542.6	2,746.9	583.0
Stockton, CA M.S.A.	754,858									
Includes San Joaquin County										
City of Stockton	313,604	4,380	34	181	1,158	3,007	12,367	2,209	8,480	1,678
Total area actually reporting	100.0%	5,952	50	301	1,560	4,041	21,409	3,771	14,560	3,078
Rate per 100,000 inhabitants		788.5	6.6	39.9	206.7	535.3	2,836.2	499.6	1,928.8	407.8
Sumter, SC M.S.A.	140,002									
Includes Clarendon and Sumter Counties										
City of Sumter	39,546	418	8	11	48	351	1,796	397	1,291	108
Total area actually reporting	100.0%	1,006	17	52	96	841	4,411	1,093	2,989	329
Rate per 100,000 inhabitants		718.6	12.1	37.1	68.6	600.7	3,150.7	780.7	2,135.0	235.0

Table 6. Crime in the United States, by Selected Metropolitan Statistical Area, 2019—Continued

(Number, percent, rate per 100,000 population.)

Area	Population	Violent crime	Murder and nonnegligent manslaughter	Rape[1]	Robbery	Aggravated assault	Property crime	Burglary	Larceny-theft	Motor vehicle theft
Syracuse, NY M.S.A.	645,385									
Includes Madison, Onondaga, and Oswego Counties										
City of Syracuse	142,438	1,129	19	105	246	759	4,464	850	3,051	563
Total area actually reporting	100.0%	1,807	20	370	330	1,087	10,822	1,626	8,318	878
Rate per 100,000 inhabitants		280.0	3.1	57.3	51.1	168.4	1,676.8	251.9	1,288.8	136.0
Tallahassee, FL M.S.A.	384,437									
Includes Gadsden, Jefferson, Leon, and Wakulla Counties										
City of Tallahassee	195,104	1,359	20	197	252	890	7,763	1,187	5,897	679
Total area actually reporting	99.2%	2,019	25	272	311	1,411	11,200	2,141	8,119	940
Estimated total	100.0%	2,028	25	273	312	1,418	11,266	2,154	8,167	945
Rate per 100,000 inhabitants		527.5	6.5	71.0	81.2	368.9	2,930.5	560.3	2,124.4	245.8
Tampa-St. Petersburg-Clearwater, FL M.S.A.	3,167,603									
Includes Hernando, Hillsborough, Pasco, and Pinellas Counties										
City of Tampa	400,501	1,622	31	120	285	1,186	6,523	1,022	4,978	523
City of St. Petersburg	267,696	1,594	17	125	297	1,155	8,592	1,044	6,765	783
City of Clearwater	117,458	469	2	80	98	289	2,810	268	2,370	172
City of Largo	85,740	329	5	71	74	179	2,348	202	1,991	155
City of Pinellas Park	53,589	206	3	40	52	111	2,038	192	1,753	93
Total area actually reporting	99.9%	9,246	126	1,169	1,575	6,376	53,335	6,834	42,460	4,041
Estimated total	100.0%	9,254	126	1,170	1,576	6,382	53,394	6,845	42,503	4,046
Rate per 100,000 inhabitants		292.1	4.0	36.9	49.8	201.5	1,685.6	216.1	1,341.8	127.7
Texarkana, TX-AR M.S.A.[3]	149,595									
Includes Little River and Miller Counties, AR and Bowie County, TX										
City of Texarkana, TX	37,401	157	3	33	43	78	1,710	280	1,347	83
Total area actually reporting	100.0%	676	8	90	77	501	3,968	836	2,902	230
Rate per 100,000 inhabitants		451.9	5.3	60.2	51.5	334.9	2,652.5	558.8	1,939.9	153.7
The Villages, FL M.S.A.	132,914									
Includes Sumter County										
Total area actually reporting	100.0%	249	5	18	20	206	1,139	318	703	118
Rate per 100,000 inhabitants		187.3	3.8	13.5	15.0	155.0	856.9	239.3	528.9	88.8
Toledo, OH M.S.A.	641,535									
Includes Fulton, Lucas, Ottawa, and Wood Counties										
City of Toledo	273,505	2,604	34	205	655	1,710	9,470	2,362	6,314	794
Total area actually reporting	91.1%	2,960	35	298	707	1,920	14,757	2,880	10,879	998
Estimated total	100.0%	3,026	36	311	717	1,962	15,736	3,011	11,685	1,040
Rate per 100,000 inhabitants		471.7	5.6	48.5	111.8	305.8	2,452.9	469.3	1,821.4	162.1
Topeka, KS M.S.A.[4]	231,941									
Includes Jackson, Jefferson, Osage,[4] Shawnee, and Wabaunsee Counties										
City of Topeka	125,655	895	13	74	243	565	6,271	905	4,404	962
Total area actually reporting	97.9%	1,122	16	106	250	750			5,533	1,155
Estimated total	100.0%	1,143	16	106	254	767			5,588	1,159
Rate per 100,000 inhabitants		492.8	6.9	45.7	109.5	330.7			2,409.2	499.7
Trenton-Princeton, NJ M.S.A.	368,390									
Includes Mercer County										
City of Trenton	83,457	937	15	70	300	552	1,748	360	1,142	246
City of Princeton	31,610	10	0	1	0	9	238	45	190	3
Total area actually reporting	100.0%	1,277	17	118	389	753	5,571	931	4,139	501
Rate per 100,000 inhabitants		346.6	4.6	32.0	105.6	204.4	1,512.3	252.7	1,123.5	136.0
Tucson, AZ M.S.A.	1,047,076									
Includes Pima County										
City of Tucson	548,374	3,775	40	527	1,105	2,103	17,943	2,497	13,196	2,250
Total area actually reporting	100.0%	4,685	56	653	1,297	2,679	30,170	4,242	22,701	3,227
Rate per 100,000 inhabitants		447.4	5.3	62.4	123.9	255.9	2,881.4	405.1	2,168.0	308.2
Tulsa, OK M.S.A.	998,117									
Includes Creek, Okmulgee, Osage, Pawnee, Rogers, Tulsa, and Wagoner Counties										
City of Tulsa	401,700	3,964	55	341	718	2,850	21,336	4,846	13,457	3,033
Total area actually reporting	100.0%	5,286	82	573	828	3,803	32,217	7,356	20,556	4,305
Rate per 100,000 inhabitants		529.6	8.2	57.4	83.0	381.0	3,227.8	737.0	2,059.5	431.3
Twin Falls, ID M.S.A.	111,928									
Includes Jerome and Twin Falls Counties										
City of Twin Falls	50,463	201	1	27	10	163	1,034	152	827	55
Total area actually reporting	100.0%	321	2	62	10	247	1,519	304	1,116	99
Rate per 100,000 inhabitants		286.8	1.8	55.4	8.9	220.7	1,357.1	271.6	997.1	88.4
Tyler, TX M.S.A.	231,362									
Includes Smith County										
City of Tyler	106,851	401	0	72	58	271	3,206	439	2,597	170
Total area actually reporting	100.0%	773	7	133	83	550	5,034	926	3,680	428
Rate per 100,000 inhabitants		334.1	3.0	57.5	35.9	237.7	2,175.8	400.2	1,590.6	185.0

Table 6. Crime in the United States, by Selected Metropolitan Statistical Area, 2019—Continued

(Number, percent, rate per 100,000 population.)

Area	Population	Violent crime	Murder and nonnegligent manslaughter	Rape[1]	Robbery	Aggravated assault	Property crime	Burglary	Larceny-theft	Motor vehicle theft
Urban Honolulu, HI M.S.A.	974,902									
Includes Honolulu County										
Total area actually reporting	100.0%	2,638	27	340	954	1,317	29,263	3,864	21,562	3,837
Rate per 100,000 inhabitants		270.6	2.8	34.9	97.9	135.1	3,001.6	396.3	2,211.7	393.6
Utica-Rome, NY M.S.A.	288,854									
Includes Herkimer and Oneida Counties										
City of Utica	59,842	374	6	31	143	194	1,986	261	1,635	90
City of Rome	32,019	54	1	8	11	34	524	84	416	24
Total area actually reporting	100.0%	784	8	177	177	422	4,544	597	3,756	191
Rate per 100,000 inhabitants		271.4	2.8	61.3	61.3	146.1	1,573.1	206.7	1,300.3	66.1
Vallejo, CA M.S.A.	447,069									
Includes Solano County										
City of Vallejo	122,657	1,037	12	138	336	551	4,941	2,888	1,148	905
Total area actually reporting	100.0%	2,114	21	264	661	1,168	13,161	3,727	7,369	2,065
Rate per 100,000 inhabitants		472.9	4.7	59.1	147.9	261.3	2,943.8	833.7	1,648.3	461.9
Victoria, TX M.S.A.	99,703									
Includes Goliad and Victoria Counties										
City of Victoria	67,581	347	3	66	52	226	1,974	382	1,474	118
Total area actually reporting	100.0%	463	7	88	60	308	2,452	529	1,747	176
Rate per 100,000 inhabitants		464.4	7.0	88.3	60.2	308.9	2,459.3	530.6	1,752.2	176.5
Vineland-Bridgeton, NJ M.S.A.	149,590									
Includes Cumberland County										
City of Vineland	59,860	211	1	32	55	123	1,686	269	1,375	42
City of Bridgeton	24,331	223	2	17	114	90	848	261	549	38
Total area actually reporting	100.0%	631	7	72	235	317	4,047	816	3,103	128
Rate per 100,000 inhabitants		421.8	4.7	48.1	157.1	211.9	2,705.4	545.5	2,074.3	85.6
Virginia Beach-Norfolk-Newport News, VA-NC M.S.A.[3]	1,761,473									
Includes Camden, Currituck and Gates Counties, NC and Gloucester, Isle of Wight, James City, Mathews, Southampton, and York Counties and Chesapeake, Franklin, Hampton, Newport News, Norfolk, Poquoson, Portsmouth, Suffolk, Virginia Beach, and Williamsburg Cities, VA										
City of Virginia Beach, VA	449,038	581	30	79	196	276	7,906	530	6,797	579
City of Norfolk, VA	242,813	1,325	36	134	311	844	8,405	841	6,765	799
City of Newport News, VA	177,319	1,056	24	64	164	804	4,484	503	3,641	340
City of Hampton, VA	133,173	393	15	42	122	214	3,994	347	3,397	250
City of Portsmouth, VA	93,991	889	16	37	230	606	5,509	846	4,189	474
Total area actually reporting	99.3%	6,141	140	596	1,285	4,120	42,321	4,179	34,941	3,201
Estimated total	100.0%	6,157	141	598	1,286	4,132	42,452	4,232	35,008	3,212
Rate per 100,000 inhabitants		349.5	8.0	33.9	73.0	234.6	2,410.0	240.3	1,987.4	182.3
Visalia, CA M.S.A.	464,847									
Includes Tulare County										
City of Visalia	134,961	586	4	111	159	312	3,900	747	2,627	526
Total area actually reporting	100.0%	1,692	20	194	389	1,089	10,625	2,025	6,755	1,845
Rate per 100,000 inhabitants		364.0	4.3	41.7	83.7	234.3	2,285.7	435.6	1,453.2	396.9
Waco, TX M.S.A.[3]	272,588									
Includes Falls and McLennan Counties										
City of Waco	139,870	799	10	88	133	568	4,599	784	3,492	323
Total area actually reporting	95.0%	1,129	12	161	170	786	6,767	1,183	5,006	578
Estimated total	100.0%	1,166	13	164	172	817	6,976	1,234	5,136	606
Rate per 100,000 inhabitants		427.8	4.8	60.2	63.1	299.7	2,559.2	452.7	1,884.2	222.3
Walla Walla, WA M.S.A.	60,962									
Includes Walla Walla County										
City of Walla Walla	33,047	114	2	29	16	67	1,052	161	814	77
Total area actually reporting	100.0%	145	3	34	18	90	1,479	276	1,095	108
Rate per 100,000 inhabitants		237.9	4.9	55.8	29.5	147.6	2,426.1	452.7	1,796.2	177.2
Warner Robins, GA M.S.A.[3]	184,460									
Includes Houston and Peach Counties[3]										
City of Warner Robins[3]	76,623	420	3	44	104	269	3,609	626	2,744	239
Total area actually reporting	90.3%	709	3	86	143	477	5,278	924	4,011	343
Estimated total	100.0%	765	4	90	160	511	5,732	974	4,365	393
Rate per 100,000 inhabitants		414.7	2.2	48.8	86.7	277.0	3,107.4	528.0	2,366.4	213.1
Washington-Arlington-Alexandria, DC-VA-MD-WV M.S.A.[3, 4]	6,301,628									
Includes the Metropolitan Divisions of Frederick-Gaithersburg-Rockville, MD and Washington-Arlington-Alexandria, DC-VA-MD-WV										
City of Washington, D.C.	705,749	6,896	166	342	2,359	4,029	29,965	1,840	25,827	2,298
City of Alexandria, VA	162,258	288	2	19	80	187	2,517	117	2,005	395
City of Frederick, MD	73,030	296	2	37	54	203	1,364	199	1,112	53
Total area actually reporting	99.9%			1,839	5,623	9,306	102,402	7,856	85,833	8,713
Estimated total	100.0%			1,840	5,624	9,309	102,470	7,865	85,885	8,720
Rate per 100,000 inhabitants				29.2	89.2	147.7	1,626.1	124.8	1,362.9	138.4

Table 6. Crime in the United States, by Selected Metropolitan Statistical Area, 2019—Continued

(Number, percent, rate per 100,000 population.)

Area	Population	Violent crime	Murder and nonnegligent manslaughter	Rape[1]	Robbery	Aggravated assault	Property crime	Burglary	Larceny-theft	Motor vehicle theft
Frederick-Gaithersburg-Rockville, MD M.D.	1,314,401									
Includes Frederick and Montgomery Counties										
Total area actually reporting	100.0%	2,167	18	355	644	1,150	17,671	1,812	14,848	1,011
Rate per 100,000 inhabitants		164.9	1.4	27.0	49.0	87.5	1,344.4	137.9	1,129.6	76.9
Washington-Arlington-Alexandria, DC-VA-MD-WV M.D.[3,4]	4,987,227									
Includes District of Columbia; Calvert, Charles, and Prince George's Counties, MD; Arlington, Clarke, Culpeper, Fairfax, Fauquier, Loudoun, Madison, Prince William, Rappahannock, Spotsylvania, Stafford, and Warren Counties and Alexandria, Fairfax, Falls Church, Fredericksburg, Manassas, and Manassas Park Cities, VA; and Jefferson County, WV										
Total area actually reporting	99.9%			1,484	4,979	8,156	84,731	6,044	70,985	7,702
Estimated total	100.0%			1,485	4,980	8,159	84,799	6,053	71,037	7,709
Rate per 100,000 inhabitants				29.8	99.9	163.6	1,700.3	121.4	1,424.4	154.6
Watertown-Fort Drum, NY M.S.A.	110,566									
Includes Jefferson County										
City of Watertown	25,102	154	0	57	14	83	887	108	743	36
Total area actually reporting	100.0%	243	0	96	20	127	1,615	187	1,375	53
Rate per 100,000 inhabitants		219.8	0.0	86.8	18.1	114.9	1,460.7	169.1	1,243.6	47.9
Wausau-Weston, WI M.S.A.[3]	162,956									
Includes Lincoln and Marathon Counties										
City of Wausau[3]	38,507	156	1	42	5	108	521	81	396	44
Total area actually reporting	100.0%	360	1	88	12	259	1,499	233	1,182	84
Rate per 100,000 inhabitants		220.9	0.6	54.0	7.4	158.9	919.9	143.0	725.3	51.5
Weirton-Steubenville, WV-OH M.S.A.	115,836									
Includes Jefferson County, OH and Brooke and Hancock Counties, WV										
City of Weirton, WV	18,296	11	0	1	0	10	88	2	84	2
City of Steubenville, OH	17,768	33	3	6	9	15	803	55	735	13
Total area actually reporting	81.9%	136	3	20	10	103	1,085	86	968	31
Estimated total	100.0%	179	3	26	15	135	1,566	151	1,363	52
Rate per 100,000 inhabitants		154.5	2.6	22.4	12.9	116.5	1,351.9	130.4	1,176.7	44.9
Wenatchee, WA M.S.A.	120,654									
Includes Chelan and Douglas Counties										
City of Wenatchee	34,513	62	1	16	10	35	638	66	532	40
Total area actually reporting	100.0%	128	2	28	12	86	1,380	229	1,065	86
Rate per 100,000 inhabitants		106.1	1.7	23.2	9.9	71.3	1,143.8	189.8	882.7	71.3
Wichita, KS M.S.A.[5]	638,097									
Includes Butler, Harvey, Sedgwick, and Sumner Counties										
City of Wichita	390,080	4,451	35	367	461	3,588	20,759	2,677	15,777	2,305
Total area actually reporting	99.2%	4,962	39	472	493	3,958		3,330		2,623
Estimated total	100.0%	4,985	39	472	497	3,977		3,351		2,627
Rate per 100,000 inhabitants		781.2	6.1	74.0	77.9	623.3		525.2		411.7
Wichita Falls, TX M.S.A.	150,317									
Includes Archer, Clay, and Wichita Counties										
City of Wichita Falls	104,551	364	4	103	85	172	3,183	557	2,394	232
Total area actually reporting	95.4%	461	4	127	92	238	3,747	711	2,737	299
Estimated total	100.0%	479	4	128	93	254	3,856	738	2,804	314
Rate per 100,000 inhabitants		318.7	2.7	85.2	61.9	169.0	2,565.2	491.0	1,865.4	208.9
Wilmington, NC M.S.A.[3]	299,507									
Includes New Hanover and Pender Counties[3]										
City of Wilmington[3]	124,750	759	7	74	127	551	3,593	771	2,564	258
Total area actually reporting	80.2%	1,015	7	118	159	731	5,686	1,105	4,249	332
Estimated total	100.0%	1,138	9	132	171	826	6,534	1,380	4,746	408
Rate per 100,000 inhabitants		380.0	3.0	44.1	57.1	275.8	2,181.6	460.8	1,584.6	136.2
Winchester, VA-WV M.S.A.	140,516									
Includes Frederick County and Winchester City, VA and Hampshire County, WV										
City of Winchester, VA	28,201	80	1	39	6	34	657	76	559	22
Total area actually reporting	99.7%	225	1	66	20	138	1,794	244	1,440	110
Estimated total	100.0%	226	1	66	20	139	1,803	246	1,446	111
Rate per 100,000 inhabitants		160.8	0.7	47.0	14.2	98.9	1,283.1	175.1	1,029.1	79.0
Worcester, MA-CT M.S.A.[3]	870,501									
Includes Windham County, CT and Worcester County, MA										
City of Worcester, MA	184,945	1,165	13	40	229	883	3,792	786	2,637	369
Total area actually reporting	97.4%	2,659	17	302	336	2,004	9,100	1,590	6,778	732
Estimated total	100.0%	2,702	17	308	339	2,038	9,273	1,620	6,909	744
Rate per 100,000 inhabitants		310.4	2.0	35.4	38.9	234.1	1,065.2	186.1	793.7	85.5
Yakima, WA M.S.A.	251,470									
Includes Yakima County										

Table 6. Crime in the United States, by Selected Metropolitan Statistical Area, 2019—Continued

(Number, percent, rate per 100,000 population.)

Area	Population	Violent crime	Murder and nonnegligent manslaughter	Rape[1]	Robbery	Aggravated assault	Property crime	Burglary	Larceny-theft	Motor vehicle theft
City of Yakima	94,168	420	9	44	91	276	2,723	439	1,866	418
Total area actually reporting	95.6%	684	19	89	140	436	6,281	1,098	4,100	1,083
Estimated total	100.0%	703	19	93	142	449	6,536	1,140	4,289	1,107
Rate per 100,000 inhabitants		279.6	7.6	37.0	56.5	178.6	2,599.1	453.3	1,705.6	440.2
Yuba City, CA M.S.A.	174,368									
Includes Sutter and Yuba Counties										
City of Yuba City	67,164	241	3	28	52	158	1,823	230	1,334	259
Total area actually reporting	100.0%	644	11	73	126	434	4,291	803	2,661	827
Rate per 100,000 inhabitants		369.3	6.3	41.9	72.3	248.9	2,460.9	460.5	1,526.1	474.3
Yuma, AZ M.S.A.[3]	214,209									
Includes Yuma County										
City of Yuma	98,769	376	11	27	29	309	2,302	483	1,586	233
Total area actually reporting	100.0%	595	24	46	41	484	3,707	793	2,466	448
Rate per 100,000 inhabitants		277.8	11.2	21.5	19.1	225.9	1,730.6	370.2	1,151.2	209.1
Aguadilla-Isabela, Puerto Rico M.S.A.	289,289									
Includes Aguada, Aguadilla, Anasco, Isabela, Lares, Moca, Rincon, San Sebastian, and Utuado Municipios										
Total area actually reporting	100.0%	430	14	21	51	344	1,434	412	965	57
Rate per 100,000 inhabitants		148.6	4.8	7.3	17.6	118.9	495.7	142.4	333.6	19.7
Arecibo, Puerto Rico M.S.A.	174,606									
Includes Arecibo, Camuy, Hatillo, and Quebradillas Municipios										
Total area actually reporting	100.0%	286	18	13	74	181	799	229	485	85
Rate per 100,000 inhabitants		163.8	10.3	7.4	42.4	103.7	457.6	131.2	277.8	48.7
Guayama, Puerto Rico M.S.A.	72,914									
Includes Arroyo, Guayama, and Patillas Municipios										
Total area actually reporting	100.0%	153	10	4	22	117	354	104	234	16
Rate per 100,000 inhabitants		209.8	13.7	5.5	30.2	160.5	485.5	142.6	320.9	21.9
Mayaguez, Puerto Rico M.S.A.	94,975									
Includes Hormigueros, Las Marias, and Mayaguez Municipios										
Total area actually reporting	100.0%	107	4	7	25	71	378	71	278	29
Rate per 100,000 inhabitants		112.7	4.2	7.4	26.3	74.8	398.0	74.8	292.7	30.5
Ponce, Puerto Rico M.S.A.	215,295									
Includes Adjuntas, Juana Diaz, Ponce, and Villalba Municipios										
Total area actually reporting	100.0%	356	26	8	134	188	1,235	242	825	168
Rate per 100,000 inhabitants		165.4	12.1	3.7	62.2	87.3	573.6	112.4	383.2	78.0
San German, Puerto Rico M.S.A.	121,464									
Includes Cabo Rojo, Lajas, Sabana Grande, and San German Municipios										
Total area actually reporting	100.0%	101	13	3	7	78	403	95	290	18
Rate per 100,000 inhabitants		83.2	10.7	2.5	5.8	64.2	331.8	78.2	238.8	14.8
San Juan-Bayamon-Caguas, Puerto Rico M.S.A.	2,023,227									
Includes Aguas Buenas, Aibonito, Barceloneta, Barranquitas, Bayamon, Caguas, Canovanas, Carolina, Catano, Cayey, Ceiba, Ciales, Cidra, Comerio, Corozal, Dorado, Fajardo, Florida, Guaynabo, Gurabo, Humacao, Juncos, Las Piedras, Loiza, Luquillo, Manati, Maunabo, Morovis, Naguabo, Naranjito, Orocovis, Rio Grande, San Juan, San Lorenzo, Toa Alta, Toa Baja, Trujillo Alto, Vega Alta, Vega Baja, and Yabucoa Municipios										
Total area actually reporting	100.0%	4,599	477	138	1,754	2,230	17,097	2,896	10,966	3,235
Rate per 100,000 inhabitants		227.3	23.6	6.8	86.7	110.2	845.0	143.1	542.0	159.9
Yauco, Puerto Rico M.S.A.	85,830									
Includes Guanica, Guayanilla, Penuelas, and Yauco Municipios										
Total area actually reporting	100.0%	148	10	11	19	108	267	66	184	17
Rate per 100,000 inhabitants		172.4	11.7	12.8	22.1	125.8	311.1	76.9	214.4	19.8

1 The figures shown in this column for the offense of rape were reported using only the revised Uniform Crime Reporting (UCR) definition of rape. See the chapter notes for further explanation.   2 One or more agency(s) within this Metropolitan Statistical Area submitted rape data classified according to the legacy UCR definition. See the chapter notes for further explanation.   3 Because of changes in the state/local agency's reporting practices, figures are not comparable to previous years' data.   4 The FBI determined that the agency's data were overreported. Consequently, those data are not included in this table.   5 The FBI determined that the agency's data were underreported. Consequently, those data are not included in this table.

Table 7. Offense Analysis, United States, 2015–2019

(Number.)

Classification	2015	2016	2017	2018[1]	2019
Murder	15,883	17,413	17,294	16,374	16,425
Rape[2]	126,134	132,414	135,666	143,765	139,815
Robbery[3]	328,109	332,797	320,596	281,278	267,988
By location					
Street/highway	130,724	129,337	119,180	102,149	94,090
Commercial house	47,229	50,785	49,654	45,148	44,128
Gas or service station	8,916	9,708	9,603	8,863	8,555
Convenience store	18,661	20,656	21,048	19,647	18,312
Residence	54,142	55,102	51,260	45,408	42,806
Bank	5,691	5,914	5,441	4,461	3,834
Miscellaneous	62,747	61,296	64,410	55,602	56,264
Burglary[3]	1,587,564	1,516,405	1,397,045	1,235,013	1,117,696
By location					
Residence (dwelling)	1,136,664	1,054,470	939,509	808,611	702,449
Residence, night	328,736	311,805	285,358	257,085	238,635
Residence, day	594,668	543,930	474,495	408,349	354,398
Residence, unknown	213,260	198,735	179,656	143,178	109,415
Nonresidence (store, office, etc.)	450,900	461,935	457,536	426,402	415,247
Nonresidence, night	189,167	199,741	200,859	190,817	191,663
Nonresidence, day	159,177	159,630	157,375	151,091	152,956
Nonresidence, unknown	102,556	102,564	99,302	84,493	70,629
Larceny-theft (except motor vehicle theft)[3]	5,723,488	5,644,835	5,513,000	5,232,167	5,086,096
By type					
Pocket-picking	31,208	27,648	31,026	27,326	29,481
Purse-snatching	23,144	22,671	21,961	20,113	18,568
Shoplifting	1,276,575	1,179,137	1,144,948	1,116,664	1,113,785
From motor vehicles (except accessories)	1,373,720	1,477,587	1,477,684	1,410,567	1,379,757
Motor vehicle accessories	399,452	415,590	407,017	324,298	325,800
Bicycles	205,600	184,546	174,803	157,042	154,009
From buildings	664,381	605,765	586,612	534,418	498,121
From coin-operated machines	13,020	12,349	12,014	11,511	11,328
All others	1,736,388	1,719,542	1,656,937	1,630,232	1,555,247
By value					
Over $200	2,613,333	2,561,619	2,529,654	2,445,915	2,407,972
$50 to $200	1,278,027	1,221,246	1,169,612	1,120,011	1,079,509
Under $50	1,832,128	1,861,970	1,813,734	1,666,185	1,598,615
Motor vehicle theft	713,063	767,290	772,943	751,904	721,885

1 The crime figures have been adjusted.   2 The figures shown for this offense of rape were estimated using the revised Uniform Crime Reporting (UCR) definition of rape. See chapter notes for more detail.   3 Because of rounding, the number of offenses may not add to the total.

Table 8. Offenses Known to Law Enforcement, by Selected State and City, 2019

(Number.)

State/city	Population	Violent crime	Murder and nonnegligent manslaughter	Rape[1]	Robbery	Aggravated assault	Property crime	Burglary	Larceny-theft	Motor vehicle theft	Arson[2]
ALABAMA[3]											
Hoover	85,670	114	4	15	27	68	1,922	128	1,694	100	2
ALASKA											
Anchorage	287,731	3,581	32	540	621	2,388	12,261	1,692	9,038	1,531	93
Bethel	6,544	130	1	47	3	79	132	20	84	28	12
Bristol Bay Borough	852	2	0	0	0	2	20	5	8	7	0
Cordova	2,150	0	0	0	0	7	7	1	6	0	0
Craig	1,313	7	0	0	0	7	20	5	12	3	0
Dillingham	2,405	49	1	3	1	44	58	11	37	10	0
Fairbanks	31,493	247	3	33	52	159	1,353	163	1,006	184	23
Haines	2,441	9	0	0	0	9	13	1	10	2	0
Homer	5,913	12	0	0	0	12	146	11	118	17	
Juneau	31,810	289	3	24	45	217	1,292	187	1,012	93	16
Kenai	7,862	75	2	28	3	42	446	46	353	47	2
Ketchikan	8,316	40	0	9	1	30	421	32	368	21	2
Kodiak	5,947	49	0	14	4	31	190	37	122	31	3
Kotzebue	3,272	77	0	22	7	48	83	19	47	17	2
Nome	3,899	107	0	59	1	47	53	14	32	7	0
North Pole	2,111	16	0	3	0	13	79	12	63	4	1
North Slope Borough	9,801	123	2	6	0	115	72	18	46	8	3
Palmer	7,490	21	1	1	3	16	204	19	158	27	0
Petersburg	3,181	10	0	0	0	10	88	12	74	2	0
Seward	2,732	9	0	6	0	3	105	14	85	6	0
Sitka	8,512	16	0	2	4	10	168	18	139	11	0
Skagway	1,159	1	0	1	0	0	9	0	7	2	0
Soldotna	4,756	13	0	2	1	10	142	9	125	8	0
Unalaska	4,513	7	0	0	1	6	39	2	34	3	0
Valdez	3,816	5	0	0	0	5	40	2	34	4	0
Wasilla	10,915	48	1	5	14	28	580	115	425	40	4
Wrangell	2,489	2	0	2	0	0	11	3	7	1	0
ARIZONA											
Apache Junction[4]	42,531	95	2	12	14	67			453	88	6
Avondale	87,117	251	1	21	82	147	3,095	381	2,467	247	16
Buckeye	77,904	107	2	26	10	69	1,265	146	1,050	69	1
Bullhead City	40,532	129	2	23	25	79	1,352	235	981	136	9
Camp Verde	11,286	46	0	3	0	43	265	62	187	16	1
Casa Grande[5]	58,366	274	2	27	33	212	1,336	149	1,071	116	11
Chandler	259,881	593	4	134	102	353	5,382	547	4,458	377	19
Chino Valley	12,162	37	0	1	0	36	154	32	107	15	0
Clarkdale	4,434	3	0	0	0	3	44	16	26	2	0
Coolidge[5]	13,138	70	0	2	5	61	393	73	290	30	5
Cottonwood	12,331	45	0	0	5	40	422	37	359	26	2
Douglas	15,786	10	0	0	0	10	594	88	486	20	0
Eagar[5]	4,897	11	0	3	1	7	21	7	13	1	0
El Mirage	36,185	84	2	22	14	46	982	362	523	97	5
Flagstaff	75,013	367	1	42	43	281	2,371	140	2,169	62	33
Florence	26,385	44	1	5	1	37	74	9	58	7	0
Fredonia	1,296	1	0	0	0	1	13	3	8	2	0
Gilbert	253,619	245	1	48	45	151	3,050	403	2,493	154	11
Glendale	253,951	863	17	63	233	550	8,083	1,416	5,857	810	
Globe	7,323	134	0	0	4	130	525	70	424	31	1
Goodyear	85,305	172	1	33	19	119	2,045	330	1,608	107	0
Hayden	979	8	0	0	1	7	35	19	13	3	2
Holbrook	5,098	39	0	1	6	32	324	86	212	26	3
Huachuca City	1,723	6	1	4	0	1	20	6	12	2	0
Jerome	459	1	0	0	0	1	19	7	12	0	0
Kearny	2,170	1	0	1	0	0	14	7	6	1	1
Kingman	30,600	100	0	9	12	79	1,342	208	1,039	95	28
Lake Havasu City	55,413	87	1	29	3	54	670	108	519	43	2
Mammoth	1,669	3	0	0	1	2	14	0	12	2	0
Marana	48,816	35	0	7	9	19	1,132	70	1,020	42	2
Maricopa	50,881	85	1	11	4	69	604	58	491	55	2
Mesa	518,160	1,953	11	286	390	1,266	9,683	1,518	7,326	839	27
Miami	1,768	27	0	0	3	24	31	30	1	0	1
Nogales	20,112	41	0	0	0	41	608	66	409	133	0
Oro Valley	45,970	22	1	8	3	10	588	49	515	24	0
Page	7,588	126	1	9	9	107	537	53	456	28	0
Paradise Valley	14,733	10	0	5	2	3	161	35	119	7	0
Parker	3,219	2	0	0	1	1	81	20	56	5	0
Payson	15,760	59	0	1	4	54	288	60	208	20	3
Peoria	174,571	407	4	70	83	250	3,273	438	2,592	243	9
Phoenix	1,688,722	11,803	131	1,139	3,197	7,336	55,974	9,471	39,427	7,076	201
Pima	2,530	0	0	0	0	0	36	10	21	5	0
Pinetop-Lakeside	4,452	21	0	4	1	16	143	32	104	7	0
Prescott	43,781	214	1	20	11	182	684	134	518	32	5
Prescott Valley	46,700	93	3	11	6	73	474	51	404	19	2
Safford	9,916	21	0	0	0	21	363	33	311	19	0
Sahuarita	30,928	43	1	11	6	25	345	44	272	29	3
San Luis[5]	34,192	33	0	0	2	31	420	53	262	105	2
Scottsdale	260,464	415	3	136	110	166	5,099	662	4,173	264	15
Show Low	11,401	59	0	6	2	51	332	38	277	17	0
Sierra Vista	44,310	116	2	7	16	91	987	124	800	63	3

Table 8. Offenses Known to Law Enforcement, by Selected State and City, 2019—Continued

(Number.)

State/city	Population	Violent crime	Murder and nonnegligent manslaughter	Rape[1]	Robbery	Aggravated assault	Property crime	Burglary	Larceny-theft	Motor vehicle theft	Arson[2]
Snowflake-Taylor	10,173	53	1	0	1	51	151	51	85	15	0
Somerton[5]	16,771	36	6	1	4	25	129	25	80	24	0
Springerville	1,984	0	0	0	0	0	11	4	7	0	0
St. Johns	3,520	12	1	4	1	6	59	29	29	1	1
Surprise	140,962	138	4	28	46	60	2,083	217	1,729	137	10
Tempe	196,499	889	8	141	209	531	7,420	922	5,891	607	19
Thatcher	5,177	3	0	0	0	3	112	12	99	1	0
Tolleson	7,399	68	0	4	20	44	666	206	390	70	0
Tucson	548,374	3,775	40	527	1,105	2,103	17,943	2,497	13,196	2,250	142
Wellton	3,048	5	0	1	0	4	31	9	20	2	0
Wickenburg	7,054	17	0	4	0	13	148	32	93	23	0
Willcox	3,507	7	0	0	0	7	127	29	89	9	1
Williams	3,251	26	0	0	0	26	66	8	52	6	0
Winslow	9,393	126	0	4	9	113	445	35	380	30	2
Yuma	98,769	376	11	27	29	309	2,302	483	1,586	233	14
ARKANSAS											
Alexander	3,315	15	0	6	0	9	73	16	54	3	0
Alma	5,888	35	0	18	2	15	228	36	181	11	0
Altus	729	0	0	0	0	0	22	10	12	0	0
Amity	675	1	0	0	0	1	2	0	2	0	0
Ashdown	4,370	13	0	3	0	10	102	22	74	6	0
Ash Flat	1,095	5	0	0	0	5	40	3	36	1	0
Atkins	3,037	11	0	6	0	5	76	7	60	9	0
Augusta	1,939	12	0	5	0	7	31	4	25	2	0
Austin	3,973	4	0	0	0	4	21	7	13	1	0
Bald Knob	2,872	23	0	9	2	12	118	23	89	6	1
Barling	5,010	28	0	9	0	19	75	5	66	4	0
Batesville	10,889	29	0	5	2	22	262	37	212	13	0
Bay	1,805	3	0	0	1	2	24	5	17	2	0
Bearden	859	1	0	0	0	1	7	1	5	1	0
Beebe	8,242	23	0	9	0	14	273	38	218	17	0
Bella Vista	28,931	49	0	17	0	32	188	39	144	5	1
Benton	37,161	212	4	18	27	163	1,328	202	1,000	126	6
Bentonville	53,434	119	1	21	9	88	734	80	623	31	1
Berryville	5,547	25	0	11	4	10	193	48	135	10	2
Bethel Heights	2,810	4	0	4	0	0	18	3	14	1	0
Blytheville	13,468	109	10	5	16	78	629	98	528	3	0
Bono	2,444	6	0	3	0	3	28	6	19	3	0
Booneville	3,829	17	1	2	0	14	107	34	70	3	0
Bradford	732	2	0	0	0	2	8	0	7	1	0
Brinkley	2,623	29	0	1	1	27	80	25	42	13	2
Brookland	3,759	7	0	5	0	2	60	9	50	1	1
Bryant	21,214	32	1	5	3	23	888	45	783	60	3
Bull Shoals	1,971	2	0	0	0	2	21	6	14	1	0
Cabot	26,875	100	0	39	3	58	371	62	256	53	2
Caddo Valley	588	1	0	1	0	0	34	2	30	2	0
Camden	10,742	113	0	8	10	95	373	84	274	15	4
Cammack Village	720	0	0	0	0	0	14	1	12	1	0
Carlisle	2,184	4	0	1	2	1	51	11	39	1	0
Cave Springs	5,580	3	0	2	0	1	20	3	16	1	0
Cedarville	1,413	10	0	2	1	7	19	2	12	5	0
Centerton	16,542	53	2	21	1	29	139	35	96	8	0
Charleston	2,454	7	0	2	0	5	24	8	16	0	0
Cherokee Village	4,634	10	0	2	0	8	78	31	45	2	0
Cherry Valley	583	1	0	0	0	1	8	4	4	0	0
Clarksville	9,813	29	0	15	3	11	240	15	215	10	0
Clinton	2,489	8	0	3	1	4	113	22	85	6	0
Conway	67,336	324	2	49	51	222	1,842	177	1,567	98	8
Corning	3,093	10	0	2	0	8	41	13	22	6	0
Cotter	940	3	0	1	0	2	17	6	10	1	0
Crossett	4,846	30	0	3	2	25	187	78	102	7	0
Damascus	377	0	0	0	0	0	4	0	4	0	0
Dardanelle	4,555	28	1	10	1	16	114	35	69	10	0
Decatur	1,813	17	0	8	0	9	46	9	34	3	0
De Queen	6,593	33	0	10	0	23	172	64	104	4	0
Des Arc	1,580	8	0	0	0	8	20	9	11	0	0
DeWitt	3,019	28	0	6	1	21	84	28	51	5	4
Diaz	1,197	1	0	0	0	1	14	5	4	5	0
Dover	1,434	8	0	0	0	8	30	4	24	2	1
Dumas	4,084	15	1	1	1	12	33	14	18	1	0
Earle	2,201	15	0	1	1	13	46	20	24	2	0
El Dorado	17,820	239	3	16	23	197	996	524	431	41	4
Elkins	3,246	24	0	9	0	15	27	3	22	2	1
England	2,723	21	0	4	2	15	87	28	57	2	0
Etowah	317	0	0	0	0	0	4	1	3	0	0
Eudora	1,930	4	0	1	2	1	32	12	20	0	0
Eureka Springs	2,092	22	0	4	3	15	95	28	60	7	0
Fairfield Bay	2,202	10	1	4	0	5	40	9	29	2	2
Farmington	7,387	33	0	14	3	16	67	8	53	6	3
Fayetteville	88,500	396	3	56	52	285	3,966	398	3,146	422	2
Flippin	1,340	5	0	2	0	3	61	11	47	3	0
Fordyce	3,745	42	0	6	6	30	213	63	138	12	2

Table 8. Offenses Known to Law Enforcement, by Selected State and City, 2019—Continued

(Number.)

State/city	Population	Violent crime	Murder and nonnegligent manslaughter	Rape[1]	Robbery	Aggravated assault	Property crime	Burglary	Larceny-theft	Motor vehicle theft	Arson[2]
Forrest City	13,887	129	2	8	20	99	668	85	457	126	4
Fort Smith	88,041	863	4	97	90	672	5,127	812	3,929	386	11
Gassville	2,156	9	2	2	1	4	51	6	42	3	0
Gentry	3,924	15	0	1	0	14	21	1	18	2	0
Glenwood	2,095	2	0	0	0	2	24	9	12	3	0
Gosnell	3,148	14	0	2	1	11	46	19	25	2	0
Gravette	3,443	14	0	1	1	12	77	13	59	5	0
Greenbrier	5,660	10	0	7	0	3	16	0	11	5	0
Green Forest	2,763	18	0	6	0	12	66	18	46	2	0
Greenland	1,450	6	0	1	0	5	15	0	12	3	0
Greenwood	9,436	23	0	1	0	22	36	11	25	0	1
Gurdon	2,069	19	0	5	0	14	32	8	19	5	0
Hamburg	2,636	18	1	1	0	16	16	7	8	1	1
Harrisburg	2,368	18	0	8	0	10	37	5	28	4	0
Harrison	13,107	50	0	9	2	39	350	50	272	28	3
Haskell	4,715	16	0	5	0	11	75	14	58	3	1
Hazen	1,336	5	0	1	0	4	26	10	11	5	0
Heber Springs	6,912	24	0	8	1	15	231	45	180	6	0
Helena-West Helena	10,187	187	11	17	17	142	578	167	364	47	11
Highland	1,100	4	0	0	0	4	17	5	11	1	0
Hope	9,666	70	0	12	4	54	396	96	278	22	0
Hot Springs	37,263	241	10	38	42	151	2,674	755	1,710	209	8
Hoxie	2,588	5	0	0	0	5	24	8	15	1	1
Jacksonville	28,273	271	0	26	42	203	1,484	281	1,027	176	1
Jericho	106	0	0	0	0	0	0	0	0	0	0
Johnson	3,781	6	0	1	1	4	85	32	41	12	0
Jonesboro	78,261	537	13	74	58	392	2,982	1,092	1,758	132	2
Judsonia	1,981	12	0	3	1	8	29	6	23	0	0
Kensett	1,618	7	0	1	0	6	18	3	14	1	1
Lake City	2,598	4	0	1	1	2	19	8	9	2	0
Lakeview	715	4	1	0	0	3	12	2	8	2	0
Lake Village	2,241	20	2	4	4	10	68	16	50	2	1
Lamar	1,740	0	0	0	0	0	25	4	21	0	0
Lincoln	2,500	9	0	4	0	5	51	12	34	5	0
Little Flock	2,791	10	0	2	1	7	35	8	24	3	0
Little Rock	198,382	3,009	38	209	391	2,371	12,145	1,760	9,316	1,069	45
Lonoke	4,261	22	0	4	2	16	127	15	108	4	1
Lowell	9,723	28	0	3	1	24	117	38	71	8	0
Luxora	1,016	1	0	0	1	0	3	2	1	0	0
Madison	685	3	0	0	1	2	5	2	3	0	0
Magnolia	11,440	14	0	2	1	11	295	95	198	2	2
Marianna	3,398	28	2	5	2	19	154	52	89	13	2
Marion	12,344	122	0	12	11	99	379	61	291	27	1
Marked Tree	2,462	17	0	0	0	17	50	13	31	6	0
Marmaduke	1,264	6	0	0	1	5	47	11	35	1	0
Marshall	1,297	3	0	1	0	2	12	3	8	1	1
Maumelle	18,223	28	2	3	5	18	301	64	218	19	2
Mayflower	2,489	10	0	2	1	7	66	16	46	4	0
McCrory	1,513	11	0	2	0	9	33	9	19	5	0
McGehee	3,681	31	0	8	0	23	95	34	59	2	0
McRae	661	1	0	0	0	1	4	2	2	0	0
Mena	5,508	3	0	2	0	1	223	29	186	8	2
Menifee	316	0	0	0	0	0	2	2	0	0	0
Mineral Springs	1,148	1	0	0	0	1	13	5	6	2	0
Monette	1,603	1	0	1	0	0	22	6	16	0	0
Monticello	9,438	38	0	10	5	23	289	45	229	15	6
Morrilton	6,631	26	0	11	2	13	240	9	225	6	1
Mountainburg	608	7	0	2	0	5	28	5	21	2	0
Mountain Home	12,458	32	0	19	1	12	486	48	423	15	0
Mountain View	2,850	9	0	1	0	8	99	30	66	3	0
Mulberry	1,644	14	0	3	0	11	61	10	50	1	0
Murfreesboro	1,533	4	0	1	0	3	12	3	9	0	0
Nashville	4,403	27	0	13	0	14	130	18	108	4	0
Newport	7,485	92	1	12	3	76	369	70	289	10	1
Norfork	533	0	0	0	0	0	1	0	1	0	0
North Little Rock	66,604	562	12	23	106	421	2,479	380	1,723	376	17
Osceola	6,653	172	4	15	7	146	316	151	144	21	7
Ozark	3,573	29	0	6	1	22	86	44	40	2	0
Paragould	29,245	307	0	29	13	265	1,378	188	1,083	107	4
Paris	3,392	22	0	3	2	17	94	32	59	3	1
Pea Ridge	6,230	24	0	4	0	20	69	9	52	8	0
Perryville	1,454	3	2	0	0	1	29	3	20	6	0
Piggott	3,569	17	0	7	0	10	52	13	36	3	0
Pine Bluff[4]	41,505	644	23	23	96	502			1,448	271	39
Plumerville	773	0	0	0	0	0	11	2	9	0	1
Pocahontas	6,647	43	0	21	1	21	216	31	171	14	0
Pottsville	3,332	13	0	1	0	12	18	7	11	0	1
Prairie Grove	6,595	16	1	6	0	9	134	27	103	4	0
Prescott[4]	2,985	6	0	3	0	3			34	4	1
Quitman	711	2	0	0	0	2	22	1	21	0	0
Ravenden	443	2	0	0	0	2	5	0	5	0	0
Redfield	1,564	4	0	2	0	2	23	11	11	1	0
Rogers	69,168	330	1	87	21	221	1,968	166	1,699	103	6

Table 8. Offenses Known to Law Enforcement, by Selected State and City, 2019—Continued

(Number.)

State/city	Population	Violent crime	Murder and nonnegligent manslaughter	Rape[1]	Robbery	Aggravated assault	Property crime	Burglary	Larceny-theft	Motor vehicle theft	Arson[2]
Rose Bud	483	0	0	0	0	0	11	2	8	1	0
Russellville	29,446	140	0	13	9	118	897	109	729	59	2
Salem	1,637	2	0	1	0	1	15	7	7	1	0
Searcy	23,873	199	4	15	21	159	1,042	230	756	56	0
Shannon Hills	4,017	17	0	5	1	11	62	27	21	14	1
Sheridan[4]	4,954	14	0	4	1	9		20		7	0
Sherwood	31,435	195	1	17	13	164	928	214	625	89	4
Siloam Springs	17,235	70	0	15	4	51	458	96	307	55	4
Star City	2,058	17	1	2	2	12	48	12	30	6	0
St. Charles	208	0	0	0	0	0	3	1	2	0	0
Stuttgart	8,589	101	1	10	5	85	302	69	219	14	5
Sulphur Springs	534	10	0	1	0	9	7	3	4	0	0
Swifton	727	1	0	0	0	1	7	1	6	0	0
Texarkana	29,971	183	4	13	27	139	1,130	215	847	68	3
Trumann	7,043	41	0	15	4	22	321	72	236	13	0
Tuckerman	1,671	9	0	3	0	6	34	13	17	4	0
Van Buren	23,800	117	0	14	7	96	752	149	541	62	0
Vilonia	4,762	5	0	0	1	4	55	9	43	3	0
Waldron	3,332	15	0	4	0	11	112	37	74	1	2
Walnut Ridge	5,019	11	0	2	0	9	69	20	41	8	0
Ward	5,454	64	0	12	1	51	103	31	69	3	1
Warren	5,634	24	0	4	1	19	146	55	86	5	0
Weiner	679	4	0	1	0	3	12	4	7	1	0
West Fork	2,672	5	0	1	1	3	34	7	26	1	0
West Memphis	24,442	485	8	33	57	387	1,225	336	756	133	9
White Hall	5,014	5	0	0	2	3	69	26	34	9	0
Wilson	819	0	0	0	0	0	12	0	12	0	0
Wynne	7,812	79	1	8	4	66	292	80	194	18	4
CALIFORNIA											
Adelanto	34,491	276	1	20	42	213	459	136	209	114	14
Agoura Hills	20,490	21	0	6	4	11	306	66	223	17	0
Alameda	78,907	162	0	7	94	61	2,579	218	1,958	403	29
Albany	20,083	40	0	8	21	11	685	105	534	46	1
Alhambra	84,837	161	2	11	89	59	1,749	259	1,303	187	8
Aliso Viejo	52,247	27	1	3	13	10	433	57	351	25	1
Alturas	2,471	10	0	2	1	7	30	14	13	3	0
American Canyon	20,452	53	0	7	7	39	454	59	368	27	3
Anaheim	353,915	1,120	8	141	396	575	8,258	1,123	5,904	1,231	44
Anderson	10,545	61	1	5	12	43	363	63	208	92	1
Angels Camp	3,909	6	0	2	1	3	74	19	45	10	0
Antioch	112,641	648	12	55	238	343	3,199	511	2,078	610	59
Apple Valley	74,051	339	4	19	68	248	1,105	230	660	215	11
Arcadia	58,899	84	1	10	35	38	1,348	301	973	74	3
Arcata	18,332	72	1	12	16	43	605	122	425	58	21
Arroyo Grande	18,188	27	0	2	7	18	275	35	219	21	3
Artesia	16,779	72	1	2	28	41	284	90	161	33	0
Arvin	21,811	196	3	3	16	174	437	115	178	144	16
Atascadero	30,579	65	0	7	7	51	493	96	360	37	3
Atherton	7,222	12	0	2	4	6	110	32	74	4	0
Atwater	29,632	206	1	10	22	173	1,031	140	708	183	0
Auburn	14,201	50	0	8	5	37	237	72	146	19	5
Avalon	3,722	10	0	2	0	8	40	7	28	5	0
Avenal	12,991	69	0	7	3	59	58	26	28	4	0
Azusa	50,405	144	5	17	46	76	959	174	646	139	12
Bakersfield	388,080	1,766	34	116	701	915	16,074	3,888	9,277	2,909	470
Baldwin Park	75,862	188	1	24	50	113	1,110	196	606	308	5
Banning	31,450	136	2	16	27	91	532	179	210	143	0
Barstow	24,121	274	5	10	82	177	986	285	527	174	37
Bear Valley	5,507	11	0	7	0	4	44	6	36	2	0
Beaumont	50,990	92	2	14	38	38	922	178	548	196	11
Bell	35,759	168	0	11	37	120	441	127	224	90	0
Bellflower	77,196	327	1	29	107	190	1,506	326	860	320	7
Bell Gardens	42,366	147	0	4	69	74	630	78	334	218	4
Belmont	27,272	45	1	8	1	35	392	50	312	30	2
Belvedere	2,114	1	0	0	0	1	15	2	13	0	0
Benicia	28,471	16	0	1	13	2	377	72	250	55	2
Berkeley	122,788	618	0	74	369	175	6,256	771	4,993	492	17
Beverly Hills	34,211	103	1	6	52	44	1,499	257	1,197	45	6
Big Bear	5,311	76	0	7	4	65	135	30	92	13	0
Biggs	1,726	3	0	1	0	2	17	3	10	4	0
Bishop	3,731	34	0	9	6	19	183	29	150	4	0
Blythe	19,889	92	0	7	29	56	644	177	434	33	44
Bradbury	1,089	1	0	0	1	0	10	2	6	2	0
Brawley	26,379	121	2	4	8	107	618	95	468	55	15
Brea	44,155	72	0	10	29	33	1,450	169	1,209	72	3
Brentwood	65,483	166	0	16	67	83	1,335	142	1,095	98	11
Brisbane	4,746	10	0	2	0	8	137	64	52	21	1
Broadmoor	4,446	11	0	2	7	2	82	15	55	12	0
Buellton	5,142	3	0	0	0	3	54	15	31	8	0
Buena Park	82,627	246	1	15	91	139	2,061	230	1,567	264	1
Burbank	103,738	189	1	11	54	123	2,617	299	2,107	211	4
Burlingame	30,677	74	0	9	25	40	1,185	162	937	86	4

Table 8. Offenses Known to Law Enforcement, by Selected State and City, 2019—Continued

(Number.)

State/city	Population	Violent crime	Murder and nonnegligent manslaughter	Rape[1]	Robbery	Aggravated assault	Property crime	Burglary	Larceny-theft	Motor vehicle theft	Arson[2]
Calabasas	24,016	35	1	6	15	13	331	81	226	24	1
Calexico	40,327	94	0	3	21	70	894	244	470	180	56
California City	14,319	83	0	13	15	55	281	102	120	59	3
Calimesa	9,073	22	0	0	7	15	280	51	193	36	0
Calistoga	5,341	6	0	0	0	6	70	7	54	9	0
Camarillo	69,628	58	0	22	16	20	817	100	676	41	2
Campbell	42,697	89	0	22	21	46	1,357	209	990	158	13
Canyon Lake	11,353	15	0	0	1	14	74	15	47	12	0
Capitola	10,101	30	0	3	6	21	528	53	454	21	2
Carlsbad	117,220	240	3	40	39	158	2,135	297	1,671	167	11
Carmel	3,877	11	0	0	0	11	103	20	81	2	0
Carpinteria	13,514	11	1	0	3	7	155	19	116	20	0
Carson	91,947	444	5	31	122	286	2,004	328	1,277	399	14
Cathedral City	55,346	144	7	19	48	70	602	182	227	193	4
Central Marin	34,793	32	0	6	10	16	1,094	360	684	50	0
Ceres	49,134	209	1	12	59	137	1,158	239	628	291	20
Cerritos	50,642	127	1	10	65	51	1,634	314	1,198	122	0
Chico	95,826	557	0	100	104	353	2,406	272	1,753	381	48
Chino	93,348	329	3	35	96	195	2,224	376	1,649	199	5
Chino Hills	84,577	95	1	10	20	64	891	222	606	63	5
Chowchilla	18,792	39	0	2	3	34	234	71	109	54	7
Chula Vista	275,230	904	3	61	265	575	3,816	486	2,503	827	36
Citrus Heights	88,496	313	1	46	76	190	2,248	372	1,607	269	7
Claremont	36,681	51	0	6	23	22	774	191	552	31	7
Clayton	12,356	1	0	0	1	0	155	14	137	4	0
Clearlake	15,400	119	1	19	36	63	460	146	210	104	11
Cloverdale	8,910	16	0	1	0	15	116	25	87	4	1
Clovis	114,170	243	0	54	32	157	2,276	307	1,810	159	6
Coachella	46,485	126	0	9	43	74	894	135	580	179	5
Coalinga	16,356	41	0	2	4	35	217	38	159	20	4
Colma	1,512	28	0	0	20	8	325	36	263	26	2
Colton	55,059	215	1	9	103	102	1,517	317	836	364	8
Colusa	5,903	6	0	4	1	1	78	28	34	16	0
Commerce	12,804	138	1	5	49	83	1,004	128	624	252	16
Compton	96,638	1,104	18	40	427	619	2,346	334	1,285	727	44
Concord	130,615	541	2	67	234	238	4,560	434	3,512	614	23
Corcoran	21,353	118	1	8	12	97	272	65	157	50	5
Corning	7,537	28	0	6	4	18	211	51	127	33	1
Corona	170,875	291	4	43	103	141	3,482	646	2,251	585	28
Coronado	21,115	9	0	1	7	1	324	34	276	14	2
Costa Mesa	114,047	312	0	52	104	156	3,739	450	2,934	355	16
Cotati	7,641	40	1	6	5	28	95	15	68	12	1
Covina	47,985	171	2	25	43	101	1,189	239	779	171	11
Crescent City	6,716	23	0	2	8	13	311	59	238	14	6
Cudahy	23,828	89	2	2	29	56	214	39	111	64	3
Culver City	39,252	182	0	2	102	78	1,647	172	1,380	95	1
Cupertino	60,357	55	1	6	14	34	1,018	175	803	40	1
Cypress	49,085	52	1	7	21	23	596	98	424	74	2
Daly City	107,748	232	0	44	91	97	1,868	170	1,517	181	12
Dana Point	33,779	52	0	0	18	34	399	61	311	27	0
Danville	44,997	23	1	5	7	10	296	36	247	13	1
Davis	69,767	107	2	21	44	40	2,190	274	1,816	100	4
Delano	53,002	205	8	8	33	156	1,118	203	603	312	40
Del Mar	4,369	7	0	1	2	4	67	17	37	13	0
Del Rey Oaks	1,674	7	0	0	6	1	39	8	30	1	0
Desert Hot Springs	29,107	255	5	13	59	178	680	301	216	163	4
Diamond Bar	56,364	72	1	4	25	42	908	282	574	52	2
Dinuba	24,685	161	1	5	25	130	530	58	405	67	20
Dixon	20,775	54	0	4	14	36	389	35	284	70	3
Dorris	897	4	0	0	0	4	11	8	2	1	0
Dos Palos	5,594	64	0	0	2	62	169	36	89	44	3
Downey	112,330	352	4	30	151	167	2,473	344	1,566	563	4
Duarte	21,550	55	0	2	10	43	305	48	215	42	1
Dublin	66,072	107	0	7	43	57	1,259	114	1,052	93	3
Dunsmuir	1,564	14	0	4	0	10	18	6	11	1	0
East Palo Alto	29,686	144	1	22	57	64	533	67	360	106	6
Eastvale	66,310	83	0	3	23	57	944	151	676	117	0
El Cajon	103,686	552	3	38	201	310	2,046	371	1,316	359	15
El Centro	44,303	143	3	9	41	90	1,184	228	861	95	7
El Cerrito	25,857	152	1	4	91	56	1,300	166	1,054	80	7
Elk Grove	175,492	372	0	35	114	223	2,599	292	2,107	200	10
El Monte	115,830	304	2	34	126	142	1,787	347	1,046	394	17
El Segundo	16,727	82	0	5	30	47	625	164	387	74	1
Emeryville	12,380	166	0	12	114	40	2,623	95	2,415	113	3
Encinitas	63,320	86	2	10	15	59	605	115	422	68	1
Escalon	7,644	16	0	1	0	15	135	25	102	8	1
Escondido	153,215	536	4	51	143	338	2,373	379	1,599	395	8
Etna	716	2	0	1	0	1	0	0	0	0	0
Eureka	26,973	195	3	29	63	100	1,350	187	977	186	24
Exeter	10,557	26	0	5	5	16	265	52	188	25	1
Fairfax	7,569	9	0	3	0	6	92	13	77	2	0
Fairfield	118,383	442	5	48	162	227	3,782	359	2,780	643	23
Farmersville	10,781	35	0	0	5	30	190	24	138	28	3

Table 8. Offenses Known to Law Enforcement, by Selected State and City, 2019—Continued

(Number.)

State/city	Population	Violent crime	Murder and nonnegligent manslaughter	Rape[1]	Robbery	Aggravated assault	Property crime	Burglary	Larceny-theft	Motor vehicle theft	Arson[2]
Ferndale	1,363	4	0	0	0	4	24	2	17	5	0
Fillmore	15,911	20	0	5	3	12	123	24	89	10	4
Firebaugh	8,433	11	0	2	2	7	103	15	51	37	0
Folsom	79,927	82	0	12	29	41	1,484	278	1,127	79	3
Fontana	215,883	739	6	83	206	444	3,094	483	1,846	765	9
Fort Bragg	7,366	32	0	5	7	20	316	38	262	16	1
Fort Jones	690	2	0	1	0	1	34	12	21	1	0
Fortuna	12,317	28	0	2	9	17	317	50	231	36	7
Foster City	34,624	39	0	10	8	21	425	63	341	21	2
Fountain Valley	55,858	53	0	5	23	25	1,163	163	914	86	7
Fowler	6,904	29	1	2	5	21	104	42	43	19	0
Fremont	240,887	400	1	36	159	204	4,523	547	3,408	568	17
Fullerton	140,194	373	2	80	108	183	3,157	318	2,479	360	13
Galt	26,796	77	0	10	15	52	449	71	340	38	7
Gardena	59,833	324	3	20	131	170	1,202	236	658	308	6
Garden Grove	172,832	505	6	54	185	260	3,909	627	2,778	504	17
Gilroy	60,106	251	5	37	69	140	1,479	186	1,034	259	23
Glendale	202,601	231	5	16	93	117	3,305	480	2,562	263	13
Glendora	52,211	155	1	21	38	95	1,501	187	1,241	73	6
Goleta	30,930	40	0	2	6	32	509	114	355	40	0
Gonzales	8,408	17	0	1	4	12	73	12	40	21	1
Grand Terrace	12,651	37	1	4	8	24	237	55	149	33	4
Grass Valley	12,919	73	3	0	6	64	463	76	326	61	1
Greenfield	17,809	54	1	9	9	35	165	31	98	36	12
Gridley	6,618	29	0	15	3	11	205	47	136	22	3
Grover Beach	13,574	13	0	3	1	9	239	56	151	32	1
Guadalupe	7,696	15	0	2	3	10	82	32	34	16	2
Gustine	5,896	21	0	2	4	15	116	32	54	30	3
Hanford	57,232	257	0	18	40	199	1,242	131	900	211	15
Hawaiian Gardens	14,320	76	0	5	24	47	225	68	101	56	3
Hawthorne	87,305	636	3	34	190	409	1,485	199	930	356	7
Hayward	161,588	552	5	54	275	218	4,886	448	3,197	1,241	27
Healdsburg	12,208	17	1	1	3	12	176	17	142	17	0
Hemet	86,082	343	5	23	121	194	2,877	757	1,547	573	21
Hercules	25,789	31	0	5	15	11	341	31	278	32	0
Hermosa Beach	19,460	51	0	7	9	35	449	97	326	26	4
Hesperia	95,915	462	8	35	111	308	1,664	443	893	328	17
Hidden Hills	1,903	1	0	1	0	0	18	10	7	1	0
Highland	55,686	362	7	19	90	246	906	167	511	228	8
Hillsborough	11,521	5	0	0	1	4	97	46	49	2	0
Hollister	40,399	114	1	15	27	71	311	61	174	76	5
Holtville	6,774	14	0	1	2	11	70	13	53	4	4
Hughson	7,671	5	0	0	0	5	46	8	29	9	0
Huntington Beach	201,843	386	2	61	99	224	4,144	535	3,280	329	22
Huntington Park	58,181	458	3	31	249	175	1,595	214	861	520	9
Huron	7,359	83	0	1	10	72	56	13	25	18	13
Imperial	18,090	5	0	0	1	4	56	10	36	10	0
Imperial Beach	27,583	72	0	5	16	51	331	57	195	79	1
Indian Wells	5,500	13	0	1	2	10	138	44	89	5	0
Indio	92,803	530	1	45	118	366	1,880	304	1,218	358	6
Industry	201	72	0	1	41	30	1,180	156	899	125	7
Inglewood	109,386	671	2	51	358	260	2,321	308	1,356	657	8
Ione	8,454	11	0	1	1	9	46	9	35	2	0
Irvine	292,673	188	1	52	66	69	3,823	574	3,086	163	9
Irwindale	1,469	26	0	1	8	17	240	73	139	28	3
Isleton	849	7	1	0	0	6	4	1	2	1	0
Jackson	4,797	30	0	3	0	27	133	15	107	11	9
Jurupa Valley	110,111	317	6	7	86	218	2,494	406	1,346	742	8
Kensington	5,407	5	0	1	1	3	48	15	25	8	0
Kerman	15,223	23	0	3	4	16	308	58	214	36	0
King City	14,170	19	0	3	9	7	148	43	80	25	10
Kingsburg	12,123	18	0	2	3	13	219	76	107	36	1
La Canada Flintridge	20,223	15	0	2	6	7	323	114	198	11	0
Lafayette	26,872	4	0	1	3	0	358	42	286	30	0
Laguna Beach	23,020	38	1	17	5	15	326	43	261	22	3
Laguna Hills	31,123	32	0	3	15	14	405	82	288	35	2
Laguna Niguel	66,671	43	1	9	12	21	607	105	463	39	2
Laguna Woods	16,043	7	0	0	2	5	124	20	96	8	0
La Habra	62,416	140	0	20	41	79	1,122	188	789	145	0
La Habra Heights	5,357	4	0	0	1	3	79	29	45	5	1
Lake Elsinore	70,262	173	3	3	43	124	2,005	233	1,409	363	4
Lake Forest	86,691	66	1	7	14	44	684	108	503	73	2
Lakeport	4,959	34	0	3	7	24	160	29	110	21	0
Lake Shastina	2,566	3	0	0	0	3	10	2	6	2	0
Lakewood	80,151	222	0	20	104	98	1,846	303	1,354	189	3
La Mesa	59,865	174	1	22	76	75	1,000	138	715	147	2
La Mirada	48,702	86	0	6	28	52	701	145	463	93	3
Lancaster	159,335	1,359	7	114	374	864	3,346	792	1,916	638	49
La Palma	15,571	17	0	1	7	9	302	41	242	19	1
La Puente	39,916	151	3	6	53	89	449	75	248	126	5
La Quinta	42,044	68	5	5	17	41	1,032	158	809	65	1
La Verne	32,344	51	1	6	13	31	627	133	447	47	2
Lawndale	32,751	125	1	6	40	78	411	83	228	100	4

Table 8. Offenses Known to Law Enforcement, by Selected State and City, 2019—Continued

(Number.)

State/city	Population	Violent crime	Murder and nonnegligent manslaughter	Rape[1]	Robbery	Aggravated assault	Property crime	Burglary	Larceny-theft	Motor vehicle theft	Arson[2]
Lemon Grove	27,175	167	2	4	54	107	552	67	365	120	1
Lemoore	26,728	126	1	17	14	94	372	71	264	37	6
Lincoln	48,625	32	0	4	4	24	468	78	351	39	2
Lindsay	13,708	69	0	5	13	51	250	48	119	83	8
Livermore	91,418	193	2	30	39	122	1,554	139	1,279	136	4
Livingston	14,607	40	0	1	11	28	315	85	164	66	0
Lodi	67,612	237	3	16	88	130	1,658	358	1,016	284	15
Loma Linda	24,512	77	0	7	17	53	559	125	336	98	5
Lomita	20,553	67	0	4	26	37	254	53	161	40	2
Lompoc	42,818	291	7	29	32	223	1,057	238	583	236	18
Long Beach	467,974	2,369	34	249	958	1,128	11,297	2,185	6,754	2,358	153
Los Alamitos	11,541	6	0	1	3	2	130	41	73	16	1
Los Altos	30,716	21	0	3	4	14	310	107	181	22	3
Los Altos Hills	8,622	3	0	1	0	2	67	29	38	0	0
Los Angeles	4,015,546	29,400	258	2,274	9,652	17,216	95,704	13,809	66,253	15,642	1,672
Los Banos	40,607	143	2	12	36	93	886	231	506	149	5
Los Gatos	30,793	14	0	2	6	6	419	57	332	30	0
Lynwood	70,619	454	1	21	218	214	1,419	189	723	507	14
Madera	66,250	334	2	32	77	223	1,301	235	824	242	10
Malibu	12,794	44	1	5	16	22	416	86	311	19	3
Mammoth Lakes	8,114	42	0	15	1	26	131	17	105	9	2
Manhattan Beach	35,583	55	0	5	33	17	851	160	648	43	1
Manteca	83,523	199	3	27	66	103	1,848	239	1,327	282	18
Marina	22,911	43	0	6	10	27	361	67	242	52	1
Martinez	38,692	83	0	17	26	40	570	99	386	85	11
Marysville	12,572	116	2	20	23	71	541	81	324	136	9
Maywood	27,286	90	2	7	23	58	296	60	143	93	3
McFarland	15,529	67	3	14	9	41	163	52	53	58	21
Mendota	11,433	83	1	4	4	74	155	45	50	60	1
Menifee	94,595	145	2	4	47	92	1,892	269	1,273	350	0
Menlo Park	34,871	50	0	16	13	21	774	110	633	31	0
Merced	83,854	540	5	34	103	398	2,342	396	1,439	507	70
Mill Valley	14,343	20	0	1	9	10	223	36	177	10	1
Milpitas	82,344	102	2	15	48	37	2,193	201	1,791	201	2
Mission Viejo	95,453	65	1	8	22	34	866	121	689	56	5
Modesto	216,542	1,758	13	94	399	1,252	7,183	1,149	4,849	1,185	95
Monrovia	36,730	43	1	9	16	17	845	87	686	72	10
Montague	1,399	8	0	1	0	7	32	15	13	4	0
Montclair	39,787	234	2	35	70	127	1,469	355	868	246	24
Montebello	62,650	178	0	11	90	77	1,448	480	580	388	81
Monterey	28,337	78	0	11	23	44	975	127	774	74	4
Monterey Park	60,424	126	0	7	59	60	1,355	267	929	159	0
Monte Sereno	3,507	0	0	0	0	0	12	2	9	1	0
Moorpark	36,826	26	0	7	7	12	228	34	183	11	0
Moraga	17,908	23	0	1	3	19	124	36	79	9	3
Moreno Valley	210,979	847	15	19	290	523	5,534	966	3,489	1,079	9
Morgan Hill	46,118	52	2	3	14	33	703	102	507	94	0
Morro Bay	10,624	21	0	1	3	17	127	15	102	10	0
Mountain View	84,599	165	0	20	49	96	2,463	321	2,030	112	6
Mount Shasta	3,274	12	1	0	2	9	35	5	24	6	0
Murrieta	116,413	77	3	19	26	29	1,512	206	1,080	226	4
Napa	79,526	280	1	66	55	158	1,232	248	847	137	46
National City	61,791	364	0	26	130	208	1,123	114	735	274	5
Needles	5,001	71	1	4	6	60	174	66	97	11	10
Nevada City	3,150	15	0	4	1	10	89	26	49	14	1
Newark	48,945	85	0	13	40	32	1,399	187	1,090	122	6
Newman	11,844	16	0	2	3	11	113	25	68	20	1
Newport Beach	85,325	135	5	29	32	69	1,764	273	1,344	147	7
Norco	26,557	49	0	3	14	32	669	136	434	99	0
Norwalk	105,067	432	5	21	138	268	1,571	343	922	306	18
Novato	56,134	148	0	6	26	116	890	102	711	77	3
Oakdale	23,808	40	1	5	9	25	531	99	342	90	0
Oakland	434,036	5,520	78	372	2,859	2,211	27,868	2,599	20,228	5,041	207
Oakley	43,014	51	0	7	17	27	497	74	336	87	3
Oceanside	177,129	712	4	97	163	448	3,736	426	2,858	452	23
Ojai	7,499	8	0	5	0	3	74	15	56	3	1
Ontario	183,322	659	10	85	223	341	4,290	710	2,652	928	31
Orange	139,830	180	3	18	76	83	2,184	387	1,546	251	7
Orange Cove	9,635	18	0	0	2	16	61	12	38	11	0
Orinda	20,071	17	0	2	7	3	195	52	125	18	0
Orland	7,679	33	0	4	8	21	134	23	86	25	0
Oroville	19,268	122	2	24	30	66	822	176	435	211	19
Oxnard	211,349	724	13	62	275	374	4,242	670	2,987	585	48
Pacifica	38,938	79	1	22	14	42	533	81	408	44	2
Pacific Grove	15,605	14	0	1	1	12	169	27	136	6	0
Palmdale	157,138	658	8	55	194	401	2,230	447	1,384	399	17
Palm Desert	53,776	136	3	7	24	102	1,848	338	1,382	128	6
Palm Springs	48,846	267	7	38	66	156	1,966	502	1,210	254	4
Palo Alto	66,938	86	1	10	46	29	1,983	179	1,722	82	8
Palos Verdes Estates	13,400	4	0	0	1	3	88	36	49	3	0
Paradise	26,879	22	0	5	1	16	202	83	51	68	1
Paramount	54,422	347	4	16	151	176	1,246	187	775	284	6
Parlier	15,384	62	0	2	9	51	179	24	106	49	7

Table 8. Offenses Known to Law Enforcement, by Selected State and City, 2019—Continued

(Number.)

State/city	Population	Violent crime	Murder and nonnegligent manslaughter	Rape[1]	Robbery	Aggravated assault	Property crime	Burglary	Larceny-theft	Motor vehicle theft	Arson[2]
Pasadena	141,913	613	4	46	147	416	2,866	570	2,036	260	34
Paso Robles	32,528	53	0	9	13	31	646	78	523	45	3
Patterson	22,584	46	0	6	14	26	434	81	249	104	3
Perris	80,500	262	4	6	97	155	2,071	268	1,248	555	5
Petaluma	62,425	190	3	22	28	137	789	109	626	54	9
Pico Rivera	62,880	234	3	16	67	148	1,052	198	581	273	11
Piedmont	11,307	14	0	3	5	6	227	46	162	19	1
Pinole	19,439	59	0	2	17	40	866	77	726	63	0
Pismo Beach	8,285	29	0	0	6	23	341	89	236	16	1
Pittsburg	73,637	446	7	41	157	241	1,660	256	983	421	19
Placentia	51,756	192	0	13	28	151	889	275	511	103	0
Placerville	11,123	39	0	2	6	31	281	67	164	50	0
Pleasant Hill	35,125	88	0	11	41	36	1,484	112	1,276	96	6
Pleasanton	84,017	112	0	12	56	44	1,632	149	1,386	97	4
Pomona	152,776	940	12	101	342	485	4,208	816	2,529	863	15
Porterville	60,209	192	2	7	47	136	1,297	213	835	249	3
Port Hueneme	22,232	43	0	5	14	24	415	63	305	47	3
Poway	49,928	51	2	2	12	35	490	91	354	45	1
Rancho Cordova	75,869	225	5	12	56	152	1,422	233	1,004	185	4
Rancho Cucamonga	179,247	500	4	39	108	349	3,456	590	2,560	306	13
Rancho Mirage	18,481	45	0	1	7	37	628	120	459	49	0
Rancho Palos Verdes	41,961	29	2	3	2	22	313	102	199	12	1
Rancho Santa Margarita	48,377	30	0	4	12	14	296	34	250	12	0
Red Bluff	14,308	133	1	26	14	92	787	205	467	115	21
Redlands	71,941	257	1	40	70	146	2,108	330	1,534	244	20
Redondo Beach	67,473	160	1	5	53	101	1,370	260	992	118	1
Redwood City	87,427	189	0	32	70	87	1,343	165	1,014	164	13
Reedley	25,740	117	1	7	12	97	235	69	117	49	5
Rialto	103,965	595	8	65	185	337	3,149	403	2,179	567	16
Richmond	110,988	1,034	16	36	307	675	4,188	469	2,480	1,239	36
Ridgecrest	29,101	142	3	31	7	101	401	119	243	39	4
Rio Dell	3,392	11	1	1	1	8	61	21	36	4	1
Rio Vista	9,502	11	0	2	3	6	140	31	87	22	0
Ripon	16,103	13	0	6	4	3	248	23	206	19	0
Riverbank	25,045	24	1	3	7	13	375	49	273	53	3
Riverside	333,260	1,686	17	139	476	1,054	9,790	1,302	6,997	1,491	75
Rocklin	68,554	67	0	22	13	32	983	168	738	77	6
Rohnert Park	44,131	267	0	28	28	211	786	93	615	78	8
Rolling Hills	1,868	1	0	0	0	1	8	6	2	0	0
Rolling Hills Estates	8,151	10	0	0	3	7	126	35	82	9	1
Rosemead	54,489	175	1	11	74	89	942	196	552	194	8
Roseville	141,744	259	4	32	96	127	3,154	389	2,518	247	19
Ross	2,470	2	0	0	0	2	25	5	19	1	0
Sacramento	513,934	3,223	34	127	1,039	2,023	16,354	2,993	10,644	2,717	179
Salinas	156,943	782	8	66	241	467	3,532	742	1,709	1,081	26
San Bernardino	216,715	2,858	46	140	906	1,766	9,081	2,029	4,974	2,078	75
San Bruno	43,297	138	0	17	34	87	1,139	116	948	75	5
San Clemente	65,018	87	1	3	29	54	918	160	700	58	4
Sand City	407	9	0	0	2	7	77	4	70	3	0
San Diego	1,441,737	5,215	50	561	1,346	3,258	27,141	3,543	18,426	5,172	122
San Dimas	34,059	78	0	15	15	48	833	113	659	61	1
San Fernando	24,621	80	1	4	25	50	243	52	112	79	2
San Francisco	886,007	5,933	40	324	3,055	2,514	48,780	4,644	39,887	4,249	275
San Gabriel	40,422	98	0	2	58	38	715	202	468	45	3
Sanger	25,443	156	0	9	15	132	304	59	178	67	0
San Jacinto	49,452	108	2	1	68	37	1,637	334	1,018	285	5
San Jose	1,040,008	4,559	32	671	1,339	2,517	25,164	4,114	14,924	6,126	135
San Juan Capistrano	36,209	63	2	4	20	37	297	69	201	27	2
San Leandro	90,297	454	0	18	283	153	4,105	375	2,941	789	16
San Luis Obispo	47,735	192	0	44	34	114	1,738	277	1,387	74	25
San Marcos	98,598	193	0	17	46	130	955	163	649	143	3
San Marino	13,196	14	0	1	3	10	208	77	126	5	0
San Mateo	106,020	266	2	45	68	151	2,217	516	1,523	178	9
San Pablo	31,336	194	2	7	102	83	1,009	101	589	319	11
San Rafael	58,819	230	0	23	87	120	1,686	299	1,173	214	13
San Ramon	76,387	58	0	4	21	33	1,099	179	869	51	3
Santa Ana	333,664	1,453	13	207	472	761	6,808	854	4,611	1,343	49
Santa Barbara	91,717	400	2	72	82	244	2,118	254	1,686	178	15
Santa Clara	131,173	214	0	35	73	106	4,748	363	4,013	372	18
Santa Clarita	218,103	277	2	49	89	137	2,059	392	1,448	219	17
Santa Cruz	65,263	389	0	29	88	272	2,932	348	2,363	221	34
Santa Fe Springs	18,041	105	2	10	42	51	1,035	205	654	176	6
Santa Monica	91,621	664	3	40	247	374	3,964	577	3,143	244	19
Santa Paula	30,098	91	2	6	21	62	404	103	272	29	3
Santa Rosa	177,884	857	3	146	126	582	2,874	486	2,077	311	28
Santee	58,701	98	0	8	29	61	806	74	659	73	7
Saratoga	30,666	16	0	4	2	10	240	104	122	14	5
Sausalito	7,118	7	0	0	1	6	258	21	224	13	0
Scotts Valley	11,875	13	0	2	1	10	141	31	102	8	2
Seal Beach	24,120	19	0	1	10	8	551	62	458	31	0
Seaside	34,036	78	3	11	12	52	439	44	329	66	5
Sebastopol	7,815	21	0	3	7	11	177	51	110	16	2
Selma	24,983	85	3	6	25	51	605	204	280	121	0

Table 8. Offenses Known to Law Enforcement, by Selected State and City, 2019—Continued

(Number.)

State/city	Population	Violent crime	Murder and nonnegligent manslaughter	Rape[1]	Robbery	Aggravated assault	Property crime	Burglary	Larceny-theft	Motor vehicle theft	Arson[2]
Shafter	20,456	53	0	3	9	41	513	127	298	88	8
Sierra Madre	10,917	15	0	1	0	14	79	29	46	4	0
Signal Hill	11,624	95	0	1	27	67	678	110	491	77	3
Simi Valley	126,025	146	1	15	35	95	1,188	208	889	91	7
Solana Beach	13,440	13	0	3	4	6	173	39	115	19	0
Soledad	26,015	53	0	4	14	35	136	24	83	29	5
Solvang	5,962	10	0	0	2	8	68	18	46	4	0
Sonoma	11,323	38	0	6	1	31	122	21	95	6	1
Sonora	4,867	26	0	6	6	14	269	69	180	20	4
South El Monte	20,852	102	1	11	32	58	500	132	254	114	3
South Gate	94,445	622	4	21	179	418	2,754	351	1,663	740	26
South Lake Tahoe	22,116	111	2	10	20	79	449	79	335	35	0
South Pasadena	25,612	29	0	2	11	16	566	94	434	38	0
South San Francisco	68,251	166	2	19	64	81	1,484	230	1,074	180	7
Stallion Springs	2,648	7	1	1	0	5	19	5	13	1	0
Stanton	38,276	95	3	10	31	51	526	83	344	99	7
St. Helena	6,195	12	0	1	1	10	67	21	43	3	0
Stockton	313,604	4,380	34	181	1,158	3,007	12,367	2,209	8,480	1,678	128
Suisun City	29,922	114	0	11	35	68	664	69	479	116	11
Sunnyvale	154,859	259	0	37	84	138	3,380	458	2,598	324	32
Susanville	14,878	196	0	7	10	179	207	45	157	5	0
Sutter Creek	2,624	3	0	1	0	2	44	8	30	6	2
Taft	9,413	67	0	6	4	57	244	70	149	25	0
Tehachapi	12,211	60	2	8	7	43	327	70	231	26	0
Temecula	116,630	166	1	8	72	85	2,626	318	2,018	290	5
Temple City	36,192	64	1	7	23	33	331	122	175	34	1
Thousand Oaks	127,811	88	0	27	23	38	1,392	244	1,084	64	2
Tiburon	9,135	0	0	0	0	0	82	13	67	2	0
Torrance	145,183	280	3	26	114	137	2,853	399	2,161	293	12
Tracy	92,895	166	5	35	62	64	1,843	156	1,411	276	14
Truckee	16,611	31	0	3	4	24	114	36	66	12	1
Tulare	65,134	261	4	27	69	161	1,469	225	951	293	11
Tulelake	985	3	0	1	0	2	4	1	3	0	0
Turlock	74,120	426	1	29	138	258	2,323	402	1,483	438	34
Tustin	80,356	141	1	16	61	63	2,118	241	1,694	183	6
Twentynine Palms	26,588	117	0	10	15	92	265	96	134	35	4
Ukiah	16,197	110	1	9	24	76	298	117	147	34	23
Union City	75,202	277	2	8	79	188	1,718	192	1,300	226	9
Upland	77,398	298	3	20	107	168	1,821	368	1,206	247	11
Vacaville	101,147	331	3	47	80	201	2,442	162	2,120	160	8
Vallejo	122,657	1,037	12	138	336	551	4,941	2,888	1,148	905	52
Ventura	111,596	458	3	56	106	293	2,969	353	2,362	254	7
Vernon	112	27	0	1	12	14	485	133	272	80	5
Victorville	123,089	988	5	45	255	683	2,271	590	1,061	620	21
Villa Park	5,840	4	0	0	0	4	44	9	35	0	0
Visalia	134,961	586	4	111	159	312	3,900	747	2,627	526	20
Vista	102,227	354	2	38	93	221	1,438	251	945	242	6
Walnut	30,108	38	0	4	14	20	386	152	207	27	0
Walnut Creek	70,546	120	0	6	40	74	2,496	307	2,034	155	4
Waterford	9,021	13	0	1	5	7	143	17	76	50	0
Watsonville	54,261	328	1	37	53	237	971	148	589	234	8
Weed	2,673	34	0	3	4	27	55	8	38	9	0
West Covina	106,335	260	6	21	129	104	2,369	354	1,660	355	15
West Hollywood	37,173	294	0	24	139	131	1,898	215	1,566	117	9
Westlake Village	8,358	13	0	5	6	2	189	44	140	5	0
Westminster	91,086	259	0	19	122	118	2,611	511	1,824	276	22
West Sacramento	54,372	212	1	34	79	98	1,603	236	1,158	209	26
Wheatland	3,940	6	0	0	1	5	43	8	26	9	0
Whittier	86,158	213	1	27	93	92	1,901	318	1,278	305	7
Wildomar	37,939	61	0	1	12	48	637	101	375	161	1
Williams	5,348	20	0	3	4	13	76	28	34	14	2
Willits	4,937	16	0	2	6	8	92	28	51	13	2
Windsor	27,981	58	0	8	8	42	257	30	212	15	0
Winters	7,374	11	0	0	1	10	115	19	81	15	3
Woodlake	7,682	28	0	4	2	22	88	14	61	13	0
Woodland	61,176	224	3	18	44	159	1,488	231	1,062	195	52
Yorba Linda	68,225	42	0	3	17	22	627	140	433	54	1
Yountville	2,988	5	0	0	0	5	42	5	36	1	1
Yreka	7,527	28	0	0	1	27	235	34	172	29	0
Yuba City	67,164	241	3	28	52	158	1,823	230	1,334	259	7
Yucaipa	53,964	200	3	14	31	152	641	172	365	104	0
Yucca Valley	21,858	160	0	9	25	126	292	84	157	51	3
COLORADO											
Alamosa	10,086	63	1	17	5	40	511	94	392	25	5
Arvada	122,312	266	1	42	58	165	3,642	316	2,951	375	9
Aspen	7,461	9	0	2	2	5	240	16	220	4	0
Aurora	380,600	2,799	28	438	638	1,695	11,106	1,554	7,258	2,294	104
Avon	6,496	10	0	3	0	7	93	1	82	10	0
Basalt	4,209	1	0	0	0	1	10	0	10	0	0
Bayfield	2,754	1	0	1	0	0	41	15	26	0	0
Black Hawk	128	8	0	0	0	8	211	4	200	7	0
Boulder	108,519	278	1	41	37	199	3,284	405	2,628	251	6

Table 8. Offenses Known to Law Enforcement, by Selected State and City, 2019—Continued

(Number.)

State/city	Population	Violent crime	Murder and nonnegligent manslaughter	Rape[1]	Robbery	Aggravated assault	Property crime	Burglary	Larceny-theft	Motor vehicle theft	Arson[2]
Bow Mar	959	0	0	0	0	0	10	3	6	1	0
Breckenridge	5,079	16	1	4	1	10	189	7	176	6	0
Brighton	42,267	138	0	36	5	97	1,119	93	859	167	3
Broomfield	70,798	75	2	13	9	51	2,046	205	1,710	131	3
Buena Vista	2,857	1	0	0	1	0	23	0	22	1	0
Burlington	3,072	14	0	4	0	10	71	10	50	11	0
Canon City	16,793	103	3	37	2	61	818	136	635	47	6
Carbondale	6,941	9	0	2	0	7	77	4	69	4	0
Castle Rock	67,208	30	0	16	4	10	962	96	806	60	2
Center	2,312	6	0	4	2	0	63	21	39	3	1
Cherry Hills Village	6,734	3	0	2	0	1	74	17	52	5	0
Colorado Springs	479,648	2,806	23	431	485	1,867	17,587	2,400	12,095	3,092	115
Columbine Valley	1,519	0	0	0	0	0	7	1	6	0	0
Commerce City	60,198	272	5	76	44	147	1,845	212	1,258	375	11
Cortez	8,748	43	0	10	4	29	282	26	246	10	3
Craig	8,886	14	0	2	3	9	251	33	209	9	2
Crested Butte	1,708	2	0	0	0	2	11	4	7	0	0
Cripple Creek	1,271	8	0	0	0	8	63	11	50	2	1
Dacono	6,074	5	0	3	1	1	69	22	40	7	0
Delta	8,929	10	0	0	2	8	337	69	244	24	5
Denver	728,941	5,459	67	713	1,205	3,474	27,288	3,967	18,027	5,294	107
Dillon	981	3	0	0	0	3	25	3	19	3	0
Durango	19,271	75	0	13	7	55	611	73	508	30	3
Eaton	5,690	3	0	1	0	2	41	2	34	5	0
Edgewater	5,363	9	0	2	4	3	352	34	288	30	1
Elizabeth	1,424	2	1	1	0	0	15	2	13	0	0
Englewood	35,273	72	1	8	19	44	1,843	108	1,432	303	13
Erie	26,523	28	0	4	3	21	239	33	192	14	3
Estes Park	6,406	10	0	0	0	10	58	13	42	3	0
Evans[5]	21,585	47	0	32	4	11	406	61	287	58	7
Fairplay	773	0	0	0	0	0	11	3	8	0	0
Firestone	15,558	6	1	2	0	3	127	16	94	17	4
Florence	3,965	3	0	1	0	2	44	3	33	8	0
Fort Collins	170,889	371	1	41	36	293	3,713	350	3,135	228	7
Fort Morgan	11,355	43	0	24	3	16	271	38	203	30	2
Fountain	31,041	127	2	23	15	87	665	98	479	88	2
Fowler	1,139	0	0	0	0	0	7	4	2	1	0
Fraser/Winter Park	2,371	14	0	5	0	9	60	4	53	3	0
Frederick	14,238	0	0	0	0	0	14	3	4	7	0
Frisco	3,220	11	0	2	0	9	84	2	77	5	0
Fruita	13,504	22	1	3	1	17	208	24	174	10	2
Glendale	5,289	50	1	5	14	30	936	22	833	81	1
Glenwood Springs	10,027	27	0	7	1	19	469	33	416	20	2
Granby	2,133	0	0	0	0	0	25	1	23	1	0
Grand Junction	63,949	235	3	43	30	159	2,463	278	2,034	151	20
Greeley	109,255	386	2	71	67	246	2,542	338	1,898	306	20
Green Mountain Falls	714	0	0	0	0	0	2	2	0	0	0
Gunnison	6,689	20	0	5	0	15	91	5	78	8	1
Hayden	1,992	1	0	0	0	1	30	5	22	3	0
Holyoke	2,204	0	0	0	0	0	6	1	5	0	0
Hotchkiss	932	2	0	2	0	0	20	3	16	1	0
Hudson	1,806	7	0	2	1	4	33	3	23	7	1
Idaho Springs	1,803	14	0	3	0	11	92	6	78	8	0
Ignacio	892	4	0	0	0	4	14	3	11	0	0
Johnstown	15,547	17	0	5	1	11	291	16	256	19	3
Kersey	1,679	3	0	0	0	3	1	0	0	1	0
Lafayette	29,522	63	0	28	4	31	731	77	605	49	4
La Junta	6,983	32	1	15	3	13	386	83	279	24	1
Lakeside	8	0	0	0	0	0	205	1	202	2	0
Lamar	7,619	0	0	0	0	0	82	15	67	0	0
La Salle	2,400	6	0	0	0	6	30	11	16	3	0
Leadville	2,785	8	0	3	0	5	27	6	16	5	0
Limon	1,929	0	0	0	0	0	2	0	1	1	0
Littleton	48,831	43	0	20	13	10	1,372	211	974	187	6
Lone Tree	15,129	47	1	5	10	31	1,051	40	976	35	3
Longmont	97,928	422	1	124	31	266	2,548	294	1,935	319	43
Louisville	21,532	16	0	5	0	11	301	40	244	17	3
Loveland	78,856	222	0	54	18	150	1,571	157	1,289	125	10
Mancos	1,429	2	0	0	0	2	17	3	13	1	0
Manitou Springs	5,388	5	1	1	0	3	72	12	53	7	0
Mead	4,924	4	0	4	0	0	55	6	38	11	0
Meeker	2,238	5	0	2	0	3	22	1	21	0	1
Milliken	7,978	1	0	1	0	0	29	3	20	6	1
Monte Vista	4,084	19	0	4	2	13	157	25	123	9	2
Montrose	19,564	40	0	0	9	31	689	68	571	50	5
Mountain View	541	0	0	0	0	0	11	0	10	1	0
Mountain Village	1,450	1	0	0	0	1	19	0	15	4	0
Mount Crested Butte	859	7	0	2	0	5	15	0	14	1	0
Nederland	1,560	2	0	0	0	2	4	0	3	1	0
New Castle	5,095	4	0	0	0	4	46	5	39	2	1
Northglenn	39,420	180	1	48	21	110	1,229	119	868	242	12
Oak Creek	975	4	0	3	0	1	7	0	6	1	0
Olathe	1,824	0	0	0	0	0	6	1	2	3	0

Table 8. Offenses Known to Law Enforcement, by Selected State and City, 2019—Continued

(Number.)

State/city	Population	Violent crime	Murder and nonnegligent manslaughter	Rape[1]	Robbery	Aggravated assault	Property crime	Burglary	Larceny-theft	Motor vehicle theft	Arson[2]
Pagosa Springs	2,044	5	0	1	0	4	44	7	36	1	0
Palisade	2,723	6	0	3	0	3	34	4	30	0	0
Parachute	1,125	16	0	4	0	12	34	6	18	10	1
Parker	57,050	55	1	12	5	37	826	150	610	66	3
Platteville	3,922	5	0	2	0	3	55	7	36	12	0
Pueblo[6]	112,381		5	110		481	4,801	894	3,208	699	61
Rangely	2,278	3	0	1	0	2	5	1	4	0	0
Rifle	9,782	38	1	6	3	28	221	25	180	16	4
Salida	6,061	5	0	0	0	5	184	7	166	11	0
Severance	5,362	2	0	2	0	0	15	3	11	1	0
Sheridan	6,233	28	0	4	7	17	450	37	369	44	2
Silt	3,215	10	0	0	0	10	20	4	12	4	0
Silverthorne	4,948	2	0	0	0	2	90	8	76	6	0
Simla	642	2	0	0	0	2	3	1	2	0	0
Snowmass Village	2,767	0	0	0	0	0	14	0	14	0	0
South Fork	348	1	0	1	0	0	8	2	3	3	0
Springfield	1,369	1	0	0	0	1	3	1	2	0	0
Sterling	13,573	107	1	35	5	66	462	99	344	19	7
Telluride	2,518	3	0	0	0	3	17	1	15	1	0
Thornton	142,168	388	1	130	74	183	4,303	393	3,279	631	18
Timnath	5,027	2	0	1	1	0	99	20	74	5	0
Trinidad	8,116	38	0	0	9	29	350	67	263	20	3
Walsh	513	1	0	0	0	1	0	0	0	0	0
Westminster	114,392	316	2	53	77	184	3,713	376	2,703	634	10
Woodland Park	7,863	11	0	3	0	8	111	5	105	1	0
Wray	2,331	1	0	1	0	0	1	0	1	0	1
Yuma	3,452	4	0	1	0	3	19	3	8	8	0
CONNECTICUT											
Ansonia	18,656	36	1	10	11	14	277	14	220	43	1
Avon	18,320	4	0	0	1	3	209	15	182	12	0
Berlin	20,500	19	0	2	5	12	251	40	196	15	1
Bethel	19,855	6	2	1	1	2	125	13	108	4	0
Bloomfield	21,406	27	1	5	5	16	500	21	431	48	0
Branford	28,002	9	0	2	4	3	386	30	326	30	0
Bridgeport	144,908	843	17	71	392	363	2,465	555	1,292	618	13
Bristol	59,977	53	1	8	21	23	822	113	603	106	2
Brookfield	17,071	4	0	1	1	2	143	6	134	3	0
Canton	10,267	5	0	1	0	4	56	4	45	7	0
Cheshire	29,167	13	1	4	2	6	207	14	172	21	0
Clinton	12,914	12	0	5	3	4	232	21	207	4	0
Coventry	12,411	12	0	6	1	5	132	16	103	13	0
Cromwell	13,894	5	0	1	2	2	363	21	326	16	3
Danbury	85,167	97	1	15	28	53	1,045	132	827	86	4
Darien	21,880	3	0	0	1	2	267	29	206	32	0
Derby	12,468	24	0	4	11	9	240	39	179	22	2
East Hampton	12,842	3	0	0	3	0	104	10	84	10	0
East Hartford	49,842	76	1	18	31	26	775	109	525	141	8
East Haven	28,635	36	0	7	11	18	572	58	454	60	0
East Lyme	18,588	8	0	1	1	6	83	12	54	17	1
Easton	7,519	0	0	0	0	0	42	13	21	8	0
East Windsor	11,399	14	1	1	4	8	275	39	219	17	0
Enfield[5]	44,443	49	1	12	6	30	606	59	497	50	2
Fairfield	62,239	31	1	3	13	14	941	96	791	54	0
Farmington	25,525	6	0	2	3	1	599	107	464	28	1
Glastonbury	34,497	22	0	3	5	14	327	35	270	22	1
Granby	11,386	0	0	0	0	0	64	3	58	3	0
Greenwich	62,905	22	0	4	4	14	471	65	348	58	0
Groton	8,967	16	0	4	0	12	99	26	70	3	2
Groton Long Point	509	0	0	0	0	0	3	1	2	0	0
Groton Town	29,046	34	1	10	2	21	304	37	249	18	2
Guilford	22,194	10	0	4	1	5	201	14	176	11	3
Hamden	60,855	199	2	9	45	143	1,328	109	1,047	172	1
Hartford	122,245	1,049	21	31	271	726	3,424	427	2,464	533	50
Ledyard	14,698	6	0	4	0	2	73	15	53	5	1
Madison	18,087	0	0	0	0	0	65	3	50	12	1
Manchester[5]	57,630	100	1	16	46	37	1,376	143	1,135	98	1
Meriden	59,378	157	3	19	38	97	1,020	178	719	123	7
Middlebury	7,750	2	0	0	0	2	64	9	47	8	0
Middletown	45,963	38	0	5	10	23	613	62	474	77	0
Milford	54,898	29	1	0	16	12	1,028	95	853	80	1
Monroe	19,466	3	0	2	1	0	84	12	66	6	1
Naugatuck	31,214	30	0	10	9	11	441	48	372	21	3
New Britain[5]	72,354	306	3	44	66	193	1,195	188	826	181	7
New Canaan	20,268	2	0	0	0	2	101	14	80	7	0
New Haven	130,494	1,168	13	45	321	789	4,958	659	3,580	719	28
Newington	30,060	24	0	2	14	8	646	65	530	51	0
New London	26,856	79	0	19	32	28	461	90	329	42	4
New Milford	26,835	15	0	9	0	6	181	2	173	6	1
Newtown	27,795	6	0	0	1	5	57	11	45	1	1
North Branford	14,127	8	0	4	3	1	99	10	79	10	0
North Haven	23,642	11	0	0	5	6	361	57	268	36	1
Norwalk	89,440	183	1	8	29	145	1,247	133	989	125	4

Table 8. Offenses Known to Law Enforcement, by Selected State and City, 2019—Continued

(Number.)

State/city	Population	Violent crime	Murder and nonnegligent manslaughter	Rape[1]	Robbery	Aggravated assault	Property crime	Burglary	Larceny-theft	Motor vehicle theft	Arson[2]
Norwich	38,964	149	0	26	22	101	533	112	368	53	5
Old Saybrook	10,069	2	0	0	0	2	69	5	59	5	0
Orange	13,948	4	0	0	3	1	370	25	326	19	0
Plainfield	15,145	18	1	9	1	7	37	3	29	5	0
Plainville	17,610	33	0	1	3	29	348	18	309	21	0
Plymouth	11,573	2	0	0	1	1	110	10	84	16	0
Portland	9,281	4	0	1	0	3	38	3	26	9	0
Putnam	9,374	18	0	9	0	9	72	9	56	7	2
Redding	9,120	2	0	1	1	0	35	9	26	0	0
Ridgefield	25,050	1	0	0	0	1	72	12	53	7	0
Rocky Hill	20,199	12	1	7	2	2	212	21	166	25	0
Seymour	16,505	9	0	2	4	3	104	20	73	11	2
Shelton	41,287	22	0	8	7	7	304	61	219	24	1
Simsbury	25,169	3	0	1	2	0	146	5	121	20	0
Southington	43,886	26	0	2	6	18	542	87	407	48	1
South Windsor	26,097	13	0	5	4	4	332	50	255	27	2
Stamford	130,678	264	5	27	87	145	1,803	196	1,446	161	1
Stonington	18,439	15	2	3	0	10	159	31	126	2	0
Stratford	52,034	71	1	13	25	32	859	97	654	108	4
Suffield	15,740	5	0	2	1	2	62	13	39	10	0
Thomaston	7,521	4	0	1	1	2	58	6	46	6	0
Torrington	33,972	36	0	12	5	19	372	53	289	30	2
Trumbull	35,772	45	0	7	15	23	778	53	692	33	1
Vernon	29,318	16	0	5	3	8	307	50	211	46	0
Wallingford	44,457	17	0	6	1	10	291	35	237	19	1
Waterbury	107,812	325	5	53	124	143	3,263	450	2,272	541	12
Waterford	18,812	8	0	4	1	3	189	10	174	5	0
Watertown	21,534	13	3	3	2	5	284	26	221	37	0
West Hartford	62,875	36	0	1	30	5	1,406	130	1,192	84	1
West Haven	54,794	85	1	21	29	34	1,091	96	828	167	3
Weston	10,254	0	0	0	0	0	15	1	14	0	0
Westport	28,332	4	0	0	2	2	193	20	152	21	0
Wethersfield	26,009	23	0	4	8	11	351	39	272	40	1
Willimantic	17,660	22	0	7	6	9	119	18	85	16	1
Wilton	18,439	4	0	0	0	4	109	13	89	7	0
Winchester	10,585	7	0	3	3	1	85	24	56	5	0
Windsor	28,717	12	0	3	2	7	605	43	502	60	1
Windsor Locks	12,924	8	1	1	6	0	140	16	98	26	0
Wolcott	16,642	7	0	3	4	0	195	30	139	26	0
Woodbridge	8,782	6	1	3	1	1	89	13	66	10	0
DELAWARE											
Bethany Beach	1,244	3	0	1	2	0	79	3	76	0	1
Blades	1,469	4	0	1	1	2	23	3	20	0	0
Bridgeville	2,407	12	0	1	2	9	77	9	66	2	0
Camden	3,507	5	0	2	2	1	173	7	163	3	0
Cheswold	1,639	6	0	0	0	6	27	2	21	4	0
Clayton	3,448	7	0	0	0	7	35	11	24	0	0
Dagsboro	916	2	0	1	0	1	15	2	13	0	0
Delaware City	1,830	11	0	1	0	10	52	11	41	0	0
Delmar	1,822	17	0	1	3	13	51	10	41	0	0
Dewey Beach	394	7	0	0	0	7	16	2	13	1	0
Dover	38,361	334	4	13	49	268	2,057	82	1,886	89	8
Ellendale	444	2	0	0	0	2	13	0	12	1	0
Elsmere	5,963	11	0	0	5	6	133	37	74	22	0
Felton	1,420	2	0	1	0	1	17	2	15	0	0
Georgetown	7,558	43	0	1	11	31	312	46	256	10	0
Greenwood	1,138	6	0	1	1	4	19	6	10	3	0
Harrington	3,652	35	2	3	6	24	77	12	63	2	0
Laurel	4,469	62	0	3	15	44	225	42	179	4	0
Lewes	3,286	4	0	1	0	3	45	6	38	1	0
Middletown	23,079	48	0	3	8	37	470	70	386	14	0
Milford	11,592	84	0	5	20	59	585	68	505	12	0
Millsboro	4,524	27	0	4	0	23	221	23	196	2	0
Milton	3,017	4	0	0	0	4	40	6	33	1	0
Newark	33,957	85	1	11	21	52	708	76	596	36	0
New Castle	5,558	21	0	0	5	16	225	19	196	10	0
Newport	1,026	3	0	1	1	1	31	3	27	1	0
Ocean View	2,180	1	0	0	1	0	19	4	15	0	0
Rehoboth Beach	1,546	10	0	4	0	6	128	11	113	4	0
Seaford	7,987	68	0	8	11	49	477	45	422	10	1
Selbyville	2,540	12	0	2	0	10	37	9	25	3	0
Smyrna	11,768	32	0	5	3	24	246	39	201	6	0
Wilmington	70,624	1,058	24	19	326	689	3,150	569	2,121	460	2
Wyoming	1,565	4	0	0	0	4	23	7	14	2	0
DISTRICT OF COLUMBIA											
Washington	705,749	6,896	166	342	2,359	4,029	29,965	1,840	25,827	2,298	
FLORIDA											
Alachua	10,070	41	0	4	7	30	230	32	191	7	1
Altamonte Springs	44,582	107	0	14	31	62	1,408	111	1,212	85	1
Altha	504	0	0	0	0	0	0	0	0	0	0

Table 8. Offenses Known to Law Enforcement, by Selected State and City, 2019—Continued

(Number.)

State/city	Population	Violent crime	Murder and nonnegligent manslaughter	Rape[1]	Robbery	Aggravated assault	Property crime	Burglary	Larceny-theft	Motor vehicle theft	Arson[2]
Apopka	55,072	206	0	25	41	140	1,931	375	1,406	150	1
Arcadia	8,274	55	3	2	7	43	106	30	70	6	2
Astatula	2,091	3	0	0	0	3	10	2	6	2	0
Atlantic Beach	13,983	36	1	2	6	27	197	37	145	15	1
Atlantis	2,126	6	0	0	2	4	54	6	41	7	0
Auburndale	16,679	55	0	6	16	33	715	101	596	18	0
Aventura	38,259	69	1	6	26	36	1,815	87	1,677	51	1
Bal Harbour Village	3,086	0	0	0	0	0	98	3	92	3	0
Bartow	20,296	77	2	9	10	56	613	98	491	24	2
Bay Harbor Islands	6,018	3	0	2	0	1	51	4	36	11	0
Belleair	4,253	1	0	0	0	1	32	8	21	3	0
Belleair Beach	1,618	1	0	0	1	0	18	4	14	0	0
Belleair Bluffs	2,209	2	1	0	0	1	33	6	25	2	0
Belle Glade	20,301	200	4	9	16	171	405	81	292	32	5
Belle Isle	7,326	16	0	0	9	7	119	23	70	26	0
Belleview	5,086	20	0	3	6	11	208	71	129	8	2
Biscayne Park	3,169	6	0	0	0	6	30	5	25	0	0
Blountstown	2,473	6	0	0	0	6	36	8	23	5	0
Boca Raton	101,163	186	3	36	63	84	2,183	244	1,769	170	6
Bonifay	2,683	3	1	0	0	2	5	3	0	2	0
Bowling Green	2,899	5	0	0	0	5	46	16	27	3	0
Boynton Beach	79,360	566	4	30	120	412	2,618	254	2,147	217	3
Bradenton	58,782	360	6	22	57	275	1,474	204	1,191	79	2
Bradenton Beach	1,292	2	0	0	1	1	21	3	17	1	0
Brooksville	8,373	50	0	8	10	32	332	60	255	17	4
Bunnell	2,865	33	0	1	3	29	105	26	62	17	0
Cape Coral	194,183	226	5	16	36	169	2,176	274	1,739	163	6
Casselberry	29,244	90	0	7	18	65	936	96	788	52	2
Cedar Key	685	1	0	0	0	1	10	3	6	1	0
Center Hill	1,472	1	0	0	0	1	5	2	3	0	0
Chattahoochee	3,004	16	2	2	0	12	92	15	47	30	0
Chiefland	2,162	0	0	0	0	0	55	27	26	2	0
Chipley	3,567	26	0	2	5	19	115	13	88	14	0
Clearwater	117,458	469	2	80	98	289	2,810	268	2,370	172	5
Clermont	37,818	79	1	11	11	56	678	80	555	43	0
Clewiston	8,098	26	1	1	5	19	211	73	130	8	0
Cocoa	18,807	151	2	5	58	86	965	137	768	60	3
Cocoa Beach	11,806	64	1	6	7	50	300	21	266	13	0
Coconut Creek	62,471	82	2	13	19	48	1,010	89	802	119	0
Cooper City	36,890	26	0	7	8	11	360	34	303	23	1
Coral Gables	51,530	50	0	4	17	29	1,343	157	1,103	83	4
Coral Springs	134,967	195	2	40	55	98	2,309	163	1,977	169	2
Crescent City	1,540	10	0	0	2	8	40	7	31	2	0
Crestview	25,152	96	3	11	20	62	644	107	478	59	1
Cross City	1,710	2	0	0	0	2	2	0	2	0	0
Cutler Bay	45,452	94	3	7	28	56	1,328	63	1,172	93	1
Dade City	7,337	36	0	8	5	23	287	32	245	10	0
Dania Beach	32,593	221	2	31	59	129	1,006	112	780	114	2
Davenport	5,814	5	0	0	0	5	76	22	44	10	0
Davie	108,486	276	2	21	63	190	2,796	203	2,316	277	11
Daytona Beach	69,834	794	13	18	109	654	2,833	380	2,213	240	10
Daytona Beach Shores	4,579	9	0	0	2	7	107	19	80	8	0
Deerfield Beach	81,602	351	6	31	99	215	2,161	211	1,703	247	2
DeFuniak Springs	6,940	29	0	3	0	26	188	23	144	21	2
DeLand	34,468	198	4	1	26	167	1,126	182	873	71	4
Delray Beach	70,509	336	5	33	87	211	2,418	299	1,914	205	1
Doral	64,168	62	1	9	13	39	1,475	66	1,287	122	0
Dunedin	36,743	39	0	6	5	28	472	46	391	35	1
Dunnellon	1,830	8	0	1	1	6	92	22	70	0	0
Eatonville	2,317	39	0	3	4	32	114	29	73	12	0
Edgewater	22,926	22	0	0	1	21	361	108	224	29	0
Edgewood	3,044	3	0	0	1	2	66	12	48	6	0
El Portal	2,479	2	0	0	2	0	25	4	21	0	0
Eustis	21,432	53	1	3	12	37	536	72	402	62	6
Fellsmere	5,830	5	1	0	1	3	48	5	39	4	0
Fernandina Beach	12,710	25	1	4	0	20	152	13	130	9	1
Flagler Beach	5,157	3	0	1	0	2	41	5	33	3	0
Florida City	12,180	319	4	5	70	240	885	77	756	52	1
Fort Lauderdale	184,765	1,098	21	93	408	576	9,082	1,275	6,945	862	10
Fort Myers	85,127	486	9	34	94	349	1,952	245	1,553	154	6
Fort Pierce	46,597	259	10	19	66	164	1,342	151	1,051	140	3
Fort Walton Beach	22,645	68	2	18	1	47	475	59	372	44	1
Fruitland Park	11,410	25	1	2	1	21	119	53	65	1	0
Gainesville	135,085	928	2	153	185	588	4,712	501	3,803	408	6
Golden Beach	964	1	0	1	0	0	15	0	12	3	0
Graceville	2,191	15	0	0	0	15	53	35	15	3	0
Greenacres City	41,525	117	1	10	35	71	740	63	640	37	0
Green Cove Springs	8,505	30	0	8	3	19	182	27	144	11	0
Gretna	1,509	5	0	1	3	1	10	10	0	0	0
Groveland	15,667	26	0	6	3	17	235	33	190	12	0
Gulf Breeze	6,843	5	1	0	0	4	71	11	58	2	1
Gulfport	12,449	28	0	4	5	19	391	30	322	39	1
Gulf Stream	891	2	0	0	0	2	15	2	12	1	0

Table 8. Offenses Known to Law Enforcement, by Selected State and City, 2019—Continued

(Number.)

State/city	Population	Violent crime	Murder and nonnegligent manslaughter	Rape[1]	Robbery	Aggravated assault	Property crime	Burglary	Larceny-theft	Motor vehicle theft	Arson[2]
Haines City	25,746	45	1	2	16	26	493	50	407	36	1
Hallandale Beach	40,297	178	2	12	57	107	1,244	97	1,028	119	1
Havana	1,701	2	0	0	0	2	59	17	29	13	0
Hialeah	240,688	503	6	30	159	308	4,893	342	3,985	566	11
Hialeah Gardens	24,337	30	0	1	2	27	624	52	524	48	1
Highland Beach	3,951	4	0	2	0	2	40	6	28	6	0
High Springs	6,252	28	0	3	1	24	152	34	110	8	0
Hillsboro Beach	2,038	2	0	0	1	1	12	0	11	1	0
Holly Hill	12,403	46	0	2	10	34	335	59	236	40	1
Hollywood	156,643	456	10	45	148	253	4,159	536	3,187	436	5
Holmes Beach	4,355	0	0	0	0	0	42	5	36	1	0
Homestead	71,757	684	4	35	303	342	2,272	184	1,957	131	8
Howey-in-the-Hills	1,185	3	0	0	0	3	15	2	12	1	0
Hypoluxo	2,808	2	0	0	2	0	38	3	29	6	0
Indialantic	2,937	4	0	0	1	3	63	6	50	7	0
Indian Creek Village	92	0	0	0	0	0	85	5	76	4	0
Indian Harbour Beach	8,616	4	0	0	1	3	9	0	9	0	0
Indian River Shores	4,302	0	0	0	0	0	67	6	55	6	0
Indian Rocks Beach	4,315	8	0	2	0	6	23	1	21	1	0
Indian Shores	3,816	1	0	0	0	1	23	1	21	1	0
Jacksonville	909,142	5,886	129	554	1,294	3,909	30,088	4,906	22,373	2,809	82
Jacksonville Beach	23,974	113	1	24	21	67	856	58	743	55	1
Jasper	4,057	5	0	0	0	5	40	7	31	2	0
Jay	632	2	0	1	1	0	7	1	5	1	0
Jennings	862	3	0	0	0	3	5	1	4	0	0
Juno Beach	3,709	1	0	0	1	0	37	8	25	4	0
Jupiter	66,906	118	2	17	22	77	1,035	79	895	61	4
Jupiter Inlet Colony	459	1	0	0	0	1	0	0	0	0	0
Jupiter Island	934	1	0	0	0	1	6	0	6	0	0
Kenneth City	5,074	18	0	4	3	11	134	7	117	10	0
Key Biscayne	13,248	5	0	1	2	2	175	11	146	18	0
Key Colony Beach	816	0	0	0	0	0	7	1	6	0	0
Key West	24,554	96	0	17	11	68	734	72	591	71	1
Kissimmee	75,544	368	3	42	54	269	1,899	257	1,504	138	4
Lady Lake	15,835	16	0	1	0	15	281	19	237	25	0
Lake Alfred	6,123	3	0	0	0	3	37	12	21	4	0
Lake City	12,141	161	2	4	28	127	781	129	639	13	2
Lake Clarke Shores	3,657	4	0	0	0	4	43	7	33	3	0
Lake Hamilton	1,472	2	0	0	0	2	55	20	30	5	0
Lake Helen	2,837	3	0	0	0	3	28	5	18	5	0
Lakeland	112,237	350	7	63	97	183	3,230	438	2,589	203	7
Lake Mary	17,778	20	0	2	1	17	204	35	154	15	0
Lake Park	8,670	86	2	7	32	45	700	40	605	55	2
Lake Placid	2,459	14	0	1	5	8	105	14	91	0	0
Lake Wales	16,901	55	0	1	8	46	358	54	275	29	1
Lake Worth	38,703	409	6	37	145	221	1,201	183	884	134	4
Lantana	12,033	78	0	8	23	47	561	48	470	43	0
Largo	85,740	329	5	71	74	179	2,348	202	1,991	155	10
Lauderdale-by-the-Sea	6,745	17	1	3	0	13	96	6	82	8	0
Lauderdale Lakes	36,784	329	2	28	77	222	965	103	750	112	8
Lauderhill	72,746	571	13	42	103	413	2,131	361	1,541	229	6
Lawtey	722	4	0	0	0	4	5	2	3	0	1
Leesburg	23,527	172	1	20	31	120	1,194	199	895	100	3
Lighthouse Point	11,403	9	0	1	4	4	183	13	153	17	0
Live Oak	6,988	64	0	0	8	56	160	76	71	13	0
Longboat Key	7,379	0	0	0	0	0	59	7	52	0	0
Longwood	15,320	44	0	4	9	31	399	65	305	29	0
Loxatachee Groves	3,614	11	0	1	1	9	102	9	76	17	0
Lynn Haven	21,859	29	0	5	4	20	310	38	250	22	0
Madeira Beach	4,346	14	0	2	1	11	142	9	129	4	0
Maitland	18,222	28	0	2	3	23	339	85	225	29	0
Manalapan	474	3	0	0	0	3	18	3	15	0	0
Mangonia Park	2,033	33	0	3	11	19	177	10	160	7	1
Marco Island	18,124	7	0	1	2	4	83	7	74	2	0
Margate	59,371	99	1	9	28	61	935	99	731	105	2
Marianna	7,034	65	0	6	7	52	185	57	110	18	0
Mascotte	5,977	49	2	1	3	43	129	52	72	5	1
Medley	896	11	0	0	3	8	179	28	130	21	0
Melbourne	83,668	579	1	80	87	411	2,802	439	2,219	144	15
Melbourne Beach	3,313	2	0	0	0	2	30	3	26	1	0
Melbourne Village	702	0	0	0	0	0	14	1	12	1	0
Mexico Beach	1,243	4	0	0	0	4	29	8	19	2	0
Miami	480,505	2,850	43	152	769	1,886	17,624	1,771	14,219	1,634	37
Miami Beach	92,185	852	6	92	284	470	6,977	717	5,894	366	10
Miami Gardens	113,786	841	26	14	244	557	4,311	371	3,467	473	12
Miami Lakes	31,907	33	0	3	14	16	600	34	499	67	0
Miami Shores	10,572	23	0	1	11	11	572	57	493	22	0
Miami Springs	14,374	36	0	6	11	19	381	39	301	41	0
Milton	10,460	20	0	6	3	11	187	73	102	12	0
Minneola	12,506	15	0	2	3	10	108	21	71	16	1
Miramar	143,334	310	3	29	71	207	1,947	191	1,490	266	3
Monticello	2,413	6	0	0	2	4	60	23	35	2	0
Mount Dora	14,491	64	0	2	10	52	568	103	426	39	0

Table 8. Offenses Known to Law Enforcement, by Selected State and City, 2019—Continued

(Number.)

State/city	Population	Violent crime	Murder and nonnegligent manslaughter	Rape[1]	Robbery	Aggravated assault	Property crime	Burglary	Larceny-theft	Motor vehicle theft	Arson[2]
Naples	22,369	11	1	2	1	7	323	29	275	19	0
Neptune Beach	7,332	12	0	0	3	9	112	14	90	8	0
New Port Richey	16,703	132	0	10	22	100	505	79	407	19	1
New Smyrna Beach	27,743	67	0	0	10	57	562	107	424	31	0
Niceville	15,947	11	0	1	0	10	204	24	169	11	0
North Bay Village	8,425	13	0	1	4	8	104	3	78	23	0
North Lauderdale	44,808	230	7	32	71	120	817	81	639	97	2
North Miami	63,547	507	4	28	166	309	2,425	275	1,890	260	5
North Miami Beach	46,307	279	1	21	94	163	1,566	176	1,254	136	3
North Palm Beach	13,273	10	0	1	2	7	111	14	80	17	0
North Port	70,181	95	1	22	8	64	967	89	847	31	3
North Redington Beach	1,485	1	0	1	0	0	7	0	6	1	0
Oakland	3,160	17	0	0	3	14	63	36	21	6	0
Oakland Park	45,857	294	3	28	86	177	1,770	229	1,400	141	2
Ocala	60,932	493	7	52	108	326	2,548	252	2,131	165	17
Ocean Ridge	1,978	1	0	0	0	1	31	6	20	5	0
Ocoee	49,451	155	3	14	38	100	1,333	196	1,052	85	3
Okeechobee	5,741	13	0	0	3	10	196	15	166	15	0
Oldsmar	14,990	17	0	5	4	8	215	17	188	10	1
Opa Locka	16,501	323	11	10	67	235	1,013	188	712	113	4
Orange City	11,920	24	0	2	4	18	645	42	573	30	0
Orange Park	8,852	13	0	4	1	8	153	19	123	11	1
Orlando	292,120	2,157	25	204	536	1,392	14,100	1,464	11,362	1,274	15
Ormond Beach	44,005	133	1	13	15	104	1,119	158	894	67	2
Oviedo	42,684	56	0	17	11	28	292	58	219	15	0
Pahokee	6,335	59	0	6	3	50	160	34	116	10	2
Palatka	10,450	53	0	1	11	41	499	71	408	20	0
Palm Bay	115,520	396	8	71	59	258	1,981	334	1,499	148	5
Palm Beach	8,884	8	0	0	0	8	97	15	69	13	0
Palm Beach Gardens	57,236	78	1	9	22	46	1,295	71	1,173	51	0
Palm Beach Shores	1,278	2	0	0	0	2	21	6	13	2	0
Palmetto	13,855	78	1	8	8	61	353	39	297	17	0
Palmetto Bay	24,730	43	0	9	12	22	649	71	540	38	1
Palm Springs	25,303	161	1	5	35	120	957	131	757	69	0
Panama City	37,199	228	2	5	42	179	1,914	384	1,308	222	7
Panama City Beach	13,266	133	2	20	16	95	842	90	748	4	0
Parker	4,616	21	0	5	2	14	100	25	68	7	0
Parkland	35,244	9	0	2	2	5	189	16	151	22	0
Pembroke Park	6,798	51	2	4	10	35	216	31	162	23	1
Pembroke Pines	174,641	355	7	36	71	241	3,344	205	2,873	266	1
Pensacola	52,801	312	3	35	38	236	1,888	287	1,508	93	3
Perry	6,918	70	0	2	3	65	288	98	174	16	0
Pinellas Park	53,589	206	3	40	52	111	2,038	192	1,753	93	4
Plantation	95,474	211	2	10	91	108	2,578	161	2,152	265	4
Plant City	39,725	162	3	6	31	122	1,073	90	872	111	7
Pompano Beach	113,536	900	8	73	317	502	4,277	661	3,058	558	8
Ponce Inlet	3,315	0	0	0	0	0	32	6	24	2	0
Port Orange	65,278	30	0	1	6	23	1,178	157	946	75	0
Port St. Joe	3,579	7	0	0	1	6	40	11	28	1	0
Port St. Lucie	199,433	293	7	43	47	196	1,696	177	1,438	81	4
Punta Gorda	20,458	18	0	0	4	14	278	11	260	7	0
Quincy	7,143	55	1	4	11	39	345	242	96	7	1
Redington Beaches	1,488	0	0	0	0	0	26	2	20	4	0
Riviera Beach	35,130	346	7	20	71	248	1,466	186	1,141	139	7
Rockledge	28,078	62	1	6	7	48	389	59	289	41	3
Royal Palm Beach	40,802	57	1	7	10	39	655	31	581	43	1
Safety Harbor	18,178	17	1	3	1	12	165	20	139	6	0
Sanford	60,844	497	2	62	116	317	2,127	315	1,689	123	1
Sanibel	7,525	3	0	0	0	3	45	3	42	0	0
Sarasota	58,470	319	4	28	66	221	1,857	264	1,462	131	1
Satellite Beach	11,219	11	0	2	1	8	69	16	45	8	0
Sea Ranch Lakes	626	0	0	0	0	0	11	0	11	0	0
Sebastian	26,232	19	0	6	4	9	297	20	262	15	0
Sebring	11,008	57	6	9	13	29	481	131	339	11	2
Seminole	19,073	24	0	4	4	16	507	35	457	15	1
Sewall's Point	2,244	2	0	0	2	0	12	0	11	1	0
Sneads	1,792	4	0	0	0	4	26	15	3	8	0
South Bay	5,225	36	1	2	6	27	92	13	73	6	1
South Daytona	13,159	30	0	1	6	23	211	54	132	25	0
South Miami	12,284	39	1	1	10	27	475	84	366	25	0
South Palm Beach	1,486	0	0	0	0	0	3	0	3	0	0
South Pasadena	5,137	4	0	0	0	4	130	8	119	3	0
Southwest Ranches	8,061	7	0	1	1	5	146	29	94	23	0
Springfield	9,517	51	0	5	13	33	309	87	192	30	1
Starke	5,402	43	1	0	3	39	212	14	185	13	0
St. Augustine	14,778	107	1	19	14	73	440	58	357	25	3
St. Augustine Beach	7,137	4	0	1	0	3	85	9	75	1	0
St. Cloud	56,560	106	2	16	5	83	636	102	498	36	4
St. Pete Beach	9,689	15	0	5	2	8	205	16	177	12	0
St. Petersburg	267,696	1,594	17	125	297	1,155	8,592	1,044	6,765	783	27
Stuart	16,424	53	2	13	9	29	402	27	355	20	1
Sunny Isles Beach	22,476	33	1	7	7	18	355	20	307	28	0
Sunrise	96,919	191	4	17	63	107	2,014	157	1,673	184	3

Table 8. Offenses Known to Law Enforcement, by Selected State and City, 2019—Continued

(Number.)

State/city	Population	Violent crime	Murder and nonnegligent manslaughter	Rape[1]	Robbery	Aggravated assault	Property crime	Burglary	Larceny-theft	Motor vehicle theft	Arson[2]
Surfside	5,829	6	0	1	0	5	130	11	113	6	0
Sweetwater	21,747	16	0	0	4	12	228	2	209	17	0
Tallahassee	195,104	1,359	20	197	252	890	7,763	1,187	5,897	679	9
Tamarac	66,799	186	3	17	51	115	1,381	126	1,112	143	1
Tampa	400,501	1,622	31	120	285	1,186	6,523	1,022	4,978	523	38
Tarpon Springs	25,841	102	3	14	10	75	537	70	439	28	2
Tavares	17,962	47	0	8	4	35	273	79	166	28	0
Temple Terrace	26,725	71	0	11	14	46	565	99	424	42	0
Tequesta	6,195	7	1	0	0	6	43	16	27	0	0
Titusville	46,866	377	2	37	52	286	1,492	289	1,031	172	5
Treasure Island	6,978	17	1	2	1	13	173	16	150	7	0
Trenton	2,141	4	0	0	1	3	14	7	6	1	0
Umatilla	3,852	7	0	0	0	7	92	24	59	9	2
Valparaiso	5,218	7	0	1	0	6	48	17	26	5	0
Venice	23,726	20	1	1	3	15	283	30	242	11	0
Vero Beach	17,503	54	0	6	8	40	343	46	275	22	1
Village of Pinecrest	19,760	18	0	2	4	12	414	58	333	23	0
Virginia Gardens	2,460	5	0	0	2	3	40	5	31	4	0
Wauchula	4,890	20	0	2	3	15	172	58	106	8	0
Welaka	712	1	0	0	1	0	7	1	6	0	0
Wellington	66,331	65	0	14	11	40	787	59	669	59	1
Westlake	380	2	0	0	0	2	3	3	0	0	0
West Melbourne	24,077	32	0	3	5	24	521	53	449	19	0
West Miami	8,362	12	0	0	2	10	93	11	73	9	0
Weston	71,946	33	1	12	8	12	362	34	288	40	0
West Palm Beach	112,798	859	17	79	304	459	4,231	464	3,314	453	18
West Park	15,246	85	3	8	18	56	430	59	300	71	1
White Springs	766	6	0	0	0	6	23	5	16	2	0
Wildwood	7,310	48	0	3	7	38	250	122	111	17	0
Williston	2,713	14	0	2	0	12	95	22	62	11	1
Wilton Manors	12,948	62	1	7	25	29	434	67	334	33	1
Windermere	3,588	7	0	0	0	7	33	17	10	6	0
Winter Garden	46,750	181	2	13	27	139	1,112	111	918	83	3
Winter Haven	44,211	187	3	22	25	137	1,126	181	884	61	4
Winter Park	31,494	70	2	9	13	46	759	139	551	69	2
Winter Springs	37,854	46	0	12	4	30	249	65	157	27	0
Zephyrhills	15,836	49	1	8	7	33	602	67	513	22	3
GEORGIA[5]											
Acworth	22,921	16	0	2	1	13	437	24	399	14	0
Adairsville	4,953	7	0	2	0	5	83	15	59	9	0
Albany	74,989	790	12	32	165	581	3,452	729	2,489	234	17
Alma	3,438	10	0	0	2	8	111	36	69	6	0
Alpharetta	67,411	75	1	7	11	56	991	97	849	45	0
Americus	15,110	127	4	13	27	83	835	124	677	34	3
Bainbridge	11,986	81	1	4	13	63	469	100	351	18	2
Barnesville	6,714	18	0	0	2	16	138	12	124	2	1
Blackshear	3,471	10	0	2	1	7	169	17	147	5	0
Blakely	4,573	41	0	2	3	36	120	24	89	7	0
Braselton	12,297	8	0	0	2	6	128	15	99	14	0
Braswell	382	0	0	0	0	0	0	0	0	0	0
Brookhaven	54,734	212	2	10	74	126	1,338	221	976	141	3
Calhoun	17,069	51	0	2	3	46	369	33	320	16	0
Canon	837	0	0	0	0	0	1	0	1	0	2
Centerville	7,854	22	0	0	1	21	192	19	160	13	1
Clarkston	12,840	73	4	2	37	30	377	78	246	53	0
Claxton	2,218	19	0	2	1	16	90	19	68	3	0
College Park	15,278	177	6	8	64	99	1,038	114	712	212	0
Coolidge	525	0	0	0	0	0	2	1	0	1	0
Dillard	370	0	0	0	0	0	4	0	4	0	1
Donalsonville	2,539	11	0	0	1	10	48	11	36	1	6
Douglasville	34,609	182	0	17	37	128	2,013	135	1,805	73	0
Dunwoody	49,868	64	2	6	25	31	1,915	201	1,611	103	0
Eatonton	6,625	15	0	1	1	13	142	28	110	4	0
Edison	1,430	3	0	0	1	2	8	1	6	1	0
Elberton	4,321	27	0	4	5	18	228	47	170	11	0
Ellijay	1,722	2	0	0	0	2	29	7	22	0	0
Emerson	1,603	7	0	0	2	5	37	3	27	7	1
Eton	917	0	0	0	0	0	14	0	14	0	0
Fairburn	16,264	77	0	6	15	56	496	42	385	69	1
Folkston	4,662	31	0	0	1	30	87	9	74	4	0
Forest Park	20,273	146	2	9	66	69	903	131	654	118	3
Franklin Springs	1,232	0	0	0	0	0	1	0	0	1	0
Glennville	5,084	5	0	0	1	4	76	12	63	1	0
Grantville	3,295	24	0	2	2	20	42	6	30	6	0
Grovetown	14,918	22	0	6	3	13	168	17	132	19	0
Hampton	8,044	8	0	1	2	5	64	5	52	7	1
Homerville	2,348	2	0	0	1	1	87	22	62	3	0
Kennesaw	34,641	48	1	8	8	31	484	34	417	33	1
Lake City	2,858	5	0	0	2	3	106	18	70	18	0
Lavonia	2,162	15	0	2	3	10	68	6	57	5	0
Lilburn	12,769	23	0	3	8	12	354	52	266	36	2
Manchester	3,958	16	1	0	2	13	143	30	105	8	2

Table 8. Offenses Known to Law Enforcement, by Selected State and City, 2019—Continued

(Number.)

State/city	Population	Violent crime	Murder and nonnegligent manslaughter	Rape[1]	Robbery	Aggravated assault	Property crime	Burglary	Larceny-theft	Motor vehicle theft	Arson[2]
Marietta	61,324	262	1	14	84	163	1,930	221	1,518	191	6
Maysville	2,033	0	0	0	0	0	11	2	9	0	0
McDonough	26,277	72	2	5	12	53	731	103	565	63	3
McIntyre	602	0	0	0	0	0	12	1	10	1	0
Millen	2,718	31	0	2	4	25	59	12	45	2	0
Milton	40,067	15	0	10	1	4	291	29	254	8	1
Monroe	13,662	72	0	7	12	53	354	56	277	21	
Morrow	7,636	32	0	5	16	11	692	33	608	51	0
Mount Zion	1,826	6	0	0	0	6	7	0	4	3	0
Nahunta	1,109	0	0	0	0	0	15	2	13	0	0
Nashville	4,799	36	0	1	4	31	285	57	225	3	1
Newnan	40,720	222	3	18	18	183	1,090	116	894	80	9
Oxford	2,337	2	0	0	0	2	11	4	6	1	0
Palmetto	4,743	13	2	1	3	7	109	13	80	16	
Pelham	3,474	20	1	1	4	14	150	24	116	10	3
Pine Mountain	1,411	9	0	1	1	7	38	4	30	4	0
Pooler	24,917	45	2	9	6	28	628	42	528	58	3
Rincon	10,260	21	0	2	5	14	144	26	116	2	0
Sandersville	5,420	22	0	0	2	20	200	18	174	8	0
Sandy Springs	110,760	143	1	11	39	92	1,972	286	1,527	159	4
Shiloh	485	1	0	0	0	1	5	0	5	0	0
Snellville	20,113	55	0	2	8	45	641	32	585	24	
Sparta	1,209	7	0	0	1	6	10	3	7	0	0
Springfield	4,260	4	0	0	0	4	50	12	34	4	0
Suwanee	21,331	39	0	10	6	23	393	35	334	24	1
Sylvania	2,427	7	0	0	1	6	102	22	77	3	0
Tallapoosa	3,154	14	0	1	0	13	85	19	59	7	0
Thomasville	18,533	52	2	3	11	36	733	152	546	35	1
Thunderbolt	2,677	4	0	0	0	4	30	5	22	3	0
Tyrone	7,451	5	0	0	2	3	66	18	45	3	0
Warner Robins	76,623	420	3	44	104	269	3,609	626	2,744	239	13
Waynesboro	5,387	23	3	2	5	13	211	42	162	7	0
Woodstock	33,470	39	0	5	7	27	438	11	405	22	0
HAWAII											
Honolulu	974,902	2,638	27	340	954	1,317	29,263	3,864	21,562	3,837	272
IDAHO											
Aberdeen	1,946	4	0	0	0	4	21	4	14	3	1
American Falls	4,354	2	0	1	0	1	73	7	64	2	0
Ashton	1,052	6	0	1	0	5	9	1	8	0	0
Bellevue	2,441	7	0	1	0	6	11	3	8	0	0
Blackfoot	11,938	42	0	11	4	27	253	59	180	14	2
Boise	231,314	649	4	164	44	437	3,653	470	2,952	231	23
Bonners Ferry	2,606	1	0	0	0	1	48	16	30	2	0
Buhl	4,440	16	0	4	0	12	56	13	36	7	0
Caldwell	57,940	203	0	18	3	182	997	154	718	125	6
Challis	1,087	2	0	1	0	1	8	1	7	0	0
Chubbuck	15,490	37	0	4	6	27	553	41	497	15	1
Coeur d'Alene	52,256	132	0	38	8	86	712	83	579	50	10
Cottonwood	935	0	0	0	0	0	2	1	1	0	0
Emmett	6,950	25	0	4	0	21	73	15	55	3	2
Fruitland	5,472	3	0	1	1	1	36	10	25	1	0
Garden City	12,033	53	0	7	3	43	268	50	203	15	4
Gooding	3,457	2	0	0	0	2	45	12	30	3	1
Grangeville	3,205	7	0	1	0	6	5	1	4	0	0
Hagerman	883	1	0	0	0	1	5	2	2	1	0
Hailey	8,575	20	0	1	0	19	29	8	18	3	0
Heyburn	3,460	2	0	1	0	1	30	4	24	2	0
Idaho Falls	62,088	172	1	37	11	123	940	264	608	68	8
Jerome	11,921	42	1	17	0	24	157	30	119	8	0
Kellogg	2,117	4	0	0	0	4	38	14	20	4	2
Ketchum	2,843	12	0	1	0	11	19	3	15	1	0
Kimberly	4,052	5	0	2	0	3	26	13	13	0	0
Lewiston	32,931	42	0	15	2	25	955	145	755	55	2
McCall	3,541	13	0	2	0	11	51	15	30	6	0
Meridian	111,196	177	4	48	7	118	1,188	182	964	42	12
Middleton	8,395	11	0	1	0	10	75	12	54	9	0
Montpelier	2,514	5	0	2	0	3	35	4	29	2	0
Moscow	26,018	7	0	1	0	6	345	53	285	7	1
Mountain Home	14,476	54	0	9	0	45	229	17	196	16	3
Nampa	98,208	306	0	87	18	201	1,767	304	1,323	140	8
Osburn	1,549	1	0	0	0	1	7	3	2	2	0
Parma	2,152	7	0	2	0	5	35	4	26	5	0
Payette	7,535	23	0	7	1	15	122	14	95	13	5
Pinehurst	1,616	1	0	0	0	1	14	0	11	3	0
Pocatello	56,514	233	1	30	9	193	1,326	226	1,012	88	7
Ponderay	1,145	2	0	1	0	1	51	5	45	1	0
Post Falls	35,649	68	0	14	3	51	585	61	486	38	5
Preston	5,533	5	1	4	0	0	51	21	30	0	0
Priest River	1,868	6	0	2	0	4	30	4	24	2	0
Rathdrum	8,968	8	0	1	1	6	69	14	53	2	0
Rexburg	29,109	6	0	0	0	6	121	8	112	1	0

Table 8. Offenses Known to Law Enforcement, by Selected State and City, 2019—Continued

(Number.)

State/city	Population	Violent crime	Murder and nonnegligent manslaughter	Rape[1]	Robbery	Aggravated assault	Property crime	Burglary	Larceny-theft	Motor vehicle theft	Arson[2]
Rigby	4,225	3	0	0	0	3	35	10	24	1	0
Rupert	5,791	4	0	0	0	4	71	19	51	1	0
Salmon	3,141	17	0	0	0	17	17	3	14	0	0
Sandpoint	8,873	16	1	1	1	13	185	59	116	10	0
Shelley	4,423	1	0	1	0	0	50	8	35	7	0
Soda Springs	3,029	7	0	1	1	5	20	4	16	0	1
Spirit Lake	2,596	5	0	0	0	5	26	5	19	2	1
St. Anthony	3,572	4	0	1	0	3	24	4	20	0	0
Sun Valley	1,482	2	0	0	0	2	7	0	7	0	0
Twin Falls	50,463	201	1	27	10	163	1,034	152	827	55	8
Weiser	5,369	0	0	0	0	0	0	0	0	0	0
Wendell	2,707	5	0	3	0	2	21	5	11	5	0
ILLINOIS											
Addison	36,676	73	0	25	23	25	423	52	344	27	0
Aledo	3,448	0	0	0	0	0	39	7	30	2	0
Alexis	785	1	0	0	0	1	12	1	10	1	0
Algonquin	31,016	23	0	6	3	14	303	16	285	2	1
Alsip[6]	18,830	53	0	8	13	32		61	378		0
Altamont	2,278	3	0	3	0	0	21	4	16	1	0
Alton	26,360	268	2	34	28	204	1,101	203	813	85	4
Amboy	2,301	6	0	2	0	4	17	6	10	1	0
Anna	4,110	30	0	2	0	28	162	42	117	3	0
Annawan	853	1	0	0	0	1	5	0	4	1	0
Antioch	14,229	17	0	2	6	9	138	4	126	8	0
Arcola	2,831	4	0	2	0	2	30	19	9	2	0
Arlington Heights	75,249	33	2	9	7	15	600	41	539	20	8
Arthur	2,220	1	0	0	0	1	17	3	13	1	1
Ashland	1,181	3	0	1	0	2	25	2	23	0	0
Assumption	1,071	4	0	0	1	3	17	6	7	4	0
Athens	1,913	2	0	0	0	2	9	2	7	0	0
Auburn	4,664	4	0	0	0	4	3	0	3	0	0
Aurora	199,784	516	12	59	89	356	2,014	232	1,638	144	17
Aviston	2,128	1	0	1	0	0	6	0	5	1	0
Bannockburn	1,605	0	0	0	0	0	32	2	30	0	0
Barrington	10,268	2	0	0	0	2	87	14	66	7	0
Barrington Hills	4,205	0	0	0	0	0	18	0	18	0	0
Barry	1,244	2	0	1	1	0	15	1	14	0	0
Bartlett	40,898	23	1	7	3	12	188	22	157	9	1
Bartonville	6,137	22	0	8	8	6	179	28	127	24	0
Batavia	26,330	33	0	7	11	15	337	15	317	5	0
Beardstown	5,425	45	0	3	0	42	256	39	215	2	0
Bedford Park	602	9	0	3	0	6	388	2	366	20	0
Beecher	4,471	8	0	2	2	4	24	0	22	2	0
Belgium	366	0	0	0	0	0	0	0	0	0	0
Belleville	40,930	227	2	57	45	123	1,093	213	778	102	13
Bellwood	18,811	127	3	7	42	75	433	81	305	47	4
Belvidere	25,143	64	0	15	7	42	258	39	202	17	1
Bensenville	18,208	17	0	8	3	6	195	26	154	15	1
Berkeley	5,056	6	0	0	1	5	64	1	60	3	1
Berwyn	54,702	114	2	30	40	42	595	127	421	47	4
Bethalto	9,270	10	3	3	2	2	75	10	61	4	0
Bethany	1,258	1	0	0	0	1	12	5	7	0	0
Blandinsville	597	0	0	0	0	0	0	0	0	0	0
Bloomingdale	21,872	19	0	8	3	8	432	25	396	11	0
Bloomington	78,107	387	1	49	57	280	1,096	171	851	74	8
Blue Island	23,037	127	1	17	54	55	329	79	201	49	1
Blue Mound	1,073	0	0	0	0	0	5	1	4	0	0
Bluffs	649	0	0	0	0	0	2	1	1	0	0
Bolingbrook	75,394	123	1	28	19	75	650	65	501	84	0
Bourbonnais	19,588	57	0	9	12	36	253	15	232	6	0
Bradley	15,205	41	0	1	14	26	500	29	463	8	1
Braidwood	6,199	10	0	5	0	5	34	4	30	0	0
Breese	4,498	5	0	1	0	4	36	0	35	1	2
Bridgeview	16,153	42	0	6	12	24	315	35	272	8	0
Brighton	2,137	1	0	0	0	1	9	3	6	0	0
Broadview	7,664	20	0	0	9	11	343	23	280	40	1
Brooklyn	700	16	0	1	2	13	12	2	6	4	1
Buffalo Grove	40,768	11	2	2	2	5	288	35	245	8	1
Bunker Hill	1,675	0	0	0	0	0	21	3	17	1	0
Burbank	28,483	54	0	5	17	32	244	51	182	11	2
Burr Ridge	10,828	7	0	1	2	4	160	20	129	11	0
Byron	3,585	3	0	0	0	3	30	3	24	3	0
Cahokia	13,864	83	3	15	15	50	629	195	376	58	6
Calumet City	36,128	186	8	30	99	49	1,040	158	680	202	4
Cambria	1,281	1	0	0	0	1	5	2	3	0	0
Cambridge	2,078	2	0	0	0	2	11	1	10	0	0
Campton Hills	11,202	1	0	0	1	0	7	5	1	1	0
Canton	13,600	39	0	11	1	27	130	64	57	9	1
Carbondale	25,242	208	1	48	38	121	932	113	779	40	17
Carlinville	5,498	23	0	6	0	17	195	16	170	9	1
Carlyle	3,168	7	0	1	1	5	53	2	51	0	0
Carol Stream	39,599	29	0	7	4	18	412	40	342	30	1

Table 8. Offenses Known to Law Enforcement, by Selected State and City, 2019—Continued

(Number.)

State/city	Population	Violent crime	Murder and nonnegligent manslaughter	Rape[1]	Robbery	Aggravated assault	Property crime	Burglary	Larceny-theft	Motor vehicle theft	Arson[2]
Carpentersville	37,744	21	0	6	10	5	380	25	343	12	1
Carrollton	2,404	10	0	4	0	6	32	7	23	2	0
Carthage	2,448	1	0	0	0	1	20	5	15	0	0
Cary	17,728	8	0	2	0	6	138	7	130	1	0
Casey	2,618	8	0	2	0	6	38	6	32	0	0
Caseyville	4,088	23	0	6	1	16	68	14	42	12	0
Catlin	1,941	1	0	0	0	1	16	11	5	0	0
Centralia	12,288	181	2	34	22	123	570	144	388	38	8
Centreville	4,922	38	1	3	16	18	236	55	128	53	9
Champaign	88,891	827	2	73	94	658	2,203	300	1,777	126	5
Channahon	13,146	7	0	2	1	4	79	8	65	6	0
Charleston	19,987	31	0	3	2	26	84	23	61	0	3
Chatham	12,809	6	0	2	0	4	90	12	69	9	0
Chenoa	3,143	2	0	0	0	2	11	1	8	2	0
Cherry Valley	2,877	15	0	3	1	11	170	12	153	5	0
Chester	8,224	10	0	2	0	8	22	4	18	0	0
Chicago	2,707,064	25,532	492	1,761	7,983	15,296	80,742	9,578	62,083	9,081	416
Chicago Heights	29,471	228	2	29	78	119	576	220	274	82	1
Chicago Ridge	14,017	17	0	4	6	7	346	31	302	13	5
Chillicothe	6,071	25	0	5	0	20	43	23	18	2	0
Christopher	2,716	3	0	0	0	3	26	9	17	0	0
Cicero	81,270	258	3	47	85	123	1,579	283	1,175	121	18
Clarendon Hills	8,829	5	0	0	0	5	44	6	34	4	0
Clinton	6,869	12	0	8	4	0	193	74	114	5	0
Coal City	5,340	4	0	2	1	1	29	5	24	0	0
Coal Valley	3,760	5	0	0	1	4	60	7	52	1	0
Colchester	1,287	1	0	1	0	0	7	0	7	0	0
Colfax	1,017	1	0	0	0	1	7	4	3	0	0
Collinsville	24,496	64	0	12	7	45	493	68	388	37	1
Colona	5,122	13	1	1	0	11	61	10	51	0	0
Columbia	10,491	17	0	1	1	15	62	23	36	3	0
Cortland	4,369	2	0	0	0	2	43	1	41	1	0
Country Club Hills	16,491	44	0	8	15	21	553	31	471	51	1
Countryside	5,957	9	0	2	5	2	181	14	163	4	0
Cowden	576	0	0	0	0	0	4	0	3	1	0
Crest Hill	20,534	55	2	12	11	30	220	25	166	29	1
Crete	8,096	19	0	2	5	12	146	28	108	10	1
Crystal Lake	39,944	45	1	11	9	24	491	25	459	7	0
Dallas City	870	2	0	1	0	1	9	7	2	0	0
Dana	152	0	0	0	0	0	1	1	0	0	0
Danvers	1,107	1	0	0	0	1	1	0	1	0	0
Danville	30,642	536	7	50	65	414	1,370	341	957	72	9
Darien	21,935	11	0	5	3	3	219	40	166	13	0
Decatur	70,710	375	11	52	65	247	1,954	442	1,339	173	32
Deer Creek	661	1	0	1	0	0	4	0	2	2	0
Deerfield	18,848	7	0	0	0	7	131	13	102	16	0
DeKalb	42,428	245	1	41	33	170	1,284	162	1,081	41	12
Delavan	1,605	2	0	0	0	2	37	10	27	0	2
De Soto	1,510	5	0	0	0	5	9	4	5	0	0
Des Plaines	59,023	56	2	11	13	30	650	66	550	34	12
Diamond	2,527	0	0	0	0	0	0	0	0	0	0
Divernon	1,112	0	0	0	0	0	0	0	0	0	0
Dixon	15,096	37	1	25	2	9	278	27	244	7	0
Downers Grove	49,444	46	0	10	10	26	732	46	666	20	2
Dupo	3,810	7	0	0	1	6	77	11	57	9	3
Du Quoin	5,705	14	0	0	4	10	27	4	16	7	1
Durand	1,392	1	0	1	0	0	5	1	4	0	0
Dwight	3,962	4	0	2	1	1	40	3	37	0	0
Earlville	1,588	1	0	1	0	0	24	4	17	3	0
East Alton	5,995	24	0	8	10	6	137	23	103	11	0
East Dubuque	1,571	6	0	0	0	6	38	7	24	7	0
East Dundee	3,236	2	0	0	1	1	38	13	21	4	0
East Hazel Crest	1,507	2	0	0	2	0	53	14	38	1	0
East Peoria	22,454	70	0	10	4	56	409	43	357	9	2
East St. Louis	26,277	268	36	27	32	173	415	169	139	107	7
Edinburg	1,012	3	0	2	0	1	16	1	15	0	0
Edwardsville	25,047	16	3	0	0	13	193	15	169	9	0
Effingham	12,662	69	0	13	1	55	324	31	285	8	6
Elburn	5,967	1	0	0	1	0	20	1	14	5	0
Eldorado	3,941	7	0	0	0	7	103	36	61	6	1
Elgin	112,112	223	1	42	68	112	1,429	177	1,195	57	3
Elizabeth	721	0	0	0	0	0	2	0	1	1	0
Elk Grove Village	32,371	30	0	6	6	18	452	47	363	42	0
Elmhurst	46,857	35	0	12	11	12	478	71	391	16	3
Elmwood	2,021	2	0	1	0	1	7	0	7	0	0
Elmwood Park	24,185	65	0	0	12	53	268	46	210	12	1
El Paso	2,726	30	0	9	0	21	39	11	27	1	0
Elwood	2,257	3	0	2	0	1	24	4	19	1	0
Energy	1,126	0	0	0	0	0	22	5	16	1	0
Erie	1,506	0	0	0	0	0	4	1	3	0	0
Essex	759	0	0	0	0	0	0	0	0	0	0
Eureka	5,276	25	0	9	0	16	40	6	30	4	1
Evanston	74,047	115	1	7	42	65	1,937	292	1,575	70	0

Table 8. Offenses Known to Law Enforcement, by Selected State and City, 2019—Continued

(Number.)

State/city	Population	Violent crime	Murder and nonnegligent manslaughter	Rape[1]	Robbery	Aggravated assault	Property crime	Burglary	Larceny-theft	Motor vehicle theft	Arson[2]
Evergreen Park	19,260	62	1	19	10	32	842	32	802	8	0
Fairbury	3,602	7	0	0	0	7	13	5	8	0	0
Fairfield	4,961	8	0	2	2	4	126	39	85	2	0
Fairmont City	2,452	0	0	0	0	0	25	11	11	3	0
Fairmount	602	0	0	0	0	0	0	0	0	0	0
Fairview Heights[4]	16,368	41	0	8	8	25	591	45	516	30	
Farmington	2,236	12	0	4	0	8	41	17	21	3	0
Findlay	639	1	0	1	0	0	3	0	0	3	0
Fisher	1,966	0	0	0	0	0	20	4	16	0	0
Fithian	455	0	0	0	0	0	2	2	0	0	0
Flora	4,860	6	0	0	2	4	73	3	65	5	0
Flossmoor	9,211	14	0	3	6	5	213	10	191	12	0
Forest City	227	0	0	0	0	0	2	0	2	0	0
Forest Park	13,761	60	1	9	23	27	571	66	466	39	0
Forest View	675	4	0	0	0	4	30	2	21	7	0
Fox Lake	10,457	20	0	9	1	10	259	29	218	12	1
Fox River Grove	4,610	2	0	2	0	0	48	2	43	3	1
Frankfort	19,352	16	0	3	4	9	212	22	168	22	0
Franklin Park	17,745	41	0	5	4	32	183	50	119	14	1
Freeburg	4,240	3	0	0	1	2	24	5	18	1	0
Freeport	23,721	50	2	10	17	21	498	94	401	3	2
Fulton	3,330	5	0	0	0	5	60	10	40	10	0
Galena	3,155	6	0	2	0	4	119	6	112	1	0
Galesburg	30,220	138	0	35	13	90	1,249	234	979	36	1
Geneva	21,905	16	0	1	2	13	145	15	128	2	2
Genoa	5,211	8	0	3	0	5	49	3	43	3	0
Georgetown	3,205	19	0	6	1	12	23	6	14	3	0
Germantown	1,279	0	0	0	0	0	28	5	20	3	1
Gibson City	3,283	5	0	1	1	3	13	3	8	2	0
Gifford	1,100	1	0	0	0	1	0	0	0	0	0
Gilberts	8,259	1	0	0	0	1	35	5	26	4	0
Gillespie	3,097	23	0	7	0	16	99	19	76	4	0
Gilman	1,666	1	0	0	1	0	35	2	33	0	0
Glasford	961	0	0	0	0	0	2	2	0	0	0
Glen Carbon	12,958	4	0	0	0	4	85	8	69	8	0
Glencoe	8,887	2	0	0	0	2	64	11	41	12	0
Glendale Heights	33,878	28	0	11	8	9	373	25	329	19	1
Glen Ellyn	27,942	20	0	4	6	10	244	21	219	4	1
Glenview	47,581	50	0	5	14	31	393	66	307	20	12
Glenwood	8,767	15	1	0	7	7	98	18	51	29	1
Godley	756	2	0	2	0	0	4	0	4	0	0
Golf	496	0	0	0	0	0	2	0	2	0	0
Goodfield	998	1	0	0	0	1	23	0	23	0	0
Grafton	632	3	0	0	0	3	14	2	12	0	0
Grand Ridge	522	0	0	0	0	0	2	1	1	0	0
Granite City	28,315	233	1	34	29	169	655	222	320	113	15
Grantfork	338	0	0	0	0	0	10	8	0	2	0
Grant Park	1,233	1	0	0	1	0	4	0	4	0	0
Grayslake	20,883	13	0	4	3	6	178	20	151	7	2
Grayville	1,563	7	0	0	1	6	33	8	20	5	1
Greenfield	981	6	0	1	0	5	6	0	3	3	0
Greenup	1,486	3	0	0	1	2	20	5	14	1	0
Greenville	6,384	5	0	0	1	4	41	10	27	4	1
Gurnee	30,493	40	0	15	11	14	994	63	904	27	0
Hainesville	3,599	4	0	2	1	1	39	4	35	0	0
Hamel	813	3	0	1	1	1	5	0	4	1	0
Hampshire	6,425	10	0	1	2	7	26	14	12	0	0
Hampton	1,757	1	0	0	0	1	23	4	16	3	0
Hanover Park	37,699	30	0	7	12	11	253	36	205	12	2
Harrisburg	8,621	57	1	7	6	43	234	79	145	10	1
Hartford	1,344	3	0	1	1	1	15	1	12	2	0
Harvard	9,092	19	0	2	0	17	127	7	116	4	0
Harwood Heights	8,388	33	0	4	16	13	105	9	89	7	1
Havana	3,009	32	0	14	0	18	63	10	44	9	0
Hawthorn Woods	8,651	2	0	0	2	0	16	2	14	0	0
Hazel Crest	13,654	61	1	10	18	32	492	64	336	92	0
Henning	233	0	0	0	0	0	0	0	0	0	0
Herrin	12,878	43	2	3	3	35	251	77	154	20	3
Herscher	1,502	1	0	0	0	1	2	0	2	0	0
Hickory Hills	13,806	21	0	11	6	4	193	24	162	7	0
Highland	9,836	9	0	0	1	8	92	6	82	4	1
Highland Park	29,602	29	0	6	3	20	206	47	142	17	0
Hillsboro	5,972	14	1	4	0	9	98	23	72	3	2
Hillside	7,932	29	0	4	7	18	201	26	161	14	0
Hinckley	2,033	0	0	0	0	0	4	2	2	0	0
Hinsdale	17,756	5	0	0	2	3	177	17	148	12	1
Hodgkins	1,883	7	0	1	0	6	257	2	253	2	0
Hoffman Estates	51,105	65	0	25	4	36	432	57	353	22	1
Homer	1,165	0	0	0	0	0	2	0	2	0	0
Homer Glen	24,623	6	0	0	2	4	124	15	98	11	0
Homewood	18,831	35	1	10	8	16	806	36	727	43	1
Hoopeston	5,046	37	0	11	2	24	167	55	108	4	2
Hopedale	821	0	0	0	0	0	6	2	4	0	0

Table 8. Offenses Known to Law Enforcement, by Selected State and City, 2019—Continued

(Number.)

State/city	Population	Violent crime	Murder and nonnegligent manslaughter	Rape[1]	Robbery	Aggravated assault	Property crime	Burglary	Larceny-theft	Motor vehicle theft	Arson[2]
Hudson	1,816	0	0	0	0	0	6	1	5	0	0
Huntley	27,849	4	0	0	1	3	127	10	112	0	0
Hurst	789	0	0	0	0	0	2	0	2	5	0
Ina[4]	2,266	0	0	0	0	0		0	5	0	0
Indian Head Park	3,742	1	1	0	0	0	30	3	27	0	0
Indianola	261	0	0	0	0	0	0	0	0	0	0
Inverness	7,442	0	0	0	0	0	18	2	16	0	0
Island Lake	8,071	7	0	1	2	4	39	1	37	1	0
Itasca	10,032	8	0	3	0	5	109	16	91	2	0
Jacksonville	18,667	77	1	13	7	56	568	95	471	2	1
Jerseyville	8,208	33	0	14	14	5	146	24	116	6	0
Joliet	148,155	751	18	53	99	581	2,160	256	1,736	168	47
Justice	12,682	4	0	2	2	0	59	24	32	3	0
Kankakee	25,872	236	4	29	53	150	873	156	675	42	6
Kansas	721	0	0	0	0	0	1	0	1	0	0
Kenilworth	2,492	0	0	0	0	0	37	4	30	3	0
Kewanee	12,338	55	0	12	3	40	484	47	431	6	1
Kildeer	4,033	0	0	0	0	0	42	9	33	0	0
Kincaid	1,376	5	0	0	0	5	21	4	16	1	0
Kingston	1,159	0	0	0	0	0	1	0	1	0	0
Lacon	1,727	3	0	0	0	3	4	1	3	0	0
Ladd	1,199	0	0	0	0	0	6	1	5	0	0
La Grange	15,424	10	0	0	4	6	162	20	139	3	1
La Grange Park	13,260	6	0	0	1	5	81	12	68	1	0
La Harpe	1,147	0	0	0	0	0	10	6	4	0	0
Lake Bluff	5,606	1	0	0	0	1	54	3	48	3	0
Lake Forest	19,564	8	0	1	2	5	123	17	99	7	1
Lake in the Hills	28,811	19	0	12	1	6	105	16	88	1	2
Lakemoor	6,008	1	0	0	0	1	34	3	31	0	0
Lake Villa	8,625	5	0	0	0	5	41	3	36	2	0
Lakewood	4,006	1	0	0	0	1	22	1	19	2	1
Lake Zurich	20,060	8	0	4	1	3	248	15	231	2	3
Lanark	1,319	1	0	1	0	0	6	2	4	0	0
Lansing	27,570	104	2	9	59	34	1,495	130	1,259	106	4
La Salle	8,997	5	1	0	1	3	104	10	90	4	0
Lebanon	4,257	3	0	0	0	3	55	9	45	1	2
Lemont	17,297	17	0	7	3	7	153	15	126	12	2
Lenzburg	487	0	0	0	0	0	5	0	4	1	2
Le Roy	3,542	6	0	2	0	4	24	5	17	2	0
Lincoln	13,584	44	0	7	2	35	240	29	198	13	0
Lincolnwood	12,318	14	0	1	5	8	203	25	156	22	0
Lindenhurst	14,296	5	0	4	0	1	42	2	39	1	0
Lisle	23,506	9	0	4	1	4	149	26	116	7	1
Litchfield	6,708	7	0	0	1	6	229	33	192	4	1
Loami	746	0	0	0	0	0	14	7	7	0	0
Lockport	25,587	21	0	7	1	13	212	25	174	13	3
Lombard	44,672	43	0	6	10	27	949	61	875	13	1
Loves Park	23,265	74	0	20	9	45	400	55	293	52	3
Lovington	1,044	4	0	1	0	3	9	4	5	0	1
Lyons	10,436	16	1	3	6	6	99	8	83	8	2
Machesney Park	22,594	56	2	11	2	41	418	52	350	16	0
Mackinaw	1,901	3	0	0	0	3	43	22	20	1	0
Macomb	17,353	59	0	10	4	45	252	42	204	6	2
Mahomet	8,795	10	0	2	1	7	49	12	35	2	0
Manhattan	8,121	1	0	0	0	1	42	5	35	2	0
Manteno	8,965	30	0	10	2	18	136	11	118	7	0
Maple Park	1,341	0	0	0	0	0	11	0	11	0	0
Marissa	1,807	13	0	0	1	12	44	9	27	8	0
Marquette Heights	2,644	0	0	0	0	0	7	0	6	1	0
Marseilles	4,844	10	0	0	0	10	50	10	37	3	1
Marshall	3,833	4	0	0	0	4	35	5	29	1	0
Martinsville	1,097	0	0	0	0	0	20	0	20	0	0
Maryville	8,033	10	0	1	0	9	62	7	50	5	0
Mascoutah	8,091	2	0	0	0	2	48	4	40	4	0
Mason City	2,133	9	0	2	0	7	24	11	12	1	0
Matteson	19,517	253	2	18	19	214	546	48	424	74	2
Mattoon	17,629	82	2	28	5	47	174	52	122	0	3
Maywood	23,277	135	11	19	48	57	470	88	277	105	3
Mazon	972	1	0	1	0	0	4	1	3	0	0
McCook	220	2	0	1	0	1	12	2	10	0	0
McHenry	27,020	40	0	8	0	32	229	14	210	5	0
McLean	797	1	0	0	0	1	7	0	5	2	0
McLeansboro	2,760	4	0	1	0	3	38	2	35	1	0
Melrose Park	24,863	74	0	14	17	43	317	66	198	53	2
Mendota	7,020	11	0	3	3	5	60	9	48	3	0
Metropolis	5,986	33	0	12	2	19	265	57	194	14	1
Midlothian	14,433	21	1	1	11	8	295	55	199	41	0
Milan	5,012	21	0	2	3	16	75	24	47	4	0
Milledgeville	945	1	0	1	0	0	6	1	5	0	0
Millstadt	3,869	16	0	2	1	13	20	6	14	0	0
Minier	1,188	1	0	0	0	1	9	4	4	1	0
Mokena	20,573	16	0	3	3	10	306	30	244	32	0
Moline	41,701	219	1	36	26	156	978	190	727	61	3

Table 8. Offenses Known to Law Enforcement, by Selected State and City, 2019—Continued

(Number.)

State/city	Population	Violent crime	Murder and nonnegligent manslaughter	Rape[1]	Robbery	Aggravated assault	Property crime	Burglary	Larceny-theft	Motor vehicle theft	Arson[2]
Momence	3,089	1	0	0	0	1	48	4	41	3	0
Monee	5,118	4	1	1	0	2	75	19	50	6	0
Monmouth	8,944	23	0	7	0	16	175	43	124	8	2
Montgomery	19,927	30	0	8	3	19	269	24	233	12	3
Monticello	5,577	12	0	1	0	11	27	8	18	1	0
Morris	15,083	17	1	5	3	8	284	22	256	6	1
Morrison	4,026	19	0	3	1	15	64	16	43	5	3
Morrisonville	1,003	1	0	0	0	1	2	0	2	0	0
Morton	16,209	30	0	2	2	26	77	12	63	2	0
Morton Grove	22,904	19	1	0	3	15	194	41	129	24	0
Mount Carmel	6,988	8	0	0	3	5	127	16	110	1	0
Mount Morris	2,786	1	0	0	0	1	23	2	20	1	0
Mount Olive	1,941	3	0	1	0	2	29	5	24	0	0
Mount Prospect	54,089	29	0	10	9	10	464	42	408	14	2
Mount Pulaski	1,471	0	0	0	0	0	14	8	6	0	0
Mount Vernon	14,802	214	3	18	17	176	731	102	608	21	8
Mount Zion	5,799	11	0	6	0	5	60	9	47	4	0
Moweaqua	1,715	0	0	0	0	0	1	0	0	1	0
Mundelein	31,260	23	0	5	3	15	222	18	194	10	0
Murphysboro	7,417	54	0	2	5	47	115	31	82	2	0
Neoga	1,608	3	0	0	0	3	9	1	6	2	0
New Athens[4]	1,885	2	0	1	0	1	10	4	5	1	
New Baden	3,252	2	0	0	1	1	19	0	17	2	1
New Berlin	1,324	0	0	0	0	0	5	2	2	1	0
New Lenox	27,103	29	0	15	0	14	383	21	342	20	1
Newton	2,855	15	0	4	0	11	19	4	13	2	0
Niles	29,104	36	0	5	15	16	624	70	542	12	0
Nokomis	2,110	9	0	2	0	7	33	9	22	2	0
Normal	55,013	152	2	41	23	86	936	102	790	44	3
Norridge	14,244	13	0	0	4	9	402	29	360	13	0
North Aurora	18,317	26	0	3	2	21	257	36	216	5	1
Northbrook	33,158	9	0	4	4	1	480	58	402	20	1
Northfield	5,418	2	0	0	0	2	61	7	50	4	1
Northlake	12,223	20	0	4	5	11	277	20	242	15	0
North Pekin	1,526	1	0	0	0	1	13	0	13	0	0
North Riverside[6]	6,466	37	0	0	6	31		5		10	0
North Utica	1,345	0	0	0	0	0	0	0	0	0	0
Oak Brook	8,096	6	0	3	1	2	468	15	433	20	0
Oakbrook Terrace	2,120	11	0	3	4	4	109	9	96	4	0
Oak Forest	27,336	51	2	9	15	25	283	57	186	40	0
Oak Lawn	55,361	83	0	11	26	46	826	95	719	12	3
Oak Park	52,311	156	0	13	95	48	1,594	244	1,280	70	3
Oakwood	1,496	1	0	0	0	1	11	1	8	2	0
Oblong	1,368	8	0	0	0	8	23	10	13	0	1
O'Fallon	29,686	53	1	12	8	32	423	41	367	15	1
Okawville	1,362	5	0	0	1	4	16	4	10	2	0
Olney	8,800	35	0	10	0	25	205	47	155	3	1
Olympia Fields	4,821	13	0	4	7	2	490	11	471	8	0
Onarga	1,276	1	0	1	0	0	8	7	1	0	1
Orion	1,790	1	0	0	0	1	9	1	8	0	0
Orland Hills	7,066	1	0	0	0	1	25	0	23	2	0
Orland Park	58,519	26	1	2	9	14	948	35	887	26	0
Oswego	35,856	23	0	7	6	10	339	15	318	6	0
Ottawa	18,047	27	2	0	0	25	273	28	240	5	2
Palatine	67,984	42	0	13	9	20	308	31	266	11	2
Palestine	1,272	3	0	0	0	3	22	9	13	0	0
Palos Heights	12,639	5	0	1	1	3	102	6	84	12	0
Palos Hills	17,158	19	0	3	1	15	113	19	81	13	0
Palos Park	4,768	1	0	0	0	1	16	1	14	1	0
Paris	8,288	68	0	5	4	59	155	83	60	12	5
Park City	7,442	19	2	10	1	6	90	13	70	7	0
Park Forest	21,358	85	1	16	29	39	323	70	210	43	3
Park Ridge	37,206	11	1	2	4	4	295	36	245	14	0
Pawnee	2,640	3	0	1	0	2	6	4	2	0	0
Paxton	4,196	12	0	3	0	9	42	8	32	2	0
Pekin	32,033	132	0	18	8	106	618	102	490	26	3
Peoria	110,955	1,158	25	65	268	800	4,160	758	2,959	443	41
Peoria Heights	5,742	30	0	11	2	17	65	25	22	18	0
Peotone	4,135	0	0	0	0	0	41	8	20	13	0
Peru	9,738	19	0	7	1	11	162	13	149	0	2
Petersburg	2,214	1	0	0	0	1	21	1	17	3	0
Phoenix	1,919	12	0	0	1	11	49	9	28	12	0
Pierron	548	0	0	0	0	0	0	0	0	0	0
Pinckneyville	5,404	11	0	0	0	11	26	5	21	0	0
Pingree Grove	9,765	6	0	5	0	1	52	5	46	1	0
Pittsfield	4,228	5	1	1	0	3	44	4	38	2	3
Plainfield	44,691	55	0	16	4	35	252	25	208	19	1
Plano[4]	11,772		0		5	13	71	16	55	0	1
Pleasant Hill	924	1	1	0	0	0	1	0	1	0	1
Pleasant Plains	794	0	0	0	0	0	3	1	2	0	0
Polo	2,180	5	0	2	0	3	16	2	12	2	0
Pontiac	11,211	28	0	0	1	27	148	25	119	4	0
Pontoon Beach	5,648	18	0	3	0	15	69	13	48	8	0

Table 8. Offenses Known to Law Enforcement, by Selected State and City, 2019—Continued

(Number.)

State/city	Population	Violent crime	Murder and nonnegligent manslaughter	Rape[1]	Robbery	Aggravated assault	Property crime	Burglary	Larceny-theft	Motor vehicle theft	Arson[2]
Posen	5,834	17	0	2	9	6	71	15	38	18	0
Potomac	696	2	0	0	0	2	5	3	1	1	0
Princeton	7,500	11	0	3	0	8	139	10	128	1	0
Prophetstown	1,941	0	0	0	0	0	0	0	0	0	0
Prospect Heights	15,982	17	1	4	1	11	79	16	60	3	1
Quincy	39,954	243	3	54	12	174	1,210	191	977	42	6
Rankin	516	0	0	0	0	0	0	0	0	0	0
Rantoul	12,657	32	0	15	14	3	317	58	246	13	0
Raymond	941	0	0	0	0	0	0	0	0	0	0
Red Bud	3,505	8	0	0	0	8	13	5	8	0	0
Richmond	1,921	3	0	1	0	2	20	5	13	2	0
Richton Park	13,375	60	0	13	21	26	295	35	227	33	0
Ridge Farm	817	0	0	0	0	0	7	2	5	0	0
Riverdale	13,161	114	4	11	50	49	354	93	189	72	0
River Forest	10,869	12	0	0	4	8	232	26	195	11	0
River Grove	9,946	32	1	7	5	19	159	41	103	15	0
Riverside	8,616	9	0	5	3	1	90	19	67	4	0
Riverton	3,398	27	0	1	0	26	82	21	56	5	1
Riverwoods	3,585	1	0	1	0	0	21	4	16	1	0
Robbins	5,479	49	1	7	13	28	64	13	28	23	2
Rochelle	9,048	22	1	11	3	7	109	20	84	5	1
Rochester	3,714	4	0	1	2	1	23	1	22	0	0
Rockdale	1,924	9	0	0	0	9	13	4	7	2	0
Rock Falls	8,744	7	0	0	0	7	79	29	49	1	0
Rockford	145,719	1,711	14	125	282	1,290	4,848	1,001	3,458	389	70
Rock Island	37,517	139	1	14	29	95	878	166	599	113	5
Rockton	7,436	8	0	7	0	1	128	5	121	2	1
Rolling Meadows	23,703	19	0	2	5	12	253	16	229	8	2
Romeoville	39,616	78	1	16	18	43	402	38	335	29	2
Roscoe	10,492	11	0	1	0	10	64	12	49	3	0
Roselle	22,642	16	1	7	3	5	146	14	122	10	1
Rosemont	4,094	36	0	16	6	14	504	11	488	5	0
Rossville	1,223	1	0	0	0	1	14	6	6	2	0
Round Lake	18,266	16	0	1	3	12	120	17	96	7	0
Round Lake Beach	27,228	40	0	8	9	23	553	20	507	26	0
Round Lake Heights	2,662	4	0	1	0	3	24	3	17	4	0
Roxana	1,439	9	0	6	0	3	25	1	24	0	0
Royalton	1,116	2	0	0	0	2	6	1	5	0	0
Ruma	307	1	0	0	0	1	2	0	2	0	0
Rushville	2,867	5	0	0	0	5	71	14	57	0	0
Salem	7,053	21	0	7	2	12	334	34	288	12	0
Sandoval	1,207	7	0	3	1	3	34	12	18	4	25
Sandwich	7,364	12	0	2	1	9	25	5	18	2	0
San Jose	602	0	0	0	0	0	1	0	0	1	0
Sauget	164	3	0	0	2	1	66	12	31	23	0
Sauk Village	10,319	566	2	8	66	490	227	52	156	19	1
Savanna	2,767	25	0	4	1	20	71	19	50	2	0
Schaumburg	73,412	73	2	29	21	21	1,561	100	1,396	65	1
Schiller Park	11,480	26	0	1	6	19	192	18	163	11	1
Shawneetown	1,116	1	0	0	0	1	13	4	9	0	1
Sherman	4,753	4	0	0	0	4	27	5	22	0	0
Shiloh	13,177	13	0	3	2	8	189	14	167	8	1
Shorewood	17,606	25	0	12	2	11	150	11	127	12	0
Sidell	570	0	0	0	0	0	1	0	1	0	0
Silvis	7,538	53	0	4	1	48	168	28	128	12	0
Skokie	63,082	150	1	18	58	73	1,870	188	1,619	63	1
Sleepy Hollow	3,273	0	0	0	0	0	11	2	9	0	0
Smithton	3,836	0	0	0	0	0	15	3	12	0	0
Somonauk	1,870	0	0	0	0	0	2	0	2	0	0
South Barrington	5,047	1	0	0	0	1	32	9	22	1	0
South Beloit	7,636	13	0	1	1	11	142	16	117	9	0
South Chicago Heights	4,029	18	0	5	3	10	163	11	143	9	0
South Elgin	23,634	16	0	4	1	11	104	12	88	4	1
South Holland	21,438	77	0	30	31	16	574	89	353	132	3
South Pekin	1,088	4	0	0	0	4	21	5	13	3	0
South Roxana	1,991	8	0	4	2	2	49	21	23	5	0
Springfield	114,393	889	9	108	208	564	5,080	1,039	3,776	265	24
Spring Grove	5,702	3	0	0	0	3	18	2	15	1	0
Spring Valley	5,156	13	1	6	1	5	37	4	33	0	0
Stanford	586	1	0	0	0	1	2	1	1	0	0
St. Charles	33,118	43	0	10	2	31	208	30	167	11	0
Steger	9,301	38	0	10	6	22	227	44	171	12	2
St. Elmo	1,389	1	0	0	0	1	19	4	15	0	0
Sterling	14,510	26	1	13	3	9	491	45	416	30	3
Stickney	6,599	4	0	1	2	1	50	6	41	3	0
Stockton	1,707	2	0	0	0	2	12	4	8	0	0
Stone Park	4,831	23	0	6	4	13	55	11	42	2	0
Streamwood	39,529	60	0	18	13	29	415	55	342	18	1
Streator	13,100	36	0	31	1	4	271	16	248	7	1
Sullivan	4,487	52	0	1	0	51	51	0	49	2	0
Summit	11,205	54	0	13	18	23	175	23	128	24	1
Sumner	2,949	5	0	1	0	4	12	6	4	2	0
Swansea	13,432	20	0	7	6	7	216	27	174	15	1

Table 8. Offenses Known to Law Enforcement, by Selected State and City, 2019—Continued

(Number.)

State/city	Population	Violent crime	Murder and nonnegligent manslaughter	Rape[1]	Robbery	Aggravated assault	Property crime	Burglary	Larceny-theft	Motor vehicle theft	Arson[2]
Sycamore	18,154	22	0	5	1	16	200	10	186	4	2
Taylorville	10,398	11	1	0	1	9	166	42	123	1	0
Thayer	658	1	0	0	0	1	2	0	2	0	0
Thomasboro	1,094	1	0	0	0	1	9	2	7	0	0
Thornton	2,423	4	0	4	0	0	34	5	27	2	0
Tilton	2,638	8	0	2	1	5	88	20	66	2	0
Tinley Park	56,119	22	0	6	7	9	712	75	592	45	0
Tolono	3,447	2	0	2	0	0	20	7	13	0	0
Toluca	1,267	1	0	0	0	1	8	2	5	1	0
Tower Lakes	1,230	0	0	0	0	0	0	0	0	0	0
Trenton	2,593	2	0	0	0	2	10	3	7	0	0
Troy	10,345	15	0	11	0	4	73	5	62	6	0
Tuscola	4,336	15	0	2	0	13	54	15	33	6	1
Union	553	0	0	0	0	0	0	0	0	0	0
Urbana	42,080	124	1	30	36	57	1,090	161	890	39	5
Valmeyer	1,244	0	0	0	0	0	5	1	4	0	0
Vandalia	6,664	26	0	6	3	17	120	24	95	1	1
Vernon Hills	26,847	18	0	5	7	6	435	13	412	10	0
Vienna	1,443	0	0	0	0	0	12	3	8	1	0
Villa Park	21,651	34	0	10	7	17	295	17	263	15	1
Viola	889	0	0	0	0	0	0	0	0	0	0
Virden	3,333	10	0	4	0	6	93	15	74	4	1
Warren	1,301	1	0	1	0	0	2	1	1	0	0
Warrensburg	1,124	3	0	0	0	3	4	0	4	0	0
Warrenville	13,268	10	0	2	7	1	90	14	70	6	0
Washington	16,897	27	0	9	1	17	168	19	147	2	0
Watseka	4,809	16	1	8	3	4	138	25	102	11	0
Waukegan	86,505	331	1	20	127	183	1,929	350	1,498	81	20
Waverly	1,200	0	0	0	0	0	10	9	1	0	0
Wayne	2,426	1	0	0	0	1	4	0	4	0	0
Westchester	16,224	19	1	2	5	11	148	43	105	0	1
West Chicago	27,019	38	0	13	7	18	219	35	172	12	0
West City	640	1	0	0	0	1	78	4	70	4	0
West Dundee	8,388	3	0	3	0	0	108	7	98	3	0
Western Springs	13,460	3	0	0	0	3	131	14	112	5	0
Westfield	556	0	0	0	0	0	2	1	1	0	0
Westmont	24,642	16	0	3	2	11	317	50	248	19	1
Westville	2,964	18	0	4	3	11	54	20	33	1	0
Wheaton	53,160	44	1	12	5	26	611	51	551	9	2
Wheeling	39,028	29	0	9	5	15	418	41	363	14	1
Willow Springs	5,658	2	0	1	0	1	53	4	49	0	0
Wilmette	27,289	9	0	2	1	6	220	32	181	7	0
Winnebago	2,963	1	0	0	0	1	33	3	30	0	0
Winnetka	12,407	1	0	0	0	1	79	13	63	3	0
Witt	847	0	0	0	0	0	2	1	1	0	0
Wood Dale	13,709	13	0	3	3	7	204	14	180	10	0
Woodridge	33,635	37	0	10	10	17	301	78	201	22	3
Woodstock	25,324	18	0	7	2	9	285	19	254	12	1
Worth	10,534	31	0	14	6	11	70	30	32	8	1
Yates City	653	0	0	0	0	0	4	0	4	0	0
Yorkville	20,541	28	0	16	5	7	142	13	124	5	0
Zion	23,617	130	2	32	25	71	640	96	461	83	8
INDIANA											
Anderson	54,899	242	4	62	62	114	2,096	375	1,526	195	
Bedford	13,271	28	0	3	1	24	293	34	238	21	0
Bluffton[5]	10,134	9	0	2	5	2	163	17	138	8	0
Brownsburg	27,005	40	0	2	6	32	255	25	206	24	3
Carmel	95,388	30	3	9	9	9	807	56	684	67	
Chesterton	13,929	9	0	5	0	4	125	15	101	9	
Clarksville	21,630	118	0	5	8	105	1,263	80	1,102	81	
Clinton	4,701	42	0	0	1	41	127	23	103	1	0
Columbia City	9,203	12	0	4	0	8	137	6	124	7	0
Columbus	47,991	67	0	40	17	10	1,439	130	1,254	55	6
Crawfordsville	16,136	65	3	8	3	51	345	53	269	23	2
Crown Point	30,341	7	0	1	2	4	290	3	271	16	0
Cumberland[5]	5,894	11	0	0	8	3	220	18	192	10	
East Chicago	27,717	201	7	8	78	108	1,094	80	859	155	2
Edinburgh[5]	4,590	29	0	2	1	26	221	14	202	5	0
Ellettsville	6,731	10	0	3	1	6	85	18	61	6	0
Elwood	8,379	24	0	9	3	12	170	29	128	13	3
Evansville	117,700	721	11	90	153	467	4,917	588	3,926	403	44
Fairmount	2,754	9	0	1	0	8	17	13	4	0	0
Fishers	95,506	51	0	10	9	32	734	49	636	49	7
Fort Wayne	269,366	974	26	145	357	446	7,437	990	5,879	568	49
Franklin[5]	25,443	94	0	13	5	76	516	48	436	32	0
Gary	74,687	414	57	21	175	161	2,656	567	1,599	490	21
Greenfield	22,800	21	0	5	6	10	304	31	247	26	3
Greenwood	59,797	97	1	9	26	61	1,528	72	1,332	124	1
Griffith	15,957	11	2	4	4	1	286	26	227	33	0
Hagerstown	1,670	11	0	4	0	7	4	2	2	0	
Hammond	75,201	315	9	27	110	169	2,792	334	2,194	264	13
Hartford City	5,716	15	0	0	0	15	33	8	22	3	0

Table 8. Offenses Known to Law Enforcement, by Selected State and City, 2019—Continued

(Number.)

State/city	Population	Violent crime	Murder and nonnegligent manslaughter	Rape[1]	Robbery	Aggravated assault	Property crime	Burglary	Larceny-theft	Motor vehicle theft	Arson[2]
Highland[5]	22,220	19	0	3	11	5	393	37	344	12	1
Hobart[5]	27,880	39	0	10	20	9	964	50	863	51	0
Jasper	15,629	48	0	4	0	44	189	26	149	14	1
Jeffersonville	47,723	114	1	19	22	72	1,341	138	994	209	7
Kokomo	57,845	392	5	25	48	314	1,493	312	1,081	100	1
Lafayette	72,585	352	5	38	55	254	2,388	387	1,844	157	7
La Porte	21,557	116	1	8	10	97	464	79	343	42	0
Lawrence	49,432	178	4	16	78	80	1,087	157	743	187	3
Ligonier	4,371	1	0	0	0	1	25	2	13	10	
Loogootee	2,717	7	0	0	0	7	9	0	8	1	0
Marion	27,829	103	4	5	30	64	870	102	709	59	0
Merrillville[5]	34,724	50	3	15	19	13	580	67	443	70	0
Munster[5]	22,412	22	0	3	13	6	329	31	278	20	1
New Haven	15,821	47	2	6	15	24	326	42	244	40	3
New Whiteland[5]	6,242	3	0	0	1	2	44	7	35	2	1
Noblesville	64,567	32	0	16	7	9	618	29	552	37	0
Plainfield[5]	35,317	50	0	2	7	41	634	59	516	59	
Plymouth	9,872	13	0	6	2	5	222	10	200	12	0
Portage	36,800	73	1	10	5	57	583	55	493	35	
Porter	4,821	8	0	1	0	7	23	3	19	1	0
Portland	6,069	12	0	3	0	9	65	0	65	0	0
Rensselaer	5,820	12	0	1	3	8	203	30	173	0	0
Sellersburg	8,949	5	0	2	2	1	76	13	49	14	0
Seymour	19,941	41	2	9	3	27	868	83	724	61	1
Shelbyville	19,362	146	0	3	6	137	407	48	325	34	0
South Bend	101,944	1,357	14	56	267	1,020	4,296	867	2,868	561	75
Speedway	12,202	38	1	1	22	14	486	43	395	48	0
St. John[5]	18,478	4	0	1	3	0	124	11	105	8	0
Tipton	5,074	9	0	1	1	7	34	6	27	1	0
Westfield	43,212	16	0	6	6	4	338	13	313	12	1
West Lafayette	49,154	32	0	5	3	24	357	42	304	11	0
Westville	5,619	12	0	1	0	11	38	5	32	1	0
Whitestown	9,810	22	0	2	1	19	114	2	98	14	0
Zionsville	27,630	4	0	0	0	4	78	4	67	7	0
IOWA											
Adel	5,136	11	0	3	0	8	110	23	73	14	0
Albia	3,725	14	0	3	0	11	64	22	36	6	1
Algona	5,413	21	0	0	0	21	30	6	19	5	0
Ames	68,237	135	1	44	21	69	1,171	138	975	58	2
Atlantic	6,514	22	0	2	0	20	182	31	144	7	2
Audubon	1,883	6	0	4	0	2	31	4	26	1	0
Bettendorf	36,972	46	1	8	7	30	474	62	375	37	0
Bloomfield	2,700	4	0	0	0	4	21	4	14	3	0
Boone	12,448	36	0	2	0	34	141	23	107	11	2
Carlisle	4,334	7	0	2	0	5	42	9	32	1	0
Carroll	9,775	9	0	2	1	6	175	27	142	6	2
Cedar Rapids	134,007	345	2	27	83	233	4,470	837	3,268	365	13
Centerville	5,459	13	0	2	1	10	129	35	88	6	0
Charles City	7,334	8	1	2	1	4	71	15	55	1	0
Clarinda	5,352	24	0	5	1	18	83	12	59	12	0
Clarion	2,729	2	0	0	0	2	32	10	15	7	0
Clear Lake	7,555	31	0	0	0	31	132	29	100	3	0
Clinton	24,982	77	0	11	12	54	911	182	685	44	3
Clive	17,305	7	0	1	2	4	121	10	93	18	0
Coralville	22,035	69	3	10	15	41	689	49	613	27	3
Council Bluffs	62,427	493	6	39	57	391	3,649	529	2,629	491	22
Creston	7,784	26	0	2	0	24	164	40	117	7	1
Davenport	102,392	609	2	84	124	399	3,918	745	2,830	343	17
Decorah	7,529	9	0	4	0	5	74	2	70	2	1
Denison	8,415	19	0	5	0	14	58	10	35	13	0
Des Moines	218,384	1,555	14	117	283	1,141	8,933	2,284	5,336	1,313	53
DeWitt	5,153	8	0	3	0	5	104	24	65	15	1
Dubuque	57,973	110	0	34	9	67	949	138	747	64	12
Dyersville	4,245	5	0	0	0	5	29	12	16	1	0
Eldridge	6,972	2	0	0	1	1	42	10	27	5	0
Emmetsburg	3,691	8	0	0	0	8	32	16	15	1	0
Estherville	5,609	9	0	0	0	9	31	9	18	4	0
Evansdale	4,758	18	0	1	0	17	101	29	59	13	0
Forest City	4,036	7	0	3	0	4	9	3	5	1	0
Fort Dodge	23,973	101	2	15	12	72	724	117	566	41	6
Fort Madison	10,392	69	0	8	0	61	205	38	152	15	2
Glenwood	5,321	26	0	4	0	22	65	15	43	7	0
Grinnell	9,333	39	0	24	0	15	167	16	149	2	0
Hampton	4,207	4	0	0	0	4	16	2	14	0	0
Harlan	4,796	7	0	2	0	5	9	2	6	1	2
Hawarden	2,479	8	0	3	0	5	6	3	3	0	1
Hiawatha	7,441	28	0	1	0	27	113	24	81	8	3
Humboldt	4,578	0	0	0	0	0	48	3	41	4	0
Independence	6,086	22	0	0	2	20	80	20	53	7	1
Indianola	16,235	115	0	28	2	85	316	57	238	21	6
Iowa City	77,390	167	1	40	25	101	1,252	314	867	71	2
Iowa Falls	5,006	11	0	3	0	8	83	4	73	6	0

Table 8. Offenses Known to Law Enforcement, by Selected State and City, 2019—Continued

(Number.)

State/city	Population	Violent crime	Murder and nonnegligent manslaughter	Rape[1]	Robbery	Aggravated assault	Property crime	Burglary	Larceny-theft	Motor vehicle theft	Arson[2]
Jefferson	4,123	3	0	0	0	3	42	4	38	0	0
Johnston	22,708	29	0	6	1	22	272	55	194	23	4
Lake City	1,649	8	0	0	0	8	16	1	15	0	0
Lansing	941	1	0	0	0	1	22	4	17	1	0
Le Mars	10,018	24	0	5	0	19	166	30	122	14	1
Manchester	4,958	10	0	2	0	8	86	17	63	6	1
Maquoketa	5,972	15	0	2	0	13	138	27	98	13	1
Marion	40,612	68	0	9	4	55	519	119	350	50	1
Marshalltown	27,002	105	0	19	4	82	674	176	445	53	12
Mason City	26,976	176	0	20	1	155	789	116	617	56	3
Missouri Valley	2,609	13	0	2	0	11	45	10	33	2	0
Monticello	3,898	6	0	3	1	2	51	11	37	3	0
Mount Pleasant	8,749	12	0	0	0	12	155	38	110	7	0
Mount Vernon	4,449	2	0	2	0	0	29	8	19	2	1
Muscatine	23,823	47	0	6	2	39	320	71	221	28	4
Nevada	6,744	28	0	3	1	24	85	25	52	8	0
North Liberty	20,086	70	0	20	0	50	121	21	97	3	0
Norwalk	11,871	4	0	1	0	3	89	12	72	5	1
Oelwein	5,886	18	0	0	0	18	91	24	62	5	0
Onawa	2,762	11	0	4	0	7	33	6	20	7	1
Osage	3,538	4	0	1	0	3	7	4	3	0	0
Osceola	5,224	24	0	5	0	19	125	30	84	11	0
Oskaloosa	11,415	54	0	7	4	43	204	54	131	19	0
Ottumwa	24,488	134	2	18	5	109	1,009	182	748	79	11
Pella	10,334	10	0	8	0	2	128	7	110	11	0
Perry	7,421	20	0	3	1	16	91	17	70	4	0
Polk City	5,013	1	0	0	0	1	25	2	20	3	0
Postville	2,065	4	0	1	1	2	43	5	37	1	0
Prairie City	1,736	1	0	0	0	1	3	2	1	0	0
Red Oak	5,287	33	0	7	0	26	123	39	75	9	0
Sac City	2,056	2	0	1	0	1	35	5	28	2	0
Sergeant Bluff	4,993	9	0	0	0	9	43	9	30	4	0
Shenandoah	4,859	7	1	0	0	6	41	12	26	3	0
Sioux Center	7,688	3	0	2	0	1	21	1	19	1	0
Sioux City	82,339	366	2	50	57	257	3,203	645	2,310	248	15
Spencer	11,008	7	0	6	1	0	183	42	135	6	0
Spirit Lake	5,097	30	0	4	0	26	72	13	53	6	0
Storm Lake	10,430	41	0	7	0	34	169	27	131	11	6
Story City	3,362	7	0	2	0	5	41	3	33	5	0
Tama	2,730	21	0	2	0	19	22	8	11	3	0
Urbandale	44,541	28	0	7	3	18	455	54	365	36	1
Vinton	5,074	10	0	1	0	9	32	8	21	3	0
Washington	7,315	48	0	8	0	40	132	22	102	8	0
Waterloo	67,723	306	1	12	38	255	1,682	515	1,038	129	14
Waukee	24,255	15	0	8	1	6	184	28	143	13	1
Waukon	3,654	10	0	0	0	10	77	15	60	2	0
Waverly[4]	10,187	44	0	5	0	39			83	6	0
Webster City	7,684	32	0	5	1	26	84	20	48	16	1
West Burlington[4]	2,882	16	0	0	2	14			189	5	1
Williamsburg	3,159	4	0	0	0	4	25	8	17	0	0
Windsor Heights	4,896	13	0	5	2	6	265	13	240	12	0
KANSAS											
Abilene	6,235	10	0	2	1	7	85	14	62	9	0
Alma	773	0	0	0	0	0	0	0	0	0	0
Alta Vista	419	0	0	0	0	0	0	0	0	0	0
Anthony	2,081	8	0	3	0	5	24	11	12	1	1
Arkansas City	11,718	65	0	11	5	49	434	81	326	27	1
Arma	1,427	5	0	0	0	5	17	4	12	1	0
Atchison	10,509	41	0	6	0	35	280	32	236	12	0
Attica	556	4	0	0	0	4	10	2	8	0	0
Atwood	1,204	6	0	1	1	4	21	5	13	3	1
Augusta	9,334	29	1	3	2	23	329	32	272	25	0
Basehor	6,418	1	0	0	0	1	55	10	41	4	1
Baxter Springs	3,907	6	0	2	0	4	90	20	59	11	0
Bel Aire	8,252	11	0	1	1	9	126	13	97	16	0
Belleville	1,877	1	0	0	0	1	25	7	16	2	1
Beloit	3,715	8	0	2	0	6	50	17	27	6	0
Bonner Springs	7,850	20	0	2	0	18	150	15	114	21	1
Bronson	308	0	0	0	0	0	0	0	0	0	0
Burlington	2,545	9	0	1	0	8	33	13	19	1	0
Carbondale	1,371	0	0	0	0	0	29	8	19	2	0
Cheney	2,181	2	0	0	0	2	31	6	23	2	0
Cherryvale	2,127	5	0	2	1	2	37	12	18	7	1
Claflin	608	0	0	0	0	0	4	0	4	0	0
Clay Center	3,946	23	0	1	0	22	89	15	66	8	0
Clearwater	2,550	4	0	0	0	4	34	5	28	1	0
Coffeyville	9,260	60	1	10	5	44	325	69	234	22	4
Colby	5,305	14	0	1	0	13	75	8	61	6	1
Colony	410	1	0	0	0	1	2	2	0	0	0
Columbus	3,042	4	0	0	1	3	49	12	32	5	2
Concordia	4,904	40	0	4	0	36	92	13	73	6	2
Derby[6]	25,012	25	0	12	1	12		32		32	2

Table 8. Offenses Known to Law Enforcement, by Selected State and City, 2019—Continued

(Number.)

State/city	Population	Violent crime	Murder and nonnegligent manslaughter	Rape[1]	Robbery	Aggravated assault	Property crime	Burglary	Larceny-theft	Motor vehicle theft	Arson[2]
Dodge City	27,314	129	0	13	9	107	613	85	474	54	
Edwardsville	4,505	22	0	4	1	17	112	16	86	10	4
El Dorado	12,899	17	0	3	5	9	361	102	225	34	1
Elkhart	1,775	4	0	1	0	3	16	4	12	0	2
Ellinwood	1,950	2	0	1	0	1	20	3	14	3	0
Ellsworth	2,983	8	0	1	0	7	16	1	13	2	0
Emporia	24,747	36	0	12	1	23	517	63	436	18	1
Eudora	6,414	13	0	5	0	8	61	9	50	2	0
Fort Scott	7,729	39	0	2	2	35	78	3	68	7	0
Frontenac	3,406	7	0	2	0	5	63	10	47	6	0
Galena	2,848	6	0	0	0	6	65	16	38	11	0
Garden City[4]	26,509	130	1	33	11	85			451	42	4
Garden Plain	907	0	0	0	0	0	8	3	5	0	0
Gardner	22,229	32	0	5	3	24	175	7	149	19	2
Garnett	3,244	7	1	0	0	6	67	21	40	6	0
Goddard	4,764	4	0	0	0	4	33	3	28	2	0
Goessel	496	0	0	0	0	0	3	0	3	0	0
Goodland	4,374	15	0	2	0	13	80	10	67	3	0
Grandview Plaza	1,563	18	0	1	0	17	21	6	15	0	1
Halstead	2,018	1	0	0	0	1	11	1	7	3	0
Haven	1,189	1	0	1	0	0	18	2	15	1	1
Havensville	157	0	0	0	0	0	0	0	0	0	0
Hays	20,894	56	1	8	6	41	358	30	313	15	2
Herington	2,277	7	0	0	0	7	58	12	43	3	0
Hesston	3,736	6	0	0	0	6	30	9	20	1	0
Hiawatha	3,119	8	0	7	0	1	120	22	95	3	0
Highland	999	4	0	3	0	1	4	1	3	0	0
Hillsboro	2,814	2	0	0	0	2	35	8	21	6	0
Hoisington	2,486	6	0	3	0	3	35	9	26	0	1
Holton	3,239	5	0	0	0	5	48	8	37	3	0
Holyrood	419	0	0	0	0	0	0	0	0	0	0
Horton	1,679	3	0	1	0	2	22	5	16	1	0
Hutchinson	40,431	153	1	25	20	107	1,290	259	970	61	11
Independence	8,497	84	1	6	6	71	399	93	293	13	3
Inman	1,327	5	0	0	0	5	10	4	6	0	0
Iola	5,265	23	0	4	1	18	170	39	119	12	0
Junction City	21,921	219	2	24	16	177	554	106	425	23	7
Kanopolis	457	0	0	0	0	0	1	1	0	0	0
Kingman	2,874	10	0	0	0	10	42	10	27	5	0
La Harpe	523	0	0	0	0	0	0	0	0	0	0
Lake Quivira	942	0	0	0	0	0	4	0	4	0	0
Lansing	12,051	32	0	3	1	28	61	11	45	5	3
Larned	3,739	15	0	3	0	12	29	7	22	0	0
Leawood	35,052	19	1	4	0	14	401	57	316	28	0
Lebo	889	0	0	0	0	0	4	0	4	0	0
Lenexa	56,240	87	0	17	4	66	761	69	606	86	0
Le Roy	538	0	0	0	0	0	0	0	0	0	0
Lindsborg	3,269	1	0	1	0	0	43	5	36	2	0
Little River	518	0	0	0	0	0	0	0	0	0	0
Louisburg	4,532	6	0	1	1	4	42	4	34	4	0
Lyndon	1,016	5	0	0	0	5	18	4	13	1	0
Macksville	530	0	0	0	0	0	1	0	1	0	0
Maize	4,836	8	0	1	0	7	57	11	41	5	1
Marion	1,770	1	0	0	0	1	20	3	17	0	0
Mayetta	349	0	0	0	0	0	1	0	1	0	0
McLouth	839	1	0	0	0	1	3	1	1	1	0
McPherson	13,070	24	0	6	0	18	234	30	198	6	1
Meade	1,546	6	0	1	1	4	12	4	8	0	0
Merriam	11,197	43	0	6	7	30	484	27	388	69	0
Minneapolis	1,920	3	0	0	0	3	25	5	18	2	0
Mission Hills	3,588	1	0	0	0	1	44	14	21	9	0
Montezuma	961	0	0	0	0	0	0	0	0	0	0
Mound City	685	0	0	0	0	0	0	0	0	0	0
Mulberry	522	0	0	0	0	0	14	4	10	0	0
Mulvane	6,451	15	0	2	1	12	122	14	103	5	0
Neodesha	2,289	7	0	1	0	6	20	5	14	1	0
Newton	18,697	91	1	21	9	60	415	77	316	22	7
North Newton	1,752	0	0	0	0	0	7	2	5	0	0
Norton	2,754	6	0	1	1	4	42	11	28	3	1
Olathe[5]	141,371	290	4	76	35	175	1,604	123	1,290	191	8
Osage City	2,807	19	0	0	0	19	28	9	15	4	0
Osawatomie	4,245	13	0	2	1	10	32	8	22	2	1
Oswego	1,682	1	0	0	0	1	11	2	6	3	0
Ottawa[6]	12,221	28	0	9	1	18		28		14	2
Ozawkie	618	0	0	0	0	0	0	0	0	0	0
Paola	5,676	13	0	3	1	9	76	3	65	8	0
Park City	7,779	18	0	4	2	12	147	33	105	9	1
Peabody	1,098	3	0	2	0	1	27	12	14	1	0
Perry	902	0	0	0	0	0	1	0	1	0	0
Pittsburg[6]	20,168	91	0	17	4	70		71		101	6
Prairie Village	22,508	29	0	2	3	24	243	33	182	28	0
Pratt	6,606	18	0	5	1	12	112	27	81	4	0
Rose Hill	3,969	6	0	1	0	5	32	3	27	2	0

Table 8. Offenses Known to Law Enforcement, by Selected State and City, 2019—Continued

(Number.)

State/city	Population	Violent crime	Murder and nonnegligent manslaughter	Rape[1]	Robbery	Aggravated assault	Property crime	Burglary	Larceny-theft	Motor vehicle theft	Arson[2]
Russell	4,455	18	0	0	2	16	61	21	36	4	1
Salina	46,567	213	2	30	27	154	1,726	212	1,382	132	9
Scott City	3,799	8	0	0	0	8	14	1	13	0	1
Sedgwick	1,635	4	0	1	0	3	16	1	14	1	0
Seneca	2,058	7	0	0	0	7	28	2	26	0	2
Shawnee[6]	66,300	141	1	7	10	123		96		119	7
Spearville	795	0	0	0	0	0					0
Sterling	2,194	3	0	2	0	1	32	13	18	1	0
St. Marys[4]	2,636	1	0	0	0	1			13	2	0
Tonganoxie[4]	5,591	4	0	0	0	4			26	4	0
Topeka	125,655	895	13	74	243	565	6,271	905	4,404	962	3
Troy	969	0	0	0	0	0	4	0	4	0	0
Ulysses	5,709	15	1	0	0	14	36	10	25	1	0
Valley Center	7,376	6	0	4	0	2	38	8	28	2	0
Wamego	4,808	14	0	1	3	10	76	6	61	9	0
Waverly	548	0	0	0	0	0	0	0	0	0	3
Wellington	7,698	29	0	2	0	27	218	41	168	9	0
Wellsville	1,795	4	0	0	0	4	22	2	18	2	0
Wichita	390,080	4,451	35	367	461	3,588	20,759	2,677	15,777	2,305	125
Winfield	12,023	33	1	0	2	30	403	62	309	32	3
KENTUCKY											
Adairville	873	0	0	0	0	0	0	0	0	0	0
Albany	2,001	0	0	0	0	0	3	0	1	2	0
Alexandria	9,692	7	2	0	0	5	112	10	95	7	0
Anchorage	2,443	0	0	0	0	0	10	0	7	3	2
Ashland	20,222	59	3	11	14	31	740	96	608	36	1
Auburn	1,376	1	0	0	0	1	10	4	6	0	1
Audubon Park	1,504	1	0	0	0	1	27	5	20	2	0
Augusta	1,135	1	0	0	0	1	11	2	8	1	0
Barbourville	3,090	8	0	0	2	6	67	33	25	9	5
Bardstown	13,239	15	1	7	2	5	348	62	263	23	5
Bardwell	671	0	0	0	0	0	3	2	1	0	0
Beattyville	1,194	3	0	1	0	2	3	1	1	1	0
Beaver Dam	3,600	1	0	0	0	1	51	0	47	4	0
Bellefonte	827	0	0	0	0	0	0	0	0	0	0
Bellevue	5,749	6	0	1	2	3	78	4	67	7	0
Benton	4,461	4	0	1	1	2	168	16	148	4	0
Berea	16,074	19	0	9	1	9	208	36	141	31	0
Bloomfield	1,063	0	0	0	0	0	1	0	0	1	0
Bowling Green	69,627	203	4	63	55	81	3,250	386	2,610	254	1
Brandenburg	2,902	3	0	0	2	1	62	6	30	26	0
Brodhead	1,182	1	0	0	0	1	7	4	2	1	0
Brownsville	835	0	0	0	0	0	3	0	3	0	0
Burgin	981	0	0	0	0	0	0	0	0	0	0
Burkesville	1,459	0	0	0	0	0	14	2	11	1	0
Burnside	905	1	0	0	1	0	64	14	47	3	0
Cadiz	2,673	5	0	0	2	3	43	9	30	4	0
Calvert City	2,492	0	0	0	0	0	5	0	5	0	0
Campbellsville	11,488	29	0	3	14	12	417	101	286	30	1
Carlisle	1,954	2	0	1	0	1	32	5	21	6	0
Carrollton	3,817	3	0	0	0	3	42	5	31	6	0
Catlettsburg	1,746	2	0	1	0	1	33	9	18	6	0
Cave City	2,451	3	0	2	0	1	0	0	0	0	0
Centertown	432	0	0	0	0	0	1	0	1	0	0
Central City	5,726	9	0	4	1	4	88	7	75	6	0
Clarkson	882	0	0	0	0	0	10	2	5	3	0
Clay City	1,107	0	0	0	0	0	5	2	3	0	0
Clinton	1,249	2	0	0	1	1	22	4	17	1	0
Coal Run Village	1,486	0	0	0	0	0	90	5	80	5	0
Cold Spring	6,509	3	0	0	0	3	26	12	11	3	0
Columbia	4,645	4	0	2	1	1	133	27	88	18	0
Corbin	7,255	9	0	0	2	7					
Covington	40,350	188	2	40	67	79	1,175	199	809	167	3
Crab Orchard	831	0	0	0	0	0	10	0	9	1	0
Cumberland	1,936	2	0	0	1	1	92	9	77	6	1
Cynthiana	6,354	6	0	3	1	2	277	62	182	33	1
Danville	16,873	26	0	8	6	12	46	15	27	4	1
Dawson Springs	2,633	2	0	0	0	2	75	19	44	12	1
Dayton	5,527	5	0	1	2	2	42	4	37	1	0
Dry Ridge	2,229	0	0	0	0	0	32	2	29	1	0
Eddyville	2,525	0	0	0	0	0	60	6	48	6	2
Edgewood	8,749	4	0	1	1	2	28	20	7	1	0
Edmonton	1,567	0	0	0	0	0					3
Elizabethtown	30,383	49	3	13	15	18	452	140	239	73	3
Elkhorn City	889	0	0	0	0	0	0	0	0	0	0
Elkton	2,115	1	0	0	0	1	35	7	22	6	0
Elsmere	8,673	9	0	1	3	5	83	14	58	11	0
Eminence	2,594	1	1	0	0	0					2
Erlanger	23,116	16	0	5	2	9	155	23	108	24	2
Eubank	331	0	0	0	0	0	2	1	1	0	0
Evarts	808	0	0	0	0	0					0
Falmouth	2,089	4	1	0	1	2	27	4	21	2	0

Table 8. Offenses Known to Law Enforcement, by Selected State and City, 2019—Continued

(Number.)

State/city	Population	Violent crime	Murder and nonnegligent manslaughter	Rape[1]	Robbery	Aggravated assault	Property crime	Burglary	Larceny-theft	Motor vehicle theft	Arson[2]
Ferguson	945	0	0	0	0	0	10	2	6	2	0
Flatwoods	7,041	1	0	1	0	0	26	7	12	7	0
Fleming-Neon	673	0	0	0	0	0	0	0	0	0	0
Flemingsburg	2,801	2	0	1	0	1	41	7	32	2	0
Florence	32,848	55	1	12	29	13	1,415	141	1,202	72	1
Fort Mitchell	8,252	7	0	2	2	3	70	7	54	9	1
Fort Thomas	16,386	5	0	1	3	1	84	9	65	10	0
Fort Wright	5,744	4	0	1	2	1	72	7	58	7	0
Frankfort	27,723	81	3	11	23	44	950	181	698	71	5
Franklin	9,036	21	0	9	3	9	250	20	212	18	0
Fulton	2,145	6	0	2	2	2	118	17	100	1	1
Georgetown	35,106	41	0	14	11	16	999	90	821	88	0
Glasgow	14,475	26	0	8	4	14	433	64	339	30	4
Graymoor-Devondale	2,976	1	0	0	0	1	40	5	28	7	1
Grayson	3,923	5	0	3	0	2	73	15	51	7	0
Greensburg	2,087	2	0	1	0	1	28	5	20	3	0
Greenup	1,107	0	0	0	0	0	9	1	4	4	0
Greenville	4,224	5	0	2	1	2	19	4	10	5	0
Guthrie	1,398	0	0	0	0	0	6	2	2	2	0
Hardinsburg	2,346	2	0	0	0	2	28	15	11	2	0
Harlan	1,507	6	0	0	3	3	47	7	38	2	1
Harrodsburg	8,509	9	0	2	0	7	115	43	57	15	1
Hartford	2,749	0	0	0	0	0	16	5	11	0	0
Hawesville	993	0	0	0	0	0	6	2	4	0	0
Hazard	4,938	14	1	3	1	9	144	20	110	14	3
Henderson	28,368	65	2	19	9	35	698	112	490	96	4
Heritage Creek	1,148	0	0	0	0	0	10	0	10	0	0
Hickman	2,128	0	0	0	0	0	2	2	0	0	0
Highland Heights	7,114	5	0	3	0	2	65	5	55	5	1
Hillview	9,235	8	0	2	1	5	112	14	74	24	0
Hodgenville	3,239	4	0	2	1	1	74	26	44	4	0
Hopkinsville	30,895	90	3	19	28	40	1,083	236	783	64	1
Horse Cave	2,402	1	0	0	1	0	12	1	9	2	0
Hurstbourne Acres	1,910	0	0	0	0	0	20	2	17	1	0
Hyden	334	0	0	0	0	0	0	0	0	0	0
Independence	28,541	13	0	5	3	5	125	20	90	15	2
Indian Hills	2,998	0	0	0	0	0	28	2	25	1	0
Irvine	2,307	2	0	0	0	2	9	4	5	0	0
Irvington	1,187	2	0	0	0	2	13	2	4	7	0
Jackson	1,954	0	0	0	0	0	52	8	40	4	0
Jamestown	1,787	0	0	0	0	0	34	9	24	1	0
Jeffersontown	28,015	31	0	7	19	5	596	94	414	88	0
Jenkins	1,930	0	0	0	0	0	0	0	0	0	0
Junction City	2,315	0	0	0	0	0	18	7	9	2	0
La Center	970	0	0	0	0	0	0	0	0	0	0
La Grange	9,080	10	0	1	4	5	157	27	117	13	1
Lakeside Park-Crestview Hills	6,046	3	0	0	2	1	73	3	68	2	0
Lancaster	3,862	8	0	0	0	8	82	25	49	8	0
Lawrenceburg	11,538	4	0	1	0	3	123	35	56	32	1
Lebanon	5,716	12	0	4	1	7	88	20	58	10	1
Lebanon Junction	1,973	1	0	0	1	0	1	0	1	0	0
Leitchfield	6,852	13	0	2	1	10	176	28	132	16	0
Lewisburg	802	0	0	0	0	0	2	1	1	0	0
Lewisport	1,698	0	0	0	0	0	4	2	2	0	0
Lexington	326,070	967	26	175	362	404	9,776	1,537	7,333	906	43
Liberty	2,113	3	0	0	0	3	8	2	5	1	0
Livingston	218	0	0	0	0	0	1	0	1	0	0
London	8,050	5	0	0	2	3	375	63	268	44	0
Louisa	2,365	5	0	0	1	4	11	3	3	5	0
Louisville Metro	675,501	4,640	94	201	1,008	3,337	26,287	4,316	18,037	3,934	7
Loyall	606	0	0	0	0	0	3	2	1	0	0
Ludlow	4,495	9	0	5	2	2	80	17	54	9	0
Madisonville	18,711	17	1	6	5	5	266	62	175	29	5
Manchester	1,318	3	0	1	0	2	23	7	11	5	1
Marion	2,853	2	0	0	0	2	41	1	38	2	0
Martin	552	0	0	0	0	0	3	0	2	1	0
Mayfield	9,851	40	2	11	8	19	433	79	328	26	0
Maysville	8,750	19	0	6	6	7	258	36	207	15	2
McKee	785	0	0	0	0	0	0	0	0	0	0
Meadow Vale	766	0	0	0	0	0	1	1	0	0	0
Middlesboro	9,223	24	0	4	3	17	366	50	284	32	2
Middletown	7,957	6	0	1	3	2	139	14	113	12	0
Millersburg	799	0	0	0	0	0	6	0	6	0	0
Monticello	6,015	9	0	0	4	5	120	24	83	13	1
Morehead	7,736	7	0	5	2	0	166	19	139	8	0
Morganfield	3,387	2	0	0	1	1	49	12	35	2	0
Morgantown	2,402	2	0	2	0	0	15	5	8	2	0
Mount Sterling	7,326	15	0	6	4	5	285	24	247	14	1
Mount Vernon	2,442	0	0	0	0	0	8	2	5	1	2
Mount Washington	14,855	8	0	3	1	4	102	12	76	14	0
Muldraugh	1,000	2	0	0	2	0	24	7	11	6	0
Munfordville	1,663	1	0	0	1	0	14	6	5	3	0
Murray	19,545	20	3	4	4	9	378	65	299	14	0

Table 8. Offenses Known to Law Enforcement, by Selected State and City, 2019—Continued

(Number.)

State/city	Population	Violent crime	Murder and nonnegligent manslaughter	Rape[1]	Robbery	Aggravated assault	Property crime	Burglary	Larceny-theft	Motor vehicle theft	Arson[2]
New Haven	894	0	0	0	0	0	0	0	0	0	0
Newport	14,965	37	1	9	15	12	547	83	422	42	2
Nicholasville	31,188	47	0	11	16	20	758	122	601	35	4
Northfield	1,060	0	0	0	0	0	7	0	7	0	0
Oak Grove	7,359	24	0	5	2	17	312	40	246	26	0
Olive Hill	1,560	1	0	0	0	1	41	9	28	4	1
Owensboro	60,107	135	6	30	33	66	2,432	358	1,874	200	6
Owenton	1,546	0	0	0	0	0	2	0	2	0	0
Owingsville	1,566	1	0	0	0	1	10	2	7	1	0
Paducah	24,832	71	0	16	23	32	1,305	110	1,135	60	8
Paintsville	4,013	4	0	1	0	3	31	4	18	9	1
Paris	9,879	16	0	3	4	9	204	26	167	11	0
Park Hills	2,980	2	0	1	1	0	23	8	10	5	0
Pembroke	893	1	0	0	0	1	4	1	3	0	0
Perryville	754	0	0	0	0	0	0	0	0	0	0
Pewee Valley	1,576	0	0	0	0	0	2	0	2	0	0
Pikeville	6,592	18	0	8	3	7	366	59	295	12	2
Pineville	1,763	2	0	0	1	1	27	8	15	4	0
Pioneer Village	2,945	0	0	0	0	0	21	6	10	5	0
Pippa Passes	677	0	0	0	0	0	0	0	0	0	0
Prestonsburg	3,550	6	0	1	0	5	32	4	21	7	0
Princeton	6,105	9	0	2	1	6	165	26	128	11	0
Prospect	4,954	1	0	0	0	1	45	6	38	1	0
Providence	3,021	0	0	0	0	0	14	3	10	1	0
Raceland	2,337	2	0	2	0	0	15	6	8	1	1
Radcliff	22,998	58	2	15	12	29	789	186	552	51	6
Ravenna	562	0	0	0	0	0	4	1	3	0	0
Richmond	36,458	75	0	22	14	39	804	129	609	66	2
Russell	3,221	5	0	3	1	1	42	5	35	2	0
Russell Springs	2,632	8	0	1	1	6	91	19	62	10	1
Russellville	7,068	15	0	6	2	7	224	39	175	10	0
Sadieville	364	0	0	0	0	0	0	0	0	0	0
Salyersville	1,712	5	0	0	1	4	7	0	4	3	0
Science Hill	697	0	0	0	0	0	3	1	1	1	0
Scottsville	4,520	8	1	0	1	6	151	28	107	16	2
Sebree	1,549	0	0	0	0	0	1	0	0	1	0
Shelbyville	16,531	21	0	6	11	4	294	56	218	20	0
Shepherdsville	12,515	22	0	5	6	11	317	78	184	55	0
Shively	15,845	54	5	9	21	19	531	65	344	122	1
Simpsonville	2,945	6	0	1	1	4	80	3	74	3	0
Smiths Grove	803	0	0	0	0	0	2	0	2	0	0
Somerset	11,519	35	1	6	5	23	258	60	166	32	3
Southgate	3,962	4	0	3	0	1	32	4	23	5	0
South Shore	1,055	0	0	0	0	0	1	0	0	1	0
Springfield	2,965	6	0	1	2	3	31	10	18	3	1
Stamping Ground	802	0	0	0	0	0	3	0	2	1	0
Stanford	3,679	2	0	0	0	2	23	4	11	8	1
Stanton	2,651	2	0	0	0	2	72	30	38	4	2
St. Matthews	18,275	22	0	3	15	4	974	71	823	80	0
Sturgis	1,794	1	0	0	1	0	10	2	7	1	0
Taylor Mill	6,810	2	0	0	0	2	42	5	34	3	0
Taylorsville	1,286	0	0	0	0	0	11	2	9	0	0
Tompkinsville	2,279	5	0	0	0	5	4	1	2	1	0
Trenton	375	0	0	0	0	0	0	0	0	0	0
Uniontown	930	0	0	0	0	0	18	5	11	2	2
Vanceburg	1,387	1	0	0	0	1	10	2	8	0	0
Versailles	26,625	23	0	10	4	9	328	61	245	22	1
Villa Hills	7,465	6	0	1	2	3	83	22	55	6	1
Vine Grove	6,468	3	0	0	1	2	49	14	29	6	0
Warsaw	1,699	0	0	0	0	0	11	2	8	1	0
Wayland	377	0	0	0	0	0	0	0	0	0	0
West Buechel	1,285	6	0	0	4	2	50	6	31	13	0
West Liberty	3,563	2	0	1	0	1	3	1	2	0	0
West Point	870	0	0	0	0	0	7	1	4	2	0
Wheelwright	464	0	0	0	0	0	0	0	0	0	0
Whitesburg	1,845	1	0	0	0	1	3	2	0	1	0
Wilder	3,074	0	0	0	0	0	37	2	31	4	0
Williamsburg	5,298	10	1	3	1	5	54	13	38	3	1
Williamstown	3,946	0	0	0	0	0	25	4	17	4	0
Wilmore	6,489	0	0	0	0	0	76	3	65	8	0
Winchester	18,605	44	0	6	13	25	823	119	621	83	1
Woodburn	381	0	0	0	0	0	8	4	4	0	0
Worthington	1,505	1	0	0	0	1	0	0	0	0	0
LOUISIANA											
Abbeville	12,142	101	1	2	23	75	315	91	222	2	0
Addis	5,747	9	0	0	0	9	1	0	1	0	0
Alexandria	46,630	732	9	16	132	575	4,180	892	3,056	232	0
Baker	13,240	51	1	6	8	36	326	45	271	10	0
Bastrop	10,156	102	0	4	14	84	827	302	499	26	1
Baton Rouge	220,648	2,066	70	52	645	1,299	11,673	2,258	8,616	799	133
Bernice	1,611	6	0	0	1	5	34	16	15	3	0
Berwick	4,416	4	0	1	2	1	64	17	46	1	0

Table 8. Offenses Known to Law Enforcement, by Selected State and City, 2019—Continued

(Number.)

State/city	Population	Violent crime	Murder and nonnegligent manslaughter	Rape[1]	Robbery	Aggravated assault	Property crime	Burglary	Larceny-theft	Motor vehicle theft	Arson[2]
Blanchard	3,147	0	0	0	0	0	39	6	30	3	0
Bogalusa	11,681	147	2	16	14	115	539	128	374	37	1
Bossier City	69,044	546	2	52	72	420	3,225	461	2,382	382	1
Breaux Bridge	8,237	42	1	2	10	29	605	73	516	16	0
Broussard	12,985	32	0	3	6	23	429	100	315	14	0
Brusly	2,737	11	0	1	0	10	24	5	18	1	0
Carencro	9,387	34	3	0	0	31	216	43	173	0	0
Church Point	4,424	39	1	1	0	37	78	18	57	3	0
Crowley	12,621	158	1	8	14	135	528	132	372	24	0
Cullen	1,069	2	0	0	0	2	3	0	3	0	0
Epps	819	0	0	0	0	0	0	0	0	0	0
Erath	2,059	7	0	0	0	7	25	5	19	1	0
Eunice	9,939	51	2	3	5	41	550	104	417	29	0
Farmerville	3,725	19	0	0	2	17	174	46	125	3	1
Franklinton	3,761	44	0	0	4	40	140	32	98	10	0
French Settlement	1,182	1	0	0	0	1	11	1	9	1	0
Georgetown	326	0	0	0	0	0	0	0	0	0	0
Gonzales	10,940	61	2	4	13	42	933	39	849	45	0
Gramercy	3,307	4	0	0	0	4	79	7	65	7	0
Greensburg	653	3	0	1	0	2	12	3	9	0	0
Greenwood	3,141	8	0	0	0	8	77	15	52	10	0
Gretna	17,729	119	2	5	7	105	717	84	580	53	1
Harahan	9,298	12	0	0	0	12	82	6	68	8	2
Houma	32,771	209	4	17	22	166	1,489	169	1,260	60	6
Ida	205	0	0	0	0	0	0	0	0	0	0
Independence	1,921	26	0	1	1	24	99	25	69	5	1
Iowa	3,262	11	0	2	0	9	133	31	93	9	0
Jena	3,370	3	0	0	0	3	3	0	3	0	0
Kaplan	4,465	32	0	3	0	29	43	11	29	3	0
Kenner	66,653	149	4	28	37	80	1,955	123	1,689	143	2
Kinder	2,388	10	0	2	3	5	94	12	76	6	0
Krotz Springs	1,208	8	0	2	0	6	35	1	32	2	0
Lafayette	126,694	664	14	16	148	486	5,454	1,032	4,101	321	31
Lake Arthur	2,778	7	0	2	0	5	46	7	35	4	0
Lake Charles	78,733	413	11	52	83	267	2,907	1,212	1,467	228	0
Leesville	5,617	55	0	13	4	38	243	55	177	11	0
Lutcher	3,192	4	0	0	0	4	36	8	26	2	0
Mandeville	12,331	18	0	2	1	3	12	224	23	195	6	0
Many	2,704	0	0	0	0	0	4	1	3	0	0
Marksville	5,369	119	0	1	4	114	333	90	242	1	0
Minden	11,984	105	1	5	19	80	397	110	273	14	2
Monroe	47,746	843	9	37	171	626	3,141	623	2,339	179	11
Natchitoches	17,747	177	4	12	23	138	1,221	441	741	39	3
New Orleans[6]	394,498	4,516	121	774	1,013	2,608	20,879	2,143	15,785	2,951	
Norwood	295	0	0	0	0	0	0	0	0	0	0
Oil City	980	1	0	0	0	1	18	2	16	0	0
Olla	1,349	0	0	0	0	0	2	0	0	2	0
Opelousas	16,049	394	6	25	48	315	1,287	405	831	51	2
Pearl River	2,631	19	0	0	1	18	48	10	33	5	0
Pineville	14,261	114	0	11	6	97	736	138	554	44	0
Ponchatoula	7,478	78	0	5	23	50	523	118	379	26	0
Port Allen	4,940	33	2	0	1	30	131	23	100	8	0
Port Vincent	751	2	0	0	0	2	8	4	3	1	0
Rayne	8,088	20	0	0	3	17	186	24	157	5	2
Rayville	3,492	0	0	0	0	0	2	0	1	1	0
Ruston	22,148	85	3	0	10	72	677	105	565	7	0
Scott	8,725	12	0	2	0	10	259	61	179	19	0
Shreveport	187,556	1,462	35	133	294	1,000	9,189	1,626	6,915	648	73
Sibley	1,144	0	0	0	0	0	0	0	0	0	0
Slidell	27,768	75	1	4	11	59	791	73	674	44	0
Springhill	4,792	19	0	0	0	19	67	9	53	5	0
Sulphur	20,200	66	0	7	15	44	885	107	707	71	0
Tallulah	6,701	35	0	2	2	31	35	9	25	1	0
Thibodaux	14,587	81	4	5	0	72	515	63	432	20	2
Vidalia	3,871	16	0	7	1	8	174	17	154	3	0
Ville Platte	7,029	9	0	0	9	0	410	112	282	16	0
Vinton	3,291	17	0	2	2	13	100	20	73	7	0
Walker	6,296	33	0	4	2	27	328	33	292	3	0
Welsh	3,254	20	1	1	1	17	74	16	56	2	0
Westlake	4,959	3	0	0	0	3	124	70	43	11	0
West Monroe	12,350	113	0	8	17	88	905	146	718	41	1
Westwego	8,415	20	0	3	6	11	179	25	144	10	1
Winnfield	4,307	24	0	0	3	21	130	37	84	9	1
Youngsville	15,020	14	0	3	1	10	157	34	122	1	0
Zachary	18,009	79	0	5	3	71	635	39	562	34	0
MAINE											
Ashland	1,206	2	0	0	0	2	2	0	2	0	0
Auburn	23,214	34	1	13	5	15	511	56	445	10	1
Augusta	18,629	49	0	20	12	17	587	59	519	9	2
Baileyville	1,442	15	0	1	1	13	11	5	5	1	0
Bangor	31,872	35	1	1	15	18	1,168	64	1,076	28	4
Bar Harbor	7,682	3	0	1	0	2	62	10	49	3	0

Table 8. Offenses Known to Law Enforcement, by Selected State and City, 2019—Continued

(Number.)

State/city	Population	Violent crime	Murder and nonnegligent manslaughter	Rape[1]	Robbery	Aggravated assault	Property crime	Burglary	Larceny-theft	Motor vehicle theft	Arson[2]
Bath[5]	8,309	4	0	0	0	4	136	8	126	2	0
Belfast[5]	6,720	3	0	0	0	3	38	8	27	3	0
Berwick[5]	7,860	5	0	1	1	3	60	22	35	3	0
Biddeford	21,545	92	0	24	9	59	578	53	511	14	1
Boothbay Harbor	2,204	3	0	2	0	1	13	0	12	1	0
Brewer	9,000	3	0	0	0	3	302	11	286	5	0
Bridgton	5,388	6	0	2	0	4	44	6	38	0	0
Brunswick	20,510	10	0	6	1	3	319	16	297	6	0
Bucksport	4,926	2	0	0	0	2	55	5	46	4	1
Buxton	8,345	12	0	3	0	9	40	4	34	2	0
Calais	2,973	6	0	2	0	4	61	9	50	2	0
Camden	4,823	0	0	0	0	0	3	0	3	0	0
Cape Elizabeth	9,352	1	0	1	0	0	46	11	34	1	1
Caribou	7,548	8	0	0	2	6	126	19	97	10	0
Carrabassett Valley	777	1	0	0	0	1	10	1	9	0	0
Clinton	3,329	12	0	8	0	4	15	0	14	1	0
Cumberland	8,295	0	0	0	0	0	17	2	14	1	0
Damariscotta	2,151	1	0	1	0	0	46	1	44	1	0
Dexter	3,671	1	0	0	1	0	44	10	33	1	0
Dixfield	2,465	3	0	3	0	0	25	13	10	2	0
Dover-Foxcroft	4,033	2	0	0	0	2	43	8	34	1	0
East Millinocket	2,919	0	0	0	0	0	43	12	28	3	0
Eastport	1,251	3	0	1	0	2	7	2	5	0	0
Eliot	6,817	7	0	4	1	2	23	5	17	1	0
Ellsworth	8,088	6	0	5	0	1	174	11	153	10	0
Fairfield	6,534	11	0	6	1	4	108	27	75	6	0
Falmouth	12,378	3	0	0	0	3	136	5	130	1	0
Farmington	7,603	8	0	4	0	4	90	15	74	1	0
Fort Fairfield	3,256	1	0	1	0	0	11	5	3	3	0
Fort Kent	3,816	0	0	0	0	0	20	0	20	0	0
Freeport	8,593	1	0	1	0	0	93	6	85	2	0
Fryeburg	3,398	1	0	1	0	0	49	7	41	1	0
Gardiner	5,645	4	1	0	1	2	42	2	37	3	0
Gorham	17,818	7	0	2	0	5	131	7	121	3	1
Gouldsboro	1,745	0	0	0	0	0	6	1	5	0	0
Greenville	1,595	0	0	0	0	0	21	1	18	2	0
Hallowell[5]	2,371	4	0	0	2	2	12	3	9	0	0
Hampden	7,352	1	0	1	0	0	52	6	46	0	0
Holden	3,081	3	0	0	0	3	21	3	15	3	0
Houlton	5,720	20	0	4	0	16	160	18	134	8	1
Islesboro[5]	565	0	0	0	0	0	13	1	12	0	0
Jay	4,586	7	0	3	0	4	30	4	23	3	0
Kennebunk	11,622	8	0	4	0	4	46	2	43	1	1
Kennebunkport	3,660	2	0	1	0	1	29	5	24	0	0
Kittery	9,890	8	0	7	0	1	92	12	78	2	1
Lewiston	35,865	107	0	31	18	58	716	122	555	39	3
Limestone	2,200	2	0	0	0	2	18	5	12	1	0
Lincoln	4,886	1	0	0	1	0	113	14	94	5	0
Lisbon	8,975	10	0	6	1	3	55	4	46	5	1
Livermore Falls	3,134	16	0	6	0	10	32	3	28	1	0
Machias	2,055	2	0	1	0	1	35	6	28	1	0
Madawaska	3,662	0	0	0	0	0	35	1	33	1	0
Mechanic Falls	2,973	5	0	4	0	1	26	3	22	1	0
Mexico	2,605	6	0	6	0	0	118	20	97	1	0
Milbridge	1,255	1	0	0	0	1	4	1	2	1	0
Millinocket	4,241	1	0	0	0	1	81	14	63	4	0
Milo	2,270	1	0	0	0	1	24	1	21	2	0
Monmouth	4,131	1	0	0	0	1	16	4	11	1	0
Newport	3,269	0	0	0	0	0	55	13	40	2	0
North Berwick	4,731	2	0	0	0	2	19	3	16	0	0
Norway	4,979	2	0	0	1	1	78	15	62	1	1
Oakland	6,296	7	0	5	0	2	60	12	45	3	0
Ogunquit	931	0	0	0	0	0	27	1	25	1	0
Old Orchard Beach	8,946	25	1	6	2	16	107	17	86	4	3
Old Town	7,413	8	0	2	1	5	74	9	63	2	0
Orono	10,722	7	0	3	0	4	77	6	67	4	0
Oxford	4,100	4	0	1	2	1	110	10	97	3	0
Paris	5,112	6	2	2	2	0	55	14	37	4	0
Phippsburg	2,259	1	0	0	0	1	6	2	4	0	0
Pittsfield	3,999	1	0	0	1	0	24	3	21	0	0
Portland	66,458	161	3	29	43	86	1,715	181	1,460	74	5
Presque Isle	8,918	23	1	3	1	18	225	42	171	12	1
Rangeley	1,143	0	0	0	0	0	10	0	9	1	0
Richmond	3,440	2	1	1	0	0	23	12	7	4	0
Rockland	7,128	4	0	1	0	3	118	8	102	8	1
Rockport	3,378	1	0	0	0	1	18	2	15	1	0
Rumford	5,670	18	0	12	1	5	150	28	119	3	1
Sabattus	5,064	1	0	0	0	1	14	6	5	3	0
Saco	19,908	21	0	12	1	8	300	46	234	20	1
Sanford	21,233	41	0	13	9	19	578	109	456	13	4
Scarborough	20,542	11	1	3	0	7	253	15	234	4	0
Searsport	2,648	1	0	0	0	1	12	4	8	0	2
Skowhegan	8,214	25	0	10	2	13	199	21	170	8	2

Table 8. Offenses Known to Law Enforcement, by Selected State and City, 2019—Continued

(Number.)

State/city	Population	Violent crime	Murder and nonnegligent manslaughter	Rape[1]	Robbery	Aggravated assault	Property crime	Burglary	Larceny-theft	Motor vehicle theft	Arson[2]
South Berwick	7,564	4	0	2	0	2	37	11	23	3	0
South Portland	25,686	48	0	17	8	23	563	39	505	19	3
Southwest Harbor	1,795	1	0	0	0	1	18	0	17	1	3
Thomaston	2,767	0	0	0	0	0	65	4	54	7	1
Topsham[5]	8,863	5	0	2	0	3	89	7	81	1	0
Van Buren	1,972	2	0	0	0	2	8	0	7	1	0
Veazie	1,814	2	0	0	0	2	29	10	19	0	1
Waldoboro	5,041	3	0	1	1	1	45	10	35	0	0
Washburn	1,533	2	0	2	0	0	34	5	24	5	2
Waterville	16,765	37	1	17	2	17	442	33	398	11	1
Wells	10,670	14	0	4	2	8	51	5	44	2	0
Westbrook	19,166	34	0	7	3	24	265	55	194	16	1
Wilton	3,924	6	0	1	0	5	17	2	14	1	0
Windham	18,627	12	0	2	3	7	170	11	154	5	0
Winslow	7,598	7	0	6	1	0	68	9	56	3	1
Winter Harbor	513	0	0	0	0	0	0	0	0	0	0
Winthrop	5,979	5	0	0	0	5	45	12	31	2	0
Wiscasset	3,697	2	0	1	0	1	23	2	20	1	0
Yarmouth	8,540	3	0	2	1	0	38	4	33	1	0
York	13,231	11	0	5	2	4	86	11	71	4	2
MARYLAND											
Aberdeen	16,194	120	0	9	28	83	326	60	254	12	2
Annapolis	39,277	252	4	11	67	170	924	98	734	92	15
Baltimore	597,239	11,101	348	324	4,856	5,573	25,748	5,414	16,395	3,939	108
Baltimore City Sheriff	0	0	0	0	0	0	0	0	0	0	0
Bel Air	10,031	21	0	2	5	14	175	8	167	0	0
Berlin	4,862	3	0	1	0	2	67	6	61	0	0
Berwyn Heights	3,278	7	0	0	6	1	64	7	49	8	0
Bladensburg	9,476	59	3	3	18	35	308	17	221	70	0
Boonsboro	3,596	1	0	0	0	1	16	5	11	0	
Bowie	59,093	59	1	8	26	24	896	55	759	82	
Brentwood	3,494	15	0	1	7	7	51	7	27	17	0
Brunswick	6,426	15	0	0	3	12	124	18	104	2	0
Cambridge	12,264	119	2	10	20	87	659	138	507	14	5
Capitol Heights	4,551	19	1	1	10	7	60	7	37	16	0
Centreville	4,882	4	0	2	0	2	39	6	32	1	1
Chestertown	5,027	13	0	1	6	6	71	17	52	2	1
Cheverly	6,482	24	0	0	14	10	124	15	94	15	0
Chevy Chase Village	2,073	0	0	0	0	0	40	11	27	2	0
Colmar Manor	1,468	6	0	0	1	5	42	2	38	2	
Cottage City	1,363	2	0	0	1	1	26	4	17	5	0
Crisfield	2,554	3	1	0	0	2	11	2	9	0	1
Cumberland	19,321	151	0	9	33	109	869	216	627	26	5
Delmar	3,248	12	0	0	3	9	58	6	50	2	0
Denton	4,504	11	0	1	4	6	156	19	135	2	1
District Heights	6,015	20	0	1	10	9	55	10	38	7	
Easton	16,523	49	1	8	10	30	332	29	297	6	0
Edmonston	1,499	1	0	0	0	1	29	3	16	10	0
Elkton	15,662	151	0	11	39	101	1,039	109	877	53	0
Fairmount Heights	1,533	10	3	0	5	2	42	11	23	8	0
Federalsburg	2,652	14	1	2	3	8	67	15	49	3	0
Forest Heights	2,583	9	2	0	4	3	24	2	11	11	0
Frederick	73,030	296	2	37	54	203	1,364	199	1,112	53	11
Frostburg	8,510	14	0	0	4	10	153	28	114	11	
Fruitland	5,346	15	0	2	0	13	228	17	208	3	0
Glenarden	6,234	4	0	1	0	3	54	4	42	8	0
Greenbelt	23,417	110	1	3	41	65	726	63	588	75	0
Greensboro	1,874	3	0	0	0	3	46	12	32	2	0
Hagerstown	40,258	213	3	22	81	107	960	239	613	108	26
Hampstead	6,397	7	0	0	0	7	31	12	19	0	2
Hancock	1,539	0	0	0	0	0	6	0	5	1	0
Havre de Grace	13,890	36	0	3	7	26	165	19	145	1	0
Hurlock	2,013	2	0	0	0	2	81	6	68	7	0
Hyattsville	18,331	85	4	3	53	25	1,112	54	996	62	0
Landover Hills	1,656	9	1	0	6	2	77	3	64	10	0
La Plata	9,538	47	0	0	9	38	316	20	285	11	2
Laurel	25,814	123	1	8	51	63	887	69	739	79	0
Luke	61	0	0	0	0	0	0	0	0	0	0
Manchester	4,858	0	0	0	0	0	11	1	10	0	0
Morningside	1,296	9	0	1	5	3	27	1	25	1	0
Mount Airy	9,472	5	0	0	0	5	115	15	96	4	0
Mount Rainier	8,143	33	1	1	19	12	255	24	199	32	0
New Carrollton	13,036	33	0	2	10	21	165	19	118	28	0
North East	3,639	12	0	0	6	6	85	17	63	5	0
Oakland	1,816	2	0	0	0	2	114	3	111	0	0
Ocean City	6,905	91	0	5	18	68	720	94	615	11	0
Ocean Pines	12,264	8	0	0	0	8	72	22	49	1	0
Oxford	598	0	0	0	0	0	3	2	1	0	0
Perryville	4,431	15	0	0	2	13	80	12	66	2	0
Pocomoke City	4,025	3	0	1	2	0	106	15	89	2	0
Princess Anne	3,549	29	0	5	6	18	178	46	132	0	0
Ridgely	1,652	4	0	1	1	2	42	3	39	0	0

Table 8. Offenses Known to Law Enforcement, by Selected State and City, 2019—Continued

(Number.)

State/city	Population	Violent crime	Murder and nonnegligent manslaughter	Rape[1]	Robbery	Aggravated assault	Property crime	Burglary	Larceny-theft	Motor vehicle theft	Arson[2]
Rising Sun	2,799	6	0	0	0	6	23	3	20	0	1
Riverdale Park	7,258	22	1	0	7	14	192	19	149	24	0
Rock Hall	1,264	2	0	0	0	2	8	2	6	0	0
Salisbury	33,132	294	0	19	58	217	1,422	207	1,170	45	2
Seat Pleasant	4,803	36	1	0	15	20	104	12	74	18	1
Smithsburg	2,967	1	0	0	0	1	13	2	11	0	0
Snow Hill	2,029	5	0	0	1	4	19	3	16	0	0
St. Michaels	1,025	6	0	0	1	5	17	3	13	1	0
Sykesville	3,959	33	0	1	0	32	24	4	16	4	0
Takoma Park	17,893	71	0	5	30	36	409	50	333	26	0
Taneytown	6,824	13	0	0	0	13	64	5	59	0	0
Thurmont	6,824	15	0	0	2	13	42	5	37	0	0
University Park	2,651	0	0	0	0	0	31	2	20	9	0
Upper Marlboro	675	0	0	0	0	0	14	1	13	0	0
Westminster	18,664	68	0	9	13	46	575	66	493	16	0
MASSACHUSETTS											
Abington	16,448	23	4	5	3	11	153	23	122	8	1
Acton	23,780	32	0	6	2	24	66	13	50	3	0
Acushnet	10,533	12	0	5	0	7	35	14	19	2	0
Adams	8,028	26	0	10	2	14	94	34	59	1	2
Agawam	28,736	82	0	13	8	61	376	133	228	15	1
Amesbury	17,595	25	0	3	3	19	132	18	107	7	0
Amherst	39,603	99	0	28	2	69	173	55	103	15	2
Andover	36,547	8	0	6	1	1	215	28	180	7	0
Aquinnah	328	2	0	0	0	2	0	0	0	0	0
Arlington	45,614	34	0	5	8	21	167	16	139	12	3
Ashburnham	6,330	8	0	2	0	6	28	7	18	3	0
Ashland	17,742	21	0	4	1	16	77	9	60	8	0
Athol	11,679	47	1	7	2	37	101	9	88	4	1
Attleboro	44,959	123	0	27	14	82	522	69	427	26	1
Auburn	16,724	28	0	0	1	27	305	29	263	13	3
Avon[5]	4,504	10	0	1	2	7	111	9	98	4	
Ayer	8,192	14	0	1	1	12	57	14	40	3	0
Barnstable	44,032	178	2	22	14	140	425	61	350	14	7
Barre	5,573	16	0	1	1	14	18	1	10	7	0
Becket[5]	1,724	3	0	0	0	3	4	1	3	0	0
Bedford	14,193	7	0	0	1	6	40	2	37	1	0
Belchertown	15,195	16	0	1	1	14	55	12	38	5	0
Bellingham	17,143	25	0	3	2	20	194	16	170	8	2
Belmont	26,331	6	0	1	0	5	179	76	98	5	2
Berkley	6,799	8	0	2	0	6	19	9	9	1	0
Berlin	3,241	4	0	2	1	1	31	4	26	1	0
Bernardston	2,113	5	0	3	0	2	12	3	9	0	0
Beverly	42,317	47	0	4	2	41	206	19	177	10	1
Billerica	43,882	22	0	2	2	18	169	21	135	13	0
Blackstone	9,294	13	0	1	2	10	21	5	12	4	0
Bolton[5,6]	5,393	2	0	0	0	2	25	2	23	0	0
Boston[5,6]	698,941	4,244	42	231	1,039	2,932		1,703	10,590	13	0
Bourne	19,734	54	0	13	2	39	213	43	157	4	0
Boxborough	6,540	4	0	0	0	4	26	1	21	4	0
Boxford	8,352	0	0	0	0	0	13	2	11	0	0
Boylston	4,694	4	0	0	0	4	2	0	2	0	0
Braintree	37,145	45	0	3	4	38	486	52	417	17	1
Brewster	9,725	25	0	4	0	21	38	9	28	1	0
Bridgewater	27,270	59	0	4	3	52	95	23	62	10	0
Brockton	95,287	782	5	63	148	566	1,853	248	1,317	288	16
Brookfield	3,440	6	0	2	1	3	26	4	20	2	0
Brookline	58,928	57	1	2	14	40	503	44	453	6	0
Burlington	29,082	45	0	12	3	30	451	15	424	12	8
Cambridge	119,908	334	1	26	67	240	1,983	161	1,724	98	1
Canton	23,706	85	0	0	5	80	157	18	132	7	0
Carlisle	5,255	1	0	1	0	0	22	4	18	0	0
Carver	11,721	26	0	6	3	17	68	13	49	6	1
Charlton	13,679	8	0	2	0	6	55	16	36	3	0
Chatham	6,117	8	0	2	1	5	59	12	47	0	0
Chelmsford	35,218	34	0	4	1	29	397	17	364	16	2
Chelsea	40,496	270	0	27	65	178	594	105	406	83	2
Cheshire	3,133	1	0	0	0	1	1	0	0	1	0
Chicopee	55,293	340	2	35	57	246	1,320	245	971	104	4
Chilmark	920	3	0	0	0	3	6	0	6	0	0
Clinton	13,964	4	1	0	0	3	14	1	11	2	0
Cohasset	8,609	3	0	0	0	3	53	10	40	3	1
Concord	19,253	17	0	4	1	12	89	6	82	1	1
Dalton	6,546	6	0	1	0	5	22	8	12	2	1
Danvers	27,664	39	0	2	4	33	357	26	315	16	3
Dartmouth	34,035	77	0	4	16	57	502	40	444	18	1
Dedham	25,203	7	0	5	1	1	327	8	297	22	0
Deerfield	5,032	5	0	2	0	3	43	15	27	1	1
Dennis	13,738	88	0	17	1	70	194	45	144	5	0
Douglas	8,946	8	0	2	1	5	24	6	15	3	0
Dover	6,118	1	0	0	0	1	13	3	10	0	0
Dracut	31,786	30	0	2	4	24	141	24	107	10	1

Table 8. Offenses Known to Law Enforcement, by Selected State and City, 2019—Continued

(Number.)

State/city	Population	Violent crime	Murder and nonnegligent manslaughter	Rape[1]	Robbery	Aggravated assault	Property crime	Burglary	Larceny-theft	Motor vehicle theft	Arson[2]
Dudley	11,754	32	0	7	2	23	52	9	38	5	1
Dunstable	3,405	3	0	0	0	3	7	3	3	1	0
Duxbury	15,934	9	0	2	0	7	57	9	47	1	1
East Bridgewater	14,472	27	0	3	2	22	64	12	46	6	2
East Brookfield	2,202	4	0	0	0	4	7	0	3	4	0
Eastham	4,823	5	0	2	0	3	38	2	35	1	0
Easthampton	15,979	37	0	7	2	28	156	25	122	9	0
East Longmeadow	16,269	24	1	6	6	11	172	28	132	12	2
Easton	25,079	43	0	9	3	31	145	24	110	11	2
Edgartown	4,362	20	0	3	1	16	60	9	47	4	0
Erving	1,771	0	0	0	0	0	15	5	9	1	0
Everett	47,195	245	3	19	19	204	623	104	445	74	1
Fairhaven	15,996	51	0	11	2	38	214	29	178	7	0
Fall River	89,066	773	5	51	113	604	1,074	412	499	163	21
Falmouth	30,717	110	0	17	5	88	357	112	231	14	3
Fitchburg	40,621	217	1	26	36	154	538	94	399	45	3
Foxborough	17,631	35	0	5	4	26	158	18	122	18	1
Framingham	73,127	297	1	20	29	247	800	158	609	33	2
Franklin	33,149	2	0	0	1	1	41	5	31	5	0
Freetown	9,388	15	0	5	2	8	51	16	28	7	1
Gardner	20,628	70	0	13	8	49	309	60	228	21	2
Georgetown	8,777	2	0	0	0	2	33	5	27	1	0
Gill	1,490	0	0	0	0	0	10	1	9	0	0
Gloucester	30,362	58	0	7	1	50	164	21	130	13	0
Goshen	1,065	0	0	0	0	0	4	2	2	0	0
Grafton	18,880	15	0	4	1	10	46	10	34	2	0
Granby	6,360	9	0	1	0	8	21	3	15	3	0
Great Barrington	6,822	11	0	2	1	8	28	5	23	0	2
Greenfield	17,464	84	0	11	10	63	342	84	248	10	0
Groton	11,388	8	1	5	0	2	23	4	19	0	0
Groveland	6,846	2	1	0	0	1	9	1	6	2	0
Hadley	5,358	26	0	7	0	19	170	6	157	7	0
Halifax	7,874	8	0	1	0	7	51	9	37	5	1
Hamilton	8,075	1	0	0	0	1	26	4	19	3	0
Hampden	5,199	1	0	0	0	1	20	6	13	1	0
Hanover	14,485	3	0	0	0	3	121	4	116	1	0
Hanson	10,876	17	0	1	2	14	47	9	37	1	0
Hardwick	3,039	14	0	2	0	12	15	4	11	0	0
Harvard	6,569	5	0	3	0	2	26	6	20	0	0
Harwich	12,028	22	0	2	1	19	103	26	72	5	1
Hatfield	3,286	2	0	0	0	2	35	12	23	0	0
Haverhill	63,935	335	1	15	15	304	838	179	570	89	7
Hingham	23,960	30	0	6	0	24	183	45	134	4	0
Holbrook	10,990	33	0	4	4	25	129	26	94	9	0
Holland	2,484	2	0	2	0	0	9	1	5	3	0
Holliston	14,996	13	0	0	1	12	41	8	31	2	0
Holyoke	40,178	345	4	36	53	252	1,494	213	1,184	97	4
Hopedale	5,929	12	0	1	1	10	13	2	11	0	0
Hopkinton	18,585	0	0	0	0	0	30	1	28	1	0
Hull	10,402	47	0	4	1	42	81	7	70	4	0
Ipswich	14,095	19	0	8	2	9	46	6	33	7	0
Kingston	13,758	21	0	4	3	14	108	8	96	4	1
Lakeville	11,419	16	0	3	1	12	84	20	62	2	0
Lancaster	8,136	5	0	0	0	5	43	7	32	4	0
Lawrence	80,243	541	3	32	87	419	954	113	677	164	1
Lee	5,686	10	0	3	0	7	65	5	58	2	0
Leicester	11,368	23	0	2	1	20	232	9	222	1	1
Lenox	4,951	7	0	2	0	5	71	11	59	1	0
Leominster	41,631	239	0	31	20	188	599	64	495	40	2
Lexington	33,824	17	1	2	0	14	77	5	72	0	0
Lincoln	6,798	4	0	1	0	3	16	2	14	0	0
Littleton	10,334	11	0	5	0	6	48	5	43	0	0
Longmeadow	15,737	10	0	3	0	7	120	28	82	10	1
Lowell	111,423	405	4	20	100	281	1,652	292	1,190	170	10
Ludlow	21,395	63	0	5	4	54	199	37	142	20	1
Lunenburg	11,781	23	0	4	4	15	128	13	115	0	0
Lynn	94,449	465	8	33	103	321	1,347	302	908	137	1
Lynnfield	13,130	2	0	0	0	2	77	8	68	1	0
Malden	60,746	162	1	9	26	126	719	103	521	95	0
Manchester-by-the-Sea	5,423	2	0	0	0	2	24	4	19	1	0
Mansfield	23,987	65	0	11	5	49	167	15	144	8	0
Marblehead	20,574	22	0	7	0	15	114	10	99	5	0
Marion	5,132	4	0	1	0	3	32	4	28	0	0
Marlborough	39,673	149	0	17	15	117	530	70	435	25	1
Marshfield	25,794	32	0	2	3	27	71	9	56	6	0
Mashpee	14,094	39	0	6	0	33	133	17	104	12	0
Mattapoisett	6,372	12	0	1	0	11	40	5	33	2	0
Maynard	10,654	24	0	3	2	19	39	7	29	3	0
Medford	57,484	116	0	7	17	92	526	51	442	33	1
Medway	13,405	6	0	0	0	6	27	6	21	0	0
Melrose	28,120	32	0	0	3	29	172	25	131	16	0
Mendon	6,176	3	0	0	0	3	16	2	9	5	0
Merrimac	7,001	2	0	0	0	2	15	5	9	1	0

Table 8. Offenses Known to Law Enforcement, by Selected State and City, 2019—Continued

(Number.)

State/city	Population	Violent crime	Murder and nonnegligent manslaughter	Rape[1]	Robbery	Aggravated assault	Property crime	Burglary	Larceny-theft	Motor vehicle theft	Arson[2]
Methuen	50,727	95	1	1	11	82	552	58	446	48	0
Middleboro	25,183	128	0	17	9	102	188	14	151	23	5
Middleton	10,113	5	0	0	0	5	41	3	35	3	0
Milford	29,015	48	0	11	4	33	171	38	120	13	2
Millbury	13,837	24	0	2	1	21	139	13	115	11	1
Millville	3,249	5	0	3	0	2	14	1	13	0	0
Milton	27,471	11	0	2	5	4	61	13	40	8	0
Monson	8,851	27	0	4	0	23	43	12	24	7	0
Montague	8,298	49	0	4	4	41	84	18	64	2	0
Nahant	3,511	12	0	1	0	11	12	2	9	1	0
Nantucket	11,393	27	0	2	0	25	154	17	133	4	1
Natick	36,358	37	0	7	4	26	383	22	350	11	2
Needham	31,275	10	0	2	0	8	135	22	112	1	1
New Bedford	94,613	628	3	66	176	383	2,127	465	1,513	149	5
New Braintree	1,024	3	0	0	0	3	4	2	1	1	0
Newburyport	18,158	23	0	5	0	18	126	13	111	2	0
Newton	88,658	49	0	4	10	35	510	75	424	11	1
Norfolk	11,992	1	0	0	0	1	23	3	20	0	0
North Adams	12,800	72	0	13	9	50	400	88	301	11	0
Northampton	28,735	119	1	25	9	84	448	53	375	20	8
North Andover	31,428	17	0	4	3	10	163	14	139	10	0
North Attleboro	29,202	24	3	6	0	15	420	21	394	5	2
Northborough	15,075	3	0	0	0	3	88	12	76	0	1
Northbridge	16,732	31	0	2	0	29	140	21	113	6	1
Northfield	2,988	0	0	0	0	0	10	1	9	0	0
North Reading	15,687	16	0	3	1	12	60	10	44	6	0
Norton	19,894	23	0	3	0	20	13	7	5	1	1
Norwell	11,105	11	0	0	0	11	51	8	38	5	0
Norwood	29,185	47	0	9	8	30	215	33	173	9	2
Oak Bluffs	4,681	26	0	1	1	24	64	11	49	4	0
Oakham	1,955	0	0	0	0	0	4	0	3	1	0
Orange	7,643	22	0	3	2	17	93	17	72	4	1
Orleans	5,742	5	0	1	0	4	50	6	44	0	0
Oxford	13,973	29	0	11	0	18	162	12	144	6	0
Palmer	12,258	50	0	2	3	45	115	34	71	10	3
Paxton	4,944	8	0	2	0	6	12	1	9	2	0
Peabody	53,104	123	0	21	8	94	435	55	350	30	2
Pelham	1,322	0	0	0	0	0	3	2	1	0	0
Pembroke	18,378	13	0	2	3	8	80	12	60	8	1
Pepperell	12,146	15	0	5	1	9	58	5	50	3	0
Pittsfield	42,268	300	2	36	31	231	796	263	490	43	6
Plainville	9,281	6	1	0	0	5	48	7	40	1	0
Plymouth	60,870	199	0	38	11	150	594	73	490	31	5
Plympton	2,980	4	0	0	1	3	15	5	9	1	0
Princeton	3,459	1	0	0	0	1	13	3	10	0	0
Provincetown	2,939	16	0	2	1	13	51	8	41	2	2
Quincy	94,113	375	1	31	61	282	1,146	216	875	55	1
Randolph	34,385	82	1	6	10	65	409	69	307	33	0
Raynham	14,322	28	0	4	4	20	210	12	183	15	0
Reading	25,305	3	0	0	0	3	116	15	94	7	0
Rehoboth	12,252	8	0	0	1	7	46	16	26	4	1
Revere	53,654	173	2	11	38	122	653	68	524	61	3
Rockland	17,879	53	0	8	4	41	59	16	39	4	0
Rockport	7,280	7	0	2	1	4	16	4	11	1	0
Rowley	6,372	6	0	1	0	5	26	4	21	1	0
Rutland	8,888	35	0	10	1	24	22	5	15	2	0
Salem	43,443	108	0	14	21	73	727	87	594	46	6
Salisbury	9,575	17	0	5	0	12	74	25	44	5	1
Sandwich	20,016	40	0	5	1	34	97	16	79	2	2
Saugus	28,378	72	0	9	10	53	360	28	305	27	1
Scituate	18,774	14	0	2	0	12	62	7	50	5	1
Seekonk	15,841	27	0	1	3	23	244	27	206	11	1
Sharon	18,973	9	0	4	0	5	47	10	33	4	1
Shirley	7,633	19	0	1	0	18	42	10	28	4	0
Shrewsbury	37,983	4	0	1	2	1	126	15	92	19	0
Somerset	18,036	43	0	3	4	36	130	8	114	8	0
Somerville	81,668	166	0	16	38	112	1,025	140	796	89	4
Southampton	6,247	9	0	1	0	8	37	12	23	2	0
Southborough	10,140	3	0	0	0	3	29	14	12	3	0
Southbridge	16,826	79	0	21	3	55	238	50	172	16	0
South Hadley	17,816	27	0	4	0	23	156	28	120	8	3
Southwick	9,772	10	0	3	0	7	65	21	39	5	0
Spencer	11,911	11	0	4	0	7	65	16	40	9	0
Springfield	154,306	1,397	20	81	358	938	4,005	746	2,766	493	31
Sterling	8,175	4	0	3	0	1	16	2	13	1	0
Stockbridge	1,898	1	0	0	0	1	24	4	19	1	0
Stoneham	22,732	33	0	9	5	19	175	44	115	16	0
Stoughton	28,961	58	1	9	7	41	286	33	231	22	1
Stow	7,234	4	0	0	0	4	12	4	8	0	1
Sturbridge	9,611	17	0	3	0	14	113	12	94	7	3
Sudbury	19,727	15	0	6	1	8	67	6	58	3	0
Sunderland	3,656	4	0	2	0	2	21	5	13	3	0
Sutton	9,551	12	0	2	0	10	53	18	33	2	0

Table 8. Offenses Known to Law Enforcement, by Selected State and City, 2019—Continued

(Number.)

State/city	Population	Violent crime	Murder and nonnegligent manslaughter	Rape[1]	Robbery	Aggravated assault	Property crime	Burglary	Larceny-theft	Motor vehicle theft	Arson[2]
Swampscott	15,296	8	0	1	1	6	113	12	100	1	0
Swansea	16,681	34	0	5	1	28	118	17	97	4	0
Taunton	57,028	217	2	15	17	183	345	86	238	21	3
Templeton	8,109	13	0	2	0	11	22	6	12	4	0
Tewksbury	31,424	81	0	23	7	51	345	19	308	18	1
Tisbury	4,116	30	0	3	0	27	31	6	23	2	1
Topsfield	6,644	5	0	1	0	4	10	2	7	1	0
Townsend	9,546	10	0	2	0	8	32	4	21	7	0
Truro	1,984	5	0	1	0	4	5	0	5	0	0
Tyngsboro	12,456	19	0	4	3	12	47	5	31	11	0
Uxbridge	14,066	20	0	3	2	15	74	18	48	8	1
Wakefield	27,178	37	0	3	3	31	164	25	127	12	0
Wales	1,894	2	0	1	0	1	5	3	2	0	1
Walpole	25,150	49	0	11	1	37	257	25	220	12	0
Waltham	62,737	102	0	13	7	82	512	70	420	22	5
Ware	9,804	49	0	1	6	42	83	9	64	10	0
Wareham	22,592	161	1	23	9	128	322	51	251	20	0
Watertown	36,189	29	0	10	2	17	319	36	269	14	0
Wayland	13,891	0	0	0	0	0	1	1	0	0	0
Webster	16,925	122	0	16	3	103	208	39	158	11	0
Wellesley	29,651	7	0	0	0	7	120	15	104	1	0
Wellfleet	2,705	0	0	0	0	0	25	6	19	0	0
Wenham	5,295	0	0	0	0	0	8	1	6	1	0
Westborough	19,155	24	0	8	0	16	200	33	163	4	1
West Boylston	8,216	11	0	0	2	9	47	13	27	7	0
West Bridgewater	7,248	9	0	1	0	8	71	16	48	7	1
Westfield	41,507	83	3	15	7	58	398	52	324	22	1
Westford	24,403	10	0	0	1	9	54	5	45	4	0
Westminster	7,902	20	0	1	0	19	43	5	36	2	0
Weston	12,138	9	0	2	0	7	28	3	24	1	0
Westport	15,920	21	0	4	0	17	111	27	74	10	1
West Springfield	28,628	138	0	18	15	105	969	101	814	54	2
West Tisbury	2,911	7	0	1	0	6	17	2	11	4	0
Westwood	16,199	10	0	1	3	6	166	14	148	4	0
Weymouth	57,776	170	0	21	9	140	462	44	386	32	0
Whately	1,589	1	0	0	0	1	17	2	10	5	0
Whitman	15,134	33	0	3	3	27	104	21	76	7	2
Wilbraham	14,730	21	0	1	0	20	220	58	155	7	0
Williamsburg	2,489	2	0	1	0	1	18	4	14	0	0
Williamstown	8,021	6	0	4	0	2	71	3	66	2	0
Wilmington	23,915	32	0	5	1	26	154	15	124	15	0
Winchendon	10,897	37	0	9	0	28	100	30	57	13	1
Winchester	22,850	7	0	0	0	7	88	10	74	4	1
Winthrop	18,692	37	0	2	6	29	129	11	102	16	0
Woburn	40,251	70	0	2	10	58	414	46	323	45	1
Worcester	184,945	1,165	13	40	229	883	3,792	786	2,637	369	6
Worthington	1,191	0	0	0	0	0	0	0	0	0	0
Wrentham	11,989	4	0	2	0	2	178	18	153	7	0
Yarmouth	23,076	96	0	19	3	74	229	38	186	5	0
MICHIGAN											
Addison Township	6,653	6	0	2	2	2	15	4	9	2	0
Adrian	20,334	140	0	37	12	91	477	94	366	17	1
Adrian Township	6,239	2	0	1	0	1	20	14	6	0	0
Akron	374	0	0	0	0	0	4	1	3	0	0
Albion	8,462	80	1	6	8	65	299	75	210	14	1
Allegan	5,038	10	0	4	1	5	47	1	42	4	1
Allen Park	26,945	48	0	10	10	28	496	54	399	43	2
Alma	8,866	20	0	5	2	13	109	12	94	3	0
Almont	2,814	11	0	2	0	9	29	7	19	3	0
Alpena	9,901	58	0	20	1	37	159	30	122	7	0
Ann Arbor	122,893	309	2	77	46	184	2,124	197	1,789	138	8
Argentine Township	6,506	3	0	1	0	2	19	3	13	3	1
Auburn Hills	24,393	82	0	25	11	46	536	32	487	17	2
Au Gres	834	0	0	0	0	0	0	0	0	0	0
Augusta	902	3	0	2	1	0	14	0	14	0	0
Bad Axe	2,923	7	0	5	1	1	42	1	40	1	0
Bancroft	494	0	0	0	0	0	1	0	1	0	0
Bangor	1,823	20	0	3	0	17	24	6	15	3	1
Baroda-Lake Township	3,859	6	0	1	0	5	41	6	30	5	0
Barryton	353	0	0	0	0	0	0	0	0	0	0
Barry Township	3,510	1	0	0	0	1	13	4	9	0	0
Bath Township	13,131	14	0	7	0	7	114	18	86	10	0
Battle Creek	60,607	568	5	60	67	436	1,969	460	1,377	132	27
Bay City	32,793	271	2	35	20	214	654	135	476	43	4
Beaverton	1,176	1	0	0	0	1	7	0	7	0	0
Belding	5,747	6	0	3	1	2	66	8	56	2	0
Bellaire	1,067	0	0	0	0	0	0	0	0	0	0
Belleville	3,873	12	0	3	1	8	47	9	35	3	0
Bellevue	1,291	0	0	0	0	0	0	0	0	0	0
Benton Harbor	9,801	190	3	18	19	150	320	73	198	49	1
Benton Township	14,372	287	2	32	25	228	813	105	621	87	7
Berkley	15,482	9	0	3	1	5	54	6	48	0	0

Table 8. Offenses Known to Law Enforcement, by Selected State and City, 2019—Continued

(Number.)

State/city	Population	Violent crime	Murder and nonnegligent manslaughter	Rape[1]	Robbery	Aggravated assault	Property crime	Burglary	Larceny-theft	Motor vehicle theft	Arson[2]
Berrien Springs-Oronoko Township	8,940	12	0	5	1	6	88	15	64	9	0
Beverly Hills	10,429	2	0	0	0	2	78	10	60	8	0
Big Rapids	10,389	26	0	6	0	20	135	18	114	3	1
Birch Run	1,462	3	0	0	0	3	55	3	52	0	0
Birmingham	21,479	10	0	2	1	7	127	20	100	7	0
Blackman Township	37,002	85	1	34	8	42	1,236	94	1,073	69	2
Blissfield	3,250	7	0	3	0	4	21	5	15	1	0
Bloomfield Hills	4,027	5	0	1	1	3	25	4	19	2	0
Bloomfield Township	42,326	11	0	1	1	9	324	41	267	16	0
Boyne City	3,752	13	0	3	0	10	26	0	25	1	0
Brandon Township	16,121	12	0	2	0	10	50	10	36	4	0
Breckenridge	1,261	0	0	0	0	0	7	0	6	1	0
Bridgeport Township	9,778	49	0	5	3	41	124	36	80	8	0
Bridgman	2,224	3	0	0	0	3	16	0	14	2	0
Brighton	7,684	9	1	4	0	4	154	8	143	3	0
Bronson	2,308	11	0	5	1	5	50	6	39	5	0
Brown City	1,240	2	0	0	0	2	15	0	14	1	0
Brownstown Township	32,083	75	0	12	4	59	296	49	210	37	7
Buchanan	4,274	21	0	7	0	14	108	13	88	7	2
Buena Vista Township	8,095	92	2	8	8	74	171	59	98	14	0
Burton[4]	28,496	136	2	20	18	96			524	88	4
Cadillac	10,466	52	0	17	1	34	355	30	310	15	0
Calumet	691	0	0	0	0	0	3	1	2	0	0
Cambridge Township	5,657	5	0	3	0	2	27	6	18	3	0
Canton Township	93,406	120	1	30	6	83	1,086	113	919	54	5
Capac	1,822	5	0	0	0	5	23	8	14	1	0
Caro	3,969	12	0	4	0	8	77	4	68	5	0
Carrollton Township	5,626	10	2	0	0	8	64	22	41	1	1
Carson City	1,117	3	0	3	0	0	3	0	3	0	0
Caseville	731	0	0	0	0	0	14	2	12	0	1
Caspian-Gaastra	1,165	4	0	0	0	4	3	1	2	0	0
Cass City	2,268	1	0	1	0	0	38	3	35	0	0
Cassopolis	1,695	2	0	2	0	0	14	1	11	2	0
Center Line	8,232	28	0	4	4	20	135	13	112	10	0
Central Lake	938	0	0	0	0	0	0	0	0	0	0
Charlevoix	2,498	10	0	6	0	4	36	6	27	3	1
Charlotte	9,088	28	0	7	3	18	175	20	143	12	0
Cheboygan	4,695	18	0	8	0	10	88	7	80	1	1
Chelsea	5,543	4	0	0	0	4	72	3	66	3	0
Chesaning	2,238	2	0	0	0	2	7	1	6	0	0
Chesterfield Township	46,774	87	0	12	10	65	559	68	470	21	5
Chikaming Township	3,108	5	0	2	1	2	50	19	30	1	0
Chocolay Township	5,931	11	0	0	0	11	27	2	25	0	1
Clare	3,061	10	0	5	0	5	39	5	34	0	1
Clarkston	925	1	0	0	0	1	3	0	3	0	0
Clawson	11,948	7	0	2	1	4	52	8	42	2	0
Clayton Township	7,110	9	0	0	0	9	45	26	18	1	0
Clay Township	8,844	23	0	5	0	18	55	4	46	5	1
Clinton	2,274	2	0	1	0	1	14	4	9	1	0
Clinton Township	101,308	298	0	39	18	241	1,370	171	1,043	156	7
Clio	2,483	9	0	1	2	6	30	6	23	1	0
Coldwater	12,098	47	1	14	2	30	275	29	225	21	2
Coleman	1,188	0	0	0	0	0	3	1	2	0	0
Coloma Township	6,362	14	0	7	0	7	126	24	96	6	0
Colon	1,159	2	1	1	0	0	6	1	5	0	0
Columbia Township	7,359	12	0	1	0	11	49	4	40	5	0
Commerce Township	39,690	26	1	4	4	17	201	19	176	6	1
Constantine	2,105	6	0	2	0	4	22	5	15	2	1
Corunna	3,337	10	0	4	0	6	23	5	18	0	2
Covert Township	2,853	12	0	4	0	8	56	19	33	4	0
Croswell	2,262	14	0	8	1	5	21	1	19	1	0
Crystal Falls	1,359	3	0	0	0	3	20	4	13	3	0
Davison	4,874	10	0	8	0	2	38	4	31	3	0
Davison Township	19,207	26	0	8	0	18	208	41	158	9	0
Dearborn	93,902	305	4	36	56	209	2,104	201	1,637	266	8
Dearborn Heights	55,368	227	0	24	34	169	874	190	590	94	4
Decatur	1,731	8	0	2	0	6	37	7	29	1	0
Denton Township	5,379	2	0	2	0	0	45	0	44	1	0
Detroit	663,502	13,040	275	952	2,346	9,467	28,550	6,820	14,844	6,886	789
DeWitt	4,790	4	0	2	0	2	19	2	17	0	1
DeWitt Township	15,613	23	0	8	4	11	125	27	90	8	0
Dowagiac	5,719	45	0	11	1	33	195	23	152	20	0
Dryden Township	4,734	2	1	1	0	0	25	4	18	3	0
Durand	3,825	6	0	1	2	3	16	0	14	2	0
East Grand Rapids	12,040	4	0	2	1	1	99	13	75	11	0
East Jordan	2,351	4	0	2	0	2	24	3	21	0	0
East Lansing	47,913	88	0	40	11	37	840	113	563	164	24
Eastpointe	32,340	223	3	27	37	156	828	165	553	110	5
Eaton Rapids	5,216	31	0	9	0	22	81	8	62	11	0
Eau Claire	599	0	0	0	0	0	1	1	0	0	0
Ecorse	9,601	117	2	2	21	92	106	24	70	12	6
Elk Rapids	1,618	0	0	0	0	0	0	0	0	0	0

Table 8. Offenses Known to Law Enforcement, by Selected State and City, 2019—Continued
(Number.)

State/city	Population	Violent crime	Murder and nonnegligent manslaughter	Rape[1]	Robbery	Aggravated assault	Property crime	Burglary	Larceny-theft	Motor vehicle theft	Arson[2]
Elkton	751	0	0	0	0	0	4	0	4	0	0
Elsie	983	0	0	0	0	0	1	0	0	1	0
Emmett Township	11,668	43	0	6	4	33	601	77	507	17	1
Escanaba	12,129	60	0	16	3	41	222	14	202	6	1
Essexville	3,296	0	0	0	0	0	21	5	14	2	1
Evart	1,865	13	0	4	1	8	21	8	11	2	1
Fair Haven Township	1,038	0	0	0	0	0	2	0	2	0	0
Farmington	10,587	6	0	2	0	4	83	15	64	4	0
Farmington Hills	81,262	87	0	17	7	63	759	145	547	67	5
Fennville	1,421	0	0	0	0	0	3	0	3	0	0
Fenton	11,281	21	0	5	4	12	203	18	179	6	1
Ferndale	20,097	50	0	4	5	41	443	45	352	46	1
Flat Rock	10,024	17	0	1	4	12	146	4	117	25	1
Flint	95,212	1,284	23	64	78	1,119	1,986	559	1,220	207	25
Flint Township[4]	30,319	241	2	30	36	173			936	82	9
Flushing	7,860	6	0	3	0	3	65	7	55	3	0
Flushing Township	10,174	11	0	7	1	3	46	14	31	1	0
Forsyth Township	6,197	12	0	4	0	8	28	5	22	1	0
Fowlerville	2,869	5	0	4	0	1	62	5	56	1	0
Frankenmuth	5,458	5	0	3	0	2	54	10	43	1	0
Frankfort	1,289	3	0	0	0	3	9	0	9	0	0
Franklin	3,268	2	0	0	0	2	36	7	27	2	0
Fraser	14,578	33	0	7	4	22	220	28	180	12	1
Fremont	4,103	11	0	5	0	6	82	2	77	3	0
Fruitport Township	14,346	16	0	3	8	5	536	30	499	7	1
Gagetown	360	0	0	0	0	0	0	0	0	0	0
Gaines Township	6,080	3	0	1	0	2	15	4	10	1	0
Galien	533	0	0	0	0	0	0	0	0	0	0
Garden City	26,420	96	1	11	14	70	293	65	188	40	0
Garfield Township	838	0	0	0	0	0	0	0	0	0	0
Gaylord	3,709	14	0	2	0	12	186	10	170	6	0
Genesee Township	20,410	63	0	12	4	47	341	172	141	28	2
Gerrish Township	2,922	2	0	0	1	1	11	2	9	0	0
Gibraltar	4,467	4	0	2	0	2	41	10	26	5	0
Gladstone	4,699	5	0	0	0	5	51	8	43	0	1
Gladwin	2,880	18	0	5	0	13	48	13	33	2	1
Grand Blanc	7,865	11	0	1	0	10	68	11	53	4	0
Grand Blanc Township	36,523	61	0	19	3	39	402	54	320	28	1
Grand Haven	11,155	28	1	11	3	13	173	14	155	4	0
Grand Ledge	7,862	5	0	3	1	1	92	11	75	6	0
Grand Rapids	201,799	1,286	8	144	274	860	3,850	595	2,754	501	35
Grandville	16,021	39	0	9	8	22	575	37	518	20	1
Grant	892	1	0	1	0	0	13	2	10	1	0
Grayling	1,833	7	0	4	0	3	73	10	63	0	0
Green Oak Township	19,075	15	0	4	2	9	124	14	101	9	0
Greenville	8,447	29	0	8	2	19	311	33	269	9	2
Grosse Ile Township	10,135	1	0	1	0	0	18	3	14	1	0
Grosse Pointe	5,141	6	0	0	2	4	91	10	73	8	0
Grosse Pointe Farms	9,108	9	0	1	3	5	80	4	64	12	0
Grosse Pointe Park	11,041	14	0	6	4	4	165	12	138	15	0
Grosse Pointe Shores	2,836	1	0	0	0	1	28	2	25	1	0
Grosse Pointe Woods	15,350	25	0	2	6	17	191	9	153	29	0
Hamburg Township	21,755	5	0	0	0	5	38	6	30	2	1
Hampton Township	9,428	16	0	7	1	8	76	11	59	6	0
Hamtramck	21,633	174	1	8	53	112	414	113	230	71	7
Hancock	4,533	5	0	5	0	0	31	0	29	2	0
Harbor Beach	1,584	9	0	5	0	4	35	5	30	0	0
Harbor Springs	1,208	1	0	0	0	1	6	0	6	0	0
Harper Woods	13,746	110	1	4	18	87	606	91	425	90	2
Hart	2,089	17	0	2	0	15	131	7	121	3	1
Hartford	2,589	6	0	0	0	6	13	4	9	0	0
Hastings	7,313	18	0	5	0	13	151	14	133	4	1
Hazel Park	16,478	40	1	8	2	29	261	20	212	29	1
Hesperia	941	3	0	0	0	3	22	4	18	0	0
Highland Park	10,703	221	2	16	43	160	328	57	203	68	26
Highland Township	20,302	8	0	2	0	6	75	13	52	10	0
Hillsdale	8,020	23	0	7	0	16	128	13	108	7	0
Holland	33,356	127	1	25	12	89	613	94	498	21	4
Holly	6,185	5	0	4	0	1	40	13	26	1	0
Hopkins	611	0	0	0	0	0	0	0	0	0	0
Houghton	8,029	3	0	2	0	1	113	1	108	4	0
Howell	9,637	32	1	9	2	20	76	10	57	9	1
Hudson	2,207	9	0	2	0	7	34	6	24	4	0
Huntington Woods	6,321	0	0	0	0	0	23	7	14	2	0
Huron Township	16,089	26	0	7	2	17	106	16	81	9	0
Imlay City	3,575	6	0	1	0	5	30	6	22	2	0
Independence Township	37,101	34	0	2	3	29	179	18	149	12	0
Inkster	24,268	242	7	22	32	181	595	176	318	101	9
Ionia	10,907	44	0	30	0	14	139	14	114	11	2
Iron Mountain	7,320	7	0	2	0	5	4	0	4	0	0
Iron River	2,816	15	0	1	0	14	38	6	25	7	0
Ironwood	4,883	8	0	1	1	6	90	8	77	5	1
Ishpeming	6,426	12	0	2	1	9	65	3	56	6	0

Table 8. Offenses Known to Law Enforcement, by Selected State and City, 2019—Continued

(Number.)

State/city	Population	Violent crime	Murder and nonnegligent manslaughter	Rape[1]	Robbery	Aggravated assault	Property crime	Burglary	Larceny-theft	Motor vehicle theft	Arson[2]
Ishpeming Township	3,528	3	0	0	0	3	2	2	0	0	0
Jackson	32,503	360	4	51	37	268	1,344	206	1,025	113	17
Jonesville	2,204	6	0	2	0	4	95	3	88	4	0
Kalamazoo	76,827	949	9	110	182	648	3,578	703	2,546	329	44
Kalamazoo Township	24,613	96	1	14	25	56	670	135	455	80	4
Kalkaska	2,086	1	0	1	0	0	24	1	21	2	0
Keego Harbor	3,462	1	0	1	0	0	21	2	18	1	0
Kentwood	52,274	162	0	23	20	119	1,111	170	850	91	5
Kinde	417	0	0	0	0	0	0	0	0	0	0
Kingsford	4,950	10	0	6	0	4	37	6	29	2	0
Kinross Township	7,288	8	1	2	0	5	6	2	4	0	0
Laingsburg	1,281	2	0	2	0	0	8	4	2	2	2
Lake Angelus	309	0	0	0	0	0	0	0	0	0	0
Lake Linden	962	0	0	0	0	0	3	1	1	1	0
Lake Odessa	2,036	2	0	1	0	1	16	3	13	0	1
Lake Orion	3,177	6	0	2	0	4	27	5	21	1	1
Lakeview	1,007	1	0	0	0	1	43	2	41	0	0
Lansing	118,953	1,313	12	140	178	983	3,355	763	2,225	367	21
Lansing Township	8,294	70	1	13	11	45	441	52	353	36	3
Lapeer	8,597	35	1	12	5	17	279	24	252	3	0
Lapeer Township	5,032	1	0	0	0	1	6	1	5	0	0
Lathrup Village	4,124	3	0	2	0	1	35	6	29	0	0
Laurium	1,912	0	0	0	0	0	21	4	17	0	1
Lawton	1,799	4	0	1	0	3	48	12	33	3	0
Lennon	482	0	0	0	0	0	6	2	4	0	0
Leslie	1,909	1	0	0	0	1	22	4	16	2	0
Lexington	1,099	0	0	0	0	0	3	0	3	0	0
Lincoln Park	36,336	224	1	24	35	164	812	127	620	65	5
Lincoln Township	14,615	14	0	6	1	7	171	11	151	9	0
Linden	3,908	3	0	0	1	2	15	1	14	0	0
Litchfield	1,333	1	0	0	1	0	10	2	8	0	0
Livonia	93,644	167	0	22	18	127	1,411	126	1,173	112	7
Lowell	4,198	7	0	0	0	7	104	16	77	11	0
Ludington	8,144	32	0	17	0	15	136	21	112	3	0
Lyon Township	21,540	13	0	2	1	10	125	26	96	3	0
Mackinac Island	468	2	0	0	0	2	94	0	93	1	0
Mackinaw City	797	0	0	0	0	0	23	2	21	0	0
Madison Heights	30,081	53	0	11	13	29	593	92	461	40	2
Madison Township	8,287	11	2	1	0	8	100	4	92	4	0
Mancelona	1,364	0	0	0	0	0	0	0	0	0	0
Manistee	6,103	23	0	17	0	6	99	9	87	3	0
Manistique	2,915	16	0	3	0	13	44	5	37	2	0
Manton	1,544	0	0	0	0	0	0	0	0	0	0
Marenisco Township	1,434	0	0	0	0	0	1	0	1	0	0
Marine City	4,061	9	0	1	0	8	21	1	18	2	0
Marlette	1,756	6	0	0	1	5	16	0	16	0	0
Marquette	20,599	26	0	15	3	8	182	12	165	5	0
Marshall	6,997	10	0	4	1	5	81	6	71	4	0
Marysville	9,656	9	1	0	1	7	73	7	63	3	1
Mason	8,483	19	0	2	0	17	82	10	71	1	1
Mattawan	1,970	15	0	1	0	14	44	10	30	4	0
Mayville	882	4	0	4	0	0	3	0	3	0	0
Melvindale	10,264	47	0	5	2	40	236	35	172	29	1
Memphis	1,184	1	0	1	0	0	0	0	0	0	0
Mendon	854	1	0	0	0	1	7	1	6	0	0
Menominee	8,052	33	0	13	1	19	144	18	117	9	3
Meridian Township	43,790	108	1	40	12	55	900	96	759	45	7
Metamora Township	4,287	4	0	1	0	3	14	1	11	2	0
Metro Police Authority of Genesee County	19,931	49	0	8	5	36	268	81	178	9	1
Midland	41,791	56	1	21	4	30	392	36	344	12	3
Milan	6,106	13	0	6	1	6	45	7	35	3	0
Milford	16,984	12	0	4	2	6	62	11	45	6	0
Millington	995	0	0	0	0	0	16	1	15	0	0
Montague	2,359	3	1	0	0	2	33	2	28	3	0
Montrose Township	7,447	6	0	1	1	4	59	16	37	6	1
Morenci	2,146	9	0	2	0	7	19	6	13	0	0
Morrice	894	1	0	1	0	0	7	0	7	0	0
Mount Morris	2,834	25	0	9	3	13	31	9	22	0	0
Mount Morris Township	20,274	130	2	18	7	103	344	111	187	46	5
Mount Pleasant	25,315	48	0	22	2	24	384	36	332	16	1
Munising	2,177	7	1	0	0	6	40	6	33	1	0
Muskegon	37,178	308	8	27	46	227	1,293	252	911	130	11
Muskegon Heights	10,717	232	5	15	36	176	544	113	395	36	11
Muskegon Township	17,937	45	0	11	6	28	494	56	417	21	0
Napoleon Township	6,757	5	0	2	0	3	17	3	12	2	0
Nashville	1,678	4	0	1	0	3	21	8	12	1	0
Negaunee	4,544	9	0	3	1	5	40	2	38	0	1
Newaygo	2,068	6	0	1	0	5	39	6	32	1	2
New Baltimore	12,444	8	0	6	0	2	47	9	38	0	1
New Buffalo	1,877	2	0	0	0	2	13	2	11	0	0
New Era	446	0	0	0	0	0	2	0	2	0	0
New Lothrop	552	0	0	0	0	0	4	1	3	0	0

Table 8. Offenses Known to Law Enforcement, by Selected State and City, 2019—Continued

(Number.)

State/city	Population	Violent crime	Murder and nonnegligent manslaughter	Rape[1]	Robbery	Aggravated assault	Property crime	Burglary	Larceny-theft	Motor vehicle theft	Arson[2]
Niles	11,106	86	0	20	17	49	366	49	274	43	1
Northfield Township	8,788	16	0	4	0	12	81	19	56	6	0
North Muskegon	3,797	2	0	2	0	0	51	1	49	1	0
Northville	5,971	8	0	0	0	8	44	2	42	0	1
Northville Township	29,170	20	0	6	0	14	297	31	250	16	2
Norton Shores	24,702	37	0	11	5	21	477	44	405	28	2
Norway	2,756	1	0	1	0	0	0	0	0	0	0
Novi	61,699	48	1	8	2	37	514	21	466	27	0
Oakland Township	19,649	2	0	2	0	0	38	14	23	1	0
Oak Park	29,654	72	2	12	15	43	510	125	323	62	6
Olivet	1,857	2	0	1	0	1	13	0	13	0	0
Ontwa Township-Edwardsburg	6,553	19	0	4	1	14	128	21	93	14	1
Orchard Lake	2,483	2	0	0	0	2	20	3	16	1	1
Orion Township	36,878	24	1	3	2	18	172	18	147	7	0
Oscoda Township	6,746	19	1	1	1	16	79	27	49	3	2
Otisville	823	0	0	0	0	0	0	0	0	0	0
Otsego	4,007	0	0	0	0	0	37	10	24	3	1
Ovid	1,611	0	0	0	0	0	4	1	2	1	0
Owendale	224	0	0	0	0	0	0	0	0	0	0
Owosso	14,399	97	1	21	7	68	197	44	140	13	3
Oxford	3,574	1	0	0	1	0	10	2	7	1	0
Oxford Township	19,467	14	0	6	0	8	82	13	65	4	0
Paw Paw	3,370	17	0	9	1	7	177	20	152	5	0
Peck	591	0	0	0	0	0	0	0	0	0	0
Pentwater	853	2	0	0	1	1	5	0	5	0	0
Perry	2,075	7	0	0	1	6	18	7	10	1	0
Petoskey	5,747	2	0	0	1	1	30	8	21	1	0
Pigeon	1,123	0	0	0	0	0	0	0	0	0	0
Pinckney	2,410	2	0	0	0	2	11	2	9	0	0
Pinconning	1,238	3	0	2	0	1	12	3	9	0	0
Pittsfield Township	39,417	69	1	16	11	41	629	54	512	63	2
Plainwell	3,804	11	0	2	0	9	53	5	45	3	0
Pleasant Ridge	2,465	0	0	0	0	0	15	1	14	0	0
Plymouth	9,175	6	0	4	1	1	61	9	46	6	1
Plymouth Township	27,020	18	1	4	1	12	184	21	141	22	1
Pontiac	59,791	769	10	66	108	585	1,300	315	875	110	15
Portage	49,583	136	0	30	14	92	1,549	204	1,279	66	7
Port Austin	620	1	0	0	0	1	9	3	6	0	0
Port Huron	28,783	218	2	25	26	165	662	124	491	47	9
Portland	3,932	11	0	5	0	6	47	2	40	5	1
Potterville	2,712	0	0	0	0	0	2	0	1	1	0
Prairieville Township	3,525	2	0	2	0	0	16	0	15	1	0
Quincy	1,616	4	0	0	0	4	25	3	21	1	0
Raisin Township	7,760	6	0	4	0	2	6	4	2	0	0
Reading	1,042	0	0	0	0	0	0	0	0	0	0
Redford Township	46,742	244	4	33	20	187	953	218	551	184	5
Reed City	2,377	18	0	4	0	14	39	13	26	0	0
Reese	1,364	2	0	0	0	2	8	4	4	0	0
Richfield Township, Genesee County	8,358	6	0	3	0	3	63	19	33	11	0
Richfield Township, Roscommon County	3,630	4	0	3	0	1	8	4	4	0	0
Richland	806	1	0	0	0	1	3	0	3	0	0
Richland Township, Saginaw County	3,925	1	0	0	0	1	9	2	7	0	0
Richmond	5,904	26	0	6	0	20	29	1	28	0	0
River Rouge	7,404	80	3	10	11	56	155	26	107	22	8
Riverview	12,027	20	0	2	4	14	102	14	72	16	2
Rochester	13,429	6	0	2	1	3	51	5	44	2	0
Rochester Hills	75,167	39	0	5	3	31	461	42	405	14	1
Rockford	6,377	9	0	6	1	2	60	5	52	3	0
Rockwood	3,165	3	0	1	0	2	19	2	15	2	0
Rogers City	2,663	1	0	0	0	1	26	3	21	2	0
Romeo	3,608	3	0	0	0	3	5	1	4	0	1
Romulus	23,507	231	2	34	18	177	671	117	446	108	1
Roosevelt Park	3,793	3	0	0	0	3	254	1	250	3	1
Roseville	47,381	180	3	18	45	114	1,361	141	1,086	134	7
Rothbury	448	0	0	0	0	0	9	0	9	0	0
Royal Oak	59,742	61	1	9	4	47	439	38	369	32	1
Saginaw	47,954	707	9	34	51	613	743	245	421	77	20
Saginaw Township	39,022	82	2	15	14	51	707	70	615	22	2
Saline	9,431	6	0	1	0	5	62	2	54	6	0
Sandusky	2,508	7	0	0	0	7	50	10	40	0	0
Saugatuck-Douglas	2,307	0	0	0	0	0	8	0	7	1	0
Sault Ste. Marie	13,478	33	0	16	0	17	182	19	155	8	0
Schoolcraft	1,559	0	0	0	0	0	29	3	23	3	0
Scottville	1,210	2	0	0	0	2	32	0	32	0	0
Sebewaing	1,629	2	0	2	0	0	6	1	5	0	0
Shelby	2,032	10	0	0	0	10	42	5	37	0	0
Shelby Township	80,806	99	0	33	3	63	475	55	371	49	1
Shepherd	1,489	3	0	1	0	2	7	0	7	0	0
Somerset Township	4,541	3	0	1	0	2	12	1	11	0	0
Southfield	73,335	200	1	33	45	121	1,508	358	898	252	3

Table 8. Offenses Known to Law Enforcement, by Selected State and City, 2019—Continued

(Number.)

State/city	Population	Violent crime	Murder and nonnegligent manslaughter	Rape[1]	Robbery	Aggravated assault	Property crime	Burglary	Larceny-theft	Motor vehicle theft	Arson[2]
Southgate	28,979	74	1	14	15	44	731	57	628	46	2
South Haven	4,326	24	0	7	1	16	258	14	237	7	0
South Lyon	11,896	6	0	3	0	3	33	4	29	0	0
Sparta	4,391	8	0	4	0	4	72	7	64	1	0
Spring Arbor Township	8,009	1	0	0	0	1	10	2	8	0	0
Springfield Township	14,554	5	0	2	0	3	38	10	24	4	0
Springport Township	2,148	3	0	0	0	3	11	4	7	0	0
Stanton	1,435	1	0	0	0	1	17	2	15	0	0
St. Charles	1,891	1	0	0	0	1	9	4	5	0	0
St. Clair	5,286	12	0	5	0	7	65	13	48	4	1
St. Clair Shores	59,365	107	2	24	10	71	552	80	415	57	0
Sterling Heights	133,377	167	0	25	17	125	1,140	92	952	96	7
St. Ignace	2,309	5	0	1	0	4	16	1	15	0	1
St. Johns	7,938	18	0	10	1	7	43	9	31	3	0
St. Joseph	8,355	17	0	6	2	9	169	8	156	5	1
St. Joseph Township	9,738	12	0	1	1	10	162	15	139	8	0
St. Louis	7,104	20	0	9	0	11	59	7	51	1	0
Stockbridge	1,257	2	0	1	0	1	23	5	17	1	0
Sturgis	10,779	44	0	17	4	23	310	29	244	37	5
Sumpter Township	9,407	15	0	0	1	14	54	13	34	7	0
Sylvan Lake	1,864	2	0	0	0	2	14	1	13	0	0
Tawas	4,471	8	0	2	0	6	69	3	63	3	0
Taylor	60,923	378	1	35	41	301	1,386	242	998	146	12
Tecumseh	8,382	15	0	1	1	13	78	14	61	3	1
Thetford Township	6,689	0	0	0	0	0	0	0	0	0	0
Thomas Township	11,438	20	0	3	0	17	88	21	61	6	0
Three Oaks	1,549	3	0	0	1	2	32	6	25	1	0
Three Rivers	7,643	75	1	16	8	50	352	52	269	31	1
Tittabawassee Township	9,863	6	0	0	0	6	40	9	28	3	0
Traverse City	15,772	66	3	15	4	44	231	27	197	7	1
Trenton	18,147	20	0	7	1	12	135	14	101	20	0
Troy	84,688	67	2	10	8	47	1,042	70	918	54	2
Tuscarora Township	2,934	6	0	1	0	5	51	4	45	2	0
Ubly	785	4	0	4	0	0	8	2	6	0	0
Unadilla Township	3,425	8	0	1	0	7	13	4	8	1	0
Utica	5,195	11	0	4	1	6	186	5	176	5	0
Van Buren Township	28,294	80	1	9	5	65	579	58	456	65	0
Vassar	2,534	10	0	1	0	9	7	0	7	0	0
Vernon	770	0	0	0	0	0	4	0	4	0	0
Vicksburg	3,490	4	0	0	0	4	58	6	49	3	0
Walker	25,051	45	0	15	9	21	604	59	518	27	3
Walled Lake	7,184	10	0	0	1	9	49	4	43	2	0
Warren	134,653	648	8	89	83	468	2,465	569	1,540	356	17
Waterford Township	73,105	135	2	43	10	80	646	122	472	52	9
Watervliet	1,652	6	0	2	0	4	23	5	17	1	0
Wayland	4,272	14	0	6	1	7	58	13	43	2	5
Wayne	16,816	120	0	17	17	86	296	73	174	49	1
West Bloomfield Township	66,067	40	0	10	6	24	344	42	276	26	1
West Branch	2,048	0	0	0	0	0	28	2	26	0	1
Westland	81,444	307	1	80	29	197	1,178	164	904	110	8
White Cloud	1,395	10	0	6	0	4	22	3	18	1	0
Whitehall	2,785	3	0	1	0	2	46	4	40	2	1
White Lake Township	31,556	25	0	6	2	17	210	14	188	8	1
White Pigeon	1,521	2	0	0	0	2	40	5	26	9	0
Williamston	3,972	7	0	2	0	5	26	6	18	2	0
Wixom	14,074	24	0	4	4	16	187	22	155	10	0
Wolverine Lake	4,825	1	0	0	0	1	15	0	15	0	0
Woodhaven	12,438	13	0	0	4	9	164	8	143	13	0
Woodland Township	2,115	0	0	0	0	0	0	0	0	0	0
Wyandotte	24,829	59	1	11	6	41	354	47	279	28	3
Wyoming	76,295	368	3	61	51	253	1,122	125	800	197	9
Yale	1,875	9	0	0	0	9	22	8	14	0	1
Ypsilanti	21,178	216	2	26	26	162	736	119	553	64	0
Zeeland	5,572	11	1	4	0	6	49	15	32	2	0
Zilwaukee	1,523	0	0	0	0	0	6	3	3	0	0
MINNESOTA											
Adrian	1,220	0	0	0	0	0	5	1	2	2	0
Aitkin[5]	1,985	2	0	0	0	2	45	2	40	3	0
Akeley	442	2	0	0	0	2	22	5	16	1	0
Albany	2,752	1	0	0	0	1	9	0	9	0	0
Albert Lea	17,597	38	0	5	4	29	506	101	381	24	3
Alexandria	13,914	29	0	7	2	20	385	26	346	13	1
Annandale	3,415	3	0	0	0	3	44	2	41	1	0
Anoka[5]	17,591	44	0	4	8	32	323	36	259	28	1
Appleton	1,322	6	0	0	0	6	38	4	30	4	0
Apple Valley	54,779	51	0	24	10	17	1,062	58	963	41	3
Arlington	2,163	0	0	0	0	0	5	0	5	0	0
Atwater	1,110	0	0	0	0	0	1	0	1	0	1
Austin	25,224	54	0	6	6	42	487	80	378	29	0
Avon	1,597	1	0	0	0	1	18	2	10	6	0
Babbitt	1,498	0	0	0	0	0	8	2	6	0	0
Barnesville	2,608	3	0	0	0	3	0	0	0	0	0

Table 8. Offenses Known to Law Enforcement, by Selected State and City, 2019—Continued

(Number.)

State/city	Population	Violent crime	Murder and nonnegligent manslaughter	Rape[1]	Robbery	Aggravated assault	Property crime	Burglary	Larceny-theft	Motor vehicle theft	Arson[2]
Battle Lake	938	0	0	0	0	0	5	0	5	0	0
Baxter	8,401	11	0	4	0	7	303	13	281	9	1
Bayport	3,834	1	0	1	0	0	19	0	14	5	0
Becker	4,957	8	0	4	0	4	39	13	26	0	1
Belgrade/Brooten	1,524	0	0	0	0	0	13	0	10	3	0
Belle Plaine	7,232	2	0	0	0	2	66	3	59	4	0
Bemidji	15,550	83	0	13	11	59	1,187	91	1,039	57	2
Benson	3,050	0	0	0	0	0	0	0	0	0	0
Big Lake	11,236	5	0	0	0	5	55	7	38	10	1
Blackduck	838	2	0	1	0	1	10	2	8	0	0
Blaine[5]	66,260	61	1	20	16	24	1,586	126	1,369	91	3
Blooming Prairie	1,956	0	0	0	0	0	5	1	2	2	0
Bloomington	85,902	203	3	54	61	85	3,079	183	2,731	165	17
Blue Earth	3,113	2	0	1	0	1	24	13	10	1	0
Braham	1,791	1	0	0	0	1	1	1	0	0	0
Brainerd	13,449	63	0	19	2	42	461	57	383	21	0
Breckenridge	3,175	6	0	2	0	4	69	13	54	2	1
Breezy Point	2,418	0	0	0	0	0	5	0	5	0	0
Breitung Township	612	1	0	0	0	1	0	0	0	0	0
Brooklyn Center	31,000	108	1	21	45	41	1,223	79	944	200	2
Brooklyn Park	81,211	299	2	52	97	148	2,760	299	2,160	301	7
Brownton	723	0	0	0	0	0	4	0	4	0	0
Buffalo	16,421	16	0	8	1	7	268	16	244	8	0
Buffalo Lake	680	1	0	1	0	0	8	2	6	0	0
Burnsville	61,306	103	1	12	27	63	1,621	130	1,379	112	5
Caledonia[5]	2,718	0	0	0	0	0	3	0	3	0	0
Cambridge	9,008	6	0	1	1	4	361	19	331	11	0
Canby	1,674	0	0	0	0	0	0	0	0	0	0
Cannon Falls	4,063	1	0	0	1	0	74	9	62	3	0
Centennial Lakes[5]	11,025	15	0	6	0	9	111	13	89	9	1
Champlin	25,636	25	0	7	5	13	231	20	203	8	0
Chaska	27,143	16	0	4	2	10	253	26	220	7	1
Chisholm	4,875	6	0	1	0	5	59	5	50	4	0
Clara City	1,282	1	0	1	0	0	3	0	3	0	0
Clearbrook	520	3	0	1	0	2	24	9	15	0	0
Cleveland	726	0	0	0	0	0	12	0	12	0	0
Cloquet	12,009	10	0	1	1	8	277	9	258	10	0
Cold Spring/Richmond	5,656	3	0	1	0	2	29	3	24	2	0
Columbia Heights[5]	20,632	60	0	10	25	25	486	51	386	49	2
Comfrey[5]	353	0	0	0	0	0	2	0	2	0	0
Corcoran	6,195	0	0	0	0	0	41	8	29	4	0
Cottage Grove	37,534	29	0	16	5	8	590	50	509	31	0
Crookston[5]	7,794	23	0	6	0	17	179	24	151	4	0
Crosby	2,335	0	0	0	0	0	14	1	12	1	0
Crosslake	2,294	0	0	0	0	0	8	3	5	0	0
Crystal	23,184	60	1	14	19	26	602	51	506	45	1
Danube	457	3	0	0	0	3	5	1	4	0	0
Dawson/Boyd[5]	1,547	0	0	0	0	0	4	1	3	0	0
Dayton	6,542	1	0	0	0	1	42	6	25	11	0
Deephaven	3,980	1	0	0	0	1	26	3	22	1	0
Deer River[5]	933	3	0	1	0	2	18	2	16	0	0
Detroit Lakes	9,362	14	0	3	3	8	269	18	243	8	0
Dilworth	4,491	6	0	1	5	0	275	15	250	10	0
Duluth	85,846	292	2	37	69	184	3,670	481	2,977	212	16
Dundas	1,623	0	0	0	0	0	12	1	11	0	0
Eagan	66,824	39	0	12	12	15	1,294	93	1,129	72	1
Eagle Lake	3,195	4	0	2	0	2	15	5	8	2	0
East Grand Forks[5]	8,597	11	0	1	1	9	100	17	70	13	1
East Range	3,590	8	0	3	0	5	37	7	26	4	0
Eden Prairie	64,777	52	0	13	14	25	700	68	610	22	3
Eden Valley	1,035	0	0	0	0	0	1	0	1	0	3
Edina	53,076	47	0	15	15	17	983	140	794	49	3
Elko New Market	4,783	1	0	0	0	1	21	1	18	2	0
Elk River	25,081	15	0	5	1	9	403	36	350	17	0
Ely	3,344	2	0	2	0	0	40	6	31	3	0
Eveleth	3,582	11	0	5	1	5	108	20	81	7	0
Fairfax	1,127	3	0	0	0	3	14	0	14	0	1
Fairmont	10,023	26	0	10	1	15	212	39	164	9	0
Faribault	23,913	61	0	15	8	38	470	99	337	34	5
Farmington	23,335	12	0	0	1	11	177	24	138	15	0
Fergus Falls	13,900	47	0	10	4	33	613	60	527	26	1
Floodwood	523	1	0	0	0	1	7	0	7	0	0
Foley	2,671	0	0	0	0	0	36	9	27	0	0
Forest Lake	20,457	30	0	15	3	12	624	69	527	28	1
Fridley[5]	27,805	88	1	17	20	50	1,036	103	856	77	5
Fulda[5]	1,209	0	0	0	0	0	7	2	5	0	0
Gaylord	2,236	9	0	5	0	4	39	11	27	1	1
Gilbert	1,788	3	0	2	0	1	56	5	50	1	1
Glencoe	5,444	5	0	0	0	5	49	12	36	1	0
Glenwood	2,593	3	0	0	0	3	35	3	32	0	0
Golden Valley	21,934	18	0	5	7	6	463	65	362	36	1
Goodview	4,149	3	0	0	0	3	50	10	36	4	0
Grand Rapids[5]	11,267	20	0	4	0	16	171	11	154	6	3

Table 8. Offenses Known to Law Enforcement, by Selected State and City, 2019—Continued

(Number.)

State/city	Population	Violent crime	Murder and nonnegligent manslaughter	Rape[1]	Robbery	Aggravated assault	Property crime	Burglary	Larceny-theft	Motor vehicle theft	Arson[2]
Granite Falls	2,700	3	0	0	0	3	51	4	42	5	0
Hallock	899	0	0	0	0	0	0	0	0	0	0
Hastings	22,774	39	0	10	2	27	451	58	360	33	0
Hawley	2,223	1	0	0	0	1	6	4	2	0	0
Hector	1,045	0	0	0	0	0	10	0	9	1	1
Henning	814	0	0	0	0	0	2	0	2	0	0
Hermantown	9,770	9	0	4	0	5	618	25	581	12	1
Hibbing	15,895	41	1	12	0	28	166	19	126	21	1
Hill City[5]	585	1	0	0	0	1	18	1	16	1	0
Hokah[5]	543	0	0	0	0	0	0	0	0	0	0
Hopkins	18,735	33	1	9	5	18	292	47	218	27	1
Houston[5]	963	0	0	0	0	0	4	0	4	0	0
Howard Lake	2,091	1	0	0	0	1	4	0	4	0	0
Hutchinson	13,960	31	0	7	4	20	236	32	197	7	0
International Falls	5,871	13	0	2	1	10	74	8	64	2	1
Inver Grove Heights	35,668	78	0	23	9	46	650	90	487	73	4
Isanti	5,985	6	0	1	0	5	80	8	70	2	0
Isle	803	3	0	0	0	3	62	7	52	3	0
Janesville	2,261	5	0	1	0	4	37	14	21	2	0
Jordan	6,384	4	0	1	1	2	45	5	38	2	0
Kasson[5]	6,514	6	0	0	0	6	51	3	45	3	0
Kimball	797	0	0	0	0	0	0	0	0	0	1
La Crescent[5]	4,981	2	0	0	0	2	23	3	20	0	0
Lake City	5,140	4	0	2	0	2	58	7	48	3	0
Lake Crystal	2,496	5	0	1	0	4	30	6	22	2	0
Lakes Area	9,833	11	0	5	0	6	163	23	130	10	0
Lake Shore[5]	1,056	0	0	0	0	0	6	3	3	0	0
Lakeville	67,206	45	0	18	6	21	564	52	496	16	4
Lamberton	766	0	0	0	0	0	0	0	0	0	0
Lauderdale	2,548	3	0	1	0	2	50	10	36	4	0
Le Center	2,482	0	0	0	0	0	8	1	7	0	0
Lester Prairie	1,722	0	0	0	0	0	14	2	11	1	0
Le Sueur	4,016	0	0	0	0	0	32	6	25	1	0
Lewiston	1,558	0	0	0	0	0	6	3	3	0	0
Lino Lakes[5]	21,925	19	0	5	2	12	130	18	103	9	0
Litchfield	6,632	12	0	2	0	10	128	12	105	11	1
Little Falls	8,669	7	0	0	0	7	199	23	166	10	0
Long Prairie	3,297	5	0	1	0	4	50	2	48	0	0
Lonsdale	4,141	1	0	1	0	0	12	1	10	1	0
Madelia[5]	2,266	3	0	3	0	0	21	2	19	0	0
Mankato	42,955	110	0	29	12	69	1,462	186	1,217	59	3
Maple Grove	73,170	58	2	20	8	28	1,107	72	998	37	4
Mapleton	2,203	1	0	1	0	0	19	3	16	0	0
Maplewood	41,341	158	1	18	32	107	2,080	276	1,627	177	6
Marshall[5]	13,511	21	0	8	0	13	161	31	122	8	0
McGregor[5]	363	0	0	0	0	0	0	0	0	0	0
Medina	6,852	1	0	0	0	1	91	11	79	1	0
Melrose	3,642	2	0	0	1	1	27	2	22	3	0
Mendota Heights	11,373	15	0	2	2	11	153	32	114	7	0
Milaca	2,909	10	0	1	1	8	122	6	103	13	0
Minneapolis[5]	431,016	3,990	46	459	1,289	2,196	19,469	3,397	13,172	2,900	75
Minneota[5]	1,360	1	0	0	0	1	5	0	5	0	0
Minnetonka	54,497	30	0	8	7	15	772	91	643	38	0
Minnetrista	10,527	3	0	0	1	2	76	7	64	5	0
Montevideo	5,071	9	0	3	0	6	24	10	11	3	0
Montgomery	2,995	0	0	0	0	0	17	3	13	1	0
Moose Lake	2,821	4	0	0	0	4	51	2	48	1	0
Morris	5,360	2	0	2	0	0	70	16	51	3	0
Motley	650	0	0	0	0	0	54	8	46	0	
Mounds View	13,307	27	0	4	4	19	303	31	250	22	2
Mountain Lake[5]	2,047	2	0	1	0	1	14	4	6	4	1
New Brighton	23,058	31	1	2	7	21	442	48	360	34	2
New Hope	21,147	20	0	1	12	7	581	64	468	49	1
New Prague	8,326	8	0	3	1	4	69	12	57	0	1
New Richland	1,188	0	0	0	0	0	32	6	26	0	0
New Ulm[5]	13,205	8	0	2	0	6	116	12	96	8	1
New York Mills	1,228	0	0	0	0	0	7	1	3	3	0
Nisswa	2,066	0	0	0	0	0	1	0	1	0	0
North Branch	10,641	14	0	1	1	12	174	29	135	10	0
Northfield	20,707	12	0	7	1	4	152	17	129	6	0
North Mankato	13,977	14	0	5	2	7	124	16	99	9	0
North St. Paul	12,595	20	0	5	8	7	312	36	240	36	0
Oakdale	28,097	36	0	8	15	13	719	70	586	63	0
Oak Park Heights	4,972	2	0	2	0	0	241	14	217	10	0
Olivia	2,328	8	0	4	0	4	48	6	39	3	0
Onamia	861	3	0	1	0	2	28	4	22	2	0
Orono	20,349	14	1	6	2	5	126	25	101	0	0
Ortonville	1,774	1	0	1	0	0	19	6	10	3	0
Osakis	1,750	2	0	0	0	2	15	3	11	1	0
Osseo	2,801	0	0	0	0	0	1	0	1	0	0
Owatonna	25,792	27	0	8	1	18	403	31	339	33	1
Park Rapids	4,262	16	0	5	0	11	260	23	230	7	0
Paynesville	2,510	2	1	0	0	1	1	1	0	0	0

Table 8. Offenses Known to Law Enforcement, by Selected State and City, 2019—Continued

(Number.)

State/city	Population	Violent crime	Murder and nonnegligent manslaughter	Rape[1]	Robbery	Aggravated assault	Property crime	Burglary	Larceny-theft	Motor vehicle theft	Arson[2]
Pelican Rapids	2,507	3	0	1	0	2	5	1	2	2	0
Pequot Lakes	2,328	2	0	0	0	2	60	1	59	0	0
Perham	3,625	5	0	2	0	3	5	0	3	2	0
Pillager[5]	482	0	0	0	0	0	13	3	10	0	0
Pine River[5]	925	1	0	1	0	0	56	5	51	0	0
Plainview	3,295	1	0	1	0	0	22	6	15	1	0
Plymouth	80,616	37	0	8	5	24	938	152	742	44	2
Preston	1,290	0	0	0	0	0	3	0	3	0	0
Princeton	4,711	5	0	1	1	3	159	8	149	2	0
Prior Lake	27,362	42	0	12	7	23	603	50	528	25	0
Proctor	3,038	5	0	3	0	2	91	9	80	2	0
Ramsey[5]	27,358	24	0	12	0	12	286	21	246	19	0
Red Wing	16,408	38	1	3	4	30	426	66	323	37	3
Redwood Falls	4,951	12	0	3	0	9	143	15	121	7	0
Renville	1,177	2	0	1	0	1	19	2	12	5	0
Rice	1,389	0	0	0	0	0	11	2	8	1	0
Richfield	36,100	73	0	12	23	38	850	113	649	88	2
Robbinsdale	14,555	56	0	10	14	32	426	47	337	42	0
Rochester[5]	118,267	254	1	62	34	157	2,225	282	1,816	127	3
Rogers	13,417	11	0	3	2	6	225	13	200	12	0
Roseau	2,665	2	0	0	0	2	25	1	20	4	0
Rosemount	24,961	21	0	8	1	12	146	17	126	3	0
Roseville	36,750	83	0	14	34	35	2,164	162	1,885	117	6
Rushford	1,703	0	0	0	0	0	0	0	0	0	0
Sauk Centre	4,492	4	0	1	0	3	102	6	92	4	0
Sauk Rapids	14,015	13	0	1	0	12	284	30	243	11	0
Savage	32,336	35	0	12	3	20	404	63	327	14	4
Shakopee	41,892	81	0	31	9	41	745	75	627	43	1
Silver Bay	1,764	0	0	0	0	0	0	0	0	0	0
Silver Lake	813	0	0	0	0	0	12	0	11	1	0
Slayton[5]	1,979	0	0	0	0	0	2	1	1	0	0
Sleepy Eye[5]	3,347	6	0	3	0	3	17	3	12	2	1
South Lake Minnetonka	12,762	12	0	5	2	5	88	16	68	4	0
South St. Paul	20,148	46	0	18	5	23	481	71	355	55	2
Springfield[5]	1,999	0	0	0	0	0	20	2	17	1	0
Spring Grove[5]	1,264	0	0	0	0	0	19	1	17	1	0
Spring Lake Park[5]	6,994	19	1	2	2	14	195	29	151	15	0
St. Anthony	9,172	9	0	4	2	3	197	31	154	12	1
Staples	2,945	5	0	3	0	2	62	6	53	3	0
Starbuck	1,255	2	0	2	0	0	46	5	40	1	0
St. Charles	3,773	3	0	1	0	2	37	4	29	4	0
St. Cloud	68,311	298	0	73	50	175	2,443	225	2,044	174	10
St. Francis[5]	7,894	19	0	3	0	16	95	12	81	2	0
St. James[5]	4,426	6	0	1	0	5	73	11	55	7	1
St. Joseph	7,227	7	0	1	0	6	49	6	39	4	0
St. Louis Park	49,535	89	0	19	20	50	1,396	130	1,175	91	2
St. Paul	310,263	1,752	28	236	542	946	11,208	2,038	6,751	2,419	118
St. Paul Park	5,410	11	0	1	1	9	147	20	116	11	1
St. Peter	12,032	16	0	6	0	10	128	13	112	3	0
Thief River Falls	8,825	6	0	4	0	2	132	23	104	5	1
Tracy[5]	2,094	2	0	0	0	2	30	10	19	1	0
Twin Valley	761	0	0	0	0	0	0	0	0	0	0
Two Harbors	3,523	0	0	0	0	0	5	0	5	0	0
Virginia	8,398	41	0	7	3	31	315	51	239	25	0
Wabasha	2,471	5	0	0	0	5	39	8	25	6	0
Wadena	4,097	10	0	4	0	6	76	4	69	3	0
Waite Park	7,764	33	0	0	7	26	644	39	579	26	1
Walker[5]	930	2	0	0	0	2	42	4	35	3	0
Warroad	1,796	4	0	0	0	4	25	1	24	0	0
Waseca	8,841	15	0	4	0	11	159	15	141	3	0
Waterville	1,874	2	0	0	0	2	11	1	9	1	0
Wayzata	6,560	1	0	0	1	0	98	13	77	8	1
Wells	2,170	2	0	0	0	2	6	0	4	2	0
West Concord[5]	768	0	0	0	0	0	10	5	4	1	0
West Hennepin	5,670	2	0	0	0	2	28	5	22	1	0
West St. Paul	19,694	82	1	8	28	45	1,373	101	1,184	88	4
Wheaton[5]	1,295	1	0	1	0	0	26	4	20	2	0
White Bear Lake	26,176	35	0	8	12	15	609	93	461	55	4
Willmar	19,684	84	0	29	6	49	419	53	335	31	2
Windom[5]	4,393	33	0	6	1	26	61	8	45	8	0
Winona	26,720	30	0	10	6	14	644	51	573	20	1
Winsted	2,247	1	0	0	0	1	16	1	14	1	0
Woodbury	72,527	45	2	26	10	7	1,264	145	1,092	27	2
Worthington	13,329	31	0	10	2	19	130	31	80	19	0
Wyoming	7,993	4	0	0	0	4	68	6	56	6	0
Zumbrota	3,477	2	0	1	0	1	42	5	33	4	0
MISSISSIPPI											
Ackerman	1,443	2	0	0	1	1	39	15	24	0	0
Batesville	7,234	24	0	4	1	19	328	48	278	2	1
Biloxi	46,185	188	3	35	65	85	2,663	619	1,877	167	6
Booneville[7]	8,742		0		8	22	281	79	191	11	0
Brandon	24,426	26	0	3	2	21	269	49	193	27	1

Table 8. Offenses Known to Law Enforcement, by Selected State and City, 2019—Continued

(Number.)

State/city	Population	Violent crime	Murder and nonnegligent manslaughter	Rape[1]	Robbery	Aggravated assault	Property crime	Burglary	Larceny-theft	Motor vehicle theft	Arson[2]
Brookhaven	12,037	45	6	3	5	31	387	198	166	23	1
Byram	11,672	17	2	1	3	11	271	20	240	11	0
D'Iberville	14,125	10	0	1	3	6	895	38	828	29	0
Edwards	991	21	0	1	0	20	14	4	10	0	0
Florence[5]	4,500	3	0	0	0	3	284	14	257	13	1
Flowood	9,401	19	0	6	0	13	140	15	121	4	0
Fulton[7]	4,044		0		1	36	488	97	347	44	2
Gautier	18,563	53	3	6	8	36	3,492	419	2,805	268	10
Gulfport	72,383	236	12	25	65	134	2,065	269	1,622	174	4
Hattiesburg	45,971	106	2	27	23	54	676	81	509	86	4
Horn Lake	27,256	31	3	0	18	10	78	24	51	3	0
Iuka[7]	2,945		0		1						
Jackson[7]	163,297		76		478	675	7,411	1,806	4,693	912	82
Kosciusko	6,774	23	3	4	6	10	106	38	63	5	1
Laurel	18,471	125	2	14	21	88	800	255	490	55	1
Madison	25,862	10	0	0	3	7	269	17	251	1	0
Meridian	36,878	181	14	16	72	79	1,475	441	904	130	11
Ocean Springs[5]	17,864	23	0	4	4	15	492	67	390	35	4
Olive Branch	38,761	89	4	26	21	38	893	111	696	86	8
Pascagoula	21,610	56	4	12	19	21	1,241	167	993	81	0
Pass Christian	6,285	16	0	6	7	3	202	52	145	5	0
Petal	10,702	3	0	1	0	2	61	36	19	6	1
Ridgeland	24,171	66	1	3	25	37	485	44	407	34	2
Southaven[5]	55,718	92	5	4	26	57	1,778	206	1,393	179	0
Summit[7]	1,577		0		0	0	68	47	17	4	7
Vicksburg[7]	21,928		3		4	123	1,111	174	862	75	3
West Point	10,430	39	1	5	8	25	292	68	221	3	3
Wiggins	4,618	5	0	0	0	5	205	34	162	9	0
MISSOURI											
Adrian	1,599	4	0	1	0	3	65	27	35	3	0
Advance	1,337	4	0	1	0	3	21	5	15	1	0
Alma	381	0	0	0	0	0	1	0	1	0	0
Annapolis	338	0	0	0	0	0	2	1	1	0	0
Appleton City	1,068	2	0	0	0	1	13	7	4	2	0
Archie	1,210	1	0	0	0	1	11	4	6	1	0
Arnold	21,102	32	0	1	3	28	629	30	544	55	1
Ash Grove	1,447	2	0	0	0	2	28	4	23	1	0
Ashland	3,975	3	0	0	0	3	59	7	47	5	0
Aurora	7,455	36	0	3	0	33	374	64	279	31	6
Ava	2,902	8	0	0	0	8	47	7	38	2	0
Battlefield	6,348	0	0	0	0	0	72	13	55	4	0
Bella Villa	726	3	0	1	0	2	8	1	5	2	
Bellefontaine Neighbors	10,416	124	3	6	19	96	354	106	168	80	
Bel-Nor	1,398	1	0	0	0	1	25	4	10	11	
Belton	23,657	67	3	18	15	31	730	60	598	72	5
Berkeley	8,868	91	1	4	31	55	377	80	196	101	9
Bernie	1,884	1	0	0	0	1	23	4	18	1	0
Bertrand	745	0	0	0	0	0	19	11	8	0	0
Bethany	3,065	1	0	0	0	1	51	14	32	5	0
Billings	1,114	3	0	0	0	3	0	0	0	0	0
Blackburn	238	0	0	0	0	0	0	0	0	0	
Blue Springs[5]	55,415	99	0	26	9	64	1,216	118	961	137	
Bolivar[5]	11,129	30	0	9	4	17	416	45	349	22	0
Boonville[5]	8,410	16	0	3	1	12	189	35	144	10	
Branson	11,688	73	0	10	16	47	1,173	118	993	62	7
Branson West	449	3	0	1	0	2	102	1	101	0	0
Bucklin	437	0	0	0	0	0	0	0	0	0	0
Buffalo	3,073	2	0	0	0	2	93	15	67	11	1
Butler	4,017	15	1	4	0	10	132	31	88	13	0
Cabool	2,103	5	0	0	0	5	55	9	45	1	
Calverton Park	1,269	10	3	0	1	6	29	7	19	3	
Camdenton	4,138	18	0	0	2	16	199	46	148	5	1
Cameron[5]	9,674	32	0	2	1	29	172	16	152	4	0
Campbell	1,812	3	0	1	0	2	33	3	27	3	0
Canalou	301	0	0	0	0	0	1	1	0	0	0
Cape Girardeau	40,077	233	6	24	46	157	1,432	215	1,145	72	1
Carthage	14,808	38	0	15	2	21	505	35	410	60	2
Caruthersville	5,451	65	0	5	5	55	221	78	129	14	0
Cassville	3,327	15	0	1	1	13	265	17	240	8	
Charleston	5,490	42	1	1	3	37	99	16	76	7	2
Chillicothe	9,700	31	0	1	2	28	217	55	144	18	1
Clayton	16,936	12	0	1	3	8	234	23	176	35	0
Cleveland	663	0	0	0	0	0	4	0	3	1	0
Clever	2,787	2	0	0	0	2	12	1	9	2	0
Columbia[5]	125,017	401	11	69	74	247	3,243	499	2,431	313	13
Conway	775	0	0	0	0	0	0	0	0	0	0
Corder	397	0	0	0	0	0	2	2	0	0	0
Cottleville	5,849	5	0	0	1	4	36	1	30	5	0
Country Club Hills	1,265	14	0	1	4	9	44	5	26	13	0
Creve Coeur	18,829	14	0	1	2	11	289	31	224	34	2
Crystal City	4,698	5	2	0	1	2	161	20	129	12	2
Delta	438	0	0	0	0	0	0	0	0	0	0

Table 8. Offenses Known to Law Enforcement, by Selected State and City, 2019—Continued

(Number.)

State/city	Population	Violent crime	Murder and nonnegligent manslaughter	Rape[1]	Robbery	Aggravated assault	Property crime	Burglary	Larceny-theft	Motor vehicle theft	Arson[2]
De Soto	6,355	6	0	2	0	4	118	11	106	1	0
Dexter	7,861	15	0	7	1	7	193	42	146	5	0
Diamond	923	1	0	0	0	1	7	1	5	1	0
Dixon	1,421	15	0	0	0	15	42	6	36	0	0
Doolittle	600	0	0	0	0	0	0	0	0	0	0
Duenweg	1,378	3	0	2	0	1	25	4	18	3	2
Duquesne	1,577	1	0	0	0	1	52	11	36	5	0
East Lynne	303	0	0	0	0	0	0	0	0	0	0
Edgar Springs	193	0	0	0	0	0	1	0	0	1	0
Edina	1,111	1	0	0	0	1	6	5	0	1	0
Edmundson	830	3	0	2	0	1	46	0	30	16	0
Eldon[5]	4,649	14	1	2	1	10	113	17	89	7	0
El Dorado Springs	3,594	19	1	4	1	13	237	44	178	15	7
Ellisville	9,946	14	0	2	1	11	123	12	97	14	
Eminence	578	0	0	0	0	0	0	0	0	0	0
Excelsior Springs	11,715	15	0	8	0	7	253	32	201	20	0
Exeter	773	0	0	0	0	0	0	0	0	0	0
Farber	313	0	0	0	0	0	0	0	0	0	0
Farmington	19,178	27	1	6	3	17	641	49	561	31	0
Fayette	2,719	6	1	1	1	3	19	5	14	0	0
Ferguson[6]	20,664			4	10	42	1,001	178	694	129	
Fleming	125	0	0	0	0	0	0	0	0	0	0
Flordell Hills	776	6	0	0	1	5	34	12	20	2	0
Fordland	850	2	0	0	0	2	15	2	12	1	2
Foristell	589	3	0	0	0	3	19	0	18	1	0
Forsyth	2,582	5	0	0	0	5	56	6	49	1	0
Frontenac	3,851	5	0	2	1	2	95	6	79	10	0
Gladstone	27,553	89	1	12	14	62	725	102	504	119	3
Glasgow	1,095	0	0	0	0	0	0	0	0	0	0
Glendale	5,873	1	0	0	1	0	57	6	42	9	0
Goodman	1,257	0	0	0	0	0	11	6	2	3	0
Grain Valley	14,464	21	0	4	3	14	208	26	145	37	0
Grandview	25,022	192	4	12	37	139	969	113	701	155	
Greenfield	1,309	5	0	0	0	5	21	6	13	2	0
Hamilton[5]	1,694	5	0	3	0	2	14	1	11	2	0
Hardin	533	1	0	1	0	0	2	1	1	0	0
Harrisonville	10,095	28	0	4	2	22	395	68	286	41	0
Hayti	2,548	23	0	1	0	22	125	31	88	6	5
Hazelwood	25,146	113	2	5	33	73	695	127	432	136	
Herculaneum	4,149	5	0	1	0	4	121	5	98	18	0
Hermann[5]	2,325	3	0	0	0	3	33	7	23	3	1
Higginsville[5]	4,588	3	0	0	0	3	44	6	32	6	0
Highlandville	1,052	0	0	0	0	0	0	0	0	0	0
Hillsboro	3,231	17	0	0	3	14	69	6	53	10	6
Hillsdale	1,568	15	1	0	4	10	29	15	10	4	0
Hollister	4,608	7	0	0	0	7	51	0	51	0	
Hornersville	596	1	0	0	0	1	7	5	0	2	0
Houston	2,091	6	0	0	0	6	119	19	97	3	0
Howardville	339	1	0	0	0	1	0	0	0	0	0
Humansville	1,059	3	0	0	0	3	6	3	3	0	0
Huntsville	1,513	1	0	0	0	1	3	0	3	0	0
Iberia	749	1	0	0	0	1	7	1	4	2	0
Independence[5]	116,931	689	6	125	106	452	5,443	559	3,877	1,007	19
Jackson	15,151	16	0	1	0	15	228	28	185	15	
Jasper	969	1	0	0	0	1	15	2	13	0	0
Jefferson City	42,793	119	2	30	23	64	1,101	125	910	66	4
Jonesburg	709	0	0	0	0	0	16	3	12	1	0
Joplin	50,635	307	2	63	63	179	3,677	521	2,815	341	22
Kansas City	495,964	7,099	150	347	1,443	5,159	19,124	3,070	12,253	3,801	160
Kearney	10,736	7	0	5	0	2	109	3	96	10	0
Kimberling City	2,286	8	0	2	0	6	33	0	29	4	0
Kimmswick	151	0	0	0	0	0	0	0	0	0	0
Ladue	8,650	8	0	0	2	6	143	17	106	20	0
La Grange	902	0	0	0	0	0	7	1	6	0	0
Lake Lotawana	2,126	1	0	0	0	1	28	8	14	6	0
Lake Ozark	1,832	1	0	0	0	1	47	1	46	0	0
Lakeshire	1,393	1	0	0	0	1	4	3	1	0	0
Lake St. Louis	16,444	22	0	0	2	20	267	14	234	19	0
Lake Tapawingo	720	3	0	0	0	3	10	3	6	1	0
La Plata	1,312	3	0	1	0	2	7	3	3	1	0
Lathrop	2,009	2	0	1	0	1	12	2	8	2	0
Laurie	947	4	0	0	0	4	26	5	21	0	0
Lawson[5]	2,389	9	0	6	1	2	19	3	14	2	0
Lebanon	14,841	60	0	15	5	40	709	93	567	49	10
Lee's Summit	99,365	115	0	33	28	54	2,095	212	1,702	181	3
Licking[5]	3,087	8	0	1	0	7	25	7	16	2	0
Lilbourn	1,060	0	0	0	0	0	0	0	0	0	0
Lone Jack	1,342	5	0	1	0	4	19	2	12	5	0
Louisiana	3,241	12	0	3	0	9	88	10	72	6	0
Maplewood	8,108	26	0	0	7	19	594	39	523	32	3
Marble Hill	1,463	1	0	0	0	1	20	4	14	2	0
Marshall	12,915	59	1	14	5	39	263	45	204	14	3
Marshfield	7,566	7	0	0	1	6	236	46	179	11	0

Table 8. Offenses Known to Law Enforcement, by Selected State and City, 2019—Continued

(Number.)

State/city	Population	Violent crime	Murder and nonnegligent manslaughter	Rape[1]	Robbery	Aggravated assault	Property crime	Burglary	Larceny-theft	Motor vehicle theft	Arson[2]
Martinsburg	297	0	0	0	0	0	0	0	0	0	0
Maryland Heights	26,964	56	0	12	13	31	761	68	614	79	1
Maryville	11,643	8	0	0	2	6	130	15	109	6	0
Matthews	597	1	0	0	0	1	15	2	12	1	0
Merriam Woods	1,870	1	0	0	0	1	10	4	5	1	0
Mexico	11,529	9	1	4	1	3	398	55	328	15	0
Moberly	13,559	83	0	3	1	79	275	67	197	11	1
Moline Acres	2,352	22	1	2	3	16	90	17	56	17	
Monroe City	2,439	2	0	0	0	2	12	2	10	0	0
Montgomery City	2,647	0	0	0	0	0	36	10	22	4	1
Morehouse	865	0	0	0	0	0	5	2	3	0	1
Moscow Mills[5]	3,298	4	0	1	0	3	48	8	34	6	0
Mound City	1,025	0	0	0	0	0	25	9	14	2	0
Mountain Grove	4,681	20	0	1	0	19	82	15	55	12	0
Mount Vernon	4,504	0	0	0	0	0	132	13	107	12	1
Neosho	12,076	29	0	6	4	19	394	60	315	19	3
Nevada	8,237	21	1	8	1	11	461	50	389	22	
New Florence	708	0	0	0	0	0	11	4	7	0	
New Franklin	1,072	0	0	0	0	0	0	0	0	0	0
New Haven	2,071	2	0	0	0	2	20	1	18	1	0
Niangua	426	0	0	0	0	0	0	0	0	0	0
Nixa[5]	22,235	29	1	5	1	22	209	12	175	22	0
Noel	1,833	5	0	0	0	5	45	14	23	8	0
North Kansas City	4,573	29	1	7	7	14	377	19	278	80	0
Northmoor	349	4	0	0	1	3	16	6	8	2	0
Oak Grove	8,226	17	0	3	3	11	138	18	108	12	0
Odessa[5]	5,190	9	0	0	1	8	43	7	33	3	0
O'Fallon	89,611	114	1	16	9	88	1,015	75	867	73	1
Old Monroe	285	0	0	0	0	0	2	1	1	0	0
Oregon	755	0	0	0	0	0	5	2	3	0	0
Oronogo	2,694	1	0	1	0	0	22	2	16	4	0
Osage Beach[5]	4,598	25	0	7	0	18	283	28	232	23	0
Osceola	900	0	0	0	0	0	0	0	0	0	0
Owensville	2,574	3	0	2	0	1	115	18	82	15	0
Ozark	20,490	60	0	5	7	48	457	32	403	22	1
Pacific	7,265	4	0	0	0	4	176	23	134	19	0
Pagedale	3,293	64	3	3	10	48	99	17	62	20	
Palmyra	3,606	0	0	0	0	0	113	4	106	3	0
Park Hills	8,484	36	2	8	3	23	191	25	141	25	1
Parkville	7,143	6	1	0	1	4	133	12	110	11	0
Peculiar	5,417	7	0	1	0	6	99	27	62	10	
Perry	694	0	0	0	0	0	2	2	0	0	0
Perryville	8,466	28	0	5	2	21	231	38	184	9	0
Piedmont	1,915	3	0	0	0	3	47	17	27	3	1
Pilot Grove	758	3	0	0	0	3	3	0	3	0	0
Pilot Knob	719	1	0	0	0	1	11	3	7	1	1
Pineville	801	0	0	0	0	0	0	0	0	0	0
Platte City	5,002	7	0	1	2	4	58	6	37	15	0
Platte Woods	409	0	0	0	0	0	0	0	0	0	0
Pleasant Valley	3,073	1	0	0	0	1	35	4	20	11	0
Portageville	2,964	16	0	1	0	15	50	5	40	5	0
Potosi[5]	2,609	15	0	5	1	9	174	12	146	16	1
Raymore	22,121	17	0	3	3	11	291	26	251	14	0
Raytown	28,932	200	9	20	49	122	1,294	255	826	213	6
Republic	16,715	31	0	5	2	24	277	25	237	15	0
Rich Hill	1,323	0	0	0	0	0	0	0	0	0	0
Richland	1,757	9	0	0	1	8	54	12	39	3	0
Richmond	5,615	42	0	3	0	39	210	53	151	6	3
Risco	310	0	0	0	0	0	0	0	0	0	0
Riverside	3,522	15	0	2	1	12	218	21	164	33	0
Riverview	2,836	50	4	2	4	40	96	30	42	24	7
Rockaway Beach	880	1	0	0	0	1	0	0	0	0	0
Rock Hill	4,620	6	1	0	0	5	63	11	46	6	0
Rogersville	3,888	4	0	0	0	4	54	9	40	5	0
Rolla	20,482	109	0	16	6	87	814	164	604	46	
Rutledge	111	0	0	0	0	0	0	0	0	0	0
Salem[5]	4,895	6	0	0	0	6	90	10	77	3	0
Sarcoxie	1,321	2	0	0	0	2	50	9	36	5	1
Savannah	5,212	1	0	0	0	1	43	6	28	9	0
Scott City[6]	4,493	11	0	3	0	8	90	18	68	4	0
Sedalia	21,742	188	1	16	9	162	954	175	714	65	7
Seligman	848	1	0	0	0	1	12	4	6	2	0
Seneca	2,392	0	0	0	0	0	51	8	38	5	1
Smithville	10,503	15	0	1	0	14	109	15	87	7	0
Sparta	1,937	1	0	0	0	1	18	5	11	2	0
Springfield	169,235	2,571	11	356	319	1,885	13,188	2,068	9,436	1,684	64
Ste. Genevieve	4,445	9	0	0	0	9	45	2	41	2	0
St. Joseph	75,872	431	2	124	54	251	4,355	584	3,132	639	11
St. Louis	300,521	5,792	194	265	1,475	3,858	18,582	3,044	12,540	2,998	169
St. Marys	348	0	0	0	0	0	0	0	0	0	0
St. Peters	57,697	139	0	21	13	105	1,162	99	969	94	6
Strasburg	140	0	0	0	0	0	0	0	0	0	0
St. Robert	6,034	21	0	2	4	15	406	71	319	16	

Table 8. Offenses Known to Law Enforcement, by Selected State and City, 2019—Continued

(Number.)

State/city	Population	Violent crime	Murder and nonnegligent manslaughter	Rape[1]	Robbery	Aggravated assault	Property crime	Burglary	Larceny-theft	Motor vehicle theft	Arson[2]
Sugar Creek	3,269	24	0	6	4	14	110	26	60	24	0
Sullivan	7,111	41	0	10	6	25	323	74	216	33	2
Summersville	487	6	0	0	0	6	3	1	2	0	0
Sunrise Beach	500	0	0	0	0	0	4	1	3	0	0
Sunset Hills	8,480	11	0	0	4	7	175	13	144	18	0
Sweet Springs	1,414	0	0	0	0	0	2	0	2	0	0
Tarkio	1,422	0	0	0	0	0	4	1	3	0	0
Terre du Lac	2,382	12	1	0	0	11	13	4	9	0	0
Trenton	5,779	14	0	2	0	12	114	28	75	11	0
Truesdale	870	0	0	0	0	0	11	1	9	1	0
Van Buren	800	6	0	0	0	6	10	2	6	2	0
Vandalia	4,072	1	0	0	0	1	30	0	28	2	0
Velda City	1,373	14	0	0	2	12	41	17	18	6	0
Verona	606	6	0	2	1	3	2	0	1	1	0
Versailles	2,450	9	0	1	0	8	55	1	54	0	0
Vinita Park	10,979	159	7	6	33	113	600	153	366	81	2
Walnut Grove	803	0	0	0	0	0	15	8	7	0	0
Warrensburg	20,435	60	0	18	6	36	616	60	521	35	8
Warsaw	2,206	16	0	5	0	11	78	9	66	3	1
Warson Woods	1,925	0	0	0	0	0	16	2	14	0	0
Washburn	439	0	0	0	0	0	0	0	0	0	0
Washington[5]	14,064	37	0	5	4	28	481	38	411	32	0
Waynesville	5,265	23	1	8	2	12	92	17	67	8	0
Wellsville	1,144	3	0	0	0	3	12	3	8	1	0
Wentzville	42,892	88	0	11	7	70	450	45	378	27	0
Weston	1,829	0	0	0	0	0	15	4	10	1	0
West Plains	12,284	52	0	10	2	40	709	126	496	87	0
Wheaton	693	0	0	0	0	0	0	0	0	0	0
Willard	5,616	7	0	1	0	6	74	14	55	5	0
Willow Springs[5]	2,103	13	0	4	0	9	71	22	41	8	1
MONTANA											
Baker	1,928	3	0	0	0	3	7	1	6	0	0
Belgrade	9,204	35	0	10	1	24	175	8	153	14	1
Billings[4]	110,198			75	98	499	4,499	608	3,266	625	15
Boulder	1,278	2	0	0	0	2	10	0	9	1	0
Bozeman[4]	50,152			46	10	67	849	57	747	45	4
Bridger	760	0	0	0	0	0	6	1	4	1	0
Colstrip	2,271	2	0	0	0	2	5	0	3	2	0
Columbia Falls	5,695	11	0	1	2	8	69	7	61	1	0
Cut Bank	3,038	36	0	4	0	32	114	9	97	8	0
Deer Lodge	2,888	7	0	1	1	5	17	2	14	1	0
Dillon	4,276	8	0	1	0	7	13	3	9	1	0
East Helena	2,098	11	0	2	0	9	55	7	35	13	0
Ennis	1,019	3	0	0	0	3	4	0	4	0	0
Eureka	1,125	1	0	0	0	1	8	0	8	0	0
Glasgow	3,334	14	0	4	0	10	35	3	30	2	1
Glendive	4,964	5	0	0	0	5	14	4	9	1	0
Great Falls	58,637	302	0	39	18	245	3,405	318	2,826	261	11
Hamilton	4,879	18	1	6	0	11	148	14	128	6	0
Havre[4]	9,738			3	0	49	360	38	275	47	0
Helena	32,806	190	0	57	8	125	1,400	125	1,201	74	6
Hot Springs	570	0	0	0	0	0	3	1	2	0	0
Kalispell	24,473	102	1	14	2	85	821	68	698	55	1
Laurel	6,768	28	0	3	1	24	177	7	163	7	5
Libby	2,750	4	0	1	0	3	62	5	56	1	1
Manhattan	1,865	7	0	0	0	7	20	2	18	0	0
Miles City	8,393	22	0	2	0	20	244	11	230	3	0
Missoula	75,422	310	3	75	27	205	3,082	342	2,565	175	6
Polson	5,075	26	0	2	0	24	197	13	162	22	1
Red Lodge	2,316	5	0	0	0	5	23	2	20	1	0
Ronan City	2,113	19	0	1	0	18	50	3	42	5	0
Sidney	6,376	30	2	5	0	23	76	18	51	7	1
Stevensville	2,051	9	0	1	0	8	24	3	21	0	0
Troy	936	1	0	0	0	1	13	0	13	0	0
West Yellowstone	1,396	8	0	0	0	8	25	5	20	0	0
Wolf Point	2,761	26	0	0	2	24	54	9	44	1	0
NEBRASKA											
Ashland	2,604	2	0	0	0	2	11	3	8	0	
Aurora	4,539	4	0	1	0	3	28	3	24	1	0
Beatrice	12,227	22	0	12	0	10	194	28	150	16	0
Bellevue	53,880	110	2	37	26	45	961	99	697	165	7
Blair	7,836	10	0	5	2	3	119	11	87	21	2
Boys Town	579	8	0	6	0	2	8	0	8	0	
Broken Bow	3,532	7	0	1	0	6	20	2	17	1	0
Central City	2,868	6	0	1	0	5	6	0	5	1	0
Chadron	5,446	10	0	4	1	5	104	7	82	15	0
Columbus	23,406	28	0	12	3	13	359	38	288	33	1
Cozad	3,757	6	0	0	0	6	12	1	10	1	0
Crete	7,094	46	0	16	0	30	127	12	106	9	0
Emerson	796	0	0	0	0	0	3	0	3	0	0
Falls City	4,130	8	0	2	0	6	44	2	36	6	0

Table 8. Offenses Known to Law Enforcement, by Selected State and City, 2019—Continued

(Number.)

State/city	Population	Violent crime	Murder and nonnegligent manslaughter	Rape[1]	Robbery	Aggravated assault	Property crime	Burglary	Larceny-theft	Motor vehicle theft	Arson[2]
Fremont	26,523	49	0	24	7	18	589	127	414	48	4
Gering	8,189	9	0	2	2	5	95	7	82	6	0
Gothenburg	3,433	0	0	0	0	0	47	2	41	4	0
Grand Island	51,821	236	1	55	14	166	1,323	189	1,034	100	12
Hastings	24,778	45	0	17	2	26	727	119	557	51	4
Holdrege	5,394	14	2	10	0	2	75	7	63	5	0
Imperial	2,074	0	0	0	0	0	4	0	4	0	0
La Vista	17,223	19	0	6	2	11	181	19	128	34	0
Lexington	10,108	20	1	5	0	14	164	18	139	7	0
Lincoln	291,128	1,115	5	323	166	621	8,008	988	6,566	454	
Madison	2,378	2	0	2	0	0	13	4	7	2	0
McCook	7,533	11	0	5	0	6	168	41	109	18	0
Minden	2,985	3	0	2	0	1	45	2	41	2	1
Nebraska City	7,273	18	0	2	0	16	306	68	227	11	5
Norfolk	24,698	32	1	11	1	19	381	32	323	26	2
North Platte	23,705	89	0	23	4	62	800	106	643	51	12
Ogallala	4,476	10	0	2	0	8	111	9	100	2	0
Omaha	470,481	2,883	23	379	519	1,962	17,144	1,684	12,307	3,153	
O'Neill[5]	3,615	8	0	5	0	3	17	3	12	2	
Ord	2,087	5	0	1	0	4	10	1	9	0	0
Papillion	20,580	40	1	10	2	27	433	17	394	22	10
Plattsmouth	6,478	17	0	9	0	8	85	14	64	7	0
Ralston	7,468	12	0	9	2	1	108	12	76	20	0
Ravenna	1,369	0	0	0	0	0	20	3	15	2	1
Schuyler	6,396	3	0	0	0	3	25	5	19	1	0
Scottsbluff	15,862	53	0	13	4	36	433	55	359	19	2
Seward	7,250	2	0	1	0	1	40	3	34	3	0
Sidney	6,331	22	0	2	1	19	151	15	124	12	0
South Sioux City	12,771	30	0	3	3	24	359	29	289	41	1
Superior	1,812	2	0	1	0	1	18	2	16	0	
Tekamah[5]	1,692	2	0	0	0	2	13	4	9	0	
Tilden	934	0	0	0	0	0	0	0	0	0	
Valentine	2,751	9	1	1	0	7	27	1	23	3	0
Valley	2,904	1	0	0	0	1	16	4	11	1	0
Wahoo	4,513	2	0	1	0	1	18	0	16	2	0
West Point	3,307	1	0	0	0	1	17	4	11	2	0
York	7,877	13	0	9	2	2	179	27	145	7	
NEVADA											
Boulder City	16,102	19	1	2	3	13	114	27	71	16	0
Carlin	2,259	15	0	1	0	14	29	16	8	5	0
Elko	20,601	69	4	18	14	33	530	117	340	73	
Henderson	317,732	543	9	75	191	268	5,554	907	4,093	554	19
Las Vegas Metropolitan Police Department	1,666,803	8,854	84	1,439	2,118	5,213	46,197	10,646	28,240	7,311	125
Lovelock	1,806	6	0	1	0	5	39	12	24	3	0
Mesquite	19,612	26	0	20	2	4	224	47	158	19	
North Las Vegas	249,854	2,158	18	118	457	1,565	5,086	1,200	2,773	1,113	
Reno[5]	254,349	1,419	12	178	308	921	5,344	822	3,343	1,179	15
Sparks[5]	106,010	450	1	76	76	297	2,426	513	1,537	376	4
Winnemucca	7,800	8	0	0	1	7	204	56	136	12	0
Yerington	3,185	6	0	5	0	1	5	0	5	0	0
NEW HAMPSHIRE											
Alexandria	1,620	0	0	0	0	0	15	3	11	1	0
Allenstown	4,435	10	0	4	0	6	26	3	22	1	1
Alstead	1,931	3	0	2	0	1	1	0	1	0	0
Alton	5,339	10	2	5	0	3	34	8	24	2	0
Amherst	11,344	3	0	2	1	0	108	12	95	1	1
Antrim	2,702	3	1	1	0	1	21	4	16	1	0
Ashland	2,053	1	0	0	0	1	40	5	35	0	0
Atkinson	7,037	0	0	0	0	0	29	13	15	1	0
Auburn	5,608	2	0	0	0	2	37	7	27	3	0
Barnstead	4,668	3	0	3	0	0	20	5	13	2	0
Barrington	9,263	6	0	5	0	1	36	11	20	5	0
Bartlett	2,809	2	0	1	1	0	23	6	16	1	0
Bath	1,093	0	0	0	0	0	1	0	0	1	0
Bedford	22,887	12	0	5	3	4	174	11	161	2	1
Belmont	7,293	19	0	3	0	16	128	17	104	7	0
Bennington	1,512	1	0	1	0	0	5	0	4	1	1
Berlin	10,230	22	0	8	4	10	110	13	94	3	4
Bethlehem	2,569	5	0	4	0	1	20	5	13	2	0
Boscawen	4,095	8	0	0	0	8	32	3	25	4	1
Bow	8,004	5	0	0	1	4	30	3	20	7	1
Bradford	1,710	0	0	0	0	0	19	0	16	3	1
Bristol	3,057	6	1	3	1	1	49	7	39	3	0
Brookline	5,461	0	0	0	0	0	21	2	17	2	0
Campton	3,305	5	0	4	0	1	36	2	32	2	0
Candia	3,945	1	0	0	0	1	32	2	30	0	0
Canterbury	2,468	2	0	0	0	2	26	3	21	2	2
Carroll	740	0	0	0	0	0	16	1	12	3	0
Center Harbor	1,099	0	0	0	0	0	8	1	6	1	0
Charlestown	4,998	8	0	0	0	8	18	5	13	0	1

Table 8. Offenses Known to Law Enforcement, by Selected State and City, 2019—Continued

(Number.)

State/city	Population	Violent crime	Murder and nonnegligent manslaughter	Rape[1]	Robbery	Aggravated assault	Property crime	Burglary	Larceny-theft	Motor vehicle theft	Arson[2]
Chester	5,295	9	0	3	0	6	28	4	23	1	2
Chichester	2,709	2	0	1	0	1	27	4	23	0	0
Colebrook	2,114	1	0	0	0	1	28	14	13	1	0
Concord	43,509	65	4	10	25	26	805	49	710	46	2
Conway	10,287	22	0	15	1	6	222	21	194	7	0
Cornish	1,623	0	0	0	0	0	7	2	5	0	1
Dalton	868	0	0	0	0	0	0	0	0	0	0
Danville	4,584	0	0	0	0	0	11	3	5	3	0
Deerfield	4,562	1	0	1	0	0	17	6	11	0	0
Deering	1,967	2	0	0	0	2	20	2	15	3	0
Derry	33,672	33	1	18	3	11	279	22	247	10	5
Dover	31,950	25	0	8	6	11	347	38	295	14	1
Dublin	1,538	1	0	0	0	1	7	0	7	0	0
Dunbarton	2,870	3	0	2	0	1	21	1	19	1	0
Durham	16,810	6	0	2	2	2	42	10	31	1	1
East Kingston	2,430	1	0	0	0	1	8	0	7	1	0
Effingham	1,480	1	0	1	0	0	1	0	1	0	0
Enfield	4,563	5	0	2	0	3	27	3	24	0	0
Epping	7,117	3	0	2	0	1	74	2	68	4	0
Epsom	4,777	3	0	2	0	1	26	3	23	0	0
Exeter	15,425	28	0	9	0	19	99	11	85	3	0
Farmington	6,932	8	0	5	0	3	103	26	65	12	2
Fitzwilliam	2,373	0	0	0	0	0	12	3	7	2	0
Franconia	1,111	1	0	0	0	1	14	0	13	1	1
Freedom	1,562	0	0	0	0	0	3	0	3	0	0
Fremont	4,803	0	0	0	0	0	37	3	32	2	1
Gilford	7,197	5	0	2	0	3	111	16	90	5	0
Gilmanton	3,754	7	0	4	0	3	23	5	18	0	0
Goffstown	18,163	18	1	9	4	4	114	13	98	3	0
Gorham	2,579	3	0	1	0	2	20	2	18	0	0
Grantham	2,946	0	0	0	0	0	14	4	10	0	0
Greenland	4,195	0	0	0	0	0	16	2	12	2	0
Hampstead	8,662	7	0	3	0	4	48	1	45	2	0
Hampton	15,616	31	1	3	4	23	138	13	114	11	2
Hampton Falls	2,385	2	0	2	0	0	18	2	16	0	0
Hancock	1,658	1	0	0	0	1	2	0	2	0	0
Hanover	11,531	7	0	4	0	3	95	12	81	2	2
Haverhill	4,568	16	0	5	1	10	71	9	57	5	1
Henniker	5,009	12	0	5	0	7	45	5	35	5	0
Hillsborough	5,990	12	1	5	0	6	56	13	39	4	1
Hinsdale	3,888	5	2	1	0	2	94	11	80	3	0
Holderness	2,109	0	0	0	0	0	14	2	11	1	0
Hollis	7,976	5	1	3	0	1	29	7	19	3	1
Hooksett	14,554	12	2	3	4	3	162	13	139	10	1
Hopkinton	5,759	1	0	1	0	0	20	2	16	2	0
Hudson	25,695	19	0	3	2	14	210	27	174	9	1
Jackson	856	0	0	0	0	0	6	1	5	0	0
Keene	22,999	42	0	17	12	13	488	31	434	23	0
Kensington	2,118	1	0	1	0	0	3	0	2	1	0
Kingston	6,362	5	0	2	0	3	11	2	7	2	0
Laconia	16,534	37	1	17	4	15	535	32	461	42	1
Lancaster	3,219	5	0	0	0	5	29	7	22	0	2
Lebanon	13,661	16	0	8	2	6	299	21	265	13	1
Lee	4,494	1	0	1	0	0	17	1	14	2	1
Lincoln	1,775	1	0	0	0	1	27	6	21	0	1
Lisbon	1,583	0	0	0	0	0	11	3	6	2	0
Litchfield	8,660	3	0	1	0	2	31	3	23	5	1
Littleton	5,889	16	1	7	4	4	106	16	85	5	2
Londonderry	26,567	20	1	6	2	11	173	16	139	18	0
Loudon	5,660	4	1	1	1	1	43	4	31	8	0
Lyndeborough	1,740	0	0	0	0	0	6	1	4	1	0
Madbury	1,868	0	0	0	0	0	2	0	2	0	0
Madison	2,613	3	1	0	0	2	28	3	25	0	0
Manchester	112,895	678	6	62	133	477	2,678	299	2,225	154	14
Marlborough	2,068	1	0	0	0	1	7	1	6	0	0
Mason	1,441	1	0	0	0	1	5	1	4	0	0
Meredith	6,424	16	0	8	0	8	107	23	76	8	0
Merrimack	26,028	4	0	0	2	2	207	21	177	9	0
Middleton	1,827	0	0	0	0	0	17	3	12	2	0
Milford	16,121	11	0	6	1	4	78	5	71	2	0
Milton	4,652	7	0	2	0	5	42	7	27	8	1
Mont Vernon	2,603	2	0	1	0	1	5	0	5	0	0
Moultonborough	4,174	0	0	0	0	0	26	4	22	0	0
Nashua	89,586	129	1	69	20	39	1,151	81	1,016	54	10
New Boston	5,856	2	0	1	0	1	15	1	13	1	0
Newbury	2,245	0	0	0	0	0	15	3	11	1	0
New Castle	982	0	0	0	0	0	1	0	1	0	0
New Durham	2,704	3	0	0	0	3	24	3	19	2	2
Newfields	1,735	1	0	0	0	1	14	0	14	0	0
New Hampton	2,216	4	0	2	0	2	12	2	7	3	0
Newington	810	5	0	0	1	4	113	2	110	1	0
New Ipswich	5,408	3	0	2	0	1	20	4	14	2	0
Newmarket	9,161	8	0	2	0	6	43	5	37	1	1

Table 8. Offenses Known to Law Enforcement, by Selected State and City, 2019—Continued

(Number.)

State/city	Population	Violent crime	Murder and nonnegligent manslaughter	Rape[1]	Robbery	Aggravated assault	Property crime	Burglary	Larceny-theft	Motor vehicle theft	Arson[2]
Newport	6,348	6	1	0	2	3	94	8	72	14	1
Northfield	4,940	7	0	2	1	4	67	15	46	6	0
North Hampton	4,512	3	0	2	0	1	35	6	26	3	2
Northumberland	2,111	4	0	1	0	3	24	2	21	1	0
Northwood	4,302	2	0	0	0	2	31	3	26	2	0
Nottingham	5,149	3	0	0	0	3	7	0	7	0	0
Orford	1,302	1	0	0	0	1	3	0	3	0	0
Ossipee	4,401	5	0	3	1	1	35	4	27	4	2
Pelham	14,198	10	0	4	1	5	94	8	83	3	2
Pembroke	7,240	12	0	9	0	3	59	10	45	4	0
Peterborough	6,669	11	0	4	1	6	48	4	42	2	0
Pittsburg	807	0	0	0	0	0	5	0	4	1	0
Pittsfield	4,142	15	0	5	1	9	21	3	16	2	0
Plainfield	2,381	1	0	0	0	1	12	0	12	0	0
Plaistow	7,734	4	0	0	0	4	97	5	87	5	1
Plymouth	6,755	10	0	5	0	5	76	7	65	4	1
Portsmouth	21,951	28	0	10	2	16	359	28	309	22	1
Raymond	10,475	14	0	8	0	6	114	5	101	8	0
Rindge	6,308	12	0	5	0	7	60	8	48	4	14
Rochester	31,527	94	0	21	11	62	976	111	828	37	3
Rollinsford	2,591	3	0	1	1	1	17	5	11	1	1
Rye	5,464	0	0	0	0	0	42	2	35	5	0
Salem	29,612	25	0	5	13	7	448	25	403	20	2
Sanbornton	2,975	4	0	0	0	4	24	2	20	2	1
Sandown	6,501	2	1	0	0	1	20	7	11	2	0
Sandwich	1,358	0	0	0	0	0	13	2	11	0	0
Seabrook	8,880	4	0	1	1	2	137	16	116	5	0
Somersworth	11,979	15	0	8	5	2	353	25	317	11	2
South Hampton	829	0	0	0	0	0	5	2	3	0	0
Springfield	1,342	0	0	0	0	0	0	0	0	0	0
Strafford	4,205	0	0	0	0	0	7	2	4	1	0
Stratham	7,479	2	0	0	0	2	44	1	41	2	0
Sugar Hill	579	0	0	0	0	0	1	0	0	1	0
Sunapee	3,489	0	0	0	0	0	19	1	16	2	1
Tamworth	3,077	2	0	0	1	1	14	0	12	2	0
Thornton	2,513	1	0	0	1	0	9	3	6	0	0
Tilton	3,557	12	0	3	2	7	200	8	184	8	1
Troy	2,091	2	0	0	0	2	13	1	12	0	0
Tuftonboro	2,414	1	0	0	0	1	12	5	6	1	0
Wakefield	5,789	13	0	7	0	6	34	7	24	3	1
Warner	2,953	1	0	0	0	1	34	4	28	2	0
Washington	1,104	0	0	0	0	0	2	1	1	0	0
Waterville Valley	243	1	0	1	0	0	12	0	12	0	0
Weare	9,111	4	0	2	0	2	26	11	12	3	0
Webster	1,962	3	0	1	0	2	24	5	14	5	0
Whitefield	2,201	4	0	0	1	3	7	1	6	0	0
Wilton	3,768	6	0	5	0	1	20	7	13	0	2
Winchester	4,192	8	0	4	1	3	34	6	23	5	0
Windham	14,876	5	0	2	0	3	59	8	51	0	0
Wolfeboro	6,403	4	0	1	0	3	34	4	26	4	0
Woodstock	1,369	0	0	0	0	0	9	4	4	1	1
NEW JERSEY											
Aberdeen Township	18,700	15	0	3	5	7	164	7	145	12	0
Absecon	8,436	8	0	1	2	5	236	24	207	5	0
Allendale	6,795	0	0	0	0	0	38	8	26	4	0
Allenhurst	484	0	0	0	0	0	11	1	9	1	0
Allentown	1,784	0	0	0	0	0	8	2	6	0	0
Alpha	2,262	1	0	0	0	1	37	7	30	0	0
Alpine	1,856	1	0	0	0	1	15	4	2	9	0
Andover Township	5,870	0	0	0	0	0	17	3	13	1	0
Asbury Park	15,437	179	2	10	47	120	525	59	457	9	2
Atlantic City	37,593	323	11	29	182	101	1,738	130	1,519	89	0
Atlantic Highlands	4,308	3	0	0	1	2	50	2	48	0	0
Audubon	8,601	5	0	0	2	3	296	21	268	7	0
Audubon Park	997	1	0	0	0	1	5	0	5	0	0
Avalon	1,236	5	0	0	0	5	157	12	145	0	0
Avon-by-the-Sea	1,766	1	0	0	0	1	36	5	31	0	0
Barnegat Light	587	0	0	0	0	0	6	1	5	0	0
Barnegat Township	23,399	12	0	0	4	8	124	13	108	3	0
Barrington	6,620	3	0	1	1	1	62	8	49	5	0
Bay Head	976	0	0	0	0	0	15	3	12	0	0
Bayonne	65,032	145	2	11	52	80	704	120	519	65	4
Beach Haven	1,191	0	0	0	0	0	141	5	136	0	0
Beachwood	11,275	5	0	3	0	2	79	14	65	0	0
Bedminster Township	8,043	2	0	0	0	2	39	6	29	4	0
Belleville	36,531	78	1	9	24	44	508	70	351	87	1
Bellmawr	11,294	13	0	0	2	11	133	28	97	8	1
Belmar	5,562	8	0	0	0	8	86	4	78	4	0
Belvidere	2,564	8	0	1	0	7	32	13	19	0	0
Bergenfield	27,432	15	1	1	0	13	75	11	62	2	0
Berkeley Heights Township	13,592	4	0	3	1	0	58	12	36	10	0
Berkeley Township	41,738	44	0	9	10	25	385	68	310	7	1

Table 8. Offenses Known to Law Enforcement, by Selected State and City, 2019—Continued

(Number.)

State/city	Population	Violent crime	Murder and nonnegligent manslaughter	Rape[1]	Robbery	Aggravated assault	Property crime	Burglary	Larceny-theft	Motor vehicle theft	Arson[2]
Berlin	7,510	10	0	0	2	8	126	21	100	5	1
Berlin Township	5,651	3	0	0	3	0	126	11	111	4	1
Bernards Township	27,228	0	0	0	0	0	83	15	54	14	0
Bernardsville	7,670	2	0	0	0	2	43	3	34	6	0
Beverly	2,476	11	0	0	1	10	35	9	20	6	0
Blairstown Township	5,703	5	0	1	0	4	19	8	10	1	0
Bloomfield	50,307	32	0	0	11	21	567	58	447	62	0
Bloomingdale	8,089	5	0	3	0	2	32	3	29	0	0
Bogota	8,403	2	0	0	2	0	33	5	26	2	0
Boonton	8,157	11	0	1	2	8	82	8	70	4	0
Boonton Township	4,279	2	0	1	0	1	18	4	12	2	0
Bordentown City	3,786	2	0	0	1	1	26	1	24	1	0
Bordentown Township	12,018	11	0	0	0	11	66	3	53	10	2
Bound Brook	10,257	16	1	0	6	9	112	11	98	3	0
Bradley Beach	4,158	6	0	0	0	6	68	7	60	1	0
Branchburg Township	14,551	4	0	2	1	1	83	13	63	7	1
Brick Township	75,592	83	3	18	9	53	805	128	665	12	4
Bridgeton	24,331	223	2	17	114	90	848	261	549	38	1
Bridgewater Township	44,610	7	0	0	3	4	435	32	382	21	1
Brielle	4,683	2	0	1	0	1	15	3	11	1	0
Brigantine	8,684	1	0	0	0	1	165	31	129	5	0
Brooklawn	1,899	16	0	1	5	10	149	13	134	2	0
Buena	4,316	4	0	1	0	3	47	16	28	3	0
Burlington City	9,877	51	2	2	14	33	150	40	94	16	0
Burlington Township	22,516	31	0	7	6	18	261	30	210	21	1
Butler	7,613	1	0	0	0	1	26	3	22	1	0
Byram Township	7,875	10	0	4	1	5	63	9	48	6	0
Caldwell	7,943	7	0	1	0	6	57	15	41	1	0
Califon	1,055	0	0	0	0	0	3	1	1	1	0
Camden County Police Department	73,270	1,159	25	67	302	765	2,101	372	1,194	535	41
Cape May	3,428	4	0	1	0	3	94	3	86	5	0
Cape May Point	274	0	0	0	0	0	4	3	1	0	0
Carlstadt	6,170	8	0	0	2	6	73	4	61	8	0
Carney's Point Township	7,664	17	0	10	3	4	104	18	80	6	1
Carteret	23,645	32	0	5	11	16	265	40	201	24	0
Cedar Grove Township	12,508	6	0	0	1	5	56	4	50	2	0
Chatham	8,696	0	0	0	0	0	63	5	52	6	0
Chatham Township	10,219	0	0	0	0	0	24	1	20	3	0
Cherry Hill Township	70,716	59	0	0	30	29	1,694	148	1,497	49	1
Chesilhurst	1,616	4	0	0	0	4	43	20	19	4	0
Chester	1,635	0	0	0	0	0	13	1	12	0	0
Chesterfield Township	7,474	3	0	0	0	3	6	0	6	0	0
Chester Township	7,731	0	0	0	0	0	35	11	20	4	0
Cinnaminson Township	16,477	16	0	2	3	11	352	28	310	14	0
Clark Township	16,022	14	0	4	3	7	224	13	207	4	1
Clayton	8,709	13	0	2	1	10	85	16	65	4	1
Clementon	4,919	13	0	0	8	5	132	43	83	6	0
Cliffside Park	26,115	18	0	1	5	12	102	8	94	0	0
Clifton	85,021	95	0	0	50	45	1,272	115	1,046	111	0
Clinton	2,679	4	0	1	0	3	12	1	11	0	0
Clinton Township	12,801	2	0	0	0	2	33	12	18	3	0
Closter	8,562	5	0	1	0	4	43	0	39	4	0
Collingswood	13,850	16	1	0	6	9	393	53	322	18	3
Colts Neck Township	9,846	4	0	1	2	1	58	9	40	9	0
Cranbury Township	4,013	3	0	0	0	3	34	6	25	3	0
Cranford Township	24,251	4	0	0	1	3	202	11	175	16	0
Cresskill	8,761	2	0	1	1	0	28	6	18	4	0
Deal	719	0	0	0	0	0	28	3	13	12	0
Delanco Township	4,463	2	0	1	0	1	53	3	46	4	0
Delaware Township	4,419	0	0	0	0	0	7	0	6	1	0
Delran Township	16,473	8	0	0	3	5	212	23	182	7	0
Demarest	4,912	2	0	0	0	2	12	4	5	3	0
Denville Township	16,590	6	0	1	0	5	65	4	57	4	0
Deptford Township	30,258	40	0	4	18	18	1,174	122	1,024	28	1
Dover	17,852	40	0	2	11	27	157	49	94	14	1
Dumont	17,649	6	0	0	1	5	54	2	52	0	0
Dunellen	7,244	14	0	3	2	9	122	9	105	8	0
Eastampton Township	5,938	3	0	2	1	0	50	12	34	4	0
East Brunswick Township	47,857	27	0	6	9	12	530	35	491	4	1
East Greenwich Township	10,658	0	0	0	0	0	103	16	82	5	0
East Hanover Township	10,990	3	0	0	1	2	126	10	107	9	0
East Newark	2,661	1	0	0	0	0	24	3	18	3	0
East Orange	64,200	275	3	26	102	144	894	151	581	162	11
East Rutherford	9,831	4	0	0	2	2	127	9	106	12	0
East Windsor Township	27,343	16	1	1	4	10	182	17	151	14	1
Eatontown	12,215	34	0	7	9	18	274	18	247	9	0
Edgewater	12,821	4	0	1	2	1	160	13	142	5	0
Edgewater Park Township	8,644	16	1	4	3	8	132	28	88	16	0
Edison Township	100,282	84	1	9	19	55	1,371	138	1,143	90	2
Egg Harbor City	4,085	21	0	1	11	9	195	42	144	9	1
Egg Harbor Township	42,475	52	0	0	10	42	672	91	558	23	4
Elizabeth	128,753	926	7	50	384	485	3,898	365	2,776	757	1

Table 8. Offenses Known to Law Enforcement, by Selected State and City, 2019—Continued

(Number.)

State/city	Population	Violent crime	Murder and nonnegligent manslaughter	Rape[1]	Robbery	Aggravated assault	Property crime	Burglary	Larceny-theft	Motor vehicle theft	Arson[2]
Elk Township	4,154	0	0	0	0	0	39	8	25	6	1
Elmer	1,300	1	1	0	0	0	5	0	5	0	0
Elmwood Park	20,104	25	0	0	12	13	274	37	215	22	0
Elsinboro Township	967	2	0	0	0	2	11	1	10	0	1
Emerson	7,640	1	0	0	0	1	31	2	25	4	0
Englewood	28,683	71	2	10	18	41	343	64	257	22	0
Englewood Cliffs	5,368	1	0	0	0	1	48	27	12	9	0
Englishtown	1,937	3	0	0	0	3	12	2	9	1	0
Essex Fells	2,072	0	0	0	0	0	16	2	10	4	0
Evesham Township	44,999	29	0	5	8	16	510	55	440	15	0
Ewing Township	36,338	60	0	4	20	36	507	76	385	46	1
Fairfield Township, Essex County	7,472	0	0	0	0	0	177	8	158	11	0
Fair Haven	5,784	1	0	0	0	1	16	4	10	2	0
Fair Lawn	33,064	7	0	0	1	6	236	32	187	17	2
Fairview	14,285	27	1	1	11	14	152	38	104	10	0
Fanwood	7,718	2	0	1	0	1	25	5	17	3	0
Far Hills	909	0	0	0	0	0	3	0	3	0	0
Fieldsboro	539	0	0	0	0	0	2	0	2	0	0
Flemington	4,590	10	0	1	0	9	58	9	47	2	1
Florence Township	12,593	17	0	7	2	8	81	25	51	5	1
Florham Park	11,522	1	0	0	0	1	111	19	85	7	0
Fort Lee	38,062	25	0	2	6	17	323	57	239	27	1
Franklin	4,699	10	0	1	1	8	48	3	44	1	0
Franklin Lakes	11,109	5	0	0	1	4	59	4	44	11	2
Franklin Township, Gloucester County	16,264	15	0	1	2	12	169	32	123	14	0
Franklin Township, Hunterdon County	3,560	0	0	0	0	0	8	1	7	0	0
Franklin Township, Somerset County	66,173	58	4	10	18	26	625	76	517	32	0
Freehold Borough	11,733	22	0	0	11	11	129	20	105	4	0
Freehold Township	34,560	34	2	1	9	22	487	21	455	11	1
Frenchtown	1,348	0	0	0	0	0	3	0	3	0	1
Galloway Township	35,813	62	0	2	2	58	367	94	252	21	2
Garfield	31,888	51	1	9	16	25	620	58	532	30	0
Garwood	4,361	1	0	0	0	1	35	5	30	0	0
Gibbsboro	2,212	1	0	0	0	1	23	4	17	2	0
Glassboro	20,082	31	0	5	3	23	303	83	205	15	1
Glen Ridge	7,574	4	0	2	0	2	108	21	82	5	0
Glen Rock	11,803	0	0	0	0	0	60	13	43	4	0
Gloucester City	11,168	20	2	1	3	14	281	41	230	10	3
Gloucester Township	63,500	63	1	9	18	35	880	67	789	24	1
Green Brook Township	7,071	1	0	0	0	1	56	8	44	4	0
Greenwich Township, Gloucester County	4,777	2	0	1	0	1	58	6	50	2	0
Greenwich Township, Warren County	5,447	1	0	0	1	0	126	11	110	5	0
Guttenberg	11,289	27	0	0	13	14	71	12	53	6	0
Hackensack	44,505	103	1	6	15	81	594	54	506	34	2
Hackettstown	9,431	3	0	0	0	3	28	2	25	1	1
Haddonfield	11,261	5	0	0	2	3	135	13	119	3	0
Haddon Heights	7,515	3	0	0	1	2	54	12	39	3	0
Haddon Township	14,489	33	0	1	19	13	288	26	250	12	0
Haledon	8,277	31	0	0	4	27	141	25	101	15	0
Hamburg	3,102	0	0	0	0	0	17	4	13	0	0
Hamilton Township, Atlantic County	25,667	49	0	1	21	27	769	91	641	37	2
Hamilton Township, Mercer County	87,027	122	1	20	47	54	1,585	264	1,215	106	5
Hammonton	14,003	25	0	1	4	20	115	25	78	12	1
Hanover Township	14,447	12	0	4	1	7	136	7	120	9	0
Harding Township	3,805	3	0	0	0	3	20	10	9	1	0
Hardyston Township	7,760	1	0	0	1	0	26	4	22	0	0
Harrington Park	4,751	0	0	0	0	0	5	0	4	1	0
Harrison	18,374	47	0	5	14	28	341	49	262	30	2
Harrison Township	13,125	1	0	0	0	1	57	8	45	4	0
Harvey Cedars	339	0	0	0	0	0	7	2	5	0	0
Hasbrouck Heights	12,049	3	0	0	0	3	63	3	60	0	0
Haworth	3,420	1	0	0	0	1	8	2	3	3	0
Hawthorne	18,699	0	0	0	0	0	139	9	116	14	0
Hazlet Township	19,739	31	0	5	2	24	199	16	171	12	0
Helmetta	2,173	0	0	0	0	0	10	2	7	1	0
High Bridge	3,427	1	0	0	0	1	25	3	21	1	0
Highland Park	13,791	14	0	5	2	7	222	33	181	8	1
Highlands	4,739	2	0	0	0	2	9	4	5	0	0
Hightstown	5,264	6	0	3	1	2	22	2	19	1	0
Hillsborough Township	39,813	13	0	7	1	5	191	29	158	4	0
Hillsdale	10,382	2	0	0	0	2	45	4	40	1	0
Hillside Township	22,024	64	0	5	26	33	533	51	398	84	0
Hi-Nella	855	2	0	0	0	2	4	0	4	0	1
Hoboken	53,641	79	0	2	14	63	666	73	562	31	0
Ho-Ho-Kus	4,091	0	0	0	0	0	20	7	11	2	0

Table 8. Offenses Known to Law Enforcement, by Selected State and City, 2019—Continued

(Number.)

State/city	Population	Violent crime	Murder and nonnegligent manslaughter	Rape[1]	Robbery	Aggravated assault	Property crime	Burglary	Larceny-theft	Motor vehicle theft	Arson[2]
Holland Township	5,081	2	0	1	0	1	9	4	4	1	0
Holmdel Township	16,648	17	0	1	1	15	194	16	168	10	0
Hopatcong	14,091	8	0	0	1	7	39	0	37	2	1
Hopewell Borough	1,905	0	0	0	0	0	13	2	10	1	0
Hopewell Township	17,854	7	0	1	0	6	73	14	55	4	0
Howell Township	52,242	31	1	14	1	15	376	43	321	12	0
Independence Township	5,420	2	0	1	0	1	5	4	0	1	0
Interlaken	789	0	0	0	0	0	3	0	3	0	0
Irvington	54,034	280	7	17	190	66	1,016	178	565	273	7
Island Heights	1,675	0	0	0	0	0	7	3	4	0	0
Jackson Township	57,380	25	0	3	5	17	391	71	298	22	3
Jamesburg	5,931	10	2	1	2	5	19	3	15	1	1
Jefferson Township	20,877	10	1	2	0	7	72	12	54	6	0
Jersey City	266,508	1,393	13	81	431	868	5,074	890	3,514	670	18
Keansburg	9,674	21	0	2	6	13	176	18	157	1	0
Kearny	41,314	54	0	0	13	41	661	36	541	84	0
Kenilworth	8,218	10	0	4	2	4	109	8	86	15	0
Keyport	7,032	12	0	0	4	8	92	10	73	9	0
Kinnelon	9,984	1	0	1	0	0	22	11	9	2	0
Lacey Township	29,247	25	0	4	4	17	265	29	233	3	1
Lake Como	1,685	1	0	0	1	0	16	2	11	3	0
Lakehurst	2,701	5	0	0	2	3	18	0	16	2	0
Lakewood Township	105,403	148	1	11	45	91	965	253	675	37	4
Lambertville	3,782	1	0	1	0	0	26	2	24	0	0
Laurel Springs	1,860	2	0	0	1	1	19	6	12	1	0
Lavallette	1,846	0	0	0	0	0	39	2	34	3	0
Lawnside	2,874	6	0	0	0	6	104	10	92	2	0
Lawrence Township, Mercer County	32,415	45	0	10	11	24	493	83	388	22	2
Lebanon Township	6,061	2	0	0	0	2	17	3	12	2	0
Leonia	9,088	3	0	1	0	2	51	11	38	2	0
Lincoln Park	10,162	2	0	0	0	2	46	8	32	6	0
Linden	42,592	159	0	21	44	94	1,228	110	1,079	39	4
Lindenwold	17,197	123	0	16	50	57	492	124	334	34	3
Linwood	6,697	2	0	0	0	2	92	10	78	4	0
Little Egg Harbor Township	21,508	18	0	2	3	13	206	36	164	6	1
Little Falls Township	14,513	20	0	0	0	20	89	12	70	7	0
Little Ferry	10,794	9	1	0	2	6	83	12	55	16	0
Little Silver	5,793	2	0	0	0	2	34	1	25	8	0
Livingston Township	29,998	6	0	3	1	2	353	26	301	26	0
Loch Arbour	179	0	0	0	0	0	14	1	13	0	0
Lodi	24,488	35	0	2	6	27	273	31	200	42	1
Logan Township	5,854	5	0	1	2	2	105	13	85	7	0
Long Beach Township	3,060	10	0	5	0	5	78	6	70	2	0
Long Branch	30,352	109	0	11	23	75	625	60	538	27	0
Long Hill Township	8,500	3	0	1	0	2	45	3	40	2	0
Longport	854	1	0	0	0	1	10	3	7	0	0
Lopatcong Township	8,350	4	0	0	0	4	99	5	90	4	0
Lower Alloways Creek Township	1,663	1	0	0	0	1	3	0	3	0	0
Lower Township	21,325	41	0	10	2	29	149	30	113	6	0
Lumberton Township	12,162	22	0	2	4	16	174	11	153	10	0
Lyndhurst Township	22,741	13	0	0	6	7	150	5	127	18	0
Madison	16,533	1	0	0	0	1	70	11	52	7	0
Magnolia	4,247	13	0	0	5	8	76	26	46	4	0
Mahwah Township	26,317	8	0	3	0	5	115	10	90	15	1
Manalapan Township	39,662	18	1	11	2	4	226	36	173	17	0
Manasquan	5,839	7	0	3	0	4	88	3	82	3	0
Manchester Township	43,369	12	3	0	3	6	278	51	215	12	2
Mansfield Township, Burlington County	8,520	8	0	0	3	5	46	10	26	10	0
Mansfield Township, Warren County	7,347	3	0	1	0	2	83	5	76	2	0
Mantoloking	252	0	0	0	0	0	5	0	3	2	0
Mantua Township	14,779	3	0	0	0	3	212	30	169	13	2
Manville	10,205	6	0	4	1	1	218	14	197	7	0
Maple Shade Township	18,451	54	1	8	17	28	344	41	272	31	0
Maplewood Township	25,297	22	2	3	13	4	435	22	365	48	0
Margate City	5,912	6	0	0	2	4	140	55	84	1	1
Marlboro Township	39,850	9	0	0	2	7	273	38	212	23	1
Matawan	8,716	0	0	0	0	0	5	0	5	0	0
Maywood	9,667	6	0	0	2	4	62	7	54	1	0
Medford Lakes	3,922	3	0	0	0	3	16	4	12	0	0
Medford Township	23,393	19	0	4	1	14	134	30	101	3	1
Mendham	4,876	0	0	0	0	0	20	1	14	5	0
Mendham Township	5,700	1	0	0	0	1	11	3	6	2	0
Merchantville	3,687	4	0	0	0	4	59	9	48	2	0
Metuchen	14,423	11	0	0	4	7	165	31	124	10	0
Middlesex Borough	13,659	6	0	0	2	4	55	4	47	4	1
Middle Township	18,225	34	0	6	7	21	303	54	232	17	2
Middletown Township	65,361	22	0	4	2	16	354	38	294	22	0
Midland Park	7,246	2	0	0	0	2	38	0	34	4	0
Millburn Township	20,085	6	0	0	5	1	434	23	374	37	0

Table 8. Offenses Known to Law Enforcement, by Selected State and City, 2019—Continued

(Number.)

State/city	Population	Violent crime	Murder and nonnegligent manslaughter	Rape[1]	Robbery	Aggravated assault	Property crime	Burglary	Larceny-theft	Motor vehicle theft	Arson[2]
Milltown	7,020	2	0	0	2	0	84	2	80	2	0
Millville	27,528	130	2	14	50	64	1,107	154	925	28	6
Mine Hill Township	3,501	2	0	0	1	1	12	3	8	1	0
Monmouth Beach	3,222	2	0	0	0	2	8	0	8	0	0
Monroe Township, Gloucester County	36,884	26	1	1	12	12	425	88	313	24	1
Monroe Township, Middlesex County	45,342	19	0	0	0	19	116	18	89	9	0
Montclair	38,625	58	1	9	17	31	476	106	335	35	1
Montgomery Township	23,364	5	0	0	0	5	111	62	39	10	0
Montvale	8,657	1	0	0	0	1	172	11	137	24	0
Montville Township	21,208	4	0	0	0	4	28	1	26	1	1
Moonachie	2,736	0	0	0	0	0	200	24	166	10	0
Moorestown Township	20,307	18	0	3	4	11	71	3	65	3	0
Morris Plains	5,935	2	0	0	0	2	170	9	157	4	2
Morristown	19,153	41	0	5	9	27	96	22	70	4	0
Morris Township	22,080	8	0	0	0	8	28	10	11	7	0
Mountain Lakes	4,269	0	0	0	0	0	52	9	36	7	1
Mountainside	6,888	3	0	0	0	3	27	3	23	1	0
Mount Arlington	5,964	0	0	0	0	0	179	7	169	3	0
Mount Ephraim	4,567	5	0	0	1	4	190	20	163	7	0
Mount Holly Township	9,568	27	0	8	7	12	597	45	524	28	0
Mount Laurel Township	41,109	57	1	15	17	24	112	19	92	1	0
Mount Olive Township	29,025	14	0	5	3	6	71	22	43	6	0
Mullica Township	5,897	2	0	0	1	1	23	8	15	0	0
National Park	2,934	3	1	0	0	2	118	6	112	0	0
Neptune City	4,625	11	0	0	2	9	871	72	786	13	4
Neptune Township	27,549	95	2	2	18	73	28	2	25	1	0
Netcong	3,151	11	0	5	0	6	4,618	721	2,356	1,541	21
Newark	281,422	1,742	57	120	636	929	1,111	223	823	65	0
New Brunswick	55,995	262	3	11	96	152	8	2	5	1	0
Newfield	1,537	2	0	0	0	2	0	0	0	0	0
New Hanover Township	8,123	1	0	0	0	1	64	8	53	3	0
New Milford	16,506	1	0	0	0	0	35	5	29	1	0
New Providence	13,592	0	0	0	0	10	63	8	55	0	0
Newton	7,916	14	0	4	0	13	158	9	132	17	0
North Arlington	15,710	19	0	0	6	56	404	54	306	44	1
North Bergen Township	61,447	90	1	16	17	40	605	52	517	36	0
North Brunswick Township	41,706	61	0	4	17	4	22	10	8	4	0
North Caldwell	6,645	5	0	1	0	4	86	13	66	7	0
Northfield	8,163	4	0	0	0	2	49	5	39	5	0
North Haledon	8,379	3	0	1	0	3	18	3	13	2	0
North Hanover Township	7,476	3	0	0	0	10	281	36	234	11	0
North Plainfield	21,474	47	1	10	26	0	9	0	8	1	0
Northvale	4,937	0	0	0	0	4	144	12	131	1	0
North Wildwood	3,763	6	0	1	1	0	19	6	10	3	0
Norwood	5,816	1	0	1	0	22	164	26	117	21	0
Nutley Township	28,384	28	0	0	6	4	53	5	46	2	0
Oakland	12,992	5	0	0	1	3	127	39	83	5	0
Oaklyn	3,936	5	0	1	1	4	323	37	285	1	0
Ocean City	10,962	6	0	0	2	4	24	7	17	0	0
Ocean Gate	2,025	1	0	0	1	0	43	8	33	2	0
Oceanport	5,739	12	0	2	2	8	582	60	499	23	1
Ocean Township, Monmouth County	26,638	17	1	0	4	12	38	6	32	0	0
Ocean Township, Ocean County	9,134	4	0	1	0	3	10	0	9	1	0
Ogdensburg	2,247	0	0	0	0	0	477	60	378	39	1
Old Bridge Township	65,659	39	2	1	12	24	12	2	6	4	0
Old Tappan	5,944	0	0	0	0	0	21	7	13	1	0
Oradell	8,181	2	0	0	0	2	635	140	337	158	10
Orange City	30,558	190	4	13	96	77	6	2	4	0	0
Oxford Township	2,423	1	0	0	0	1	106	19	81	6	0
Palisades Park	20,877	16	0	1	4	11	120	17	100	3	2
Palmyra	7,134	8	1	1	0	6	919	24	871	24	0
Paramus	26,460	44	0	2	8	34	9	2	6	1	0
Park Ridge	8,761	1	0	0	1	0	326	59	233	34	0
Parsippany-Troy Hills Township	51,907	23	1	9	3	10	1,215	133	923	159	2
Passaic	69,639	369	1	6	166	196	3,132	847	1,829	456	24
Paterson	144,866	1,219	19	54	464	682	114	23	79	12	0
Paulsboro	5,828	14	0	0	5	9	18	8	5	5	0
Peapack-Gladstone	2,591	0	0	0	0	0	28	9	19	0	6
Pemberton Borough	1,321	3	0	0	2	1	435	114	299	22	0
Pemberton Township	26,966	72	1	2	11	58	8	1	5	2	1
Pennington	2,516	0	0	0	0	0	848	197	578	73	2
Pennsauken Township	35,506	111	1	2	41	67	154	31	110	13	0
Penns Grove	4,746	51	1	8	14	28	198	19	171	8	0
Pennsville Township	12,345	18	0	0	3	15	73	13	60	0	2
Pequannock Township	15,045	7	0	0	3	4	697	110	511	76	3
Perth Amboy	51,816	147	0	2	30	115	304	37	254	13	0
Phillipsburg	14,228	30	0	14	5	11	23	3	20	0	
Pine Beach	2,173	1	0	0	0	1					

Table 8. Offenses Known to Law Enforcement, by Selected State and City, 2019—Continued

(Number.)

State/city	Population	Violent crime	Murder and nonnegligent manslaughter	Rape[1]	Robbery	Aggravated assault	Property crime	Burglary	Larceny-theft	Motor vehicle theft	Arson[2]
Pine Hill	10,419	30	0	1	4	25	143	29	110	4	0
Pine Valley	12	0	0	0	0	0	0	0	0	0	0
Piscataway Township	56,783	47	0	7	5	35	443	45	376	22	0
Pitman	8,709	4	0	0	2	2	55	12	42	1	0
Plainfield	50,576	192	3	2	90	97	805	140	607	58	10
Plainsboro Township	22,976	9	1	0	0	8	151	12	135	4	0
Pleasantville	20,388	65	1	4	26	34	271	90	156	25	0
Plumsted Township	8,545	5	0	1	0	4	32	12	19	1	0
Pohatcong Township	3,181	0	0	0	0	0	230	21	208	1	0
Point Pleasant	18,684	15	0	0	0	15	116	24	87	5	0
Point Pleasant Beach	4,516	5	0	0	1	4	54	20	24	10	0
Pompton Lakes	10,953	8	0	1	0	7	58	5	51	2	0
Princeton	31,610	10	0	1	0	9	238	45	190	3	4
Prospect Park	5,831	5	0	2	1	2	83	12	62	9	0
Rahway	30,072	32	1	1	10	20	157	25	103	29	0
Ramsey	14,978	3	0	0	2	1	161	3	155	3	0
Randolph Township	25,490	8	0	1	1	6	99	10	81	8	0
Raritan	7,999	6	0	3	1	2	61	11	45	5	0
Raritan Township	22,220	8	0	0	1	7	64	7	55	2	0
Readington Township	15,805	11	0	1	0	10	61	15	40	6	1
Red Bank	12,016	13	0	4	4	5	126	14	108	4	0
Ridgefield	11,240	6	0	0	0	6	49	3	38	8	0
Ridgefield Park	12,983	7	0	0	2	5	124	6	108	10	1
Ridgewood	25,192	13	0	0	2	11	143	22	108	13	0
Ringwood	12,165	5	0	1	0	4	42	6	34	2	0
Riverdale	4,255	2	0	0	0	2	96	9	83	4	1
River Edge	11,500	2	0	1	1	0	72	7	62	3	0
Riverside Township	7,806	14	0	1	1	12	36	4	31	1	0
Riverton	2,675	0	0	0	0	0	25	2	23	0	0
River Vale Township	10,063	0	0	0	0	0	20	1	18	1	0
Robbinsville Township	14,635	2	0	2	0	0	51	6	43	2	0
Rochelle Park Township	5,598	4	0	0	3	1	66	11	53	2	0
Rockaway	6,325	1	0	0	1	0	53	13	37	3	0
Rockaway Township	25,756	13	0	0	2	11	231	20	203	8	1
Rockleigh	531	0	0	0	0	0	2	0	2	0	0
Roseland	5,826	2	0	0	0	2	34	0	26	8	0
Roselle	21,903	67	1	1	16	49	339	51	255	33	2
Roselle Park	13,630	2	0	2	0	0	135	11	115	9	0
Roxbury Township	22,755	3	0	0	2	1	101	13	88	0	0
Rumson	6,740	0	0	0	0	0	57	7	36	14	0
Runnemede	8,262	7	0	0	0	7	144	24	112	8	0
Rutherford	18,423	12	0	2	2	8	181	20	145	16	0
Saddle Brook Township	13,897	1	0	0	1	0	220	5	214	1	0
Saddle River	3,186	2	0	0	0	2	30	5	22	3	0
Salem	4,702	73	2	3	19	49	227	77	124	26	12
Sayreville	44,581	34	0	0	8	26	310	42	231	37	0
Scotch Plains Township	24,383	14	0	2	3	9	162	50	105	7	0
Sea Bright	1,352	2	0	1	0	1	11	2	9	0	0
Sea Girt	1,764	1	0	0	0	1	12	1	11	0	0
Sea Isle City	2,035	0	0	0	0	0	89	16	73	0	0
Seaside Heights	2,902	12	0	0	1	11	166	21	141	4	0
Seaside Park	1,538	3	0	0	1	2	20	6	14	0	0
Secaucus	21,217	41	0	3	11	27	516	31	466	19	1
Ship Bottom	1,144	0	0	0	0	0	18	0	18	0	0
Shrewsbury	4,122	6	0	0	1	5	88	4	79	5	0
Somerdale	5,492	12	0	0	2	10	263	23	236	4	2
Somers Point	10,224	11	0	2	2	7	260	22	229	9	0
Somerville	12,198	11	0	0	8	3	138	11	117	10	0
South Amboy	8,922	2	0	0	0	2	67	10	46	11	0
South Bound Brook	4,570	1	0	0	1	0	43	6	36	1	0
South Brunswick Township	46,038	17	0	4	5	8	254	36	204	14	3
South Hackensack Township	2,465	13	1	0	3	9	43	5	31	7	0
South Harrison Township	3,122	1	0	0	0	1	13	1	11	1	0
South Orange Village	16,740	13	0	0	9	4	279	21	233	25	0
South Plainfield	24,114	30	0	0	8	22	394	34	343	17	1
South River	15,945	35	0	7	6	22	102	13	80	9	0
South Toms River	3,780	7	0	0	2	5	32	6	24	2	0
Sparta Township	18,532	4	0	0	0	4	31	2	27	2	0
Spotswood	8,276	2	0	0	1	1	52	8	43	1	0
Springfield Township, Burlington County	3,252	2	0	0	0	2	18	1	15	2	0
Springfield Township, Union County	17,661	3	0	0	2	1	134	19	105	10	0
Spring Lake	2,917	0	0	0	0	0	34	4	29	1	0
Spring Lake Heights	4,538	1	0	0	0	1	13	2	10	1	0
Stafford Township	27,609	32	0	4	1	27	232	19	205	8	1
Stanhope	3,281	1	0	1	0	0	27	7	18	2	0
Stone Harbor	804	2	0	0	0	2	106	14	91	1	1
Stratford	6,926	10	0	1	6	3	60	8	51	1	0
Summit	21,980	3	0	1	2	0	136	9	118	9	0
Surf City	1,193	2	0	2	0	0	8	3	5	0	0
Swedesboro	2,565	0	0	0	0	0	36	4	31	1	0
Tavistock	5	0	0	0	0	0	0	0	0	0	0

Table 8. Offenses Known to Law Enforcement, by Selected State and City, 2019—Continued

(Number.)

State/city	Population	Violent crime	Murder and nonnegligent manslaughter	Rape[1]	Robbery	Aggravated assault	Property crime	Burglary	Larceny-theft	Motor vehicle theft	Arson[2]
Teaneck Township	40,533	56	1	11	12	32	364	49	304	11	1
Tenafly	14,586	1	0	0	1	0	89	14	63	12	1
Teterboro	68	0	0	0	0	0	102	0	99	3	0
Tewksbury Township	5,765	2	0	0	0	2	23	6	14	3	0
Tinton Falls	17,506	8	0	0	4	4	243	7	227	9	0
Toms River Township	93,836	72	1	13	18	40	1,248	136	1,070	42	3
Totowa	10,754	15	0	1	2	12	166	16	134	16	0
Trenton	83,457	937	15	70	300	552	1,748	360	1,142	246	11
Tuckerton	3,370	1	0	0	0	1	36	7	23	6	0
Union Beach	5,396	11	0	0	0	11	14	5	8	1	1
Union City	68,459	193	0	12	52	129	1,080	101	891	88	3
Union Township	58,736	43	0	4	27	12	912	44	792	76	1
Upper Saddle River	8,245	2	0	0	0	2	27	4	14	9	0
Ventnor City	9,966	15	0	4	2	9	364	66	282	16	0
Vernon Township	21,912	3	0	0	0	3	81	12	68	1	0
Verona	13,355	1	0	0	0	1	49	5	39	5	8
Vineland	59,860	211	1	32	55	123	1,686	269	1,375	42	1
Voorhees Township	29,099	30	0	0	10	20	352	34	309	9	0
Waldwick	10,240	2	0	0	0	2	57	5	48	4	1
Wallington	11,568	9	0	0	2	7	143	6	124	13	0
Wall Township	25,648	22	0	0	0	22	178	21	144	13	0
Wanaque	11,772	4	0	1	0	3	34	2	27	5	0
Warren Township	15,772	0	0	0	0	0	42	11	25	6	0
Washington	6,453	8	0	0	0	8	44	9	33	2	0
Washington Township, Bergen County	9,219	1	0	0	0	1	19	1	14	4	0
Washington Township, Gloucester County	47,126	72	0	2	3	67	652	91	543	18	1
Washington Township, Morris County	18,296	12	0	3	0	9	80	13	63	4	0
Washington Township, Warren County	6,391	6	2	0	0	4	64	8	51	5	0
Watchung	6,054	1	0	0	0	1	320	13	301	6	0
Waterford Township	10,664	12	0	3	1	8	54	6	48	0	0
Wayne Township	53,279	30	0	0	8	22	894	78	777	39	0
Weehawken Township	15,115	22	0	5	4	13	231	41	178	12	0
Wenonah	2,204	1	0	0	0	1	32	5	27	0	0
Westampton Township	8,666	30	0	9	6	15	159	17	131	11	0
West Amwell Township	2,727	1	0	0	0	1	27	3	23	1	0
West Caldwell Township	10,840	2	0	1	0	1	54	7	42	5	1
West Cape May	1,003	1	0	1	0	0	11	4	7	0	0
West Deptford Township	20,902	16	0	1	7	8	244	57	167	20	0
Westfield	29,688	4	0	0	2	2	141	9	112	20	0
West Long Branch	7,889	0	0	0	0	0	89	7	75	7	0
West Milford Township	26,287	13	0	2	1	10	127	18	104	5	1
West New York	53,145	128	1	13	58	56	692	85	580	27	0
West Orange	47,696	92	0	17	16	59	673	80	532	61	1
Westville	4,128	9	0	1	1	7	120	29	84	7	0
West Wildwood	553	2	0	0	0	2	9	2	7	0	2
West Windsor Township	28,026	11	0	0	4	7	310	46	259	5	0
Westwood	11,129	0	0	0	0	0	75	23	49	3	0
Wharton	6,417	10	0	0	3	7	57	9	47	1	0
Wildwood	4,959	29	0	0	8	21	318	47	267	4	0
Wildwood Crest	3,051	17	0	2	0	15	63	19	44	0	3
Willingboro Township	31,920	102	5	13	25	59	421	114	274	33	0
Winfield Township	1,507	0	0	0	0	0	9	3	6	0	6
Winslow Township	38,390	67	0	3	13	51	492	99	345	48	1
Woodbridge Township	100,125	111	2	13	24	72	1,413	117	1,197	99	4
Woodbury	9,768	28	0	1	4	23	299	46	241	12	0
Woodbury Heights	2,949	1	0	0	1	0	53	7	42	4	0
Woodcliff Lake	5,853	2	0	0	1	1	29	4	25	0	0
Woodland Park	12,657	14	0	1	0	13	167	18	136	13	0
Woodlynne	2,901	12	0	0	3	9	55	5	45	5	0
Wood-Ridge	9,328	1	0	0	0	1	45	1	43	1	0
Woodstown	3,440	1	0	0	0	0	34	10	23	1	1
Woolwich Township	13,075	2	0	1	1	0	54	5	45	4	0
Wyckoff Township	17,030	5	0	2	0	3	81	10	64	7	0
NEW MEXICO											
Alamogordo	31,832	109	0	6	4	99	796	103	618	75	
Albuquerque[4]	561,920	7,596	84	486	1,699	5,327			20,634	5,425	98
Angel Fire	1,072	2	0	0	0	2	23	4	18	1	
Anthony	9,284	32	0	3	0	29	67	40	19	8	
Artesia	12,366	65	0	10	4	51	376	79	264	33	
Bayard	2,137	20	0	0	0	20	27	12	13	2	
Belen	7,094	144	0	1	8	135	372	64	262	46	
Bernalillo	10,353	85	1	0	10	74	232	65	137	30	
Bosque Farms	3,809	18	0	0	1	17	42	9	19	14	
Capitan	1,417	3	0	0	0	3	10	6	2	2	
Carrizozo	935	3	0	0	0	3	8	3	5	0	
Clayton	2,691	3	0	0	0	3	9	2	7	0	
Cloudcroft	700	1	0	0	0	1	6	3	2	1	
Clovis	38,734	261	2	54	28	177	1,474	300	979	195	

Table 8. Offenses Known to Law Enforcement, by Selected State and City, 2019—Continued

(Number.)

State/city	Population	Violent crime	Murder and nonnegligent manslaughter	Rape[1]	Robbery	Aggravated assault	Property crime	Burglary	Larceny-theft	Motor vehicle theft	Arson[2]
Corrales	8,715	12	0	1	1	10	62	18	36	8	
Cuba	756	11	0	0	1	10	2	1	0	1	
Deming	14,011	135	1	17	16	101	722	218	457	47	
Dexter	1,236	0	0	0	0	0	2	0	1	1	
Edgewood	6,161	20	1	1	8	10	76	18	52	6	
Estancia	1,586	1	0	0	0	1	6	6	0	0	
Eunice	2,997	1	0	0	0	1	56	30	14	12	
Gallup	21,935	437	1	20	84	332	1,397	250	987	160	
Grants	8,937	49	2	1	2	44	185	82	88	15	
Hatch	1,605	16	0	0	0	16	31	11	19	1	
Hope	106	0	0	0	0	0	2	1	1	0	
Hurley	1,181	3	0	0	0	3	5	1	4	0	
Jal	2,097	14	0	1	1	12	34	5	21	8	
Las Cruces	103,520	514	10	64	57	383	3,707	654	2,746	307	3
Logan	959	4	0	0	0	4	12	2	10	0	
Lordsburg	2,385	12	0	0	0	12	43	16	23	4	
Los Alamos[6]	19,220		0	10	1		72	8	59	5	
Los Lunas	15,929	205	0	4	16	185	649	134	415	100	
Lovington	11,322	12	3	0	3	6	260	86	140	34	
Magdalena	873	3	1	0	0	2	13	3	9	1	
Mesilla	1,826	0	0	0	0	0	0	0	0	0	
Milan	3,632	4	0	0	0	4	4	2	2	0	
Moriarty	1,792	5	0	2	0	3	54	20	25	9	
Peralta	3,586	22	0	0	0	22	37	11	23	3	
Portales	11,675	55	1	6	2	46	305	92	179	34	
Questa	1,753	3	0	1	2		10	0	10	0	
Raton	5,939	16	0	0	0	16	50	10	39	1	
Rio Rancho	99,359	189	3	32	20	134	1,474	261	1,084	129	
Roswell	47,533	404	9	61	36	298	1,793	301	1,362	130	27
Ruidoso	7,826	31	2	4	1	24	206	77	120	9	
Ruidoso Downs	2,575	19	0	0	1	18	112	32	73	7	
Santa Clara	1,765	5	0	0	0	5	12	4	7	1	
Santa Rosa	2,639	18	0	0	0	18	60	18	39	3	
San Ysidro	199	1	0	0	0	1	0	0	0	0	
Springer	898	7	0	0	0	7	12	3	6	3	
Sunland Park	18,103	65	0	9	2	54	189	58	114	17	1
Taos	5,963	19	0	0	4	15	317	50	249	18	
Taos Ski Valley	69	0	0	0	0	0	5	1	4	0	
Tatum	823	0	0	0	0	0	0	0	0	0	
Texico	1,078	0	0	0	0	0	4	2	2	0	
Truth or Consequences	5,791	20	0	0	0	20	65	16	46	3	
Tularosa	2,988	7	1	0	0	6	56	21	34	1	
NEW YORK											
Adams Village	1,735	0	0	0	0	0	0	0	0	0	
Addison Town and Village	2,471	3	0	0	0	3	5	0	5	0	0
Afton Village	796	0	0	0	0	0	0	0	0	0	0
Akron Village	2,851	1	0	0	0	1	5	1	4	0	0
Albany	97,221	736	4	60	189	483	2,919	445	2,315	159	16
Albion Village	5,802	17	0	2	1	14	147	27	115	5	2
Alfred Village	3,988	1	0	0	0	1	23	5	18	0	0
Allegany Village	1,707	1	0	0	0	1	9	0	8	1	0
Amherst Town	120,864	141	2	11	42	86	1,840	157	1,640	43	5
Amityville Village	9,430	3	1	0	0	2	68	12	52	4	0
Amsterdam	17,773	40	1	3	7	29	220	49	158	13	3
Angelica Village	818	0	0	0	0	0	0	0	0	0	0
Arcade Village	1,933	2	0	0	0	2	6	1	5	0	0
Ardsley Village	4,538	1	0	1	0	0	21	3	17	1	0
Asharoken Village	644	0	0	0	0	0	0	0	0	0	0
Attica Village	2,411	0	0	0	0	0	5	0	5	0	0
Baldwinsville Village	7,931	0	0	0	0	0	46	4	41	1	3
Ballston Spa Village	5,257	2	0	1	0	1	31	3	27	1	0
Barker	505	0	0	0	0	0	0	0	0	0	0
Bath Village	5,446	12	0	2	3	7	73	14	59	0	0
Beacon	14,510	24	1	4	6	13	150	15	128	7	0
Bedford Town	17,791	1	0	0	0	1	57	4	52	1	0
Belmont Village	904	0	0	0	0	0	3	0	3	0	0
Bethlehem Town	35,275	29	0	11	2	16	438	41	391	6	0
Binghamton	44,475	355	2	42	66	245	1,907	417	1,429	61	16
Black River	1,253	0	0	0	0	0	8	0	8	0	0
Blasdell Village	2,665	5	0	0	2	3	39	7	30	2	0
Blooming Grove Town	11,816	6	0	1	0	5	54	8	45	1	0
Bolton Town	2,251	0	0	0	0	0	10	1	8	1	0
Boonville Village	1,995	1	0	1	0	0	11	2	8	1	
Brant Town	2,055	0	0	0	0	0	5	0	4	1	0
Brewster	2,345	0	0	0	0	0	5	0	5	0	0
Briarcliff Manor Village	8,267	0	0	0	0	0	30	1	29	0	0
Brighton Town	36,036	25	0	5	4	16	611	85	507	19	0
Brockport Village	8,241	10	0	3	1	6	59	5	52	2	0
Bronxville Village	6,459	0	0	0	0	0	34	5	28	1	0
Brownville Village	1,093	0	0	0	0	0	1	0	1	0	0
Buchanan Village	2,243	2	0	1	1	0	6	0	6	0	0
Buffalo	255,686	2,533	47	121	802	1,563	8,298	1,610	6,009	679	143

Table 8. Offenses Known to Law Enforcement, by Selected State and City, 2019—Continued

(Number.)

State/city	Population	Violent crime	Murder and nonnegligent manslaughter	Rape[1]	Robbery	Aggravated assault	Property crime	Burglary	Larceny-theft	Motor vehicle theft	Arson[2]
Cairo Town	6,413	1	0	0	0	1	30	5	24	1	0
Cambridge Village	1,794	0	0	0	0	0	19	2	17	0	0
Camden Village	2,164	0	0	0	0	0	24	1	22	1	0
Camillus Town and Village	24,160	17	0	7	2	8	277	22	245	10	2
Canajoharie Village	2,136	1	0	1	0	0	15	2	12	1	0
Canandaigua	10,217	45	0	22	3	20	178	22	148	8	0
Canastota Village	4,513	7	0	3	1	3	33	7	24	2	1
Canisteo Village	2,131	4	0	2	0	2	3	0	3	0	0
Canton Village	6,407	3	0	1	0	2	18	2	16	0	0
Cape Vincent Village	702	0	0	0	0	0	0	0	0	0	0
Carmel Town	34,251	8	0	0	0	8	76	5	69	2	0
Carroll Town	3,329	0	0	0	0	0	19	5	14	0	0
Carthage Village	3,336	1	0	1	0	0	45	3	41	1	0
Catskill Village	3,797	6	0	0	1	5	71	18	52	1	0
Cattaraugus Village	907	0	0	0	0	0	0	0	0	0	0
Cayuga Heights Village	3,666	0	0	0	0	0	7	1	6	0	0
Cazenovia Village	2,842	2	0	1	0	1	18	3	15	0	0
Central Square Village	1,749	0	0	0	0	0	63	1	62	0	1
Centre Island Village	410	0	0	0	0	0	1	1	0	0	0
Chatham Village	1,619	0	0	0	0	0	3	0	3	0	0
Cheektowaga Town	76,821	187	2	15	57	113	2,153	208	1,856	89	4
Chester Town	8,043	8	0	1	3	4	7	0	7	0	0
Chester Village	4,120	0	0	0	0	0	16	0	16	0	0
Chittenango Village	4,835	1	0	0	0	1	19	1	16	2	0
Cicero Town	28,732	5	0	1	1	3	174	18	150	6	0
Clarkstown Town	80,599	56	0	12	11	33	985	33	918	34	2
Clayton Village	1,828	0	0	0	0	0	12	1	11	0	0
Clyde Village	1,937	3	0	0	1	2	23	8	15	0	1
Cobleskill Village	4,329	15	0	2	1	12	51	2	48	1	1
Coeymans Town	7,297	17	0	2	1	14	71	4	65	2	0
Cohocton Town	2,452	0	0	0	0	0	0	0	0	0	1
Cohoes	16,717	37	2	5	3	27	153	14	127	12	1
Colchester Town	1,965	5	0	1	1	3	14	3	9	2	0
Cold Spring Village	1,955	1	0	0	0	1	2	1	1	0	0
Colonie Town	79,509	62	0	10	19	33	1,870	120	1,716	34	5
Cornwall-on-Hudson Village	2,914	1	0	0	0	1	15	1	14	0	0
Cornwall Town	9,502	2	0	1	0	1	7	2	5	0	0
Cortland	18,655	55	0	27	6	22	325	77	246	2	1
Coxsackie Village	2,653	0	0	0	0	0	1	0	1	0	0
Crawford Town	9,171	1	0	0	1	0	64	13	49	2	1
Croton-on-Hudson Village	8,131	3	0	0	0	3	36	2	32	2	0
Cuba Town	3,083	1	0	0	0	1	27	3	24	0	0
Dansville Village	4,389	1	0	0	0	1	52	7	44	1	0
Deerpark Town	7,714	11	0	2	0	9	49	8	35	6	0
Delhi Village	3,094	8	0	1	0	7	22	6	16	0	0
Depew Village	15,008	15	0	5	2	8	193	27	156	10	1
Deposit Village	1,524	1	0	0	1	0	10	1	8	1	0
DeWitt Town	25,000	36	0	3	12	21	608	62	514	32	1
Dexter Village	1,011	0	0	0	0	0	1	0	1	0	0
Dobbs Ferry Village	10,990	4	0	0	2	2	44	2	38	4	0
Dryden Village	2,121	4	0	2	1	1	24	3	21	0	0
Dunkirk	11,712	21	1	0	5	15	210	37	168	5	0
Durham Town	2,659	0	0	0	0	0	3	0	3	0	0
East Aurora-Aurora Town	13,785	2	0	0	1	1	67	10	52	5	0
Eastchester Town	20,073	3	0	0	2	1	67	8	52	7	0
East Greenbush Town	16,324	10	0	1	2	7	400	37	358	5	0
East Rochester Village	6,522	6	0	0	1	5	69	18	47	4	0
Eden Town	7,621	2	0	1	0	1	36	8	25	3	0
Ellenville Village	3,980	9	0	0	1	8	50	4	44	2	0
Ellicott Town	5,014	13	0	2	2	9	241	30	210	1	0
Ellicottville	1,575	0	0	0	0	0	9	2	7	0	0
Elmira	26,958	83	1	0	40	42	831	172	643	16	0
Elmira Heights Village	3,819	4	0	0	1	3	73	13	58	2	0
Elmira Town	5,589	0	0	0	0	0	2	1	1	0	0
Elmsford Village	5,295	3	0	0	1	2	11	3	8	0	0
Evans Town	16,118	20	0	6	4	10	171	8	154	9	1
Fairport Village	5,334	2	0	0	1	1	24	1	22	1	0
Fishkill Town	21,307	8	0	0	2	6	190	5	184	1	0
Fishkill Village	2,071	1	0	0	0	1	20	1	19	0	0
Floral Park Village	15,927	8	0	0	4	4	26	2	22	2	0
Florida Village	2,851	0	0	0	0	0	5	3	2	0	0
Fort Edward Village	3,253	2	0	2	0	0	4	2	2	0	0
Fort Plain Village	2,224	9	0	4	0	5	53	7	46	0	0
Frankfort Town	4,817	3	0	1	0	2	20	3	16	1	1
Frankfort Village	2,432	6	0	1	0	5	12	1	9	2	0
Franklinville Village	1,632	0	0	0	0	0	2	0	2	0	0
Freeport Village	43,064	72	0	1	23	48	428	45	361	22	0
Friendship Town	1,869	0	0	0	0	0	0	0	0	0	0
Galway Village	194	0	0	0	0	0	0	0	0	0	1
Garden City Village	22,514	9	0	0	3	6	267	25	234	8	2
Gates Town	28,366	55	0	11	11	33	776	66	669	41	0
Geddes Town	10,038	4	0	0	2	2	162	22	135	5	1
Geneseo Village	8,158	3	0	3	0	0	83	7	76	0	

Table 8. Offenses Known to Law Enforcement, by Selected State and City, 2019—Continued

(Number.)

State/city	Population	Violent crime	Murder and nonnegligent manslaughter	Rape[1]	Robbery	Aggravated assault	Property crime	Burglary	Larceny-theft	Motor vehicle theft	Arson[2]
Geneva	12,708	20	0	8	4	8	234	47	185	2	1
Glen Cove	27,228	5	0	0	4	1	84	5	77	2	0
Glen Park Village	481	0	0	0	0	0	0	0	0	0	0
Glens Falls	14,306	28	0	8	1	19	100	18	80	2	1
Glenville Town	21,634	12	0	5	0	7	309	23	281	5	0
Gloversville	14,738	66	0	24	2	40	401	36	349	16	1
Goshen Town	8,798	2	0	0	0	2	27	3	23	1	0
Goshen Village	5,337	2	0	0	0	2	29	5	23	1	0
Gowanda Village	2,575	4	0	0	0	4	26	2	24	0	0
Granville Village	2,422	3	0	0	1	2	12	3	9	0	0
Great Neck Estates Village	2,884	0	0	0	0	0	12	8	1	3	0
Greece Town	95,777	167	0	27	43	97	1,847	194	1,576	77	2
Greenburgh Town	45,040	43	0	8	8	27	438	22	403	13	0
Greene Village	1,415	0	0	0	0	0	22	5	16	1	0
Greenport Town	4,286	0	0	0	0	0	56	0	55	1	0
Greenwich Village	1,708	0	0	0	0	0	16	3	13	0	0
Greenwood Lake Village	3,074	2	0	0	0	2	7	2	5	0	0
Groton Village	2,278	0	0	0	0	0	36	2	34	0	0
Guilderland Town	34,133	23	0	5	9	9	841	51	785	5	0
Hamburg Town	46,445	43	2	0	8	33	742	66	659	17	3
Hamburg Village	9,725	2	0	0	0	2	76	10	63	3	0
Hamilton Village	4,081	0	0	0	0	0	3	0	3	0	0
Hancock Village	934	2	0	1	0	1	5	1	4	0	0
Harriman Village	2,439	3	0	0	0	3	28	2	26	0	0
Harrison Town	27,946	0	0	0	0	0	147	20	120	7	0
Hastings-on-Hudson Village	7,916	2	0	0	0	2	58	4	53	1	1
Hempstead Village	55,404	297	7	11	101	178	579	120	348	111	2
Herkimer Village	7,291	41	0	11	2	28	201	19	179	3	0
Highlands Town	8,444	0	0	0	0	0	7	2	5	0	0
Holley Village	1,676	1	0	1	0	0	9	4	5	0	2
Homer Village	3,100	1	0	0	0	1	2	0	2	0	0
Hoosick Falls Village	3,359	5	0	0	0	5	21	3	17	1	0
Horseheads Village	6,390	4	0	1	1	2	101	8	91	2	0
Hudson Falls Village	7,023	14	0	4	0	10	45	8	35	2	1
Huntington Bay Village	1,434	0	0	0	0	0	7	0	7	0	0
Hyde Park Town	20,808	4	0	0	1	3	84	10	73	1	0
Ilion Village	7,685	38	0	14	2	22	163	21	136	6	0
Independence Town	1,137	2	0	0	0	2	4	1	3	0	0
Inlet Town	302	0	0	0	0	0	1	1	0	0	0
Irvington Village	6,506	0	0	0	0	0	33	3	28	2	0
Ithaca	31,122	41	1	5	9	26	840	56	768	16	2
Jamestown	29,102	199	0	31	19	149	863	203	621	39	13
Johnson City Village	14,196	61	1	19	10	31	765	76	681	8	1
Johnstown	8,198	13	0	8	0	5	138	13	123	2	1
Jordan Village	1,298	0	0	0	0	0	0	0	0	0	0
Kenmore Village	15,025	11	0	0	4	7	175	23	147	5	0
Kensington Village	1,189	0	0	0	0	0	5	0	3	2	0
Kent Town	13,235	5	0	4	1	0	27	2	23	2	1
Kings Point Village	5,312	2	0	0	1	1	24	4	2	18	0
Kingston	22,844	68	2	13	10	43	498	59	419	20	2
Kirkland Town	8,329	0	0	0	0	0	4	0	3	1	0
Lackawanna	17,724	81	0	12	9	60	378	53	291	34	1
Lake Placid Village	2,369	3	0	2	1	0	19	3	16	0	0
Lake Success Village	3,153	0	0	0	0	0	16	2	12	2	0
Lakewood-Busti	7,193	5	0	2	2	1	332	42	284	6	1
Lancaster Town	37,571	21	0	5	8	8	398	37	351	10	0
Larchmont Village	6,096	2	0	1	1	0	84	2	78	4	0
Lewisboro Town	12,582	0	0	0	0	0	0	0	0	0	0
Lewiston Town and Village	15,763	4	0	2	0	2	87	4	72	11	3
Liberty Village	4,083	29	0	7	4	18	119	15	103	1	0
Little Falls	4,642	15	0	2	1	12	39	4	34	1	2
Liverpool Village	2,202	0	0	0	0	0	9	0	8	1	0
Lloyd Harbor Village	3,667	3	0	0	0	3	7	0	6	1	0
Lloyd Town	10,463	7	0	2	1	4	99	9	88	2	1
Long Beach	33,552	19	0	0	2	17	66	5	53	8	1
Lowville Village	3,315	3	0	0	0	3	14	2	12	0	0
Lynbrook Village	19,492	13	0	2	2	9	95	8	81	6	0
Macedon Town and Village	8,877	5	0	2	0	3	72	6	63	3	0
Malone Village	5,581	12	0	6	1	5	112	12	96	4	0
Malverne Village	8,514	2	0	0	0	2	10	3	7	0	0
Mamaroneck Town	12,088	2	0	0	0	2	79	10	67	2	0
Mamaroneck Village	19,183	16	0	1	2	13	157	21	122	14	0
Manchester Village	1,618	0	0	0	0	0	0	0	0	0	0
Manlius Town	24,168	19	0	5	4	10	254	24	216	14	2
Marcellus Village	1,717	0	0	0	0	0	4	0	4	0	0
Marlborough Town	8,601	3	0	0	0	3	45	4	37	4	0
Massena Village	10,177	11	0	0	3	8	246	29	209	8	0
Maybrook Village	3,791	1	0	0	0	1	7	2	4	1	0
Mechanicville	5,072	7	0	0	0	7	32	6	23	3	0
Medina Village	5,631	12	0	2	3	7	90	20	66	4	4
Menands Village	3,885	4	0	0	1	3	92	14	74	4	0
Middleport Village	1,745	1	0	0	0	1	10	2	8	0	0
Middletown	27,801	87	3	16	16	52	308	45	249	14	2

Table 8. Offenses Known to Law Enforcement, by Selected State and City, 2019—Continued

(Number.)

State/city	Population	Violent crime	Murder and nonnegligent manslaughter	Rape[1]	Robbery	Aggravated assault	Property crime	Burglary	Larceny-theft	Motor vehicle theft	Arson[2]
Millerton Village	2,958	0	0	0	0	0	10	6	3	1	0
Mohawk Village	2,533	3	0	1	0	2	24	4	20	0	1
Monroe Village	8,593	7	0	0	1	6	119	4	114	1	1
Montgomery Village	4,621	0	0	0	0	0	13	1	12	0	0
Monticello Village	6,392	25	0	2	4	19	113	27	82	4	
Moravia Village	1,200	0	0	0	0	0	11	1	10	0	0
Moriah Town	4,557	1	0	0	0	1	1	0	1	0	0
Mount Hope Town	6,624	1	0	0	0	1	6	0	6	0	6
Mount Vernon	67,619	381	2	20	98	261	842	91	642	109	0
Nassau Village	1,101	0	0	0	0	0	7	1	6	0	0
Newark Village	8,799	28	0	2	10	16	228	20	202	6	0
New Berlin Town	1,510	0	0	0	0	0	15	2	12	1	3
Newburgh	28,070	317	3	19	82	213	640	137	484	19	4
Newburgh Town	31,128	22	0	2	6	14	911	34	864	13	0
New Castle Town	17,896	1	0	0	0	1	53	5	48	0	3
New Hartford Town and Village	20,294	17	0	2	6	9	617	21	587	9	
New Rochelle	78,936	98	0	9	34	55	762	35	696	31	2
New Windsor Town	27,971	28	2	3	1	22	271	34	235	2	
New York	8,379,043	47,821	319	2,770	13,396	31,336	122,299	9,846	106,931	5,522	0
New York Mills Village	3,217	0	0	0	0	0	39	5	32	2	25
Niagara Falls	47,900	431	2	32	101	296	1,848	266	1,471	111	1
Niagara Town	7,958	4	0	0	2	2	212	9	194	9	0
Niskayuna Town	22,407	11	0	1	4	6	308	23	275	10	0
Nissequogue Village	1,731	0	0	0	0	1	5	1	3	1	0
Norfolk Town	4,375	1	0	0	0	1	4	2	2	0	0
North Castle Town	12,248	4	0	0	0	4	75	5	66	4	0
Northport Village	7,288	0	0	0	0	0	7	0	7	0	1
North Syracuse Village	6,637	14	0	0	5	9	70	5	61	4	0
North Tonawanda	30,228	44	0	11	13	20	351	47	288	16	1
Norwich	6,581	28	0	15	0	13	186	31	153	2	0
Norwood Village	1,553	2	0	0	0	2	6	2	4	0	2
Ocean Beach Village	83	0	0	0	0	0	9	0	9	0	0
Ogdensburg	10,484	36	0	3	2	31	296	56	237	3	0
Ogden Town	20,144	10	1	0	2	7	141	2	129	10	1
Old Brookville Village	2,202	1	0	0	0	1	45	9	27	9	2
Old Westbury Village	4,752	1	0	0	0	1	47	13	20	14	0
Olean	13,499	45	0	9	4	32	310	36	266	8	1
Oneida	10,864	41	0	15	4	22	372	44	326	2	1
Oneonta City	13,915	34	0	10	3	21	145	29	108	8	0
Orangetown Town	37,371	34	0	5	12	17	265	27	234	4	0
Orchard Park Town	29,599	24	0	9	4	11	345	31	306	8	0
Oriskany Village	1,329	0	0	0	0	0	10	0	10	0	1
Ossining Village	24,991	20	1	1	4	14	157	13	141	3	0
Oswego City	17,239	51	0	17	4	30	583	56	503	24	
Owego Village	3,887	17	0	8	2	7	114	19	94	1	0
Oxford Village	1,379	0	0	0	0	0	2	0	2	0	0
Oyster Bay Cove Village	4,296	1	0	0	0	1	7	1	4	2	0
Painted Post Village	1,953	1	0	0	0	1	8	3	4	1	0
Palmyra Village	3,316	4	0	2	1	1	7	0	6	1	0
Peekskill	24,243	30	0	1	7	22	209	7	196	6	0
Pelham Manor Village	5,567	7	0	0	2	5	149	10	134	5	0
Pelham Village	6,911	4	0	0	1	3	45	3	41	1	1
Penn Yan Village	4,910	5	0	4	0	1	51	8	42	1	0
Perry Village	3,442	4	0	3	0	1	36	7	27	2	0
Philmont Village	1,260	0	0	0	0	0	3	0	3	0	0
Phoenix Village	2,242	4	0	0	0	4	15	0	15	0	0
Piermont Village	2,538	0	0	0	0	0	4	1	3	0	0
Pine Plains Town	2,402	0	0	0	0	0	0	0	0	0	0
Plattekill Town	10,160	2	0	0	0	2	22	7	15	0	3
Plattsburgh City	19,367	36	0	13	1	22	243	22	219	2	0
Pleasantville Village	7,261	6	3	0	3	0	38	3	35	0	1
Port Chester Village	29,317	21	1	2	7	11	200	18	172	10	1
Port Jervis	8,523	37	1	7	3	26	137	14	117	6	1
Port Washington	19,396	6	0	0	2	4	91	6	82	3	0
Potsdam Village	8,917	2	0	0	1	1	67	8	58	1	5
Poughkeepsie	30,422	235	3	26	63	143	513	73	402	38	3
Poughkeepsie Town	38,889	70	2	12	20	36	991	65	893	33	0
Pound Ridge Town	5,159	1	0	1	0	0	34	2	32	0	0
Pulaski Village	2,227	0	0	0	0	0	22	2	20	1	1
Quogue Village	1,015	1	0	0	0	1	29	0	28	20	4
Ramapo Town	94,633	68	1	16	5	46	436	36	380	0	0
Red Hook Village	1,956	1	0	0	0	1	38	9	29	0	0
Rhinebeck Village	2,556	1	0	0	0	1	21	3	18	9	4
Riverhead Town	33,536	33	1	3	10	19	568	43	516	651	83
Rochester	205,769	1,540	33	102	429	976	7,142	1,269	5,222	17	0
Rockville Centre Village	24,669	10	0	0	3	7	175	19	139	24	2
Rome	32,019	54	1	8	11	34	524	84	416	0	0
Rosendale Town	5,826	1	0	0	0	1	26	3	23	31	0
Rotterdam Town	29,855	32	0	4	3	25	754	54	669	3	0
Rye	15,756	1	0	0	1	0	15	1	11	5	0
Rye Brook Village	9,530	0	0	0	0	0	69	6	58	0	0
Sackets Harbor Village	1,413	0	0	0	0	0	0	0	0	0	0
Sag Harbor Village	2,298	0	0	0	0	0	0	0	0		

Table 8. Offenses Known to Law Enforcement, by Selected State and City, 2019—Continued

(Number.)

State/city	Population	Violent crime	Murder and nonnegligent manslaughter	Rape[1]	Robbery	Aggravated assault	Property crime	Burglary	Larceny-theft	Motor vehicle theft	Arson[2]
Salamanca	5,439	24	0	0	4	20	54	8	43	3	1
Sands Point Village	2,912	1	0	1	0	0	29	5	12	12	0
Saranac Lake Village	5,221	4	0	2	0	2	35	8	26	1	0
Saratoga Springs	28,186	64	0	19	5	40	448	51	390	7	3
Saugerties Town	19,095	27	0	8	0	19	165	28	132	5	1
Scarsdale Village	17,954	6	0	0	0	6	117	12	104	1	0
Schenectady	65,504	528	3	56	133	336	1,770	248	1,392	130	20
Schodack Town	11,722	9	0	2	2	5	74	11	59	4	0
Schoharie Village	818	0	0	0	0	0	0	0	0	0	0
Scotia Village	7,641	15	0	4	5	6	111	11	94	6	0
Seneca Falls Town	8,632	9	0	3	1	5	205	15	187	3	0
Shandaken Town	2,947	0	0	0	0	0	9	1	8	0	0
Shawangunk Town	13,853	2	0	1	0	1	41	8	30	3	0
Sherburne Village	1,302	0	0	0	0	0	13	0	13	0	0
Sherrill	2,991	0	0	0	0	0	6	3	3	0	0
Shortsville Village	1,419	0	0	0	0	0	1	0	1	0	0
Sidney Village	3,573	16	0	6	2	8	119	7	109	3	1
Skaneateles Village	2,464	0	0	0	0	0	40	1	39	0	0
Sleepy Hollow Village	10,080	0	0	0	0	0	0	0	0	0	0
Solvay Village	6,227	13	0	2	1	10	65	17	40	8	0
Southampton Town	51,090	46	0	9	6	31	474	42	411	21	0
Southampton Village	3,326	1	0	0	0	1	48	6	38	4	0
South Glens Falls Village	3,677	4	0	0	1	3	35	3	31	1	0
Southold Town	19,915	15	0	4	0	11	209	30	172	7	2
Spring Valley Village	32,367	115	1	15	38	61	425	40	380	5	2
Stillwater Town	7,300	1	0	1	0	0	16	1	14	1	0
St. Johnsville Village	1,679	1	0	0	0	1	22	1	20	1	0
Stony Point Town	15,413	10	0	4	1	5	51	9	41	1	1
Syracuse	142,438	1,129	19	105	246	759	4,464	850	3,051	563	39
Tarrytown Village	11,416	6	0	2	2	2	58	14	38	6	0
Theresa Village	788	0	0	0	0	0	0	0	0	0	0
Ticonderoga Town	4,790	10	0	0	1	9	30	3	23	4	1
Tonawanda	14,754	38	0	11	4	23	188	20	158	10	0
Tonawanda Town	56,717	83	4	5	34	40	725	132	552	41	4
Troy	49,286	296	3	25	73	195	1,365	225	1,035	105	11
Trumansburg Village	1,757	1	0	1	0	0	31	2	29	0	0
Tuckahoe Village	6,584	0	0	0	0	0	28	3	21	4	0
Tuxedo Town	2,901	0	0	0	0	0	1	1	0	0	0
Ulster Town	12,625	16	1	4	2	9	208	15	190	3	0
Utica	59,842	374	6	31	143	194	1,986	261	1,635	90	16
Vernon Village	1,156	0	0	0	0	0	6	0	6	0	0
Walden Village	6,670	2	0	0	0	2	36	2	32	2	0
Wallkill Town	29,236	37	0	2	8	27	557	27	514	16	0
Warsaw Village	3,251	5	0	2	0	3	43	4	36	3	0
Washingtonville Village	5,740	1	0	0	0	1	20	2	17	1	0
Waterford Town and Village	8,574	2	0	0	0	2	27	10	13	4	0
Waterloo Village	4,885	0	0	0	0	0	51	11	38	2	0
Watertown	25,102	154	0	57	14	83	887	108	743	36	6
Watervliet	9,954	44	0	5	7	32	198	25	162	11	2
Watkins Glen Village	1,905	1	0	0	0	1	24	3	21	0	0
Waverly Village	4,119	3	0	1	0	2	10	2	8	0	0
Webb Town	1,790	1	0	0	0	1	3	0	2	1	0
Weedsport Village	1,711	0	0	0	0	0	14	2	12	0	0
Wellsville Village	4,366	9	0	6	0	3	32	2	30	0	0
West Carthage Village	1,957	0	0	0	0	0	10	1	9	0	0
Westfield Village	2,981	0	0	0	0	0	11	0	11	0	0
Westhampton Beach Village	1,811	0	0	0	0	0	26	4	21	1	1
West Seneca Town	45,399	67	1	16	13	37	601	83	491	27	1
Whitestown Town	9,096	0	0	0	0	0	28	5	14	9	0
Windham Town	1,675	2	0	0	0	2	5	1	4	0	0
Woodbury Town	11,006	3	0	0	1	2	460	5	450	5	0
Woodridge Village	776	4	0	0	1	3	17	8	9	0	0
Woodstock Town	5,781	3	0	0	1	2	32	7	24	1	1
Yonkers	200,075	708	6	42	224	436	1,826	208	1,466	152	15
Yorktown Town	36,426	8	0	1	3	4	214	20	186	8	0
Youngstown Village	1,879	0	0	0	0	0	3	0	3	0	0
NORTH CAROLINA[5]											
Aberdeen	7,892	41	0	3	7	31	301	54	229	18	0
Ahoskie	4,772	56	2	1	20	33	253	68	174	11	2
Albemarle	16,134	146	1	4	23	118	882	179	667	36	14
Apex	56,276	53	0	13	3	37	527	79	432	16	0
Asheville	93,641	695	6	59	163	467	5,923	833	4,552	538	20
Atlantic Beach	1,506	9	0	3	1	5	114	43	66	5	1
Bailey	560	2	1	1	0	0	15	7	8	0	0
Bald Head Island	182	0	0	0	0	0	24	4	19	1	0
Banner Elk	1,101	5	0	1	1	3	11	2	8	1	0
Beech Mountain	324	0	0	0	0	0	15	6	9	0	0
Belhaven	1,567	0	0	0	0	0	21	3	16	2	1
Benson	3,901	31	0	4	5	22	200	51	136	13	1
Bessemer City	5,552	13	0	0	2	11	85	18	58	9	1
Biltmore Forest	1,410	0	0	0	0	0	16	4	12	0	2
Biscoe	1,724	6	0	0	2	4	186	9	175	2	0

Table 8. Offenses Known to Law Enforcement, by Selected State and City, 2019—Continued

(Number.)

State/city	Population	Violent crime	Murder and nonnegligent manslaughter	Rape[1]	Robbery	Aggravated assault	Property crime	Burglary	Larceny-theft	Motor vehicle theft	Arson[2]
Black Mountain	8,187	8	0	0	3	5	189	32	137	20	2
Boiling Spring Lakes	6,238	10	1	3	0	6	83	19	63	1	1
Boone	19,893	26	0	6	5	15	261	34	214	13	3
Brevard	7,928	18	0	6	4	8	188	23	162	3	1
Bunn	377	1	0	0	0	1	18	2	14	2	0
Burgaw	4,176	13	0	5	3	5	130	17	111	2	2
Burlington	54,108	460	10	42	66	342	2,490	534	1,815	141	5
Butner	7,847	33	0	4	4	25	113	19	91	3	0
Canton	4,349	16	0	3	0	13	226	71	132	23	0
Cape Carteret	2,076	4	0	0	0	4	30	3	25	2	0
Carolina Beach	6,437	29	0	4	2	23	187	27	153	7	0
Carthage	2,524	4	0	1	2	1	72	15	52	5	0
Cary	172,525	114	1	12	34	67	1,560	185	1,298	77	1
Chapel Hill	61,457	58	0	10	17	31	926	184	706	36	4
Charlotte-Mecklenburg	944,260	6,982	103	317	1,975	4,587	37,070	5,426	28,304	3,340	151
Cherryville	6,062	16	0	2	1	13	153	30	117	6	0
Chocowinity	794	6	0	2	1	3	23	1	21	1	0
Clayton	23,842	40	1	7	8	24	497	49	434	14	1
Cleveland	882	4	0	1	1	2	14	2	11	1	0
Columbus	995	1	0	0	0	1	47	9	33	5	1
Concord	96,138	117	4	1	28	84	1,586	149	1,338	99	8
Cooleemee	969	0	0	0	0	0	20	4	14	2	1
Creedmoor	4,636	10	0	2	0	8	55	19	33	3	0
Dallas	4,787	20	0	2	5	13	153	24	109	20	1
Davidson	13,193	8	0	2	1	5	121	17	94	10	0
Drexel	1,849	0	0	0	0	0	33	9	15	9	0
Duck	390	0	0	0	0	0	21	7	14	0	0
Dunn	9,768	56	1	5	23	27	514	111	374	29	2
Durham	280,282	2,046	37	121	626	1,262	10,672	1,972	7,942	758	39
East Spencer	1,550	7	1	0	1	5	25	3	16	6	0
Eden	14,773	88	4	9	9	66	513	154	339	20	3
Edenton	4,631	39	2	3	5	29	145	37	99	9	0
Elizabeth City	17,424	89	1	10	16	62	762	243	468	51	3
Elizabethtown	3,447	17	0	2	0	15	225	47	168	10	0
Elon	12,214	8	0	1	3	4	82	34	44	4	3
Enfield	2,288	23	0	0	6	17	65	21	37	7	1
Erwin	5,148	10	0	2	3	5	109	40	66	3	0
Fair Bluff	882	1	0	1	0	0	14	2	12	0	0
Fairmont	2,601	14	0	4	2	8	125	31	88	6	1
Farmville	4,679	27	0	4	4	19	183	38	140	5	0
Fayetteville	209,614	1,835	24	117	281	1,413	7,391	1,365	5,641	385	59
Forest City	7,116	34	1	3	8	22	585	207	357	21	1
Four Oaks	2,224	7	0	0	1	6	35	1	32	2	0
Fuquay-Varina	30,977	26	0	3	10	13	295	48	234	13	0
Garner	31,137	79	2	7	27	43	1,076	110	912	54	3
Gibsonville	7,356	17	0	5	2	10	136	84	46	6	2
Goldsboro	34,085	267	2	7	50	208	1,985	380	1,506	99	3
Granite Falls	4,629	4	0	0	2	2	332	124	191	17	1
Greensboro	298,025	2,440	43	113	621	1,663	10,994	2,215	7,792	987	90
Greenville	94,193	437	5	17	94	321	2,837	415	2,308	114	11
Havelock	20,128	52	0	11	6	35	536	146	376	14	5
Haw River	2,525	5	0	0	1	4	46	12	29	5	1
Henderson	14,883	242	8	9	30	195	828	211	576	41	10
Hendersonville	14,234	61	2	9	17	33	680	124	515	41	2
Hertford	2,109	13	0	1	5	7	75	25	47	3	2
Hickory	41,040	165	4	16	39	106	1,793	235	1,410	148	6
Highlands	974	4	0	2	0	2	69	23	43	3	1
High Point	113,307	828	19	44	133	632	3,726	621	2,705	400	18
Hillsborough	7,321	38	0	1	11	26	392	30	350	12	0
Holly Ridge	2,829	9	0	1	4	4	86	50	31	5	0
Holly Springs	38,577	25	1	7	1	16	256	22	225	9	1
Hope Mills	15,878	111	1	5	22	83	773	94	655	24	2
Hudson	3,704	8	0	0	1	7	89	11	76	2	1
Huntersville	58,512	79	1	4	23	51	948	114	769	65	0
Indian Beach	119	0	0	0	0	0	21	2	19	0	0
Kannapolis	50,725	132	1	20	36	75	1,154	182	872	100	2
Kenansville	855	2	0	1	1	0	9	3	6	0	0
Kernersville	24,980	65	0	8	20	37	1,141	113	989	39	3
Kill Devil Hills	7,268	19	0	5	2	12	281	55	219	7	0
King	6,878	9	2	0	2	5	222	14	207	1	1
Kings Mountain	10,965	15	1	3	5	6	343	67	246	30	0
Kitty Hawk	3,563	4	0	2	1	1	127	17	109	1	0
Knightdale	18,351	42	0	10	9	23	326	23	285	18	1
Laurinburg	14,928	160	3	5	27	125	762	386	328	48	28
Lenoir	17,904	78	0	17	13	48	799	234	476	89	3
Lexington	18,917	121	2	1	27	91	812	149	627	36	3
Long View	4,921	5	0	2	0	3	88	20	55	13	0
Louisburg	3,549	23	0	2	5	16	149	30	116	3	1
Lowell	3,709	9	0	2	0	7	36	5	18	13	0
Maggie Valley	1,230	14	0	1	0	13	103	50	45	8	0
Manteo	1,453	5	0	0	1	4	34	4	28	2	0
Marion	7,837	12	0	1	1	10	419	95	301	23	0
Marshville	2,748	16	0	3	3	10	130	67	58	5	0

Table 8. Offenses Known to Law Enforcement, by Selected State and City, 2019—Continued

(Number.)

State/city	Population	Violent crime	Murder and nonnegligent manslaughter	Rape[1]	Robbery	Aggravated assault	Property crime	Burglary	Larceny-theft	Motor vehicle theft	Arson[2]
Matthews	33,372	58	3	8	18	29	1,112	111	959	42	0
Maysville	955	0	0	0	0	0	8	4	4	0	0
Mebane	16,203	45	0	5	9	31	691	53	611	27	1
Middlesex	824	0	0	0	0	0	12	3	7	2	0
Mint Hill	27,776	59	4	8	11	36	383	67	268	48	3
Mocksville	5,322	14	0	5	4	5	109	16	90	3	4
Monroe	35,630	332	2	37	70	223	1,881	343	1,407	131	9
Mooresville	38,967	65	1	11	9	44	1,050	81	913	56	8
Morehead City[4]	9,721	28	0	1	2	25			380	14	1
Morganton	16,524	82	1	13	4	64	613	182	402	29	1
Morrisville	28,796	12	0	1	2	9	379	39	324	16	2
Mount Olive	4,652	28	0	1	8	19	132	27	100	5	0
Murfreesboro	3,072	5	0	1	4	0	74	28	43	3	0
Murphy	1,657	15	0	2	1	12	119	43	68	8	0
Nags Head	2,963	18	2	2	1	13	107	23	81	3	1
New Bern	30,187	125	0	5	21	99	999	195	787	17	5
Newland	684	1	0	1	0	0	17	2	10	5	0
Newport	4,666	7	0	3	0	4	51	10	38	3	0
Newton	13,153	46	0	6	8	32	458	97	338	23	2
North Wilkesboro	4,220	16	0	1	4	11	131	3	114	14	0
Oak Island	8,244	15	0	3	1	11	135	28	99	8	0
Ocean Isle Beach	644	3	0	2	0	1	44	16	27	1	0
Oxford	8,851	91	4	0	15	72	231	31	190	10	2
Pinehurst	16,522	11	1	4	0	6	113	22	87	4	0
Pine Level	2,016	8	0	2	1	5	25	5	19	1	1
Pineville	9,088	68	1	4	21	42	1,131	115	956	60	3
Pittsboro	4,359	26	0	2	2	22	82	19	61	2	1
Plymouth	3,400	37	1	4	4	28	139	57	68	14	2
Princeton	1,402	0	0	0	0	0	16	4	11	1	0
Raeford	5,001	17	2	3	4	8	107	23	78	6	0
Raleigh	477,828	1,222	5	164	322	731	8,520	1,200	6,572	748	36
Red Springs	3,341	52	1	2	6	43	197	57	128	12	3
Reidsville	13,959	105	0	7	19	79	890	121	704	65	2
Roanoke Rapids	14,354	128	4	8	32	84	706	166	518	22	1
Robersonville	1,348	9	0	1	2	6	35	12	20	3	0
Rockingham	8,687	39	1	6	13	19	431	146	269	16	3
Rockwell	2,151	7	0	2	1	4	30	4	24	2	0
Rocky Mount	53,827	424	16	20	103	285	1,627	420	1,098	109	9
Rowland	1,002	8	1	2	2	3	45	13	29	3	1
Roxboro	8,299	61	1	3	12	45	365	89	269	7	3
Rutherfordton	4,047	0	0	0	0	0	145	1	142	2	0
Salisbury	33,877	249	2	15	69	163	1,413	220	1,094	99	9
Selma	7,018	55	1	3	9	42	204	36	138	30	0
Shallotte	4,396	9	2	1	3	3	315	31	277	7	0
Siler City	8,237	67	1	13	10	43	325	44	255	26	1
Smithfield	12,882	71	2	5	15	49	461	56	387	18	1
Snow Hill	1,513	5	0	1	0	4	58	24	34	0	0
Southern Pines	14,524	46	1	3	11	31	366	57	295	14	0
Southern Shores	2,940	1	0	1	0	0	19	7	11	1	2
Southport	3,961	4	0	3	0	1	97	6	90	1	0
Spencer	3,238	11	0	1	5	5	73	17	48	8	0
Stallings	16,173	20	0	5	2	13	199	43	139	17	1
Sugar Mountain	197	0	0	0	0	0	8	3	5	0	0
Swansboro	3,354	2	1	0	0	1	127	16	106	5	0
Sylva	2,742	9	0	3	0	6	149	14	127	8	0
Troutman	2,755	4	0	2	2	0	67	16	49	2	0
Troy	3,326	19	0	0	3	16	98	30	63	5	0
Valdese	4,435	15	0	0	0	15	67	12	44	11	0
Wadesboro	5,228	99	0	6	16	77	336	77	247	12	4
Wake Forest	46,145	24	1	3	4	16	393	33	344	16	0
Warrenton	837	4	0	0	1	3	40	11	28	1	0
Washington	9,497	71	0	4	10	57	357	62	281	14	2
Waxhaw	17,203	25	0	4	4	17	156	46	107	3	0
Waynesville	10,146	62	4	3	2	53	685	143	508	34	4
Weaverville	4,013	4	0	2	0	2	153	1	146	6	0
Wendell	8,096	6	0	1	2	3	77	22	45	10	0
West Jefferson	1,311	2	0	1	0	1	70	6	62	2	0
Whispering Pines	3,385	0	0	0	0	0	31	3	28	0	0
Whiteville	5,338	78	2	2	10	64	509	88	402	19	0
Wilkesboro	3,491	15	0	4	2	9	229	12	204	13	2
Williamston	5,217	66	1	6	3	56	348	80	260	8	2
Wilmington	124,750	759	7	74	127	551	3,593	771	2,564	258	18
Wilson	49,344	220	2	18	60	140	1,545	364	1,066	115	8
Windsor	3,310	18	0	2	0	16	22	2	18	2	0
Winterville	9,922	9	0	2	1	6	86	21	63	2	3
Wrightsville Beach	2,550	30	0	7	2	21	96	15	77	4	1
Youngsville	1,365	2	0	0	0	2	36	3	32	1	0
Zebulon	5,814	24	0	1	6	17	234	24	199	11	1
NORTH DAKOTA											
Belfield	1,028	1	0	0	0	1	25	9	16	0	0
Berthold	497	1	0	0	0	1	2	0	2	0	0
Beulah	3,200	4	0	0	0	4	17	4	11	2	0

Table 8. Offenses Known to Law Enforcement, by Selected State and City, 2019—Continued

(Number.)

State/city	Population	Violent crime	Murder and nonnegligent manslaughter	Rape[1]	Robbery	Aggravated assault	Property crime	Burglary	Larceny-theft	Motor vehicle theft	Arson[2]
Bismarck	74,705	228	1	64	36	127	2,079	225	1,647	207	4
Bowman	1,604	0	0	0	0	0	15	2	10	3	0
Burlington	1,233	5	0	0	0	5	4	1	3	0	0
Carrington	1,980	1	0	0	0	1	9	3	4	2	0
Cavalier	1,253	0	0	0	0	0	9	0	9	0	0
Devils Lake	7,294	20	0	7	2	11	271	26	229	16	0
Dickinson	23,428	52	0	3	2	47	446	43	370	33	2
Ellendale	1,223	0	0	0	0	0	5	0	5	0	0
Emerado	456	0	0	0	0	0	9	3	6	0	1
Fargo	127,423	574	5	111	78	380	3,978	830	2,757	391	26
Fessenden	442	0	0	0	0	0	1	0	0	1	0
Grafton	4,144	6	0	2	0	4	65	17	47	1	0
Grand Forks	57,459	166	0	25	23	118	1,422	218	1,101	103	5
Harvey	1,683	0	0	0	0	0	8	3	4	1	0
Hazen	2,321	1	0	0	0	1	3	0	2	1	0
Jamestown	15,198	37	0	11	0	26	315	45	252	18	0
Kenmare	1,010	0	0	0	0	0	5	2	3	0	0
Killdeer	1,213	3	0	1	0	2	12	4	7	1	0
Lincoln	3,986	3	0	2	0	1	9	1	7	1	0
Lisbon	2,036	2	0	1	0	1	28	4	20	4	0
Mandan	23,012	85	4	23	8	50	660	70	492	98	6
Medora	130	0	0	0	0	0	0	0	0	0	0
Minot	48,185	130	1	33	12	84	984	204	608	172	10
Napoleon	763	1	0	1	0	0	0	0	0	0	0
New Town	2,621	0	0	0	0	0	16	0	10	6	0
Northwood	904	1	0	0	0	1	7	2	3	2	0
Oakes	1,694	3	0	1	0	2	8	0	7	1	0
Powers Lake	279	0	0	0	0	0	0	0	0	0	0
Ray	866	0	0	0	0	0	2	2	0	0	0
Rolette	599	0	0	0	0	0	2	0	2	0	0
Rugby	2,661	1	0	1	0	0	30	5	21	4	1
Stanley	2,813	2	0	0	0	2	2	0	2	0	0
Steele	709	4	0	0	0	4	3	1	2	0	0
Surrey	1,445	0	0	0	0	0	1	0	0	1	0
Thompson	1,021	0	0	0	0	0	1	0	1	0	0
Tioga	1,639	3	0	1	1	1	9	1	7	1	0
Valley City	6,351	18	0	3	0	15	138	14	110	14	1
Wahpeton	7,752	15	2	3	0	10	216	29	159	28	0
Watford City	8,488	42	0	7	1	34	128	14	95	19	0
West Fargo	38,171	55	0	9	4	42	584	114	417	53	1
Williston	28,966	133	6	25	5	97	795	82	630	83	7
Wishek	921	2	0	1	0	1	5	1	4	0	0
OHIO											
Ada	5,509	3	0	2	1	0	24	6	17	1	0
Akron	197,882	1,782	27	181	328	1,246	6,568	1,686	4,305	577	65
Alliance	21,536	28	0	4	1	23	558	61	474	23	10
Amberley Village	3,791	2	0	0	0	2	35	3	29	3	0
American Township	12,050	0	0	0	0	0	97	5	88	4	0
Amherst	12,166	4	0	0	3	1	147	20	123	4	1
Arcanum	2,006	0	0	0	0	0	9	0	9	0	0
Archbold	4,320	5	0	1	1	3	80	6	68	6	0
Ashland	20,410	33	1	18	2	12	384	50	331	3	1
Ashville	4,331	4	0	2	0	2	53	1	39	13	0
Athens	24,745	16	0	0	5	11	398	30	349	19	3
Aurora	16,319	1	0	0	0	1	128	5	120	3	1
Bainbridge Township	11,493	4	0	2	1	1	241	34	203	4	0
Barberton	26,015	69	2	15	10	42	689	111	546	32	4
Barnesville	4,020	1	0	1	0	0	12	2	8	2	0
Batavia	1,680	3	0	0	0	3	35	8	25	2	0
Bath Township, Summit County	9,659	5	0	1	1	3	145	13	130	2	0
Bay Village	15,235	4	1	0	0	3	72	11	56	5	0
Bazetta Township	5,530	7	0	1	0	6	210	4	204	2	0
Beachwood	11,612	7	0	2	1	4	438	16	413	9	0
Beavercreek	47,672	33	0	11	10	12	1,193	78	1,088	27	4
Beaver Township	6,415	3	0	2	0	1	74	21	51	2	0
Bedford	12,485	19	0	1	8	10	157	22	103	32	1
Bellaire	4,039	12	0	4	0	8	30	4	25	1	1
Bellbrook	7,326	0	0	0	0	0	36	3	33	0	0
Bellefontaine	13,145	25	0	6	0	19	202	32	167	3	0
Bellville	1,895	1	0	0	1	0	15	0	14	1	0
Belpre	6,386	4	0	0	0	4	105	21	70	14	0
Berea	18,573	9	0	0	3	6	79	16	59	4	1
Bethel	2,809	8	0	1	0	7	77	14	60	3	1
Bexley	13,956	12	0	4	3	5	300	63	229	8	0
Blanchester	4,251	3	0	1	0	2	99	20	78	1	0
Blue Ash	12,307	14	0	3	2	9	204	17	179	8	0
Bowling Green	31,719	37	0	18	4	15	547	42	489	16	1
Brewster	2,158	2	0	1	0	1	23	6	17	0	0
Bridgeport	1,741	1	0	1	0	0	10	1	7	2	0
Brimfield Township	10,388	7	1	1	2	3	204	16	185	3	0
Brunswick	34,977	17	0	2	1	14	189	20	157	12	2

Table 8. Offenses Known to Law Enforcement, by Selected State and City, 2019—Continued

(Number.)

State/city	Population	Violent crime	Murder and nonnegligent manslaughter	Rape[1]	Robbery	Aggravated assault	Property crime	Burglary	Larceny-theft	Motor vehicle theft	Arson[2]
Bucyrus	11,712	25	0	6	3	16	287	49	230	8	1
Burton[7]	1,454		0		0	1	2	0	2	0	0
Butler Township	7,819	23	0	9	5	9	386	30	345	11	2
Cambridge[7]	10,318		0		3	6	349	36	302	11	0
Campbell	7,815	9	0	1	2	6	53	25	21	7	0
Canal Fulton	5,450	7	0	0	2	5	52	10	40	2	0
Canfield	7,199	0	0	0	0	0	47	3	43	1	0
Canton	70,139	981	6	135	188	652	3,712	962	2,429	321	24
Cardington	2,056	2	0	0	0	2	15	5	9	1	0
Carroll Township	2,096	1	0	0	0	1	15	2	11	2	0
Centerville	23,744	15	0	5	1	9	285	37	242	6	0
Chagrin Falls	3,941	1	0	0	1	0	41	16	25	6	0
Chardon	5,183	9	0	0	1	8	94	3	91	0	0
Chester Township	10,322	0	0	0	0	0	15	2	12	1	0
Cheviot	8,269	23	0	5	7	11	221	55	143	23	0
Chillicothe	21,670	103	0	23	17	63	1,575	183	1,337	55	5
Cincinnati[8]	303,335	2,562	64	280	872	1,346	13,051	2,765	8,935	1,351	
Circleville	14,025	47	1	13	13	20	609	81	493	35	3
Clayton	13,221	2	0	0	1	1	83	8	70	5	0
Clearcreek Township	16,070	2	0	1	0	1	37	11	26	0	0
Cleveland	381,829	5,791	92	479	1,895	3,325	17,057	4,311	9,968	2,778	157
Cleveland Heights[5]	44,098	95	1	6	31	57	696	105	526	65	0
Cleves	3,443	2	0	0	0	2	31	3	25	3	0
Clyde	6,147	3	0	0	0	3	66	14	51	1	0
Coitsville Township	1,324	3	0	0	0	2	21	4	14	3	0
Colerain Township	59,479	67	1	4	40	22	1,342	138	1,157	47	5
Columbiana	6,209	2	0	0	0	2	49	8	40	1	1
Columbus[6]	906,120	4,561	81	882	1,810	1,788	29,974	5,809	20,606	3,559	
Copley Township	17,309	14	0	6	0	8	192	20	155	17	0
Cortland	6,769	3	0	0	1	2	46	10	36	0	0
Covington	2,694	0	0	0	0	0	10	1	9	0	0
Cuyahoga Falls	49,236	50	0	14	10	26	980	92	860	28	2
Dayton	140,427	1,351	48	200	347	756	5,673	1,533	3,393	747	8
Deer Park	5,654	2	0	1	0	1	36	1	28	7	1
Defiance	16,601	22	1	11	0	10	225	21	201	3	1
Delaware	40,616	60	0	45	4	11	477	94	371	12	1
Delhi Township	29,811	21	0	6	7	8	303	36	255	12	0
Delphos[7]	6,930		0	0	2	3	106	17	77	12	2
Dennison	2,596	0	0	0	0	0	8	1	7	0	0
Dover	12,741	14	1	7	1	5	77	8	65	4	1
Dublin	49,626	26	0	13	3	10	429	59	345	25	0
East Cleveland	17,001	97	3	1	49	44	369	115	123	131	6
Eastlake	18,074	12	0	0	6	6	327	31	275	21	0
East Liverpool	10,653	13	0	3	5	5	124	31	86	7	1
East Palestine	4,435	8	0	2	0	6	69	18	46	5	0
Eaton	8,136	6	0	2	2	2	213	12	194	7	0
Elyria	53,806	137	4	35	37	61	921	207	665	49	7
Englewood	13,478	16	0	1	8	7	367	16	341	10	3
Euclid	46,659	243	3	28	74	138	1,285	202	895	188	5
Evendale	2,839	5	0	0	0	5	143	5	131	7	0
Fairborn	33,726	88	0	25	8	55	627	132	457	38	9
Fairfax	1,710	5	0	0	4	1	358	2	355	1	0
Fairfield	42,620	84	1	16	17	50	879	93	748	38	0
Fairfield Township	22,956	21	0	3	0	18	507	24	477	6	2
Fairview Park	16,201	7	0	0	2	5	142	5	134	3	0
Fayette	1,242	1	0	0	0	1	13	3	9	1	0
Findlay	41,350	106	0	46	17	43	902	114	760	28	3
Forest Park	18,673	49	1	21	17	10	276	43	208	25	3
Franklin	11,675	34	0	13	6	15	501	57	413	31	2
Frazeysburg	1,309	3	0	0	0	3	9	1	7	1	0
Fredericktown	2,517	5	0	1	0	4	20	4	15	1	0
Fremont[7]	15,958		0		1	31	637	94	519	24	0
Gahanna	35,847	44	1	10	13	20	719	51	640	28	3
Gallipolis	3,553	8	1	3	0	4	243	39	195	9	0
Gates Mills	2,227	0	0	0	0	0	4	0	3	1	0
Georgetown	4,253	6	0	3	0	3	85	16	67	2	0
Germantown	5,500	11	1	0	0	10	71	12	57	2	0
Glouster	1,796	3	0	0	0	3	34	6	28	0	0
Goshen Township, Clermont County	16,300	16	0	6	2	8	140	19	108	13	3
Goshen Township, Mahoning County	3,102	3	0	0	0	3	46	13	30	3	0
Grafton	5,808	2	0	0	1	1	14	1	13	0	0
Grandview Heights	8,581	9	1	4	1	3	179	53	120	6	0
Granville	5,917	5	0	4	0	1	27	3	24	0	0
Greenfield	4,544	14	0	3	1	10	85	12	65	8	0
Greenhills	3,591	1	0	0	0	1	35	4	31	0	0
Green Township	59,273	37	0	15	16	6	808	111	680	17	5
Grove City	42,423	41	1	16	18	6	1,193	84	1,060	49	0
Groveport	5,679	10	0	1	3	6	104	9	67	28	1
Hamilton	62,155	265	4	40	65	156	2,228	417	1,521	290	47
Hamilton Township, Warren County	23,791	13	0	4	0	9	78	7	68	3	1

Table 8. Offenses Known to Law Enforcement, by Selected State and City, 2019—Continued

(Number.)

State/city	Population	Violent crime	Murder and nonnegligent manslaughter	Rape[1]	Robbery	Aggravated assault	Property crime	Burglary	Larceny-theft	Motor vehicle theft	Arson[2]
Harrison	11,837	6	0	2	2	2	108	6	102	0	0
Hartville	3,068	0	0	0	0	0	32	0	32	0	0
Heath	10,933	24	0	7	4	13	461	61	382	18	3
Hilliard	37,578	26	0	6	5	15	242	30	195	17	0
Hillsboro	6,518	11	0	4	0	7	113	12	91	10	1
Hinckley Township[5]	8,076	3	0	1	1	1	10	2	8	0	0
Howland Township	16,420	20	0	1	4	15	281	36	232	13	0
Hubbard Township	5,306	6	0	1	2	3	90	22	65	3	3
Huber Heights	38,183	76	0	20	16	40	890	169	668	53	3
Hudson	22,286	6	0	2	1	3	117	13	101	3	1
Huron	6,863	6	1	3	0	2	98	14	79	5	1
Indian Hill	5,897	0	0	0	0	0	25	5	20	0	0
Ironton	10,576	19	1	2	3	13	191	50	131	10	0
Jackson	6,222	6	0	1	1	4	193	32	152	9	0
Jackson Township, Montgomery County	3,685	8	0	1	0	7	12	3	9	0	0
Jackson Township, Stark County	40,347	52	0	15	12	25	986	170	793	23	1
Jamestown	2,136	5	0	2	0	3	51	13	36	2	0
Johnstown	5,119	0	0	0	0	0	26	2	23	1	0
Kent	29,761	30	0	3	8	19	393	65	315	13	1
Kenton	8,198	22	0	8	4	10	263	37	215	11	1
Kettering	54,974	56	1	27	13	15	794	139	604	51	1
Kirtland	6,823	6	0	0	1	5	21	2	18	1	0
Kirtland Hills[7]	644		0		0		0	0	0	0	2
Lakemore	3,082	8	0	3	0	5	99	12	85	2	0
Lakewood	49,802	61	0	6	28	27	643	77	511	55	15
Lancaster	40,622	110	0	35	22	53	1,540	215	1,244	81	0
Lawrence Township	8,255	6	0	1	0	5	58	17	40	1	0
Lexington	4,666	0	0	0	0	0	5	0	5	0	0
Lima	36,653	259	4	59	64	132	1,493	392	1,037	64	71
Lockland	3,455	24	0	1	12	11	97	22	67	8	3
Logan	7,039	24	0	11	5	8	433	68	350	15	2
London	10,320	26	2	7	3	14	216	19	185	12	2
Lorain	64,022	289	3	29	65	192	1,437	394	967	76	16
Lordstown	3,248	3	0	0	0	3	28	4	23	1	0
Loudonville	2,628	10	0	5	0	5	40	5	34	1	0
Louisville	9,329	6	0	2	1	3	78	8	68	2	0
Loveland	13,245	16	0	9	1	6	73	14	55	4	0
Lyndhurst	13,407	14	0	1	2	11	139	8	131	0	1
Madison Township, Franklin County	19,682	18	0	1	3	14	177	39	114	24	2
Madison Township, Lake County	15,646	9	0	0	0	9	200	28	169	3	0
Mansfield	46,418	187	3	48	38	98	1,996	396	1,523	77	17
Mariemont	3,473	0	0	0	0	0	27	0	27	0	1
Marietta	13,547	17	0	8	0	9	192	22	167	3	0
Martins Ferry	6,558	12	0	1	2	9	351	46	292	13	0
Marysville	24,544	14	0	5	2	7	218	18	193	7	0
Mason	33,939	10	0	2	2	6	743	116	610	17	4
Massillon	32,433	72	1	26	14	31	361	27	323	11	5
Maumee	13,656	14	0	4	2	8	230	8	220	2	0
Mayfield Heights	18,519	12	0	1	3	8	17	1	16	0	0
McConnelsville	1,760	0	0	0	0	0	18	3	12	3	0
Mechanicsburg	1,579	1	0	0	0	1	13	1	12	0	0
Mentor	47,289	63	0	9	13	41	703	60	620	23	0
Mentor-on-the-Lake	7,400	11	0	2	4	5	61	7	52	2	0
Miamisburg	19,913	40	0	13	11	16	264	46	190	28	2
Miami Township, Clermont County	42,764	22	1	10	0	11	472	42	409	21	2
Miami Township, Montgomery County	29,188	63	2	12	16	33	848	41	769	38	2
Middlefield[7]	2,713		0		0		55	3	52	0	0
Middleport	2,434	0	0	0	0	0	13	7	5	1	0
Middletown	48,878	206	1	29	50	126	1,459	285	1,034	140	5
Milford	6,880	12	0	8	1	3	134	13	113	8	2
Milton Township	2,439	1	0	0	0	1	13	6	6	1	0
Mingo Junction	3,202	44	0	0	0	44	43	8	30	5	2
Mogadore[7]	3,832		0		1		34	4	29	1	0
Monroe	16,531	14	0	0	1	13	450	34	407	9	0
Monroeville	1,356	3	0	0	0	3	18	0	17	1	0
Montgomery	10,867	4	0	3	0	1	97	8	89	0	1
Montpelier	3,932	11	0	8	0	3	137	20	113	4	3
Moraine	6,455	41	3	7	12	19	516	45	451	20	3
Mount Healthy	6,052	25	0	7	5	13	304	62	219	23	3
Mount Orab	3,454	6	0	3	1	2	50	3	44	3	1
Mount Vernon	16,663	27	0	11	0	16	315	29	284	2	0
Munroe Falls	5,080	0	0	0	0	0	23	1	22	0	1
Napoleon	8,188	23	0	7	1	15	186	25	160	1	0
Navarre	1,846	7	0	2	0	5	15	4	10	1	0
Nelsonville	5,158	9	0	1	1	7	183	50	117	16	0
New Albany	11,332	4	0	0	0	4	112	23	87	2	0
Newark	50,340	149	1	34	31	83	1,676	330	1,209	137	21

Table 8. Offenses Known to Law Enforcement, by Selected State and City, 2019—Continued

(Number.)

State/city	Population	Violent crime	Murder and nonnegligent manslaughter	Rape[1]	Robbery	Aggravated assault	Property crime	Burglary	Larceny-theft	Motor vehicle theft	Arson[2]
New Boston	2,093	18	0	0	6	12	302	19	277	6	1
New Bremen	2,977	1	0	0	0	1	19	3	16	0	0
Newcomerstown[7]	3,743		0		0		1	63	9	45	9	1
New Franklin	14,162	8	0	2	2	4	84	21	58	5	0
New Lebanon	4,001	3	0	1	0	2	54	11	39	4	1
New Lexington	4,654	16	0	5	2	9	114	15	90	9	0
New Philadelphia	17,434	8	0	0	0	8	242	4	232	6	1
New Richmond	2,700	6	0	2	0	4	26	4	19	3	0
Newton Falls	4,481	11	0	3	1	7	47	8	35	4	0
Newtown	2,666	0	0	0	0	0	20	1	19	0	0
Niles	18,222	70	2	8	16	44	465	46	400	19	0
North Baltimore	3,557	3	0	2	0	1	14	6	7	1	0
North Canton	17,251	15	0	5	1	9	234	26	204	4	1
North College Hill	9,271	31	0	3	13	15	252	38	193	21	0
Northfield	3,670	5	0	1	1	3	29	2	26	1	0
North Olmsted	31,421	8	0	0	0	8	389	22	354	13	1
North Ridgeville	34,469	13	0	3	1	9	112	23	80	9	1
North Royalton	30,177	17	0	6	1	10	119	22	93	4	1
Northwood	5,445	12	0	6	3	3	107	21	79	7	1
Norton	12,007	18	0	3	2	13	190	36	134	20	0
Norwalk	16,903	15	0	8	1	6	262	40	218	4	2
Oak Harbor	2,728	1	1	0	0	0	25	2	22	1	0
Oberlin	8,302	16	0	8	7	1	172	31	140	1	5
Olmsted Falls	8,861	4	1	0	1	2	18	5	12	1	1
Olmsted Township	13,432	1	0	0	0	1	30	2	26	2	0
Ontario	6,067	7	0	2	0	5	246	3	241	2	0
Oregon	19,868	45	0	11	7	27	645	44	581	20	0
Orrville	8,461	21	0	8	2	11	78	13	61	4	1
Ottawa	4,317	1	0	0	0	1	8	1	6	1	0
Ottawa Hills	4,471	0	0	0	0	0	34	3	24	7	0
Oxford Township	2,224	0	0	0	0	0	13	2	9	2	0
Parma	78,322	112	0	28	11	73	759	130	572	57	6
Peninsula	558	0	0	0	0	0	9	0	9	0	0
Pepper Pike	6,371	5	0	0	1	4	28	6	22	0	0
Perrysburg	21,672	3	0	3	0	0	123	9	112	2	0
Perrysburg Township	13,013	3	0	0	0	3	127	13	109	5	0
Perry Township, Franklin County	3,788	2	0	0	0	2	32	4	27	1	0
Perry Township, Stark County	28,121	42	0	12	7	23	411	101	283	27	2
Pickerington	21,590	29	0	9	7	13	222	23	187	12	1
Pierce Township	11,742	11	0	7	1	3	228	14	209	5	1
Pioneer	1,395	1	0	0	0	1	40	13	26	1	0
Poland Township	11,859	6	0	0	0	6	35	11	24	0	1
Poland Village	2,420	0	0	0	0	0	6	0	6	0	0
Port Clinton	5,914	15	0	7	1	7	109	13	91	5	1
Powell	13,545	2	0	2	0	0	84	7	75	2	0
Reading	10,995	20	0	2	8	10	261	36	217	8	0
Reminderville	4,528	0	0	0	0	0	10	3	7	0	0
Reynoldsburg	38,578	73	2	21	26	24	988	91	833	64	1
Richmond Heights	10,346	32	1	1	10	20	168	36	109	23	3
Rio Grande	766	2	0	1	0	1	10	3	6	1	0
Ripley	1,695	4	0	1	0	3	13	2	10	1	0
Riverside	25,148	35	0	9	12	14	343	69	231	43	1
Ross Township	8,944	7	0	3	0	4	69	16	45	8	0
Russells Point	1,377	2	0	0	0	2	22	4	18	0	0
Russell Township	5,219	1	0	0	0	1	13	0	13	0	0
Sabina	2,544	5	0	1	1	3	86	15	71	0	0
Sagamore Hills	10,934	0	0	0	0	0	30	5	24	1	0
Salem	11,644	22	0	3	2	17	341	35	299	7	0
Salineville	1,219	2	0	0	0	2	44	8	29	7	1
Sandusky	24,572	74	0	31	22	21	925	175	710	40	4
Sebring	4,200	5	0	0	0	5	94	10	80	4	2
Seven Hills	11,621	7	0	1	4	2	37	6	30	1	0
Shawnee Township	12,056	10	0	3	1	6	98	12	84	2	0
Sheffield Lake	8,939	6	1	5	0	0	70	17	53	0	1
Shelby	8,997	16	0	6	1	9	231	53	169	9	0
Sidney	20,437	39	0	20	8	11	631	85	514	32	6
Solon	22,830	11	0	3	1	7	217	19	190	8	0
Somerset	1,456	0	0	0	0	0	15	3	10	2	0
South Bloomfield	1,997	5	0	0	2	3	29	3	24	2	0
South Euclid	21,351	27	0	9	6	12	583	42	496	45	0
South Russell	3,767	0	0	0	0	0	4	0	4	0	0
Springboro	18,975	1	0	0	0	1	66	15	50	1	0
Springfield	59,128	292	3	14	124	151	2,992	763	1,978	251	49
Springfield Township, Hamilton County	36,696	50	2	4	18	26	485	85	368	32	5
Springfield Township, Mahoning County	6,415	10	0	2	1	7	47	13	31	3	0
Springfield Township, Summit County	14,555	36	1	10	9	16	631	88	528	15	2
St. Clair Township	7,482	5	0	1	1	3	51	5	46	0	0
Steubenville	17,768	33	3	6	9	15	803	55	735	13	5
St. Marys	8,212	1	0	0	0	1	82	17	64	1	0

Table 8. Offenses Known to Law Enforcement, by Selected State and City, 2019—Continued

(Number.)

State/city	Population	Violent crime	Murder and nonnegligent manslaughter	Rape[1]	Robbery	Aggravated assault	Property crime	Burglary	Larceny-theft	Motor vehicle theft	Arson[2]
Stow	34,862	15	0	8	1	6	537	56	475	6	1
Strasburg	2,691	1	0	0	0	1	11	1	9	1	0
Streetsboro	16,561	20	0	2	8	10	227	16	193	18	3
Strongsville	44,814	18	0	1	6	11	585	36	541	8	0
Struthers	10,148	18	0	5	7	6	152	31	119	2	2
Sugarcreek Township	8,494	5	0	3	1	1	166	10	154	2	0
Swanton	3,857	2	0	0	0	2	36	1	34	1	1
Sylvania	19,046	13	0	4	0	9	166	17	142	7	0
Sylvania Township	29,754	34	0	2	10	22	678	61	596	21	0
Tallmadge	17,583	12	0	5	2	5	239	37	192	10	0
Tiffin	17,498	9	0	3	3	3	354	37	312	5	2
Toledo[8]	273,505	2,604	34	205	655	1,710	9,470	2,362	6,314	794	
Toronto	4,919	9	0	2	0	7	13	5	8	0	0
Trotwood	24,435	133	2	18	40	73	659	169	392	98	7
Troy	26,250	23	0	6	4	13	433	56	369	8	1
Twinsburg	19,103	17	1	1	4	11	92	9	80	3	0
Uhrichsville	5,317	9	0	3	1	5	53	12	38	3	1
Uniontown	3,353	1	0	0	0	1	67	10	52	5	0
Union Township, Clermont County	48,486	48	0	17	11	20	1,040	61	949	30	1
University Heights	12,852	19	0	2	9	8	237	20	203	14	2
Upper Arlington	35,754	12	5	1	5	1	366	52	299	15	1
Upper Sandusky	6,467	15	0	8	0	7	123	11	110	2	0
Urbana	11,309	15	0	8	2	5	275	28	237	10	7
Utica	2,253	2	0	0	1	1	18	3	13	2	0
Van Wert	10,662	23	0	10	0	13	336	63	267	6	3
Vermilion	10,420	2	0	1	0	1	91	15	75	1	0
Vienna Township	3,784	3	0	0	0	3	48	13	28	7	0
Village of Leesburg	1,308	0	0	0	0	0	39	12	25	2	0
Wadsworth	24,058	15	1	9	0	5	413	69	338	6	1
Waite Hill	454	0	0	0	0	0	0	0	0	0	0
Wapakoneta	9,717	2	0	2	0	0	137	9	124	4	0
Warren	38,012	212	5	35	68	104	1,478	431	941	106	7
Warren Township	5,169	24	0	0	0	24	83	27	51	5	2
Washington Court House	14,150	39	0	21	3	15	504	55	430	19	1
Waterville	5,518	3	0	0	1	2	28	5	21	2	0
Waterville Township	1,705	0	0	0	0	0	3	1	2	0	0
Wauseon	7,428	14	0	4	1	9	142	9	127	6	0
Waverly	4,253	6	0	0	4	2	90	6	78	6	0
Weathersfield	8,017	9	0	3	1	5	86	23	61	2	1
Wellston	5,488	13	0	0	1	12	194	54	128	12	1
West Carrollton[5]	12,886	45	0	9	17	19	233	47	163	23	2
West Chester Township	62,517	67	4	22	22	19	1,220	124	1,048	48	5
Westerville	40,903	74	3	18	16	37	767	53	692	22	3
West Union	3,153	3	0	0	0	3	21	7	11	3	0
Whitehall	19,121	114	6	23	45	40	1,102	139	884	79	6
Whitehouse	4,887	2	0	0	0	2	9	2	6	1	0
Wickliffe	12,758	16	0	6	2	8	174	13	149	12	1
Willard	6,021	3	0	0	0	3	144	16	123	5	0
Williamsburg	2,569	5	0	0	1	4	44	7	35	2	1
Willoughby	23,081	19	0	5	5	9	321	30	276	15	2
Wilmington	12,391	26	0	9	6	11	651	90	537	24	1
Windham	2,210	4	0	1	0	3	16	5	11	0	0
Wintersville	3,665	6	0	0	1	5	46	4	41	1	0
Woodlawn	3,346	6	0	2	0	4	81	7	72	2	0
Wooster	26,615	110	0	29	15	66	738	97	614	27	7
Worthington	14,875	10	0	5	0	5	236	31	200	5	1
Wyoming	8,596	2	0	0	0	2	121	7	109	5	0
Xenia	26,926	74	0	23	10	41	676	79	556	41	2
Yellow Springs	3,727	7	0	0	2	5	94	20	72	2	1
Zanesville	25,346	89	1	23	16	49	1,071	126	912	33	3
OKLAHOMA											
Achille	541	0	0	0	0	0	12	4	5	3	0
Ada	17,321	71	1	20	6	44	673	159	442	72	3
Adair	817	1	0	0	0	1	7	3	4	0	0
Allen	930	2	0	0	1	1	9	6	3	0	3
Altus	18,572	42	1	9	4	28	398	90	277	31	0
Alva	5,022	6	0	1	0	5	36	11	24	1	0
Amber	467	0	0	0	0	0	2	1	1	0	8
Anadarko	6,540	48	0	6	2	40	223	64	146	13	0
Antlers	2,296	0	0	0	0	0	26	8	13	5	0
Apache	1,399	7	0	1	0	6	38	15	20	3	6
Ardmore	24,830	205	1	20	25	159	1,046	195	773	78	0
Atoka	3,131	8	0	0	1	7	122	36	78	8	0
Avant	304	0	0	0	0	0	1	1	0	0	0
Barnsdall	1,143	3	0	0	0	3	18	4	14	0	1
Bartlesville	36,502	111	2	16	10	83	1,145	234	811	100	0
Beaver	1,390	1	0	0	0	1	4	1	3	0	0
Beggs	1,227	1	0	0	0	1	26	6	16	4	0
Bernice	579	0	0	0	0	0	7	2	5	0	0
Bethany	19,346	73	2	7	17	47	688	177	445	66	9
Big Cabin	252	3	0	0	0	3	7	2	5	0	0

Table 8. Offenses Known to Law Enforcement, by Selected State and City, 2019—Continued

(Number.)

State/city	Population	Violent crime	Murder and nonnegligent manslaughter	Rape[1]	Robbery	Aggravated assault	Property crime	Burglary	Larceny-theft	Motor vehicle theft	Arson[2]
Bixby	28,383	30	1	9	2	18	401	72	297	32	0
Blackwell	6,610	13	1	2	0	10	71	28	38	5	3
Blanchard	9,028	1	1	0	0	0	80	16	52	12	0
Boise City	1,077	3	0	0	0	3	13	7	6	0	0
Bokchito	688	4	0	1	0	3	13	2	9	2	0
Boley	1,175	3	0	0	0	3	1	0	1	0	0
Bristow	4,195	10	0	2	2	6	120	32	76	12	1
Broken Arrow	110,480	138	0	44	20	74	1,977	293	1,507	177	7
Broken Bow	4,053	37	1	6	3	27	223	61	140	22	5
Butler	299	0	0	0	0	0	1	1	0	0	0
Cache	2,814	18	1	2	2	13	36	7	25	4	0
Caddo	1,091	0	0	0	0	0	5	1	2	2	0
Calera	2,375	4	0	2	0	2	24	4	16	4	0
Caney	196	0	0	0	0	0	6	0	5	1	0
Canton	592	3	0	0	0	3	18	6	8	4	0
Carnegie	1,651	3	0	0	0	3	33	9	17	7	1
Carney	656	0	0	0	0	0	3	0	3	0	0
Cashion	883	0	0	0	0	0	0	0	0	0	0
Catoosa	6,975	38	0	6	7	25	418	67	272	79	0
Cement	481	0	0	0	0	0	5	4	0	1	0
Chandler	3,094	15	0	1	1	13	52	9	37	6	0
Chattanooga	441	0	0	0	0	0	1	0	0	1	0
Checotah	3,143	15	0	1	1	13	120	23	85	12	0
Chelsea	1,902	3	0	2	0	1	33	2	25	6	0
Cherokee	1,509	2	0	0	0	2	20	8	10	2	0
Chickasha	16,395	71	3	10	5	53	451	122	274	55	3
Choctaw	12,812	14	0	4	0	10	179	56	98	25	1
Chouteau	2,086	2	0	1	0	1	46	4	35	7	0
Claremore	18,786	23	1	7	1	14	495	73	395	27	0
Clayton	794	0	0	0	0	0	7	2	3	2	0
Cleveland	3,136	7	0	3	0	4	17	2	10	5	0
Clinton	9,179	46	2	4	9	31	191	52	112	27	1
Coalgate	1,779	4	0	0	0	4	12	2	9	1	0
Colbert	1,250	8	0	0	0	8	6	3	2	1	0
Colcord	838	1	0	0	0	1	29	9	17	3	1
Collinsville	7,271	11	0	2	2	7	72	13	52	7	1
Comanche	1,555	5	0	1	0	4	27	10	13	4	1
Commerce	2,392	9	1	0	0	8	20	9	8	3	0
Cordell	2,753	1	0	0	0	1	35	7	21	7	0
Covington	533	1	0	0	0	1	2	0	2	0	0
Coweta	10,016	23	0	6	2	15	135	18	98	19	0
Crescent	1,547	2	0	0	0	2	15	5	10	0	0
Cushing	7,639	10	0	3	1	6	309	60	230	19	3
Cyril	1,022	1	0	0	1	0	9	1	6	2	0
Davenport	816	0	0	0	0	0	15	2	12	1	0
Davis	2,911	6	0	2	1	3	78	18	53	7	0
Del City	21,794	188	3	20	42	123	942	184	667	91	4
Depew	479	0	0	0	0	0	4	2	1	1	0
Dewar	847	2	0	0	0	2	7	1	3	3	0
Dewey	3,405	5	0	2	0	3	57	21	29	7	0
Dibble	871	2	0	0	0	2	11	3	8	0	0
Dickson	1,251	1	0	0	0	1	8	1	5	2	0
Drumright	2,816	2	0	0	1	1	74	32	39	3	0
Duncan	22,296	37	2	8	8	19	733	214	475	44	4
Durant	18,478	67	1	8	5	53	781	190	534	57	2
Edmond	94,699	138	5	41	15	77	1,599	235	1,245	119	1
Eldorado	410	0	0	0	0	0	0	0	0	0	0
Elgin	3,294	0	0	0	0	0	7	0	6	1	0
Elk City	11,509	13	0	2	1	10	251	40	190	21	3
Elmore City	706	10	0	1	0	9	24	3	21	0	0
El Reno	19,830	42	0	16	8	18	374	84	226	64	8
Enid	49,598	204	1	44	9	150	1,625	364	1,148	113	3
Erick	988	0	0	0	0	0	5	1	1	3	0
Eufaula	2,907	10	0	3	0	7	87	29	48	10	0
Fairfax	1,268	5	0	0	0	5	24	12	12	0	1
Fairview	2,601	8	0	5	0	3	25	7	15	3	0
Forest Park	1,075	0	0	0	0	0	7	3	3	1	0
Fort Cobb	613	0	0	0	0	0	8	4	2	2	0
Fort Gibson	3,972	12	0	2	1	9	28	7	18	3	0
Fort Towson	486	4	1	0	0	3	13	7	6	0	3
Frederick	3,558	22	0	3	1	18	101	43	51	7	0
Gans	298	1	0	1	0	0	0	0	0	0	0
Geary	1,276	6	0	0	0	6	86	30	55	1	1
Glenpool	14,356	78	0	11	5	62	299	85	186	28	0
Goodwell	1,289	0	0	0	0	0	17	5	12	0	0
Gore	939	2	0	1	0	1	7	3	3	1	0
Grandfield	938	1	0	0	0	1	9	2	6	1	0
Granite	1,968	4	0	0	0	4	10	5	4	1	0
Grove	7,129	17	0	3	0	14	267	48	199	20	0
Guthrie	11,597	22	1	3	4	14	254	61	170	23	2
Guymon	11,247	36	0	2	3	31	145	51	84	10	0
Haileyville	753	2	0	0	0	2	5	1	2	2	0
Harrah	6,602	5	0	2	0	3	136	32	93	11	1

Table 8. Offenses Known to Law Enforcement, by Selected State and City, 2019—Continued

(Number.)

State/city	Population	Violent crime	Murder and nonnegligent manslaughter	Rape[1]	Robbery	Aggravated assault	Property crime	Burglary	Larceny-theft	Motor vehicle theft	Arson[2]
Hartshorne	1,930	3	0	0	0	3	71	34	30	7	1
Haskell	1,913	3	0	0	1	2	9	2	5	2	1
Healdton	2,688	7	0	2	0	5	36	17	12	7	0
Heavener	3,285	9	0	0	0	9	43	11	27	5	1
Hennessey	2,241	5	0	2	1	2	27	5	16	6	0
Henryetta	5,517	11	0	7	0	4	165	57	90	18	1
Hinton	3,228	2	0	0	0	2	28	6	17	5	1
Hobart	3,403	8	0	1	1	6	56	22	25	9	2
Holdenville	5,518	20	0	0	1	19	150	42	97	11	5
Hollis	1,856	6	0	0	1	5	42	20	17	5	0
Hominy	3,381	14	0	4	0	10	51	15	32	4	2
Hooker	1,882	1	0	0	0	1	22	3	18	1	0
Howe	786	4	0	0	0	4	11	1	10	0	0
Hugo	5,081	24	0	2	3	19	232	55	158	19	6
Hulbert	584	1	0	0	0	0	1	0	1	0	0
Hydro	937	0	0	0	0	0	5	3	2	0	1
Idabel	6,816	43	3	10	0	30	431	78	334	19	2
Jay	2,532	11	0	1	0	10	65	16	41	8	0
Jenks	24,264	27	2	3	2	20	298	49	223	26	0
Jennings	357	0	0	0	0	0	2	1	0	1	0
Jones	3,196	5	0	2	0	3	77	24	44	9	1
Kiefer	2,039	2	0	2	0	0	25	7	13	5	0
Kingfisher	4,962	17	0	7	0	10	106	22	69	15	1
Kingston	1,676	0	0	0	0	0	4	1	0	3	0
Kiowa	668	5	0	0	1	4	31	5	24	2	0
Konawa	1,211	6	0	0	1	5	64	22	41	1	2
Krebs	1,922	2	0	0	0	2	49	16	31	2	2
Lahoma	621	6	0	0	0	6	3	3	0	0	0
Lamont	390	1	0	0	0	1	0	0	0	0	0
Langley	823	2	0	0	0	2	24	4	12	8	0
Langston	1,842	1	0	1	0	0	10	3	7	0	0
Lawton	92,256	854	15	97	91	651	2,972	877	1,836	259	12
Lexington	2,152	5	0	0	0	5	42	7	33	2	0
Lindsay	2,798	8	0	3	0	5	86	23	55	8	0
Locust Grove	1,401	1	0	0	0	1	41	5	31	5	0
Lone Grove	5,111	0	0	0	0	0	13	5	5	3	2
Luther	1,834	4	0	0	0	4	10	2	6	2	2
Madill	4,056	10	1	3	1	5	127	5	116	6	0
Mangum	2,735	9	0	1	0	8	50	22	24	4	0
Mannford	3,210	5	0	0	0	5	26	7	10	9	1
Marietta	2,771	5	0	1	1	3	82	16	57	9	0
Marlow	4,398	10	0	1	4	5	99	32	60	7	0
Maysville	1,208	5	0	0	0	5	34	18	14	2	0
McAlester[5]	17,840	99	1	19	14	65	1,039	199	780	60	3
McCurtain	503	1	0	0	0	1	1	0	1	0	0
McLoud	4,746	8	0	2	1	5	49	5	33	11	0
Meeker	1,149	5	0	0	0	5	8	4	1	3	0
Miami	13,078	70	1	8	8	53	377	111	242	24	3
Midwest City	57,678	156	4	31	42	79	1,905	302	1,408	195	9
Minco	1,641	1	0	0	0	1	12	2	9	1	0
Moore	62,998	110	1	22	23	64	1,423	252	1,026	145	1
Mooreland	1,176	5	0	0	1	4	4	0	3	1	0
Morris	1,416	2	0	2	0	0	27	7	17	3	0
Mounds	1,253	6	0	0	0	6	8	3	4	1	0
Mountain View	726	0	0	0	0	0	8	3	4	1	0
Muldrow	3,226	20	0	0	0	20	83	21	56	6	0
Muskogee	37,174	389	2	35	43	309	1,333	359	861	113	12
Mustang	22,630	47	0	8	2	37	223	35	168	20	0
Nash	194	0	0	0	0	0	2	1	1	0	0
Newcastle	10,649	8	0	3	0	5	232	52	136	44	1
Newkirk	2,181	6	1	0	0	5	30	7	20	3	1
Nichols Hills	3,945	3	0	0	2	1	81	18	52	11	0
Nicoma Park	2,481	4	0	1	0	3	81	18	51	12	1
Ninnekah	1,041	0	0	0	0	0	12	4	3	5	0
Noble	6,922	17	0	2	2	13	139	55	63	21	1
Norman	125,076	335	4	80	42	209	3,267	498	2,424	345	10
North Enid	932	1	0	0	0	1	10	1	9	0	0
Nowata	3,598	13	0	2	1	10	81	31	47	3	1
Oilton	1,012	0	0	0	0	0	5	3	0	2	0
Okarche	1,351	0	0	0	0	0	14	1	12	1	0
Okemah	3,168	13	0	0	2	11	180	72	91	17	2
Oklahoma City[5]	657,890	4,751	75	539	888	3,249	26,918	6,206	16,922	3,790	96
Okmulgee	11,702	72	2	9	5	56	563	139	377	47	3
Olustee	563	0	0	0	0	0	0	0	0	0	0
Oologah	1,176	0	0	0	0	0	2	0	1	1	0
Owasso	37,654	80	2	13	10	55	782	77	647	58	2
Paoli	613	1	0	0	0	1	2	0	1	1	0
Pauls Valley	6,157	30	0	3	2	25	356	132	206	18	0
Pawhuska	3,410	19	0	3	0	16	118	34	77	7	2
Pawnee	2,107	6	0	0	0	6	38	16	21	1	0
Perkins	2,833	1	0	0	0	1	72	20	47	5	1
Perry	4,905	12	1	0	2	9	104	39	60	5	0
Piedmont	8,553	8	0	0	0	8	41	10	27	4	0

Table 8. Offenses Known to Law Enforcement, by Selected State and City, 2019—Continued

(Number.)

State/city	Population	Violent crime	Murder and nonnegligent manslaughter	Rape[1]	Robbery	Aggravated assault	Property crime	Burglary	Larceny-theft	Motor vehicle theft	Arson[2]
Pocola	4,124	4	0	1	0	3	28	9	12	7	1
Ponca City	23,876	152	0	33	25	94	933	217	665	51	8
Pond Creek	822	1	0	0	0	1	2	1	1	0	0
Porum	702	0	0	0	0	0	1	0	1	0	0
Poteau	8,961	37	0	5	1	31	337	79	237	21	1
Prague	2,385	6	1	0	1	4	52	14	30	8	0
Pryor Creek	9,395	56	1	3	1	51	207	42	130	35	2
Purcell	6,481	20	0	3	1	16	222	52	155	15	1
Ramona	543	0	0	0	0	0	5	3	2	0	1
Rattan	297	0	0	0	0	0	2	1	0	1	0
Ringling	966	2	0	1	0	1	15	1	13	1	0
Roland	3,894	7	0	0	2	5	85	13	63	9	0
Rush Springs	1,262	8	0	8	0	0	29	6	19	4	0
Salina	1,396	5	0	1	1	3	23	4	14	5	1
Sallisaw	8,391	27	0	6	1	20	250	50	179	21	1
Sand Springs	20,024	22	0	5	8	9	878	88	710	80	1
Sapulpa	20,888	58	0	8	9	41	545	153	282	110	3
Savanna	649	2	0	0	0	2	23	5	13	5	0
Sawyer	311	0	0	0	0	0	2	2	0	0	0
Sayre	4,476	8	0	0	0	8	39	14	18	7	1
Seiling	861	0	0	0	0	0	6	1	4	1	0
Seminole	7,134	22	1	1	2	18	207	34	152	21	1
Shady Point	998	1	0	0	1	0	2	0	0	2	0
Shattuck	1,280	4	0	4	0	0	14	8	6	0	0
Shawnee	31,627	156	1	25	13	117	1,517	345	1,018	154	4
Skiatook	8,041	12	0	5	1	6	196	54	123	19	1
Snyder	1,271	3	0	0	0	3	23	10	12	1	0
South Coffeyville	740	2	0	1	0	1	11	0	10	1	0
Sparks	170	0	0	0	0	0	2	2	0	0	0
Spencer	3,989	12	0	2	1	9	84	31	38	15	0
Sperry	1,329	10	0	0	0	10	48	15	22	11	0
Spiro	2,171	6	0	0	1	5	17	5	10	2	1
Sportsmen Acres	307	0	0	0	0	0	0	0	0	0	0
Stigler	2,719	5	0	0	1	4	51	13	35	3	0
Stillwater	51,008	160	5	37	10	108	1,086	189	838	59	12
Stilwell	4,054	21	0	2	2	17	146	28	102	16	2
Stratford	1,535	2	0	0	0	2	14	8	4	2	1
Stringtown	397	0	0	0	0	0	2	1	1	0	0
Stroud	2,713	8	2	0	0	6	51	19	27	5	0
Sulphur	5,028	10	1	3	0	6	127	27	96	4	0
Tahlequah	16,861	11	0	1	1	9	749	104	607	38	0
Talala	278	0	0	0	0	0	0	0	0	0	0
Talihina	1,086	4	0	0	1	3	40	11	24	5	1
Tecumseh	6,667	27	0	6	1	20	194	52	101	41	1
Texhoma	917	2	0	0	0	2	0	0	0	0	0
Thackerville	488	0	0	0	0	0	9	0	7	2	0
The Village	9,535	21	0	1	6	14	228	54	166	8	1
Thomas	1,205	0	0	0	0	0	9	3	5	1	0
Tipton	762	2	0	2	0	0	7	3	4	0	0
Tishomingo	3,040	6	0	2	1	3	37	18	17	2	2
Tonkawa	3,006	7	0	0	0	7	56	18	34	4	0
Tryon	499	0	0	0	0	0	0	0	0	0	0
Tulsa	401,700	3,964	55	341	718	2,850	21,336	4,846	13,457	3,033	209
Tupelo	303	1	0	0	0	1	0	0	0	0	0
Tushka	303	0	0	0	0	0	8	3	5	0	0
Tuttle[5]	7,553	13	0	1	2	10	99	21	68	10	1
Tyrone	760	0	0	0	0	0	11	3	8	0	0
Union City	2,193	3	0	0	0	3	12	2	7	3	2
Valley Brook	776	3	0	0	0	3	24	7	14	3	0
Valliant	731	0	0	0	0	0	12	3	6	3	0
Velma	595	0	0	0	0	0	0	0	0	0	0
Verden	535	0	0	0	0	0	10	3	5	2	0
Verdigris	4,603	4	0	0	0	4	31	3	22	6	0
Vian	1,351	12	0	2	0	10	27	3	21	3	0
Vici	708	1	0	1	0	0	7	1	6	0	0
Vinita	5,343	11	0	3	1	7	95	28	60	7	1
Wagoner	9,154	14	0	4	1	9	223	40	169	14	2
Wakita	324	0	0	0	0	0	1	0	1	0	0
Walters	2,379	1	0	0	1	0	38	16	17	5	0
Warner	1,588	1	0	0	0	1	5	2	2	1	0
Warr Acres	10,331	71	1	5	10	55	344	139	164	41	0
Washington	664	0	0	0	0	0	3	3	0	0	0
Watonga	2,837	3	0	0	0	3	32	7	20	5	0
Watts	310	1	0	0	0	1	2	2	0	0	0
Waukomis	1,290	1	0	0	0	1	15	5	9	1	1
Waurika	1,919	2	0	1	0	1	21	7	12	2	0
Waynoka	913	1	0	0	0	1	11	0	9	2	1
Weatherford	12,186	25	0	5	3	17	270	51	202	17	0
Weleetka	964	7	0	0	0	7	16	4	11	1	0
Wellston	783	0	0	0	0	0	8	3	3	2	0
West Siloam Springs	870	3	0	0	0	3	69	7	49	13	1
Westville	1,543	8	0	1	0	7	64	17	45	2	0
Wetumka	1,198	5	0	3	0	2	32	13	16	3	0

Table 8. Offenses Known to Law Enforcement, by Selected State and City, 2019—Continued

(Number.)

State/city	Population	Violent crime	Murder and nonnegligent manslaughter	Rape[1]	Robbery	Aggravated assault	Property crime	Burglary	Larceny-theft	Motor vehicle theft	Arson[2]
Wewoka	3,252	19	0	2	0	17	103	45	50	8	1
Wilburton	2,560	14	0	1	0	13	51	19	25	7	0
Wilson	1,697	2	0	1	0	1	24	7	13	4	0
Woodward	12,195	31	0	9	1	21	253	85	155	13	0
Wyandotte	330	1	0	0	0	1	1	0	8	0	0
Wynnewood	2,207	13	0	1	0	12	12	4	8	0	0
Wynona	434	0	0	0	0	0	1	0	1	0	0
Yale	1,192	0	0	0	0	0	15	5	9	1	2
Yukon	28,184	45	0	5	3	37	438	56	355	27	5
OREGON											
Albany	54,993	70	1	10	16	43	1,467	128	1,242	97	17
Ashland[4]	21,415	29	0	4	5	20			460	23	4
Astoria	10,040	75	0	9	11	55	336	66	255	15	3
Baker City	9,750	22	0	2	8	12	324	28	283	13	3
Banks	2,055	1	0	1	0	0	21	4	17	0	0
Beaverton	100,130	217	1	53	49	114	1,988	185	1,601	202	14
Bend	100,588	154	0	30	21	103	1,919	135	1,678	106	14
Boardman	3,425	13	0	3	0	10	43	9	31	3	1
Burns	2,781	13	0	2	6	5	45	5	39	1	0
Canby	17,962	32	0	8	0	24	187	17	156	14	3
Cannon Beach	1,756	0	0	0	0	0	23	1	21	1	0
Carlton	2,206	2	0	2	0	0	41	6	35	0	1
Central Point	18,753	31	1	9	2	19	362	48	297	17	4
Coburg	1,156	4	0	1	1	2	21	11	8	2	0
Columbia City	2,048	1	0	0	0	1	11	0	10	1	0
Coos Bay	16,471	76	0	20	14	42	795	172	587	36	10
Coquille	3,933	19	0	2	2	15	87	19	66	2	0
Cornelius	12,827	35	0	5	7	23	271	35	218	18	3
Dallas	16,983	48	0	7	1	40	326	35	273	18	2
Eagle Point	9,530	16	0	1	1	14	224	22	197	5	1
Eugene	173,183	675	2	123	180	370	6,184	964	4,614	606	42
Florence	9,183	17	1	4	1	11	227	20	202	5	5
Forest Grove	25,063	52	0	10	3	39	466	57	366	43	2
Gearhart	1,612	0	0	0	0	0	20	1	19	0	0
Gervais	2,783	2	0	1	1	0	13	0	11	2	0
Gladstone	12,340	24	0	7	3	14	245	38	177	30	6
Grants Pass	38,475	121	0	24	21	76	1,235	151	958	126	7
Gresham	110,692	490	3	77	113	297	3,442	407	1,992	1,043	29
Hermiston	17,780	47	0	3	8	36	541	67	443	31	1
Hillsboro	110,549	274	0	77	56	141	2,164	175	1,779	210	19
Hines	1,549	1	0	0	0	1	17	0	15	2	0
Hood River	7,876	13	0	2	3	8	229	9	201	19	1
Hubbard	3,598	7	0	0	1	6	42	5	31	6	3
Independence	10,367	19	0	2	1	16	145	14	123	8	2
Jacksonville	2,919	3	0	0	0	3	67	2	62	3	2
Keizer	40,109	61	0	9	9	43	648	78	508	62	2
King City	4,072	1	0	0	0	1	64	21	40	3	0
Klamath Falls	22,447	105	4	18	15	68	741	117	543	81	11
La Grande	13,294	14	1	4	2	7	321	68	233	20	4
Lake Oswego	39,888	24	1	7	6	10	481	55	380	46	2
Lebanon	17,304	29	0	11	0	18	372	22	323	27	4
Madras	7,028	21	1	2	4	14	250	33	192	25	1
McMinnville	34,935	69	1	22	7	39	758	88	632	38	6
Milton-Freewater	7,051	14	1	2	3	8	163	25	113	25	1
Molalla	9,328	9	0	4	1	4	67	10	55	2	2
Monmouth	10,630	15	0	4	2	9	128	13	106	9	2
Mount Angel	3,621	4	0	0	0	4	42	5	33	4	1
Myrtle Creek	3,508	4	0	2	0	2	125	23	94	8	0
Newberg-Dundee	27,378	33	0	14	1	18	381	29	331	21	4
Newport	10,772	37	1	8	1	27	279	16	239	24	3
North Bend	9,775	16	1	2	3	10	444	43	380	21	2
North Plains	2,226	3	0	0	0	3	31	1	29	1	0
Ontario	11,044	82	2	10	11	59	673	75	541	57	5
Oregon City	37,723	107	0	13	10	84	644	54	516	74	9
Pendleton	16,796	54	0	9	7	38	483	33	405	45	5
Phoenix	4,627	15	2	1	3	9	248	14	226	8	1
Pilot Rock	1,510	5	0	1	0	4	12	4	8	0	0
Portland	662,114	3,606	29	368	979	2,230	34,452	4,200	23,820	6,432	252
Prineville	10,479	38	0	5	3	30	223	26	187	10	0
Rainier	2,017	2	0	1	0	1	48	7	40	1	0
Redmond	31,558	71	0	7	7	57	1,113	86	954	73	10
Reedsport	4,123	16	0	3	1	12	145	17	116	12	1
Rockaway Beach	1,415	6	0	0	0	6	24	11	12	1	0
Rogue River	2,365	7	1	3	0	3	103	6	87	10	2
Roseburg	23,447	78	0	18	20	40	1,345	151	1,084	110	9
Salem	175,867	670	0	35	152	483	6,488	680	4,966	842	43
Scappoose	7,592	11	0	3	0	8	65	3	57	5	1
Sherwood	19,865	12	0	0	0	12	217	19	188	10	0
Silverton	10,831	16	0	5	3	8	229	30	183	16	2
Springfield	63,438	190	1	34	32	123	1,978	169	1,640	169	16
Stanfield	2,094	6	0	0	1	5	42	12	26	4	1
Stayton	8,318	16	0	0	1	15	236	26	186	24	1

Table 8. Offenses Known to Law Enforcement, by Selected State and City, 2019—Continued

(Number.)

State/city	Population	Violent crime	Murder and nonnegligent manslaughter	Rape[1]	Robbery	Aggravated assault	Property crime	Burglary	Larceny-theft	Motor vehicle theft	Arson[2]
St. Helens	13,900	41	0	9	4	28	139	14	111	14	4
Sunriver		1	0	0	0	1	54	9	43	2	0
Sutherlin	8,136	24	0	4	1	19	223	30	173	20	1
Talent	6,604	9	0	1	0	8	160	7	142	11	1
The Dalles	15,752	28	0	9	0	19	491	81	358	52	5
Tigard	55,621	119	0	13	29	77	1,410	137	1,158	115	9
Toledo	3,648	1	0	0	0	1	41	3	37	1	1
Tualatin	27,788	63	0	8	17	38	765	62	641	62	2
Umatilla	7,202	8	0	2	0	6	88	14	62	12	0
Vernonia	2,288	2	0	0	0	2	7	2	5	0	0
Warrenton	5,772	21	0	3	8	10	407	23	374	10	4
West Linn	26,962	19	0	9	2	8	231	21	196	14	2
Winston	5,515	10	0	1	0	9	145	19	89	37	0
Woodburn	26,338	90	0	19	20	51	918	137	640	141	3
PENNSYLVANIA											
Abington Township, Montgomery County	55,476	53	0	6	15	32	934	32	883	19	2
Adamstown	1,855	5	0	1	2	2	4	1	2	1	0
Adams Township, Butler County	14,330	13	0	0	1	12	20	4	16	0	0
Akron	4,033	2	0	0	0	2	16	0	15	1	0
Aleppo Township	1,867	0	0	0	0	0	13	1	11	1	0
Allegheny Township, Blair County	6,512	22	0	2	1	19	114	12	102	0	0
Allentown	121,855	471	7	64	170	230	2,782	521	2,018	243	5
Altoona	43,429	264	0	83	22	159	675	142	481	52	9
Armagh Township	3,794	2	0	0	0	2	8	2	6	0	0
Ashland	2,670	4	0	0	0	4	5	0	5	0	0
Athens	3,191	5	0	0	0	5	24	3	21	0	0
Athens Township	5,077	12	0	2	1	9	168	6	159	3	0
Avalon	4,539	18	0	2	1	15	51	8	41	2	0
Baldwin Borough	19,426	18	0	3	3	12	105	18	81	6	0
Baldwin Township	1,926	4	0	0	0	4	9	0	8	1	0
Bangor	5,234	15	0	1	1	13	38	7	29	2	0
Bedford	2,691	6	0	2	1	3	22	4	18	0	0
Bellwood	1,741	1	0	0	0	1	18	3	14	1	0
Ben Avon Heights	362	0	0	0	0	0	3	0	3	0	0
Bethel Township, Berks County	4,178	1	0	0	0	1	23	1	19	3	0
Bigler Township Regional	1,225	0	0	0	0	0	12	0	10	2	0
Birmingham Township	4,210	3	0	0	0	3	9	1	8	0	0
Blacklick Township	1,877	0	0	0	0	0	0	0	0	0	0
Blair Township	4,500	6	0	0	1	5	35	6	28	1	0
Blawnox	1,379	2	0	0	0	2	1	0	1	0	0
Blossburg	1,489	2	0	0	0	2	4	1	2	1	0
Blythe Township	887	0	0	0	0	0	0	0	0	0	0
Bonneauville	1,838	1	0	0	0	1	3	0	3	0	0
Brackenridge	3,140	7	0	1	1	5	33	1	29	3	0
Braddock	2,107	3	0	0	1	2	48	13	26	9	0
Brecknock Township, Berks County	4,669	0	0	0	0	0	11	3	7	1	0
Brentwood	9,291	20	0	1	2	17	96	17	73	6	0
Bristol Township	53,508	93	1	20	42	30	752	77	583	92	10
Buckingham Township	20,279	0	0	0	0	0	55	13	39	3	1
Butler	12,901	49	0	0	9	40	229	38	181	10	2
Butler Township, Butler County	16,447	24	0	8	2	14	236	6	227	3	0
Caernarvon Township, Berks County	4,174	8	0	0	1	7	73	5	67	1	0
Caln Township	14,363	28	0	1	3	24	261	10	242	9	0
Cambridge Springs	2,648	5	0	1	0	4	16	5	11	0	0
Canonsburg	8,789	7	0	0	1	6	31	1	30	0	2
Carnegie	7,828	26	0	0	8	18	180	13	154	13	0
Carrolltown	789	1	0	0	0	1	5	3	2	0	0
Catasauqua	6,619	14	0	1	0	13	118	19	90	9	0
Central Bucks Regional	15,494	8	0	0	1	7	72	6	63	3	1
Chambersburg	21,131	59	4	9	12	34	491	51	429	11	4
Chartiers Township	8,031	3	0	0	1	2	35	2	33	0	1
Chester	33,905	469	18	29	142	280	1,019	254	597	168	17
Cleona	2,221	0	0	0	0	0	10	0	10	0	
Cochranton	1,077	2	0	0	0	2	1	0	1	0	0
Collegeville	5,115	1	0	0	0	1	18	1	17	0	0
Covington Township	2,255	7	0	0	1	6	19	3	13	3	0
Crafton	6,178	12	0	0	1	11	168	5	160	3	0
Cresson Township	2,492	1	0	0	0	1	5	0	5	0	0
Cumberland Township, Greene County	6,180	9	0	0	0	9	77	8	65	4	1
Cumru Township	15,496	16	0	0	3	13	232	20	202	10	2
Dallas Township	9,354	1	0	0	1	0	33	4	28	1	0
Danville	4,613	18	0	0	0	18	51	4	46	1	0
Darby Township	9,256	68	2	2	7	57	176	16	138	22	0
Derry	2,512	0	0	0	0	0	4	0	4	0	0
Doylestown Township	17,397	12	0	3	0	9	88	10	77	1	0
Dublin Borough	2,140	4	0	0	2	2	7	1	5	1	0

Table 8. Offenses Known to Law Enforcement, by Selected State and City, 2019—Continued

(Number.)

State/city	Population	Violent crime	Murder and nonnegligent manslaughter	Rape[1]	Robbery	Aggravated assault	Property crime	Burglary	Larceny-theft	Motor vehicle theft	Arson[2]
Duncansville	1,162	1	0	0	0	1	6	0	5	1	0
Dunnstable Township	1,010	0	0	0	0	0	0	0	0	0	0
East Bangor	1,699	0	0	0	0	0	2	0	2	0	0
East Brandywine Township	9,123	4	0	0	0	4	16	0	15	1	0
East Franklin Township	3,849	0	0	0	0	0	27	0	27	0	0
East Greenville	2,962	0	0	0	0	0	10	1	9	0	0
East Taylor Township	2,488	2	0	0	0	2	13	4	8	1	0
Eddystone	2,404	21	0	1	4	16	176	6	164	6	1
Edgeworth	1,647	0	0	0	0	0	0	0	0	0	0
Elderton	338	0	0	0	0	0	1	0	1	0	0
Elizabeth	1,966	3	0	0	0	3	84	14	68	2	1
Elizabeth Township	12,991	12	0	3	1	8	17	3	13	1	1
Elkland	1,742	3	0	0	0	3	14	1	13	0	0
Emporium	1,806	5	0	0	0	5	149	8	133	8	0
Ephrata Township	10,483	8	0	1	2	5	44	4	35	5	0
Erie	95,834	476	9	54	93	320	1,817	342	1,379	96	33
Etna	3,324	6	0	0	1	5	12	1	9	2	0
Fawn Township	2,304	2	0	0	0	2	1	0	1	0	0
Fayette City	555	0	0	0	0	0	1	0	1	0	0
Ford City	2,770	4	0	1	2	1	31	3	25	3	2
Forest City	1,741	1	0	0	0	1	13	2	11	0	0
Forks Township	15,741	4	0	4	0	0	141	2	137	2	0
Foster Township, McKean County	4,047	4	0	1	1	2	21	6	15	0	1
Frackville	3,609	6	0	0	0	6	20	4	16	0	0
Franklin Township, Columbia County	583	3	0	0	1	2	0	0	0	0	0
Greene County Regional Police Department	5,250	1	0	0	0	1	40	9	28	3	0
Grove City	7,840	9	1	2	0	6	31	5	25	1	0
Hanover	15,707	37	0	1	13	23	300	26	269	5	2
Harrisburg	49,195	443	13	36	160	234	1,069	229	728	112	13
Harveys Lake	2,768	0	0	0	0	0	13	1	11	1	0
Hastings	1,171	0	0	0	0	0	8	1	7	0	0
Highspire	2,371	12	0	0	3	9	42	2	40	0	0
Hilltown Township	15,589	13	0	5	1	7	116	8	103	5	0
Hughestown	1,375	1	0	0	0	1	5	1	4	0	0
Independence Township, Beaver County	2,342	2	0	0	0	2	11	1	10	0	0
Indiana	12,974	88	0	10	6	72	142	19	122	1	0
Ingram	3,212	5	0	0	1	4	19	4	15	0	0
Ivyland	1,039	0	0	0	0	0	4	2	2	0	0
Jackson Township, Cambria County	4,041	4	0	0	0	4	7	0	7	0	1
Jackson Township, Luzerne County	4,638	0	0	0	0	0	7	1	5	1	0
Jefferson Hills Borough	11,211	25	0	0	1	24	62	6	53	3	0
Kingston Township	6,882	4	0	0	0	4	34	2	31	1	0
Lancaster Township, Butler County	2,683	1	0	0	0	1	2	2	0	0	0
Lancaster Township, Lancaster County	17,176	21	1	2	3	15	343	16	299	28	0
Langhorne Borough	1,580	2	0	0	0	2	6	0	6	0	0
Langhorne Manor	1,428	0	0	0	0	0	2	1	1	0	0
Lansdale	16,759	23	0	3	3	17	177	10	164	3	0
Lansdowne	10,621	18	0	3	9	6	244	23	201	20	0
Lansford	3,800	26	0	1	2	23	82	14	62	6	0
Latimore Township	2,621	4	0	0	1	3	15	8	7	0	0
Lawrence Park Township	3,755	5	0	0	0	5	2	1	1	0	0
Lebanon	25,959	65	1	5	21	38	528	77	430	21	1
Leetsdale	1,173	2	0	0	0	2	28	5	21	2	0
Lehighton	5,309	23	0	1	2	20	79	21	49	9	1
Lower Allen Township	19,650	26	0	7	3	16	255	12	240	3	1
Lower Burrell	11,077	16	0	5	1	10	105	2	102	1	0
Lower Heidelberg Township	6,192	7	0	0	1	6	13	2	11	0	0
Lower Merion Township	59,796	29	0	2	19	8	874	78	762	34	1
Lower Salford Township	15,534	0	0	0	0	0	49	3	45	1	0
Luzerne Township	5,896	0	0	0	0	0	0	0	0	0	0
Mahoning Township, Carbon County	4,232	20	0	0	1	19	102	10	90	2	0
Mahoning Township, Lawrence County	2,875	1	0	0	0	1	0	0	0	0	0
Malvern	3,506	2	0	0	0	2	15	3	10	2	0
Manheim	4,859	25	0	4	2	19	70	11	53	6	0
Manor Township, Armstrong County	4,053	1	0	0	0	1	2	0	2	0	0
Manor Township, Lancaster County	21,059	8	0	1	2	5	119	23	91	5	0
Mansfield	2,940	2	0	0	0	2	4	0	4	0	0
Marion Township, Beaver County	872	0	0	0	0	0	3	1	2	0	0
Marple Township	23,859	7	0	0	1	6	317	15	300	2	0
Masontown	3,287	1	0	0	0	1	18	6	11	1	0

Table 8. Offenses Known to Law Enforcement, by Selected State and City, 2019—Continued

(Number.)

State/city	Population	Violent crime	Murder and nonnegligent manslaughter	Rape[1]	Robbery	Aggravated assault	Property crime	Burglary	Larceny-theft	Motor vehicle theft	Arson[2]
McDonald Borough	2,058	4	0	0	1	3	34	2	32	0	0
McKeesport	20,765	318	7	10	32	269	573	160	371	42	14
McSherrystown	3,091	2	0	0	0	2	1	0	1	0	0
Mechanicsburg	8,994	13	0	5	1	7	144	10	131	3	0
Middleburg	1,289	0	0	0	0	0	15	4	11	0	3
Midland	2,469	7	0	2	1	4	28	6	20	2	0
Midway	875	1	0	0	0	1	0	0	0	0	0
Millcreek Township, Lebanon County	5,783	0	0	0	0	0	17	2	14	1	0
Monongahela	9,795	12	0	0	1	11	83	14	61	8	0
Montoursville	4,404	4	0	0	2	2	82	6	76	0	0
Moon Township	25,647	13	0	2	4	7	208	28	171	9	0
Moscow	2,061	19	0	0	0	19	17	3	13	1	0
Mount Carmel Township	2,970	16	0	0	0	16	8	3	5	0	0
Mount Pleasant Township	3,529	1	0	0	0	1	11	0	10	1	0
Nazareth	5,717	2	0	0	0	2	61	5	55	1	1
Newberry Township	15,885	21	0	2	0	19	255	39	204	12	0
New Britain Township	11,444	2	0	0	0	2	54	4	49	1	1
New Kensington	12,273	65	1	8	19	37	325	48	258	19	0
Newport Township	5,386	3	0	1	0	2	28	7	21	0	0
New Sewickley Township	7,175	12	0	2	0	10	81	8	72	1	0
New Wilmington	2,178	3	0	0	0	3	11	2	9	0	0
Norristown	34,430	170	4	4	100	62	543	70	411	62	1
Northampton Township	39,171	6	0	3	2	1	131	13	114	4	0
North Coventry Township	8,004	1	0	1	0	0	128	7	119	2	0
North Middleton Township	11,713	4	1	1	0	2	43	3	36	4	0
North Sewickley Township	5,392	7	0	0	0	7	27	1	24	2	0
North Strabane Township	14,751	35	0	2	1	32	88	2	85	1	0
Northumberland	3,605	4	0	0	0	4	16	6	7	3	0
North Versailles Township	12,034	31	0	1	6	24	47	6	36	5	0
Old Forge	7,891	6	0	0	0	6	31	2	28	1	0
Palmerton	5,334	2	0	0	0	2	89	10	77	2	0
Palmyra	7,609	35	0	1	0	34	61	5	56	0	0
Palo Alto	977	0	0	0	0	0	0	0	0	0	0
Patton	1,609	2	0	0	0	2	3	0	3	0	0
Penndel	2,140	5	0	0	1	4	4	0	2	2	0
Penn Hills	40,809	165	7	18	42	98	820	145	588	87	12
Penn Township, Butler County	4,887	0	0	0	0	0	26	1	19	6	0
Pequea Township	5,108	9	0	3	0	6	52	13	37	2	0
Pine Creek Township	3,242	0	0	0	0	0	6	0	2	4	0
Plymouth	5,780	46	0	5	7	34	79	18	51	10	1
Point Township	3,598	2	0	0	0	2	27	5	22	0	0
Portage	2,391	1	0	1	0	0	22	4	18	0	0
Port Allegany	2,001	1	0	1	0	0	3	1	2	0	0
Port Carbon	1,772	1	0	0	0	1	1	0	1	0	0
Portersville	225	0	0	0	0	0	0	0	0	0	0
Pottstown	22,705	163	5	31	27	100	705	108	556	41	5
Prospect	1,116	0	0	0	0	0	2	1	1	0	0
Pymatuning Township	3,057	11	0	0	1	10	38	6	28	4	1
Ralpho Township	4,214	12	0	1	0	11	9	0	9	0	0
Ridley Park	7,046	7	0	1	1	5	47	7	35	5	1
Roaring Brook Township	1,970	0	0	0	0	0	4	1	3	0	0
Robinson Township, Allegheny County	13,711	17	1	1	0	15	283	0	280	3	0
Robinson Township, Washington County	1,890	4	0	1	0	3	17	0	16	1	0
Rosslyn Farms	413	0	0	0	0	0	0	0	0	0	0
Rostraver Township	11,005	8	0	1	3	4	245	12	229	4	1
Royersford	4,770	8	0	1	2	5	38	3	33	2	0
Ryan Township	2,547	0	0	0	0	0	4	0	4	0	0
Salisbury Township	13,991	7	0	0	3	4	124	8	113	3	2
Sandy Township	10,445	25	0	4	0	21	158	23	130	5	0
Scottdale	4,093	9	0	0	2	7	59	8	48	3	1
Scranton	77,323	1,199	0	45	66	1,088	1,347	239	1,026	82	6
Selinsgrove	5,962	20	0	6	2	12	123	16	104	3	1
Shamokin Dam	1,723	2	0	0	0	2	3	2	1	0	0
Sharpsville	4,091	14	0	3	0	11	53	10	43	0	0
Sinking Spring	4,132	7	0	0	1	6	48	11	32	5	0
Smethport	1,530	1	0	0	0	1	11	2	9	0	0
Smith Township	4,362	12	0	0	0	12	25	9	14	2	0
South Beaver Township	2,648	2	0	0	0	2	15	0	11	4	0
South Buffalo Township	2,520	1	0	0	0	1	10	1	9	0	0
South Centre Township	4,169	2	0	0	0	2	6	0	5	1	0
South Heights	443	0	0	0	0	0	0	0	0	0	0
South Strabane Township	9,464	13	0	3	4	6	404	9	388	7	0
Southwest Greensburg	2,016	5	0	0	1	4	15	1	14	0	0
Southwest Regional, Washington County	131	2	0	0	0	2	10	2	8	0	0
Springdale	3,294	12	0	2	3	7	45	14	30	1	1
Springettsbury Township	26,888	28	0	5	7	16	685	35	626	24	1
Spring Township, Centre County	7,944	3	0	0	0	3	17	0	17	0	0
State College	58,633	54	3	11	8	32	548	36	497	15	3

Table 8. Offenses Known to Law Enforcement, by Selected State and City, 2019—Continued

(Number.)

State/city	Population	Violent crime	Murder and nonnegligent manslaughter	Rape[1]	Robbery	Aggravated assault	Property crime	Burglary	Larceny-theft	Motor vehicle theft	Arson[2]
St. Clair Township	1,425	0	0	0	0	0	0	0	0	0	0
St. Marys City	12,277	26	0	9	1	16	118	19	95	4	1
Stockertown	923	0	0	0	0	0	1	0	1	0	0
Stowe Township	6,141	29	3	2	1	23	122	15	98	9	0
Sugarloaf Township, Luzerne County	3,920	1	0	0	0	1	34	6	27	1	0
Summit Township	2,116	0	0	0	0	0	0	0	0	0	0
Sunbury	9,352	16	0	5	2	9	117	17	91	9	5
Susquehanna Township, Dauphin County	25,238	73	1	10	12	50	274	39	217	18	2
Swarthmore	6,428	2	0	1	0	1	30	2	27	1	0
Swatara Township	26,643	76	2	9	17	48	786	47	718	21	2
Swissvale	8,652	17	1	0	4	12	149	20	120	9	1
Sykesville	1,117	0	0	0	0	0	0	0	0	0	0
Throop	3,902	12	0	0	0	12	36	12	23	1	0
Tiadaghton Valley Regional	7,578	8	0	1	0	7	34	2	32	0	0
Tinicum Township, Bucks County	3,956	3	0	1	1	1	15	3	11	1	0
Tioga	646	0	0	0	0	0	4	0	4	0	0
Tulpehocken Township	3,412	1	0	0	0	1	5	0	4	1	0
Tyrone	5,160	9	0	0	2	7	69	13	56	0	0
Union City	3,126	3	0	1	0	2	35	2	33	0	0
Union Township, Lawrence County	4,863	15	0	0	2	13	187	22	165	0	0
Upper Burrell Township	2,220	0	0	0	0	0	10	0	10	0	0
Upper Chichester Township	16,925	28	0	5	7	16	265	19	230	16	0
Upper Dublin Township	26,624	7	2	1	0	4	147	11	130	6	0
Upper Perkiomen	3,876	1	0	1	0	0	41	4	34	3	0
Upper Providence Township, Delaware County	10,437	2	0	1	0	1	21	2	14	5	0
Upper St. Clair Township	19,741	1	0	0	0	1	149	5	142	2	0
Valley Township	7,934	14	0	0	3	11	77	15	61	1	0
Vandling	705	1	0	1	0	0	0	0	0	1	0
Vintondale	376	0	0	0	0	0	0	0	0	0	0
Wampum	665	0	0	0	0	0	6	1	5	0	0
Warminster Township	32,293	27	0	9	12	6	284	14	253	17	
Warren	9,054	60	0	3	1	56	134	12	119	3	0
Warrington Township	24,607	23	0	1	4	18	164	11	149	4	0
Wayne Township	2,458	0	0	0	0	0	9	1	8	0	1
Weissport	396	0	0	0	0	0	1	0	1	0	0
West Brandywine Township	7,508	4	0	2	0	2	54	6	42	6	0
West Caln Township	9,113	27	0	3	1	23	52	13	30	9	0
West Carroll Township	1,203	5	0	1	0	4	4	2	2	0	0
West Cocalico Township	7,446	3	0	1	0	2	16	7	9	0	0
West Conshohocken	1,435	5	0	2	1	2	20	6	12	2	0
West Cornwall Township	2,058	0	0	0	0	0	0	0	0	0	0
West Hazleton	4,463	9	0	0	1	8	73	17	50	6	0
West Kittanning	1,095	0	0	0	0	0	0	0	0	0	0
West Leechburg	1,222	0	0	0	0	0	2	0	2	0	0
West Manchester Township	18,860	27	1	3	6	17	480	19	441	20	0
West Norriton Township	15,650	38	2	1	13	22	227	20	192	15	0
West Nottingham Township	2,700	0	0	0	0	0	0	0	0	0	0
West Pikeland Township	4,086	0	0	0	0	0	16	2	12	2	0
West Pottsgrove Township	3,876	5	0	0	1	4	81	7	70	4	0
West Reading	4,224	30	0	0	3	27	128	9	113	6	0
Westtown-East Goshen Regional	32,366	44	0	6	2	36	173	11	155	7	0
West Vincent Township	5,887	2	0	0	0	2	16	5	11	0	0
West Whiteland Township	18,389	9	0	6	1	2	373	8	359	6	1
Whitpain Township	19,294	9	0	0	8	1	132	9	122	1	0
Wilkes-Barre	40,722	242	3	24	68	147	852	194	616	42	2
Wilkinsburg	15,389	120	11	6	22	81	403	75	262	66	1
Wilkins Township	6,137	3	0	0	2	1	129	10	108	11	0
Williamsburg	1,174	0	0	0	0	0	16	5	10	1	0
Wilson	7,822	21	1	4	2	14	144	11	126	7	0
Womelsdorf	2,899	1	0	0	0	1	10	1	9	0	0
Worthington	592	0	0	0	0	0	0	0	0	0	0
Wyomissing	10,504	18	1	4	6	7	199	8	188	3	1
RHODE ISLAND											
Barrington	16,090	4	0	2	1	1	89	14	74	1	0
Bristol	22,070	16	0	7	0	9	103	6	94	3	1
Burrillville	16,859	9	1	2	0	6	79	17	57	5	2
Central Falls	19,423	82	1	11	13	57	289	44	192	53	1
Charlestown	7,819	6	0	1	1	4	48	14	32	2	1
Coventry	34,751	31	0	11	0	20	386	73	294	19	3
Cranston	81,471	127	1	26	20	80	1,110	113	912	85	13
Cumberland	35,206	25	0	8	5	12	252	30	203	19	2
East Greenwich	13,119	5	0	0	2	3	91	9	78	4	0
East Providence	47,590	62	0	20	6	36	498	75	353	70	3
Foster	4,730	3	0	1	0	2	27	9	18	0	0
Glocester	10,281	4	0	0	0	4	26	5	17	4	1
Hopkinton	8,110	4	0	3	0	1	39	7	31	1	0

Table 8. Offenses Known to Law Enforcement, by Selected State and City, 2019—Continued

(Number.)

State/city	Population	Violent crime	Murder and nonnegligent manslaughter	Rape[1]	Robbery	Aggravated assault	Property crime	Burglary	Larceny-theft	Motor vehicle theft	Arson[2]
Jamestown	5,508	4	0	2	0	2	24	2	21	1	0
Johnston	29,424	32	0	8	6	18	326	62	225	39	0
Lincoln	21,891	25	0	6	8	11	380	33	325	22	0
Little Compton	3,488	2	0	0	0	2	21	6	14	1	0
Middletown	15,934	11	0	5	0	6	151	14	129	8	2
Narragansett	15,411	14	0	6	1	7	103	13	84	6	2
Newport	24,584	68	0	19	8	41	537	79	437	21	3
New Shoreham	1,032	3	0	0	0	3	23	7	15	1	0
North Kingstown	26,286	23	0	15	0	8	214	29	180	5	2
North Providence	32,655	44	1	6	2	35	208	48	117	43	2
North Smithfield	12,568	6	0	2	0	4	272	12	251	9	1
Pawtucket	72,030	293	1	57	47	188	1,640	315	1,146	179	13
Portsmouth	17,330	11	0	4	0	7	76	16	57	3	1
Providence	179,762	892	13	106	241	532	5,413	715	4,224	474	5
Richmond	7,701	3	0	0	0	3	37	4	30	3	0
Scituate	10,707	6	0	4	0	2	38	2	34	2	1
Smithfield	21,790	6	0	3	0	3	195	21	171	3	1
South Kingstown	30,656	19	0	8	1	10	214	31	172	11	1
Tiverton	15,745	11	0	5	2	4	180	21	148	11	1
Warren	10,419	18	0	5	1	12	133	24	104	5	0
Warwick	80,749	76	2	29	8	37	1,239	108	1,073	58	2
Westerly	22,475	15	1	9	0	5	243	36	193	14	1
West Greenwich	6,375	4	0	0	1	3	37	10	24	3	0
West Warwick	28,847	54	0	14	2	38	238	58	161	19	2
Woonsocket	41,709	237	2	34	40	161	865	197	580	88	15
SOUTH CAROLINA											
Abbeville	5,017	47	9	4	4	30	123	29	89	5	0
Aiken	30,922	178	4	23	32	119	1,499	162	1,239	98	6
Allendale	2,924	76	1	2	4	69	136	52	68	16	5
Aynor	994	3	0	0	1	2	27	0	23	4	0
Bamberg	3,195	16	2	2	3	9	147	37	99	11	1
Barnwell	4,321	89	0	8	5	76	206	55	140	11	1
Batesburg-Leesville	5,389	61	2	6	3	50	221	23	189	9	0
Beaufort	13,485	58	3	3	22	30	460	58	391	11	0
Belton	4,434	15	1	1	2	11	156	34	100	22	0
Bennettsville	7,726	53	2	0	3	48	311	39	263	9	0
Bishopville	2,927	86	1	2	11	72	194	40	142	12	0
Blacksburg	1,883	10	0	0	0	10	68	9	53	6	0
Blackville	2,194	23	2	1	2	18	130	62	61	7	0
Bluffton	24,812	46	1	9	10	26	220	35	175	10	3
Bowman	904	16	0	0	5	11	38	16	17	5	0
Branchville	952	1	0	0	0	1	19	6	13	0	0
Burnettown	2,751	1	0	0	0	1	23	5	15	3	0
Calhoun Falls	1,912	14	2	0	0	12	31	11	17	3	0
Camden	7,242	86	2	4	7	73	385	39	318	28	2
Cameron	396	0	0	0	0	0	8	3	3	2	0
Cayce	14,211	138	0	11	12	115	804	64	644	96	1
Central	5,380	1	0	1	0	0	136	3	126	7	0
Chapin	1,653	3	0	0	1	2	56	9	41	6	0
Charleston	138,254	516	8	51	95	362	3,124	292	2,335	497	7
Cheraw	5,589	61	0	3	8	50	413	57	343	13	2
Chesnee	948	3	0	1	0	2	53	15	34	4	0
Chester	5,368	82	5	5	2	70	213	29	174	10	0
Chesterfield	1,415	4	0	0	0	4	57	13	44	0	0
Clemson	17,547	32	0	7	5	20	425	27	298	100	0
Clinton	8,412	66	0	6	6	54	349	57	270	22	3
Clio	660	2	0	0	1	1	13	4	8	1	0
Clover	6,575	19	0	0	2	17	157	13	124	20	1
Columbia	133,790	1,037	29	88	220	700	7,027	916	5,216	895	15
Conway	26,127	111	1	14	11	85	884	90	739	55	2
Coward	767	4	0	2	0	2	16	4	12	0	0
Cowpens	2,408	4	0	0	1	3	57	7	47	3	0
Darlington	5,886	87	1	7	12	67	505	73	416	16	2
Denmark	2,924	31	3	0	4	24	132	64	60	8	0
Due West	1,240	0	0	0	0	0	18	3	15	0	0
Duncan	3,573	7	0	1	3	3	67	7	53	7	0
Easley	21,390	98	0	3	9	86	1,098	128	910	60	3
Edisto Beach	406	1	0	0	0	1	10	1	8	1	0
Ehrhardt	481	3	0	0	0	3	13	0	12	1	0
Elgin	1,612	6	0	0	0	6	76	7	68	1	0
Estill	1,855	37	2	0	3	32	93	37	50	6	1
Eutawville	292	2	0	0	1	1	7	0	5	2	0
Florence	37,640	447	7	29	58	353	2,496	388	1,909	199	4
Forest Acres	10,320	64	0	5	9	50	637	87	508	42	0
Fort Mill	21,219	22	0	3	2	17	233	27	204	2	0
Fountain Inn	10,375	45	2	7	2	34	201	32	148	21	0
Gaffney	12,528	102	0	5	12	85	733	88	596	49	1
Gaston	1,692	4	0	0	0	4	50	7	37	6	0
Georgetown	8,733	107	0	8	10	89	543	61	453	29	2
Great Falls	1,875	7	0	1	0	6	72	19	49	4	1
Greenville	69,830	402	4	44	82	272	2,805	352	2,236	217	1
Greenwood	23,427	350	2	29	32	287	1,292	254	1,016	22	11

Table 8. Offenses Known to Law Enforcement, by Selected State and City, 2019—Continued

(Number.)

State/city	Population	Violent crime	Murder and nonnegligent manslaughter	Rape[1]	Robbery	Aggravated assault	Property crime	Burglary	Larceny-theft	Motor vehicle theft	Arson[2]
Greer	32,976	143	1	18	26	98	1,021	157	787	77	3
Hampton	2,499	26	1	0	2	23	168	37	124	7	0
Hanahan	26,941	55	2	17	6	30	345	37	266	42	3
Hardeeville	7,075	53	1	4	14	34	208	25	160	23	1
Hartsville	7,524	108	0	6	15	87	668	119	523	26	2
Hemingway	400	2	0	0	2	0	37	6	28	3	0
Holly Hill	1,181	10	0	1	2	7	44	4	36	4	0
Honea Path	3,810	12	0	1	1	10	146	17	109	20	2
Inman	2,404	3	0	1	0	2	59	16	42	1	1
Irmo	12,516	39	0	3	4	32	413	51	340	22	1
Isle of Palms	4,366	1	0	0	0	1	86	20	51	15	0
Iva	1,311	4	0	2	0	2	42	8	28	6	0
Jackson	1,792	4	0	1	1	2	33	5	26	2	0
Jamestown	83	1	0	0	1	0	4	1	3	0	0
Johnsonville	1,494	1	0	0	0	1	25	13	9	3	0
Jonesville	834	2	0	0	0	2	17	6	9	2	0
Kingstree	3,026	17	1	2	4	10	180	25	148	7	4
Lake City	6,541	112	1	4	9	98	283	49	212	22	0
Lamar	937	6	1	0	4	1	20	5	14	1	0
Latta	1,288	20	0	1	2	17	95	15	79	1	1
Laurens	8,823	80	0	8	13	59	450	63	362	25	2
Lexington	22,160	72	0	8	11	53	632	29	571	32	1
Liberty	3,152	21	0	1	2	18	70	11	53	6	0
Loris	2,740	34	1	1	3	29	85	17	63	5	0
Lyman	3,661	24	1	0	2	21	77	11	56	10	0
Manning	3,921	58	1	2	6	49	341	45	292	4	1
Marion	6,373	55	1	2	14	38	363	65	275	23	2
Mauldin	25,453	57	0	9	13	35	413	52	331	30	1
McColl	1,981	28	1	0	4	23	76	14	56	6	0
McCormick	2,298	10	0	0	0	10	52	12	35	5	2
Moncks Corner	11,986	55	1	10	10	34	416	47	338	31	1
Mount Pleasant	92,448	105	1	11	14	79	1,135	114	919	102	1
Mullins	4,290	41	2	2	7	30	226	99	119	8	2
Myrtle Beach	34,860	415	3	52	98	262	3,916	304	3,384	228	6
Newberry	10,333	72	2	4	9	57	406	55	341	10	2
New Ellenton	2,145	20	1	2	1	16	23	3	18	2	0
Ninety Six	2,039	2	0	0	0	2	41	2	37	2	1
North Augusta	23,875	55	1	8	13	33	651	80	537	34	1
North Charleston	115,312	1,114	26	103	229	756	6,941	853	5,123	965	14
North Myrtle Beach	16,942	71	1	15	10	45	1,115	108	910	97	1
Pacolet	2,502	9	0	2	0	7	46	8	35	3	2
Pamplico	1,221	7	0	0	1	6	15	12	2	1	0
Pelion	704	2	0	0	0	2	18	2	15	1	0
Pickens	3,171	19	0	5	0	14	187	22	155	10	3
Port Royal	13,368	40	0	0	16	24	232	28	189	15	0
Prosperity	1,219	4	0	0	0	4	14	3	10	1	0
Quinby	927	0	0	0	0	0	0	0	0	0	0
Ridge Spring	758	6	0	0	1	5	13	6	6	1	0
Rock Hill	75,342	498	4	50	63	381	2,521	329	2,006	186	10
Salem	152	0	0	0	0	0	0	0	0	0	0
Saluda	3,641	9	0	2	2	5	85	26	55	4	0
Scranton	864	4	0	0	0	4	15	4	10	1	0
Seneca	8,525	50	1	4	5	40	222	40	161	21	2
Simpsonville	23,682	46	1	7	11	27	635	74	523	38	3
Society Hill	533	0	0	0	0	0	4	0	2	2	0
South Congaree	2,483	2	0	0	0	2	73	13	53	7	0
Spartanburg	37,754	448	6	24	77	341	2,450	440	1,839	171	8
Springdale	2,753	11	0	2	3	6	96	9	74	13	0
St. Matthews	1,900	9	0	0	1	8	100	34	61	5	0
St. Stephen	1,809	18	1	1	1	15	69	11	55	3	0
Sullivans Island	1,938	1	0	0	0	1	32	2	25	5	0
Summerton	939	9	0	0	2	7	47	16	31	0	2
Summerville	52,886	186	5	34	21	126	1,662	244	1,313	105	5
Sumter	39,546	418	8	11	48	351	1,796	397	1,291	108	0
Swansea	959	5	0	0	4	1	37	2	28	7	1
Tega Cay	11,322	5	0	0	1	4	164	1	162	1	1
Travelers Rest	5,339	5	1	1	1	2	312	7	294	11	0
Union	7,694	76	1	6	10	59	534	86	423	25	1
Wagener	838	1	0	0	0	1	6	1	4	1	0
Walhalla	4,384	7	0	1	1	5	76	22	52	2	0
Walterboro	5,429	21	0	3	4	14	316	23	279	14	0
Ware Shoals	2,156	23	0	0	1	22	105	17	79	9	0
Wellford	2,697	1	0	1	0	0	32	4	25	3	2
West Columbia	17,986	127	0	23	28	76	1,199	148	944	107	1
Westminster	2,570	10	0	0	3	7	76	17	55	4	0
West Union	325	0	0	0	0	0	24	5	19	0	1
Whitmire	1,469	3	0	0	1	2	51	10	41	0	1
Williamston	4,249	31	0	2	5	24	85	6	69	10	1
Williston	2,907	17	2	3	6	6	145	31	97	17	0
Winnsboro	3,165	23	0	0	2	21	78	10	66	2	0
Woodruff	4,356	3	0	0	0	3	35	11	23	1	0
Yemassee	954	17	0	2	3	12	45	6	35	4	1
York	8,294	67	0	8	8	51	421	34	372	15	2

Table 8. Offenses Known to Law Enforcement, by Selected State and City, 2019—Continued

(Number.)

State/city	Population	Violent crime	Murder and nonnegligent manslaughter	Rape[1]	Robbery	Aggravated assault	Property crime	Burglary	Larceny-theft	Motor vehicle theft	Arson[2]
SOUTH DAKOTA											
Aberdeen	28,870	160	0	41	4	115	629	117	468	44	0
Alcester	744	0	0	0	0	0	11	4	6	1	0
Avon	597	0	0	0	0	0	0	0	0	0	0
Belle Fourche	5,600	11	0	3	0	8	87	7	75	5	0
Beresford	1,989	0	0	0	0	0	12	4	8	0	0
Box Elder	10,077	42	0	5	1	36	216	54	137	25	0
Brandon	10,244	7	0	1	0	6	27	4	22	1	0
Brookings	24,823	54	0	12	1	41	316	28	271	17	0
Burke	586	0	0	0	0	0	0	0	0	0	0
Canton	3,521	12	0	2	0	10	59	17	39	3	0
Centerville	879	0	0	0	0	0	7	2	4	1	1
Chamberlain	2,345	16	0	3	1	12	77	18	57	2	0
Clark	1,056	0	0	0	0	0	2	1	1	0	0
Deadwood	1,307	3	0	0	0	3	0	0	0	0	0
Elk Point	1,857	4	0	0	0	4	1	0	0	1	0
Faith	413	0	0	0	0	0	1	0	0	1	0
Flandreau	2,323	18	0	3	0	15	78	19	52	7	1
Freeman	1,290	1	0	1	0	0	9	1	4	4	0
Groton	1,506	0	0	0	0	0	0	0	0	0	0
Hot Springs	3,485	11	0	1	0	10	33	4	28	1	0
Huron	13,840	58	0	11	0	47	349	29	311	9	1
Kadoka	714	2	0	0	0	2	5	1	1	3	0
Kimball	662	0	0	0	0	0	2	2	0	0	0
Lead	2,958	2	0	0	0	2	16	2	12	2	0
Lennox	2,476	5	0	1	0	4	11	5	4	2	0
Madison	7,558	17	0	3	0	14	78	16	57	5	0
Martin	1,071	27	0	3	2	22	80	20	59	1	0
Menno	622	0	0	0	0	0	0	0	0	0	0
Mitchell	15,733	59	1	13	1	44	538	61	437	40	4
Mobridge	3,550	13	0	2	0	11	26	4	20	2	0
Murdo	442	0	0	0	0	0	2	2	0	0	0
North Sioux City	2,932	6	0	1	0	5	55	7	41	7	0
Philip	773	1	0	0	0	1	5	2	2	1	0
Pierre	14,018	65	1	15	3	46	383	42	318	23	0
Platte	1,263	4	0	2	0	2	2	1	1	0	0
Rapid City	76,343	540	4	114	64	358	2,454	488	1,646	320	9
Rosholt	434	0	0	0	0	0	0	0	0	0	0
Scotland	814	0	0	0	0	0	0	0	0	0	0
Sioux Falls	185,628	897	4	116	68	709	5,653	695	4,300	658	29
Sisseton	2,423	3	0	1	0	2	16	2	10	4	0
Spearfish	11,842	23	0	4	1	18	268	29	229	10	1
Springfield	1,935	0	0	0	0	0	0	0	0	0	0
Sturgis	6,983	14	0	2	1	11	151	21	125	5	0
Summerset	2,796	5	0	1	0	4	57	4	52	1	0
Tea	5,898	8	0	3	0	5	96	9	79	8	0
Tripp	630	1	0	1	0	0	1	1	0	0	0
Tyndall	1,036	0	0	0	0	0	0	0	0	0	0
Vermillion	10,833	21	0	5	0	16	209	13	187	9	0
Wagner	1,561	4	0	1	0	3	16	0	13	3	0
Watertown	22,233	67	1	20	3	43	367	58	292	17	0
Yankton	14,730	86	1	20	2	63	375	33	301	41	1
TENNESSEE											
Adamsville	2,171	6	0	2	0	4	27	2	22	3	1
Alamo	2,294	12	0	3	0	9	89	13	66	10	0
Alcoa	10,798	85	2	17	7	59	431	27	361	43	0
Alexandria	1,006	4	0	0	1	3	4	2	2	0	0
Algood	4,549	13	0	3	0	10	172	7	157	8	0
Ardmore	1,229	0	0	0	0	0	28	1	23	4	0
Ashland City	4,708	12	0	0	0	12	264	13	243	8	0
Athens	13,879	116	0	7	9	100	881	120	688	73	1
Atoka	9,510	12	0	2	1	9	67	5	58	4	0
Baileyton	445	2	0	0	0	2	12	1	10	1	0
Bartlett	59,610	188	1	12	30	145	1,046	100	878	68	2
Baxter	1,514	4	0	0	2	2	38	7	27	4	0
Bean Station	3,085	8	0	0	0	8	33	8	20	5	0
Belle Meade	2,879	1	0	0	0	1	27	5	20	2	0
Bells	2,455	7	0	0	2	5	31	11	16	4	0
Benton	1,258	4	0	1	0	3	34	3	29	2	0
Berry Hill	515	15	0	0	7	8	120	19	97	4	0
Big Sandy	522	0	0	0	0	0	10	3	5	2	0
Blaine	1,871	0	0	0	0	0	30	2	24	4	0
Bluff City	1,661	4	0	0	0	4	25	6	15	4	0
Bolivar	4,888	73	0	3	4	66	141	45	87	9	1
Bradford	983	3	0	0	1	2	12	1	10	1	1
Brentwood	43,217	38	0	12	12	14	374	38	318	18	1
Brighton	2,926	4	0	0	1	3	9	4	5	0	0
Bristol	26,900	135	1	15	12	107	813	138	604	71	3
Brownsville	9,336	151	2	13	9	127	329	63	251	15	0
Bruceton	1,400	4	0	0	0	4	25	5	16	4	0
Burns	1,456	0	0	0	0	0	10	1	6	3	0
Calhoun	498	0	0	0	0	0	3	0	3	0	0

Table 8. Offenses Known to Law Enforcement, by Selected State and City, 2019—Continued

(Number.)

State/city	Population	Violent crime	Murder and nonnegligent manslaughter	Rape[1]	Robbery	Aggravated assault	Property crime	Burglary	Larceny-theft	Motor vehicle theft	Arson[2]
Camden	3,573	2	0	0	0	2	31	3	28	0	0
Carthage	2,276	6	0	0	0	6	49	0	45	4	0
Caryville	2,146	3	0	1	0	2	42	8	23	11	0
Celina	1,453	4	0	0	0	4	25	3	19	3	0
Centerville	3,564	10	0	0	0	6	61	12	46	3	0
Chapel Hill	1,532	6	0	0	0	6	12	6	6	0	0
Charleston	695	0	0	0	0	0	3	0	0	3	0
Chattanooga	181,848	1,946	33	161	196	1,556	10,106	1,098	7,694	1,314	25
Church Hill	6,671	0	0	0	0	0	10	1	8	1	0
Clarksburg	376	0	0	0	0	0	0	0	0	0	0
Clarksville	159,996	926	14	103	116	693	4,467	543	3,457	467	12
Cleveland	45,453	464	2	35	42	385	2,403	371	1,845	187	2
Clifton	2,665	2	0	0	0	2	15	4	11	0	0
Clinton	10,062	45	0	2	6	37	324	39	249	36	0
Collegedale	11,929	10	0	1	4	5	222	14	198	10	0
Collierville	51,273	119	3	9	22	85	688	49	610	29	1
Collinwood	939	0	0	0	0	0	8	0	6	2	0
Columbia	40,001	257	0	13	19	225	1,202	124	980	98	3
Cookeville	34,373	121	1	28	7	85	1,047	140	779	128	1
Coopertown	4,590	4	0	0	0	4	44	12	28	4	1
Cornersville	1,271	3	0	0	0	3	8	1	7	0	0
Covington	8,755	126	0	6	8	112	479	64	357	58	1
Cowan	1,657	1	0	0	0	1	16	3	13	0	0
Cross Plains	1,827	0	0	0	0	0	5	0	4	1	0
Crossville	11,643	42	0	16	0	26	499	88	380	31	1
Cumberland City	308	2	0	1	0	1	5	1	4	0	0
Dandridge	3,168	12	0	1	0	11	68	15	50	3	1
Dayton	7,408	20	0	2	0	18	197	34	156	7	0
Decatur	1,646	11	1	1	1	8	37	5	29	3	0
Decaturville	860	0	0	0	0	0	10	6	4	0	0
Decherd	2,386	19	1	2	0	16	87	8	72	7	0
Dickson	15,703	112	1	15	4	92	672	60	557	55	1
Dover	1,489	2	1	0	0	1	18	3	13	2	0
Dresden	2,908	2	0	0	1	1	30	9	17	4	0
Dunlap	5,155	23	0	0	0	23	150	31	102	17	0
Dyer	2,204	4	0	0	0	4	32	2	28	2	0
Dyersburg	16,300	180	3	7	30	140	905	235	618	52	5
Eagleville	714	0	0	0	0	0	0	0	0	0	0
East Ridge	21,027	91	0	10	10	71	714	97	555	62	0
Elizabethton	13,409	81	0	5	1	75	639	103	471	65	2
Elkton	528	0	0	0	0	0	4	1	3	0	0
Englewood	1,524	14	0	0	0	14	31	4	24	3	0
Erin	1,287	2	0	0	0	2	16	3	12	1	0
Erwin	5,826	30	0	4	0	26	89	12	61	16	0
Estill Springs	2,030	16	0	0	0	16	23	4	15	4	0
Ethridge	489	2	0	0	0	2	10	1	7	2	0
Etowah	3,482	15	0	0	0	15	87	10	65	12	0
Fairview	9,153	18	0	3	0	15	127	15	99	13	0
Fayetteville	7,047	53	0	4	2	47	224	24	189	11	1
Franklin	83,517	138	0	15	10	113	926	58	814	54	3
Friendship	670	5	0	1	0	4	3	0	3	0	1
Gadsden	461	0	0	0	0	0	7	3	3	1	0
Gainesboro	944	0	0	0	0	0	1	0	1	0	0
Gallatin	41,918	117	4	6	10	97	451	33	387	31	1
Gallaway	644	1	0	0	0	1	7	0	5	2	0
Gates	621	2	0	1	0	1	17	7	9	1	0
Gatlinburg	4,163	20	0	3	0	17	192	25	152	15	0
Germantown	39,127	36	0	8	5	23	492	44	422	26	1
Gibson	394	0	0	0	0	0	2	0	2	0	0
Gleason	1,364	5	0	0	0	5	21	4	14	3	0
Goodlettsville	16,976	53	0	3	16	34	517	39	422	56	1
Gordonsville	1,239	3	0	0	0	3	10	3	7	0	0
Grand Junction	266	1	0	0	0	1	1	0	1	0	0
Graysville	1,564	11	0	0	0	11	31	4	22	5	0
Greenbrier	6,887	23	0	2	2	19	57	12	37	8	0
Greeneville	14,881	50	1	4	1	44	521	51	405	65	4
Greenfield	2,063	9	0	0	0	9	43	6	36	1	0
Halls	2,079	3	0	0	0	3	12	4	4	4	1
Harriman	6,121	29	0	1	1	27	180	30	130	20	0
Henderson	6,314	41	0	6	2	33	104	16	78	10	0
Hendersonville	58,388	100	0	2	12	86	652	44	574	34	0
Henry	466	0	0	0	0	0	3	1	0	2	0
Hohenwald	3,680	22	0	4	0	18	125	8	106	11	0
Hollow Rock	675	0	0	0	0	0	4	3	1	0	0
Hornbeak	394	0	0	0	0	0	0	0	0	0	0
Humboldt	8,165	63	1	2	5	55	272	65	189	18	1
Huntingdon	3,805	1	0	0	0	1	49	7	39	3	0
Huntland	839	0	0	0	0	0	0	0	0	0	0
Jacksboro	1,919	5	0	0	0	5	95	0	94	1	0
Jackson	66,915	650	17	30	97	506	2,473	374	1,904	195	15
Jamestown	1,960	10	0	0	1	9	72	7	64	1	0
Jasper	3,361	8	1	0	0	7	63	10	44	9	0
Jefferson City	8,193	14	0	2	1	11	207	28	167	12	3

Table 8. Offenses Known to Law Enforcement, by Selected State and City, 2019—Continued

(Number.)

State/city	Population	Violent crime	Murder and nonnegligent manslaughter	Rape[1]	Robbery	Aggravated assault	Property crime	Burglary	Larceny-theft	Motor vehicle theft	Arson[2]
Jellico	2,161	7	0	0	0	7	61	13	44	4	0
Johnson City	67,197	286	1	28	38	219	2,390	301	1,904	185	8
Jonesborough	5,487	20	1	2	1	16	105	17	74	14	0
Kenton	1,195	4	0	1	0	3	28	3	25	0	0
Kimball	1,421	5	0	0	0	5	58	5	49	4	1
Kingsport	54,218	332	3	22	35	272	2,829	324	2,232	273	5
Kingston	5,809	7	0	2	1	4	72	13	55	4	1
Kingston Springs	2,750	1	0	0	0	1	11	3	8	0	0
Knoxville	188,666	1,259	22	146	232	859	8,207	1,157	6,067	983	10
Lafayette	5,309	34	0	0	3	31	115	21	80	14	1
La Follette	6,651	52	0	3	4	45	339	84	232	23	0
La Vergne	36,227	142	4	17	22	99	650	103	472	75	1
Lawrenceburg	10,877	50	0	10	3	37	427	62	339	26	1
Lebanon	36,337	149	2	24	9	114	929	106	763	60	1
Lenoir City	9,392	37	0	2	2	33	272	33	215	24	0
Lexington	7,723	45	0	1	2	42	238	25	201	12	0
Livingston	4,014	12	0	1	1	10	65	18	45	2	0
Lookout Mountain	1,866	0	0	0	0	0	20	1	18	1	0
Loretto	1,789	7	0	0	0	7	9	3	5	1	0
Loudon	5,869	5	0	2	0	3	52	6	42	4	0
Madisonville	4,949	21	0	0	2	19	199	20	163	16	0
Manchester	11,020	61	0	6	1	54	435	65	351	19	0
Martin	10,488	18	1	0	1	16	327	38	279	10	0
Maryville	29,415	44	1	4	1	38	463	53	375	35	1
Mason	1,549	2	0	0	1	1	2	2	0	0	0
Maury City	664	1	0	0	0	1	14	2	10	2	0
Maynardville	2,397	7	0	0	1	6	42	5	34	3	0
McEwen	1,733	4	0	0	0	4	33	11	22	0	1
McKenzie	5,509	23	0	0	1	22	86	21	61	4	3
McMinnville	13,696	130	2	13	8	107	478	87	350	41	0
Medina	4,334	13	0	0	0	13	14	6	8	0	0
Memphis	650,410	12,367	190	468	2,432	9,277	39,860	7,833	27,981	4,046	336
Metropolitan Nashville Police Department	687,361	7,376	83	438	1,978	4,877	27,777	3,374	21,655	2,748	60
Middleton	637	0	0	0	0	0	2	1	1	0	0
Milan	7,613	42	0	4	3	35	194	48	136	10	0
Millersville	6,829	29	1	3	0	25	85	26	51	8	1
Millington	10,669	105	2	6	13	84	552	97	397	58	3
Minor Hill	532	0	0	0	0	0	0	0	0	0	0
Monteagle	1,225	8	0	0	1	7	41	15	19	7	0
Monterey	2,888	9	0	0	0	9	51	14	32	5	0
Morristown	30,044	255	2	16	18	219	1,423	169	1,140	114	1
Moscow	559	4	0	1	0	3	11	1	9	1	0
Mountain City	2,407	1	0	0	0	1	34	3	31	0	0
Mount Carmel	5,295	2	0	0	0	2	29	7	14	8	0
Mount Juliet	37,359	59	1	2	9	47	523	24	456	43	0
Mount Pleasant	4,934	8	0	1	0	7	45	8	33	4	0
Munford	6,083	17	1	3	1	12	81	18	58	5	0
Murfreesboro	145,929	611	4	96	106	405	4,228	510	3,454	264	6
Newbern	3,312	11	0	1	1	9	58	12	42	4	0
New Johnsonville	1,900	4	0	0	0	4	31	9	16	6	0
New Market	1,372	1	0	0	1	0	8	0	7	1	0
Newport	6,786	66	0	6	1	59	593	52	480	61	1
New Tazewell	2,702	7	0	0	0	7	76	6	64	6	0
Niota	727	2	0	0	0	2	15	3	8	4	0
Nolensville	9,488	16	0	1	3	12	94	23	61	10	2
Norris	1,609	6	0	0	0	6	16	3	11	2	0
Oakland	8,323	1	0	0	0	1	65	4	60	1	0
Oak Ridge	29,084	112	0	22	9	81	671	97	523	51	6
Obion	1,042	0	0	0	0	0	5	1	4	0	0
Oliver Springs	3,419	2	0	0	0	2	59	13	32	14	2
Oneida	3,704	10	0	1	0	9	116	28	85	3	0
Paris	10,047	31	1	1	4	25	271	61	199	11	0
Parsons	2,304	5	0	0	0	5	28	1	16	11	0
Petersburg	564	0	0	0	0	0	2	0	2	0	0
Pigeon Forge	6,383	47	1	12	4	30	334	54	241	39	0
Pikeville	1,626	6	0	0	0	6	17	6	5	6	0
Piperton	1,887	0	0	0	0	0	11	4	7	0	0
Pittman Center	581	0	0	0	0	0	1	0	1	0	0
Plainview	2,126	2	0	0	0	2	16	7	8	1	0
Pleasant View	4,686	0	0	0	0	0	53	10	40	3	0
Portland	12,995	41	0	4	7	30	235	41	166	28	3
Pulaski	7,628	54	0	10	5	39	349	32	301	16	1
Puryear	666	2	0	0	0	2	10	4	5	1	0
Red Bank	11,779	49	0	10	3	36	262	52	180	30	0
Red Boiling Springs	1,140	8	0	0	0	8	30	6	22	2	0
Ridgely	1,641	15	0	1	1	13	19	1	17	1	0
Ridgetop	2,079	1	0	1	0	0	2	0	2	0	0
Ripley	7,818	120	1	1	9	109	287	70	205	12	1
Rockwood	5,439	31	1	0	2	28	298	23	246	29	1
Rocky Top	1,766	16	1	0	1	14	113	8	85	20	1
Rogersville	4,277	13	0	1	2	10	208	18	170	20	1
Rossville	950	0	0	0	0	0	4	1	3	0	0

Table 8. Offenses Known to Law Enforcement, by Selected State and City, 2019—Continued

(Number.)

State/city	Population	Violent crime	Murder and nonnegligent manslaughter	Rape[1]	Robbery	Aggravated assault	Property crime	Burglary	Larceny-theft	Motor vehicle theft	Arson[2]
Rutherford	1,066	1	0	0	0	1	6	2	4	0	0
Rutledge	1,352	0	0	0	0	0	25	6	18	1	0
Saltillo	528	0	0	0	0	0	12	4	8	0	0
Savannah	6,941	69	1	6	6	56	412	76	300	36	3
Scotts Hill	977	1	0	0	0	1	10	5	3	2	0
Selmer	4,401	19	1	2	0	16	118	12	93	13	0
Sevierville	16,760	108	1	6	8	93	830	78	677	75	1
Sharon	911	4	0	0	1	3	17	5	7	5	1
Shelbyville	22,062	183	0	15	15	153	667	103	514	50	2
Signal Mountain	8,605	4	0	2	0	2	39	7	29	3	0
Smithville	4,828	21	0	1	2	18	118	19	89	10	0
Smyrna	52,225	204	0	11	29	164	1,464	163	1,193	108	6
Soddy-Daisy	13,818	33	0	1	2	30	339	55	256	28	2
Somerville	3,213	14	1	1	1	11	52	7	40	5	2
South Carthage	1,386	20	1	0	0	19	13	6	5	2	0
South Fulton	2,214	13	0	0	0	13	41	5	30	6	0
South Pittsburg	3,008	8	0	0	0	8	20	3	14	3	0
Sparta	4,957	6	0	1	0	5	207	24	158	25	0
Spencer	1,646	2	0	0	0	2	10	0	8	2	0
Spring City	1,865	5	0	2	0	3	24	0	21	3	0
Springfield	17,022	115	1	7	5	102	392	41	318	33	2
Spring Hill	43,303	53	0	7	4	42	381	45	320	16	1
St. Joseph	814	1	0	0	0	1	8	1	5	2	0
Surgoinsville	1,772	1	0	0	0	1	8	1	5	2	0
Sweetwater	5,875	29	0	0	1	28	295	46	219	30	1
Tazewell	2,273	6	0	0	0	6	64	11	36	17	0
Tellico Plains	921	6	0	0	0	6	22	5	14	3	1
Tiptonville	4,286	15	0	0	4	11	29	9	18	2	1
Toone	334	1	0	0	0	1	3	2	1	0	0
Townsend	446	0	0	0	0	0	12	1	11	0	0
Tracy City	1,389	8	0	1	0	7	36	4	24	8	0
Trenton	4,022	33	0	1	3	29	178	17	151	10	1
Trezevant	842	2	0	0	0	2	2	0	1	1	0
Trimble	613	2	0	0	1	1	0	0	0	0	0
Troy	1,317	5	0	0	0	5	13	1	9	3	0
Tullahoma	19,468	143	0	14	12	117	638	83	510	45	4
Tusculum	2,805	0	0	0	0	0	4	1	3	0	0
Union City	10,340	83	1	8	6	68	522	77	419	26	5
Vonore	1,539	8	0	1	0	7	71	8	58	5	0
Wartburg	896	1	0	1	0	0	9	0	7	2	0
Wartrace	692	2	0	0	0	2	1	0	1	0	0
Watertown	1,519	1	0	0	0	1	13	6	6	1	0
Waverly	4,081	4	0	0	0	4	60	9	50	1	1
Waynesboro	2,307	12	0	0	0	12	18	10	4	4	0
Westmoreland	2,431	6	0	0	0	6	6	0	4	2	0
White Bluff	3,659	7	0	1	0	6	40	7	29	4	0
White House	12,822	19	0	1	2	16	161	9	144	8	0
White Pine	2,356	2	0	0	0	2	72	5	63	4	0
Whiteville	4,466	4	0	0	1	3	23	14	9	0	0
Whitwell	1,723	3	0	1	0	2	21	2	11	8	1
Winchester	8,733	42	1	2	2	37	293	26	253	14	0
Woodbury	2,878	15	0	0	0	15	29	5	22	2	0
TEXAS											
Abernathy[5]	2,713	2	0	0	0	2	20	5	12	3	0
Abilene	123,665	458	6	87	68	297	3,112	576	2,330	206	7
Addison[5]	16,339	80	1	10	18	51	702	89	499	114	1
Alamo	19,903	91	1	11	10	69	979	108	842	29	2
Alamo Heights[5]	8,808	7	0	1	2	4	157	19	134	4	0
Alba	539	0	0	0	0	0	7	1	5	1	0
Alice	18,858	103	0	7	7	89	830	149	653	28	8
Allen	105,961	88	0	19	15	54	1,154	95	997	62	0
Alpine	6,021	12	1	1	0	10	36	21	11	4	1
Alvarado	4,468	17	0	5	4	8	71	19	43	9	0
Alvin[5]	27,159	65	1	25	12	27	666	80	513	73	7
Amarillo	201,036	1,447	15	161	246	1,025	7,835	1,439	5,425	971	39
Andrews[5]	14,133	59	0	10	1	48	219	47	151	21	1
Angleton	19,660	50	0	15	8	27	278	39	218	21	1
Anna	15,253	18	1	3	2	12	135	16	110	9	0
Anthony	5,738	16	0	0	3	13	98	11	75	12	0
Archer City	1,732	6	0	3	0	3	2	2	0	0	0
Arcola	2,627	1	0	0	1	0	53	12	28	13	0
Arlington	402,304	2,055	16	241	402	1,396	11,291	1,305	8,738	1,248	14
Athens	12,807	47	0	10	8	29	283	75	170	38	0
Atlanta	5,497	45	0	14	4	27	158	26	130	2	0
Atlanta	3,786	7	0	0	1	6	12	5	7	0	0
Aubrey	986,062	3,953	32	534	971	2,416	36,588	4,344	29,216	3,028	103
Austin[5]	13,691	14	0	0	4	10	236	41	177	18	5
Azle	1,508	2	0	0	0	2	17	10	5	2	1
Baird	25,511	165	2	14	33	116	905	100	581	224	2
Balch Springs	3,366	38	1	0	8	29	304	23	244	37	0
Balcones Heights	3,615	2	0	0	0	2	30	12	17	1	0
Ballinger[5]	1,540	1	0	1	0	0	4	1	2	1	0
Bangs											

Table 8. Offenses Known to Law Enforcement, by Selected State and City, 2019—Continued

(Number.)

State/city	Population	Violent crime	Murder and nonnegligent manslaughter	Rape[1]	Robbery	Aggravated assault	Property crime	Burglary	Larceny-theft	Motor vehicle theft	Arson[2]
Bartonville[5]	1,752	2	0	0	1	1	8	1	6	1	0
Baytown	77,707	325	3	49	91	182	2,838	447	2,005	386	5
Beaumont	118,562	1,241	19	97	323	802	4,287	950	2,999	338	28
Bedford	49,771	145	1	34	30	80	1,010	94	823	93	2
Bee Cave	7,217	5	0	1	1	3	155	15	126	14	0
Beeville	12,866	28	2	0	5	21	347	98	239	10	3
Bellaire	19,233	21	1	5	11	4	341	56	266	19	1
Bellmead	10,817	99	0	13	13	73	640	68	514	58	3
Bellville	4,288	12	0	3	1	8	40	2	38	0	0
Belton	22,741	44	0	20	9	15	431	57	365	9	5
Benbrook	23,872	38	0	5	10	23	368	44	290	34	2
Beverly Hills	1,989	5	0	0	2	3	60	14	39	7	0
Big Sandy	1,385	1	0	0	0	1	3	1	0	2	0
Big Spring	28,278	152	3	11	21	117	1,049	173	731	145	7
Bishop	3,069	2	0	0	0	2	50	12	32	6	0
Blanco	2,040	3	0	0	1	2	13	4	4	5	0
Blue Mound[5]	2,485	5	0	0	0	5	29	9	13	7	1
Boerne	18,135	23	0	5	2	16	340	22	283	35	0
Bogata	1,060	3	0	1	0	2	24	9	15	0	1
Bonham	10,404	20	1	9	1	9	168	22	136	10	0
Bowie	5,040	28	0	0	3	25	142	70	71	1	1
Boyd	1,510	1	0	0	1	0	4	2	2	0	0
Brady[5]	5,288	9	0	1	0	8	44	20	21	3	2
Brazoria[5]	3,123	10	0	2	1	7	77	6	59	12	0
Breckenridge	5,453	14	0	0	1	13	101	20	72	9	1
Brenham	17,375	93	0	15	6	72	361	63	276	22	1
Bridgeport	6,670	22	0	1	0	21	84	24	50	10	1
Brookshire[5]	5,592	22	0	4	4	14	82	12	60	10	1
Brownfield	9,270	25	0	6	0	19	121	26	80	15	2
Brownsboro	1,283	1	0	1	0	0	1	0	1	0	0
Brownsville	184,418	776	0	82	143	551	4,553	631	3,801	121	27
Brownwood	18,646	61	0	19	6	36	649	121	486	42	1
Bryan	86,632	370	2	90	57	221	1,928	336	1,444	148	9
Buda	18,146	20	0	3	3	14	271	28	223	20	1
Bullard	3,722	7	0	0	1	6	22	12	9	1	0
Bulverde	5,311	3	0	0	0	3	81	8	66	7	1
Burkburnett	11,305	24	0	7	5	12	215	50	150	15	0
Burleson[5]	48,743	113	1	17	19	76	726	67	580	79	0
Burnet	6,452	20	0	5	3	12	70	28	37	5	0
Cactus	3,194	16	0	5	1	10	40	14	21	5	0
Caldwell	4,433	3	0	0	0	3	13	2	11	0	0
Calvert	1,143	6	0	0	0	6	10	3	5	2	0
Cameron	5,530	10	0	1	0	9	64	23	34	7	1
Canton	3,909	0	0	0	0	0	128	0	126	2	0
Canyon	16,312	14	0	3	3	8	153	35	113	5	0
Carthage	6,491	39	1	1	2	35	187	21	152	14	1
Castle Hills	4,515	17	1	2	1	13	290	39	227	24	1
Castroville	3,144	8	0	0	2	6	60	20	36	4	0
Cedar Hill[5]	48,866	99	4	12	24	59	1,252	76	1,097	79	2
Cedar Park[5]	80,170	57	2	24	8	23	674	65	558	51	4
Celina	13,977	12	0	3	0	9	93	17	69	7	0
Center	5,271	30	0	8	1	21	181	45	132	4	1
Chandler[5]	3,142	0	0	0	0	0	12	2	8	2	0
Childress[5]	6,034	4	0	1	0	3	34	13	18	3	0
Cibolo[5]	32,112	39	0	10	1	28	280	36	232	12	0
Cisco	3,735	12	0	1	0	11	42	16	25	1	0
Cleburne	30,860	101	0	25	8	68	588	147	396	45	0
Cleveland	8,284	49	1	0	7	41	484	54	393	37	1
Clifton[5]	3,454	1	0	0	0	1	24	4	18	2	0
Clute[5]	11,740	46	0	13	7	26	264	68	166	30	0
Clyde	3,868	1	0	0	0	1	66	36	28	2	0
Coleman	4,341	24	1	3	0	20	33	17	15	1	0
College Station[5]	119,246	225	1	48	43	133	2,098	391	1,529	178	0
Colleyville[5]	27,499	5	0	0	0	5	169	22	137	10	0
Collinsville	1,951	0	0	0	0	0	3	1	1	1	0
Colorado City	3,831	13	0	0	2	11	130	40	81	9	0
Comanche[5]	4,151	13	2	1	1	9	101	16	80	5	0
Converse	28,598	152	0	6	10	136	460	54	360	46	1
Coppell[5]	42,181	25	1	9	5	10	525	52	457	16	0
Copperas Cove	32,693	129	0	9	6	114	691	112	557	22	5
Corinth[5]	22,090	16	0	3	2	11	168	33	125	10	1
Corpus Christi[5]	329,320	2,616	31	266	496	1,823	11,347	1,961	8,494	892	73
Corrigan	1,605	12	0	2	0	10	30	5	17	8	0
Corsicana[5]	23,823	176	1	51	16	108	744	116	575	53	2
Crandall[5]	3,861	16	0	6	3	7	78	18	54	6	0
Crane	3,725	6	0	3	0	3	13	4	5	4	0
Crockett	6,484	34	1	1	0	32	129	23	101	5	0
Crowley[5]	16,027	38	0	5	6	27	418	36	369	13	0
Crystal City	7,283	9	0	0	0	9	41	22	19	0	0
Cuero	8,259	49	0	4	0	45	184	28	148	8	6
Cumby	796	0	0	0	0	0	0	0	0	0	0
Daingerfield[5]	2,360	14	0	0	2	12	52	7	38	7	0
Dalhart[5]	8,338	35	0	5	0	30	186	58	108	20	1

Table 8. Offenses Known to Law Enforcement, by Selected State and City, 2019—Continued

(Number.)

State/city	Population	Violent crime	Murder and nonnegligent manslaughter	Rape[1]	Robbery	Aggravated assault	Property crime	Burglary	Larceny-theft	Motor vehicle theft	Arson[2]
Dallas	1,363,295	11,764	198	797	4,400	6,369	45,279	9,210	25,812	10,257	144
Dalworthington Gardens[5]	2,403	2	0	0	0	2	22	6	12	4	0
Dawson[5]	796	0	0	0	0	0	13	5	8	0	1
Dayton	8,464	14	0	1	3	10	228	47	151	30	0
Decatur	7,116	8	1	0	2	5	247	6	230	11	0
Deer Park[5]	34,167	48	4	22	5	17	551	52	462	37	1
De Kalb	1,615	5	0	1	0	4	26	12	13	1	0
De Leon	2,162	2	0	1	0	1	42	16	22	4	1
Del Rio	35,947	38	2	10	9	17	610	112	456	42	2
Denison[5]	25,432	106	1	22	5	78	464	103	304	57	1
Denton	141,492	331	3	125	66	137	2,665	316	2,148	201	1
Denver City	4,933	1	0	1	0	0	63	24	34	5	0
DeSoto[5]	54,026	176	3	18	58	97	1,188	172	846	170	2
Devine	4,931	5	0	0	0	5	57	10	40	7	1
Dickinson[5]	21,101	66	0	25	15	26	374	72	234	68	0
Dilley	4,475	10	0	0	0	10	48	25	20	3	1
Dimmitt[5]	4,146	23	0	4	0	19	25	11	12	2	0
Donna	16,715	139	0	19	19	101	787	85	668	34	6
Double Oak	3,073	0	0	0	0	0	2	0	1	1	0
Dumas	14,290	25	1	6	1	17	252	35	180	37	1
Duncanville[5]	39,430	174	1	12	80	81	1,096	148	770	178	0
Eagle Lake	3,719	6	0	0	0	6	51	17	30	4	1
Eagle Pass	29,847	37	1	0	5	31	687	154	485	48	0
Early[5]	3,105	27	0	1	0	26	51	8	41	2	0
Eastland	3,913	8	1	5	1	1	84	34	47	3	0
Edinburg	100,896	281	6	53	40	182	2,959	335	2,577	47	14
Edna	5,924	7	1	1	2	3	64	10	51	3	1
El Campo	11,615	41	0	3	8	30	347	64	266	17	0
Electra	2,696	6	0	0	1	5	48	17	26	5	0
Elgin	10,475	8	0	2	3	3	97	25	68	4	2
El Paso[5]	686,793	2,422	40	310	338	1,734	10,378	1,048	8,479	851	29
Elsa	7,226	20	0	2	3	15	252	21	231	0	0
Ennis	20,096	17	0	3	4	10	333	43	266	24	1
Euless	58,136	107	1	12	45	49	1,186	126	924	136	3
Fairfield	2,936	6	1	0	0	5	41	6	31	4	7
Fair Oaks Ranch[5]	10,151	6	0	3	0	3	28	4	20	4	0
Fairview	9,350	12	0	0	2	10	42	9	28	5	0
Falfurrias	4,819	15	0	0	1	14	111	48	62	1	0
Farmers Branch[5]	41,932	63	1	10	26	26	940	141	626	173	1
Farmersville[5]	3,494	7	0	2	0	5	42	4	34	4	0
Farwell	1,314	2	0	0	0	2	8	2	5	1	0
Fate	15,378	6	0	2	0	4	73	16	54	3	1
Ferris	2,876	6	0	0	1	5	66	16	36	14	0
Flatonia	1,471	1	0	0	0	1	18	7	9	2	0
Floresville	7,970	19	0	0	1	18	147	47	89	11	2
Flower Mound	79,052	43	0	13	5	25	730	83	624	23	2
Floydada[5]	2,711	17	0	2	0	15	31	10	18	3	0
Forest Hill	13,034	36	4	1	18	13	413	73	278	62	0
Forney	25,374	32	0	8	4	20	302	38	227	37	0
Fort Stockton[5]	8,402	27	0	3	1	23	72	26	37	9	0
Fort Worth	915,237	4,068	69	470	972	2,557	24,605	3,969	17,301	3,335	85
Frankston	1,180	2	0	1	0	1	27	4	19	4	0
Fredericksburg	11,562	13	0	0	1	12	131	11	117	3	0
Freeport	12,213	45	0	4	5	36	257	52	205	0	2
Friendswood[5]	40,735	26	0	12	8	6	264	53	193	18	3
Friona	3,888	3	0	1	0	2	17	5	11	1	0
Frisco	199,445	160	1	46	30	83	2,390	249	2,037	104	9
Fulshear	13,967	0	0	0	0	0	87	4	76	7	0
Gainesville[5]	16,688	89	0	12	5	72	370	59	299	12	1
Galena Park	10,934	22	1	7	3	11	141	27	92	22	1
Galveston[5]	50,801	243	3	81	71	88	1,642	201	1,179	262	0
Ganado	2,063	3	0	2	0	1	18	8	7	3	0
Garden Ridge	4,124	0	0	0	0	0	36	9	23	4	0
Garland	244,277	738	11	139	250	338	6,311	1,003	4,337	971	9
Gatesville	12,311	23	0	13	0	10	202	62	135	5	2
Georgetown	78,332	81	0	25	8	48	730	103	586	41	1
Giddings[5]	5,124	26	0	7	2	17	103	0	97	6	0
Gilmer[5]	5,164	32	0	4	2	26	147	15	120	12	2
Gladewater	6,349	14	0	2	2	10	180	41	127	12	1
Glenn Heights	13,520	45	0	2	10	33	249	54	179	16	0
Gonzales	7,655	81	1	11	1	68	168	25	130	13	0
Graham	8,670	10	1	3	1	5	69	9	55	5	2
Granbury[5]	10,752	26	1	4	6	15	444	34	390	20	0
Grand Prairie	196,971	428	5	45	135	243	4,140	504	3,133	503	11
Grand Saline	3,171	4	0	1	0	3	34	13	18	3	0
Granite Shoals	5,137	7	0	1	1	5	35	5	23	7	6
Greenville[5]	28,613	77	2	8	22	45	635	102	484	49	0
Gregory	1,917	3	1	2	0	0	18	3	8	7	0
Groesbeck	4,302	5	0	0	0	5	55	6	46	3	1
Groves	15,601	85	0	8	9	68	304	58	215	31	0
Gun Barrel City	6,273	10	0	2	1	7	110	35	59	16	0
Gunter	1,614	2	0	0	0	2	10	3	7	0	1
Hallettsville	2,634	13	0	1	0	12	39	5	32	2	1

Table 8. Offenses Known to Law Enforcement, by Selected State and City, 2019—Continued

(Number.)

State/city	Population	Violent crime	Murder and nonnegligent manslaughter	Rape[1]	Robbery	Aggravated assault	Property crime	Burglary	Larceny-theft	Motor vehicle theft	Arson[2]
Haltom City	44,582	126	2	46	21	57	1,171	210	792	169	3
Hamilton	3,008	10	0	3	0	7	35	12	22	1	0
Hamlin	1,982	2	0	0	0	2	9	2	6	1	0
Harker Heights[5]	32,527	65	0	14	17	34	529	68	419	42	4
Harlingen	65,481	273	0	54	54	165	3,152	443	2,613	96	10
Haskell[5]	3,234	8	0	1	0	7	34	10	15	9	0
Hawkins	1,331	4	0	0	0	4	3	0	2	1	0
Hearne	4,510	16	0	0	4	12	171	55	97	19	1
Heath	9,179	12	0	5	1	6	46	9	34	3	0
Hedwig Village	2,684	6	0	0	6	0	205	6	193	6	0
Helotes[5]	9,881	2	0	1	0	1	81	13	63	5	1
Henderson	13,226	74	4	8	3	59	512	60	428	24	1
Hereford	14,733	81	0	1	5	75	310	67	217	26	2
Hewitt	15,019	13	1	3	2	7	139	20	107	12	0
Hickory Creek	4,933	5	0	4	0	1	57	5	48	4	0
Hidalgo	14,281	50	0	8	0	42	125	14	103	8	0
Highland Park	9,251	9	0	3	1	5	192	35	143	14	1
Highland Village	16,721	8	0	5	0	3	108	9	96	3	0
Hill Country Village[5]	1,109	3	0	0	0	3	22	3	18	1	0
Hillsboro	8,476	17	0	0	3	14	262	15	232	15	0
Hollywood Park	3,406	4	0	1	3	0	31	3	23	5	0
Hondo	9,459	36	0	8	2	26	173	23	137	13	1
Honey Grove[5]	1,718	2	0	1	1	0	23	10	11	2	0
Hooks	2,743	2	0	0	0	2	18	4	10	4	0
Horizon City	20,131	7	0	0	1	6	101	12	85	4	1
Horseshoe Bay	4,030	7	0	2	0	5	28	10	17	1	0
Houston	2,355,606	25,257	275	1,249	9,147	14,586	101,750	17,038	71,614	13,098	485
Howe	3,432	3	1	0	0	2	20	5	13	2	0
Hudson	4,909	6	0	0	0	6	66	30	31	5	0
Hudson Oaks	2,515	6	0	0	3	3	66	5	56	5	0
Humble	16,157	189	1	34	58	96	1,681	110	1,394	177	1
Huntington	2,107	3	0	0	0	3	26	13	11	2	0
Hurst[5]	39,196	82	1	17	30	34	1,402	93	1,220	89	2
Hutchins	5,776	23	1	0	10	12	212	49	122	41	1
Idalou[5]	2,289	10	0	6	0	4	9	1	6	2	0
Ingleside	10,366	23	0	11	0	12	174	41	115	18	0
Ingram	1,888	1	0	0	0	1	28	10	16	2	0
Iowa Park	6,369	3	0	1	0	2	48	8	36	4	0
Irving	245,423	617	5	56	294	262	5,982	719	4,552	711	16
Jacinto City	10,632	13	0	0	5	8	228	20	176	32	0
Jacksboro	4,353	6	0	2	0	4	34	10	21	3	0
Jarrell	1,800	1	0	1	0	0	12	4	6	2	0
Jasper	7,647	28	1	0	0	27	363	80	259	24	1
Jefferson	1,945	6	0	0	1	5	12	10	1	1	0
Jersey Village[5]	8,006	18	0	0	8	10	185	58	97	30	1
Jones Creek	2,110	2	0	0	1	1	13	2	11	0	0
Jonestown	2,118	9	0	3	2	4	37	6	29	2	0
Joshua[5]	8,115	6	0	0	1	5	54	12	36	6	0
Jourdanton	4,537	1	0	0	0	1	10	2	7	1	0
Karnes City	3,439	9	0	0	0	9	47	17	29	1	0
Katy	19,966	60	0	20	19	21	793	61	693	39	0
Kaufman	7,580	17	0	4	2	11	149	19	115	15	0
Keene	6,584	10	0	1	2	7	46	19	23	4	0
Keller	48,387	25	0	4	3	18	349	33	302	14	0
Kenedy[5]	3,465	43	0	2	2	39	140	37	87	16	1
Kennedale[5]	8,792	19	0	5	3	11	133	27	97	9	1
Kerens[5]	1,532	9	0	0	0	9	13	7	5	1	1
Kermit	6,321	22	1	0	1	20	135	58	61	16	2
Kerrville[5]	23,902	50	1	8	1	40	301	19	264	18	2
Kilgore	15,047	46	2	6	7	31	316	59	231	26	0
Killeen	151,832	583	14	105	124	340	3,432	818	2,296	318	29
Kingsville	25,401	130	1	26	14	89	753	183	553	17	2
Kirby	8,841	22	0	2	4	16	158	53	76	29	1
Knox City	1,110	2	0	1	0	1	26	14	11	1	0
Kountze	2,094	6	0	0	0	6	28	10	16	2	0
Kyle	49,855	68	1	12	14	41	659	61	537	61	1
Lacy-Lakeview	6,720	17	0	9	2	6	194	36	145	13	1
La Feria	7,341	19	0	1	1	17	135	30	104	1	1
Lago Vista	7,255	18	0	10	0	8	56	19	36	1	0
La Grange	4,630	19	0	9	0	10	85	10	70	5	2
La Grulla	1,709	6	0	0	0	6	3	2	1	0	1
Laguna Vista	3,163	5	0	2	2	1	27	8	17	2	0
Lake Dallas[5]	8,052	22	1	3	2	16	117	20	84	13	1
Lake Jackson	27,624	57	2	10	12	33	703	84	597	22	2
Lakeside	1,614	3	0	0	0	3	26	5	16	5	0
Lakeview, Harrison County[5]	6,361	5	0	1	0	4	48	5	39	4	0
Lakeway	16,248	9	0	1	3	5	146	21	120	5	0
Lake Worth	4,993	6	0	1	2	3	337	53	272	12	0
La Marque	17,088	71	2	10	17	42	776	103	617	56	0
Lamesa	8,997	74	2	7	12	53	398	109	271	18	1
Lampasas	8,067	15	0	3	1	11	206	20	180	6	1
Lancaster	39,795	147	0	8	53	86	1,014	155	680	179	2
La Porte[5]	35,622	83	1	15	15	52	520	73	392	55	0

Table 8. Offenses Known to Law Enforcement, by Selected State and City, 2019—Continued

(Number.)

State/city	Population	Violent crime	Murder and nonnegligent manslaughter	Rape[1]	Robbery	Aggravated assault	Property crime	Burglary	Larceny-theft	Motor vehicle theft	Arson[2]
Laredo[5]	264,916	836	4	104	164	564	4,692	708	3,726	258	39
La Vernia	1,472	1	0	0	0	1	11	4	6	1	0
Lavon	3,755	4	0	0	1	3	22	1	21	0	0
League City[5]	109,401	121	3	56	14	48	1,487	192	1,209	86	4
Leander[5]	61,314	67	0	32	7	28	520	48	439	33	4
Leon Valley	11,644	14	1	0	4	9	539	51	436	52	0
Levelland	13,530	140	2	22	8	108	405	113	269	23	0
Lewisville	108,000	239	2	54	67	116	2,125	266	1,623	236	14
Liberty	9,471	26	0	5	2	19	216	29	181	6	1
Liberty Hill	2,757	2	0	1	0	1	17	7	8	2	0
Linden	1,926	3	0	0	1	2	32	8	22	2	0
Littlefield	5,911	30	0	5	3	22	126	30	86	10	0
Live Oak	16,280	33	0	2	9	22	645	41	570	34	2
Livingston	5,112	16	1	6	2	7	297	13	254	30	3
Lockhart	14,079	2	0	1	1	0	154	29	116	9	2
Longview	81,783	374	4	62	63	245	2,410	411	1,809	190	4
Lorena	1,776	11	0	2	0	9	32	1	28	3	0
Los Fresnos	7,992	53	0	1	1	51	124	12	108	4	0
Lubbock	259,208	2,613	10	268	468	1,867	11,940	2,391	8,324	1,225	85
Lufkin[5]	35,555	184	1	28	35	120	1,558	261	1,181	116	3
Luling	6,027	25	0	7	0	18	107	12	90	5	0
Lumberton	13,084	22	1	2	1	18	151	18	122	11	0
Lyford	2,545	4	0	3	0	1	22	6	14	2	0
Lytle	3,073	1	0	0	1	0	93	11	69	13	1
Madisonville	4,776	20	0	1	3	16	28	6	17	5	0
Manor	12,379	48	0	11	3	34	249	28	203	18	6
Mansfield[5]	72,979	65	1	24	13	27	766	87	633	46	1
Manvel	12,721	10	0	0	1	9	104	37	56	11	2
Marble Falls	7,047	23	0	5	1	17	251	52	191	8	1
Marfa	1,682	5	0	1	0	4					
Marshall[4]	23,036	121	3	3	16	99			207	45	3
Mathis	4,768	21	1	2	3	15	112	31	72	9	3
McAllen	144,915	140	1	33	39	67	3,595	152	3,415	28	3
McGregor	5,235	21	0	5	2	14	34	11	22	1	0
McKinney	200,615	287	2	61	42	182	1,993	255	1,572	166	8
Meadows Place	4,616	5	0	0	1	4	148	14	121	13	0
Melissa	11,195	7	0	2	0	5	76	10	65	1	0
Memorial Villages	12,472	8	0	0	1	7	75	18	56	1	0
Mercedes	16,882	67	0	7	8	52	667	83	559	25	0
Merkel	2,623	17	0	8	2	7	17	7	7	3	1
Mesquite	143,078	685	6	45	244	390	5,197	661	3,660	876	7
Mineola	4,804	5	0	0	0	5	87	8	70	9	0
Mineral Wells	14,872	22	1	3	3	15	457	153	274	30	3
Mission	85,705	105	1	37	23	44	1,618	161	1,387	70	3
Missouri City[5]	75,747	107	1	13	26	67	811	109	645	57	4
Monahans	7,770	36	1	5	1	29	135	18	106	11	0
Mont Belvieu	6,647	11	0	1	1	9	168	16	121	31	0
Morgans Point Resort	4,637	5	0	3	1	1	10	3	5	2	0
Mount Pleasant[5]	16,307	90	2	26	11	51	465	72	369	24	2
Muleshoe	5,029	3	0	0	0	3	20	5	14	1	0
Murphy	20,962	9	0	2	2	5	105	9	92	4	0
Mustang Ridge[5]	1,001	11	0	2	0	9	35	3	23	9	0
Nacogdoches	33,613	111	2	12	27	70	864	159	647	58	2
Naples[5]	1,302	1	0	0	0	1	8	4	4	0	0
Nash	3,783	41	0	2	1	37	58	15	43	0	0
Natalia	1,602	4	0	1	0	3	16	3	10	3	0
Navasota	7,795	37	0	8	3	26	212	82	100	30	0
Nederland	17,557	62	1	13	6	42	332	52	243	37	0
Needville	3,094	1	0	0	1	0	2	0	2	0	0
New Boston	4,663	72	0	0	0	72	211	37	172	2	0
New Braunfels	88,706	219	2	21	25	171	1,120	209	805	106	3
Newton[5]	2,346	6	0	3	0	3	38	15	21	2	2
Nixon	2,482	6	0	0	0	6	11	5	3	3	0
Nocona	2,975	2	0	0	0	2	20	10	10	0	0
Nolanville	5,879	5	0	0	2	3	66	11	50	5	0
Northeast[5]	3,404	1	0	1	0	0	49	6	39	4	2
Northlake	3,341	5	0	2	0	3	58	8	43	7	1
North Richland Hills	71,816	143	1	39	24	79	1,279	153	990	136	0
Oak Ridge North	3,174	3	0	0	1	2	37	2	33	2	0
Odessa	123,468	1,282	13	141	128	1,000	3,624	469	2,656	499	17
Olmos Park[5]	2,478	1	0	0	0	1	31	8	23	0	0
Olney	3,091	14	0	1	1	12	48	25	19	4	4
Olton	2,090	4	0	2	0	2	35	18	16	1	0
Onalaska	2,852	9	0	1	0	8	61	27	20	14	0
Orange	18,468	86	1	7	18	60	335	93	205	37	1
Ore City[5]	1,230	5	0	0	0	5	25	17	7	1	0
Overton[5]	2,510	1	0	0	0	1	18	7	10	1	0
Ovilla	4,232	1	0	0	0	1	12	2	10	0	0
Oyster Creek[5]	1,170	15	0	0	0	15	29	7	19	3	0
Palacios	4,561	15	0	2	0	13	95	14	81	0	0
Palestine	18,062	99	0	19	10	70	449	95	322	32	0
Palmer	2,079	0	0	0	0	0	33	4	29	0	0
Palm Valley	1,249	0	0	0	0	0	4	0	4	0	0

Table 8. Offenses Known to Law Enforcement, by Selected State and City, 2019—Continued

(Number.)

State/city	Population	Violent crime	Murder and nonnegligent manslaughter	Rape[1]	Robbery	Aggravated assault	Property crime	Burglary	Larceny-theft	Motor vehicle theft	Arson[2]
Pampa	17,150	127	0	17	6	104	654	143	483	28	0
Panhandle	2,322	7	0	0	0	7	25	12	8	5	0
Pantego	2,556	11	1	0	4	6	134	7	96	31	0
Paris	24,787	252	0	29	19	204	714	178	476	60	0
Parker	4,951	0	0	0	0	0	30	3	27	0	0
Pasadena[5]	153,689	839	8	82	182	567	3,861	530	2,789	542	7
Patton Village	2,095	5	0	1	0	4	21	2	13	6	0
Pearland	126,206	113	3	24	46	40	2,071	247	1,719	105	1
Pearsall	10,604	6	0	0	1	5	133	51	69	13	0
Pecos[5]	10,451	93	3	3	3	84	186	42	120	24	5
Pelican Bay[5]	1,818	0	0	0	0	0	36	14	22	0	1
Penitas[5]	4,915	7	0	1	0	6	95	27	63	5	2
Perryton	8,577	11	0	2	0	9	104	24	74	6	0
Petersburg	1,133	3	0	0	0	3	4	2	0	2	0
Pflugerville	66,729	64	1	0	19	44	829	74	664	91	1
Pharr	80,896	235	0	50	28	157	1,423	235	1,135	53	3
Pittsburg	4,720	20	0	4	1	15	64	7	53	4	1
Plano	291,611	431	3	90	144	194	4,908	630	3,831	447	14
Pleasanton[5]	10,911	36	0	8	8	20	289	30	239	20	0
Ponder	2,542	2	0	1	0	1	16	7	9	0	0
Port Aransas	4,260	7	0	0	0	7	205	14	164	27	0
Port Arthur[5]	55,084	344	9	29	84	222	1,203	326	757	120	11
Port Isabel	5,058	8	1	0	0	7	148	26	122	0	0
Portland	17,604	20	0	1	5	14	318	33	269	16	1
Port Neches	12,808	37	0	6	1	30	198	35	146	17	0
Poteet	3,524	6	0	1	0	5	76	20	54	2	3
Prairie View	6,543	5	0	0	2	3	31	11	19	1	0
Premont	2,540	16	0	0	1	15	61	34	25	2	1
Primera	5,103	3	0	0	0	3	59	8	47	4	0
Prosper[5]	24,814	14	0	0	2	12	218	23	184	11	0
Queen City	1,450	14	1	2	0	11	26	10	15	1	0
Ralls	1,814	3	0	0	0	3	12	8	4	0	0
Rancho Viejo	2,480	1	0	0	0	1	7	2	5	0	0
Raymondville	10,894	126	0	7	4	115	243	108	130	5	3
Red Oak[5]	13,429	17	0	0	9	8	307	77	210	20	0
Refugio	2,757	3	0	0	0	3	21	5	13	3	0
Reno, Lamar County	3,333	8	0	0	1	7	49	5	42	2	0
Reno, Parker County	3,333	16	0	2	1	13	28	9	14	5	0
Richardson[5]	123,893	178	4	28	63	83	2,279	292	1,742	245	3
Richland Hills	8,060	39	1	7	13	18	286	32	213	41	0
Richmond	12,086	45	0	8	6	31	224	36	178	10	1
Richwood	4,007	3	0	3	0	0	69	13	49	7	2
Rio Grande City[5]	14,607	14	0	0	0	14	269	59	186	24	2
Rio Hondo[5]	2,806	7	1	0	0	6	17	8	9	0	0
Roanoke[5]	9,563	12	0	2	3	7	113	17	91	5	0
Rockdale	5,665	15	1	1	1	12	135	22	95	18	0
Rockport[5]	10,854	26	0	6	3	17	441	106	303	32	2
Rockwall	46,096	50	0	13	8	29	740	70	605	65	0
Roma	11,527	24	0	5	1	18	108	27	63	18	2
Roman Forest	2,031	3	0	0	0	3	9	0	8	1	0
Rosenberg	38,936	148	0	33	22	93	684	131	489	64	0
Round Rock	132,747	165	3	21	51	90	2,235	165	2,017	53	4
Royse City	13,539	22	2	7	1	12	168	15	134	19	0
Runaway Bay	1,579	0	0	0	0	0	3	1	2	0	0
Rusk	5,582	5	0	0	0	5	93	23	65	5	0
Sabinal	1,675	0	0	0	0	0	21	7	14	0	0
Sachse	26,926	13	0	3	1	9	185	24	146	15	0
Saginaw	24,382	45	0	29	9	7	409	47	313	49	0
Salado	2,375	2	0	0	0	2	32	20	9	3	0
San Angelo	101,072	357	5	56	32	264	3,173	512	2,437	224	7
San Antonio	1,559,166	11,046	105	1,630	1,965	7,346	67,422	8,172	51,469	7,781	181
San Augustine	1,850	0	0	0	0	0	0	0	0	0	0
San Benito	24,394	161	1	25	14	121	946	164	746	36	3
San Diego	4,226	7	0	0	0	7	0	0	0	0	0
San Elizario	9,129	9	0	1	0	8	34	4	26	4	0
San Juan	37,542	173	1	22	18	132	859	101	711	47	1
San Marcos	66,279	241	8	78	26	129	1,530	228	1,176	126	1
San Saba	3,152	8	0	1	0	7	57	24	29	4	0
Sansom Park Village	6,000	8	0	0	3	5	113	41	50	22	1
Santa Fe[5]	13,657	15	0	5	4	6	127	21	89	17	2
Santa Rosa	2,767	0	0	0	0	0	9	3	5	1	0
Schertz	42,337	78	0	22	9	47	559	67	458	34	1
Schulenburg	2,929	25	0	2	0	23	43	14	28	1	0
Seabrook[5]	14,611	20	0	10	2	8	198	32	146	20	0
Seagoville[5]	17,120	14	0	2	5	7	355	73	186	96	0
Seagraves	2,904	16	0	1	1	14	31	9	20	2	0
Sealy	6,593	11	0	0	2	9	121	36	73	12	0
Seguin	30,244	84	1	11	18	54	714	104	567	43	1
Selma	12,054	19	1	5	1	12	258	21	220	17	1
Seminole	7,784	11	0	2	0	9	83	18	58	7	0
Seven Points	1,534	8	0	1	0	7	47	11	29	7	0
Seymour	2,600	5	0	1	0	4	25	5	16	4	0
Shavano Park	4,052	2	0	0	0	2	20	4	16	0	0

Table 8. Offenses Known to Law Enforcement, by Selected State and City, 2019—Continued

(Number.)

State/city	Population	Violent crime	Murder and nonnegligent manslaughter	Rape[1]	Robbery	Aggravated assault	Property crime	Burglary	Larceny-theft	Motor vehicle theft	Arson[2]
Shenandoah	3,077	12	0	5	3	4	265	17	227	21	0
Sherman[5]	43,002	179	3	32	27	117	1,122	241	790	91	4
Shiner	2,181	2	0	1	0	1	3	1	2	0	0
Silsbee	6,650	14	1	0	1	12	69	7	47	15	1
Sinton[5]	5,373	46	0	10	2	34	190	40	136	14	0
Slaton	5,877	24	0	2	2	20	203	40	139	24	2
Smithville[5]	4,565	2	0	0	0	2	62	11	48	3	3
Snyder[5]	11,161	160	0	7	3	150	226	74	134	18	4
Socorro	34,841	43	0	5	4	34	299	38	232	29	1
Sonora[5]	2,736	3	0	1	0	2	14	3	7	4	0
Sour Lake[5]	1,887	9	0	2	0	7	25	6	14	5	0
South Houston	17,655	82	1	6	33	42	453	85	268	100	0
Southlake	33,049	10	0	0	5	5	387	30	337	20	0
South Padre Island	2,805	44	0	20	6	18	365	18	318	29	0
Southside Place	1,902	3	0	0	2	1	13	2	10	1	0
Spearman	3,275	3	0	0	0	3	8	3	3	2	0
Splendora	2,199	8	0	1	2	5	29	11	6	12	0
Springtown	3,102	3	0	0	0	3	63	8	55	0	0
Spring Valley	4,414	1	0	0	1	0	85	3	70	12	0
Stafford	18,380	109	1	24	31	53	592	60	490	42	0
Stamford	2,898	4	0	0	0	4	40	15	24	1	0
Stephenville	21,748	39	0	16	7	16	393	69	313	11	0
Stratford	2,103	0	0	0	0	0	5	1	4	0	0
Sullivan City[5]	4,152	44	0	4	0	40	59	10	47	2	0
Sulphur Springs[5]	16,220	33	0	6	7	20	169	20	118	31	0
Sunset Valley	683	5	0	0	2	3	135	4	126	5	0
Surfside Beach	594	1	0	1	0	0	24	3	19	2	0
Sweeny	3,745	8	0	1	3	4	68	12	55	1	0
Taft	2,904	9	0	3	1	5	34	10	22	2	0
Tahoka	2,624	1	0	0	0	1	16	6	5	5	0
Tatum[5]	1,394	2	0	0	0	2	40	19	17	4	0
Taylor	17,405	42	0	2	7	33	431	89	314	28	2
Teague	3,524	15	0	4	0	11	54	20	30	4	0
Temple	77,558	217	4	61	39	113	1,718	244	1,276	198	1
Tenaha	1,153	4	0	0	1	3	9	4	2	3	0
Terrell	18,395	44	2	4	8	30	631	103	465	63	0
Terrell Hills	5,496	2	0	1	1	0	83	52	28	3	0
Texarkana	37,401	157	3	33	43	78	1,710	280	1,347	83	19
Texas City[5]	49,659	199	5	29	52	113	1,400	184	1,090	126	3
The Colony	44,356	122	1	62	13	46	641	74	509	58	6
Thrall	968	3	0	1	0	2	10	4	6	0	0
Tioga	1,035	0	0	0	0	0	2	0	2	0	0
Tool	2,337	1	0	0	0	1	15	3	10	2	0
Trophy Club	13,031	1	0	0	1	0	64	12	49	3	1
Troup	2,059	8	0	1	0	7	41	9	26	6	0
Troy	2,044	4	0	0	0	4	30	4	23	3	0
Tulia	4,644	29	0	3	6	20	138	33	101	4	0
Tye	1,318	6	0	0	1	5	16	5	11	0	0
Tyler	106,851	401	0	72	58	271	3,206	439	2,597	170	0
Universal City[5]	21,062	74	0	9	22	43	577	116	416	45	4
University Park	25,434	6	0	1	3	2	189	18	135	36	0
Uvalde	16,233	53	1	10	4	38	611	69	528	14	0
Van	2,713	5	0	5	0	0	41	11	29	1	0
Van Alstyne	4,437	9	0	1	1	7	47	5	40	2	1
Venus[5]	3,986	6	0	3	0	3	20	2	17	1	1
Vernon[5]	10,312	48	0	9	4	35	191	44	137	10	1
Victoria	67,581	347	3	66	52	226	1,974	382	1,474	118	1
Vidor	10,499	20	0	1	5	14	222	74	132	16	0
Waco	139,870	799	10	88	133	568	4,599	784	3,492	323	9
Wake Village[5]	5,417	28	0	4	1	23	78	16	52	10	1
Waller	3,611	4	0	0	0	4	50	5	38	7	0
Wallis[5]	1,322	10	0	0	0	10	8	2	6	0	0
Watauga	24,685	39	2	4	8	25	383	29	320	34	0
Weatherford	32,656	50	1	22	4	23	482	53	383	46	0
Weimar	2,180	5	0	2	0	3	20	1	17	2	0
Weslaco	41,729	155	2	33	29	91	1,528	161	1,313	54	2
West Columbia	3,881	11	0	4	1	6	64	11	44	9	1
West Lake Hills	3,349	3	0	0	2	1	83	8	73	2	0
West Orange	3,299	13	0	3	0	10	133	7	121	5	0
Westover Hills	685	0	0	0	0	0	15	3	11	1	0
West University Place	15,818	6	0	1	4	1	124	49	68	7	0
Westworth[5]	2,720	10	0	2	2	6	207	13	188	6	2
Wharton	8,627	40	0	4	13	23	212	40	159	13	1
Whitehouse	8,945	12	0	1	2	9	72	11	59	2	0
White Oak[5]	6,345	4	0	0	1	3	95	16	70	9	0
Whitesboro	4,115	6	0	0	0	6	29	10	15	4	2
White Settlement	18,127	26	1	0	8	17	359	56	243	60	2
Whitney	2,188	8	0	0	0	8	55	9	40	6	2
Wichita Falls	104,551	364	4	103	85	172	3,183	557	2,394	232	2
Willis	6,587	27	0	6	5	16	156	28	116	12	0
Willow Park	5,808	5	0	0	2	3	43	8	33	2	0
Wills Point	3,684	8	0	0	1	7	52	20	24	8	1
Wilmer	4,916	8	0	0	5	3	111	15	84	12	1

Table 8. Offenses Known to Law Enforcement, by Selected State and City, 2019—Continued

(Number.)

State/city	Population	Violent crime	Murder and nonnegligent manslaughter	Rape[1]	Robbery	Aggravated assault	Property crime	Burglary	Larceny-theft	Motor vehicle theft	Arson[2]
Winnsboro	3,289	5	0	2	0	3	49	26	20	3	0
Winters	2,448	10	0	0	1	9	16	9	7	0	0
Wolfforth	5,445	3	0	0	1	2	53	8	39	6	0
Woodway	9,033	16	0	6	0	10	91	5	80	6	1
Wortham	1,000	7	0	1	0	6	22	11	9	2	0
Wylie	52,921	37	0	13	9	15	381	21	340	20	0
Yoakum[5]	5,962	20	0	3	3	14	101	69	32	0	1
UTAH											
Alta	383	0	0	0	0	0	18	0	17	1	0
American Fork/Cedar Hills[5]	43,610	18	0	2	4	12	817	51	736	30	2
Aurora	1,053	0	0	0	0	0	0	0	0	0	0
Big Water	506	3	0	0	0	3	0	0	0	0	0
Bluffdale	15,976	25	0	9	6	10	129	35	79	15	0
Bountiful	44,280	36	0	14	1	21	447	55	372	20	0
Brigham City[5]	19,592	41	0	18	1	22	338	63	247	28	1
Cedar City	33,614	93	0	22	2	69	632	78	510	44	0
Centerville	18,018	21	0	13	2	6	289	61	215	13	3
Clearfield	32,217	56	0	12	5	39	369	38	292	39	3
Clinton	22,544	17	0	1	1	15	300	15	266	19	0
Cottonwood Heights[5]	34,183	54	0	16	10	28	806	90	688	28	2
Draper	49,112	69	0	27	5	37	906	129	722	55	9
Enoch	7,199	20	0	1	0	19	30	7	18	5	0
Ephraim	7,449	21	0	18	0	3	46	4	41	1	0
Farmington	25,409	19	0	9	0	10	350	28	296	26	1
Grantsville	11,942	36	0	12	1	23	162	27	112	23	4
Harrisville	6,845	11	0	5	4	2	237	40	188	9	1
Heber	17,142	11	0	4	1	6	146	18	116	12	
Helper	2,077	5	0	2	0	3	49	13	34	2	0
Hurricane	18,850	36	0	12	1	23	267	40	209	18	0
Kanab	4,850	8	0	2	0	6	55	5	46	4	0
Kaysville	32,691	23	0	10	1	12	274	44	214	16	1
La Verkin	4,442	8	0	4	0	4	57	7	47	3	0
Layton	78,585	129	0	46	11	72	1,558	238	1,240	80	6
Logan	52,029	113	3	35	5	70	691	105	549	37	1
Mapleton	10,463	2	0	1	0	1	41	4	35	2	0
Moab	5,349	42	0	20	2	20	132	21	109	2	3
Monticello	1,998	7	0	1	0	6	14	1	10	3	0
Mount Pleasant	3,517	4	0	4	0	0	44	4	40	0	1
Murray	49,642	218	0	49	31	138	2,890	423	2,062	405	1
Naples	2,113	2	0	1	0	1	12	3	9	0	0
Nephi	6,207	5	0	3	0	2	74	12	57	5	0
North Ogden	20,352	17	0	6	0	11	203	44	142	17	0
North Park	16,411	10	1	7	0	2	207	11	184	12	
North Salt Lake	21,501	25	1	10	4	10	343	48	260	35	0
Ogden	87,875	384	6	84	63	231	3,211	484	2,382	345	22
Orem	98,686	89	2	37	11	39	1,970	156	1,673	141	5
Park City	8,620	54	0	3	2	49	276	15	252	9	0
Payson	19,981	20	0	6	3	11	323	31	272	20	
Pleasant Grove	39,066	39	0	10	1	28	365	50	291	24	0
Pleasant View	11,137	4	0	1	0	3	85	19	56	10	0
Provo	117,189	135	1	44	13	77	1,767	163	1,476	128	1
Richfield[5]	7,952	6	0	0	0	6	245	47	190	8	1
Riverdale	8,821	26	0	6	8	12	559	39	491	29	0
Roosevelt	7,189	30	0	24	0	6	213	23	169	21	2
Roy	39,001	55	0	20	8	27	466	62	345	59	1
Salem[5]	8,760	0	0	0	0	0	29	2	27	0	0
Salina[5]	2,573	4	0	0	0	4	78	14	58	6	1
Salt Lake City	202,426	1,442	13	234	403	792	11,452	1,290	8,902	1,260	30
Sandy	97,797	187	3	48	35	101	2,368	334	1,841	193	6
Santa Clara/Ivins	17,346	9	0	3	0	6	135	36	97	2	0
Santaquin/Genola	14,288	8	1	3	1	3	71	11	57	3	0
Saratoga Springs	33,647	53	0	21	4	28	259	96	152	11	0
South Jordan	77,645	73	2	16	9	46	1,124	167	879	78	1
South Ogden	17,215	25	0	14	1	10	263	30	200	33	0
South Salt Lake	25,599	205	1	24	49	131	1,865	255	1,260	350	4
Spanish Fork	40,604	7	0	2	1	4	332	38	278	16	0
Springdale	620	0	0	0	0	0	16	2	13	1	0
Springville	33,542	19	1	6	3	9	501	47	413	41	0
St. George	89,160	181	2	48	13	118	1,397	229	1,023	145	3
Sunset	5,364	12	0	0	0	12	57	13	40	4	0
Syracuse	31,230	25	0	14	1	10	196	32	153	11	5
Tooele	35,719	73	1	45	7	20	860	106	690	64	2
Tremonton	9,038	14	0	6	0	8	140	40	90	10	
Washington	29,047	29	0	8	2	19	432	52	361	19	0
West Bountiful	5,790	11	0	7	0	4	102	10	77	15	1
West Jordan	117,644	264	1	39	35	189	2,555	268	2,083	204	7
West Valley	137,269	960	11	159	136	654	4,378	644	3,030	704	15
Woods Cross	11,531	42	1	10	3	28	160	21	104	35	2
VERMONT											
Barre	8,551	64	0	18	3	43	203	20	183	0	3
Barre Town	7,679	6	0	1	0	5	67	3	62	2	1

Table 8. Offenses Known to Law Enforcement, by Selected State and City, 2019—Continued

(Number.)

State/city	Population	Violent crime	Murder and nonnegligent manslaughter	Rape[1]	Robbery	Aggravated assault	Property crime	Burglary	Larceny-theft	Motor vehicle theft	Arson[2]
Bellows Falls	2,988	7	0	0	2	5	54	11	42	1	0
Bennington	14,912	63	0	3	9	51	514	67	431	16	0
Berlin	2,789	9	0	2	0	7	122	4	117	1	0
Bradford	2,701	0	0	0	0	0	19	4	14	1	0
Brandon	3,744	6	0	2	0	4	63	10	50	3	0
Brattleboro	11,401	48	0	3	6	39	616	53	554	9	2
Brighton	1,184	0	0	0	0	0	6	2	3	1	0
Bristol	3,883	1	0	1	0	0	17	3	13	1	0
Burlington	42,958	174	2	41	13	118	1,110	109	976	25	2
Castleton	4,507	3	0	0	0	3	32	8	23	1	0
Chester	3,018	6	0	0	0	6	16	7	4	5	0
Colchester	17,548	26	0	10	4	12	234	21	212	1	1
Dover	1,057	3	0	0	0	3	73	2	70	1	0
Essex	22,213	19	0	2	1	16	286	42	238	6	0
Fair Haven	2,554	4	0	1	0	3	35	1	32	2	0
Hardwick	2,852	5	0	2	0	3	28	3	25	0	0
Hartford	9,654	38	0	12	4	22	168	30	132	6	0
Hinesburg	4,601	5	1	3	0	1	23	11	9	3	0
Killington	757	0	0	0	0	0	1	0	1	0	0
Ludlow	1,876	7	0	0	1	6	13	2	11	0	0
Lyndonville	1,160	3	0	0	0	3	30	1	29	0	0
Manchester	4,242	6	0	2	1	3	54	7	47	0	0
Middlebury	8,776	16	0	5	0	11	118	15	101	2	0
Milton	11,064	11	0	5	1	5	117	14	101	2	0
Montpelier	7,386	11	0	6	0	5	171	7	164	0	1
Morristown	5,465	14	0	7	0	7	121	10	111	0	0
Newport	4,216	34	0	8	0	26	87	15	69	3	0
Northfield	5,990	13	0	1	0	12	37	3	31	3	0
Norwich	3,307	1	0	0	0	1	13	3	9	1	0
Pittsford	2,786	0	0	0	0	0	10	1	9	0	0
Richmond	4,178	1	0	0	0	1	13	0	13	0	0
Royalton	2,864	0	0	0	0	0	10	0	9	1	0
Rutland	15,191	67	0	13	5	49	415	64	330	21	6
Rutland Town	4,096	7	0	4	0	3	53	12	38	3	0
Shelburne	7,857	1	0	0	0	1	110	8	99	3	0
South Burlington	19,687	22	0	6	4	12	687	32	647	8	2
Springfield	8,900	25	0	8	0	17	159	25	133	1	1
St. Albans	6,800	51	0	6	2	43	332	19	310	3	3
St. Johnsbury	7,158	17	0	5	1	11	142	21	118	3	2
Stowe	4,452	1	0	0	0	1	48	5	42	1	4
Swanton	6,595	10	0	0	2	8	60	7	48	5	0
Thetford	2,545	2	0	1	0	1	12	4	8	0	0
Vergennes	2,596	5	0	1	0	4	27	3	24	0	0
Weathersfield	2,753	2	0	0	0	2	7	3	3	1	0
Williston	10,026	8	0	0	2	6	205	8	193	4	0
Wilmington	1,801	6	0	1	0	5	15	5	7	5	2
Windsor	3,324	3	0	0	0	3	26	5	18	3	0
Winhall	731	0	0	0	0	0	11	2	9	0	2
Winooski	7,346	23	1	7	0	15	128	31	93	4	2
Woodstock	2,925	2	0	1	0	1	23	7	15	1	0
VIRGINIA											
Abingdon	7,933	7	0	1	1	5	118	6	104	8	0
Alexandria	162,258	288	2	19	80	187	2,517	117	2,005	395	2
Amherst	2,179	3	0	1	0	2	14	3	11	0	0
Appalachia	1,544	6	0	2	0	4	48	8	34	6	1
Ashland	7,916	19	0	1	4	14	158	8	142	8	1
Bedford	6,588	9	0	3	0	6	198	6	187	5	1
Berryville	4,363	1	0	0	0	1	33	6	27	0	0
Big Stone Gap	5,170	4	0	3	0	1	84	6	74	4	1
Blacksburg	44,948	50	0	26	1	23	275	38	228	9	0
Bluefield	4,822	9	0	3	1	5	274	9	254	11	0
Bowling Green	1,187	0	0	0	0	0	0	0	0	0	0
Bridgewater	6,167	0	0	0	0	0	23	2	21	0	0
Bristol	16,234	52	0	14	6	32	388	66	287	35	0
Broadway	3,973	0	0	0	0	0	13	4	9	0	0
Brookneal	1,098	2	0	0	1	1	9	0	9	0	0
Buena Vista	6,156	7	0	3	0	4	18	3	15	0	0
Cape Charles	1,002	4	0	0	0	4	3	0	3	0	0
Cedar Bluff	1,003	1	0	1	0	0	7	2	4	1	0
Charlottesville	48,453	157	0	32	22	103	1,124	122	924	78	5
Chase City	2,212	5	0	0	1	4	35	9	25	1	0
Chatham	1,433	0	0	0	0	0	9	0	9	0	0
Chesapeake	243,726	1,112	7	111	139	855	5,541	510	4,641	390	12
Chilhowie	1,710	0	0	0	0	0	20	1	17	2	0
Chincoteague	2,872	4	0	2	1	1	50	8	39	3	0
Christiansburg	22,700	31	0	7	4	20	466	28	424	14	2
Clifton Forge	3,465	8	0	1	0	7	43	5	35	3	0
Clintwood	1,287	0	0	0	0	0	25	2	23	0	0
Coeburn	1,857	2	0	0	0	2	39	9	24	6	0
Colonial Beach	3,593	11	0	2	1	8	48	5	41	2	0
Colonial Heights	17,793	71	1	20	6	44	720	37	663	20	4
Covington	5,372	5	0	3	0	2	116	10	98	8	1

Table 8. Offenses Known to Law Enforcement, by Selected State and City, 2019—Continued

(Number.)

State/city	Population	Violent crime	Murder and nonnegligent manslaughter	Rape[1]	Robbery	Aggravated assault	Property crime	Burglary	Larceny-theft	Motor vehicle theft	Arson[2]
Crewe	2,148	9	0	0	2	7	43	11	31	1	1
Culpeper	18,873	32	0	4	13	15	340	9	315	16	0
Damascus	787	0	0	0	0	0	56	3	49	4	0
Danville	40,191	112	8	11	25	68	1,467	180	1,205	82	10
Dayton	1,636	1	0	0	1	0	8	2	6	0	0
Dublin	2,604	3	0	2	0	1	33	6	25	2	1
Dumfries	5,265	7	1	0	4	2	41	3	34	4	0
Elkton	2,900	3	0	0	0	3	71	34	35	2	1
Emporia	5,000	12	1	3	5	3	195	19	168	8	1
Exmore	1,368	9	0	2	2	5	33	5	25	3	0
Fairfax City	24,689	18	0	4	11	3	345	11	308	26	2
Falls Church	15,008	10	0	1	5	4	230	12	173	45	1
Farmville	7,830	31	0	5	3	23	167	16	146	5	1
Franklin	7,899	16	2	3	7	4	292	24	248	20	3
Front Royal	15,336	28	0	9	3	16	293	27	242	24	2
Galax	6,320	29	0	12	1	16	255	17	226	12	2
Gate City	1,857	4	0	1	0	3	22	1	19	2	0
Glade Spring	1,426	0	0	0	0	0	11	2	6	3	0
Glasgow	1,111	0	0	0	0	0	2	0	2	0	0
Gordonsville	1,621	6	0	1	0	5	19	3	16	0	0
Gretna	1,197	1	0	0	0	1	9	1	6	2	0
Grottoes	2,860	1	0	1	0	0	25	2	21	2	0
Grundy	900	1	0	0	0	1	23	1	21	1	0
Halifax	1,217	2	0	0	0	2	22	9	11	2	0
Hampton	133,173	393	15	42	122	214	3,994	347	3,397	250	25
Harrisonburg	54,387	112	0	32	17	63	924	68	813	43	5
Haymarket	1,740	0	0	0	0	0	8	0	8	0	0
Haysi	472	0	0	0	0	0	7	3	4	0	0
Herndon	24,693	64	2	5	25	32	270	15	230	25	0
Hillsville	2,644	7	0	2	0	5	54	4	49	1	0
Honaker	1,330	2	0	0	1	1	16	4	12	0	0
Hopewell	22,461	75	5	3	22	45	480	80	349	51	3
Hurt	1,226	2	0	2	0	0	9	0	8	1	0
Independence	896	0	0	0	0	0	5	1	3	1	0
Jonesville	931	1	0	1	0	0	15	0	15	0	0
Kenbridge	1,180	0	0	0	0	0	0	0	0	0	0
Kilmarnock	1,410	1	0	0	0	1	21	1	20	0	1
La Crosse	573	0	0	0	0	0	1	1	0	0	0
Lawrenceville	993	1	0	0	0	1	10	1	8	1	0
Lebanon	3,148	9	0	4	1	4	128	6	120	2	0
Leesburg	55,461	102	0	20	19	63	570	21	530	19	1
Lexington	7,107	7	0	1	1	5	27	3	24	0	0
Louisa	1,721	1	0	0	0	1	44	0	41	3	0
Luray	4,853	11	0	1	0	10	136	13	122	1	0
Lynchburg	82,512	316	2	35	60	219	1,802	261	1,382	159	11
Manassas	41,850	103	2	19	26	56	623	53	528	42	13
Manassas Park	17,602	21	0	13	2	6	154	12	131	11	1
Marion	5,593	24	0	3	1	20	224	33	184	7	1
Martinsville	12,726	66	2	9	13	42	343	49	260	34	0
Middleburg	864	0	0	0	0	0	4	0	4	0	0
Middletown	1,396	0	0	0	0	0	5	0	4	1	0
Mount Jackson	2,115	3	0	2	0	1	21	3	18	0	0
Narrows	1,955	1	0	0	0	1	25	6	16	3	1
New Market	2,256	1	0	0	0	1	18	1	17	0	0
Newport News	177,319	1,056	24	64	164	804	4,484	503	3,641	340	40
Norfolk	242,813	1,325	36	134	311	844	8,405	841	6,765	799	8
Norton	3,940	6	0	2	0	4	134	8	120	6	0
Occoquan	1,109	1	0	0	0	1	2	0	2	0	0
Onancock	1,210	3	0	1	1	1	24	7	15	2	1
Onley	500	1	0	0	1	0	21	1	18	2	0
Orange	5,092	15	0	3	0	12	81	12	68	1	0
Parksley	810	0	0	0	0	0	4	0	2	2	0
Pearisburg	2,639	2	0	1	0	1	67	3	57	7	0
Pembroke	1,085	1	0	0	0	1	14	3	10	1	0
Pennington Gap	1,716	1	0	0	0	1	38	1	36	1	0
Petersburg	31,273	234	19	12	48	155	1,034	131	760	143	2
Pocahontas	354	0	0	0	0	0	1	0	1	0	0
Poquoson	12,126	23	0	6	1	16	91	18	72	1	1
Portsmouth	93,991	889	16	37	230	606	5,509	846	4,189	474	11
Pulaski	8,683	34	0	14	5	15	278	43	214	21	1
Purcellville	10,346	8	0	1	0	7	37	3	31	3	0
Radford	18,487	45	1	11	1	32	179	24	152	3	0
Rich Creek	743	1	0	0	0	1	15	1	13	1	0
Richlands	5,198	16	0	8	0	8	100	16	76	8	2
Richmond	230,721	1,068	55	45	385	583	8,074	986	6,234	854	44
Roanoke	99,752	386	13	41	106	226	4,402	519	3,585	298	25
Rocky Mount	4,744	20	2	9	3	6	268	10	248	10	1
Rural Retreat	1,453	0	0	0	0	0	7	2	5	0	0
Salem	25,590	23	1	3	5	14	559	46	473	40	1
Saltville	1,910	3	0	0	0	3	16	0	14	2	0
Shenandoah	2,335	0	0	0	0	0	35	5	27	3	0
Smithfield	8,485	17	1	0	2	14	150	7	128	15	0
South Boston	7,601	28	2	3	4	19	339	52	281	6	0

Table 8. Offenses Known to Law Enforcement, by Selected State and City, 2019—Continued

(Number.)

State/city	Population	Violent crime	Murder and nonnegligent manslaughter	Rape[1]	Robbery	Aggravated assault	Property crime	Burglary	Larceny-theft	Motor vehicle theft	Arson[2]
South Hill	4,335	8	0	0	7	1	135	15	114	6	0
Stanley	1,670	1	0	0	0	1	8	0	8	0	0
Staunton	24,931	51	0	18	5	28	473	35	419	19	5
Stephens City	2,069	1	0	0	0	1	35	6	28	1	0
St. Paul	862	1	0	0	0	1	19	2	16	1	1
Strasburg	6,686	12	0	2	0	10	66	9	53	4	0
Suffolk	91,486	270	6	29	67	168	2,266	196	1,925	145	5
Tappahannock	2,391	19	0	1	0	18	71	3	66	2	0
Tazewell	4,140	9	1	3	0	5	58	10	44	4	0
Timberville	2,697	4	0	1	0	3	17	1	16	0	0
Victoria	1,603	3	0	0	0	3	6	1	5	0	1
Vienna	16,660	20	0	1	5	14	163	2	154	7	0
Vinton	8,110	27	0	1	2	24	194	18	168	8	0
Virginia Beach	449,038	581	30	79	196	276	7,906	530	6,797	579	34
Warrenton	9,977	14	0	9	0	5	109	9	95	5	0
Warsaw	1,488	0	0	0	0	0	10	2	8	0	0
Waverly	1,949	4	0	1	2	1	28	4	20	4	0
Waynesboro	22,711	57	2	12	3	40	475	38	397	40	4
Weber City	1,204	1	0	0	1	0	13	0	13	0	0
West Point	3,254	3	0	1	0	2	27	9	18	0	0
White Stone	334	0	0	0	0	0	0	0	0	0	0
Williamsburg	14,965	22	0	3	5	14	197	13	179	5	0
Winchester	28,201	80	1	39	6	34	657	76	559	22	5
Windsor	2,763	4	0	1	0	3	23	2	17	4	0
Wise	2,926	3	0	1	0	2	58	6	47	5	0
Woodstock	5,267	10	0	4	0	6	125	3	121	1	0
Wytheville	7,909	5	0	4	1	0	196	22	168	6	1
WASHINGTON											
Aberdeen	16,627	71	1	25	14	31	680	123	519	38	6
Airway Heights	9,545	27	0	8	5	14	408	58	304	46	2
Algona	3,247	6	0	2	2	2	52	8	39	5	1
Anacortes	17,483	20	1	2	6	11	387	67	306	14	0
Arlington	20,043	47	1	7	5	34	703	93	570	40	3
Bainbridge Island	25,080	10	0	3	0	7	226	42	179	5	0
Battle Ground	21,375	17	0	8	5	4	444	53	365	26	0
Beaux Arts	331	0	0	0	0	0	2	1	1	0	0
Bellevue	150,200	185	1	28	76	80	4,263	426	3,498	339	3
Bellingham	91,906	251	4	28	61	158	2,689	323	2,251	115	6
Bingen	740	1	0	0	0	1	9	4	5	0	0
Bonney Lake	21,574	35	0	10	7	18	362	62	268	32	2
Bothell	47,565	30	0	11	8	11	964	102	776	86	5
Bremerton	41,675	168	1	26	34	107	1,358	234	984	140	6
Brier	7,070	2	0	1	0	1	68	5	58	5	0
Buckley	5,534	10	0	3	0	7	77	32	40	5	3
Burien	52,388	180	3	21	56	100	1,744	341	964	439	12
Burlington	9,219	19	1	8	5	5	597	56	513	28	2
Camas	24,388	10	1	4	2	3	221	30	180	11	0
Castle Rock	2,291	1	0	0	0	1	43	7	32	4	0
Centralia	17,603	60	1	14	13	32	670	102	525	43	1
Chehalis	7,682	22	0	3	7	12	377	46	309	22	0
Cheney	12,632	39	0	16	5	18	204	56	137	11	0
Chewelah	2,673	1	0	0	0	1	33	4	28	1	0
Cle Elum	2,989	5	0	1	1	3	77	17	57	3	1
Clyde Hill	3,436	0	0	0	0	0	38	4	32	2	1
College Place	9,428	11	0	1	1	9	161	27	129	5	1
Connell	5,772	11	0	3	0	8	39	14	24	1	0
Covington	21,698	36	0	5	10	21	582	88	447	47	0
Darrington	1,429	4	0	0	0	4	11	4	7	0	0
Des Moines	32,708	86	1	17	31	37	1,007	139	691	177	6
Dupont	9,672	20	0	0	0	20	123	26	88	9	3
Duvall	8,244	5	0	4	0	1	46	0	43	3	0
East Wenatchee	14,293	8	1	0	1	6	192	13	171	8	1
Eatonville	3,061	19	0	2	0	17	31	4	20	7	0
Edgewood	11,981	24	0	2	4	18	202	83	101	18	4
Edmonds	43,152	87	1	10	24	52	909	138	723	48	2
Ellensburg	21,324	45	0	11	5	29	652	79	545	28	2
Enumclaw	11,975	6	0	1	0	5	208	29	146	33	3
Ephrata	8,253	17	0	4	1	12	394	105	258	31	2
Everett	112,302	341	6	40	87	208	3,991	498	2,669	824	13
Everson	4,428	1	0	0	0	1	40	2	38	0	1
Federal Way	98,025	330	4	35	147	144	4,164	519	3,041	604	13
Fife	10,324	78	1	10	23	44	664	89	401	174	3
Fircrest	6,852	11	0	2	0	9	98	23	72	3	2
Forks	3,903	11	0	1	0	10	65	11	51	3	0
Gig Harbor	10,931	14	0	2	5	7	447	44	383	20	1
Gold Bar	2,370	5	0	3	1	1	40	16	21	3	0
Goldendale	3,508	9	0	1	1	7	145	24	109	12	1
Grand Coulee	2,079	8	0	5	0	3	62	21	33	8	0
Grandview	11,179	10	0	1	3	6	204	29	137	38	0
Ilwaco	967	2	0	0	0	2	4	1	2	1	0
Issaquah	40,651	20	0	9	2	9	1,138	78	980	80	2
Kalama	2,766	3	0	0	0	3	30	4	24	2	0

Table 8. Offenses Known to Law Enforcement, by Selected State and City, 2019—Continued

(Number.)

State/city	Population	Violent crime	Murder and nonnegligent manslaughter	Rape[1]	Robbery	Aggravated assault	Property crime	Burglary	Larceny-theft	Motor vehicle theft	Arson[2]
Kelso	12,354	33	1	11	6	15	392	47	330	15	5
Kenmore	23,430	18	0	4	6	8	242	42	171	29	0
Kennewick	84,072	253	2	54	49	148	2,487	378	1,907	202	12
Kent	131,003	486	4	94	242	146	5,200	754	3,598	848	14
La Center	3,324	3	0	0	1	2	41	11	29	1	6
Lacey	51,816	105	0	29	17	59	1,436	180	1,136	120	3
Lake Forest Park	13,690	3	0	0	2	1	196	30	147	19	0
Lake Stevens	34,081	44	0	10	4	30	284	74	170	40	2
Lakewood	60,916	461	2	49	101	309	2,296	385	1,607	304	8
Liberty Lake	11,043	8	0	0	2	6	166	22	135	9	0
Long Beach	1,441	1	0	0	0	1	15	1	13	1	0
Longview	38,282	101	1	30	19	51	1,102	159	841	102	8
Lynden	15,116	14	0	4	2	8	263	30	229	4	1
Lynnwood	38,847	113	0	15	38	60	1,855	145	1,499	211	4
Maple Valley	27,705	15	1	4	4	6	311	77	208	26	4
Marysville	71,081	144	0	27	38	79	1,404	206	973	225	7
Medina	3,337	0	0	0	0	0	53	14	36	3	0
Mercer Island	26,408	8	1	2	1	4	371	64	287	20	1
Mill Creek	21,360	17	0	2	2	13	290	26	238	26	0
Milton	8,381	32	0	3	6	23	210	57	126	27	2
Monroe	19,630	58	1	15	1	41	559	58	449	52	3
Montesano	4,033	3	0	0	1	2	37	8	25	4	0
Mountlake Terrace	21,617	37	0	6	13	18	466	92	311	63	0
Mount Vernon	36,274	55	0	13	17	25	1,140	126	899	115	5
Moxee	4,151	1	0	1	0	0	21	5	13	3	0
Mukilteo	21,704	22	0	5	3	14	351	62	259	30	1
Newcastle	12,015	10	0	2	2	6	196	45	123	28	1
Newport	2,156	2	0	0	1	1	44	0	41	3	0
Normandy Park	6,699	1	0	1	0	0	124	20	98	6	0
North Bend	7,314	5	1	1	0	3	199	12	182	5	1
Oak Harbor	23,554	31	0	8	2	21	134	26	95	13	0
Oakville	690	2	0	1	0	1	9	4	4	1	0
Olympia	53,286	254	2	25	70	157	1,854	244	1,409	201	10
Orting	8,629	12	0	2	3	7	129	17	99	13	1
Othello	8,388	7	0	2	1	4	145	27	91	27	1
Pacific	7,297	6	0	3	2	1	133	21	80	32	0
Port Angeles	20,207	117	0	38	14	65	719	127	529	63	3
Port Orchard	14,684	66	0	7	14	45	492	74	376	42	0
Port Townsend	9,780	41	0	8	1	32	172	39	124	9	6
Poulsbo	11,154	19	0	6	5	8	265	48	196	21	0
Prosser	6,388	7	0	0	2	5	124	38	76	10	2
Pullman	34,585	42	0	14	5	23	273	44	213	16	2
Puyallup	42,509	133	0	16	55	62	2,187	284	1,652	251	18
Quincy	7,977	13	0	0	2	11	144	38	78	28	0
Raymond	2,976	6	0	1	0	5	31	11	16	4	0
Redmond	69,501	71	1	11	17	42	1,846	163	1,563	120	4
Renton	103,452	325	2	44	109	170	4,182	456	2,913	813	10
Richland	58,514	100	2	24	9	65	1,199	195	949	55	10
Ridgefield	8,955	10	0	3	1	6	74	16	58	0	0
Ritzville	1,645	1	0	1	0	0	57	18	38	1	0
Roy	828	3	0	0	0	3	6	1	5	0	0
Royal City	2,240	2	0	1	0	1	21	8	9	4	0
Ruston	855	1	0	0	0	1	39	5	28	6	0
Sammamish	66,820	23	2	5	3	13	404	68	312	24	2
SeaTac	29,533	130	3	22	52	53	1,098	175	624	299	3
Seattle	763,706	4,471	28	358	1,339	2,746	34,333	7,210	23,478	3,645	98
Sedro Woolley	12,184	11	0	1	0	10	219	29	174	16	0
Selah	8,110	7	0	2	2	3	127	24	90	13	0
Sequim	7,599	16	2	4	0	10	316	45	263	8	2
Shelton	10,432	53	0	20	5	28	583	66	485	32	1
Shoreline	57,216	95	0	17	25	53	1,104	229	737	138	4
Skykomish	225	0	0	0	0	0	2	2	0	0	0
Snoqualmie	14,183	6	0	1	3	2	170	15	145	10	1
Soap Lake	1,613	4	0	0	1	3	59	14	43	2	0
South Bend	1,680	0	0	0	0	0	1	0	0	1	0
Spokane	220,432	1,520	6	230	311	973	13,048	1,743	10,026	1,279	45
Spokane Valley	100,983	311	1	38	82	190	4,465	483	3,626	356	4
Stanwood	7,330	11	0	0	1	10	155	20	124	11	0
Steilacoom	6,423	13	0	0	1	12	77	19	51	7	2
Sultan	5,266	8	0	0	2	6	73	9	54	10	0
Sumas	1,529	1	0	1	0	0	8	1	7	0	0
Sumner	10,270	34	0	6	9	19	451	104	282	65	9
Sunnyside	16,839	24	0	3	6	15	540	51	379	110	0
Tacoma	218,650	1,848	16	160	422	1,250	11,415	1,768	8,021	1,626	91
Tenino	1,873	3	0	0	0	3	26	4	18	4	0
Toledo	765	0	0	0	0	0	12	1	11	0	0
Toppenish	8,886	54	1	6	13	34	541	100	311	130	2
Tukwila	20,439	158	1	26	74	57	3,350	189	2,681	480	2
Tumwater	24,167	73	0	14	18	41	648	99	483	66	1
Twisp	964	0	0	0	0	0	11	4	5	2	0
Union Gap	6,162	15	1	1	8	5	580	46	493	41	0
University Place	34,085	88	0	18	18	52	541	103	397	41	0
Vancouver	185,034	889	3	206	185	495	5,998	888	4,302	808	36

Table 8. Offenses Known to Law Enforcement, by Selected State and City, 2019—Continued

(Number.)

State/city	Population	Violent crime	Murder and nonnegligent manslaughter	Rape[1]	Robbery	Aggravated assault	Property crime	Burglary	Larceny-theft	Motor vehicle theft	Arson[2]
Walla Walla	33,047	114	2	29	16	67	1,052	161	814	77	5
Washougal	16,305	24	1	9	4	10	235	34	183	18	1
Wenatchee	34,513	62	1	16	10	35	638	66	532	40	1
Westport	2,080	7	0	0	0	7	64	8	55	1	0
West Richland	15,343	15	0	5	1	9	103	23	76	4	2
White Salmon	2,655	0	0	0	0	0	19	3	10	6	0
Winlock	1,392	1	0	0	0	1	13	1	11	1	0
Winthrop	457	3	0	0	0	3	5	0	5	0	0
Woodinville	13,068	10	0	1	4	5	270	23	225	22	2
Woodland	6,469	11	0	7	0	4	205	42	146	17	1
Yakima	94,168	420	9	44	91	276	2,723	439	1,866	418	15
Yarrow Point	1,166	0	0	0	0	0	8	2	6	0	0
Yelm	9,741	32	0	2	5	25	392	36	327	29	3
WEST VIRGINIA											
Charles Town	6,171	9	1	1	4	3	75	30	43	2	0
Glen Dale	1,375	1	0	1	0	0	16	6	9	1	0
Huntington	45,675	330	4	56	59	211	1,792	456	1,147	189	21
Lewisburg	3,830	3	0	0	0	3	81	1	79	1	1
Milton	2,588	9	0	0	3	6	69	13	54	2	0
Moorefield	2,418	24	1	1	1	21	153	5	145	3	0
Morgantown	31,281	67	0	9	5	53	489	71	383	35	1
Moundsville	8,323	29	0	8	0	21	103	0	103	0	0
New Martinsville	5,114	2	0	0	0	2	14	5	7	2	0
Nitro	6,406	15	0	0	1	14	220	20	187	13	0
Oak Hill	8,140	5	2	1	0	2	14	0	14	0	0
Ranson	5,288	8	0	1	1	6	76	11	64	1	1
Ronceverte	1,674	2	0	0	0	2	13	2	9	2	0
St. Albans	9,956	33	2	2	1	28	304	59	227	18	1
Summersville	3,292	1	0	0	0	1	107	4	100	3	0
Weirton	18,296	11	0	1	0	10	88	2	84	2	1
Wellsburg	2,531	1	0	0	0	1	17	1	14	2	0
Weston	3,887	4	0	0	0	4	2	0	1	1	0
White Sulphur Springs	2,395	5	0	2	1	2	12	3	8	1	1
Williamson	2,694	6	0	0	0	6	2	0	2	0	1
Winfield	2,378	0	0	0	0	0	12	0	11	1	0
WISCONSIN											
Adams	1,886	9	0	6	1	2	67	4	60	3	1
Albany[5]	994	1	0	0	0	1	9	0	8	1	0
Algoma	3,030	2	0	2	0	0	17	0	17	0	0
Altoona	7,939	9	0	4	0	5	109	16	90	3	0
Amery	2,792	8	0	2	1	5	37	4	31	2	0
Appleton	74,757	206	2	32	23	149	1,073	107	910	56	10
Arcadia	3,044	4	0	0	0	4	5	0	5	0	0
Ashland	7,859	25	0	4	0	21	291	29	240	22	1
Ashwaubenon	17,311	21	0	9	1	11	477	20	445	12	0
Athens	1,078	3	0	2	0	1	8	0	8	0	0
Avoca	625	0	0	0	0	0	0	0	0	0	0
Bangor	1,468	0	0	0	0	0	2	1	1	0	0
Baraboo	12,151	28	0	15	2	11	345	43	284	18	0
Barneveld	1,256	1	0	0	0	1	7	0	7	0	0
Barron[5]	3,306	10	0	2	0	8	25	3	20	2	0
Bayfield	476	1	0	0	0	1	19	6	12	1	0
Bayside	4,342	3	0	0	0	3	17	3	13	1	0
Beaver Dam	16,375	27	1	5	0	21	260	27	224	9	2
Belleville	2,459	2	0	1	0	1	16	0	15	1	0
Beloit[5]	37,025	154	4	19	31	100	1,114	122	921	71	11
Beloit Town	7,707	7	0	2	2	3	126	23	95	8	0
Berlin	5,401	1	0	0	0	1	68	8	53	7	0
Big Bend	1,460	0	0	0	0	0	26	3	19	4	0
Birchwood	433	0	0	0	0	0	2	1	1	0	0
Black River Falls	3,454	5	0	3	1	1	76	2	70	4	0
Blair	1,345	2	0	1	0	1	3	2	1	0	0
Blanchardville	791	1	0	1	0	0	3	0	2	1	0
Bloomer[5]	3,499	11	0	2	0	9	29	2	24	3	0
Bloomfield	6,342	10	0	2	1	7	35	5	30	0	0
Boyceville	1,130	3	0	2	1	0	14	3	11	0	0
Brandon-Fairwater	1,212	0	0	0	0	0	0	0	0	0	0
Brillion	3,100	5	0	3	0	2	14	1	13	0	0
Brodhead[5]	3,240	0	0	0	0	0	22	1	19	2	0
Brookfield	38,879	31	0	6	14	11	691	72	604	15	0
Brookfield Township	6,281	6	0	0	0	6	102	4	93	5	0
Brooklyn	1,474	1	0	0	0	1	4	0	3	1	0
Brown Deer	11,869	40	0	4	14	22	451	25	400	26	1
Brownsville	573	0	0	0	0	0	2	0	2	0	0
Burlington	11,057	6	0	0	0	6	87	5	78	4	1
Butler	1,807	2	0	0	1	1	65	2	55	8	1
Caledonia	25,123	21	0	1	0	20	127	22	95	10	0
Campbellsport	1,969	0	0	0	0	0	13	0	13	0	0
Campbell Township	4,337	1	0	0	0	1	44	6	34	4	0
Cascade	692	0	0	0	0	0	2	0	2	0	0
Cashton	1,111	2	0	0	0	2	2	0	2	0	0

Table 8. Offenses Known to Law Enforcement, by Selected State and City, 2019—Continued

(Number.)

State/city	Population	Violent crime	Murder and nonnegligent manslaughter	Rape[1]	Robbery	Aggravated assault	Property crime	Burglary	Larceny-theft	Motor vehicle theft	Arson[2]
Cedarburg	11,548	2	0	1	0	1	89	6	82	1	0
Chenequa	604	0	0	0	0	0	1	0	1	0	0
Chetek[5]	2,097	6	0	0	0	6	12	0	10	2	0
Chilton	3,774	2	0	1	0	1	32	4	27	1	0
Chippewa Falls	14,237	50	0	8	2	40	180	25	133	22	1
Cleveland	1,450	0	0	0	0	0	2	0	2	0	0
Clinton	2,154	6	0	0	2	4	12	1	11	0	0
Colby-Abbotsford	4,152	2	0	0	0	2	25	2	22	1	0
Colfax	1,154	2	0	0	0	2	6	0	5	1	0
Columbus	5,090	10	0	4	0	6	53	6	44	3	0
Cornell[5]	1,396	0	0	0	0	0	23	2	21	0	0
Cottage Grove	7,203	3	0	0	0	3	22	0	21	1	0
Crandon	1,826	3	0	0	0	3	21	2	17	2	0
Cross Plains	4,346	4	0	1	0	3	23	3	17	3	0
Cuba City	2,034	0	0	0	0	0	0	0	0	0	0
Cudahy[5]	18,164	29	0	2	5	22	205	42	137	26	3
Cumberland	2,099	0	0	0	0	0	0	0	0	0	0
Darlington[5]	2,324	4	0	2	0	2	18	0	18	0	0
Deforest	10,766	10	0	1	1	8	97	6	85	6	1
Delafield	7,610	4	0	2	1	1	108	4	101	3	0
Delavan	9,889	17	2	2	0	13	212	4	206	2	1
Delavan Town	5,339	8	1	2	0	5	22	1	20	1	0
De Pere	25,163	20	1	2	0	17	217	19	194	4	6
Dodgeville	4,713	6	0	3	1	2	114	13	98	3	0
Durand	1,810	2	0	2	0	0	6	2	4	0	0
Eagle River	1,548	2	0	1	0	1	47	0	41	6	0
Eagle Village	2,112	1	0	1	0	0	12	2	10	0	0
East Troy	4,327	7	0	0	0	7	25	1	24	0	0
Eau Claire	69,195	191	0	58	22	111	1,634	252	1,317	65	2
Edgar	1,439	1	0	0	0	1	7	1	6	0	0
Edgerton	5,646	1	0	0	0	1	56	1	53	2	0
Elkhart Lake[5]	1,018	0	0	0	0	0	8	0	6	2	0
Elkhorn[5]	9,989	12	0	5	4	3	95	10	79	6	0
Elk Mound	878	3	0	0	0	3	21	1	20	0	0
Ellsworth	3,306	5	0	1	2	2	21	3	18	0	0
Elm Grove	6,195	4	0	0	0	4	48	3	45	0	0
Endeavor	461	0	0	0	0	0	1	0	1	0	0
Everest Metropolitan[5]	17,340	76	0	10	3	63	201	40	151	10	4
Fall Creek	1,308	1	0	0	0	1	9	1	8	0	0
Fall River	1,715	1	0	0	0	1	0	0	0	0	0
Fennimore	2,465	6	0	6	0	0	11	0	8	3	0
Fitchburg	30,854	93	1	13	23	56	529	89	378	62	1
Fond du Lac	42,954	134	0	28	14	92	797	59	697	41	3
Fontana[5]	1,729	2	0	1	0	1	5	1	4	0	0
Fort Atkinson	12,519	26	0	7	3	16	178	21	151	6	0
Fox Crossing[5]	18,992	25	0	6	2	17	159	22	130	7	1
Fox Lake	1,445	0	0	0	0	0	2	2	0	0	0
Fox Point	6,599	3	0	0	3	0	61	4	51	6	0
Fox Valley Metro	22,190	25	0	9	0	16	87	5	75	7	0
Franklin	35,875	25	2	4	3	16	576	24	529	23	0
Fulton	3,410	0	0	0	0	0	4	1	2	1	0
Galesville	1,571	0	0	0	0	0	9	2	7	0	0
Geneva Town	5,045	2	0	0	0	2	19	2	17	0	0
Genoa City	2,992	0	0	0	0	0	10	0	9	1	0
Germantown	19,983	16	0	3	1	12	450	11	434	5	0
Gillett	1,295	0	0	0	0	0	14	1	12	1	0
Gilman	393	0	0	0	0	0	9	0	9	0	0
Glendale	12,792	33	1	2	10	20	661	22	597	42	1
Grafton	11,798	8	1	0	3	4	141	5	134	2	0
Grand Chute	23,450	69	0	13	3	53	734	29	674	31	2
Grand Rapids	7,405	3	0	2	0	1	22	7	14	1	0
Grantsburg	1,283	6	0	0	0	6	9	0	8	1	0
Green Bay	104,992	529	3	78	49	399	1,724	245	1,355	124	10
Greendale	14,057	13	0	4	0	9	160	9	149	2	0
Greenfield	37,387	64	1	3	18	42	946	62	842	42	3
Green Lake	961	1	0	0	0	1	3	1	2	0	0
Hales Corners	7,578	6	0	2	0	4	94	11	81	2	0
Hammond	1,885	0	0	0	0	0	8	0	6	2	0
Hancock	401	0	0	0	0	0	0	0	0	0	0
Hartford	15,460	10	0	5	1	4	219	11	203	5	0
Hartford Township	3,570	0	0	0	0	0	0	0	0	0	0
Hartland	9,366	9	0	3	0	6	46	6	39	1	0
Hayward	2,296	8	2	1	0	5	49	5	42	2	0
Hazel Green	1,225	0	0	0	0	0	14	5	9	0	0
Highland	833	1	0	0	1	0	5	1	3	1	0
Hillsboro	1,398	4	0	2	0	2	8	0	8	0	0
Hobart-Lawrence	15,460	8	0	2	0	6	44	8	35	1	0
Holmen	10,217	9	0	0	0	9	100	19	78	3	0
Horicon	3,587	2	0	0	0	2	57	0	52	5	0
Hortonville[5]	2,805	1	0	0	0	1	29	1	27	1	0
Hudson	14,074	19	0	2	1	16	381	29	331	21	0
Hurley	1,426	0	0	0	0	0	7	0	6	1	0
Independence	1,295	1	0	0	0	1	3	0	3	0	0

Table 8. Offenses Known to Law Enforcement, by Selected State and City, 2019—Continued

(Number.)

State/city	Population	Violent crime	Murder and nonnegligent manslaughter	Rape[1]	Robbery	Aggravated assault	Property crime	Burglary	Larceny-theft	Motor vehicle theft	Arson[2]
Iron Ridge	891	0	0	0	0	0	0	0	0	0	0
Iron River	1,135	1	0	1	0	0	12	2	8	2	0
Jackson	7,218	9	0	2	0	7	95	5	89	1	0
Janesville	64,687	148	1	38	28	81	1,577	137	1,397	43	6
Jefferson	8,042	9	0	4	0	5	129	9	104	16	1
Juneau	2,639	4	0	0	0	4	15	1	14	0	0
Kaukauna	16,341	14	0	5	1	8	110	13	88	9	0
Kenosha	100,255	311	5	58	53	195	1,582	188	1,222	172	7
Kewaskum	4,244	2	0	1	0	1	27	1	26	0	0
Kewaunee	2,836	5	0	1	1	3	17	0	17	0	0
Kiel	3,808	11	2	0	0	9	24	0	23	1	0
Kohler[5]	2,063	0	0	0	0	0	35	0	35	0	0
Kronenwetter[5]	8,095	7	0	5	0	2	40	10	29	1	0
La Crosse	51,591	122	2	27	26	67	1,850	226	1,561	63	1
Ladysmith	3,111	3	0	1	0	2	25	3	22	0	1
La Farge	760	0	0	0	0	0	6	3	3	0	0
Lake Delton	3,005	24	0	4	3	17	458	23	417	18	0
Lake Geneva[5]	8,001	9	0	4	1	4	147	14	130	3	0
Lake Hallie[5]	6,724	12	1	2	2	7	159	3	148	8	0
Lake Mills	5,949	10	0	2	1	7	15	0	9	6	0
Lancaster	3,716	8	0	3	0	5	30	1	26	3	0
Lena	538	0	0	0	0	0	5	0	5	0	0
Linden	531	0	0	0	0	0	0	0	0	0	0
Linn Township[5]	2,406	0	0	0	0	0	11	4	7	0	0
Lodi	3,070	2	0	0	0	2	24	4	16	4	0
Lomira	2,469	2	0	2	0	0	7	0	7	0	0
Luxemburg	2,557	3	0	2	1	0	11	0	9	2	0
Madison	261,270	940	4	107	217	612	6,464	1,046	4,873	545	9
Manawa	1,286	10	0	5	0	5	11	1	10	0	0
Manitowoc	32,497	73	0	6	4	63	631	47	566	18	1
Maple Bluff	1,319	0	0	0	0	0	10	3	5	2	0
Marathon City	1,500	2	0	1	0	1	7	0	7	0	0
Marinette	10,569	11	0	3	1	7	184	20	158	6	1
Marion	1,183	0	0	0	0	0	3	1	2	0	0
Markesan	1,395	2	0	1	0	1	16	1	15	0	0
Marshall Village	3,967	6	0	2	0	4	33	8	22	3	0
Marshfield	18,216	29	0	15	1	13	312	32	268	12	1
Mauston[5]	4,364	14	1	6	1	6	126	70	53	3	0
Mayville	4,859	8	1	1	0	6	53	1	48	4	0
McFarland	8,961	5	0	0	0	5	52	7	43	2	0
Medford	4,313	14	0	0	0	14	81	8	66	7	0
Menasha[5]	17,809	48	0	12	1	35	238	27	201	10	2
Menomonee Falls	37,936	28	0	2	6	20	331	33	287	11	0
Menomonie	16,573	36	0	7	1	28	280	20	241	19	2
Mequon	24,548	14	0	3	1	10	176	22	147	7	0
Merrill	9,017	14	0	3	0	11	169	9	156	4	0
Middleton	20,072	12	0	2	5	5	268	43	202	23	0
Milton	5,621	8	0	0	2	6	69	12	53	4	0
Milton Town	3,152	0	0	0	0	0	5	1	4	0	0
Milwaukee	590,923	7,874	97	427	1,911	5,439	15,097	3,594	8,053	3,450	198
Mineral Point	2,477	3	0	0	0	3	28	4	21	3	0
Minocqua	4,409	9	0	4	0	5	41	1	39	1	0
Mishicot	1,382	0	0	0	0	0	4	1	3	0	0
Monona	8,106	9	0	1	4	4	624	11	594	19	0
Monroe[5]	10,537	7	0	5	0	2	123	11	110	2	0
Montello	1,461	1	0	0	0	1	8	0	8	0	0
Mosinee	4,072	4	0	2	0	2	39	3	32	4	0
Mount Horeb	7,481	7	0	3	1	3	23	1	21	1	0
Mount Pleasant	27,070	40	0	7	6	27	536	46	465	25	1
Mukwonago	8,144	3	1	1	0	1	89	2	86	1	0
Mukwonago Town	8,167	5	0	0	0	5	5	1	4	0	0
Muscoda	1,252	5	0	1	0	4	20	2	16	2	0
Muskego	25,224	5	0	1	0	4	85	3	78	4	0
Neenah[5]	26,133	45	1	10	0	34	330	28	288	14	1
Neillsville	2,388	1	0	0	0	1	27	3	24	0	0
Nekoosa	2,432	0	0	0	0	0	58	4	52	2	0
Neshkoro	426	0	0	0	0	0	2	1	1	0	0
New Berlin	39,752	20	1	6	3	10	452	32	407	13	0
New Glarus	2,187	2	0	0	0	2	30	1	29	0	0
New Holstein	3,056	1	0	0	0	1	8	1	7	0	0
New London	7,118	7	0	1	1	5	121	8	106	7	0
New Richmond	9,268	22	0	7	1	14	115	14	101	0	1
Niagara	1,545	3	0	3	0	0	7	0	6	1	1
North Fond du Lac	5,098	7	0	2	0	5	29	3	25	1	0
North Hudson	3,813	2	0	0	0	2	9	0	8	1	0
North Prairie	2,249	2	0	0	0	2	7	0	7	0	0
Norwalk	632	0	0	0	0	0	0	0	0	0	1
Oak Creek	36,679	40	0	11	5	24	722	73	615	34	1
Oconomowoc	16,980	13	0	6	1	6	125	7	115	3	0
Oconomowoc Lake	604	0	0	0	0	0	4	0	4	0	0
Oconomowoc Town	8,741	3	0	2	0	1	17	1	16	0	0
Oconto	4,517	14	0	1	0	13	72	5	65	2	2
Oconto Falls	2,793	4	0	2	0	2	43	2	39	2	2

Table 8. Offenses Known to Law Enforcement, by Selected State and City, 2019—Continued

(Number.)

State/city	Population	Violent crime	Murder and nonnegligent manslaughter	Rape[1]	Robbery	Aggravated assault	Property crime	Burglary	Larceny-theft	Motor vehicle theft	Arson[2]
Omro[5]	3,587	5	0	1	0	4	15	2	13	0	0
Onalaska	18,825	10	0	2	2	6	522	24	491	7	0
Oregon	10,677	8	0	2	3	3	53	14	38	1	0
Osceola	2,511	21	0	1	0	20	15	0	15	0	0
Oshkosh[5]	66,797	190	0	50	16	124	1,067	213	794	60	3
Osseo	1,672	0	0	0	0	0	30	1	25	4	0
Oxford	603	1	0	0	0	1	11	1	9	1	0
Palmyra	1,767	1	0	0	0	1	10	0	10	0	0
Park Falls	2,212	6	0	0	1	5	6	0	6	0	0
Pepin	758	4	0	0	0	4	17	1	16	0	0
Peshtigo	3,333	4	0	2	0	2	28	2	25	1	0
Pewaukee Village	8,190	6	0	5	0	1	87	11	75	1	1
Phillips	1,339	1	0	0	0	1	13	2	11	0	0
Pittsville	829	1	0	0	0	1	40	0	40	0	0
Plainfield	824	0	0	0	0	0	0	0	0	0	0
Platteville	12,115	19	0	4	1	14	230	16	201	13	0
Pleasant Prairie	21,074	13	1	3	2	7	419	15	384	20	0
Plover	13,164	20	0	4	1	15	198	14	181	3	0
Plymouth	8,765	5	0	5	0	0	114	5	106	3	0
Portage	10,452	17	0	2	2	13	164	7	143	14	1
Port Edwards	1,772	0	0	0	0	0	5	1	3	1	0
Port Washington	11,908	29	0	2	0	27	88	4	80	4	0
Poynette	2,499	4	0	2	0	2	4	0	4	0	0
Prairie du Chien	5,636	4	0	3	0	1	82	4	77	1	0
Prescott	4,278	7	0	0	2	5	41	11	24	6	0
Princeton	1,167	3	0	0	0	3	18	1	15	2	0
Pulaski	3,598	8	0	0	0	8	16	0	15	1	0
Racine	77,269	291	4	45	53	189	990	212	682	96	4
Readstown	418	0	0	0	0	0	0	0	0	0	0
Reedsburg	9,554	5	0	3	0	2	159	6	147	6	0
Rhinelander	7,615	13	0	0	0	13	133	5	126	2	1
Rib Lake	867	0	0	0	0	0	3	0	3	0	0
Rice Lake	8,369	21	0	12	0	9	284	12	269	3	0
Richland Center	4,923	11	0	4	0	7	55	6	44	5	0
Rio	1,033	0	0	0	0	0	0	0	0	0	0
Ripon	7,820	15	0	11	0	4	68	11	55	2	0
Ripon Town	1,374	0	0	0	0	0	0	0	0	0	0
River Falls	16,069	13	0	5	2	6	188	25	157	6	0
River Hills	1,579	1	0	0	0	1	8	2	6	0	0
Rome Town	2,727	4	0	4	0	0	24	6	17	1	0
Rosendale	1,029	0	0	0	0	0	0	0	0	0	0
Rothschild[5]	5,266	7	0	3	0	4	51	6	41	4	0
Sauk Prairie	4,633	4	0	2	0	2	45	5	34	6	1
Saukville	4,428	1	0	1	0	0	58	2	53	3	0
Seymour	3,474	12	2	5	0	5	36	1	35	0	0
Sharon	1,559	2	0	0	0	2	0	0	0	0	0
Sheboygan	48,035	172	0	48	10	114	783	88	676	19	3
Sheboygan Falls	7,947	3	0	2	0	1	59	10	45	4	0
Shiocton	919	0	0	0	0	0	0	0	0	0	0
Shorewood[5]	13,217	20	0	1	6	13	210	24	176	10	0
Shorewood Hills	2,079	1	0	0	0	1	40	5	33	2	0
Shullsburg	1,189	0	0	0	0	0	22	2	19	1	0
Siren	770	0	0	0	0	0	15	0	14	1	0
Slinger	5,527	5	0	0	0	5	65	4	60	1	0
South Milwaukee	20,731	29	1	7	0	21	347	22	308	17	0
Sparta	9,823	15	0	7	1	7	87	5	79	3	0
Spencer	1,883	5	0	5	0	0	9	4	5	0	0
Spooner	2,598	13	1	3	1	8	42	3	39	0	0
Spring Green	1,644	0	0	0	0	0	3	0	3	0	0
Spring Valley	1,352	0	0	0	0	0	4	0	4	0	0
Stanley[5]	3,710	5	0	4	0	1	30	2	27	1	0
St. Croix Falls	2,032	13	0	1	0	12	101	4	88	9	0
Stevens Point	26,095	55	1	8	1	45	260	26	229	5	2
St. Francis	9,526	14	0	3	4	7	118	26	83	9	0
Stoughton	13,110	30	0	0	8	22	190	30	156	4	0
Strum	1,088	0	0	0	0	0	7	1	5	1	0
Sturgeon Bay	8,937	4	0	0	0	4	93	4	89	0	1
Sturtevant[5]	6,645	5	0	0	1	4	32	2	26	4	0
Summit	4,944	13	0	6	0	7	32	4	28	0	0
Sun Prairie	34,562	33	0	1	11	21	498	35	412	51	1
Superior	25,967	72	0	14	4	54	1,101	122	918	61	0
Theresa	1,204	0	0	0	0	0	21	0	20	1	0
Thiensville	3,139	0	0	0	0	0	23	1	21	1	0
Thorp	1,618	0	0	0	0	0	0	0	0	0	0
Three Lakes	2,101	1	0	0	0	1	12	4	8	0	0
Tomah	9,406	26	1	5	1	19	191	15	171	5	0
Tomahawk	3,130	3	0	2	0	1	49	14	32	3	0
Town of East Troy	4,064	4	0	0	0	4	9	3	6	0	0
Town of Madison	6,934	16	0	4	5	7	143	18	101	24	0
Trempealeau	1,652	1	0	0	0	1	6	2	4	0	0
Twin Lakes	6,157	17	0	0	0	17	39	10	28	1	0
Two Rivers	11,027	28	0	2	0	26	117	5	109	3	0
Verona	13,510	18	0	5	1	12	189	35	145	9	0

Table 8. Offenses Known to Law Enforcement, by Selected State and City, 2019—Continued

(Number.)

State/city	Population	Violent crime	Murder and nonnegligent manslaughter	Rape[1]	Robbery	Aggravated assault	Property crime	Burglary	Larceny-theft	Motor vehicle theft	Arson[2]
Viroqua	4,412	3	0	1	0	2	57	2	52	3	0
Walworth	2,837	2	0	0	1	1	16	1	14	1	0
Washburn	2,039	10	0	0	0	10	10	1	9	0	0
Waterford Town	6,505	0	0	0	0	0	24	4	18	2	0
Waterloo	3,350	1	0	1	0	0	32	2	29	1	0
Watertown	23,596	47	0	14	2	31	241	31	201	9	0
Waukesha	72,718	67	1	25	8	33	690	77	575	38	5
Waunakee	14,163	15	0	4	1	10	134	20	106	8	0
Waupaca	5,874	8	0	4	0	4	124	9	108	7	0
Waupun	11,315	3	1	1	0	1	62	9	51	2	2
Wausau[5]	38,507	156	1	42	5	108	521	81	396	44	3
Wautoma	2,118	1	0	0	1	0	94	2	91	1	0
Wauwatosa	48,562	57	0	7	28	22	1,331	88	1,178	65	1
Webster	616	0	0	0	0	0	22	9	13	0	0
West Allis	59,302	211	2	30	69	110	1,686	262	1,282	142	9
West Bend	31,638	67	0	10	3	54	512	24	473	15	1
Westby	2,238	5	0	0	0	5	36	4	31	1	1
Westfield	1,254	0	0	0	0	0	13	0	13	0	0
West Milwaukee[5]	4,107	30	1	0	11	18	1,467	31	1,411	25	0
West Salem	5,087	5	0	0	0	5	38	3	31	4	0
Whitefish Bay	13,816	3	0	1	1	1	145	6	130	9	0
Whitehall	1,569	0	0	0	0	0	17	2	14	1	0
Whitewater[5]	14,997	31	0	13	0	18	159	11	139	9	0
Wild Rose	691	0	0	0	0	0	1	0	1	0	0
Williams Bay	2,638	1	0	0	0	1	10	0	10	0	0
Wind Point	1,702	1	0	0	1	0	2	0	2	0	0
Winneconne[5]	2,506	2	0	0	0	2	19	1	17	1	0
Wisconsin Rapids	17,613	28	0	23	1	4	549	36	501	12	0
Woodruff	1,962	5	0	0	0	5	8	0	7	1	0
WYOMING											
Afton	2,017	0	0	0	0	0	12	1	11	0	0
Buffalo	4,571	8	0	1	0	7	52	13	30	9	0
Casper	57,752	169	2	58	18	91	1,677	285	1,271	121	2
Cheyenne	64,501	220	5	43	27	145	1,999	211	1,613	175	11
Cody[5]	9,865	17	0	7	1	9	107	10	94	3	2
Diamondville	756	1	0	0	0	1	1	0	1	0	0
Douglas	6,294	8	1	0	1	6	87	8	72	7	0
Evanston[5]	11,624	29	0	21	1	7	183	22	152	9	1
Evansville	2,977	7	0	0	3	4	73	13	52	8	2
Gillette	31,960	43	1	9	0	33	626	62	529	35	2
Glenrock	2,544	3	0	0	0	3	20	1	18	1	0
Green River	11,927	22	0	0	0	22	97	11	84	2	0
Greybull	1,857	0	0	0	0	0	5	1	4	0	0
Hanna	766	0	0	0	0	0	1	0	0	1	0
Kemmerer	2,745	1	0	0	0	1	8	0	8	0	0
Lander	7,489	0	0	0	0	0	253	15	226	12	0
Laramie	32,669	58	0	17	2	39	318	50	252	16	6
Lusk	1,537	5	0	2	0	3	8	0	7	1	0
Mills	3,975	3	0	0	2	1	71	22	39	10	4
Moorcroft	1,068	1	0	0	0	1	4	2	1	1	0
Newcastle	3,386	10	0	5	0	5	49	12	31	6	0
Pine Bluffs	1,170	2	0	1	1	0	5	2	3	0	2
Powell[5]	6,310	22	0	12	0	10	76	12	58	6	2
Rawlins	8,589	26	0	4	1	21	122	31	84	7	0
Riverton	11,004	38	3	19	1	15	426	52	332	42	6
Rock Springs	23,092	44	0	14	1	29	309	36	259	14	1
Saratoga	1,615	1	0	0	0	1	6	1	4	1	3
Sheridan	17,895	9	0	4	0	5	369	75	278	16	3
Thermopolis[5]	2,830	13	0	0	0	13	34	7	22	5	0
Torrington	6,709	13	0	4	1	8	48	8	40	0	0
Wheatland	3,544	7	0	1	0	6	72	24	45	3	0
Worland	5,026	8	0	5	0	3	56	14	30	12	2
Kermit	6,131	28	0	2	1	25	56	14	30	12	1
Kerrville	23,532	68	1	6	6	55	409	80	292	37	0
Kilgore[4]	14,978	42	0	6	4	32	400	41	343	16	1
Killeen	148,007	577	7	117	146	307	3,336	854	2,233	249	30
Kingsville	25,383	81	0	0	8	73	754	162	571	21	1
Kirby[4]	8,807	29	0	2	9	18	194	48	111	35	1
Knox City[4]	1,137	1	0	0	1	0	17	13	4	0	1
Kountze	2,111	6	0	1	2	3	52	22	28	2	1
Kress	689	1	0	0	0	1	1	0	1	0	2
Kyle[4]	46,155	80	1	20	7	52	538	42	452	44	0
La Feria	7,384	31	0	0	0	31	138	41	92	5	0
Lago Vista	6,923	12	0	2	1	9	69	18	45	6	0
La Grange[4]	4,686	21	0	2	3	16	115	25	86	4	0
La Grulla[4]	1,711	4	0	0	0	4	8	0	6	2	0
Laguna Vista[4]	3,206	6	0	0	0	6	21	14	6	1	0
La Joya	4,328	40	0	5	2	33	61	10	51	0	1
Lake Dallas	8,084	37	0	8	1	28	102	25	65	12	1
Lake Jackson	27,568	50	0	21	7	22	553	61	459	33	2
Lakeside	1,404	2	0	2	0	0	18	0	13	5	0
Lakeview, Harrison County	6,388	6	0	2	2	2	54	8	41	5	0

Table 8. Offenses Known to Law Enforcement, by Selected State and City, 2019—Continued

(Number.)

State/city	Population	Violent crime	Murder and nonnegligent manslaughter	Rape[1]	Robbery	Aggravated assault	Property crime	Burglary	Larceny-theft	Motor vehicle theft	Arson[2]
Lakeway	15,722	22	0	10	1	11	154	14	131	9	1
Lake Worth	5,002	15	0	0	9	6	356	65	279	12	0
La Marque	17,107	73	1	6	24	42	904	129	729	46	1
Lamesa	9,183	43	1	10	3	29	374	98	257	19	1
Lampasas	7,992	21	0	10	1	10	183	24	155	4	1
Lancaster	39,772	171	4	12	64	91	983	149	652	182	1
La Porte	35,591	65	2	21	10	32	457	71	334	52	2
Laredo	264,214	890	10	145	141	594	6,367	692	5,506	169	37
La Vernia	1,464	2	0	0	0	2	28	2	26	0	0
Lavon	3,299	3	0	1	0	2	27	1	26	0	0
League City	108,275	109	1	41	20	47	1,814	215	1,485	114	12
Leander	53,637	48	0	27	3	18	501	44	443	14	3
Leon Valley[4]	11,598	34	0	2	6	26	489	55	388	46	1
Levelland[4]	13,646	124	1	23	3	97	426	120	275	31	3
Lewisville	107,560	275	4	57	71	143	2,396	354	1,807	235	6
Liberty	9,334	33	0	5	4	24	184	21	145	18	0
Liberty Hill	2,119	2	0	0	0	2	33	10	19	4	0
Lindale	6,268	12	0	2	1	9	142	35	102	5	0
Linden	1,927	3	0	0	0	3	37	6	28	3	0
Little Elm	50,547	88	1	37	7	43	275	39	216	20	1
Littlefield	5,934	36	0	7	2	27	142	30	104	8	2
Live Oak	16,230	42	0	10	7	25	505	38	428	39	3
Livingston	5,128	36	0	7	8	21	259	34	209	16	1
Lockhart[4]	13,944	12	1	1	0	10	171	44	120	7	0
Log Cabin	752	2	0	0	0	2	12	8	4	0	0
Lone Star	1,497	15	0	1	0	14	16	3	13	0	0
Longview	81,660	326	8	53	46	219	2,506	584	1,722	200	6
Lorena[4]	1,771	8	0	1	2	5	34	6	28	0	0
Los Fresnos	7,947	42	0	2	0	40	132	10	115	7	1
Lubbock	257,372	2,565	13	239	443	1,870	11,743	2,312	8,228	1,203	57
Lufkin	35,937	134	1	20	16	97	1,403	260	1,067	76	5
Luling	5,979	35	0	5	4	26	97	17	75	5	0
Lumberton	12,948	18	0	5	2	11	153	15	118	20	0
Lyford	2,546	11	0	0	1	10	35	7	25	3	0
Lytle[4]	2,992	3	0	2	0	1	93	5	73	15	0
Madisonville	4,709	16	0	0	4	12	118	31	80	7	0
Magnolia	2,143	3	0	0	1	2	18	4	13	1	0
Manor[4]	10,102	41	0	4	3	34	220	27	182	11	2
Mansfield	70,851	73	0	31	15	27	766	93	624	49	1
Manvel[4]	11,097	13	0	3	0	10	72	30	36	6	0
Marble Falls	6,579	9	0	2	1	6	236	45	184	7	0
Marfa	1,742	6	0	0	0	6	2	1	1	0	0
Marshall	23,146	136	2	6	17	111	687	143	493	51	10
Mathis	4,797	53	0	3	2	48	89	32	47	10	6
McAllen	144,363	122	0	39	26	57	3,856	203	3,598	55	7
McGregor	5,134	18	0	11	0	7	45	11	29	5	2
McKinney	189,555	288	0	63	77	148	1,980	251	1,573	156	15
Meadows Place	4,621	12	0	1	7	4	111	16	85	10	0
Melissa[4]	10,107	9	0	3	0	6	58	16	41	1	0
Memorial Villages	12,402	4	0	0	2	2	72	15	54	3	0
Memphis[4]	2,062	7	0	0	0	7	33	17	11	5	0
Mercedes	16,869	81	1	17	9	54	646	92	510	44	1
Merkel	2,601	9	0	4	0	5	23	12	10	1	0
Mesquite[4]	144,558	573	6	54	210	303	5,238	811	3,603	824	10
Midland	140,072	403	5	60	59	279	2,764	378	2,108	278	16
Midlothian	26,346	22	0	6	4	12	336	34	290	12	1
Mineola	4,713	9	0	0	0	9	96	10	82	4	0
Mineral Wells	14,729	52	0	5	10	37	396	121	246	29	2
Mission	85,368	94	0	35	27	32	1,594	150	1,380	64	22
Missouri City	75,628	102	5	21	27	49	815	96	674	45	5
Monahans	7,611	10	1	3	1	5	84	23	59	2	0
Mont Belvieu	6,301	6	0	2	0	4	102	15	74	13	0
Montgomery	1,034	4	0	0	0	4	8	2	6	0	0
Morgans Point Resort	4,499	0	0	0	0	0	0	0	0	0	0
Mount Pleasant	16,291	63	1	14	8	40	555	72	460	23	3
Muleshoe[4]	5,073	7	0	0	0	7	44	6	34	4	0
Murphy	21,084	10	0	1	2	7	113	6	102	5	1
Nacogdoches	33,703	102	3	13	29	57	979	199	749	31	1
Nash	3,483	9	0	1	0	8	97	18	66	13	0
Nassau Bay	4,058	16	0	4	5	7	102	10	84	8	0
Natalia	1,567	5	0	0	0	5	19	10	7	2	1
Navasota[4]	7,677	34	0	5	3	26	162	64	65	33	0
Nederland[4]	17,563	47	1	11	1	34	309	50	234	25	0
Needville	3,083	4	0	1	0	3	18	2	14	2	0
New Boston	4,642	39	0	0	0	39	182	16	164	2	0
New Braunfels[4]	82,739	241	2	43	22	174	1,197	215	892	90	0
Nixon	2,506	21	0	1	1	19	13	3	10	0	0
Nocona	2,966	8	0	2	0	6	16	11	5	0	0
Nolanville	5,380	8	0	6	0	2	70	17	53	0	0
Northeast	3,106	2	0	0	1	1	67	4	60	3	0
Northlake[4]	2,946	14	0	2	3	7	63	4	51	8	0
North Richland Hills[4]	71,498	104	1	13	26	64	1,387	151	1,113	123	0
Oak Ridge North	3,143	2	0	0	1	1	33	5	23	5	0

Table 8. Offenses Known to Law Enforcement, by Selected State and City, 2019—Continued

(Number.)

State/city	Population	Violent crime	Murder and nonnegligent manslaughter	Rape[1]	Robbery	Aggravated assault	Property crime	Burglary	Larceny-theft	Motor vehicle theft	Arson[2]
Odessa	119,545	1,049	8	118	104	819	2,996	504	2,123	369	8
Olmos Park	2,434	1	0	0	0	1	24	5	17	2	0
Olney[4]	3,078	4	0	1	1	2	60	15	42	3	0
Olton	2,097	6	0	1	0	5	28	16	12	0	5
Omaha	980	1	0	0	0	1	4	2	1	1	0
Onalaska[4]	2,771	8	0	0	0	8	22	13	5	4	0
Overton	2,490	12	0	1	1	10	22	9	12	1	0
Ovilla	4,207	2	0	0	0	2	21	1	17	3	0
Oyster Creek	1,163	16	0	0	1	15	27	6	16	5	0
Palacios[4]	4,634	12	0	1	2	9	94	40	51	3	1
Palmer	2,083	3	0	0	1	2	15	5	9	1	0
Palmhurst	2,765	6	0	0	0	6	158	0	158	0	0
Palmview[4]	5,842	48	0	1	9	38	262	43	201	18	2
Pampa	17,412	103	1	8	8	86	653	157	453	43	0
Panhandle	2,337	11	1	0	0	10	15	7	6	2	0
Pantego	2,564	11	0	0	2	9	83	9	71	3	1
Paris	24,736	218	1	4	23	190	725	173	507	45	0
Parker[4]	4,746	2	0	1	0	1	27	4	22	1	0
Pasadena	154,101	679	7	109	159	404	3,467	519	2,603	345	9
Patton Village	2,016	3	0	1	0	2	14	5	7	2	0
Pearland	124,179	118	2	19	32	65	1,841	215	1,532	94	3
Pearsall[4]	10,525	14	0	1	1	12	209	69	129	11	1
Pecos	10,094	124	0	17	5	102	164	26	135	3	1
Pelican Bay	1,780	1	0	0	0	1	25	14	10	1	0
Penitas	4,961	16	0	3	1	12	64	12	48	4	0
Perryton	8,675	30	0	6	0	24	164	47	109	8	0
Petersburg	1,128	3	0	0	1	2	6	4	2	0	0
Pharr	80,814	238	2	58	26	152	1,585	244	1,280	61	12
Pilot Point	4,387	0	0	0	0	0	11	3	7	1	0
Pinehurst	2,070	9	0	0	1	8	56	2	49	5	0
Pittsburg[4]	4,668	22	0	3	0	19	90	27	54	9	0
Plainview[4]	20,569	59	0	8	5	46	503	108	376	19	0
Plano	289,897	402	5	77	112	208	4,955	671	3,911	373	16
Pleasanton	10,627	30	0	9	1	20	406	70	315	21	0
Ponder	2,049	12	4	2	0	6	19	3	14	2	0
Port Aransas	4,245	15	0	3	1	11	279	38	216	25	0
Port Arthur	55,643	390	13	20	96	261	1,445	504	807	134	7
Port Isabel[4]	5,064	18	0	1	0	17	168	17	142	9	0
Portland	17,547	25	0	8	5	12	376	33	323	20	1
Port Neches	12,881	56	0	11	2	43	178	49	114	15	0
Poteet	3,436	11	0	1	0	10	99	25	65	9	0
Pottsboro	2,381	1	0	0	0	1	6	1	4	1	0
Prairie View	6,526	6	1	3	1	1	22	3	18	1	0
Primera	4,954	3	0	2	0	1	30	7	21	2	0
Princeton	10,749	19	0	8	3	8	183	14	157	12	0
Prosper	22,570	63	0	7	0	56	188	31	154	3	0
Queen City	1,449	10	0	1	0	9	18	2	15	1	0
Quitman	1,826	9	0	5	0	4	25	10	14	1	0
Ralls[4]	1,852	6	0	0	1	5	11	4	3	4	2
Rancho Viejo	2,483	2	0	0	0	2	14	6	8	0	0
Ranger	2,454	22	0	1	0	21	37	19	16	2	0
Raymondville	10,959	106	0	9	7	90	318	91	216	11	6
Red Oak	13,095	22	0	0	9	13	336	59	257	20	1
Refugio	2,826	3	0	0	0	3	12	3	7	2	0
Reno, Lamar County	3,318	2	0	0	0	2	72	8	54	10	0
Reno, Parker County	2,971	27	0	0	0	27	31	10	18	3	0
Richardson	119,480	135	2	18	52	63	2,522	364	1,944	214	3
Richland Hills	8,089	38	0	8	15	15	283	38	207	38	0
Richmond	12,130	46	1	9	7	29	255	58	187	10	1
Richwood	3,967	4	0	2	2	0	35	7	24	4	0
Riesel	1,026	0	0	0	0	0	4	3	0	1	0
Rio Bravo	4,755	0	0	0	0	0	0	0	0	0	1
Rio Grande City	14,617	59	0	1	3	55	194	29	151	14	1
Rio Hondo	2,835	4	0	0	0	4	30	10	20	0	0
River Oaks	7,743	5	0	0	0	5	101	11	85	5	0
Roanoke	8,489	21	0	0	3	18	99	15	78	6	0
Robinson	11,774	25	0	0	1	24	156	23	125	8	0
Rockdale	5,663	12	1	2	3	6	146	28	108	10	2
Rockport	10,734	22	0	5	1	16	443	114	309	20	2
Rockwall	45,183	42	1	15	6	20	750	34	653	63	0
Rollingwood	1,585	0	0	0	0	0	17	1	14	2	0
Roma	11,506	25	0	4	2	19	82	16	48	18	0
Roman Forest	1,968	1	0	0	0	1	1	0	0	1	0
Rosenberg[4]	38,541	157	1	26	29	101	615	97	433	85	5
Round Rock	127,354	154	1	34	29	90	2,494	288	2,148	58	0
Rowlett	63,863	114	1	18	16	79	912	94	744	74	0
Royse City	13,104	20	0	3	1	16	129	17	101	11	1
Runaway Bay[4]	1,524	0	0	0	0	0	8	3	4	1	1
Rusk	5,539	18	0	3	4	11	84	27	51	6	0
Sabinal	1,696	0	0	0	0	0	10	2	7	1	0
Sachse	26,839	15	0	8	2	5	208	26	167	15	0
Salado[4]	2,308	5	0	1	1	3	15	5	9	1	0
San Angelo	101,084	373	2	82	52	237	3,383	583	2,567	233	3

Table 8. Offenses Known to Law Enforcement, by Selected State and City, 2019—Continued

(Number.)

State/city	Population	Violent crime	Murder and nonnegligent manslaughter	Rape[1]	Robbery	Aggravated assault	Property crime	Burglary	Larceny-theft	Motor vehicle theft	Arson[2]
San Antonio	1,539,328	9,647	107	1,346	1,767	6,427	61,478	9,118	46,271	6,089	186
San Augustine	1,856	0	0	0	0	0	6	4	2	0	0
San Benito	24,559	65	0	33	9	23	1,018	193	798	27	3
San Diego	4,261	13	0	0	1	12	3	3	0	0	0
San Elizario	9,161	4	0	0	1	3	28	11	10	7	0
Sanger[5]	8,457	27	0	6	0	21		23		12	0
San Juan	37,398	155	1	19	14	121	858	98	715	45	1
San Marcos[4]	66,157	263	1	83	42	137	1,415	270	1,044	101	3
San Saba	3,059	8	0	0	0	8	46	15	28	3	2
Sansom Park Village	6,034	12	0	0	4	8	120	43	58	19	0
Santa Fe	13,600	17	0	7	4	6	171	45	108	18	1
Santa Rosa	2,797	0	0	0	0	0	8	4	4	0	0
Schertz	41,383	95	1	23	13	58	670	117	517	36	1
Schulenburg[4]	2,915	18	0	0	0	18	52	12	37	3	1
Seabrook	13,958	25	0	12	2	11	144	34	98	12	0
Seagoville	16,981	12	0	0	4	8	384	72	210	102	0
Seagraves	2,875	5	0	1	0	4	13	2	10	1	0
Sealy[4]	6,544	14	0	2	3	9	91	28	55	8	0
Seguin[4]	29,487	88	1	6	18	63	745	78	633	34	1
Selma	11,742	24	0	8	5	11	240	33	178	29	1
Seminole	7,725	52	0	2	2	48	112	26	80	6	2
Seven Points	1,504	5	0	2	0	3	28	3	21	4	0
Seymour	2,606	7	0	0	0	7	30	3	25	2	0
Shavano Park	3,913	2	0	0	0	2	22	6	16	0	0
Shenandoah	3,008	9	0	1	4	4	229	12	197	20	1
Sherman	42,448	147	0	29	28	90	1,068	224	778	66	5
Shiner	2,173	1	0	0	0	1	14	3	10	1	0
Silsbee	6,734	18	0	2	2	14	129	27	88	14	0
Sinton	5,424	46	0	11	0	35	190	41	144	5	2
Smithville	4,322	15	1	3	1	10	87	18	63	6	0
Snyder	11,337	34	0	3	2	29	198	55	140	3	0
Socorro	34,327	45	0	6	8	31	251	24	202	25	0
Somerset	1,893	2	0	0	0	2	6	1	3	2	0
Somerville	1,445	6	0	1	1	4	23	6	14	3	0
Sonora	2,737	7	0	2	1	4	25	0	23	2	0
Sour Lake	1,860	0	0	0	0	0	23	2	17	4	0
South Houston	17,619	73	1	6	35	31	422	71	245	106	2
Southlake	32,639	11	0	3	4	4	450	21	414	15	0
South Padre Island[4]	2,830	55	0	21	1	33	457	33	394	30	0
Southside Place[4]	1,874	0	0	0	0	0	16	2	13	1	0
Spearman[4]	3,267	4	0	0	0	4	11	9	1	1	0
Splendora	2,109	4	0	0	2	2	44	21	16	7	0
Springtown	2,950	7	0	1	0	6	78	12	66	0	0
Spring Valley[4]	4,363	3	0	0	1	2	73	11	57	5	0
Spur	1,187	0	0	0	0	0	3	3	0	0	0
Stagecoach	600	0	0	0	0	0	0	0	0	0	0
Stamford	2,933	4	0	0	2	2	50	10	37	3	0
Stanton	3,016	9	0	3	1	5	32	5	17	10	1
Stephenville	21,400	30	0	8	3	19	404	64	316	24	1
Sugar Land	89,919	82	0	15	45	22	1,537	186	1,288	63	0
Sullivan City	4,172	29	0	5	1	23	91	25	62	4	0
Sulphur Springs	16,111	37	2	6	9	20	157	33	98	26	2
Sunset Valley	693	6	0	0	3	3	138	11	122	5	0
Surfside Beach[4]	582	6	0	2	1	3	32	7	24	1	0
Sweeny[4]	3,753	13	0	5	1	7	82	10	68	4	1
Sweetwater	10,530	50	0	4	5	41	307	139	152	16	1
Taft[4]	2,924	5	0	0	0	5	60	24	32	4	0
Tahoka[4]	2,617	1	0	0	0	1	26	7	15	4	0
Tatum	1,386	4	0	0	0	4	25	14	9	2	0
Taylor	17,225	50	0	8	5	37	387	92	281	14	7
Teague[4]	3,498	4	0	0	2	2	45	15	26	4	0
Temple	75,706	236	12	70	51	103	1,940	342	1,408	190	9
Terrell	18,104	73	3	9	14	47	581	97	424	60	2
Terrell Hills	5,473	4	0	1	0	3	43	15	28	0	0
Texarkana	37,460	171	3	28	45	95	1,914	348	1,427	139	16
Texas City	49,044	236	5	46	62	123	1,489	278	1,100	111	2
The Colony	43,697	100	0	61	5	34	477	60	382	35	5
Thorndale	1,302	7	0	3	0	4	21	6	13	2	0
Tioga[4]	1,009	2	0	0	0	2	4	3	1	0	0
Tool[4]	2,299	0	0	0	0	0	9	4	3	2	0
Trophy Club	13,090	2	0	1	1	0	69	5	58	6	1
Troup	2,019	9	0	2	2	5	66	28	38	0	0
Troy	2,030	6	0	0	2	4	35	4	29	2	0
Tulia[4]	4,690	34	0	2	1	31	132	34	89	9	1
Tye[4]	1,300	3	0	1	0	2	30	5	23	2	0
Tyler	106,159	412	7	71	82	252	3,133	386	2,596	151	1
Universal City	20,825	63	0	15	20	28	546	120	391	35	1
University Park[4]	25,516	5	0	1	4	0	302	33	232	35	3
Uvalde	16,375	36	0	11	7	18	621	109	499	13	4
Van	2,742	5	0	4	0	1	48	8	36	4	0
Van Alstyne	4,115	10	0	0	3	7	59	17	40	2	0
Venus	3,683	3	0	0	0	3	30	2	27	1	0
Vernon	10,259	46	0	5	3	38	269	64	195	10	1

Table 8. Offenses Known to Law Enforcement, by Selected State and City, 2019—Continued

(Number.)

State/city	Population	Violent crime	Murder and nonnegligent manslaughter	Rape[1]	Robbery	Aggravated assault	Property crime	Burglary	Larceny-theft	Motor vehicle theft	Arson[2]
Victoria	67,766	280	4	51	46	179	1,885	358	1,440	87	4
Waco[4]	138,091	878	3	129	122	624	4,851	1,194	3,329	328	20
Waelder	1,129	4	0	1	2	1	2	1	1	0	0
Wake Village	5,416	9	2	0	2	5	99	17	71	11	0
Waller[4]	3,546	2	0	1	0	1	43	10	31	2	0
Wallis	1,304	5	0	0	0	5	5	1	4	0	0
Watauga[4]	24,757	48	0	13	10	25	319	40	244	35	0
Waxahachie	36,225	73	1	4	17	51	527	65	417	45	2
Weatherford	31,389	58	0	15	10	33	508	67	407	34	0
Webster	11,194	47	0	12	16	19	774	84	594	96	0
Weimar	2,189	3	0	2	0	1	23	5	17	1	0
Weslaco	40,856	162	0	29	42	91	1,595	162	1,404	29	3
West[4]	2,990	5	0	2	0	3	40	8	30	2	0
West Columbia	3,899	3	0	2	0	1	97	24	69	4	0
West Lake Hills	3,444	7	0	0	0	7	89	9	79	1	0
West Orange	3,414	9	0	1	2	6	97	10	80	7	0
Westover Hills[4]	701	1	0	0	0	1	12	6	6	0	0
West University Place	15,759	2	0	1	1	0	111	35	71	5	0
Westworth	2,763	1	0	0	0	1	239	31	208	0	0
Wharton[4]	8,754	31	0	0	4	27	256	60	187	9	5
Whitehouse	8,406	9	0	1	0	8	53	10	40	3	0
White Oak	6,332	3	0	0	0	3	72	21	47	4	0
Whitesboro	4,039	3	0	0	1	2	44	6	34	4	0
White Settlement	18,082	33	0	0	14	19	338	56	231	51	0
Whitewright	1,689	1	0	0	0	1	8	3	5	0	0
Whitney	2,146	6	0	0	0	6	27	8	18	1	0
Wichita Falls	104,738	387	5	78	139	165	3,234	602	2,381	251	1
Willis	6,515	40	0	7	6	27	141	25	101	15	5
Willow Park	5,569	9	0	3	0	6	49	6	36	7	0
Wills Point[4]	3,639	9	0	3	0	6	22	8	13	1	0
Wilmer	4,199	9	0	0	2	7	93	16	68	9	0
Windcrest	5,936	11	0	1	8	2	252	19	206	27	1
Winnsboro[4]	3,337	6	0	1	0	5	36	8	28	0	0
Winters[4]	2,461	9	0	0	1	8	28	20	8	0	0
Wolfforth	5,131	0	0	0	0	0	32	10	22	0	0
Woodville	2,488	4	0	1	2	1	10	5	5	0	0
Woodway	8,878	5	0	1	1	3	109	5	100	4	1
Wortham[4]	994	1	0	0	0	1	12	2	9	1	0
Wylie	51,051	52	0	16	9	27	398	31	347	20	4
Yoakum	5,983	14	0	3	0	11	51	18	30	3	0
UTAH											
Alta	385	0	0	0	0	0	15	1	14	0	0
American Fork/Cedar Hills	40,366	22	0	8	1	13	702	36	641	25	2
Aurora	1,047	0	0	0	0	0	0	0	0	0	0
Big Water	500	1	0	0	0	1	0	0	0	0	0
Bluffdale	14,648	13	0	3	0	10	177	51	100	26	0
Bountiful	44,317	43	1	25	7	10	642	87	500	55	1
Brigham City	19,362	28	0	7	2	19	362	72	261	29	0
Cedar City	32,242	70	1	8	2	59	751	119	571	61	4
Centerville	18,013	23	0	18	1	4	380	32	317	31	0
Clearfield	31,558	59	0	15	8	36	462	68	341	53	2
Clinton	22,179	13	1	2	2	8	301	17	265	19	0
Cottonwood Heights	34,054	43	0	7	12	24	787	103	638	46	2
Draper	48,518	84	0	35	6	43	976	114	729	133	4
Enoch	6,892	31	0	2	0	29	38	8	24	6	0
Ephraim	7,302	16	0	7	1	8	90	6	83	1	0
Farmington	25,006	15	0	6	1	8	306	38	245	23	4
Garland	2,541	5	0	2	1	2	51	14	35	2	0
Grantsville	11,326	29	0	9	2	18	192	34	142	16	4
Harrisville	6,678	7	0	5	1	1	224	21	184	19	2
Heber	16,527	26	0	4	2	20	228	17	194	17	0
Helper	2,075	4	0	0	0	4	47	12	33	2	0
Hurricane	17,676	22	0	8	0	14	283	60	201	22	0
Kanab	4,729	3	0	0	0	3	32	5	26	1	2
Kaysville	32,404	24	0	13	2	9	246	41	190	15	0
La Verkin[4]	4,387	9	0	6	0	3	61	11	42	8	5
Layton	78,052	134	1	58	17	58	1,561	249	1,238	74	4
Lehi	65,125	59	0	28	1	30	694	97	563	34	4
Logan	51,508	70	1	35	3	31	852	145	675	32	4
Lone Peak	29,969	7	0	6	0	1	151	28	112	11	0
Mapleton	10,041	1	0	0	0	1	56	11	42	3	0
Moab	5,274	33	1	7	2	23	175	15	138	22	2
Monticello	1,995	0	0	0	0	0	18	3	13	2	0
Mount Pleasant	3,440	4	0	2	0	2	49	4	43	2	0
Murray	49,675	216	1	56	41	118	3,027	431	2,188	408	4
Nephi	6,037	9	0	5	1	3	100	21	72	7	0
North Ogden	19,771	6	0	3	1	2	232	34	173	25	0
North Park	15,713	6	0	3	1	2	169	12	150	7	0
North Salt Lake	21,190	27	1	8	7	11	405	49	314	42	1
Ogden	87,616	417	5	74	81	257	3,218	500	2,319	399	10
Orem	99,221	69	1	20	12	36	1,827	152	1,576	99	0
Park City	8,491	51	0	2	2	47	225	14	193	18	0

Table 8. Offenses Known to Law Enforcement, by Selected State and City, 2019—Continued

(Number.)

State/city	Population	Violent crime	Murder and nonnegligent manslaughter	Rape[1]	Robbery	Aggravated assault	Property crime	Burglary	Larceny-theft	Motor vehicle theft	Arson[2]
Parowan	3,073	14	0	12	0	2	50	7	36	7	
Payson	20,079	10	0	3	1	6	318	54	254	10	
Pleasant Grove	39,641	29	1	6	0	22	424	62	335	27	0
Pleasant View	10,663	11	0	3	1	7	108	21	74	13	1
Price	8,201	34	0	4	2	28	486	57	420	9	0
Provo	117,986	207	2	70	22	113	2,090	209	1,747	134	3
Richfield	7,777	4	0	2	0	2	247	27	205	15	
Riverdale	8,795	23	0	1	6	16	530	38	476	16	0
Roosevelt	6,962	22	0	14	2	6	201	28	150	23	0
Roy	38,834	53	0	19	6	28	514	90	369	55	0
Salem	8,496	1	0	0	0	1	69	10	57	2	
Salina	2,560	4	0	1	1	2	91	21	59	11	0
Salt Lake City	202,633	1,480	10	245	414	811	12,516	1,601	9,422	1,493	32
Sandy	97,057	159	0	54	21	84	2,613	405	1,940	268	5
Santa Clara/Ivins	16,671	9	0	0	0	9	126	28	87	11	0
Santaquin/Genola	13,584	4	0	3	0	1	114	21	78	15	0
Saratoga Springs	31,786	32	0	14	0	18	226	47	169	10	0
South Jordan	74,321	77	1	17	16	43	1,453	160	1,165	128	3
South Ogden	17,174	25	1	12	3	9	329	80	226	23	1
South Salt Lake	25,160	242	6	50	57	129	1,796	237	1,246	313	2
Spanish Fork	40,095	12	0	4	2	6	352	29	294	29	0
Spring City	1,053	0	0	0	0	0	20	6	14	0	0
Springdale	601	1	0	0	0	1	21	4	16	1	0
Springville	33,824	23	0	9	3	11	627	52	538	37	
St. George	86,202	196	3	48	19	126	1,388	228	1,049	111	7
Sunset	5,304	15	0	3	0	12	83	14	64	5	1
Syracuse	30,301	23	0	13	2	8	235	39	180	16	0
Tooele	35,065	104	1	35	17	51	1,143	110	939	94	6
Tremonton	8,764	9	1	3	0	5	151	30	107	14	
Vernal	10,484	32	2	8	1	21	261	28	221	12	0
Washington	27,705	35	0	16	2	17	477	51	410	16	0
West Bountiful	5,705	18	0	13	1	4	147	10	115	22	0
West Jordan	115,392	298	1	39	50	208	3,036	352	2,374	310	3
West Valley	137,132	945	8	183	148	606	4,915	741	3,353	821	15
Willard	1,872	6	0	0	0	6	35	10	21	4	0
Woods Cross	11,600	11	0	1	7	3	176	27	129	20	2
VERMONT											
Barre	8,605	72	1	28	3	40	237	24	212	1	2
Barre Town	7,693	8	0	3	2	3	44	8	36	0	0
Bellows Falls	2,993	3	0	0	0	3	56	9	44	3	0
Bennington	14,900	31	0	5	4	22	415	51	351	13	0
Berlin	2,796	4	0	0	1	3	120	6	113	1	0
Bradford	2,697	0	0	0	0	0	22	7	14	1	0
Brandon	3,766	9	0	1	0	8	41	7	34	0	0
Brattleboro	11,410	40	0	2	9	29	457	67	368	22	0
Bristol	3,891	4	0	0	1	3	17	4	10	3	0
Burlington	42,212	115	1	22	10	82	837	120	704	13	3
Castleton	4,595	0	0	0	0	0	0	0	0	0	0
Chester	3,006	3	0	1	0	2	28	8	19	1	0
Colchester	17,313	16	0	6	1	9	196	21	175	0	1
Dover	1,057	5	0	1	0	4	52	6	46	0	0
Essex	21,803	13	0	0	3	10	297	59	227	11	2
Hardwick	2,849	7	0	2	1	4	33	6	27	0	0
Hartford	9,567	25	0	12	0	13	127	25	92	10	0
Hinesburg	4,577	3	0	1	0	2	18	2	14	2	0
Ludlow	1,870	3	0	1	0	2	12	1	11	0	0
Lyndonville	1,157	4	0	0	1	3	23	1	22	0	0
Manchester	4,230	5	0	0	0	5	46	8	38	0	1
Middlebury	8,613	5	0	1	0	4	96	11	82	3	0
Milton	11,024	16	0	8	1	7	104	20	84	0	0
Montpelier	7,434	7	0	4	1	2	161	28	132	1	1
Morristown	5,450	6	0	3	1	2	73	5	68	0	0
Newport	4,248	22	0	5	1	16	104	13	88	3	1
Northfield	6,006	16	0	4	2	10	46	8	35	3	0
Norwich	3,304	2	0	1	0	1	13	5	7	1	0
Pittsford	2,806	1	0	0	0	1	6	2	4	0	0
Royalton	2,835	0	0	0	0	0	9	1	7	1	0
Rutland	15,300	60	0	3	5	52	383	56	312	15	2
Rutland Town	4,078	5	0	3	0	2	48	4	44	0	0
Shelburne	7,817	3	0	1	0	2	48	8	36	4	0
South Burlington	19,318	32	1	17	1	13	572	51	520	1	1
Springfield	8,864	16	0	5	2	9	185	42	142	1	1
St. Albans	6,777	39	0	6	0	33	431	36	393	2	1
St. Johnsbury	7,158	15	0	3	0	12	98	12	85	1	1
Stowe	4,495	3	0	2	0	1	51	4	47	0	0
Swanton	6,560	8	0	0	0	8	55	12	40	3	0
Thetford	2,557	0	0	0	0	0	5	0	5	0	0
Vergennes	2,547	2	0	1	0	1	37	2	34	1	0
Weathersfield	2,745	4	0	1	0	3	15	4	11	0	0
Williston	9,778	7	0	2	0	5	193	17	174	2	0
Wilmington	1,796	2	0	2	0	0	11	2	7	2	0
Windsor	3,377	8	0	0	0	8	34	5	26	3	0

Table 8. Offenses Known to Law Enforcement, by Selected State and City, 2019—Continued

(Number.)

State/city	Population	Violent crime	Murder and nonnegligent manslaughter	Rape[1]	Robbery	Aggravated assault	Property crime	Burglary	Larceny-theft	Motor vehicle theft	Arson[2]
Winhall	730	1	0	0	0	1	9	0	9	0	0
Winooski	7,233	28	0	5	2	21	121	26	95	0	2
Woodstock	2,917	3	0	1	0	2	23	2	20	1	0
VIRGINIA											
Abingdon	7,949	6	0	2	2	2	129	7	112	10	0
Alexandria	162,588	260	4	24	78	154	2,482	128	1,967	387	5
Altavista	3,417	7	0	1	1	5	86	5	77	4	0
Amherst	2,194	4	0	0	0	4	8	1	7	0	0
Appalachia	1,568	2	0	0	0	2	18	10	5	3	3
Ashland	7,876	37	1	3	6	27	199	13	177	9	0
Bedford	6,532	20	0	9	1	10	199	14	178	7	2
Berryville	4,361	1	0	0	0	1	36	4	32	0	1
Big Stone Gap	5,215	3	0	2	0	1	110	12	94	4	3
Blacksburg	44,853	41	0	20	4	17	322	28	285	9	0
Blackstone	3,367	14	0	4	3	7	83	16	64	3	0
Bluefield	4,624	6	1	3	1	1	218	16	198	4	0
Bridgewater	6,125	3	0	1	0	2	25	2	23	0	0
Bristol	16,613	42	2	9	3	28	513	68	395	50	2
Broadway	3,908	1	0	0	1	0	9	2	6	1	0
Buena Vista	6,272	5	0	1	0	4	54	10	39	5	0
Burkeville	402	0	0	0	0	0	10	0	10	0	0
Cape Charles	1,009	1	0	0	0	1	4	0	3	1	0
Cedar Bluff	1,011	1	0	1	0	0	5	1	4	0	1
Charlottesville	48,585	174	1	36	30	107	1,161	116	961	84	0
Chase City	2,219	4	1	0	0	3	46	12	29	5	0
Chatham	1,434	0	0	0	0	0	4	0	4	0	0
Chesapeake	242,310	979	7	99	143	730	5,191	596	4,285	310	11
Chilhowie	1,718	1	0	1	0	0	17	3	13	1	0
Chincoteague	2,881	11	0	2	2	7	73	8	64	1	0
Christiansburg	22,444	43	0	15	2	26	532	34	485	13	1
Clarksville	1,175	0	0	0	0	0	12	1	11	0	0
Clifton Forge	3,524	7	0	0	0	7	48	6	35	7	0
Clintwood	1,311	2	0	0	0	2	15	2	13	0	0
Coeburn	1,881	9	0	2	0	7	38	5	32	1	0
Colonial Heights	17,857	50	0	17	8	25	676	29	620	27	2
Covington	5,462	4	0	1	0	3	107	10	93	4	2
Crewe	2,151	8	0	0	2	6	52	5	36	11	1
Culpeper	18,671	31	0	6	9	16	296	17	266	13	0
Damascus	788	0	0	0	0	0	16	3	13	0	0
Danville	40,781	216	11	26	61	118	1,632	222	1,326	84	14
Dayton	1,615	3	0	0	0	3	6	0	6	0	0
Dublin	2,667	3	0	2	0	1	23	4	19	0	0
Dumfries	5,265	9	0	0	5	4	74	14	45	15	0
Elkton	2,860	2	0	0	0	2	29	5	21	3	0
Emporia	5,184	26	0	2	8	16	192	14	176	2	0
Exmore	1,386	1	0	0	0	1	24	5	18	1	0
Fairfax City	24,259	24	0	5	13	6	405	13	366	26	1
Falls Church	14,884	12	0	1	3	8	176	15	148	13	1
Farmville	7,778	10	1	3	0	6	162	16	135	11	0
Franklin	8,100	25	1	6	7	11	348	38	290	20	2
Fredericksburg	28,919	108	2	13	16	77	999	58	905	36	4
Front Royal	15,356	33	0	16	6	11	279	25	239	15	1
Galax	6,559	27	0	5	3	19	292	20	259	13	1
Gate City	1,888	0	0	0	0	0	41	3	33	5	0
Glade Spring	1,424	0	0	0	0	0	2	0	2	0	0
Glasgow	1,106	0	0	0	0	0	2	0	2	0	0
Gordonsville	1,606	3	0	0	2	1	16	2	14	0	0
Gretna	1,205	0	0	0	0	0	3	0	3	0	0
Grottoes	2,813	1	0	0	0	1	29	1	27	1	0
Grundy	917	1	0	0	0	1	36	0	35	1	0
Halifax	1,219	1	0	0	0	1	14	2	11	1	0
Hampton[6]	133,965	316	16	24	120	156		491		231	21
Harrisonburg	54,869	110	4	17	12	77	834	98	711	25	3
Haymarket	1,744	5	0	1	0	4	11	0	9	2	0
Haysi	480	0	0	0	0	0	7	1	6	0	0
Herndon	24,697	32	1	10	18	3	259	28	226	5	0
Hillsville	2,644	3	0	2	0	1	63	10	50	3	0
Hopewell	22,562	99	6	7	25	61	553	119	403	31	2
Hurt	1,235	0	0	0	0	0	14	1	11	2	0
Independence	895	1	0	0	0	1	9	1	6	2	0
Jonesville	938	1	0	1	0	0	5	0	5	0	0
Kenbridge	1,198	0	0	0	0	0	0	0	0	0	0
Kilmarnock	1,407	1	0	0	0	1	25	7	18	0	0
La Crosse	574	2	0	0	2	0	5	4	1	0	0
Lawrenceville	1,004	2	0	0	1	1	4	1	3	0	0
Lebanon	3,184	8	0	6	1	1	154	30	120	4	0
Leesburg	56,030	100	0	18	16	66	626	24	571	31	0
Lexington	7,098	3	0	0	1	2	36	2	33	1	0
Louisa	1,678	2	0	0	0	2	53	2	51	0	0
Luray	4,806	7	0	2	1	4	137	14	112	11	1
Lynchburg	81,603	275	8	33	41	193	1,627	181	1,278	168	11
Manassas	41,888	105	1	23	16	65	636	72	525	39	4

Table 8. Offenses Known to Law Enforcement, by Selected State and City, 2019—Continued

(Number.)

State/city	Population	Violent crime	Murder and nonnegligent manslaughter	Rape[1]	Robbery	Aggravated assault	Property crime	Burglary	Larceny-theft	Motor vehicle theft	Arson[2]
Manassas Park	16,882	25	0	9	6	10	111	10	90	11	0
Marion	5,615	29	0	2	5	22	183	27	147	9	1
Martinsville	13,025	54	2	3	8	41	471	72	366	33	0
Middleburg	879	0	0	0	0	0	9	0	9	0	0
Middletown	1,365	1	0	1	0	0	15	3	12	0	0
Mount Jackson	2,100	1	0	0	0	1	50	3	44	3	0
Narrows	1,950	1	0	0	0	1	7	1	6	0	0
New Market	2,245	3	0	0	1	2	8	1	6	1	1
Newport News	178,734	942	24	89	187	642	5,148	693	3,961	494	31
Norfolk	244,347	1,134	36	117	321	660	8,463	703	6,972	788	14
Norton	3,914	9	0	3	1	5	138	6	127	5	0
Occoquan	1,097	0	0	0	0	0	2	0	2	0	0
Onancock	1,218	3	0	0	2	1	31	4	26	1	0
Onley	502	0	0	0	0	0	20	3	15	2	0
Orange	5,016	9	0	2	0	7	49	9	36	4	0
Parksley	817	1	0	0	0	1	6	0	4	2	0
Pearisburg	2,643	3	0	2	0	1	49	5	38	6	0
Pennington Gap	1,732	3	1	1	0	1	47	2	44	1	1
Petersburg	31,568	224	14	13	53	144	916	141	681	94	7
Pocahontas	357	0	0	0	0	0	0	0	0	0	0
Poquoson	12,011	19	0	6	1	12	101	18	80	3	1
Portsmouth	94,218	749	20	44	203	482	4,977	958	3,651	368	11
Pound	939	3	0	1	0	2	3	0	3	0	0
Pulaski	8,720	27	1	11	8	7	258	32	213	13	1
Purcellville	10,090	13	0	3	1	9	46	2	38	6	0
Radford	17,797	52	0	20	4	28	237	38	192	7	2
Rich Creek	744	2	0	2	0	0	16	2	13	1	0
Richlands	5,256	16	0	3	0	13	136	29	99	8	2
Richmond	229,927	1,190	52	77	428	633	8,807	1,121	6,518	1,168	50
Roanoke	100,042	427	12	48	103	264	4,434	488	3,579	367	26
Rocky Mount	4,762	12	0	1	4	7	143	4	137	2	0
Rural Retreat	1,459	0	0	0	0	0	15	1	14	0	0
Salem	25,942	24	1	8	8	7	503	29	438	36	2
Saltville	1,927	1	0	1	0	0	11	3	8	0	0
Shenandoah	2,316	2	0	0	1	1	22	1	19	2	0
Smithfield	8,392	7	0	0	0	7	127	14	98	15	2
South Boston	7,721	28	0	2	8	18	335	40	291	4	1
South Hill	4,345	12	0	2	3	7	121	9	105	7	0
Stanley	1,651	1	0	0	0	1	19	4	15	0	0
Staunton	24,584	46	1	7	11	27	608	63	523	22	3
Stephens City	2,024	1	0	0	0	1	49	2	46	1	0
St. Paul	877	1	0	1	0	0	16	1	12	3	0
Strasburg	6,643	15	0	2	1	12	82	14	64	4	1
Suffolk	90,817	251	2	30	69	150	2,340	296	1,892	152	10
Tappahannock	2,417	17	0	1	0	16	46	7	37	2	0
Tazewell	4,185	6	0	1	0	5	35	10	21	4	0
Timberville	2,662	2	0	0	1	1	22	1	19	2	0
Victoria	1,631	1	0	0	0	1	30	4	25	1	0
Vienna	16,660	8	0	2	2	4	149	15	125	9	0
Vinton	8,077	9	0	0	0	9	180	15	146	19	0
Virginia Beach	451,001	528	7	81	174	266	7,772	584	6,611	577	39
Warrenton	9,912	12	0	4	2	6	215	8	204	3	1
Warsaw	1,484	0	0	0	0	0	13	2	11	0	0
Waverly	1,976	9	0	1	0	8	32	8	22	2	1
Waynesboro	22,470	50	1	10	12	27	477	53	382	42	0
Weber City	1,224	2	0	0	0	2	15	1	12	2	0
West Point	3,311	3	0	0	0	3	28	1	26	1	0
White Stone	332	0	0	0	0	0	2	0	2	0	0
Williamsburg	15,191	20	0	3	7	10	193	5	180	8	0
Winchester	28,128	93	0	38	15	40	692	86	567	39	2
Windsor	2,731	4	0	0	0	4	15	3	12	0	0
Wise	2,965	1	0	0	0	1	36	10	23	3	1
Woodstock	5,232	9	0	0	1	8	97	4	91	2	0
Wytheville	7,969	5	0	1	1	3	194	12	168	14	0
WASHINGTON											
Aberdeen	16,404	85	0	15	16	54	834	159	614	61	3
Airway Heights	9,085	33	0	8	4	21	480	72	347	61	2
Algona	3,207	2	0	0	1	1	31	11	18	2	0
Anacortes	17,130	30	0	8	3	19	380	64	308	8	1
Arlington	19,394	60	0	15	8	37	662	118	473	71	1
Auburn	82,381	360	1	59	120	180	3,334	605	2,116	613	21
Bainbridge Island	24,739	25	1	10	2	12	242	48	188	6	2
Battle Ground	21,002	32	2	9	4	17	404	56	314	34	3
Bellevue	146,913	194	0	27	82	85	4,294	519	3,395	380	16
Bellingham	90,208	204	0	34	53	117	3,346	459	2,722	165	5
Black Diamond	4,476	0	0	0	0	0	16	3	12	1	0
Bonney Lake	21,192	33	0	10	2	21	451	77	330	44	3
Bothell	46,387	65	0	17	19	29	1,017	165	774	78	6
Brier	6,975	3	0	0	0	3	47	9	34	4	1
Buckley	5,402	6	0	2	1	3	66	21	36	9	2
Burien[4,8]	52,189			4	66	113	1,900	332	1,005	563	17
Burlington	8,839	17	0	4	5	8	705	82	584	39	0

Table 8. Offenses Known to Law Enforcement, by Selected State and City, 2019—Continued

(Number.)

State/city	Population	Violent crime	Murder and nonnegligent manslaughter	Rape[1]	Robbery	Aggravated assault	Property crime	Burglary	Larceny-theft	Motor vehicle theft	Arson[2]
Camas	23,865	19	1	10	2	6	219	35	169	15	1
Carnation[4,8]	2,224		0		0	0	17	1	12	4	2
Castle Rock	2,251	3	0	1	0	2	70	10	51	9	0
Centralia	17,299	88	0	19	23	46	794	145	590	59	1
Chehalis	7,573	17	0	1	2	14	454	68	365	21	0
Cheney	12,715	43	0	18	0	25	203	55	135	13	0
Chewelah	2,643	5	0	0	0	5	33	5	26	2	0
Clarkston	7,417	17	0	5	4	8	342	70	264	8	2
Cle Elum	2,966	4	0	0	0	4	78	18	56	4	0
Colville	4,777	4	0	2	0	2	55	5	48	2	0
Connell	5,765	3	0	0	0	3	25	7	16	2	0
Coulee Dam	1,076	0	0	0	0	0	18	7	11	0	0
Covington[4,8]	21,436		1		13	10	584	111	433	40	3
Darrington	1,414	9	0	2	0	7	28	9	13	6	1
Des Moines	31,460	111	2	11	55	43	1,092	197	652	243	9
Dupont	9,678	31	0	4	0	27	113	15	91	7	1
Duvall	7,980	5	1	0	2	2	39	7	28	4	1
East Wenatchee	14,097	14	0	4	2	8	377	33	328	16	1
Eatonville	3,027	4	0	1	1	2	44	13	23	8	1
Edgewood	11,510	15	0	2	2	11	231	60	140	31	1
Edmonds	42,565	65	3	15	16	31	842	140	632	70	2
Ellensburg	20,616	42	0	14	5	23	601	84	489	28	5
Elma	3,089	6	0	1	0	5	82	17	58	7	1
Enumclaw	11,882	9	0	5	3	1	229	38	170	21	0
Ephrata	8,062	12	0	1	3	8	407	90	289	28	2
Everett	111,091	373	5	55	110	203	4,683	650	3,077	956	13
Federal Way	97,762	458	0	51	210	197	4,480	668	3,042	770	14
Ferndale	14,439	16	0	2	1	13	308	50	240	18	2
Fircrest	6,839	16	0	1	4	11	105	24	74	7	1
Forks	3,874	11	0	3	0	8	71	11	52	8	0
Gig Harbor	9,909	22	0	4	4	14	511	47	441	23	2
Gold Bar	2,323	2	0	0	0	2	44	20	22	2	1
Goldendale	3,496	2	0	1	0	1	57	7	47	3	0
Grand Coulee	2,047	1	0	0	0	1	79	31	38	10	0
Grandview	11,163	7	0	1	2	4	205	43	142	20	3
Granite Falls	3,634	3	0	0	0	3	73	22	45	6	0
Hoquiam	8,469	13	0	2	3	8	268	55	201	12	2
Index	210	0	0	0	0	0	1	0	1	0	0
Issaquah	38,606	30	0	16	7	7	1,357	133	1,134	90	2
Kalama	2,737	2	0	1	1	0	40	11	28	1	0
Kelso	12,164	52	0	13	4	35	486	76	365	45	6
Kenmore[4,8]	23,219		1		4	5	259	58	161	40	1
Kennewick	82,687	158	3	36	35	84	2,126	293	1,680	153	21
Kent	129,870	452	5	92	196	159	5,953	854	3,949	1,150	13
Kettle Falls	1,616	4	0	0	1	3	23	12	11	0	0
Kirkland	89,805	101	0	26	17	58	2,004	288	1,538	178	12
La Center	3,258	2	0	0	0	2	17	2	9	6	0
Lacey	50,844	96	4	15	17	60	1,374	190	1,087	97	3
Lake Forest Park	13,504	14	0	5	6	3	262	37	205	20	3
Lake Stevens	33,491	63	0	20	9	34	356	76	239	41	5
Lakewood	60,694	393	9	34	80	270	2,818	486	1,939	393	13
Liberty Lake	10,272	10	0	3	0	7	125	13	99	13	0
Long Beach	1,416	2	0	1	0	1	29	4	22	3	0
Longview	37,720	110	2	36	21	51	1,350	230	948	172	14
Lynden	14,612	18	0	7	3	8	205	32	163	10	4
Lynnwood	38,620	101	0	17	36	48	1,646	159	1,286	201	3
Maple Valley[4,8]	26,212		0		7	8	354	86	221	47	1
Marysville	70,204	170	1	21	38	110	1,549	235	1,061	253	9
Medina	3,311	1	0	0	0	1	51	6	41	4	1
Mercer Island	25,641	10	0	4	4	2	452	63	366	23	1
Mill Creek	21,234	19	0	6	8	5	333	52	254	27	3
Milton	8,366	27	0	1	5	21	257	36	192	29	0
Monroe	19,003	69	0	17	6	46	458	50	377	31	1
Montesano	3,959	10	0	1	0	9	77	16	58	3	0
Morton	1,164	0	0	0	0	0	13	2	11	0	0
Moses Lake	23,763	80	1	11	9	59	1,049	174	804	71	3
Mossyrock	794	0	0	0	0	0	9	1	7	1	0
Mountlake Terrace	21,549	39	1	12	9	17	538	121	365	52	1
Mount Vernon	35,550	99	2	16	26	55	1,308	233	964	111	6
Moxee	4,114	8	0	1	0	7	20	4	12	4	0
Mukilteo	21,638	37	2	11	3	21	433	87	308	38	1
Napavine	1,908	0	0	0	0	0	41	2	36	3	0
Newcastle[4,8]	11,878		0		2	4	243	54	150	39	0
North Bend	6,971	2	0	0	1	1	181	11	162	8	1
Oak Harbor	23,330	24	0	8	1	15	162	19	122	21	0
Oakville	683	1	0	1	0	0	14	7	6	1	0
Ocean Shores	5,977	9	0	1	1	7	120	42	74	4	0
Olympia	52,312	246	1	38	50	157	2,020	320	1,473	227	12
Oroville	1,669	3	0	1	0	2	48	5	39	4	0
Orting	8,179	11	0	0	4	7	132	23	90	19	3
Othello	8,247	9	0	1	0	8	177	32	106	39	0
Pacific	7,269	11	0	1	8	2	107	13	57	37	3
Pasco	74,582	166	5	33	34	94	1,328	252	936	140	15

Table 8. Offenses Known to Law Enforcement, by Selected State and City, 2019—Continued

(Number.)

State/city	Population	Violent crime	Murder and nonnegligent manslaughter	Rape[1]	Robbery	Aggravated assault	Property crime	Burglary	Larceny-theft	Motor vehicle theft	Arson[2]
Port Angeles	19,992	106	0	20	11	75	823	162	612	49	1
Port Orchard	14,269	67	1	8	7	51	633	100	489	44	1
Port Townsend	9,615	29	3	5	2	19	179	33	133	13	7
Poulsbo	10,886	19	0	7	1	11	227	34	182	11	1
Prosser	6,342	12	0	1	0	11	176	49	110	17	0
Pullman	33,896	41	0	16	5	20	371	65	292	14	5
Puyallup	41,572	108	1	17	33	57	2,337	336	1,770	231	25
Quincy	7,598	16	0	5	2	9	376	80	258	38	3
Raymond	2,928	7	0	1	1	5	30	9	20	1	0
Redmond	65,827	89	1	6	32	50	1,854	186	1,577	91	14
Renton	102,749	331	5	53	110	163	4,915	542	3,447	926	14
Richland	57,450	127	0	17	18	92	1,281	177	1,039	65	7
Ridgefield	8,552	8	0	2	1	5	90	15	72	3	2
Ritzville	1,631	3	0	0	0	3	82	32	46	4	1
Roy	826	9	0	2	0	7	24	6	16	2	0
Royal City	2,212	4	0	0	2	2	20	2	13	5	0
Ruston	840	1	0	0	0	1	34	12	20	2	0
Sammamish[4,8]	65,604		1		6	6	371	86	260	25	5
SeaTac[4,8]	29,463		4		55	71	1,402	227	785	390	5
Seattle	742,759	5,052	32	292	1,649	3,079	38,246	7,985	26,219	4,042	109
Sedro Woolley	11,953	10	0	1	0	9	309	57	233	19	0
Selah	7,932	8	0	2	1	5	196	29	148	19	0
Sequim	7,183	18	0	7	2	9	295	29	258	8	1
Shelton	10,188	52	0	13	3	36	657	103	504	50	3
Shoreline[4,8]	56,637		1		22	45	1,100	230	715	155	8
Snohomish	10,227	25	0	2	4	19	265	42	193	30	0
Snoqualmie	13,947	3	0	1	1	1	169	10	148	11	2
Soap Lake	1,583	1	0	0	0	1	35	0	30	5	0
Spokane	218,222	1,742	8	351	297	1,086	15,439	2,130	11,631	1,678	45
Spokane Valley	99,020	346	1	79	59	207	4,165	484	3,328	353	3
Stanwood	7,225	13	0	3	3	7	132	21	97	14	0
Steilacoom	6,389	6	1	0	1	4	95	18	74	3	0
Sultan	5,204	7	0	1	3	3	60	20	36	4	1
Sumas	1,488	0	0	0	0	0	14	5	8	1	0
Sumner	10,191	26	0	2	8	16	532	101	362	69	2
Sunnyside	16,468	37	2	4	6	25	422	74	282	66	0
Tacoma	215,687	1,869	17	198	503	1,151	11,362	1,912	7,573	1,877	90
Toppenish	8,898	33	1	8	5	19	491	89	282	120	0
Tukwila	20,288	148	3	20	72	53	3,401	273	2,556	572	4
Tumwater	23,405	84	1	15	9	59	703	155	481	67	2
Union Gap	6,163	19	1	4	9	5	661	61	553	47	0
University Place	33,743	72	3	10	23	36	719	137	524	58	5
Vancouver	177,580	819	3	150	155	511	5,852	789	3,987	1,076	52
Walla Walla	32,906	128	0	25	12	91	1,194	162	972	60	15
Warden	2,733	4	0	0	0	4	79	19	34	26	0
Washougal	15,949	25	0	10	0	15	251	35	193	23	2
Wenatchee	34,169	100	0	20	17	63	851	97	698	56	5
Westport	2,047	3	0	1	0	2	40	13	26	1	0
West Richland	15,012	11	1	3	1	6	125	21	95	9	1
White Salmon	2,583	1	0	0	0	1	14	0	12	2	0
Winthrop	444	0	0	0	0	0	7	0	7	0	0
Woodinville[4,8]	12,153		0		2	7	308	42	241	25	1
Woodland	6,228	6	0	3	2	1	234	41	176	17	3
Woodway	1,390	0	0	0	0	0	8	5	3	0	0
Yakima	93,959	421	16	49	121	235	3,343	625	2,212	506	23
Yarrow Point	1,144	1	0	0	0	1	3	0	2	1	0
Zillah	3,139	2	0	2	0	0	68	11	53	4	0
WEST VIRGINIA											
Alderson	1,151	3	0	0	0	3	32	5	25	2	0
Barboursville	4,256	3	0	1	2	0	208	11	193	4	0
Beckley	16,234	147	3	24	11	109	836	136	669	31	2
Bluefield	9,789	92	0	3	1	88	103	32	66	5	1
Bridgeport	8,708	9	0	1	2	6	204	7	192	5	0
Buckhannon	5,516	4	0	2	0	2	176	7	165	4	0
Ceredo	1,339	1	0	0	0	1	4	0	3	1	0
Charleston	47,470	331	10	50	48	223	2,853	660	1,947	246	25
Charles Town	6,060	10	0	2	2	6	37	13	22	2	0
Dunbar	7,262	44	1	3	0	40	299	67	190	42	2
Fairmont	18,430	63	2	11	9	41	261	48	182	31	8
Glen Dale	1,398	6	0	0	0	6	5	3	2	0	0
Hinton	2,417	1	0	0	1	0	38	14	20	4	1
Kenova	2,979	6	0	4	2	0	38	5	28	5	0
Lewisburg	3,917	3	0	0	0	3	93	0	93	0	0
Madison	2,764	0	0	0	0	0	48	19	25	4	1
Marmet	1,397	2	0	0	0	2	23	4	18	1	0
Martinsburg	17,428	55	0	10	6	39	540	69	456	15	3
Mason	941	0	0	0	0	0	83	2	79	2	1
Moorefield	2,417	20	0	1	0	19	69	2	66	1	0
Morgantown	30,855	82	0	11	6	65	500	85	386	29	4
Moundsville	8,417	17	0	4	1	12	212	31	173	8	2
Mount Hope	1,297	0	0	0	0	0	10	2	8	0	0
Nitro	6,509	25	0	3	0	22	259	25	218	16	1

Table 8. Offenses Known to Law Enforcement, by Selected State and City, 2019—Continued

(Number.)

State/city	Population	Violent crime	Murder and nonnegligent manslaughter	Rape[1]	Robbery	Aggravated assault	Property crime	Burglary	Larceny-theft	Motor vehicle theft	Arson[2]
Oak Hill	8,264	13	1	1	1	10	147	40	97	10	0
Point Pleasant	4,126	4	0	3	0	1	61	7	45	9	0
Ranson	5,292	15	1	1	1	12	27	2	22	3	1
Ravenswood	3,720	16	0	0	1	15	34	6	26	2	0
Shepherdstown	1,757	2	0	0	0	2	6	2	4	0	0
South Charleston	12,357	47	0	10	4	33	577	52	503	22	4
St. Albans	10,161	19	0	4	4	11	187	41	126	20	0
Summersville	3,332	4	0	0	0	4	78	3	73	2	0
Vienna	10,306	23	0	4	0	19	351	17	329	5	1
Weirton	18,542	9	0	2	0	7	166	21	137	8	4
Wellsburg	2,560	1	0	0	1	0	22	2	17	3	1
Weston	3,953	11	0	0	0	11	6	1	2	3	0
Weston	3,953	11	0	0	0	11	6	1	2	3	0
Wheeling	26,855	229	1	16	12	200	321	81	219	21	1
Williamson	2,745	16	0	0	1	15	34	8	24	2	0
WISCONSIN											
Adams	1,852	7	0	4	1	2	77	6	69	2	1
Albany	999	2	0	0	0	2	6	2	4	0	0
Algoma	3,071	1	0	1	0	0	23	4	19	0	0
Altoona[4]	7,827	12	0	8	1	3	105	23	78	4	0
Amery	2,809	26	0	4	0	22	34	4	29	1	0
Antigo	7,720	25	0	1	0	24	351	29	307	15	0
Appleton	74,931	165	0	26	23	116	1,151	131	973	47	5
Arcadia	3,065	0	0	0	0	0	6	1	5	0	0
Ashland	7,770	31	1	3	1	26	254	23	214	17	4
Ashwaubenon	17,316	13	0	6	2	5	528	36	474	18	2
Athens	1,086	0	0	0	0	0	3	0	3	0	0
Avoca	627	0	0	0	0	0	0	0	0	0	0
Bangor	1,472	1	0	0	0	1	5	0	5	0	0
Baraboo	12,178	24	0	15	0	9	358	35	317	6	1
Barneveld	1,240	0	0	0	0	0	11	6	5	0	0
Barron	3,300	0	0	0	0	0	1	1	0	0	0
Bayfield	471	2	0	0	0	2	24	11	10	3	0
Bayside	4,375	0	0	0	0	0	19	2	14	3	0
Beaver Dam[4]	16,394	25	0	11	4	10	239	21	210	8	0
Beaver Dam Township	3,912	0	0	0	0	0	2	0	2	0	0
Belleville	2,432	0	0	0	0	0	13	2	10	1	0
Beloit	36,746	171	1	38	41	91	979	125	815	39	9
Beloit Town	7,688	7	0	1	1	5	103	25	70	8	0
Berlin	5,365	3	0	0	0	3	72	7	61	4	0
Big Bend	1,395	3	0	1	0	2	22	2	19	1	0
Birchwood	428	1	0	0	0	1	10	1	9	0	0
Black River Falls	3,488	6	0	3	1	2	115	11	97	7	0
Blair	1,365	0	0	0	0	0	6	1	5	0	0
Blanchardville	795	0	0	0	0	0	3	0	2	1	0
Bloomer	3,491	2	0	0	0	2	27	3	21	3	0
Bloomfield	6,323	11	0	3	0	8	50	11	37	2	1
Boscobel	3,104	10	0	2	0	8	17	4	13	0	0
Boyceville	1,098	4	0	2	0	2	6	1	5	0	0
Brandon-Fairwater	1,208	0	0	0	0	0	1	0	1	0	0
Brillion	3,116	4	0	0	1	3	11	0	11	0	0
Brodhead	3,247	3	0	0	0	3	58	3	52	3	0
Brookfield	38,065	28	1	1	20	6	815	62	734	19	0
Brookfield Township	6,295	10	1	1	4	4	110	6	102	2	0
Brooklyn[4]	1,464	0	0	0	0	0	20	1	19	0	0
Brown Deer	11,963	51	0	2	6	43	548	34	440	74	2
Brownsville	573	0	0	0	0	0	9	3	6	0	0
Burlington[4]	11,039	15	0	2	0	13	108	13	92	3	2
Butler	1,812	9	0	2	1	6	82	1	70	11	1
Caledonia	25,047	21	0	0	3	18	151	37	110	4	1
Campbellsport	1,963	0	0	0	0	0	12	2	10	0	0
Campbell Township	4,366	3	0	0	0	3	37	2	34	1	0
Cascade	697	0	0	0	0	0	1	0	1	0	0
Cashton	1,103	0	0	0	0	0	1	0	1	0	0
Cedarburg	11,469	3	0	0	0	3	54	1	53	0	0
Chenequa	597	0	0	0	0	0	3	0	3	0	0
Chetek	2,141	2	0	1	0	1	26	2	18	6	0
Chilton	3,798	4	0	1	0	3	11	0	10	1	0
Chippewa Falls	14,084	26	0	11	1	14	175	20	144	11	1
Cleveland	1,457	0	0	0	0	0	2	0	2	0	0
Clinton	2,124	0	0	0	0	0	21	7	12	2	1
Clintonville	4,332	7	0	3	1	3	154	15	134	5	2
Colby-Abbotsford	4,085	6	2	0	0	4	18	2	15	1	0
Colfax	1,142	1	0	1	0	0	11	3	7	1	0
Columbus	5,037	19	0	7	0	12	21	1	19	1	1
Cornell	1,412	0	0	0	0	0	35	3	30	2	0
Cottage Grove	7,024	6	0	2	0	4	21	0	21	0	0
Crandon	1,833	1	0	0	0	1	16	1	15	0	0
Cross Plains	4,331	2	0	0	0	2	25	2	23	0	0
Cuba City	2,037	0	0	0	0	0	2	0	2	0	0
Cudahy	18,290	24	1	3	6	14	221	30	174	17	0
Cumberland	2,112	0	0	0	0	0	0	0	0	0	0
Darlington	2,351	10	0	0	0	10	26	2	24	0	0

Table 8. Offenses Known to Law Enforcement, by Selected State and City, 2019—Continued

(Number.)

State/city	Population	Violent crime	Murder and nonnegligent manslaughter	Rape[1]	Robbery	Aggravated assault	Property crime	Burglary	Larceny-theft	Motor vehicle theft	Arson[2]
Deforest	10,557	9	0	3	0	6	98	8	85	5	0
Delafield	7,588	3	0	0	1	2	96	6	87	3	0
Delavan[4]	9,938	21	0	6	1	14	251	19	222	10	2
Delavan Town	5,322	1	0	0	0	1	37	9	24	4	5
De Pere	25,199	38	0	10	0	28	205	16	182	7	0
Dodgeville	4,734	6	0	2	1	3	88	3	83	2	0
Durand	1,805	2	0	1	0	1	2	2	0	0	0
Eagle River	1,514	1	0	1	0	0	57	5	48	4	0
Eagle Village	2,086	0	0	0	0	0	8	1	7	0	0
East Troy	4,333	4	0	0	1	3	43	2	41	0	0
Eau Claire[4]	68,923	199	0	58	23	118	1,688	292	1,332	64	7
Edgar	1,452	0	0	0	0	0	2	1	1	0	0
Edgerton[4]	5,602	2	0	0	1	1	51	7	44	0	0
Elkhart Lake	1,022	0	0	0	0	0	9	1	8	0	0
Elkhorn	9,934	13	0	3	1	9	113	16	93	4	0
Elk Mound	875	1	0	1	0	0	9	3	4	2	0
Ellsworth	3,287	5	0	4	0	1	33	3	29	1	0
Elm Grove[4]	6,205	3	0	2	0	1	58	1	53	4	1
Elroy	1,355	0	0	0	0	0	6	1	5	0	1
Endeavor	460	2	0	2	0	0	1	0	1	0	0
Evansville[4]	5,379	2	0	0	0	2	40	1	37	2	0
Everest Metropolitan	17,392	19	0	7	0	12	198	20	173	5	1
Fall Creek	1,309	0	0	0	0	0	7	0	7	0	0
Fall River	1,703	2	0	0	0	2	0	0	0	0	0
Fennimore	2,478	5	0	3	0	2	7	1	6	0	0
Fitchburg	30,151	86	1	10	19	56	581	66	461	54	0
Fond du Lac	42,777	101	4	29	14	54	1,012	78	887	47	3
Fontana	1,719	0	0	0	0	0	14	4	10	0	3
Fort Atkinson	12,495	25	1	7	3	14	169	17	152	0	0
Fox Crossing	19,323	20	0	8	1	11	189	31	138	20	0
Fox Lake[4]	1,452	1	0	1	0	0	2	0	0	2	0
Fox Point	6,671	8	0	0	1	7	68	5	50	13	0
Fox Valley Metro	22,006	16	0	2	1	13	82	3	76	3	0
Franklin	36,251	13	0	3	5	5	527	30	472	25	0
Frederic	1,098	0	0	0	0	0	5	3	2	0	1
Fulton	3,379	0	0	0	0	0	1	0	1	0	0
Galesville	1,585	2	0	1	0	1	6	0	6	0	0
Geneva Town	5,032	0	0	0	0	0	23	4	18	1	0
Genoa City	3,005	2	0	0	2	0	18	2	15	1	0
Germantown	20,014	8	0	1	2	5	422	25	391	6	1
Gillett	1,313	4	0	0	0	4	22	2	20	0	0
Gilman	392	0	0	0	0	0	2	0	2	0	0
Glendale	12,710	53	1	7	20	25	965	41	844	80	0
Grafton	11,662	7	0	3	1	3	136	2	131	3	0
Grand Chute	22,865	52	0	16	2	34	683	24	633	26	0
Grand Rapids	7,385	2	0	1	0	1	49	12	37	0	0
Grantsburg	1,287	0	0	0	0	0	37	1	36	0	0
Green Bay	105,281	483	1	78	56	348	1,798	250	1,448	100	7
Greendale	14,181	12	0	2	2	8	251	15	231	5	0
Greenfield	36,850	64	0	6	16	42	898	80	772	46	1
Green Lake	925	0	0	0	0	0	13	0	13	0	0
Hales Corners	7,640	8	0	2	0	6	97	7	87	3	0
Hammond	1,887	1	0	1	0	0	7	0	7	0	0
Hancock	404	0	0	0	0	0	0	0	0	0	0
Hartford	15,183	17	0	12	4	1	204	10	191	3	0
Hartford Township	3,561	0	0	0	0	0	0	0	0	0	0
Hartland	9,302	3	0	1	1	1	61	8	52	1	0
Hayward	2,296	5	0	0	0	5	62	13	46	3	1
Hazel Green	1,230	1	0	0	0	1	4	1	2	1	0
Highland	834	0	0	0	0	0	3	1	2	0	0
Hobart-Lawrence[4]	14,667	7	0	4	1	2	69	31	36	2	1
Holmen	9,993	7	0	1	0	6	69	18	50	1	0
Horicon[4]	3,605	11	0	7	0	4	28	1	24	3	0
Hortonville	2,776	1	0	0	0	1	22	1	21	0	0
Hudson	13,848	19	0	2	1	16	383	20	349	14	0
Hurley	1,426	1	0	0	0	1	11	0	9	2	0
Independence	1,305	0	0	0	0	0	6	3	3	0	0
Iron Ridge	895	0	0	0	0	0	9	1	8	0	0
Iron River	1,133	1	0	0	0	1	4	1	3	0	0
Jackson	7,156	7	0	3	4	0	74	1	73	0	1
Janesville[4]	64,471	167	1	41	28	97	1,800	282	1,454	64	4
Jefferson	8,021	13	0	7	0	6	141	4	132	5	2
Juneau[4]	2,662	4	0	1	0	3	28	1	27	0	0
Kaukauna	16,172	25	0	6	0	19	135	24	104	7	0
Kenosha	99,948	338	4	48	80	206	1,495	248	1,196	51	3
Kewaskum	4,139	1	0	1	0	0	29	1	27	1	0
Kewaunee	2,856	2	0	2	0	0	12	0	11	1	0
Kiel	3,780	12	0	1	0	11	18	2	15	1	0
Kohler	2,077	0	0	0	0	0	36	0	35	1	0
Kronenwetter	7,813	10	0	4	0	6	36	12	24	0	1
La Crosse	51,901	145	1	41	22	81	1,924	260	1,600	64	3
Ladysmith	3,120	6	0	1	0	5	24	3	21	0	1
La Farge	766	1	0	0	0	1	5	1	3	1	1

Table 8. Offenses Known to Law Enforcement, by Selected State and City, 2019—Continued

(Number.)

State/city	Population	Violent crime	Murder and nonnegligent manslaughter	Rape[1]	Robbery	Aggravated assault	Property crime	Burglary	Larceny-theft	Motor vehicle theft	Arson[2]
Lake Delton	3,005	17	0	5	2	10	421	8	408	5	2
Lake Geneva	7,907	13	0	7	1	5	177	5	172	0	0
Lake Hallie	6,742	0	0	0	0	0	260	6	245	9	0
Lake Mills	5,925	9	0	0	0	9	14	1	13	0	0
Lancaster	3,717	14	0	3	0	11	39	4	34	1	0
Lena	539	0	0	0	0	0	7	0	7	0	0
Linden	532	0	0	0	0	0	0	0	0	0	0
Linn Township	2,403	1	0	0	0	1	6	0	3	3	0
Lodi	3,058	2	0	0	0	2	7	1	5	1	0
Lomira	2,366	3	0	1	0	2	9	0	9	0	0
Luxemburg	2,562	0	0	0	0	0	8	0	8	0	0
Madison	258,455	1,043	5	116	240	682	6,722	1,061	5,129	532	16
Manawa	1,284	8	0	4	0	4	14	2	12	0	1
Manitowoc	32,557	71	3	6	5	57	661	103	532	26	0
Maple Bluff	1,333	0	0	0	0	0	11	3	7	1	0
Marathon City	1,506	1	0	0	0	1	14	3	11	0	0
Marinette	10,561	9	0	3	2	4	182	17	160	5	0
Marion	1,191	1	0	0	0	1	6	2	4	0	0
Markesan	1,399	0	0	0	0	0	14	0	12	2	0
Marshall Village	3,988	10	0	2	0	8	9	0	8	1	0
Marshfield	18,309	12	0	9	0	3	382	31	343	8	0
Mauston	4,390	16	0	0	0	16	34	2	29	3	0
Mayville	4,862	3	0	1	1	1	50	4	42	4	1
McFarland	8,544	9	0	0	1	8	82	17	59	6	0
Medford	4,294	6	0	0	0	6	103	6	91	6	1
Menasha	17,788	45	0	9	5	31	367	44	297	26	1
Menomonee Falls	37,712	21	1	1	9	10	408	24	355	29	0
Menomonie	16,450	28	1	6	1	20	306	27	263	16	1
Mequon	24,311	5	0	0	1	4	241	34	192	15	0
Merrill	9,091	19	0	3	1	15	139	15	120	4	2
Middleton	19,970	52	0	2	9	41	276	39	218	19	0
Milton[4]	5,585	6	0	0	0	6	58	4	52	2	0
Milton Town	3,114	0	0	0	0	0	6	1	4	1	0
Milwaukee	595,619	8,416	99	489	2,279	5,549	17,699	4,259	8,851	4,589	251
Mineral Point	2,478	2	0	0	0	2	28	6	22	0	0
Minocqua	4,380	7	0	0	0	7	33	2	31	0	0
Mishicot	1,381	5	0	0	0	5	4	2	2	0	0
Mondovi	2,613	1	0	1	0	0	16	3	12	1	0
Monona	8,183	9	0	0	6	3	495	9	478	8	0
Monroe	10,575	11	0	3	0	8	127	9	110	8	0
Montello	1,439	1	0	0	0	1	19	2	16	1	0
Monticello	1,204	0	0	0	0	0	1	0	1	0	0
Mosinee	4,003	5	0	4	0	1	46	7	34	5	0
Mount Horeb	7,462	8	0	2	0	6	71	14	57	0	1
Mount Pleasant	26,571	23	0	3	5	15	569	70	474	25	1
Mukwonago	8,034	6	0	2	1	3	114	9	103	2	0
Mukwonago Town	8,146	3	0	0	0	3	7	4	3	0	0
Muscoda	1,253	2	0	0	0	2	20	2	18	0	0
Muskego	25,118	9	1	1	0	7	143	14	124	5	0
Neillsville	2,410	2	0	1	0	1	35	3	26	6	0
Nekoosa	2,408	0	0	0	0	0	49	1	47	1	0
Neshkoro	426	0	0	0	0	0	2	0	2	0	0
New Berlin	39,763	15	0	1	3	11	432	54	365	13	0
New Glarus	2,148	1	0	0	0	1	21	1	19	1	1
New Holstein	3,098	2	0	0	0	2	16	1	14	1	0
New Lisbon	2,500	8	0	0	0	8	8	0	8	0	0
New London	7,083	18	0	2	0	16	62	3	58	1	0
New Richmond	9,052	18	0	0	1	17	153	9	135	9	0
Niagara	1,543	0	0	0	0	0	14	4	9	1	0
North Fond du Lac	5,079	9	0	1	1	7	66	8	55	3	0
North Hudson	3,801	0	0	0	0	0	26	0	24	2	0
North Prairie	2,236	0	0	0	0	0	4	1	3	0	0
Norwalk	628	0	0	0	0	0	1	0	1	0	0
Oak Creek	36,643	46	0	10	11	25	739	52	662	25	0
Oconomowoc	16,850	7	0	1	0	6	133	12	118	3	0
Oconomowoc Lake	600	0	0	0	0	0	8	0	8	0	0
Oconomowoc Town	8,692	1	0	0	0	1	10	2	6	2	0
Oconto	4,421	2	0	0	0	2	71	6	61	4	0
Oconto Falls	2,810	1	0	0	0	1	34	1	30	3	0
Omro	3,590	4	0	1	0	3	27	8	18	1	0
Onalaska	18,841	6	0	0	0	6	415	22	386	7	0
Oregon	10,549	4	0	1	0	3	97	14	82	1	0
Osceola	2,500	7	0	0	1	6	19	4	15	0	0
Oshkosh	66,736	115	1	5	17	92	1,107	126	913	68	3
Osseo	1,671	2	0	0	1	1	30	5	23	2	0
Oxford	599	1	0	0	0	1	9	1	8	0	0
Palmyra	1,766	2	0	0	0	2	15	3	12	0	0
Park Falls	2,227	7	0	0	0	7	1	0	1	0	0
Pepin	775	1	0	0	0	1	12	0	10	2	0
Peshtigo	3,355	2	0	1	0	1	29	4	24	1	0
Pewaukee Village	8,172	8	1	5	0	2	103	8	89	6	0
Phillips	1,345	1	0	0	0	1	19	2	16	1	0
Pittsville	833	0	0	0	0	0	31	0	30	1	0

Table 8. Offenses Known to Law Enforcement, by Selected State and City, 2019—Continued

(Number.)

State/city	Population	Violent crime	Murder and nonnegligent manslaughter	Rape[1]	Robbery	Aggravated assault	Property crime	Burglary	Larceny-theft	Motor vehicle theft	Arson[2]
Platteville	12,642	31	0	8	0	23	208	11	194	3	0
Pleasant Prairie	20,911	36	0	22	5	9	390	29	358	3	0
Plover	12,853	14	0	3	0	11	175	13	156	6	3
Plymouth	8,554	10	0	5	2	3	96	8	85	3	0
Portage	10,496	25	1	4	3	17	156	26	127	3	1
Port Edwards	1,772	1	0	0	0	1	14	4	10	0	0
Port Washington	11,831	19	0	6	1	12	73	5	64	4	0
Poynette	2,489	4	0	2	0	2	8	0	8	0	0
Prairie du Chien	5,618	9	0	4	0	5	117	7	110	0	1
Prescott	4,273	9	0	2	0	7	24	5	11	8	0
Princeton	1,165	1	0	1	0	0	16	1	15	0	0
Pulaski	3,581	3	0	0	0	3	21	1	19	1	0
Racine	77,373	435	8	54	81	292	1,662	347	1,196	119	16
Reedsburg	9,518	8	0	5	0	3	125	4	118	3	0
Rhinelander	7,535	21	0	6	0	15	192	22	168	2	0
Rib Lake	875	0	0	0	0	0	0	0	0	0	0
Rice Lake	8,332	25	0	13	0	12	239	17	215	7	0
Richland Center	4,968	7	0	2	0	5	58	10	46	2	0
Rio	1,040	0	0	0	0	0	3	0	3	0	0
Ripon	7,823	9	0	0	1	8	83	7	74	2	0
Ripon Town	1,381	0	0	0	0	0	1	1	0	0	0
River Falls	15,578	16	0	6	1	9	259	43	203	13	1
River Hills	1,590	0	0	0	0	0	15	3	10	2	0
Rome Town	2,670	2	0	0	0	2	5	0	5	0	1
Rosendale	1,032	0	0	0	0	0	0	0	0	0	0
Rothschild	5,334	9	0	6	0	3	44	4	40	0	0
Sauk Prairie	4,611	1	0	0	0	1	78	1	74	3	0
Saukville	4,415	2	0	1	0	1	50	0	50	0	0
Seymour	3,460	5	0	0	0	5	29	1	26	2	0
Sharon	1,572	0	0	0	0	0	3	0	3	0	0
Shawano	8,936	34	0	2	2	30	300	31	256	13	1
Sheboygan	48,195	183	0	27	10	146	826	89	715	22	8
Sheboygan Falls	7,945	2	0	1	0	1	77	8	67	2	0
Shiocton	920	0	0	0	0	0	15	0	15	0	0
Shorewood	13,368	18	0	0	6	12	374	12	331	31	0
Shorewood Hills	2,101	2	0	0	1	1	42	2	36	4	0
Shullsburg	1,203	1	0	1	0	0	19	2	17	0	0
Siren	773	2	0	0	0	2	45	10	34	1	1
Slinger	5,476	10	0	3	3	4	52	5	43	4	0
South Milwaukee	20,972	35	0	5	8	22	366	28	320	18	1
Sparta	9,681	20	0	9	2	9	100	16	81	3	0
Spencer	1,908	4	0	2	0	2	3	1	2	0	0
Spooner	2,583	13	0	3	0	10	30	3	27	0	0
Spring Green	1,641	0	0	0	0	0	4	1	3	0	0
Spring Valley	1,374	0	0	0	0	0	0	0	0	0	0
St. Croix Falls	2,036	4	0	0	0	4	112	6	97	9	0
Stevens Point	26,233	40	0	4	4	32	392	41	341	10	3
St. Francis	9,459	14	0	1	3	10	115	15	94	6	0
Stoughton	13,149	22	0	1	2	19	238	16	216	6	0
Strum	1,094	0	0	0	0	0	4	2	2	0	0
Sturgeon Bay	8,889	6	1	2	0	3	78	7	70	1	1
Sturtevant	6,966	3	0	0	0	3	42	8	31	3	0
Summit	4,947	6	0	1	0	5	35	5	28	2	0
Sun Prairie	33,390	27	0	4	7	16	676	62	570	44	4
Superior	26,054	76	0	11	16	49	1,114	150	882	82	0
Theresa	1,206	2	0	0	0	2	12	0	12	0	0
Thiensville	3,137	0	0	0	0	0	14	1	12	1	0
Three Lakes	2,088	3	0	0	0	3	26	9	17	0	0
Tomah	9,394	13	0	1	0	12	213	10	199	4	1
Tomahawk	3,147	1	0	1	0	0	62	11	50	1	0
Town of East Troy	4,058	2	0	1	0	1	11	4	7	0	0
Town of Madison	6,942	50	0	4	9	37	148	29	93	26	0
Trempealeau	1,645	0	0	0	0	0	7	4	3	0	0
Twin Lakes	6,077	6	0	1	0	5	25	6	17	2	0
Two Rivers	11,077	36	0	1	1	34	136	19	110	7	2
Verona	13,490	19	0	7	1	11	207	30	166	11	1
Viroqua	4,461	6	0	2	0	4	63	13	48	2	0
Walworth	2,849	1	0	0	0	1	19	2	17	0	0
Washburn	2,039	6	0	1	0	5	16	1	12	3	0
Waterloo	3,337	8	0	3	0	5	24	1	23	0	0
Watertown	23,628	46	0	11	4	31	220	30	185	5	0
Waukesha	72,672	92	2	37	13	40	750	83	618	49	1
Waunakee	14,000	20	1	4	0	15	92	28	55	9	0
Waupaca	5,859	14	0	4	1	9	189	12	174	3	0
Waupun	11,260	12	0	7	0	5	92	13	75	4	0
Wausau	38,682	119	1	21	11	86	626	94	491	41	1
Wautoma	2,130	3	0	1	0	2	127	5	121	1	0
Wauwatosa[4]	48,562	55	3	6	34	12	1,249	123	1,008	118	2
Webster	619	1	0	1	0	0	9	1	8	0	0
West Allis	59,887	195	1	31	84	79	1,673	258	1,292	123	6
West Bend[4]	31,651	56	0	7	4	45	528	29	485	14	0
Westby	2,255	4	0	0	0	4	34	2	31	1	0
Westfield	1,244	0	0	0	0	0	12	1	11	0	0

Table 8. Offenses Known to Law Enforcement, by Selected State and City, 2019—Continued

(Number.)

State/city	Population	Violent crime	Murder and nonnegligent manslaughter	Rape[1]	Robbery	Aggravated assault	Property crime	Burglary	Larceny-theft	Motor vehicle theft	Arson[2]
West Milwaukee	4,152	51	0	2	25	24	434	22	376	36	0
West Salem	5,055	5	0	1	0	4	21	3	17	1	0
Whitefish Bay	13,933	10	0	3	3	4	191	24	139	28	0
Whitehall	1,582	1	0	1	0	0	15	1	14	0	0
Whitewater	14,561	24	0	8	3	13	104	20	74	10	0
Wild Rose	700	0	0	0	0	0	1	0	1	0	0
Williams Bay	2,600	0	0	0	0	0	11	1	10	0	0
Wilton	498	0	0	0	0	0	2	0	2	0	0
Wind Point	1,705	0	0	0	0	0	4	2	2	0	0
Winneconne	2,429	1	0	0	0	1	20	0	20	0	0
Wisconsin Dells	3,018	10	0	4	0	6	146	9	131	6	0
Wisconsin Rapids	17,725	27	2	12	2	11	599	54	518	27	4
Woodruff	1,952	1	0	0	0	1	8	0	8	0	0
WYOMING											
Afton	2,018	0	0	0	0	0	28	2	26	0	0
Buffalo	4,583	10	0	2	0	8	65	8	52	5	0
Casper	58,200	117	2	60	4	51	1,630	327	1,165	138	5
Cheyenne	64,178	207	2	30	23	152	2,559	280	2,063	216	10
Cody	9,935	23	0	4	0	19	146	15	125	6	0
Diamondville	761	0	0	0	0	0	0	0	0	0	0
Douglas	6,386	11	1	0	0	10	73	5	63	5	0
Evanston	11,797	11	0	3	1	7	212	11	193	8	0
Evansville	3,001	17	0	1	0	16	57	8	41	8	0
Gillette	30,659	56	0	13	3	40	667	83	561	23	2
Glenrock	2,584	2	0	0	0	2	17	2	15	0	0
Green River	12,025	14	0	0	0	14	102	22	78	2	0
Greybull	1,864	9	0	1	0	8	10	5	4	1	0
Hanna	787	0	0	0	0	0	6	2	4	0	0
Kemmerer	2,761	2	0	0	0	2	17	1	15	1	0
Lander	7,542	0	0	0	0	0	257	12	234	11	0
Laramie	32,509	32	1	8	1	22	395	44	332	19	6
Lusk	1,539	10	0	1	0	9	7	3	4	0	0
Mills	3,966	2	1	0	0	1	89	28	50	11	0
Moorcroft	1,060	1	0	0	0	1	9	0	9	0	0
Newcastle	3,370	14	0	4	0	10	39	6	27	6	0
Pine Bluffs	1,143	1	0	0	0	1	17	5	11	1	0
Powell	6,458	17	0	10	0	7	113	20	89	4	0
Rawlins	8,806	37	0	8	0	29	171	19	135	17	3
Riverton	11,076	26	0	5	7	14	332	29	278	25	1
Rock Springs	23,405	43	0	21	0	22	314	53	257	4	0
Saratoga	1,651	1	0	0	0	1	8	0	8	0	0
Sheridan	17,919	17	1	2	0	14	313	39	261	13	1
Thermopolis	2,919	13	0	0	0	13	64	10	48	6	0
Torrington	6,699	35	0	0	0	35	73	12	57	4	0
Wheatland	3,557	3	0	0	0	3	56	19	33	4	1
Worland	5,148	2	0	2	0	0	69	18	46	5	1

1 The figures shown in this column for the offense of rape were reported using only the revised Uniform Crime Reporting (UCR) definition of rape. See the chapter notes for further explanation.   2 The FBI does not publish arson data unless it receives data from either the agency or the state for all 12 months of the calendar year.   3 Limited 2019 data were available for Alabama.   4 The FBI determined that the agency's data were overreported. Consequently, those data are not included in this table.   5 Because of changes in the state/local agency's reporting practices, figures are not comparable to previous years' data.   6 The FBI determined that the agency's data were underreported. Consequently, those data are not included in this table.   7 This agency submits rape data classified according to the legacy UCR definition; therefore the rape offense and violent crime total, which rape is a part of, is not included in this table. See the chapter notes for further explanation.   8 Arson offenses are reported by the Toledo Fire Department; therefore, those figures are not included in this report.

Table 9. Offenses Known to Law Enforcement, by Selected State and University and College, 2019

(Number.)

State and university/college	Student enrollment[1]	Violent crime	Murder and nonnegligent manslaughter	Rape[2]	Robbery	Aggravated assault	Property crime	Burglary	Larceny-theft	Motor vehicle theft	Arson[3]
ALABAMA[4]											
ALASKA											
University of Alaska											
Anchorage	24,144	1	0	0	0	1	70	3	62	5	0
Fairbanks	12,738	3	0	3	0	0	43	3	34	6	0
ARIZONA											
Arizona State University, Main Campus	127,582	49	0	21	5	23	739	56	667	16	1
Arizona Western College	11,492	0	0	0	0	0	11	0	11	0	0
Central Arizona College	8,086	0	0	0	0	0	17	2	15	0	0
Northern Arizona University	34,803	13	0	9	1	3	233	11	220	2	1
University of Arizona	48,318	32	0	19	3	10	656	45	597	14	1
ARKANSAS											
Beebe	5,423	0	0	0	0	0	10	1	8	1	0
Jonesboro	19,032	5	0	3	0	2	47	10	36	1	0
Newport	4,794	0	0	0	0	0	0	0	0	0	0
Arkansas Tech University	13,487	3	0	2	0	1	78	4	73	1	0
Henderson State University	3,850	2	0	1	1	0	34	4	29	1	0
Southern Arkansas University	5,467	0	0	0	0	0	23	1	22	0	0
University of Arkansas											
Fayetteville	30,378	4	0	4	0	0	163	20	114	29	0
Little Rock	14,429	1	0	0	1	0	49	5	42	2	0
Medical Sciences	3,106	8	0	0	0	8	82	1	76	5	0
Monticello	4,302	4	0	4	0	0	12	2	10	0	0
Pine Bluff	2,872	0	0	0	0	0	67	6	60	1	0
University of Central Arkansas	12,948	4	0	2	1	1	55	2	52	1	0
CALIFORNIA											
Allan Hancock College	17,070	0	0	0	0	0	9	0	9	0	0
California State Polytechnic University											
Pomona	28,093	8	0	2	1	5	165	24	130	11	0
San Luis Obispo	23,630	4	0	3	0	1	122	15	105	2	0
California State University											
Bakersfield	12,128	2	0	1	0	1	67	14	52	1	0
Channel Islands	8,336	4	0	3	1	0	64	0	62	2	0
Chico	19,754	6	0	3	1	2	127	2	119	6	1
Dominguez Hills	17,926	6	0	2	3	1	21	4	17	0	0
East Bay	19,613	4	0	3	0	1	96	15	78	3	0
Fresno	27,251	11	0	3	2	6	162	17	129	16	4
Fullerton	47,158	6	1	3	0	2	204	8	194	2	0
Long Beach	41,221	4	0	0	2	2	125	0	111	14	0
Los Angeles	30,038	4	0	1	1	2	99	4	89	6	0
Monterey Bay	8,502	9	0	2	1	6	48	6	41	1	0
Northridge	44,639	8	0	3	2	3	220	2	214	4	0
Sacramento	35,173	3	0	0	1	2	162	13	145	4	0
San Bernardino	22,286	4	0	2	1	1	69	4	57	8	0
San Jose	39,002	23	0	8	4	11	287	22	255	10	3
San Marcos	17,042	1	0	0	1	0	21	1	20	0	0
Stanislaus	11,767	1	0	1	0	0	44	0	38	6	0
Chaffey College	29,808	3	0	0	1	2	35	3	28	4	0
College of the Sequoias	15,686	0	0	0	0	0	40	5	30	5	0
Contra Costa Community College	53,483	1	0	0	1	0	111	14	94	3	0
Cuesta College	15,212	0	0	0	0	0	7	0	7	0	0
El Camino College	33,616	3	0	0	2	1	60	2	57	1	1
Foothill-De Anza College	61,553	2	0	1	1	0	28	4	24	0	0
Humboldt State University	9,262	5	0	1	1	3	120	15	103	2	1
Irvine Valley College	20,065	0	0	0	0	0	11	2	9	0	0
Marin Community College	8,140	3	0	0	0	3	17	0	17	0	0
Mt. San Jacinto College	20,992	2	0	0	1	1	22	3	13	6	0
Pasadena Community College	37,252	0	0	0	0	0	74	4	64	6	0
Riverside Community College	60,699	2	0	0	2	0	39	3	32	4	1
San Bernardino Community College	28,807	1	0	1	0	0	40	1	34	5	0
San Diego State University	37,748	20	0	7	4	9	441	38	389	14	5
San Francisco State University	33,506	14	0	5	7	2	196	22	168	6	0
San Jose/Evergreen Community College	28,801	0	0	0	0	0	27	8	18	1	0
Sonoma County Junior College	30,597	2	0	1	0	1	55	2	53	0	0
Sonoma State University	10,468	12	0	10	0	2	68	26	42	0	0
State Center Community College District	63,592	0	0	0	0	0	136	11	120	5	2
University of California											
Berkeley	44,235	70	1	13	22	34	763	56	646	61	0
Davis	39,783	14	0	6	2	6	906	86	794	26	2
Irvine	37,170	21	0	7	1	13	464	19	437	8	3
Los Angeles	46,592	89	0	23	8	58	756	132	608	16	2
Medical Center, Sacramento[5]		7	0	1	1	5	141	3	131	7	1
Merced	8,388	6	0	4	0	2	89	8	77	4	0
Riverside	24,907	11	0	5	3	3	305	32	267	6	0
San Diego	37,744	10	0	2	0	8	502	24	419	59	1
San Francisco	3,201	11	0	1	7	3	371	15	351	5	2
Santa Barbara	26,561	61	0	37	2	22	341	17	320	4	0
Santa Cruz	20,592	15	0	8	0	7	184	20	162	2	1

Table 9. Offenses Known to Law Enforcement, by Selected State and University and College, 2019—Continued

(Number.)

State and university/college	Student enrollment[1]	Violent crime	Murder and nonnegligent manslaughter	Rape[2]	Robbery	Aggravated assault	Property crime	Burglary	Larceny-theft	Motor vehicle theft	Arson[3]
Ventura County Community College District	50,436	2	0	0	1	1	52	15	35	2	1
West Valley-Mission College	24,612	1	0	0	1	0	26	4	22	0	0
COLORADO											
Adams State University	4,217	1	0	1	0	0	30	0	28	2	0
Aims Community College	8,436	0	0	0	0	0	1	0	1	0	0
Araphoe Community College	14,803	0	0	0	0	0	8	0	7	1	0
Auraria Higher Education Center[5]		10	0	0	3	7	139	15	116	8	1
Colorado School of Mines	6,994	1	0	0	0	1	79	6	69	4	0
Colorado State University, Fort Collins	37,676	10	0	2	1	7	393	11	378	4	1
Fort Lewis College	3,730	5	0	5	0	0	27	7	20	0	0
Pikes Peak Community College	18,604	1	0	0	0	1	8	0	7	1	0
University of Colorado											
Boulder	39,302	20	0	14	2	4	465	28	423	14	2
Colorado Springs	16,899	8	0	7	0	1	48	1	45	2	0
Denver	31,912	2	0	0	1	1	101	7	82	12	0
University of Northern Colorado	15,825	2	0	1	1	0	119	5	111	3	2
CONNECTICUT											
Central Connecticut State University	14,006	1	0	0	1	0	25	6	19	0	0
Eastern Connecticut State University	5,899	1	0	1	0	0	33	0	31	2	0
Southern Connecticut State University	11,642	1	0	1	0	0	30	0	30	0	0
University of Connecticut, Storrs, Avery Point, and Hartford[5]		3	0	2	0	1	112	15	94	3	2
Western Connecticut State University	6,675	1	0	1	0	0	14	1	12	1	1
Yale University	13,972	3	0	1	0	2	258	40	216	2	0
DELAWARE											
Delaware State University	4,633	8	0	1	2	5	65	5	60	0	0
University of Delaware	25,534	7	0	4	0	3	177	7	169	1	2
FLORIDA											
Florida A&M University	10,986	1	0	0	1	0	65	29	34	2	0
Florida Atlantic University	37,588	8	0	5	0	3	116	6	106	4	0
Florida Gulf Coast University	16,878	3	0	3	0	0	21	0	16	5	0
Florida International University	70,581	15	0	10	2	3	192	9	180	3	0
Florida Polytechnic University	1,519	0	0	0	0	0	4	0	4	0	0
Florida SouthWestern State College	22,279	2	0	2	0	0	7	0	7	0	0
Florida State University											
Panama City[5]		0	0	0	0	0	2	1	1	0	0
Tallahassee	46,946	17	0	5	10	2	350	29	296	25	1
New College of Florida	896	0	0	0	0	0	12	0	12	0	0
Northwest Florida State College	7,962	0	0	0	0	0	10	0	10	0	0
Pensacola State College	13,734	2	0	0	0	2	24	1	23	0	0
Santa Fe College	19,571	3	0	1	0	2	17	2	15	0	0
Tallahassee Community College	16,944	0	0	0	0	0	43	7	35	1	0
University of Central Florida	78,073	15	0	9	2	4	246	34	203	9	2
University of Florida	59,603	16	0	10	1	5	302	22	258	22	1
University of North Florida	19,547	3	0	3	0	0	72	10	62	0	0
University of South Florida											
St. Petersburg	5,864	1	0	1	0	0	29	3	25	1	0
Tampa	51,282	12	0	7	1	4	237	11	220	6	0
University of West Florida	16,374	1	0	1	0	0	52	0	52	0	0
GEORGIA[6]											
Abraham Baldwin Agricultural College	6,347	2	0	2	0	0	12	2	10	0	0
Albany Technical College	4,587	0	0	0	0	0	2	0	2	0	0
Augusta University	9,278	7	0	0	5	2	127	2	120	5	0
Bainbridge State College[5]		0	0	0	0	0	3	0	3	0	0
Chattahoochee Technical College	14,886	0	0	0	0	0	356	18	335	3	0
Emory University	15,831	18	0	13	3	2	356	18	335	3	0
Fort Valley State University	3,044	0	0	0	0	0	20	3	17	0	0
Georgia College and State University	7,977	2	0	1	0	1	26	4	20	2	0
Georgia Gwinnett College	15,116	4	0	0	0	4	40	2	38	0	0
Georgia Institute of Technology	34,108	7	0	1	4	2	322	36	255	31	2
Georgia Southern University	31,503	7	0	7	0	0	90	2	88	0	2
Georgia Southwestern State University	3,794	3	0	1	0	2	36	0	35	1	0
Georgia State University	38,731	15	0	2	9	4	195	4	184	7	1
Gordon State College	4,696	1	0	1	0	0	12	1	10	1	0
Kennesaw State University	41,439	5	0	4	0	1	92	6	85	1	0
Mercer University	9,692	3	0	3	0	0	55	3	46	6	0
Middle Georgia State University	9,182	1	0	0	1	0	25	1	22	2	0
Morehouse College	2,326	2	0	0	1	1	45	21	24	0	0
Savannah Technical College	5,819	0	0	0	0	0	10	0	8	2	0
Southern Crescent Technical College	6,610	0	0	0	0	0	2	1	1	0	0
Spelman College	2,171	0	0	0	0	0	9	1	8	0	0
University of Georgia	41,538	16	0	11	2	3	259	35	220	4	0
West Georgia Technical College	9,627	0	0	0	0	0	17	1	16	0	0
Young Harris College	1,366	0	0	0	0	0	4	0	4	0	0
ILLINOIS											
Chicago State University	3,702	1	0	1	0	0	8	0	8	0	0
College of DuPage	43,669	3	0	3	0	0	11	0	11	0	0
College of Lake County	23,794	0	0	0	0	0	15	0	15	0	0

Table 9. Offenses Known to Law Enforcement, by Selected State and University and College, 2019—Continued

(Number.)

State and university/college	Student enrollment[1]	Violent crime	Murder and nonnegligent manslaughter	Rape[2]	Robbery	Aggravated assault	Property crime	Burglary	Larceny-theft	Motor vehicle theft	Arson[3]
Eastern Illinois University	8,991	16	0	5	0	11	30	4	24	2	0
Elgin Community College	15,074	0	0	0	0	0	11	0	11	0	0
Illinois State University	22,948	20	0	11	1	8	102	12	90	0	1
John Wood Community College	2,838	0	0	0	0	0	0	0	0	0	0
Joliet Junior College	23,177	1	0	0	0	1	12	0	12	0	0
Lake Land College	14,957	0	0	0	0	0	0	0	0	0	0
Lewis University	7,939	3	0	2	0	1	17	0	17	0	0
Lincoln Land Community College	11,135	0	0	0	0	0	1	0	1	0	0
McHenry County College	10,668	0	0	0	0	0	12	0	12	0	0
Moraine Valley Community College	23,362	0	0	0	0	0	6	0	6	0	0
Morton College	6,254	0	0	0	0	0	4	0	4	0	0
Northeastern Illinois University	11,220	0	0	0	0	0	14	2	11	1	0
Northern Illinois University	20,443	11	0	6	0	5	78	6	72	0	1
Oakton Community College	18,251	2	0	0	1	1	6	0	6	0	0
Parkland College	12,238	3	0	0	0	3	12	1	11	0	0
Prairie State College	8,719	0	0	0	0	0	6	0	6	0	0
Rend Lake College	4,908	0	0	0	0	0	0	0	0	0	0
Rock Valley College	10,387	1	0	0	1	0	17	2	14	1	0
Southern Illinois University											
Carbondale	16,271	7	0	4	0	3	89	14	74	1	3
School of Medicine[4]		0	0	0	0	0	1	0	1	0	0
South Suburban College	9,136	0	0	0	0	0	8	2	6	0	0
Southwestern Illinois College	16,187	0	0	0	0	0	22	3	18	1	0
Triton College	17,777	1	0	0	0	1	14	0	14	0	0
University of Illinois											
Springfield	5,878	0	0	0	0	0	7	0	7	0	0
Urbana	52,986	21	0	5	2	14	261	14	244	3	2
Waubonsee Community College	17,229	0	0	0	0	0	10	0	10	0	0
Western Illinois University	10,905	5	0	4	0	1	53	2	51	0	0
INDIANA											
Ball State University	27,369	10	0	6	4	0	237	42	195	0	0
Indiana State University[7]	16,180	14	0	2	3	9		1		3	
Indiana University											
Bloomington	46,723	31	0	18	3	10	257	17	226	14	
Indianapolis	34,699	20	0	9	4	7	217	13	197	7	1
Northwest	5,152	7	1	0	3	3	22	8	14	0	0
South Bend	6,406	4	0	2	0	2	17	0	16	1	0
Southeast	6,415	2	0	1	0	1	8	0	8	0	0
Purdue University	45,685	13	0	7	5	1	293	28	262	3	0
IOWA											
Iowa State University	39,108	11	0	9	0	2	141	5	135	1	0
University of Iowa	35,876	26	0	7	2	17	178	14	163	1	0
University of Northern Iowa	14,221	4	0	3	1	0	47	2	42	3	0
KANSAS											
Fort Hays State University	17,953	4	0	3	0	1	30	7	22	1	0
Kansas State University	25,450	4	0	3	0	1	67	11	54	2	0
Pittsburg State University	8,330	0	0	0	0	0	56	1	54	1	0
University of Kansas											
Main Campus	31,136	2	0	1	0	1	97	6	88	3	1
Medical Center[5]		19	0	1	2	16	111	0	108	3	0
Washburn University	7,745	4	0	3	0	1	56	2	53	1	0
KENTUCKY											
Eastern Kentucky University	19,355	5	0	4	1	0	97	10	85	2	1
Kentucky State University	2,919	0	0	0	0	0	1	0	1	0	0
Morehead State University	12,217	1	0	1	0	0	33	1	31	1	0
Murray State University	11,095	4	0	3	0	1	63	11	52	0	0
Northern Kentucky University	16,539	6	0	6	0	0	26	0	26	0	0
University of Kentucky	31,102	11	0	5	2	4	426	20	394	12	3
University of Louisville	24,828	13	0	7	6	0	292	27	251	14	0
Western Kentucky University	24,560	4	0	2	0	2	85	5	76	4	0
LOUISIANA											
Delgado Community College	20,393	0	0	0	0	0	7	2	4	1	0
Grambling State University	6,424	12	0	3	1	8	76	21	53	2	0
Louisiana State University											
Baton Rouge	33,554	24	0	11	4	9	302	45	240	17	2
Health Sciences Center, Shreveport	1,113	18	0	1	0	17	89	1	84	4	0
Shreveport	7,981	2	0	0	0	2	15	0	15	0	0
Louisiana Tech University	13,893	1	0	0	0	1	75	12	62	1	0
McNeese State University	8,567	6	0	1	2	3	23	2	21	0	0
Nicholls State University	7,486	1	0	1	0	0	27	2	25	0	0
Southeastern Louisiana University	17,714	11	0	6	1	4	95	8	86	1	0
Southern University and A&M College											
Baton Rouge	6,988	6	0	0	0	6	124	13	110	1	3
New Orleans	3,111	0	0	0	0	0	0	0	0	0	0
Shreveport	4,380	0	0	0	0	0	0	0	0	0	0
Tulane University	14,286	7	0	1	2	4	171	16	148	7	2
University of Louisiana											
Lafayette	19,517	13	0	1	1	11	111	16	94	1	0

Table 9. Offenses Known to Law Enforcement, by Selected State and University and College, 2019—Continued

(Number.)

State and university/college	Student enrollment[1]	Violent crime	Murder and nonnegligent manslaughter	Rape[2]	Robbery	Aggravated assault	Property crime	Burglary	Larceny-theft	Motor vehicle theft	Arson[3]
Monroe	10,337	4	0	2	0	2	35	3	31	1	0
University of New Orleans	9,910	1	0	0	0	1	58	8	50	0	0
MAINE											
University of Maine											
Farmington	2,477	0	0	0	0	0	8	0	7	1	0
Orono	12,722	0	0	0	0	0	70	3	67	0	2
University of Southern Maine	10,213	1	0	0	0	1	33	0	33	0	0
MARYLAND											
Bowie State University	6,998	10	0	2	0	8	40	12	26	2	0
Coppin State University	3,357	4	0	0	0	4	32	13	18	1	0
Frostburg State University	6,122	4	0	3	0	1	22	0	22	0	0
Hagerstown Community College	5,761	1	0	0	1	0	0	0	0	0	0
Morgan State University	8,375	12	0	1	10	1	51	4	45	2	0
Prince George's County Community College	16,868	2	0	1	1	0	33	0	33	0	0
Salisbury University	9,529	3	0	2	0	1	64	4	60	0	0
St. Mary's College	1,690	6	0	5	0	1	33	8	25	0	0
Towson University	25,744	13	0	2	4	7	74	10	64	0	1
University of Baltimore	6,666	1	0	0	1	0	21	0	19	2	0
University of Maryland											
Baltimore City	7,495	8	0	0	7	1	63	2	60	1	1
Baltimore County	15,681	4	0	0	4	0	76	15	58	3	0
College Park	44,052	8	0	3	3	2	296	29	243	24	0
Eastern Shore	3,875	4	0	0	4	0	14	7	5	2	0
MASSACHUSETTS											
Assumption College	2,728	5	0	5	0	0	23	5	17	1	0
Babson College[6]	4,079	4	0	2	0	2	28	0	28	0	
Becker College	2,290	0	0	0	0	0	10	1	9	0	0
Bentley University	5,810	7	0	2	0	5	30	3	27	0	0
Boston College[6]	15,903	2	0	1	0	1	91	3	88	0	0
Boston University	41,418	11	0	8	1	2	389	17	365	7	0
Brandeis University	6,330	1	0	0	0	1	25	1	24	0	
Bridgewater State University	13,215	9	0	4	0	5	22	0	21	1	0
Bristol Community College	10,513	0	0	0	0	0	4	0	4	0	
Bunker Hill Community College	17,830	1	0	0	0	1	25	0	25	0	
Clark University	3,596	1	0	1	0	0	12	3	9	0	
College of the Holy Cross	2,922	1	0	1	0	0	33	9	24	0	
Dean College	1,595	0	0	0	0	0	19	5	14	0	0
Emerson College	4,815	7	0	7	0	0	21	1	20	0	
Endicott College	6,789	1	0	0	0	1	17	0	17	0	
Fitchburg State University[6]	11,496	3	0	3	0	0	10	1	9	0	0
Framingham State University	9,007	0	0	0	0	0	26	0	26	0	
Gordon College	2,424	1	0	1	0	0	23	0	23	0	
Harvard University	40,803	9	0	2	2	5	442	48	391	3	
Holyoke Community College	7,113	2	0	1	0	1	19	0	19	0	0
Lasell College[6]	2,351	3	0	2	0	1	6	1	5	0	0
Massachusetts Bay Community College	7,227	0	0	0	0	0	1	0	1	0	0
Massachusetts College of Liberal Arts	2,157	2	0	2	0	0	9	0	9	0	0
Massachusetts Institute of Technology	12,168	2	0	0	0	2	285	13	271	1	0
Massasoit Community College	10,323	1	0	0	1	0	6	0	6	0	0
MCPHS University	7,534	0	0	0	0	0	3	0	3	0	
Merrimack College	5,061	8	0	1	0	7	26	5	21	0	
Mount Holyoke College	2,571	3	0	1	1	1	30	3	27	0	0
Mount Wachusett Community College	5,194	0	0	0	0	0	5	0	5	0	
Northeastern University	27,795	19	0	10	2	7	292	17	267	8	
North Shore Community College	8,491	1	0	0	0	1	8	0	8	0	
Quinsigamond Community College	10,234	1	0	0	0	1	14	2	12	0	0
Salem State University	10,556	1	0	0	0	1	26	2	24	0	1
Smith College	3,259	2	0	2	0	0	48	6	42	0	0
Springfield College	3,366	3	0	2	1	0	28	5	22	1	
Springfield Technical Community College	7,431	0	0	0	0	0	16	0	16	0	0
Stonehill College	2,592	3	0	1	0	2	11	0	11	0	
University of Massachusetts											
Amherst	35,156	10	0	6	2	2	161	7	154	0	3
Harbor Campus, Boston	19,783	0	0	0	0	0	31	1	30	0	0
Medical Center, Worcester	1,120	21	0	0	0	21	53	0	52	1	0
Wellesley College	2,674	1	0	0	0	1	26	3	23	0	
Wentworth Institute of Technology	4,763	1	0	1	0	0	34	1	31	2	
Western New England University	4,130	4	0	3	0	1	21	1	20	0	
Westfield State University	7,598	5	0	4	0	1	12	2	10	0	0
Worcester Polytechnic Institute	7,338	3	0	0	0	3	25	1	24	0	
Worcester State University[6]	10,276	2	0	0	0	2	8	1	6	1	1
MICHIGAN											
Central Michigan University	26,971	4	0	4	0	0	48	5	43	0	0
Delta College	11,644	0	0	0	0	0	12	2	10	0	0
Eastern Michigan University	23,715	18	0	11	2	5	99	8	88	3	0
Ferris State University	16,549	8	0	1	0	7	36	3	31	2	0
Grand Rapids Community College	19,969	0	0	0	0	0	50	1	49	0	0
Grand Valley State University	28,190	4	0	2	0	2	90	7	82	1	0
Kalamazoo Valley Community College	12,039	0	0	0	0	0	11	0	11	0	0

Table 9. Offenses Known to Law Enforcement, by Selected State and University and College, 2019—Continued

(Number.)

State and university/college	Student enrollment[1]	Violent crime	Murder and nonnegligent manslaughter	Rape[2]	Robbery	Aggravated assault	Property crime	Burglary	Larceny-theft	Motor vehicle theft	Arson[3]
Kellogg Community College	7,236	1	0	0	0	1	3	0	3	0	0
Kirtland Community College	1,929	0	0	0	0	0	0	0	0	0	0
Lansing Community College	17,503	0	0	0	0	0	22	0	22	0	0
Macomb Community College	29,245	0	0	0	0	0	18	0	18	0	0
Michigan State University	55,423	23	0	10	0	13	492	50	406	36	0
Michigan Technological University	7,727	3	0	3	0	0	18	0	18	0	0
Mott Community College	10,504	1	0	0	1	0	8	0	8	0	0
Northern Michigan University	9,073	1	0	1	0	0	26	0	26	0	0
Oakland Community College	27,113	1	0	0	0	1	10	0	9	1	0
Oakland University	22,694	4	0	2	0	2	39	3	36	0	0
Saginaw Valley State University	9,688	5	0	1	0	4	30	2	27	1	0
Schoolcraft College	17,002	1	0	0	0	1	19	1	12	6	0
University of Michigan											
Ann Arbor	47,543	15	0	5	1	9	523	9	507	7	4
Flint	9,138	4	0	0	2	2	47	4	43	0	0
Washtenaw Community College	21,041	2	0	1	0	1	32	0	32	0	0
Western Michigan University	25,645	11	0	4	1	6	71	3	66	2	1
MINNESOTA											
University of Minnesota											
Duluth	11,777	2	0	1	0	1	45	1	44	0	1
Morris	1,778	0	0	0	0	0	0	0	0	0	0
Twin Cities[6]	64,115	32	0	8	11	13	667	48	573	46	1
MISSISSIPPI											
Coahoma Community College	2,596	0	0	0	0	0	23	21	2	0	0
Jackson State University	10,000	20	0	2	1	17	104	33	66	5	0
Mississippi State University[6]	24,054	3	0	0	0	3	79	9	65	5	0
University of Mississippi, Oxford	25,416	3	0	2	0	1	33	1	32	0	0
MISSOURI											
Jefferson College	5,663	1	0	0	0	1	5	1	4	0	0
Metropolitan Community College	24,011	1	0	0	0	1	29	1	24	4	0
Missouri University of Science and Technology	9,466	4	0	4	0	0	43	4	38	1	0
Southeast Missouri State University	13,245	3	0	1	0	2	25	1	24	0	0
St. Charles Community College	9,349	1	0	1	0	0	11	0	11	0	0
St. Louis Community College, Meramec	28,937	0	0	0	0	0	47	3	43	1	0
Truman State University[6]	6,810	2	0	0	1	1	49	1	44	4	0
University of Central Missouri[6]	16,665	0	0	0	0	0	101	6	93	2	0
University of Missouri											
Columbia	34,329	17	0	10	0	7	226	14	193	19	0
St. Louis	20,888	1	0	0	0	1	63	12	51	0	0
Washington University	16,962	0	0	0	0	0	83	11	72	0	0
					1						
MONTANA											
Montana State University	18,722	7	0	0	1	6	101	3	94	4	0
NEBRASKA											
University of Nebraska											
Kearney	8,041	0	0	0	0	0	22	2	20	0	1
Lincoln	28,642	6	0	5	0	1	180	2	173	5	1
NEVADA											
University Police Services	90,603	20	0	7	6	7	286	35	225	26	1
NEW HAMPSHIRE											
Plymouth State University	5,931	6	0	6	0	0	18	0	18	0	0
University of New Hampshire	16,859	8	0	6	2	0	112	12	100	0	1
NEW JERSEY											
Brookdale Community College	18,316	0	0	0	0	0	8	0	8	0	0
Essex County College	11,840	0	0	0	0	0	24	0	24	0	0
Kean University	16,577	3	0	1	1	1	76	0	74	2	0
Middlesex County College	16,876	0	0	0	0	0	14	0	14	0	0
Monmouth University	6,936	3	0	3	0	0	21	2	17	2	0
Montclair State University	24,022	4	0	3	0	1	105	4	100	1	0
New Jersey Institute of Technology	13,158	8	0	3	2	3	72	4	64	4	0
Princeton University	8,593	2	0	0	1	1	221	5	179	37	4
Rowan University	21,305	6	0	2	1	3	91	11	78	2	2
Rutgers University											
Camden	7,904	2	0	0	1	1	81	1	79	1	0
Newark	15,220	15	0	3	5	7	197	2	190	5	0
New Brunswick	55,698	32	0	13	4	15	345	27	316	2	0
Stevens Institute of Technology	8,015	2	0	2	0	0	17	1	16	0	1
Stockton University	10,976	2	0	1	0	1	44	1	43	0	0
The College of New Jersey	8,630	4	0	3	0	1	55	3	48	4	1
William Paterson University	12,422	5	0	4	0	1	54	12	42	0	0
NEW MEXICO											
Eastern New Mexico University	7,502	3	0	2	0	1	26	4	19	3	0
New Mexico Military Institute	450	2	0	2	0	0	12	0	12	0	0
New Mexico State University	16,383	7	0	6	0	1	207	21	178	8	0

Table 9. Offenses Known to Law Enforcement, by Selected State and University and College, 2019—Continued

(Number.)

State and university/college	Student enrollment[1]	Violent crime	Murder and nonnegligent manslaughter	Rape[2]	Robbery	Aggravated assault	Property crime	Burglary	Larceny-theft	Motor vehicle theft	Arson[3]
University of New Mexico	30,280	100	0	14	2	84	478	56	373	49	
Western New Mexico University	4,257	1	0	0	0	1	11	2	9	0	
NEW YORK											
Ithaca College	7,036	12	0	11	1	0	62	3	56	3	0
State University of New York Police											
Alfred	4,060	2	0	1	0	1	40	3	36	1	0
Binghamton	18,892	4	0	3	0	1	158	12	146	0	1
Brockport	9,539	2	0	2	0	0	47	5	41	1	0
Buffalo	34,183	12	0	6	1	5	208	18	189	1	0
Buffalo State College	11,048	7	0	2	2	3	122	3	118	1	0
Canton	4,981	1	0	1	0	0	26	3	23	0	0
Cobleskill	3,277	3	0	3	0	0	15	3	12	0	0
Cortland	7,886	1	0	1	0	0	39	6	33	0	0
Delhi	4,207	1	0	0	1	0	21	2	19	0	1
Downstate Medical	2,033	1	0	0	1	0	44	0	44	0	0
Farmingdale	19,903	2	0	2	0	0	19	1	18	0	0
Geneseo	6,000	1	0	1	0	0	38	6	32	0	0
Maritime	1,998	0	0	0	0	0	31	15	16	0	0
Morrisville	3,741	4	0	3	0	1	39	6	33	0	1
Nanoscale Science and Engineering[5]		0	0	0	0	0	7	0	7	0	0
New Paltz	9,669	0	0	0	0	0	38	1	37	0	0
Oneonta	7,171	4	0	4	0	0	31	4	27	0	0
Optometry	413	0	0	0	0	0	3	1	2	0	1
Oswego	11,159	2	0	1	0	1	45	3	42	0	0
Plattsburgh	6,558	1	0	1	0	0	57	0	57	0	0
Polytechnic Institute	3,307	0	0	0	0	0	7	0	6	1	0
Potsdam	4,365	2	0	2	0	0	42	4	38	0	0
Purchase	4,789	3	0	3	0	0	32	5	27	0	0
Stony Brook	30,012	7	0	0	1	6	173	12	160	1	0
Upstate Medical	1,608	4	0	0	0	4	100	3	94	3	0
NORTH CAROLINA[6]											
Duke University	18,107	5	0	2	2	1	417	15	381	21	2
Elizabeth City State University	1,586	2	0	1	0	1	48	21	27	0	0
Elon University	7,088	1	0	1	0	0	51	8	41	2	0
Fayetteville State University	7,662	4	0	0	1	3	37	5	32	0	0
North Carolina State University, Raleigh	39,136	10	0	1	5	4	175	28	142	5	0
University of North Carolina											
Chapel Hill	32,180	9	0	4	3	2	151	13	137	1	0
Charlotte	33,673	9	2	3	1	3	137	2	131	4	0
Wake Forest University	8,740	1	0	0	0	1	160	14	138	8	0
Western Carolina University	12,501	10	0	10	0	0	76	4	69	3	0
Winston-Salem State University	5,881	6	0	0	0	6	132	25	104	3	0
NORTH DAKOTA											
Bismarck State College	4,948	1	0	1	0	0	1	0	1	0	0
North Dakota State College of Science	3,657	0	0	0	0	0	8	1	7	0	0
North Dakota State University	15,065	2	0	2	0	0	80	6	72	2	0
University of North Dakota	17,646	5	0	2	0	3	106	5	98	3	0
OHIO											
Bowling Green State University	20,459	9	0	7	0	2	81	8	72	1	1
Cuyahoga Community College	35,558	4	0	0	2	2	29	0	29	0	0
Kent State University	34,023	3	0	2	0	1	107	1	106	0	0
Lakeland Community College	10,085	0	0	0	0	0	4	0	4	0	0
Miami University	21,731	34	0	25	0	9	183	6	160	17	5
Ohio State University, Columbus	64,924	16	0	8	2	6	378	22	350	6	1
University of Akron	23,217	4	0	3	0	1	78	1	75	2	0
University of Toledo	22,945	5	0	3	1	1	124	18	102	4	0
OKLAHOMA											
Bacone College	1,048	0	0	0	0	0	4	1	3	0	0
Cameron University[6]	5,750	1	0	1	0	0	6	1	5	0	0
East Central University	4,491	1	0	1	0	0	17	2	14	1	0
Eastern Oklahoma State College	1,977	0	0	0	0	0	4	2	2	0	0
Langston University	2,598	7	0	4	0	3	61	25	34	2	1
Mid-America Christian University	2,618	0	0	0	0	0	5	2	3	0	0
Northeastern Oklahoma A&M College	2,663	2	0	1	0	1	32	16	15	1	0
Northeastern State University, Tahlequah	9,269	3	0	2	0	1	20	6	13	1	0
Northwestern Oklahoma State University	2,456	0	0	0	0	0	1	0	0	1	0
Oklahoma City Community College	17,875	1	0	0	0	1	11	1	10	0	0
Oklahoma City University	3,247	0	0	0	0	0	36	5	27	4	0
Oklahoma State University											
Main Campus	27,791	7	0	6	0	1	145	11	132	2	0
Okmulgee	3,290	1	0	1	0	0	8	0	8	0	0
Tulsa	1,087	1	0	0	0	1	7	0	7	0	0
Rogers State University	4,612	0	0	0	0	0	3	1	2	0	0
Seminole State College	2,155	0	0	0	0	0	5	1	4	0	0
Southeastern Oklahoma State University	5,039	0	0	0	0	0	20	6	11	3	0
Southwestern Oklahoma State University	6,341	0	0	0	0	0	11	1	10	0	0
Tulsa Community College	23,778	2	0	0	0	2	21	0	21	0	0
University of Central Oklahoma	18,751	1	0	1	0	0	35	8	27	0	0

Table 9. Offenses Known to Law Enforcement, by Selected State and University and College, 2019—Continued

(Number.)

State and university/college	Student enrollment[1]	Violent crime	Murder and nonnegligent manslaughter	Rape[2]	Robbery	Aggravated assault	Property crime	Burglary	Larceny-theft	Motor vehicle theft	Arson[3]
University of Oklahoma											
Health Sciences Center	3,695	4	0	0	1	3	102	4	95	3	0
Norman	32,373	22	0	19	2	1	253	8	240	5	0
PENNSYLVANIA											
Bloomsburg University	10,288	4	0	2	0	2	15	1	14	0	0
Clarion University	6,125	0	0	0	0	0	15	2	13	0	0
Edinboro University	6,573	1	0	0	0	1	13	1	12	0	0
Kutztown University	8,997	7	0	7	0	0	29	1	28	0	0
Lock Haven University	4,215	2	0	1	0	1	9	3	6	0	0
Mansfield University	2,055	0	0	0	0	0	4	1	3	0	0
Pennsylvania State University											
Abington	4,576	2	0	1	0	1	3	0	3	0	0
Altoona	3,690	4	0	3	0	1	21	5	16	0	0
Dubois	672	0	0	0	0	0	0	0	0	0	0
Fayette	719	0	0	0	0	0	0	0	0	0	0
Greater Allegheny	553	0	0	0	0	0	5	1	4	0	0
Mont Alto	1,038	0	0	0	0	0	1	0	1	0	0
Wilkes-Barre	562	0	0	0	0	0	0	0	0	0	0
Worthington Scranton	1,131	0	0	0	0	0	1	0	1	0	0
Shippensburg University	7,345	5	0	5	0	0	21	4	17	0	0
University of Pittsburgh, Bradford	1,478	0	0	0	0	0	6	0	6	0	0
RHODE ISLAND											
Brown University	10,694	0	0	0	0	0	132	24	108	0	0
University of Rhode Island	20,502	2	0	2	0	0	53	5	48	0	1
SOUTH CAROLINA											
Bob Jones University	3,383	0	0	0	0	0	1	0	1	0	0
Clemson University	27,796	6	0	6	0	0	165	8	134	23	1
Coastal Carolina University	12,015	1	0	1	0	0	107	14	92	1	0
College of Charleston	13,258	1	0	0	1	0	44	0	44	0	0
Denmark Technical College	863	0	0	0	0	0	0	0	0	0	0
Erskine College	883	0	0	0	0	0	0	0	0	0	0
Francis Marion University	4,384	0	0	0	0	0	9	0	9	0	0
Greenville Technical College	15,700	2	0	0	1	1	21	4	16	1	0
Medical University of South Carolina	3,421	5	0	1	1	3	114	2	109	3	0
Midlands Technical College	14,571	0	0	0	0	0	3	0	3	0	0
Orangeburg-Calhoun Technical College	3,324	0	0	0	0	0	1	0	0	1	0
South Carolina State University	3,205	6	0	1	1	4	42	3	37	2	0
The Citadel	4,305	0	0	0	0	0	49	5	44	0	0
University of South Carolina											
Aiken	4,281	0	0	0	0	0	4	0	3	1	0
Columbia	37,348	5	0	4	1	0	214	13	184	17	0
Upstate	7,147	2	0	2	0	0	30	2	25	3	0
Winthrop University	7,009	2	0	2	0	0	23	2	21	0	0
SOUTH DAKOTA											
South Dakota State University	15,244	2	0	1	1	0	21	0	20	1	0
TENNESSEE											
Austin Peay State University	12,156	5	1	2	0	2	28	6	17	5	0
Chattanooga State Community College	10,770	5	0	0	0	5	4	0	4	0	0
Cleveland State Community College	3,883	0	0	0	0	0	5	1	3	1	0
Columbia State Community College	7,703	0	0	0	0	0	0	0	0	0	0
East Tennessee State University	16,151	9	0	7	0	2	75	1	72	2	1
Jackson State Community College	6,263	1	0	1	0	0	4	0	4	0	0
Lincoln Memorial University	5,118	1	0	0	0	1	7	1	6	0	0
Middle Tennessee State University	25,602	6	0	3	0	3	78	2	73	3	0
Motlow State Community College	8,014	0	0	0	0	0	3	1	2	0	0
Nashville State Community College	11,197	0	0	0	0	0	0	0	0	0	0
Northeast State Community College	7,407	0	0	0	0	0	4	1	3	0	0
Pellissippi State Community College	15,428	0	0	0	0	0	20	0	18	2	0
Roane State Community College	7,014	0	0	0	0	0	4	2	2	0	0
Southwest Tennessee Community College	12,720	0	0	0	0	0	7	0	7	0	0
Tennessee State University	11,251	9	0	3	2	4	60	2	58	0	0
Tennessee Technological University	11,451	0	0	0	0	0	59	4	55	0	0
University of Memphis	24,847	7	0	2	0	5	132	14	110	8	1
University of Tennessee											
Chattanooga	12,766	11	0	2	1	8	140	19	117	4	0
Health Science Center	3,355	0	0	0	0	0	20	2	18	0	0
Knoxville	30,845	6	0	2	1	3	138	15	102	21	0
Martin	7,837	1	0	1	0	0	23	0	23	0	0
University of the South	1,984	4	0	3	0	1	66	11	52	3	0
Vanderbilt University	13,431	29	0	1	6	22	448	3	436	9	0
Volunteer State Community College	11,419	0	0	0	0	0	9	0	9	0	0
Walters State Community College	7,471	0	0	0	0	0	2	0	2	0	0
TEXAS											
Abilene Christian University	5,709	1	0	1	0	0	88	13	70	5	0
Alamo Colleges District	109,114	3	0	0	1	2	131	9	111	11	7
Angelo State University	11,820	1	0	1	0	0	32	0	31	1	0
Austin Community College District	62,493	1	0	1	0	0	117	6	80	31	1

Table 9. Offenses Known to Law Enforcement, by Selected State and University and College, 2019—Continued

(Number.)

State and university/college	Student enrollment[1]	Violent crime	Murder and nonnegligent manslaughter	Rape[2]	Robbery	Aggravated assault	Property crime	Burglary	Larceny-theft	Motor vehicle theft	Arson[3]
Baylor Health Care System[5]		8	0	1	5	2	403	10	361	32	0
Baylor University, Waco	18,261	4	0	2	0	2	144	13	129	2	1
El Paso Community College	38,006	1	0	1	0	0	16	1	15	0	0
Hardin-Simmons University	2,483	0	0	0	0	0	17	8	9	0	0
Houston Community College	82,166	4	0	0	3	1	134	7	118	9	1
Lamar University, Beaumont	19,508	2	0	0	0	2	51	1	49	1	0
Lubbock Christian University	2,217	0	0	0	0	0	4	2	2	0	0
Prairie View A&M University	9,945	18	0	11	3	4	106	18	76	12	0
Rice University	7,362	3	0	1	1	1	180	2	170	8	0
Southern Methodist University	13,062	10	0	4	3	3	158	11	139	8	0
Southwestern University[6]	1,430	0	0	0	0	0	14	2	12	0	0
Stephen F. Austin State University	14,561	8	0	4	0	4	34	3	31	0	0
St. Mary's University	3,926	4	0	2	0	2	32	2	29	1	0
St. Thomas University	3,727	0	0	0	0	0	35	3	32	0	0
Sul Ross State University	3,672	0	0	0	0	0	6	5	1	0	0
Tarleton State University[6]	14,950	6	0	6	0	0	48	3	45	0	1
Texas A&M International University	8,818	1	0	1	0	0	17	2	15	0	0
Texas A&M University											
Central Texas	3,319	0	0	0	0	0	1	0	0	1	0
College Station[6]	72,775	11	0	5	3	3	413	33	351	29	0
Commerce	15,596	4	0	3	0	1	74	6	68	0	0
Corpus Christi	14,307	2	0	0	0	2	76	8	67	1	0
Galveston[5]		0	0	0	0	0	14	0	14	0	0
San Antonio	7,534	0	0	0	0	0	11	0	11	0	0
Texas Christian University	11,044	2	0	0	1	1	76	7	64	5	0
Texas Southern University	11,485	15	0	5	4	6	95	14	71	10	0
Texas State Technical College											
Harlingen[5]		1	0	1	0	0	3	0	3	0	0
Waco[5,6]		6	1	3	2	0	50	12	35	3	1
Texas State University, San Marcos[6]	42,924	14	0	8	3	3	147	16	129	2	1
Texas Tech University, Lubbock	39,987	7	0	3	0	4	245	7	236	2	0
Texas Woman's University	18,773	0	0	0	0	0	43	2	41	0	0
Trinity Valley Community College	9,678	1	0	0	0	1	6	4	2	0	0
University of Houston, Central Campus[6]	51,371	23	0	9	9	5	464	50	393	21	0
University of North Texas, Denton	43,730	7	0	6	0	1	161	12	148	1	0
University of Texas											
Arlington	60,075	16	0	7	6	3	129	11	112	6	0
Austin[6]	55,097	8	0	1	1	6	449	17	429	3	0
Dallas[6]	30,572	6	0	4	0	2	124	7	115	2	0
El Paso	29,598	5	0	1	0	4	84	14	68	2	1
Health Science Center, San Antonio	3,960	0	0	0	0	0	21	1	19	1	0
Health Science Center, Tyler	59	1	0	0	0	1	7	0	7	0	0
Houston	6,948	8	0	5	3	0	293	9	279	5	1
Medical Branch	4,189	6	0	1	0	5	74	0	66	8	0
Permian Basin	9,651	0	0	0	0	0	30	14	15	1	0
Rio Grande Valley	33,012	2	0	2	0	0	64	3	61	0	0
San Antonio	34,473	10	0	4	0	6	102	3	95	4	0
Southwestern Medical School	2,506	1	0	0	0	1	228	5	219	4	0
West Texas A&M University	11,753	2	0	1	0	1	33	3	28	2	0
UTAH											
Brigham Young University	39,515	1	0	1	0	0	107	0	105	2	0
Dixie State University	12,920	2	0	1	1	0	13	0	12	1	0
University of Utah	38,229	5	0	1	0	4	353	20	314	19	
Utah State University	37,585	11	1	0	3	7	409	31	360	18	
Utah State University, Logan	34,904	1	0	0	1	0	45	8	37	0	0
Eastern[5]		2	0	2	0	0	8	0	7	1	0
Logan	32,944	1	0	1	0	0	30	1	27	2	0
Weber State University	35,447	0	0	0	0	0	17	0	16	1	0
VERMONT											
University of Vermont	15,629	3	0	2	0	1	93	7	86	0	0
VIRGINIA											
Bridgewater College	1,936	3	0	0	0	3	9	1	8	0	0
College of William and Mary	9,805	0	0	0	0	0	80	11	69	0	0
Eastern Virginia Medical School	1,376	1	0	0	1	0	36	0	36	0	0
George Mason University	47,049	5	0	4	1	0	87	5	82	0	0
Germanna Community College	9,077	0	0	0	0	0	4	0	4	0	0
Hampton University	4,698	2	0	0	1	1	41	5	35	1	1
James Madison University	24,133	2	0	2	0	0	89	5	84	0	0
J. Sargeant Reynolds Community College	13,875	0	0	0	0	0	8	0	7	1	0
Longwood University	5,909	2	0	0	0	2	27	0	27	0	0
Lord Fairfax Community College	9,112	0	0	0	0	0	5	0	5	0	0
Norfolk State University	5,855	8	0	4	4	0	79	12	64	3	0
Northern Virginia Community College	73,657	0	0	0	0	0	30	0	30	0	0
Old Dominion University	28,297	34	0	9	4	21	251	13	232	6	1
Radford University	10,296	11	0	11	0	0	55	2	53	0	1
Richard Bland College	2,882	1	0	1	0	0	19	2	17	0	0
University of Mary Washington	5,373	3	0	2	0	1	34	0	34	0	2
University of Richmond	4,740	4	0	4	0	0	84	12	71	1	0
University of Virginia	28,244	19	0	9	2	8	180	8	166	6	0
University of Virginia's College at Wise	3,325	0	0	0	0	0	12	1	11	0	0

Table 9. Offenses Known to Law Enforcement, by Selected State and University and College, 2019—Continued

(Number.)

State and university/college	Student enrollment[1]	Violent crime	Murder and nonnegligent manslaughter	Rape[2]	Robbery	Aggravated assault	Property crime	Burglary	Larceny-theft	Motor vehicle theft	Arson[3]
Virginia Commonwealth University	33,636	14	0	4	3	7	606	15	586	5	1
Virginia Military Institute	1,769	3	0	3	0	0	18	2	16	0	0
Virginia Polytechnic Institute and State University	36,115	5	0	2	1	2	195	11	182	2	0
Virginia State University	5,156	4	0	3	0	1	41	4	35	2	0
Virginia Western Community College	10,130	0	0	0	0	0	2	0	2	0	0
WASHINGTON											
Central Washington University	17,638	0	0	0	0	0	93	5	87	1	0
Eastern Washington University	16,208	0	0	0	0	0	38	4	32	2	0
Evergreen State College	4,587	2	0	2	0	0	30	0	29	1	0
University of Washington	55,508	18	0	2	3	13	616	68	540	8	0
Washington State University											
Pullman	34,356	8	0	7	0	1	47	5	41	1	0
Vancouver[5]		0	0	0	0	0	0	0	0	0	0
Western Washington University	17,782	3	0	1	1	1	89	3	85	1	1
WEST VIRGINIA											
West Virginia University, Morgantown	31,994	9	0	5	1	3	197	27	168	2	0
WISCONSIN											
Marquette University	12,162	42	0	6	13	23	263	23	215	25	0
University of Wisconsin											
Eau Claire[6]	11,790	2	0	2	0	0	36	7	29	0	0
Green Bay	8,534	1	0	1	0	0	16	0	16	0	0
La Crosse	11,751	0	0	0	0	0	64	0	64	0	0
Milwaukee	28,921	4	0	2	1	1	107	12	93	2	0
Oshkosh	16,057	5	0	4	0	1	30	2	27	1	0
Parkside	4,911	0	0	0	0	0	11	1	10	0	0
Platteville	9,511	4	0	0	0	4	15	4	11	0	0
River Falls	6,798	1	0	0	0	1	36	2	34	0	0
Stevens Point	9,144	1	0	1	0	0	54	1	53	0	0
Superior	3,168	0	0	0	0	0	16	0	16	0	0
Whitewater	14,196	0	0	0	0	0	31	0	31	0	0
WYOMING											
University of Wyoming	13,963	3	0	0	0	3	77	2	74	1	0

Note: Caution should be exercised in making any intercampus comparisons or ranking schools because university/college crime statistics are affected by a variety of factors. These include demographic characteristics of the surrounding community, ratio of male to female students, number of on-campus residents, accessibility of the campus to outside visitors, size of enrollment, etc. 1 The student enrollment figures provided by the United States Department of Education are for the 2018 school year, the most recent available. The enrollment figures include full-time and part-time students. 2 The figures shown in this column for the offense of rape were reported using only the revised Uniform Crime Reporting (UCR) definition of rape. See chapter notes for more detail. 3 The FBI does not publish arson data unless it receives data from either the agency or the state for all 12 months of the calendar year. 4 Limited data for 2019 were available for Alabama. 5 Student enrollment figures were not available. 6 Because of changes in the state/local agency's reporting practices, figures are not comparable to previous years' data. 7 The FBI determined that the agency's data were underreported. Consequently, those data are not included in this table.

Table 10. Offenses Known to Law Enforcement, by Selected State Metropolitan and Nonmetropolitan Counties, 2019

(Number.)

State/county	Violent crime	Murder and nonnegligent manslaughter	Rape[1]	Robbery	Aggravated assault	Property crime	Burglary	Larceny-theft	Motor vehicle theft	Arson[2]
ALABAMA[3]										
ARIZONA										
Metropolitan Counties										
Cochise	47	0	1	3	43	531	195	273	63	5
Coconino	127	6	17	1	103	264	59	180	25	6
Mohave	135	3	6	19	107	1,983	573	1,197	213	13
Pinal	197	3	5	18	171	1,469	321	987	161	
Yavapai	193	5	0	4	184	860	155	608	97	10
Yuma	136	7	17	6	106	807	223	502	82	7
Nonmetropolitan Counties										
Gila	176	1	3	5	167	384	65	252	67	
Graham	61	4	0	0	57	104	20	76	8	12
La Paz	40	1	2	3	34	310	87	181	42	1
Navajo	43	1	0	5	37	341	192	115	34	5
Santa Cruz	1	0	0	0	1	117	35	66	16	0
ARKANSAS										
Metropolitan Counties										
Benton[4]	159	3	32	3	121			188	61	1
Cleveland	20	0	4	0	16	162	90	56	16	2
Craighead	48	2	16	1	29	315	108	168	39	3
Crawford	55	1	1	1	52	254	37	188	29	0
Crittenden	123	3	9	8	103	286	83	182	21	1
Faulkner	116	1	18	5	92	749	176	476	97	6
Garland[4]	279	0	25	8	246			675	145	0
Grant	28	0	3	1	24	167	53	86	28	1
Jefferson	78	4	12	2	60	414	110	247	57	7
Lincoln	14	0	7	0	7	40	15	20	5	0
Little River	10	0	1	1	8	93	27	58	8	1
Lonoke	75	1	8	0	66	374	68	220	86	4
Madison	44	1	5	1	37	169	48	99	22	3
Miller	57	0	8	1	48	199	68	113	18	0
Perry	29	0	7	0	22	95	23	72	0	0
Poinsett	42	0	4	0	38	138	60	50	28	0
Pulaski	428	4	31	27	366	1,638	353	1,123	162	9
Saline[4]	187	7	31	2	147			376	81	2
Sebastian	45	0	6	0	39	223	83	127	13	1
Washington	177	5	6	1	165	572	139	346	87	8
Nonmetropolitan Counties										
Arkansas	15	0	1	1	13	58	14	42	2	1
Ashley	22	0	1	2	19	153	38	98	17	3
Baxter	70	1	15	1	53	616	81	472	63	5
Boone	199	0	30	1	168	269	79	150	40	1
Bradley	8	0	0	0	8	51	31	12	8	0
Calhoun	11	0	0	0	11	68	22	34	12	0
Carroll	45	0	5	1	39	209	52	111	46	1
Chicot	13	0	2	0	11	76	18	58	0	0
Clark	11	0	0	0	11	70	19	42	9	0
Cleburne	142	0	21	4	117	297	86	185	26	6
Columbia	23	1	2	0	20	67	21	37	9	0
Conway	46	2	13	1	30	234	43	164	27	9
Drew	16	0	4	0	12	66	23	37	6	0
Fulton	29	0	3	0	26	51	0	45	6	0
Hempstead	29	0	6	1	22	143	41	75	27	1
Howard	20	0	4	0	16	57	29	25	3	0
Independence	153	1	44	2	106	367	110	209	48	14
Izard	33	0	8	0	25	197	55	130	12	5
Jackson	45	1	6	1	37	119	10	80	29	5
Johnson	40	0	7	0	33	114	47	51	16	2
Lee	13	1	4	0	8	101	26	64	11	1
Logan	36	0	10	0	26	162	35	117	10	6
Marion	32	0	9	0	23	243	80	150	13	0
Mississippi	23	0	3	2	18	247	81	133	33	3
Monroe	1	0	1	0	0	32	3	14	15	1
Pike	10	0	3	0	7	73	22	49	2	1
Pope	91	2	15	1	73	309	102	163	44	4
Prairie	3	0	1	1	1	67	24	39	4	0
Randolph	40	1	16	0	23	112	24	75	13	2
Scott	22	0	2	1	19	65	28	29	8	0
Sevier	26	0	6	0	20	88	21	53	14	2
St. Francis	40	0	7	6	27	286	80	206	0	2
Union	60	3	2	3	52	273	76	174	23	2
Van Buren	44	2	5	0	37	141	24	82	35	11
White	200	0	61	8	131	598	154	354	90	6
Woodruff	6	0	0	0	6	62	18	41	3	0
Yell	30	0	5	0	25	177	66	90	21	1
CALIFORNIA										
Metropolitan Counties										
Alameda	633	5	27	210	391	2,169	354	1,324	491	21
Butte	283	5	32	28	218	1,290	524	724	42	3

Table 10. Offenses Known to Law Enforcement, by Selected State Metropolitan and Nonmetropolitan Counties, 2019—Continued

(Number.)

State/county	Violent crime	Murder and nonnegligent manslaughter	Rape[1]	Robbery	Aggravated assault	Property crime	Burglary	Larceny-theft	Motor vehicle theft	Arson[2]
Contra Costa	332	8	28	89	207	1,499	411	1,053	35	11
El Dorado	173	3	47	29	94	1,695	482	1,186	27	4
Fresno	1,082	14	38	102	928	3,281	1,378	1,304	599	129
Imperial	211	2	11	7	191	588	178	324	86	22
Kern	2,864	29	244	433	2,158	9,449	2,756	4,680	2,013	275
Kings	125	2	19	19	85	432	114	297	21	1
Los Angeles	5,564	68	300	1,443	3,753	15,040	2,798	8,595	3,647	220
Madera	457	1	34	14	408	1,017	375	621	21	7
Marin	63	1	5	12	45	738	143	591	4	1
Merced	500	4	19	24	453	1,515	487	956	72	8
Monterey	258	3	25	36	194	1,125	361	733	31	7
Napa	69	0	11	7	51	269	55	212	2	0
Orange	247	2	11	21	213	881	142	642	97	4
Placer	183	3	28	13	139	1,077	278	769	30	9
Riverside	932	24	37	179	692	7,220	1,454	4,320	1,446	24
Sacramento	2,408	36	161	685	1,526	8,067	2,276	5,634	157	67
San Benito	33	0	7	2	24	152	34	105	13	0
San Bernardino	1,503	27	115	189	1,172	3,945	1,142	1,875	928	53
San Diego	1,499	10	104	224	1,161	4,300	901	2,498	901	30
San Joaquin	903	5	35	162	701	2,439	719	1,589	131	24
San Luis Obispo	181	5	26	5	145	963	331	614	18	7
San Mateo	324	3	71	62	188	3,245	297	2,612	336	5
Santa Barbara	232	2	17	26	187	1,257	305	938	14	8
Santa Clara	356	2	40	25	289	1,518	178	1,154	186	4
Santa Cruz	331	5	58	34	234	1,630	439	1,174	17	7
Shasta	386	4	41	34	307	824	415	332	77	12
Solano	109	1	13	18	77	377	110	192	75	7
Sonoma	497	1	45	36	415	1,089	350	733	6	22
Stanislaus	370	8	17	90	255	1,602	559	1,000	43	13
Sutter	77	1	4	13	59	576	167	350	59	1
Tulare[5]	334	9	30	64	231	1,893	637	1,254	2	0
Ventura	159	5	18	25	111	543	112	363	68	13
Yolo	69	0	8	6	55	294	79	204	11	1
Yuba	204	5	21	37	141	847	316	520	11	11
Nonmetropolitan Counties										
Alpine	13	0	2	0	11	29	12	14	3	0
Amador	66	1	3	8	54	416	146	268	2	4
Calaveras	139	1	32	8	98	668	274	380	14	0
Colusa	26	0	8	4	14	169	53	111	5	3
Del Norte	84	2	11	18	53	424	192	228	4	12
Glenn	55	2	8	8	37	362	86	239	37	3
Humboldt	310	1	21	59	229	1,092	398	661	33	17
Inyo	60	1	9	3	47	192	86	105	1	0
Lake	193	3	21	19	150	435	204	225	6	5
Lassen	78	0	8	0	70	172	100	65	7	1
Mariposa	79	0	8	2	69	171	53	115	3	0
Mendocino	178	2	29	14	133	414	174	225	15	18
Modoc	31	0	2	1	28	29	6	22	1	0
Mono	25	0	3	0	22	53	21	32	0	1
Nevada	118	0	9	6	103	424	191	226	7	1
Plumas	128	1	9	5	113	294	116	167	11	3
Sierra	1	0	0	0	1	31	15	16	0	0
Siskiyou	70	5	2	2	61	146	69	69	8	1
Tehama	95	2	14	12	67	472	179	278	15	0
Trinity	61	2	10	9	40	190	83	101	6	2
Tuolumne	169	2	62	7	98	669	306	355	8	6
COLORADO										
Metropolitan Counties										
Adams	513	7	94	76	336	2,845	350	1,608	887	23
Boulder	85	1	11	8	65	617	143	431	43	3
Douglas	318	2	99	21	196	2,098	328	1,610	160	20
Elbert	5	0	1	0	4	5	1	2	2	1
El Paso	484	7	112	50	315	2,351	402	1,509	440	23
Gilpin	25	0	2	4	19	83	21	55	7	1
Larimer	211	2	24	7	178	753	134	531	88	8
Mesa	164	5	36	18	105	1,059	249	694	116	17
Park	41	1	6	1	33	65	17	42	6	2
Pueblo	45	2	0	5	38	1,058	183	720	155	1
Teller	13	0	1	0	12	53	14	31	8	1
Weld	136	2	24	10	100	664	128	415	121	8
Nonmetropolitan Counties										
Archuleta	46	0	13	1	32	125	38	73	14	1
Baca	3	0	0	0	3	2	0	1	1	0
Bent	17	1	3	1	12	166	57	96	13	1
Chaffee	3	0	2	0	1	57	10	38	9	0
Cheyenne	3	0	0	0	3	14	2	12	0	0
Crowley	5	0	1	0	4	61	25	30	6	1
Custer	8	0	0	0	8	67	7	53	7	0
Dolores	1	0	0	0	1	22	13	5	4	0

Table 10. Offenses Known to Law Enforcement, by Selected State Metropolitan and Nonmetropolitan Counties, 2019—Continued

(Number.)

State/county	Violent crime	Murder and nonnegligent manslaughter	Rape[1]	Robbery	Aggravated assault	Property crime	Burglary	Larceny-theft	Motor vehicle theft	Arson[2]
Eagle	28	0	12	0	16	190	25	154	11	2
Fremont	35	1	9	1	24	198	51	110	37	0
Garfield	70	0	15	4	51	205	55	130	20	4
Gunnison	6	0	1	0	5	21	2	15	4	0
Huerfano	24	0	4	1	19	151	51	78	22	1
Kiowa	2	0	0	0	2	14	4	8	2	0
Kit Carson	4	1	1	0	2	42	19	21	2	1
La Plata	50	1	19	0	30	197	54	125	18	3
Las Animas	16	1	1	0	14	53	18	31	4	2
Logan	33	1	7	0	25	109	51	42	16	1
Moffat	15	0	0	0	15	10	1	9	0	0
Montezuma	15	1	1	1	12	136	52	71	13	1
Montrose	20	0	3	0	17	176	59	108	9	1
Morgan	21	1	9	0	11	127	49	66	12	3
Otero	21	4	7	0	10	92	24	47	21	0
Phillips	2	0	0	0	2	2	0	2	0	0
Pitkin	2	0	2	0	0	23	2	19	2	0
Prowers	2	0	0	0	2	16	3	9	4	0
Rio Grande	3	0	0	1	2	55	17	31	7	0
Routt	5	1	1	0	3	48	8	37	3	0
San Juan	1	0	0	0	1	9	0	6	3	0
San Miguel	2	0	0	0	2	5	2	3	0	0
Summit	36	0	16	1	19	237	44	189	4	2
Washington	3	1	0	1	1	74	7	52	15	0
Yuma	4	0	3	0	1	44	15	28	1	0
DELAWARE										
Metropolitan Counties										
New Castle County Police Department	912	8	103	112	689	4,125	668	2,955	502	0
FLORIDA										
Metropolitan Counties										
Alachua	738	4	111	99	524	1,817	414	1,260	143	19
Baker	121	0	14	7	100	275	63	181	31	0
Bay	360	4	51	26	279	2,192	464	1,544	184	6
Brevard	540	8	52	54	426	3,548	656	2,589	303	14
Broward	349	2	26	93	228	694	99	527	68	1
Charlotte	301	2	41	16	242	1,833	262	1,445	126	9
Citrus	366	4	29	40	293	2,046	394	1,466	186	14
Clay	510	4	86	64	356	2,876	496	2,213	167	10
Collier	864	8	124	144	588	3,884	433	3,177	274	7
Escambia	1,451	24	149	299	979	7,196	1,540	5,117	539	3
Flagler	172	3	36	8	125	1,022	150	803	69	3
Gadsden	77	0	15	7	55	264	114	138	12	1
Gilchrist	33	0	8	1	24	145	53	68	24	0
Hernando	465	6	58	43	358	2,258	397	1,690	171	9
Highlands	209	5	20	40	144	1,755	401	1,279	75	5
Hillsborough	1,752	32	248	278	1,194	11,353	1,460	8,948	945	33
Indian River	274	5	24	18	227	1,398	177	1,123	98	0
Jefferson	69	1	2	1	65	157	61	82	14	1
Lake	445	3	66	51	325	2,231	567	1,404	260	11
Lee	1,236	9	191	256	780	4,632	806	3,398	428	29
Leon	322	1	35	22	264	1,447	273	1,059	115	1
Levy	462	1	17	2	442	527	225	243	59	4
Manatee	1,368	10	179	173	1,006	4,650	648	3,659	343	15
Marion	1,014	24	171	96	723	3,987	853	2,614	520	4
Martin	293	3	83	34	173	1,528	199	1,265	64	3
Miami-Dade	5,353	90	478	1,294	3,491	31,822	2,869	25,805	3,148	74
Nassau	174	1	35	4	134	919	332	514	73	5
Okaloosa	535	7	82	39	407	2,375	271	1,912	192	2
Orange	4,874	58	437	1,112	3,267	20,832	3,236	15,470	2,126	0
Osceola	678	9	80	86	503	4,509	830	3,408	271	5
Palm Beach	1,589	31	215	290	1,053	9,137	1,073	7,255	809	26
Pasco	1,452	13	225	259	955	6,456	993	4,969	494	46
Pinellas	466	7	91	62	306	3,831	507	3,090	234	11
Polk	1,166	10	63	128	965	5,089	971	3,572	546	6
Santa Rosa	209	4	54	14	137	1,360	276	973	111	7
Sarasota	475	3	26	64	382	4,183	583	3,398	202	6
Seminole	445	4	83	45	313	2,551	392	1,977	182	5
St. Johns	281	5	24	32	220	2,104	297	1,657	150	4
St. Lucie	259	2	42	36	179	1,160	210	842	108	8
Sumter	176	5	15	13	143	884	194	589	101	4
Volusia	546	7	60	87	392	2,205	421	1,572	212	14
Wakulla	75	0	11	2	62	503	124	346	33	1
Walton	114	1	15	4	94	755	130	569	56	0
Nonmetropolitan Counties										
Bradford	65	0	12	3	50	226	82	123	21	1
Calhoun	30	1	0	1	28	78	27	42	9	0
Columbia	158	1	17	19	121	894	361	483	50	2
DeSoto	104	0	17	6	81	512	147	321	44	2

Table 10. Offenses Known to Law Enforcement, by Selected State Metropolitan and Nonmetropolitan Counties, 2019—Continued

(Number.)

State/county	Violent crime	Murder and nonnegligent manslaughter	Rape[1]	Robbery	Aggravated assault	Property crime	Burglary	Larceny-theft	Motor vehicle theft	Arson[2]
Dixie	85	1	14	2	68	147	88	44	15	1
Franklin	59	0	1	0	58	211	33	169	9	2
Glades	24	0	2	0	22	124	20	92	12	0
Gulf	29	1	1	0	27	156	47	97	12	0
Hamilton	41	1	4	4	32	186	56	119	11	1
Hardee	47	1	4	4	38	270	79	167	24	0
Hendry	126	7	19	11	89	630	254	328	48	3
Holmes	72	0	12	3	57	158	54	97	7	0
Lafayette	13	0	1	0	12	37	12	20	5	0
Liberty	19	1	0	1	17	66	22	35	9	0
Madison	109	0	14	3	92	174	71	101	2	0
Monroe	186	2	19	23	142	681	86	557	38	6
Okeechobee	162	2	21	25	114	780	153	549	78	0
Putnam	124	4	21	10	89	797	217	528	52	0
Suwannee	148	2	17	2	127	432	137	269	26	0
Taylor	71	0	9	4	58	229	91	108	30	0
Union	47	0	12	3	32	83	30	47	6	0
Washington	32	0	0	1	31	132	44	74	14	0
GEORGIA										
Metropolitan Counties[6]										
Brooks	50	0	5	1	44	196	47	122	27	0
Bryan	47	1	5	9	32	277	45	217	15	0
Burke	27	0	2	3	22	225	57	142	26	0
Butts	57	2	6	3	46	329	40	266	23	1
Cherokee	74	0	19	12	43	1,145	149	902	94	0
Clayton County Police Department	1,440	33	220	422	765	7,364	1,627	4,595	1,142	20
Cobb	6	0	0	0	6	74	0	71	3	0
Coweta	596	5	53	10	528	1,007	179	730	98	3
Dougherty	0	0	0	0	0	56	0	55	1	0
Dougherty County Police Department	38	0	5	9	24	284	84	173	27	0
Echols	3	0	1	0	2	19	9	10	0	0
Fayette	50	4	7	5	34	346	93	222	31	2
Forsyth	123	1	22	7	93	1,377	180	1,077	120	0
Hall	252	4	37	20	191	1,315	288	876	151	4
Haralson	146	1	8	2	135	384	102	234	48	3
Heard	18	0	1	2	15	96	25	60	11	2
Jasper	69	0	2	2	65	193	34	144	15	1
Jones	22	0	2	2	18	303	81	192	30	1
Lanier	22	0	0	1	21	117	33	71	13	0
Lee	41	0	6	11	24	494	103	356	35	1
Madison	99	1	3	2	93	363	60	280	23	4
Marion	2	0	0	0	2	29	9	17	3	0
McDuffie	28	0	3	6	19	178	67	101	10	0
Meriwether	42	2	5	2	33	257	64	173	20	1
Murray	47	0	5	3	39	85	16	51	18	
Newton	81	3	8	32	38	821	303	408	110	12
Paulding	320	5	27	22	266	1,862	314	1,272	276	11
Peach	25	0	6	3	16	156	32	106	18	0
Pike	20	0	1	2	17	193	24	160	9	0
Walton	39	1	10	7	21	444	74	322	48	0
Nonmetropolitan Counties[6]										
Berrien	51	1	3	0	47	132	31	92	9	2
Bleckley	21	0	3	0	18	100	34	61	5	0
Candler	9	0	1	3	5	41	9	31	1	1
Cook	36	0	1	1	34	131	25	89	17	0
Fannin	31	2	8	1	20	274	61	179	34	3
Franklin	16	2	3	0	11	221	53	153	15	0
Gilmer	72	0	16	0	56	327	73	226	28	2
Hancock	15	0	0	0	15	50	15	28	7	0
Jefferson	27	0	2	0	25	70	23	36	11	0
Laurens	92	1	12	8	71	523	175	291	57	3
Mitchell	28	0	2	2	24	265	40	196	29	0
Pierce	31	0	5	2	24	321	72	219	30	2
Pulaski	50	2	2	1	45	209	55	151	3	
Screven	37	0	0	4	33	112	41	59	12	2
Thomas	60	0	17	11	32	477	106	322	49	3
Towns	23	0	3	0	20	88	17	67	4	0
Treutlen	5	0	1	0	4	34	10	22	2	1
Ware	83	1	3	3	76	432	62	354	16	
White	22	0	1	1	20	136	51	77	8	1
Wilkes	22	0	1	0	21	30	6	20	4	0
Wilkinson	10	0	0	1	9	34	16	14	4	0
HAWAII										
Metropolitan Counties										
Maui Police Department	449	1	110	67	271	4,984	577	3,746	661	128
IDAHO										
Metropolitan Counties										
Ada	257	0	67	4	186	595	131	443	21	10
Bannock	5	0	2	0	3	37	9	20	8	0

Table 10. Offenses Known to Law Enforcement, by Selected State Metropolitan and Nonmetropolitan Counties, 2019—Continued

(Number.)

State/county	Violent crime	Murder and nonnegligent manslaughter	Rape[1]	Robbery	Aggravated assault	Property crime	Burglary	Larceny-theft	Motor vehicle theft	Arson[2]
Boise	17	0	1	1	15	62	7	51	4	0
Bonneville	109	1	15	3	90	607	157	409	41	5
Butte	7	0	0	0	7	1	0	1	0	0
Canyon	117	1	28	3	85	430	139	200	91	3
Franklin	8	1	0	0	7	34	20	14	0	0
Gem	22	1	3	0	18	64	25	32	7	0
Jefferson	19	0	2	0	17	68	12	50	6	0
Jerome	13	0	2	0	11	95	32	52	11	0
Kootenai	149	1	15	4	129	707	175	490	42	3
Nez Perce	8	0	4	0	4	83	11	67	5	0
Owyhee	30	0	6	0	24	60	14	39	7	0
Power	10	0	5	0	5	29	5	21	3	0
Twin Falls	42	0	9	0	33	136	60	62	14	2
Nonmetropolitan Counties										
Adams	10	0	0	0	10	43	6	37	0	0
Benewah	25	1	1	1	22	36	7	22	7	1
Bingham	27	1	4	1	21	154	44	95	15	0
Blaine	5	0	2	0	3	18	7	10	1	0
Bonner	26	0	1	0	25	342	111	190	41	2
Camas	3	0	0	0	3	8	2	6	0	0
Cassia	34	0	1	1	32	257	23	209	25	0
Clark	1	0	1	0	0	5	0	5	0	0
Custer	4	1	1	0	2	16	4	11	1	0
Elmore	29	1	3	0	25	55	7	38	10	2
Fremont	2	0	1	0	1	42	5	34	3	0
Gooding	19	1	2	0	16	41	11	19	11	0
Idaho	26	0	3	1	22	63	20	35	8	0
Latah	14	1	7	0	6	89	22	63	4	0
Lemhi	6	0	0	0	6	9	4	3	2	0
Lewis	5	0	0	0	5	49	11	29	9	0
Lincoln	17	0	2	0	15	26	9	15	2	0
Madison	22	0	7	0	15	54	12	34	8	0
Minidoka	12	0	1	0	11	82	21	53	8	0
Oneida	5	0	1	0	4	19	8	8	3	0
Payette	14	0	3	0	11	85	7	66	12	0
Shoshone	14	0	2	0	12	106	34	62	10	0
Teton	15	0	2	0	13	33	4	28	1	0
Valley	22	0	6	0	16	58	22	35	1	0
Washington	5	0	1	0	4	16	8	7	1	0
ILLINOIS										
Metropolitan Counties										
Alexander	6	0	1	0	5	53	15	37	1	0
Boone	27	0	12	1	14	146	34	103	9	0
Champaign	48	0	24	9	15	405	130	251	24	1
Clinton	9	0	1	1	7	73	12	58	3	0
Cook	231	4	61	37	129	1,035	156	745	134	11
DeKalb	28	0	3	7	18	85	42	42	1	0
DuPage	81	1	21	12	47	434	120	272	42	2
Fulton	29	0	2	4	23	155	60	87	8	0
Grundy	20	1	6	2	11	79	19	58	2	2
Henry	6	0	0	0	6	51	11	36	4	0
Jackson	29	0	8	1	20	299	115	163	21	0
Jersey	25	0	15	0	10	115	37	67	11	0
Johnson	26	0	2	1	23	93	29	50	14	0
Kane	87	1	12	9	65	280	87	171	22	0
Kankakee	56	1	9	8	38	250	80	151	19	6
Kendall	52	0	19	7	26	225	27	193	5	1
Lake	104	1	27	13	63	771	194	501	76	3
Macon	38	0	5	3	30	282	60	210	12	3
Macoupin	10	0	0	4	6	250	55	180	15	1
Madison	126	0	22	8	96	1,059	223	751	85	1
Marshall	3	0	1	0	2	24	14	7	3	1
McHenry	65	1	17	3	44	257	63	179	15	1
McLean	30	0	12	1	17	117	27	77	13	3
Menard	10	0	3	0	7	51	8	40	3	22
Monroe	9	0	3	0	6	34	16	15	3	0
Peoria	55	0	12	8	35	866	162	616	88	4
Piatt	16	0	5	0	11	63	37	20	6	0
Rock Island	54	0	17	2	35	222	53	154	15	1
Sangamon	204	1	21	22	160	467	209	196	62	1
Stark	9	0	0	0	9	33	18	12	3	0
Vermilion	87	0	19	2	66	403	135	249	19	4
Will	125	2	24	21	78	658	119	411	128	7
Williamson	8	2	4	1	1	248	45	183	20	1
Winnebago	123	3	27	9	84	517	161	314	42	4
Woodford	24	5	3	1	15	104	37	62	5	1
Nonmetropolitan Counties										
Brown	1	0	0	0	1	10	2	8	0	0
Bureau	29	0	10	0	19	113	28	73	12	4
Carroll	9	0	1	0	8	21	8	12	1	1

Table 10. Offenses Known to Law Enforcement, by Selected State Metropolitan and Nonmetropolitan Counties, 2019—Continued

(Number.)

State/county	Violent crime	Murder and nonnegligent manslaughter	Rape[1]	Robbery	Aggravated assault	Property crime	Burglary	Larceny-theft	Motor vehicle theft	Arson[2]
Cass	2	0	0	0	2	30	9	20	1	0
Clay	5	0	0	0	5	43	17	19	7	1
Coles	16	0	5	0	11	98	21	66	11	1
Crawford	6	0	1	0	5	76	15	59	2	0
Cumberland	1	0	0	0	1	13	7	5	1	0
Douglas	8	0	2	0	6	30	13	15	2	0
Edgar	4	0	1	0	3	32	11	17	4	0
Effingham	16	0	0	0	16	107	23	69	15	0
Fayette	14	0	4	0	10	50	14	23	13	0
Ford	11	0	1	0	10	52	18	34	0	0
Franklin	14	0	0	0	14	217	56	151	10	0
Gallatin	5	0	0	0	5	38	8	23	7	0
Greene	9	0	0	0	9	20	4	15	1	1
Hamilton	7	0	3	0	4	42	6	33	3	0
Iroquois	19	3	2	0	14	142	48	74	20	1
Jasper	48	0	13	1	34	56	32	18	6	1
Jefferson	59	0	4	2	53	286	102	156	28	4
Jo Daviess	6	0	2	1	3	74	27	43	4	0
Knox	51	0	9	0	42	171	72	81	18	1
La Salle	33	0	12	0	21	167	45	110	12	2
Lee	21	0	0	0	21	81	11	63	7	1
Livingston	28	0	8	2	18	96	33	57	6	1
Logan	11	0	1	0	10	63	29	31	3	0
Marion	43	1	10	4	28	202	100	86	16	0
Mason	12	0	2	0	10	85	16	66	3	1
McDonough	8	0	0	0	8	19	9	9	1	0
Montgomery	42	0	5	0	37	133	51	79	3	1
Morgan	11	0	3	2	6	108	57	45	6	0
Moultrie	8	0	2	0	6	38	15	20	3	0
Ogle	13	0	0	0	13	149	46	101	2	0
Perry	7	0	3	0	4	67	26	37	4	0
Pike	15	0	6	1	8	37	14	22	1	0
Putnam	1	0	0	0	1	19	5	14	0	0
Randolph	4	0	1	0	3	18	5	12	1	0
Schuyler	3	0	0	0	3	14	0	14	0	0
Scott	0	0	0	0	0	15	5	6	4	0
Shelby	1	0	1	0	0	49	16	33	0	0
Stephenson	36	2	13	1	20	87	21	62	4	1
Wabash	0	0	0	0	0	2	1	1	0	0
Wayne	15	0	4	1	10	108	40	56	12	0
Whiteside	17	1	8	0	8	79	36	37	6	0
INDIANA										
Metropolitan Counties										
Allen	184	2	36	29	117	642	128	436	78	1
Bartholomew	51	0	18	2	31	402	75	287	40	
Floyd	16	2	1	1	12	281	37	200	44	
Franklin	4	0	0	0	4	137	30	89	18	0
Hancock	60	0	2	5	53	233	50	145	38	1
Howard	56	0	3	4	49	126	29	86	11	
La Porte	57	1	2	10	44	416	130	233	53	1
Madison	37	0	16	6	15	369	95	249	25	3
Porter	38	2	10	2	24	350	77	248	25	
Shelby	58	1	4	3	50	154	46	90	18	2
Tippecanoe	41	1	12	6	22	500	120	344	36	3
Vanderburgh	51	1	9	4	37	482	61	399	22	1
Vigo[7]	218	0	11	10	197		190		91	10
Warrick	88	2	6	6	74	508	84	386	38	0
Nonmetropolitan Counties										
Blackford[6]	8	1	0	1	6	16	5	11	0	1
Clinton	19	1	6	0	12	175	47	121	7	0
Gibson	32	0	7	0	25	116	23	81	12	1
Grant	36	0	4	1	31	254	89	158	7	0
Jackson	12	0	1	0	11	277	67	189	21	
Jay	7	1	0	0	6	53	4	43	6	
Jennings	10	3	5	0	2	89	70	19	0	1
Lawrence	27	0	1	10	16	142	55	53	34	
Pulaski	41	0	2	2	37	118	23	83	12	0
Scott	6	0	4	0	2	219	70	144	5	1
Starke[6]	36	1	1	3	31	196	38	137	21	0
Steuben[6]	12	0	4	0	8	322	63	207	52	1
Wayne	6	1	3	0	2	147	37	92	18	
White	12	0	0	0	12	44	20	19	5	
IOWA										
Metropolitan Counties										
Black Hawk	20	0	0	0	20	123	58	48	17	1
Boone	17	0	0	0	17	48	13	27	8	1
Bremer	4	0	2	0	2	24	14	9	1	0
Dubuque	13	1	7	0	5	114	30	68	16	0

Table 10. Offenses Known to Law Enforcement, by Selected State Metropolitan and Nonmetropolitan Counties, 2019—Continued

(Number.)

State/county	Violent crime	Murder and nonnegligent manslaughter	Rape[1]	Robbery	Aggravated assault	Property crime	Burglary	Larceny-theft	Motor vehicle theft	Arson[2]
Grundy	7	0	0	0	7	63	40	18	5	1
Guthrie	2	0	0	0	2	45	19	23	3	0
Harrison	7	0	0	0	7	43	12	25	6	2
Jasper	6	0	2	0	4	44	20	17	7	0
Johnson	65	0	8	1	56	196	60	116	20	4
Madison	2	0	0	0	2	26	14	11	1	0
Mills	17	0	1	0	16	98	28	53	17	2
Polk	112	0	14	9	89	822	211	486	125	4
Pottawattamie	57	1	7	3	46	251	54	173	24	4
Scott	40	2	6	0	32	170	53	100	17	0
Story	13	1	3	0	9	105	43	46	16	1
Warren	54	0	7	0	47	136	37	82	17	4
Washington	35	0	2	0	33	61	25	27	9	0
Woodbury	22	0	3	0	19	186	98	78	10	0
Nonmetropolitan Counties										
Adair	0	0	0	0	0	24	7	14	3	0
Adams	3	0	0	0	3	20	8	10	2	0
Allamakee	7	0	1	0	6	20	5	13	2	0
Appanoose	8	0	0	0	8	70	24	30	16	1
Buchanan	33	0	8	0	25	115	41	57	17	5
Buena Vista	12	0	1	0	11	41	29	10	2	0
Butler	7	0	4	0	3	25	15	6	4	1
Calhoun	8	0	0	0	8	31	12	14	5	1
Cass	10	1	2	0	7	38	6	25	7	0
Cedar	12	0	2	0	10	43	14	24	5	1
Cerro Gordo	10	0	2	0	8	98	26	53	19	0
Cherokee	2	0	1	0	1	12	7	5	0	0
Chickasaw	10	0	1	0	9	29	9	15	5	0
Clarke	7	0	2	0	5	36	11	16	9	1
Clay	13	0	1	0	12	11	7	3	1	0
Clayton	11	0	7	0	4	41	11	27	3	0
Clinton	17	0	6	1	10	92	25	61	6	0
Crawford	3	0	0	0	3	3	0	2	1	1
Davis	4	0	0	0	4	1	0	1	0	0
Delaware	4	0	3	0	1	46	7	30	9	2
Des Moines	14	0	1	0	13	118	70	46	2	0
Dickinson	5	0	0	0	5	29	12	13	4	0
Emmet	0	0	0	0	0	7	0	5	2	0
Franklin	0	0	0	0	0	1	0	0	1	0
Fremont	11	0	2	1	8	43	16	22	5	1
Hamilton	6	0	0	0	6	54	28	19	7	0
Hancock	6	0	2	0	4	31	17	14	0	0
Hardin	11	0	4	0	7	83	36	38	9	0
Henry	20	0	0	0	20	69	20	46	3	2
Howard	0	0	0	0	0	35	20	12	3	0
Humboldt	0	0	0	0	0	41	11	28	2	1
Ida	10	0	2	0	8	68	17	44	7	0
Iowa	8	0	0	0	8	55	12	31	12	0
Jackson	3	0	0	0	3	23	6	12	5	0
Jefferson	2	0	1	0	1	26	11	12	3	0
Kossuth	6	3	3	0	0	32	22	8	2	0
Lee	15	0	2	0	13	108	42	49	17	0
Louisa	23	0	6	0	17	58	18	35	5	0
Lucas	12	0	2	2	8	68	29	34	5	0
Lyon	11	0	2	0	9	57	21	26	10	0
Mahaska	23	0	1	0	22	64	22	31	11	0
Marion	19	0	10	0	9	44	12	28	4	0
Marshall	42	0	3	0	39	94	31	49	14	3
Mitchell	0	0	0	0	0	5	2	3	0	0
Monona	16	0	1	0	15	37	15	15	7	0
Monroe	5	0	3	0	2	20	5	8	7	0
Muscatine	21	1	7	1	12	56	29	20	7	1
O'Brien	21	0	5	0	16	57	12	41	4	0
Osceola	14	0	1	0	13	73	14	57	2	0
Page	3	0	1	0	2	26	9	11	6	0
Palo Alto	15	0	2	0	13	48	23	21	4	0
Plymouth	13	0	3	0	10	45	15	23	7	0
Ringgold	4	0	0	0	4	21	4	16	1	0
Sac	6	0	1	0	5	32	10	20	2	1
Shelby	3	0	0	0	3	14	6	7	1	1
Sioux	7	0	3	0	4	50	12	35	3	0
Tama	23	0	1	0	22	57	22	23	12	0
Taylor	8	0	0	0	8	14	3	8	3	1
Union	4	0	0	0	4	46	14	28	4	0
Van Buren	4	0	0	0	4	58	24	31	3	0
Wapello	25	0	2	0	23	91	33	45	13	2
Wayne	8	0	0	0	8	28	13	12	3	1
Webster	27	0	4	0	23	113	41	59	13	2
Winneshiek	9	0	2	0	7	12	1	8	3	0
Worth	6	0	1	0	5	27	7	19	1	0
Wright	4	0	1	0	3	21	4	14	3	1

Table 10. Offenses Known to Law Enforcement, by Selected State Metropolitan and Nonmetropolitan Counties, 2019—Continued

(Number.)

State/county	Violent crime	Murder and nonnegligent manslaughter	Rape[1]	Robbery	Aggravated assault	Property crime	Burglary	Larceny-theft	Motor vehicle theft	Arson[2]
KANSAS										
Metropolitan Counties										
Butler	49	0	12	1	36	301	61	201	39	3
Doniphan	1	0	0	0	1	8	3	4	1	0
Geary	15	1	1	0	13	32	8	19	5	0
Harvey	11	0	0	1	10	24	12	11	1	0
Jackson	15	0	3	0	12	122	17	96	9	1
Jefferson	33	0	11	1	21	224	25	164	35	1
Johnson	50	0	10	2	38	220	24	163	33	1
Linn	13	1	2	0	10	86	26	52	8	1
Osage[4]	14	0	1	1	12			31	10	1
Pottawatomie	27	0	5	1	21	177	42	111	24	4
Riley County Police Department[4]	263	1	32	21	209			998	105	13
Sedgwick	94	2	21	3	68	205	61	109	35	3
Shawnee	87	1	8	3	75	958	250	589	119	2
Sumner	12	0	2	2	8	156	65	75	16	3
Wabaunsee	14	0	2	0	12	77	29	45	3	2
Wyandotte	21	0	4	2	15	92	6	82	4	0
Nonmetropolitan Counties										
Allen	14	0	3	0	11	51	22	22	7	0
Anderson	8	0	0	0	8	31	13	14	4	0
Barber	6	0	0	1	5	19	4	13	2	0
Barton	20	1	3	0	16	69	15	52	2	0
Bourbon	10	0	0	0	10	33	7	19	7	1
Brown	5	0	0	0	5	16	5	8	3	0
Clark	3	0	0	0	3	14	1	13	0	0
Clay	2	0	0	1	1	5	0	5	0	0
Cowley	30	0	8	0	22	125	45	67	13	1
Crawford	22	1	2	1	18	157	1	125	31	2
Dickinson	23	0	2	0	21	106	33	64	9	1
Edwards	0	0	0	0	0	15	5	9	1	0
Ellis	14	0	0	2	12	32	10	20	2	1
Ellsworth	8	0	1	0	7	47	26	16	5	1
Finney	28	1	5	2	20	135	28	83	24	1
Ford	13	0	0	0	13	59	15	34	10	0
Franklin	52	0	6	1	45	155	54	81	20	4
Gove	4	0	2	0	2	7	2	4	1	0
Grant	2	0	0	0	2	13	5	7	1	0
Gray	4	0	2	0	2	42	6	33	3	0
Greenwood	25	0	4	0	21	72	18	46	8	1
Hamilton	9	0	1	1	7	21	3	16	2	0
Haskell	0	0	0	0	0	22	5	15	2	0
Jewell	2	0	1	0	1	16	10	5	1	0
Kearny	12	0	3	0	9	74	14	55	5	0
Kingman	3	0	0	0	3	30	8	19	3	0
Kiowa	3	0	0	0	3	18	9	8	1	0
Labette	6	0	0	0	6	55	22	29	4	0
Logan	1	0	0	0	1	10	0	9	1	0
Lyon	17	0	7	0	10	57	18	36	3	0
Marion	9	0	1	0	8	40	17	17	6	0
McPherson	14	0	1	0	13	37	15	20	2	0
Mitchell	2	0	0	0	2	29	12	12	5	0
Montgomery[4]	27	0	2	1	24			76	17	3
Morris	7	0	0	0	7	21	8	10	3	0
Nemaha	5	0	0	0	5	51	4	39	8	1
Neosho	8	0	1	0	7	30	13	14	3	1
Ness	8	0	0	0	8	18	5	11	2	0
Osborne	1	0	0	0	1	26	14	10	2	0
Phillips	5	0	0	0	5	5	2	2	1	0
Pratt	5	0	1	0	4	20	13	5	2	0
Reno	32	0	4	0	28	178	64	96	18	0
Rice	4	0	0	0	4	28	3	20	5	0
Rooks	3	1	1	0	1	16	5	10	1	1
Rush	11	0	0	1	10	31	11	18	2	0
Russell	5	0	1	0	4	40	13	22	5	0
Seward	4	1	0	0	3	19	6	8	5	2
Thomas	4	0	0	0	4	19	2	15	2	0
Washington	3	0	0	0	3	5	3	0	2	0
Wichita	4	0	0	0	4	5	1	3	1	0
Wilson	10	0	2	0	8	47	14	28	5	1
Woodson	1	0	0	0	1	19	7	11	1	0
KENTUCKY										
Metropolitan Counties										
Allen	8	0	2	1	5	86	38	37	11	2
Boone	66	0	24	15	27	817	152	553	112	5
Bourbon	3	0	1	0	2	55	16	31	8	0
Boyd	20	0	5	0	15	181	67	94	20	0
Bracken	2	0	0	1	1	50	12	25	13	0
Bullitt	20	0	5	5	10	347	90	205	52	1

Table 10. Offenses Known to Law Enforcement, by Selected State Metropolitan and Nonmetropolitan Counties, 2019—Continued

(Number.)

State/county	Violent crime	Murder and nonnegligent manslaughter	Rape[1]	Robbery	Aggravated assault	Property crime	Burglary	Larceny-theft	Motor vehicle theft	Arson[2]
Butler	2	0	0	0	2	32	10	15	7	0
Campbell	0	0	0	0	0	0	0	0	0	0
Campbell County Police Department	13	0	7	1	5	141	38	79	24	0
Carter	6	1	0	1	4	57	13	24	20	0
Christian	18	0	6	2	10	258	88	133	37	1
Clark	6	0	2	2	2	142	54	67	21	0
Daviess	20	2	9	1	8	374	93	242	39	4
Edmonson	9	0	0	0	9	22	4	12	6	0
Fayette	0	0	0	0	0	0	0	0	0	0
Gallatin	2	0	0	0	2	17	11	3	3	0
Grant	6	0	2	1	3	135	33	79	23	0
Greenup	3	0	0	1	2	34	4	18	12	0
Hancock	2	0	1	0	1	27	8	12	7	0
Hardin	16	1	3	3	9	140	39	79	22	3
Henderson	19	1	4	0	14	163	48	93	22	1
Henry	1	0	0	0	1	8	4	1	3	0
Jefferson	1	0	0	0	1	0	0	0	0	0
Jessamine	14	0	7	1	6	206	59	121	26	2
Kenton	0	0	0	0	0	6	0	5	1	0
Kenton County Police Department	19	0	7	5	7	116	41	69	6	2
Larue	3	0	0	1	2	18	4	5	9	0
McLean	2	0	1	0	1	53	27	18	8	0
Meade	14	0	0	2	12	122	48	52	22	1
Oldham	0	0	0	0	0	3	2	1	0	0
Oldham County Police Department	25	0	13	4	8	455	87	337	31	6
Pendleton	4	0	0	1	3	60	15	40	5	1
Scott	8	1	0	2	5	161	35	104	22	0
Shelby	18	0	3	4	11	244	56	162	26	1
Spencer	0	0	0	0	0	43	13	24	6	0
Trigg	6	0	1	0	5	98	42	51	5	0
Warren	39	1	16	5	17	537	165	313	59	0
Woodford	0	0	0	0	0	14	1	12	1	0
Nonmetropolitan Counties										
Adair	1	0	0	0	1	5	1	3	1	0
Anderson	2	0	0	0	2	15	4	7	4	0
Ballard	9	0	1	0	8	62	21	32	9	0
Barren	30	1	2	3	24	84	22	43	19	0
Bath	4	0	0	0	4	33	11	17	5	0
Bell	18	0	0	0	18	137	54	66	17	0
Boyle	6	0	1	2	3	34	12	18	4	1
Breathitt	2	2	0	0	0	10	6	3	1	0
Breckinridge	7	1	0	1	5	40	13	13	14	1
Caldwell	2	0	0	0	2	22	4	12	6	0
Calloway	10	0	4	1	5	194	68	110	16	4
Carlisle	2	0	0	1	1	19	5	13	1	1
Carroll	5	0	1	3	1	54	18	27	9	1
Casey	1	0	0	0	1	44	27	9	8	0
Clay	4	1	0	0	3	95	30	32	33	1
Clinton	0	0	0	0	0	15	2	6	7	0
Crittenden	1	0	1	0	0	24	10	9	5	0
Cumberland	0	0	0	0	0	10	6	1	3	0
Elliott	0	0	0	0	0	0	0	0	0	0
Estill	2	0	0	1	1	29	6	18	5	0
Fleming	2	0	0	0	2	12	4	8	0	0
Floyd	5	0	1	0	4	50	6	30	14	0
Franklin	25	1	4	2	18	209	43	119	47	0
Fulton	0	0	0	0	0	13	4	7	2	0
Garrard	0	0	0	0	0	0	0	0	0	0
Garrard County Police Department	3	0	0	0	3	69	21	36	12	0
Graves	28	0	15	3	10	223	81	120	22	1
Grayson	4	0	0	3	1	84	25	45	14	1
Green	2	0	1	0	1	2	2	0	0	0
Harlan	1	0	1	0	0	39	21	14	4	1
Harrison	7	0	0	2	5	73	23	41	9	1
Hart	3	0	1	1	1	79	32	30	17	0
Hickman	0	0	0	0	0	13	5	6	2	0
Hopkins	18	0	2	0	16	204	56	128	20	1
Jackson	4	0	0	0	4	76	23	30	23	0
Johnson	4	0	1	0	3	45	20	13	12	0
Knott	2	0	0	1	1	26	4	17	5	0
Knox	17	0	1	4	12	81	23	27	31	0
Laurel	25	1	1	6	17	460	112	229	119	0
Lawrence	3	0	0	2	1	42	11	16	15	0
Lee	1	0	0	1	0	5	2	2	1	0
Leslie	1	0	0	0	1	17	2	6	9	0
Letcher	1	0	0	0	1	13	0	11	2	0
Lewis	4	0	1	0	3	18	10	5	3	0
Lincoln	5	0	0	0	5	57	16	21	20	0
Livingston	2	0	0	0	2	52	19	26	7	2
Logan	26	0	10	1	15	80	39	36	5	0

Table 10. Offenses Known to Law Enforcement, by Selected State Metropolitan and Nonmetropolitan Counties, 2019—Continued

(Number.)

State/county	Violent crime	Murder and nonnegligent manslaughter	Rape[1]	Robbery	Aggravated assault	Property crime	Burglary	Larceny-theft	Motor vehicle theft	Arson[2]
Lyon	3	0	0	2	1	60	22	34	4	0
Madison	18	0	4	3	11	226	60	139	27	0
Magoffin	1	0	1	0	0	19	3	8	8	0
Marion	3	0	0	2	1	49	22	23	4	1
Marshall	19	0	7	2	10	204	61	119	24	0
Martin	4	0	0	0	4	13	2	4	7	0
Mason	4	0	0	0	0	73	36	26	11	0
McCracken	38	1	16	5	16	472	137	289	46	2
McCreary	1	0	0	0	1	58	12	30	16	0
Menifee	0	0	0	0	0	10	2	4	4	0
Mercer	2	0	0	0	2	49	17	30	2	0
Metcalfe	2	0	0	0	2	34	21	9	4	0
Monroe	0	0	0	0	0	9	1	6	2	0
Montgomery	10	1	2	1	6	285	96	150	39	0
Morgan	2	0	0	0	2	14	5	7	2	0
Muhlenberg	14	0	0	2	12	66	24	31	11	2
Nelson	22	0	6	0	16	213	57	122	34	3
Nicholas	0	0	0	0	0	2	1	0	1	1
Ohio	19	0	10	0	9	116	33	56	27	1
Owen	2	0	1	0	1	28	14	9	5	0
Owsley	0	0	0	0	0	16	3	3	10	0
Perry	8	1	2	0	5	51	15	17	19	0
Pike	2	0	1	0	1	33	4	24	5	0
Powell	0	0	0	0	0	8	2	4	2	0
Pulaski	30	0	13	3	14	315	135	124	56	2
Robertson	0	0	0	0	0	8	1	6	1	0
Rockcastle	3	0	1	1	1	40	15	15	10	1
Rowan	8	0	4	1	3	65	27	31	7	1
Russell	3	0	2	0	1	63	15	42	6	2
Simpson	2	0	1	0	1	40	11	19	10	0
Taylor	13	1	4	1	7	148	63	74	11	0
Todd	1	0	0	0	1	45	24	13	8	0
Trimble	0	0	0	0	0	11	4	4	3	1
Union	3	0	0	0	3	35	12	19	4	0
Washington	6	0	1	1	4	43	25	13	5	0
Wayne	8	0	5	1	2	35	7	23	5	2
Webster	0	0	0	0	0	21	7	9	5	0
Whitley	9	0	0	1	8	176	78	67	31	0
Wolfe	0	0	0	0	0	18	7	7	4	0
LOUISIANA										
Metropolitan Counties										
Acadia	109	4	10	8	87	514	192	271	51	0
Ascension	340	3	21	37	279	1,519	260	1,150	109	8
Assumption	70	1	6	0	63	215	25	182	8	0
Bossier	64	2	4	1	57	467	99	345	23	1
Caddo	8	1	1	0	6	309	46	245	18	1
Calcasieu	583	4	80	26	473	3,819	869	2,669	281	3
De Soto	72	1	6	4	61	358	92	245	21	0
East Baton Rouge	609	18	53	149	389	6,475	729	5,433	313	4
East Feliciana	70	4	2	2	62	131	32	85	14	0
Iberville	206	0	2	6	198	335	55	279	1	0
Jefferson	1,240	45	99	264	832	9,618	1,079	8,014	525	45
Lafourche	231	12	24	0	195	2,084	451	1,530	103	6
Livingston	550	9	53	16	472	2,948	681	2,094	173	0
Morehouse	30	2	4	4	20	226	58	142	26	0
Ouachita	425	7	42	39	337	2,512	599	1,724	189	7
Plaquemines	37	0	2	1	34	108	20	82	6	1
Pointe Coupee	154	3	3	1	147	286	66	194	26	0
Rapides	326	5	40	21	260	1,512	554	850	108	8
St. Charles	133	3	4	19	107	762	133	592	37	5
St. Helena	54	5	1	1	47	137	27	101	9	0
St. James	59	2	0	0	57	371	124	226	21	1
St. John the Baptist	93	10	2	0	81	965	175	755	35	1
St. Martin	156	3	21	8	124	627	153	417	57	0
St. Tammany	259	8	32	13	206	1,485	286	1,076	123	3
Tangipahoa	688	10	36	78	564	2,350	647	1,463	240	8
West Baton Rouge	85	2	6	15	62	545	66	427	52	6
West Feliciana	34	0	3	1	30	60	13	42	5	0
Nonmetropolitan Counties										
Allen[7]	19	1	8	0	10		26		28	0
Beauregard	18	1	5	0	12	241	55	166	20	1
Bienville	83	0	12	3	68	196	60	118	18	1
Caldwell	38	1	0	0	37	207	60	132	15	0
Claiborne	16	0	0	1	15	51	12	35	4	1
Concordia	73	0	4	18	51	304	95	196	13	0
East Carroll	21	5	3	0	13	28	8	18	2	1
Franklin	58	2	0	1	55	143	32	102	9	0
Jackson	6	0	0	0	6	52	14	34	4	0
La Salle	30	0	2	1	27	66	28	31	7	0

Table 10. Offenses Known to Law Enforcement, by Selected State Metropolitan and Nonmetropolitan Counties, 2019—Continued

(Number.)

State/county	Violent crime	Murder and nonnegligent manslaughter	Rape[1]	Robbery	Aggravated assault	Property crime	Burglary	Larceny-theft	Motor vehicle theft	Arson[2]
Lincoln	79	0	7	0	72	197	39	147	11	0
Madison	11	1	0	0	10	27	8	18	1	1
Natchitoches	79	2	7	4	66	371	92	245	34	0
Red River	33	0	0	1	32	136	45	84	7	0
Richland	12	1	3	1	7	40	20	18	2	2
Sabine	27	1	8	0	18	194	8	186	0	0
St. Landry	159	4	0	13	142	746	326	370	50	1
St. Mary	121	0	12	9	100	563	121	400	42	0
Tensas	6	0	1	1	4	18	8	9	1	1
Vernon	58	1	8	4	45	451	87	327	37	1
Washington	274	0	48	13	213	657	174	418	65	4
Webster	21	2	7	1	11	151	64	65	22	0
West Carroll	33	1	5	1	26	57	4	48	5	0
Winn	32	2	2	1	27	63	21	24	18	0
MAINE										
Metropolitan Counties										
Androscoggin	13	0	5	1	7	100	25	69	6	1
Cumberland	29	0	9	2	18	285	57	207	21	0
Penobscot	5	0	0	2	3	226	46	163	17	0
Sagadahoc[6]	8	0	1	1	6	58	17	36	5	1
York	20	0	4	4	12	291	70	209	12	0
Nonmetropolitan Counties										
Aroostook	6	0	0	0	6	77	25	48	4	0
Franklin	6	0	4	0	2	38	7	30	1	0
Hancock	4	0	1	0	3	72	16	49	7	0
Kennebec	21	0	4	1	16	174	51	117	6	0
Knox	5	0	0	0	5	156	21	122	13	1
Lincoln	25	0	19	0	6	128	29	92	7	0
Oxford	25	0	13	3	9	223	56	156	11	0
Piscataquis	4	0	2	0	2	45	10	32	3	0
Somerset	33	0	14	3	16	296	59	212	25	6
Waldo[6]	13	0	0	1	12	75	33	38	4	0
Washington	14	0	1	0	13	82	26	54	2	0
MARYLAND										
Metropolitan Counties										
Allegany	43	0	8	4	31	178	51	119	8	
Anne Arundel	0	0	0	0	0	0	0	0	0	0
Anne Arundel County Police Department	1,580	16	148	371	1,045	9,594	1,045	7,986	563	31
Baltimore County	0	0	0	0	0	0	0	0	0	0
Baltimore County Police Department	4,718	50	382	1,155	3,131	20,246	2,539	16,114	1,593	144
Calvert	111	0	18	18	75	760	109	618	33	3
Cecil	69	2	5	12	50	398	95	273	30	1
Charles	539	5	64	118	352	2,213	284	1,778	151	9
Frederick	196	0	20	23	153	1,183	153	979	51	9
Harford	252	5	32	45	170	1,624	257	1,275	92	1
Howard	0	0	0	0	0	1	0	1	0	0
Howard County Police Department	512	8	57	167	280	4,303	428	3,612	263	26
Montgomery	7	0	0	0	7	0	0	0	0	0
Montgomery County Police Department	1,491	15	288	512	676	14,209	1,329	12,016	864	6
Prince George's County Police Department[6]	1,983	50	185	831	917	10,750	1,253	7,426	2,071	44
Queen Anne's	45	0	5	4	36	317	52	249	16	3
Somerset	6	0	1	0	5	40	2	38	0	0
St. Mary's	202	1	20	39	142	1,663	301	1,297	65	6
Washington	254	0	19	30	205	1,081	261	787	33	0
Wicomico	50	0	6	10	34	486	119	350	17	1
Worcester	15	0	4	2	9	248	33	207	8	1
Nonmetropolitan Counties										
Caroline	12	0	2	6	4	184	61	112	11	1
Dorchester	15	0	2	1	12	137	31	98	8	0
Garrett	60	0	11	0	49	159	37	119	3	0
Kent	5	0	2	1	2	94	33	58	3	1
Talbot	19	0	5	0	14	111	39	70	2	0
MICHIGAN										
Metropolitan Counties										
Bay	68	1	15	7	45	422	80	324	18	1
Berrien	117	0	37	7	73	689	106	532	51	8
Cass	0	0	0	0	0	0	0	0	0	0
Clinton	14	0	5	0	9	97	19	62	16	0
Eaton	154	2	46	21	85	981	114	808	59	2
Genesee[4]	155	1	16	5	133			347	32	3
Ingham	182	2	50	12	118	479	104	336	39	0
Ionia	61	1	31	1	28	217	35	164	18	1
Kalamazoo	290	2	56	34	198	2,529	493	1,814	222	5
Kent	390	4	135	30	221	2,325	333	1,850	142	7
Lapeer	55	1	26	1	27	180	44	112	24	0
Livingston	63	0	23	5	35	416	48	347	21	3

Table 10. Offenses Known to Law Enforcement, by Selected State Metropolitan and Nonmetropolitan Counties, 2019—Continued

(Number.)

State/county	Violent crime	Murder and nonnegligent manslaughter	Rape[1]	Robbery	Aggravated assault	Property crime	Burglary	Larceny-theft	Motor vehicle theft	Arson[2]
Macomb	272	1	69	30	172	1,046	193	758	95	6
Midland	47	0	24	0	23	259	53	196	10	0
Montcalm	18	0	6	0	12	109	30	74	5	2
Muskegon	68	1	29	2	36	421	87	314	20	2
Oakland	23	0	6	5	12	37	2	30	5	1
Ottawa	571	3	216	32	320	2,081	331	1,650	100	22
Saginaw	99	0	28	10	61	522	74	435	13	1
Shiawassee	15	0	5	0	10	152	49	95	8	1
St. Clair	146	1	38	9	98	540	129	372	39	7
Washtenaw	574	3	71	55	445	1,655	268	1,218	169	8
Wayne	20	0	1	0	19	1	0	1	0	0
Nonmetropolitan Counties										
Alcona	10	0	1	0	9	62	12	50	0	0
Alger	3	0	0	0	3	2	1	1	0	0
Allegan	100	0	14	3	83	535	112	369	54	3
Alpena	23	0	9	0	14	51	12	39	0	0
Antrim	33	1	12	0	20	130	36	85	9	2
Arenac	25	0	7	1	17	71	35	33	3	2
Baraga	3	0	0	0	3	15	4	9	2	0
Barry	83	2	53	2	26	304	78	205	21	0
Benzie	19	0	4	0	15	38	6	28	4	1
Branch	13	0	3	0	10	119	38	67	14	1
Charlevoix	30	0	12	0	18	96	41	52	3	1
Cheboygan	22	0	9	0	13	30	8	21	1	0
Chippewa	6	0	3	0	3	11	3	8	0	1
Crawford	21	0	5	0	16	95	40	50	5	1
Delta	4	0	1	0	3	46	2	41	3	0
Dickinson	1	0	1	0	0	0	0	0	0	0
Emmet	50	0	10	0	40	72	10	60	2	1
Gladwin	31	0	2	0	29	115	49	61	5	2
Gogebic	4	0	1	0	3	29	6	22	1	1
Grand Traverse	145	2	57	4	82	510	65	430	15	4
Gratiot	34	1	12	1	20	273	19	239	15	2
Hillsdale	70	0	18	0	52	133	57	60	16	6
Huron	16	0	7	1	8	91	31	57	3	1
Iosco	3	0	0	0	3	1	0	1	0	0
Iron	0	0	0	0	0	0	0	0	0	0
Isabella	47	0	20	3	24	256	51	186	19	2
Keweenaw	1	0	1	0	0	13	5	8	0	0
Leelanau	7	0	2	0	5	39	11	27	1	0
Lenawee	45	2	19	2	22	169	54	105	10	4
Luce	35	0	1	0	34	84	15	67	2	0
Mackinac	10	0	2	0	8	107	9	97	1	0
Manistee	39	0	17	0	22	118	19	94	5	2
Marquette	15	0	6	1	8	87	3	77	7	1
Mason	36	2	7	0	27	138	29	106	3	0
Mecosta	99	1	15	1	82	378	85	269	24	9
Menominee	19	1	5	0	13	63	34	28	1	0
Missaukee	26	0	5	0	21	51	8	40	3	2
Montmorency	9	0	1	0	8	17	5	10	2	1
Newaygo	40	0	8	0	32	241	80	152	9	2
Oceana	46	0	5	0	41	186	56	122	8	1
Ogemaw	12	0	4	0	8	138	42	94	2	1
Ontonagon	8	0	0	0	8	14	3	8	3	0
Osceola	31	0	13	0	18	140	34	98	8	0
Oscoda	18	0	7	0	11	74	18	47	9	1
Otsego	0	0	0	0	0	2	1	1	0	0
Presque Isle	10	0	2	0	8	33	6	23	4	0
Sanilac	34	0	3	2	29	87	34	41	12	0
Schoolcraft	1	0	0	0	1	4	0	3	1	0
St. Joseph	67	1	15	2	49	224	81	113	30	2
Tuscola	61	1	18	1	41	160	56	91	13	1
Van Buren	97	1	32	1	63	376	114	231	31	3
Wexford	25	0	15	0	10	260	92	153	15	0
MINNESOTA										
Metropolitan Counties										
Anoka[6]	75	0	18	7	50	936	112	731	93	0
Benton	9	0	5	1	3	173	41	101	31	1
Blue Earth	24	0	8	0	16	105	25	66	14	0
Carlton	12	0	4	0	8	166	56	93	17	1
Carver	38	0	16	4	18	497	77	401	19	1
Chisago	12	0	0	2	10	152	18	119	15	0
Clay	7	0	1	2	4	58	22	29	7	0
Dakota	17	0	2	0	15	48	13	34	1	1
Dodge[6]	11	0	1	0	10	104	27	71	6	0
Fillmore	9	0	2	0	7	59	11	46	2	1
Hennepin	20	0	0	0	20	44	5	35	4	0
Houston[6]	5	0	0	0	5	29	15	13	1	0
Isanti	15	0	4	0	11	232	43	165	24	1

Table 10. Offenses Known to Law Enforcement, by Selected State Metropolitan and Nonmetropolitan Counties, 2019—Continued

(Number.)

State/county	Violent crime	Murder and nonnegligent manslaughter	Rape[1]	Robbery	Aggravated assault	Property crime	Burglary	Larceny-theft	Motor vehicle theft	Arson[2]
Lake	0	0	0	0	0	19	14	5	0	0
Le Sueur	4	0	2	0	2	60	4	53	3	0
Mille Lacs	34	0	14	2	18	354	94	225	35	0
Nicollet	7	0	6	1	0	52	13	37	2	0
Olmsted[6]	40	1	3	3	33	228	57	153	18	2
Polk[6]	34	1	4	0	29	167	49	112	6	0
Ramsey	141	1	22	27	91	1,249	158	930	161	8
Scott	4	0	0	0	4	25	8	15	2	0
Sherburne	30	2	5	1	22	272	26	226	20	2
Stearns	21	0	12	1	8	164	32	124	8	0
St. Louis[6]	50	1	22	0	27	566	208	303	55	5
Wabasha	7	0	1	0	6	22	3	16	3	0
Washington	52	0	27	7	18	579	116	428	35	2
Wright	98	0	45	3	50	1,396	127	1,204	65	3
Nonmetropolitan Counties										
Aitkin[6]	11	1	3	0	7	167	59	99	9	0
Becker	29	0	11	0	18	134	57	59	18	2
Beltrami	50	2	13	2	33	268	74	164	30	3
Big Stone	0	0	0	0	0	14	5	7	2	0
Brown[6]	5	0	2	0	3	31	6	21	4	0
Cass[6]	37	1	5	3	28	486	143	293	50	1
Chippewa	2	0	0	0	2	1	0	1	0	0
Clearwater	10	0	1	0	9	47	19	24	4	1
Cook	10	0	5	0	5	47	6	36	5	0
Cottonwood[6]	2	0	0	0	2	13	6	3	4	0
Crow Wing	15	0	6	0	9	210	71	121	18	1
Douglas	18	0	4	1	13	180	50	114	16	1
Faribault	12	0	0	0	12	27	8	11	8	0
Freeborn	11	0	1	0	10	84	28	48	8	6
Goodhue	10	0	4	0	6	171	39	103	29	0
Grant	2	0	0	0	2	6	1	5	0	0
Hubbard	18	0	9	0	9	170	46	105	19	1
Itasca[6]	46	1	15	0	30	134	35	79	20	3
Jackson[6]	6	0	0	0	6	30	11	16	3	0
Kandiyohi	25	0	10	1	14	170	32	121	17	1
Kittson	0	0	0	0	0	0	0	0	0	0
Koochiching	6	0	1	0	5	32	7	19	6	0
Lac qui Parle[6]	0	0	0	0	0	20	3	14	3	0
Lake of the Woods	6	0	1	0	5	9	4	3	2	0
Lyon[6]	4	0	1	0	3	34	13	15	6	1
Mahnomen	10	0	1	0	9	42	14	23	5	1
Martin	0	0	0	0	0	14	5	7	2	0
McLeod	11	0	6	0	5	55	10	40	5	0
Meeker	4	0	0	1	3	103	21	77	5	0
Morrison	10	0	0	0	10	195	45	128	22	1
Mower	9	0	2	0	7	68	18	40	10	0
Murray[6]	2	0	0	0	2	6	1	5	0	0
Nobles	6	0	1	0	5	35	10	21	4	0
Norman	0	0	0	0	0	0	0	0	0	0
Otter Tail	30	0	8	1	21	214	65	135	14	0
Pennington	2	0	0	1	1	45	21	20	4	0
Pine	138	0	42	3	93	563	126	374	63	4
Pipestone	5	0	0	0	5	80	14	64	2	0
Pope	6	0	1	1	4	49	18	26	5	0
Red Lake[6]	3	0	2	0	1	16	0	15	1	0
Redwood	6	0	0	0	6	44	9	32	3	0
Renville	5	0	2	0	3	81	18	55	8	0
Rice	18	0	7	1	10	142	42	92	8	0
Rock	7	0	1	0	6	57	14	29	14	0
Roseau	6	0	2	0	4	31	2	27	2	0
Sibley	2	0	0	0	2	1	1	0	0	0
Steele	12	0	3	2	7	76	17	48	11	0
Stevens	2	0	1	0	1	33	9	24	0	0
Swift	2	0	0	1	1	2	0	1	1	0
Todd[6]	17	2	7	0	8	140	39	91	10	1
Traverse[6]	6	0	1	0	5	12	1	6	5	0
Wadena	10	0	2	0	8	10	1	8	1	0
Waseca	4	0	3	0	1	55	13	41	1	0
Watonwan[6]	8	0	5	0	3	26	15	10	1	1
Wilkin	0	0	0	0	0	20	6	11	3	0
Winona	6	0	2	0	4	79	14	60	5	0
Yellow Medicine	3	0	1	0	2	35	8	24	3	1
MISSISSIPPI										
Metropolitan Counties										
DeSoto	35	2	7	4	22	359	86	228	45	1
Hancock	28	0	2	6	20	516	108	354	54	1
Harrison	60	2	12	17	29	869	172	559	138	4
Hinds	111	5	6	6	94	383	150	169	64	0
Jackson	135	1	30	11	93	1,388	292	860	236	7

Table 10. Offenses Known to Law Enforcement, by Selected State Metropolitan and Nonmetropolitan Counties, 2019—Continued

(Number.)

State/county	Violent crime	Murder and nonnegligent manslaughter	Rape[1]	Robbery	Aggravated assault	Property crime	Burglary	Larceny-theft	Motor vehicle theft	Arson[2]
Lamar	87	3	20	10	54	637	166	434	37	2
Madison[8]		2		3	28	223	78	125	20	2
Stone	47	1	15	1	30	174	56	96	22	3
Tunica[8]		4		7	25	383	72	261	50	2
Nonmetropolitan Counties										
Choctaw	6	1	1	0	4	57	14	40	3	0
Claiborne	21	2	1	1	17	87	62	8	17	0
George[6]	21	0	7	0	14	315	82	184	49	5
Lauderdale	27	2	4	8	13	410	230	139	41	10
Leflore[8]		4		15	67	250	71	163	16	4
Lincoln	31	0	1	11	19	299	86	203	10	0
Oktibbeha[8]		0		3	33	464	319	135	10	5
Tishomingo	15	0	6	1	8	115	43	57	15	0
MISSOURI										
Metropolitan Counties										
Andrew	1	0	0	0	1	41	12	24	5	0
Bates	34	0	6	1	27	120	51	69	0	0
Buchanan	41	0	17	2	22	213	38	113	62	4
Caldwell	20	2	0	0	18	87	21	54	12	0
Christian	64	0	5	1	58	250	85	137	28	
Clinton	16	0	4	1	11	53	12	36	5	0
Cole	34	1	0	1	32	381	62	286	33	1
Dallas	5	0	0	0	5	23	6	12	5	0
DeKalb	5	1	0	0	4	51	16	25	10	1
Franklin[7]	37	0	4	2	31			135	55	3
Howard[6]	17	0	2	1	14	35	8	22	5	0
Jefferson	386	3	36	27	320	2,722	621	1,656	445	12
Platte	48	0	15	1	32	290	54	186	50	1
Polk	34	0	9	0	25	326	100	201	25	0
St. Charles[6]	0	0	0	0	0	0	0	0	0	0
St. Charles County Police Department[6]	139	2	22	13	102	757	129	547	81	6
St. Louis County Police Department	1,821	44	188	342	1,247	8,077	1,365	5,390	1,322	58
Webster	9	1	0	0	8	178	61	97	20	0
Nonmetropolitan Counties										
Adair	5	0	0	0	5	97	45	45	7	1
Benton	22	2	1	0	19	214	70	114	30	
Camden[6]	89	1	18	2	68	413	187	186	40	2
Carroll	6	0	1	0	5	32	12	9	11	0
Carter[6]	21	0	2	0	19	54	23	20	11	0
Cedar	36	0	3	0	33	53	16	37	0	1
Dade	45	0	0	0	45	65	25	36	4	1
Daviess	17	0	0	0	17	29	10	14	5	0
Dent	12	1	5	1	5	71	46	22	3	
Gasconade	49	1	0	1	47	178	51	94	33	0
Gentry	1	0	0	0	1	30	14	11	5	0
Grundy	2	0	0	0	2	15	7	7	1	0
Harrison	3	0	0	0	3	33	17	12	4	0
Henry	78	0	5	1	72	267	117	112	38	9
Hickory	1	0	0	0	1	81	29	43	9	0
Howell	70	1	0	2	67	349	69	188	92	0
Iron	4	0	1	0	3	63	21	28	14	
Laclede	49	0	13	1	35	333	86	197	50	1
Lawrence	17	1	2	3	11	224	69	130	25	0
Linn	8	0	0	0	8	20	7	11	2	0
Livingston	2	0	0	0	2	26	8	17	1	0
Macon	4	0	2	1	1	66	30	35	1	0
Madison	0	0	0	0	0	0	0	0	0	0
Mercer	0	0	0	0	0	2	1	1	0	0
Oregon	29	0	3	0	26	91	43	33	15	0
Ozark	20	0	2	0	18	45	21	18	6	0
Pemiscot	22	2	4	2	14	80	26	43	11	
Perry	31	0	0	0	31	39	19	13	7	0
Pulaski	157	0	12	4	141	346	103	205	38	0
Ralls	30	0	0	1	29	82	30	43	9	0
Randolph	11	0	1	0	10	101	31	57	13	1
Schuyler	4	1	0	0	3	36	6	25	5	0
Shannon	17	0	2	0	15	22	4	13	5	1
Shelby	3	0	1	0	2	8	3	4	1	0
St. Clair	15	0	2	2	11	111	32	64	15	2
Ste. Genevieve	53	0	7	0	46	128	23	88	17	0
Stoddard[6]	52	0	5	3	44	214	66	126	22	0
Taney	82	0	4	6	72	298	73	174	51	2
Texas	39	1	1	2	35	131	46	54	31	1
Wayne	23	0	2	0	21	171	58	91	22	2
Worth	6	0	0	0	6	6	0	4	2	0
MONTANA										
Metropolitan Counties										
Carbon	21	0	2	1	18	43	10	25	8	0
Cascade[4]		4		3	69	248	57	157	34	4

Table 10. Offenses Known to Law Enforcement, by Selected State Metropolitan and Nonmetropolitan Counties, 2019—Continued

(Number.)

State/county	Violent crime	Murder and nonnegligent manslaughter	Rape[1]	Robbery	Aggravated assault	Property crime	Burglary	Larceny-theft	Motor vehicle theft	Arson[2]
Stillwater	18	0	3	0	15	52	8	36	8	1
Yellowstone	143	3	18	6	116	656	85	482	89	4
Nonmetropolitan Counties										
Beaverhead	3	0	0	0	3	4	2	2	0	0
Big Horn	53	0	6	2	45	46	2	36	8	1
Broadwater	27	0	5	0	22	31	6	22	3	0
Butte-Silver Bow	120	0	9	6	105	1,372	154	1,070	148	4
Carter	0	0	0	0	0	0	0	0	0	0
Custer	6	0	0	0	6	29	2	21	6	0
Dawson	10	0	2	0	8	12	4	7	1	1
Deer Lodge	13	0	1	0	12	268	66	176	26	1
Fergus	13	0	2	0	11	32	3	20	9	2
Flathead	191	2	36	6	147	862	141	622	99	4
Gallatin	86	0	25	0	61	392	25	333	34	1
Garfield	0	0	0	0	0	0	0	0	0	0
Golden Valley	2	0	0	0	2	7	3	4	0	0
Hill	22	1	3	1	17	146	10	119	17	4
Jefferson	23	0	2	0	21	83	27	42	14	0
Lake	81	3	10	1	67	260	52	163	45	3
Lewis and Clark	63	1	12	1	49	330	74	201	55	3
Lincoln	22	0	2	0	20	69	6	56	7	0
Madison	10	0	2	0	8	50	11	31	8	1
McCone	0	0	0	0	0	4	1	3	0	0
Meagher	6	0	0	0	6	8	3	5	0	0
Musselshell	11	0	1	0	10	28	2	21	5	2
Park	12	0	6	0	6	26	2	21	3	0
Phillips	15	0	2	0	13	52	8	34	10	0
Powell	12	1	3	0	8	19	4	8	7	1
Prairie	11	0	0	0	11	1	0	1	0	1
Ravalli	65	0	11	0	54	266	50	196	20	3
Richland	14	0	1	0	13	32	7	20	5	0
Roosevelt	60	0	3	3	54	65	26	26	13	2
Sanders	5	0	1	0	4	35	5	27	3	0
Sweet Grass	20	1	3	0	16	46	2	36	8	0
Teton	9	0	3	0	6	28	5	18	5	0
Toole	30	0	4	0	26	51	4	43	4	0
Valley	22	0	3	0	19	15	1	13	1	0
Wheatland	9	0	0	0	9	7	0	6	1	0
NEBRASKA										
Metropolitan Counties										
Cass	27	0	12	1	14	138	13	104	21	1
Dixon	2	0	0	0	2	30	8	18	4	0
Douglas	71	1	18	6	46	605	155	384	66	5
Hall	35	0	2	1	32	113	31	73	9	0
Lancaster	20	0	15	0	5	146	41	86	19	
Merrick	3	0	1	0	2	3	1	1	1	0
Sarpy	35	0	17	3	15	798	57	631	110	0
Saunders	8	0	1	0	7	65	23	34	8	0
Seward	3	0	0	0	3	16	7	4	5	1
Washington	2	0	0	0	2	79	15	56	8	0
Nonmetropolitan Counties										
Adams	4	0	2	0	2	72	13	54	5	0
Arthur	0	0	0	0	0	0	0	0	0	
Boone	2	0	1	0	1	15	4	10	1	1
Box Butte	4	0	0	0	4	14	2	8	4	
Buffalo	13	1	4	0	8	87	20	58	9	2
Burt[6]	3	0	1	0	2	20	10	7	3	
Butler	6	0	2	0	4	28	8	15	5	0
Cedar	3	0	0	0	3	27	0	23	4	
Chase[6]	2	1	0	0	1	6	3	2	1	0
Cherry	2	0	0	0	2	9	2	3	4	
Cheyenne	7	0	1	0	6	14	1	11	2	1
Colfax	9	0	3	0	6	27	4	21	2	1
Cuming	6	0	4	0	2	3	1	1	1	0
Custer	6	0	2	0	4	35	3	29	3	0
Dawson	18	1	4	0	13	36	16	19	1	0
Deuel	4	0	0	0	4	5	0	5	0	0
Dodge	3	0	1	0	2	92	26	59	7	
Fillmore	5	0	3	0	2	16	4	11	1	0
Franklin	0	0	0	0	0	10	2	6	2	
Frontier	3	0	1	0	2	24	3	20	1	0
Furnas	7	0	2	0	5	57	13	35	9	0
Gage	11	0	0	1	10	77	16	54	7	0
Gosper	2	0	0	0	2	9	1	7	1	0
Greeley[6]	0	0	0	0	0	0	0	0	0	0
Hamilton	2	0	1	0	1	20	5	12	3	0
Holt[6]	1	0	1	0	0	2	0	2	0	0
Hooker[6]	0	0	0	0	0	0	0	0	0	0
Jefferson	14	0	2	0	12	95	28	62	5	0

Table 10. Offenses Known to Law Enforcement, by Selected State Metropolitan and Nonmetropolitan Counties, 2019—Continued

(Number.)

State/county	Violent crime	Murder and nonnegligent manslaughter	Rape[1]	Robbery	Aggravated assault	Property crime	Burglary	Larceny-theft	Motor vehicle theft	Arson[2]
Johnson	5	0	2	0	3	39	6	25	8	1
Kearney	6	0	4	0	2	40	13	23	4	0
Keith	3	0	0	0	3	17	1	14	2	0
Keya Paha	2	0	0	0	2	0	0	0	0	
Knox[6]	0	0	0	0	0	29	3	16	10	
Lincoln	16	0	5	2	9	66	20	36	10	0
Madison	10	0	3	0	7	19	4	14	1	0
Nemaha	10	0	3	2	5	17	5	8	4	0
Perkins	0	0	0	0	0	24	4	17	3	0
Platte	8	0	2	0	6	69	11	50	8	0
Polk	0	0	0	0	0	20	1	19	0	0
Saline	7	0	0	0	7	46	13	29	4	1
Scotts Bluff	10	0	2	0	8	54	16	28	10	0
Sherman	5	0	0	0	5	23	5	18	0	0
Stanton	2	1	0	0	1	29	1	22	6	
Thayer[6]	4	0	2	0	2	25	8	12	5	0
Thurston	7	0	1	0	6	13	5	7	1	0
Valley	5	0	3	0	2	4	0	1	3	0
Wayne	6	0	1	0	5	10	5	2	3	1
Wheeler	0	0	0	0	0	1	0	1	0	0
York	3	0	3	0	0	21	2	14	5	0
NEVADA										
Metropolitan Counties										
Storey	31	0	5	1	25	74	20	47	7	0
Washoe[6]	223	2	32	18	171	616	160	370	86	7
Nonmetropolitan Counties										
Churchill	20	0	11	0	9	186	56	113	17	2
Elko	57	1	11	0	45	176	40	111	25	1
Esmeralda	6	0	1	1	4	6	1	4	1	1
Eureka	22	0	4	0	18	27	13	11	3	0
Humboldt	26	0	1	2	23	76	41	29	6	
Lander	62	2	23	0	37	56	25	26	5	2
Lyon	179	0	18	7	154	522	102	349	71	4
Mineral	4	0	1	0	3	48	3	38	7	3
Nye	113	2	5	21	85	715	167	404	144	0
Pershing	26	1	11	1	13	39	11	22	6	
NEW HAMPSHIRE										
Metropolitan Counties										
Rockingham	0	0	0	0	0	3	0	3	0	0
Strafford	3	0	1	0	2	4	0	3	1	1
Nonmetropolitan Counties										
Carroll	4	0	0	0	4	49	7	38	4	0
Cheshire	0	0	0	0	0	7	2	5	0	0
Grafton	4	0	4	0	0	4	0	4	0	0
Merrimack	1	0	1	0	0	1	1	0	0	0
NEW JERSEY										
Metropolitan Counties										
Atlantic	0	0	0	0	0	0	0	0	0	0
Bergen	2	0	2	0	0	46	2	44	0	0
Burlington	0	0	0	0	0	0	0	0	0	0
Camden	2	0	0	0	2	44	4	38	2	0
Cape May	0	0	0	0	0	0	0	0	0	0
Cumberland	0	0	0	0	0	1	0	1	0	0
Essex	131	0	9	35	87	135	5	127	3	8
Gloucester	0	0	0	0	0	0	0	0	0	0
Hudson	0	0	0	0	0	0	0	0	0	0
Hunterdon	0	0	0	0	0	0	0	0	0	0
Mercer	2	0	0	0	2	14	1	6	7	0
Middlesex	0	0	0	0	0	0	0	0	0	0
Monmouth	7	0	0	0	7	1	0	1	0	0
Morris	0	0	0	0	0	0	0	0	0	0
Ocean	0	0	0	0	0	8	0	8	0	0
Passaic	0	0	0	0	0	0	0	0	0	0
Salem	0	0	0	0	0	0	0	0	0	0
Somerset	1	0	0	0	1	1	0	1	0	0
Sussex	0	0	0	0	0	0	0	0	0	0
Union	0	0	0	0	0	0	0	0	0	0
Warren	0	0	0	0	0	0	0	0	0	0
NEW MEXICO										
Metropolitan Counties										
Sandoval	144	0	1	1	142	102	43	59	0	
Santa Fe	103	0	6	7	90	414	258	156	0	
Torrance	65	0	5	1	59	105	57	25	23	
Valencia	376	3	17	6	350	907	315	421	171	

Table 10. Offenses Known to Law Enforcement, by Selected State Metropolitan and Nonmetropolitan Counties, 2019—Continued

(Number.)

State/county	Violent crime	Murder and nonnegligent manslaughter	Rape[1]	Robbery	Aggravated assault	Property crime	Burglary	Larceny-theft	Motor vehicle theft	Arson[2]
Nonmetropolitan Counties										
Catron	1	0	0	0	1	15	9	6	0	
Chaves	54	3	9	3	39	223	90	98	35	
Cibola	12	0	2	0	10	37	14	16	7	
Colfax	3	0	0	0	3	8	5	3	0	
De Baca	4	0	1	0	3	15	11	2	2	
Grant	24	0	5	0	19	112	52	60	0	
Guadalupe	0	0	0	0	0	6	0	6	0	
Hidalgo	10	0	0	0	10	17	5	7	5	
Lea	60	4	4	5	47	342	112	160	70	
Lincoln	43	2	1	2	38	118	52	55	11	
Luna	63	0	1	1	61	222	97	98	27	
McKinley	183	1	0	7	175	222	89	86	47	
Otero	149	0	13	2	134	272	108	138	26	
Quay	1	0	0	0	1	13	6	7	0	
San Miguel	0	0	0	0	0	2	0	2	0	
Sierra	43	1	7	0	35	71	26	41	4	
Socorro	15	0	0	1	14	61	13	42	6	
Taos	28	2	2	2	22	93	43	30	20	
Union	2	0	0	0	2	15	3	10	2	
NEW YORK										
Metropolitan Counties										
Albany	25	1	4	1	19	121	21	90	10	0
Broome	51	0	22	11	18	486	60	403	23	1
Chemung	9	0	2	0	7	221	18	198	5	0
Dutchess	38	0	12	6	20	353	48	279	26	2
Erie	50	0	0	2	48	505	72	411	22	7
Herkimer	0	0	0	0	0	1	1	0	0	0
Jefferson	28	0	5	0	23	227	18	204	5	1
Livingston	32	0	14	3	15	283	31	250	2	1
Madison	20	0	6	0	14	85	15	68	2	0
Monroe	209	0	44	42	123	2,341	264	2,001	76	2
Nassau	1,179	9	40	339	791	9,655	583	8,677	395	35
Niagara	56	0	14	6	36	475	78	372	25	0
Oneida	70	0	48	3	19	309	53	240	16	0
Onondaga	191	0	49	29	113	1,518	210	1,204	104	9
Ontario	69	2	26	5	36	669	87	571	11	0
Orleans	15	0	6	1	8	115	19	87	9	0
Oswego	33	1	17	3	12	268	40	202	26	0
Putnam	18	0	4	4	10	127	15	108	4	0
Rensselaer	18	0	5	5	8	230	21	199	10	1
Schoharie	5	0	1	0	4	18	2	13	3	3
Suffolk	34	0	0	0	34	0	0	0	0	0
Suffolk County Police Department	1,183	24	159	281	719	14,828	891	13,161	776	42
Tioga	7	0	5	1	1	140	45	89	6	1
Ulster	21	0	6	1	14	145	25	115	5	0
Washington	30	0	26	1	3	67	12	55	0	0
Wayne	63	0	16	7	40	333	81	237	15	3
Westchester Public Safety	30	0	1	2	27	199	10	182	7	2
Yates	12	0	3	0	9	98	31	66	1	0
Nonmetropolitan Counties										
Allegany	3	0	0	0	3	7	0	3	4	0
Cattaraugus	48	0	13	0	35	202	44	136	22	6
Chautauqua	33	1	16	2	14	428	148	266	14	9
Chenango	32	0	15	1	16	274	71	194	9	1
Clinton	11	0	0	0	11	34	3	31	0	0
Columbia	25	1	6	1	17	251	54	189	8	3
Delaware	22	0	12	0	10	151	46	100	5	0
Essex	2	0	0	0	2	4	0	4	0	0
Franklin	0	0	0	0	0	0	0	0	0	0
Fulton	22	0	9	1	12	288	34	247	7	0
Greene	13	0	2	3	8	26	7	19	0	2
Hamilton	1	0	0	0	1	6	1	5	0	0
Lewis	12	0	4	0	8	54	18	33	3	0
Montgomery	6	0	0	1	5	212	8	192	12	1
Otsego	13	0	5	0	8	29	3	24	2	1
Schuyler	5	0	1	0	4	10	2	7	1	0
Seneca	2	0	1	0	1	43	2	41	0	0
Steuben	9	0	2	0	7	47	13	31	3	1
St. Lawrence	11	0	2	1	8	25	8	15	2	0
Sullivan	27	0	6	1	20	273	34	234	5	1
Wyoming	17	0	7	1	9	96	20	76	0	0
NORTH CAROLINA[6]										
Metropolitan Counties										
Alamance	118	3	11	10	94	649	230	368	51	4
Alexander	86	8	27	1	50	429	138	247	44	3
Anson	26	3	4	3	16	181	92	82	7	1
Buncombe	219	0	14	27	178	1,830	520	1,071	239	19

Table 10. Offenses Known to Law Enforcement, by Selected State Metropolitan and Nonmetropolitan Counties, 2019—Continued

(Number.)

State/county	Violent crime	Murder and nonnegligent manslaughter	Rape[1]	Robbery	Aggravated assault	Property crime	Burglary	Larceny-theft	Motor vehicle theft	Arson[2]
Burke	110	4	16	9	81	1,045	349	553	143	3
Cabarrus	38	2	3	8	25	640	156	435	49	6
Caldwell	75	2	18	9	46	1,199	439	594	166	13
Camden	11	0	0	1	10	74	32	38	4	1
Chatham	60	0	13	6	41	478	173	278	27	9
Craven	119	4	8	11	96	919	399	436	84	3
Cumberland	458	3	43	65	347	1,964	494	1,324	146	63
Currituck	63	0	8	1	54	268	69	187	12	2
Franklin	77	1	8	5	63	616	198	368	50	4
Gaston	17	0	0	0	17	5	0	4	1	0
Granville	57	1	5	3	48	316	99	198	19	3
Guilford	206	3	8	28	167	1,063	399	561	103	14
Haywood	118	0	21	2	95	835	366	405	64	6
Iredell	121	2	5	10	104	780	361	356	63	7
Johnston	152	3	16	17	116	1,463	404	950	109	11
Lincoln	131	1	14	10	106	943	214	655	74	5
Madison	14	0	2	0	12	178	74	82	22	4
New Hanover	179	0	25	24	130	1,593	264	1,269	60	14
Onslow	214	3	26	19	166	1,773	504	1,161	108	13
Pamlico	25	0	5	0	20	206	60	127	19	1
Person	56	0	2	2	52	357	151	185	21	6
Pitt	138	3	8	22	105	915	315	541	59	6
Rockingham	70	1	22	10	37	700	232	415	53	0
Rowan	149	4	16	16	113	999	265	636	98	11
Union	235	3	77	23	132	1,987	419	1,449	119	7
Wake	215	6	16	24	169	1,376	375	857	144	22
Wayne	206	2	2	24	178	1,181	458	574	149	6
Yadkin	66	1	11	4	50	451	130	286	35	4
Nonmetropolitan Counties										
Alleghany	19	0	11	1	7	72	26	39	7	
Ashe	57	0	14	1	42	151	68	71	12	
Avery	18	0	2	0	16	179	92	79	8	
Bladen	65	0	3	4	58	481	158	273	50	
Carteret	69	2	16	3	48	640	199	408	33	
Cherokee	68	0	13	4	51	763	228	477	58	
Chowan	21	0	3	1	17	95	47	42	6	
Dare	12	1	3	0	8	239	53	176	10	
Greene	60	4	24	2	30	304	131	145	28	
Hertford	28	5	4	11	8	184	62	102	20	
Macon	25	0	5	1	19	476	136	307	33	
McDowell	59	1	8	5	45	881	380	411	90	
Mitchell	2	0	0	1	1	55	24	28	3	
Moore	62	1	9	7	45	580	173	385	22	
Pasquotank	64	0	6	7	51	233	93	118	22	
Richmond	178	2	21	27	128	1,007	411	505	91	
Robeson	717	22	12	90	593	2,525	1,238	1,110	177	
Sampson	195	4	22	24	145	877	425	385	67	
Scotland	59	1	5	12	41	325	170	128	27	
Stanly	24	1	3	2	18	481	203	240	38	
Swain	27	2	4	2	19	242	118	91	33	
Transylvania	38	0	14	0	24	257	78	163	16	
Tyrrell	4	0	1	0	3	23	10	12	1	
Vance	125	4	12	8	101	546	206	299	41	
Warren	40	4	8	5	23	216	101	101	14	
Watauga	30	4	2	1	23	266	85	159	22	
Wilkes	132	3	27	8	94	676	241	349	86	
Yancey	5	0	0	1	4	47	17	26	4	
NORTH DAKOTA										
Metropolitan Counties										
Burleigh	12	0	5	0	7	97	23	60	14	1
Cass	18	0	4	2	12	141	49	71	21	1
Grand Forks	15	0	4	0	11	89	18	52	19	0
Morton	3	0	0	0	3	113	18	85	10	1
Oliver	0	0	0	0	0	3	1	1	1	0
Nonmetropolitan Counties										
Adams	2	0	1	0	1	9	2	6	1	0
Barnes	2	0	0	0	2	18	6	10	2	0
Benson	1	0	0	0	1	13	2	7	4	0
Billings	0	0	0	0	0	6	1	5	0	0
Bottineau	4	0	4	0	0	55	14	29	12	0
Bowman	1	0	0	1	0	10	3	3	4	0
Burke	0	0	0	0	0	2	2	0	0	0
Cavalier	2	0	1	0	1	11	3	6	2	0
Dickey	0	0	0	0	0	8	4	4	0	0
Divide	2	0	1	0	1	6	0	5	1	0
Dunn	5	0	1	0	4	14	3	9	2	0
Eddy	1	0	1	0	0	20	3	13	4	0
Emmons	3	0	1	0	2	28	7	20	1	0

Table 10. Offenses Known to Law Enforcement, by Selected State Metropolitan and Nonmetropolitan Counties, 2019—Continued

(Number.)

State/county	Violent crime	Murder and nonnegligent manslaughter	Rape[1]	Robbery	Aggravated assault	Property crime	Burglary	Larceny-theft	Motor vehicle theft	Arson[2]
Foster	0	0	0	0	0	10	1	4	5	0
Golden Valley	0	0	0	0	0	0	0	0	0	0
Grant	1	0	1	0	0	5	1	4	0	0
Griggs	3	0	2	0	1	6	1	4	1	0
Hettinger	1	0	0	0	1	22	2	15	5	0
Kidder	0	0	0	0	0	7	3	4	0	0
Lamoure	3	0	0	0	3	4	1	2	1	0
Logan	2	0	0	0	2	0	0	0	0	0
McHenry	6	0	2	0	4	34	7	20	7	1
McIntosh	0	0	0	0	0	0	0	0	0	0
McKenzie	15	0	8	0	7	167	25	114	28	1
McLean	12	0	3	0	9	79	21	52	6	0
Mercer	1	0	1	0	0	16	10	5	1	0
Mountrail	2	1	1	0	0	58	4	48	6	0
Nelson	5	0	0	0	5	15	4	9	2	0
Pembina	6	0	0	0	6	36	11	20	5	0
Pierce	0	0	0	0	0	11	3	7	1	0
Ramsey	3	0	1	0	2	18	2	12	4	0
Ransom	3	1	0	0	2	26	11	9	6	1
Renville	2	0	1	0	1	24	5	17	2	0
Richland	8	0	0	0	8	94	27	51	16	0
Rolette	4	0	1	0	3	38	9	23	6	0
Sargent	7	0	1	0	6	21	10	10	1	2
Sheridan	1	0	0	0	1	4	1	3	0	0
Sioux	0	0	0	0	0	0	0	0	0	0
Slope	0	0	0	0	0	1	1	0	0	0
Stark	5	0	0	0	5	55	9	42	4	1
Steele	0	0	0	0	0	1	0	1	0	0
Stutsman	2	0	1	0	1	33	11	12	10	0
Towner	0	0	0	0	0	16	3	9	4	1
Traill	3	0	1	0	2	54	18	28	8	2
Walsh	7	1	2	0	4	96	35	52	9	0
Ward	38	1	9	2	26	182	65	82	35	5
Wells	3	0	1	0	2	7	5	1	1	1
Williams	15	0	5	0	10	166	37	102	27	1
OHIO										
Metropolitan Counties										
Allen	38	1	14	13	10	582	115	437	30	4
Belmont	42	0	12	3	27	205	35	151	19	2
Carroll	2	0	0	0	2	71	21	41	9	0
Clermont	111	0	23	3	85	897	269	582	46	1
Fairfield	52	0	14	5	33	1,039	139	855	45	2
Fulton	14	0	5	2	7	167	32	132	3	1
Geauga	10	0	6	1	3	134	28	94	12	0
Greene	36	0	12	4	20	348	86	240	22	3
Hamilton	176	4	69	22	81	2,025	235	1,621	169	13
Hocking	28	4	6	2	16	346	108	210	28	3
Jefferson	10	0	1	0	9	44	10	33	1	1
Lawrence	65	2	18	6	39	446	112	303	31	4
Licking	53	0	16	3	34	793	179	555	59	1
Lorain	60	0	16	9	35	509	167	323	19	1
Lucas	93	0	8	18	67	801	110	640	51	1
Madison	20	0	12	2	6	264	56	183	25	2
Mahoning	1	0	1	0	0	57	8	44	5	0
Medina	11	0	4	0	7	166	98	64	4	0
Miami	38	0	10	2	26	280	98	166	16	4
Montgomery	279	3	43	76	157	1,051	288	615	148	17
Perry	13	0	7	2	4	124	38	75	11	1
Pickaway	22	1	1	3	17	546	130	386	30	5
Portage[8]		1		39	304	916	190	688	38	4
Richland	61	1	34	6	20	757	166	562	29	1
Stark	107	2	36	10	59	1,544	401	1,019	124	12
Summit	80	0	22	14	44	944	176	705	63	3
Union	21	0	3	2	16	126	28	86	12	1
Wood	13	0	6	0	7	301	42	240	19	0
Nonmetropolitan Counties										
Adams	8	0	3	1	4	186	45	119	22	2
Ashland	37	1	23	0	13	103	25	74	4	0
Ashtabula	32	0	2	3	27	457	104	320	33	1
Auglaize	3	0	1	0	2	45	10	31	4	0
Champaign	25	0	4	0	21	153	39	102	12	0
Columbiana	37	1	15	1	20	315	63	222	30	3
Coshocton	40	4	15	1	20	345	73	244	28	11
Crawford	3	0	1	0	2	92	32	58	2	0
Defiance	14	0	6	1	7	117	25	90	2	1
Erie	1	0	0	0	1	189	40	144	5	1
Fayette	19	0	8	4	7	307	76	219	12	2
Gallia	32	1	9	0	22	294	77	192	25	2
Hancock	14	0	4	1	9	127	31	91	5	1

Table 10. Offenses Known to Law Enforcement, by Selected State Metropolitan and Nonmetropolitan Counties, 2019—Continued

(Number.)

State/county	Violent crime	Murder and nonnegligent manslaughter	Rape[1]	Robbery	Aggravated assault	Property crime	Burglary	Larceny-theft	Motor vehicle theft	Arson[2]
Hardin	13	0	2	0	11	68	22	42	4	1
Henry	13	0	3	1	9	109	36	64	9	0
Highland	38	4	17	3	14	305	91	199	15	0
Jackson	26	0	14	1	11	229	82	125	22	1
Knox	56	0	21	2	33	330	58	272	0	4
Logan	31	0	8	1	22	171	45	114	12	0
Marion	38	0	13	2	23	935	136	763	36	4
Meigs	16	1	1	1	13	230	76	125	29	0
Monroe	12	0	3	0	9	64	36	24	4	0
Morgan	29	0	2	1	26	80	22	47	11	0
Noble	5	0	3	0	2	36	7	27	2	0
Paulding	30	1	1	0	28	104	23	80	1	0
Pike	33	3	7	1	22	464	93	270	101	5
Putnam	15	1	9	2	3	90	19	66	5	0
Ross	114	3	33	5	73	1,041	285	631	125	12
Scioto	48	0	12	7	29	633	177	394	62	6
Shelby	12	1	1	1	9	131	27	97	7	2
Tuscarawas	22	0	9	1	12	241	83	130	28	3
Van Wert	16	0	6	0	10	106	40	60	6	1
Vinton	10	0	1	0	9	78	23	43	12	0
Washington	34	4	8	3	19	172	51	102	19	0
Wayne	44	0	14	5	25	473	164	277	32	1
Wyandot	3	0	0	0	3	3	2	0	1	0
OKLAHOMA										
Metropolitan Counties										
Canadian	19	1	6	1	11	151	31	93	27	2
Cleveland	30	1	5	1	23	245	79	135	31	1
Comanche	17	0	4	0	13	215	100	79	36	4
Cotton	0	0	0	0	0	21	3	16	2	1
Creek	65	2	14	3	46	374	126	178	70	3
Garfield	12	0	3	0	9	157	38	107	12	2
Grady	24	0	4	1	19	321	86	177	58	4
Lincoln	48	1	12	4	31	289	110	132	47	4
Logan	36	0	9	3	24	384	136	194	54	1
McClain	27	1	4	1	21	280	109	134	37	3
Oklahoma	35	1	2	2	30	227	72	94	61	0
Okmulgee	42	2	10	2	28	216	111	70	35	2
Osage	56	5	8	3	40	332	140	153	39	7
Rogers	109	3	11	2	93	472	187	216	69	4
Sequoyah	88	2	16	1	69	301	122	155	24	7
Tulsa	228	6	18	16	188	924	321	416	187	7
Wagoner	48	1	5	5	37	295	115	150	30	10
Nonmetropolitan Counties										
Adair	38	1	11	1	25	159	59	79	21	4
Alfalfa	1	0	0	0	1	26	10	13	3	0
Atoka	5	0	1	0	4	68	24	27	17	0
Beaver	0	0	0	0	0	14	4	8	2	0
Beckham	9	0	2	0	7	77	34	33	10	3
Blaine	10	0	3	0	7	104	38	56	10	1
Bryan	30	0	7	1	22	321	138	137	46	2
Caddo	12	0	1	0	11	165	72	73	20	5
Carter	29	0	16	3	10	208	64	119	25	4
Cherokee	69	4	6	5	54	461	169	213	79	4
Choctaw	47	0	0	0	47	79	28	34	17	0
Cimarron	0	0	0	0	0	10	2	4	4	0
Coal	0	0	0	0	0	4	2	1	1	0
Craig	13	0	4	0	9	106	45	48	13	5
Custer	12	1	2	0	9	113	44	56	13	0
Delaware	46	0	8	3	35	263	67	156	40	5
Dewey	2	0	2	0	0	40	16	19	5	1
Ellis	7	0	1	0	6	51	16	30	5	2
Garvin	30	0	8	1	21	269	80	167	22	11
Grant	3	0	0	0	3	31	11	14	6	1
Harmon	2	0	1	0	1	9	2	7	0	0
Haskell	7	0	1	0	6	66	29	29	8	1
Hughes	8	0	1	0	7	121	27	81	13	2
Jackson	15	0	3	0	12	46	15	22	9	1
Jefferson	11	0	2	0	9	18	8	6	4	0
Johnston	14	2	4	1	7	32	14	11	7	1
Kay	24	0	0	0	24	68	33	28	7	0
Kingfisher	13	0	3	0	10	84	9	66	9	1
Kiowa	5	0	1	0	4	26	10	12	4	1
Latimer	15	0	1	1	13	85	34	36	15	3
Le Flore	37	0	4	2	31	281	88	152	41	3
Love	18	0	4	4	10	100	19	65	16	2
Major	5	0	2	0	3	30	10	13	7	1
Marshall	19	3	2	2	12	209	78	92	39	0
Mayes	38	0	12	1	25	327	90	170	67	7
McCurtain	29	0	8	1	20	318	124	145	49	15

Table 10. Offenses Known to Law Enforcement, by Selected State Metropolitan and Nonmetropolitan Counties, 2019—Continued

(Number.)

State/county	Violent crime	Murder and nonnegligent manslaughter	Rape[1]	Robbery	Aggravated assault	Property crime	Burglary	Larceny-theft	Motor vehicle theft	Arson[2]
McIntosh	37	1	7	1	28	221	104	87	30	3
Murray	10	0	2	0	8	10	6	3	1	0
Muskogee	73	0	7	2	64	295	124	144	27	5
Noble	6	0	1	0	5	76	25	36	15	2
Nowata	12	0	1	0	11	65	20	28	17	2
Okfuskee	13	1	3	1	8	145	63	63	19	3
Ottawa	15	0	5	0	10	122	31	63	28	1
Payne	25	3	1	0	21	221	64	116	41	5
Pittsburg	55	3	9	1	42	422	195	186	41	2
Pontotoc	21	0	4	0	17	143	65	64	14	0
Pottawatomie	65	1	20	4	40	540	188	271	81	1
Pushmataha	14	0	0	0	14	91	44	39	8	6
Roger Mills	9	0	0	0	9	31	5	23	3	2
Seminole	29	0	8	1	20	257	103	123	31	7
Stephens	19	0	3	0	16	152	49	80	23	0
Texas	9	0	3	0	6	51	13	34	4	1
Tillman	1	0	0	0	1	27	14	11	2	0
Washita	14	0	2	0	12	52	8	37	7	1
Woods	6	0	1	0	5	23	4	14	5	0
Woodward	12	0	2	0	10	68	23	35	10	1
OREGON										
Metropolitan Counties										
Clackamas	446	8	80	92	266	4,651	600	3,461	590	17
Deschutes	86	1	19	3	63	654	109	475	70	5
Jackson	128	10	20	12	86	1,274	312	833	129	10
Josephine	45	0	11	3	31	394	76	148	170	3
Linn	56	5	9	8	34	705	167	451	87	14
Marion[8]		6			34	48	2,409	332	1,666	411	
Multnomah	165	3	30	23	109	1,696	155	1,255	286	4
Polk	52	0	3	5	44	295	88	187	20	4
Washington	349	3	108	31	207	2,480	406	1,791	283	30
Yamhill	41	0	13	5	23	473	100	327	46	8
Nonmetropolitan Counties										
Baker	10	0	1	0	9	59	14	39	6	0
Clatsop	28	0	6	0	22	166	34	125	7	2
Coos	40	0	4	4	32	506	108	346	52	6
Crook	17	3	0	0	14	126	23	93	10	1
Curry	42	0	3	0	39	254	59	163	32	1
Douglas	153	0	23	10	120	889	235	455	199	12
Gilliam[6]	9	0	3	0	6	52	14	36	2	0
Harney	1	0	1	0	0	21	6	12	3	0
Jefferson	8	1	2	1	4	172	44	109	19	3
Lake	9	0	1	0	8	88	30	49	9	0
Lincoln	44	1	6	0	37	271	91	165	15	4
Malheur	17	0	3	1	13	192	35	116	41	2
Morrow	20	0	4	0	16	112	26	70	16	2
Sherman	0	0	0	0	0	42	6	33	3	0
Umatilla	43	0	7	3	33	410	152	207	51	10
Union	8	0	1	0	7	209	64	129	16	5
Wasco	22	0	2	1	19	132	32	89	11	0
PENNSYLVANIA										
Metropolitan Counties										
Allegheny	3	0	0	0	3	0	0	0	0	0
Berks	5	0	0	0	5	0	0	0	0	0
Bucks	0	0	0	0	0	1	0	1	0	0
Erie	5	0	0	0	5	1	0	1	0	0
Lancaster	1	0	0	0	1	0	0	0	0	0
Monroe	0	0	0	0	0	0	0	0	0	0
Montgomery	0	0	0	0	0	0	0	0	0	0
Nonmetropolitan Counties										
Elk	0	0	0	0	0	0	0	0	0	0
Snyder	0	0	0	0	0	0	0	0	0	0
Wayne	0	0	0	0	0	0	0	0	0	0
SOUTH CAROLINA										
Metropolitan Counties										
Aiken	549	7	74	44	424	2,639	700	1,574	365	7
Anderson	693	12	73	63	545	4,585	882	3,073	630	27
Beaufort	577	6	52	73	446	1,879	347	1,384	148	9
Calhoun	62	0	5	4	53	294	107	146	41	0
Charleston	280	12	27	32	209	1,698	356	1,060	282	6
Chester	111	3	8	7	93	529	122	362	45	2
Clarendon	137	3	16	10	108	668	206	412	50	1
Darlington	386	12	26	39	309	1,853	674	1,034	145	10
Dorchester	292	2	1	33	256	1,871	380	1,305	186	1
Fairfield	154	3	8	8	135	465	130	294	41	3
Florence	516	12	66	82	356	2,325	586	1,512	227	19

Table 10. Offenses Known to Law Enforcement, by Selected State Metropolitan and Nonmetropolitan Counties, 2019—Continued

(Number.)

State/county	Violent crime	Murder and nonnegligent manslaughter	Rape[1]	Robbery	Aggravated assault	Property crime	Burglary	Larceny-theft	Motor vehicle theft	Arson[2]
Greenville	1,705	24	214	250	1,217	7,923	1,585	5,510	828	52
Horry	10	0	6	0	4	1	0	0	1	0
Horry County Police Department	834	8	148	88	590	6,144	1,089	4,493	562	18
Kershaw	160	1	26	18	115	1,201	240	845	116	11
Lancaster	284	7	52	19	206	1,677	366	1,235	76	7
Laurens	219	4	30	15	170	978	281	547	150	8
Lexington	554	13	69	87	385	5,086	1,000	3,324	762	18
Pickens	228	4	22	8	194	1,408	383	846	179	7
Richland	2,206	21	138	263	1,784	8,709	1,422	6,137	1,150	38
Saluda	43	0	8	1	34	198	63	115	20	1
Spartanburg	1,042	16	65	83	878	5,420	1,357	3,487	576	28
Sumter	384	5	23	30	326	1,543	421	955	167	6
York	377	3	46	42	286	2,565	515	1,842	208	9
Nonmetropolitan Counties										
Allendale	12	0	0	2	10	48	18	26	4	1
Bamberg	24	0	1	3	20	146	41	87	18	3
Barnwell	57	1	2	2	52	292	78	174	40	3
Colleton	214	11	15	15	173	726	201	439	86	8
Dillon	138	5	6	18	109	576	229	301	46	12
Georgetown	187	6	17	15	149	986	213	677	96	6
Hampton	61	0	7	3	51	269	92	164	13	3
Lee	64	0	1	3	60	306	96	185	25	0
Marion	71	0	5	13	53	462	120	265	77	2
Marlboro	106	3	13	6	84	342	115	211	16	4
McCormick	8	0	0	0	8	77	23	41	13	0
Newberry	91	4	5	4	78	299	64	214	21	0
Oconee	199	4	46	13	136	1,553	351	1,047	155	22
Orangeburg	744	16	18	41	669	2,661	791	1,502	368	5
Union	53	0	7	3	43	376	87	256	33	4
SOUTH DAKOTA										
Metropolitan Counties										
Lincoln	32	1	7	2	22	274	141	113	20	0
McCook	7	0	2	0	5	19	8	8	3	0
Meade	26	1	3	1	21	151	50	87	14	1
Minnehaha	54	0	17	1	36	319	96	172	51	0
Pennington	122	0	57	2	63	352	76	235	41	1
Turner	18	0	2	0	16	45	11	26	8	1
Union	7	0	1	0	6	46	11	33	2	2
Nonmetropolitan Counties										
Aurora	5	0	0	0	5	1	1	0	0	0
Beadle	4	0	0	0	4	7	3	3	1	0
Bennett	0	0	0	0	0	6	4	0	2	1
Bon Homme	2	0	0	0	2	13	2	3	8	0
Brookings	9	1	2	0	6	45	11	33	1	0
Brown	9	0	2	0	7	40	19	17	4	2
Brule	3	0	1	0	2	1	0	1	0	0
Butte	6	0	0	0	6	29	3	26	0	0
Charles Mix	11	0	3	0	8	19	8	11	0	0
Clark	1	0	0	0	1	5	0	3	2	0
Clay	7	0	1	0	6	50	6	32	12	1
Codington	9	0	0	0	9	16	1	12	3	1
Corson	1	0	0	0	1	26	10	8	8	1
Custer	8	0	2	0	6	135	54	74	7	1
Davison	3	0	0	0	3	14	8	6	0	1
Day	4	0	1	0	3	33	13	14	6	0
Deuel	1	0	0	0	1	16	4	10	2	0
Edmunds	0	0	0	0	0	0	0	0	0	0
Faulk	0	0	0	0	0	7	4	3	0	0
Gregory	0	0	0	0	0	7	0	5	2	0
Hamlin	5	0	1	0	4	29	7	20	2	0
Hand	4	0	3	0	1	1	0	1	0	0
Hanson	1	0	0	0	1	10	5	1	4	0
Hughes	4	0	0	0	4	9	2	5	2	1
Hutchinson	0	0	0	0	0	6	5	0	1	0
Jerauld	1	0	0	0	1	9	3	5	1	0
Jones	0	0	0	0	0	2	1	1	0	0
Kingsbury	0	0	0	0	0	4	1	3	0	0
Lake	2	0	1	0	1	19	4	14	1	0
Lawrence	7	0	1	0	6	39	14	21	4	0
Lyman	2	0	0	0	2	11	7	3	1	0
Marshall	6	0	0	0	6	23	8	14	1	0
McPherson	3	0	0	0	3	18	4	14	0	0
Mellette	0	0	0	0	0	6	1	5	0	0
Miner	0	0	0	0	0	6	4	2	0	0
Moody	3	0	0	0	3	2	2	0	0	1
Perkins	2	0	2	0	0	10	1	9	0	0
Potter	3	0	1	0	2	3	0	2	1	0
Roberts	11	0	1	0	10	7	0	5	2	0

Table 10. Offenses Known to Law Enforcement, by Selected State Metropolitan and Nonmetropolitan Counties, 2019—Continued

(Number.)

State/county	Violent crime	Murder and nonnegligent manslaughter	Rape[1]	Robbery	Aggravated assault	Property crime	Burglary	Larceny-theft	Motor vehicle theft	Arson[2]
Sanborn	3	0	0	0	3	7	1	6	0	0
Spink	13	0	0	0	13	84	26	49	9	0
Stanley	0	0	0	0	0	10	3	6	1	0
Sully	4	0	0	0	4	9	7	0	2	2
Tripp	2	0	1	0	1	4	0	3	1	0
Walworth	0	0	0	0	0	5	0	5	0	0
Yankton	7	1	2	0	4	53	10	27	16	0
Ziebach	0	0	0	0	0	0	0	0	0	0
Anderson	144	0	11	4	129	472	136	253	83	12
Blount	322	0	55	14	253	1,103	256	711	136	3
Bradley	205	1	15	13	176	808	190	508	110	1
Campbell	62	0	22	1	39	335	106	178	51	2
Cannon	12	0	1	0	11	96	42	27	27	1
Carter	63	0	3	3	57	334	67	236	31	0
Cheatham	87	1	6	2	78	280	57	174	49	2
Chester	25	1	6	0	18	79	30	37	12	0
Crockett	29	0	0	1	28	106	35	57	14	0
Dickson	121	0	15	4	102	334	88	195	51	0
Fayette	55	1	1	4	49	209	60	121	28	0
Gibson	56	2	7	3	44	160	51	88	21	0
Grainger	43	0	3	1	39	160	38	104	18	0
Hamblen	120	1	11	8	100	462	100	288	74	5
Hartsville/Trousdale	30	0	5	1	24	142	24	105	13	0
Hawkins	77	2	6	2	67	587	163	335	89	3
Jefferson	97	1	14	0	82	428	135	230	63	1
Knox	577	2	62	30	483	3,413	588	2,331	494	15
Loudon	72	3	3	3	63	375	79	243	53	1
Macon	41	0	0	0	41	159	54	91	14	1
Madison	103	0	4	12	87	380	73	251	56	0
Marion	59	0	3	1	55	220	43	135	42	3
Maury	140	1	24	1	114	431	94	260	77	3
Montgomery	104	2	10	1	91	571	136	378	57	2
Morgan	40	0	3	1	36	320	100	168	52	1
Polk	25	0	1	2	22	311	61	192	58	3
Roane	63	2	5	1	55	235	70	123	42	1
Robertson	75	1	6	1	67	243	48	164	31	2
Rutherford	205	1	19	16	169	746	153	506	87	10
Sequatchie	31	0	1	1	29	153	40	84	29	3
Shelby	569	3	34	72	460	2,473	551	1,703	219	11
Smith	43	0	7	1	35	148	54	82	12	0
Stewart	18	0	3	0	15	92	35	39	18	0
Sullivan	228	5	28	7	188	1,043	225	656	162	12
Sumner	118	9	11	4	94	404	85	267	52	4
Tipton	123	0	11	3	109	465	131	273	61	1
Unicoi	21	0	0	0	21	116	31	75	10	1
Union	22	1	4	0	17	204	63	116	25	0
Washington	159	1	10	4	144	762	182	446	134	3
Williamson	119	2	14	2	101	289	66	196	27	4
Wilson	85	0	2	4	79	555	105	384	66	1
TENNESSEE										
Metropolitan Counties										
Anderson	144	0	11	4	129	472	136	253	83	12
Blount	322	0	55	14	253	1,103	256	711	136	3
Bradley	205	1	15	13	176	808	190	508	110	1
Campbell	62	0	22	1	39	335	106	178	51	2
Cannon	12	0	1	0	11	96	42	27	27	1
Carter	63	0	3	3	57	334	67	236	31	0
Cheatham	87	1	6	2	78	280	57	174	49	2
Chester	25	1	6	0	18	79	30	37	12	0
Crockett	29	0	0	1	28	106	35	57	14	0
Dickson	121	0	15	4	102	334	88	195	51	0
Fayette	55	1	1	4	49	209	60	121	28	0
Gibson	56	2	7	3	44	160	51	88	21	0
Grainger	43	0	3	1	39	160	38	104	18	0
Hamblen	120	1	11	8	100	462	100	288	74	5
Hartsville/Trousdale	30	0	5	1	24	142	24	105	13	0
Hawkins	77	2	6	2	67	587	163	335	89	3
Jefferson	97	1	14	0	82	428	135	230	63	1
Knox	577	2	62	30	483	3,413	588	2,331	494	15
Loudon	72	3	3	3	63	375	79	243	53	1
Macon	41	0	0	0	41	159	54	91	14	0
Madison	103	0	4	12	87	380	73	251	56	3
Marion	59	0	3	1	55	220	43	135	42	3
Maury	140	1	24	1	114	431	94	260	77	2
Montgomery	104	2	10	1	91	571	136	378	57	1
Morgan	40	0	3	1	36	320	100	168	52	3
Polk	25	0	1	2	22	311	61	192	58	1
Roane	63	2	5	1	55	235	70	123	42	2
Robertson	75	1	6	1	67	243	48	164	31	10
Rutherford	205	1	19	16	169	746	153	506	87	

Table 10. Offenses Known to Law Enforcement, by Selected State Metropolitan and Nonmetropolitan Counties, 2019—Continued

(Number.)

State/county	Violent crime	Murder and nonnegligent manslaughter	Rape[1]	Robbery	Aggravated assault	Property crime	Burglary	Larceny-theft	Motor vehicle theft	Arson[2]
Sequatchie	31	0	1	1	29	153	40	84	29	3
Shelby	569	3	34	72	460	2,473	551	1,703	219	11
Smith	43	0	7	1	35	148	54	82	12	0
Stewart	18	0	3	0	15	92	35	39	18	0
Sullivan	228	5	28	7	188	1,043	225	656	162	12
Sumner	118	9	11	4	94	404	85	267	52	4
Tipton	123	0	11	3	109	465	131	273	61	1
Unicoi	21	0	0	0	21	116	31	75	10	1
Union	22	1	4	0	17	204	63	116	25	0
Washington	159	1	10	4	144	762	182	446	134	3
Williamson	119	2	14	2	101	289	66	196	27	4
Wilson	85	0	2	4	79	555	105	384	66	1
Nonmetropolitan Counties										
Bedford	75	0	8	0	67	250	59	165	26	3
Benton	18	0	6	1	11	114	47	50	17	0
Bledsoe	11	0	0	0	11	62	16	28	18	1
Carroll	44	1	7	2	34	154	63	73	18	0
Claiborne	58	4	3	2	49	283	80	162	41	5
Clay	14	0	0	2	12	40	18	20	2	0
Coffee	87	0	6	3	78	403	102	261	40	2
Cumberland	42	1	1	4	36	737	198	440	99	2
Decatur	30	0	3	0	27	100	43	43	14	0
DeKalb	17	1	1	0	15	117	34	68	15	2
Dyer	18	0	2	0	16	184	51	112	21	0
Fentress	27	1	3	0	23	189	46	120	23	3
Franklin	98	3	8	1	86	238	41	163	34	0
Giles	51	1	7	2	41	184	44	114	26	3
Greene	168	0	8	5	155	888	258	487	143	12
Grundy	77	2	7	0	68	245	47	149	49	4
Hancock	21	0	3	0	18	110	24	74	12	0
Hardeman	46	0	2	3	41	178	57	92	29	1
Hardin	35	1	4	2	28	348	121	181	46	1
Haywood	36	1	2	1	32	133	47	64	22	1
Henderson	83	0	9	2	72	295	87	161	47	2
Henry	47	0	8	1	38	298	89	168	41	3
Hickman	84	0	8	1	75	394	108	201	85	0
Houston	23	0	0	0	23	75	21	48	6	0
Humphreys	30	0	0	0	30	93	28	52	13	1
Jackson	24	1	1	1	21	83	21	50	12	2
Johnson	34	1	3	2	28	132	41	69	22	0
Lake	4	0	1	0	3	25	9	12	4	0
Lauderdale	45	2	3	1	39	192	68	104	20	3
Lawrence	49	0	5	1	43	267	97	133	37	3
Lewis	17	0	0	0	17	71	24	40	7	2
Lincoln	62	0	7	2	53	286	101	152	33	1
Marshall	28	0	0	1	27	72	10	43	19	0
McMinn	93	1	8	5	79	549	180	255	114	5
McNairy	55	1	5	1	48	276	93	145	38	4
Meigs	61	0	6	4	51	284	78	157	49	7
Monroe	234	0	10	7	217	873	284	465	124	6
Moore	7	0	2	0	5	58	4	51	3	0
Obion	34	0	1	1	32	177	35	114	28	1
Overton	13	0	1	0	12	135	16	90	29	1
Perry	13	0	0	0	13	59	14	40	5	2
Pickett	8	0	2	0	6	28	4	22	2	0
Putnam	85	0	13	0	72	518	136	317	65	5
Rhea	67	0	5	2	60	191	57	112	22	0
Scott	27	1	2	0	24	161	104	41	16	0
Sevier	153	0	19	10	124	836	203	460	173	1
Van Buren	3	0	0	0	3	30	3	20	7	0
Wayne	14	2	0	0	12	93	21	54	18	1
Weakley	27	0	7	1	19	116	45	53	18	0
White	55	0	2	5	48	251	45	165	41	8
TEXAS										
Metropolitan Counties										
Austin	13	0	2	0	11	87	40	29	18	0
Bandera[6]	12	0	2	1	9	268	95	143	30	1
Bastrop	212	6	46	18	142	649	192	349	108	5
Bell	82	0	27	1	54	631	152	445	34	0
Bexar	692	13	145	88	446	5,297	990	3,801	506	39
Bowie	102	1	25	2	74	331	131	170	30	6
Brazoria	170	4	13	34	119	1,325	306	851	168	3
Brazos	29	0	13	1	15	306	93	200	13	2
Burleson	20	1	7	2	10	100	34	63	3	1
Caldwell[6]	51	0	6	2	43	88	26	53	9	0
Callahan	5	0	0	0	5	44	12	22	10	1
Cameron	162	1	46	15	100	937	298	586	53	4
Carson	22	1	2	3	16	25	9	15	1	0
Chambers	93	3	8	8	74	544	132	408	4	4

Table 10. Offenses Known to Law Enforcement, by Selected State Metropolitan and Nonmetropolitan Counties, 2019—Continued

(Number.)

State/county	Violent crime	Murder and nonnegligent manslaughter	Rape[1]	Robbery	Aggravated assault	Property crime	Burglary	Larceny-theft	Motor vehicle theft	Arson[2]
Clay	16	0	8	0	8	103	33	49	21	2
Collin	66	0	22	4	40	338	102	187	49	2
Comal	135	0	40	9	86	601	179	373	49	0
Coryell	4	0	0	1	3	54	11	43	0	0
Dallas	43	0	11	4	28	307	54	206	47	0
Denton[6]	95	0	43	7	45	440	88	299	53	3
Ector	116	4	14	19	79	1,579	228	985	366	0
Ellis[6]	83	1	19	4	59	362	85	238	39	0
El Paso[6]	259	1	44	17	197	641	145	395	101	4
Fort Bend	841	10	119	120	592	4,643	691	3,653	299	1
Galveston	123	2	30	16	75	727	179	454	94	15
Goliad	22	1	3	2	16	79	19	49	11	0
Grayson	32	0	15	7	10	401	109	237	55	4
Gregg	84	3	26	4	51	373	106	212	55	2
Guadalupe	69	2	32	3	32	424	113	279	32	19
Hardin	38	1	1	5	31	285	91	148	46	5
Harris	7,329	97	860	2,249	4,123	42,526	7,044	29,466	6,016	85
Harrison	52	3	0	3	46	445	138	246	61	1
Hays	111	0	37	12	62	672	141	479	52	1
Hidalgo[6]	518	5	139	103	271	3,241	909	2,012	320	10
Hudspeth	8	0	0	0	8	14	3	9	2	1
Hunt[6]	350	4	16	9	321	570	166	293	111	0
Jefferson	59	1	1	8	49	358	78	224	56	1
Johnson[6]	205	0	53	4	148	660	167	397	96	3
Jones	4	0	0	1	3	60	20	35	5	0
Kaufman	126	2	30	15	79	767	237	425	105	1
Kendall	19	0	2	2	15	104	23	67	14	2
Lampasas[6]	12	1	1	0	10	83	21	55	7	1
Lubbock	16	1	4	0	11	331	89	191	51	0
Lynn[6]	0	0	0	0	0	3	0	3	0	1
McLennan	69	0	24	0	45	500	149	227	124	5
Medina	101	2	14	4	81	351	79	202	70	0
Montgomery	736	12	74	103	547	4,976	1,052	3,366	558	15
Nueces	61	1	10	9	41	160	49	108	3	0
Oldham	0	0	0	0	0	6	4	2	0	0
Parker	100	2	24	4	70	751	188	474	89	2
Randall	61	0	26	3	32	249	94	122	33	1
Robertson	8	1	1	0	6	116	37	65	14	0
Rockwall	13	0	4	0	9	91	15	50	26	1
Rusk	33	1	7	2	23	442	145	240	57	2
San Patricio	37	0	0	4	33	166	60	80	26	0
Smith	335	7	58	18	252	1,453	412	800	241	7
Tarrant[6]	123	0	28	18	77	742	214	456	72	2
Taylor	39	0	5	0	34	89	45	37	7	0
Tom Green	32	1	25	1	5	254	89	140	25	5
Travis[6]	790	2	117	71	600	3,240	762	2,192	286	16
Victoria	94	3	19	6	66	399	128	224	47	0
Wichita	38	0	1	1	36	126	42	62	22	0
Williamson	152	1	57	4	90	1,377	295	975	107	9
Wilson[6]	20	0	7	0	13	228	94	111	23	3
Wise	83	2	22	4	55	323	114	170	39	1
Nonmetropolitan Counties										
Anderson	30	2	3	2	23	363	150	171	42	0
Angelina	97	1	27	5	64	567	183	330	54	1
Aransas	60	0	13	3	44	240	62	164	14	0
Bailey[6]	3	0	1	0	2	36	15	20	1	0
Bee	21	0	3	0	18	159	56	93	10	1
Borden[6]	1	0	1	0	0	10	5	4	1	0
Bosque[6]	27	0	3	0	24	71	38	24	9	1
Brewster	7	0	1	0	6	10	4	3	3	0
Briscoe	0	0	0	0	0	3	2	0	1	0
Brooks	1	0	0	0	1	0	0	0	0	0
Brown[6]	31	0	7	1	23	189	62	114	13	4
Burnet	54	0	11	2	41	219	65	119	35	2
Calhoun	22	0	8	0	14	103	26	71	6	0
Camp[6]	9	0	2	0	7	67	31	29	7	2
Cass	32	0	3	1	28	174	61	92	21	5
Castro	6	0	0	0	6	47	13	26	8	0
Cherokee	61	1	7	2	51	362	117	198	47	2
Childress	1	0	0	0	1	7	1	5	1	0
Cochran[6]	3	0	0	0	3	27	12	15	0	1
Coke	2	0	0	0	2	14	10	0	4	0
Colorado	19	1	7	1	10	117	29	77	11	2
Comanche	3	0	0	0	3	58	11	41	6	0
Concho	11	0	0	0	11	8	8	0	0	0
Cooke[6]	33	3	8	3	19	100	38	51	11	2
Crockett	2	0	0	1	1	18	9	5	4	0
Culberson	0	0	0	0	0	0	0	0	0	0
Dallam	0	0	0	0	0	1	0	0	1	0
Dawson[6]	2	0	0	0	2	64	27	25	12	0

Table 10. Offenses Known to Law Enforcement, by Selected State Metropolitan and Nonmetropolitan Counties, 2019—Continued

(Number.)

State/county	Violent crime	Murder and nonnegligent manslaughter	Rape[1]	Robbery	Aggravated assault	Property crime	Burglary	Larceny-theft	Motor vehicle theft	Arson[2]
Deaf Smith	8	0	1	0	7	60	18	32	10	0
Delta	1	0	0	0	1	27	10	16	1	1
DeWitt	33	1	7	0	25	120	47	66	7	2
Dimmit	11	1	2	0	8	139	39	93	7	0
Donley[6]	4	2	0	0	2	30	12	16	2	0
Duval	12	0	0	0	12	104	24	41	39	0
Eastland[6]	5	2	2	0	1	22	9	5	8	0
Edwards	2	0	1	0	1	5	1	2	2	2
Erath[6]	50	2	9	2	37	93	52	30	11	0
Fannin	42	1	8	0	33	194	51	114	29	1
Fayette	11	0	6	1	4	123	41	76	6	0
Floyd[6]	12	0	0	1	11	25	5	19	1	2
Freestone[6]	22	0	3	3	16	131	55	68	8	2
Frio	9	0	0	0	9	60	17	34	9	0
Gaines	11	2	2	1	6	88	29	49	10	10
Garza	15	0	5	0	10	30	17	11	2	0
Gillespie	12	1	3	0	8	55	6	46	3	1
Gonzales	25	0	7	0	18	116	27	83	6	2
Gray[6]	15	0	1	2	12	59	19	36	4	0
Hale	16	0	0	0	16	64	25	38	1	1
Hall	3	1	0	0	2	7	2	5	0	0
Hamilton[6]	4	0	2	0	2	15	4	8	3	0
Hansford[6]	1	0	0	0	1	11	4	3	4	0
Hardeman	5	0	0	0	5	13	3	10	0	0
Hartley	0	0	0	0	0	10	3	3	4	0
Haskell	1	0	0	0	1	8	2	6	0	0
Hemphill[6]	2	0	0	0	2	13	1	12	0	0
Henderson	141	2	58	5	76	584	281	242	61	0
Hill	31	1	12	1	17	234	56	154	24	2
Hockley[6]	13	0	2	2	9	71	30	34	7	0
Hood	55	0	11	2	42	356	99	205	52	2
Hopkins[6]	27	1	9	0	17	61	17	26	18	0
Houston	2	0	0	0	2	102	43	53	6	0
Howard[6]	53	0	4	0	49	273	53	172	48	4
Hutchinson	11	0	3	0	8	71	26	42	3	0
Jack	9	0	0	2	7	36	15	13	8	0
Jackson	6	0	1	0	5	51	10	34	7	0
Jasper	72	2	18	2	50	403	155	197	51	1
Jim Hogg[6]	5	0	0	0	5	20	10	7	3	1
Karnes[6]	3	1	0	0	2	99	45	42	12	0
Kenedy	0	0	0	0	0	8	2	3	3	0
Kerr	51	0	21	0	30	199	51	133	15	2
Kimble	2	0	1	1	0	4	2	2	0	1
Kinney	0	0	0	0	0	1	1	0	0	0
Lamar	28	1	9	1	17	135	39	88	8	0
Lamb	6	0	2	1	3	61	24	31	6	0
La Salle	5	0	0	1	4	44	7	37	0	0
Lavaca	10	2	2	0	6	63	16	41	6	0
Lee[6]	25	0	2	1	22	86	28	49	9	0
Leon	11	0	0	0	11	116	36	70	10	0
Limestone	14	0	2	0	12	76	63	10	3	0
Llano[6]	29	1	3	0	25	145	41	88	16	2
Madison[6]	8	0	0	1	7	66	34	15	17	0
Mason[6]	8	0	1	0	7	10	4	5	1	0
Matagorda	62	0	19	6	37	332	91	214	27	0
McCulloch[6]	3	0	0	0	3	41	17	19	5	0
Menard	3	0	0	1	2	1	1	0	0	0
Milam	13	0	2	0	11	87	19	60	8	1
Mills[6]	14	0	1	0	13	20	11	9	0	0
Mitchell	1	0	0	0	1	25	5	15	5	0
Montague[6]	33	0	7	0	26	83	28	48	7	0
Moore[6]	6	1	0	0	5	39	12	20	7	0
Morris	10	0	4	2	4	72	21	48	3	0
Nacogdoches	58	2	10	1	45	270	85	148	37	1
Navarro	58	1	15	3	39	242	105	118	19	2
Newton[6]	22	0	1	1	20	98	49	38	11	2
Nolan[6]	4	0	0	0	4	31	10	21	0	1
Ochiltree[6]	0	0	0	0	0	22	7	12	3	0
Palo Pinto[6]	9	0	4	1	4	68	22	34	12	0
Panola	26	1	12	3	10	260	75	165	20	2
Pecos	1	0	0	0	1	98	15	66	17	0
Polk	76	5	33	7	31	671	212	379	80	8
Rains	8	0	0	0	8	48	19	24	5	0
Reagan	7	0	0	0	7	32	11	18	3	0
Real	3	0	0	0	3	59	15	39	5	1
Refugio	3	0	2	0	1	52	30	19	3	0
Roberts[6]	0	0	0	0	0	2	1	1	0	0
Runnels	1	0	0	0	1	11	5	6	0	0
Sabine[6]	14	0	5	0	9	73	39	24	10	0
San Augustine[6]	13	0	1	0	12	57	34	16	7	0
San Jacinto	44	0	26	1	17	330	115	173	42	0

Table 10. Offenses Known to Law Enforcement, by Selected State Metropolitan and Nonmetropolitan Counties, 2019—Continued

(Number.)

State/county	Violent crime	Murder and nonnegligent manslaughter	Rape[1]	Robbery	Aggravated assault	Property crime	Burglary	Larceny-theft	Motor vehicle theft	Arson[2]
Schleicher[6]	4	0	0	0	4	13	6	6	1	0
Scurry	7	0	2	0	5	44	15	28	1	0
Shelby	40	1	0	2	37	189	61	90	38	3
Sherman	0	0	0	0	0	3	2	1	0	0
Somervell	4	0	0	0	4	30	11	16	3	0
Starr	79	1	11	6	61	232	72	126	34	3
Stephens	1	0	1	0	0	21	9	9	3	0
Stonewall	1	0	0	0	1	0	0	0	0	0
Sutton[6]	0	0	0	0	0	1	0	0	1	0
Swisher[6]	7	0	1	1	5	24	7	13	4	0
Terry	1	0	0	0	1	30	15	9	6	0
Titus[6]	50	0	3	3	44	162	55	88	19	2
Tyler[6]	67	5	6	1	55	252	121	92	39	4
Upton[6]	2	0	0	0	2	31	3	25	3	0
Uvalde	16	1	0	0	15	85	30	46	9	2
Val Verde	29	0	3	1	25	87	41	41	5	0
Walker[6]	52	0	11	3	38	186	61	93	32	2
Ward	27	0	3	3	21	218	38	173	7	0
Washington	50	0	11	2	37	140	47	79	14	1
Wharton	68	0	12	4	52	230	73	127	30	2
Wheeler[6]	5	0	0	0	5	11	1	7	3	0
Wilbarger[6]	2	0	2	0	0	13	2	10	1	0
Willacy[6]	24	0	8	0	16	123	43	75	5	1
Winkler	9	1	2	0	6	80	10	55	15	0
Wood	75	0	39	6	30	225	65	127	33	0
Yoakum	3	0	1	0	2	18	9	5	4	0
Young[6]	12	0	7	1	4	35	16	13	6	0
Zapata	52	0	1	5	46	183	76	105	2	0
Zavala	12	0	4	0	8	32	19	8	5	0
UTAH										
Metropolitan Counties										
Box Elder[6]	12	1	5	0	6	131	40	81	10	0
Cache	32	0	23	1	8	150	15	95	40	4
Davis	50	0	14	1	35	213	28	173	12	0
Juab	3	0	1	0	2	54	8	39	7	0
Morgan[4]	4	0	2	0	2			21	3	0
Salt Lake County Unified Police Department	731	5	156	145	425	8,002	983	6,028	991	20
Tooele	12	0	4	1	7	218	25	173	20	1
Utah	87	2	30	3	52	323	38	260	25	2
Washington	28	1	5	3	19	138	31	94	13	0
Weber	94	0	32	6	56	963	291	583	89	2
Nonmetropolitan Counties										
Carbon	10	0	5	0	5	93	25	63	5	0
Grand	16	0	1	1	14	79	5	70	4	0
Iron[6]	49	0	8	0	41	119	37	65	17	1
Kane	7	0	0	0	7	24	6	13	5	0
Millard	20	1	4	0	15	213	34	154	25	0
Rich	3	0	0	0	3	18	1	17	0	0
San Juan	6	1	1	1	3	38	7	25	6	0
Sanpete	21	0	4	1	16	94	21	65	8	2
Sevier[6]	8	0	2	0	6	98	17	73	8	1
Summit	33	0	2	4	27	399	58	320	21	0
Uintah	55	0	22	1	32	158	48	91	19	4
Wasatch	31	0	20	0	11	91	14	67	10	0
VERMONT										
Metropolitan Counties										
Franklin	6	0	1	0	5	26	7	18	1	0
Grand Isle	4	0	0	1	3	27	8	16	3	0
Nonmetropolitan Counties										
Bennington	2	0	1	0	1	6	1	4	1	0
Caledonia	2	0	0	0	2	1	0	1	0	0
Essex	0	0	0	0	0	18	7	10	1	0
Lamoille	9	0	2	0	7	59	3	56	0	0
Orange	6	0	6	0	0	18	3	15	0	0
Orleans	0	0	0	0	0	75	6	68	1	0
Rutland	2	0	0	0	2	13	2	11	0	0
Washington	1	0	0	0	1	1	0	1	0	0
Windham	2	0	0	0	2	23	5	18	0	0
Windsor	0	0	0	0	0	15	12	3	0	0
VIRGINIA										
Metropolitan Counties										
Albemarle County Police Department	116	2	28	14	72	1,267	113	1,104	50	6
Amelia	26	0	3	4	19	172	35	107	30	1
Amherst	74	5	7	5	57	356	36	296	24	2
Appomattox	20	0	5	2	13	85	9	76	0	0
Arlington County Police Department	298	2	55	92	149	3,085	158	2,721	206	6

Table 10. Offenses Known to Law Enforcement, by Selected State Metropolitan and Nonmetropolitan Counties, 2019—Continued

(Number.)

State/county	Violent crime	Murder and nonnegligent manslaughter	Rape[1]	Robbery	Aggravated assault	Property crime	Burglary	Larceny-theft	Motor vehicle theft	Arson[2]
Augusta	90	0	15	5	70	801	182	539	80	3
Bedford	63	1	13	2	47	475	95	349	31	1
Botetourt	29	0	5	1	23	247	47	182	18	2
Charles City	4	1	2	0	1	40	13	23	4	0
Chesterfield County Police Department	458	12	115	146	185	5,841	642	4,887	312	30
Clarke	6	0	2	0	4	64	11	49	4	1
Craig	5	0	1	0	4	17	1	12	4	0
Dinwiddie	86	0	9	10	67	294	43	229	22	5
Fairfax County Police Department	957	14	167	346	430	13,279	619	11,822	838	30
Fauquier	40	1	14	1	24	284	30	246	8	1
Fluvanna	33	1	14	0	18	160	23	128	9	1
Franklin	56	2	14	4	36	565	98	384	83	3
Frederick	80	0	17	13	50	910	97	748	65	1
Giles	12	0	2	0	10	127	36	76	15	0
Gloucester	32	1	10	9	12	399	20	359	20	1
Goochland	13	1	7	0	5	160	17	135	8	1
Greene	19	1	10	0	8	195	21	164	10	3
Hanover	168	0	28	7	133	884	52	796	36	10
Henrico County Police Department	456	7	42	120	287	7,887	561	6,833	493	17
Isle of Wight	23	0	3	0	20	200	27	158	15	3
James City County Police Department	83	0	12	13	58	696	44	633	19	0
King and Queen	13	0	1	1	11	30	2	27	1	2
King William	13	0	1	2	10	85	14	68	3	0
Loudoun	393	0	168	36	189	2,309	136	2,019	154	24
Madison	12	0	7	0	5	67	7	52	8	0
Mathews	5	0	2	0	3	57	15	39	3	2
Montgomery	61	0	11	6	44	308	53	223	32	2
Nelson	26	0	8	0	18	166	27	123	16	0
New Kent	40	3	6	3	28	198	16	180	2	0
Powhatan	25	0	13	2	10	284	41	234	9	0
Prince George County Police Department	73	0	15	6	52	339	35	280	24	1
Prince William County Police Department	787	14	147	155	471	4,723	425	3,954	344	13
Pulaski	51	0	18	2	31	728	76	629	23	6
Rappahannock	4	0	1	0	3	16	2	13	1	0
Roanoke County Police Department	187	0	25	22	140	1,207	146	979	82	0
Rockingham	41	0	25	1	15	369	88	265	16	4
Scott	21	0	8	4	9	201	39	140	22	3
Southampton	19	2	10	0	7	203	42	138	23	3
Spotsylvania	168	4	31	32	101	803	69	671	63	1
Stafford	338	6	73	47	212	1,427	156	1,203	68	7
Sussex	8	1	0	2	5	74	23	46	5	3
Warren	34	1	20	1	12	154	14	135	5	4
Washington	37	3	10	4	20	603	92	456	55	2
York	78	0	20	7	51	875	50	793	32	5
Nonmetropolitan Counties										
Accomack	100	6	10	25	59	333	81	243	9	2
Alleghany	14	0	5	1	8	88	25	59	4	2
Bath	3	0	0	0	3	7	0	7	0	1
Bland	5	0	1	0	4	37	7	26	4	1
Brunswick	9	0	1	1	7	81	17	59	5	3
Buchanan	47	1	11	4	31	281	51	199	31	4
Buckingham	13	1	5	0	7	122	31	80	11	2
Caroline	58	0	14	4	40	223	25	198	0	5
Carroll	36	3	5	0	28	166	27	117	22	0
Charlotte	20	0	5	3	12	122	29	77	16	1
Cumberland	11	1	0	1	9	41	9	27	5	1
Dickenson	17	2	0	0	15	33	5	20	8	1
Essex	19	0	0	0	19	44	17	17	10	0
Floyd	19	2	9	0	8	82	16	59	7	2
Grayson	26	3	6	0	17	169	35	103	31	2
Greensville	10	0	4	2	4	79	20	56	3	0
Halifax	45	2	14	8	21	209	56	137	16	4
Henry	126	2	18	22	84	1,115	220	785	110	10
Highland	0	0	0	0	0	11	1	9	1	0
King George	29	0	7	2	20	213	34	159	20	0
Lancaster	29	1	8	0	20	50	10	38	2	0
Lee	27	1	5	2	19	122	12	109	1	1
Louisa	39	5	10	2	22	333	32	271	30	4
Lunenburg	17	3	3	1	10	40	18	20	2	0
Mecklenburg	53	1	22	0	30	185	45	126	14	3
Middlesex	13	1	4	0	8	112	18	89	5	4
Northampton	12	0	2	2	8	53	11	34	8	0
Northumberland	20	1	6	0	13	70	21	45	4	2
Nottoway	15	1	3	1	10	71	16	46	9	0
Orange	23	0	12	1	10	125	17	97	11	0
Page	29	0	9	2	18	152	34	110	8	1
Patrick	37	0	11	3	23	284	62	201	21	3
Pittsylvania	79	9	18	10	42	425	107	292	26	2
Prince Edward	19	0	5	2	12	57	16	37	4	0
Rockbridge	32	1	7	0	24	238	60	164	14	1

Table 10. Offenses Known to Law Enforcement, by Selected State Metropolitan and Nonmetropolitan Counties, 2019—Continued

(Number.)

State/county	Violent crime	Murder and nonnegligent manslaughter	Rape[1]	Robbery	Aggravated assault	Property crime	Burglary	Larceny-theft	Motor vehicle theft	Arson[2]
Russell	54	2	16	2	34	159	35	112	12	3
Shenandoah	46	2	7	0	37	237	54	174	9	0
Smyth	29	0	12	1	16	186	27	139	20	2
Surry	3	0	1	0	2	16	2	11	3	0
Tazewell	36	1	18	3	14	288	39	221	28	4
Westmoreland	12	0	4	0	8	68	15	50	3	2
Wise	64	1	39	3	21	249	51	163	35	5
Wythe	26	3	15	2	6	193	31	139	23	3
WASHINGTON										
Metropolitan Counties										
Asotin	15	1	4	0	10	126	28	91	7	0
Benton	73	2	6	5	60	386	81	259	46	5
Chelan	43	0	3	0	40	322	90	219	13	0
Clark	230	4	64	27	135	2,189	402	1,410	377	10
Cowlitz	64	3	23	1	37	285	85	150	50	5
Douglas	15	0	9	1	5	225	59	141	25	1
Franklin	16	1	1	4	10	126	45	68	13	3
King	607	5	64	176	362	3,621	796	2,132	693	77
Kitsap	445	3	115	28	299	3,036	590	2,196	250	4
Pierce	1,152	9	144	183	816	6,822	1,718	4,029	1,075	48
Skagit	74	0	11	13	50	757	222	474	61	1
Skamania	12	1	3	0	8	132	32	88	12	2
Snohomish	535	1	82	74	378	4,328	917	2,619	792	30
Spokane	195	5	51	20	119	2,666	555	1,900	211	11
Stevens	35	1	8	2	24	338	115	176	47	2
Thurston	246	3	27	19	197	1,546	545	808	193	11
Walla Walla	20	1	4	1	14	266	88	152	26	2
Yakima	153	8	31	17	97	1,466	383	759	324	7
Nonmetropolitan Counties										
Adams	18	0	4	0	14	93	36	45	12	2
Clallam	49	1	14	3	31	461	119	315	27	1
Columbia	9	0	1	0	8	72	22	46	4	1
Ferry	3	0	2	1	0	26	4	19	3	0
Grant	95	0	25	6	64	837	179	537	121	16
Grays Harbor	47	1	18	1	27	250	96	134	20	2
Island	56	1	14	1	40	373	124	230	19	2
Jefferson	33	0	4	3	26	222	91	117	14	1
Kittitas	8	1	3	0	4	142	43	88	11	0
Klickitat	4	1	0	0	3	76	68	5	3	0
Lewis	86	2	22	3	59	473	146	269	58	1
Lincoln	10	0	3	0	7	87	26	51	10	5
Mason	85	0	11	9	65	956	334	510	112	2
Okanogan	38	1	12	0	25	158	43	106	9	2
Pacific	21	0	0	2	19	137	59	71	7	1
Pend Oreille	5	0	2	0	3	140	35	93	12	0
San Juan	9	0	0	0	9	105	20	76	9	0
Wahkiakum	4	0	2	0	2	32	9	20	3	0
Whitman	7	0	0	0	7	35	13	14	8	0
WEST VIRGINIA										
Metropolitan Counties										
Berkeley	55	2	5	0	48	88	5	81	2	0
Brooke	4	0	3	0	1	7	1	6	0	1
Fayette	49	2	0	2	45	347	108	194	45	5
Hampshire	25	0	2	1	22	118	42	61	15	1
Hancock	7	0	1	0	6	2	0	2	0	0
Jackson	44	0	3	0	41	26	7	14	5	1
Jefferson	40	1	8	7	24	214	27	167	20	1
Kanawha	380	10	31	13	326	1,361	463	688	210	17
Marshall	9	0	0	0	9	67	25	35	7	0
Mineral	2	0	0	0	2	40	8	32	0	0
Monongalia	136	0	10	2	124	487	161	297	29	1
Morgan	59	0	4	2	53	71	15	50	6	0
Preston	10	1	3	3	3	133	2	119	12	0
Wirt	14	0	1	0	13	22	12	8	2	0
Wood	105	3	10	4	88	489	146	292	51	4
Nonmetropolitan Counties										
Calhoun	0	0	0	0	0	10	3	5	2	0
Doddridge	1	0	0	1	0	32	15	17	0	0
Greenbrier	14	1	2	1	10	63	26	32	5	1
Hardy	33	0	0	0	33	13	5	5	3	0
Lewis	3	0	0	1	2	22	10	6	6	0
Logan	131	1	4	0	126	4	0	4	0	3
McDowell	3	0	0	0	3	4	3	1	0	1
Mercer	83	4	8	10	61	306	106	163	37	7
Monroe	1	0	1	0	0	33	11	18	4	0
Nicholas	120	0	4	0	116	13	0	13	0	2
Randolph	80	0	4	0	76	174	66	102	6	3

Table 10. Offenses Known to Law Enforcement, by Selected State Metropolitan and Nonmetropolitan Counties, 2019—Continued

(Number.)

State/county	Violent crime	Murder and nonnegligent manslaughter	Rape[1]	Robbery	Aggravated assault	Property crime	Burglary	Larceny-theft	Motor vehicle theft	Arson[2]
Roane	4	0	0	0	4	2	0	2	0	1
Summers	10	0	0	0	10	25	3	17	5	0
Upshur	3	0	2	0	1	11	1	9	1	0
Wetzel	41	0	2	0	39	22	9	8	5	1
Wyoming	66	0	1	1	64	70	24	39	7	0
WISCONSIN										
Metropolitan Counties										
Brown	83	1	28	3	51	623	36	557	30	2
Calumet	10	0	4	0	6	74	12	53	9	0
Chippewa	53	4	22	0	27	199	48	141	10	1
Columbia	34	1	8	0	25	201	47	136	18	2
Dane	98	0	20	5	73	684	181	453	50	2
Douglas	15	0	5	2	8	156	45	99	12	0
Eau Claire	29	0	16	0	13	192	65	108	19	1
Fond du Lac	26	0	9	1	16	204	102	92	10	0
Green[6]	7	0	3	0	4	56	8	45	3	0
Iowa	8	0	1	0	7	43	11	31	1	0
Kenosha	50	0	12	7	31	253	26	216	11	6
Kewaunee	13	0	3	0	10	42	7	34	1	0
La Crosse	15	0	2	0	13	126	39	78	9	0
Lincoln	38	0	4	0	34	56	17	36	3	1
Marathon[6]	41	0	8	4	29	319	45	264	10	0
Milwaukee	107	2	7	5	93	92	0	68	24	1
Oconto	19	0	4	1	14	212	80	124	8	0
Outagamie	37	0	8	0	29	265	82	165	18	3
Ozaukee	13	0	8	0	5	76	18	51	7	0
Pierce	4	0	0	0	4	99	29	67	3	2
Rock	56	0	16	4	36	244	57	163	24	1
Sheboygan	27	0	4	1	22	271	22	233	16	1
St. Croix	22	0	1	1	20	278	82	182	14	1
Washington	7	0	5	1	1	192	37	148	7	0
Waukesha	58	0	1	0	57	305	37	250	18	0
Winnebago	18	0	3	1	14	155	45	97	13	0
Nonmetropolitan Counties										
Adams	21	0	0	0	21	255	109	134	12	2
Ashland	22	0	3	0	19	41	11	29	1	0
Barron	20	1	13	0	6	127	35	83	9	2
Bayfield	19	0	3	0	16	80	33	40	7	0
Buffalo	4	0	1	0	3	6	1	3	2	0
Burnett	20	0	4	0	16	237	78	144	15	3
Clark	14	0	1	0	13	97	25	57	15	3
Crawford	25	0	2	0	23	90	10	79	1	0
Dodge	39	0	14	3	22	149	16	123	10	0
Door	10	0	4	0	6	57	10	44	3	0
Dunn	47	0	6	1	40	82	17	51	14	0
Florence[6]	11	0	1	0	10	16	0	15	1	0
Forest	8	0	2	0	6	52	9	37	6	2
Grant	38	1	10	0	27	133	34	84	15	1
Green Lake	4	0	2	0	2	49	4	41	4	0
Iron	7	0	0	0	7	42	1	38	3	0
Jackson	11	0	1	2	8	131	35	78	18	0
Jefferson	35	0	1	2	32	231	58	162	11	0
Juneau	50	1	10	0	39	141	49	83	9	0
Manitowoc	32	0	1	0	31	131	35	91	5	0
Marinette	10	1	4	2	3	198	81	105	12	1
Marquette	9	1	1	1	6	69	10	57	2	1
Monroe	30	0	0	0	30	101	26	59	16	1
Oneida	28	0	7	0	21	150	37	107	6	1
Pepin	6	0	4	0	2	30	7	23	0	0
Polk	35	0	15	2	18	167	34	110	23	0
Portage	40	0	10	0	30	138	56	75	7	1
Price	4	0	0	0	4	73	33	38	2	0
Rusk	13	0	4	1	8	44	14	27	3	0
Sauk	27	2	13	4	8	304	103	181	20	0
Sawyer	38	0	7	0	31	105	21	79	5	0
Taylor	21	0	5	0	16	56	7	48	1	0
Trempealeau	11	0	0	0	11	82	17	60	5	0
Vernon	3	1	0	0	2	77	12	58	7	0
Vilas	4	0	0	0	4	101	20	76	5	0
Walworth	10	0	3	2	5	152	65	79	8	1
Washburn	19	0	6	0	13	123	51	63	9	0
Waupaca	52	0	8	0	44	298	58	221	19	0
Waushara	36	1	3	1	31	158	42	102	14	1
Wood	18	1	14	0	3	123	27	85	11	1
WYOMING										
Metropolitan Counties										
Natrona	48	0	10	2	36	145	50	79	16	1

Table 10. Offenses Known to Law Enforcement, by Selected State Metropolitan and Nonmetropolitan Counties, 2019—Continued

(Number.)

State/county	Violent crime	Murder and nonnegligent manslaughter	Rape[1]	Robbery	Aggravated assault	Property crime	Burglary	Larceny-theft	Motor vehicle theft	Arson[2]
Nonmetropolitan Counties										
Albany	6	0	1	0	5	28	4	22	2	0
Big Horn	3	0	2	0	1	20	3	16	1	1
Campbell	73	0	8	0	65	118	19	83	16	0
Carbon	9	0	1	0	8	38	4	33	1	0
Converse	11	0	0	0	11	34	1	32	1	0
Crook	4	0	1	0	3	17	2	14	1	0
Fremont	13	0	4	0	9	183	22	144	17	0
Goshen	10	0	1	0	9	27	9	16	2	0
Hot Springs	2	0	0	0	2	8	1	7	0	0
Johnson	4	0	1	0	3	22	5	13	4	0
Lincoln	16	0	7	0	9	119	37	77	5	1
Niobrara	4	0	0	0	4	10	2	8	0	0
Park[6]	13	0	8	0	5	67	20	43	4	1
Platte	0	0	0	0	0	44	8	32	4	0
Sheridan	3	0	0	0	3	47	7	31	9	0
Sublette	3	0	0	0	3	45	2	40	3	0
Sweetwater	16	0	4	0	12	83	16	58	9	1
Uinta	2	0	0	0	2	40	5	34	1	0
Washakie	2	0	1	0	1	22	3	13	6	0
Weston	0	0	0	0	0	1	0	0	1	0

1 The figures shown in this column for the offense of rape were reported using only the revised Uniform Crime Reporting (UCR) definition of rape. See chapter notes for more detail.   2 The FBI does not publish arson data unless it receives data from either the agency or the state for all 12 months of the calendar year.   3 Limited data for 2019 were available for Alabama.   4 The FBI determined that the agency's data were overreported. Consequently, those data are not included in this table.   5 The Tulare County Highway Patrol collects the motor vehicle thefts for this county. These data can be found in Table 11.   6 Because of changes in the state/local agency's reporting practices, figures are not comparable to previous years' data.   7 The FBI determined that the agency's data were underreported. Consequently, those data are not included in this table.   8 This agency/state submits rape data classified according to the legacy UCR definition; therefore the rape offense and violent crime total, which rape is a part of, is not included in this table. See the chapter notes for more detail.

Table 11. Offenses Known to Law Enforcement, by Selected State, Tribal, and Other Agencies, 2019

(Number.)

State/other agency unit/office	Violent crime	Murder and nonnegligent manslaughter	Rape[1]	Robbery	Aggravated assault	Property crime	Burglary	Larceny-theft	Motor vehicle theft	Arson[2]
ALABAMA[3]										
Tribal Agencies										
Poarch Creek Tribal	10	0	0	5	5	398	6	377	15	0
ALASKA										
State Agencies										
Alaska State Troopers	1,369	23	278	65	1,003	2,985	1,073	1,446	466	47
Tribal Agencies										
Metlakatla Tribal	0	0	0	0	0	0	0	0	0	0
Other Agencies										
Fairbanks International Airport		1	0	0	0	1	16	0	14	2
Ted Stevens Anchorage International Airport		6	0	0	0	6	107	8	83	16
ARIZONA										
Tribal Agencies										
Ak-Chin Tribal	2	0	0	0	2	7	2	4	1	0
Cocopah Tribal	9	0	0	0	9	7	0	5	2	0
Fort McDowell Tribal	11	0	0	1	10	26	3	19	4	
Fort Mojave Tribal	11	0	0	1	10	14	1	11	2	
Kaibab Paiute Tribal	1	0	0	0	1	0	0	0	0	0
Navajo Nation	2,171	20	193	17	1,941	957	260	351	346	41
Pascua Yaqui Tribal	20	1	0	1	18	271	23	231	17	0
Salt River Tribal	351	1	5	9	336	653	89	528	36	3
San Carlos Apache	759	1	14	7	737	373	186	165	22	36
Tonto Apache Tribal	2	0	0	0	2	13	1	12	0	0
Truxton Canon Agency	13	0	0	0	13	0	0	0	0	0
White Mountain Apache Tribal	395	1	35	4	355	412	130	267	15	37
Yavapai-Apache Nation	7	0	0	1	6	4	0	4	0	0
Yavapai-Prescott Tribal	4	0	0	0	4	104	1	101	2	0
Other Agencies										
Tucson Airport Authority	1	0	0	0	1	52	4	12	36	0
ARKANSAS										
State Agencies										
Camp Robinson	1	0	0	0	1	7	1	5	1	0
State Capitol Police	0	0	0	0	0	44	6	38	0	0
Other Agencies										
Northwest Arkansas Regional Airport	1	0	1	0	0	33	0	27	6	0
CALIFORNIA										
State Agencies										
Atascadero State Hospital	43	0	0	0	43	1	1	0	0	0
California State Fair	5	0	1	2	2	49	5	41	3	0
Coalinga State Hospital	202	0	3	0	199	11	1	10	0	1
Department of Parks and Recreation										
Angeles	2	0	1	0	1	22	0	22	0	0
Bay Area	0	0	0	0	0	0	0	0	0	0
Calaveras County	0	0	0	0	0	4	4	0	0	0
Capital	5	0	0	0	5	3	0	2	1	0
Channel Coast	0	0	0	0	0	64	5	59	0	0
Colorado	0	0	0	0	0	1	1	0	0	0
Four Rivers District	0	0	0	0	0	3	3	0	0	0
Gold Fields District	4	0	2	1	1	31	0	31	0	0
Hollister Hills	0	0	0	0	0	0	0	0	0	0
Hungry Valley	1	0	0	0	1	0	0	0	0	0
Inland Empire	1	0	0	0	1	2	0	2	0	0
Marin County	1	0	0	0	1	10	7	3	0	0
Monterey County	0	0	0	0	0	24	7	15	2	0
North Coast Redwoods	0	0	0	0	0	40	0	40	0	0
Northern Buttes	1	0	0	0	1	7	2	5	0	0
Oceano Dunes	2	0	0	1	1	35	2	31	2	1
Ocotillo Wells	1	0	0	0	1	0	0	0	0	0
Orange Coast	0	0	0	0	0	147	102	45	0	0
San Diego Coast	13	0	0	1	12	59	1	57	1	0
San Joaquin	3	0	0	0	3	5	1	4	0	0
San Luis Obispo Coast	0	0	0	0	0	22	0	21	1	0
Santa Cruz Mountains	0	0	0	0	0	118	0	116	2	0
Sierra	0	0	0	0	0	17	0	17	0	0
Sonoma	0	0	0	0	0	0	0	0	0	0
Sonoma-Mendocino Coast	1	0	0	1	0	19	2	17	0	0
Tehachapi District	0	0	0	0	0	3	1	1	1	0
Twin Cities	0	0	0	0	0	1	0	1	0	0
Fairview Developmental Center	1	0	0	0	1	0	0	0	0	0
Highway Patrol										
Alameda County	0	0	0	0	0	207	0	40	167	0
Alpine County	0	0	0	0	0	3	1	1	1	0
Amador County	0	0	0	0	0	31	0	15	16	0
Butte County	1	0	0	0	1	230	1	95	134	0
Calaveras County	0	0	0	0	0	92	0	47	45	0
Colusa County	6	0	0	0	6	24	0	3	21	0
Contra Costa County	0	0	0	0	0	487	0	40	447	0
Del Norte County	2	0	0	0	2	69	0	40	29	0

Table 11. Offenses Known to Law Enforcement, by Selected State, Tribal, and Other Agencies, 2019—Continued

(Number.)

State/other agency unit/office	Violent crime	Murder and nonnegligent manslaughter	Rape[1]	Robbery	Aggravated assault	Property crime	Burglary	Larceny-theft	Motor vehicle theft	Arson[2]
El Dorado County	0	0	0	0	0	134	1	99	34	0
Fresno County	0	0	0	0	0	152	0	22	130	0
Glenn County	3	0	0	0	3	30	0	9	21	0
Humboldt County	1	0	0	0	1	317	1	105	211	0
Imperial County	1	0	0	0	1	66	1	24	41	0
Inyo County	0	0	0	0	0	18	0	5	13	0
Kern County	3	1	0	0	2	238	1	40	197	0
Kings County	0	0	0	0	0	85	0	14	71	0
Lake County	1	1	0	0	0	173	0	38	135	0
Lassen County	0	0	0	0	0	39	0	9	30	0
Los Angeles County	48	0	0	0	48	507	5	139	363	0
Madera County	0	0	0	0	0	140	0	41	99	0
Marin County	0	0	0	0	0	313	0	266	47	0
Mariposa County	0	0	0	0	0	11	0	9	2	0
Mendocino County	0	0	0	0	0	135	0	51	84	0
Merced County	0	0	0	0	0	430	0	94	336	0
Modoc County	2	0	0	0	2	7	0	3	4	0
Mono County	0	0	0	0	0	3	0	1	2	0
Monterey County	1	0	0	0	1	310	0	94	216	0
Napa County	0	0	0	0	0	26	0	16	10	0
Nevada County	1	0	0	0	1	101	0	18	83	0
Orange County	21	0	0	2	19	144	2	35	107	0
Placer County	6	0	0	0	6	193	6	58	129	0
Plumas County	0	0	0	0	0	19	0	7	12	0
Riverside County	13	0	0	0	13	83	7	20	56	0
Sacramento County	13	1	0	0	12	3,105	3	1,374	1,728	0
San Benito County	0	0	0	0	0	8	0	4	4	0
San Bernardino County	34	0	0	1	33	152	0	65	87	1
San Diego County	43	0	0	0	43	143	1	50	92	0
San Francisco County	1	0	0	0	1	40	0	17	23	0
San Joaquin County	0	0	0	0	0	571	0	172	399	0
San Luis Obispo County	0	0	0	0	0	108	0	42	66	0
San Mateo County	1	0	0	0	1	38	1	24	13	0
Santa Barbara County	0	0	0	0	0	181	0	52	129	0
Santa Clara County	0	0	0	0	0	65	0	28	37	0
Santa Cruz County	0	0	0	0	0	501	0	178	323	0
Shasta County	0	0	0	0	0	284	1	78	205	0
Sierra County	0	0	0	0	0	0	0	0	0	0
Siskiyou County	1	0	0	0	1	54	1	21	32	0
Solano County	0	0	0	0	0	31	0	12	19	0
Sonoma County	0	0	0	0	0	136	1	88	47	0
Stanislaus County	0	0	0	0	0	318	0	116	202	0
Sutter County	0	0	0	0	0	47	0	13	34	0
Tehama County	0	0	0	0	0	149	1	57	91	0
Trinity County	0	0	0	0	0	47	0	21	26	0
Tulare County	0	0	0	0	0	701	1	146	554	21
Tuolumne County	0	0	0	0	0	136	0	63	73	0
Ventura County	0	0	0	0	0	36	0	9	27	0
Yolo County	0	0	0	0	0	47	0	16	31	0
Yuba County	0	0	0	0	0	411	0	92	319	0
Metropolitan State Hospital	1,181	0	10	1	1,170	8	2	6	0	1
Napa State Hospital	328	0	5	0	323	2	0	2	0	0
Patton State Hospital	356	0	2	0	354	1	1	0	0	0
Porterville Developmental Center	62	0	2	0	60	4	2	2	0	0
Tribal Agencies										
Hoopa Valley Tribal	32	0	0	0	32	54	25	25	4	0
La Jolla Tribal	8	0	0	1	7	9	2	7	0	1
Sycuan Tribal	38	0	0	1	37	68	18	29	21	0
Table Mountain Rancheria	3	0	0	1	2	249	20	205	24	0
Yurok Tribal	1	0	0	0	1	15	3	12	0	0
Other Agencies										
Clovis Unified School District	13	0	0	0	13	20	3	17	0	0
East Bay Regional Park District	44	0	3	21	20	357	73	274	10	12
Fontana Unified School District	31	0	3	10	18	70	8	56	6	1
Kern High School District	41	0	0	4	37	158	48	101	9	6
Los Angeles County Metropolitan Transportation Authority	6	0	0	0	6	21	0	20	1	0
Los Angeles Transportation Services Bureau	150	0	7	74	69	155	5	131	19	1
Monterey Peninsula Airport	0	0	0	0	0	9	0	6	3	0
Port of San Diego Harbor	75	0	8	20	47	655	65	585	5	0
San Bernardino Unified School District	67	0	3	53	11	264	124	129	11	10
San Fransisco Bay Area Rapid Transit										
Alameda County	282	2	2	227	51	1,796	13	1,634	149	4
Contra Costa County	61	0	4	34	23	676	2	592	82	0
San Francisco County	132	0	0	104	28	624	4	619	1	0
San Mateo County	24	0	1	13	10	345	1	332	12	0
Santa Clara Transit District	92	0	3	36	53	116	4	97	15	0
Shasta County Marshal	2	0	0	0	2	0	0	0	0	0
Stockton Unified School District	38	0	0	20	18	130	31	98	1	0
Twin Rivers Unified School District	21	0	0	16	5	103	70	25	8	0
Union Pacific Railroad Alameda County	1	0	0	0	1	29	20	9	0	0

Table 11. Offenses Known to Law Enforcement, by Selected State, Tribal, and Other Agencies, 2019—Continued

(Number.)

State/other agency unit/office	Violent crime	Murder and nonnegligent manslaughter	Rape[1]	Robbery	Aggravated assault	Property crime	Burglary	Larceny-theft	Motor vehicle theft	Arson[2]
Amador County	0	0	0	0	0	0	0	0	0	0
Butte County	0	0	0	0	0	16	1	15	0	0
Calaveras County	0	0	0	0	0	0	0	0	0	0
Colusa County	0	0	0	0	0	0	0	0	0	0
Contra Costa County	0	0	0	0	0	2	0	2	0	0
El Dorado County	0	0	0	0	0	0	0	0	0	0
Fresno County	0	0	0	0	0	3	0	3	0	0
Glenn County	0	0	0	0	0	0	0	0	0	0
Humboldt County	0	0	0	0	0	0	0	0	0	0
Imperial County	0	0	0	0	0	0	0	0	0	0
Inyo County	0	0	0	0	0	0	0	0	0	0
Kern County	0	0	0	0	0	71	19	52	0	0
Kings County	0	0	0	0	0	1	1	0	0	0
Lassen County	0	0	0	0	0	1	0	1	0	0
Los Angeles County	1	0	0	0	1	1,933	1,462	471	0	2
Madera County	0	0	0	0	0	1	1	0	0	0
Marin County	0	0	0	0	0	0	0	0	0	0
Mendocino County	0	0	0	0	0	0	0	0	0	0
Merced County	0	0	0	0	0	2	0	2	0	0
Modoc County	0	0	0	0	0	0	0	0	0	0
Monterey County	0	0	0	0	0	2	1	1	0	0
Napa County	0	0	0	0	0	0	0	0	0	0
Nevada County	0	0	0	0	0	0	0	0	0	0
Orange County	1	0	0	1	0	4	2	2	0	0
Placer County	0	0	0	0	0	9	1	8	0	0
Plumas County	0	0	0	0	0	1	0	1	0	0
Riverside County	1	0	0	0	1	25	13	12	0	1
Sacramento County	0	0	0	0	0	2	1	1	0	0
San Benito County	0	0	0	0	0	1	1	0	0	0
San Bernardino County	2	0	0	0	2	43	33	10	0	0
San Francisco County	1	0	0	0	1	1	0	1	0	0
San Joaquin County	0	0	0	0	0	170	11	159	0	3
San Luis Obispo County	0	0	0	0	0	2	0	2	0	0
San Mateo County	0	0	0	0	0	0	0	0	0	0
Santa Barbara County	0	0	0	0	0	1	0	1	0	0
Santa Clara County	1	0	0	0	1	3	0	3	0	0
Santa Cruz County	0	0	0	0	0	0	0	0	0	0
Shasta County	0	0	0	0	0	5	1	4	0	0
Sierra County	0	0	0	0	0	0	0	0	0	0
Siskiyou County	0	0	0	0	0	2	0	2	0	0
Solano County	0	0	0	0	0	18	1	17	0	0
Sonoma County	0	0	0	0	0	1	0	1	0	0
Stanislaus County	0	0	0	0	0	4	0	4	0	0
Sutter County	0	0	0	0	0	1	1	0	0	0
Tehama County	0	0	0	0	0	4	0	4	0	0
Trinity County	0	0	0	0	0	0	0	0	0	0
Tulare County	0	0	0	0	0	2	1	1	0	0
Ventura County	0	0	0	0	0	1	0	1	0	0
Yolo County	0	0	0	0	0	1	0	1	0	0
Yuba County	0	0	0	0	0	2	0	2	0	0
COLORADO										
State Agencies										
Colorado Bureau of Investigation	0	0	0	0	0	1	0	0	1	0
Colorado Mental Health Institute	0	0	0	0	0	0	0	0	0	0
State Patrol	24	0	0	1	23	16	1	3	12	0
Tribal Agencies										
Southern Ute Tribal	14	0	1	0	13	26	4	20	2	0
Ute Mountain Tribal	29	0	1	0	28	33	5	17	11	4
Other Agencies										
All Crimes Enforcement Team	0	0	0	0	0	0	0	0	0	0
Delta Montrose Drug Task Force	0	0	0	0	0	0	0	0	0	0
Southwest Drug Task Force	0	0	0	0	0	0	0	0	0	0
CONNECTICUT										
State Agencies										
Connecticut State Police	237	9	67	34	127	1,717	365	1,060	292	13
Department of Energy and Environmental Protection[4]	5	0	1	0	4	27	0	27	0	0
Department of Motor Vehicles	0	0	0	0	0	0	0	0	0	0
State Capitol Police	0	0	0	0	0	2	0	2	0	0
Tribal Agencies										
Mashantucket Pequot Tribal	15	0	8	0	7	175	0	173	2	0
Mohegan Tribal	9	0	3	1	5	243	4	237	2	0
Other Agencies										
Metropolitan Transportation Authority	5	0	0	1	4	62	0	61	1	0
DELAWARE										
State Agencies										
Alcohol and Tobacco Enforcement	0	0	0	0	0	1	0	1	0	0
Animal Welfare										
Kent County	0	0	0	0	0	0	0	0	0	0
New Castle County	0	0	0	0	0	0	0	0	0	0
Sussex County	0	0	0	0	0	0	0	0	0	0

Table 11. Offenses Known to Law Enforcement, by Selected State, Tribal, and Other Agencies, 2019—Continued

(Number.)

State/other agency unit/office	Violent crime	Murder and nonnegligent manslaughter	Rape[1]	Robbery	Aggravated assault	Property crime	Burglary	Larceny-theft	Motor vehicle theft	Arson[2]
Attorney General, New Castle County	2	0	0	0	2	4	0	4	0	0
Environmental Control	0	0	0	0	0	9	1	8	0	0
Fish and Wildlife	0	0	0	0	0	22	3	19	0	0
Park Rangers	3	0	0	1	2	88	20	67	1	2
River and Bay Authority	8	0	0	0	8	8	3	5	0	0
State Capitol Police	0	0	0	0	0	19	1	18	0	0
State Fire Marshal	8	0	0	0	8	3	3	0	0	110
State Police										
Headquarters	0	0	0	0	0	1	0	1	0	0
Kent County	287	0	44	25	218	909	204	608	97	0
New Castle County	434	6	28	137	263	4,275	255	3,814	206	0
Sussex County	410	3	37	19	351	2,377	551	1,734	92	1
Other Agencies										
Amtrak Police	0	0	0	0	0	16	0	14	2	0
DISTRICT OF COLUMBIA										
Other Agencies										
District of Columbia Fire and Emergency Medical Services, Arson Investigation Unit	0	0	0	0	0	0	0	0	0	159
Metro Transit Police	507	0	3	354	150	856	3	818	35	3
FLORIDA										
State Agencies										
Capitol Police	0	0	0	0	0	14	2	11	1	0
Department of Corrections, Office of the Inspector General										
Alachua County	0	0	0	0	0	0	0	0	0	0
Baker County	0	0	0	0	0	0	0	0	0	0
Bay County	0	0	0	0	0	0	0	0	0	0
Bradford County	0	0	0	0	0	0	0	0	0	0
Brevard County	0	0	0	0	0	0	0	0	0	0
Broward County	0	0	0	0	0	0	0	0	0	0
Calhoun County	0	0	0	0	0	0	0	0	0	0
Charlotte County	0	0	0	0	0	0	0	0	0	0
Citrus County	0	0	0	0	0	0	0	0	0	0
Clay County	0	0	0	0	0	0	0	0	0	0
Collier County	0	0	0	0	0	0	0	0	0	0
Columbia County	0	0	0	0	0	0	0	0	0	0
DeSoto County	0	0	0	0	0	0	0	0	0	0
Dixie County	0	0	0	0	0	0	0	0	0	0
Duval County	0	0	0	0	0	0	0	0	0	0
Escambia County	0	0	0	0	0	0	0	0	0	0
Flagler County	0	0	0	0	0	0	0	0	0	0
Franklin County	0	0	0	0	0	0	0	0	0	0
Gadsden County	0	0	0	0	0	0	0	0	0	0
Gilchrist County	0	0	0	0	0	0	0	0	0	0
Glades County	0	0	0	0	0	0	0	0	0	0
Gulf County	0	0	0	0	0	0	0	0	0	0
Hamilton County	0	0	0	0	0	0	0	0	0	0
Hardee County	0	0	0	0	0	0	0	0	0	0
Hendry County	0	0	0	0	0	0	0	0	0	0
Hernando County	0	0	0	0	0	0	0	0	0	0
Highlands County	0	0	0	0	0	0	0	0	0	0
Hillsborough County	0	0	0	0	0	0	0	0	0	0
Holmes County	0	0	0	0	0	0	0	0	0	0
Indian River County	0	0	0	0	0	0	0	0	0	0
Jackson County	0	0	0	0	0	0	0	0	0	0
Jefferson County	0	0	0	0	0	0	0	0	0	0
Lafayette County	0	0	0	0	0	0	0	0	0	0
Lake County	0	0	0	0	0	0	0	0	0	0
Lee County	0	0	0	0	0	0	0	0	0	0
Leon County	0	0	0	0	0	0	0	0	0	0
Levy County	0	0	0	0	0	0	0	0	0	0
Liberty County	0	0	0	0	0	0	0	0	0	0
Madison County	0	0	0	0	0	0	0	0	0	0
Manatee County	0	0	0	0	0	0	0	0	0	0
Marion County	0	0	0	0	0	0	0	0	0	0
Martin County	0	0	0	0	0	0	0	0	0	0
Miami-Dade County	0	0	0	0	0	0	0	0	0	0
Monroe County	0	0	0	0	0	0	0	0	0	0
Nassau County	0	0	0	0	0	0	0	0	0	0
Okaloosa County	0	0	0	0	0	0	0	0	0	0
Okeechobee County	0	0	0	0	0	0	0	0	0	0
Orange County	0	0	0	0	0	0	0	0	0	0
Osceola County	0	0	0	0	0	0	0	0	0	0
Palm Beach County	0	0	0	0	0	0	0	0	0	0
Pasco County	0	0	0	0	0	0	0	0	0	0
Pinellas County	0	0	0	0	0	0	0	0	0	0
Polk County	0	0	0	0	0	0	0	0	0	0
Putnam County	0	0	0	0	0	0	0	0	0	0
Santa Rosa County	0	0	0	0	0	0	0	0	0	0
Sarasota County	0	0	0	0	0	0	0	0	0	0

Table 11. Offenses Known to Law Enforcement, by Selected State, Tribal, and Other Agencies, 2019—Continued

(Number.)

State/other agency unit/office	Violent crime	Murder and nonnegligent manslaughter	Rape[1]	Robbery	Aggravated assault	Property crime	Burglary	Larceny-theft	Motor vehicle theft	Arson[2]
Seminole County	0	0	0	0	0	0	0	0	0	0
St. Johns County	0	0	0	0	0	0	0	0	0	0
St. Lucie County	0	0	0	0	0	0	0	0	0	0
Sumter County	0	0	0	0	0	0	0	0	0	0
Suwannee County	0	0	0	0	0	0	0	0	0	0
Taylor County	0	0	0	0	0	0	0	0	0	0
Union County	0	0	0	0	0	0	0	0	0	0
Volusia County	0	0	0	0	0	0	0	0	0	0
Wakulla County	0	0	0	0	0	0	0	0	0	0
Walton County	0	0	0	0	0	0	0	0	0	0
Washington County	0	0	0	0	0	0	0	0	0	0
Department of Law Enforcement										
Duval County, Jacksonville	0	0	0	0	0	4	0	0	4	0
Escambia County, Pensacola	2	0	1	0	1	0	0	0	0	0
Hillsborough County, Tampa	0	0	0	0	0	2	0	2	0	0
Lee County, Fort Myers	1	0	0	0	1	0	0	0	0	0
Leon County, Tallahassee	0	0	0	0	0	4	0	4	0	0
Miami-Dade County, Miami	0	0	0	0	0	0	0	0	0	0
Orange County, Orlando	3	1	2	0	0	9	0	9	0	0
Division of Alcoholic Beverages and Tobacco										
Alachua County	0	0	0	0	0	0	0	0	0	0
Baker County	0	0	0	0	0	0	0	0	0	0
Bay County	0	0	0	0	0	0	0	0	0	0
Bradford County	0	0	0	0	0	0	0	0	0	0
Brevard County	0	0	0	0	0	0	0	0	0	0
Broward County	0	0	0	0	0	0	0	0	0	0
Calhoun County	0	0	0	0	0	0	0	0	0	0
Charlotte County	0	0	0	0	0	0	0	0	0	0
Citrus County	0	0	0	0	0	0	0	0	0	0
Clay County	0	0	0	0	0	0	0	0	0	0
Collier County	0	0	0	0	0	0	0	0	0	0
Columbia County	0	0	0	0	0	0	0	0	0	0
DeSoto County	0	0	0	0	0	0	0	0	0	0
Dixie County	0	0	0	0	0	0	0	0	0	0
Duval County	0	0	0	0	0	0	0	0	0	0
Escambia County	0	0	0	0	0	0	0	0	0	0
Flagler County	0	0	0	0	0	0	0	0	0	0
Franklin County	0	0	0	0	0	0	0	0	0	0
Gadsden County	0	0	0	0	0	0	0	0	0	0
Gilchrist County	0	0	0	0	0	0	0	0	0	0
Glades County	0	0	0	0	0	0	0	0	0	0
Gulf County	0	0	0	0	0	0	0	0	0	0
Hamilton County	0	0	0	0	0	0	0	0	0	0
Hardee County	0	0	0	0	0	0	0	0	0	0
Hendry County	0	0	0	0	0	0	0	0	0	0
Hernando County	0	0	0	0	0	0	0	0	0	0
Highlands County	0	0	0	0	0	0	0	0	0	0
Hillsborough County	0	0	0	0	0	0	0	0	0	0
Holmes County	0	0	0	0	0	0	0	0	0	0
Indian River County	0	0	0	0	0	0	0	0	0	0
Jackson County	0	0	0	0	0	0	0	0	0	0
Jefferson County	0	0	0	0	0	0	0	0	0	0
Lafayette County	0	0	0	0	0	0	0	0	0	0
Lake County	0	0	0	0	0	0	0	0	0	0
Lee County	0	0	0	0	0	0	0	0	0	0
Leon County	0	0	0	0	0	0	0	0	0	0
Levy County	0	0	0	0	0	0	0	0	0	0
Liberty County	0	0	0	0	0	0	0	0	0	0
Madison County	0	0	0	0	0	0	0	0	0	0
Manatee County	0	0	0	0	0	0	0	0	0	0
Marion County	0	0	0	0	0	0	0	0	0	0
Martin County	0	0	0	0	0	0	0	0	0	0
Miami-Dade County	0	0	0	0	0	0	0	0	0	0
Monroe County	0	0	0	0	0	0	0	0	0	0
Nassau County	0	0	0	0	0	0	0	0	0	0
Okaloosa County	0	0	0	0	0	0	0	0	0	0
Okeechobee County	0	0	0	0	0	0	0	0	0	0
Orange County	0	0	0	0	0	0	0	0	0	0
Osceola County	0	0	0	0	0	0	0	0	0	0
Palm Beach County	0	0	0	0	0	0	0	0	0	0
Pasco County	0	0	0	0	0	0	0	0	0	0
Pinellas County	0	0	0	0	0	0	0	0	0	0
Polk County	0	0	0	0	0	0	0	0	0	0
Putnam County	0	0	0	0	0	0	0	0	0	0
Santa Rosa County	0	0	0	0	0	0	0	0	0	0
Sarasota County	0	0	0	0	0	0	0	0	0	0
Seminole County	0	0	0	0	0	0	0	0	0	0
St. Johns County	0	0	0	0	0	0	0	0	0	0
St. Lucie County	0	0	0	0	0	0	0	0	0	0
Sumter County	0	0	0	0	0	0	0	0	0	0
Suwannee County	0	0	0	0	0	0	0	0	0	0
Taylor County	0	0	0	0	0	0	0	0	0	0

Table 11. Offenses Known to Law Enforcement, by Selected State, Tribal, and Other Agencies, 2019—Continued

(Number.)

State/other agency unit/office	Violent crime	Murder and nonnegligent manslaughter	Rape[1]	Robbery	Aggravated assault	Property crime	Burglary	Larceny-theft	Motor vehicle theft	Arson[2]
Union County	0	0	0	0	0	0	0	0	0	0
Volusia County	0	0	0	0	0	0	0	0	0	0
Wakulla County	0	0	0	0	0	0	0	0	0	0
Walton County	0	0	0	0	0	0	0	0	0	0
Washington County	0	0	0	0	0	0	0	0	0	0
Division of Investigative and Forensic Services										
Broward County	0	0	0	0	0	0	0	0	0	0
Duval County	0	0	0	0	0	0	0	0	0	0
Escambia County	0	0	0	0	0	0	0	0	0	0
Hillsborough County	0	0	0	0	0	0	0	0	0	0
Lee County	0	0	0	0	0	0	0	0	0	0
Leon County	0	0	0	0	0	0	0	0	0	0
Miami-Dade County	0	0	0	0	0	0	0	0	0	0
Orange County	0	0	0	0	0	0	0	0	0	0
Palm Beach County	0	0	0	0	0	0	0	0	0	0
Pinellas County	0	0	0	0	0	0	0	0	0	0
Fish and Wildlife Conservation Commission										
Alachua County	0	0	0	0	0	0	0	0	0	0
Baker County	0	0	0	0	0	0	0	0	0	0
Bay County	0	0	0	0	0	0	0	0	0	0
Bradford County	0	0	0	0	0	0	0	0	0	0
Brevard County	0	0	0	0	0	0	0	0	0	0
Broward County	0	0	0	0	0	0	0	0	0	0
Calhoun County	0	0	0	0	0	0	0	0	0	0
Charlotte County	0	0	0	0	0	0	0	0	0	0
Citrus County	0	0	0	0	0	0	0	0	0	0
Clay County	0	0	0	0	0	0	0	0	0	0
Collier County	0	0	0	0	0	0	0	0	0	0
Columbia County	0	0	0	0	0	0	0	0	0	0
DeSoto County	0	0	0	0	0	0	0	0	0	0
Dixie County	0	0	0	0	0	0	0	0	0	0
Duval County	0	0	0	0	0	0	0	0	0	0
Escambia County	0	0	0	0	0	0	0	0	0	0
Flagler County	0	0	0	0	0	0	0	0	0	0
Franklin County	0	0	0	0	0	0	0	0	0	0
Gadsden County	0	0	0	0	0	0	0	0	0	0
Gilchrist County	0	0	0	0	0	0	0	0	0	0
Glades County	0	0	0	0	0	0	0	0	0	0
Gulf County	0	0	0	0	0	0	0	0	0	0
Hamilton County	0	0	0	0	0	0	0	0	0	0
Hardee County	0	0	0	0	0	0	0	0	0	0
Hendry County	0	0	0	0	0	0	0	0	0	0
Hernando County	0	0	0	0	0	0	0	0	0	0
Highlands County	0	0	0	0	0	0	0	0	0	0
Hillsborough County	0	0	0	0	0	0	0	0	0	0
Holmes County	0	0	0	0	0	0	0	0	0	0
Indian River County	0	0	0	0	0	0	0	0	0	0
Jackson County	0	0	0	0	0	0	0	0	0	0
Jefferson County	0	0	0	0	0	0	0	0	0	0
Lafayette County	0	0	0	0	0	0	0	0	0	0
Lake County	0	0	0	0	0	0	0	0	0	0
Lee County	0	0	0	0	0	0	0	0	0	0
Leon County	0	0	0	0	0	0	0	0	0	0
Levy County	0	0	0	0	0	0	0	0	0	0
Liberty County	0	0	0	0	0	0	0	0	0	0
Madison County	0	0	0	0	0	0	0	0	0	0
Manatee County	0	0	0	0	0	0	0	0	0	0
Marion County	0	0	0	0	0	0	0	0	0	0
Martin County	0	0	0	0	0	0	0	0	0	0
Miami-Dade County	0	0	0	0	0	0	0	0	0	0
Monroe County	0	0	0	0	0	0	0	0	0	0
Nassau County	0	0	0	0	0	0	0	0	0	0
Okaloosa County	0	0	0	0	0	0	0	0	0	0
Okeechobee County	0	0	0	0	0	0	0	0	0	0
Orange County	0	0	0	0	0	0	0	0	0	0
Osceola County	0	0	0	0	0	0	0	0	0	0
Palm Beach County	0	0	0	0	0	0	0	0	0	0
Pasco County	0	0	0	0	0	0	0	0	0	0
Pinellas County	0	0	0	0	0	0	0	0	0	0
Polk County	0	0	0	0	0	0	0	0	0	0
Putnam County	0	0	0	0	0	0	0	0	0	0
Santa Rosa County	0	0	0	0	0	0	0	0	0	0
Sarasota County	0	0	0	0	0	0	0	0	0	0
Seminole County	0	0	0	0	0	0	0	0	0	0
St. Johns County	0	0	0	0	0	0	0	0	0	0
St. Lucie County	0	0	0	0	0	0	0	0	0	0
Sumter County	0	0	0	0	0	0	0	0	0	0
Suwannee County	0	0	0	0	0	0	0	0	0	0
Taylor County	0	0	0	0	0	0	0	0	0	0
Union County	0	0	0	0	0	0	0	0	0	0
Volusia County	0	0	0	0	0	0	0	0	0	0

Table 11. Offenses Known to Law Enforcement, by Selected State, Tribal, and Other Agencies, 2019—Continued

(Number.)

State/other agency unit/office	Violent crime	Murder and nonnegligent manslaughter	Rape[1]	Robbery	Aggravated assault	Property crime	Burglary	Larceny-theft	Motor vehicle theft	Arson[2]
Wakulla County	0	0	0	0	0	0	0	0	0	0
Walton County	0	0	0	0	0	0	0	0	0	0
Washington County	0	0	0	0	0	0	0	0	0	0
Highway Patrol										
Alachua County	11	0	0	0	11	15	3	6	6	0
Baker County	0	0	0	0	0	0	0	0	0	0
Bay County	0	0	0	0	0	1	0	1	0	0
Bradford County	0	0	0	0	0	0	0	0	0	0
Brevard County	1	0	0	0	1	0	0	0	0	0
Broward County	51	0	0	0	51	27	0	27	0	0
Calhoun County	0	0	0	0	0	0	0	0	0	0
Charlotte County	48	0	0	0	48	3	0	3	0	0
Citrus County	7	0	0	0	7	9	0	0	9	0
Clay County	1	0	0	0	1	0	0	0	0	0
Collier County	14	0	0	0	14	18	0	4	14	0
Columbia County	36	0	0	0	36	2	0	2	0	0
DeSoto County	0	0	0	0	0	0	0	0	0	0
Dixie County	2	0	0	0	2	0	0	0	0	0
Duval County	9	0	0	1	8	27	0	12	15	0
Escambia County	9	0	0	0	9	42	0	24	18	0
Flagler County	0	0	0	0	0	3	0	0	3	0
Franklin County	0	0	0	0	0	0	0	0	0	0
Gadsden County	14	0	0	0	14	3	0	3	0	0
Gilchrist County	3	0	0	0	3	0	0	0	0	0
Glades County	0	0	0	0	0	1	0	1	0	0
Gulf County	0	0	0	0	0	0	0	0	0	0
Hamilton County	0	0	0	0	0	0	0	0	0	0
Hardee County	0	0	0	0	0	3	0	0	3	0
Hendry County	0	0	0	0	0	0	0	0	0	0
Hernando County	3	0	0	0	3	0	0	0	0	0
Highlands County	0	0	0	0	0	0	0	0	0	0
Hillsborough County	31	0	0	0	31	47	2	23	22	1
Holmes County	0	0	0	0	0	3	0	0	3	0
Indian River County	0	0	0	0	0	0	0	0	0	0
Jackson County	9	0	0	0	9	0	0	0	0	0
Jefferson County	0	0	0	0	0	4	0	1	3	0
Lafayette County	0	0	0	0	0	0	0	0	0	0
Lake County	3	0	0	0	3	2	0	2	0	0
Lee County	22	0	0	0	22	17	15	0	2	1
Leon County	0	0	0	0	0	17	8	6	3	0
Levy County	0	0	0	0	0	0	0	0	0	0
Liberty County	0	0	0	0	0	0	0	0	0	0
Madison County	2	0	0	0	2	0	0	0	0	0
Manatee County	12	0	0	0	12	3	0	0	3	0
Marion County	21	0	0	0	21	6	0	3	3	0
Martin County	0	0	0	0	0	3	0	3	0	0
Miami-Dade County	96	0	0	0	96	22	0	11	11	0
Monroe County	0	0	0	0	0	0	0	0	0	0
Nassau County	0	0	0	0	0	0	0	0	0	0
Okaloosa County	22	0	0	0	22	0	0	0	0	0
Okeechobee County	17	0	0	0	17	7	0	0	7	0
Orange County	7	0	0	0	7	16	0	7	9	0
Osceola County	0	0	0	0	0	2	0	2	0	0
Palm Beach County	152	0	0	0	152	18	0	5	13	0
Pasco County	24	0	0	0	24	24	0	21	3	0
Pinellas County	5	0	0	0	5	0	0	0	0	0
Polk County	45	0	0	0	45	1	0	1	0	0
Putnam County	0	0	0	0	0	4	0	4	0	0
Santa Rosa County	24	0	0	0	24	0	0	0	0	0
Sarasota County	3	0	0	0	3	0	0	0	0	0
Seminole County	0	0	0	0	0	1	0	1	0	0
St. Johns County	0	0	0	0	0	0	0	0	0	0
St. Lucie County	1	0	0	0	1	35	0	20	15	0
Sumter County	24	0	0	0	24	0	0	0	0	0
Suwannee County	0	0	0	0	0	0	0	0	0	0
Taylor County	12	0	0	0	12	13	0	1	12	0
Union County	0	0	0	0	0	0	0	0	0	0
Volusia County	0	0	0	0	0	0	0	0	0	0
Wakulla County	1	0	0	0	1	0	0	0	0	0
Walton County	0	0	0	0	0	0	0	0	0	0
Washington County	3	0	0	0	3	0	0	0	0	0
Tribal Agencies										
Miccosukee Tribal	6	0	0	0	6	192	6	184	2	0
Seminole Tribal	73	0	6	27	40	550	24	469	57	0
Other Agencies										
Clay County School Board	0	0	0	0	0	44	2	42	0	0
Duval County Schools	28	0	1	6	21	201	67	130	4	2
Florida School for the Deaf and Blind	0	0	0	0	0	1	0	1	0	0
Fort Lauderdale Airport	10	0	1	0	9	347	9	289	49	0
Jackson County School District	7	0	0	0	7	4	1	3	0	0
Jacksonville Aviation Authority	0	0	0	0	0	66	4	26	36	0
Lee County Port Authority	0	0	0	0	0	40	0	37	3	0
Melbourne International Airport	1	0	0	0	1	10	0	3	7	0

Table 11. Offenses Known to Law Enforcement, by Selected State, Tribal, and Other Agencies, 2019—Continued

(Number.)

State/other agency unit/office	Violent crime	Murder and nonnegligent manslaughter	Rape[1]	Robbery	Aggravated assault	Property crime	Burglary	Larceny-theft	Motor vehicle theft	Arson[2]
Miami-Dade County Public Schools	101	0	18	23	60	151	76	70	5	1
Northwest Florida Beaches International Airport	0	0	0	0	0	8	0	8	0	0
Palm Beach County School District	40	0	5	10	25	320	20	297	3	3
Port Everglades	15	0	7	0	8	43	0	42	1	0
Sarasota County Schools	13	0	0	2	11	20	1	19	0	0
Sarasota-Manatee Airport Authority	0	0	0	0	0	20	0	0	20	0
St. Petersburg-Clearwater International Airport	0	0	0	0	0	1	0	1	0	0
Tampa International Airport	6	0	0	0	6	145	5	108	32	0
Volusia County Beach Safety	10	0	0	2	8	75	0	73	2	0
GEORGIA										
State Agencies[4]										
Georgia Department of Transportation, Office of Investigations	0	0	0	0	0	0	0	0	0	0
Georgia Forestry Commission	0	0	0	0	0	3	1	2	0	45
Georgia Public Safety Training Center	0	0	0	0	0	0	0	0	0	0
Georgia World Congress	2	0	0	0	2	203	1	201	1	0
Ports Authority, Savannah	0	0	0	0	0	8	1	7	0	0
Other Agencies[4]										
Atlanta Public Schools	23	0	16	4	3	198	33	156	9	3
Augusta Board of Education	2	0	2	0	0	48	3	45	0	
Bibb County Board of Education	5	0	0	2	3	43	2	40	1	0
Cherokee County Board of Education	9	0	3	0	6	67	0	67	0	1
Cherokee County Marshal	0	0	0	0	0	0	0	0	0	0
Fulton County Marshal	4	0	0	0	4	30	0	15	15	0
Fulton County School System	9	0	2	4	3	111	12	95	4	1
Glynn County School System	4	0	0	1	3	18	0	18	0	0
Gwinnett County Public Schools	39	0	24	3	12	151	4	145	2	5
Hall County Marshal	0	0	0	0	0	0	0	0	0	0
Stone Mountain Park	0	0	0	0	0	22	5	15	2	0
IDAHO										
State Agencies										
Idaho State Police	38	9	5	0	24	10	2	3	5	0
Tribal Agencies										
Coeur d'Alene Tribal	8	0	1	3	4	68	16	45	7	0
Fort Hall Tribal	56	0	8	0	48	177	17	137	23	5
Kootenai Tribal	1	0	0	0	1	0	0	0	0	0
ILLINOIS										
State Agencies										
Illinois Department of Natural Resources	186	21	74	10	81	67	21	33	13	2
Secretary of State Police	2	0	1	0	1	15	2	12	1	340
Other Agencies										
Alton & Southern Railway	0	0	0	0	0	3	1	2	0	1
Belt Railway	0	0	0	0	0	0	0	0	0	0
Canton Park District	0	0	0	0	0	0	0	0	0	0
Capitol Airport Authority	0	0	0	0	0	0	0	0	0	0
Cook County Forest Preserve	14	1	5	2	6	88	3	85	0	1
Crystal Lake Park District	1	0	0	0	1	6	5	1	0	0
Decatur Park District	6	0	0	3	3	13	3	9	1	1
Fox Valley Park District	2	0	1	1	0	14	0	14	0	1
Indiana Harbor Belt Railroad	0	0	0	0	0	4	2	2	0	0
Kane County Forest Preserve	0	0	0	0	0	7	1	6	0	0
Lake County Forest Preserve	2	0	0	1	1	14	1	13	0	0
McHenry County Conservation District	1	0	0	0	1	0	0	0	0	0
Pekin Park District	1	0	0	0	1	6	0	6	0	0
Rockford Park District	16	1	1	2	12	55	26	29	0	0
Springfield Park District	28	0	2	3	23	31	18	9	4	0
Terminal Railroad Association	0	0	0	0	0	0	0	0	0	0
Tri-County Drug Enforcement Narcotics Team	0	0	0	0	0	1	0	1	0	0
Union Pacific Railroad, Cook County	0	0	0	0	0	1,434	264	1,170	0	0
Will County Forest Preserve	2	0	0	0	2	17	3	14	0	0
Zion Park District	0	0	0	0	0	1	0	1	0	0
INDIANA										
State Agencies										
Indiana State Excise Police	1	0	0	0	1	6	0	6	0	0
Northern Indiana Commuter Transportation District	0	0	0	0	0	20	0	16	4	0
State Police										
Adams County	0	0	0	0	0	1	0	1	0	0
Allen County	5	0	1	0	4	19	0	15	4	0
Bartholomew County	2	0	0	0	2	5	2	1	2	0
Cass County	3	0	2	0	1	10	1	8	1	0
Clark County	11	0	2	0	9	32	3	22	7	0
Clay County	6	0	3	0	3	4	0	3	1	0
Clinton County	2	0	0	0	2	5	1	1	3	0
Crawford County	13	0	2	1	10	11	1	9	1	0
Daviess County	1	0	0	0	1	13	2	10	1	0

Table 11. Offenses Known to Law Enforcement, by Selected State, Tribal, and Other Agencies, 2019—Continued

(Number.)

State/other agency unit/office	Violent crime	Murder and nonnegligent manslaughter	Rape[1]	Robbery	Aggravated assault	Property crime	Burglary	Larceny-theft	Motor vehicle theft	Arson[2]
Dearborn County	7	0	5	0	2	5	0	5	0	0
Decatur County	3	0	0	0	3	3	1	2	0	0
DeKalb County	6	0	6	0	0	12	5	2	5	0
Delaware County	2	0	0	0	2	3	0	2	1	0
Dubois County	7	1	1	0	5	19	3	13	3	0
Elkhart County	1	0	0	0	1	18	0	13	5	0
Floyd County	6	0	2	0	4	19	1	7	11	0
Fountain County	7	0	0	1	6	3	2	1	0	0
Franklin County	2	0	0	0	2	6	0	6	0	0
Fulton County	1	0	1	0	0	4	2	0	2	1
Gibson County	17	0	3	0	14	8	0	6	2	0
Grant County	4	1	0	0	3	4	0	3	1	0
Greene County	6	0	0	0	6	15	2	10	3	0
Hamilton County	2	0	1	0	1	4	0	3	1	0
Hancock County	0	0	0	0	0	6	0	4	2	0
Harrison County	7	0	1	0	6	13	0	10	3	0
Hendricks County	1	0	0	0	1	27	0	12	15	0
Henry County	12	0	0	0	12	8	1	7	0	0
Howard County	7	0	3	1	3	6	1	5	0	0
Huntington County	1	0	0	1	0	4	0	4	0	0
Jackson County	10	0	2	1	7	13	2	7	4	0
Jasper County	2	0	0	0	2	4	1	2	1	0
Jefferson County	12	0	0	0	12	12	3	9	0	0
Knox County	2	0	1	0	1	12	1	9	2	0
Kosciusko County	4	0	1	0	3	8	1	6	1	0
LaGrange County	2	0	0	0	2	11	1	9	1	0
Lake County	18	0	1	1	16	59	1	25	33	0
La Porte County	9	1	0	2	6	14	1	11	2	0
Lawrence County	6	0	0	0	6	10	3	5	2	0
Madison County	14	1	0	0	13	10	2	5	3	0
Marion County	42	1	10	4	27	286	4	135	147	0
Marshall County	3	0	2	0	1	10	2	5	3	1
Martin County	9	0	3	0	6	4	0	4	0	0
Miami County	20	1	3	0	16	27	5	18	4	0
Monroe County	4	1	1	0	2	29	3	18	8	0
Montgomery County	7	0	0	1	6	5	1	4	0	0
Morgan County	3	0	3	0	0	24	0	5	19	0
Noble County	1	0	0	0	1	8	1	5	2	0
Orange County	7	0	5	0	2	12	1	11	0	0
Perry County	2	0	0	0	2	5	0	3	2	1
Pike County	5	0	0	0	5	6	2	4	0	0
Porter County	5	0	1	0	4	27	0	23	4	0
Posey County	13	0	1	0	12	5	1	4	0	0
Putnam County	7	0	5	0	2	6	0	4	2	0
Ripley County	14	0	2	0	12	24	7	12	5	1
Rush County	0	0	0	0	0	3	2	1	0	1
Scott County	10	1	5	1	3	10	0	7	3	0
Spencer County	6	1	2	0	3	15	2	10	3	0
Steuben County	5	0	0	0	5	13	1	9	3	2
St. Joseph County	3	0	0	0	3	14	1	8	5	0
Sullivan County	11	0	5	1	5	8	2	5	1	0
Tippecanoe County	10	1	4	0	5	29	1	22	6	0
Vanderburgh County	6	0	1	0	5	13	1	11	1	0
Vigo County	13	0	1	0	12	31	6	18	7	0
Wabash County	2	0	0	1	1	2	0	2	0	0
Warren County	0	0	0	0	0	3	2	0	1	0
Warrick County	1	0	0	0	1	4	1	2	1	0
Washington County	8	0	2	0	6	12	4	7	1	0
Wayne County	3	0	0	0	3	4	0	4	0	0
White County	0	0	0	0	0	6	0	6	0	1
Whitley County	4	0	3	0	1	7	0	5	2	0
KANSAS										
State Agencies										
Highway Patrol										
Capitol	0	0	0	0	0	17	3	14	0	0
Troop A	29	0	0	0	29	6	1	4	1	0
Troop B	10	1	0	0	9	4	1	1	2	0
Troop C	4	0	0	0	4	2	0	0	2	0
Troop D	2	0	0	0	2	2	0	0	2	0
Troop E	3	0	0	0	3	1	0	0	1	0
Troop F	9	0	0	0	9	5	0	2	3	0
Troop G	7	1	0	0	6	25	1	14	10	0
Troop H	17	1	0	0	16	1	0	1	0	0
Troop N	0	0	0	0	0	1	0	0	1	0
Troop S	0	0	0	0	0	1	0	0	1	0
Kansas Alcoholic Beverage Control	0	0	0	0	0	0	0	0	0	0
Kansas Bureau of Investigation	18	2	4	1	11	2	0	2	0	0
Kansas Department of Wildlife and Parks	1	0	0	0	1	12	2	10	0	0
Securities Office, Investigation Section	0	0	0	0	0	0	0	0	0	0
Tribal Agencies										
Iowa Tribal	0	0	0	0	0	2	1	0	1	0
Kickapoo Tribal	3	0	0	1	2	9	5	1	3	0

Table 11. Offenses Known to Law Enforcement, by Selected State, Tribal, and Other Agencies, 2019—Continued

(Number.)

State/other agency unit/office	Violent crime	Murder and nonnegligent manslaughter	Rape[1]	Robbery	Aggravated assault	Property crime	Burglary	Larceny-theft	Motor vehicle theft	Arson[2]
Potawatomi Tribal	4	0	0	1	3	21	5	14	2	0
Sac and Fox Tribal	3	0	1	0	2	16	2	13	1	0
Other Agencies										
El Dorado School District	0	0	0	0	0	0	0	0	0	0
Johnson County Park	0	0	0	0	0	36	2	33	1	0
Unified School District, Kansas City	1	0	0	0	1	16	2	14	0	0
KENTUCKY										
State Agencies										
Alcohol Beverage Control										
Enforcement Division	0	0	0	0	0	0	0	0	0	0
Investigative Division	0	0	0	0	0	0	0	0	0	0
Department of Agriculture Animal Health										
Enforcement Division	0	0	0	0	0	1	0	1	0	0
Fish and Wildlife Enforcement	1	0	0	0	1	10	1	7	2	0
Kentucky Horse Park	0	0	0	0	0	23	2	21	0	0
Motor Vehicle Enforcement	0	0	0	0	0	9	1	6	2	0
Park Security	0	0	0	0	0	16	1	13	2	0
State Police										
Ashland	32	0	23	0	9	168	40	96	32	2
Bowling Green	39	2	16	0	21	92	30	41	21	2
Campbellsburg	43	3	23	1	16	172	54	92	26	2
Cannabis Suppression Section	0	0	0	0	0	0	0	0	0	0
Columbia	59	4	32	0	23	108	43	56	9	2
Drug Enforcement Area[2]	0	0	0	0	0	4	0	3	1	0
Dry Ridge	36	0	27	1	8	75	19	47	9	1
Electronic Crimes	1	0	1	0	0	0	0	0	0	0
Elizabethtown	49	1	19	2	27	116	30	55	31	1
Frankfort	27	4	7	0	16	84	20	49	15	3
Harlan	56	2	26	4	24	197	76	74	47	2
Hazard	42	1	10	6	25	189	83	62	44	3
Headquarters	0	0	0	0	0	0	0	0	0	0
Henderson	25	0	11	1	13	79	26	42	11	0
London	63	8	35	2	18	228	72	97	59	7
Madisonville	31	3	18	0	10	64	18	30	16	3
Mayfield	38	0	21	3	14	128	37	67	24	0
Morehead[5]			38	1	23	156	64	75	17	4
Pikeville	94	3	32	12	47	344	134	114	96	6
Richmond	39	1	17	0	21	119	40	51	28	9
Special Operations	0	0	0	0	0	0	0	0	0	0
Vehicle Investigations	0	0	0	0	0	3	0	3	0	0
West Drug Enforcement Branch	0	0	0	0	0	3	1	1	1	0
Unlawful Narcotics Investigation										
Treatment and Education	0	0	0	0	0	0	0	0	0	0
Other Agencies										
Barren County Drug Task Force	0	0	0	0	0	0	0	0	0	0
Bluegrass Narcotics Task Force	0	0	0	0	0	4	1	3	0	0
Cincinnati-Northern Kentucky										
International Airport	0	0	0	0	0	60	0	44	16	0
Clark County School System	2	0	0	0	2	6	0	6	0	0
Fayette County Schools	18	0	1	0	17	119	11	107	1	0
FIVCO Area Drug Task Force	0	0	0	0	0	1	0	1	0	0
Gateway Area Drug Task Force	0	0	0	0	0	0	0	0	0	0
Greater Hardin County Narcotics Task										
Force	1	0	0	0	1	1	1	0	0	0
Jefferson County School District	21	0	0	2	19	92	33	58	1	0
Lake Cumberland Area Drug Enforcement										
Task Force	0	0	0	0	0	0	0	0	0	0
Lexington Bluegrass Airport	0	0	0	0	0	23	0	8	15	0
Louisville Fire Department Arson Division	0	0	0	0	0	0	0	0	0	122
Louisville Regional Airport Authority	1	0	0	1	0	66	1	10	55	0
McCracken County Public Schools	0	0	0	0	0	3	0	3	0	0
Montgomery County School District	0	0	0	0	0	1	0	1	0	0
Northern Kentucky Drug Strike Force	0	0	0	0	0	0	0	0	0	0
Pennyrile Narcotics Task Force	0	0	0	0	0	2	0	2	0	0
Pulaski County Constable District[4]	0	0	0	0	0	0	0	0	0	0
South Central Kentucky Drug Task Force	2	0	1	0	1	1	0	1	0	0
LOUISIANA										
State Agencies										
Tensas Basin Levee District	0	0	0	0	0	0	0	0	0	0
MAINE										
State Agencies										
Bureau of Capitol Police	0	0	0	0	0	2	0	2	0	0
Drug Enforcement Agency[4]	0	0	0	0	0	0	0	0	0	0
State Fire Marshal[4]	3	0	0	0	3	5	4	0	1	89
State Police[4]	164	7	79	9	69	834	212	529	93	1
Tribal Agencies										
Passamaquoddy Indian Township	7	0	0	0	7	11	8	1	2	1
Passamaquoddy Pleasant Point Tribal	1	0	0	0	1	7	7	0	0	0
Penobscot Nation	0	0	0	0	0	3	0	3	0	0

Table 11. Offenses Known to Law Enforcement, by Selected State, Tribal, and Other Agencies, 2019—Continued

(Number.)

State/other agency unit/office	Violent crime	Murder and nonnegligent manslaughter	Rape[1]	Robbery	Aggravated assault	Property crime	Burglary	Larceny-theft	Motor vehicle theft	Arson[2]
MARYLAND										
State Agencies										
Comptroller of the Treasury Field Enforcement Division	0	0	0	0	0	0	0	0	0	0
Department of Public Safety and Correctional Services, Internal Investigation Division	481	0	0	0	481	0	0	0	0	0
General Services										
Annapolis, Anne Arundel County	0	0	0	0	0	2	0	2	0	0
Baltimore City	2	0	0	1	1	21	1	18	2	0
Maryland State Police Statewide	6	0	1	2	3	13	5	7	1	0
Natural Resources Police	4	0	2	0	2	103	8	93	2	13
Springfield Hospital	0	0	0	0	0	1	0	1	0	0
State Fire Marshal	1	0	0	0	1	2	0	0	2	
State Police										
Allegany County	16	0	4	3	9	299	54	229	16	9
Baltimore City	0	0	0	0	0	0	0	0	0	0
Baltimore County	3	1	0	0	2	38	2	30	6	0
Calvert County	22	0	0	1	21	80	13	60	7	4
Caroline County	1	0	0	0	1	3	1	2	0	0
Carroll County	19	1	2	7	9	174	24	138	12	3
Cecil County	54	0	4	4	46	461	97	311	53	9
Charles County	3	0	0	0	3	4	0	4	0	0
Dorchester County	0	0	0	0	0	0	0	0	0	
Frederick County	47	1	3	5	38	135	37	88	10	0
Garrett County	17	0	7	0	10	80	25	53	2	2
Harford County	42	0	3	5	34	159	2	146	11	4
Howard County	5	0	0	0	5	11	0	10	1	0
Kent County	1	0	0	0	1	9	4	5	0	4
Montgomery County	2	0	0	0	2	4	0	3	1	0
Prince George's County	4	0	0	0	4	26	0	11	15	0
Queen Anne's County	23	0	3	1	19	76	12	53	11	4
Somerset County	27	0	1	4	22	76	34	40	2	4
St. Mary's County	23	0	4	7	12	184	24	154	6	5
Talbot County	1	0	0	0	1	1	0	1	0	0
Washington County	24	0	2	5	17	187	23	154	10	8
Wicomico County	52	1	7	6	38	148	39	87	22	3
Worcester County	5	0	1	1	3	80	15	57	8	0
Transit Administraion	58	0	0	28	30	97	0	95	2	0
Transportation Authority	8	0	1	1	6	148	0	123	25	0
Other Agencies										
Maryland-National Capital Park Police										
Montgomery County	25	0	2	15	8	114	4	110	0	0
Prince George's County	60	3	4	34	19	143	10	129	4	3
MASSACHUSETTS										
State Agencies										
Division of Law Enforcement, Environmental Police	5	0	0	0	5	20	7	9	4	0
Massachusetts Bay Transportation Authority										
Bristol County	0	0	0	0	0	3	0	3	0	
Essex County	1	1	0	0	0	15	0	15	0	
Middlesex County	34	0	0	8	26	181	2	177	2	
Norfolk County	12	0	0	5	7	73	0	70	3	
Plymouth County	0	0	0	0	0	13	0	12	1	
Suffolk County	217	2	1	87	127	241	7	231	3	
Worcester County	0	0	0	0	0	2	0	2	0	
State Police										
Berkshire County	1	0	0	0	1	32	9	20	3	
Bristol County	1	0	0	0	1	0	0	0	0	
Franklin County	4	0	0	0	4	0	0	0	0	
Hampden County	15	0	0	0	15	11	0	2	9	
Hampshire County	5	0	0	0	5	1	0	1	0	
Middlesex County	0	0	0	0	0	0	0	0	0	
Norfolk County	1	0	0	0	1	0	0	0	0	
Suffolk County	5	0	0	0	5	29	2	15	12	
Worcester County	12	0	0	0	12	1	0	1	0	
Tribal Agencies										
Wampanoag Tribe of Gay Head	0	0	0	0	0	0	0	0	0	0
Other Agencies										
Massachusetts General Hospital	97	0	0	1	96	135	0	135	0	
MICHIGAN										
State Agencies										
State Police										
Alcona County	4	0	0	0	4	3	0	3	0	0
Alger County	11	0	5	0	6	24	9	13	2	0
Allegan County	82	0	32	0	50	243	62	156	25	2
Alpena County	23	0	14	0	9	106	16	83	7	1
Antrim County	15	0	10	0	5	12	2	9	1	0
Arenac County	9	0	5	0	4	4	1	2	1	0
Baraga County	14	0	4	0	10	13	7	4	2	1

Table 11. Offenses Known to Law Enforcement, by Selected State, Tribal, and Other Agencies, 2019—Continued

(Number.)

State/other agency unit/office	Violent crime	Murder and nonnegligent manslaughter	Rape[1]	Robbery	Aggravated assault	Property crime	Burglary	Larceny-theft	Motor vehicle theft	Arson[2]
Barry County	34	0	12	0	22	117	26	83	8	1
Bay County	38	0	19	1	18	97	30	51	16	1
Benzie County	7	0	4	0	3	10	1	8	1	0
Berrien County	50	0	24	4	22	137	43	83	11	1
Branch County	51	0	20	1	30	115	45	43	27	2
Calhoun County[5]	36	0	9	2	25			62	17	3
Cass County	13	0	8	0	5	15	6	8	1	0
Charlevoix County	7	0	4	0	3	5	1	4	0	0
Cheboygan County	8	0	7	0	1	14	6	6	2	1
Chippewa County	39	0	11	0	28	35	17	17	1	1
Clare County	13	0	9	0	4	35	12	20	3	1
Clinton County	11	0	7	0	4	11	2	7	2	0
Crawford County	11	0	6	0	5	8	5	2	1	0
Delta County	23	0	9	0	14	46	10	34	2	0
Dickinson County	7	1	4	0	2	20	6	14	0	0
Eaton County[5]	45	0	15	2	28			47	7	0
Emmet County	12	0	7	0	5	47	9	34	4	1
Genesee County	67	0	24	6	37	83	27	34	22	7
Gladwin County	29	1	21	0	7	20	5	13	2	0
Gogebic County	15	0	4	0	11	19	4	14	1	1
Grand Traverse County	47	0	35	1	11	48	11	33	4	0
Gratiot County	11	2	5	0	4	3	0	2	1	0
Hillsdale County	68	0	26	0	42	131	46	66	19	0
Houghton County	16	0	7	0	9	79	25	44	10	0
Ingham County	16	0	11	0	5	46	21	24	1	1
Ionia County	73	0	27	1	45	104	30	62	12	1
Iosco County	29	0	14	0	15	95	49	36	10	1
Iron County	16	0	7	0	9	14	4	6	4	0
Isabella County	52	0	38	0	14	122	38	75	9	1
Jackson County	85	0	46	0	39	106	38	55	13	2
Kalamazoo County	28	0	9	2	17	43	9	28	6	0
Kalkaska County	22	0	21	0	1	25	4	17	4	1
Kent County	21	0	13	0	8	27	2	23	2	0
Lake County	9	0	3	0	6	20	11	7	2	1
Lapeer County	22	0	11	0	11	39	20	14	5	0
Lenawee County	55	1	30	0	24	56	21	30	5	3
Livingston County	60	0	30	0	30	147	36	106	5	0
Luce County	13	0	10	0	3	11	6	2	3	0
Mackinac County	8	0	5	0	3	23	4	18	1	0
Macomb County	44	1	13	0	30	32	9	19	4	0
Manistee County	24	2	16	0	6	40	15	23	2	0
Marquette County	77	0	19	1	57	103	20	66	17	0
Mason County	29	1	9	0	19	43	9	33	1	0
Mecosta County	20	0	13	0	7	66	16	47	3	0
Menominee County	7	1	2	0	4	15	3	9	3	0
Midland County	15	0	13	0	2	7	2	4	1	0
Missaukee County	4	0	1	0	3	10	2	3	5	0
Monroe County	60	0	12	2	46	114	32	69	13	0
Montcalm County[5]	161	2	72	3	84			152	56	2
Montmorency County	5	0	5	0	0	7	2	4	1	0
Muskegon County[5]	69	2	28	0	39			126	13	3
Newaygo County	66	1	27	0	38	147	55	77	15	1
Oakland County	79	0	22	4	53	141	37	82	22	0
Oceana County	51	0	13	0	38	78	26	45	7	1
Ogemaw County	47	1	14	1	31	54	21	31	2	1
Ontonagon County	9	0	3	0	6	14	5	8	1	0
Osceola County	16	0	6	0	10	18	9	7	2	0
Oscoda County	5	0	5	0	0	7	3	3	1	0
Otsego County	33	0	16	0	17	54	14	31	9	1
Ottawa County	6	0	6	0	0	3	0	3	0	1
Presque Isle County	4	0	2	0	2	2	0	2	0	0
Roscommon County	14	0	9	0	5	47	11	31	5	1
Saginaw County	98	2	30	0	66	94	19	58	17	5
Sanilac County	31	0	25	0	6	30	12	18	0	0
Schoolcraft County	14	3	7	0	4	36	11	22	3	2
Shiawassee County	51	0	26	2	23	121	29	86	6	0
St. Clair County	21	1	7	1	12	36	10	23	3	0
St. Joseph County	49	1	18	0	30	149	62	66	21	1
Tuscola County	48	0	28	0	20	77	29	44	4	1
Van Buren County	69	0	36	0	33	143	57	65	21	2
Washtenaw County	91	0	35	1	55	148	59	74	15	2
Wayne County	104	3	30	3	68	116	2	98	16	1
Wexford County	40	1	19	1	19	101	24	70	7	1
Tribal Agencies										
Grand Traverse Tribal	1	0	0	1	0	20	0	19	1	0
Gun Lake Tribal	0	0	0	0	0	181	0	179	2	0
Hannahville Tribal	18	1	5	1	11	29	3	22	4	0
Lac Vieux Desert Tribal	2	0	0	0	2	0	0	0	0	0
Little River Band of Ottawa Indians	2	0	2	0	0	40	1	38	1	0
Nottawaseppi Huron Band of Potawatomi	3	0	0	3	0	138	2	131	5	1
Pokagon Tribal	0	0	0	0	0	164	0	162	2	0
Saginaw Chippewa Tribal	31	0	21	0	10	125	13	105	7	0

Table 11. Offenses Known to Law Enforcement, by Selected State, Tribal, and Other Agencies, 2019—Continued

(Number.)

State/other agency unit/office	Violent crime	Murder and nonnegligent manslaughter	Rape[1]	Robbery	Aggravated assault	Property crime	Burglary	Larceny-theft	Motor vehicle theft	Arson[2]
Other Agencies										
Bishop International Airport	0	0	0	0	0	10	0	3	7	0
Capitol Region Airport Authority	0	0	0	0	0	1	0	0	1	0
Genesee County Parks and Recreation	0	0	0	0	0	7	0	5	2	0
Gerald R. Ford International Airport	0	0	0	0	0	0	0	0	0	0
Huron-Clinton Metropolitan Authority										
Hudson Mills Metropark	0	0	0	0	0	0	0	0	0	0
Kensington Metropark	2	0	0	0	2	3	0	3	0	0
Lower Huron Metropark	1	0	0	0	1	6	0	6	0	1
Stony Creek Metropark	3	0	0	0	3	14	2	12	0	0
Wayne County Airport	1	0	0	0	1	242	0	171	71	0
MINNESOTA										
State Agencies										
Bureau of Criminal Apprehension	0	0	0	0	0	0	0	0	0	0
Capitol Security, St. Paul[4]	1	0	0	0	1	23	0	23	0	0
Department of Natural Resources										
Enforcement Division	0	0	0	0	0	0	0	0	0	0
Minnesota State Patrol[4]	0	0	0	0	0	0	0	0	0	0
State Patrol										
Brainerd[4]	0	0	0	0	0	0	0	0	0	0
Detroit Lakes[4]	0	0	0	0	0	0	0	0	0	0
Duluth[4]	0	0	0	0	0	0	0	0	0	0
Golden Valley[4]	0	0	0	0	0	0	0	0	0	0
Mankato[4]	0	0	0	0	0	0	0	0	0	0
Marshall[4]	0	0	0	0	0	0	0	0	0	0
Oakdale[4]	0	0	0	0	0	0	0	0	0	0
Rochester[4]	0	0	0	0	0	0	0	0	0	0
St. Cloud[4]	0	0	0	0	0	0	0	0	0	0
Thief River Falls[4]	0	0	0	0	0	0	0	0	0	0
Virginia[4]	0	0	0	0	0	0	0	0	0	0
Tribal Agencies										
Fond du Lac Tribal	19	0	3	0	16	120	13	88	19	2
Mille Lacs Tribal	39	0	4	7	28	180	27	140	13	0
Nett Lake Tribal	6	0	0	0	6	3	0	2	1	0
Upper Sioux Community	1	0	0	0	1	23	0	19	4	0
White Earth Tribal	33	0	2	2	29	170	32	109	29	1
Other Agencies										
Metropolitan Transit Commission	355	0	2	210	143	624	1	614	9	7
Minneapolis-St. Paul International Airport	7	0	0	0	7	301	1	265	35	0
Three Rivers Park District	0	0	0	0	0	79	0	79	0	0
MISSISSIPPI										
Tribal Agencies										
Choctaw Tribal	165	2	5	0	158	178	17	161	0	2
MISSOURI										
State Agencies										
Capitol Police	0	0	0	0	0	21	0	20	1	0
Department of Conservation	0	0	0	0	0	0	0	0	0	0
Missouri State Highway Patrol	113	6	2	1	104	200	10	137	53	3
Other Agencies										
Clay County Park Authority	2	0	0	0	2	11	0	11	0	0
Jackson County Park Rangers	0	0	0	0	0	0	0	0	0	0
Kansas City International Airport	2	0	0	0	2	113	4	38	71	0
Logan-Rogersville School District	2	0	0	0	2	4	0	4	0	0
Springfield-Branson Airport	0	0	0	0	0	16	0	10	6	0
Springfield-Greene County Park Rangers	1	0	0	0	1	14	3	11	0	0
Terminal Railroad	0	0	0	0	0	1	0	1	0	0
MONTANA										
Tribal Agencies										
Blackfeet Agency	332	0	16	0	316	125	28	47	50	2
Crow Agency	59	0	13	0	46	203	39	96	68	0
Fort Belknap Tribal	25	0	2	0	23	32	11	15	6	0
Fort Peck Assiniboine and Sioux Tribes	89	1	1	3	84	58	34	0	24	2
Northern Cheyenne Agency	79	0	11	0	68	99	24	50	25	0
Rocky Boy's Tribal	58	2	10	0	46	91	34	30	27	3
NEBRASKA										
State Agencies										
Nebraska State Patrol	7	1	0	0	6	4	1	3	0	
State Police										
Adams County	1	0	0	0	1	0	0	0	0	
Antelope County	0	0	0	0	0	1	0	1	0	
Arthur County	0	0	0	0	0	0	0	0	0	
Banner County	0	0	0	0	0	0	0	0	0	
Blaine County	0	0	0	0	0	0	0	0	0	
Boone County	0	0	0	0	0	0	0	0	0	
Box Butte County	0	0	0	0	0	1	0	1	0	
Boyd County	0	0	0	0	0	0	0	0	0	
Brown County	0	0	0	0	0	0	0	0	0	
Buffalo County	0	0	0	0	0	1	0	0	1	

Table 11. Offenses Known to Law Enforcement, by Selected State, Tribal, and Other Agencies, 2019—Continued

(Number.)

State/other agency unit/office	Violent crime	Murder and nonnegligent manslaughter	Rape[1]	Robbery	Aggravated assault	Property crime	Burglary	Larceny-theft	Motor vehicle theft	Arson[2]
Burt County	0	0	0	0	0	0	0	0	0	
Butler County	0	0	0	0	0	1	0	0	1	
Cass County	0	0	0	0	0	1	0	1	0	
Cedar County	0	0	0	0	0	0	0	0	0	
Chase County	0	0	0	0	0	1	0	0	1	
Cherry County	0	0	0	0	0	1	0	0	1	
Cheyenne County	0	0	0	0	0	1	0	1	0	
Clay County	0	0	0	0	0	0	0	0	0	
Colfax County	0	0	0	0	0	0	0	0	0	
Cuming County	0	0	0	0	0	0	0	0	0	
Custer County	0	0	0	0	0	1	0	0	1	
Dawes County	0	0	0	0	0	0	0	0	0	
Deuel County	0	0	0	0	0	0	0	0	0	
Dixon County	0	0	0	0	0	0	0	0	0	
Dodge County	0	0	0	0	0	0	0	0	0	
Douglas County	1	0	1	0	0	9	1	5	3	
Dundy County	0	0	0	0	0	0	0	0	0	
Fillmore County	0	0	0	0	0	0	0	0	0	
Franklin County	1	0	0	0	1	0	0	0	0	
Frontier County	0	0	0	0	0	0	0	0	0	
Furnas County	0	0	0	0	0	0	0	0	0	
Gage County	0	0	0	0	0	0	0	0	0	
Garden County	0	0	0	0	0	0	0	0	0	
Garfield County	0	0	0	0	0	0	0	0	0	
Gosper County	0	0	0	0	0	0	0	0	0	
Grant County	0	0	0	0	0	0	0	0	0	
Greeley County	0	0	0	0	0	0	0	0	0	
Hall County	3	0	1	0	2	2	0	1	2	
Hamilton County	0	0	0	0	0	1	0	0	0	
Harlan County	0	0	0	0	0	0	0	0	0	
Hayes County	1	0	0	0	1	2	0	1	1	
Hitchcock County	0	0	0	0	0	1	0	1	0	
Holt County	0	0	0	0	0	0	0	0	0	
Hooker County	0	0	0	0	0	1	1	0	0	
Howard County	0	0	0	0	0	0	0	0	0	
Jefferson County	0	0	0	0	0	0	0	0	0	
Kearney County	1	0	0	0	1	0	0	0	0	
Keya Paha County	0	0	0	0	0	1	0	1	0	
Kimball County	0	0	0	0	0	0	0	0	0	
Knox County	0	0	0	0	0	0	0	0	0	
Lincoln County	2	0	0	0	2	0	0	0	0	
Logan County	0	0	0	0	0	0	0	0	0	
Loup County	1	0	1	0	0	0	0	0	2	
Madison County	1	0	0	0	1	2	0	0	0	
McPherson County	0	0	0	0	0	0	0	0	0	
Merrick County	0	0	0	0	0	0	0	0	0	
Morrill County	1	0	0	1	0	0	0	0	0	
Nance County	0	0	0	0	0	0	0	0	0	
Nemaha County	0	0	0	0	0	0	0	0	0	
Nuckolls County	0	0	0	0	0	0	0	0	0	
Otoe County	1	1	0	0	0	0	0	0	0	
Pawnee County	0	0	0	0	0	0	0	0	0	
Perkins County	0	0	0	0	0	0	0	0	0	
Phelps County	0	0	0	0	0	1	0	1	0	
Pierce County	0	0	0	0	0	0	0	0	0	
Platte County	0	0	0	0	0	0	0	0	0	
Polk County	0	0	0	0	0	0	0	0	0	
Richardson County	0	0	0	0	0	0	0	0	0	
Rock County	0	0	0	0	0	0	0	0	0	
Saline County	0	0	0	0	0	0	0	0	0	
Sarpy County	0	0	0	0	0	0	0	0	0	
Saunders County	0	0	0	0	0	0	0	0	0	
Scotts Bluff County	2	0	0	0	2	0	0	0	0	
Seward County	0	0	0	0	0	0	0	0	0	
Sherman County	0	0	0	0	0	0	0	0	0	
Sioux County	0	0	0	0	0	0	0	0	0	
Thayer County	0	0	0	0	0	0	0	0	0	
Thomas County	0	0	0	0	0	1	0	0	1	
Thurston County	0	0	0	0	0	0	0	0	0	
Valley County	0	0	0	0	0	1	0	0	1	
Washington County	0	0	0	0	0	1	0	0	0	
Wayne County	0	0	0	0	0	0	0	0	0	
Webster County	0	0	0	0	0	0	0	0	0	
Wheeler County	0	0	0	0	0	1	0	0	1	
York County	1	0	0	1	0	1	0	0	0	
NEVADA										
State Agencies										
Capitol Police	14	0	1	0	13	64	22	26	16	
Department of Public Safety, Investigative Division	0	0	0	0	0	0	0	0	0	0
Department of Wildlife, Law Enforcement Division	0	0	0	0	0	0	0	0	0	0

Table 11. Offenses Known to Law Enforcement, by Selected State, Tribal, and Other Agencies, 2019—Continued
(Number.)

State/other agency unit/office	Violent crime	Murder and nonnegligent manslaughter	Rape[1]	Robbery	Aggravated assault	Property crime	Burglary	Larceny-theft	Motor vehicle theft	Arson[2]
Highway Patrol										
Northwestern Division	2	0	0	0	2	1	0	1	0	0
Southern Division	2	0	0	0	2	0	0	0	0	0
Secretary of State Securities Division, Enforcement Section	0	0	0	0	0	0	0	0	0	0
State Fire Marshal	0	0	0	0	0	0	0	0	0	6
Tribal Agencies										
Ely Shoshone Tribal	2	1	0	0	1	1	1	0	0	0
Fallon Tribal	4	0	0	0	4	9	6	1	2	0
Lovelock Paiute Tribal	2	0	0	0	2	0	0	0	0	0
Reno-Sparks Indian Colony	6	0	2	1	3	123	8	111	4	
Walker River Tribal	0	0	0	0	0	5	1	1	3	0
Western Shoshone Tribal	1	0	0	0	1	0	0	0	0	0
Other Agencies										
Clark County School District	314	0	0	31	283	728	141	567	20	5
Las Vegas Fire and Rescue, Arson Bomb Unit	0	0	0	0	0	0	0	0	0	48
Reno Municipal Court Marshal[4]	0	0	0	0	0	0	0	0	0	0
Reno Tahoe Airport Authority	0	0	0	0	0	41	2	29	10	
NEW HAMPSHIRE										
State Agencies										
Liquor Commission	1	0	0	1	0	50	0	50	0	0
State Police										
Belknap County	0	0	0	0	0	2	0	1	1	0
Carroll County	0	0	0	0	0	7	0	2	5	0
Cheshire County	6	0	3	1	2	16	8	5	3	0
Coos County	6	0	2	0	4	39	7	28	4	0
Grafton County	3	0	2	1	0	32	11	19	2	0
Hillsborough County	2	0	0	0	2	3	0	2	1	0
Merrimack County	6	0	1	1	4	21	3	14	4	1
Rockingham County	2	1	0	1	1	2	0	1	1	0
Strafford County	0	0	0	0	0	2	1	1	0	0
Sullivan County	4	0	1	0	3	15	7	5	3	0
NEW JERSEY										
State Agencies										
Department of Corrections	80	3	0	0	77	0	0	0	0	0
Department of Human Services	45	0	2	0	43	24	1	23	0	2
Division of Fish and Wildlife	0	0	0	0	0	7	1	6	0	0
New Jersey Transit Police	16	0	0	3	13	295	0	289	6	4
Palisades Interstate Parkway	1	0	0	0	1	1	0	1	0	0
Port Authority of New York and New Jersey	51	0	0	14	37	612	9	578	25	0
State Park Police	5	0	0	0	5	18	3	13	2	0
State Police										
Atlantic County	19	1	2	7	9	672	31	630	11	0
Bergen County	9	0	0	1	8	59	6	47	6	0
Burlington County	20	0	3	2	15	254	47	195	12	2
Camden County	9	0	1	0	8	18	0	13	5	0
Cape May County	14	0	3	3	8	139	38	91	10	1
Cumberland County	67	2	9	16	40	405	132	253	20	9
Essex County	5	0	0	0	5	13	3	6	4	0
Gloucester County	6	0	0	1	5	7	1	4	2	0
Hudson County	2	0	0	0	2	5	0	3	2	0
Hunterdon County	14	1	2	1	10	92	16	66	10	0
Mercer County	8	0	1	1	6	27	5	21	1	0
Middlesex County	9	0	1	2	6	32	1	31	0	0
Monmouth County	10	1	2	1	6	108	30	74	4	1
Morris County	9	1	1	0	7	16	3	11	2	0
Ocean County	2	0	0	0	2	21	5	16	0	0
Passaic County	1	0	0	0	1	5	1	3	1	0
Salem County	17	0	5	3	9	182	43	122	17	2
Somerset County	1	0	0	0	1	7	2	4	1	0
Sussex County	25	0	8	2	15	213	52	146	15	1
Union County	3	0	0	0	3	5	1	2	2	0
Warren County	6	0	2	2	2	104	28	68	8	2
Other Agencies										
Park Police										
Morris County	0	0	0	0	0	16	1	15	0	0
Union County	22	0	3	10	9	32	0	32	0	0
Prosecutor										
Atlantic County	0	0	0	0	0	0	0	0	0	0
Bergen County	0	0	0	0	0	0	0	0	0	0
Burlington County	0	0	0	0	0	0	0	0	0	0
Camden County	0	0	0	0	0	0	0	0	0	0
Cape May County	0	0	0	0	0	0	0	0	0	0
Cumberland County	0	0	0	0	0	0	0	0	0	0
Essex County	0	0	0	0	0	0	0	0	0	0
Gloucester County	0	0	0	0	0	0	0	0	0	0
Hudson County	0	0	0	0	0	0	0	0	0	0
Hunterdon County	0	0	0	0	0	0	0	0	0	0
Mercer County	0	0	0	0	0	0	0	0	0	0

Table 11. Offenses Known to Law Enforcement, by Selected State, Tribal, and Other Agencies, 2019—Continued

(Number.)

State/other agency unit/office	Violent crime	Murder and nonnegligent manslaughter	Rape[1]	Robbery	Aggravated assault	Property crime	Burglary	Larceny-theft	Motor vehicle theft	Arson[2]
Middlesex County	0	0	0	0	0	0	0	0	0	0
Monmouth County	0	0	0	0	0	0	0	0	0	0
Morris County	0	0	0	0	0	0	0	0	0	2
Ocean County	0	0	0	0	0	0	0	0	0	0
Passaic County	0	0	0	0	0	0	0	0	0	0
Salem County	0	0	0	0	0	0	0	0	0	0
Somerset County	0	0	0	0	0	0	0	0	0	0
Sussex County	0	0	0	0	0	0	0	0	0	0
Union County	0	0	0	0	0	0	0	0	0	0
Warren County	0	0	0	0	0	0	0	0	0	0
NEW MEXICO										
Tribal Agencies										
Acoma Tribal	17	0	1	3	13	23	4	13	6	0
Isleta Tribal	12	0	0	0	12	18	2	12	4	0
Jemez Pueblo	4	0	0	0	4	12	4	8	0	0
Jicarilla Apache Tribal	77	0	0	0	77	5	0	2	3	0
Laguna Tribal	53	1	9	4	39	84	9	70	5	0
Mescalero Tribal	21	0	2	0	19	4	1	0	3	1
Northern Pueblos Agency	4	0	0	0	4	6	3	3	0	0
Ohkay Owingeh Tribal	11	1	0	0	10	27	7	13	7	0
Pojoaque Tribal	8	0	2	0	6	62	15	44	3	0
Ramah Navajo Tribal	24	0	2	0	22	15	8	7	0	0
Santa Ana Tribal	8	0	0	2	6	106	10	85	11	0
Santa Clara Pueblo	4	0	1	1	2	28	7	17	4	0
Southern Pueblos Agency	7	0	1	0	6	31	14	10	7	1
Taos Pueblo	16	1	0	2	13	12	4	7	1	0
Tesuque Pueblo	3	1	0	0	2	9	1	7	1	0
Zuni Tribal	15	0	0	0	15	0	0	0	0	0
NEW YORK										
State Agencies										
State Police										
Albany County	30	0	22	3	5	120	3	116	1	0
Allegany County	44	2	23	0	19	247	79	147	21	
Broome County	65	1	30	1	33	380	72	279	29	6
Cattaraugus County	32	0	12	0	20	181	32	138	11	
Cayuga County	51	0	25	1	25	168	30	126	12	0
Chautauqua County	31	0	18	2	11	137	38	94	5	
Chemung County	78	0	16	3	59	217	26	183	8	0
Chenango County	51	0	30	1	20	154	40	109	5	
Clinton County	80	1	49	3	27	694	103	573	18	10
Columbia County	31	0	17	1	13	187	35	147	5	
Cortland County	15	0	11	0	4	113	13	97	3	0
Delaware County	30	0	18	1	11	128	27	97	4	2
Dutchess County	160	0	49	9	102	416	39	362	15	2
Erie County	38	0	20	3	15	261	31	220	10	0
Essex County	32	0	23	0	9	226	51	169	6	
Franklin County	46	0	32	2	12	227	51	162	14	
Fulton County	24	1	16	0	7	59	11	47	1	
Genesee County	12	0	7	2	3	114	9	98	7	0
Greene County	156	0	39	4	113	259	57	192	10	0
Hamilton County	2	0	1	0	1	19	4	13	2	0
Herkimer County	34	0	13	1	20	171	54	105	12	2
Jefferson County	60	0	33	6	21	422	56	355	11	6
Lewis County	13	0	7	0	6	62	19	39	4	1
Livingston County	15	0	12	1	2	20	2	17	1	1
Madison County	31	0	24	1	6	153	35	115	3	0
Monroe County	57	0	53	2	2	74	2	63	9	0
Montgomery County	22	0	14	1	7	83	6	69	8	0
Nassau County	9	1	1	2	5	7	0	5	2	0
New York County	13	0	8	0	5	68	17	31	20	0
Niagara County	38	0	25	6	7	186	27	154	5	1
Oneida County	119	1	44	1	73	298	52	235	11	1
Onondaga County	89	0	56	10	23	562	55	476	31	4
Ontario County	32	0	19	2	11	219	27	186	6	
Orange County	114	1	81	5	27	532	38	482	12	3
Orleans County	13	0	10	0	3	61	7	44	10	
Oswego County	78	0	52	0	26	441	91	318	32	2
Otsego County	47	1	22	1	23	313	25	281	7	
Putnam County	17	0	10	1	6	81	7	68	6	
Rensselaer County	37	0	23	2	12	398	69	317	12	3
Rockland County	6	0	2	0	4	4	0	4	0	0
Saratoga County	58	1	39	2	16	514	33	468	13	2
Schenectady County	8	0	5	0	3	57	7	48	2	0
Schoharie County	23	0	12	0	11	105	28	72	5	1
Schuyler County	4	0	3	0	1	19	6	11	2	0
Seneca County	33	0	17	0	16	89	7	80	2	0
Steuben County	48	0	34	1	13	304	63	222	19	5
St. Lawrence County	36	0	23	2	11	276	68	183	25	
Suffolk County	16	1	8	0	7	16	0	14	2	0
Sullivan County	93	1	53	2	37	215	65	140	10	5
Tioga County	31	2	19	1	9	74	9	57	8	0

Table 11. Offenses Known to Law Enforcement, by Selected State, Tribal, and Other Agencies, 2019—Continued

(Number.)

State/other agency unit/office	Violent crime	Murder and nonnegligent manslaughter	Rape[1]	Robbery	Aggravated assault	Property crime	Burglary	Larceny-theft	Motor vehicle theft	Arson[2]
Tompkins County	42	0	22	1	19	231	42	184	5	1
Ulster County	89	1	38	3	47	362	63	277	22	2
Warren County	25	0	19	0	6	173	19	150	4	0
Washington County	25	0	20	1	4	77	15	58	4	0
Wayne County	55	0	35	3	17	379	84	275	20	4
Westchester County	63	0	17	3	43	276	25	243	8	0
Wyoming County	18	0	5	0	13	25	1	20	4	1
Yates County	6	0	5	0	1	14	3	11	0	0
Tribal Agencies										
Oneida Indian Nation	7	0	3	1	3	61	4	54	3	1
St. Regis Tribal	8	0	3	1	4	22	1	19	2	0
Other Agencies										
New York City Department of Environmental Protection Police										
Ashokan Precinct	0	0	0	0	0	0	0	0	0	0
Beerston Precinct	0	0	0	0	0	4	0	4	0	0
Eastview Precinct	0	0	0	0	0	10	0	10	0	0
Gilboa Precinct	0	0	0	0	0	0	0	0	0	0
Grahamsville Precinct	1	0	0	0	1	0	0	0	0	0
Hillview Precinct	0	0	0	0	0	0	0	0	0	0
New York City Metropolitan Transportation Authority	63	0	0	28	35	378	14	358	6	0
Onondaga County Parks	2	0	0	1	1	26	1	25	0	0
NORTH CAROLINA										
State Agencies[4]										
State Capitol Police	8	0	4	0	4	12	2	10	0	2
State Park Rangers										
Hanging Rock	0	0	0	0	0	4	0	4	0	0
Jockey's Ridge	0	0	0	0	0	0	0	0	0	0
Lake Norman	0	0	0	0	0	16	7	9	0	0
New River-Mount Jefferson	0	0	0	0	0	0	0	0	0	0
Other Agencies[4]										
Raleigh-Durham International Airport	3	0	1	0	2	120	2	95	23	0
Triad Municipal Alcoholic Beverage Control Law Enforcement	0	0	0	0	0	9	0	9	0	0
WakeMed Campus Police	34	0	2	0	32	99	6	88	5	0
NORTH DAKOTA										
State Agencies										
North Dakota Highway Patrol	11	0	0	0	11	21	0	3	18	0
OHIO										
State Agencies										
Ohio Department of Natural Resources	31	2	3	0	26	283	16	259	8	4
Ohio Investigative Unit	0	0	0	0	0	0	0	0	0	0
Ohio State Highway Patrol	217	4	24	2	187	147	4	108	35	5
Other Agencies										
Greater Cleveland Regional Transit Authority	28	0	1	18	9	134	0	134	0	2
Hamilton County Park District	1	0	1	0	0	60	0	56	4	0
Lake Metroparks	0	0	0	0	0	1	0	1	0	0
Toledo Fire Department Fire Investigation Unit	0	0	0	0	0	0	0	0	0	86
University Hospitals Portage Medical Center	1	0	0	1	0	6	0	6	0	0
OKLAHOMA										
State Agencies										
Capitol Park Police	0	0	0	0	0	0	0	0	0	0
Oklahoma Highway Patrol	2	2	0	0	0	0	0	0	0	0
State Park Rangers	6	0	1	0	5	99	22	73	4	2
Tribal Agencies										
Absentee Shawnee Tribal	4	0	0	0	4	19	8	10	1	0
Anadarko Agency	5	0	1	0	4	57	5	47	5	0
Cherokee Nation	13	0	2	1	10	36	6	27	3	0
Chickasaw Nation	25	0	0	9	16	928	68	837	23	0
Choctaw Nation	49	0	2	3	44	306	16	267	23	0
Citizen Potawatomi Nation	6	0	2	1	3	202	8	178	16	1
Comanche Nation	5	0	0	0	5	130	10	112	8	0
Concho Agency	6	0	0	0	6	32	1	26	5	0
Eastern Shawnee Tribal	3	0	0	0	3	80	0	72	8	0
Iowa Tribal[4]	0	0	0	0	0	25	2	23	0	0
Kaw Tribal	0	0	0	0	0	7	1	6	0	0
Kickapoo Tribal	4	2	0	0	2	27	6	17	4	1
Miami Agency	4	0	0	0	4	51	2	38	11	0
Miami Tribal	0	0	0	0	0	10	3	7	0	0
Muscogee Nation Tribal	22	0	3	0	19	231	21	169	41	0
Osage Nation[4]	5	0	1	0	4	183	40	101	42	1
Otoe-Missouria Tribal	3	0	0	0	3	9	5	2	2	0
Pawnee Tribal	1	0	0	0	1	9	3	5	1	0
Ponca Tribal	1	0	0	0	1	11	5	5	1	0
Quapaw Tribal[4]	13	0	1	3	9	157	15	134	8	4

Table 11. Offenses Known to Law Enforcement, by Selected State, Tribal, and Other Agencies, 2019—Continued

(Number.)

State/other agency unit/office	Violent crime	Murder and nonnegligent manslaughter	Rape[1]	Robbery	Aggravated assault	Property crime	Burglary	Larceny-theft	Motor vehicle theft	Arson[2]
Sac and Fox Tribal	11	0	1	0	10	42	15	22	5	0
Seminole Nation Lighthorse	3	0	1	0	2	24	3	19	2	0
Tonkawa Tribal	1	0	0	0	1	11	0	10	1	0
Wyandotte Nation	6	0	0	1	5	17	4	12	1	1
Other Agencies										
District 1 Narcotics Task Force	0	0	0	0	0	0	0	0	0	0
Jenks Public Schools	1	0	0	0	1	3	0	3	0	0
Lawton Public Schools	4	0	1	2	1	26	2	24	0	1
Muskogee City Schools	4	0	0	0	4	2	0	2	0	1
Putnam City Campus	8	0	2	0	6	6	1	5	0	0
Victory Life	0	0	0	0	0	0	0	0	0	0
OREGON										
State Agencies										
State Police										
Baker County	3	0	1	0	2	5	0	4	1	2
Benton County	6	0	0	2	4	333	17	313	3	1
Clackamas County	17	0	0	0	17	22	0	17	5	0
Clatsop County	3	0	1	0	2	4	0	2	2	0
Columbia County	6	0	0	0	6	6	0	4	2	0
Coos County	6	0	0	0	6	31	4	25	2	1
Crook County	3	0	0	0	3	0	0	0	0	0
Curry County	6	0	1	0	5	18	0	17	1	0
Deschutes County	12	0	1	0	11	7	0	6	1	0
Douglas County	23	1	1	0	21	34	3	24	7	1
Grant County	4	0	1	0	3	4	1	3	0	0
Harney County	3	0	0	0	3	3	0	2	1	0
Hood River County	5	0	0	0	5	6	0	6	0	1
Jackson County[5]			0	0	14	29	0	24	5	1
Jefferson County	2	0	1	0	1	3	0	3	0	0
Josephine County	43	0	2	0	41	14	2	8	4	6
Klamath County	17	1	3	0	13	8	1	7	0	1
Lake County	5	0	0	0	5	2	0	1	1	0
Lane County[5]			1	0	23	52	3	38	11	2
Lincoln County	4	0	1	0	3	18	0	18	0	0
Linn County	8	0	1	0	7	20	0	17	3	1
Malheur County	9	0	0	0	9	4	0	4	0	1
Marion County	52	0	4	1	47	93	7	70	16	0
Multnomah County	6	0	1	0	5	10	0	6	4	0
Polk County	5	0	0	0	5	1	0	1	0	0
Sherman County	9	0	0	0	9	2	0	2	0	0
Tillamook County	4	0	0	0	4	13	0	12	1	1
Umatilla County	17	0	3	1	13	6	1	5	0	0
Union County	1	0	0	0	1	4	0	3	1	0
Wasco County	7	0	0	0	7	8	0	5	3	0
Washington County	4	0	1	0	3	3	0	1	2	0
Yamhill County	9	0	0	0	9	2	0	2	0	0
Tribal Agencies										
Burns Paiute Tribal	0	0	0	0	0	0	0	0	0	0
Columbia River Inter-Tribal Fisheries										
Enforcement	8	0	1	0	7	10	2	6	2	0
Coos, Lower Umpqua, and Siuslaw Tribal	0	0	0	0	0	15	0	15	0	
Coquille Tribal	2	0	1	1	0	5	3	1	1	0
Grand Ronde Tribal	3	0	1	0	2	53	6	44	3	0
Siletz Tribal	1	0	0	0	1	3	1	1	1	0
Umatilla Tribal	37	3	6	0	28	132	24	92	16	0
Other Agencies										
Hillsboro School District	0	0	0	0	0	0	0	0	0	0
Port of Portland	6	0	0	0	6	554	8	490	56	0
PENNSYLVANIA										
State Agencies										
Bureau of Forestry										
Adams County	0	0	0	0	0	0	0	0	0	0
Allegheny County	0	0	0	0	0	0	0	0	0	0
Chester County	0	0	0	0	0	0	0	0	0	0
Columbia County	0	0	0	0	0	0	0	0	0	0
Cumberland County	0	0	0	0	0	0	0	0	0	0
Delaware County	0	0	0	0	0	0	0	0	0	3
Fayette County	0	0	0	0	0	0	0	0	0	0
McKean County	0	0	0	0	0	0	0	0	0	1
Snyder County	0	0	0	0	0	0	0	0	0	0
Bureau of Narcotics										
Adams County	0	0	0	0	0	0	0	0	0	0
Allegheny County	1	0	0	0	1	0	0	0	0	0
Beaver County	0	0	0	0	0	0	0	0	0	0
Berks County	0	0	0	0	0	0	0	0	0	0
Bradford County	0	0	0	0	0	0	0	0	0	0
Clearfield County	0	0	0	0	0	0	0	0	0	0
Columbia County	0	0	0	0	0	0	0	0	0	0
Erie County	0	0	0	0	0	0	0	0	0	0
Franklin County	0	0	0	0	0	0	0	0	0	0
Huntingdon County	0	0	0	0	0	0	0	0	0	0

Table 11. Offenses Known to Law Enforcement, by Selected State, Tribal, and Other Agencies, 2019—Continued

(Number.)

State/other agency unit/office	Violent crime	Murder and nonnegligent manslaughter	Rape[1]	Robbery	Aggravated assault	Property crime	Burglary	Larceny-theft	Motor vehicle theft	Arson[2]
Jefferson County	0	0	0	0	0	0	0	0	0	0
Lancaster County	0	0	0	0	0	0	0	0	0	0
Lebanon County	0	0	0	0	0	0	0	0	0	0
Lehigh County	0	0	0	0	0	0	0	0	0	0
Mifflin County	0	0	0	0	0	0	0	0	0	0
Montgomery County	0	0	0	0	0	0	0	0	0	0
Montour County	0	0	0	0	0	0	0	0	0	0
Northampton County	0	0	0	0	0	0	0	0	0	0
Tioga County	0	0	0	0	0	0	0	0	0	0
Union County	0	0	0	0	0	0	0	0	0	0
Venango County	0	0	0	0	0	0	0	0	0	0
Warren County	0	0	0	0	0	0	0	0	0	0
Wyoming County	0	0	0	0	0	0	0	0	0	0
State Capitol Police	1	0	0	0	1	16	0	16	0	0
State Park Rangers										
Cowans Gap	0	0	0	0	0	1	0	1	0	0
Fort Washington	0	0	0	0	0	0	0	0	0	0
Frances Slocum	0	0	0	0	0	1	0	1	0	0
Keystone	0	0	0	0	0	2	0	2	0	0
Kings Gap Environmental Education Center	0	0	0	0	0	0	0	0	0	0
Little Pine	0	0	0	0	0	0	0	0	0	0
Maurice K. Goddard	0	0	0	0	0	0	0	0	0	0
Pymatuning	0	0	0	0	0	1	1	0	0	0
Sinnemahoning	0	0	0	0	0	0	0	0	0	0
Sizerville	0	0	0	0	0	0	0	0	0	0
Worlds End	0	0	0	0	0	0	0	0	0	0
State Police, Bureau of Criminal Investigation										
Adams County	0	0	0	0	0	0	0	0	0	0
Allegheny County	0	0	0	0	0	0	0	0	0	0
Armstrong County	0	0	0	0	0	0	0	0	0	0
Beaver County	0	0	0	0	0	0	0	0	0	0
Bedford County	0	0	0	0	0	0	0	0	0	0
Berks County	0	0	0	0	0	0	0	0	0	0
Blair County	0	0	0	0	0	0	0	0	0	0
Bradford County	0	0	0	0	0	0	0	0	0	0
Bucks County	0	0	0	0	0	0	0	0	0	0
Cambria County	0	0	0	0	0	4	0	4	0	0
Cameron County	0	0	0	0	0	0	0	0	0	0
Carbon County	0	0	0	0	0	0	0	0	0	0
Centre County	0	0	0	0	0	0	0	0	0	0
Chester County	2	0	2	0	0	0	0	0	0	0
Clearfield County	0	0	0	0	0	0	0	0	0	0
Clinton County	0	0	0	0	0	0	0	0	0	0
Columbia County	0	0	0	0	0	0	0	0	0	0
Crawford County	0	0	0	0	0	0	0	0	0	0
Cumberland County	0	0	0	0	0	0	0	0	0	0
Dauphin County	0	0	0	0	0	1	0	1	0	0
Delaware County	0	0	0	0	0	0	0	0	0	0
Elk County	0	0	0	0	0	0	0	0	0	0
Erie County	0	0	0	0	0	0	0	0	0	0
Fayette County	0	0	0	0	0	1	0	1	0	0
Forest County	0	0	0	0	0	0	0	0	0	0
Franklin County	0	0	0	0	0	0	0	0	0	0
Fulton County	0	0	0	0	0	0	0	0	0	0
Greene County	0	0	0	0	0	0	0	0	0	0
Huntingdon County	0	0	0	0	0	2	0	2	0	0
Indiana County	0	0	0	0	0	0	0	0	0	0
Jefferson County	0	0	0	0	0	0	0	0	0	0
Juniata County	0	0	0	0	0	0	0	0	0	0
Lackawanna County	2	0	2	0	0	0	0	0	0	0
Lancaster County	0	0	0	0	0	0	0	0	0	0
Lawrence County	0	0	0	0	0	0	0	0	0	0
Lebanon County	2	0	2	0	0	0	0	0	0	0
Lehigh County	0	0	0	0	0	0	0	0	0	0
Lycoming County	0	0	0	0	0	0	0	0	0	0
Mercer County	0	0	0	0	0	1	0	1	0	0
Mifflin County	0	0	0	0	0	0	0	0	0	0
Montgomery County	0	0	0	0	0	0	0	0	0	0
Montour County	0	0	0	0	0	0	0	0	0	0
Northampton County	0	0	0	0	0	0	0	0	0	0
Northumberland County	0	0	0	0	0	0	0	0	0	0
Perry County	0	0	0	0	0	0	0	0	0	0
Philadelphia County	0	0	0	0	0	0	0	0	0	0
Pike County	0	0	0	0	0	0	0	0	0	0
Potter County	0	0	0	0	0	0	0	0	0	0
Schuylkill County	0	0	0	0	0	0	0	0	0	0
Snyder County	0	0	0	0	0	0	0	0	0	0
Sullivan County	0	0	0	0	0	0	0	0	0	0
Susquehanna County	0	0	0	0	0	0	0	0	0	0
Union County	0	0	0	0	0	0	0	0	0	0
Warren County	0	0	0	0	0	0	0	0	0	0

Table 11. Offenses Known to Law Enforcement, by Selected State, Tribal, and Other Agencies, 2019—Continued

(Number.)

State/other agency unit/office	Violent crime	Murder and nonnegligent manslaughter	Rape[1]	Robbery	Aggravated assault	Property crime	Burglary	Larceny-theft	Motor vehicle theft	Arson[2]
Washington County	0	0	0	0	0	2	1	1	0	0
Wayne County	0	0	0	0	0	0	0	0	0	0
Westmoreland County	0	0	0	0	0	1	0	1	0	0
York County	0	0	0	0	0	0	0	0	0	0
State Police										
Allegheny County	30	1	2	3	24	224	10	205	9	
Armstrong County	105	0	26	9	70	228	58	159	11	5
Beaver County	35	0	12	2	21	67	13	47	7	1
Bedford County	61	3	29	3	26	355	97	237	21	4
Bradford County	69	3	32	1	33	317	75	211	31	1
Bucks County	25	0	9	3	13	237	39	182	16	1
Cameron County	13	0	3	0	10	32	7	24	1	0
Delaware County	34	0	6	5	23	498	34	443	21	4
Elizabethville	199	3	51	6	139	681	97	546	38	4
Elk County	13	0	3	0	10	186	23	157	6	1
Fulton County	23	0	8	0	15	129	34	85	10	0
Jefferson County	49	0	31	2	16	180	76	95	9	1
Juniata County	66	1	24	3	38	121	34	84	3	2
Luzerne County	69	3	26	5	35	506	99	374	33	5
Mifflin County	21	1	11	0	9	52	12	36	4	2
Northumberland County	67	2	25	3	37	182	73	100	9	2
Potter County	72	0	6	0	66	89	29	59	1	0
Snyder County	33	0	7	3	23	265	38	216	11	1
Susquehanna County	30	0	17	6	7	268	103	132	33	1
Tioga County	44	0	15	0	29	253	81	135	37	3
Tionesta	11	0	6	0	5	52	22	28	2	0
Washington County	74	0	16	7	51	375	65	280	30	
Westmoreland County	138	2	41	17	78	800	167	580	53	11
York County	125	2	37	17	69	473	93	358	22	3
Other Agencies										
Allegheny County District Attorney, Criminal Investigation Division	4	0	0	0	4	34	0	34	0	0
Allegheny County Housing Authority	5	1	0	0	4	29	4	22	3	0
County Detective										
Chester County	5	0	2	0	3	7	1	6	0	0
Dauphin County	8	0	0	0	8	9	0	9	0	0
Lackawanna County	18	0	2	0	16	0	0	0	0	0
Lawrence County	0	0	0	0	0	0	0	0	0	0
Lebanon County	2	0	2	0	0	0	0	0	0	0
Lehigh County	3	0	0	3	0	54	0	0	54	0
Pike County	13	0	0	0	13	2	1	1	0	0
Delaware County Park	16	0	0	0	16	78	2	76	0	0
Fort Indiantown Gap	1	0	1	0	0	4	0	4	0	0
Lehigh Valley International Airport	0	0	0	0	0	22	0	9	13	0
Westmoreland County Park	1	0	0	0	1	10	0	10	0	0
Wyoming Area School District	0	0	0	0	0	0	0	0	0	0
RHODE ISLAND										
State Agencies										
Department of Environmental Management	0	0	0	0	0	13	0	12	1	1
Rhode Island State Police Headquarters	44	2	30	0	12	57	0	41	16	1
State Police										
Chepachet/Scituate	10	0	3	1	6	23	3	7	13	0
Hope Valley	8	0	5	0	3	32	3	22	7	0
Lincoln	19	0	8	1	10	31	2	21	8	0
Portsmouth	0	0	0	0	0	4	1	3	0	0
Wickford	4	0	4	0	0	24	4	15	5	0
T.F. Green Airport	0	0	0	0	0	46	0	33	13	0
SOUTH CAROLINA										
State Agencies										
Department of Mental Health	1	0	0	0	1	3	0	3	0	0
Department of Natural Resources										
Allendale County	0	0	0	0	0	0	0	0	0	0
Anderson County	0	0	0	0	0	0	0	0	0	0
Barnwell County	0	0	0	0	0	0	0	0	0	0
Beaufort County	0	0	0	0	0	0	0	0	0	0
Berkeley County	0	0	0	0	0	0	0	0	0	0
Calhoun County	0	0	0	0	0	0	0	0	0	0
Charleston County	0	0	0	0	0	0	0	0	0	0
Cherokee County	0	0	0	0	0	0	0	0	0	0
Chester County	0	0	0	0	0	0	0	0	0	0
Darlington County	0	0	0	0	0	0	0	0	0	0
Dillon County	0	0	0	0	0	0	0	0	0	0
Dorchester County	0	0	0	0	0	0	0	0	0	0
Fairfield County	0	0	0	0	0	0	0	0	0	0
Florence County	0	0	0	0	0	0	0	0	0	0
Georgetown County	0	0	0	0	0	0	0	0	0	0
Greenville County	0	0	0	0	0	0	0	0	0	0
Greenwood County	0	0	0	0	0	0	0	0	0	0
Hampton County	0	0	0	0	0	0	0	0	0	0
Horry County	0	0	0	0	0	0	0	0	0	0

Table 11. Offenses Known to Law Enforcement, by Selected State, Tribal, and Other Agencies, 2019—Continued

(Number.)

State/other agency unit/office	Violent crime	Murder and nonnegligent manslaughter	Rape[1]	Robbery	Aggravated assault	Property crime	Burglary	Larceny-theft	Motor vehicle theft	Arson[2]
Jasper County	0	0	0	0	0	0	0	0	0	0
Kershaw County	0	0	0	0	0	0	0	0	0	0
Lancaster County	0	0	0	0	0	0	0	0	0	0
Laurens County	0	0	0	0	0	0	0	0	0	0
Lee County	0	0	0	0	0	0	0	0	0	0
Lexington County	0	0	0	0	0	0	0	0	0	0
Marion County	0	0	0	0	0	0	0	0	0	0
McCormick County	0	0	0	0	0	0	0	0	0	0
Newberry County	0	0	0	0	0	0	0	0	0	0
Oconee County	0	0	0	0	0	0	0	0	0	0
Orangeburg County	0	0	0	0	0	0	0	0	0	0
Pickens County	0	0	0	0	0	0	0	0	0	0
Richland County	0	0	0	0	0	0	0	0	0	0
Saluda County	0	0	0	0	0	0	0	0	0	0
Spartanburg County	0	0	0	0	0	0	0	0	0	0
Sumter County	0	0	0	0	0	0	0	0	0	0
Union County	0	0	0	0	0	0	0	0	0	0
Williamsburg County	0	0	0	0	0	0	0	0	0	0
York County	0	0	0	0	0	0	0	0	0	0
Highway Patrol	2	0	1	1	0	46	1	44	1	0
Anderson County	0	0	0	0	0	0	0	0	0	0
Berkeley County	0	0	0	0	0	0	0	0	0	0
Cherokee County	1	0	0	0	1	0	0	0	0	0
Chester County	0	0	0	0	0	0	0	0	0	0
Dillon County	0	0	0	0	0	0	0	0	0	0
Fairfield County	0	0	0	0	0	1	0	1	0	0
Florence County	0	0	0	0	0	0	0	0	0	0
Greenville County	0	0	0	0	0	4	1	3	0	0
Horry County	0	0	0	0	0	0	0	0	0	0
Kershaw County	0	0	0	0	0	0	0	0	0	0
Lexington County	0	0	0	0	0	0	0	0	0	0
Richland County	0	0	0	0	0	1	0	0	1	0
Spartanburg County	0	0	0	0	0	0	0	0	0	0
Union County	0	0	0	0	0	0	0	0	0	0
York County	1	1	0	0	0	0	0	0	0	0
South Carolina School for the Deaf and Blind	0	0	0	0	0	0	0	0	0	0
State Museum	0	0	0	0	0	0	0	0	0	0
State Ports Authority	0	0	0	0	0	0	0	0	0	0
United States Department of Energy Savannah River Plant	0	0	0	0	0	8	0	8	0	0
Other Agencies										
Charleston County Aviation Authority	0	0	0	0	0	30	1	22	7	0
Columbia Metropolitan Airport	0	0	0	0	0	19	0	12	7	0
Greenville Hospital										
Greenville	5	0	0	0	5	129	1	127	1	0
Laurens	5	0	0	0	5	5	0	5	0	0
Oconee	1	0	0	0	1	13	1	12	0	0
Greenville-Spartanburg International Airport	1	0	0	0	1	31	0	11	20	0
Lexington County Medical Center	0	0	0	0	0	50	0	47	3	0
SOUTH DAKOTA										
State Agencies										
Highway Patrol	5	0	0	0	5	18	0	10	8	0
TENNESSEE										
State Agencies										
Alcoholic Beverage Commission	0	0	0	0	0	0	0	0	0	0
Department of Agriculture, Agricultural Crime Unit	0	0	0	0	0	1	1	0	0	0
Department of Safety	125	1	0	0	124	126	1	27	98	0
State Park Rangers										
Bicentennial Capitol Mall	0	0	0	0	0	2	0	2	0	0
Big Hill Pond	0	0	0	0	0	0	0	0	0	0
Big Ridge	0	0	0	0	0	2	1	1	0	0
Bledsoe Creek	0	0	0	0	0	0	0	0	0	0
Booker T. Washington	0	0	0	0	0	1	0	1	0	0
Burgess Falls Natural Area	0	0	0	0	0	0	0	0	0	0
Cedars of Lebanon	0	0	0	0	0	0	0	0	0	0
Chickasaw	0	0	0	0	0	3	0	3	0	0
Cordell Hull Birthplace	0	0	0	0	0	0	0	0	0	0
Cove Lake	0	0	0	0	0	1	0	1	0	0
Cumberland Mountain	0	0	0	0	0	1	0	1	0	0
Cumberland Trail	0	0	0	0	0	7	0	7	0	1
Cummins Falls	0	0	0	0	0	0	0	0	0	0
David Crockett	0	0	0	0	0	3	0	3	0	0
Davy Crockett Birthplace	0	0	0	0	0	1	0	1	0	0
Dunbar Cave Natural Area	0	0	0	0	0	2	0	2	0	0
Edgar Evins	0	0	0	0	0	3	0	3	0	0
Fall Creek Falls	0	0	0	0	0	2	0	2	0	0
Fort Loudon State Historic Park	0	0	0	0	0	1	1	0	0	0
Fort Pillow State Historic Park	0	0	0	0	0	0	0	0	0	0
Frozen Head Natural Area	0	0	0	0	0	1	0	1	0	0

Table 11. Offenses Known to Law Enforcement, by Selected State, Tribal, and Other Agencies, 2019—Continued

(Number.)

State/other agency unit/office	Violent crime	Murder and nonnegligent manslaughter	Rape[1]	Robbery	Aggravated assault	Property crime	Burglary	Larceny-theft	Motor vehicle theft	Arson[2]
Harrison Bay	1	0	0	0	1	6	0	6	0	0
Henry Horton	1	0	0	0	1	1	0	1	0	0
Hiwassee/Ocoee State Scenic Rivers	0	0	0	0	0	0	0	0	0	0
Indian Mountain	0	0	0	0	0	0	0	0	0	0
Johnsonville State Historic Park	0	0	0	0	0	0	0	0	0	0
Long Hunter	0	0	0	0	0	15	0	15	0	0
Meeman-Shelby Forest	0	0	0	0	0	1	0	1	0	0
Montgomery Bell	1	0	0	0	1	6	0	6	0	0
Mousetail Landing	0	0	0	0	0	1	0	1	0	0
Natchez Trace	0	0	0	0	0	1	0	1	0	0
Nathan Bedford Forrest	0	0	0	0	0	1	0	1	0	0
Norris Dam	0	0	0	0	0	1	0	1	0	0
Old Stone Fort State Archaeological Park	0	0	0	0	0	1	0	1	0	0
Panther Creek	0	0	0	0	0	1	0	1	0	0
Paris Landing	0	0	0	0	0	2	0	2	0	0
Pickett	0	0	0	0	0	0	0	0	0	0
Pickwick Landing	0	0	0	0	0	6	1	5	0	0
Pinson Mounds State Archaeological Park	0	0	0	0	0	0	0	0	0	0
Radnor Lake Natural Area	0	0	0	0	0	3	0	3	0	0
Red Clay State Historic Park	0	0	0	0	0	0	0	0	0	0
Reelfoot Lake	0	0	0	0	0	1	0	1	0	0
Roan Mountain	0	0	0	0	0	7	1	6	0	0
Rock Island	0	0	0	0	0	0	0	0	0	0
Rocky Fork	0	0	0	0	0	0	0	0	0	0
Seven Islands Birding Park	0	0	0	0	0	0	0	0	0	0
Sgt. Alvin C. York	0	0	0	0	0	1	0	1	0	0
South Cumberland Recreation Area	0	0	0	0	0	0	0	0	0	0
Standing Stone	0	0	0	0	0	0	0	0	0	0
Sycamore Shoals State Historic Park	0	0	0	0	0	4	0	4	0	0
Tim's Ford	0	0	0	0	0	1	0	1	0	0
T.O. Fuller	0	0	0	0	0	5	0	5	0	0
Warrior's Path	0	0	0	0	0	0	0	0	0	0
TennCare Office of Inspector General	0	0	0	0	0	0	0	0	0	0
Tennessee Bureau of Investigation	2	0	2	0	0	4	0	4	0	0
Tennessee Department of Revenue, Special Investigations Unit	0	0	0	0	0	0	0	0	0	0
Wildlife Resources Agency										
Region 1	1	0	0	0	1	0	0	0	0	0
Region 2	4	0	0	0	4	0	0	0	0	0
Region 3	0	0	0	0	0	0	0	0	0	0
Region 4	0	0	0	0	0	0	0	0	0	0
Other Agencies										
7th Judicial District Crime Task Force	0	0	0	0	0	1	0	1	0	0
Chattanooga Housing Authority	0	0	0	0	0	0	0	0	0	0
Chattanooga Metropolitan Airport	0	0	0	0	0	0	0	0	0	0
Dickson City Park Ranger Division	0	0	0	0	0	1	0	1	0	0
Drug Task Force										
1st Judicial District	0	0	0	0	0	0	0	0	0	0
2nd Judicial District	0	0	0	0	0	0	0	0	0	0
3rd Judicial District	0	0	0	0	0	0	0	0	0	0
4th Judicial District	0	0	0	0	0	0	0	0	0	0
5th Judicial District	0	0	0	0	0	0	0	0	0	0
8th Judicial District	0	0	0	0	0	7	0	7	0	0
9th Judicial District	0	0	0	0	0	0	0	0	0	0
10th Judicial District	0	0	0	0	0	0	0	0	0	0
12th Judicial District	0	0	0	0	0	0	0	0	0	0
14th Judicial District	0	0	0	0	0	0	0	0	0	0
15th Judicial District	0	0	0	0	0	0	0	0	0	0
17th Judicial District	0	0	0	0	0	0	0	0	0	0
18th Judicial District	0	0	0	0	0	1	0	1	0	0
19th Judicial District	0	0	0	0	0	0	0	0	0	0
21st Judicial District	0	0	0	0	0	0	0	0	0	0
22nd Judicial District	0	0	0	0	0	2	0	1	1	0
23rd Judicial District	0	0	0	0	0	0	0	0	0	0
24th Judicial District	0	0	0	0	0	0	0	0	0	0
25th Judicial District	0	0	0	0	0	0	0	0	0	0
27th Judicial District	0	0	0	0	0	0	0	0	0	0
31st Judicial District	1	0	0	0	1	10	0	7	3	0
Knoxville Metropolitan Airport	1	0	0	0	1	455	0	160	295	0
Memphis-Shelby County Airport Authority	1	0	0	1	0	112	4	106	2	0
Metropolitan Nashville Park Police	2	0	0	0	2	76	0	50	26	0
Nashville International Airport	0	0	0	0	0	2	0	0	2	0
Tri-Cities Regional Airport	0	0	0	0	0	0	0	0	0	0
West Tennessee Violent Crime Task Force	0	0	0	0	0	0	0	0	0	0
TEXAS										
Tribal Agencies										
Ysleta del Sur Pueblo Tribal	5	0	0	0	5	61	0	57	4	0
Other Agencies										
Dallas-Fort Worth International Airport	10	0	0	2	8	475	4	428	43	1
Hospital District Dallas County	12	0	0	3	9	290	5	272	13	0

Table 11. Offenses Known to Law Enforcement, by Selected State, Tribal, and Other Agencies, 2019—Continued

(Number.)

State/other agency unit/office	Violent crime	Murder and nonnegligent manslaughter	Rape[1]	Robbery	Aggravated assault	Property crime	Burglary	Larceny-theft	Motor vehicle theft	Arson[2]
Tarrant County	3	0	1	0	2	105	0	103	2	0
Houston Metropolitan Transit Authority	9	0	0	2	7	52	0	47	5	0
Independent School District										
Aldine	9	0	0	3	6	85	21	55	9	0
Alief	34	0	0	11	23	48	1	44	3	0
Alvin	28	0	1	0	27	140	2	135	3	0
Angleton[4]	9	0	0	1	8	9	0	9	0	0
Austin[4]	27	0	11	5	11	333	16	308	9	8
Barbers Hill	0	0	0	0	0	4	0	4	0	0
Bay City	14	0	0	0	14	7	3	4	0	1
Brownsville	68	0	0	0	68	157	3	154	0	0
Calhoun County	2	0	0	1	1	0	0	0	0	0
Conroe[4]	122	0	19	2	101	99	4	95	0	2
Corpus Christi	212	0	0	3	209	72	19	51	2	0
Duncanville[4]	4	0	0	1	3	51	3	47	1	0
Ector County	76	0	0	2	74	37	4	33	0	0
Edinburg	46	0	0	0	46	55	4	50	1	2
El Paso	30	0	6	0	24	217	19	197	1	0
Floresville[4]	5	0	2	0	3	17	2	15	0	0
Fort Bend	153	0	4	3	146	240	5	232	3	0
Houston	91	0	44	14	33	362	112	237	13	10
Humble	5	0	2	1	2	49	0	47	2	2
Hutto[4]	2	0	0	0	2	7	3	4	0	0
Katy	33	0	20	9	4	231	2	228	1	0
Klein[4]	19	0	4	1	14	131	0	130	1	1
Mansfield[4]	4	0	0	0	4	171	4	167	0	0
Midland	40	0	0	0	40	12	0	12	0	0
Pflugerville	19	0	0	0	19	65	4	59	2	1
Rio Grande City	22	0	1	0	21	21	1	20	0	0
Santa Fe	21	0	0	0	21	9	0	9	0	0
Socorro	6	0	0	0	6	15	0	15	0	0
Spring	53	0	3	3	47	70	6	62	2	2
Spring Branch	13	0	1	1	11	72	7	57	8	0
United	1	0	0	0	1	21	1	20	0	1
Port of Houston Authority[4]	1	0	1	0	0	8	1	6	1	0
UTAH										
State Agencies										
Parks and Recreation	3	1	1	0	1	25	3	19	3	1
Utah Highway Patrol	53	6	3	2	42	125	1	106	18	0
Wildlife Resources	1	1	0	0	0	12	0	8	4	2
Tribal Agencies										
Goshute Tribal	0	0	0	0	0	0	0	0	0	
Uintah and Ouray Tribal	5	0	1	0	4	8	1	1	6	0
Other Agencies										
Cache-Rich Drug Task Force	0	0	0	0	0	5	1	4	0	0
Davis Metropolitan Narcotics Strike Force	0	0	0	0	0	0	0	0	0	0
Granite School District	42	0	0	9	33	112	1	104	7	7
Utah County Attorney, Investigations Division	0	0	0	0	0	0	0	0	0	0
Utah County Major Crimes Task Force	0	0	0	0	0	0	0	0	0	0
Utah Transit Authority	22	0	0	8	14	2,132	0	2,083	49	4
Weber Morgan Narcotics Strike Force	2	0	0	0	2	3	0	3	0	0
VERMONT										
State Agencies										
Department of Motor Vehicles	0	0	0	0	0	5	0	5	0	0
Fish and Wildlife Department, Law Enforcement Division	0	0	0	0	0	3	0	3	0	0
State Police										
Derby[5]			6	2	41	209	76	116	17	0
Middlesex	39	0	8	1	30	222	62	141	19	1
New Haven	20	1	5	0	14	125	43	71	11	2
Royalton	35	0	10	0	25	92	32	52	8	2
Rutland	25	1	5	1	18	84	27	52	5	0
Shaftsbury	27	0	2	1	24	78	21	47	10	0
St. Albans	39	1	11	2	25	206	42	143	21	3
St. Johnsbury	54	1	5	1	47	261	73	168	20	1
Westminster	36	0	6	1	29	153	50	93	10	3
Williston	23	0	2	0	21	128	40	81	7	5
Vermont State Police	3	2	0	0	1	2	0	2	0	0
Vermont State Police Headquarters, Bureau of Criminal Investigations	1	1	0	0	0	0	0	0	0	0
Other Agencies										
Chittenden Unit for Special Investigations	18	0	18	0	0	0	0	0	0	0
VIRGINIA										
State Agencies										
Alcoholic Beverage Control Commission	0	0	0	0	0	24	1	23	0	0
Department of Conservation and Recreation	1	0	1	0	0	40	2	38	0	0
Department of Game and Inland Fisheries, Enforcement Division	5	0	0	0	5	39	0	37	2	0
Department of Motor Vehicles	0	0	0	0	0	52	0	10	42	1

Table 11. Offenses Known to Law Enforcement, by Selected State, Tribal, and Other Agencies, 2019—Continued

(Number.)

State/other agency unit/office	Violent crime	Murder and nonnegligent manslaughter	Rape[1]	Robbery	Aggravated assault	Property crime	Burglary	Larceny-theft	Motor vehicle theft	Arson[2]
State Police										
Accomack County	17	3	0	0	14	14	0	13	1	5
Albemarle County	2	0	0	0	2	5	0	3	2	0
Alexandria	5	0	0	0	5	5	0	4	0	0
Alleghany County	11	0	0	0	11	4	0	2	0	0
Amelia County	0	0	0	0	0	1	0	1	0	0
Amherst County	0	0	0	0	0	2	0	2	0	0
Appomattox County	1	0	0	0	1	3	0	1	2	0
Arlington County	1	0	0	0	1	6	0	5	1	2
Augusta County	7	0	0	0	7	0	0	0	0	0
Bath County	0	0	0	0	0	5	0	4	1	0
Bedford County	15	0	1	0	14	2	0	1	1	0
Bland County	7	0	2	0	5	3	0	1	1	0
Botetourt County	6	0	0	0	6	2	0	1	1	0
Bristol	1	0	0	0	1	0	0	0	0	0
Brunswick County	1	0	0	0	1	11	0	10	1	10
Buchanan County	3	0	0	0	3	3	1	2	0	1
Buckingham County	6	0	1	0	5	0	0	0	0	0
Buena Vista	0	0	0	0	0	4	0	4	0	1
Campbell County	5	0	0	0	5	23	1	11	11	0
Caroline County	12	0	0	0	12	10	1	7	2	1
Carroll County	2	1	0	0	1	0	0	0	0	0
Charles City County	0	0	0	0	0	3	0	2	1	1
Charlotte County	1	0	0	0	1	1	0	1	0	0
Charlottesville	1	0	1	0	0	10	0	3	7	0
Chesapeake	8	0	0	0	8	14	0	9	5	0
Chesterfield County	8	0	0	2	6	0	0	0	0	0
Clarke County[5]										
Clifton Forge	0	0	0	0	0	1	0	0	1	0
Colonial Heights	4	0	1	0	3	0	0	0	0	0
Covington	0	0	0	0	0	4	1	2	1	0
Craig County	1	0	1	0	0	1	0	1	0	1
Culpeper County	0	0	0	0	0	0	0	0	0	0
Cumberland County	1	1	0	0	0	2	0	2	0	0
Danville	2	0	0	0	2	3	0	3	0	1
Dickenson County	3	0	1	0	2	1	0	1	0	0
Dinwiddie County	10	0	5	0	5	0	0	0	0	0
Emporia	0	0	0	0	0	0	0	0	0	0
Essex County	1	0	0	0	1	0	0	0	0	0
Fairfax City	0	0	0	0	0	0	0	0	0	0
Fairfax County	44	0	1	1	42	24	0	11	13	0
Falls Church	0	0	0	0	0	3	0	1	2	0
Fauquier County	3	1	0	0	2	5	1	3	1	0
Floyd County	3	1	0	0	2	3	0	2	1	1
Fluvanna County	5	0	0	0	5	0	0	0	0	1
Franklin	0	0	0	0	0	4	0	4	0	1
Franklin County	2	0	0	1	1	8	0	5	3	0
Frederick County	6	0	1	0	5	1	0	1	0	0
Fredericksburg	1	0	1	0	0	0	0	0	0	0
Galax	0	0	0	0	0	0	0	0	0	1
Giles County	2	0	0	0	2	5	1	3	1	1
Gloucester County	7	0	1	0	6	0	0	0	0	0
Goochland County	1	0	0	0	1	0	0	0	0	1
Grayson County	0	0	0	0	0	2	0	1	1	0
Greene County	0	0	0	0	0	0	0	0	0	0
Greensville County	6	0	0	0	6	6	0	4	2	0
Halifax County	0	0	0	0	0	10	0	4	6	0
Hampton	3	0	0	0	3	2	0	1	1	1
Hanover County	3	0	0	0	3	3	0	2	1	0
Harrisonburg	2	0	0	0	2	7	0	5	2	0
Henrico County	5	0	0	0	5	7	0	5	2	0
Henry County	1	0	0	1	0	1	0	1	0	0
Highland County	1	0	0	0	1	2	0	2	0	0
Hopewell	1	0	0	1	0	1	0	1	0	0
Isle of Wight County	2	0	1	0	1	0	0	0	0	0
James City County	5	0	3	0	2	1	0	1	0	0
King and Queen County	1	0	0	0	1	0	0	0	0	0
King George County	0	0	0	0	0	0	0	0	0	0
King William County	1	1	0	0	0	0	0	0	0	0
Lancaster County	2	0	0	0	2	10	0	5	5	5
Lee County	1	1	0	0	0	0	0	0	0	0
Lexington	0	0	0	0	0	2	1	1	0	0
Loudoun County	1	0	0	0	1	2	0	2	0	0
Louisa County	0	0	0	0	0	1	0	1	0	0
Lunenburg County	5	0	0	0	5	0	0	0	0	0
Lynchburg	0	0	0	0	0	0	0	0	0	0
Madison County	2	0	0	0	2	0	0	0	0	0
Manassas	0	0	0	0	0	0	0	0	0	0
Manassas Park	0	0	0	0	0	1	0	0	1	0
Martinsville	0	0	0	0	0	1	0	1	0	0
Mathews County	6	1	0	0	5	5	0	3	2	1
Mecklenburg County	3	0	0	0	3	1	0	1	0	0
Middlesex County	3	0	0	0	3	1	0	1	0	0
Montgomery County	2	0	0	0	2	3	0	1	2	0

Table 11. Offenses Known to Law Enforcement, by Selected State, Tribal, and Other Agencies, 2019—Continued

(Number.)

State/other agency unit/office	Violent crime	Murder and nonnegligent manslaughter	Rape[1]	Robbery	Aggravated assault	Property crime	Burglary	Larceny-theft	Motor vehicle theft	Arson[2]
Nelson County	7	1	0	0	6	1	0	1	0	
New Kent County	6	0	0	0	6	4	1	3	0	1
Newport News	3	0	0	0	3	3	0	1	2	1
Norfolk	9	0	0	0	9	2	0	1	1	0
Northampton County	0	0	0	0	0	1	0	1	0	0
Northumberland County	1	0	0	0	1	0	0	0	0	0
Norton	0	0	0	0	0	0	0	0	0	0
Nottoway County	2	1	1	0	0	4	1	3	0	0
Orange County	4	0	1	0	3	2	1	1	0	0
Page County	1	0	0	0	1	3	1	1	1	0
Patrick County	1	0	0	0	1	4	0	3	1	0
Petersburg	1	0	0	0	1	0	0	0	0	0
Pittsylvania County	3	0	0	0	3	29	0	5	24	0
Poquoson	0	0	0	0	0	0	0	0	0	0
Portsmouth	16	0	0	0	16	9	0	2	7	1
Powhatan County	0	0	0	0	0	0	0	0	0	0
Prince Edward County	5	1	0	0	4	1	0	0	1	0
Prince George County	1	0	0	0	1	6	0	6	0	0
Prince William County	7	0	0	0	7	17	0	7	10	1
Pulaski County	11	1	1	0	9	13	2	8	3	0
Radford	0	0	0	0	0	0	0	0	0	0
Rappahannock County	1	0	0	0	1	3	0	2	1	0
Richmond	4	1	0	0	3	7	1	4	2	0
Richmond County	2	0	0	0	2	3	1	2	0	0
Roanoke	3	0	0	0	3	8	0	6	2	0
Roanoke County	2	0	1	0	1	1	0	0	1	0
Rockbridge County	6	0	0	0	6	1	0	1	0	0
Rockingham County	3	0	1	0	2	32	1	16	15	0
Russell County	3	0	2	0	1	6	0	6	0	0
Salem	1	0	0	0	1	6	0	5	1	0
Scott County	3	0	1	0	2	11	0	7	4	1
Shenandoah County	3	1	0	0	2	2	0	1	1	0
Smyth County	1	0	0	0	1	8	0	5	3	1
Southampton County	0	0	0	0	0	2	0	1	1	0
South Boston	0	0	0	0	0	0	0	0	0	0
Spotsylvania County	3	0	0	0	3	4	0	4	0	0
Stafford County	6	2	1	0	3	2	0	1	1	0
Staunton	5	0	1	0	4	0	0	0	0	1
Suffolk	2	0	0	0	2	4	0	0	4	0
Surry County	0	0	0	0	0	0	0	0	0	0
Sussex County	0	0	0	0	0	1	1	0	0	0
Tazewell County	8	0	0	0	8	16	3	9	4	1
Virginia Beach	11	0	0	0	11	0	0	0	0	0
Warren County	3	0	0	0	3	3	0	3	0	0
Washington County	1	0	0	0	1	11	0	10	1	2
Waynesboro	0	0	0	0	0	1	0	0	1	2
Westmoreland County	3	0	0	0	3	1	0	1	0	0
Williamsburg	0	0	0	0	0	0	0	0	0	0
Winchester	0	0	0	0	0	1	0	1	0	0
Wise County	0	0	0	0	0	7	1	3	3	0
Wythe County	7	0	2	0	5	18	0	12	6	2
York County	3	0	0	0	3	2	0	1	1	0
Virginia State Capitol	0	0	0	0	0	22	0	22	0	0
Other Agencies										
Norfolk Airport Authority	1	0	0	0	1	77	0	68	9	0
Port Authority, Norfolk	0	0	0	0	0	4	0	4	0	0
Reagan National Airport	2	0	0	0	2	320	0	280	40	0
Richmond International Airport	0	0	0	0	0	32	0	28	4	0
WASHINGTON										
State Agencies										
State Insurance Commissioner, Special Investigations Unit	0	0	0	0	0	6	0	6	0	0
Washington State Patrol	0	0	0	0	0	0	0	0	0	0
Tribal Agencies										
Chehalis Tribal	40	0	1	1	38	81	28	41	12	0
Colville Tribal	35	0	9	5	21	245	88	125	32	6
Jamestown S'Klallam Tribal	0	0	0	0	0	14	0	13	1	0
Kalispel Tribal	2	0	0	1	1	182	7	162	13	0
La Push Tribal	1	0	0	0	1	6	2	4	0	0
Lower Elwha Klallam Tribal	1	0	0	0	1	0	0	0	0	0
Makah Tribal	5	0	1	0	4	4	2	1	1	0
Muckleshoot Tribal	6	0	0	0	6	51	17	31	3	0
Nooksack Tribal	3	0	0	0	3	26	6	20	0	0
Port Gamble S'Klallam Tribal	1	0	0	0	1	15	1	13	1	0
Puyallup Tribal	66	0	9	23	34	671	107	365	199	0
Quinault Indian Nation	11	0	1	1	9	9	6	2	1	0
Shoalwater Bay Tribal	0	0	0	0	0	0	0	0	0	0
Skokomish Tribal	3	0	0	0	3	33	6	23	4	0
Snoqualmie Tribal	0	0	0	0	0	0	0	0	0	0
Spokane Agency	11	0	1	1	9	107	23	67	17	0
Squaxin Island Tribal	13	0	1	1	11	107	1	95	11	0
Stillaguamish Tribal	2	0	0	0	2	28	3	23	2	
Swinomish Tribal	4	0	4	0	0	37	2	34	1	0
Tulalip Tribal	31	0	5	5	21	1,142	37	972	133	2

Table 11. Offenses Known to Law Enforcement, by Selected State, Tribal, and Other Agencies, 2019—Continued

(Number.)

State/other agency unit/office	Violent crime	Murder and nonnegligent manslaughter	Rape[1]	Robbery	Aggravated assault	Property crime	Burglary	Larceny-theft	Motor vehicle theft	Arson[2]
Upper Skagit Tribal	18	0	1	1	16	41	4	33	4	0
Yakama Nation	65	1	35	7	22	807	188	400	219	45
Other Agencies	0	0	0	0	0	0	0	0	0	0
Port of Seattle	11	0	1	5	5	915	33	814	68	0
WEST VIRGINIA										
State Agencies										
State Police, Bureau of Criminal Investigations										
Beckley	0	0	0	0	0	0	0	0	0	0
Charleston	0	0	0	0	0	5	0	5	0	0
State Police	0	0	0	0	0	0	0	0	0	0
Beckley	19	2	4	0	13	166	24	120	22	0
Berkeley Springs	2	0	1	0	1	26	7	16	3	0
Bridgeport	10	0	7	0	3	118	27	73	18	0
Clay	15	0	4	2	9	57	24	24	9	0
Elkins	7	0	1	0	6	58	14	38	6	0
Fairmont	6	0	1	0	5	59	23	30	6	0
Franklin	5	0	1	0	4	33	13	20	0	1
Gauley Bridge	2	0	0	0	2	8	0	6	2	0
Glenville	12	0	4	0	8	24	9	12	3	0
Hamlin	21	0	9	0	12	168	42	79	47	1
Harrisville	7	1	3	0	3	41	12	26	3	1
Hinton	3	0	2	0	1	15	4	10	1	0
Jesse	10	0	7	0	3	27	13	9	5	0
Keyser	16	0	2	0	14	97	14	74	9	0
Kingwood	8	0	4	0	4	69	28	31	10	0
Lewisburg	6	0	1	0	5	79	17	49	13	1
Logan	25	0	10	2	13	76	20	38	18	0
Madison	5	0	2	0	3	66	17	34	15	0
Marlinton	7	0	3	0	4	36	12	19	5	2
Martinsburg	36	1	28	2	5	205	33	154	18	1
Moorefield	22	0	5	1	16	101	28	54	19	0
Morgantown	13	0	9	0	4	140	20	100	20	0
New Cumberland	6	0	2	0	4	0	0	0	0	0
Paden City	9	0	5	0	4	33	10	17	6	0
Parkersburg	9	0	9	0	0	29	3	19	7	0
Parsons	1	0	0	0	1	18	4	13	1	0
Philippi	11	0	2	0	9	36	12	20	4	0
Point Pleasant	5	0	0	0	5	31	7	13	11	1
Princeton	22	1	5	1	15	147	17	118	12	0
Quincy	7	1	4	0	2	98	19	64	15	0
Rainelle	3	0	0	0	3	33	11	22	0	1
Richwood	1	1	0	0	0	26	4	16	6	0
Ripley	7	0	4	0	3	44	12	25	7	0
Romney	10	0	6	0	4	47	20	25	2	0
South Charleston	26	0	20	0	6	299	38	229	32	0
Spencer	6	0	0	0	6	23	6	11	6	0
Summersville	6	2	0	0	4	60	9	41	10	0
Sutton	7	0	4	0	3	76	13	50	13	1
Union	1	0	0	0	1	18	7	6	5	0
Wayne	31	0	7	1	23	237	82	100	55	4
Welch	14	1	5	0	8	42	20	15	7	0
Weston	4	0	2	0	2	84	16	63	5	0
Wheeling	2	0	2	0	0	5	2	3	0	0
Whitesville	2	0	1	0	1	44	16	21	7	0
Winfield	8	0	3	0	5	99	16	70	13	1
Other Agencies										
Hancock/Brooke/Weirton Drug Task Force	0	0	0	0	0	0	0	0	0	0
Metropolitan Drug Enforcement Network Team	0	0	0	0	0	1	0	1	0	0
Mon Metro Drug Task Force	0	0	0	0	0	0	0	0	0	0
WISCONSIN										
State Agencies										
Capitol Police	0	0	0	0	0	9	0	9	0	0
Department of Natural Resources	0	0	0	0	0	0	0	0	0	0
State Fair Park Police	0	0	0	0	0	31	0	30	1	0
Wisconsin State Patrol	0	0	0	0	0	0	0	0	0	0
Tribal Agencies										
Lac Courte Oreilles Tribal	26	0	7	0	19	55	8	38	9	1
Lac du Flambeau Tribal	41	0	11	1	29	136	8	119	9	0
Menominee Tribal	85	2	4	1	78	57	13	34	10	1
Oneida Tribal	31	0	4	0	27	111	6	100	5	0
WYOMING										
Tribal Agencies										
Wind River Agency	78	1	21	0	56	90	16	38	36	1
PUERTO RICO AND OTHER OUTLYING AREAS										
Puerto Rico	6,479	606	215	2,121	3,537	22,441	4,291	14,483	3,667	5

1 The figures shown in this column for the offense of rape were reported using the revised Uniform Crime Reporting (UCR) definition of rape. See notes for further explanation.   2 The FBI does not publish arson data unless it receives data from either the agency or the state for all 12 months of the calendar year.   3 Limited data for 2019 were available for Alabama.   4 Because of changes in the state/local agency's reporting practices, figures are not comparable to previous years' data.   5 The FBI determined that the agency's data were overreported. Consequently, those data are not included in this table.

Table 12. Crime Trends, by Population Group, 2018–2019

(Number, percent change.)

Population group	Violent crime	Murder and nonnegligent manslaughter	Rape[1]	Robbery	Aggravated assault	Property crime	Burglary	Larceny-theft	Motor vehicle theft	Arson	Number of agencies	Estimated population, 2019
Total, All Agencies												
2018	1,142,958	14,915	131,959	261,241	734,843	6,621,258	1,104,712	4,785,340	696,099	35,107		
2019	1,135,093	15,020	126,958	248,681	744,434	6,358,176	998,474	4,659,007	667,300	33,395	15,261	307,140,768
Percent change	-0.7	+0.7	-3.8	-4.8	+1.3	-4.0	-9.6	-2.6	-4.1	-4.9		
Total, Cities												
2018	916,541	11,646	98,794	230,353	575,748	5,322,104	829,649	3,904,823	560,635	26,997		
2019	911,416	11,762	94,778	219,080	585,796	5,133,915	751,526	3,819,909	536,344	26,136	11,023	210,976,208
Percent change	-0.6	+1.0	-4.1	-4.9	+1.7	-3.5	-9.4	-2.2	-4.3	-3.2		
Group I (250,000 and over)												
2018	445,300	6,067	38,088	131,006	270,139	1,965,032	312,400	1,381,781	259,944	10,907		
2019	444,396	6,185	36,109	125,730	276,372	1,934,133	289,121	1,382,779	251,510	10,723	86	62,641,973
Percent change	-0.2	+1.9	-5.2	-4.0	+2.3	-1.6	-7.5	+0.1	-3.2	-1.7		
1,000,000 and over (Group I subset)												
2018	190,674	2,224	15,452	60,259	112,739	713,836	108,420	508,266	93,478	3,672		
2019	192,648	2,209	15,071	58,737	116,631	707,846	99,871	513,190	91,185	3,600	11	27,806,004
Percent change	+1.0	-0.7	-2.5	-2.5	+3.5	-0.8	-7.9	+1.0	-2.5	-2.0		
500,000 to 999,999 (Group I subset)												
2018	145,955	2,141	11,403	42,090	90,321	707,239	113,298	497,820	92,324	3,797		
2019	143,997	2,289	10,505	39,402	91,801	684,426	105,433	487,358	88,038	3,597	26	18,474,842
Percent change	-1.3	+6.9	-7.9	-6.4	+1.6	-3.2	-6.9	-2.1	-4.6	-5.3		
250,000 to 499,999 (Group I subset)												
2018	108,671	1,702	11,233	28,657	67,079	543,957	90,682	375,695	74,142	3,438		
2019	107,751	1,687	10,533	27,591	67,940	541,861	83,817	382,231	72,287	3,526	49	16,361,127
Percent change	-0.8	-0.9	-6.2	-3.7	+1.3	-0.4	-7.6	+1.7	-2.5	+2.6		
Group II (100,000 to 249,999)												
2018	139,303	1,833	15,785	35,875	85,810	885,077	138,400	637,127	105,333	4,217		
2019	140,053	1,841	14,772	33,871	89,569	844,779	124,271	618,458	98,007	4,043	220	31,945,830
Percent change	+0.5	+0.4	-6.4	-5.6	+4.4	-4.6	-10.2	-2.9	-7.0	-4.1		
Group III (50,000 to 99,999)												
2018	112,336	1,282	13,372	26,923	70,759	778,839	120,597	579,227	75,119	3,896		
2019	110,416	1,254	13,028	25,385	70,749	748,189	107,498	566,010	71,055	3,626	492	34,283,540
Percent change	-1.7	-2.2	-2.6	-5.7	*	-3.9	-10.9	-2.3	-5.4	-6.9		
Group IV (25,000 to 49,999)												
2018	81,996	1,004	11,829	17,120	52,043	633,847	94,717	486,908	49,495	2,727		
2019	80,560	1,016	11,167	15,829	52,548	605,639	84,376	470,766	47,792	2,705	888	30,781,974
Percent change	-1.8	+1.2	-5.6	-7.5	+1.0	-4.5	-10.9	-3.3	-3.4	-0.8		
Group V (10,000 to 24,999)												
2018	72,343	809	10,304	11,906	49,324	578,557	90,127	445,525	40,532	2,373		
2019	70,475	838	10,112	11,004	48,521	544,868	79,393	424,801	38,339	2,335	1,799	28,730,692
Percent change	-2.6	+3.6	-1.9	-7.6	-1.6	-5.8	-11.9	-4.7	-5.4	-1.6		
Group VI (under 10,000)												
2018												
2019	65,263	651	9,416	7,523	47,673	480,752	73,408	374,255	30,212	2,877		
Percent change	65,516	628	9,590	7,261	48,037	456,307	66,867	357,095	29,641	2,704	7,538	22,592,199
	+0.4	-3.5	+1.8	-3.5	+0.8	-5.1	-8.9	-4.6	-1.9	-6.0		
Metropolitan Counties												
2018												
2019	180,792	2,457	24,343	28,695	125,297	1,060,896	205,351	737,843	111,565	6,137		
Percent change	177,882	2,442	23,472	27,477	124,491	1,002,794	183,458	706,947	106,956	5,433	1,922	73,179,304
	-1.6	-0.6	-3.6	-4.2	-0.6	-5.5	-10.7	-4.2	-4.1	-11.5		
Nonmetropolitan Counties[2]												
2018												
2019	45,625	812	8,822	2,193	33,798	238,258	69,712	142,674	23,899	1,973		
Percent change	45,795	816	8,708	2,124	34,147	221,467	63,490	132,151	24,000	1,826	2,316	22,985,256
	+0.4	+0.5	-1.3	-3.1	+1.0	-7.0	-8.9	-7.4	+0.4	-7.5		
Suburban Areas[3]												
2018	314,980	3,972	43,742	54,668	212,598	2,179,059	361,192	1,611,305	195,519	11,043		
2019	309,842	3,917	42,129	52,030	211,766	2,069,523	322,835	1,548,496	188,088	10,104	8,421	133,848,983
Percent change	-1.6	-1.4	-3.7	-4.8	-0.4	-5.0	-10.6	-3.9	-3.8	-8.5		

* = Less than one-tenth of one percent.
1 The figures shown in the rape (revised definition) column include only those reported by law enforcement agencies that used the revised Uniform Crime Reporting (UCR) definition of rape. See chapter notes for more detail.   2 Includes state police agencies that report aggregately for the entire state.   3 Suburban areas include law enforcement agencies in cities with less than 50,000 inhabitants and county law enforcement agencies that are within a Metropolitan Statistical Area. Suburban areas exclude all metropolitan agencies associated with a principal city. The agencies associated with suburban areas also appear in other groups within this table.

Table 13. Crime Trends, by Suburban and Nonsuburban Cities,[1] by Population Group, 2018–2019

(Number, percent change.)

Population group	Violent crime	Murder and nonnegligent manslaughter	Rape[2]	Robbery	Aggravated assault	Property crime	Burglary	Larceny-theft	Motor vehicle theft	Arson	Number of agencies	Estimated population, 2019
Suburban Cities												
2018	134,188	1,515	19,399	25,973	87,301	1,118,163	155,841	873,462	83,954	4,906		
2019	131,960	1,475	18,657	24,553	87,275	1,066,729	139,377	841,549	81,132	4,671	6,499	60,669,679
Percent change	-1.7	-2.6	-3.8	-5.5	*	-4.6	-10.6	-3.7	-3.4	-4.8		
Group IV (25,000 to 49,999)												
2018	51,525	611	7,672	11,700	31,542	433,170	59,594	336,590	35,337	1,649		
2019	50,043	611	7,088	10,892	31,452	415,472	53,148	326,158	34,539	1,627	706	24,251,769
Percent change	-2.9	0.0	-7.6	-6.9	-0.3	-4.1	-10.8	-3.1	-2.3	-1.3		
Group V (10,000 to 24,999)												
2018	47,134	542	6,668	8,798	31,126	388,036	55,998	300,948	29,557	1,533		
2019	45,719	529	6,361	8,195	30,634	366,792	49,206	288,126	28,010	1,450	1,385	22,249,907
Percent change	-3.0	-2.4	-4.6	-6.9	-1.6	-5.5	-12.1	-4.3	-5.2	-5.4		
Group VI (under 10,000)												
2018	35,529	362	5,059	5,475	24,633	296,957	40,249	235,924	19,060	1,724		
2019	36,198	335	5,208	5,466	25,189	284,465	37,023	227,265	18,583	1,594	4,408	14,168,003
Percent change	+1.9	-7.5	+2.9	-0.2	+2.3	-4.2	-8.0	-3.7	-2.5	-7.5		
Nonsuburban Cities												
2018	59,815	614	8,886	5,599	44,716	408,315	73,350	307,683	25,098	2,184		
2019	58,940	655	9,035	5,049	44,201	381,483	65,109	289,848	24,322	2,204	3,553	16,030,361
Percent change	-1.5	+6.7	+1.7	-9.8	-1.2	-6.6	-11.2	-5.8	-3.1	+0.9		
Group IV (25,000 to 49,999)												
2018	8,094	91	1,278	1,017	5,708	58,916	10,234	44,206	4,202	274		
2019	7,709	97	1,236	943	5,433	54,294	8,674	41,311	4,034	275	63	2,044,018
Percent change	-4.8	+6.6	-3.3	-7.3	-4.8	-7.8	-15.2	-6.5	-4.0	+0.4		
Group V (10,000 to 24,999)												
2018	22,037	234	3,258	2,538	16,007	165,926	29,997	125,415	9,757	757		
2019	21,967	265	3,424	2,315	15,963	155,662	26,604	118,971	9,267	820	365	5,579,822
Percent change	-0.3	+13.2	+5.1	-8.8	-0.3	-6.2	-11.3	-5.1	-5.0	+8.3		
Group VI (under 10,000)												
2018	29,684	289	4,350	2,044	23,001	183,473	33,119	138,062	11,139	1,153		
2019	29,264	293	4,375	1,791	22,805	171,527	29,831	129,566	11,021	1,109	3,125	8,406,521
Percent change	-1.4	+1.4	+0.6	-12.4	-0.9	-6.5	-9.9	-6.2	-1.1	-3.8		

* = Less than one-tenth of one percent.
1 Suburban cities include law enforcement agencies in cities with less than 50,000 inhabitants that are within a Metropolitan Statistical Area. Suburban cities exclude all metropolitan agencies associated with a principal city. Nonsuburban cities include law enforcement agencies in cities with less than 50,000 inhabitants that are not associated with a Metropolitan Statistical Area.   2 The figures shown in the rape column include only those reported by law enforcement agencies that used the revised Uniform Crime Reporting (UCR) definition of rape. See chapter notes for more detail.

Table 14. Crime Trends, by Metropolitan and Nonmetropolitan Counties,[1] by Population Group, 2018–2019

(Number, percent change.)

Population group and range	Violent crime	Murder and nonnegligent manslaughter	Rape[2]	Robbery	Aggravated assault	Property crime	Burglary	Larceny-theft	Motor vehicle theft	Arson	Number of agencies	Estimated population, 2019
Metropolitan Counties												
100,000 and over												
2018	118,955	1,600	14,098	23,969	79,288	708,584	123,965	508,062	72,761	3,796		
2019	117,124	1,635	13,773	23,015	78,701	674,508	109,877	491,569	69,716	3,346	167	45,594,677
Percent change	-1.5	+2.2	-2.3	-4.0	-0.7	-4.8	-11.4	-3.2	-4.2	-11.9		
25,000 to 99,999												
2018	42,928	605	6,842	3,466	32,015	257,498	63,113	169,694	23,193	1,498		
2019	41,664	591	6,329	3,255	31,489	239,363	55,566	159,427	23,054	1,316	435	22,755,761
Percent change	-2.9	-2.3	-7.5	-6.1	-1.6	-7.0	-12.0	-6.1	-0.6	-12.1		
Under 25,000												
2018	18,909	252	3,403	1,260	13,994	94,814	18,273	60,087	15,611	843		
2019	19,094	216	3,370	1,207	14,301	88,923	18,015	55,951	14,186	771	1,320	4,828,866
Percent change	+1.0	-14.3	-1.0	-4.2	+2.2	-6.2	-1.4	-6.9	-9.1	-8.5		
Nonmetropolitan Counties												
25,000 and over												
2018	18,655	289	3,322	1,161	13,883	104,916	30,768	63,382	10,032	734		
2019	19,237	323	3,376	1,199	14,339	97,586	27,871	59,165	9,825	725	252	10,171,234
Percent change	+3.1	+11.8	+1.6	+3.3	+3.3	-7.0	-9.4	-6.7	-2.1	-1.2		
10,000 to 24,999												
2018	14,821	259	2,500	721	11,341	83,050	24,974	49,695	7,715	666		
2019	14,800	252	2,485	661	11,402	77,391	23,032	45,907	7,814	638	542	8,683,253
Percent change	-0.1	-2.7	-0.6	-8.3	+0.5	-6.8	-7.8	-7.6	+1.3	-4.2		
Under 10,000												
2018	12,149	264	3,000	311	8,574	50,292	13,970	29,597	6,152	573		
2019	11,758	241	2,847	264	8,406	46,490	12,587	27,079	6,361	463	1,522	4,130,769
Percent change	-3.2	-8.7	-5.1	-15.1	-2.0	-7.6	-9.9	-8.5	+3.4	-19.2		

1 Metropolitan counties include sheriffs and county law enforcement agencies associated with a Metropolitan Statistical Area. Nonmetropolitan counties include sheriffs and county law enforcement agencies that are not associated with a Metropolitan Statistical Area.   2 The figures shown in the rape column include only those reported by law enforcement agencies that used the revised Uniform Crime Reporting (UCR) definition of rape. See notes for further detail.

Table 15. Crime Trends, Additional Information About Selected Offenses, by Population Group, 2018–2019

(Number, percent change.)

Population group	Rape[1]	Assault to rape-attempts	Robbery Firearm	Knife or cutting instrument	Other weapon	Strong-arm	Aggravated assault Firearm	Knife or cutting instrument	Other weapon	Hands, fists, feet, etc.
Total, All Agencies										
2018	120,678	5,564	95,281	20,995	25,716	105,557	186,543	123,370	217,585	178,904
2019	116,254	5,008	87,716	19,963	24,438	104,551	195,787	123,179	212,518	183,137
Percent change	-3.7	-10.0	-7.9	-4.9	-5.0	-1.0	+5.0	-0.2	-2.3	+2.4
Total, Cities										
2018	89,442	4,342	81,667	18,739	22,473	93,982	149,769	100,921	167,381	131,066
2019	85,889	3,852	74,991	17,738	21,395	93,170	157,606	100,962	164,329	135,021
Percent change	-4.0	-11.3	-8.2	-5.3	-4.8	-0.9	+5.2	*	-1.8	+3.0
Group I (250,000 and over)										
2018	34,329	1,902	47,906	10,362	11,955	51,102	82,879	48,837	79,353	43,755
2019	32,664	1,684	44,436	10,177	11,610	51,524	87,885	49,373	77,823	45,995
Percent change	-4.9	-11.5	-7.2	-1.8	-2.9	+0.8	+6.0	+1.1	-1.9	+5.1
1,000,000 and over (Group I subset)										
2018	12,745	850	17,362	4,806	4,932	23,478	24,120	21,244	30,613	21,447
2019	12,546	764	16,464	4,994	5,369	23,927	25,861	21,817	30,032	23,625
Percent change	-1.6	-10.1	-5.2	+3.9	+8.9	+1.9	+7.2	+2.7	-1.9	+10.2
500,000 to 999,999 (Group I subset)										
2018	10,856	547	18,767	3,342	4,606	15,375	33,727	15,911	28,813	11,870
2019	10,023	482	16,644	3,082	3,999	15,677	35,987	15,873	28,332	11,609
Percent change	-7.7	-11.9	-11.3	-7.8	-13.2	+2.0	+6.7	-0.2	-1.7	-2.2
250,000 to 499,999 (Group I subset)										
2018	10,728	505	11,777	2,214	2,417	12,249	25,032	11,682	19,927	10,438
2019	10,095	438	11,328	2,101	2,242	11,920	26,037	11,683	19,459	10,761
Percent change	-5.9	-13.3	-3.8	-5.1	-7.2	-2.7	+4.0	*	-2.3	+3.1
Group II (100,000 to 249,999)										
2018	14,838	605	12,816	3,192	3,825	15,332	23,034	16,218	25,693	18,735
2019	13,919	507	11,836	2,918	3,407	14,959	25,297	16,378	25,178	20,255
Percent change	-6.2	-16.2	-7.6	-8.6	-10.9	-2.4	+9.8	+1.0	-2.0	+8.1
Group III (50,000 to 99,999)										
2018	12,378	517	8,553	2,303	2,824	12,377	16,217	12,641	22,116	17,804
2019	11,963	559	7,783	2,146	2,766	11,875	16,525	12,343	21,611	18,163
Percent change	-3.4	+8.1	-9.0	-6.8	-2.1	-4.1	+1.9	-2.4	-2.3	+2.0
Group IV (25,000 to 49,999)										
2018	10,454	436	5,750	1,360	1,867	7,088	11,086	8,930	14,963	14,102
2019	9,894	334	5,128	1,155	1,650	6,901	11,436	8,855	14,649	14,450
Percent change	-5.4	-23.4	-10.8	-15.1	-11.6	-2.6	+3.2	-0.8	-2.1	+2.5
Group V (10,000 to 24,999)										
2018	9,058	353	4,141	928	1,156	4,760	9,662	7,591	13,844	15,700
2019	8,917	297	3,637	849	1,215	4,383	9,290	7,487	13,511	15,173
Percent change	-1.6	-15.9	-12.2	-8.5	+5.1	-7.9	-3.9	-1.4	-2.4	-3.4
Group VI (under 10,000)										
2018	8,385	529	2,501	594	846	3,323	6,891	6,704	11,412	20,970
2019	8,532	471	2,171	493	747	3,528	7,173	6,526	11,557	20,985
Percent change	+1.8	-11.0	-13.2	-17.0	-11.7	+6.2	+4.1	-2.7	+1.3	+0.1
Metropolitan Counties										
2018	22,974	868	12,664	2,081	2,926	10,853	29,857	18,453	40,371	35,324
2019	22,232	806	11,766	2,065	2,760	10,684	30,889	18,098	38,403	35,844
Percent change	-3.2	-7.1	-7.1	-0.8	-5.7	-1.6	+3.5	-1.9	-4.9	+1.5
Nonmetropolitan Counties										
2018	8,262	354	950	175	317	722	6,917	3,996	9,833	12,514
2019	8,133	350	959	160	283	697	7,292	4,119	9,786	12,272
Percent change	-1.6	-1.1	+0.9	-8.6	-10.7	-3.5	+5.4	+3.1	-0.5	-1.9
Suburban Areas[2]										
2018	39,927	1,663	21,358	4,020	5,712	21,609	45,744	31,958	64,310	64,716
2019	38,503	1,476	19,347	3,761	5,428	21,468	46,581	31,198	62,048	65,325
Percent change	-3.6	-11.2	-9.4	-6.4	-5.0	-0.7	+1.8	-2.4	-3.5	+0.9

Table 15. Crime Trends, Additional Information About Selected Offenses, by Population Group, 2018–2019 —Continued

(Number, percent change.)

Population group	Burglary: Forcible entry	Unlawful entry	Attempted forcible entry	Motor vehicle theft: Autos	Trucks and buses	Other vehicles	Arson: Structure	Mobile	Other	Number of agencies	Estimated population, 2019
Total, All Agencies											
2018	602,997	397,190	68,966	506,780	107,769	62,901	14,280	8,117	11,484		
2019	540,947	364,119	62,244	485,731	103,152	60,659	13,589	7,288	11,322	14,558	295,229,669
Percent change	-10.3	-8.3	-9.7	-4.2	-4.3	-3.6	-4.8	-10.2	-1.4		
Total, Cities											
2018	450,959	292,682	54,690	412,527	86,614	44,082	10,862	5,947	9,069		
2019	405,033	270,051	49,460	394,680	82,979	42,158	10,563	5,347	9,138	10,415	200,825,277
Percent change	-10.2	-7.7	-9.6	-4.3	-4.2	-4.4	-2.8	-10.1	+0.8		
Group I (250,000 and over)											
2018	184,885	94,719	21,071	182,988	49,181	17,660	4,053	2,659	3,770		
2019	168,328	91,562	19,653	178,229	47,578	16,622	3,912	2,405	3,990	85	59,934,909
Percent change	-9.0	-3.3	-6.7	-2.6	-3.3	-5.9	-3.5	-9.6	+5.8		
1,000,000 and over (Group I subset)											
2018	62,598	27,388	6,709	53,213	24,330	5,820	974	669	1,604		
2019	57,736	26,054	6,503	50,136	26,303	5,665	964	539	1,681	10	25,098,940
Percent change	-7.8	-4.9	-3.1	-5.8	+8.1	-2.7	-1.0	-19.4	+4.8		
500,000 to 999,999 (Group I subset)											
2018	69,286	35,973	8,039	72,204	13,561	6,559	1,487	1,058	1,252		
2019	61,795	36,193	7,445	69,756	11,421	6,861	1,402	976	1,219	26	18,474,842
Percent change	-10.8	+0.6	-7.4	-3.4	-15.8	+4.6	-5.7	-7.8	-2.6		
250,000 to 499,999 (Group I subset)											
2018	53,001	31,358	6,323	57,571	11,290	5,281	1,592	932	914		
2019	48,797	29,315	5,705	58,337	9,854	4,096	1,546	890	1,090	49	16,361,127
Percent change	-7.9	-6.5	-9.8	+1.3	-12.7	-22.4	-2.9	-4.5	+19.3		
Group II (100,000 to 249,999)											
2018	76,058	49,386	9,788	80,941	15,332	7,990	1,651	1,020	1,391		
2019	67,834	44,849	9,008	75,208	14,270	7,395	1,615	932	1,362	214	31,111,370
Percent change	-10.8	-9.2	-8.0	-7.1	-6.9	-7.4	-2.2	-8.6	-2.1		
Group III (50,000 to 99,999)											
2018	62,944	46,606	7,780	57,379	10,217	6,487	1,545	839	1,415		
2019	56,218	41,340	6,911	54,020	9,605	6,219	1,450	710	1,341	471	32,899,487
Percent change	-10.7	-11.3	-11.2	-5.9	-6.0	-4.1	-6.1	-15.4	-5.2		
Group IV (25,000 to 49,999)											
2018	47,252	36,065	6,361	38,041	4,894	4,495	1,090	484	954		
2019	41,516	32,800	5,431	36,321	4,890	4,616	1,151	468	923	827	28,743,747
Percent change	-12.1	-9.1	-14.6	-4.5	-0.1	+2.7	+5.6	-3.3	-3.2		
Group V (10,000 to 24,999)											
2018	44,387	35,802	5,083	30,439	4,117	3,880	1,036	443	747		
2019	39,132	31,518	4,488	28,711	3,915	3,601	1,011	364	823	1,679	26,741,149
Percent change	-11.8	-12.0	-11.7	-5.7	-4.9	-7.2	-2.4	-17.8	+10.2		
Group VI (under 10,000)											
2018	35,433	30,104	4,607	22,739	2,873	3,570	1,487	502	792		
2019	32,005	27,982	3,969	22,191	2,721	3,705	1,424	468	699	7,139	21,394,615
Percent change	-9.7	-7.0	-13.8	-2.4	-5.3	+3.8	-4.2	-6.8	-11.7		
Metropolitan Counties											
2018	112,819	77,920	11,661	78,268	17,403	14,927	2,455	1,761	1,841		
2019	100,720	69,376	10,423	75,308	16,287	14,415	2,161	1,532	1,657	1,876	71,943,603
Percent change	-10.7	-11.0	-10.6	-3.8	-6.4	-3.4	-12.0	-13.0	-10.0		
Nonmetropolitan Counties											
2018	39,219	26,588	2,615	15,985	3,752	3,892	963	409	574		
2019	35,194	24,692	2,361	15,743	3,886	4,086	865	409	527	2,267	22,460,789
Percent change	-10.3	-7.1	-9.7	-1.5	+3.6	+5.0	-10.2	0.0	-8.2		
Suburban Areas[2]											
2018	188,763	137,461	22,709	141,711	25,661	22,920	4,596	2,720	3,370		
2019	169,061	122,556	20,038	136,226	24,282	22,376	4,244	2,396	3,121	7,953	128,292,366
Percent change	-10.4	-10.8	-11.8	-3.9	-5.4	-2.4	-7.7	-11.9	-7.4		

* = Less than one-tenth of one percent.
1 The figures shown in the rape column include only those reported by law enforcement agencies that used the revised Uniform Crime Reporting (UCR) definition of rape. See notes for more detail.   2 Suburban areas include law enforcement agencies in cities with less than 50,000 inhabitants and county law enforcement agencies that are within a Metropolitan Statistical Area. Suburban areas exclude all metropolitan agencies associated with a principal city. The agencies associated with suburban areas also appear in other groups within this table.

Table 16. Rate: Number of Crimes Per 100,000 Population, by Population Group, 2019

(Number, rate.)

Population group	Violent crime		Murder and nonnegligent manslaughter		Rape[1]		Robbery		Aggravated assault	
	Number of offenses known	Rate	Number of offenses known	Rate	Number of offenses known	Rate	Number of offenses known	Rate	Number of offenses known	Rate
Total, All Agencies	1,081,697	387.0	14,014	5.0	122,822	44.0	237,873	85.1	706,988	253.0
Total, Cities	873,689	449.2	11,039	5.7	92,472	47.6	210,769	108.4	559,409	287.7
Group I (250,000 and over)	430,847	715.8	5,794	9.6	35,621	59.2	121,748	202.3	267,684	444.7
1,000,000 and over (Group I subset)	181,251	691.3	1,944	7.4	14,291	54.5	54,543	208.0	110,473	421.4
500,000 to 999,999 (Group I subset)	138,815	796.3	2,184	12.5	10,518	60.3	37,942	217.6	88,171	505.8
250,000 to 499,999 (Group I subset)	110,781	669.8	1,666	10.1	10,812	65.4	29,263	176.9	69,040	417.5
Group II (100,000 to 249,999)	139,414	451.9	1,817	5.9	14,924	48.6	33,469	108.9	89,204	289.1
Group III (50,000 to 99,999)	106,412	333.2	1,196	3.8	12,654	39.6	24,217	75.8	68,345	214.0
Group IV (25,000 to 49,999)	75,729	270.5	933	3.3	10,763	38.4	14,944	53.4	49,089	175.3
Group V (10,000 to 24,999)	63,994	254.8	753	3.0	9,636	38.5	10,057	40.0	43,548	173.6
Group VI (under 10,000)	57,293	310.9	546	3.0	8,874	48.3	6,334	34.4	41,539	225.4
Metropolitan Counties	166,611	255.7	2,224	3.4	22,200	34.2	25,201	38.7	116,986	179.5
Nonmetropolitan Counties[2]	41,397	208.4	751	3.8	8,150	41.1	1,903	9.6	30,593	154.0
Suburban Areas[3]	287,940	243.3	3,569	3.0	40,024	33.9	48,063	40.6	196,284	165.9

Table 16. Rate: Number of Crimes Per 100,000 Population, by Population Group, 2019—Continued

(Number, rate.)

Population group	Property crime		Burglary		Larceny-theft		Motor vehicle theft	
	Number of offenses known	Rate	Number of offenses known	Rate	Number of offenses known	Rate	Number of offenses known	Rate
Total, All Agencies	5,954,888	2,130.3	937,367	336.7	4,383,165	1,569.2	634,356	227.6
Total, Cities	4,847,733	2,492.2	713,134	368.1	3,620,225	1,862.7	514,374	265.5
Group I (250,000 and over)	1,853,455	3,079.4	276,877	464.4	1,334,313	2,216.9	242,265	407.2
1,000,000 and over (Group I subset)	667,672	2,546.7	95,427	364.0	485,179	1,850.6	87,066	332.1
500,000 to 999,999 (Group I subset)	645,353	3,701.9	97,495	577.9	465,157	2,668.2	82,701	494.2
250,000 to 499,999 (Group I subset)	540,430	3,267.7	83,955	507.6	383,977	2,321.7	72,498	438.4
Group II (100,000 to 249,999)	834,255	2,704.2	124,515	403.6	612,218	1,984.5	97,522	316.1
Group III (50,000 to 99,999)	706,211	2,211.6	101,485	317.8	537,090	1,685.5	67,636	212.3
Group IV (25,000 to 49,999)	562,852	2,010.4	79,048	284.1	438,758	1,568.6	45,046	160.9
Group V (10,000 to 24,999)	489,238	1,947.6	71,688	285.7	382,237	1,525.0	35,313	140.7
Group VI (under 10,000)	401,722	2,180.2	59,521	323.4	315,609	1,713.9	26,592	144.3
Metropolitan Counties	910,152	1,396.9	166,581	257.1	645,121	990.8	98,450	151.1
Nonmetropolitan Counties[2]	197,003	991.6	57,652	290.3	117,819	593.4	21,532	108.4
Suburban Areas[3]	1,885,710	1,593.5	295,785	251.0	1,415,616	1,197.3	174,309	147.3

NOTE: Due to a system upgrade, the rates in this table are now caculated using aggregate popualtion for each individual offense. The agency counts and population are provided for each individual offense. See Appendix V for further explanations of these changes.

1 The figures shown in this column for the offense of rape were reported using only the revised Uniform Crime Reporting definition of rape. See the chapter notes for further explanation.   2 Includes state police agencies that report aggregately for the entire state.   3 Suburban areas include law enforcement agencies in cities with less than 50,000 inhabitants and county law enforcement agencies that are within a Metropolitan Statistical Area. Suburban areas exclude all metropolitan agencies associated with a principal city. The agencies associated with suburban areas also appear in other groups within this table.

Table 17. Rate: Number of Crimes Per 100,000 Inhabitants, by Suburban and Nonsuburban Cities,[1] by Population Group, 2019

(Number, rate.)

Population group	Violent crime		Murder and nonnegligent manslaughter		Rape[2]		Robbery		Aggravated assault	
	Number of offenses known	Rate	Number of offenses known	Rate	Number of offenses known	Rate	Number of offenses known	Rate	Number of offenses known	Rate
Total, Suburban Cities	121,329	228.1	1,345	2.5	17,824	33.5	22,862	43.0	79,298	149.2
Group IV (25,000 to 49,999)	47,626	215.1	576	2.6	6,920	31.3	10,373	46.8	29,757	134.4
Group V (10,000 to 24,999)	42,665	217.6	490	2.5	6,141	31.3	7,673	39.1	28,361	144.8
Group VI (under 10,000)	31,038	271.4	279	2.4	4,763	41.7	4,816	42.1	21,180	185.2
Total, Nonsuburban Cities	52,516	386.0	577	4.2	8,491	62.7	4,387	32.2	39,061	287.5
Group IV (25,000 to 49,999)	7,011	391.9	85	4.8	1,182	66.1	865	48.4	4,879	272.7
Group V (10,000 to 24,999)	19,367	401.2	228	4.7	3,207	67.1	2,005	41.5	13,927	289.7
Group VI (under 10,000)	26,138	374.0	264	3.8	4,102	58.9	1,517	21.7	20,255	289.9

Population group	Property crime		Burglary		Larceny-theft		Motor vehicle theft	
	Number of offenses known	Rate	Number of offenses known	Rate	Number of offenses known	Rate	Number of offenses known	Rate
Total, Suburban Cities	975,558	1,834.3	129,204	243.6	770,495	1,450.4	75,859	142.7
Group IV (25,000 to 49,999)	388,141	1,752.9	50,516	229.2	304,725	1,377.7	32,900	148.6
Group V (10,000 to 24,999)	335,631	1,712.1	45,846	234.2	263,570	1,346.1	26,215	133.9
Group VI (under 10,000)	251,786	2,201.3	32,842	287.3	202,200	1,769.6	16,744	146.4
Total, Nonsuburban Cities	334,822	2,461.2	58,026	427.9	255,141	1,880.0	21,655	159.2
Group IV (25,000 to 49,999)	49,151	2,747.5	8,030	455.6	37,486	2,095.4	3,635	203.2
Group V (10,000 to 24,999)	136,190	2,821.4	23,338	483.5	104,648	2,182.6	8,204	170.0
Group VI (under 10,000)	149,481	2,139.2	26,658	382.3	113,007	1,617.2	9,816	140.5

NOTE: Due to a system upgrade, the rates in this table are now caculated using aggregate popualtion for each individual offense. The agency counts and population are provided for each individual offense. See Appendix V for further explanations of these changes.

1 Suburban cities include law enforcement agencies in cities with less than 50,000 inhabitants that are within a Metropolitan Statistical Area. Suburban cities exclude all metropolitan agencies associated with a principal city. Nonsuburban cities include law enforcement agencies in cities with less than 50,000 inhabitants that are not associated with a Metropolitan Statistical Area.   2 The figures shown in this column for the offense of rape were reported using only the revised Uniform Crime Reporting definition of rape. See chapter notes for more detail.

Table 18. Rate: Number of Crimes Per 100,000 Inhabitants, by Metropolitan and Nonmetropolitan Counties,[1] by Population Group, 2019

(Number, rate.)

Population group	Violent crime		Murder and nonnegligent manslaughter		Rape[2]		Robbery		Aggravated assault	
	Number of offenses known	Rate	Number of offenses known	Rate	Number of offenses known	Rate	Number of offenses known	Rate	Number of offenses known	Rate
Metropolitan Counties										
100,000 and over	111,997	266.0	1,484	3.5	13,465	32.0	21,215	50.4	75,833	180.1
25,000 to 99,999	37,116	198.1	543	2.9	5,597	30.2	2,869	15.3	28,107	150.0
Under 25,000	17,498	404.5	197	4.6	3,138	72.7	1,117	25.8	13,046	301.6
Nonmetropolitan Counties										
25,000 and over	17,302	200.3	290	3.4	3,099	35.9	1,085	12.6	12,828	148.5
10,000 to 24,999	13,589	177.0	234	3.1	2,344	30.7	582	7.6	10,429	135.8
Under 10,000	10,506	295.9	227	6.4	2,707	76.2	236	6.6	7,336	206.6

Table 18. Rate: Number of Crimes Per 100,000 Inhabitants, by Metropolitan and Nonmetropolitan Counties,[1] by Population Group, 2019—Continued

(Number, rate.)

Population group	Property crime		Burglary		Larceny-theft		Motor vehicle theft	
	Number of offenses known	Rate	Number of offenses known	Rate	Number of offenses known	Rate	Number of offenses known	Rate
Metropolitan Counties								
100,000 and over	622,188	1,477.9	101,511	241.1	456,313	1,083.9	64,364	152.9
25,000 to 99,999	206,045	1,100.0	48,555	263.9	136,982	733.0	20,508	109.5
Under 25,000	81,919	1,893.5	16,515	383.5	51,826	1,198.0	13,578	313.9
Nonmetropolitan Counties								
25,000 and over	85,656	991.4	25,281	292.6	51,615	597.4	8,760	101.4
10,000 to 24,999	69,370	903.6	21,026	273.9	41,338	539.4	7,006	91.3
Under 10,000	41,977	1,182.2	11,345	320.4	24,866	700.3	5,766	162.4

NOTE: Due to a system upgrade, the rates in this table are now caculated using aggregate popualtion for each individual offense. The agency counts and population are provided for each individual offense. See Appendix V for further explanations of these changes.

1 Metropolitan counties include sheriffs and county law enforcement agencies associated with a Metropolitan Statistical Area. Nonmetropolitan counties include sheriffs and county law enforcement agencies that are not associated with a Metropolitan Statistical Area.   2 The figures shown in this column for the offense of rape were reported using only the revised Uniform Crime Reporting definition of rape. See the chapter notes for further explanation.

Table 19. Rate: Number of Crimes Per 100,000 Inhabitants, Additional Information About Selected Offenses, by Population Group, 2019

(Number, rate.)

Population group	Rape[1]		Robbery			Aggravated assault			
	Rape by force	Assault to rape-attempts	Firearm	Knife or cutting instrument	Other weapon	Strong-arm	Firearm	Knife or cutting instrument	Other weapon
Total, All Agencies									
Number of offenses known	112,482	4,738	82,285	19,157	23,196	101,268	186,874	118,227	201,578
Rate	42.0	1.8	30.7	7.2	8.7	37.8	69.7	44.1	75.2
Total, Cities									
Number of offenses known	83,832	3,673	70,906	17,066	20,446	90,609	151,179	96,983	156,286
Rate	45.5	2.0	38.4	9.2	11.1	49.1	81.9	52.5	84.7
Group I (250,000 and over)									
Number of offenses known	32,208	1,652	42,158	9,790	11,180	50,637	84,985	47,876	75,061
Rate	56.0	2.9	73.3	17.0	19.4	88.1	147.8	83.3	130.6
1,000,000 and over (Group I subset)									
Number of offenses known	11,820	710	14,893	4,696	5,050	21,921	23,915	20,630	27,990
Rate	50.3	3.0	63.3	20.0	21.5	93.2	101.7	87.8	119.1
500,000 to 999,999 (Group I subset)									
Number of offenses known	10,037	481	15,968	2,986	3,894	15,094	34,514	15,343	27,337
Rate	57.6	2.8	91.6	17.1	22.3	86.6	198.0	88.0	156.8
250,000 to 499,999 (Group I subset)									
Number of offenses known	10,351	461	11,297	2,108	2,236	13,622	26,556	11,903	19,734
Rate	62.6	2.8	68.3	12.7	13.5	82.4	160.6	72.0	119.3
Group II (100,000 to 249,999)									
Number of offenses known	14,087	510	11,669	2,890	3,344	14,834	25,123	16,227	25,085
Rate	47.0	1.7	38.8	9.6	11.1	49.4	83.3	53.8	83.2
Group III (50,000 to 99,999)									
Number of offenses known	11,614	534	7,373	2,054	2,571	11,404	15,929	11,945	20,432
Rate	38.0	1.7	24.1	6.7	8.4	37.3	52.1	39.1	66.9
Group IV (25,000 to 49,999)									
Number of offenses known	9,500	315	4,685	1,104	1,587	6,569	10,741	8,333	13,639
Rate	36.6	1.2	18.0	4.3	6.1	25.3	41.4	32.1	52.5
Group V (10,000 to 24,999)									
Number of offenses known	8,503	277	3,212	792	1,102	4,044	8,254	6,838	11,862
Rate	36.7	1.2	13.8	3.4	4.8	17.4	35.6	29.5	51.2
Group VI (under 10,000)									
Number of offenses known	7,920	385	1,809	436	662	3,121	6,147	5,764	10,207
Rate	45.9	2.2	10.5	2.5	3.8	18.0	35.5	33.3	59.0
Metropolitan Counties									
Number of offenses known	21,008	768	10,528	1,949	2,489	10,035	29,069	17,456	36,231
Rate	33.0	1.2	16.5	3.0	3.9	15.7	45.4	27.3	56.6
Nonmetropolitan Counties									
Number of offenses known	7,642	297	851	142	261	624	6,626	3,788	9,061
Rate	39.5	1.5	4.4	0.7	1.3	3.2	34.2	19.5	46.7
Suburban Areas[2]									
Number of offenses known	36,556	1,369	17,355	3,551	5,014	20,144	43,329	29,621	58,251
Rate	32.4	1.2	15.4	3.1	4.4	17.8	38.4	26.2	51.6

Table 19. Rate: Number of Crimes Per 100,000 Inhabitants, Additional Information About Selected Offenses, by Population Group, 2019—Continued

(Number, rate.)

Population group	Burglary				Motor vehicle theft		
	Hands, fists, feet, etc.	Forcible entry	Unlawful entry	Attempted forcible entry	Autos	Trucks and buses	Other vehicles
Total, All Agencies							
Number of offenses known	170,619	505,122	342,830	58,569	459,395	100,113	57,246
Rate	63.7	189.3	128.5	21.9	171.9	37.5	21.4
Total, Cities							
Number of offenses known	127,095	382,177	257,251	46,887	376,503	81,154	40,322
Rate	68.8	207.9	139.9	25.5	204.8	44.1	21.9
Group I (250,000 and over)							
Number of offenses known	44,466	160,326	88,405	18,568	170,190	46,926	16,068
Rate	77.4	281.7	155.3	32.6	299.7	82.6	28.3
1,000,000 and over (Group I subset)							
Number of offenses known	22,642	55,083	24,619	6,147	46,332	26,231	5,422
Rate	96.3	234.3	104.7	26.1	197.1	111.6	23.1
500,000 to 999,999 (Group I subset)							
Number of offenses known	10,977	56,315	34,578	6,602	65,237	10,881	6,583
Rate	63.0	333.8	205.0	39.1	389.8	65.0	39.3
250,000 to 499,999 (Group I subset)							
Number of offenses known	10,847	48,928	29,208	5,819	58,621	9,814	4,063
Rate	65.6	295.8	176.6	35.2	354.5	59.3	24.6
Group II (100,000 to 249,999)							
Number of offenses known	20,356	66,814	46,194	9,045	74,850	14,130	7,465
Rate	67.5	221.5	153.1	30.0	248.1	46.8	24.7
Group III (50,000 to 99,999)							
Number of offenses known	17,932	53,079	38,682	6,567	51,234	9,174	6,017
Rate	58.7	173.8	126.6	21.5	168.1	30.1	19.7
Group IV (25,000 to 49,999)							
Number of offenses known	13,186	38,719	30,426	5,187	34,018	4,724	4,327
Rate	50.8	150.1	118.0	20.1	131.0	18.2	16.7
Group V (10,000 to 24,999)							
Number of offenses known	13,485	35,046	28,460	4,080	26,365	3,680	3,216
Rate	58.2	151.3	122.8	17.6	113.6	15.9	13.9
Group VI (under 10,000)							
Number of offenses known	17,670	28,193	25,084	3,440	19,846	2,520	3,229
Rate	102.2	163.2	145.2	19.9	114.7	14.6	18.7
Metropolitan Counties							
Number of offenses known	32,997	90,860	63,203	9,634	68,686	15,348	13,482
Rate	51.6	142.8	99.4	15.1	107.4	24.0	21.1
Nonmetropolitan Counties							
Number of offenses known	10,527	32,085	22,376	2,048	14,206	3,611	3,442
Rate	54.3	165.6	115.5	10.6	73.3	18.6	17.8
Suburban Areas[2]							
Number of offenses known	58,415	153,856	112,509	18,454	125,321	23,055	20,798
Rate	51.7	136.9	100.1	16.4	111.0	20.4	18.4

NOTE: Due to a system upgrade, the rates in this table are now calculated using aggregate population for each individual offense. The agency counts and population are provided for each individual offense. See Appendix V for further explanations of these changes.

1 The figures shown in this column for the offense of rape were reported using only the revised Uniform Crime Reporting definition of rape. See the chapter notes for further explanation.   2 Suburban areas include law enforcement agencies in cities with less than 50,000 inhabitants and county law enforcement agencies that are within a Metropolitan Statistical Area. Suburban areas exclude all metropolitan agencies associated with a principal city. The agencies associated with suburban areas also appear in other groups within this table.

Table 20. Murder, by Selected State, Territory, and Type of Weapon, 2019

(Number.)

State/territory	Total murders[1]	Total firearms	Handguns	Rifles	Shotguns	Firearms (type unknown)	Knives or cutting instruments	Other weapons	Hands, fists, feet, etc.[2]
Alabama[3]	4	3	3	0	0	0	0	1	0
Alaska	69	44	17	1	6	20	8	5	12
Arizona	337	213	170	6	6	31	47	67	10
Arkansas	231	177	87	10	5	75	21	29	4
California	1,679	1,142	762	34	26	320	252	183	102
Colorado	209	135	83	5	3	44	32	30	12
Connecticut	104	65	11	1	0	53	15	17	7
Delaware	48	40	13	0	0	27	2	3	3
District of Columbia	166	136	52	0	0	84	18	2	10
Florida[4]	1	0	0	0	0	0	0	1	0
Georgia	445	367	305	14	3	45	34	35	9
Hawaii	32	9	5	0	0	4	7	11	5
Idaho	35	16	9	0	0	7	3	13	3
Illinois[5]	771	647	564	7	4	72	70	44	10
Indiana	247	185	118	3	1	63	25	29	8
Iowa	58	36	21	0	0	15	8	8	6
Kansas	93	56	37	1	0	18	12	13	12
Kentucky	221	174	101	9	5	59	23	20	4
Louisiana	522	433	200	21	3	209	24	54	11
Maine	20	13	6	0	3	4	2	4	1
Maryland	551	460	414	3	4	39	43	34	14
Massachusetts	146	86	33	0	0	53	38	14	8
Michigan	551	379	172	13	5	189	44	104	24
Minnesota	114	79	61	0	0	18	10	15	10
Mississippi	189	153	117	4	3	29	11	23	2
Missouri	566	486	255	26	10	195	31	37	12
Montana	27	16	11	1	1	3	4	4	3
Nebraska	45	35	26	2	2	5	2	4	4
Nevada	147	94	49	5	3	37	20	23	10
New Hampshire	33	16	12	0	0	4	5	7	5
New Jersey	262	176	118	2	1	55	45	25	16
New Mexico	146	96	51	1	3	41	21	24	5
New York	550	298	255	3	5	35	119	89	44
North Carolina	516	383	224	26	8	125	52	68	13
North Dakota	26	13	5	2	1	5	5	4	4
Ohio	521	382	178	13	3	188	26	88	25
Oklahoma	264	189	129	11	12	37	27	37	11
Oregon	98	61	31	1	4	25	19	14	4
Pennsylvania	556	429	350	11	11	57	46	66	15
Rhode Island	25	10	1	0	0	9	7	6	2
South Carolina	445	381	224	9	8	140	22	27	15
South Dakota	19	7	4	1	0	2	3	6	3
Tennessee	498	391	173	13	7	198	41	46	20
Texas	1,379	1,064	568	72	21	403	127	130	58
Utah	66	41	18	1	6	16	8	13	4
Vermont	11	8	3	2	0	3	0	1	2
Virginia	427	323	150	15	9	149	40	49	15
Washington	194	135	89	5	3	38	23	24	12
West Virginia	72	48	23	7	2	16	6	15	3
Wisconsin	178	119	53	3	3	60	25	27	7
Wyoming	13	9	7	0	0	2	3	0	1

1 Total number of murders for which supplemental homicide data were received.   2 Pushed is included in hands, fists, feet, etc.   3 Limited data for 2019 were available for Alabama.   4 Data submitted through the Bureau of Indian Affairs.   5 Limited supplemental homicide data were received.

Table 21. Robbery, by State and Type of Weapon, 2019

(Number.)

State	Total robberies[1]	Firearms	Knives or cutting instruments	Other weapons	Strong-arm	Agency count	Population
Alabama[2]	32	15	2	2	13	2	85,670
Alaska	826	167	89	119	451	33	727,792
Arizona	6,042	2,207	759	688	2,388	96	6,308,226
Arkansas	1,351	651	83	122	495	243	2,501,782
California	51,196	12,181	4,635	5,964	28,416	731	38,767,853
Colorado	3,227	1,242	290	422	1,273	183	4,798,277
Connecticut	1,863	575	193	206	889	106	3,492,933
Delaware	789	288	88	78	335	52	970,535
District of Columbia	2,713	897	258	158	1,400	3	705,749
Florida	16,199	6,194	1,097	1,574	7,334	678	21,424,937
Georgia	1,626	912	64	104	546	168	3,026,506
Hawaii	1,021	160	92	162	607	2	1,142,377
Idaho	155	35	20	18	82	101	1,751,712
Illinois[3]	282	127	23	22	110	1	145,719
Indiana	1,840	809	93	312	626	169	3,004,084
Iowa	808	336	62	95	315	183	2,584,085
Kansas	924	430	69	79	346	219	1,821,596
Kentucky	2,158	1,007	154	207	790	398	4,456,082
Louisiana	3,760	1,841	183	304	1,432	150	3,988,385
Maine	188	40	21	26	101	135	1,344,212
Maryland	9,195	4,018	895	727	3,555	151	6,043,312
Massachusetts	3,590	790	594	669	1,537	346	6,726,719
Michigan	5,239	2,275	265	468	2,231	612	9,492,862
Minnesota	3,097	908	206	612	1,371	368	5,433,467
Mississippi	1,003	611	44	108	240	55	1,273,580
Missouri	4,547	2,617	228	353	1,349	327	4,271,657
Montana	191	46	17	45	83	78	855,718
Nebraska	781	353	61	52	315	198	1,767,262
Nevada	3,259	1,307	289	365	1,298	42	2,948,674
New Hampshire	297	74	42	42	139	182	1,281,465
New Jersey	5,730	1,653	526	399	3,152	577	8,882,190
New Mexico	2,063	909	282	246	626	99	1,480,451
New York	17,917	2,950	2,332	1,752	10,883	497	18,382,202
North Carolina	6,374	3,611	480	478	1,805	253	7,678,759
North Dakota	176	46	31	24	75	103	759,718
Ohio	8,211	2,504	347	598	4,762	414	9,215,222
Oklahoma	2,364	1,101	194	197	872	406	3,909,106
Oregon	2,136	452	220	319	1,145	151	3,680,010
Pennsylvania	1,476	589	145	94	648	438	3,297,344
Rhode Island	418	114	94	33	177	48	1,059,361
South Carolina	3,044	1,749	201	233	861	260	4,660,637
South Dakota	159	45	25	21	68	107	816,216
Tennessee	6,133	3,794	284	460	1,595	456	6,643,476
Texas	28,432	14,877	1,949	2,790	8,816	823	27,151,685
Utah	1,098	302	136	143	517	109	2,883,845
Vermont	69	20	10	4	35	79	599,538
Virginia	3,487	1,754	320	279	1,134	400	8,403,438
Washington	4,914	1,091	455	639	2,729	219	7,114,406
West Virginia	134	59	18	17	40	103	953,873
Wisconsin	2,905	1,349	160	312	1,084	409	5,649,131
Wyoming	62	20	4	9	29	55	512,713

1 The number of robberies from agencies that submitted 12 months of data in 2019 for which breakdowns by type of weapon were included.   2 Limited data for 2019 were available for Alabama.   3 Limited data were received.

Table 22. Aggravated Assault, by State and Type of Weapon, 2019

(Number.)

State	Total aggravated assaults[1]	Firearms	Knives or cutting instruments	Other weapons	Personal weapons	Agency count	Population
Alabama[2]	73	17	6	17	33	2	85,670
Alaska	4,342	834	801	1,484	1,223	33	727,792
Arizona	20,173	5,206	3,033	4,327	7,607	96	6,308,226
Arkansas	11,551	3,657	1,456	2,546	3,892	243	2,501,782
California	102,822	17,341	16,098	34,424	34,959	731	38,767,853
Colorado	12,619	4,066	2,608	3,122	2,823	184	4,910,658
Connecticut	3,549	692	810	1,268	779	106	3,492,933
Delaware	2,962	1,102	552	1,029	279	52	970,535
District of Columbia	4,179	1,089	1,175	1,520	395	3	705,749
Florida	55,333	17,196	10,213	18,648	9,276	678	21,424,937
Georgia	6,171	2,122	794	1,359	1,896	168	3,026,506
Hawaii	1,588	219	385	595	389	2	1,142,377
Idaho	2,978	524	489	928	1,037	101	1,751,712
Illinois[3]	1,290	553	173	206	358	1	145,719
Indiana	5,488	1,142	510	1,252	2,584	169	3,004,084
Iowa	5,584	803	846	1,281	2,654	183	2,584,085
Kansas	6,893	2,308	1,074	1,752	1,759	219	1,821,596
Kentucky	5,722	2,160	660	2,323	579	398	4,456,082
Louisiana	16,346	5,699	2,461	4,564	3,622	150	3,988,385
Maine	824	72	147	253	352	135	1,344,212
Maryland	15,727	2,840	3,490	5,898	3,499	151	6,043,312
Massachusetts	16,375	1,666	3,562	7,502	3,645	346	6,726,719
Michigan	29,325	8,993	5,580	8,934	5,818	612	9,492,862
Minnesota	7,338	1,820	1,516	1,954	2,048	368	5,433,467
Mississippi	2,424	1,163	308	553	400	55	1,273,580
Missouri	18,379	7,896	1,898	5,217	3,368	327	4,271,657
Montana	3,043	387	278	929	1,449	78	855,718
Nebraska	3,531	867	697	1,173	794	198	1,767,262
Nevada	9,246	2,594	1,922	2,576	2,154	42	2,948,674
New Hampshire	1,091	204	217	285	385	182	1,281,465
New Jersey	10,852	1,729	2,038	3,352	3,733	577	8,882,190
New Mexico	9,356	2,475	1,390	2,483	3,008	99	1,480,451
New York	43,967	4,535	11,626	12,825	14,981	497	18,382,202
North Carolina	21,191	10,813	2,892	3,915	3,571	253	7,678,759
North Dakota	1,243	28	141	517	557	103	759,718
Ohio	16,947	6,636	3,247	4,931	2,133	414	9,215,222
Oklahoma	12,122	3,342	1,956	3,627	3,197	406	3,909,106
Oregon	6,933	1,031	1,244	2,382	2,276	151	3,680,010
Pennsylvania	5,959	962	599	812	3,586	438	3,297,344
Rhode Island	1,408	228	403	444	333	48	1,059,361
South Carolina	18,207	8,598	2,675	4,145	2,789	260	4,660,637
South Dakota	2,005	277	463	471	794	107	816,216
Tennessee	30,687	13,807	5,270	9,587	2,023	456	6,643,476
Texas	73,258	25,970	14,156	20,714	12,418	823	27,151,685
Utah	4,281	692	812	1,321	1,456	109	2,883,845
Vermont	861	131	137	148	445	79	599,538
Virginia	10,823	3,535	1,601	3,132	2,555	400	8,403,438
Washington	12,990	2,667	2,047	4,311	3,965	219	7,114,406
West Virginia	1,996	474	239	453	830	103	953,873
Wisconsin	11,351	2,814	1,058	3,090	4,389	409	5,649,131
Wyoming	739	102	101	247	289	55	512,713

1 The number of aggravated assaults from agencies that submitted 12 months of data in 2019 for which breakdowns by type of weapon were included.   2 Limited data for 2019 were available for Alabama.   3 Limited data were received.

Table 23. Offense Analysis, Number and Percent Change, 2018–2019

(Number, percent, dollars; 13,848 agencies; 2019 estimated population 273,654,275.)

Classification	Number of offenses, 2019	Percent change from 2018	Percent distribution[1]	Average value (dollars)
Murder	13,002	+1.5	NA	X
Rape[2]	114,810	-3.0	NA	X
Robbery	211,113	-4.4	100.0	$1,797
By location				
Street/highway	74,121	-6.3	35.1	1,529
Commercial house	34,763	-3.6	16.5	1,772
Gas or service station	6,739	-3.1	3.2	1,248
Convenience store	14,426	-6.9	6.8	1,006
Residence	33,721	-5.0	16.0	2,560
Bank	3,020	-15.2	1.4	4,213
Miscellaneous	44,323	+0.3	21.0	1,864
Burglary	917,464	-8.6	100.0	2,661
By location				
Residence (dwelling)	576,607	-40.7	62.8	8,290
Residence, night	195,884	-5.9	21.4	2,345
Residence, day	290,909	-12.0	31.7	2,507
Residence, unknown	89,814	-22.8	9.8	3,439
Nonresidence (store, office, etc.)	340,857	-13.1	37.2	8,781
Nonresidence, night	157,327	+0.8	17.1	2,667
Nonresidence, day	125,554	+1.5	13.7	2,510
Nonresidence, unknown	57,976	-15.4	6.3	3,604
Larceny-theft (except motor vehicle theft)	4,132,566	-1.8	100.0	1,162
By type				
Pocket-picking	23,954	+10.3	0.6	1,235
Purse-snatching	15,087	-6.2	0.4	651
Shoplifting	904,975	+1.2	21.9	338
From motor vehicles (except accessories)	1,121,083	-1.6	27.1	1,012
Motor vehicle accessories	264,720	+1.0	6.4	690
Bicycles	125,136	-2.9	3.0	569
From buildings	404,734	-6.1	9.8	1,663
From coin-operated machines	9,204	-0.8	0.2	829
All others	1,263,673	-3.3	30.6	1,888
By value				
Over $200	1,956,531	-0.7	47.3	2,395
$50 to $200	877,125	-2.4	21.2	107
Under $50	1,298,910	-3.0	31.4	14
Motor Vehicle Theft	612,187	-3.8	NA	8,886

NA = Not available.
X = Not applicable.
* = Less than one-tenth of one percent.
1 Because of rounding, the percentages may not add to 100.0. 2 The rape figure in this table is an aggregate total of the data submitted using both the revised and legacy Uniform Crime Reporting definitions. See the chapter notes for further explanation.

Table 24. Property Stolen and Recovered, by Type and Value, 2019

(Dollars, percent; 14,165 agencies; 2019 estimated population 285,731,352.)

Type of property	Value of property (dollars)		Percent recovered
	Stolen	Recovered	
Total	$13,339,804,036	$3,861,187,443	28.9
Currency, notes, etc.	1,423,559,757	36,980,933	2.6
Jewelry and precious metals	1,057,763,740	36,890,088	3.5
Clothing and furs	383,191,187	31,171,004	8.1
Locally stolen motor vehicles	5,752,240,315	3,228,870,193	56.1
Office equipment	420,417,080	23,237,884	5.5
Televisions, radios, stereos, etc.	323,393,740	14,009,033	4.3
Firearms	116,159,390	13,495,262	11.6
Household goods	186,264,170	8,179,579	4.4
Consumable goods	160,368,125	13,380,144	8.3
Livestock	14,350,714	1,570,468	10.9
Miscellaneous	3,502,095,818	453,402,855	12.9

SECTION III

OFFENSES CLEARED

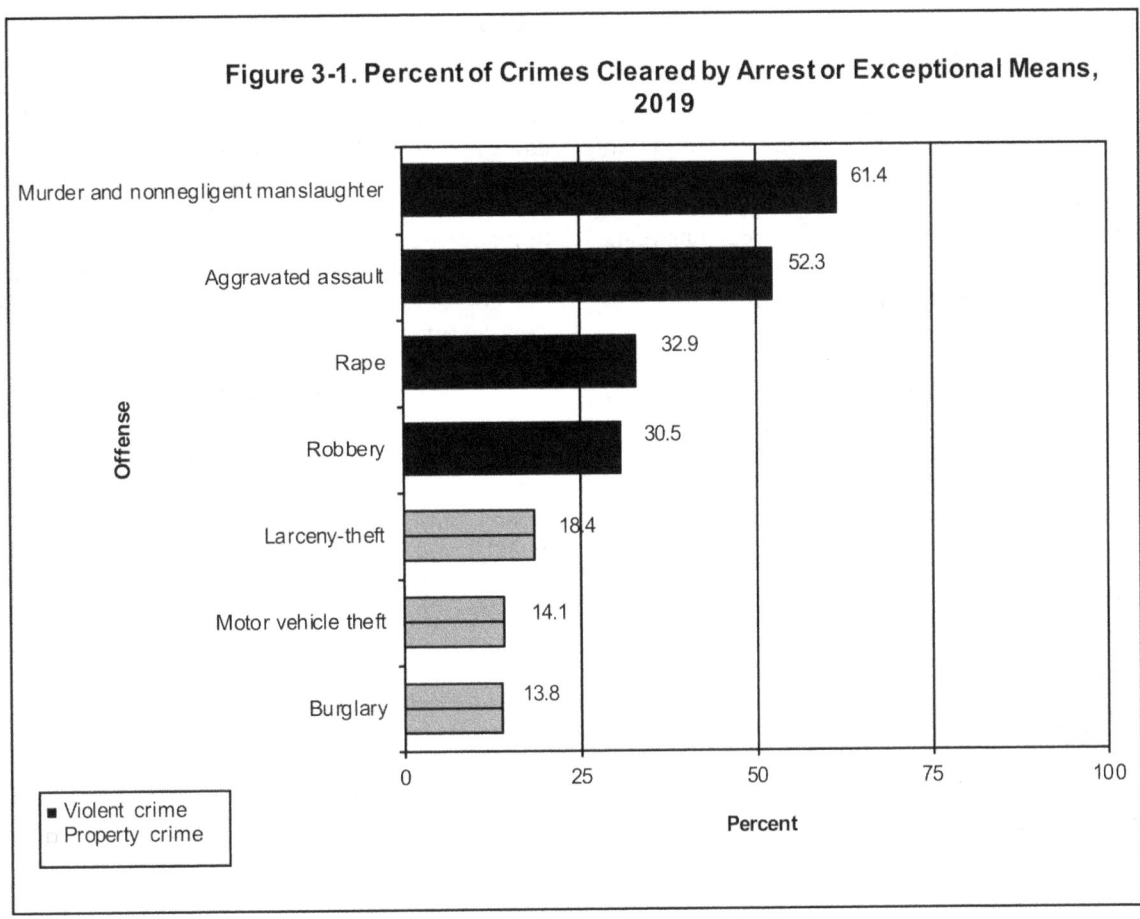

Figure 3-1. Percent of Crimes Cleared by Arrest or Exceptional Means, 2019

Law enforcement agencies that report crime to the Federal Bureau of Investigation (FBI) can clear, or "close," offenses in one of two ways: by arrest or by exceptional means. However, the administrative closing of a case by a local law enforcement agency does not necessarily mean that the agency can clear an offense for Uniform Crime Reporting (UCR) purposes. To clear an offense within the program's guidelines, the reporting agency must adhere to certain criteria, which are outlined in this section. (*Note:* The UCR program does not distinguish between offenses cleared by arrest and those cleared by exceptional means in its data presentations. The distinction is made solely for the purpose of a definition and not for data collection and publication.) See Appendix I for information on the UCR program's statistical methodology.

Important Note: Rape Data

In 2013, the FBI UCR Program initiated the collection of rape data within the Summary Reporting System under a revised definition. The changes bring uniformity to the offense in both the Summary Reporting System (SRS) and the National Incident-Based Reporting System (NIBRS) by capturing data (1) without regard to

gender, (2) including penetration of any bodily orifice by any object or body part, and (3) including offenses where physical force is not involved. The term "forcible" was removed, and the definition changed to the revised UCR definition below.

- Legacy UCR definition of rape: The carnal knowledge of a female forcibly and against her will. This definition has ceased to be used by the FBI.

- Revised UCR definition of rape: Penetration, no matter how slight, of the vagina or anus with any body part or object, or oral penetration by a sex organ of another person, without the consent of the victim. This is the definition currently in use; unless specified otherwise, "rape" refers to this definition.

Cleared by Arrest

In the UCR program, a law enforcement agency reports that an offense is cleared by arrest, or solved for crime reporting purposes, when at least one person is arrested, charged with the commission of the offense, and turned over to the court for prosecution (whether following

285

arrest, court summons, or police notice). To qualify as a clearance, *all* of these conditions must be met.

In its calculations, the UCR program counts the number of offenses that are cleared, not the number of arrestees. Therefore, the arrest of one person may clear several crimes, and the arrest of many persons may clear only one offense. In addition, some clearances recorded by an agency during a particular calendar year, such as 2019, may pertain to offenses that occurred in previous years.

Cleared by Exceptional Means

In certain situations, elements beyond law enforcement's control prevent the agency from arresting and formally charging the offender. When this occurs, the agency can clear the offense *exceptionally*. There are four UCR program requirements that law enforcement must meet in order to clear an offense by exceptional means. The agency must have:

- Identified the offender

- Gathered enough evidence to support an arrest, make a charge, and turn over the offender to the court for prosecution

- Identified the offender's exact location so that the suspect could be taken into custody immediately

- Encountered a circumstance outside the control of law enforcement that prohibits the agency from arresting, charging, and prosecuting the offender

Examples of exceptional clearances include, but are not limited to, the death of the offender (e.g., suicide or justifiably killed by a law enforcement officer or a citizen), the victim's refusal to cooperate with the prosecution after the offender has been identified, or the denial of extradition because the offender committed a crime in another jurisdiction and is being prosecuted for that offense. In the UCR program, the recovery of property does not clear an offense.

National Clearances

A review of the data for 2019 revealed law enforcement agencies in the United States cleared 45.5 percent of violent crimes (murder, rape, robbery, and aggravated assault) and 17.2 percent of property crimes (burglary, larceny-theft, and motor vehicle theft) brought to their attention. In addition, law enforcement cleared 23.8 percent of arson offenses, which are reported in a slightly different manner than the other property crimes. (Table 25) More details concerning this offense are furnished in the arson text in this section.

As in most years, law enforcement agencies cleared a higher percentage of violent crimes than property crimes in 2019.

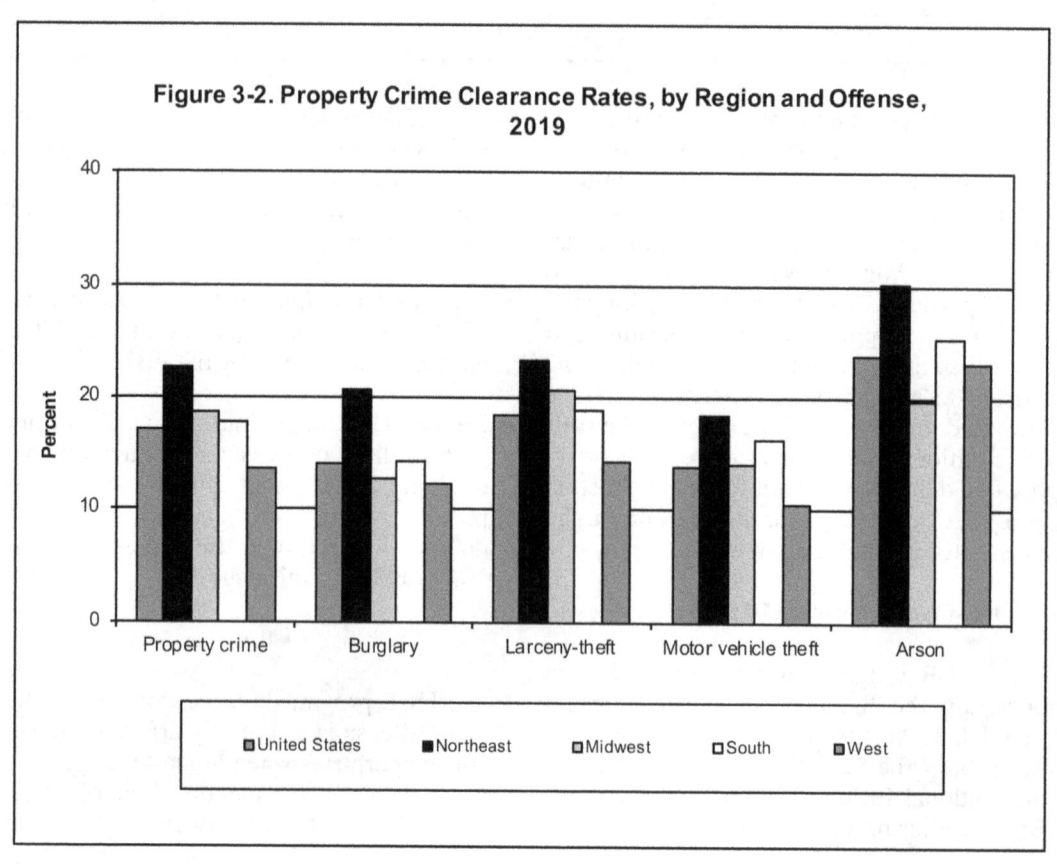

Figure 3-2. Property Crime Clearance Rates, by Region and Offense, 2019

As a rule, clearance rates generally rise due to the more vigorous investigative efforts put forth for violent crimes. In addition, violent crimes more often involve victims and/or witnesses who are able to identify the perpetrators.

A breakdown of the clearances for violent crimes for 2019 revealed that the nation's law enforcement agencies cleared 61.4 percent of murder offenses, 52.3 percent of aggravated assault offenses, 32.9 percent of rape offenses, and 30.5 percent of robbery offenses. These numbers were similar to the clearances in 2018. (Table 25)

For property crime offenses in 2019, law enforcement agencies throughout the nation collectively 14.1 percent of burglary offenses, 18.4 percent of larceny-theft offenses, and 13.8 percent of motor vehicle theft offenses. These clearances were also similar to 2018. (Table 25)

Regional Clearances

The UCR program divides the nation into four regions: the Northeast, the Midwest, the South, and the West. (See Appendix III for further details.) A review of clearance data for 2019 by region showed that agencies in the Northeast cleared the greatest proportion of their violent crime offenses (54.8 percent). Law enforcement agencies in the West cleared 46.1 percent of their violent crimes, while agencies in the Midwest and South cleared 43.3 percent and 42.8 percent of their violent crimes, respectively. (Table 26)

For murder and nonnegligent manslaughter in 2019, the Northeast cleared 66.1 percent of offenses, followed by the West (63.7 percent). The South cleared 60.7 percent and the Midwest cleared 57.2 percent of these offenses. Rape offenses were cleared 36.7 percent of the time in the Northeast, 34.9 percent of the time in the South, 30.4 percent of the time in the West, and 30.0 percent of the time in the Midwest. For robbery, the Northeast had the highest clearance rate, at 38.4 percent, while the Midwest had the lowest clearance rate, at 26.0 percent. The Northeast also had the highest proportion of clearances for aggravated assault (64.0 percent). The South had the lowest proportion of aggravated assault clearances (48.0 percent). (Table 26)

Clearance data for 2019 showed that, among the regions, law enforcement agencies in the Northeast cleared the highest percentage of their property crimes (22.6 percent). Agencies in the Midwest and South cleared 18.6 percent and 17.8 percent, respectively. Agencies in the West cleared 13.6 percent of their property crimes. (Table 26)

Agencies in the Northeast cleared the highest percentage of burglary offenses at 20.6 percent, followed by the South at 14.3 percent, the Midwest at 12.8 percent, and the West at 12.4 percent. For larceny-theft, the Northeast

(23.2 percent) was followed by the Midwest at 20.6 percent, the South at 18.8 percent, and the West at 14.3 percent. The Northeast and South cleared the highest proportion of motor vehicle thefts at 18.4 and 16.2 percent, respectively, followed by the Midwest at 14.0 percent and the West at 10.5 percent. The Northeast cleared the greatest percentage of arson offenses (30.1 percent), followed by the South (25.2 percent), West (23.0 percent), and Midwest (19.8 percent). (Table 26)

Clearances by Population Groups

The UCR program uses the following population group designations in its data presentations: cities (grouped according to population size) and counties (classified as either metropolitan or nonmetropolitan counties). A breakdown of these classifications is furnished in Appendix III.

CITIES

In 2019, the clearance data collected showed that law enforcement agencies in the nation's cities cleared 43.5 percent of their violent crime offenses. Among the city population groups and subsets, agencies in the smallest cities, those with fewer than 10,000 inhabitants, cleared the greatest proportion of their violent crime offenses (53.8 percent), and law enforcement in cities with 250,000 to 499,999 inhabitants cleared the smallest proportion of their violent crime offenses (35.1 percent). (Table 25)

The clearance data for murder showed that among the city population groups and subsets, cities with populations of 1,000,000 or more inhabitants cleared the greatest percentage of their murders (67.3 percent). Law enforcement agencies in cities with 250,000 to 499,999 inhabitants cleared the lowest percentage of their murders (51.5 percent). For rape, cities with 50,000 to 99,999 inhabitants cleared the largest percentage of offenses at 34.0 percent, while cities with 250,000 to 499,999 inhabitants cleared the lowest percentage of offenses at 25.6 percent. Cities with under 10,000 inhabitants cleared the greatest percentage of their robbery offenses at 40.1 percent, and cities with 250,000 to 49,999 inhabitants cleared the lowest proportion of their robbery offenses at 23.8 percent. For aggravated assault, cities with fewer than 10,000 inhabitants cleared the highest proportion of offenses (60.3 percent); cities with 500,000 to 999,999 inhabitants cleared the lowest percentage of offenses (40.8 percent). (Table 25)

In 2019, agencies in the nation's cities collectively cleared 17.2 percent of their property crime offenses. Law enforcement in cities with 10,000 to 24,999 inhabitants cleared the highest proportion of the property crimes (25.3 percent) brought to their attention; cities with 500,000 to 999,999 inhabitants cleared the smallest proportion of their property crimes (10.2 percent). (Table 25)

Law enforcement agencies in cities cleared 14.1 percent of burglaries, 18.4 percent of larceny-thefts, 13.8 percent of motor vehicle thefts, and 23.8 percent of arsons in 2019. For burglaries, cities with fewer than 10,000 inhabitants cleared the largest percentage of their offenses at 18.8 percent, while cities with 500,000 to 999,999 inhabitants cleared the smallest percentage of their offenses at 10.7 percent. Cities with 10,000 to 24,999 inhabitants cleared the greatest percentage of their larceny-theft offenses (27.5 percent), and cities with 500,000 to 999,999 inhabitants cleared the lowest proportion of larceny-theft offenses (10.4 percent). For motor vehicle theft, cities with fewer than 10,000 inhabitants cleared the highest percentages of their offenses at 22.3 percent, while cities with 1,000,000 or more inhabitants cleared the lowest percentage (9.5 percent). Cities with 10,000 to 24,999 inhabitants cleared the greatest percentage of their arson offenses, at 30.4 percent, and cities with 1,000,000 or more inhabitants cleared the lowest percentage (12.7 percent). (Table 25)

METROPOLITAN AND NONMETROPOLITAN COUNTIES

In 2019, law enforcement agencies in metropolitan counties cleared 52.9 percent of their violent crime offenses. Of the violent crimes made known to law enforcement agencies in metropolitan counties, murder offenses had the highest proportion of clearance (69.4 percent), followed by aggravated assaults (59.0 percent), rapes (39.4 percent), and robberies (35.1 percent). Law enforcement agencies in metropolitan counties cleared 17.9 percent of their total property crimes, 15.4 percent of burglaries, 18.6 percent of larceny-thefts, 17.5 percent of motor vehicle thefts, and 27.8 percent of their arsons. (Table 25)

Like their counterparts in metropolitan counties, non-metropolitan counties collectively cleared a greater proportion of their violent crimes than did the nation as a whole in 2019. Nonmetropolitan counties cleared 54.6 percent of their violent crime offenses and 19.7 percent of property crimes. Of the violent crimes known to them, law enforcement in nonmetropolitan counties had the highest number of clearances for murder (66.9 percent), with 36.9 percent of rapes, 40.3 percent of robberies, and 59.8 percent of aggravated assaults being cleared. Agencies in nonmetropolitan counties reported clearing 18.2 percent of property crimes, including 15.7 percent of their burglaries, 19.9 percent of their larceny-thefts, 22.6 percent of their motor vehicle thefts, and 29.0 percent of their arsons. In suburban areas, 52.7 percent of violent crimes (66.6 percent of murders, 36.6 percent of rapes, 35.9 percent of robberies, and 59.7 percent of aggravated assaults) and 20.5 percent of property crimes (15.9 percent of burglaries, 21.8 percent of larceny-thefts, 17.2 percent of motor vehicle thefts, and 28.2 percent of arsons) were cleared in 2019. (Table 25)

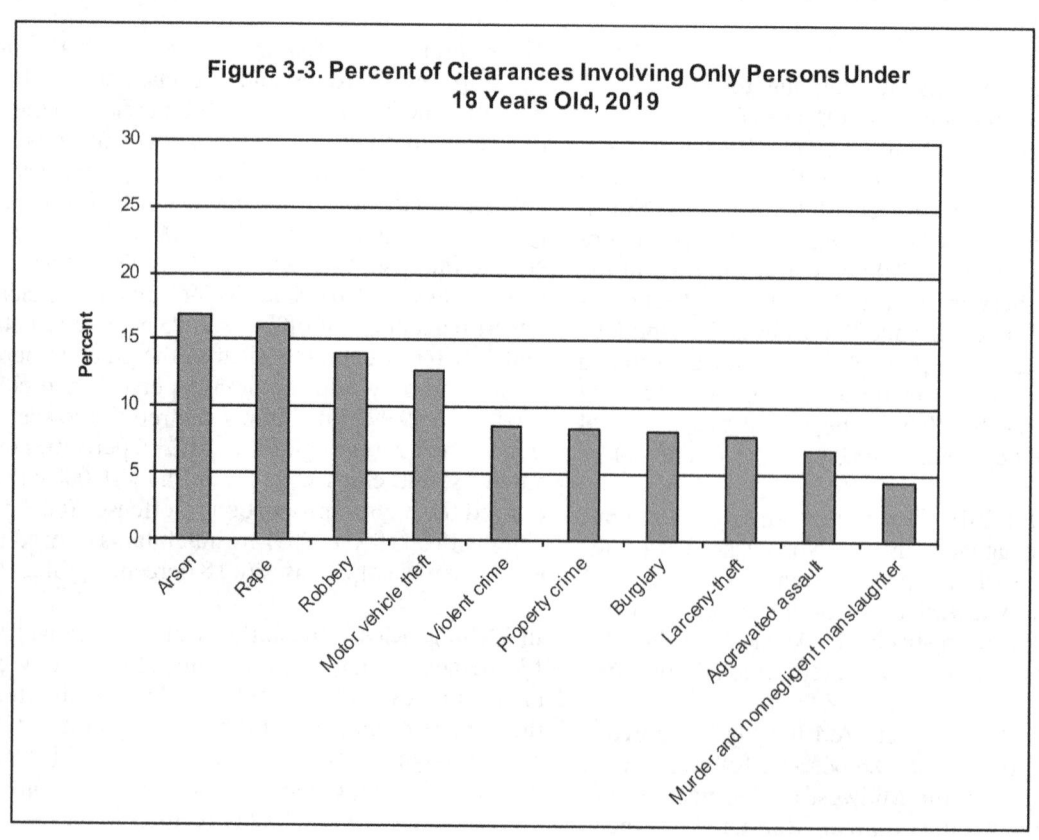

Figure 3-3. Percent of Clearances Involving Only Persons Under 18 Years Old, 2019

Clearances by Classification Group and Type

For rape, by classification group and type, law enforcement agencies cleared 37.1 percent of assault-to-rape attempts and 32.6 percent of rapes in 2019. Cleared robbery offenses included 33.4 percent of offenses involving knives or other cutting instruments, 31.2 percent of offenses involving strong-arm tactics, 29.9 percent of offenses involving other weapons, and 22.2 percent of offenses involving firearms. For aggravated assaults, agencies cleared 58.6 percent of offenses involving hands, feet, fists, etc.; 55.7 percent of offenses involving knives or other cutting instruments; 49.8 percent of offenses involving other weapons; and 31.3 percent of offenses involving firearms. (Table 27)

For property crime clearances grouped by classification and type, data showed that the highest percentage of burglary clearances in the nation in 2019 (16.1 percent) were for offenses that involved unlawful entry. Law enforcement agencies cleared 12.7 percent of burglaries involving forcible entry and 13.8 percent of burglaries involving attempted forcible entry. For motor vehicle theft, agencies cleared 14.6 percent of motor vehicle theft offenses involving automobiles, 11.5 percent of motor vehicle theft offenses involving trucks and buses, and 11.3 percent of motor vehicle offenses involving other vehicles. (Table 27)

In 2019, 28.2 percent of structural arson offenses were cleared by arrest or exceptional means, while 11.9 percent of mobile arson offenses and 26.2 percent of other arson crimes were cleared. (Table 27)

CLEARANCES AND JUVENILES

When an offender under 18 years of age is cited to appear in juvenile court or before other juvenile authorities, the UCR program considers the incident for which the juvenile is being held responsible to be cleared by arrest, although a physical arrest may not have occurred. In addition, according to program definitions, clearances that include both adult and juvenile offenders are classified as clearances for crimes committed by adults. Therefore, the juvenile clearance data are limited to those clearances involving juveniles only, and the figures in this publication should not be used to present a definitive picture of juvenile involvement in crime.

Of the clearances for violent crimes that were reported in the nation in 2019, 8.5 percent involved only juveniles. In the nation's cities, collectively, 8.5 percent of violent crime clearances also involved only juveniles, with juveniles in cities exclusively involved in 4.9 percent of murder clearances, 16.2 percent of rape clearances, 14.0 percent of robbery clearances, and 6.7 percent of aggravated assault clearances. Of the nation's city population groups and subsets, cities with under 10,000 inhabitants had the highest percentage of overall clearances for violent crime only involving juveniles (10.9 percent); cities with 1,000,000 or more inhabitants had the lowest percentage, 7.5 percent. (Table 28)

Law enforcement agencies in metropolitan counties reported that 8.8 percent of their violent crime clearances—including 3.5 percent of their murder clearances, 19.8 percent of their rape clearances, 14.1 percent of their robbery clearances, and 6.9 percent of their aggravated assault clearances—involved only juveniles. Agencies in nonmetropolitan counties reported that 7.1 percent of their clearances for violent crime involved only juveniles, including 3.2 percent of their murder clearances, 17.8 percent of their rape clearances, 6.5 percent of their robbery clearances, and 5.6 percent of their aggravated assault clearances. In suburban areas, 9.5 percent of violent crimes, 3.5 percent of murders, 18.7 percent of rapes, 14.4 percent of robberies, and 7.8 percent of aggravated assaults involved only juveniles. (Table 28)

In 2019, 8.4 percent of clearances for property crime involved only juveniles. In cities collectively, 8.3 percent of the clearances for property crime, 8.2 percent of clearances for burglary, 7.9 percent of clearances for larceny-theft, 12.7 percent of clearances for motor vehicle theft, and 16.8 percent of clearances for arson involved juveniles only. Among the population groups and subsets labeled *city*, the percentages of clearances involving only juveniles for overall property crime ranged from a low of 5.9 percent in cities with more than 1,000,000 inhabitants to a high of 10.1 percent in cities with populations of 250,000 to 499,999 inhabitants. (Table 28)

Metropolitan counties reported that 9.5 percent of all property crime clearances, 9.1 percent of burglary clearances, 9.1 percent of larceny-theft clearances, 12.3 percent of motor vehicle theft clearances, and 19.5 percent of arson clearances involved persons under 18 years of age. In nonmetropolitan counties, 6.2 percent of property crime clearances, 6.3 percent of burglary clearances, 5.7 percent of larceny-theft clearances, 7.7 percent of motor vehicle theft clearances, and 12.2 percent of arson clearances involved juveniles exclusively. In suburban areas, 21.0 percent of arson clearances involved only juveniles, as did 8.7 percent of property crimes, 9.2 percent of burglaries, 8.3 percent of larceny-thefts, and 12.5 percent of motor vehicle thefts. (Table 28)

Table 25. Number and Percent of Offenses Cleared by Arrest or Exceptional Means, by Population Group, 2019

(Number, percent.)

Population group	Violent crime	Murder and nonnegligent manslaughter	Rape[1]	Robbery	Aggravated assault	Property crime	Burglary	Larceny-theft	Motor vehicle theft	Arson[2]	Number of agencies	Estimated population, 2019
Total, All Agencies												
Offenses known	1,105,563	14,325	124,817	239,643	726,778	6,203,201	981,264	4,533,178	655,778	32,981	15,008	297,524,524
Percent cleared by arrest	45.5	61.4	32.9	30.5	52.3	17.2	14.1	18.4	13.8	23.8		
Total Cities												
Offenses known	878,923	11,020	92,241	209,959	565,703	4,976,072	733,199	3,693,498	523,739	25,636	10,779	201,853,210
Percent cleared by arrest	43.5	59.2	30.8	29.7	50.4	17.0	13.6	18.3	12.6	22.6		
Group I (250,000 and over)												
Offenses known	422,438	5,693	34,899	119,642	262,204	1,853,997	280,302	1,320,696	242,429	10,570	85	59,934,909
Percent cleared by arrest	38.2	57.6	29.5	27.1	44.0	11.4	11.2	11.7	9.8	16.5		
1,000,000 and over (Group I subset)												
Offenses known	167,116	1,717	13,310	50,754	101,335	626,897	90,293	451,107	82,104	3,393	10	25,098,940
Percent cleared by arrest	42.5	67.3	33.8	31.0	49.0	11.6	11.7	12.0	9.4	12.7		
500,000 to 999,999 (Group I subset)												
Offenses known	144,314	2,289	10,822	39,402	91,801	685,236	106,192	487,358	88,038	3,648	26	18,474,842
Percent cleared by arrest	35.6	54.7	28.0	24.4	40.8	10.2	10.7	10.2	9.5	19.1		
250,000 to 499,999 (Group I subset)												
Offenses known	111,008	1,687	10,767	29,486	69,068	541,864	83,817	382,231	72,287	3,529	49	16,361,127
Percent cleared by arrest	35.1	51.5	25.6	23.8	41.0	12.8	11.2	13.5	10.7	17.3		
Group II (100,000 to 249,999)												
Offenses known	140,059	1,817	14,997	33,820	89,425	848,193	125,498	619,505	99,211	3,979	217	31,723,575
Percent cleared by arrest	43.3	60.9	30.6	29.9	50.2	15.4	12.8	16.4	12.1	25.9		
Group III (50,000 to 99,999)												
Offenses known	107,657	1,155	12,721	24,308	69,473	725,084	104,499	547,385	69,667	3,533	467	32,634,179
Percent cleared by arrest	48.8	60.7	34.0	33.9	56.5	18.9	14.2	20.5	13.7	24.3		
Group IV (25,000 to 49,999)												
Offenses known	75,927	937	10,486	14,925	49,579	575,373	80,395	446,492	45,900	2,586	827	28,786,886
Percent cleared by arrest	48.7	58.2	30.2	34.5	56.7	22.2	15.0	24.1	15.6	25.7		
Group V (10,000 to 24,999)												
Offenses known	66,748	783	9,561	10,148	46,256	521,268	76,010	406,489	36,529	2,240	1,689	26,893,861
Percent cleared by arrest	52.7	64.0	33.0	36.7	60.1	25.3	16.8	27.5	19.0	30.4		
Group VI (under 10,000)												
Offenses known	66,094	635	9,577	7,116	48,766	452,157	66,495	352,931	30,003	2,728	7,494	21,879,800
Percent cleared by arrest	53.8	62.0	30.0	40.1	60.3	23.9	18.8	25.0	22.3	29.9		
Metropolitan Counties												
Offenses known	180,344	2,475	23,744	27,531	126,594	1,003,685	183,893	706,656	107,686	5,450	1,905	72,761,754
Percent cleared by arrest	52.9	69.4	39.4	35.1	59.0	17.9	15.4	18.6	17.5	27.8		
Nonmetropolitan Counties												
Offenses known	46,296	830	8,832	2,153	34,481	223,444	64,172	133,024	24,353	1,895	2,324	22,909,560
Percent cleared by arrest	54.6	66.9	36.9	40.3	59.8	18.1	15.7	18.2	22.6	29.0		
Suburban Areas[3]												
Offenses known	305,904	3,834	41,324	50,446	210,300	2,020,200	317,024	1,507,725	185,517	9,934	8,144	129,507,894
Percent cleared by arrest	52.7	66.6	36.6	35.9	59.7	20.5	15.9	21.8	17.2	28.2		

1 The figures shown in the rape column include only those reported by law enforcement agencies that used the revised Uniform Crime Reporting definition of rape. 2 Not all agencies submit reports for arson to the FBI. As a result, the number of reports the FBI uses to compute the percent of offenses cleared for arson is less than the number it uses to compute the percent of offenses cleared for all other offenses. 3 Suburban area includes law enforcement agencies in cities with less than 50,000 inhabitants and county law enforcement agencies that are within a Metropolitan Statistical Area. Suburban area excludes all metropolitan agencies associated with a principal city. The agencies associated with suburban areas also appear in other groups within this table.

Table 26. Number and Percent of Offenses Cleared by Arrest or Exceptional Means, by Region and Geographic Division, 2019

(Number, percent.)

Geographic region/division	Violent crime	Murder and nonnegligent manslaughter	Rape[1]	Robbery	Aggravated assault	Property crime	Burglary	Larceny-theft	Motor vehicle theft	Arson[2]	Number of agencies	Estimated population, 2019
Total, All Agencies												
Offenses known	1,105,563	14,325	124,817	239,643	726,778	6,203,201	981,264	4,533,178	655,778	32,981	15,008	297,524,524
Percent cleared by arrest	45.5	61.4	32.9	30.5	52.3	17.2	14.1	18.4	13.8	23.8		
Northeast												
Offenses known	154,840	1,713	16,457	37,778	98,892	718,402	89,056	578,548	47,642	3,156	3,428	54,697,418
Percent cleared by arrest	54.8	66.1	36.7	38.4	64.0	22.6	20.6	23.2	18.4	30.1		
New England												
Offenses known	35,436	342	4,743	6,410	23,941	187,987	26,049	146,325	14,696	917	919	14,583,362
Percent cleared by arrest	49.5	54.4	27.4	27.6	59.7	19.1	17.2	19.9	14.5	30.8		
Middle Atlantic												
Offenses known	119,404	1,371	11,714	31,368	74,951	530,415	63,007	432,223	32,946	2,239	2,509	40,114,056
Percent cleared by arrest	56.4	69.1	40.5	40.6	65.3	23.8	22.0	24.3	20.2	29.9		
Midwest												
Offenses known	175,381	2,325	25,460	29,855	117,741	976,939	160,566	710,807	99,633	5,933	3,788	50,060,213
Percent cleared by arrest	43.3	57.2	30.0	26.0	50.3	18.6	12.8	20.6	14.0	19.8		
East North Central												
Offenses known	103,566	1,416	15,691	18,806	67,653	525,118	90,217	382,466	48,838	3,597	1,807	29,505,571
Percent cleared by arrest	40.7	55.0	28.5	24.3	47.7	17.7	12.2	19.7	11.8	18.7		
West North Central												
Offenses known	71,815	909	9,769	11,049	50,088	451,821	70,349	328,341	50,795	2,336	1,981	20,554,642
Percent cleared by arrest	47.2	60.6	32.4	29.0	53.8	19.8	13.5	21.7	16.0	21.5		
South												
Offenses known	461,709	7,209	47,954	94,205	312,341	2,659,800	435,961	1,959,101	254,276	10,462	5,710	116,465,809
Percent cleared by arrest	42.8	60.7	34.9	28.0	48.0	17.8	14.3	18.8	16.2	25.2		
South Atlantic												
Offenses known	220,936	3,764	21,166	47,327	148,679	1,288,580	194,059	979,378	110,151	4,992	2,633	60,684,647
Percent cleared by arrest	47.2	60.5	42.8	33.6	51.8	19.7	17.4	20.4	17.9	29.4		
East South Central												
Offenses known	63,338	1,028	5,610	10,375	46,325	355,347	62,327	254,194	37,389	1,437	1,200	16,103,086
Percent cleared by arrest	46.3	59.6	42.2	27.8	50.6	21.8	16.7	22.8	23.4	26.7		
West South Central												
Offenses known	177,435	2,417	21,178	36,503	117,337	1,015,873	179,575	725,529	106,736	4,033	1,877	39,678,076
Percent cleared by arrest	36.0	61.4	25.0	20.7	42.2	13.9	10.1	15.2	11.8	19.5		
West												
Offenses known	313,633	3,078	34,946	77,805	197,804	1,848,060	295,681	1,284,722	254,227	13,430	2,082	76,301,084
Percent cleared by arrest	46.1	63.7	30.4	31.3	54.4	13.6	12.4	14.3	10.5	23.0		
Mountain												
Offenses known	97,639	1,006	13,757	16,588	66,288	555,312	88,293	396,597	67,685	2,737	877	23,524,310
Percent cleared by arrest	46.1	63.2	27.2	29.7	53.8	17.8	13.4	19.8	11.9	28.0		
Pacific												
Offenses known	215,994	2,072	21,189	61,217	131,516	1,292,748	207,388	888,125	186,542	10,693	1,205	52,776,774
Percent cleared by arrest	46.1	63.9	32.4	31.8	54.7	11.7	12.0	11.9	10.0	21.7		

1 The figures shown in the rape column include only those reported by law enforcement agencies that used the revised Uniform Crime Reporting definition of rape.   2 Not all agencies submit reports for arson to the FBI. As a result, the number of reports the FBI uses to compute the percent of offenses cleared for arson is less than the number it uses to compute the percent of offenses cleared for all other offenses.

Table 27. Number and Percent of Offenses Cleared by Arrest or Exceptional Means, Additional Information About Selected Offenses, by Population Group, 2019

(Number, percent.)

Population group	Rape[1]		Robbery				Aggravated assault			
	Rape by force	Assault to rape-attempts	Firearm	Knife or cutting instrument	Other weapon	Strong-arm	Firearm	Knife or cutting instrument	Other weapon	Hands, fists, feet, etc.
Total, All Agencies										
Offenses known	119,685	5,132	88,254	20,003	24,580	106,806	198,807	124,593	215,897	187,481
Percent cleared by arrest	32.6	37.1	22.2	33.4	29.9	31.2	31.3	55.7	49.8	58.6
Total Cities										
Offenses known	88,292	3,949	75,357	17,763	21,499	95,340	159,141	101,850	166,451	138,261
Percent cleared by arrest	30.5	36.5	22.2	33.5	29.8	31.3	29.8	56.0	49.7	59.6
Group I (250,000 and over)										
Offenses known	33,188	1,711	44,436	10,177	11,610	53,419	88,231	49,605	78,235	46,133
Percent cleared by arrest	28.9	40.2	20.4	32.2	27.3	29.7	26.2	54.3	45.5	55.4
1,000,000 and over (Group I subset)										
Offenses known	12,546	764	16,464	4,994	5,369	23,927	25,861	21,817	30,032	23,625
Percent cleared by arrest	32.8	50.7	21.4	37.3	30.3	36.5	27.9	58.7	50.4	61.5
500,000 to 999,999 (Group I subset)										
Offenses known	10,325	497	16,644	3,082	3,999	15,677	35,987	15,873	28,332	11,609
Percent cleared by arrest	27.7	33.4	19.8	27.6	24.4	26.1	26.1	51.7	43.9	49.7
250,000 to 499,999 (Group I subset)										
Offenses known	10,317	450	11,328	2,101	2,242	13,815	26,383	11,915	19,871	10,899
Percent cleared by arrest	25.4	30.0	20.0	27.1	25.5	22.0	24.6	49.5	40.1	48.5
Group II (100,000 to 249,999)										
Offenses known	14,474	523	12,233	2,952	3,466	15,169	25,901	16,703	25,812	21,009
Percent cleared by arrest	30.3	37.1	22.2	31.7	30.0	30.0	30.3	54.8	49.1	57.7
Group III (50,000 to 99,999)										
Offenses known	12,159	562	7,633	2,123	2,742	11,810	16,439	12,244	21,550	19,240
Percent cleared by arrest	33.7	39.5	25.0	34.7	32.5	32.7	32.5	57.1	53.6	62.2
Group IV (25,000 to 49,999)										
Offenses known	10,143	343	5,182	1,155	1,668	6,920	11,654	8,865	14,678	14,382
Percent cleared by arrest	30.1	32.1	24.5	37.1	32.2	35.0	35.2	57.3	54.9	61.4
Group V (10,000 to 24,999)										
Offenses known	9,254	307	3,633	851	1,242	4,422	9,479	7,609	13,750	15,418
Percent cleared by arrest	32.9	32.6	29.6	40.7	36.4	36.0	40.6	61.4	57.0	63.6
Group VI (under 10,000)										
Offenses known	9,074	503	2,240	505	771	3,600	7,437	6,824	12,426	22,079
Percent cleared by arrest	30.2	25.0	30.6	42.8	40.6	42.1	43.3	62.3	56.3	64.1
Metropolitan Counties										
Offenses known	22,906	838	11,922	2,076	2,783	10,750	32,006	18,502	39,281	36,805
Percent cleared by arrest	39.2	42.6	21.1	31.9	29.9	29.5	34.2	52.2	48.2	55.2
Nonmetropolitan Counties										
Offenses known	8,487	345	975	164	298	716	7,660	4,241	10,165	12,415
Percent cleared by arrest	37.0	31.3	32.6	40.9	36.9	42.2	49.1	62.6	58.5	57.3
Suburban Areas[3]										
Offenses known	39,797	1,527	19,554	3,780	5,501	21,611	48,033	31,810	63,708	66,749
Percent cleared by arrest	36.5	37.1	22.9	34.9	32.3	33.6	35.8	55.7	51.4	59.3

Table 27. Number and Percent of Offenses Cleared by Arrest or Exceptional Means, Additional Information About Selected Offenses, by Population Group, 2019—Continued

(Number, percent.)

| Population group | Burglary | | | Motor vehicle theft | | | Arson[2] | | | Number of agencies | Estimated population, 2019 |
	Forcible entry	Unlawful entry	Attempted forcible entry	Autos	Trucks and buses	Other vehicles	Structure	Mobile	Other		
Total, All Agencies											
Offenses known	547,328	370,786	63,150	490,712	103,692	61,374	13,898	7,484	11,599	15,008	297,524,524
Percent cleared by arrest	12.7	16.1	13.8	14.6	11.5	11.3	28.2	11.9	26.2		
Total Cities											
Offenses known	408,259	274,872	50,068	397,870	83,253	42,616	10,796	5,503	9,337	10,779	201,853,210
Percent cleared by arrest	12.2	15.7	13.6	13.5	10.2	9.7	26.1	11.6	25.0		
Group I (250,000 and over)											
Offenses known	168,552	92,058	19,692	178,229	47,578	16,622	4,009	2,493	4,068	85	59,934,909
Percent cleared by arrest	9.9	13.2	12.4	10.5	8.0	7.7	19.6	8.5	18.2		
1,000,000 and over (Group I subset)											
Offenses known	57,736	26,054	6,503	50,136	26,303	5,665	1,037	610	1,746	10	25,098,940
Percent cleared by arrest	10.0	14.7	15.7	11.0	6.6	8.8	20.6	10.2	8.8		
500,000 to 999,999 (Group I subset)											
Offenses known	62,019	36,689	7,484	69,756	11,421	6,861	1,424	993	1,231	26	18,474,842
Percent cleared by arrest	9.5	12.6	11.1	9.7	10.1	6.6	19.3	8.6	27.5		
250,000 to 499,999 (Group I subset)											
Offenses known	48,797	29,315	5,705	58,337	9,854	4,096	1,548	890	1,091	49	16,361,127
Percent cleared by arrest	10.4	12.5	10.4	11.0	9.5	8.2	19.1	7.4	22.9		
Group II (100,000 to 249,999)											
Offenses known	68,798	47,458	9,242	77,297	14,309	7,605	1,648	944	1,387	217	31,723,575
Percent cleared by arrest	11.6	14.5	13.9	12.7	11.1	8.2	28.3	13.5	31.5		
Group III (50,000 to 99,999)											
Offenses known	55,976	41,623	6,900	53,739	9,618	6,310	1,451	713	1,369	467	32,634,179
Percent cleared by arrest	12.9	15.9	13.5	14.3	12.6	9.5	25.9	12.3	28.8		
Group IV (25,000 to 49,999)											
Offenses known	42,003	32,822	5,570	36,425	4,918	4,557	1,172	476	938	827	28,786,886
Percent cleared by arrest	14.0	16.5	13.9	16.4	14.2	10.4	30.2	12.8	26.7		
Group V (10,000 to 24,999)											
Offenses known	39,539	31,914	4,557	28,853	3,996	3,680	1,022	379	839	1,689	26,893,861
Percent cleared by arrest	15.4	18.7	16.0	20.1	16.5	13.2	32.0	16.9	34.7		
Group VI (under 10,000)											
Offenses known	33,391	28,997	4,107	23,327	2,834	3,842	1,494	498	736	7,494	21,879,800
Percent cleared by arrest	17.4	20.8	15.9	23.6	17.4	17.8	34.1	17.7	29.6		
Metropolitan Counties											
Offenses known	102,625	70,609	10,659	76,646	16,402	14,638	2,198	1,557	1,695	1,905	72,761,754
Percent cleared by arrest	13.9	17.7	14.4	18.2	16.8	14.2	36.6	10.9	31.8		
Nonmetropolitan Counties											
Offenses known	36,444	25,305	2,423	16,196	4,037	4,120	904	424	567	2,324	22,909,560
Percent cleared by arrest	15.1	16.8	14.2	25.3	17.9	16.5	32.6	19.1	30.5		
Suburban Areas[3]											
Offenses known	171,951	124,603	20,470	138,232	24,551	22,734	4,309	2,439	3,186	8,144	129,507,894
Percent cleared by arrest	14.4	18.1	14.4	18.0	15.8	13.8	35.3	12.4	30.8		

1 The figures shown in the rape column include only those reported by law enforcement agencies that used the revised Uniform Crime Reporting definition of rape.   2 Not all agencies submit reports for arson to the FBI. As a result, the number of reports the FBI uses to compute the percent of offenses cleared for arson is less than the number it uses to compute the percent of offenses cleared for all other offenses. Agencies must report arson clearances by detailed property classification as specified on the Monthly Return of Arson Offenses Known to Law Enforcement to be included in this table; therefore, clearances in this table may differ from other clearance tables.   3 Suburban area includes law enforcement agencies in cities with less than 50,000 inhabitants and county law enforcement agencies that are within a Metropolitan Statistical Area. Suburban area excludes all metropolitan agencies associated with a principal city. The agencies associated with suburban areas also appear in other groups within this table.

Table 28. Number of Offenses Cleared by Arrest or Exceptional Means and Percent Involving Persons Under 18 Years of Age, by Population Group, 2019

(Number, percent.)

Population group	Violent crime	Murder and nonnegligent manslaughter	Rape[1]	Robbery	Aggravated assault	Property crime	Burglary	Larceny-theft	Motor vehicle theft	Arson[2]	Number of agencies	Estimated population, 2019
Total, All Agencies												
Total clearances	502,833	8,795	41,011	72,993	380,034	1,067,978	137,970	831,637	90,519	7,852	15,008	297,524,524
Percent under 18 years	8.5	4.5	16.2	14.0	6.7	8.4	8.2	7.9	12.7	16.8		
Total Cities												
Total clearances	382,297	6,524	28,399	62,453	284,921	848,134	99,585	676,551	66,209	5,789	10,779	201,853,210
Percent under 18 years	8.5	4.9	14.8	14.1	6.7	8.3	8.2	7.8	13.2	16.5		
Group I (250,000 and over)												
Total clearances	161,396	3,277	10,283	32,364	115,472	212,030	31,325	155,113	23,853	1,739	85	59,934,909
Percent under 18 years	7.7	5.4	12.5	14.8	5.4	7.9	6.9	7.3	13.0	9.9		
1,000,000 and over (Group I subset)												
Total clearances	71,095	1,156	4,497	15,750	49,692	72,866	10,604	54,085	7,747	430	10	25,098,940
Percent under 18 years	7.5	6.4	9.8	15.9	4.6	5.9	5.3	5.6	8.9	8.1		
500,000 to 999,999 (Group I subset)												
Total clearances	51,350	1,252	3,031	9,606	37,461	69,933	11,357	49,485	8,393	698	26	18,474,842
Percent under 18 years	7.6	5.2	16.5	13.3	5.6	7.7	7.7	6.5	14.4	8.7		
250,000 to 499,999 (Group I subset)												
Total clearances	38,951	869	2,755	7,008	28,319	69,231	9,364	51,543	7,713	611	49	16,361,127
Percent under 18 years	8.3	4.3	12.6	14.3	6.6	10.1	7.6	9.7	15.7	12.6		
Group II (100,000 to 249,999)												
Total clearances	60,712	1,106	4,595	10,104	44,907	131,005	16,122	101,812	12,041	1,030	217	31,723,575
Percent under 18 years	8.6	5.8	15.0	14.2	6.8	9.4	8.7	8.8	15.3	15.0		
Group III (50,000 to 99,999)												
Total clearances	52,500	701	4,327	8,251	39,221	137,195	14,792	112,025	9,520	858	467	32,634,179
Percent under 18 years	8.7	3.9	16.9	12.4	7.1	9.0	8.1	8.7	12.7	17.4		
Group IV (25,000 to 49,999)												
Total clearances	36,982	545	3,172	5,156	28,109	127,703	12,057	107,815	7,166	665	827	28,786,886
Percent under 18 years	8.9	3.1	17.7	12.7	7.3	8.4	8.3	7.9	13.9	22.4		
Group V (10,000 to 24,999)												
Total clearances	35,159	501	3,151	3,725	27,782	132,127	12,798	111,702	6,945	682	1,689	26,893,861
Percent under 18 years	8.8	5.0	15.7	10.7	7.8	7.3	8.4	6.9	11.5	20.5		
Group VI (under 10,000)												
Total clearances	35,548	394	2,871	2,853	29,430	108,074	12,491	88,084	6,684	815	7,494	21,879,800
Percent under 18 years	10.9	2.3	15.8	18.6	9.8	8.0	10.7	7.2	11.8	23.6		
Metropolitan Counties												
Total clearances	95,247	1,716	9,353	9,672	74,506	179,476	28,307	130,841	18,814	1,514	1,905	72,761,754
Percent under 18 years	8.8	3.5	19.8	14.1	6.9	9.5	9.1	9.1	12.3	19.5		
Nonmetropolitan Counties												
Total clearances	25,289	555	3,259	868	20,607	40,368	10,078	24,245	5,496	549	2,324	22,909,560
Percent under 18 years	7.1	3.2	17.8	6.5	5.6	6.2	6.3	5.7	7.7	12.2		
Suburban Areas[3]												
Total clearances	161,158	2,550	15,140	18,092	125,376	413,481	50,358	328,396	31,923	2,804	8,144	129,507,894
Percent under 18 years	9.5	3.5	18.7	14.4	7.8	8.9	9.2	8.3	12.5	21.0		

1 The figures shown in the rape column include only those reported by law enforcement agencies that used the revised Uniform Crime Reporting definition of rape.   2 Not all agencies submit reports for arson to the FBI. As a result, the number of reports the FBI uses to compute the percent of offenses cleared for arson is less than the number it uses to compute the percent of offenses cleared for all other offenses.   3 Suburban area includes law enforcement agencies in cities with less than 50,000 inhabitants and county law enforcement agencies that are within a Metropolitan Statistical Area. Suburban area excludes all metropolitan agencies associated with a principal city. The agencies associated with suburban areas also appear in other groups within this table.

SECTION IV

PERSONS ARRESTED

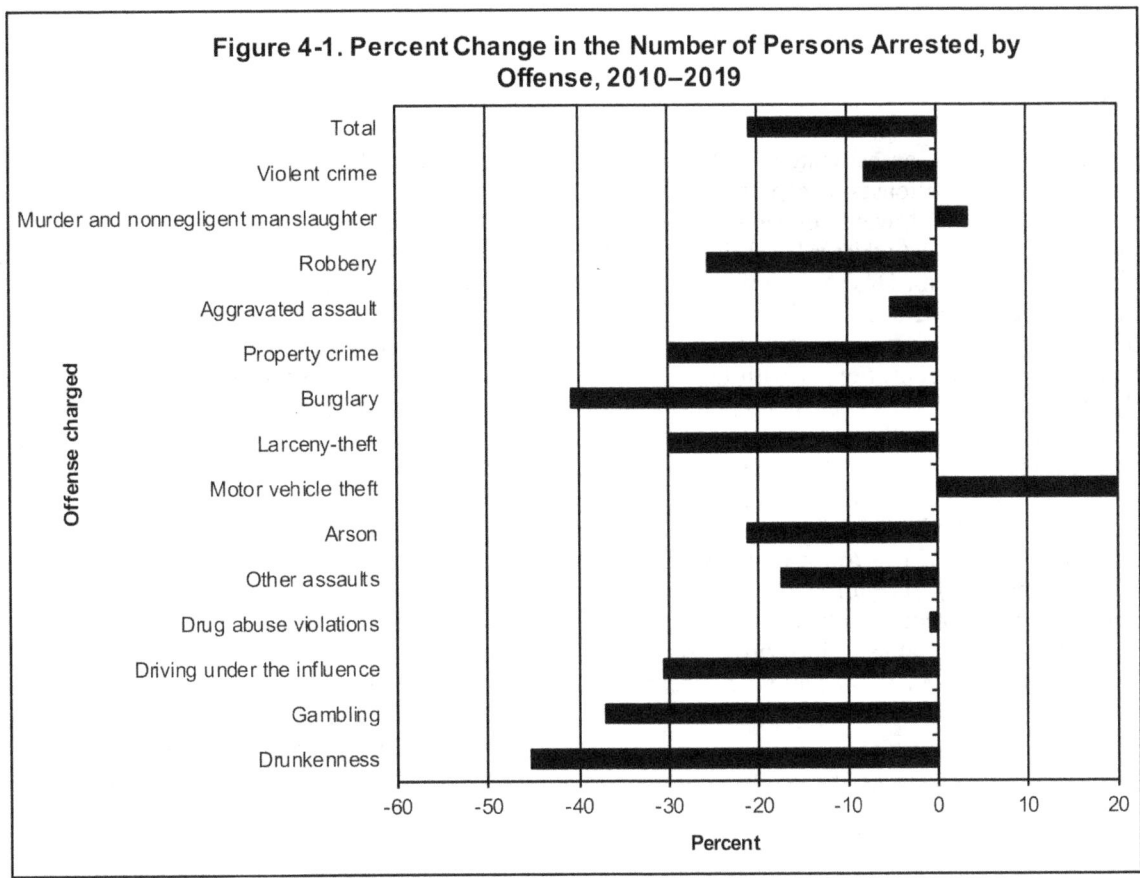

Figure 4-1. Percent Change in the Number of Persons Arrested, by Offense, 2010–2019

In the Uniform Crime Reporting (UCR) program, one arrest is counted for each separate instance in which an individual is arrested, cited, or summoned for criminal acts in Part I and Part II crimes. (See Appendix I for additional information concerning Part I and Part II crimes.) One person may be arrested multiple times during the year; as a result, the arrest figures in this section should not be taken as the total number of individuals arrested. Instead, it provides the number of *arrest occurrences* reported by law enforcement. Information regarding the UCR program's statistical methodology and table construction can be found in Appendix I.

Important Note: Rape Data

In 2013, the UCR Program initiated the collection of rape data under a revised definition and removed the term "forcible" from the offense name. The UCR Program now defines rape as follows:

Rape (revised definition): Penetration, no matter how slight, of the vagina or anus with any body part or object, or oral penetration by a sex organ of another person,

without the consent of the victim. (This includes the offenses of rape, sodomy, and sexual assault with an object as converted from data submitted via the National Incident-Based Reporting System.)

Rape (legacy definition): The carnal knowledge of a female forcibly and against her will. For tables within this publication that present data for 2018 only or provide a 2-year trend, the rape figures are an aggregate total of the data submitted based on both the legacy and revised UCR definitions. For 5- and 10-year trend tables, the rape figures for the previous year (2014 or 2009) are based on the legacy definition and the 2018 rape figures are an aggregate total based on both the legacy and revised definitions. For this reason, a percent change is not provided.

Data Collection: Juveniles

The UCR Program considers a juvenile to be an individual under 18 years of age regardless of state definition. The program does not collect data regarding police contact with a juvenile who has not committed an offense, nor does it collect data on situations in which police take

297

a juvenile into custody for his or her protection, e.g., neglect cases.

National Volume, Trends, and Rates

VOLUME

The FBI estimated that an estimated 10,085,207 arrests occurred in 2019 for all offenses (except traffic violations). Of these arrests, 495,871 were for violent crimes, and 1,074,367 were for property crimes UCR does not collect data for traffic violations. Of the total violent crimes in 2019, aggravated assaults accounted for nearly 77.7 percent of the violent crime total, or 385,278 incidents. Robbery had the next highest proportion with 15.0 percent, or 74,547 incidents; followed by rape at 5.0 percent (24,986 incidents) and murder and non-negligent manslaughter, at 2.2 percent (11,060 incidents). Of the estimated arrests for property crimes in 2019, 813,073 (75.7 percent) were for larceny-theft, 171,590 (16.0 percent) were for burglary, 80,636 (7.5 percent) were for motor vehicle theft, and 9,068 (0.8 percent) were for arson. Outside of these categories, the most frequent identifiable arrests made in 2019 were for drug abuse violations (estimated at 1,558,862 arrests). These arrests comprised 15.5 percent of the total number of all arrests. (Table 29)

A comparison of arrest figures from 2018 to 2019 revealed a 3.7 percent decrease. Arrests for violent crimes decreased 0.9 percent and arrests for property crimes decreased 3.4 percent over this time period. An examination of the 5-year and 10-year arrest trends showed that the total number of arrests in 2018 fell 6.7 percent from the 2014 total. Arrests for violent crimes showed a 3.4 percent increase from 2015 to 2019 and property crimes showed a 25.3 percent decrease. In the 10-year trend data (2010 to 2019), the number of arrests decreased 21.9 percent. For violent crimes, the number of arrests fell 11.0 percent, while arrests for property crimes decreased 31.2 percent. (Tables 32, 34, and 36)

TRENDS

The number of adults arrested for violent crime (arrestees age 18 years and over) decreased 1.1 percent from 2018 to 2019, increased 1.1 percent from 2015 to 2019, and decreased 4.3 percent from 2010 to 2019. The number of juveniles arrested for violent crime (arrestees under 18 years of age) increased 1.2 percent from 2018 to 2019, decreased 1.6 percent from 2015 to 2019, and decreased 31.3 percent from 2010 to 2019. (Tables 32, 34, and 36)

The trend data for murder and nonnegligent manslaughter showed that the number of arrests for this offense decreased 0.3 percent from 2018 to 2019, increased 5.9 percent from 2015 to 2019, and increased 3.5 percent from 2010 to 2019. The number of adults arrested for murder decreased 0.2 percent from 2018 to 2019, increased 1.1 percent from 2015 to 2019, and rose 5.5 percent from 2010 to 2019. The number of juveniles arrested for murder decreased 2.3 percent from 2018 to 2019, increased 18.5 percent from 2015 to 2019, and fell 15.7 percent from 2010 to 2019. (Tables 32, 34, and 36)

For rape, the trend data showed that arrests decreased 2.5 percent from 2018 to 2019, with adult arrests decreasing 2.6 percent and juvenile arrests falling 1.6 percent. The five-year data (2015 to 2019) shows arrests increasing 7.4 percent overall, with adult arrests increasing 6.1 percent and juvenile arrests increasing 14.1 percent. The 10-year trend data percentages were not calculated due to the program changes in the classification of rape data. (Tables 32, 34, and 36)

For robbery, the data showed that arrests decreased 4.5 percent from 2018 to 2019, with adult arrests decreasing 6.8 percent and juvenile arrests rising 5.1 percent. The 5-year trend data showed that total robbery arrests fell 13.2 percent from 2015 to 2019; adult arrests decreased 16.1 percent and juvenile arrests dropped 0.2 percent during this period. The 10-year trend data showed that arrests fell 25.4 percent from 2010 to 2019, with adult arrests dropping 23.1 percent and juvenile arrests falling by 32.8 percent. (Tables 32, 34, and 36)

The aggravated assault trend data showed that the number of arrests for this offense fell 0.1 percent from 2018 to 2019, increased 3.5 percent from 2015 to 2019, and fell 5.0 percent from 2010 to 2019. The number of adults arrested for aggravated assault remained static from 2018 to 2019, rose 4.2 percent from 2015 to 2019, and decreased 1.4 percent from 2010 to 2019. The number of juveniles arrested for aggravated assault decreased 0.6 percent from 2018 to 2019, fell 5.0 percent from 2015 to 2019, and dropped 35.8 percent from 2010 to 2019. (Tables 32, 34, and 36)

The 2-year, 5-year, and 10-year trend data showed that the number of arrests for property crime decreased 3.4 percent from 2018 to 2019, decreased 22.7 percent from 2015 to 2019, and decreased 29.6 percent from 2010 to 2019. The number of adults arrested for property crime offenses (arrestees age 18 years and over) decreased 3.0 percent from 2018 to 2019, decreased 19.7 percent from 2015 to 2019, and decreased 18.62 percent from 2010 to 2019. The number of juveniles arrested for property crime (arrestees under 18 years of age) decreased 6.9 percent from 2018 to 2019, decreased 40.6 percent from 2015 to 2019, and decreased 66.0 percent from 2010 to 2019. (Tables 32, 34, and 36)

The trend data for burglary showed that the number of arrests for this offense decreased 5.1 percent from 2018 to 2019, decreased 21.3 percent from 2015 to 2019, and decreased 40.8 percent from 2010 to 2019. The number of adults arrested for burglary fell 4.5 percent from 2018 to 2019, fell 17.3 percent from 2015 to 2019, and decreased 32.8 percent from 2010 to 2019. The number of juveniles arrested for burglary decreased 8.7 percent from 2018 to 2019, decreased 41.4 percent from 2015 to 2019, and fell 68.1 percent from 2010 to 2019. (Tables 32, 34, and 36)

For larceny-theft, the 2-year trend data showed that arrests fell 2.9 percent from 2018 to 2019, with adult arrests decreasing 2.4 percent and juvenile arrests decreasing 7.1 percent. The 5-year trend data showed that total larceny-theft arrests decreased 25.3 percent from 2015 to 2019; adult arrests fell 22.3 percent, while juvenile arrests dropped by 44.3 percent during this period. The 10-year trend data showed that larceny-theft arrests fell 29.8 percent from 2010 to 2019, with adult arrests decreasing by 18.1 percent and juvenile arrests falling by 68.5 percent. (Tables 32, 34, and 36)

For motor vehicle theft, the 2-year trend data showed that arrests fell 5.9 percent from 2018 to 2019, with adult arrests decreasing 6.5 percent and juvenile arrests decreasing 2.8 percent. The 5-year trend data showed that total motor vehicle theft arrests rose 11.3 percent from 2015 to 2019; juvenile arrests increased 7.8 percent and adult arrests increased 12.1 percent during this period. The 10-year trend data showed that arrests rose 21.7 percent from 2010 to 2019, with adult arrests rising 29.7 percent and juvenile arrests dropping 7.2 percent. (Tables 32, 34, and 36)

The arson trend data showed that the number of arrests for this offense decreased 3.4 percent from 2018 to 2019, rose 0.1 percent from 2015 to 2019, and fell 21.3 percent from 2010 to 2019. The number of adults arrested for arson fell 2.8 percent from 2018 to 2019, increased 18.7 percent from 2015 to 2019, and increased 11.5 percent from 2010 to 2019. The number of juveniles arrested for arson dropped 5.7 percent from 2018 to 2019, dropped 39.3 percent from 2015 to 2019, and dropped 63.9 percent from 2010 to 2019. (Tables 32, 34, and 36)

Figure 4-2A. Arrest Distribution, Violent Crime, by Age, 2019

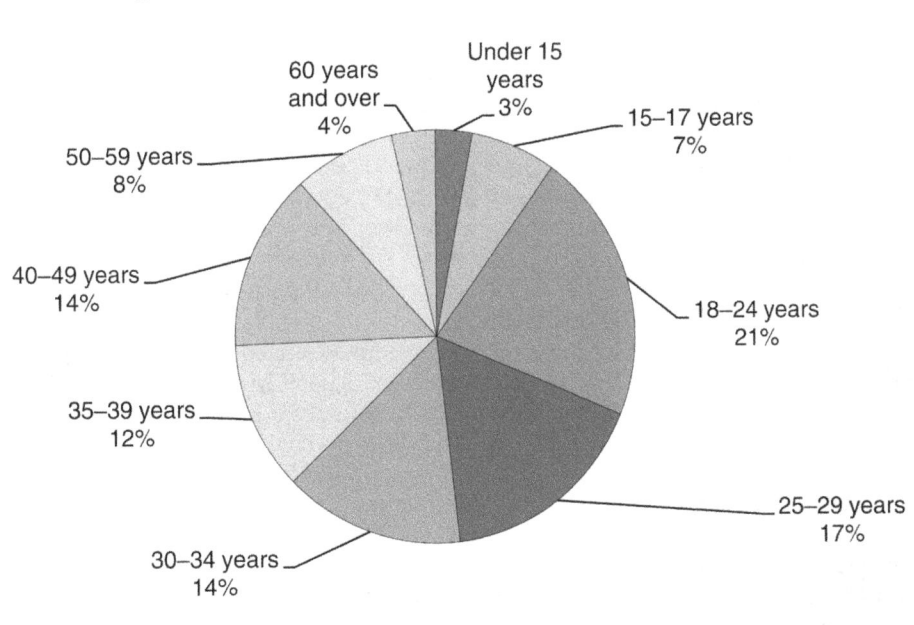

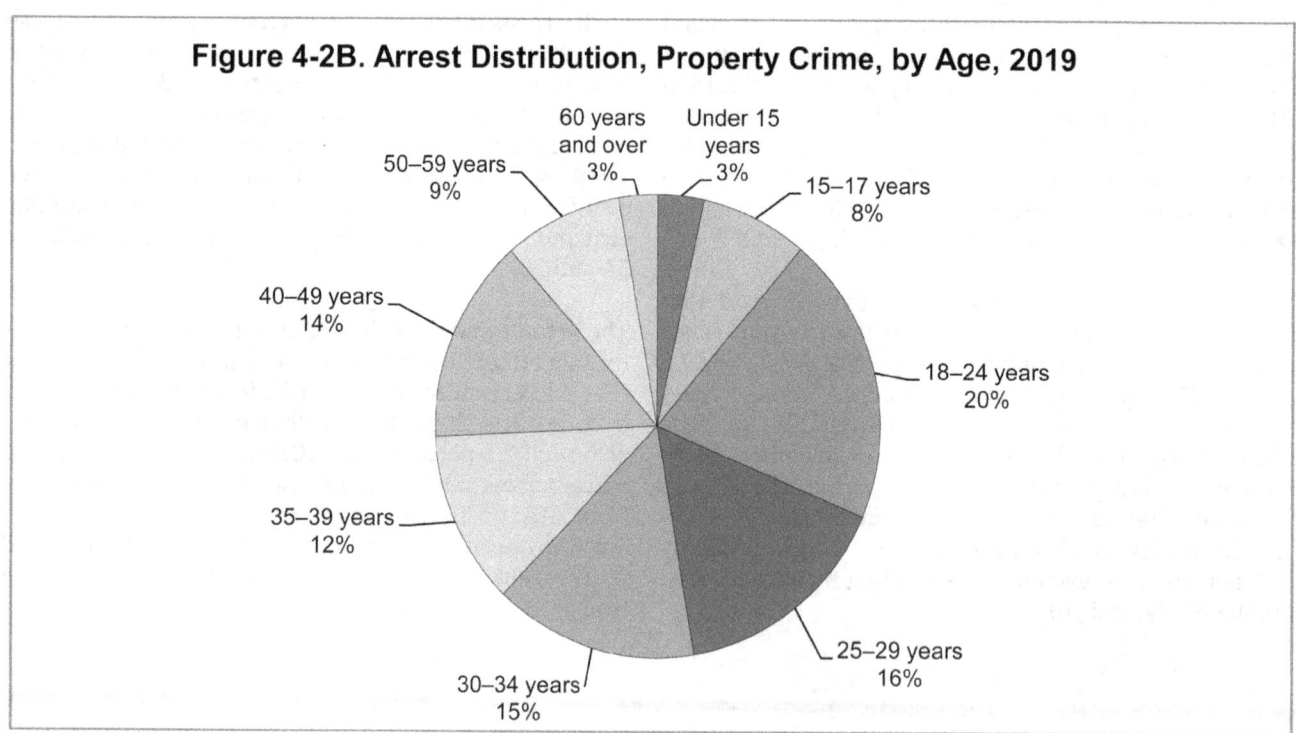

Figure 4-2B. Arrest Distribution, Property Crime, by Age, 2019

RATES

The rate of arrests was estimated at 3,011.0 arrests per 100,000 inhabitants in 2019. The arrest rate for violent crime was 156.3 arrests per 100,000 inhabitants, and the arrest rate for property crime was 343.3 arrests per 100,000 inhabitants. Law enforcement agencies throughout the nation reported 3.4 murder arrests, 7.4 rape arrests, 24.7 robbery arrests, and 120.8 aggravated assault arrests per 100,000 inhabitants in 2019. Law enforcement agencies throughout the nation reported 52.3 burglary arrests, 263.0 larceny-theft arrests, 25.1 motor vehicle theft arrests, and 2.8 arson arrests per 100,000 inhabitants in 2019. (Table 30)

By Age, Sex, and Race

Law enforcement agencies that contributed arrest data to the UCR program reported information on the age, sex, and race of the persons they arrested. According to the data for 2019, adults accounted for 93.0 percent of arrestees nationally. (Table 38)

A review of arrest data by age from 2018 to 2019 showed that arrests of adults decreased 3.7 percent during this period, with a 0.9 percent decrease in arrests for violent crime and a 3.4 percent drop in arrests for property crimes. The arrest total for juveniles (those under 18 years of age) decreased 3.4 percent from 2018 to 2019. Over the 2-year period, arrests of juveniles for violent crimes rose 1.2 percent; juvenile arrests for property crimes decreased 6.9 percent. (Table 36)

By sex, males accounted for 72.5 percent of all persons arrested in 2019. Males represented 78.9 percent of arrestees for violent crime, 88.0 percent of arrestees for murder, 96.6 percent of arrestees for rape, 84.2 percent for robbery, and 76.5 percent for aggravated assault. Females accounted for 21.1 percent of violent crime arrestees, 12.0 percent of murder arrestees, 3.4 percent of rape arrestees, 15.8 percent of robbery arrestees, and 23.5 percent of aggravated assault arrestees. (Table 42)

Most arrestees for property crime in 2019 (88.9 percent) were over 18 years of age. By sex, males accounted for 62.3

percent of arrestees for property crime, 79.3 percent of arrestees for burglary, 57.4 percent of arrestees for larceny-theft, 76.8 percent of arrestees for motor vehicle theft, and 78.4 percent of arrestees for arson. Females accounted for 37.7 percent of property crime arrestees. Of the four property crimes, larceny-theft had the highest proportion of female arrestees at 42.6 percent. (Tables 38 and 42)

In 2019, 69.4 percent of all persons arrested were White, 26.6 percent were Black, and the remaining 4.0 percent were of other races (American Indian or Alaskan Native, Asian, and Native Hawaiian or Pacific Islander). Of all arrestees for violent crimes, 59.1 percent were White, 36.4 percent were Black, and 4.5 percent were of other races. For murder, 45.8 percent of arrestees were White, 51.2 percent were Black, and 3.0 percent were of other races. For rape, 69.8 percent of arrestees were White, 52.7 percent were Black, and 3.6 percent of arrestees were of other races. For robbery, 44.7 percent of arrestees were White, 54.2 percent of arrestees were Black, and 2.6 percent of arrestees were of other races. For aggravated assault, 61.8 percent of arrestees were White, 33.2 percent of arrestees were Black, and 5.0 percent were of other races. (Table 43)

Of all arrestees for property crimes in 2019, 66.8 percent were White, 29.8 percent were Black, and 3.4 percent were of other races. For burglary, 68.2 percent of arrestees were White, 28.8 percent were Black, and 3.0 percent were of other races. For larceny-theft, 66.3 percent of

arrestees were White, 30.2 percent were Black, and 3.5 percent were of other races. For motor vehicle theft, 67.6 percent of arrestees were White, 28.6 percent of arrestees were Black, and 3.8 percent were of other races. For arson, 70.8 percent of arrestees were White, 24.7 percent of arrestees were Black, and 4.5 percent were of other races. (Table 43)

Outside of the scope of violent and property crimes, White adults were most commonly arrested for drug abuse violations (748,874 arrests) and driving under the influence (526,928 arrests). Black adults were most frequently arrested for drug abuse violations (274,670 arrests) and other assaults (219,400 arrests). (Table 43)

Regional Arrest Rates

The UCR program divides the United States into four regions: the Northeast, the Midwest, the South, and the West. (Appendix III provides more information about the regions.) Law enforcement agencies in the Northeast had an overall arrest rate of 2,476.8 arrests per 100,000 inhabitants, below the national rate (3,011.0 arrests per 100,000 inhabitants). In this region, the arrest rate for violent crimes was 104.3 arrests per 100,000 inhabitants, and for property crime, the arrest rate was 296.2 arrests per 100,000 inhabitants. In the Midwest, law enforcement agencies reported an arrest rate of 2,973.1 arrests per 100,000 inhabitants. The arrest rate for violent crimes was 128.0 and the arrest rate for property crime

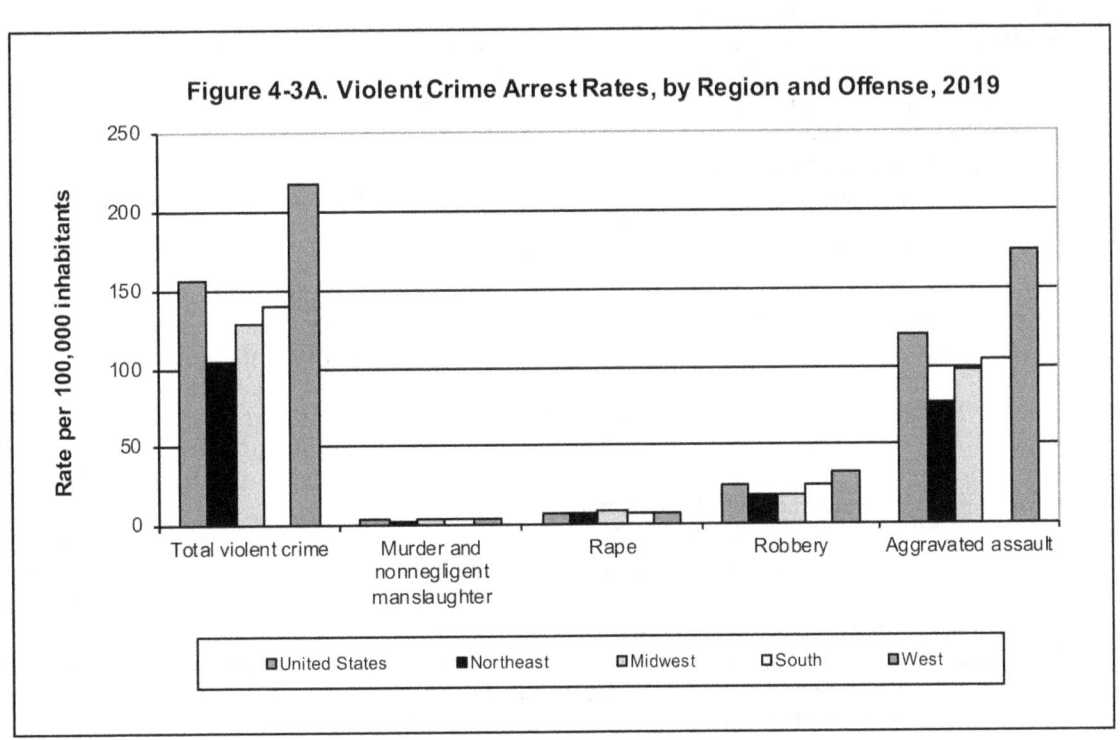

Figure 4-3A. Violent Crime Arrest Rates, by Region and Offense, 2019

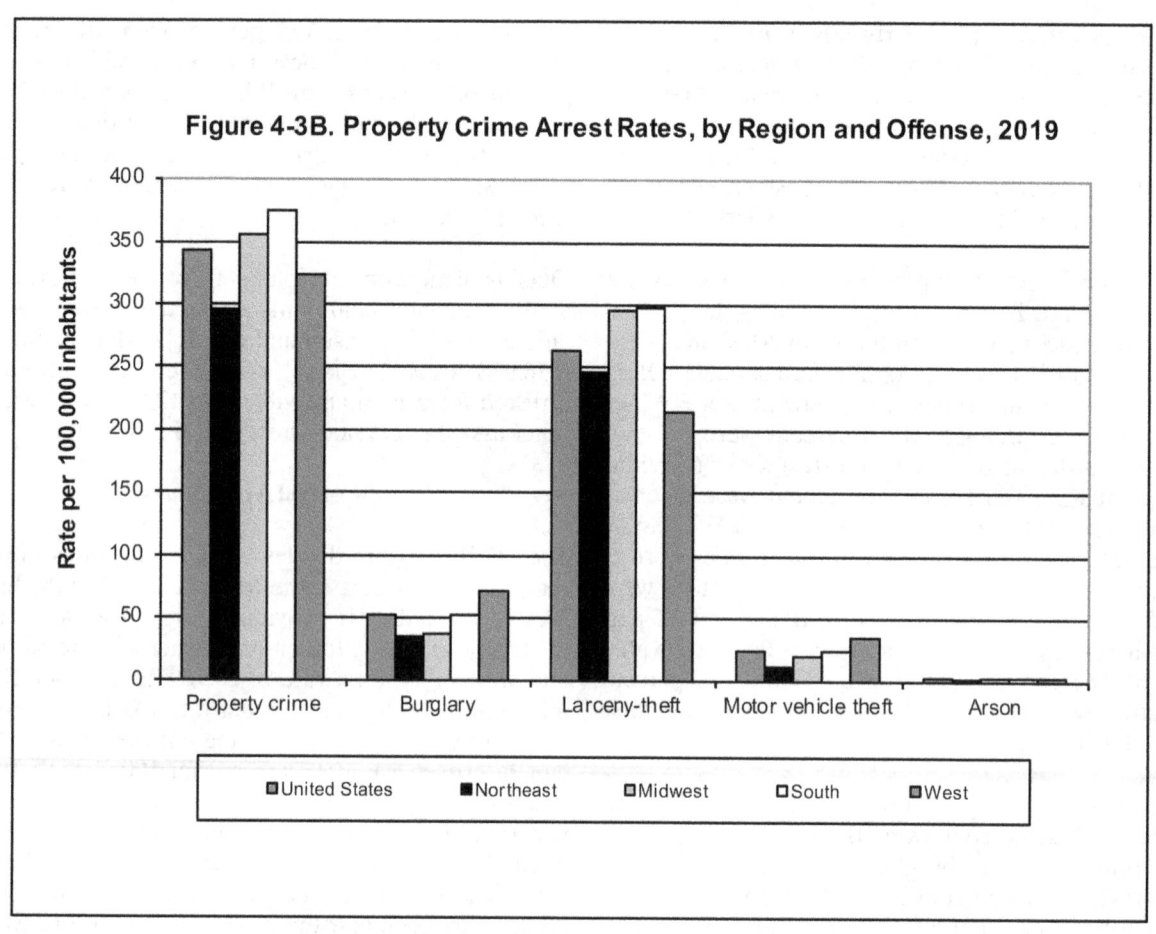

Figure 4-3B. Property Crime Arrest Rates, by Region and Offense, 2019

was 355.3. Law enforcement agencies in the South, the nation's most populous region, reported an arrest rate of 3,217.8 per 100,000 inhabitants. Arrests for violent crime occurred at a rate of 140.3 arrests per 100,000 residents, and for property crime, the arrest rate was 375.2 arrests per 100,000 inhabitants. In the West, law enforcement agencies reported an overall arrest rate of 3,075.1 arrests per 100,000 inhabitants. The region's violent crime arrest rate was 217.2, the highest of the regions, while its property crime arrest rate was 324.5. (Table 30)

The regional murder arrest rates were 1.8 in the Northeast, 3.2 in the Midwest, 4.3 in the South, and 3.2 in the West. For rape, the regional arrest rates were 6.8 in the Northeast, 9.0 in the Midwest, 7.0 in the South, and 7.1 in the West. Regional arrest rates for robbery were 18.7 in the Northeast, 17.6 in the Midwest, 24.1 in the South, and 32.8 in the West. For aggravated assault, the regional arrest rates were 77.0 in the Northeast, 98.2 in the Midwest, 104.9 in the South, and 174.0 in the West. (Table 30)

The regional burglary arrest rates were 35.6 in the Northeast, 36.3 in the Midwest, 51.4 in the South, and 71.6 in the West. For larceny-theft, the regional arrest rates were 246.1 in the Northeast, 295.5 in the Midwest, 297.0 in the South, and 214.5 in the West. Regional arrest rates for motor vehicle theft were 12.7 in the Northeast, 21.1 in the Midwest, 24.4 in the South, and 34.6 in the West. For arson, the regional arrest rates were 1.9 in the Northeast, 2.5 in the Midwest, 2.4 in the South, and 3.8 in the West. (Table 30)

Population Groups: Trends and Rates

The national UCR program aggregates data by various population groups, which include cities, metropolitan counties, and nonmetropolitan counties. Definitions of these groups can be found in Appendix III. The total number of arrests in U.S. cities fell 3.5 percent from 2018 to 2019. The number of arrests for violent crimes fell 0.1 percent and arrests for property crimes decreased 2.5 percent during the 2-year time frame. (Table 44)

In 2019, law enforcement agencies in cities collectively recorded an arrest rate of 3,133.8 arrests per 100,000 inhabitants. The nation's smallest cities, those with fewer than 10,000 inhabitants, had the highest arrest rate among the city population groups with 4.761.9 arrests per 100,000 inhabitants. Law enforcement agencies in cities with 250,000 or more inhabitants recorded the lowest rate, 2,683.8. In the nation's metropolitan counties, law enforcement agencies reported an arrest rate of 2,643.6 per 100,000 inhabitants. Agencies in nonmetropolitan counties reported an arrest rate of 2,979.1. (Table 31)

By population group, law enforcement agencies in the nation's cities collectively reported 175.7 violent crime arrests per 100,000 inhabitants in 2098. In the city population groups, cities with 250,000 or more inhabitants reported the highest violent crime arrest rate (237.8) and cities with 10,000 to 24,999 inhabitants reported the lowest violent crime arrest rate (118.6). Cities reported an overall murder arrest rate of 3.6 per 100,000 inhabitants; cities with 250,000 or more inhabitants had the highest murder arrest rate (5.8) and cities with under 10,000 inhabitants had the lowest murder arrest rate (2.0). The collective city rape arrest rate was 7.6 per 100,000 inhabitants, with the highest rate in cities with less than 10,000 inhabitants (8.6) and the lowest rate in cities with 25,000 to 49,999 inhabitants (6.5). The overall robbery arrest rate for cities was 30.1 per 100,000 inhabitants; cities with 250,000 or more inhabitants had the highest robbery arrest rate (47.8) and cities with fewer than 10,000 inhabitants had the lowest robbery arrest rate (15.3). For aggravated assault, the collective city arrest rate was 134.4 per 100,000 inhabitants, with the greatest arrest rate in cities with 250,000 or more inhabitants (176.0) and the lowest arrest ratè in cities with 10,000 to 24,999 inhabitants (93.6). (Table 31)

Agencies in metropolitan counties reported a violent crime arrest rate of 119.2 per 100,000 inhabitants, with arrest rates of 2.9 for murder, 6.6 for rape, 15.3 for robbery, and 94.4 for aggravated assault. Agencies in non-metropolitan counties reported arrest rates of 91.6 for violent crime, 2.9 for murder, 8.0 for rape, 4.3 for robbery, and 76.5 for aggravated assault. (Table 31)

By population group, law enforcement agencies in the nation's cities collectively reported 404.6 property crime arrests per 100,000 inhabitants in 2019. In the city population groups, cities with less than 10,000 inhabitants reported the highest property crime arrest rate (478.3) and cities with 250,000 or more inhabitants reported the lowest property crime arrest rate (328.4). Cities reported an overall burglary arrest rate of 57.7 per 100,000 inhabitants; cities with 100,000 to 249,999 inhabitants had the highest burglary arrest rate (66.1) and cities with 25,000 to 49,999 inhabitants had the lowest burglary arrest rate (48.4). The collective city larceny-theft arrest rate was 316.7 per 100,000 inhabitants, with the highest rate in cities with 10,000 to 24,999 inhabitants (397.0) and the lowest rate in cities with 250,000 or more inhabitants (229.9). The overall motor vehicle theft arrest rate for cities was 27.2 per 100,000 inhabitants; cities with 250,000 or more inhabitants had the highest motor vehicle theft arrest rate

(35.0), and cities with 10,000 to 24,999 inhabitants had the lowest motor vehicle theft arrest rate (19.3). For arson, the collective city arrest rate was 3.1 per 100,000 inhabitants, with the greatest arrest rate in cities with less than 10,000 inhabitants (3.9) and the lowest arrest rate in cities with 50,000 to 99,999 inhabitants (2.7). (Table 31)

Agencies in metropolitan counties reported a property crime arrest rate of 223.8 per 100,000 inhabitants, with arrest rates of 39.8 for burglary, 160.6 for larceny-theft, 21.3 for motor vehicle theft, and 2.0 for arson. Agencies in nonmetropolitan counties reported arrest rates of 145.1 for property crime, 41.5 for burglary, 83.4 for larceny-theft, 18.1 for motor vehicle theft, and 2.1 for arson. (Table 31)

In suburban areas, the rates per 100,000 inhabitants for violent crime and property crime were 113.4 and 305.6, respectively. The rate for murder was 2.3 for rape, 6.3; for robbery, 16.0; and for aggravated assault, 88.7. Specific property crime rates included 41.9 for burglary, 241.5 for larceny-theft, 20.0 for motor vehicle theft, and 2.3 for arson. (Table 31)

Community Types

In 2019, law enforcement agencies in the nation's cities reported that 92.3 percent of arrests in their jurisdictions were of adults and 7.7 percent of arrests were of juveniles. Adults accounted for 90.0 percent of arrestees for violent crimes, while juveniles accounted for 10.0 percent of these arrests. Adults made up 88.7 percent of the arrestees for property crimes, and juveniles accounted for the remaining 11.3 percent. Of all arrests in the nation's cities in 2019, 27.9 percent were of individuals under 25 years of age. In metropolitan counties, 25.0 percent of arrests were of individuals under 25 years of age. In nonmetropolitan counties, 22.3 percent of persons arrested were of individuals under 25 years of age. (Tables 46, 47, 53, and 59)

Males accounted for 72.2 percent and females accounted for 27.8 percent of arrestees in the nation's cities in 2019. In metropolitan counties, males comprised 73.2 percent of arrestees, and in nonmetropolitan counties, males represented 72.9 percent of all arrestees. (Tables 48, 54, and 60)

By race, 67.1 percent of arrestees in the nation's cities in 2019 were White, 28.4 percent were Black, and 4.4 percent were of other races (American Indian or Alaska Native and Asian or Pacific Islander). Whites accounted for 71.7 percent of arrestees in metropolitan counties in 2019, Blacks made up 25.8 percent of arrestees, and persons of other races made up 2.4 percent of the total. In nonmetropolitan counties, Whites made up 84.3 percent of arrestees, Blacks accounted for 11.8 percent of arrestees, and other races made up 4.0 percent of the total. (Tables 49, 55, and 61)

Table 29. Estimated Number of Arrests, 2019

(Number.)

Offense	Arrests
Total[1]	10,085,207
Violent crime[2]	495,871
Murder and nonnegligent manslaughter	11,060
Rape[3]	24,986
Robbery	74,547
Aggravated assault	385,278
Property crime[2]	1,074,367
Burglary	171,590
Larceny-theft	813,073
Motor vehicle theft	80,636
Arson	9,068
Other assaults	1,025,711
Forgery and counterfeiting	45,183
Fraud	112,707
Embezzlement	13,497
Stolen property; buying, receiving, possessing	88,272
Vandalism	180,501
Weapons; carrying, possessing, etc.	153,161
Prostitution and commercialized vice	26,713
Sex offenses (except forcible rape and prostitution)	40,796
Drug abuse violations	1,558,862
Gambling	2,458
Offenses against the family and children	85,687
Driving under the influence	1,024,508
Liquor laws	175,548
Drunkenness	316,032
Disorderly conduct	310,331
Vagrancy	21,896
All other offenses (except traffic)	3,318,453
Suspicion	579
Curfew and loitering law violations	14,653

1 Does not include suspicion.   2 Violent crimes are offenses of murder and nonnegligent manslaughter, rape, robbery, and aggravated assault. Property crimes are offenses of burglary, larceny-theft, motor vehicle theft, and arson.   3 The rape figures in this table are an aggregate total of the data submitted using both the revised and legacy Uniform Crime Reporting definitions.

Table 30. Number and Rate of Arrests, by Geographic Region, 2019

(Number, rate per 100,000 inhabitants.)

Offense charged	United States total (10,831 agencies; population 229,735,355) Total	Rate	Northeast (2,330 agencies; population 35,810,078) Total	Rate	Midwest (2,883 agencies; population 43,951,001) Total	Rate	South (3,792 agencies; population 78,293,710) Total	Rate	West (1,826 agencies; population 71,680,566) Total	Rate
Total[1]	6,917,223	3,011.0	886,938	2,476.8	1,306,691	2,973.1	2,519,358	3,217.8	2,204,236	3,075.1
	359,092	156.3	37,356	104.3	56,258	128.0	109,807	140.3	155,671	217.2
Violent crime[2]										
Murder and nonnegligent manslaughter	7,711	3.4	652	1.8	1,394	3.2	3,353	4.3	2,312	3.2
Rape[3]	16,966	7.4	2,449	6.8	3,967	9.0	5,484	7.0	5,066	7.1
Robbery	56,854	24.7	6,690	18.7	7,749	17.6	18,874	24.1	23,541	32.8
Aggravated assault	277,561	120.8	27,565	77.0	43,148	98.2	82,096	104.9	124,752	174.0
Property crime[2]	788,636	343.3	106,085	296.2	156,168	355.3	293,751	375.2	232,632	324.5
Burglary	120,242	52.3	12,755	35.6	15,954	36.3	40,230	51.4	51,303	71.6
Larceny-theft	604,287	263.0	88,121	246.1	129,859	295.5	232,526	297.0	153,781	214.5
Motor vehicle theft	57,738	25.1	4,538	12.7	9,259	21.1	19,126	24.4	24,815	34.6
Arson	6,369	2.8	671	1.9	1,096	2.5	1,869	2.4	2,733	3.8
Other assaults	717,793	312.4	104,755	292.5	146,069	332.3	260,246	332.4	206,723	288.4
Forgery and counterfeiting	32,495	14.1	4,861	13.6	5,783	13.2	13,653	17.4	8,198	11.4
Fraud	79,954	34.8	13,032	36.4	17,856	40.6	30,457	38.9	18,609	26.0
Embezzlement	10,003	4.4	866	2.4	1,986	4.5	4,934	6.3	2,217	3.1
Stolen property; buying, receiving, possessing	64,027	27.9	7,367	20.6	12,807	29.1	19,801	25.3	24,052	33.6
Vandalism	128,474	55.9	23,884	66.7	24,702	56.2	31,930	40.8	47,958	66.9
Weapons; carrying, possessing, etc.	110,130	47.9	10,397	29.0	22,185	50.5	37,071	47.3	40,477	56.5
Prostitution and commercialized vice	20,015	8.7	2,021	5.6	1,822	4.1	6,006	7.7	10,166	14.2
Sex offenses (except forcible rape and prostitution)	28,973	12.6	4,248	11.9	4,916	11.2	5,855	7.5	13,954	19.5
Drug abuse violations	1,067,764	464.8	152,508	425.9	176,747	402.1	406,667	519.4	331,842	462.9
Gambling	1,909	0.8	273	0.8	182	0.4	726	0.9	728	1.0
Offenses against the family and children	58,720	25.6	11,747	32.8	10,902	24.8	24,606	31.4	11,465	16.0
Driving under the influence	658,902	286.8	91,365	255.1	136,193	309.9	191,198	244.2	240,146	335.0
Liquor laws	112,467	49.0	8,809	24.6	40,395	91.9	30,286	38.7	32,977	46.0
Drunkenness	219,696	95.6	15,235	42.5	12,284	27.9	118,132	150.9	74,045	103.3
Disorderly conduct	211,960	92.3	42,778	119.5	71,290	162.2	53,522	68.4	44,370	61.9
Vagrancy	16,104	7.0	1,209	3.4	2,323	5.3	3,113	4.0	9,459	13.2
All other offenses (except traffic)	2,219,328	966.0	247,423	690.9	402,626	916.1	873,940	1,116.2	695,339	970.1
Suspicion	329	0.1	100	0.3	32	0.1	80	0.1	117	0.2
Curfew and loitering law violations	10,781	4.7	719	2.0	3,197	7.3	3,657	4.7	3,208	4.5

1 Does not include suspicion.   2 Violent crimes are offenses of murder and nonnegligent manslaughter, rape, robbery, and aggravated assault. Property crimes are offenses of burglary, larceny-theft, motor vehicle theft, and arson.   3 The rape figures in this table are aggregate totals of the data submitted based on both the legacy and revised Uniform Crime Reporting definitions.

Table 31. Number and Rate of Arrests, by Population Group, 2019

(Number, rate per 100,000 inhabitants.)

Offense charged	Total (10,831 agencies; population 229,735,355)		Total cities (7,979 cities; population 159,706,353)		Group I (70 cities, 250,000 and over; population 43,703,387)		Group II (182 cities, 100,000 to 249,999; population 26,636,848)		Group III (389 cities, 50,000 to 99,999; population 27,232,262)	
	Total	Rate	Total	Rate	Total	Rate	Total	Rate	Total	Rate
Total[2]	6,917,223	3,011.0	5,004,922	3,133.8	1,172,912	2,683.8	830,531	3,118.0	799,672	2,936.5
Violent crime[3]	359,092	156.3	280,634	175.7	103,922	237.8	54,801	205.7	42,967	157.8
Murder and nonnegligent manslaughter	7,711	3.4	5,693	3.6	2,516	5.8	1,139	4.3	666	2.4
Rape[4]	16,966	7.4	12,070	7.6	3,590	8.2	2,041	7.7	1,907	7.0
Robbery	56,854	24.7	48,151	30.1	20,899	47.8	9,256	34.7	7,215	26.5
Aggravated assault	277,561	120.8	214,720	134.4	76,917	176.0	42,365	159.0	33,179	121.8
Property crime[3]	788,636	343.3	646,218	404.6	143,531	328.4	108,980	409.1	109,650	402.6
Burglary	120,242	52.3	92,073	57.7	26,367	60.3	17,610	66.1	15,599	57.3
Larceny-theft	604,287	263.0	505,838	316.7	100,466	229.9	81,614	306.4	87,196	320.2
Motor vehicle theft	57,738	25.1	43,390	27.2	15,290	35.0	8,913	33.5	6,109	22.4
Arson	6,369	2.8	4,917	3.1	1,408	3.2	843	3.2	746	2.7
Other assaults	717,793	312.4	552,879	346.2	153,670	351.6	96,157	361.0	88,852	326.3
Forgery and counterfeiting	32,495	14.1	24,813	15.5	4,404	10.1	4,083	15.3	4,178	15.3
Fraud	79,954	34.8	59,417	37.2	11,158	25.5	8,860	33.3	9,718	35.7
Embezzlement	10,003	4.4	8,061	5.0	2,017	4.6	1,148	4.3	1,557	5.7
Stolen property; buying, receiving, possessing	64,027	27.9	48,895	30.6	15,399	35.2	8,781	33.0	8,591	31.5
Vandalism	128,474	55.9	101,046	63.3	27,696	63.4	16,791	63.0	15,987	58.7
Weapons; carrying, possessing, etc.	110,130	47.9	82,918	51.9	30,274	69.3	15,026	56.4	11,841	43.5
Prostitution and commercialized vice	20,015	8.7	17,588	11.0	12,054	27.6	2,645	9.9	1,241	4.6
Sex offenses (except forcible rape and prostitution)	28,973	12.6	21,212	13.3	6,079	13.9	3,701	13.9	3,621	13.3
Drug abuse violations	1,067,764	464.8	752,471	471.2	156,387	357.8	131,398	493.3	131,982	484.7
Gambling	1,909	0.8	1,205	0.8	445	1.0	204	0.8	225	0.8
Offenses against the family and children	58,720	25.6	32,341	20.3	6,596	15.1	5,696	21.4	4,217	15.5
Driving under the influence	658,902	286.8	389,429	243.8	81,407	186.3	55,323	207.7	59,300	217.8
Liquor laws	112,467	49.0	88,737	55.6	13,155	30.1	11,405	42.8	11,485	42.2
Drunkenness	219,696	95.6	188,238	117.9	28,838	66.0	34,315	128.8	32,197	118.2
Disorderly conduct	211,960	92.3	175,498	109.9	24,400	55.8	25,957	97.4	27,164	99.7
Vagrancy	16,104	7.0	14,326	9.0	7,098	16.2	2,979	11.2	1,290	4.7
All other offenses (except traffic)	2,219,328	966.0	1,509,280	945.0	342,321	783.3	240,796	904.0	231,946	851.7
Suspicion	329	0.1	211	0.1	0	0.0	2	*	11	*
Curfew and loitering law violations	10,781	4.7	9,716	6.1	2,061	4.7	1,485	5.6	1,663	6.1

Table 31. Number and Rate of Arrests, by Population Group, 2019—Continued

(Number, rate per 100,000 inhabitants.)

Offense charged	Group IV (689 cities, 25,000 to 49,999; population 24,056,009) Total	Rate	Group V (1,355 cities, 10,000 to 24,999; population 21,714,346) Total	Rate	Group VI (5,294 cities, under 10,000; population 16,363,501) Total	Rate	Metropolitan counties (1,230 agencies; population 51,841,134) Total	Rate	Nonmetropolitan counties (1,622 agencies; population 18,187,868) Total	Rate	Suburban areas[1] (5,820 agencies; population 97,421,942) Total	Rate
Total[2]	714,256	2,969.1	708,338	3,262.1	779,213	4,761.9	1,370,463	2,643.6	541,838	2,979.1	2,713,085	2,784.9
Violent crime[3]	29,934	124.4	25,759	118.6	23,251	142.1	61,801	119.2	16,657	91.6	110,435	113.4
Murder and nonnegligent manslaughter	555	2.3	490	2.3	327	2.0	1,496	2.9	522	2.9	2,251	2.3
Rape[4]	1,557	6.5	1,570	7.2	1,405	8.6	3,446	6.6	1,450	8.0	6,183	6.3
Robbery	4,903	20.4	3,368	15.5	2,510	15.3	7,929	15.3	774	4.3	15,584	16.0
Aggravated assault	22,919	95.3	20,331	93.6	19,009	116.2	48,930	94.4	13,911	76.5	86,417	88.7
Property crime[3]	104,300	433.6	101,498	467.4	78,259	478.3	116,025	223.8	26,393	145.1	297,738	305.6
Burglary	12,246	50.9	10,505	48.4	9,746	59.6	20,629	39.8	7,540	41.5	40,785	41.9
Larceny-theft	86,640	360.2	86,200	397.0	63,722	389.4	83,278	160.6	15,171	83.4	235,319	241.5
Motor vehicle theft	4,741	19.7	4,184	19.3	4,153	25.4	11,057	21.3	3,291	18.1	19,436	20.0
Arson	673	2.8	609	2.8	638	3.9	1,061	2.0	391	2.1	2,198	2.3
Other assaults	77,162	320.8	70,595	325.1	66,443	406.0	121,001	233.4	43,913	241.4	251,819	258.5
Forgery and counterfeiting	4,108	17.1	3,949	18.2	4,091	25.0	5,998	11.6	1,684	9.3	13,438	13.8
Fraud	9,285	38.6	8,371	38.6	12,025	73.5	15,770	30.4	4,767	26.2	33,686	34.6
Embezzlement	1,377	5.7	1,177	5.4	785	4.8	1,589	3.1	353	1.9	3,697	3.8
Stolen property; buying, receiving, possessing	6,574	27.3	5,116	23.6	4,434	27.1	11,868	22.9	3,264	17.9	23,275	23.9
Vandalism	14,504	60.3	13,250	61.0	12,818	78.3	20,924	40.4	6,504	35.8	44,333	45.5
Weapons; carrying, possessing, etc.	9,302	38.7	7,942	36.6	8,533	52.1	21,245	41.0	5,967	32.8	38,587	39.6
Prostitution and commercialized vice	850	3.5	506	2.3	292	1.8	2,308	4.5	119	0.7	3,510	3.6
Sex offenses (except forcible rape and prostitution)	2,817	11.7	2,496	11.5	2,498	15.3	5,879	11.3	1,882	10.3	10,967	11.3
Drug abuse violations	107,686	447.6	102,599	472.5	122,419	748.1	225,843	435.6	89,450	491.8	443,360	455.1
Gambling	100	0.4	114	0.5	117	0.7	603	1.2	101	0.6	822	0.8
Offenses against the family and children	4,547	18.9	4,882	22.5	6,403	39.1	19,510	37.6	6,869	37.8	27,274	28.0
Driving under the influence	59,372	246.8	65,394	301.2	68,633	419.4	181,678	350.5	87,795	482.7	310,392	318.6
Liquor laws	11,282	46.9	14,743	67.9	26,667	163.0	14,407	27.8	9,323	51.3	44,448	45.6
Drunkenness	27,115	112.7	26,501	122.0	39,272	240.0	22,232	42.9	9,226	50.7	66,799	68.6
Disorderly conduct	28,176	117.1	31,277	144.0	38,524	235.4	25,038	48.3	11,424	62.8	80,244	82.4
Vagrancy	1,295	5.4	930	4.3	734	4.5	1,543	3.0	235	1.3	3,214	3.3
All other offenses (except traffic)	212,992	885.4	219,316	1,010.0	261,909	1,600.6	494,274	953.4	215,774	1,186.4	901,402	925.3
Suspicion	37	0.2	64	0.3	97	0.6	71	0.1	47	0.3	196	0.2
Curfew and loitering law violations	1,478	6.1	1,923	8.9	1,106	6.8	927	1.8	138	0.8	3,645	3.7

* = Less than one-tenth of one percent.
1 Suburban areas include law enforcement agencies in cities with less than 50,000 inhabitants and county law enforcement agencies that are within a Metropolitan Statistical Area. Suburban areas exclude all metropolitan agencies associated with a principal city. The agencies associated with suburban areas also appear in other groups within this table.   2 Does not include suspicion.   3 Violent crimes are offenses of murder and nonnegligent manslaughter, forcible rape, robbery, and aggravated assault. Property crimes are offenses of burglary, larceny-theft, motor vehicle theft, and arson.   4 The rape figures in this table are aggregate totals of the data submitted based on both the legacy and revised Uniform Crime Reporting definitions.

Table 32. Ten-Year Arrest Trends, 2010 and 2019

(Number, percent change; 8,891 agencies; 2019 estimated population 196,355,871; 2010 estimated population 185,356,420.)

Offense charged	Number of persons arrested								
	Total, all ages			Under 18 years of age			18 years of age and over		
	2010	2019	Percent change	2010	2019	Percent change	2010	2019	Percent change
Total[1]	7,595,396	6,000,327	-21.0	960,881	428,053	-55.5	6,634,515	5,572,274	-16.0
Violent crime[2]	320,464	295,421	-7.8	42,211	28,999	-31.3	278,253	266,422	-4.3
Murder and nonnegligent manslaughter	6,019	6,232	+3.5	555	468	-15.7	5,464	5,764	+5.5
Rape[3]	11,999	14,374	NA	1,754	2,494	NA	10,245	11,880	NA
Robbery	61,150	45,615	-25.4	14,338	9,635	-32.8	46,812	35,980	-23.1
Aggravated assault	241,296	229,200	-5.0	25,564	16,402	-35.8	215,732	212,798	-1.4
Property crime[2]	982,799	691,921	-29.6	227,247	77,161	-66.0	755,552	614,760	-18.6
Burglary	174,468	103,290	-40.8	39,296	12,517	-68.1	135,172	90,773	-32.8
Larceny-theft	761,675	534,836	-29.8	176,335	55,581	-68.5	585,340	479,255	-18.1
Motor vehicle theft	39,709	48,329	+21.7	8,596	7,974	-7.2	31,113	40,355	+29.7
Arson	6,947	5,466	-21.3	3,020	1,089	-63.9	3,927	4,377	+11.5
Other assaults	748,116	616,083	-17.6	121,461	77,359	-36.3	626,655	538,724	-14.0
Forgery and counterfeiting	44,102	28,678	-35.0	1,003	528	-47.4	43,099	28,150	-34.7
Fraud	107,992	71,125	-34.1	3,463	2,369	-31.6	104,529	68,756	-34.2
Embezzlement	10,800	9,153	-15.3	263	374	+42.2	10,537	8,779	-16.7
Stolen property; buying, receiving, possessing	59,261	56,957	-3.9	9,459	5,730	-39.4	49,802	51,227	+2.9
Vandalism	152,085	111,524	-26.7	47,671	20,131	-57.8	104,414	91,393	-12.5
Weapons; carrying, possessing, etc.	89,968	91,440	+1.6	18,181	9,769	-46.3	71,787	81,671	+13.8
Prostitution and commercialized vice	27,780	13,496	-51.4	543	196	-63.9	27,237	13,300	-51.2
Sex offenses (except forcible rape and prostitution)	41,298	25,684	-37.8	7,813	4,237	-45.8	33,485	21,447	-36.0
Drug abuse violations	935,117	927,704	-0.8	100,611	49,841	-50.5	834,506	877,863	+5.2
Gambling	2,402	1,514	-37.0	142	117	-17.6	2,260	1,397	-38.2
Offenses against the family and children	69,657	50,957	-26.8	2,421	1,877	-22.5	67,236	49,080	-27.0
Driving under the influence	786,469	546,213	-30.5	7,131	3,092	-56.6	779,338	543,121	-30.3
Liquor laws	312,762	98,455	-68.5	61,565	15,508	-74.8	251,197	82,947	-67.0
Drunkenness	340,974	186,298	-45.4	8,484	2,076	-75.5	332,490	184,222	-44.6
Disorderly conduct	335,720	186,342	-44.5	82,555	32,962	-60.1	253,165	153,380	-39.4
Vagrancy	16,898	15,000	-11.2	824	227	-72.5	16,074	14,773	-8.1
All other offenses (except traffic)	2,169,047	1,966,945	-9.3	176,148	86,083	-51.1	1,992,899	1,880,862	-5.6
Suspicion	634	224	-64.7	80	14	-82.5	554	210	-62.1
Curfew and loitering law violations	41,685	9,417	-77.4	41,685	9,417	-77.4	NA	NA	NA

NA = Not available.

1 Does not include suspicion.   2 Violent crimes are offenses of murder and nonnegligent manslaughter, rape, robbery, and aggravated assault. Property crimes are offenses of burglary, larceny-theft, motor vehicle theft, and arson.   3 The 2010 rape figures are based on the legacy definition, and the 2019 rape figures are aggregate totals based on both the legacy and revised Uniform Crime Reporting definitions. For this reason, a percent change is not provided.

Table 33. Ten-Year Arrest Trends, by Age and Sex, 2010 and 2019

(Number, percent change; 8,891 agencies; 2019 estimated population 196,355,871; 2010 estimated population 185,356,420.)

Offense charged	Male						Female					
	Total			Under 18			Total			Under 18		
	2010	2019	Percent change	2010	2019	Percent change	2010	2019	Percent change	2010	2019	Percent change
Total[1]	5,633,296	4,333,749	-23.1	673,608	296,739	-55.9	1,962,100	1,666,578	-15.1	287,273	131,314	-54.3
Violent crime[2]	258,262	233,368	-9.6	34,453	23,427	-32.0	62,202	62,053	-0.2	7,758	5,572	-28.2
Murder and nonnegligent manslaughter	5,320	5,461	+2.7	492	412	-16.3	699	771	+10.3	63	56	-11.1
Rape[3]	11,862	13,909		1,718	2,358		137	465		36	136	
Robbery	53,345	38,294	-28.2	12,836	8,514	-33.7	7,805	7,321	-6.2	1,502	1,121	-25.4
Aggravated assault	187,735	175,704	-6.4	19,407	12,143	-37.4	53,561	53,496	-0.1	6,157	4,259	-30.8
Property crime[2]	606,362	427,740	-29.5	139,043	51,027	-63.3	376,437	264,181	-29.8	88,204	26,134	-70.4
Burglary	145,781	81,600	-44.0	34,255	10,703	-68.8	28,687	21,690	-24.4	5,041	1,814	-64.0
Larceny-theft	422,355	304,860	-27.8	95,061	33,063	-65.2	339,320	229,976	-32.2	81,274	22,518	-72.3
Motor vehicle theft	32,468	37,001	+14.0	7,109	6,349	-10.7	7,241	11,328	+56.4	1,487	1,625	+9.3
Arson	5,758	4,279	-25.7	2,618	912	-65.2	1,189	1,187	-0.2	402	177	-56.0
Other assaults	544,274	433,813	-20.3	78,317	48,415	-38.2	203,842	182,270	-10.6	43,144	28,944	-32.9
Forgery and counterfeiting	27,312	19,022	-30.4	723	401	-44.5	16,790	9,656	-42.5	280	127	-54.6
Fraud	62,034	45,167	-27.2	2,272	1,590	-30.0	45,958	25,958	-43.5	1,191	779	-34.6
Embezzlement	5,291	4,534	-14.3	153	203	+32.7	5,509	4,619	-16.2	110	171	+55.5
Stolen property; buying, receiving, possessing	47,298	44,099	-6.8	7,875	4,697	-40.4	11,963	12,858	+7.5	1,584	1,033	-34.8
Vandalism	123,564	85,838	-30.5	40,640	16,163	-60.2	28,521	25,686	-9.9	7,031	3,968	-43.6
Weapons; carrying, possessing, etc.	82,616	82,521	-0.1	16,414	8,721	-46.9	7,352	8,919	+21.3	1,767	1,048	-40.7
Prostitution and commercialized vice	8,526	4,985	-41.5	98	58	-40.8	19,254	8,511	-55.8	445	138	-69.0
Sex offenses (except forcible rape and prostitution)	38,372	23,930	-37.6	6,994	3,781	-45.9	2,926	1,754	-40.1	819	456	-44.3
Drug abuse violations	747,597	690,794	-7.6	82,960	36,769	-55.7	187,520	236,910	+26.3	17,651	13,072	-25.9
Gambling	1,953	1,067	-45.4	119	78	-34.5	449	447	-0.4	23	39	+69.6
Offenses against the family and children	52,569	35,586	-32.3	1,593	1,105	-30.6	17,088	15,371	-10.0	828	772	-6.8
Driving under the influence	596,627	403,075	-32.4	5,248	2,307	-56.0	189,842	143,138	-24.6	1,883	785	-58.3
Liquor laws	222,348	68,341	-69.3	37,660	8,907	-76.3	90,414	30,114	-66.7	23,905	6,601	-72.4
Drunkenness	280,458	146,173	-47.9	6,144	1,406	-77.1	60,516	40,125	-33.7	2,340	670	-71.4
Disorderly conduct	242,789	131,591	-45.8	54,384	20,788	-61.8	92,931	54,751	-41.1	28,171	12,174	-56.8
Vagrancy	13,371	11,578	-13.4	665	171	-74.3	3,527	3,422	-3.0	159	56	-64.8
All other offenses (except traffic)	1,643,456	1,434,312	-12.7	129,636	60,510	-53.3	525,591	532,633	+1.3	46,512	25,573	-45.0
Suspicion	486	157	-67.7	58	13	-77.6	148	67	-54.7	22	1	-95.5
Curfew and loitering law violations	28,217	6,215	-78.0	28,217	6,215	-78.0	13,468	3,202	-76.2	13,468	3,202	-76.2

1 Does not include suspicion.   2 Violent crimes are offenses of murder and nonnegligent manslaughter, rape, robbery, and aggravated assault. Property crimes are offenses of burglary, larceny-theft, motor vehicle theft, and arson.   3 The 2010 rape figures are based on the legacy definition, and the 2019 rape figures are aggregate totals based on both the legacy and revised Uniform Crime Reporting definitions. For this reason, a percent change is not provided.

Table 34. Five-Year Arrest Trends, by Age, 2015 and 2019

(Number, percent change; 9,656 agencies; 2019 estimated population 201,599,471; 2015 estimated population 197,695,401.)

Offense charged	Number of persons arrested								
	Total, all ages			Under 18 years of age			18 years of age and over		
	2015	2019	Percent change	2015	2019	Percent change	2015	2019	Percent change
Total[1]	6,611,598	6,146,623	-7.0	562,729	431,375	-23.3	6,048,869	5,715,248	-5.5
Violent crime[2]	301,429	303,801	+0.8	29,987	29,496	-1.6	271,442	274,305	+1.1
Murder and nonnegligent manslaughter	6,254	6,620	+5.9	437	518	+18.5	5,817	6,102	+4.9
Rape[3]	13,794	14,816	+7.4	2,229	2,544	+14.1	11,565	12,272	+6.1
Robbery	53,591	46,537	-13.2	9,936	9,914	-0.2	43,655	36,623	-16.1
Aggravated assault	227,790	235,828	+3.5	17,385	16,520	-5.0	210,405	219,308	+4.2
Property crime[2]	912,536	705,257	-22.7	131,612	78,229	-40.6	780,924	627,028	-19.7
Burglary	134,310	105,699	-21.3	22,307	13,064	-41.4	112,003	92,635	-17.3
Larceny-theft	726,267	542,323	-25.3	99,528	55,457	-44.3	626,739	486,866	-22.3
Motor vehicle theft	46,430	51,698	+11.3	8,007	8,634	+7.8	38,423	43,064	+12.1
Arson	5,529	5,537	+0.1	1,770	1,074	-39.3	3,759	4,463	+18.7
Other assaults	658,483	627,873	-4.6	82,257	76,546	-6.9	576,226	551,327	-4.3
Forgery and counterfeiting	33,036	29,569	-10.5	635	552	-13.1	32,401	29,017	-10.4
Fraud	80,686	71,636	-11.2	2,546	2,260	-11.2	78,140	69,376	-11.2
Embezzlement	10,269	8,967	-12.7	373	375	+0.5	9,896	8,592	-13.2
Stolen property; buying, receiving, possessing	55,332	57,620	+4.1	6,419	5,724	-10.8	48,913	51,896	+6.1
Vandalism	120,552	113,162	-6.1	26,823	20,263	-24.5	93,729	92,899	-0.9
Weapons; carrying, possessing, etc.	85,497	93,928	+9.9	11,551	9,779	-15.3	73,946	84,149	+13.8
Prostitution and commercialized vice	18,502	11,600	-37.3	268	101	-62.3	18,234	11,499	-36.9
Sex offenses (except forcible rape and prostitution)	29,855	25,261	-15.4	5,308	4,188	-21.1	24,547	21,073	-14.2
Drug abuse violations	901,591	953,535	+5.8	61,084	49,305	-19.3	840,507	904,230	+7.6
Gambling	2,058	1,576	-23.4	189	138	-27.0	1,869	1,438	-23.1
Offenses against the family and children	61,356	53,467	-12.9	1,997	1,982	-0.8	59,359	51,485	-13.3
Driving under the influence	639,378	583,840	-8.7	4,032	3,260	-19.1	635,346	580,580	-8.6
Liquor laws	166,853	102,327	-38.7	27,353	15,904	-41.9	139,500	86,423	-38.0
Drunkenness	269,816	209,130	-22.5	3,712	2,117	-43.0	266,104	207,013	-22.2
Disorderly conduct	227,862	193,178	-15.2	41,421	33,277	-19.7	186,441	159,901	-14.2
Vagrancy	14,837	12,102	-18.4	590	236	-60.0	14,247	11,866	-16.7
All other offenses (except traffic)	2,002,856	1,979,056	-1.2	105,758	87,905	-16.9	1,897,098	1,891,151	-0.3
Suspicion	926	216	-76.7	65	11	-83.1	861	205	-76.2
Curfew and loitering law violations	18,814	9,738	-48.2	18,814	9,738	-48.2	NA	NA	NA

NA = Not available.

1 Does not include suspicion.   2 Violent crimes are offenses of murder and nonnegligent manslaughter, rape, robbery, and aggravated assault. Property crimes are offenses of burglary, larceny-theft, motor vehicle theft, and arson.   3 The rape figures in this table are aggregate totals of the data submitted based on both the legacy and revised Uniform Crime Reporting definitions.

Table 35. Five-Year Arrest Trends, by Age and Sex, 2015 and 2019

(Number, percent change; 9,656 agencies; 2019 estimated population 201,599,471; 2015 estimated population 197,695,401.)

Offense charged	Male						Female					
	Total			Under 18			Total			Under 18		
	2015	2019	Percent change	2015	2019	Percent change	2015	2019	Percent change	2015	2019	Percent change
Total[1]	4,816,901	4,449,004	-7.6	394,828	299,917	-24.0	1,794,697	1,697,619	-5.4	167,901	131,458	-21.7
Violent crime[2]	240,254	240,095	-0.1	24,438	23,944	-2.0	61,175	63,706	+4.1	5,549	5,552	+0.1
Murder and nonnegligent manslaughter	5,505	5,816	+5.6	408	457	+12.0	749	804	+7.3	29	61	+110.3
Rape[3]	13,434	14,336	+6.7	2,137	2,410	+12.8	360	480	+33.3	92	134	+45.7
Robbery	45,827	39,150	-14.6	8,832	8,783	-0.6	7,764	7,387	-4.9	1,104	1,131	+2.4
Aggravated assault	175,488	180,793	+3.0	13,061	12,294	-5.9	52,302	55,035	+5.2	4,324	4,226	-2.3
Property crime[2]	559,345	437,099	-21.9	86,412	52,121	-39.7	353,191	268,158	-24.1	45,200	26,108	-42.2
Burglary	108,903	83,782	-23.1	19,550	11,203	-42.7	25,407	21,917	-13.7	2,757	1,861	-32.5
Larceny-theft	409,720	309,327	-24.5	58,916	33,125	-43.8	316,547	232,996	-26.4	40,612	22,332	-45.0
Motor vehicle theft	36,278	39,630	+9.2	6,458	6,878	+6.5	10,152	12,068	+18.9	1,549	1,756	+13.4
Arson	4,444	4,360	-1.9	1,488	915	-38.5	1,085	1,177	+8.5	282	159	-43.6
Other assaults	471,552	443,787	-5.9	51,911	48,065	-7.4	186,931	184,086	-1.5	30,346	28,481	-6.1
Forgery and counterfeiting	21,203	19,673	-7.2	465	422	-9.2	11,833	9,896	-16.4	170	130	-23.5
Fraud	48,619	45,474	-6.5	1,658	1,508	-9.0	32,067	26,162	-18.4	888	752	-15.3
Embezzlement	5,026	4,387	-12.7	208	204	-1.9	5,243	4,580	-12.6	165	171	+3.6
Stolen property; buying, receiving, possessing	43,230	44,706	+3.4	5,356	4,678	-12.7	12,102	12,914	+6.7	1,063	1,046	-1.6
Vandalism	94,841	87,100	-8.2	22,292	16,343	-26.7	25,711	26,062	+1.4	4,531	3,920	-13.5
Weapons; carrying, possessing, etc.	77,682	84,890	+9.3	10,297	8,777	-14.8	7,815	9,038	+15.6	1,254	1,002	-20.1
Prostitution and commercialized vice	7,625	4,890	-35.9	76	57	-25.0	10,877	6,710	-38.3	192	44	-77.1
Sex offenses (except forcible rape and prostitution)	27,630	23,633	-14.5	4,656	3,717	-20.2	2,225	1,628	-26.8	652	471	-27.8
Drug abuse violations	694,191	710,306	+2.3	47,712	36,408	-23.7	207,400	243,229	+17.3	13,372	12,897	-3.6
Gambling	1,491	1,134	-23.9	161	96	-40.4	567	442	-22.0	28	42	+50.0
Offenses against the family and children	44,482	37,521	-15.6	1,278	1,173	-8.2	16,874	15,946	-5.5	719	809	+12.5
Driving under the influence	478,879	431,721	-9.8	3,012	2,421	-19.6	160,499	152,119	-5.2	1,020	839	-17.7
Liquor laws	118,298	70,834	-40.1	16,403	9,120	-44.4	48,555	31,493	-35.1	10,950	6,784	-38.0
Drunkenness	217,290	164,646	-24.2	2,637	1,435	-45.6	52,526	44,484	-15.3	1,075	682	-36.6
Disorderly conduct	163,462	136,354	-16.6	26,650	21,082	-20.9	64,400	56,824	-11.8	14,771	12,195	-17.4
Vagrancy	11,613	9,213	-20.7	448	179	-60.0	3,224	2,889	-10.4	142	57	-59.9
All other offenses (except traffic)	1,477,604	1,445,116	-2.2	76,174	61,742	-18.9	525,252	533,940	+1.7	29,584	26,163	-11.6
Suspicion	715	146	-79.6	57	11	-80.7	211	70	-66.8	8	0	-100.0
Curfew and loitering law violations	12,584	6,425	-48.9	12,584	6,425	-48.9	6,230	3,313	-46.8	6,230	3,313	-46.8

* = Less than one-tenth of one percent.
1 Does not include suspicion. 2 Violent crimes are offenses of murder and nonnegligent manslaughter, rape, robbery, and aggravated assault. Property crimes are offenses of burglary, larceny-theft, motor vehicle theft, and arson. 3 The rape figures in this table are aggregate totals of the data submitted based on both the legacy and revised uniform crime reporting definitions.

Table 36. Current Year Over Previous Year Arrest Trends, 2018–2019

(Number, percent change; 9,752 agencies; 2019 estimated population 208,476,526; 2018 estimated population 207,708,086.)

Offense charged	Number of persons arrested											
	Total, all ages			Under 15 years of age			Under 18 years of age			18 years of age and over		
	2018	2019	Percent change	2018	2019	Percent change	2018	2019	Percent change	2018	2019	Percent change
Total[1]	6,507,396	6,266,826	-3.7	137,873	144,430	+4.8	462,625	447,119	-3.4	6,044,771	5,819,707	-3.7
Violent crime[2]	333,280	330,199	-0.9	9,624	9,999	+3.9	32,060	32,439	+1.2	301,220	297,760	-1.1
Murder and nonnegligent manslaughter	6,966	6,942	-0.3	59	69	+16.9	560	547	-2.3	6,406	6,395	-0.2
Rape[3]	15,943	15,550	-2.5	1,146	1,180	+3.0	2,730	2,686	-1.6	13,213	12,864	-2.6
Robbery	54,841	52,388	-4.5	2,159	2,488	+15.2	10,859	11,408	+5.1	43,982	40,980	-6.8
Aggravated assault	255,530	255,319	-0.1	6,260	6,262	*	17,911	17,798	-0.6	237,619	237,521	*
Property crime[2]	751,830	725,934	-3.4	24,827	24,341	-2.0	86,530	80,588	-6.9	665,300	645,346	-3.0
Burglary	115,538	109,691	-5.1	4,347	4,345	*	14,412	13,161	-8.7	101,126	96,530	-4.5
Larceny-theft	572,801	556,357	-2.9	17,488	16,954	-3.1	61,757	57,391	-7.1	511,044	498,966	-2.4
Motor vehicle theft	57,392	53,995	-5.9	2,280	2,388	+4.7	9,141	8,885	-2.8	48,251	45,110	-6.5
Arson	6,099	5,891	-3.4	712	654	-8.1	1,220	1,151	-5.7	4,879	4,740	-2.8
Other assaults	652,952	644,473	-1.3	32,478	34,904	+7.5	78,790	79,903	+1.4	574,162	564,570	-1.7
Forgery and counterfeiting	32,269	29,905	-7.3	137	89	-35.0	704	566	-19.6	31,565	29,339	-7.1
Fraud	74,544	73,124	-1.9	530	578	+9.1	2,392	2,415	+1.0	72,152	70,709	-2.0
Embezzlement	9,642	9,292	-3.6	16	23	+43.8	396	380	-4.0	9,246	8,912	-3.6
Stolen property; buying, receiving, possessing	61,966	58,578	-5.5	1,341	1,288	-4.0	6,309	6,012	-4.7	55,657	52,566	-5.6
Vandalism	116,231	117,479	+1.1	7,753	9,093	+17.3	20,113	20,860	+3.7	96,118	96,619	+0.5
Weapons; carrying, possessing, etc.	101,562	100,805	-0.7	3,072	3,139	+2.2	10,462	10,737	+2.6	91,100	90,068	-1.1
Prostitution and commercialized vice	17,031	15,828	-7.1	29	22	-24.1	129	105	-18.6	16,902	15,723	-7.0
Sex offenses (except forcible rape and prostitution)	28,057	26,533	-5.4	2,230	2,196	-1.5	4,737	4,495	-5.1	23,320	22,038	-5.5
Drug abuse violations	1,044,876	969,293	-7.2	9,971	10,037	+0.7	57,734	51,048	-11.6	987,142	918,245	-7.0
Gambling	1,431	1,637	+14.4	15	9	-40.0	68	80	+17.6	1,363	1,557	+14.2
Offenses against the family and children	55,647	51,192	-8.0	713	742	+4.1	2,031	1,972	-2.9	53,616	49,220	-8.2
Driving under the influence	610,062	602,319	-1.3	71	79	+11.3	3,281	3,288	+0.2	606,781	599,031	-1.3
Liquor laws	113,734	103,181	-9.3	2,392	2,454	+2.6	17,170	15,711	-8.5	96,564	87,470	-9.4
Drunkenness	216,510	203,319	-6.1	351	313	-10.8	2,266	2,133	-5.9	214,244	201,186	-6.1
Disorderly conduct	198,993	196,190	-1.4	14,060	14,991	+6.6	34,060	34,425	+1.1	164,933	161,765	-1.9
Vagrancy	14,321	12,743	-11.0	103	77	-25.2	392	250	-36.2	13,929	12,493	-10.3
All other offenses (except traffic)	2,061,684	1,984,816	-3.7	24,956	26,695	+7.0	92,227	89,726	-2.7	1,969,457	1,895,090	-3.8
Suspicion	400	292	-27.0	10	7	-30.0	32	15	-53.1	368	277	-24.7
Curfew and loitering law violations	10,774	9,986	-7.3	3,204	3,361	+4.9	10,774	9,986	-7.3	NA	NA	NA

NA = Not available.
* = Less than one-tenth of one percent.
1 Does not include suspicion.   2 Violent crimes are offenses of murder and nonnegligent manslaughter, rape, robbery, and aggravated assault. Property crimes are offenses of burglary, larceny-theft, motor vehicle theft, and arson.   3 The rape figures in this table are aggregate totals of the data submitted based on both the legacy and revised Uniform Crime Reporting definitions.

Table 37. Current Year Over Previous Year Arrest Trends, by Age and Sex, 2018–2019

(Number, percent change; 9,752 agencies; 2019 estimated population 208,476,526; 2018 estimated population 207,708,086.)

Offense charged	Male						Female					
	Total			Under 18			Total			Under 18		
	2018	2019	Percent change	2018	2019	Percent change	2018	2019	Percent change	2018	2019	Percent change
Total[1]	4,729,317	4,548,810	-3.8	323,498	310,824	-3.9	1,778,079	1,718,016	-3.4	139,127	136,295	-2.0
Violent crime[2]	263,504	260,887	-1.0	25,779	26,252	+1.8	69,776	69,312	-0.7	6,281	6,187	-1.5
Murder and nonnegligent manslaughter	6,089	6,125	+0.6	503	487	-3.2	877	817	-6.8	57	60	+5.3
Rape[3]	15,513	15,083	-2.8	2,623	2,550	-2.8	430	467	+8.6	107	136	+27.1
Robbery	46,410	44,182	-4.8	9,617	10,075	+4.8	8,431	8,206	-2.7	1,242	1,333	+7.3
Aggravated assault	195,492	195,497	*	13,036	13,140	+0.8	60,038	59,822	-0.4	4,875	4,658	-4.5
Property crime[2]	471,286	452,028	-4.1	58,145	53,545	-7.9	280,544	273,906	-2.4	28,385	27,043	-4.7
Burglary	92,398	86,895	-6.0	12,484	11,310	-9.4	23,140	22,796	-1.5	1,928	1,851	-4.0
Larceny-theft	329,965	319,015	-3.3	37,200	34,151	-8.2	242,836	237,342	-2.3	24,557	23,240	-5.4
Motor vehicle theft	44,183	41,491	-6.1	7,440	7,107	-4.5	13,209	12,504	-5.3	1,701	1,778	+4.5
Arson	4,740	4,627	-2.4	1,021	977	-4.3	1,359	1,264	-7.0	199	174	-12.6
Other assaults	463,896	456,077	-1.7	49,429	49,947	+1.0	189,056	188,396	-0.3	29,361	29,956	+2.0
Forgery and counterfeiting	21,351	20,002	-6.3	566	429	-24.2	10,918	9,903	-9.3	138	137	-0.7
Fraud	47,142	46,910	-0.5	1,595	1,628	+2.1	27,402	26,214	-4.3	797	787	-1.3
Embezzlement	4,776	4,620	-3.3	235	203	-13.6	4,866	4,672	-4.0	161	177	+9.9
Stolen property; buying, receiving, possessing	48,125	45,455	-5.5	5,259	4,928	-6.3	13,841	13,123	-5.2	1,050	1,084	+3.2
Vandalism	89,646	90,545	+1.0	16,250	16,780	+3.3	26,585	26,934	+1.3	3,863	4,080	+5.6
Weapons; carrying, possessing, etc.	91,790	91,287	-0.5	9,280	9,627	+3.7	9,772	9,518	-2.6	1,182	1,110	-6.1
Prostitution and commercialized vice	6,689	6,427	-3.9	65	57	-12.3	10,342	9,401	-9.1	64	48	-25.0
Sex offenses (except forcible rape and prostitution)	26,217	24,861	-5.2	4,267	4,018	-5.8	1,840	1,672	-9.1	470	477	+1.5
Drug abuse violations	784,899	724,860	-7.6	42,844	37,716	-12.0	259,977	244,433	-6.0	14,890	13,332	-10.5
Gambling	1,093	1,220	+11.6	61	71	+16.4	338	417	+23.4	7	9	+28.6
Offenses against the family and children	39,386	35,509	-9.8	1,238	1,160	-6.3	16,261	15,683	-3.6	793	812	+2.4
Driving under the influence	453,626	447,456	-1.4	2,448	2,438	-0.4	156,436	154,863	-1.0	833	850	+2.0
Liquor laws	79,076	71,859	-9.1	9,841	8,990	-8.6	34,658	31,322	-9.6	7,329	6,721	-8.3
Drunkenness	171,112	160,024	-6.5	1,542	1,432	-7.1	45,398	43,295	-4.6	724	701	-3.2
Disorderly conduct	140,865	138,494	-1.7	21,741	21,653	-0.4	58,128	57,696	-0.7	12,319	12,772	+3.7
Vagrancy	10,606	9,641	-9.1	297	190	-36.0	3,715	3,102	-16.5	95	60	-36.8
All other offenses (except traffic)	1,507,080	1,454,024	-3.5	65,464	63,136	-3.6	554,604	530,792	-4.3	26,763	26,590	-0.6
Suspicion	301	202	-32.9	23	15	-34.8	99	90	-9.1	9	0	-100.0
Curfew and loitering law violations	7,152	6,624	-7.4	7,152	6,624	-7.4	3,622	3,362	-7.2	3,622	3,362	-7.2

1 Does not include suspicion.   2 Violent crimes are offenses of murder and nonnegligent manslaughter, rape, robbery, and aggravated assault. Property crimes are offenses of burglary, larceny-theft, motor vehicle theft, and arson.   3 The rape figures in this table are aggregate totals of the data submitted based on both the legacy and revised Uniform Crime Reporting definitions.

Table 38. Arrests, Distribution by Age, 2019

(Number, percent; 10,831 agencies; 2019 estimated population 229,735,355.)

Offense charged	Total, all ages	Ages under 15	Ages under 18	Ages 18 and over	Under 10	10–12	13–14	15	16	17	18	19	20
Total	6,917,552	156,886	485,964	6,431,588	2,550	36,691	117,645	94,426	108,807	125,845	170,444	192,362	192,045
Total percent distribution[1]	100.0	2.3	7.0	93.0	*	0.5	1.7	1.4	1.6	1.8	2.5	2.8	2.8
Violent crime[2]	359,092	10,870	35,253	323,839	177	2,565	8,128	7,021	8,178	9,184	10,770	10,756	10,593
Violent crime percent distribution[1]	100.0	3.0	9.8	90.2	*	0.7	2.3	2.0	2.3	2.6	3.0	3.0	2.9
Murder and nonnegligent manslaughter	7,711	74	601	7,110	0	11	63	107	165	255	400	413	389
Rape[3]	16,966	1,264	2,887	14,079	31	357	876	499	516	608	748	579	591
Robbery	56,854	2,665	12,266	44,588	8	333	2,324	2,692	3,312	3,597	3,797	3,172	2,520
Aggravated assault	277,561	6,867	19,499	258,062	138	1,864	4,865	3,723	4,185	4,724	5,825	6,592	7,093
Property crime[2]	788,636	26,629	87,710	700,926	373	5,285	20,971	18,223	20,449	22,409	26,470	25,019	22,262
Property crime percent distribution[1]	100.0	3.4	11.1	88.9	*	0.7	2.7	2.3	2.6	2.8	3.4	3.2	2.8
Burglary	120,242	4,806	14,504	105,738	88	1,024	3,694	3,089	3,286	3,323	3,953	3,872	3,310
Larceny-theft	604,287	18,480	62,200	542,087	231	3,754	14,495	12,482	14,536	16,702	20,361	19,232	17,194
Motor vehicle theft	57,738	2,626	9,742	47,996	4	260	2,362	2,442	2,450	2,224	2,010	1,793	1,653
Arson	6,369	717	1,264	5,105	50	247	420	210	177	160	146	122	105
Other assaults	717,793	38,619	88,269	629,524	736	11,229	26,654	16,913	16,818	15,919	14,660	16,145	16,496
Forgery and counterfeiting	32,495	98	611	31,884	2	23	73	93	149	271	747	1,177	1,269
Fraud	79,954	645	2,620	77,334	2	108	535	464	661	850	1,502	2,009	2,266
Embezzlement	10,003	25	400	9,603	0	5	20	26	117	232	431	545	470
Stolen property; buying, receiving, possessing	64,027	1,368	6,487	57,540	2	118	1,248	1,358	1,732	2,029	2,314	2,231	2,053
Vandalism	128,474	9,891	22,744	105,730	314	2,926	6,651	4,247	4,355	4,251	4,316	4,161	3,920
Weapons; carrying, possessing, etc.	110,130	3,347	11,563	98,567	63	863	2,421	2,092	2,705	3,419	4,186	4,342	4,232
Prostitution and commercialized vice	20,015	30	214	19,801	0	8	22	26	55	103	477	818	881
Sex offenses (except forcible rape and prostitution)	28,973	2,310	4,739	24,234	40	619	1,651	859	775	795	828	700	624
Drug abuse violations	1,067,764	10,881	55,701	1,012,063	55	1,695	9,131	9,689	13,996	21,135	36,298	41,116	38,389
Gambling	1,909	26	150	1,759	1	3	22	29	45	50	32	67	55
Offenses against the family and children	58,720	772	2,098	56,622	27	188	557	434	458	434	635	741	825
Driving under the influence	658,902	89	3,580	655,322	5	13	71	161	858	2,472	7,152	11,113	12,995
Liquor laws	112,467	2,681	17,072	95,395	6	379	2,296	2,738	4,508	7,145	14,821	15,621	13,296
Drunkenness	219,696	372	2,414	217,282	5	52	315	362	576	1,104	3,032	3,735	3,972
Disorderly conduct	211,960	16,045	36,877	175,083	224	4,335	11,486	7,733	7,029	6,070	5,379	5,212	5,439
Vagrancy	16,104	77	255	15,849	3	15	59	62	60	56	245	216	306
All other offenses (except traffic)	2,219,328	28,480	96,409	2,122,919	497	5,684	22,299	19,448	22,558	25,923	36,139	46,633	51,696
Suspicion	329	7	17	312	0	0	7	1	4	5	10	5	6
Curfew and loitering law violations	10,781	3,624	10,781	NA	18	578	3,028	2,447	2,721	1,989	NA	NA	NA

Table 38. Arrests, Distribution by Age, 2019—Continued

(Number, percent; 10,831 agencies; 2019 estimated population 229,735,355.)

Offense charged	21	22	23	24	25–29	30–34	35–39	40–44	45–49	50–54	55–59	60–64	65 and over
Total	198,861	201,462	206,878	213,855	1,164,519	1,046,118	875,810	610,752	459,614	368,597	280,854	148,619	100,798
Total percent distribution[1]	2.9	2.9	3.0	3.1	16.8	15.1	12.7	8.8	6.6	5.3	4.1	2.1	1.5
Violent crime[2]	11,069	10,890	11,162	11,497	61,075	52,192	42,142	28,612	21,157	16,758	12,746	7,041	5,379
Violent crime percent distribution[1]	3.1	3.0	3.1	3.2	17.0	14.5	11.7	8.0	5.9	4.7	3.5	2.0	1.5
Murder and nonnegligent manslaughter	370	317	299	295	1,408	950	747	501	340	223	197	127	134
Rape[3]	523	469	409	421	2,077	2,016	1,765	1,252	982	821	629	395	402
Robbery	2,245	2,034	1,831	1,849	8,733	6,548	4,511	2,777	1,739	1,372	904	385	171
Aggravated assault	7,931	8,070	8,623	8,932	48,857	42,678	35,119	24,082	18,096	14,342	11,016	6,134	4,672
Property crime[2]	21,432	20,909	21,288	22,046	125,086	116,944	96,414	64,968	48,508	39,155	28,068	13,774	8,583
Property crime percent distribution[1]	2.7	2.7	2.7	2.8	15.9	14.8	12.2	8.2	6.2	5.0	3.6	1.7	1.1
Burglary	3,281	3,232	3,548	3,746	20,129	18,695	15,020	9,419	6,665	5,130	3,456	1,498	784
Larceny-theft	16,399	15,966	15,967	16,364	94,072	88,432	73,764	50,915	38,842	31,941	23,360	11,785	7,493
Motor vehicle theft	1,630	1,600	1,653	1,782	10,017	8,986	6,845	4,092	2,648	1,758	994	361	174
Arson	122	111	120	154	868	831	785	542	353	326	258	130	132
Other assaults	19,478	19,774	20,581	21,296	115,533	102,880	86,441	60,842	45,807	36,425	27,271	14,538	11,357
Forgery and counterfeiting	906	902	887	1,037	5,856	5,570	4,805	3,174	2,161	1,533	1,079	509	272
Fraud	2,129	2,195	2,311	2,454	14,302	13,515	11,393	7,918	5,656	4,224	2,967	1,442	1,051
Embezzlement	388	408	309	350	1,667	1,412	1,114	863	630	443	336	144	93
Stolen property; buying, receiving, possessing	1,905	1,952	1,985	1,955	11,730	10,218	8,245	5,145	3,292	2,295	1,374	585	261
Vandalism	3,994	3,999	3,979	3,945	20,757	17,210	13,364	8,735	6,120	4,815	3,421	1,700	1,294
Weapons; carrying, possessing, etc.	4,308	4,230	4,160	4,241	20,241	15,171	11,690	7,529	5,146	3,800	2,767	1,452	1,072
Prostitution and commercialized vice	893	927	817	853	3,954	2,862	2,176	1,531	1,236	1,013	674	369	320
Sex offenses (except forcible rape and prostitution)	601	556	611	599	3,095	3,290	3,100	2,306	1,962	1,756	1,642	1,165	1,399
Drug abuse violations	37,432	36,358	36,652	36,982	193,061	165,241	135,033	89,556	62,814	47,410	33,345	15,620	6,756
Gambling	36	30	32	48	252	232	229	191	176	151	115	49	64
Offenses against the family and children	1,039	1,101	1,250	1,401	9,965	11,267	10,330	7,181	4,662	2,948	1,916	869	492
Driving under the influence	20,860	22,770	24,184	24,752	121,140	98,297	80,832	60,960	50,411	42,811	36,682	22,344	18,019
Liquor laws	2,745	2,084	1,642	1,608	7,072	6,453	6,013	5,005	4,884	5,042	4,692	2,733	1,684
Drunkenness	6,276	6,178	6,158	6,207	32,949	31,445	28,206	21,909	19,407	18,295	15,956	8,799	4,758
Disorderly conduct	6,489	6,030	5,767	5,753	29,318	26,167	22,237	15,820	12,967	10,870	8,730	5,056	3,849
Vagrancy	218	245	286	280	2,051	2,114	1,710	1,670	1,696	1,335	815	456
All other offenses (except traffic)	56,651	59,911	62,805	66,542	385,355	363,582	309,797	216,774	160,921	127,147	95,722	49,609	33,635
Suspicion	12	13	12	9	60	56	43	23	27	10	16	6	4
Curfew and loitering law violations	NA	NA	NA	NA	NA	NA	NA	NA	NA	NA	NA	NA	NA

NA = Not available.

* = Less than one-tenth of one percent.

1 Because of rounding, the percentages may not sum to 100 percent.   2 Violent crimes are offenses of murder and nonnegligent manslaughter, rape, robbery, and aggravated assault. Property crimes are offenses of burglary, larceny-theft, motor vehicle theft, and arson.   3 The rape figures in this table are aggregate totals of the data submitted based on both the legacy and revised Uniform Crime Reporting definitions.

Table 39. Male Arrests, Distribution by Age, 2019

(Number, percent; 10,831 agencies; 2019 estimated population 229,735,355.)

Offense charged	Total, all ages	Ages under 15	Ages under 18	Ages 18 and over	Under 10	10–12	13–14	15	16	17	18	19	20
Total	5,012,260	105,643	337,741	4,674,519	2,047	25,110	78,486	65,012	76,917	90,169	122,938	137,843	137,354
Total percent distribution[1]	100.0	2.1	6.7	93.3	*	0.5	1.6	1.3	1.5	1.8	2.5	2.8	2.7
Violent crime[2]	283,467	8,418	28,449	255,018	163	1,963	6,292	5,655	6,757	7,619	8,904	8,647	8,395
Violent crime percent distribution[1]	100.0	3.0	10.0	90.0	0.1	0.7	2.2	2.0	2.4	2.7	3.1	3.1	3.0
Murder and nonnegligent manslaughter	6,789	57	537	6,252	0	9	48	95	154	231	369	390	361
Rape[3]	16,395	1,183	2,736	13,659	30	323	830	473	493	587	732	563	570
Robbery	47,896	2,318	10,827	37,069	5	292	2,021	2,379	2,935	3,195	3,328	2,706	2,143
Aggravated assault	212,387	4,860	14,349	198,038	128	1,339	3,393	2,708	3,175	3,606	4,475	4,988	5,321
Property crime[2]	491,631	18,250	58,430	433,201	292	3,672	14,286	12,395	13,505	14,280	16,269	15,097	13,233
Property crime percent distribution[1]	100.0	3.7	11.9	88.1	0.1	0.7	2.9	2.5	2.7	2.9	3.3	3.1	2.7
Burglary	95,317	4,102	12,466	82,851	76	872	3,154	2,678	2,857	3,337	3,337	3,206	2,653
Larceny-theft	346,965	11,509	37,109	309,856	168	2,387	8,954	7,593	8,533	9,474	11,138	10,354	9,200
Motor vehicle theft	44,357	2,040	7,784	36,573	4	207	1,829	1,948	1,960	1,836	1,671	1,435	1,294
Arson	4,992	599	1,071	3,921	44	206	349	176	155	141	123	102	86
Other assaults	506,715	23,765	55,088	451,627	587	7,262	15,916	10,347	10,659	10,317	9,606	10,564	10,837
Forgery and counterfeiting	21,688	75	469	21,219	0	20	55	73	121	200	510	776	830
Fraud	51,212	426	1,754	49,458	2	71	353	311	451	566	974	1,310	1,519
Embezzlement	4,981	16	217	4,764	0	4	12	17	63	121	232	259	217
Stolen property; buying, receiving, possessing	49,688	1,082	5,332	44,356	2	92	988	1,102	1,426	1,722	1,926	1,808	1,621
Vandalism	98,712	8,056	18,269	80,443	275	2,402	5,379	3,406	3,445	3,362	3,447	3,196	2,970
Weapons; carrying, possessing, etc.	99,611	2,873	10,380	89,231	61	710	2,102	1,862	2,473	3,172	3,901	4,055	3,921
Prostitution and commercialized vice	7,404	12	63	7,341	0	3	9	10	12	29	59	123	131
Sex offenses (except forcible rape and prostitution)	26,996	2,039	4,227	22,769	30	533	1,476	757	683	748	785	662	581
Drug abuse violations	796,466	7,347	41,139	755,327	41	1,090	6,216	7,093	10,642	16,057	27,646	30,956	28,678
Gambling	1,360	18	107	1,253	1	1	16	23	31	35	24	50	40
Offenses against the family and children	40,881	457	1,237	39,644	22	103	332	251	269	418	418	479	536
Driving under the influence	488,091	63	2,667	485,424	3	9	51	111	635	1,858	5,528	8,457	9,751
Liquor laws	78,441	1,328	9,859	68,582	5	174	1,149	1,466	2,702	4,363	9,341	10,224	8,844
Drunkenness	172,813	197	1,611	171,202	2	24	171	217	382	815	2,236	2,765	3,045
Disorderly conduct	149,485	9,925	23,164	126,321	190	2,788	6,947	4,704	4,571	3,964	3,686	3,517	3,756
Vagrancy	12,401	65	192	12,209	3	14	48	39	38	50	177	157	227
All other offenses (except traffic)	1,622,846	18,937	67,924	1,554,922	354	3,796	14,787	13,543	16,191	19,253	27,261	34,738	38,217
Suspicion	224	7	16	208	0	0	7	1	4	4	8	3	5
Curfew and loitering law violations	7,147	2,287	7,147	NA	14	379	1,894	1,629	1,857	1,374	NA	NA	NA

Table 39. Male Arrests, Distribution by Age, 2019—Continued

(Number, percent; 10,831 agencies; 2019 estimated population 229,735,355.)

Offense charged	21	22	23	24	25–29	30–34	35–39	40–44	45–49	50–54	55–59	60–64	65 and over
Total	142,928	144,966	149,200	154,567	836,900	746,368	625,210	443,647	338,233	278,221	218,646	117,749	79,749
Total percent distribution[1]	2.9	2.9	3.0	3.1	16.7	14.9	12.5	8.9	6.7	5.6	4.4	2.3	1.6
Violent crime[2]	8,665	8,452	8,656	8,931	47,382	40,624	33,081	22,627	16,760	13,182	10,312	5,865	4,535
Violent crime percent distribution[1]	3.1	3.0	3.1	3.2	16.7	14.3	11.7	8.0	5.9	4.7	3.6	2.1	1.6
Murder and nonnegligent manslaughter	329	276	258	265	1,218	827	638	437	288	193	165	113	125
Rape[3]	510	452	401	403	2,009	1,965	1,696	1,209	940	803	617	390	399
Robbery	1,894	1,693	1,500	1,534	7,193	5,274	3,650	2,281	1,458	1,138	791	339	147
Aggravated assault	5,932	6,031	6,497	6,729	36,962	32,558	27,097	18,700	14,074	11,048	8,739	5,023	3,864
Property crime[2]	12,826	12,568	13,041	13,667	77,730	71,922	58,460	39,874	30,422	25,411	18,506	8,931	5,244
Property crime percent distribution[1]	2.6	2.6	2.7	2.8	15.8	14.6	11.9	8.1	6.2	5.2	3.8	1.8	1.1
Burglary	2,574	2,521	2,775	2,916	15,694	14,408	11,548	7,216	5,252	4,089	2,817	1,235	610
Larceny-theft	8,928	8,734	8,903	9,263	53,916	50,309	41,296	29,073	22,840	19,613	14,636	7,284	4,369
Motor vehicle theft	1,231	1,231	1,267	1,373	7,423	6,599	5,040	3,183	2,073	1,459	841	301	152
Arson	93	82	96	115	697	606	576	402	257	250	212	111	113
Other assaults	12,920	13,304	14,157	14,830	82,102	74,197	62,953	44,746	33,809	27,066	20,640	11,096	8,800
Forgery and counterfeiting	589	618	596	701	3,822	3,602	3,093	2,088	1,459	1,112	813	393	217
Fraud	1,362	1,423	1,475	1,589	9,117	8,306	7,090	4,988	3,665	2,761	2,160	1,020	699
Embezzlement	197	211	165	204	897	665	531	378	294	226	164	71	53
Stolen property; buying, receiving, possessing	1,484	1,534	1,507	1,482	8,793	7,639	6,162	3,997	2,613	1,923	1,140	513	214
Vandalism	3,000	3,041	3,027	2,979	15,661	12,958	10,151	6,691	4,676	3,620	2,634	1,345	1,047
Weapons; carrying, possessing, etc.	3,975	3,888	3,796	3,852	18,265	13,527	10,421	6,773	4,597	3,403	2,523	1,344	990
Prostitution and commercialized vice	168	191	175	178	1,225	1,140	999	781	639	555	420	275	282
Sex offenses (except forcible rape and prostitution)	565	516	552	554	2,879	3,049	2,877	2,193	1,832	1,657	1,567	1,128	1,372
Drug abuse violations	27,986	27,210	27,417	27,830	143,428	120,584	98,159	66,322	46,908	36,601	26,788	12,928	5,886
Gambling	29	24	22	29	173	162	160	147	120	102	81	37	53
Offenses against the family and children	643	695	755	846	6,359	7,496	7,353	5,410	3,733	2,342	1,537	682	360
Driving under the influence	15,140	16,558	17,624	18,184	89,337	72,878	59,531	45,153	36,941	31,632	27,541	17,117	14,052
Liquor laws	1,924	1,485	1,200	1,207	5,251	4,864	4,589	3,811	3,807	4,159	3,995	2,407	1,474
Drunkenness	4,872	4,842	4,803	4,867	25,587	24,440	21,510	17,197	15,134	14,854	13,354	7,488	4,208
Disorderly conduct	4,643	4,313	4,088	4,138	20,803	18,557	16,071	11,439	9,442	8,108	6,729	3,989	3,042
Vagrancy	168	187	210	209	1,548	1,587	1,666	1,276	1,274	1,358	1,128	665	372
All other offenses (except traffic)	41,761	43,895	45,923	48,284	276,499	258,135	220,331	157,745	120,092	98,143	76,602	40,450	26,846
Suspicion	11	11	11	6	42	36	22	11	16	6	12	5	3
Curfew and loitering law violations	NA	NA	NA	NA	NA	NA	NA	NA	NA	NA	NA	NA	NA

NA = Not available.

* = Less than one-tenth of one percent.

1 Because of rounding, the percentages may not sum to 100 percent.   2 Violent crimes are offenses of murder and nonnegligent manslaughter, rape, robbery, and aggravated assault. Property crimes are offenses of burglary, larceny-theft, motor vehicle theft, and arson.   3 The rape figures in this table are aggregate totals of the data submitted based on both the legacy and revised Uniform Crime Reporting definitions.

Table 40. Female Arrests, Distribution by Age, 2019

(Number, percent; 10,831 agencies; 2019 estimated population 229,735,355.)

Offense charged	Total, all ages	Ages under 15	Ages under 18	Ages 18 and over	Under 10	10–12	13–14	15	16	17	18	19	20
Total	1,905,292	51,243	148,223	1,757,069	503	11,581	39,159	29,414	31,890	35,676	47,506	54,519	54,691
Total percent distribution[1]	100.0	2.7	7.8	92.2	*	0.6	2.1	1.5	1.7	1.9	2.5	2.9	2.9
Violent crime[2]	75,625	2,452	6,804	68,821	14	602	1,836	1,366	1,421	1,565	1,866	2,109	2,198
Violent crime percent distribution[1]	100.0	3.2	9.0	91.0	*	0.8	2.4	1.8	1.9	2.1	2.5	2.8	2.9
Murder and nonnegligent manslaughter	922	17	64	858	0	2	15	12	11	24	31	23	28
Rape[3]	571	81	151	420	1	34	46	26	23	21	16	16	21
Robbery	8,958	347	1,439	7,519	3	41	303	313	377	402	469	466	377
Aggravated assault	65,174	2,007	5,150	60,024	10	525	1,472	1,015	1,010	1,118	1,350	1,604	1,772
Property crime[2]	297,005	8,379	29,280	267,725	81	1,613	6,685	5,828	6,944	8,129	10,201	9,922	9,029
Property crime percent distribution[1]	100.0	2.8	9.9	90.1	*	0.5	2.3	2.0	2.3	2.7	3.4	3.3	3.0
Burglary	24,925	704	2,038	22,887	12	152	540	411	429	494	616	666	657
Larceny-theft	257,322	6,971	25,091	232,231	63	1,367	5,541	4,889	6,003	7,228	9,223	8,878	7,994
Motor vehicle theft	13,381	586	1,958	11,423	0	53	533	494	490	388	339	358	359
Arson	1,377	118	193	1,184	6	41	71	34	22	19	23	20	19
Other assaults	211,078	14,854	33,181	177,897	149	3,967	10,738	6,566	6,159	5,602	5,054	5,581	5,659
Forgery and counterfeiting	10,807	23	142	10,665	2	3	18	20	28	71	237	401	439
Fraud	28,742	219	866	27,876	0	37	182	153	210	284	528	699	747
Embezzlement	5,022	9	183	4,839	0	1	8	9	54	111	199	286	253
Stolen property; buying, receiving, possessing	14,339	286	1,155	13,184	0	26	260	256	306	307	388	423	432
Vandalism	29,762	1,835	4,475	25,287	39	524	1,272	841	910	889	869	965	950
Weapons; carrying, possessing, etc.	10,519	474	1,183	9,336	2	153	319	230	232	247	285	287	311
Prostitution and commercialized vice	12,611	18	151	12,460	0	5	13	16	43	74	418	695	750
Sex offenses (except forcible rape and prostitution)	1,977	271	512	1,465	10	86	175	102	92	47	43	38	43
Drug abuse violations	271,298	3,534	14,562	256,736	14	605	2,915	2,596	3,354	5,078	8,652	10,160	9,711
Gambling	549	8	43	506	0	2	6	6	14	15	8	17	15
Offenses against the family and children	17,839	315	861	16,978	5	85	225	183	189	174	217	262	289
Driving under the influence	170,811	26	913	169,898	2	4	20	50	223	614	1,624	2,656	3,244
Liquor laws	34,026	1,353	7,213	26,813	1	205	1,147	1,272	1,806	2,782	5,480	5,397	4,452
Drunkenness	46,883	175	803	46,080	3	28	144	145	194	289	796	970	927
Disorderly conduct	62,475	6,120	13,713	48,762	34	1,547	4,539	3,029	2,458	2,106	1,693	1,695	1,683
Vagrancy	3,703	12	63	3,640	0	1	11	23	22	6	68	59	79
All other offenses (except traffic)	596,482	9,543	28,485	567,997	143	1,888	7,512	5,905	6,367	6,670	8,878	11,895	13,479
Suspicion	105	0	1	104	0	0	0	0	0	1	2	2	1
Curfew and loitering law violations	3,634	1,337	3,634	NA	4	199	1,134	818	864	615	NA	NA	NA

Table 40. Female Arrests, Distribution by Age, 2019—Continued

(Number, percent; 10,831 agencies; 2019 estimated population 229,735,355.)

Offense charged	21	22	23	24	25–29	30–34	35–39	40–44	45–49	50–54	55–59	60–64	65 and over
Total	55,933	56,496	57,678	59,288	327,619	299,750	250,600	167,105	121,381	90,376	62,208	30,870	21,049
Total percent distribution[1]	2.9	3.0	3.0	3.1	17.2	15.7	13.2	8.8	6.4	4.7	3.3	1.6	1.1
Violent crime[2]	2,404	2,438	2,506	2,566	13,693	11,568	9,061	5,985	4,397	3,576	2,434	1,176	844
Violent crime percent distribution[1]	3.2	3.2	3.3	3.4	18.1	15.3	12.0	7.9	5.8	4.7	3.2	1.6	1.1
Murder and nonnegligent manslaughter	41	41	41	30	190	123	109	64	52	30	32	14	9
Rape[3]	13	17	8	18	68	51	69	43	42	18	12	5	3
Robbery	351	341	331	315	1,540	1,274	861	496	281	234	113	46	24
Aggravated assault	1,999	2,039	2,126	2,203	11,895	10,120	8,022	5,382	4,022	3,294	2,277	1,111	808
Property crime[2]	8,606	8,341	8,247	8,379	47,356	45,022	37,954	25,094	18,086	13,744	9,562	4,843	3,339
Property crime percent distribution[1]	2.9	2.8	2.8	2.8	15.9	15.2	12.8	8.4	6.1	4.6	3.2	1.6	1.1
Burglary	707	711	773	830	4,435	4,287	3,472	2,203	1,413	1,041	639	263	174
Larceny-theft	7,471	7,232	7,064	7,101	40,156	38,123	32,468	21,842	16,002	12,328	8,724	4,501	3,124
Motor vehicle theft	399	369	386	409	2,594	2,387	1,805	909	575	299	153	60	22
Arson	29	29	24	39	171	225	209	140	96	76	46	19	19
Other assaults	6,558	6,470	6,424	6,466	33,431	28,683	23,488	16,096	11,998	9,359	6,631	3,442	2,557
Forgery and counterfeiting	317	284	291	336	2,034	1,968	1,712	1,086	702	421	266	116	55
Fraud	767	772	836	865	5,185	5,209	4,303	2,930	1,991	1,463	807	422	352
Embezzlement	191	197	144	146	770	747	583	485	336	217	172	73	40
Stolen property; buying, receiving, possessing	421	418	478	473	2,937	2,579	2,083	1,148	679	372	234	72	47
Vandalism	994	958	952	966	5,096	4,252	3,213	2,044	1,444	1,195	787	355	247
Weapons; carrying, possessing, etc.	333	342	364	389	1,976	1,644	1,269	756	549	397	244	108	82
Prostitution and commercialized vice	725	736	642	675	2,729	1,722	1,177	750	597	458	254	94	38
Sex offenses (except forcible rape and prostitution)	36	40	59	45	216	241	223	113	130	99	75	37	27
Drug abuse violations	9,446	9,148	9,235	9,152	49,633	44,657	36,874	23,234	15,906	10,809	6,557	2,692	870
Gambling	7	6	10	19	79	70	69	44	56	49	34	12	11
Offenses against the family and children	396	406	495	555	3,606	3,771	2,977	1,771	929	606	379	187	132
Driving under the influence	5,720	6,212	6,560	6,568	31,803	25,419	21,301	15,807	13,470	11,179	9,141	5,227	3,967
Liquor laws	821	599	442	401	1,821	1,589	1,424	1,194	1,077	883	697	326	210
Drunkenness	1,404	1,336	1,355	1,340	7,362	7,005	6,696	4,712	4,273	3,441	2,602	1,311	550
Disorderly conduct	1,846	1,717	1,679	1,615	8,515	7,610	6,166	4,381	3,525	2,762	2,001	1,067	807
Vagrancy	50	58	76	71	503	527	540	434	396	338	207	150	84
All other offenses (except traffic)	14,890	16,016	16,882	18,258	108,856	105,447	89,466	59,029	40,829	29,004	19,120	9,159	6,789
Suspicion	1	2	1	3	18	20	21	12	11	4	4	1	1
Curfew and loitering law violations	NA	NA	NA	NA	NA	NA	NA	NA	NA	NA	NA	NA	NA

NA = Not available.
* = Less than one-tenth of one percent.
1 Because of rounding, the percentages may not sum to 100 percent.   2 Violent crimes are offenses of murder and nonnegligent manslaughter, rape, robbery, and aggravated assault. Property crimes are offenses of burglary, larceny-theft, motor vehicle theft, and arson.   3 The rape figures in this table are aggregate totals of the data submitted based on both the legacy and revised Uniform Crime Reporting definitions.

Table 41. Arrests of Persons Under 15, 18, 21, and 25 Years of Age, 2019

(Number, percent; 10,831 agencies; 2019 estimated population 229,735,355.)

Offense charged	Total, all ages	Number of persons arrested				Percent of total all ages			
		Under 15	Under 18	Under 21	Under 25	Under 15	Under 18	Under 21	Under 25
Total	6,917,552	156,886	485,964	1,040,815	1,861,871	2.3	7.0	15.0	26.9
Violent crime[1]	359,092	10,870	35,253	67,372	111,990	3.0	9.8	18.8	31.2
Murder and nonnegligent manslaughter	7,711	74	601	1,803	3,084	1.0	7.8	23.4	40.0
Rape[2]	16,966	1,264	2,887	4,805	6,627	7.5	17.0	28.3	39.1
Robbery	56,854	2,665	12,266	21,755	29,714	4.7	21.6	38.3	52.3
Aggravated assault	277,561	6,867	19,499	39,009	72,565	2.5	7.0	14.1	26.1
Property crime[1]	788,636	26,629	87,710	161,461	247,136	3.4	11.1	20.5	31.3
Burglary	120,242	4,806	14,504	25,639	39,446	4.0	12.1	21.3	32.8
Larceny-theft	604,287	18,480	62,200	118,987	183,683	3.1	10.3	19.7	30.4
Motor vehicle theft	57,738	2,626	9,742	15,198	21,863	4.5	16.9	26.3	37.9
Arson	6,369	717	1,264	1,637	2,144	11.3	19.8	25.7	33.7
Other assaults	717,793	38,619	88,269	135,570	216,699	5.4	12.3	18.9	30.2
Forgery and counterfeiting	32,495	98	611	3,804	7,536	0.3	1.9	11.7	23.2
Fraud	79,954	645	2,620	8,397	17,486	0.8	3.3	10.5	21.9
Embezzlement	10,003	25	400	1,846	3,301	0.2	4.0	18.5	33.0
Stolen property; buying, receiving, possessing	64,027	1,368	6,487	13,085	20,882	2.1	10.1	20.4	32.6
Vandalism	128,474	9,891	22,744	35,141	51,058	7.7	17.7	27.4	39.7
Weapons; carrying, possessing, etc.	110,130	3,347	11,563	24,323	41,262	3.0	10.5	22.1	37.5
Prostitution and commercialized vice	20,015	30	214	2,390	5,880	0.1	1.1	11.9	29.4
Sex offenses (except forcible rape and prostitution)	28,973	2,310	4,739	6,891	9,258	8.0	16.4	23.8	32.0
Drug abuse violations	1,067,764	10,881	55,701	171,504	318,928	1.0	5.2	16.1	29.9
Gambling	1,909	26	150	304	450	1.4	7.9	15.9	23.6
Offenses against the family and children	58,720	772	2,098	4,299	9,090	1.3	3.6	7.3	15.5
Driving under the influence	658,902	89	3,580	34,840	127,406	*	0.5	5.3	19.3
Liquor laws	112,467	2,681	17,072	60,810	68,889	2.4	15.2	54.1	61.3
Drunkenness	219,696	372	2,414	13,153	37,972	0.2	1.1	6.0	17.3
Disorderly conduct	211,960	16,045	36,877	52,907	76,946	7.6	17.4	25.0	36.3
Vagrancy	16,104	77	255	1,022	2,051	0.5	1.6	6.3	12.7
All other offenses (except traffic)	2,219,328	28,480	96,409	230,877	476,786	1.3	4.3	10.4	21.5
Suspicion	329	7	17	38	84	2.1	5.2	11.6	25.5
Curfew and loitering law violations	10,781	3,624	10,781	10,781	10,781	33.6	100.0	100.0	100.0

* = Less than one-tenth of one percent.
1 Violent crimes in this table are offenses of murder and nonnegligent manslaughter, rape, robbery, and aggravated assault. Property crimes are offenses of burglary, larceny-theft, motor vehicle theft, and arson.   2 The rape figures in this table are aggregate totals of the data submitted based on both the legacy and revised Uniform Crime Reporting definitions.

Table 42. Arrests, Distribution by Sex, 2019

(Number, percent; 10,831 agencies; 2019 estimated population 229,735,355.)

Offense charged	Number of persons arrested			Percent male	Percent female	Percent distribution[1]		
	Total	Male	Female			Total	Male	Female
Total	6,917,552	5,012,260	1,905,292	72.5	27.5	100.0	100.0	100.0
Violent crime[2]	359,092	283,467	75,625	78.9	21.1	5.2	5.7	4.0
Murder and nonnegligent manslaughter	7,711	6,789	922	88.0	12.0	0.1	0.1	*
Rape[3]	16,966	16,395	571	96.6	3.4	0.2	0.3	*
Robbery	56,854	47,896	8,958	84.2	15.8	0.8	1.0	0.5
Aggravated assault	277,561	212,387	65,174	76.5	23.5	4.0	4.2	3.4
Property crime[2]	788,636	491,631	297,005	62.3	37.7	11.4	9.8	15.6
Burglary	120,242	95,317	24,925	79.3	20.7	1.7	1.9	1.3
Larceny-theft	604,287	346,965	257,322	57.4	42.6	8.7	6.9	13.5
Motor vehicle theft	57,738	44,357	13,381	76.8	23.2	0.8	0.9	0.7
Arson	6,369	4,992	1,377	78.4	21.6	0.1	0.1	0.1
Other assaults	717,793	506,715	211,078	70.6	29.4	10.4	10.1	11.1
Forgery and counterfeiting	32,495	21,688	10,807	66.7	33.3	0.5	0.4	0.6
Fraud	79,954	51,212	28,742	64.1	35.9	1.2	1.0	1.5
Embezzlement	10,003	4,981	5,022	49.8	50.2	0.1	0.1	0.3
Stolen property; buying, receiving, possessing	64,027	49,688	14,339	77.6	22.4	0.9	1.0	0.8
Vandalism	128,474	98,712	29,762	76.8	23.2	1.9	2.0	1.6
Weapons; carrying, possessing, etc.	110,130	99,611	10,519	90.4	9.6	1.6	2.0	0.6
Prostitution and commercialized vice	20,015	7,404	12,611	37.0	63.0	0.3	0.1	0.7
Sex offenses (except forcible rape and prostitution)	28,973	26,996	1,977	93.2	6.8	0.4	0.5	0.1
Drug abuse violations	1,067,764	796,466	271,298	74.6	25.4	15.4	15.9	14.2
Gambling	1,909	1,360	549	71.2	28.8	*	*	*
Offenses against the family and children	58,720	40,881	17,839	69.6	30.4	0.8	0.8	0.9
Driving under the influence	658,902	488,091	170,811	74.1	25.9	9.5	9.7	9.0
Liquor laws	112,467	78,441	34,026	69.7	30.3	1.6	1.6	1.8
Drunkenness	219,696	172,813	46,883	78.7	21.3	3.2	3.4	2.5
Disorderly conduct	211,960	149,485	62,475	70.5	29.5	3.1	3.0	3.3
Vagrancy	16,104	12,401	3,703	77.0	23.0	0.2	0.2	0.2
All other offenses (except traffic)	2,219,328	1,622,846	596,482	73.1	26.9	32.1	32.4	31.3
Suspicion	329	224	105	68.1	31.9	*	*	*
Curfew and loitering law violations	10,781	7,147	3,634	66.3	33.7	0.2	0.1	0.2

* = Less than one-tenth of 1 percent.
1 Because of rounding, the percentages may not sum to 100.   2 Violent crimes in this table are offenses of murder and nonnegligent manslaughter, rape, robbery, and aggravated assault. Property crimes are offenses of burglary, larceny-theft, motor vehicle theft, and arson.   3 The rape figures in this table are aggregate totals of the data submitted based on both the legacy and revised Uniform Crime Reporting definitions.

Table 43. Arrests, Distribution by Race, 2019

(Number, percent; 10,831 agencies; 2019 estimated population 229,735,355.)

Offense charged	Total arrests						Percent distribution[1]						Arrests under 18					
	Total	White	Black	American Indian or Alaskan Native	Asian	Native Hawaiian or Other Pacific Islander	Total	White	Black	American Indian or Alaskan Native	Asian	Native Hawaiian or Other Pacific Islander	Total	White	Black	American Indian or Alaskan Native	Asian	Native Hawaiian or Other Pacific Islander
Total	6,816,975	4,729,290	1,815,144	164,852	86,733	20,956	100.0	69.4	26.6	2.4	1.3	0.3	475,371	296,881	161,149	10,680	5,219	1,442
Violent crime[2]	355,244	209,848	129,346	8,201	5,829	2,020	100.0	59.1	36.4	2.3	1.6	0.6	34,736	17,489	16,134	584	391	138
Murder and nonnegligent manslaughter	7,964	3,650	4,078	125	83	28	100.0	45.8	51.2	1.6	1.0	0.4	629	298	314	16	1	0
Rape[3]	16,599	11,588	4,427	249	276	59	100.0	69.8	26.7	1.5	1.7	0.4	2,800	1,990	732	37	35	6
Robbery	56,305	25,143	29,677	635	568	282	100.0	44.7	52.7	1.1	1.0	0.5	12,148	4,391	7,486	69	128	74
Aggravated assault	274,376	169,467	91,164	7,192	4,902	1,651	100.0	61.8	33.2	2.6	1.8	0.6	19,159	10,810	7,602	462	227	58
Property crime[2]	775,091	517,502	231,087	14,780	9,443	2,279	100.0	66.8	29.8	1.9	1.2	0.3	85,749	47,071	35,599	1,607	1,169	303
Burglary	118,843	81,104	34,188	1,728	1,464	359	100.0	68.2	28.8	1.5	1.2	0.3	14,248	8,083	5,632	306	166	61
Larceny-theft	592,679	393,226	178,937	11,718	7,133	1,665	100.0	66.3	30.2	2.0	1.2	0.3	60,623	33,603	24,837	1,046	915	222
Motor vehicle theft	57,278	38,719	16,409	1,213	721	216	100.0	67.6	28.6	2.1	1.3	0.4	9,637	4,523	4,789	231	76	18
Arson	6,291	4,453	1,553	121	125	39	100.0	70.8	24.7	1.9	2.0	0.6	1,241	862	341	24	12	2
Other assaults	703,534	455,901	219,400	16,037	9,907	2,289	100.0	64.8	31.2	2.3	1.4	0.3	86,016	51,035	32,259	1,620	842	260
Forgery and counterfeiting	32,100	21,537	9,668	338	501	56	100.0	67.1	30.1	1.1	1.6	0.2	600	373	215	3	8	1
Fraud	78,698	51,861	24,041	1,424	1,208	164	100.0	65.9	30.5	1.8	1.5	0.2	2,547	1,274	1,181	61	30	1
Embezzlement	9,886	5,983	3,587	114	179	23	100.0	60.5	36.3	1.2	1.8	0.2	392	183	195	1	12	1
Stolen property; buying, receiving, possessing	63,035	38,751	21,998	1,108	825	353	100.0	61.5	34.9	1.8	1.3	0.6	6,355	2,201	3,962	92	57	43
Vandalism	126,161	86,360	34,670	3,198	1,598	335	100.0	68.5	27.5	2.5	1.3	0.3	22,150	15,419	6,025	492	171	43
Weapons; carrying, possessing, etc.	108,847	60,494	45,530	1,129	1,247	447	100.0	55.6	41.8	1.0	1.1	0.4	11,381	6,327	4,703	141	174	36
Prostitution and commercialized vice	19,811	10,074	8,370	73	1,205	89	100.0	50.9	42.2	0.4	6.1	0.4	213	101	108	0	2	2
Sex offenses (except forcible rape and prostitution)	28,627	21,360	5,903	596	668	100	100.0	74.6	20.6	2.1	2.3	0.3	4,651	3,471	1,013	59	86	22
Drug abuse violations	1,052,101	748,874	274,670	14,098	11,857	2,602	100.0	71.2	26.1	1.3	1.1	0.2	54,459	40,735	11,651	1,220	655	198
Gambling	1,895	1,081	553	13	214	34	100.0	57.0	29.2	0.7	11.3	1.8	149	87	57	0	5	0
Offenses against the family and children	58,042	38,196	16,454	2,821	493	78	100.0	65.8	28.3	4.9	0.8	0.1	2,056	1,377	463	206	10	0
Driving under the influence	646,607	526,928	90,888	12,373	13,071	3,347	100.0	81.5	14.1	1.9	2.0	0.5	3,460	3,093	203	107	42	15
Liquor laws	109,887	85,350	17,077	5,657	1,651	152	100.0	77.7	15.5	5.1	1.5	0.1	16,621	14,274	1,127	987	189	44
Drunkenness	218,095	164,797	32,255	18,238	2,431	374	100.0	75.6	14.8	8.4	1.1	0.2	2,306	1,784	275	222	22	3
Disorderly conduct	208,690	132,676	64,049	9,811	1,820	334	100.0	63.6	30.7	4.7	0.9	0.2	36,195	19,802	15,144	942	259	48
Vagrancy	15,952	10,763	4,497	473	201	18	100.0	67.5	28.2	3.0	1.3	0.1	255	183	65	5	2	0
All other offenses (except traffic)	2,192,791	1,532,998	577,689	54,049	22,248	5,807	100.0	69.9	26.3	2.5	1.0	0.3	94,492	63,638	27,609	2,058	958	229
Suspicion	1,316	1,008	257	49	2	0	100.0	76.6	19.5	3.7	0.2	0.0	23	16	6	1	0	0
Curfew and loitering law violations	10,565	6,948	3,155	272	135	55	100.0	65.8	29.9	2.6	1.3	0.5	10,565	6,948	3,155	272	135	55

Table 43. Arrests, Distribution by Race, 2019—Continued

(Number, percent; 10,831 agencies; 2019 estimated population 229,735,355.)

Offense charged	Percent distribution[1]						Arrests 18 and over						Percent distribution[1]					
	Total	White	Black	American Indian or Alaskan Native	Asian	Native Hawaiian or Other Pacific Islander	Total	White	Black	American Indian or Alaskan Native	Asian	Native Hawaiian or Other Pacific Islander	Total	White	Black	American Indian or Alaskan Native	Asian	Native Hawaiian or Other Pacific Islander
Total	100.0	62.5	33.9	2.2	1.1	0.3	6,341,604	4,432,409	1,653,995	154,172	81,514	19,514	100.0	69.9	26.1	2.4	1.3	0.3
Violent crime[2]	100.0	50.3	46.4	1.7	1.1	0.4	320,508	192,359	113,212	7,617	5,438	1,882	100.0	60.0	35.3	2.4	1.7	0.6
Murder and nonnegligent manslaughter	100.0	47.4	49.9	2.5	0.2	0.0	7,335	3,352	3,764	109	82	28	100.0	45.7	51.3	1.5	1.1	0.4
Rape[3]	100.0	71.1	26.1	1.3	1.3	0.2	13,799	9,598	3,695	212	241	53	100.0	69.6	26.8	1.5	1.7	0.4
Robbery	100.0	36.1	61.6	0.6	1.1	0.6	44,157	20,752	22,191	566	440	208	100.0	47.0	50.3	1.3	1.0	0.5
Aggravated assault	100.0	56.4	39.7	2.4	1.2	0.3	255,217	158,657	83,562	6,730	4,675	1,593	100.0	62.2	32.7	2.6	1.8	0.6
Property crime[2]	100.0	54.9	41.5	1.9	1.4	0.4	689,342	470,431	195,488	13,173	8,274	1,976	100.0	68.2	28.4	1.9	1.2	0.3
Burglary	100.0	56.7	39.5	2.1	1.2	0.4	104,595	73,021	28,556	1,422	1,298	298	100.0	69.8	27.3	1.4	1.2	0.3
Larceny-theft	100.0	55.4	41.0	1.7	1.5	0.4	532,056	359,623	154,100	10,672	6,218	1,443	100.0	67.6	29.0	2.0	1.2	0.3
Motor vehicle theft	100.0	46.9	49.7	2.4	0.8	0.2	47,641	34,196	11,620	982	645	198	100.0	71.8	24.4	2.1	1.4	0.4
Arson	100.0	69.5	27.5	1.9	1.0	0.2	5,050	3,591	1,212	97	113	37	100.0	71.1	24.0	1.9	2.2	0.7
Other assaults	100.0	59.3	37.5	1.9	1.0	0.3	617,518	404,866	187,141	14,417	9,065	2,029	100.0	65.6	30.3	2.3	1.5	0.3
Forgery and counterfeiting	100.0	62.2	35.8	0.5	1.3	0.2	31,500	21,164	9,453	335	493	55	100.0	67.2	30.0	1.1	1.6	0.2
Fraud	100.0	50.0	46.4	2.4	1.2	*	76,151	50,587	22,860	1,363	1,178	163	100.0	66.4	30.0	1.8	1.5	0.2
Embezzlement	100.0	46.7	49.7	0.3	3.1	0.3	9,494	5,800	3,392	113	167	22	100.0	61.1	35.7	1.2	1.8	0.2
Stolen property; buying, receiving, possessing	100.0	34.6	62.3	1.4	0.9	0.7	56,680	36,550	18,036	1,016	768	310	100.0	64.5	31.8	1.8	1.4	0.5
Vandalism	100.0	69.6	27.2	2.2	0.8	0.2	104,011	70,941	28,645	2,706	1,427	292	100.0	68.2	27.5	2.6	1.4	0.3
Weapons; carrying, possessing, etc.	100.0	55.6	41.3	1.2	1.5	0.3	97,466	54,167	40,827	988	1,073	411	100.0	55.6	41.9	1.0	1.1	0.4
Prostitution and commercialized vice	100.0	47.4	50.7	0.0	0.9	0.9	19,598	9,973	8,262	73	1,203	87	100.0	50.9	42.2	0.4	6.1	0.4
Sex offenses (except forcible rape and prostitution)	100.0	74.6	21.8	1.3	1.8	0.5	23,976	17,889	4,890	537	582	78	100.0	74.6	20.4	2.2	2.4	0.3
Drug abuse violations	100.0	74.8	21.4	2.2	1.2	0.4	997,642	708,139	263,019	12,878	11,202	2,404	100.0	71.0	26.4	1.3	1.1	0.2
Gambling	100.0	58.4	38.3	0.0	3.4	0.0	1,746	994	496	13	209	34	100.0	56.9	28.4	0.7	12.0	1.9
Offenses against the family and children	100.0	67.0	22.5	10.0	0.5	0.0	55,986	36,819	15,991	2,615	483	78	100.0	65.8	28.6	4.7	0.9	0.1
Driving under the influence	100.0	89.4	5.9	3.1	1.2	0.4	643,147	523,835	90,685	12,266	13,029	3,332	100.0	81.4	14.1	1.9	2.0	0.5
Liquor laws	100.0	85.9	6.8	5.9	1.1	0.3	93,266	71,076	15,950	4,670	1,462	108	100.0	76.2	17.1	5.0	1.6	0.1
Drunkenness	100.0	77.4	11.9	9.6	1.0	0.1	215,789	163,013	31,980	18,016	2,409	371	100.0	75.5	14.8	8.3	1.1	0.2
Disorderly conduct	100.0	54.7	41.8	2.6	0.7	0.1	172,495	112,874	48,905	8,869	1,561	286	100.0	65.4	28.4	5.1	0.9	0.2
Vagrancy	100.0	71.8	25.5	2.0	0.8	0.0	15,697	10,580	4,432	468	199	18	100.0	67.4	28.2	3.0	1.3	0.1
All other offenses (except traffic)	100.0	67.3	29.2	2.2	1.0	0.2	2,098,299	1,469,360	550,080	51,991	21,290	5,578	100.0	70.0	26.2	2.5	1.0	0.3
Suspicion	100.0	69.6	26.1	4.3	0.0	0.0	1,293	992	251	48	2	0	100.0	76.7	19.4	3.7	0.2	0.0
Curfew and loitering law violations	100.0	65.8	29.9	2.6	1.3	0.5	NA	NA	NA	NA	NA	NA	NA	NA	NA	NA	NA	NA

NA = Not available.
* = Less than one-tenth of one percent.
1 Because of rounding, the percentages may not sum to 100.   2 Violent crimes are offenses of murder and nonnegligent manslaughter, rape, robbery, and aggravated assault. Property crimes are offenses of burglary, larceny-theft, motor vehicle theft, and arson.   3 The rape figures in this table are aggregate totals of the data submitted based on both the legacy and revised Uniform Crime Reporting definitions.

Table 43A. Arrests, Distribution by Ethnicity, 2019

(Number, percent; 10,831 agencies; 2019 estimated population 229,735,355.)

Offense charged	Total arrests			Percent distribution[1]			Arrests under 18		
	Total[2]	Hispanic or Latino	Not Hispanic or Latino	Total[2]	Hispanic or Latino	Not Hispanic or Latino	Total[2]	Hispanic or Latino	Not Hispanic or Latino
Total	5,896,059	1,126,806	4,769,253	100.0	19.1	80.9	403,502	95,258	308,244
Violent crime[3]	314,630	79,712	234,918	100.0	25.3	74.7	30,609	8,245	22,364
Murder and nonnegligent manslaughter	6,474	1,341	5,133	100.0	20.7	79.3	490	158	332
Rape[4]	14,172	3,948	10,224	100.0	27.9	72.1	2,328	494	1,834
Robbery	50,705	12,002	38,703	100.0	23.7	76.3	11,015	2,861	8,154
Aggravated assault	243,279	62,421	180,858	100.0	25.7	74.3	16,776	4,732	12,044
Property crime[3]	664,276	109,950	554,326	100.0	16.6	83.4	72,497	15,532	56,965
Burglary	105,558	21,981	83,577	100.0	20.8	79.2	12,261	3,023	9,238
Larceny-theft	502,776	74,227	428,549	100.0	14.8	85.2	50,825	10,250	40,575
Motor vehicle theft	50,482	12,720	37,762	100.0	25.2	74.8	8,352	2,061	6,291
Arson	5,460	1,022	4,438	100.0	18.7	81.3	1,059	198	861
Other assaults	608,510	115,069	493,441	100.0	18.9	81.1	74,255	16,884	57,371
Forgery and counterfeiting	28,277	4,786	23,491	100.0	16.9	83.1	523	123	400
Fraud	68,160	9,984	58,176	100.0	14.6	85.4	2,165	441	1,724
Embezzlement	8,271	1,099	7,172	100.0	13.3	86.7	313	65	248
Stolen property; buying, receiving, possessing	54,930	10,331	44,599	100.0	18.8	81.2	5,509	1,087	4,422
Vandalism	109,856	21,333	88,523	100.0	19.4	80.6	19,191	4,171	15,020
Weapons; carrying, possessing, etc.	92,892	22,081	70,811	100.0	23.8	76.2	9,939	3,326	6,613
Prostitution and commercialized vice	18,191	3,506	14,685	100.0	19.3	80.7	193	32	161
Sex offenses (except forcible rape and prostitution)	25,184	7,023	18,161	100.0	27.9	72.1	3,922	1,033	2,889
Drug abuse violations	946,784	194,654	752,130	100.0	20.6	79.4	48,307	14,561	33,746
Gambling	1,682	434	1,248	100.0	25.8	74.2	136	47	89
Offenses against the family and children	49,402	6,443	42,959	100.0	13.0	87.0	1,709	405	1,304
Driving under the influence	549,292	145,127	404,165	100.0	26.4	73.6	2,846	877	1,969
Liquor laws	90,033	14,802	75,231	100.0	16.4	83.6	13,730	2,715	11,015
Drunkenness	206,492	46,634	159,858	100.0	22.6	77.4	2,145	781	1,364
Disorderly conduct	164,645	22,897	141,748	100.0	13.9	86.1	28,137	5,454	22,683
Vagrancy	14,779	2,109	12,670	100.0	14.3	85.7	193	70	123
All other offenses (except traffic)	1,870,588	306,544	1,564,044	100.0	16.4	83.6	78,393	17,157	61,236
Suspicion	410	37	373	100.0	9.0	91.0	15	1	14
Curfew and loitering law violations	8,775	2,251	6,524	100.0	25.7	74.3	8,775	2,251	6,524

Table 43A. Arrests, Distribution by Ethnicity, 2019—Continued

(Number, percent; 10,831 agencies; 2019 estimated population 229,735,355.)

Offense charged	Percent distribution[1]			Arrests 18 and over			Percent distribution[1]		
	Total[2]	Hispanic or Latino	Not Hispanic or Latino	Total[2]	Hispanic or Latino	Not Hispanic or Latino	Total[2]	Hispanic or Latino	Not Hispanic or Latino
Total	100.0	23.6	76.4	5,492,557	1,031,548	4,461,009	100.0	18.8	81.2
Violent crime[3]	100.0	26.9	73.1	284,021	71,467	212,554	100.0	25.2	74.8
Murder and nonnegligent manslaughter	100.0	32.2	67.8	5,984	1,183	4,801	100.0	19.8	80.2
Rape[4]	100.0	21.2	78.8	11,844	3,454	8,390	100.0	29.2	70.8
Robbery	100.0	26.0	74.0	39,690	9,141	30,549	100.0	23.0	77.0
Aggravated assault	100.0	28.2	71.8	226,503	57,689	168,814	100.0	25.5	74.5
Property crime[3]	100.0	21.4	78.6	591,779	94,418	497,361	100.0	16.0	84.0
Burglary	100.0	24.7	75.3	93,297	18,958	74,339	100.0	20.3	79.7
Larceny-theft	100.0	20.2	79.8	451,951	63,977	387,974	100.0	14.2	85.8
Motor vehicle theft	100.0	24.7	75.3	42,130	10,659	31,471	100.0	25.3	74.7
Arson	100.0	18.7	81.3	4,401	824	3,577	100.0	18.7	81.3
Other assaults	100.0	22.7	77.3	534,255	98,185	436,070	100.0	18.4	81.6
Forgery and counterfeiting	100.0	23.5	76.5	27,754	4,663	23,091	100.0	16.8	83.2
Fraud	100.0	20.4	79.6	65,995	9,543	56,452	100.0	14.5	85.5
Embezzlement	100.0	20.8	79.2	7,958	1,034	6,924	100.0	13.0	87.0
Stolen property; buying, receiving, possessing	100.0	19.7	80.3	49,421	9,244	40,177	100.0	18.7	81.3
Vandalism	100.0	21.7	78.3	90,665	17,162	73,503	100.0	18.9	81.1
Weapons; carrying, possessing, etc.	100.0	33.5	66.5	82,953	18,755	64,198	100.0	22.6	77.4
Prostitution and commercialized vice	100.0	16.6	83.4	17,998	3,474	14,524	100.0	19.3	80.7
Sex offenses (except forcible rape and prostitution)	100.0	26.3	73.7	21,262	5,990	15,272	100.0	28.2	71.8
Drug abuse violations	100.0	30.1	69.9	898,477	180,093	718,384	100.0	20.0	80.0
Gambling	100.0	34.6	65.4	1,546	387	1,159	100.0	25.0	75.0
Offenses against the family and children	100.0	23.7	76.3	47,693	6,038	41,655	100.0	12.7	87.3
Driving under the influence	100.0	30.8	69.2	546,446	144,250	402,196	100.0	26.4	73.6
Liquor laws	100.0	19.8	80.2	76,303	12,087	64,216	100.0	15.8	84.2
Drunkenness	100.0	36.4	63.6	204,347	45,853	158,494	100.0	22.4	77.6
Disorderly conduct	100.0	19.4	80.6	136,508	17,443	119,065	100.0	12.8	87.2
Vagrancy	100.0	36.3	63.7	14,586	2,039	12,547	100.0	14.0	86.0
All other offenses (except traffic)	100.0	21.9	78.1	1,792,195	289,387	1,502,808	100.0	16.1	83.9
Suspicion	100.0	6.7	93.3	395	36	359	100.0	9.1	90.9
Curfew and loitering law violations	100.0	25.7	74.3	NA	NA	NA	NA	NA	NA

NA = Not available.
1 Because of rounding, the percentages may not sum to 100.   2 The ethnicity totals are representative of those agencies that provided ethnicity breakdowns. Not all agencies provide ethnicity data; therefore, the race and ethnicity totals will not be equal.   3 Violent crimes are offenses of murder and nonnegligent manslaughter, rape, robbery, and aggravated assault. Property crimes are offenses of burglary, larceny-theft, motor vehicle theft, and arson.   4 The rape figures in this table are aggregate totals of the data submitted based on both the legacy and revised Uniform Crime Reporting definitions.

Table 44. Arrest Trends, Cities, 2018–2019

(Number, percent change; 7,204 agencies; 2019 estimated population 147,631,037; 2018 estimated population 146,952,334.)

Offense charged	Number of persons arrested								
	Total, all ages			Under 18 years of age			18 years of age and over		
	2018	2019	Percent change	2018	2019	Percent change	2018	2019	Percent change
Total[1]	4,738,274	4,571,745	-3.5	368,782	357,161	-3.2	4,369,492	4,214,584	-3.5
Violent crime[2]	259,160	258,817	-0.1	25,446	25,908	+1.8	233,714	232,909	-0.3
Murder and nonnegligent manslaughter	5,138	5,159	+0.4	444	439	-1.1	4,694	4,720	+0.6
Rape[3]	11,409	11,047	-3.2	1,907	1,817	-4.7	9,502	9,230	-2.9
Robbery	46,057	44,346	-3.7	9,146	9,660	+5.6	36,911	34,686	-6.0
Aggravated assault	196,556	198,265	+0.9	13,949	13,992	+0.3	182,607	184,273	+0.9
Property crime[2]	612,745	597,694	-2.5	72,010	67,216	-6.7	540,735	530,478	-1.9
Burglary	87,721	84,693	-3.5	11,381	10,411	-8.5	76,340	74,282	-2.7
Larceny-theft	478,130	467,572	-2.2	52,380	48,699	-7.0	425,750	418,873	-1.6
Motor vehicle theft	42,544	40,837	-4.0	7,323	7,210	-1.5	35,221	33,627	-4.5
Arson	4,350	4,592	+5.6	926	896	-3.2	3,424	3,696	+7.9
Other assaults	502,169	496,435	-1.1	59,848	60,122	+0.5	442,321	436,313	-1.4
Forgery and counterfeiting	24,497	23,039	-6.0	587	470	-19.9	23,910	22,569	-5.6
Fraud	55,098	54,463	-1.2	1,907	1,940	+1.7	53,191	52,523	-1.3
Embezzlement	7,726	7,494	-3.0	357	332	-7.0	7,369	7,162	-2.8
Stolen property; buying, receiving, possessing	47,247	45,087	-4.6	5,373	5,193	-3.4	41,874	39,894	-4.7
Vandalism	91,565	92,758	+1.3	15,985	16,620	+4.0	75,580	76,138	+0.7
Weapons; carrying, possessing, etc.	76,784	76,106	-0.9	8,457	8,781	+3.8	68,327	67,325	-1.5
Prostitution and commercialized vice	14,853	13,574	-8.6	94	78	-17.0	14,759	13,496	-8.6
Sex offenses (except forcible rape and prostitution)	20,391	19,287	-5.4	3,442	3,277	-4.8	16,949	16,010	-5.5
Drug abuse violations	739,737	690,707	-6.6	44,471	40,051	-9.9	695,266	650,656	-6.4
Gambling	976	1,141	+16.9	54	56	+3.7	922	1,085	+17.7
Offenses against the family and children	29,272	28,663	-2.1	1,599	1,591	-0.5	27,673	27,072	-2.2
Driving under the influence	361,381	359,408	-0.5	2,108	2,133	+1.2	359,273	357,275	-0.6
Liquor laws	89,809	81,311	-9.5	12,507	11,276	-9.8	77,302	70,035	-9.4
Drunkenness	185,925	173,989	-6.4	1,948	1,758	-9.8	183,977	172,231	-6.4
Disorderly conduct	163,836	162,778	-0.6	28,142	28,741	+2.1	135,694	134,037	-1.2
Vagrancy	12,616	11,040	-12.5	339	238	-29.8	12,277	10,802	-12.0
All other offenses (except traffic)	1,432,900	1,369,012	-4.5	74,521	72,438	-2.8	1,358,379	1,296,574	-4.5
Suspicion	152	178	+17.1	26	11	-57.7	126	167	+32.5
Curfew and loitering law violations	9,587	8,942	-6.7	9,587	8,942	-6.7	NA	NA	NA

NA = Not available.

1 Does not include suspicion.   2 Violent crimes are offenses of murder and nonnegligent manslaughter, rape, robbery, and aggravated assault. Property crimes are offenses of burglary, larceny-theft, motor vehicle theft, and arson.   3 The rape figures in this table are aggregate totals of the data submitted based on both the legacy and revised Uniform Crime Reporting definitions.

Table 45. Arrest Trends, Cities, by Age and Sex, 2018–2019

(Number, percent change; 7,204 agencies; 2019 estimated population 147,631,037; 2018 estimated population 146,952,334.)

Offense charged	Male						Female					
	Total			Under 18			Total			Under 18		
	2018	2019	Percent change	2018	2019	Percent change	2018	2019	Percent change	2018	2019	Percent change
Total[1]	3,428,489	3,304,291	-3.6	256,836	247,186	-3.8	1,309,785	1,267,454	-3.2	111,946	109,975	-1.8
Violent crime[2]	203,896	203,543	-0.2	20,465	20,968	+2.5	55,264	55,274	*	4,981	4,940	-0.8
Murder and nonnegligent manslaughter	4,492	4,549	+1.3	398	395	-0.8	646	610	-5.6	46	44	-4.3
Rape[3]	11,120	10,748	-3.3	1,828	1,734	-5.1	289	299	+3.5	79	83	+5.1
Robbery	38,946	37,323	-4.2	8,083	8,511	+5.3	7,111	7,023	-1.2	1,063	1,149	+8.1
Aggravated assault	149,338	150,923	+1.1	10,156	10,328	+1.7	47,218	47,342	+0.3	3,793	3,664	-3.4
Property crime[2]	379,252	367,761	-3.0	47,872	44,182	-7.7	233,493	229,933	-1.5	24,138	23,034	-4.6
Burglary	69,794	66,753	-4.4	9,811	8,909	-9.2	17,927	17,940	+0.1	1,570	1,502	-4.3
Larceny-theft	273,306	266,011	-2.7	31,333	28,712	-8.4	204,824	201,561	-1.6	21,047	19,987	-5.0
Motor vehicle theft	32,782	31,418	-4.2	5,957	5,799	-2.7	9,762	9,419	-3.5	1,366	1,411	+3.3
Arson	3,370	3,579	+6.2	771	762	-1.2	980	1,013	+3.4	155	134	-13.5
Other assaults	355,506	350,458	-1.4	37,268	37,431	+0.4	146,663	145,977	-0.5	22,580	22,691	+0.5
Forgery and counterfeiting	16,263	15,332	-5.7	473	349	-26.2	8,234	7,707	-6.4	114	121	+6.1
Fraud	34,892	35,120	+0.7	1,270	1,307	+2.9	20,206	19,343	-4.3	637	633	-0.6
Embezzlement	3,784	3,686	-2.6	210	180	-14.3	3,942	3,808	-3.4	147	152	+3.4
Stolen property; buying, receiving, possessing	36,588	34,843	-4.8	4,490	4,260	-5.1	10,659	10,244	-3.9	883	933	+5.7
Vandalism	70,243	71,186	+1.3	12,872	13,332	+3.6	21,322	21,572	+1.2	3,113	3,288	+5.6
Weapons; carrying, possessing, etc.	69,616	69,087	-0.8	7,542	7,917	+5.0	7,168	7,019	-2.1	915	864	-5.6
Prostitution and commercialized vice	5,634	5,278	-6.3	43	40	-7.0	9,219	8,296	-10.0	51	38	-25.5
Sex offenses (except forcible rape and prostitution)	19,037	18,035	-5.3	3,095	2,904	-6.2	1,354	1,252	-7.5	347	373	+7.5
Drug abuse violations	559,557	520,599	-7.0	33,019	29,502	-10.7	180,180	170,108	-5.6	11,452	10,549	-7.9
Gambling	747	850	+13.8	48	52	+8.3	229	291	+27.1	6	4	-33.3
Offenses against the family and children	19,014	18,302	-3.7	940	914	-2.8	10,258	10,361	+1.0	659	677	+2.7
Driving under the influence	266,765	265,308	-0.5	1,558	1,565	+0.4	94,616	94,100	-0.5	550	568	+3.3
Liquor laws	62,759	56,755	-9.6	7,218	6,452	-10.6	27,050	24,556	-9.2	5,289	4,824	-8.8
Drunkenness	147,820	137,587	-6.9	1,344	1,160	-13.7	38,105	36,402	-4.5	604	598	-1.0
Disorderly conduct	115,706	114,675	-0.9	17,751	17,862	+0.6	48,130	48,103	-0.1	10,391	10,879	+4.7
Vagrancy	9,349	8,341	-10.8	261	181	-30.7	3,267	2,699	-17.4	78	57	-26.9
All other offenses (except traffic)	1,045,672	1,001,598	-4.2	52,708	50,681	-3.8	387,228	367,414	-5.1	21,813	21,757	-0.3
Suspicion	118	117	-0.8	17	11	-35.3	34	61	+79.4	9	0	-100.0
Curfew and loitering law violations	6,389	5,947	-6.9	6,389	5,947	-6.9	3,198	2,995	-6.3	3,198	2,995	-6.3

1 Does not include suspicion.   2 Violent crimes are offenses of murder and nonnegligent manslaughter, rape, robbery, and aggravated assault. Property crimes are offenses of burglary, larceny-theft, motor vehicle theft, and arson.   3 The rape figures in this table are aggregate totals of the data submitted based on both the legacy and revised Uniform Crime Reporting definitions.

Table 46. Arrests, Cities, Distribution by Age, 2019

(Number, percent; 7,979 agencies; 2019 estimated population 159,706,353.)

Offense charged	Total, all ages	Ages under 15	Ages under 18	Ages 18 and over	Under 10	10–12	13–14	15	16	17	18	19	20
Total	5,005,133	126,702	386,458	4,618,675	1,884	29,321	95,497	75,807	86,220	97,729	129,634	145,364	141,361
Total percent distribution[1]	100.0	2.5	7.7	92.3	*	0.6	1.9	1.5	1.7	2.0	2.6	2.9	2.8
Violent crime[2]	280,634	8,607	28,164	252,470	121	1,942	6,544	5,616	6,597	7,344	8,593	8,603	8,436
Violent crime percent distribution[1]	100.0	3.1	10.0	90.0	*	0.7	2.3	2.0	2.4	2.6	3.1	3.1	3.0
Murder and nonnegligent manslaughter	5,693	61	479	5,214	0	8	53	87	124	207	313	330	294
Rape[3]	12,070	867	1,950	10,120	16	234	617	326	347	410	498	381	423
Robbery	48,151	2,262	10,398	37,753	5	281	1,976	2,296	2,796	3,044	3,176	2,694	2,133
Aggravated assault	214,720	5,417	15,337	199,383	100	1,419	3,898	2,907	3,330	3,683	4,606	5,198	5,586
Property crime[2]	646,218	22,382	73,005	573,213	295	4,442	17,645	15,094	17,017	18,512	21,561	20,480	18,034
Property crime percent distribution[1]	100.0	3.5	11.3	88.7	*	0.7	2.7	2.3	2.6	2.9	3.3	3.2	2.8
Burglary	92,073	3,835	11,400	80,673	65	830	2,940	2,451	2,562	2,552	3,004	2,977	2,511
Larceny-theft	505,838	15,797	52,747	453,091	186	3,195	12,416	10,506	12,367	14,077	16,905	16,062	14,198
Motor vehicle theft	43,390	2,177	7,880	35,510	4	215	1,958	1,977	1,963	1,763	1,535	1,347	1,239
Arson	4,917	573	978	3,939	40	202	331	160	125	120	117	94	86
Other assaults	552,879	29,230	66,219	486,660	473	8,528	20,229	12,641	12,419	11,929	11,417	13,027	13,221
Forgery and counterfeiting	24,813	79	500	24,313	2	19	58	78	119	224	609	958	977
Fraud	59,417	528	2,100	57,317	2	86	440	379	528	665	1,190	1,600	1,814
Embezzlement	8,061	22	346	7,715	0	5	17	23	103	198	359	451	394
Stolen property; buying, receiving, possessing	48,895	1,203	5,576	43,319	2	103	1,098	1,165	1,496	1,712	1,893	1,777	1,580
Vandalism	101,046	8,120	18,098	82,948	235	2,427	5,458	3,361	3,390	3,227	3,369	3,308	3,113
Weapons; carrying, possessing, etc.	82,918	2,626	9,408	73,510	49	654	1,923	1,700	2,248	2,834	3,343	3,507	3,382
Prostitution and commercialized vice	17,588	22	186	17,402	0	5	17	22	46	96	446	770	820
Sex offenses (except forcible rape and prostitution)	21,212	1,660	3,446	17,766	27	421	1,212	639	560	587	587	492	433
Drug abuse violations	752,471	8,943	43,328	709,143	40	1,409	7,494	7,762	10,899	15,724	26,306	29,425	26,273
Gambling	1,205	5	62	1,143	1	1	3	16	16	25	27	47	45
Offenses against the family and children	32,341	636	1,674	30,667	17	163	456	344	353	341	494	578	614
Driving under the influence	389,429	54	2,287	387,142	1	3	50	105	570	1,558	6,905	7,863	10,390
Liquor laws	88,737	2,132	12,281	76,456	4	299	1,829	2,086	3,179	4,884	11,632	12,224	10,390
Drunkenness	188,238	316	2,009	186,229	5	46	265	298	469	926	2,567	3,209	3,391
Disorderly conduct	175,498	13,484	30,629	144,869	175	3,644	9,665	6,453	5,729	4,963	4,513	4,489	4,635
Vagrancy	14,326	75	243	14,083	3	15	57	60	58	50	220	194	269
All other offenses (except traffic)	1,509,280	23,310	77,169	1,432,111	422	4,595	18,293	15,729	17,975	20,155	26,240	33,315	35,673
Suspicion	211	7	12	199	0	0	7	1	2	2	5	5	4
Curfew and loitering law violations	9,716	3,261	9,716	NA	10	514	2,737	2,235	2,447	1,773	NA	NA	NA

Table 46. Arrests, Cities, Distribution by Age, 2019—Continued

(Number, percent; 7,979 agencies; 2019 estimated population 159,706,353.)

Offense charged	21	22	23	24	25–29	30–34	35–39	40–44	45–49	50–54	55–59	60–64	65 and over
Total	145,521	146,572	149,384	154,190	837,175	745,039	618,022	430,230	325,198	265,437	203,979	109,101	72,468
Total percent distribution[1]	2.9	2.9	3.0	3.1	16.7	14.9	12.3	8.6	6.5	5.3	4.1	2.2	1.4
Violent crime[2]	8,819	8,732	8,873	9,163	48,403	40,910	32,587	21,974	16,006	12,747	9,553	5,244	3,827
Violent crime percent distribution[1]	3.1	3.1	3.2	3.3	17.2	14.6	11.6	7.8	5.7	4.5	3.4	1.9	1.4
Murder and nonnegligent manslaughter	290	235	232	231	1,061	688	534	355	219	137	131	89	75
Rape[3]	362	339	306	284	1,565	1,471	1,276	921	701	599	441	281	272
Robbery	1,893	1,700	1,553	1,554	7,414	5,548	3,823	2,376	1,493	1,161	767	327	141
Aggravated assault	6,274	6,458	6,782	7,094	38,363	33,203	26,954	18,322	13,593	10,850	8,214	4,547	3,339
Property crime[2]	17,610	17,156	17,472	17,912	102,313	95,515	78,861	53,058	39,579	32,131	23,113	11,418	7,000
Property crime percent distribution[1]	2.7	2.7	2.7	2.8	15.8	14.8	12.2	8.2	6.1	5.0	3.6	1.8	1.1
Burglary	2,533	2,515	2,746	2,906	15,477	14,097	11,318	7,070	5,019	3,973	2,722	1,194	611
Larceny-theft	13,732	13,366	13,405	13,568	78,736	74,140	61,862	42,575	32,405	26,615	19,483	9,868	6,171
Motor vehicle theft	1,253	1,198	1,233	1,328	7,438	6,641	5,056	2,990	1,876	1,285	721	258	112
Arson	92	77	88	110	662	637	625	423	279	258	187	98	106
Other assaults	15,630	15,811	16,439	17,013	91,670	79,656	65,688	45,966	34,445	27,210	20,370	10,903	8,194
Forgery and counterfeiting	704	682	672	788	4,442	4,317	3,604	2,405	1,600	1,142	815	393	205
Fraud	1,624	1,710	1,784	1,862	10,843	10,059	8,299	5,747	3,979	3,001	2,090	1,000	715
Embezzlement	335	347	252	288	1,339	1,153	880	683	472	348	242	104	68
Stolen property; buying, receiving, possessing	1,494	1,503	1,518	1,525	8,930	7,581	6,046	3,758	2,394	1,692	1,004	439	185
Vandalism	3,169	3,189	3,164	3,171	16,470	13,572	10,427	6,782	4,688	3,708	2,596	1,297	925
Weapons; carrying, possessing, etc.	3,328	3,263	3,217	3,166	15,297	11,241	8,543	5,437	3,633	2,581	1,850	1,015	707
Prostitution and commercialized vice	812	856	745	776	3,495	2,455	1,870	1,313	1,022	875	554	321	272
Sex offenses (except forcible rape and prostitution)	441	419	458	458	2,286	2,431	2,259	1,694	1,414	1,293	1,257	870	974
Drug abuse violations	25,647	25,105	25,085	25,470	135,171	116,448	94,540	62,835	44,113	33,731	23,329	11,042	4,623
Gambling	23	20	24	27	162	155	147	116	107	96	70	35	42
Offenses against the family and children	761	778	848	918	5,853	5,954	5,054	3,428	2,134	1,423	1,020	497	313
Driving under the influence	12,659	13,817	14,421	14,764	71,596	57,696	47,569	35,822	29,435	24,985	21,347	13,299	10,701
Liquor laws	2,242	1,685	1,293	1,259	5,625	5,133	4,802	4,011	4,054	4,282	4,047	2,337	1,440
Drunkenness	5,468	5,349	5,262	5,337	28,036	26,562	23,823	18,683	16,720	15,955	13,908	7,745	4,214
Disorderly conduct	5,609	5,136	4,818	4,833	24,447	21,618	18,220	12,845	10,540	8,858	7,176	4,102	3,030
Vagrancy	190	214	249	237	1,810	1,885	2,002	1,505	1,516	1,485	1,186	716	405
All other offenses (except traffic)	38,954	40,795	42,785	45,214	258,947	240,662	202,771	142,151	107,328	87,891	68,442	36,319	24,624
Suspicion	2	5	5	9	40	36	30	17	19	3	10	5	4
Curfew and loitering law violations	NA	NA	NA	NA	NA	NA	NA	NA	NA	NA	NA	NA	NA

NA = Not available.
* = Less than one-tenth of one percent.
1 Because of rounding, the percentages may not sum to 100.   2 Violent crimes are offenses of murder and nonnegligent manslaughter, rape, robbery, and aggravated assault. Property crimes are offenses of burglary, larceny-theft, motor vehicle theft, and arson.   3 The rape figures in this table are aggregate totals of the data submitted based on both the legacy and revised Uniform Crime Reporting definitions.

Table 47. Arrests, Cities, Persons Under 15, 18, 21, and 25 Years of Age, 2019

(Number; percent; 7,979 agencies; 2019 estimated population 159,706,353.)

Offense charged	Total, all ages	Number of persons arrested				Percent of total of all ages			
		Under 15	Under 18	Under 21	Under 25	Under 15	Under 18	Under 21	Under 25
Total	5,005,133	126,702	386,458	802,817	1,398,484	2.5	7.7	16.0	27.9
Violent crime[1]	280,634	8,607	28,164	53,796	89,383	3.1	10.0	19.2	31.9
Murder and nonnegligent manslaughter	5,693	61	479	1,416	2,404	1.1	8.4	24.9	42.2
Rape[2]	12,070	867	1,950	3,252	4,543	7.2	16.2	26.9	37.6
Robbery	48,151	2,262	10,398	18,401	25,101	4.7	21.6	38.2	52.1
Aggravated assault	214,720	5,417	15,337	30,727	57,335	2.5	7.1	14.3	26.7
Property crime[1]	646,218	22,382	73,005	133,080	203,230	3.5	11.3	20.6	31.4
Burglary	92,073	3,835	11,400	19,892	30,592	4.2	12.4	21.6	33.2
Larceny-theft	505,838	15,797	52,747	99,912	153,983	3.1	10.4	19.8	30.4
Motor vehicle theft	43,390	2,177	7,880	12,001	17,013	5.0	18.2	27.7	39.2
Arson	4,917	573	978	1,275	1,642	11.7	19.9	25.9	33.4
Other assaults	552,879	29,230	66,219	103,884	168,777	5.3	12.0	18.8	30.5
Forgery and counterfeiting	24,813	79	500	3,044	5,890	0.3	2.0	12.3	23.7
Fraud	59,417	528	2,100	6,704	13,684	0.9	3.5	11.3	23.0
Embezzlement	8,061	22	346	1,550	2,772	0.3	4.3	19.2	34.4
Stolen property; buying, receiving, possessing	48,895	1,203	5,576	10,826	16,866	2.5	11.4	22.1	34.5
Vandalism	101,046	8,120	18,098	27,888	40,581	8.0	17.9	27.6	40.2
Weapons; carrying, possessing, etc.	82,918	2,626	9,408	19,640	32,614	3.2	11.3	23.7	39.3
Prostitution and commercialized vice	17,588	22	186	2,222	5,411	0.1	1.1	12.6	30.8
Sex offenses (except forcible rape and prostitution)	21,212	1,660	3,446	4,958	6,734	7.8	16.2	23.4	31.7
Drug abuse violations	752,471	8,943	43,328	125,332	226,639	1.2	5.8	16.7	30.1
Gambling	1,205	5	62	181	275	0.4	5.1	15.0	22.8
Offenses against the family and children	32,341	636	1,674	3,360	6,665	2.0	5.2	10.4	20.6
Driving under the influence	389,429	54	2,287	21,318	76,979	*	0.6	5.5	19.8
Liquor laws	88,737	2,132	12,281	46,527	53,006	2.4	13.8	52.4	59.7
Drunkenness	188,238	316	2,009	11,176	32,592	0.2	1.1	5.9	17.3
Disorderly conduct	175,498	13,484	30,629	44,266	64,662	7.7	17.5	25.2	36.8
Vagrancy	14,326	75	243	926	1,816	0.5	1.7	6.5	12.7
All other offenses (except traffic)	1,509,280	23,310	77,169	172,397	340,145	1.5	5.1	11.4	22.5
Suspicion	211	7	12	26	47	3.3	5.7	12.3	22.3
Curfew and loitering law violations	9,716	3,261	9,716	9,716	9,716	33.6	100.0	100.0	100.0

* = Less than one-tenth of one percent.
1 Violent crimes are offenses of murder and nonnegligent manslaughter, rape, robbery, and aggravated assault. Property crimes are offenses of burglary, larceny-theft, motor vehicle theft, and arson.   2 The rape figures in this table are aggregate totals of the data submitted based on both the legacy and revised Uniform Crime Reporting definitions.

Table 48. Arrests, Cities, Distribution by Sex, 2019

(Number, percent; 7,979 agencies; 2019 estimated population 159,706,353.)

Offense charged	Number of persons arrested			Percent male	Percent female	Percent distribution[1]		
	Total	Male	Female			Total	Male	Female
Total	5,005,133	3,613,887	1,391,246	72.2	27.8	100.0	100.0	100.0
Violent crime[2]	280,634	220,491	60,143	78.6	21.4	5.6	6.1	4.3
Murder and nonnegligent manslaughter	5,693	5,003	690	87.9	12.1	0.1	0.1	*
Rape[3]	12,070	11,699	371	96.9	3.1	0.2	0.3	*
Robbery	48,151	40,510	7,641	84.1	15.9	1.0	1.1	0.5
Aggravated assault	214,720	163,279	51,441	76.0	24.0	4.3	4.5	3.7
Property crime[2]	646,218	398,141	248,077	61.6	38.4	12.9	11.0	17.8
Burglary	92,073	72,694	19,379	79.0	21.0	1.8	2.0	1.4
Larceny-theft	505,838	288,238	217,600	57.0	43.0	10.1	8.0	15.6
Motor vehicle theft	43,390	33,385	10,005	76.9	23.1	0.9	0.9	0.7
Arson	4,917	3,824	1,093	77.8	22.2	0.1	0.1	0.1
Other assaults	552,879	389,196	163,683	70.4	29.6	11.0	10.8	11.8
Forgery and counterfeiting	24,813	16,495	8,318	66.5	33.5	0.5	0.5	0.6
Fraud	59,417	38,302	21,115	64.5	35.5	1.2	1.1	1.5
Embezzlement	8,061	3,962	4,099	49.2	50.8	0.2	0.1	0.3
Stolen property; buying, receiving, possessing	48,895	37,817	11,078	77.3	22.7	1.0	1.0	0.8
Vandalism	101,046	77,310	23,736	76.5	23.5	2.0	2.1	1.7
Weapons; carrying, possessing, etc.	82,918	75,247	7,671	90.7	9.3	1.7	2.1	0.6
Prostitution and commercialized vice	17,588	6,154	11,434	35.0	65.0	0.4	0.2	0.8
Sex offenses (except forcible rape and prostitution)	21,212	19,726	1,486	93.0	7.0	0.4	0.5	0.1
Drug abuse violations	752,471	567,264	185,207	75.4	24.6	15.0	15.7	13.3
Gambling	1,205	891	314	73.9	26.1	*	*	*
Offenses against the family and children	32,341	20,652	11,689	63.9	36.1	0.6	0.6	0.8
Driving under the influence	389,429	287,415	102,014	73.8	26.2	7.8	8.0	7.3
Liquor laws	88,737	62,031	26,706	69.9	30.1	1.8	1.7	1.9
Drunkenness	188,238	148,751	39,487	79.0	21.0	3.8	4.1	2.8
Disorderly conduct	175,498	123,546	51,952	70.4	29.6	3.5	3.4	3.7
Vagrancy	14,326	11,042	3,284	77.1	22.9	0.3	0.3	0.2
All other offenses (except traffic)	1,509,280	1,102,860	406,420	73.1	26.9	30.2	30.5	29.2
Suspicion	211	138	73	65.4	34.6	*	*	*
Curfew and loitering law violations	9,716	6,456	3,260	66.4	33.6	0.2	0.2	0.2

* = Less than one-tenth of 1 percent.
1 Because of rounding, the percentages may not sum to 100.   2 Violent crimes are offenses of murder and nonnegligent manslaughter, rape, robbery, and aggravated assault. Property crimes are offenses of burglary, larceny-theft, motor vehicle theft, and arson.   3 The rape figures in this table are aggregate totals of the data submitted based on both the legacy and revised Uniform Crime Reporting definitions.

Table 49. Arrests, Cities, Distribution by Race, 2019

(Number, percent; 7,979 agencies; 2019 estimated population 159,706,353.)

Offense charged	Total arrests						Percent distribution[1]						Arrests under 18					
	Total	White	Black	American Indian or Alaskan Native	Asian	Native Hawaiian or Other Pacific Islander	Total	White	Black	American Indian or Alaskan Native	Asian	Native Hawaiian or Other Pacific Islander	Total	White	Black	American Indian or Alaskan Native	Asian	Native Hawaiian or Other Pacific Islander
Total	4,928,838	3,309,189	1,401,734	136,629	65,543	15,743	100.0	67.1	28.4	2.8	1.3	0.3	377,634	233,488	129,804	9,031	4,207	1,104
Violent crime[2]	277,231	155,876	107,896	6,791	4,884	1,784	100.0	56.2	38.9	2.4	1.8	0.6	27,696	13,689	13,097	472	321	117
Murder and nonnegligent manslaughter	5,747	2,302	3,282	77	71	15	100.0	40.1	57.1	1.3	1.2	0.3	475	208	261	5	1	0
Rape[3]	11,793	7,775	3,571	183	221	43	100.0	65.9	30.3	1.6	1.9	0.4	1,883	1,273	558	22	25	5
Robbery	47,649	21,117	25,229	568	488	247	100.0	44.3	52.9	1.2	1.0	0.5	10,294	3,800	6,260	62	109	63
Aggravated assault	212,042	124,682	75,814	5,963	4,104	1,479	100.0	58.8	35.8	2.8	1.9	0.7	15,044	8,408	6,018	383	186	49
Property crime[2]	634,350	420,628	190,677	13,341	7,846	1,858	100.0	66.3	30.1	2.1	1.2	0.3	71,273	39,022	29,623	1,382	987	259
Burglary	90,948	59,468	28,580	1,340	1,278	282	100.0	65.4	31.4	1.5	1.4	0.3	11,195	6,117	4,661	222	149	46
Larceny-theft	495,523	329,865	147,378	10,937	5,892	1,451	100.0	66.6	29.7	2.2	1.2	0.3	51,322	28,768	20,612	970	774	198
Motor vehicle theft	43,032	27,972	13,415	975	575	95	100.0	65.0	31.2	2.3	1.3	0.2	7,797	3,480	4,076	172	56	13
Arson	4,847	3,323	1,304	89	101	30	100.0	68.6	26.9	1.8	2.1	0.6	959	657	274	18	8	2
Other assaults	541,249	335,868	181,943	13,249	8,241	1,948	100.0	62.1	33.6	2.4	1.5	0.4	64,335	38,503	23,645	1,293	676	218
Forgery and counterfeiting	24,484	16,304	7,434	288	408	50	100.0	66.6	30.4	1.2	1.7	0.2	491	308	173	3	6	1
Fraud	58,434	37,385	18,823	1,193	899	134	100.0	64.0	32.2	2.0	1.5	0.2	2,035	971	984	55	24	1
Embezzlement	7,969	4,734	2,949	104	164	18	100.0	59.4	37.0	1.3	2.1	0.2	339	159	166	1	12	1
Stolen property; buying, receiving, possessing	48,059	28,194	17,950	886	697	332	100.0	58.7	37.3	1.8	1.5	0.7	5,459	1,831	3,457	81	49	41
Vandalism	99,112	65,975	28,803	2,719	1,326	289	100.0	66.6	29.1	2.7	1.3	0.3	17,595	12,194	4,820	403	141	37
Weapons; carrying, possessing, etc.	81,894	43,423	36,256	853	1,004	358	100.0	53.0	44.3	1.0	1.2	0.4	9,250	5,116	3,827	124	153	30
Prostitution and commercialized vice	17,414	8,738	7,556	66	976	78	100.0	50.2	43.4	0.4	5.6	0.4	186	79	103	0	2	2
Sex offenses (except forcible rape and prostitution)	20,930	15,062	4,685	523	567	93	100.0	72.0	22.4	2.5	2.7	0.4	3,374	2,477	755	48	73	21
Drug abuse violations	741,159	519,170	200,531	10,689	8,779	1,990	100.0	70.0	27.1	1.4	1.2	0.3	42,365	31,618	9,059	1,054	497	137
Gambling	1,194	653	370	7	153	11	100.0	54.7	31.0	0.6	12.8	0.9	61	25	35	0	1	0
Offenses against the family and children	31,814	20,101	8,917	2,363	363	70	100.0	63.2	28.0	7.4	1.1	0.2	1,638	1,032	404	194	8	0
Driving under the influence	382,803	306,754	56,868	9,270	7,368	2,543	100.0	80.1	14.9	2.4	1.9	0.7	2,211	1,935	149	86	29	12
Liquor laws	86,939	66,241	14,182	5,081	1,328	107	100.0	76.2	16.3	5.8	1.5	0.1	11,996	10,076	903	863	132	22
Drunkenness	186,891	138,266	28,502	17,727	2,069	327	100.0	74.0	15.3	9.5	1.1	0.2	1,905	1,443	224	217	20	1
Disorderly conduct	172,734	107,462	54,571	8,855	1,568	278	100.0	62.2	31.6	5.1	0.9	0.2	30,045	16,508	12,481	790	222	44
Vagrancy	14,182	9,580	3,942	465	178	17	100.0	67.6	27.8	3.3	1.3	0.1	243	174	62	5	2	0
All other offenses (except traffic)	1,490,225	1,002,433	425,855	41,859	16,630	3,448	100.0	67.3	28.6	2.8	1.1	0.2	75,610	50,125	22,874	1,703	758	150
Suspicion	262	150	67	44	1	0	100.0	57.3	25.6	16.8	0.4	0.0	18	11	6	1	0	0
Curfew and loitering law violations	9,509	6,192	2,957	256	94	10	100.0	65.1	31.1	2.7	1.0	0.1	9,509	6,192	2,957	256	94	10

Table 49. Arrests, Cities, Distribution by Race, 2019—Continued

(Number, percent; 7,979 agencies; 2019 estimated population 159,706,353.)

Offense charged	Percent distribution[1]						Arrests 18 and over						Percent distribution[1]					
	Total	White	Black	American Indian or Alaskan Native	Asian	Native Hawaiian or Other Pacific Islander	Total	White	Black	American Indian or Alaskan Native	Asian	Native Hawaiian or Other Pacific Islander	Total	White	Black	American Indian or Alaskan Native	Asian	Native Hawaiian or Other Pacific Islander
Total	100.0	61.8	34.4	2.4	1.1	0.3	4,551,204	3,075,701	1,271,930	127,598	61,336	14,639	100.0	67.6	27.9	2.8	1.3	0.3
Violent crime[2]	100.0	49.4	47.3	1.7	1.2	0.4	249,535	142,187	94,799	6,319	4,563	1,667	100.0	57.0	38.0	2.5	1.8	0.7
Murder and nonnegligent manslaughter	100.0	43.8	54.9	1.1	0.2	0.0	5,272	2,094	3,021	72	70	15	100.0	39.7	57.3	1.4	1.3	0.3
Rape[3]	100.0	67.6	29.6	1.2	1.3	0.3	9,910	6,502	3,013	161	196	38	100.0	65.6	30.4	1.6	2.0	0.4
Robbery	100.0	36.9	60.8	0.6	1.1	0.6	37,355	17,317	18,969	506	379	184	100.0	46.4	50.8	1.4	1.0	0.5
Aggravated assault	100.0	55.9	40.0	2.5	1.2	0.3	196,998	116,274	69,796	5,580	3,918	1,430	100.0	59.0	35.4	2.8	2.0	0.7
Property crime[2]	100.0	54.8	41.6	1.9	1.4	0.4	563,077	381,606	161,054	11,959	6,859	1,599	100.0	67.8	28.6	2.1	1.2	0.3
Burglary	100.0	54.6	41.6	2.0	1.3	0.4	79,753	53,351	23,919	1,118	1,129	236	100.0	66.9	30.0	1.4	1.4	0.3
Larceny-theft	100.0	56.1	40.2	1.9	1.5	0.4	444,201	301,097	126,766	9,967	5,118	1,253	100.0	67.8	28.5	2.2	1.2	0.3
Motor vehicle theft	100.0	44.6	52.3	2.2	0.7	0.2	35,235	24,492	9,339	803	519	82	100.0	69.5	26.5	2.3	1.5	0.2
Arson	100.0	68.5	28.6	1.9	0.8	0.2	3,888	2,666	1,030	71	93	28	100.0	68.6	26.5	1.8	2.4	0.7
Other assaults	100.0	59.8	36.8	2.0	1.1	0.3	476,914	297,365	158,298	11,956	7,565	1,730	100.0	62.4	33.2	2.5	1.6	0.4
Forgery and counterfeiting	100.0	62.7	35.2	0.6	1.2	0.2	23,993	15,996	7,261	285	402	49	100.0	66.7	30.3	1.2	1.7	0.2
Fraud	100.0	47.7	48.4	2.7	1.2	*	56,399	36,414	17,839	1,138	875	133	100.0	64.6	31.6	2.0	1.6	0.2
Embezzlement	100.0	46.9	49.0	0.3	3.5	0.3	7,630	4,575	2,783	103	152	17	100.0	60.0	36.5	1.3	2.0	0.2
Stolen property; buying, receiving, possessing	100.0	33.5	63.3	1.5	0.9	0.8	42,600	26,363	14,493	805	648	291	100.0	61.9	34.0	1.9	1.5	0.7
Vandalism	100.0	69.3	27.4	2.3	0.8	0.2	81,517	53,781	23,983	2,316	1,185	252	100.0	66.0	29.4	2.8	1.5	0.3
Weapons; carrying, possessing, etc.	100.0	55.3	41.4	1.3	1.7	0.3	72,644	38,307	32,429	729	851	328	100.0	52.7	44.6	1.0	1.2	0.5
Prostitution and commercialized vice	100.0	42.5	55.4	0.0	1.1	1.1	17,228	8,659	7,453	66	974	76	100.0	50.3	43.3	0.4	5.7	0.4
Sex offenses (except forcible rape and prostitution)	100.0	73.4	22.4	1.4	2.2	0.6	17,556	12,585	3,930	475	494	72	100.0	71.7	22.4	2.7	2.8	0.4
Drug abuse violations	100.0	74.6	21.4	2.5	1.2	0.3	698,794	487,552	191,472	9,635	8,282	1,853	100.0	69.8	27.4	1.4	1.2	0.3
Gambling	100.0	41.0	57.4	0.0	1.6	0.0	1,133	628	335	7	152	11	100.0	55.4	29.6	0.6	13.4	1.0
Offenses against the family and children	100.0	63.0	24.7	11.8	0.5	0.0	30,176	19,069	8,513	2,169	355	70	100.0	63.2	28.2	7.2	1.2	0.2
Driving under the influence	100.0	87.5	6.7	3.9	1.3	0.5	380,592	304,819	56,719	9,184	7,339	2,531	100.0	80.1	14.9	2.4	1.9	0.7
Liquor laws	100.0	84.0	7.5	7.2	1.1	0.2	74,943	56,165	13,279	4,218	1,196	85	100.0	74.9	17.7	5.6	1.6	0.1
Drunkenness	100.0	75.7	11.8	11.4	1.0	0.1	184,986	136,823	28,278	17,510	2,049	326	100.0	74.0	15.3	9.5	1.1	0.2
Disorderly conduct	100.0	54.9	41.5	2.6	0.7	0.1	142,689	90,954	42,090	8,065	1,346	234	100.0	63.7	29.5	5.7	0.9	0.2
Vagrancy	100.0	71.6	25.5	2.1	0.8	0.0	13,939	9,406	3,880	460	176	17	100.0	67.5	27.8	3.3	1.3	0.1
All other offenses (except traffic)	100.0	66.3	30.3	2.3	1.0	0.2	1,414,615	952,308	402,981	40,156	15,872	3,298	100.0	67.3	28.5	2.8	1.1	0.2
Suspicion	100.0	61.1	33.3	5.6	0.0	0.0	244	139	61	43	1	0	100.0	57.0	25.0	17.6	0.4	0.0
Curfew and loitering law violations	100.0	65.1	31.1	2.7	1.0	0.1	NA	NA	NA	NA	NA	NA	NA	NA	NA	NA	NA	NA

NA = Not available.
* = Less than one-tenth of one percent.
1 Because of rounding, the percentages may not sum to 100.   2 Violent crimes are offenses of murder and nonnegligent manslaughter, rape, robbery, and aggravated assault. Property crimes are offenses of burglary, larceny-theft, motor vehicle theft, and arson.   3 The rape figures in this table are aggregate totals of the data submitted based on both the legacy and revised Uniform Crime Reporting definitions.

Table 49A. Arrests, Cities, Distribution by Ethnicity, 2019

(Number, percent; 7,979 agencies; 2019 estimated population 159,706,353.)

Offense charged	Total arrests			Percent distribution[1]			Arrests under 18		
	Total[2]	Hispanic or Latino	Not Hispanic or Latino	Total[2]	Hispanic or Latino	Not Hispanic or Latino	Total[2]	Hispanic or Latino	Not Hispanic or Latino
Total	4,324,743	876,586	3,448,157	100.0	20.3	79.7	322,540	82,344	240,196
Violent crime[3]	248,972	66,736	182,236	100.0	26.8	73.2	24,782	7,141	17,641
Murder and nonnegligent manslaughter	4,834	1,015	3,819	100.0	21.0	79.0	389	129	260
Rape[4]	10,284	3,086	7,198	100.0	30.0	70.0	1,601	391	1,210
Robbery	43,139	10,579	32,560	100.0	24.5	75.5	9,378	2,548	6,830
Aggravated assault	190,715	52,056	138,659	100.0	27.3	72.7	13,414	4,073	9,341
Property crime[3]	549,117	96,332	452,785	100.0	17.5	82.5	60,569	13,732	46,837
Burglary	82,157	19,060	63,097	100.0	23.2	76.8	9,840	2,651	7,189
Larceny-theft	424,423	66,149	358,274	100.0	15.6	84.4	43,135	9,150	33,985
Motor vehicle theft	38,302	10,261	28,041	100.0	26.8	73.2	6,770	1,761	5,009
Arson	4,235	862	3,373	100.0	20.4	79.6	824	170	654
Other assaults	471,728	96,674	375,054	100.0	20.5	79.5	55,771	14,478	41,293
Forgery and counterfeiting	21,831	3,740	18,091	100.0	17.1	82.9	431	106	325
Fraud	51,175	7,780	43,395	100.0	15.2	84.8	1,737	342	1,395
Embezzlement	6,671	942	5,729	100.0	14.1	85.9	264	56	208
Stolen property; buying, receiving, possessing	42,349	8,340	34,009	100.0	19.7	80.3	4,783	947	3,836
Vandalism	86,698	18,147	68,551	100.0	20.9	79.1	15,214	3,662	11,552
Weapons; carrying, possessing, etc.	71,101	17,840	53,261	100.0	25.1	74.9	8,142	2,933	5,209
Prostitution and commercialized vice	16,153	3,152	13,001	100.0	19.5	80.5	173	29	144
Sex offenses (except forcible rape and prostitution)	18,755	5,524	13,231	100.0	29.5	70.5	2,914	890	2,024
Drug abuse violations	675,772	151,708	524,064	100.0	22.4	77.6	37,816	12,310	25,506
Gambling	1,149	269	880	100.0	23.4	76.6	55	8	47
Offenses against the family and children	27,028	4,170	22,858	100.0	15.4	84.6	1,400	340	1,060
Driving under the influence	333,695	89,187	244,508	100.0	26.7	73.3	1,854	585	1,269
Liquor laws	72,665	12,038	60,627	100.0	16.6	83.4	10,162	2,270	7,892
Drunkenness	177,409	40,212	137,197	100.0	22.7	77.3	1,789	673	1,116
Disorderly conduct	137,791	20,511	117,280	100.0	14.9	85.1	23,477	5,021	18,456
Vagrancy	13,377	1,805	11,572	100.0	13.5	86.5	181	65	116
All other offenses (except traffic)	1,293,143	229,307	1,063,836	100.0	17.7	82.3	63,057	14,612	48,445
Suspicion	207	28	179	100.0	13.5	86.5	12	0	12
Curfew and loitering law violations	7,957	2,144	5,813	100.0	26.9	73.1	7,957	2,144	5,813

Table 49A. Arrests, Cities, Distribution by Ethnicity, 2019—Continued

(Number, percent; 7,979 agencies; 2019 estimated population 159,706,353.)

Offense charged	Percent distribution[1]			Arrests 18 and over			Percent distribution[1]		
	Total[2]	Hispanic or Latino	Not Hispanic or Latino	Total[2]	Hispanic or Latino	Not Hispanic or Latino	Total[2]	Hispanic or Latino	Not Hispanic or Latino
Total	100.0	25.5	74.5	4,002,203	794,242	3,207,961	100.0	19.8	80.2
Violent crime[3]	100.0	28.8	71.2	224,190	59,595	164,595	100.0	26.6	73.4
Murder and nonnegligent manslaughter	100.0	33.2	66.8	4,445	886	3,559	100.0	19.9	80.1
Rape[4]	100.0	24.4	75.6	8,683	2,695	5,988	100.0	31.0	69.0
Robbery	100.0	27.2	72.8	33,761	8,031	25,730	100.0	23.8	76.2
Aggravated assault	100.0	30.4	69.6	177,301	47,983	129,318	100.0	27.1	72.9
Property crime[3]	100.0	22.7	77.3	488,548	82,600	405,948	100.0	16.9	83.1
Burglary	100.0	26.9	73.1	72,317	16,409	55,908	100.0	22.7	77.3
Larceny-theft	100.0	21.2	78.8	381,288	56,999	324,289	100.0	14.9	85.1
Motor vehicle theft	100.0	26.0	74.0	31,532	8,500	23,032	100.0	27.0	73.0
Arson	100.0	20.6	79.4	3,411	692	2,719	100.0	20.3	79.7
Other assaults	100.0	26.0	74.0	415,957	82,196	333,761	100.0	19.8	80.2
Forgery and counterfeiting	100.0	24.6	75.4	21,400	3,634	17,766	100.0	17.0	83.0
Fraud	100.0	19.7	80.3	49,438	7,438	42,000	100.0	15.0	85.0
Embezzlement	100.0	21.2	78.8	6,407	886	5,521	100.0	13.8	86.2
Stolen property; buying, receiving, possessing	100.0	19.8	80.2	37,566	7,393	30,173	100.0	19.7	80.3
Vandalism	100.0	24.1	75.9	71,484	14,485	56,999	100.0	20.3	79.7
Weapons; carrying, possessing, etc.	100.0	36.0	64.0	62,959	14,907	48,052	100.0	23.7	76.3
Prostitution and commercialized vice	100.0	16.8	83.2	15,980	3,123	12,857	100.0	19.5	80.5
Sex offenses (except forcible rape and prostitution)	100.0	30.5	69.5	15,841	4,634	11,207	100.0	29.3	70.7
Drug abuse violations	100.0	32.6	67.4	637,956	139,398	498,558	100.0	21.9	78.1
Gambling	100.0	14.5	85.5	1,094	261	833	100.0	23.9	76.1
Offenses against the family and children	100.0	24.3	75.7	25,628	3,830	21,798	100.0	14.9	85.1
Driving under the influence	100.0	31.6	68.4	331,841	88,602	243,239	100.0	26.7	73.3
Liquor laws	100.0	22.3	77.7	62,503	9,768	52,735	100.0	15.6	84.4
Drunkenness	100.0	37.6	62.4	175,620	39,539	136,081	100.0	22.5	77.5
Disorderly conduct	100.0	21.4	78.6	114,314	15,490	98,824	100.0	13.6	86.4
Vagrancy	100.0	35.9	64.1	13,196	1,740	11,456	100.0	13.2	86.8
All other offenses (except traffic)	100.0	23.2	76.8	1,230,086	214,695	1,015,391	100.0	17.5	82.5
Suspicion	100.0	0.0	100.0	195	28	167	100.0	14.4	85.6
Curfew and loitering law violations	100.0	26.9	73.1	NA	NA	NA	NA	NA	NA

NA = Not available.
1 Because of rounding, the percentages may not sum to 100.   2 The ethnicity totals are representative of those agencies that provided ethnicity breakdowns. Not all agencies provide ethnicity data; therefore, the race and ethnicity totals will not be equal.   3 Violent crimes are offenses of murder and nonnegligent manslaughter, rape, robbery, and aggravated assault. Property crimes are offenses of burglary, larceny-theft, motor vehicle theft, and arson.   4 The rape figures in this table are aggregate totals of the data submitted based on both the legacy and revised Uniform Crime Reporting definitions.

Table 50. Arrest Trends, Metropolitan Counties, 2018–2019

(Number, percent change; 1,095 agencies; 2019 estimated population 44,725,723; 2018 estimated population 44,615,161.)

Offense charged	Number of persons arrested								
	Total, all ages			Under 18 years of age			18 years of age and over		
	2018	2019	Percent change	2018	2019	Percent change	2018	2019	Percent change
Total[1]	1,272,399	1,220,040	-4.1	73,503	70,972	-3.4	1,198,896	1,149,068	-4.2
Violent crime[2]	58,579	56,370	-3.8	5,672	5,551	-2.1	52,907	50,819	-3.9
Murder and nonnegligent manslaughter	1,361	1,333	-2.1	81	80	-1.2	1,280	1,253	-2.1
Rape[3]	3,141	3,169	+0.9	578	624	+8.0	2,563	2,545	-0.7
Robbery	7,941	7,354	-7.4	1,666	1,687	+1.3	6,275	5,667	-9.7
Aggravated assault	46,136	44,514	-3.5	3,347	3,160	-5.6	42,789	41,354	-3.4
Property crime[2]	111,436	104,346	-6.4	12,128	11,434	-5.7	99,308	92,912	-6.4
Burglary	20,156	18,321	-9.1	2,277	2,131	-6.4	17,879	16,190	-9.4
Larceny-theft	78,622	74,911	-4.7	8,213	7,761	-5.5	70,409	67,150	-4.6
Motor vehicle theft	11,539	10,163	-11.9	1,398	1,339	-4.2	10,141	8,824	-13.0
Arson	1,119	951	-15.0	240	203	-15.4	879	748	-14.9
Other assaults	110,616	107,839	-2.5	15,265	15,881	+4.0	95,351	91,958	-3.6
Forgery and counterfeiting	5,856	5,335	-8.9	95	88	-7.4	5,761	5,247	-8.9
Fraud	14,617	14,313	-2.1	401	393	-2.0	14,216	13,920	-2.1
Embezzlement	1,528	1,461	-4.4	32	45	+40.6	1,496	1,416	-5.3
Stolen property; buying, receiving, possessing	11,763	10,686	-9.2	795	683	-14.1	10,968	10,003	-8.8
Vandalism	18,767	18,856	+0.5	3,183	3,336	+4.8	15,584	15,520	-0.4
Weapons; carrying, possessing, etc.	19,228	19,338	+0.6	1,761	1,704	-3.2	17,467	17,634	+1.0
Prostitution and commercialized vice	2,014	2,144	+6.5	29	21	-27.6	1,985	2,123	+7.0
Sex offenses (except forcible rape and prostitution)	5,762	5,485	-4.8	959	845	-11.9	4,803	4,640	-3.4
Drug abuse violations	224,203	204,582	-8.8	10,527	8,779	-16.6	213,676	195,803	-8.4
Gambling	370	404	+9.2	14	22	+57.1	356	382	+7.3
Offenses against the family and children	19,628	16,728	-14.8	344	284	-17.4	19,284	16,444	-14.7
Driving under the influence	169,086	164,939	-2.5	732	718	-1.9	168,354	164,221	-2.5
Liquor laws	15,021	13,575	-9.6	2,778	2,668	-4.0	12,243	10,907	-10.9
Drunkenness	21,563	20,679	-4.1	215	269	+25.1	21,348	20,410	-4.4
Disorderly conduct	23,839	23,048	-3.3	4,342	4,269	-1.7	19,497	18,779	-3.7
Vagrancy	1,402	1,476	+5.3	40	10	-75.0	1,362	1,466	+7.6
All other offenses (except traffic)	436,115	427,530	-2.0	13,185	13,066	-0.9	422,930	414,464	-2.0
Suspicion	228	70	-69.3	3	3	0.0	225	67	-70.2
Curfew and loitering law violations	1,006	906	-9.9	1,006	906	-9.9	NA	NA	NA

NA = Not available.

1 Does not include suspicion.   2 Violent crimes in this table are offenses of murder and nonnegligent manslaughter, rape, robbery, and aggravated assault. Property crimes are offenses of burglary, larceny-theft, motor vehicle theft, and arson.   3 The rape figures in this table are aggregate totals of the data submitted based on both the legacy and revised Uniform Crime Reporting definitions.

Table 51. Arrest Trends, Metropolitan Counties, by Age and Sex, 2018–2019

(Number, percent change; 1,095 agencies; 2019 estimated population 44,725,723; 2018 estimated population 44,615,161.)

Offense charged	Male						Female					
	Total			Under 18			Total			Under 18		
	2018	2019	Percent change	2018	2019	Percent change	2018	2019	Percent change	2018	2019	Percent change
Total[1]	937,827	898,464	-4.2	52,229	50,121	-4.0	334,572	321,576	-3.9	21,274	20,851	-2.0
Violent crime[2]	46,880	45,101	-3.8	4,539	4,488	-1.1	11,699	11,269	-3.7	1,133	1,063	-6.2
Murder and nonnegligent manslaughter	1,198	1,192	-0.5	71	67	-5.6	163	141	-13.5	10	13	+30.0
Rape[3]	3,053	3,060	+0.2	561	591	+5.3	88	109	+23.9	17	33	+94.1
Robbery	6,775	6,274	-7.4	1,490	1,512	+1.5	1,166	1,080	-7.4	176	175	-0.6
Aggravated assault	35,854	34,575	-3.6	2,417	2,318	-4.1	10,282	9,939	-3.3	930	842	-9.5
Property crime[2]	72,656	67,600	-7.0	8,424	7,855	-6.8	38,780	36,746	-5.2	3,704	3,579	-3.4
Burglary	16,388	14,783	-9.8	2,001	1,859	-7.1	3,768	3,538	-6.1	276	272	-1.4
Larceny-theft	46,480	44,246	-4.8	5,073	4,762	-6.1	32,142	30,665	-4.6	3,140	2,999	-4.5
Motor vehicle theft	8,909	7,806	-12.4	1,146	1,062	-7.3	2,630	2,357	-10.4	252	277	+9.9
Arson	879	765	-13.0	204	172	-15.7	240	186	-22.5	36	31	-13.9
Other assaults	78,860	76,105	-3.5	9,703	9,881	+1.8	31,756	31,734	-0.1	5,562	6,000	+7.9
Forgery and counterfeiting	3,871	3,675	-5.1	79	76	-3.8	1,985	1,660	-16.4	16	12	-25.0
Fraud	9,413	9,221	-2.0	266	272	+2.3	5,204	5,092	-2.2	135	121	-10.4
Embezzlement	792	768	-3.0	19	21	+10.5	736	693	-5.8	13	24	+84.6
Stolen property; buying, receiving, possessing	9,237	8,437	-8.7	653	561	-14.1	2,526	2,249	-11.0	142	122	-14.1
Vandalism	14,674	14,698	+0.2	2,592	2,694	+3.9	4,093	4,158	+1.6	591	642	+8.6
Weapons; carrying, possessing, etc.	17,224	17,430	+1.2	1,519	1,478	-2.7	2,004	1,908	-4.8	242	226	-6.6
Prostitution and commercialized vice	926	1,070	+15.6	19	15	-21.1	1,088	1,074	-1.3	10	6	-40.0
Sex offenses (except forcible rape and prostitution)	5,404	5,177	-4.2	866	777	-10.3	358	308	-14.0	93	68	-26.9
Drug abuse violations	167,897	152,252	-9.3	7,909	6,618	-16.3	56,306	52,330	-7.1	2,618	2,161	-17.5
Gambling	293	296	+1.0	13	17	+30.8	77	108	+40.3	1	5	+400.0
Offenses against the family and children	15,288	12,969	-15.2	234	175	-25.2	4,340	3,759	-13.4	110	109	-0.9
Driving under the influence	126,737	123,528	-2.5	566	549	-3.0	42,349	41,411	-2.2	166	169	+1.8
Liquor laws	10,329	9,510	-7.9	1,562	1,540	-1.4	4,692	4,065	-13.4	1,216	1,128	-7.2
Drunkenness	16,813	16,200	-3.6	134	195	+45.5	4,750	4,479	-5.7	81	74	-8.6
Disorderly conduct	17,123	16,416	-4.1	2,892	2,816	-2.6	6,716	6,632	-1.3	1,450	1,453	+0.2
Vagrancy	1,024	1,131	+10.4	25	8	-68.0	378	345	-8.7	15	2	-86.7
All other offenses (except traffic)	321,731	316,272	-1.7	9,560	9,477	-0.9	114,384	111,258	-2.7	3,625	3,589	-1.0
Suspicion	166	56	-66.3	3	3	0.0	62	14	-77.4	0	0	
Curfew and loitering law violations	655	608	-7.2	655	608	-7.2	351	298	-15.1	351	298	-15.1

1 Does not include suspicion.   2 Violent crimes are offenses of murder and nonnegligent manslaughter, rape, robbery, and aggravated assault. Property crimes are offenses of burglary, larceny-theft, motor vehicle theft, and arson.   3 The rape figures in this table are aggregate totals of the data submitted based on both the legacy and revised Uniform Crime Reporting definitions.

Table 52. Arrests, Metropolitan Counties, Distribution by Age, 2019

(Number, percent; 1,230 agencies; 2019 estimated population 51,841,134.)

Offense charged	Total, all ages	Ages under 15	Ages under 18	Ages 18 and over	Under 10	10–12	13–14	15	16	17	18	19	20
Total	1,370,534	23,951	78,478	1,292,056	500	5,727	17,724	15,020	17,893	21,614	29,198	34,003	36,264
Total percent distribution[1]	100.0	1.7	5.7	94.3	*	0.4	1.3	1.1	1.3	1.6	2.1	2.5	2.6
Violent crime[2]	61,801	1,874	6,023	55,778	44	504	1,326	1,228	1,354	1,567	1,763	1,768	1,728
Violent crime percent distribution[1]	100.0	3.0	9.7	90.3	0.1	0.8	2.1	2.0	2.2	2.5	2.9	2.9	2.8
Murder and nonnegligent manslaughter	1,496	12	90	1,406	0	3	9	11	31	36	68	67	74
Rape[3]	3,446	274	675	2,771	12	84	178	128	130	143	163	136	121
Robbery	7,929	394	1,804	6,125	3	50	341	390	495	525	572	439	355
Aggravated assault	48,930	1,194	3,454	45,476	29	367	798	699	698	863	960	1,126	1,178
Property crime[2]	116,025	3,580	12,580	103,445	59	696	2,825	2,709	2,931	3,360	4,034	3,765	3,504
Property crime percent distribution[1]	100.0	3.1	10.8	89.2	0.1	0.6	2.4	2.3	2.5	2.9	3.5	3.2	3.0
Burglary	20,629	742	2,419	18,210	18	137	587	511	563	603	680	660	589
Larceny-theft	83,278	2,372	8,432	74,846	31	492	1,849	1,779	1,930	2,351	2,977	2,727	2,576
Motor vehicle theft	11,057	347	1,498	9,559	0	30	317	376	392	383	358	356	325
Arson	1,061	119	231	830	10	37	72	43	46	23	19	22	14
Other assaults	121,001	7,650	17,870	103,131	207	2,174	5,269	3,443	3,576	3,201	2,382	2,335	2,496
Forgery and counterfeiting	5,998	14	99	5,899	0	3	11	15	28	42	106	181	244
Fraud	15,770	93	426	15,344	0	20	73	72	111	150	246	327	343
Embezzlement	1,589	3	51	1,538	0	0	3	3	13	32	66	85	67
Stolen property; buying, receiving, possessing	11,868	133	759	11,109	0	11	122	165	196	265	337	344	369
Vandalism	20,924	1,371	3,649	17,275	62	361	948	696	788	794	707	639	607
Weapons; carrying, possessing, etc.	21,245	626	1,878	19,367	11	175	440	350	398	504	702	693	714
Prostitution and commercialized vice	2,308	4	22	2,286	0	2	2	3	8	7	29	48	59
Sex offenses (except forcible rape and prostitution)	5,879	457	909	4,970	10	132	315	158	144	150	154	143	134
Drug abuse violations	225,843	1,562	9,768	216,075	11	228	1,323	1,595	2,469	4,142	7,273	8,497	8,715
Gambling	603	21	86	517	0	2	19	13	28	24	5	19	9
Offenses against the family and children	19,510	97	321	19,189	5	14	78	65	84	75	88	117	141
Driving under the influence	181,678	23	789	180,889	3	9	11	32	166	568	1,643	2,702	3,348
Liquor laws	14,407	354	2,840	11,567	1	56	297	363	778	1,345	1,763	1,941	1,584
Drunkenness	22,232	47	286	21,946	0	6	41	41	76	122	293	348	411
Disorderly conduct	25,038	1,833	4,632	20,406	30	473	1,330	984	978	837	599	509	541
Vagrancy	1,543	2	10	1,533	0	0	2	1	2	5	24	19	34
All other offenses (except traffic)	494,274	3,906	14,549	479,725	50	804	3,052	2,887	3,513	4,243	6,980	9,523	11,214
Suspicion	71	0	4	67	0	0	0	0	2	2	4	0	2
Curfew and loitering law violations	927	301	927	NA	7	57	237	197	250	179	NA	NA	NA

Table 52. Arrests, Metropolitan Counties, Distribution by Age, 2019—Continued

(Number, percent; 1,230 agencies; 2019 estimated population 51,841,134.)

Offense charged	21	22	23	24	25–29	30–34	35–39	40–44	45–49	50–54	55–59	60–64	65 and over
Total	38,820	40,050	42,132	43,797	238,030	215,208	181,549	125,896	93,895	73,173	53,842	27,323	18,876
Total percent distribution[1]	2.8	2.9	3.1	3.2	17.4	15.7	13.2	9.2	6.9	5.3	3.9	2.0	1.4
Violent crime[2]	1,824	1,754	1,891	1,877	10,031	8,866	7,361	5,040	3,922	3,048	2,434	1,344	1,127
Violent crime percent distribution[1]	3.0	2.8	3.1	3.0	16.2	14.3	11.9	8.2	6.3	4.9	3.9	2.2	1.8
Murder and nonnegligent manslaughter	66	63	55	54	262	196	150	102	84	61	48	26	30
Rape[3]	110	85	77	98	368	384	360	217	201	154	120	79	98
Robbery	323	304	256	256	1,183	890	601	351	209	191	117	54	24
Aggravated assault	1,325	1,302	1,503	1,469	8,218	7,396	6,250	4,370	3,428	2,642	2,149	1,185	975
Property crime[2]	3,124	3,066	3,145	3,448	18,505	17,277	13,933	9,444	7,110	5,784	4,063	1,970	1,273
Property crime percent distribution[1]	2.7	2.6	2.7	3.0	15.9	14.9	12.0	8.1	6.1	5.0	3.5	1.7	1.1
Burglary	550	525	609	618	3,446	3,374	2,615	1,640	1,155	852	538	229	130
Larceny-theft	2,265	2,209	2,192	2,432	12,927	11,947	9,853	6,893	5,315	4,527	3,279	1,642	1,085
Motor vehicle theft	292	308	322	367	1,988	1,813	1,344	829	585	357	199	75	41
Arson	17	24	22	31	144	143	121	82	55	48	47	24	17
Other assaults	2,886	2,946	3,057	3,177	17,549	16,752	14,837	10,527	8,001	6,552	4,879	2,567	2,188
Forgery and counterfeiting	171	178	173	202	1,116	976	892	600	422	311	192	91	44
Fraud	405	387	411	497	2,742	2,648	2,305	1,602	1,267	954	653	322	235
Embezzlement	46	53	50	48	269	223	179	142	124	74	71	29	12
Stolen property; buying, receiving, possessing	330	352	388	352	2,180	2,052	1,698	1,083	697	475	290	112	50
Vandalism	628	637	636	585	3,342	2,745	2,236	1,444	1,062	846	598	298	265
Weapons; carrying, possessing, etc.	812	778	766	868	3,991	3,032	2,357	1,537	1,089	868	633	296	231
Prostitution and commercialized vice	79	68	71	77	439	389	291	205	204	131	106	44	46
Sex offenses (except forcible rape and prostitution)	116	110	118	109	641	671	659	478	427	358	308	232	312
Drug abuse violations	8,587	8,176	8,445	8,418	41,786	34,930	28,466	18,651	12,913	9,709	7,027	3,043	1,439
Gambling	11	8	8	19	73	64	71	62	56	45	36	11	20
Offenses against the family and children	185	234	292	337	3,012	3,898	3,967	2,748	1,945	1,164	663	276	122
Driving under the influence	5,575	6,213	6,774	7,112	34,879	28,141	22,779	16,981	13,707	11,636	9,565	5,531	4,303
Liquor laws	307	227	209	219	951	880	817	667	576	529	471	271	155
Drunkenness	573	610	659	667	3,579	3,547	3,031	2,195	1,814	1,646	1,432	774	367
Disorderly conduct	625	607	686	637	3,388	3,032	2,665	1,982	1,604	1,322	1,029	644	536
Vagrancy	24	27	34	35	200	196	174	173	133	192	139	88	41
All other offenses (except traffic)	12,502	13,615	14,314	15,113	89,349	84,879	72,822	50,332	36,818	27,524	19,250	9,380	6,110
Suspicion	10	4	5	0	8	10	9	3	4	5	3	0	0
Curfew and loitering law violations	NA	NA	NA	NA	NA	NA	NA	NA	NA	NA	NA	NA	NA

NA = Not available.

* = Less than one-tenth of one percent.

1 Because of rounding, the percentages may not sum to 100.   2 Violent crimes are offenses of murder and nonnegligent manslaughter, rape, robbery, and aggravated assault. Property crimes are offenses of burglary, larceny-theft, motor vehicle theft, and arson.   3 The rape figures in this table are aggregate totals of the data submitted based on both the legacy and revised Uniform Crime Reporting definitions.

Table 53. Arrests, Metropolitan Counties, Persons Under 15, 18, 21, and 25 Years of Age, 2019

(Number, percent; 1,230 agencies; 2019 estimated population 51,841,134.)

Offense charged	Total, all ages	Number of persons arrested				Percent of total all ages			
		Under 15	Under 18	Under 21	Under 25	Under 15	Under 18	Under 21	Under 25
Total	1,370,534	23,951	78,478	177,943	342,742	1.7	5.7	13.0	25.0
Violent crime[1]	61,801	1,874	6,023	11,282	18,628	3.0	9.7	18.3	30.1
Murder and nonnegligent manslaughter	1,496	12	90	299	537	0.8	6.0	20.0	35.9
Rape[2]	3,446	274	675	1,095	1,465	8.0	19.6	31.8	42.5
Robbery	7,929	394	1,804	3,170	4,309	5.0	22.8	40.0	54.3
Aggravated assault	48,930	1,194	3,454	6,718	12,317	2.4	7.1	13.7	25.2
Property crime[1]	116,025	3,580	12,580	23,883	36,666	3.1	10.8	20.6	31.6
Burglary	20,629	742	2,419	4,348	6,650	3.6	11.7	21.1	32.2
Larceny-theft	83,278	2,372	8,432	16,712	25,810	2.8	10.1	20.1	31.0
Motor vehicle theft	11,057	347	1,498	2,537	3,826	3.1	13.5	22.9	34.6
Arson	1,061	119	231	286	380	11.2	21.8	27.0	35.8
Other assaults	121,001	7,650	17,870	25,083	37,149	6.3	14.8	20.7	30.7
Forgery and counterfeiting	5,998	14	99	630	1,354	0.2	1.7	10.5	22.6
Fraud	15,770	93	426	1,342	3,042	0.6	2.7	8.5	19.3
Embezzlement	1,589	3	51	269	466	0.2	3.2	16.9	29.3
Stolen property; buying, receiving, possessing	11,868	133	759	1,809	3,231	1.1	6.4	15.2	27.2
Vandalism	20,924	1,371	3,649	5,602	8,088	6.6	17.4	26.8	38.7
Weapons; carrying, possessing, etc.	21,245	626	1,878	3,987	7,211	2.9	8.8	18.8	33.9
Prostitution and commercialized vice	2,308	4	22	158	453	0.2	1.0	6.8	19.6
Sex offenses (except forcible rape and prostitution)	5,879	457	909	1,340	1,793	7.8	15.5	22.8	30.5
Drug abuse violations	225,843	1,562	9,768	34,253	67,879	0.7	4.3	15.2	30.1
Gambling	603	21	86	119	165	3.5	14.3	19.7	27.4
Offenses against the family and children	19,510	97	321	667	1,715	0.5	1.6	3.4	8.8
Driving under the influence	181,678	23	789	8,482	34,156	*	0.4	4.7	18.8
Liquor laws	14,407	354	2,840	8,128	9,090	2.5	19.7	56.4	63.1
Drunkenness	22,232	47	286	1,338	3,847	0.2	1.3	6.0	17.3
Disorderly conduct	25,038	1,833	4,632	6,281	8,836	7.3	18.5	25.1	35.3
Vagrancy	1,543	2	10	87	207	0.1	0.6	5.6	13.4
All other offenses (except traffic)	494,274	3,906	14,549	42,266	97,810	0.8	2.9	8.6	19.8
Suspicion	71	0	4	10	29	0.0	5.6	14.1	40.8
Curfew and loitering law violations	927	301	927	927	927	32.5	100.0	100.0	100.0

* = Less than one-tenth of one percent.
1 Violent crimes are offenses of murder and nonnegligent manslaughter, rape, robbery, and aggravated assault. Property crimes are offenses of burglary, larceny-theft, motor vehicle theft, and arson.   2 The rape figures in this table are aggregate totals of the data submitted based on both the legacy and revised Uniform Crime Reporting definitions.

Table 54. Arrests, Metropolitan Counties, Distribution by Sex, 2019

(Number, percent; 1,230 agencies; 2019 estimated population 51,841,134.)

Offense charged	Number of persons arrested			Percent male	Percent female	Percent distribution[1]		
	Total	Male	Female			Total	Male	Female
Total	1,370,534	1,003,351	367,183	73.2	26.8	100.0	100.0	100.0
Violent crime[2]	61,801	49,370	12,431	79.9	20.1	4.5	4.9	3.4
Murder and nonnegligent manslaughter	1,496	1,341	155	89.6	10.4	0.1	0.1	*
Rape[3]	3,446	3,312	134	96.1	3.9	0.3	0.3	*
Robbery	7,929	6,730	1,199	84.9	15.1	0.6	0.7	0.3
Aggravated assault	48,930	37,987	10,943	77.6	22.4	3.6	3.8	3.0
Property crime[2]	116,025	74,985	41,040	64.6	35.4	8.5	7.5	11.2
Burglary	20,629	16,574	4,055	80.3	19.7	1.5	1.7	1.1
Larceny-theft	83,278	49,079	34,199	58.9	41.1	6.1	4.9	9.3
Motor vehicle theft	11,057	8,483	2,574	76.7	23.3	0.8	0.8	0.7
Arson	1,061	849	212	80.0	20.0	0.1	0.1	0.1
Other assaults	121,001	85,297	35,704	70.5	29.5	8.8	8.5	9.7
Forgery and counterfeiting	5,998	4,093	1,905	68.2	31.8	0.4	0.4	0.5
Fraud	15,770	10,091	5,679	64.0	36.0	1.2	1.0	1.5
Embezzlement	1,589	845	744	53.2	46.8	0.1	0.1	0.2
Stolen property; buying, receiving, possessing	11,868	9,343	2,525	78.7	21.3	0.9	0.9	0.7
Vandalism	20,924	16,232	4,692	77.6	22.4	1.5	1.6	1.3
Weapons; carrying, possessing, etc.	21,245	19,065	2,180	89.7	10.3	1.6	1.9	0.6
Prostitution and commercialized vice	2,308	1,164	1,144	50.4	49.6	0.2	0.1	0.3
Sex offenses (except forcible rape and prostitution)	5,879	5,507	372	93.7	6.3	0.4	0.5	0.1
Drug abuse violations	225,843	166,220	59,623	73.6	26.4	16.5	16.6	16.2
Gambling	603	387	216	64.2	35.8	*	*	0.1
Offenses against the family and children	19,510	15,157	4,353	77.7	22.3	1.4	1.5	1.2
Driving under the influence	181,678	134,547	47,131	74.1	25.9	13.3	13.4	12.8
Liquor laws	14,407	10,068	4,339	69.9	30.1	1.1	1.0	1.2
Drunkenness	22,232	17,396	4,836	78.2	21.8	1.6	1.7	1.3
Disorderly conduct	25,038	17,781	7,257	71.0	29.0	1.8	1.8	2.0
Vagrancy	1,543	1,183	360	76.7	23.3	0.1	0.1	0.1
All other offenses (except traffic)	494,274	363,942	130,332	73.6	26.4	36.1	36.3	35.5
Suspicion	71	56	15	78.9	21.1	*	*	*
Curfew and loitering law violations	927	622	305	67.1	32.9	0.1	0.1	0.1

* = Less than one-tenth of one percent.
1 Because of rounding, the percentages may not sum to 100.   2 Violent crimes are offenses of murder and nonnegligent manslaughter, rape, robbery, and aggravated assault. Property crimes are offenses of burglary, larceny-theft, motor vehicle theft, and arson.   3 The rape figures in this table are aggregate totals of the data submitted based on both the legacy and revised Uniform Crime Reporting definitions.

Table 55. Arrests, Metropolitan Counties, Distribution by Race, 2019

(Number, percent; 1,230 agencies; 2019 estimated population 51,841,134.)

Offense charged	Total arrests						Percent distribution[1]						Arrests under 18					
	Total	White	Black	American Indian or Alaskan Native	Asian	Native Hawaiian or Other Pacific Islander	Total	White	Black	American Indian or Alaskan Native	Asian	Native Hawaiian or Other Pacific Islander	Total	White	Black	American Indian or Alaskan Native	Asian	Native Hawaiian or Other Pacific Islander
Total	1,360,157	975,178	350,940	11,505	17,866	4,668	100.0	71.7	25.8	0.8	1.3	0.3	77,606	47,117	28,517	684	956	332
Violent crime[2]	61,614	40,745	19,319	452	869	229	100.0	66.1	31.4	0.7	1.4	0.4	6,003	3,013	2,867	39	64	20
Murder and nonnegligent manslaughter	1,687	966	686	14	11	10	100.0	57.3	40.7	0.8	0.7	0.6	123	69	47	7	0	0
Rape[3]	3,387	2,571	736	14	50	16	100.0	75.9	21.7	0.4	1.5	0.5	661	491	160	0	9	1
Robbery	7,898	3,512	4,240	32	79	35	100.0	44.5	53.7	0.4	1.0	0.4	1,794	548	1,212	4	19	11
Aggravated assault	48,642	33,696	13,657	392	729	168	100.0	69.3	28.1	0.8	1.5	0.3	3,425	1,905	1,448	28	36	8
Property crime[2]	115,007	74,778	37,731	557	1,532	409	100.0	65.0	32.8	0.5	1.3	0.4	12,449	6,461	5,702	64	178	44
Burglary	20,493	15,248	4,913	92	168	72	100.0	74.4	24.0	0.4	0.8	0.4	2,392	1,455	889	16	17	15
Larceny-theft	82,457	50,753	29,921	371	1,203	209	100.0	61.6	36.3	0.4	1.5	0.3	8,339	4,055	4,093	28	139	24
Motor vehicle theft	11,001	7,973	2,687	84	138	119	100.0	72.5	24.4	0.8	1.3	1.1	1,490	792	660	15	18	5
Arson	1,056	804	210	10	23	9	100.0	76.1	19.9	0.9	2.2	0.9	228	159	60	5	4	0
Other assaults	119,586	83,810	32,988	923	1,538	327	100.0	70.1	27.6	0.8	1.3	0.3	17,657	9,466	7,837	155	159	40
Forgery and counterfeiting	5,956	3,895	1,945	22	89	5	100.0	65.4	32.7	0.4	1.5	0.1	98	57	39	0	2	0
Fraud	15,627	10,638	4,584	93	291	21	100.0	68.1	29.3	0.6	1.9	0.1	423	237	177	3	6	0
Embezzlement	1,574	953	598	4	14	5	100.0	60.5	38.0	0.3	0.9	0.3	51	23	28	0	0	0
Stolen property; buying, receiving, possessing	11,773	8,052	3,479	105	116	21	100.0	68.4	29.6	0.9	1.0	0.2	749	291	446	2	8	2
Vandalism	20,696	14,983	5,235	199	241	38	100.0	72.4	25.3	1.0	1.2	0.2	3,585	2,406	1,103	42	30	4
Weapons; carrying, possessing, etc.	21,114	12,558	8,164	100	211	81	100.0	59.5	38.7	0.5	1.0	0.4	1,860	1,010	814	9	21	6
Prostitution and commercialized vice	2,286	1,245	796	7	227	11	100.0	54.5	34.8	0.3	9.9	0.5	21	17	4	0	0	0
Sex offenses (except forcible rape and prostitution)	5,842	4,676	1,042	30	88	6	100.0	80.0	17.8	0.5	1.5	0.1	901	658	229	1	12	1
Drug abuse violations	224,555	159,139	61,005	1,275	2,589	547	100.0	70.9	27.2	0.6	1.2	0.2	9,643	7,041	2,324	68	149	61
Gambling	600	369	146	4	58	23	100.0	61.5	24.3	0.7	9.7	3.8	86	62	20	0	4	0
Offenses against the family and children	19,427	12,721	6,518	67	114	7	100.0	65.5	33.6	0.3	0.6	*	316	259	46	9	2	0
Driving under the influence	179,358	146,046	27,451	998	4,267	596	100.0	81.4	15.3	0.6	2.4	0.3	772	712	46	5	6	3
Liquor laws	14,174	11,269	2,417	200	247	41	100.0	79.5	17.1	1.4	1.7	0.3	2,798	2,519	161	46	50	22
Drunkenness	22,095	18,381	3,187	170	325	32	100.0	83.2	14.4	0.8	1.5	0.1	285	231	48	2	2	2
Disorderly conduct	24,801	16,193	8,046	307	199	56	100.0	65.3	32.4	1.2	0.8	0.2	4,597	2,213	2,304	42	34	4
Vagrancy	1,532	990	520	4	17	1	100.0	64.6	33.9	0.3	1.1	0.1	10	7	3	0	0	0
All other offenses (except traffic)	490,613	352,282	125,388	5,984	4,792	2,167	100.0	71.8	25.6	1.2	1.0	0.4	14,378	9,793	4,123	196	188	78
Suspicion	1,007	818	185	3	1	0	100.0	81.2	18.4	0.3	0.1	0.0	4	4	0	0	0	0
Curfew and loitering law violations	920	637	196	1	41	45	100.0	69.2	21.3	0.1	4.5	4.9	920	637	196	1	41	45

Table 55. Arrests, Metropolitan Counties, Distribution by Race, 2019—Continued

(Number, percent; 1,230 agencies; 2019 estimated population 51,841,134.)

Offense charged	Percent distribution[1]						Arrests 18 and over						Percent distribution[1]					
	Total	White	Black	American Indian or Alaskan Native	Asian	Native Hawaiian or Other Pacific Islander	Total	White	Black	American Indian or Alaskan Native	Asian	Native Hawaiian or Other Pacific Islander	Total	White	Black	American Indian or Alaskan Native	Asian	Native Hawaiian or Other Pacific Islander
Total	100.0	60.7	36.7	0.9	1.2	0.4	1,282,551	928,061	322,423	10,821	16,910	4,336	100.0	72.4	25.1	0.8	1.3	0.3
Violent crime[2]	100.0	50.2	47.8	0.6	1.1	0.3	55,611	37,732	16,452	413	805	209	100.0	67.8	29.6	0.7	1.4	0.4
Murder and nonnegligent manslaughter	100.0	56.1	38.2	5.7	0.0	0.0	1,564	897	639	7	11	10	100.0	57.4	40.9	0.4	0.7	0.6
Rape[3]	100.0	74.3	24.2	0.0	1.4	0.2	2,726	2,080	576	14	41	15	100.0	76.3	21.1	0.5	1.5	0.6
Robbery	100.0	30.5	67.6	0.2	1.1	0.6	6,104	2,964	3,028	28	60	24	100.0	48.6	49.6	0.5	1.0	0.4
Aggravated assault	100.0	55.6	42.3	0.8	1.1	0.2	45,217	31,791	12,209	364	693	160	100.0	70.3	27.0	0.8	1.5	0.4
Property crime[2]	100.0	51.9	45.8	0.5	1.4	0.4	102,558	68,317	32,029	493	1,354	365	100.0	66.6	31.2	0.5	1.3	0.4
Burglary	100.0	60.8	37.2	0.7	0.7	0.6	18,101	13,793	4,024	76	151	57	100.0	76.2	22.2	0.4	0.8	0.3
Larceny-theft	100.0	48.6	49.1	0.3	1.7	0.3	74,118	46,698	25,828	343	1,064	185	100.0	63.0	34.8	0.5	1.4	0.2
Motor vehicle theft	100.0	53.2	44.3	1.0	1.2	0.3	9,511	7,181	2,027	69	120	114	100.0	75.5	21.3	0.7	1.3	1.2
Arson	100.0	69.7	26.3	2.2	1.8	0.0	828	645	150	5	19	9	100.0	77.9	18.1	0.6	2.3	1.1
Other assaults	100.0	53.6	44.4	0.9	0.9	0.2	101,929	74,344	25,151	768	1,379	287	100.0	72.9	24.7	0.8	1.4	0.3
Forgery and counterfeiting	100.0	58.2	39.8	0.0	2.0	0.0	5,858	3,838	1,906	22	87	5	100.0	65.5	32.5	0.4	1.5	0.1
Fraud	100.0	56.0	41.8	0.7	1.4	0.0	15,204	10,401	4,407	90	285	21	100.0	68.4	29.0	0.6	1.9	0.1
Embezzlement	100.0	45.1	54.9	0.0	0.0	0.0	1,523	930	570	4	14	5	100.0	61.1	37.4	0.3	0.9	0.3
Stolen property; buying, receiving, possessing	100.0	38.9	59.5	0.3	1.1	0.3	11,024	7,761	3,033	103	108	19	100.0	70.4	27.5	0.9	1.0	0.2
Vandalism	100.0	67.1	30.8	1.2	0.8	0.1	17,111	12,577	4,132	157	211	34	100.0	73.5	24.1	0.9	1.2	0.2
Weapons; carrying, possessing, etc.	100.0	54.3	43.8	0.5	1.1	0.3	19,254	11,548	7,350	91	190	75	100.0	60.0	38.2	0.5	1.0	0.4
Prostitution and commercialized vice	100.0	81.0	19.0	0.0	0.0	0.0	2,265	1,228	792	7	227	11	100.0	54.2	35.0	0.3	10.0	0.5
Sex offenses (except forcible rape and prostitution)	100.0	73.0	25.4	0.1	1.3	0.1	4,941	4,018	813	29	76	5	100.0	81.3	16.5	0.6	1.5	0.1
Drug abuse violations	100.0	73.0	24.1	0.7	1.5	0.6	214,912	152,098	58,681	1,207	2,440	486	100.0	70.8	27.3	0.6	1.1	0.2
Gambling	100.0	72.1	23.3	0.0	4.7	0.0	514	307	126	4	54	23	100.0	59.7	24.5	0.8	10.5	4.5
Offenses against the family and children	100.0	82.0	14.6	2.8	0.6	0.0	19,111	12,462	6,472	58	112	7	100.0	65.2	33.9	0.3	0.6	*
Driving under the influence	100.0	92.2	6.0	0.6	0.8	0.4	178,586	145,334	27,405	993	4,261	593	100.0	81.4	15.3	0.6	2.4	0.3
Liquor laws	100.0	90.0	5.8	1.6	1.8	0.8	11,376	8,750	2,256	154	197	19	100.0	76.9	19.8	1.4	1.7	0.2
Drunkenness	100.0	81.1	16.8	0.7	0.7	0.7	21,810	18,150	3,139	168	323	30	100.0	83.2	14.4	0.8	1.5	0.1
Disorderly conduct	100.0	48.1	50.1	0.9	0.7	0.1	20,204	13,980	5,742	265	165	52	100.0	69.2	28.4	1.3	0.8	0.3
Vagrancy	100.0	70.0	30.0	0.0	0.0	0.0	1,522	983	517	4	17	1	100.0	64.6	34.0	0.3	1.1	0.1
All other offenses (except traffic)	100.0	68.1	28.7	1.4	1.3	0.5	476,235	342,489	121,265	5,788	4,604	2,089	100.0	71.9	25.5	1.2	1.0	0.4
Suspicion	100.0	100.0	0.0	0.0	0.0	0.0	1,003	814	185	3	1	0	100.0	81.2	18.4	0.3	0.1	0.0
Curfew and loitering law violations	100.0	69.2	21.3	0.1	4.5	4.9	NA	NA	NA	NA	NA	NA	NA	NA	NA	NA	NA	NA

NA = Not available.
* = Less than one-tenth of one percent.
1 Because of rounding, the percentages may not sum to 100.   2 Violent crimes are offenses of murder and nonnegligent manslaughter, rape, robbery, and aggravated assault. Property crimes are offenses of burglary, larceny-theft, motor vehicle theft, and arson.   3 The rape figures in this table are an aggregate total of the data submitted using both the revised and legacy Uniform Crime Reporting definitions.

Table 55A. Arrests, Metropolitan Counties, Distribution by Ethnicity, 2019

(Number, percent; 1,230 agencies; 2019 estimated population 51,841,134.)

Offense charged	Total arrests			Percent distribution[1]			Arrests under 18		
	Total[2]	Hispanic or Latino	Not Hispanic or Latino	Total[2]	Hispanic or Latino	Not Hispanic or Latino	Total[2]	Hispanic or Latino	Not Hispanic or Latino
Total	1,165,073	217,727	947,346	100.0	18.7	81.3	65,912	11,387	54,525
Violent crime[3]	53,283	11,852	41,431	100.0	22.2	77.8	5,089	1,031	4,058
Murder and nonnegligent manslaughter	1,264	303	961	100.0	24.0	76.0	77	27	50
Rape[4]	2,880	766	2,114	100.0	26.6	73.4	560	96	464
Robbery	6,985	1,366	5,619	100.0	19.6	80.4	1,595	307	1,288
Aggravated assault	42,154	9,417	32,737	100.0	22.3	77.7	2,857	601	2,256
Property crime[3]	95,249	12,366	82,883	100.0	13.0	87.0	10,496	1,668	8,828
Burglary	17,621	2,578	15,043	100.0	14.6	85.4	1,984	338	1,646
Larceny-theft	67,096	7,410	59,686	100.0	11.0	89.0	6,989	1,035	5,954
Motor vehicle theft	9,620	2,233	7,387	100.0	23.2	76.8	1,333	273	1,060
Arson	912	145	767	100.0	15.9	84.1	190	22	168
Other assaults	104,162	15,959	88,203	100.0	15.3	84.7	15,508	2,137	13,371
Forgery and counterfeiting	5,181	952	4,229	100.0	18.4	81.6	85	16	69
Fraud	13,372	1,920	11,452	100.0	14.4	85.6	366	92	274
Embezzlement	1,387	149	1,238	100.0	10.7	89.3	47	8	39
Stolen property; buying, receiving, possessing	9,980	1,854	8,126	100.0	18.6	81.4	615	131	484
Vandalism	18,246	2,865	15,381	100.0	15.7	84.3	3,236	457	2,779
Weapons; carrying, possessing, etc.	17,583	3,842	13,741	100.0	21.9	78.1	1,608	369	1,239
Prostitution and commercialized vice	1,985	348	1,637	100.0	17.5	82.5	18	2	16
Sex offenses (except forcible rape and prostitution)	5,084	1,389	3,695	100.0	27.3	72.7	751	131	620
Drug abuse violations	199,264	36,798	162,466	100.0	18.5	81.5	8,512	1,971	6,541
Gambling	438	144	294	100.0	32.9	67.1	79	39	40
Offenses against the family and children	16,861	1,925	14,936	100.0	11.4	88.6	239	54	185
Driving under the influence	160,962	49,535	111,427	100.0	30.8	69.2	649	246	403
Liquor laws	10,753	2,084	8,669	100.0	19.4	80.6	2,135	321	1,814
Drunkenness	21,041	5,688	15,353	100.0	27.0	73.0	263	90	173
Disorderly conduct	19,430	1,840	17,590	100.0	9.5	90.5	3,529	343	3,186
Vagrancy	1,339	301	1,038	100.0	22.5	77.5	10	5	5
All other offenses (except traffic)	408,575	65,804	342,771	100.0	16.1	83.9	11,977	2,172	9,805
Suspicion	201	9	192	100.0	4.5	95.5	3	1	2
Curfew and loitering law violations	697	103	594	100.0	14.8	85.2	697	103	594

Table 55A. Arrests, Metropolitan Counties, Distribution by Ethnicity, 2019—Continued

(Number, percent; 1,230 agencies; 2019 estimated population 51,841,134.)

Offense charged	Percent distribution[1]			Arrests 18 and over			Percent distribution[1]		
	Total[2]	Hispanic or Latino	Not Hispanic or Latino	Total[2]	Hispanic or Latino	Not Hispanic or Latino	Total[2]	Hispanic or Latino	Not Hispanic or Latino
Total	100.0	17.3	82.7	1,099,161	206,340	892,821	100.0	18.8	81.2
Violent crime[3]	100.0	20.3	79.7	48,194	10,821	37,373	100.0	22.5	77.5
Murder and nonnegligent manslaughter	100.0	35.1	64.9	1,187	276	911	100.0	23.3	76.7
Rape[4]	100.0	17.1	82.9	2,320	670	1,650	100.0	28.9	71.1
Robbery	100.0	19.2	80.8	5,390	1,059	4,331	100.0	19.6	80.4
Aggravated assault	100.0	21.0	79.0	39,297	8,816	30,481	100.0	22.4	77.6
Property crime[3]	100.0	15.9	84.1	84,753	10,698	74,055	100.0	12.6	87.4
Burglary	100.0	17.0	83.0	15,637	2,240	13,397	100.0	14.3	85.7
Larceny-theft	100.0	14.8	85.2	60,107	6,375	53,732	100.0	10.6	89.4
Motor vehicle theft	100.0	20.5	79.5	8,287	1,960	6,327	100.0	23.7	76.3
Arson	100.0	11.6	88.4	722	123	599	100.0	17.0	83.0
Other assaults	100.0	13.8	86.2	88,654	13,822	74,832	100.0	15.6	84.4
Forgery and counterfeiting	100.0	18.8	81.2	5,096	936	4,160	100.0	18.4	81.6
Fraud	100.0	25.1	74.9	13,006	1,828	11,178	100.0	14.1	85.9
Embezzlement	100.0	17.0	83.0	1,340	141	1,199	100.0	10.5	89.5
Stolen property; buying, receiving, possessing	100.0	21.3	78.7	9,365	1,723	7,642	100.0	18.4	81.6
Vandalism	100.0	14.1	85.9	15,010	2,408	12,602	100.0	16.0	84.0
Weapons; carrying, possessing, etc.	100.0	22.9	77.1	15,975	3,473	12,502	100.0	21.7	78.3
Prostitution and commercialized vice	100.0	11.1	88.9	1,967	346	1,621	100.0	17.6	82.4
Sex offenses (except forcible rape and prostitution)	100.0	17.4	82.6	4,333	1,258	3,075	100.0	29.0	71.0
Drug abuse violations	100.0	23.2	76.8	190,752	34,827	155,925	100.0	18.3	81.7
Gambling	100.0	49.4	50.6	359	105	254	100.0	29.2	70.8
Offenses against the family and children	100.0	22.6	77.4	16,622	1,871	14,751	100.0	11.3	88.7
Driving under the influence	100.0	37.9	62.1	160,313	49,289	111,024	100.0	30.7	69.3
Liquor laws	100.0	15.0	85.0	8,618	1,763	6,855	100.0	20.5	79.5
Drunkenness	100.0	34.2	65.8	20,778	5,598	15,180	100.0	26.9	73.1
Disorderly conduct	100.0	9.7	90.3	15,901	1,497	14,404	100.0	9.4	90.6
Vagrancy	100.0	50.0	50.0	1,329	296	1,033	100.0	22.3	77.7
All other offenses (except traffic)	100.0	18.1	81.9	396,598	63,632	332,966	100.0	16.0	84.0
Suspicion	100.0	33.3	66.7	198	8	190	100.0	4.0	96.0
Curfew and loitering law violations	100.0	14.8	85.2	NA	NA	NA	NA	NA	NA

NA = Not available.
1 Because of rounding, the percentages may not sum to 100.   2 The ethnicity totals are representative of those agencies that provided ethnicity breakdowns. Not all agencies provide ethnicity data; therefore, the race and ethnicity totals will not be equal.   3 Violent crimes are offenses of murder and nonnegligent manslaughter, rape, robbery, and aggravated assault. Property crimes are offenses of burglary, larceny-theft, motor vehicle theft, and arson.   4 The rape figures in this table are an aggregate total of the data submitted using both the revised and legacy Uniform Crime Reporting definitions.

Table 56. Arrest Trends, Nonmetropolitan Counties, 2018–2019

(Number, percent change; 1,453 agencies; 2019 estimated population 16,119,766; 2018 estimated population 16,140,591.)

Offense charged	Number of persons arrested								
	Total, all ages			Under 18 years of age			18 years of age and over		
	2018	2019	Percent change	2018	2019	Percent change	2018	2019	Percent change
Total[1]	496,723	475,041	-4.4	20,340	18,986	-6.7	476,383	456,055	-4.3
Violent crime[2]	15,541	15,012	-3.4	942	980	+4.0	14,599	14,032	-3.9
Murder and nonnegligent manslaughter	467	450	-3.6	35	28	-20.0	432	422	-2.3
Rape[3]	1,393	1,334	-4.2	245	245	0.0	1,148	1,089	-5.1
Robbery	843	688	-18.4	47	61	+29.8	796	627	-21.2
Aggravated assault	12,838	12,540	-2.3	615	646	+5.0	12,223	11,894	-2.7
Property crime[2]	27,649	23,894	-13.6	2,392	1,938	-19.0	25,257	21,956	-13.1
Burglary	7,661	6,677	-12.8	754	619	-17.9	6,907	6,058	-12.3
Larceny-theft	16,049	13,874	-13.6	1,164	931	-20.0	14,885	12,943	-13.0
Motor vehicle theft	3,309	2,995	-9.5	420	336	-20.0	2,889	2,659	-8.0
Arson	630	348	-44.8	54	52	-3.7	576	296	-48.6
Other assaults	40,167	40,199	+0.1	3,677	3,900	+6.1	36,490	36,299	-0.5
Forgery and counterfeiting	1,916	1,531	-20.1	22	8	-63.6	1,894	1,523	-19.6
Fraud	4,829	4,348	-10.0	84	82	-2.4	4,745	4,266	-10.1
Embezzlement	388	337	-13.1	7	3	-57.1	381	334	-12.3
Stolen property; buying, receiving, possessing	2,956	2,805	-5.1	141	136	-3.5	2,815	2,669	-5.2
Vandalism	5,899	5,865	-0.6	945	904	-4.3	4,954	4,961	+0.1
Weapons; carrying, possessing, etc.	5,550	5,361	-3.4	244	252	+3.3	5,306	5,109	-3.7
Prostitution and commercialized vice	164	110	-32.9	6	6	0.0	158	104	-34.2
Sex offenses (except forcible rape and prostitution)	1,904	1,761	-7.5	336	373	+11.0	1,568	1,388	-11.5
Drug abuse violations	80,936	74,004	-8.6	2,736	2,218	-18.9	78,200	71,786	-8.2
Gambling	85	92	+8.2	0	2		85	90	+5.9
Offenses against the family and children	6,747	5,801	-14.0	88	97	+10.2	6,659	5,704	-14.3
Driving under the influence	79,595	77,972	-2.0	441	437	-0.9	79,154	77,535	-2.0
Liquor laws	8,904	8,295	-6.8	1,885	1,767	-6.3	7,019	6,528	-7.0
Drunkenness	9,022	8,651	-4.1	103	106	+2.9	8,919	8,545	-4.2
Disorderly conduct	11,318	10,364	-8.4	1,576	1,415	-10.2	9,742	8,949	-8.1
Vagrancy	303	227	-25.1	13	2	-84.6	290	225	-22.4
All other offenses (except traffic)	192,669	188,274	-2.3	4,521	4,222	-6.6	188,148	184,052	-2.2
Suspicion	20	44	+120.0	3	1	-66.7	17	43	+152.9
Curfew and loitering law violations	181	138	-23.8	181	138	-23.8	NA	NA	NA

NA = Not available.

1 Does not include suspicion.   2 Violent crimes are offenses of murder and nonnegligent manslaughter, rape, robbery, and aggravated assault. Property crimes are offenses of burglary, larceny-theft, motor vehicle theft, and arson.   3 The rape figures in this table are aggregate totals of the data submitted based on both the legacy and revised Uniform Crime Reporting definitions.

Table 57. Arrest Trends, Nonmetropolitan Counties, by Age and Sex, 2018–2019

(Number, percent; 1,453 agencies; 2019 estimated population 16,119,766; 2018 estimated population 16,140,591.)

Offense charged	Male						Female					
	Total			Under 18			Total			Under 18		
	2018	2019	Percent change	2018	2019	Percent change	2018	2019	Percent change	2018	2019	Percent change
Total[1]	363,001	346,055	-4.7	14,433	13,517	-6.3	133,722	128,986	-3.5	5,907	5,469	-7.4
Violent crime[2]	12,728	12,243	-3.8	775	796	+2.7	2,813	2,769	-1.6	167	184	+10.2
Murder and nonnegligent manslaughter	399	384	-3.8	34	25	-26.5	68	66	-2.9	1	3	+200.0
Rape[3]	1,340	1,275	-4.9	234	225	-3.8	53	59	+11.3	11	20	+81.8
Robbery	689	585	-15.1	44	52	+18.2	154	103	-33.1	3	9	+200.0
Aggravated assault	10,300	9,999	-2.9	463	494	+6.7	2,538	2,541	+0.1	152	152	0.0
Property crime[2]	19,378	16,667	-14.0	1,849	1,508	-18.4	8,271	7,227	-12.6	543	430	-20.8
Burglary	6,216	5,359	-13.8	672	542	-19.3	1,445	1,318	-8.8	82	77	-6.1
Larceny-theft	10,179	8,758	-14.0	794	677	-14.7	5,870	5,116	-12.8	370	254	-31.4
Motor vehicle theft	2,492	2,267	-9.0	337	246	-27.0	817	728	-10.9	83	90	+8.4
Arson	491	283	-42.4	46	43	-6.5	139	65	-53.2	8	9	+12.5
Other assaults	29,530	29,514	-0.1	2,458	2,635	+7.2	10,637	10,685	+0.5	1,219	1,265	+3.8
Forgery and counterfeiting	1,217	995	-18.2	14	4	-71.4	699	536	-23.3	8	4	-50.0
Fraud	2,837	2,569	-9.4	59	49	-16.9	1,992	1,779	-10.7	25	33	+32.0
Embezzlement	200	166	-17.0	6	2	-66.7	188	171	-9.0	1	1	0.0
Stolen property; buying, receiving, possessing	2,300	2,175	-5.4	116	107	-7.8	656	630	-4.0	25	29	+16.0
Vandalism	4,729	4,661	-1.4	786	754	-4.1	1,170	1,204	+2.9	159	150	-5.7
Weapons; carrying, possessing, etc.	4,950	4,770	-3.6	219	232	+5.9	600	591	-1.5	25	20	-20.0
Prostitution and commercialized vice	129	79	-38.8	3	2	-33.3	35	31	-11.4	3	4	+33.3
Sex offenses (except forcible rape and prostitution)	1,776	1,649	-7.2	306	337	+10.1	128	112	-12.5	30	36	+20.0
Drug abuse violations	57,445	52,009	-9.5	1,916	1,596	-16.7	23,491	21,995	-6.4	820	622	-24.1
Gambling	53	74	+39.6	0	2		32	18	-43.8	0	0	
Offenses against the family and children	5,084	4,238	-16.6	64	71	+10.9	1,663	1,563	-6.0	24	26	+8.3
Driving under the influence	60,124	58,620	-2.5	324	324	0.0	19,471	19,352	-0.6	117	113	-3.4
Liquor laws	5,988	5,594	-6.6	1,061	998	-5.9	2,916	2,701	-7.4	824	769	-6.7
Drunkenness	6,479	6,237	-3.7	64	77	+20.3	2,543	2,414	-5.1	39	29	-25.6
Disorderly conduct	8,036	7,403	-7.9	1,098	975	-11.2	3,282	2,961	-9.8	478	440	-7.9
Vagrancy	233	169	-27.5	11	1	-90.9	70	58	-17.1	2	1	-50.0
All other offenses (except traffic)	139,677	136,154	-2.5	3,196	2,978	-6.8	52,992	52,120	-1.6	1,325	1,244	-6.1
Suspicion	17	29	+70.6	3	1	-66.7	3	15	+400.0	0	0	
Curfew and loitering law violations	108	69	-36.1	108	69	-36.1	73	69	-5.5	73	69	-5.5

1 Does not include suspicion.   2 Violent crimes are offenses of murder and nonnegligent manslaughter, rape, robbery, and aggravated assault. Property crimes are offenses of burglary, larceny-theft, motor vehicle theft, and arson.   3 The rape figures in this table are aggregate totals of the data submitted based on both the legacy and revised Uniform Crime Reporting definitions.

Table 58. Arrests, Nonmetropolitan Counties, Distribution by Age, 2019

(Number, percent; 1,622 agencies; 2019 estimated population 18,187,868.)

Offense charged	Total, all ages	Ages under 15	Ages under 18	Ages 18 and over	Under 10	10–12	13–14	15	16	17	18	19	20
Total	541,885	6,233	21,028	520,857	166	1,643	4,424	3,599	4,694	6,502	11,612	12,995	14,420
Total percent distribution[1]	100.0	1.2	3.9	96.1	*	0.3	0.8	0.7	0.9	1.2	2.1	2.4	2.7
Violent crime[2]	16,657	389	1,066	15,591	12	119	258	177	227	273	414	385	429
Violent crime percent distribution[1]	100.0	2.3	6.4	93.6	0.1	0.7	1.5	1.1	1.4	1.6	2.5	2.3	2.6
Murder and nonnegligent manslaughter	522	1	32	490	0	0	1	9	10	12	19	16	21
Rape[3]	1,450	123	262	1,188	3	39	81	45	39	55	87	62	47
Robbery	774	9	64	710	0	2	7	6	21	28	49	39	32
Aggravated assault	13,911	256	708	13,203	9	78	169	117	157	178	259	268	329
Property crime[2]	26,393	667	2,125	24,268	19	147	501	420	501	537	875	774	724
Property crime percent distribution[1]	100.0	2.5	8.1	91.9	0.1	0.6	1.9	1.6	1.9	2.0	3.3	2.9	2.7
Burglary	7,540	229	685	6,855	5	57	167	127	161	168	269	235	210
Larceny-theft	15,171	311	1,021	14,150	14	67	230	197	239	274	479	443	420
Motor vehicle theft	3,291	102	364	2,927	0	15	87	89	95	78	117	90	89
Arson	391	25	55	336	0	8	17	7	6	17	10	6	5
Other assaults	43,913	1,739	4,180	39,733	56	527	1,156	829	823	789	861	783	779
Forgery and counterfeiting	1,684	5	12	1,672	0	1	4	0	2	5	32	38	48
Fraud	4,767	24	94	4,673	0	2	22	13	22	35	66	82	109
Embezzlement	353	0	3	350	0	0	0	0	1	2	6	9	9
Stolen property; buying, receiving, possessing	3,264	32	152	3,112	0	4	28	28	40	52	84	110	104
Vandalism	6,504	400	997	5,507	17	138	245	190	177	230	240	214	200
Weapons; carrying, possessing, etc.	5,967	95	277	5,690	3	34	58	42	59	81	141	142	136
Prostitution and commercialized vice	119	4	6	113	0	1	3	1	1	0	2	0	2
Sex offenses (except forcible rape and prostitution)	1,882	193	384	1,498	3	66	124	62	71	58	87	65	57
Drug abuse violations	89,450	376	2,605	86,845	4	58	314	332	628	1,269	2,719	3,194	3,401
Gambling	101	0	2	99	0	0	0	0	1	1	0	1	1
Offenses against the family and children	6,869	39	103	6,766	5	11	23	25	21	18	53	46	70
Driving under the influence	87,795	12	504	87,291	1	1	10	24	122	346	1,246	1,506	1,784
Liquor laws	9,323	195	1,951	7,372	1	24	170	289	551	916	1,426	1,456	1,322
Drunkenness	9,226	9	119	9,107	0	0	9	23	31	56	172	178	170
Disorderly conduct	11,424	728	1,616	9,808	19	218	491	296	322	270	267	214	263
Vagrancy	235	0	2	233	0	0	0	1	0	1	1	3	3
All other offenses (except traffic)	215,774	1,264	4,691	211,083	25	285	954	832	1,070	1,525	2,919	3,795	4,809
Suspicion	47	0	1	46	0	0	0	0	0	1	1	0	0
Curfew and loitering law violations	138	62	138	NA	1	7	54	15	24	37	NA	NA	NA

Table 58. Arrests, Nonmetropolitan Counties, Distribution by Age, 2019—Continued

(Number, percent; 1,622 agencies; 2019 estimated population 18,187,868.)

Offense charged	21	22	23	24	25–29	30–34	35–39	40–44	45–49	50–54	55–59	60–64	65 and over
Total	14,520	14,840	15,362	15,868	89,314	85,871	76,239	54,626	40,521	29,987	23,033	12,195	9,454
Total percent distribution[1]	2.7	2.7	2.8	2.9	16.5	15.8	14.1	10.1	7.5	5.5	4.3	2.3	1.7
Violent crime[2]	426	404	398	457	2,641	2,416	2,194	1,598	1,229	963	759	453	425
Violent crime percent distribution[1]	2.6	2.4	2.4	2.7	15.9	14.5	13.2	9.6	7.4	5.8	4.6	2.7	2.6
Murder and nonnegligent manslaughter	14	19	12	10	85	66	63	44	37	25	18	12	29
Rape[3]	51	45	26	39	144	161	129	114	80	68	68	35	32
Robbery	29	30	22	39	136	110	87	50	37	20	20	4	6
Aggravated assault	332	310	338	369	2,276	2,079	1,915	1,390	1,075	850	653	402	358
Property crime[2]	698	687	671	686	4,268	4,152	3,620	2,466	1,819	1,240	892	386	310
Property crime percent distribution[1]	2.6	2.6	2.5	2.6	16.2	15.7	13.7	9.3	6.9	4.7	3.4	1.5	1.2
Burglary	198	192	193	222	1,206	1,224	1,087	709	491	305	196	75	43
Larceny-theft	402	391	370	364	2,409	2,345	2,049	1,447	1,122	799	598	275	237
Motor vehicle theft	85	94	98	87	591	532	445	273	187	116	74	28	21
Arson	13	10	10	13	62	51	39	37	19	20	24	8	9
Other assaults	962	1,017	1,085	1,106	6,314	6,472	5,916	4,349	3,361	2,663	2,022	1,068	975
Forgery and counterfeiting	31	42	42	47	298	277	309	169	139	80	72	25	23
Fraud	100	98	116	95	717	808	789	569	410	269	224	120	101
Embezzlement	7	8	7	14	59	36	55	38	34	21	23	11	13
Stolen property; buying, receiving, possessing	81	97	79	78	620	585	501	304	201	128	80	34	26
Vandalism	197	173	179	189	945	893	701	509	370	261	227	105	104
Weapons; carrying, possessing, etc.	168	189	177	207	953	898	790	555	424	351	284	141	134
Prostitution and commercialized vice	2	3	1	0	20	18	15	13	10	7	14	4	2
Sex offenses (except forcible rape and prostitution)	44	27	35	32	168	188	182	134	121	105	77	63	113
Drug abuse violations	3,198	3,077	3,122	3,094	16,104	13,863	12,027	8,070	5,788	3,970	2,989	1,535	694
Gambling	2	2	0	2	17	13	11	13	13	10	9	3	2
Offenses against the family and children	93	89	110	146	1,100	1,415	1,309	1,005	583	361	233	96	57
Driving under the influence	2,626	2,740	2,989	2,876	14,665	12,460	10,484	8,157	7,269	6,190	5,770	3,514	3,015
Liquor laws	196	172	140	130	496	440	394	327	254	231	174	125	89
Drunkenness	235	219	237	203	1,334	1,336	1,352	1,031	873	694	616	280	177
Disorderly conduct	255	287	263	283	1,483	1,517	1,352	993	823	690	525	310	283
Vagrancy	4	4	3	8	41	33	30	32	21	19	10	11	10
All other offenses (except traffic)	5,195	5,501	5,706	6,215	37,059	38,041	34,204	24,291	16,775	11,732	8,030	3,910	2,901
Suspicion	0	4	2	0	12	10	4	3	4	2	3	1	0
Curfew and loitering law violations	NA	NA	NA	NA	NA	NA	NA	NA	NA	NA	NA	NA	NA

NA = Not available.

* = Less than one-tenth of one percent.

1 Because of rounding, the percentages may not sum to 100.   2 Violent crimes are offenses of murder and nonnegligent manslaughter, rape, robbery, and aggravated assault. Property crimes are offenses of burglary, larceny-theft, motor vehicle theft, and arson.   3 The rape figures in this table are aggregate totals of the data submitted based on both the legacy and revised Uniform Crime Reporting definitions.

Table 59. Arrests, Nonmetropolitan Counties, Persons Under 15, 18, 21, and 25 Years of Age, 2019

(Number, percent; 1,622 agencies; 2019 estimated population 18,187,868.)

Offense charged	Total, all ages	Number of persons arrested				Percent of total all ages			
		Under 15	Under 18	Under 21	Under 25	Under 15	Under 18	Under 21	Under 25
Total	541,885	6,233	21,028	60,055	120,645	1.2	3.9	11.1	22.3
Violent crime[1]	16,657	389	1,066	2,294	3,979	2.3	6.4	13.8	23.9
Murder and nonnegligent manslaughter	522	1	32	88	143	0.2	6.1	16.9	27.4
Rape[2]	1,450	123	262	458	619	8.5	18.1	31.6	42.7
Robbery	774	9	64	184	304	1.2	8.3	23.8	39.3
Aggravated assault	13,911	256	708	1,564	2,913	1.8	5.1	11.2	20.9
Property crime[1]	26,393	667	2,125	4,498	7,240	2.5	8.1	17.0	27.4
Burglary	7,540	229	685	1,399	2,204	3.0	9.1	18.6	29.2
Larceny-theft	15,171	311	1,021	2,363	3,890	2.0	6.7	15.6	25.6
Motor vehicle theft	3,291	102	364	660	1,024	3.1	11.1	20.1	31.1
Arson	391	25	55	76	122	6.4	14.1	19.4	31.2
Other assaults	43,913	1,739	4,180	6,603	10,773	4.0	9.5	15.0	24.5
Forgery and counterfeiting	1,684	5	12	130	292	0.3	0.7	7.7	17.3
Fraud	4,767	24	94	351	760	0.5	2.0	7.4	15.9
Embezzlement	353	0	3	27	63	0.0	0.8	7.6	17.8
Stolen property; buying, receiving, possessing	3,264	32	152	450	785	1.0	4.7	13.8	24.1
Vandalism	6,504	400	997	1,651	2,389	6.2	15.3	25.4	36.7
Weapons; carrying, possessing, etc.	5,967	95	277	696	1,437	1.6	4.6	11.7	24.1
Prostitution and commercialized vice	119	4	6	10	16	3.4	5.0	8.4	13.4
Sex offenses (except forcible rape and prostitution)	1,882	193	384	593	731	10.3	20.4	31.5	38.8
Drug abuse violations	89,450	376	2,605	11,919	24,410	0.4	2.9	13.3	27.3
Gambling	101	0	2	4	10	0.0	2.0	4.0	9.9
Offenses against the family and children	6,869	39	103	272	710	0.6	1.5	4.0	10.3
Driving under the influence	87,795	12	504	5,040	16,271	*	0.6	5.7	18.5
Liquor laws	9,323	195	1,951	6,155	6,793	2.1	20.9	66.0	72.9
Drunkenness	9,226	9	119	639	1,533	0.1	1.3	6.9	16.6
Disorderly conduct	11,424	728	1,616	2,360	3,448	6.4	14.1	20.7	30.2
Vagrancy	235	0	2	9	28	0.0	0.9	3.8	11.9
All other offenses (except traffic)	215,774	1,264	4,691	16,214	38,831	0.6	2.2	7.5	18.0
Suspicion	47	0	1	2	8	0.0	2.1	4.3	17.0
Curfew and loitering law violations	138	62	138	138	138	44.9	100.0	100.0	100.0

* = Less than one-tenth of one percent.

1 Violent crimes are offenses of murder and nonnegligent manslaughter, rape, robbery, and aggravated assault. Property crimes are offenses of burglary, larceny-theft, motor vehicle theft, and arson.   2 The rape figures in this table are aggregate totals of the data submitted based on both the legacy and revised Uniform Crime Reporting definitions.

Table 60. Arrests, Nonmetropolitan Counties, Distribution by Sex, 2019

(Number, percent; 1,622 agencies; 2019 estimated population 18,187,868.)

Offense charged	Number of persons arrested			Percent male	Percent female	Percent distribution[1]		
	Total	Male	Female			Total	Male	Female
Total	541,885	395,022	146,863	72.9	27.1	100.0	100.0	100.0
Violent crime[2]	16,657	13,606	3,051	81.7	18.3	3.1	3.4	2.1
Murder and nonnegligent manslaughter	522	445	77	85.2	14.8	0.1	0.1	0.1
Rape[3]	1,450	1,384	66	95.4	4.6	0.3	0.4	*
Robbery	774	656	118	84.8	15.2	0.1	0.2	0.1
Aggravated assault	13,911	11,121	2,790	79.9	20.1	2.6	2.8	1.9
Property crime[2]	26,393	18,505	7,888	70.1	29.9	4.9	4.7	5.4
Burglary	7,540	6,049	1,491	80.2	19.8	1.4	1.5	1.0
Larceny-theft	15,171	9,648	5,523	63.6	36.4	2.8	2.4	3.8
Motor vehicle theft	3,291	2,489	802	75.6	24.4	0.6	0.6	0.5
Arson	391	319	72	81.6	18.4	0.1	0.1	*
Other assaults	43,913	32,222	11,691	73.4	26.6	8.1	8.2	8.0
Forgery and counterfeiting	1,684	1,100	584	65.3	34.7	0.3	0.3	0.4
Fraud	4,767	2,819	1,948	59.1	40.9	0.9	0.7	1.3
Embezzlement	353	174	179	49.3	50.7	0.1	*	0.1
Stolen property; buying, receiving, possessing	3,264	2,528	736	77.5	22.5	0.6	0.6	0.5
Vandalism	6,504	5,170	1,334	79.5	20.5	1.2	1.3	0.9
Weapons; carrying, possessing, etc.	5,967	5,299	668	88.8	11.2	1.1	1.3	0.5
Prostitution and commercialized vice	119	86	33	72.3	27.7	*	*	*
Sex offenses (except forcible rape and prostitution)	1,882	1,763	119	93.7	6.3	0.3	0.4	0.1
Drug abuse violations	89,450	62,982	26,468	70.4	29.6	16.5	15.9	18.0
Gambling	101	82	19	81.2	18.8	*	*	*
Offenses against the family and children	6,869	5,072	1,797	73.8	26.2	1.3	1.3	1.2
Driving under the influence	87,795	66,129	21,666	75.3	24.7	16.2	16.7	14.8
Liquor laws	9,323	6,342	2,981	68.0	32.0	1.7	1.6	2.0
Drunkenness	9,226	6,666	2,560	72.3	27.7	1.7	1.7	1.7
Disorderly conduct	11,424	8,158	3,266	71.4	28.6	2.1	2.1	2.2
Vagrancy	235	176	59	74.9	25.1	*	*	*
All other offenses (except traffic)	215,774	156,044	59,730	72.3	27.7	39.8	39.5	40.7
Suspicion	47	30	17	63.8	36.2	*	*	*
Curfew and loitering law violations	138	69	69	50.0	50.0	*	*	*

* = Less than one-tenth of 1 percent.
1 Because of rounding, the percentages may not sum to 100.   2 Violent crimes are offenses of murder and nonnegligent manslaughter, rape, robbery, and aggravated assault. Property crimes are offenses of burglary, larceny-theft, motor vehicle theft, and arson.   3 The rape figures in this table are aggregate totals of the data submitted based on both the legacy and revised Uniform Crime Reporting definitions.

Table 61. Arrests, Nonmetropolitan Counties, Distribution by Race, 2019

(Number, percent; 1,622 agencies; 2019 estimated population 18,187,868.)

Offense charged	Total arrests						Percent distribution[1]						Arrests under 18					
	Total	White	Black	American Indian or Alaskan Native	Asian	Native Hawaiian or Other Pacific Islander	Total	White	Black	American Indian or Alaskan Native	Asian	Native Hawaiian or Other Pacific Islander	Total	White	Black	American Indian or Alaskan Native	Asian	Native Hawaiian or Other Pacific Islander
Total	527,980	444,923	62,470	16,718	3,324	545	100.0	84.3	11.8	3.2	0.6	0.1	20,131	16,276	2,828	965	56	6
Violent crime[2]	16,399	13,227	2,131	958	76	7	100.0	80.7	13.0	5.8	0.5	*	1,037	787	170	73	6	1
Murder and nonnegligent manslaughter	530	382	110	34	1	3	100.0	72.1	20.8	6.4	0.2	0.6	31	21	6	4	0	0
Rape[3]	1,419	1,242	120	52	5	0	100.0	87.5	8.5	3.7	0.4	0.0	256	226	14	15	1	0
Robbery	758	514	208	35	1	0	100.0	67.8	27.4	4.6	0.1	0.0	60	43	14	3	0	0
Aggravated assault	13,692	11,089	1,693	837	69	4	100.0	81.0	12.4	6.1	0.5	*	690	497	136	51	5	1
Property crime[2]	25,734	22,096	2,679	882	65	12	100.0	85.9	10.4	3.4	0.3	*	2,027	1,588	274	161	4	0
Burglary	7,402	6,388	695	296	18	5	100.0	86.3	9.4	4.0	0.2	0.1	661	511	82	68	0	0
Larceny-theft	14,699	12,608	1,638	410	38	5	100.0	85.8	11.1	2.8	0.3	*	962	780	132	48	2	0
Motor vehicle theft	3,245	2,774	307	154	8	2	100.0	85.5	9.5	4.7	0.2	0.1	350	251	53	44	2	0
Arson	388	326	39	22	1	0	100.0	84.0	10.1	5.7	0.3	0.0	54	46	7	1	0	0
Other assaults	42,699	36,223	4,469	1,865	128	14	100.0	84.8	10.5	4.4	0.3	*	4,024	3,066	777	172	7	2
Forgery and counterfeiting	1,660	1,338	289	28	4	1	100.0	80.6	17.4	1.7	0.2	0.1	11	8	3	0	0	0
Fraud	4,637	3,838	634	138	18	9	100.0	82.8	13.7	3.0	0.4	0.2	89	66	20	3	0	0
Embezzlement	343	296	40	6	1	0	100.0	86.3	11.7	1.7	0.3	0.0	2	1	1	0	0	0
Stolen property; buying, receiving, possessing	3,203	2,505	569	117	12	0	100.0	78.2	17.8	3.7	0.4	0.0	147	79	59	9	0	0
Vandalism	6,353	5,402	632	280	31	8	100.0	85.0	9.9	4.4	0.5	0.1	970	819	102	47	0	2
Weapons; carrying, possessing, etc.	5,839	4,513	1,110	176	32	8	100.0	77.3	19.0	3.0	0.5	0.1	271	201	62	8	0	0
Prostitution and commercialized vice	111	91	18	0	2	0	100.0	82.0	16.2	0.0	1.8	0.0	6	5	1	0	0	0
Sex offenses (except forcible rape and prostitution)	1,855	1,622	176	43	13	1	100.0	87.4	9.5	2.3	0.7	0.1	376	336	29	10	1	0
Drug abuse violations	86,387	70,565	13,134	2,134	489	65	100.0	81.7	15.2	2.5	0.6	0.1	2,451	2,076	268	98	9	0
Gambling	101	59	37	2	3	0	100.0	58.4	36.6	2.0	3.0	0.0	2	0	2	0	0	0
Offenses against the family and children	6,801	5,374	1,019	391	16	1	100.0	79.0	15.0	5.7	0.2	*	102	86	13	3	0	0
Driving under the influence	84,446	74,128	6,569	2,105	1,436	208	100.0	87.8	7.8	2.5	1.7	0.2	477	446	8	16	7	0
Liquor laws	8,774	7,840	478	376	76	4	100.0	89.4	5.4	4.3	0.9	*	1,827	1,679	63	78	7	0
Drunkenness	9,109	8,150	566	341	37	15	100.0	89.5	6.2	3.7	0.4	0.2	116	110	3	3	0	0
Disorderly conduct	11,155	9,021	1,432	649	53	0	100.0	80.9	12.8	5.8	0.5	0.0	1,553	1,081	359	110	3	0
Vagrancy	238	193	35	4	6	0	100.0	81.1	14.7	1.7	2.5	0.0	2	2	0	0	0	0
All other offenses (except traffic)	211,953	178,283	26,446	6,206	826	192	100.0	84.1	12.5	2.9	0.4	0.1	4,504	3,720	612	159	12	1
Suspicion	47	40	5	2	0	0	100.0	85.1	10.6	4.3	0.0	0.0	1	1	0	0	0	0
Curfew and loitering law violations	136	119	2	15	0	0	100.0	87.5	1.5	11.0	0.0	0.0	136	119	2	15	0	0

Table 61. Arrests, Nonmetropolitan Counties, Distribution by Race, 2019—Continued

(Number, percent; 1,622 agencies; 2019 estimated population 18,187,868.)

Offense charged	Percent distribution[1]						Arrests 18 and over						Percent distribution[1]					
	Total	White	Black	American Indian or Alaskan Native	Asian	Native Hawaiian or Other Pacific Islander	Total	White	Black	American Indian or Alaskan Native	Asian	Native Hawaiian or Other Pacific Islander	Total	White	Black	American Indian or Alaskan Native	Asian	Native Hawaiian or Other Pacific Islander
Total	100.0	80.9	14.0	4.8	0.3	*	507,849	428,647	59,642	15,753	3,268	539	100.0	84.4	11.7	3.1	0.6	0.1
Violent crime[2]	100.0	75.9	16.4	7.0	0.6	0.1	15,362	12,440	1,961	885	70	6	100.0	81.0	12.8	5.8	0.5	*
Murder and nonnegligent manslaughter	100.0	67.7	19.4	12.9	0.0	0.0	499	361	104	30	1	3	100.0	72.3	20.8	6.0	0.2	0.6
Rape[3]	100.0	88.3	5.5	5.9	0.4	0.0	1,163	1,016	106	37	4	0	100.0	87.4	9.1	3.2	0.3	0.0
Robbery	100.0	71.7	23.3	5.0	0.0	0.0	698	471	194	32	1	0	100.0	67.5	27.8	4.6	0.1	0.0
Aggravated assault	100.0	72.0	19.7	7.4	0.7	0.1	13,002	10,592	1,557	786	64	3	100.0	81.5	12.0	6.0	0.5	*
Property crime[2]	100.0	78.3	13.5	7.9	0.2	0.0	23,707	20,508	2,405	721	61	12	100.0	86.5	10.1	3.0	0.3	0.1
Burglary	100.0	77.3	12.4	10.3	0.0	0.0	6,741	5,877	613	228	18	5	100.0	87.2	9.1	3.4	0.3	0.1
Larceny-theft	100.0	81.1	13.7	5.0	0.2	0.0	13,737	11,828	1,506	362	36	5	100.0	86.1	11.0	2.6	0.3	*
Motor vehicle theft	100.0	71.7	15.1	12.6	0.6	0.0	2,895	2,523	254	110	6	2	100.0	87.2	8.8	3.8	0.2	0.1
Arson	100.0	85.2	13.0	1.9	0.0	0.0	334	280	32	21	1	0	100.0	83.8	9.6	6.3	0.3	0.0
Other assaults	100.0	76.2	19.3	4.3	0.2	*	38,675	33,157	3,692	1,693	121	12	100.0	85.7	9.5	4.4	0.3	*
Forgery and counterfeiting	100.0	72.7	27.3	0.0	0.0	0.0	1,649	1,330	286	28	4	1	100.0	80.7	17.3	1.7	0.2	0.1
Fraud	100.0	74.2	22.5	3.4	0.0	0.0	4,548	3,772	614	135	18	9	100.0	82.9	13.5	3.0	0.4	0.2
Embezzlement	100.0	50.0	50.0	0.0	0.0	0.0	341	295	39	6	1	0	100.0	86.5	11.4	1.8	0.3	0.0
Stolen property; buying, receiving, possessing	100.0	53.7	40.1	6.1	0.0	0.0	3,056	2,426	510	108	12	0	100.0	79.4	16.7	3.5	0.4	0.0
Vandalism	100.0	84.4	10.5	4.8	0.0	0.2	5,383	4,583	530	233	31	6	100.0	85.1	9.8	4.3	0.6	0.1
Weapons; carrying, possessing, etc.	100.0	74.2	22.9	3.0	0.0	0.0	5,568	4,312	1,048	168	32	8	100.0	77.4	18.8	3.0	0.6	0.1
Prostitution and commercialized vice	100.0	83.3	16.7	0.0	0.0	0.0	105	86	17	0	2	0	100.0	81.9	16.2	0.0	1.9	0.0
Sex offenses (except forcible rape and prostitution)	100.0	89.4	7.7	2.7	0.3	0.0	1,479	1,286	147	33	12	1	100.0	87.0	9.9	2.2	0.8	0.1
Drug abuse violations	100.0	84.7	10.9	4.0	0.4	0.0	83,936	68,489	12,866	2,036	480	65	100.0	81.6	15.3	2.4	0.6	0.1
Gambling	100.0	0.0	100.0	0.0	0.0	0.0	99	59	35	2	3	0	100.0	59.6	35.4	2.0	3.0	0.0
Offenses against the family and children	100.0	84.3	12.7	2.9	0.0	0.0	6,699	5,288	1,006	388	16	1	100.0	78.9	15.0	5.8	0.2	*
Driving under the influence	100.0	93.5	1.7	3.4	1.5	0.0	83,969	73,682	6,561	2,089	1,429	208	100.0	87.7	7.8	2.5	1.7	0.2
Liquor laws	100.0	91.9	3.4	4.3	0.4	0.0	6,947	6,161	415	298	69	4	100.0	88.7	6.0	4.3	1.0	0.1
Drunkenness	100.0	94.8	2.6	2.6	0.0	0.0	8,993	8,040	563	338	37	15	100.0	89.4	6.3	3.8	0.4	0.2
Disorderly conduct	100.0	69.6	23.1	7.1	0.2	0.0	9,602	7,940	1,073	539	50	0	100.0	82.7	11.2	5.6	0.5	0.0
Vagrancy	100.0	100.0	0.0	0.0	0.0	0.0	236	191	35	4	6	0	100.0	80.9	14.8	1.7	2.5	0.0
All other offenses (except traffic)	100.0	82.6	13.6	3.5	0.3	*	207,449	174,563	25,834	6,047	814	191	100.0	84.1	12.5	2.9	0.4	0.1
Suspicion	100.0	100.0	0.0	0.0	0.0	0.0	46	39	5	2	0	0	100.0	84.8	10.9	4.3	0.0	0.0
Curfew and loitering law violations	100.0	87.5	1.5	11.0	0.0	0.0	NA	NA	NA	NA	NA	NA	NA	NA	NA	NA	NA	NA

NA = Not available.
* = Less than one-tenth of one percent.
1 Because of rounding, the percentages may not sum to 100.   2 Violent crimes are offenses of murder and nonnegligent manslaughter, rape, robbery, and aggravated assault. Property crimes are offenses of burglary, larceny-theft, motor vehicle theft, and arson.   3 The rape figures in this table are aggregate totals of the data submitted based on both the legacy and revised Uniform Crime Reporting definitions.

Table 61A. Arrests, Nonmetropolitan Counties, Distribution by Ethnicity, 2019

(Number, percent; 1,622 agencies; 2019 estimated population 18,187,868.)

Offense charged	Total arrests			Percent distribution[1]			Arrests under 18		
	Total[2]	Hispanic or Latino	Not Hispanic or Latino	Total[2]	Hispanic or Latino	Not Hispanic or Latino	Total[2]	Hispanic or Latino	Not Hispanic or Latino
Total	406,243	32,493	373,750	100.0	8.0	92.0	15,050	1,527	13,523
Violent crime[3]	12,375	1,124	11,251	100.0	9.1	90.9	738	73	665
Murder and nonnegligent manslaughter	376	23	353	100.0	6.1	93.9	24	2	22
Rape[4]	1,008	96	912	100.0	9.5	90.5	167	7	160
Robbery	581	57	524	100.0	9.8	90.2	42	6	36
Aggravated assault	10,410	948	9,462	100.0	9.1	90.9	505	58	447
Property crime[3]	19,910	1,252	18,658	100.0	6.3	93.7	1,432	132	1,300
Burglary	5,780	343	5,437	100.0	5.9	94.1	437	34	403
Larceny-theft	11,257	668	10,589	100.0	5.9	94.1	701	65	636
Motor vehicle theft	2,560	226	2,334	100.0	8.8	91.2	249	27	222
Arson	313	15	298	100.0	4.8	95.2	45	6	39
Other assaults	32,620	2,436	30,184	100.0	7.5	92.5	2,976	269	2,707
Forgery and counterfeiting	1,265	94	1,171	100.0	7.4	92.6	7	1	6
Fraud	3,613	284	3,329	100.0	7.9	92.1	62	7	55
Embezzlement	213	8	205	100.0	3.8	96.2	2	1	1
Stolen property; buying, receiving, possessing	2,601	137	2,464	100.0	5.3	94.7	111	9	102
Vandalism	4,912	321	4,591	100.0	6.5	93.5	741	52	689
Weapons; carrying, possessing, etc.	4,208	399	3,809	100.0	9.5	90.5	189	24	165
Prostitution and commercialized vice	53	6	47	100.0	11.3	88.7	2	1	1
Sex offenses (except forcible rape and prostitution)	1,345	110	1,235	100.0	8.2	91.8	257	12	245
Drug abuse violations	71,748	6,148	65,600	100.0	8.6	91.4	1,979	280	1,699
Gambling	95	21	74	100.0	22.1	77.9	2	0	2
Offenses against the family and children	5,513	348	5,165	100.0	6.3	93.7	70	11	59
Driving under the influence	54,635	6,405	48,230	100.0	11.7	88.3	343	46	297
Liquor laws	6,615	680	5,935	100.0	10.3	89.7	1,433	124	1,309
Drunkenness	8,042	734	7,308	100.0	9.1	90.9	93	18	75
Disorderly conduct	7,424	546	6,878	100.0	7.4	92.6	1,131	90	1,041
Vagrancy	63	3	60	100.0	4.8	95.2	2	0	2
All other offenses (except traffic)	168,870	11,433	157,437	100.0	6.8	93.2	3,359	373	2,986
Suspicion	2	0	2	100.0	0.0	100.0	0	0	0
Curfew and loitering law violations	121	4	117	100.0	3.3	96.7	121	4	117

Table 61A. Arrests, Nonmetropolitan Counties, Distribution by Ethnicity, 2019—Continued

(Number, percent; 1,622 agencies; 2019 estimated population 18,187,868.)

Offense charged	Percent distribution[1]			Arrests 18 and over			Percent distribution[1]		
	Total[2]	Hispanic or Latino	Not Hispanic or Latino	Total[2]	Hispanic or Latino	Not Hispanic or Latino	Total[2]	Hispanic or Latino	Not Hispanic or Latino
Total	100.0	10.1	89.9	391,193	30,966	360,227	100.0	7.9	92.1
Violent crime[3]	100.0	9.9	90.1	11,637	1,051	10,586	100.0	9.0	91.0
Murder and nonnegligent manslaughter	100.0	8.3	91.7	352	21	331	100.0	6.0	94.0
Rape[4]	100.0	4.2	95.8	841	89	752	100.0	10.6	89.4
Robbery	100.0	14.3	85.7	539	51	488	100.0	9.5	90.5
Aggravated assault	100.0	11.5	88.5	9,905	890	9,015	100.0	9.0	91.0
Property crime[3]	100.0	9.2	90.8	18,478	1,120	17,358	100.0	6.1	93.9
Burglary	100.0	7.8	92.2	5,343	309	5,034	100.0	5.8	94.2
Larceny-theft	100.0	9.3	90.7	10,556	603	9,953	100.0	5.7	94.3
Motor vehicle theft	100.0	10.8	89.2	2,311	199	2,112	100.0	8.6	91.4
Arson	100.0	13.3	86.7	268	9	259	100.0	3.4	96.6
Other assaults	100.0	9.0	91.0	29,644	2,167	27,477	100.0	7.3	92.7
Forgery and counterfeiting	100.0	14.3	85.7	1,258	93	1,165	100.0	7.4	92.6
Fraud	100.0	11.3	88.7	3,551	277	3,274	100.0	7.8	92.2
Embezzlement	100.0	50.0	50.0	211	7	204	100.0	3.3	96.7
Stolen property; buying, receiving, possessing	100.0	8.1	91.9	2,490	128	2,362	100.0	5.1	94.9
Vandalism	100.0	7.0	93.0	4,171	269	3,902	100.0	6.4	93.6
Weapons; carrying, possessing, etc.	100.0	12.7	87.3	4,019	375	3,644	100.0	9.3	90.7
Prostitution and commercialized vice	100.0	50.0	50.0	51	5	46	100.0	9.8	90.2
Sex offenses (except forcible rape and prostitution)	100.0	4.7	95.3	1,088	98	990	100.0	9.0	91.0
Drug abuse violations	100.0	14.1	85.9	69,769	5,868	63,901	100.0	8.4	91.6
Gambling	100.0	0.0	100.0	93	21	72	100.0	22.6	77.4
Offenses against the family and children	100.0	15.7	84.3	5,443	337	5,106	100.0	6.2	93.8
Driving under the influence	100.0	13.4	86.6	54,292	6,359	47,933	100.0	11.7	88.3
Liquor laws	100.0	8.7	91.3	5,182	556	4,626	100.0	10.7	89.3
Drunkenness	100.0	19.4	80.6	7,949	716	7,233	100.0	9.0	91.0
Disorderly conduct	100.0	8.0	92.0	6,293	456	5,837	100.0	7.2	92.8
Vagrancy	100.0	0.0	100.0	61	3	58	100.0	4.9	95.1
All other offenses (except traffic)	100.0	11.1	88.9	165,511	11,060	154,451	100.0	6.7	93.3
Suspicion				2	0	2	100.0	0.0	100.0
Curfew and loitering law violations	100.0	3.3	96.7	NA	NA	NA	NA	NA	NA

NA = Not available.
1 Because of rounding, the percentages may not sum to 100.   2 The ethnicity totals are representative of those agencies that provided ethnicity breakdowns. Not all agencies provide ethnicity data; therefore, the race and ethnicity totals will not be equal.   3 Violent crimes are offenses of murder and nonnegligent manslaughter, rape, robbery, and aggravated assault. Property crimes are offenses of burglary, larceny-theft, motor vehicle theft, and arson.   4 The rape figures in this table are aggregate totals of the data submitted based on both the legacy and revised Uniform Crime Reporting definitions.

Table 62. Arrest Trends, Suburban Areas,[1] 2018–2019

(Number, percent change; 5,272 agencies; 2019 estimated population 87,751,349; 2018 estimated population 87,433,861.)

Offense charged	Number of persons arrested								
	Total, all ages			Under 18 years of age			18 years of age and over		
	2018	2019	Percent change	2018	2019	Percent change	2018	2019	Percent change
Total[2]	2,591,429	2,484,062	-4.1	184,627	180,316	-2.3	2,406,802	2,303,746	-4.3
Violent crime[3]	105,996	102,508	-3.3	11,371	11,399	+0.2	94,625	91,109	-3.7
Murder and nonnegligent manslaughter	2,061	2,023	-1.8	139	143	+2.9	1,922	1,880	-2.2
Rape[4]	5,881	5,760	-2.1	1,091	1,115	+2.2	4,790	4,645	-3.0
Robbery	15,416	14,602	-5.3	3,134	3,487	+11.3	12,282	11,115	-9.5
Aggravated assault	82,638	80,123	-3.0	7,007	6,654	-5.0	75,631	73,469	-2.9
Property crime[3]	284,523	274,784	-3.4	31,977	30,481	-4.7	252,546	244,303	-3.3
Burglary	40,566	37,322	-8.0	5,298	4,727	-10.8	35,268	32,595	-7.6
Larceny-theft	222,094	217,404	-2.1	23,313	22,395	-3.9	198,781	195,009	-1.9
Motor vehicle theft	19,695	18,019	-8.5	2,786	2,840	+1.9	16,909	15,179	-10.2
Arson	2,168	2,039	-6.0	580	519	-10.5	1,588	1,520	-4.3
Other assaults	234,875	230,627	-1.8	32,368	33,495	+3.5	202,507	197,132	-2.7
Forgery and counterfeiting	13,236	12,239	-7.5	290	235	-19.0	12,946	12,004	-7.3
Fraud	31,660	31,137	-1.7	925	1,071	+15.8	30,735	30,066	-2.2
Embezzlement	3,577	3,439	-3.9	128	137	+7.0	3,449	3,302	-4.3
Stolen property; buying, receiving, possessing	23,165	21,309	-8.0	2,037	1,943	-4.6	21,128	19,366	-8.3
Vandalism	40,917	40,903	*	7,998	8,284	+3.6	32,919	32,619	-0.9
Weapons; carrying, possessing, etc.	35,762	35,780	+0.1	3,957	4,000	+1.1	31,805	31,780	-0.1
Prostitution and commercialized vice	3,229	3,312	+2.6	42	37	-11.9	3,187	3,275	+2.8
Sex offenses (except forcible rape and prostitution)	11,194	10,388	-7.2	2,084	1,867	-10.4	9,110	8,521	-6.5
Drug abuse violations	447,268	409,060	-8.5	26,978	23,888	-11.5	420,290	385,172	-8.4
Gambling	507	620	+22.3	27	54	+100.0	480	566	+17.9
Offenses against the family and children	27,126	24,067	-11.3	666	614	-7.8	26,460	23,453	-11.4
Driving under the influence	293,477	287,388	-2.1	1,414	1,391	-1.6	292,063	285,997	-2.1
Liquor laws	45,132	41,914	-7.1	7,272	6,690	-8.0	37,860	35,224	-7.0
Drunkenness	67,034	63,147	-5.8	1,017	948	-6.8	66,017	62,199	-5.8
Disorderly conduct	75,967	75,533	-0.6	14,076	14,812	+5.2	61,891	60,721	-1.9
Vagrancy	3,161	3,061	-3.2	110	54	-50.9	3,051	3,007	-1.4
All other offenses (except traffic)	839,853	809,350	-3.6	36,120	35,420	-1.9	803,733	773,930	-3.7
Suspicion	272	175	-35.7	9	6	-33.3	263	169	-35.7
Curfew and loitering law violations	3,770	3,496	-7.3	3,770	3,496	-7.3	NA	NA	NA

NA = Not available.

1 Suburban areas include law enforcement agencies in cities with less than 50,000 inhabitants and county law enforcement agencies that are within a Metropolitan Statistical Area. Suburban areas exclude all metropolitan agencies associated with a principal city.   2 Does not include suspicion.   3 Violent crimes are offenses of murder and nonnegligent manslaughter, rape, robbery, and aggravated assault. Property crimes are offenses of burglary, larceny-theft, motor vehicle theft, and arson.   4 The rape figures in this table are aggregate totals of the data submitted based on both the legacy and revised Uniform Crime Reporting definitions.

Table 63. Arrest Trends, Suburban Areas[1], by Age and Sex, 2018–2019

(Number, percent change; 5,272 agencies; 2019 estimated population 87,751,349; 2018 estimated population 87,433,861.)

Offense charged	Male						Female					
	Total			Under 18			Total			Under 18		
	2018	2019	Percent change	2018	2019	Percent change	2018	2019	Percent change	2018	2019	Percent change
Total[2]	1,880,574	1,800,596	-4.3	129,970	125,813	-3.2	710,855	683,466	-3.9	54,657	54,503	-0.3
Violent crime[3]	84,377	81,602	-3.3	9,040	9,093	+0.6	21,619	20,906	-3.3	2,331	2,306	-1.1
Murder and nonnegligent manslaughter	1,795	1,800	+0.3	121	123	+1.7	266	223	-16.2	18	20	+11.1
Rape[4]	5,723	5,578	-2.5	1,053	1,048	-0.5	158	182	+15.2	38	67	+76.3
Robbery	13,114	12,346	-5.9	2,784	3,044	+9.3	2,302	2,256	-2.0	350	443	+26.6
Aggravated assault	63,745	61,878	-2.9	5,082	4,878	-4.0	18,893	18,245	-3.4	1,925	1,776	-7.7
Property crime[3]	176,638	169,465	-4.1	21,610	20,317	-6.0	107,885	105,319	-2.4	10,367	10,164	-2.0
Burglary	32,785	30,000	-8.5	4,604	4,104	-10.9	7,781	7,322	-5.9	694	623	-10.2
Larceny-theft	126,933	123,966	-2.3	14,226	13,497	-5.1	95,161	93,438	-1.8	9,087	8,898	-2.1
Motor vehicle theft	15,228	13,860	-9.0	2,303	2,270	-1.4	4,467	4,159	-6.9	483	570	+18.0
Arson	1,692	1,639	-3.1	477	446	-6.5	476	400	-16.0	103	73	-29.1
Other assaults	166,554	162,601	-2.4	20,595	21,155	+2.7	68,321	68,026	-0.4	11,773	12,340	+4.8
Forgery and counterfeiting	8,821	8,368	-5.1	232	186	-19.8	4,415	3,871	-12.3	58	49	-15.5
Fraud	20,161	20,078	-0.4	622	738	+18.6	11,499	11,059	-3.8	303	333	+9.9
Embezzlement	1,781	1,683	-5.5	81	66	-18.5	1,796	1,756	-2.2	47	71	+51.1
Stolen property; buying, receiving, possessing	18,016	16,588	-7.9	1,687	1,577	-6.5	5,149	4,721	-8.3	350	366	+4.6
Vandalism	32,100	31,937	-0.5	6,602	6,776	+2.6	8,817	8,966	+1.7	1,396	1,508	+8.0
Weapons; carrying, possessing, etc.	32,064	32,145	+0.3	3,435	3,497	+1.8	3,698	3,635	-1.7	522	503	-3.6
Prostitution and commercialized vice	1,492	1,555	+4.2	27	28	+3.7	1,737	1,757	+1.2	15	9	-40.0
Sex offenses (except forcible rape and prostitution)	10,442	9,760	-6.5	1,853	1,652	-10.8	752	628	-16.5	231	215	-6.9
Drug abuse violations	333,507	303,263	-9.1	20,113	17,615	-12.4	113,761	105,797	-7.0	6,865	6,273	-8.6
Gambling	402	462	+14.9	23	47	+104.3	105	158	+50.5	4	7	+75.0
Offenses against the family and children	20,238	17,707	-12.5	438	369	-15.8	6,888	6,360	-7.7	228	245	+7.5
Driving under the influence	217,554	212,762	-2.2	1,069	1,051	-1.7	75,923	74,626	-1.7	345	340	-1.4
Liquor laws	31,013	29,004	-6.5	4,183	3,849	-8.0	14,119	12,910	-8.6	3,089	2,841	-8.0
Drunkenness	52,092	48,939	-6.1	667	627	-6.0	14,942	14,208	-4.9	350	321	-8.3
Disorderly conduct	53,986	53,274	-1.3	9,209	9,482	+3.0	21,981	22,259	+1.3	4,867	5,330	+9.5
Vagrancy	2,382	2,366	-0.7	80	46	-42.5	779	695	-10.8	30	8	-73.3
All other offenses (except traffic)	614,442	594,638	-3.2	25,892	25,243	-2.5	225,411	214,712	-4.7	10,228	10,177	-0.5
Suspicion	203	126	-37.9	7	6	-14.3	69	49	-29.0	2	0	-100.0
Curfew and loitering law violations	2,512	2,399	-4.5	2,512	2,399	-4.5	1,258	1,097	-12.8	1,258	1,097	-12.8

1 Suburban areas include law enforcement agencies in cities with less than 50,000 inhabitants and county law enforcement agencies that are within a Metropolitan Statistical Area. Suburban areas exclude all metropolitan agencies associated with a principal city.   2 Does not include suspicion.   3 Violent crimes are offenses of murder and nonnegligent manslaughter, rape, robbery, and aggravated assault. Property crimes are offenses of burglary, larceny-theft, motor vehicle theft, and arson.   4 The rape figures in this table are aggregate totals of the data submitted based on both the legacy and revised Uniform Crime Reporting definitions.

Table 64. Arrests, Suburban Areas,[1] Distribution by Age, 2019

(Number, percent; 5,820 agencies; 2019 estimated population 97,421,942.)

Offense charged	Total, all ages	Ages under 15	Ages under 18	Ages 18 and over	Under 10	10–12	13–14	15	16	17	18	19	20
Total	2,713,281	61,425	194,552	2,518,729	1,081	14,262	46,082	37,609	43,917	51,601	72,401	78,122	77,327
Total percent distribution[2]	100.0	2.3	7.2	92.8	*	0.5	1.7	1.4	1.6	1.9	2.7	2.9	2.8
Violent crime[3]	110,435	3,981	12,260	98,175	72	1,009	2,900	2,465	2,745	3,069	3,451	3,371	3,133
Violent crime percent distribution[2]	100.0	3.6	11.1	88.9	0.1	0.9	2.6	2.2	2.5	2.8	3.1	3.1	2.8
Murder and nonnegligent manslaughter	2,251	20	162	2,089	0	7	13	23	50	69	117	125	108
Rape[4]	6,183	476	1,196	4,987	16	132	328	213	228	279	287	237	226
Robbery	15,584	814	3,681	11,903	4	88	722	793	993	1,081	1,136	910	680
Aggravated assault	86,417	2,671	7,221	79,196	52	782	1,837	1,436	1,474	1,640	1,911	2,099	2,119
Property crime[3]	297,738	9,453	32,836	264,902	145	1,864	7,444	6,762	7,785	8,836	10,542	9,633	8,606
Property crime percent distribution[2]	100.0	3.2	11.0	89.0	*	0.6	2.5	2.3	2.6	3.0	3.5	3.2	2.9
Burglary	40,785	1,644	5,259	35,526	29	344	1,271	1,098	1,219	1,298	1,455	1,359	1,163
Larceny-theft	235,319	6,746	23,911	211,408	93	1,365	5,288	4,811	5,664	6,690	8,378	7,627	6,862
Motor vehicle theft	19,436	766	3,102	16,334	1	58	707	755	806	775	646	600	548
Arson	2,198	297	564	1,634	22	97	178	98	96	73	63	47	33
Other assaults	251,819	16,274	36,977	214,842	352	4,632	11,290	7,093	7,119	6,491	5,515	5,419	5,603
Forgery and counterfeiting	13,438	38	263	13,175	0	8	30	47	62	116	309	508	526
Fraud	33,686	300	1,146	32,540	0	49	251	191	283	372	602	812	880
Embezzlement	3,697	11	147	3,550	0	0	11	15	37	84	172	203	187
Stolen property; buying, receiving, possessing	23,275	434	2,118	21,157	0	39	395	456	559	669	771	762	712
Vandalism	44,333	3,743	8,900	35,433	129	1,020	2,594	1,668	1,783	1,706	1,749	1,513	1,388
Weapons; carrying, possessing, etc.	38,587	1,464	4,290	34,297	20	418	1,026	792	907	1,127	1,366	1,363	1,381
Prostitution and commercialized vice	3,510	9	39	3,471	0	3	6	6	14	10	38	73	86
Sex offenses (except forcible rape and prostitution)	10,967	938	1,953	9,014	18	253	667	376	316	323	329	277	254
Drug abuse violations	443,360	4,823	25,926	417,434	24	685	4,114	4,489	6,510	10,104	17,982	19,209	17,966
Gambling	822	26	118	704	1	3	22	21	35	36	17	30	24
Offenses against the family and children	27,274	204	664	26,610	10	42	152	138	158	164	220	237	286
Driving under the influence	310,392	34	1,493	308,899	3	9	22	53	304	1,102	2,935	4,622	5,674
Liquor laws	44,448	1,051	7,208	37,240	3	166	882	1,063	1,873	3,221	7,354	6,867	5,173
Drunkenness	66,799	170	996	65,803	0	31	139	149	244	433	1,194	1,437	1,418
Disorderly conduct	80,244	6,341	15,573	64,671	94	1,577	4,670	3,422	3,159	2,651	2,275	2,005	2,068
Vagrancy	3,214	17	55	3,159	1	3	13	4	16	18	74	61	74
All other offenses (except traffic)	901,402	10,937	37,938	863,464	200	2,259	8,478	7,585	9,015	10,401	15,499	19,718	21,885
Suspicion	196	1	7	189	0	0	1	0	3	3	7	2	3
Curfew and loitering law violations	3,645	1,176	3,645	NA	9	192	975	814	990	665	NA	NA	NA

Table 64. Arrests, Suburban Areas,[1] Distribution by Age, 2019—Continued

(Number, percent; 5,820 agencies; 2019 estimated population 97,421,942.)

Offense charged	21	22	23	24	25–29	30–34	35–39	40–44	45–49	50–54	55–59	60–64	65 and over
Total	79,438	79,858	82,035	84,757	454,655	407,750	341,334	237,021	178,898	141,917	107,510	56,276	39,430
Total percent distribution[2]	2.9	2.9	3.0	3.1	16.8	15.0	12.6	8.7	6.6	5.2	4.0	2.1	1.5
Violent crime[3]	3,359	3,152	3,331	3,328	17,650	15,559	12,789	8,843	6,734	5,207	4,053	2,298	1,917
Violent crime percent distribution[2]	3.0	2.9	3.0	3.0	16.0	14.1	11.6	8.0	6.1	4.7	3.7	2.1	1.7
Murder and nonnegligent manslaughter	114	86	85	79	387	282	215	155	119	79	55	40	43
Rape[4]	200	159	163	157	712	695	605	396	360	275	212	139	164
Robbery	638	546	487	482	2,230	1,712	1,198	699	422	355	245	111	52
Aggravated assault	2,407	2,361	2,596	2,610	14,321	12,870	10,771	7,593	5,833	4,498	3,541	2,008	1,658
Property crime[3]	8,152	7,742	7,975	8,399	46,704	43,865	35,720	24,304	18,530	15,015	10,868	5,385	3,462
Property crime percent distribution[2]	2.7	2.6	2.7	2.8	15.7	14.7	12.0	8.2	6.2	5.0	3.7	1.8	1.2
Burglary	1,140	1,031	1,195	1,242	6,616	6,508	4,905	3,071	2,250	1,694	1,148	484	265
Larceny-theft	6,443	6,124	6,187	6,501	36,468	34,003	28,296	19,625	15,185	12,624	9,273	4,725	3,087
Motor vehicle theft	533	545	553	603	3,343	3,101	2,277	1,435	985	616	355	126	68
Arson	36	42	40	53	277	253	242	173	110	81	92	50	42
Other assaults	6,480	6,350	6,559	6,829	37,063	34,341	30,127	21,296	16,382	13,257	9,986	5,270	4,365
Forgery and counterfeiting	386	404	403	451	2,431	2,203	1,888	1,288	905	676	450	228	119
Fraud	899	949	955	1,085	5,847	5,677	4,603	3,313	2,473	1,962	1,321	655	507
Embezzlement	131	152	108	106	610	511	393	316	270	164	128	63	36
Stolen property; buying, receiving, possessing	695	685	716	696	4,182	3,751	3,097	1,992	1,310	916	524	239	109
Vandalism	1,365	1,352	1,344	1,254	6,732	5,495	4,378	2,817	2,085	1,650	1,183	614	514
Weapons; carrying, possessing, etc.	1,457	1,435	1,379	1,497	6,957	5,255	4,070	2,665	1,890	1,446	1,132	558	446
Prostitution and commercialized vice	107	115	111	120	674	578	436	328	295	205	157	73	75
Sex offenses (except forcible rape and prostitution)	230	217	218	214	1,162	1,181	1,159	818	737	623	606	426	563
Drug abuse violations	17,162	16,248	16,076	16,029	79,725	66,347	53,256	34,625	24,076	17,945	12,574	5,639	2,575
Gambling	14	13	16	24	97	81	92	76	72	63	44	14	27
Offenses against the family and children	364	412	485	535	4,312	5,310	5,188	3,608	2,506	1,557	955	413	222
Driving under the influence	9,347	10,348	11,227	11,678	57,167	46,666	38,640	29,302	24,165	20,818	17,546	10,504	8,260
Liquor laws	944	705	607	628	2,707	2,383	2,129	1,731	1,564	1,546	1,492	865	545
Drunkenness	1,979	1,885	1,879	1,842	9,933	9,630	8,708	6,559	5,700	5,145	4,633	2,526	1,335
Disorderly conduct	2,383	2,156	2,146	2,112	10,748	9,424	7,995	5,708	4,732	4,026	3,320	1,977	1,596
Vagrancy	63	60	85	90	414	409	386	353	274	311	250	156	99
All other offenses (except traffic)	23,909	25,471	26,406	27,836	159,503	149,052	126,252	87,067	64,182	49,378	36,278	18,370	12,658
Suspicion	12	7	9	4	37	32	28	12	16	7	10	3	0
Curfew and loitering law violations	NA	NA	NA	NA	NA	NA	NA	NA	NA	NA	NA	NA	NA

NA = Not available.

* = Less than one-tenth of one percent.

1 Suburban areas include law enforcement agencies in cities with less than 50,000 inhabitants and county law enforcement agencies that are within a Metropolitan Statistical Area Suburban areas exclude all metropolitan agencies associated with a principal city.   2 Because of rounding, the percentages may not sum to 100.   3 Violent crimes are offenses of murder and nonnegligent manslaughter, rape, robbery, and aggravated assault. Property crimes are offenses of burglary, larceny-theft, motor vehicle theft, and arson.   4 The rape figures in this table are aggregate totals of the data submitted based on both the legacy and revised Uniform Crime Reporting definitions.

Table 65. Arrests, Suburban Areas,[1] Persons Under 15, 18, 21, and 25 Years of Age, 2019

(Number, percent; 5,820 agencies; 2019 estimated population 97,421,942.)

Offense charged	Total, all ages	Number of persons arrested				Percent of total all ages			
		Under 15	Under 18	Under 21	Under 25	Under 15	Under 18	Under 21	Under 25
Total	2,713,281	61,425	194,552	422,402	748,490	2.3	7.2	15.6	27.6
Violent crime[2]	110,435	3,981	12,260	22,215	35,385	3.6	11.1	20.1	32.0
Murder and nonnegligent manslaughter	2,251	20	162	512	876	0.9	7.2	22.7	38.9
Rape[3]	6,183	476	1,196	1,946	2,625	7.7	19.3	31.5	42.5
Robbery	15,584	814	3,681	6,407	8,560	5.2	23.6	41.1	54.9
Aggravated assault	86,417	2,671	7,221	13,350	23,324	3.1	8.4	15.4	27.0
Property crime[2]	297,738	9,453	32,836	61,617	93,885	3.2	11.0	20.7	31.5
Burglary	40,785	1,644	5,259	9,236	13,844	4.0	12.9	22.6	33.9
Larceny-theft	235,319	6,746	23,911	46,778	72,033	2.9	10.2	19.9	30.6
Motor vehicle theft	19,436	766	3,102	4,896	7,130	3.9	16.0	25.2	36.7
Arson	2,198	297	564	707	878	13.5	25.7	32.2	39.9
Other assaults	251,819	16,274	36,977	53,514	79,732	6.5	14.7	21.3	31.7
Forgery and counterfeiting	13,438	38	263	1,606	3,250	0.3	2.0	12.0	24.2
Fraud	33,686	300	1,146	3,440	7,328	0.9	3.4	10.2	21.8
Embezzlement	3,697	11	147	709	1,206	0.3	4.0	19.2	32.6
Stolen property; buying, receiving, possessing	23,275	434	2,118	4,363	7,155	1.9	9.1	18.7	30.7
Vandalism	44,333	3,743	8,900	13,550	18,865	8.4	20.1	30.6	42.6
Weapons; carrying, possessing, etc.	38,587	1,464	4,290	8,400	14,168	3.8	11.1	21.8	36.7
Prostitution and commercialized vice	3,510	9	39	236	689	0.3	1.1	6.7	19.6
Sex offenses (except forcible rape and prostitution)	10,967	938	1,953	2,813	3,692	8.6	17.8	25.6	33.7
Drug abuse violations	443,360	4,823	25,926	81,083	146,598	1.1	5.8	18.3	33.1
Gambling	822	26	118	189	256	3.2	14.4	23.0	31.1
Offenses against the family and children	27,274	204	664	1,407	3,203	0.7	2.4	5.2	11.7
Driving under the influence	310,392	34	1,493	14,724	57,324	*	0.5	4.7	18.5
Liquor laws	44,448	1,051	7,208	26,602	29,486	2.4	16.2	59.8	66.3
Drunkenness	66,799	170	996	5,045	12,630	0.3	1.5	7.6	18.9
Disorderly conduct	80,244	6,341	15,573	21,921	30,718	7.9	19.4	27.3	38.3
Vagrancy	3,214	17	55	264	562	0.5	1.7	8.2	17.5
All other offenses (except traffic)	901,402	10,937	37,938	95,040	198,662	1.2	4.2	10.5	22.0
Suspicion	196	1	7	19	51	0.5	3.6	9.7	26.0
Curfew and loitering law violations	3,645	1,176	3,645	3,645	3,645	32.3	100.0	100.0	100.0

* = Less than one-tenth of one percent.
1 Suburban areas include law enforcement agencies in cities with less than 50,000 inhabitants and county law enforcement agencies that are within a Metropolitan Statistical Area. Suburban areas exclude all metropolitan agencies associated with a principal city.   2 Violent crimes are offenses of murder and nonnegligent manslaughter, rape, robbery, and aggravated assault. Property crimes are offenses of burglary, larceny-theft, motor vehicle theft, and arson.   3 The rape figures in this table are aggregate totals of the data submitted based on both the legacy and revised Uniform Crime Reporting definitions.

Table 66. Arrests, Suburban Areas,[1] Distribution by Sex, 2019

(Number, percent; 5,820 agencies; 2019 estimated population 97,421,942.)

Offense charged	Number of persons arrested			Percent male	Percent female	Percent distribution[2]		
	Total	Male	Female			Total	Male	Female
Total	2,713,281	1,960,734	752,547	72.3	27.7	100.0	100.0	100.0
Violent crime[3]	110,435	87,824	22,611	79.5	20.5	4.1	4.5	3.0
Murder and nonnegligent manslaughter	2,251	2,003	248	89.0	11.0	0.1	0.1	*
Rape[4]	6,183	5,966	217	96.5	3.5	0.2	0.3	*
Robbery	15,584	13,151	2,433	84.4	15.6	0.6	0.7	0.3
Aggravated assault	86,417	66,704	19,713	77.2	22.8	3.2	3.4	2.6
Property crime[3]	297,738	183,454	114,284	61.6	38.4	11.0	9.4	15.2
Burglary	40,785	32,736	8,049	80.3	19.7	1.5	1.7	1.1
Larceny-theft	235,319	134,011	101,308	56.9	43.1	8.7	6.8	13.5
Motor vehicle theft	19,436	14,946	4,490	76.9	23.1	0.7	0.8	0.6
Arson	2,198	1,761	437	80.1	19.9	0.1	0.1	0.1
Other assaults	251,819	177,423	74,396	70.5	29.5	9.3	9.0	9.9
Forgery and counterfeiting	13,438	9,156	4,282	68.1	31.9	0.5	0.5	0.6
Fraud	33,686	21,656	12,030	64.3	35.7	1.2	1.1	1.6
Embezzlement	3,697	1,826	1,871	49.4	50.6	0.1	0.1	0.2
Stolen property; buying, receiving, possessing	23,275	18,113	5,162	77.8	22.2	0.9	0.9	0.7
Vandalism	44,333	34,527	9,806	77.9	22.1	1.6	1.8	1.3
Weapons; carrying, possessing, etc.	38,587	34,576	4,011	89.6	10.4	1.4	1.8	0.5
Prostitution and commercialized vice	3,510	1,670	1,840	47.6	52.4	0.1	0.1	0.2
Sex offenses (except forcible rape and prostitution)	10,967	10,257	710	93.5	6.5	0.4	0.5	0.1
Drug abuse violations	443,360	326,702	116,658	73.7	26.3	16.3	16.7	15.5
Gambling	822	555	267	67.5	32.5	*	*	*
Offenses against the family and children	27,274	20,168	7,106	73.9	26.1	1.0	1.0	0.9
Driving under the influence	310,392	228,378	82,014	73.6	26.4	11.4	11.6	10.9
Liquor laws	44,448	30,718	13,730	69.1	30.9	1.6	1.6	1.8
Drunkenness	66,799	51,745	15,054	77.5	22.5	2.5	2.6	2.0
Disorderly conduct	80,244	56,553	23,691	70.5	29.5	3.0	2.9	3.1
Vagrancy	3,214	2,475	739	77.0	23.0	0.1	0.1	0.1
All other offenses (except traffic)	901,402	660,322	241,080	73.3	26.7	33.2	33.7	32.0
Suspicion	196	138	58	70.4	29.6	*	*	*
Curfew and loitering law violations	3,645	2,498	1,147	68.5	31.5	0.1	0.1	0.2

* = Less than one-tenth of one percent.
1 Suburban areas include law enforcement agencies in cities with less than 50,000 inhabitants and county law enforcement agencies that are within a Metropolitan Statistical Area. Suburban areas exclude all metropolitan agencies associated with a principal city.   2 Because of rounding, the percentages may not sum to 100.   3 Violent crimes are offenses of murder and nonnegligent manslaughter, rape, robbery, and aggravated assault. Property crimes are offenses of burglary, larceny-theft, motor vehicle theft, and arson.   4 The rape figures in this table are aggregate totals of the data submitted based on both the legacy and revised Uniform Crime Reporting definitions.

Table 67. Arrests, Suburban Areas,[1] Distribution by Race, 2019

(Number, percent; 5,820 agencies; 2019 estimated population 97,421,942.)

Offense charged	Total arrests						Percent distribution[2]						Arrests under 18					
	Total	White	Black	American Indian or Alaskan Native	Asian	Native Hawaiian or Other Pacific Islander	Total	White	Black	American Indian or Alaskan Native	Asian	Native Hawaiian or Other Pacific Islander	Total	White	Black	American Indian or Alaskan Native	Asian	Native Hawaiian or Other Pacific Islander
Total	2,676,549	1,924,521	686,744	25,763	33,063	6,458	100.0	71.9	25.7	1.0	1.2	0.2	190,581	122,763	63,391	1,899	2,048	480
Violent crime[3]	109,441	71,912	34,760	935	1,513	321	100.0	65.7	31.8	0.9	1.4	0.3	12,122	6,350	5,553	83	105	31
Murder and nonnegligent manslaughter	2,493	1,352	1,091	21	19	10	100.0	54.2	43.8	0.8	0.8	0.4	200	100	92	8	0	0
Rape[4]	6,050	4,514	1,378	44	91	23	100.0	74.6	22.8	0.7	1.5	0.4	1,161	873	271	4	12	1
Robbery	15,411	7,066	8,076	80	139	50	100.0	45.9	52.4	0.5	0.9	0.3	3,643	1,211	2,375	9	30	18
Aggravated assault	85,487	58,980	24,215	790	1,264	238	100.0	69.0	28.3	0.9	1.5	0.3	7,118	4,166	2,815	62	63	12
Property crime[3]	291,106	192,823	91,804	2,435	3,459	585	100.0	66.2	31.5	0.8	1.2	0.2	31,949	17,222	13,991	242	423	71
Burglary	40,311	29,083	10,478	241	403	106	100.0	72.1	26.0	0.6	1.0	0.3	5,167	3,114	1,954	37	44	18
Larceny-theft	229,363	148,429	75,800	1,998	2,801	335	100.0	64.7	33.0	0.9	1.2	0.1	23,155	12,140	10,450	169	350	46
Motor vehicle theft	19,259	13,656	5,083	175	213	132	100.0	70.9	26.4	0.9	1.1	0.7	3,071	1,574	1,436	29	25	7
Arson	2,173	1,655	443	21	42	12	100.0	76.2	20.4	1.0	1.9	0.6	556	394	151	7	4	0
Other assaults	246,791	173,322	67,576	2,241	3,124	528	100.0	70.2	27.4	0.9	1.3	0.2	36,142	21,488	13,965	315	310	64
Forgery and counterfeiting	13,250	8,717	4,276	71	178	8	100.0	65.8	32.3	0.5	1.3	0.1	258	165	90	0	3	0
Fraud	33,166	21,586	10,771	268	496	45	100.0	65.1	32.5	0.8	1.5	0.1	1,108	575	510	10	12	1
Embezzlement	3,654	2,215	1,362	17	50	10	100.0	60.6	37.3	0.5	1.4	0.3	146	62	82	0	2	0
Stolen property; buying, receiving, possessing	22,906	15,093	7,311	229	225	48	100.0	65.9	31.9	1.0	1.0	0.2	2,068	838	1,197	11	17	5
Vandalism	43,396	31,752	10,631	466	481	66	100.0	73.2	24.5	1.1	1.1	0.2	8,628	6,131	2,318	95	71	13
Weapons; carrying, possessing, etc.	38,056	23,161	14,176	204	399	116	100.0	60.9	37.3	0.5	1.0	0.3	4,212	2,514	1,612	21	52	13
Prostitution and commercialized vice	3,451	1,913	1,128	15	378	17	100.0	55.4	32.7	0.4	11.0	0.5	38	32	6	0	0	0
Sex offenses (except forcible rape and prostitution)	10,827	8,499	2,020	80	203	25	100.0	78.5	18.7	0.7	1.9	0.2	1,921	1,451	426	8	31	5
Drug abuse violations	437,451	315,018	113,775	3,037	4,756	865	100.0	72.0	26.0	0.7	1.1	0.2	25,392	19,425	5,292	269	322	84
Gambling	815	491	222	4	74	24	100.0	60.2	27.2	0.5	9.1	2.9	117	82	31	0	4	0
Offenses against the family and children	27,004	18,426	7,961	386	213	18	100.0	68.2	29.5	1.4	0.8	0.1	647	493	121	30	3	0
Driving under the influence	306,337	251,544	45,388	2,042	6,512	851	100.0	82.1	14.8	0.7	2.1	0.3	1,458	1,328	97	13	15	5
Liquor laws	43,768	34,581	7,542	785	779	81	100.0	79.0	17.2	1.8	1.8	0.2	7,088	6,314	495	143	107	29
Drunkenness	66,246	55,211	9,340	781	818	96	100.0	83.3	14.1	1.2	1.2	0.1	974	775	172	14	11	2
Disorderly conduct	79,306	52,723	24,621	1,147	699	116	100.0	66.5	31.0	1.4	0.9	0.1	15,353	8,203	6,886	148	103	13
Vagrancy	3,189	2,027	1,101	26	32	3	100.0	63.6	34.5	0.8	1.0	0.1	55	41	10	4	0	0
All other offenses (except traffic)	891,640	640,218	229,674	10,547	8,611	2,590	100.0	71.8	25.8	1.2	1.0	0.3	37,316	26,897	9,469	456	395	99
Suspicion	1,168	920	237	10	1	0	100.0	78.8	20.3	0.9	0.1	0.0	8	8	0	0	0	0
Curfew and loitering law violations	3,581	2,369	1,068	37	62	45	100.0	66.2	29.8	1.0	1.7	1.3	3,581	2,369	1,068	37	62	45

Table 67. Arrests, Suburban Areas,[1] Distribution by Race, 2019—Continued

(Number, percent; 5,820 agencies; 2019 estimated population 97,421,942.)

Offense charged	Percent distribution[2]						Arrests 18 and over						Percent distribution[2]					
	Total	White	Black	American Indian or Alaskan Native	Asian	Native Hawaiian or Other Pacific Islander	Total	White	Black	American Indian or Alaskan Native	Asian	Native Hawaiian or Other Pacific Islander	Total	White	Black	American Indian or Alaskan Native	Asian	Native Hawaiian or Other Pacific Islander
Total	100.0	64.4	33.3	1.0	1.1	0.3	2,485,968	1,801,758	623,353	23,864	31,015	5,978	100.0	72.5	25.1	1.0	1.2	0.2
Violent crime[3]	100.0	52.4	45.8	0.7	0.9	0.3	97,319	65,562	29,207	852	1,408	290	100.0	67.4	30.0	0.9	1.4	0.3
Murder and nonnegligent manslaughter	100.0	50.0	46.0	4.0	0.0	0.0	2,293	1,252	999	13	19	10	100.0	54.6	43.6	0.6	0.8	0.4
Rape[4]	100.0	75.2	23.3	0.3	1.0	0.1	4,889	3,641	1,107	40	79	22	100.0	74.5	22.6	0.8	1.6	0.4
Robbery	100.0	33.2	65.2	0.2	0.8	0.5	11,768	5,855	5,701	71	109	32	100.0	49.8	48.4	0.6	0.9	0.3
Aggravated assault	100.0	58.5	39.5	0.9	0.9	0.2	78,369	54,814	21,400	728	1,201	226	100.0	69.9	27.3	0.9	1.5	0.3
Property crime[3]	100.0	53.9	43.8	0.8	1.3	0.2	259,157	175,601	77,813	2,193	3,036	514	100.0	67.8	30.0	0.8	1.2	0.2
Burglary	100.0	60.3	37.8	0.7	0.9	0.3	35,144	25,969	8,524	204	359	88	100.0	73.9	24.3	0.6	1.0	0.3
Larceny-theft	100.0	52.4	45.1	0.7	1.5	0.2	206,208	136,289	65,350	1,829	2,451	289	100.0	66.1	31.7	0.9	1.2	0.1
Motor vehicle theft	100.0	51.3	46.8	0.9	0.8	0.2	16,188	12,082	3,647	146	188	125	100.0	74.6	22.5	0.9	1.2	0.8
Arson	100.0	70.9	27.2	1.3	0.7	0.0	1,617	1,261	292	14	38	12	100.0	78.0	18.1	0.9	2.4	0.7
Other assaults	100.0	59.5	38.6	0.9	0.9	0.2	210,649	151,834	53,611	1,926	2,814	464	100.0	72.1	25.5	0.9	1.3	0.2
Forgery and counterfeiting	100.0	64.0	34.9	0.0	1.2	0.0	12,992	8,552	4,186	71	175	8	100.0	65.8	32.2	0.5	1.3	0.1
Fraud	100.0	51.9	46.0	0.9	1.1	0.1	32,058	21,011	10,261	258	484	44	100.0	65.5	32.0	0.8	1.5	0.1
Embezzlement	100.0	42.5	56.2	0.0	1.4	0.0	3,508	2,153	1,280	17	48	10	100.0	61.4	36.5	0.5	1.4	0.3
Stolen property; buying, receiving, possessing	100.0	40.5	57.9	0.5	0.8	0.2	20,838	14,255	6,114	218	208	43	100.0	68.4	29.3	1.0	1.0	0.2
Vandalism	100.0	71.1	26.9	1.1	0.8	0.2	34,768	25,621	8,313	371	410	53	100.0	73.7	23.9	1.1	1.2	0.2
Weapons; carrying, possessing, etc.	100.0	59.7	38.3	0.5	1.2	0.3	33,844	20,647	12,564	183	347	103	100.0	61.0	37.1	0.5	1.0	0.3
Prostitution and commercialized vice	100.0	84.2	15.8	0.0	0.0	0.0	3,413	1,881	1,122	15	378	17	100.0	55.1	32.9	0.4	11.1	0.5
Sex offenses (except forcible rape and prostitution)	100.0	75.5	22.2	0.4	1.6	0.3	8,906	7,048	1,594	72	172	20	100.0	79.1	17.9	0.8	1.9	0.2
Drug abuse violations	100.0	76.5	20.8	1.1	1.3	0.3	412,059	295,593	108,483	2,768	4,434	781	100.0	71.7	26.3	0.7	1.1	0.2
Gambling	100.0	70.1	26.5	0.0	3.4	0.0	698	409	191	4	70	24	100.0	58.6	27.4	0.6	10.0	3.4
Offenses against the family and children	100.0	76.2	18.7	4.6	0.5	0.0	26,357	17,933	7,840	356	210	18	100.0	68.0	29.7	1.4	0.8	0.1
Driving under the influence	100.0	91.1	6.7	0.9	1.0	0.3	304,879	250,216	45,291	2,029	6,497	846	100.0	82.1	14.9	0.7	2.1	0.3
Liquor laws	100.0	89.1	7.0	2.0	1.5	0.4	36,680	28,267	7,047	642	672	52	100.0	77.1	19.2	1.8	1.8	0.1
Drunkenness	100.0	79.6	17.7	1.4	1.1	0.2	65,272	54,436	9,168	767	807	94	100.0	83.4	14.0	1.2	1.2	0.1
Disorderly conduct	100.0	53.4	44.9	1.0	0.7	0.1	63,953	44,520	17,735	999	596	103	100.0	69.6	27.7	1.6	0.9	0.2
Vagrancy	100.0	74.5	18.2	7.3	0.0	0.0	3,134	1,986	1,091	22	32	3	100.0	63.4	34.8	0.7	1.0	0.1
All other offenses (except traffic)	100.0	72.1	25.4	1.2	1.1	0.3	854,324	613,321	220,205	10,091	8,216	2,491	100.0	71.8	25.8	1.2	1.0	0.3
Suspicion	100.0	100.0	0.0	0.0	0.0	0.0	1,160	912	237	10	1	0	100.0	78.6	20.4	0.9	0.1	0.0
Curfew and loitering law violations	100.0	66.2	29.8	1.0	1.7	1.3	NA	NA	NA	NA	NA	NA	NA	NA	NA	NA	NA	NA

NA = Not available.
* = Less than one-tenth of one percent.
1 Suburban areas include law enforcement agencies in cities with less than 50,000 inhabitants and county law enforcement agencies that are within a Metropolitan Statistical Area. Suburban areas exclude all metropolitan agencies associated with a principal city.   2 Because of rounding, the percentages may not sum to 100.   3 Violent crimes are offenses of murder and nonnegligent manslaughter, rape, robbery, and aggravated assault. Property crimes are offenses of burglary, larceny-theft, motor vehicle theft, and arson.   4 The rape figures in this table are aggregate totals of the data submitted based on both the legacy and revised Uniform Crime Reporting definitions.

Table 67A. Arrests, Suburban Areas,[1] Distribution by Ethnicity, 2019

(Number, percent; 5,820 agencies; 2019 estimated population 97,421,942.)

Offense charged	Total arrests			Percent distribution[2]			Arrests under 18		
	Total[3]	Hispanic or Latino	Not Hispanic or Latino	Total[3]	Hispanic or Latino	Not Hispanic or Latino	Total[3]	Hispanic or Latino	Not Hispanic or Latino
Total	2,307,837	415,979	1,891,858	100.0	18.0	82.0	161,639	33,952	127,687
Violent crime[4]	95,271	22,024	73,247	100.0	23.1	76.9	10,489	2,474	8,015
Murder and nonnegligent manslaughter	1,885	421	1,464	100.0	22.3	77.7	129	37	92
Rape[5]	5,176	1,311	3,865	100.0	25.3	74.7	976	160	816
Robbery	13,652	2,846	10,806	100.0	20.8	79.2	3,260	693	2,567
Aggravated assault	74,558	17,446	57,112	100.0	23.4	76.6	6,124	1,584	4,540
Property crime[4]	244,968	33,278	211,690	100.0	13.6	86.4	26,723	4,698	22,025
Burglary	35,321	6,128	29,193	100.0	17.3	82.7	4,395	868	3,527
Larceny-theft	190,906	23,005	167,901	100.0	12.1	87.9	19,228	3,160	16,068
Motor vehicle theft	16,838	3,823	13,015	100.0	22.7	77.3	2,621	596	2,025
Arson	1,903	322	1,581	100.0	16.9	83.1	479	74	405
Other assaults	213,599	35,546	178,053	100.0	16.6	83.4	31,479	6,320	25,159
Forgery and counterfeiting	11,663	1,986	9,677	100.0	17.0	83.0	226	50	176
Fraud	28,701	3,890	24,811	100.0	13.6	86.4	961	225	736
Embezzlement	3,071	302	2,769	100.0	9.8	90.2	128	24	104
Stolen property; buying, receiving, possessing	19,654	3,542	16,112	100.0	18.0	82.0	1,764	379	1,385
Vandalism	38,069	6,181	31,888	100.0	16.2	83.8	7,580	1,321	6,259
Weapons; carrying, possessing, etc.	32,256	7,260	24,996	100.0	22.5	77.5	3,685	1,085	2,600
Prostitution and commercialized vice	2,918	454	2,464	100.0	15.6	84.4	31	4	27
Sex offenses (except forcible rape and prostitution)	9,515	2,527	6,988	100.0	26.6	73.4	1,618	348	1,270
Drug abuse violations	390,972	73,964	317,008	100.0	18.9	81.1	22,758	6,425	16,333
Gambling	643	167	476	100.0	26.0	74.0	111	43	68
Offenses against the family and children	23,239	2,670	20,569	100.0	11.5	88.5	509	101	408
Driving under the influence	268,853	71,401	197,452	100.0	26.6	73.4	1,218	379	839
Liquor laws	35,518	5,364	30,154	100.0	15.1	84.9	5,822	999	4,823
Drunkenness	62,637	14,477	48,160	100.0	23.1	76.9	928	310	618
Disorderly conduct	63,102	7,795	55,307	100.0	12.4	87.6	12,014	1,948	10,066
Vagrancy	2,804	535	2,269	100.0	19.1	80.9	50	11	39
All other offenses (except traffic)	757,271	122,072	635,199	100.0	16.1	83.9	30,749	6,297	24,452
Suspicion	323	34	289	100.0	10.5	89.5	6	1	5
Curfew and loitering law violations	2,790	510	2,280	100.0	18.3	81.7	2,790	510	2,280

NA = Not available.

1 Suburban areas include law enforcement agencies in cities with less than 50,000 inhabitants and county law enforcement agencies that are within a Metropolitan Statistical Area. Suburban areas exclude all metropolitan agencies associated with a principal city. 2 Because of rounding, the percentages may not sum to 100. 3 The ethnicity totals are representative of those agencies that provided ethnicity breakdowns. Not all agencies provide ethnicity data; therefore, the race and ethnicity totals will not be equal. 4 Violent crimes are offenses of murder and nonnegligent manslaughter, rape, robbery, and aggravated assault. Property crimes are offenses of burglary, larceny-theft, motor vehicle theft, and arson. 5 The rape figures in this table are aggregate totals of the data submitted based on both the legacy and revised Uniform Crime Reporting definitions.

Table 67A. Arrests, Suburban Areas,[1] Distribution by Ethnicity, 2019—Continued

(Number, percent; 5,820 agencies; 2019 estimated population 97,421,942.)

Offense charged	Percent distribution[2]			Arrests 18 and over			Percent distribution[2]		
	Total[3]	Hispanic or Latino	Not Hispanic or Latino	Total[3]	Hispanic or Latino	Not Hispanic or Latino	Total[3]	Hispanic or Latino	Not Hispanic or Latino
Total	100.0	21.0	79.0	2,146,198	382,027	1,764,171	100.0	17.8	82.2
Violent crime[4]	100.0	23.6	76.4	84,782	19,550	65,232	100.0	23.1	76.9
Murder and nonnegligent manslaughter	100.0	28.7	71.3	1,756	384	1,372	100.0	21.9	78.1
Rape[5]	100.0	16.4	83.6	4,200	1,151	3,049	100.0	27.4	72.6
Robbery	100.0	21.3	78.7	10,392	2,153	8,239	100.0	20.7	79.3
Aggravated assault	100.0	25.9	74.1	68,434	15,862	52,572	100.0	23.2	76.8
Property crime[4]	100.0	17.6	82.4	218,245	28,580	189,665	100.0	13.1	86.9
Burglary	100.0	19.7	80.3	30,926	5,260	25,666	100.0	17.0	83.0
Larceny-theft	100.0	16.4	83.6	171,678	19,845	151,833	100.0	11.6	88.4
Motor vehicle theft	100.0	22.7	77.3	14,217	3,227	10,990	100.0	22.7	77.3
Arson	100.0	15.4	84.6	1,424	248	1,176	100.0	17.4	82.6
Other assaults	100.0	20.1	79.9	182,120	29,226	152,894	100.0	16.0	84.0
Forgery and counterfeiting	100.0	22.1	77.9	11,437	1,936	9,501	100.0	16.9	83.1
Fraud	100.0	23.4	76.6	27,740	3,665	24,075	100.0	13.2	86.8
Embezzlement	100.0	18.8	81.3	2,943	278	2,665	100.0	9.4	90.6
Stolen property; buying, receiving, possessing	100.0	21.5	78.5	17,890	3,163	14,727	100.0	17.7	82.3
Vandalism	100.0	17.4	82.6	30,489	4,860	25,629	100.0	15.9	84.1
Weapons; carrying, possessing, etc.	100.0	29.4	70.6	28,571	6,175	22,396	100.0	21.6	78.4
Prostitution and commercialized vice	100.0	12.9	87.1	2,887	450	2,437	100.0	15.6	84.4
Sex offenses (except forcible rape and prostitution)	100.0	21.5	78.5	7,897	2,179	5,718	100.0	27.6	72.4
Drug abuse violations	100.0	28.2	71.8	368,214	67,539	300,675	100.0	18.3	81.7
Gambling	100.0	38.7	61.3	532	124	408	100.0	23.3	76.7
Offenses against the family and children	100.0	19.8	80.2	22,730	2,569	20,161	100.0	11.3	88.7
Driving under the influence	100.0	31.1	68.9	267,635	71,022	196,613	100.0	26.5	73.5
Liquor laws	100.0	17.2	82.8	29,696	4,365	25,331	100.0	14.7	85.3
Drunkenness	100.0	33.4	66.6	61,709	14,167	47,542	100.0	23.0	77.0
Disorderly conduct	100.0	16.2	83.8	51,088	5,847	45,241	100.0	11.4	88.6
Vagrancy	100.0	22.0	78.0	2,754	524	2,230	100.0	19.0	81.0
All other offenses (except traffic)	100.0	20.5	79.5	726,522	115,775	610,747	100.0	15.9	84.1
Suspicion	100.0	16.7	83.3	317	33	284	100.0	10.4	89.6
Curfew and loitering law violations	100.0	18.3	81.7	NA	NA	NA	NA	NA	NA

NA = Not available.
1 Suburban areas include law enforcement agencies in cities with less than 50,000 inhabitants and county law enforcement agencies that are within a Metropolitan Statistical Area. Suburban areas exclude all metropolitan agencies associated with a principal city.   2 Because of rounding, the percentages may not sum to 100.   3 The ethnicity totals are representative of those agencies that provided ethnicity breakdowns. Not all agencies provide ethnicity data; therefore, the race and ethnicity totals will not be equal.   4 Violent crimes are offenses of murder and nonnegligent manslaughter, rape, robbery, and aggravated assault. Property crimes are offenses of burglary, larceny-theft, motor vehicle theft, and arson.   5 The rape figures in this table are aggregate totals of the data submitted based on both the legacy and revised Uniform Crime Reporting definitions.

Table 68. Police Disposition of Juvenile Offenders Taken into Custody, 2019

(Number, percent.)

Population group	Total[1]	Handled within department and released	Referred to juvenile court jurisdiction	Referred to welfare agency	Referred to other police agency	Referred to criminal or adult court	Referred to other authorities not specified	Number of agencies	Estimated population, 2019
Total Agencies									
Number	349,603	89,046	102,140	3,410	7,602	7,873	139,532	10,831	229,735,355
Percent[2]	100.0	25.5	29.2	1.0	2.2	2.3	39.9		
Total Cities									
Number	275,025	71,516	79,814	1,987	4,712	5,656	111,340	7,979	159,706,353
Percent[2]	100.0	26.0	29.0	0.7	1.7	2.1	40.5		
Group I (250,000 and over)									
Number	55,906	16,269	13,930	290	1,128	731	23,558	70	43,703,387
Percent[2]	100.0	29.1	24.9	0.5	2.0	1.3	42.1		
Group II (100,000 to 249,999)									
Number	43,377	9,942	12,977	48	215	106	20,089	182	26,636,848
Percent[2]	100.0	22.9	29.9	0.1	0.5	0.2	46.3		
Group III (50,000 to 99,999)									
Number	48,972	10,674	16,464	105	309	448	20,972	389	27,232,262
Percent[2]	100.0	21.8	33.6	0.2	0.6	0.9	42.8		
Group IV (25,000 to 49,999)									
Number	54,527	17,891	13,786	1,358	2,781	1,883	16,828	689	24,056,009
Percent[2]	100.0	32.8	25.3	2.5	5.1	3.5	30.9		
Group V (10,000 to 24,999)									
Number	38,827	8,338	12,403	41	112	1,260	16,673	1,355	21,714,346
Percent[2]	100.0	21.5	31.9	0.1	0.3	3.2	42.9		
Group VI (under 10,000)									
Number	33,416	8,402	10,254	145	167	1,228	13,220	5,294	16,363,501
Percent[2]	100.0	25.1	30.7	0.4	0.5	3.7	39.6		
Metropolitan Counties									
Number	54,487	11,731	18,400	143	903	598	22,712	1,230	51,841,134
Percent[2]	100.0	21.5	33.8	0.3	1.7	1.1	41.7		
Nonmetropolitan Counties									
Number	20,091	5,799	3,926	1,280	1,987	1,619	5,480	1,622	18,187,868
Percent[2]	100.0	28.9	19.5	6.4	9.9	8.1	27.3		
Suburban Areas[3]									
Number	141,261	36,352	43,865	1,575	3,834	4,066	51,569	5,820	97,421,942
Percent[2]	100.0	25.7	31.1	1.1	2.7	2.9	36.5		

1 Includes all offenses except traffic and neglect cases.   2 Because of rounding, the percentages may not sum to 100.   3 Suburban areas include law enforcement agencies in cities with less than 50,000 inhabitants and county law enforcement agencies that are within a Metropolitan Statistical Area. Suburban areas exclude all metropolitan agencies associated with a principal city. The agencies associated with suburban areas also appear in other groups within this table.

Table 69. Arrests, by State, 2019

(Number.)

State	Total, all classes[1]	Violent crime[2]	Property crime[2]	Murder and nonnegligent manslaughter	Rape[3]	Robbery	Aggravated assault	Burglary	Larceny-theft	Motor vehicle theft	Arson	Other assaults	Forgery and counterfeiting	Fraud	Embezzlement	Stolen property; buying, receiving, possessing	Vandalism
Alabama[5]																	
Under 18	103	3	70	0	0	2	1	0	68	2	0	4	0	0	0	0	6
Total, all ages	1,831	29	522	4	0	14	11	13	502	5	2	191	19	8	6	33	17
Alaska																	
Under 18	1,433	177	321	5	34	24	114	110	148	52	11	372	2	3	2	3	108
Total, all ages	27,602	2,559	3,006	46	126	310	2,077	606	1,878	473	49	4,853	78	121	43	93	1,161
Arizona																	
Under 18	18,502	1,097	2,839	19	48	296	734	489	1,992	328	30	3,583	9	69	6	87	1,473
Total, all ages	235,594	11,325	29,328	294	267	1,797	8,967	3,536	24,164	1,456	172	23,655	772	1,959	424	896	9,185
Arkansas																	
Under 18	7,809	445	1,425	11	38	78	318	230	1,090	96	9	1,700	21	27	1	155	264
Total, all ages	117,237	5,050	13,433	166	289	475	4,120	1,896	10,889	585	63	11,609	837	839	52	1,715	1,804
California																	
Under 18	38,617	6,745	6,539	64	193	2,806	3,682	2,362	2,884	1,164	129	7,292	44	159	19	781	2,112
Total, all ages	1,014,785	102,427	88,854	1,284	2,155	15,404	83,584	32,859	39,588	14,870	1,537	77,849	3,721	6,703	972	14,777	16,462
Colorado																	
Under 18	16,885	806	3,062	16	86	251	453	319	2,306	382	55	1,972	9	63	2	25	843
Total, all ages	195,870	8,058	25,261	152	532	1,148	6,226	2,518	19,662	2,883	198	16,700	722	2,771	69	487	5,084
Connecticut																	
Under 18	6,942	304	1,405	4	37	144	119	214	946	228	17	1,704	11	29	6	87	299
Total, all ages	92,925	3,060	11,932	83	223	764	1,990	1,470	9,754	646	62	16,304	475	858	134	350	1,711
Delaware																	
Under 18	2,924	316	551	1	14	107	194	145	325	74	7	836	1	60	6	81	140
Total, all ages	30,038	1,898	5,422	20	75	383	1,420	745	4,461	192	24	6,400	219	1,312	162	365	849
District of Columbia[6]																	
Under 18	807	188	65	0	0	167	21	0	65	0	0	165	0	0	0	26	9
Total, all ages	12,963	296	128	0	2	221	73	0	127	1	0	622	2	2	0	41	46
Florida[7,8]																	
Under 18	44,634	3,268	11,457	58	247	1,252	1,711	2,678	6,665	2,062	52	7,913	29	368	32	158	840
Total, all ages	679,072	33,860	85,675	787	1,765	6,006	25,302	13,560	64,087	7,776	252	80,785	1,808	11,226	1,047	1,512	5,956
Georgia																	
Under 18	5,176	270	1,032	11	12	85	162	174	783	63	12	1,018	19	24	0	79	139
Total, all ages	59,704	2,313	7,510	70	88	316	1,839	873	6,318	282	37	4,924	493	712	17	634	1,048
Hawaii																	
Under 18	1,849	107	297	0	14	61	32	36	248	9	4	355	1	0	0	45	20
Total, all ages	25,165	856	2,500	28	91	224	513	285	1,937	239	39	3,159	59	98	1	449	144
Idaho																	
Under 18	6,235	210	899	10	53	15	132	115	700	49	35	773	4	28	6	14	264
Total, all ages	57,646	1,878	4,644	84	204	83	1,507	711	3,707	179	47	4,200	97	343	40	171	760
Illinois[7]																	
Under 18	696	50	66	1	1	27	21	5	50	6	5	133	0	6	0	29	25
Total, all ages	8,248	487	565	18	19	75	375	76	461	12	16	1,516	17	33	0	93	319
Indiana																	
Under 18	5,211	282	902	5	9	57	211	98	698	101	5	934	5	18	1	14	140
Total, all ages	76,675	3,235	8,492	71	90	332	2,742	851	6,940	634	67	5,680	664	1,010	57	129	541
Iowa																	
Under 18	8,901	503	1,891	0	44	70	389	293	1,362	201	35	1,723	13	39	2	46	629
Total, all ages	87,139	4,436	10,055	35	183	274	3,944	1,271	8,118	581	85	7,173	433	558	45	239	1,874
Kansas																	
Under 18	3,632	208	552	1	25	33	149	72	423	40	17	754	1	10	5	31	210
Total, all ages	52,378	2,212	3,741	51	112	190	1,859	416	2,983	290	52	7,043	160	349	46	482	1,536
Kentucky																	
Under 18	4,798	330	1,193	15	38	130	147	262	692	192	47	933	13	33	4	355	219
Total, all ages	241,668	3,386	16,163	161	267	774	2,184	2,646	12,383	987	147	12,391	1,074	1,426	351	2,902	1,406
Louisiana																	
Under 18	12,267	962	2,546	30	79	169	684	629	1,646	237	34	2,504	8	22	3	177	380
Total, all ages	146,664	8,823	24,465	339	333	920	7,231	3,794	19,323	1,254	94	15,577	573	911	129	1,900	2,457
Maine																	
Under 18	2,470	42	543	0	11	8	23	81	413	33	16	518	1	11	6	9	212
Total, all ages	38,973	685	5,010	10	63	89	523	502	4,266	197	45	4,792	145	401	41	98	981
Maryland																	
Under 18	18,857	2,046	3,950	17	101	1,191	737	649	2,668	561	72	5,248	16	45	3	41	852
Total, all ages	181,677	10,256	21,791	254	528	3,292	6,182	3,634	16,022	1,913	222	22,532	399	843	118	275	2,738
Massachusetts																	
Under 18	4,141	486	652	1	23	85	377	155	390	91	16	1,212	9	19	3	98	242
Total, all ages	101,553	6,262	9,561	38	310	563	5,351	1,370	7,621	509	61	16,622	409	991	81	762	1,947
Michigan																	
Under 18	11,172	1,025	2,646	20	148	218	639	358	1,979	279	30	2,748	25	129	59	259	428
Total, all ages	210,905	12,521	22,003	346	846	1,272	10,057	2,528	18,012	1,246	217	28,821	695	3,708	1,121	2,193	3,001
Minnesota																	
Under 18	18,594	943	3,968	15	122	396	410	304	3,174	454	36	2,368	30	215	5	255	695
Total, all ages	145,820	5,676	25,211	104	656	1,122	3,794	1,975	21,580	1,555	101	14,981	1,066	4,486	21	1,944	2,599
Mississippi																	
Under 18	2,719	108	596	6	5	40	57	138	397	57	4	507	11	25	3	37	61
Total, all ages	64,967	1,404	7,255	133	63	323	885	944	5,909	366	36	5,338	318	724	322	625	590
Missouri																	
Under 18	10,435	722	1,799	25	76	202	419	236	1,336	215	12	1,796	5	43	11	410	424
Total, all ages	156,375	7,184	18,331	286	413	1,098	5,387	2,483	13,947	1,815	86	14,488	729	1,411	194	3,155	2,709
Montana																	
Under 18	4,355	180	658	0	14	4	162	62	535	55	6	580	3	10	1	21	245
Total, all ages	30,218	1,758	4,584	18	61	84	1,595	314	3,971	281	18	4,083	175	188	34	247	867

Table 69. Arrests, by State, 2019—Continued

(Number.)

State	Weapons; carrying, possessing, etc.	Prostitution and commercialized vice	Sex offenses (except rape and prostitution)	Drug abuse violations	Gambling	Offenses against the family and children	Driving under the influence	Liquor laws	Drunkenness[4]	Disorderly conduct	Vagrancy	All other offenses (except traffic)	Suspicion	Curfew and loitering law violations	Number of agencies	Estimated population, 2019
Alabama[5]																
Under 18	3	0	0	9	0	0	0	0	1	0	0	7	0	0	2	85,670
Total, all ages	43	0	0	378	0	3	36	1	49	24	0	472	0	0		
Alaska																
Under 18	18	0	24	156	0	0	22	43	1	11	0	170	0	0	19	684,330
Total, all ages	258	5	242	930	0	150	2,855	305	31	740	2	10,170	0	0		
Arizona																
Under 18	288	3	254	2,970	1	188	130	988	92	1,299	36	2,659	0	431	94	5,578,646
Total, all ages	2,884	242	1,239	28,254	1	2,501	18,041	5,950	11,317	13,658	421	73,083	28	431		
Arkansas																
Under 18	109	0	19	823	0	3	55	158	70	690	0	1,607	0	237	248	2,665,648
Total, all ages	1,035	83	74	17,844	24	324	6,108	1,221	5,604	2,574	320	46,450	0	237		
California																
Under 18	2,617	19	811	2,459	9	3	464	838	456	832	64	5,643	0	711	717	38,183,434
Total, all ages	26,673	5,751	8,560	212,417	562	278	120,262	5,363	53,788	3,218	4,688	260,749	0	711		
Colorado																
Under 18	339	2	135	1,920	0	28	197	899	17	1,565	0	4,496	0	505	184	4,910,658
Total, all ages	2,414	354	463	15,846	13	2,145	19,658	5,863	378	5,966	465	82,648	0	505		
Connecticut																
Under 18	151	0	51	570	0	24	22	7	0	1,328	0	935	0	9	107	3,565,287
Total, all ages	1,073	120	330	7,295	11	1,502	7,577	86	11	10,560	44	29,483	0	9		
Delaware																
Under 18	59	0	20	256	3	0	2	24	3	214	0	312	0	40	52	970,535
Total, all ages	325	82	101	3,815	20	157	452	539	356	1,138	229	6,157	0	40		
District of Columbia[6]																
Under 18	18	0	2	10	0	0	0	0	0	73	0	251	0	0	2	0
Total, all ages	62	0	22	799	0	1	7	1,385	49	409	4	9,088	0	0		
Florida[7,8]																
Under 18	871	4	321	3,881	0	0	118	282	1	0	0	15,091	0	0	618	21,418,599
Total, all ages	6,551	2,049	3,209	110,145	107	10	33,872	10,774	32	43	0	290,411	0	0		
Georgia																
Under 18	145	1	103	599	0	34	26	57	18	481	17	1,018	0	96	112	2,372,788
Total, all ages	742	148	394	10,763	15	784	5,620	461	466	2,986	322	19,252	4	96		
Hawaii																
Under 18	15	0	36	274	0	0	20	54	0	43	0	409	0	173	2	1,142,377
Total, all ages	207	107	119	1,947	103	8	4,049	343	0	573	3	10,267	0	173		
Idaho																
Under 18	100	0	90	956	0	12	82	207	29	283	0	2,185	0	93	101	1,751,712
Total, all ages	304	13	291	10,889	0	620	7,893	1,250	650	1,537	11	21,953	9	93		
Illinois[7]																
Under 18	24	0	1	123	0	1	0	8	0	95	0	111	0	24	1	145,719
Total, all ages	137	62	10	569	0	213	396	73	0	643	21	3,070	0	24		
Indiana																
Under 18	122	0	32	780	1	58	28	370	12	292	5	1,146	3	66	165	2,713,489
Total, all ages	1,202	17	283	15,134	19	532	8,524	2,434	1,771	1,883	25	24,965	12	66		
Iowa																
Under 18	123	1	33	890	0	5	75	453	84	964	0	1,305	0	122	185	2,597,154
Total, all ages	715	32	96	8,444	4	870	9,667	2,491	4,474	3,180	8	32,223	0	122		
Kansas																
Under 18	53	1	35	621	0	13	65	278	0	127	0	668	0	0	218	1,614,393
Total, all ages	767	79	129	8,475	1	216	5,672	1,751	103	1,425	0	18,191	0	0		
Kentucky																
Under 18	101	0	28	398	0	5	41	8	41	164	0	930	0	2	388	4,315,643
Total, all ages	820	100	234	24,555	19	5,202	15,570	135	14,049	4,082	50	137,751	0	2		
Louisiana																
Under 18	384	3	99	921	13	105	21	71	21	1,573	34	2,276	5	139	136	3,483,954
Total, all ages	3,119	339	562	25,900	92	1,369	5,509	1,842	2,248	5,683	323	44,684	20	139		
Maine																
Under 18	7	1	24	282	0	2	26	298	2	67	0	416	0	3	132	1,339,229
Total, all ages	137	51	175	3,600	3	154	5,444	1,577	13	1,232	2	14,427	2	3		
Maryland																
Under 18	618	2	152	1,831	17	7	45	268	0	990	9	2,680	1	36	151	6,043,312
Total, all ages	3,768	633	728	30,005	58	1,810	18,160	4,206	44	5,018	227	57,984	48	36		
Massachusetts																
Under 18	94	0	39	110	0	11	15	64	12	167	0	908	0	0	334	5,896,253
Total, all ages	891	348	327	7,119	18	1,025	9,426	1,152	4,685	3,532	53	36,341	1	0		
Michigan																
Under 18	296	8	125	403	1	5	132	187	3	408	0	2,099	0	186	619	9,590,606
Total, all ages	5,346	448	593	13,475	76	2,033	25,574	4,061	346	5,507	79	79,118	0	186		
Minnesota																
Under 18	311	0	138	1,412	5	9	146	1,525	0	1,933	0	4,006	0	630	368	5,433,467
Total, all ages	2,169	154	805	18,714	37	569	19,863	6,578	28	8,473	194	31,622	0	630		
Mississippi																
Under 18	82	0	8	214	1	124	27	17	12	362	1	460	6	57	53	1,240,709
Total, all ages	983	67	139	8,717	39	2,045	5,269	639	2,332	3,457	230	24,410	7	57		
Missouri																
Under 18	141	1	126	1,307	5	27	115	376	12	918	3	1,907	0	287	178	3,840,334
Total, all ages	2,867	145	574	28,526	11	1,222	14,237	2,360	156	5,759	980	51,050	0	287		
Montana																
Under 18	16	0	30	324	0	40	56	523	79	413	0	902	0	274	78	938,389
Total, all ages	74	4	110	2,661	1	672	3,681	1,020	309	2,385	24	7,066	1	274		

Table 69. Arrests, by State, 2019—Continued

(Number.)

State	Total, all classes[1]	Violent crime[2]	Property crime[2]	Murder and nonnegligent manslaughter	Rape[3]	Robbery	Aggravated assault	Burglary	Larceny-theft	Motor vehicle theft	Arson	Other assaults	Forgery and counterfeiting	Fraud	Embezzlement	Stolen property; buying, receiving, possessing	Vandalism
Nebraska																	
Under 18	8,282	242	1,846	2	48	130	62	93	1,565	165	23	1,605	2	72	8	123	626
Total, all ages	61,726	2,224	8,233	34	248	361	1,581	485	7,255	432	61	8,434	271	1,207	69	684	2,180
Nevada																	
Under 18	10,818	955	1,246	7	58	252	638	222	886	116	22	2,041	14	134	12	183	331
Total, all ages	145,951	7,560	10,248	124	423	1,286	5,727	3,145	6,357	670	76	18,855	476	2,033	356	1,839	1,829
New Hampshire																	
Under 18	3,243	58	241	3	7	12	36	25	197	17	2	619	3	11	6	28	193
Total, all ages	43,960	723	3,370	15	89	129	490	246	2,962	148	14	5,357	226	728	80	455	1,139
New Jersey																	
Under 18	13,360	1,041	2,199	12	53	466	510	434	1,572	173	20	1,171	26	55	15	498	501
Total, all ages	257,734	9,294	22,277	184	356	2,063	6,691	3,309	18,200	647	121	20,570	950	3,852	212	2,482	3,068
New Mexico																	
Under 18	2,852	196	265	6	9	25	156	43	206	15	1	721	0	6	1	28	94
Total, all ages	59,847	3,412	5,444	49	58	271	3,034	705	4,445	254	40	7,399	134	342	117	704	1,200
New York[7]																	
Under 18	11,606	1,143	3,263	19	183	446	495	559	2,303	352	49	1,845	29	62	0	286	1,339
Total, all ages	218,837	10,788	38,303	197	988	2,222	7,381	3,866	32,464	1,755	218	24,101	1,732	3,497	20	2,239	11,841
North Carolina																	
Under 18	12,088	792	2,798	39	34	396	323	666	1,849	248	35	2,252	22	119	20	427	472
Total, all ages	199,517	8,942	25,854	366	200	1,967	6,409	5,174	19,503	977	200	20,389	727	2,954	710	3,138	2,469
North Dakota																	
Under 18	4,152	66	559	2	6	7	51	69	423	59	8	523	4	14	5	16	183
Total, all ages	32,647	756	3,189	17	62	63	614	310	2,623	235	21	2,824	161	495	49	303	500
Ohio																	
Under 18	20,149	1,033	3,287	22	86	372	553	468	2,549	236	34	4,684	11	135	1	340	868
Total, all ages	205,987	8,752	29,869	244	438	1,830	6,240	3,583	25,142	893	251	34,495	519	1,826	22	2,393	3,656
Oklahoma																	
Under 18	7,195	403	1,513	9	28	104	262	292	1,014	179	28	868	4	32	21	204	197
Total, all ages	100,758	4,569	15,584	158	163	580	3,668	2,437	11,607	1,358	182	8,539	515	1,180	407	2,621	1,398
Oregon																	
Under 18	8,031	438	1,614	4	34	121	279	207	1,233	124	50	1,097	11	33	2	20	498
Total, all ages	124,126	4,638	18,622	47	228	814	3,549	1,716	14,836	1,802	268	10,595	653	1,858	75	523	3,520
Pennsylvania																	
Under 18	8,153	654	1,161	13	48	150	443	185	856	98	22	1,243	11	49	12	95	386
Total, all ages	91,934	4,774	11,136	105	220	701	3,748	1,250	9,371	424	91	11,187	721	1,794	131	612	1,837
Rhode Island																	
Under 18	2,176	100	340	2	19	25	54	72	227	24	17	407	2	12	6	40	189
Total, all ages	25,403	907	2,512	10	106	107	684	486	1,843	138	45	4,056	160	594	109	275	936
South Carolina																	
Under 18	9,403	582	1,918	21	86	160	315	369	1,395	133	21	2,227	12	50	12	123	334
Total, all ages	136,075	6,625	22,443	298	439	1,010	4,878	2,815	18,515	1,006	107	14,931	1,121	3,125	400	2,201	2,644
South Dakota																	
Under 18	4,791	112	546	2	9	13	88	48	413	79	6	657	2	51	4	47	156
Total, all ages	44,252	1,138	2,656	15	56	57	1,010	285	2,078	278	15	4,801	162	777	24	179	537
Tennessee																	
Under 18	19,687	1,377	3,717	28	105	461	783	532	2,379	767	39	4,059	40	139	19	122	843
Total, all ages	321,922	14,335	36,938	363	461	1,687	11,824	4,621	28,156	4,006	155	31,568	1,970	4,907	806	1,519	4,276
Texas																	
Under 18	49,409	4,400	9,351	79	330	1,438	2,553	1,414	6,802	1,041	94	10,062	104	247	24	99	1,354
Total, all ages	624,840	33,962	68,132	698	1,988	5,539	25,737	8,256	54,410	5,038	428	73,057	3,808	6,637	305	718	6,787
Utah																	
Under 18	11,334	337	2,330	5	92	59	181	182	2,016	97	35	1,473	4	50	10	68	790
Total, all ages	91,685	2,619	14,165	54	340	354	1,871	869	12,813	398	85	8,590	618	831	48	898	2,906
Vermont																	
Under 18	803	47	135	0	15	6	26	42	77	14	2	238	0	2	8	4	79
Total, all ages	15,719	863	1,984	10	94	52	707	256	1,640	74	14	1,766	43	317	58	94	424
Virginia																	
Under 18	15,992	751	2,783	21	102	311	317	260	2,317	172	34	2,810	23	115	23	142	436
Total, all ages	261,659	6,933	26,107	299	541	1,315	4,778	2,033	22,921	996	157	29,706	1,429	4,672	1,119	930	3,102
Washington																	
Under 18	10,101	937	1,905	15	84	411	427	388	1,321	162	34	2,882	5	20	2	131	755
Total, all ages	169,836	8,144	24,058	125	542	1,743	5,734	3,808	18,867	1,206	177	24,675	664	1,252	37	2,912	4,372
West Virginia																	
Under 18	292	22	29	0	3	3	16	7	19	3	0	92	2	0	0	2	18
Total, all ages	16,932	932	1,896	24	46	41	821	340	1,390	151	15	2,343	126	191	28	179	282
Wisconsin																	
Under 18	33,383	968	3,872	13	217	232	506	341	3,021	468	42	2,497	18	117	35	292	1,532
Total, all ages	224,571	7,637	23,823	173	844	1,075	5,545	1,691	20,720	1,288	124	15,813	906	1,996	338	1,013	5,250
Wyoming																	
Under 18	3,117	42	323	0	6	0	36	48	242	31	2	461	1	8	0	4	131
Total, all ages	26,028	437	1,918	7	39	23	368	231	1,556	104	27	2,110	29	110	1	56	468

Table 69. Arrests, by State, 2019—Continued

(Number.)

State	Weapons; carrying, possessing, etc.	Prostitution and commercialized vice	Sex offenses (except rape and prostitution)	Drug abuse violations	Gambling	Offenses against the family and children	Driving under the influence	Liquor laws	Drunkenness[4]	Disorderly conduct	Vagrancy	All other offenses (except traffic)	Suspicion	Curfew and loitering law violations	Number of agencies	Estimated population, 2019
Nebraska																
Under 18	115	0	67	1,111	0	106	56	521	0	398	0	1,285	0	99	127	1,761,663
Total, all ages	1,072	109	389	10,869	3	1,255	5,676	2,798	0	2,392	11	13,751	0	99		
Nevada																
Under 18	280	110	103	1,778	6	27	56	315	89	1,216	11	1,579	0	332	41	2,948,674
Total, all ages	2,355	2,960	1,157	12,092	34	962	11,170	3,033	262	2,646	3,383	62,323	46	332		
New Hampshire																
Under 18	4	0	25	337	0	1	34	186	215	88	0	1,184	0	10	182	1,281,465
Total, all ages	119	49	128	5,584	3	144	5,116	1,783	3,839	908	94	14,105	0	10		
New Jersey																
Under 18	605	2	141	2,959	61	56	67	417	4	1,101	8	2,031	0	402	577	8,882,190
Total, all ages	3,791	770	1,026	55,611	169	7,379	21,112	1,825	66	11,207	168	91,406	97	402		
New Mexico																
Under 18	71	0	6	438	0	19	34	157	26	219	1	555	1	14	60	1,366,127
Total, all ages	469	47	53	3,260	3	1,496	4,190	875	1,922	1,501	71	27,189	5	14		
New York[7]																
Under 18	236	2	224	1,510	1	4	55	50	0	257	3	1,297	0	0	491	9,909,569
Total, all ages	2,814	499	1,544	55,575	32	514	25,059	529	0	3,769	755	35,226	0	0		
North Carolina																
Under 18	372	4	41	1,400	1	21	63	175	17	670	0	2,401	0	21	252	7,210,092
Total, all ages	2,703	221	301	31,431	32	3,192	11,639	1,123	1,272	2,729	23	79,647	0	21		
North Dakota																
Under 18	22	0	31	332	0	299	23	410	0	740	0	856	0	69	103	759,718
Total, all ages	303	19	93	5,005	2	448	4,827	2,474	230	1,733	1	9,166	0	69		
Ohio																
Under 18	328	2	111	1,362	0	90	47	391	22	1,676	0	5,410	1	350	412	9,198,221
Total, all ages	4,048	381	536	33,435	19	1,045	12,301	4,595	5,060	9,427	11	53,227	20	350		
Oklahoma																
Under 18	168	0	37	1,022	1	17	62	53	168	552	0	1,296	0	577	406	3,909,106
Total, all ages	2,742	46	374	16,146	10	521	9,053	823	9,484	2,131	258	23,780	0	577		
Oregon																
Under 18	73	0	67	1,312	0	1	88	556	0	591	1	1,361	0	268	152	3,692,097
Total, all ages	2,084	151	432	13,131	4	356	12,446	2,340	28	6,574	2	45,826	0	268		
Pennsylvania																
Under 18	155	0	92	685	0	9	79	354	41	1,866	11	969	0	281	379	3,254,641
Total, all ages	1,171	138	594	14,931	32	733	12,468	1,522	6,593	8,380	89	12,810	0	281		
Rhode Island																
Under 18	90	0	7	112	0	11	6	29	0	511	0	300	0	14	48	1,059,361
Total, all ages	363	43	87	1,866	5	77	2,483	278	28	2,249	4	8,357	0	14		
South Carolina																
Under 18	389	0	43	1,375	0	10	36	169	58	865	0	1,189	0	11	254	4,344,727
Total, all ages	2,706	269	263	29,084	47	927	7,796	3,730	5,307	7,939	562	23,944	0	11		
South Dakota																
Under 18	107	0	15	754	0	237	60	516	3	476	0	986	0	62	106	816,216
Total, all ages	279	19	48	7,926	1	583	5,522	1,581	116	2,525	628	14,688	0	62		
Tennessee																
Under 18	435	0	125	2,177	3	24	94	362	144	1,403	0	3,902	0	702	450	6,521,263
Total, all ages	2,673	503	548	45,206	54	3,268	18,980	2,957	13,034	5,678	10	131,990	0	702		
Texas																
Under 18	739	22	271	8,464	13	280	281	916	492	960	8	10,101	0	1,221	791	25,983,457
Total, all ages	11,076	2,999	1,501	115,658	295	3,500	64,161	6,907	44,330	6,451	501	172,833	1	1,221		
Utah																
Under 18	175	17	220	1,968	0	34	139	574	44	330	0	2,538	0	233	106	2,858,860
Total, all ages	870	185	693	14,479	3	1,617	5,082	3,240	2,945	2,353	54	29,251	5	233		
Vermont																
Under 18	17	0	8	27	0	3	15	16	0	101	0	103	0	0	80	622,083
Total, all ages	38	3	37	927	0	219	2,680	57	0	941	0	5,268	0	0		
Virginia																
Under 18	278	3	101	1,852	2	45	68	498	108	497	0	4,944	0	513	390	8,192,933
Total, all ages	4,060	513	580	42,502	21	1,393	20,402	3,983	19,289	2,802	39	91,564	0	513		
Washington																
Under 18	228	3	88	852	0	4	139	510	11	168	2	1,458	0	1	219	7,114,406
Total, all ages	1,822	328	493	11,325	3	321	27,638	1,597	91	2,412	167	57,514	10	1		
West Virginia																
Under 18	2	0	1	53	0	1	4	3	2	8	0	48	0	5	103	953,873
Total, all ages	196	3	32	3,683	0	100	2,382	334	187	378	15	3,640	0	5		
Wisconsin																
Under 18	428	6	471	2,710	6	87	226	1,843	0	6,763	10	10,200	0	1,302	401	5,480,021
Total, all ages	3,280	357	1,360	26,175	9	1,916	23,934	9,199	0	28,343	365	71,555	0	1,302		
Wyoming																
Under 18	12	1	28	489	0	8	36	330	4	129	31	906	0	173	53	510,856
Total, all ages	63	19	102	4,611	1	339	3,181	1,798	2,324	807	168	7,300	13	173		

NOTE: Because the number of agencies submitting arrest data varies from year to year, users are cautioned about making direct comparisons between 2019 arrest totals and those published in previous years' editions of Crime in the United States. Further, arrest figures may vary widely from state to state because some Part II crimes are not considered crimes in some states.
1 Does not include traffic arrests.   2 Violent crimes are offenses of murder and nonnegligent manslaughter, rape, robbery, and aggravated assault. Property crimes are offenses of burglary, larceny-theft, motor vehicle theft, and arson.   3 The rape figures in this table are aggregate totals of the data submitted based on both the legacy and revised Uniform Crime Reporting definitions.   4 Drunkenness is not considered a crime in some states; therefore, the figures vary widely from state to state.   5 Limited data for 2019 were available for Alabama.   6 Includes arrests reported by the District of Columbia Fire and Emergency Medical Services: Arson Investigation Unit and the Metro Transit Police. These agencies have no population associated with them.
7 See 2019 arrest data for details.   8 The Florida arrest counts for offenses against the family and children, drunkenness, disorderly conduct, vagrancy, suspicion, and curfew and loitering law violations are included under the category All other offenses (except for the data submitted by two Bureau of Indian Affairs agencies that provided data using those specific breakdowns).

SECTION V

LAW ENFORCEMENT PERSONNEL

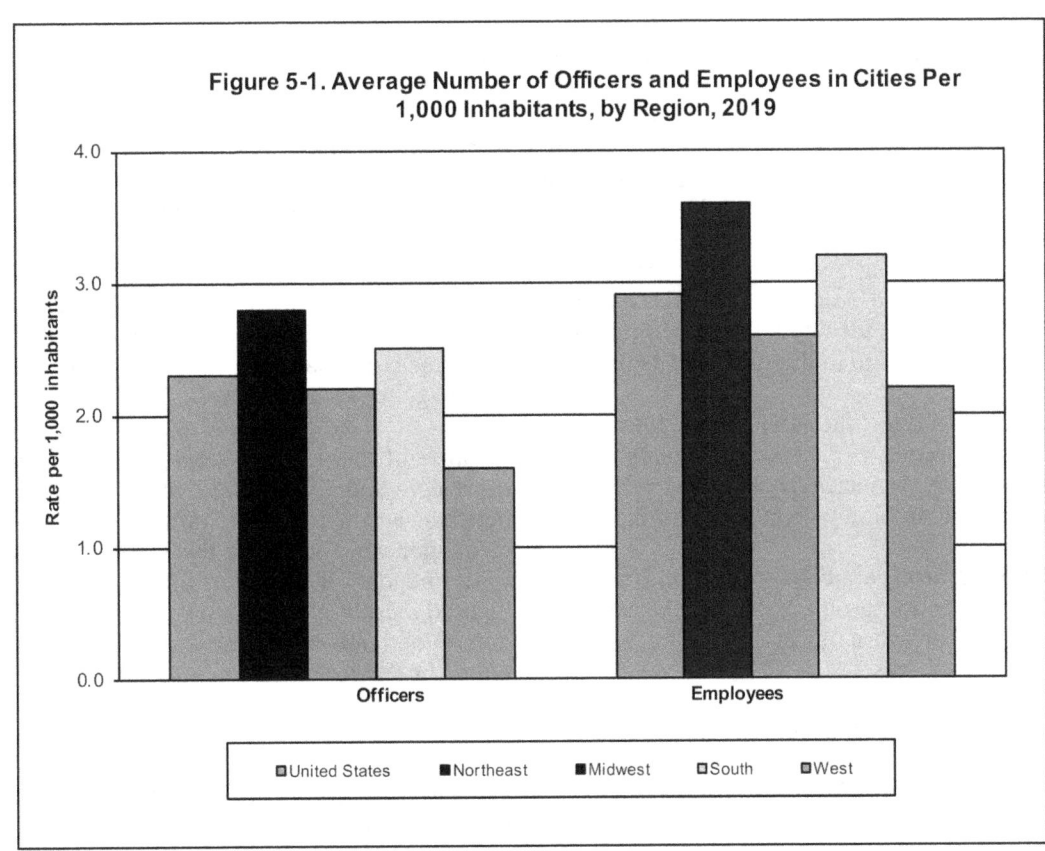

Figure 5-1. Average Number of Officers and Employees in Cities Per 1,000 Inhabitants, by Region, 2019

The Uniform Crime Reporting (UCR) program defines law enforcement officers as individuals who ordinarily carry a firearm and a badge, have full arrest powers, and are paid from government funds set aside specifically for sworn law enforcement representatives. Because of law enforcement's varied service requirements and functions, as well as the distinct demographic traits and characteristics of jurisdictions, readers should use caution when comparing staffing levels between agencies based on police employment data from the UCR program. In addition, the data presented here reflect existing staff levels and should not be interpreted as preferred officer strengths recommended by the Federal Bureau of Investigation (FBI). Also, readers should note that the totals given for sworn officers for any particular agency reflect both patrol officers on the street and officers assigned to various other duties, such as administrative and investigative positions and assignments to special teams.

Each year, law enforcement agencies across the United States report the total number of sworn law enforcement officers and civilians in their agencies as of October 31 to the UCR program. Civilian employees include personnel such as clerks, radio dispatchers, meter attendants,

stenographers, jailers, correctional officers, and mechanics, (provided that they are full-time employees of the agency).

Due to the varied service requirements and functions of law enforcement and the distinctive demographic traits and characteristics of each jurisdiction, caution should be exercised when comparing agencies' staffing levels based on the UCR Program's police employment data. The data presented here reflect existing staffing levels and should not be interpreted as FBI-preferred or FBI-recommended officer strengths. The total number of sworn officers for any particular agency reflects patrol officers on the street and officers assigned to other duties, such as those in administrative, investigative, and special-teams roles.

This section of *Crime in the United States* presents those data as the number and rate of law enforcement officers and civilian employees throughout the United States. In 2019, 697,195 sworn officers and 306,075 civilians provided law enforcement services to more than 288 million people nationwide. These law enforcement personnel were employed by 13,247 state, city, university/college, metropolitan/nonmetropolitan county, and other designated law enforcement agencies. Of the slightly more than 1 million law enforcement employees, 72.8 percent were male. (Table 74)

The data in this section are broken down by geographic region and division, population group, state, city, university/college, metropolitan/nonmetropolitan county, and other law enforcement agency groups. (Information about geographic regions and divisions and population groups can be found in Appendix III.) UCR program staff compute the rate of sworn officers and law enforcement employees by taking the number of employees (sworn officers only or in combination with civilians), dividing by the population for which the agency provides law enforcement service, and multiplying by 1,000.

- Tables 70 and 71 present the number and rate of law enforcement personnel per 1,000 inhabitants collectively employed by agencies, broken down by geographic region and division by population group

- Tables 72 and 73 provide a count of law enforcement agencies by population group, based on the employment rate ranges for sworn officer and civilian employees per 1,000 inhabitants

- Table 74 provides the number of total officers, the percentage of male and female sworn officers, and the civilian employees by population group

- Table 75 lists the percentage of full-time civilian law enforcement employees by population group

- Table 76 breaks down by state the number of sworn law enforcement officers and civilians employed by state law enforcement agencies

- Table 77 provides the number of total officers, the percentage of male and female sworn officers, and the civilian employees by state

- Tables 78 to 80 list the number of law enforcement employees for cities, universities and colleges, and metropolitan and nonmetropolitan counties

- Table 81 supplies employee data for those law enforcement agencies that serve selected transit systems, parks and forests, schools and school districts, hospitals, etc., in the nation

The demographic traits and characteristics of a jurisdiction affect its requirements for law enforcement service. For instance, a village between two large cities may require more law enforcement than a community of the same size with no urban center nearby. A town with legal gambling may have different law enforcement needs than a town near a military base. A city largely made up of college students may have different law enforcement needs than a city whose residents are mainly retirees.

Similarly, the functions of law enforcement agencies are diverse. Employees of these agencies patrol local streets and major highways, protect citizens in the nation's smallest towns and largest cities, and conduct investigations on offenses at the local and state levels. State police in one area may enforce traffic laws on state highways and interstates; in another area, they may be responsible for investigating violent crimes. Sheriff's departments may collect tax monies, serve as the enforcement authority for local and state courts, administer jail facilities, or carry out some combination of these duties. This has an impact on an agency's staffing levels.

Because of the differing service requirements and functions, care should be taken when drawing comparisons between and among the staffing levels of law enforcement agencies. The data in this section are not intended as recommended or preferred officer strength; they should be used merely as guides. Adequate staffing levels can be determined only after careful study of the conditions that affect the service requirements in a particular jurisdiction.

RATE

The UCR program computes these rates by taking the number of employees, dividing by the population of the agency's jurisdiction, and multiplying by 1,000.

An examination of the 2019 law enforcement employee data by population group showed that the nation's cities had a collective rate of 2.9 law enforcement employees per 1,000 inhabitants. Cities with fewer than 10,000 inhabitants had the highest rate of law enforcement employees, with a rate of 5.5 per 1,000 inhabitants. Cities with 25,000 to 49,999 inhabitants, 50,000 to 99,999 inhabitants, and 100,000 to 249,999 inhabitants had the lowest rate of law enforcement employees (2.1 per 1,000 in population for each). The nation's largest cities, those with 250,000 or more inhabitants, averaged 3.4 law enforcement employees for every 1,000 inhabitants. (Table 70)

Sworn Personnel

An analysis of the 2019 data showed that law enforcement agencies in the cities in the Northeast had the highest rate of sworn officers—2.8 per 1,000 inhabitants, followed by the South (2.5), the Midwest (2.2), and the West (1.6). (Table 71)

By population group in 2019, there were 2.3 sworn officers for each 1,000 resident population. Cities with fewer than 10,000 inhabitants had the highest rate at 4.2 sworn officers per 1,000 inhabitants. The nation's largest cities, those with 250,000 or more inhabitants, averaged 2.6 officers per 1,000 inhabitants, the same as in 2017 and 2018. The lowest rates were in cities with 50,000 to 99,999 inhabitants and 100,000 to 249,999 inhabitants (1.6 per 1,000 resident population for each). (Table 71)

Males accounted for 87.2 percent of all full-time sworn law enforcement officers in 2019. Cities with populations of 1 million and over employed the highest percentage (18.5 percent) of full-time female officers. Of the city population groups and subsets, cities with populations of 10,000 to 24,999 inhabitants employed the highest percentage (90.6 percent) of male officers. In metropolitan counties, 85.9 percent of officers were male; in nonmetropolitan counties, 92.0 percent of officers were male; and in suburban areas, 87.4 percent of officers were male. (Table 74)

Civilian Employees

Civilian employees provide a myriad of services to the nation's law enforcement and criminal justice agencies. Among other duties, they dispatch officers, provide administrative and record keeping support, and query local, state, and national databases.

In 2019, 30.5 percent of all law enforcement employees in the nation were civilians. Male employees accounted for 40.1 percent of all full-time civilian law enforcement employees in 2019. In cities, civilians made up 22.2 percent of law enforcement agency employees. Civilians made up 41.3 percent of law enforcement employees in metropolitan and nonmetropolitan counties and 34.5 percent of law enforcement employees in suburban areas. (Table 74)

Table 70. Full-Time Law Enforcement Employees,[1] by Region and Geographic Division and Population Group, 2019

(Number, rate per 1,000 inhabitants.)

Region/geographic division	Total (10,247 cities; population 196,900,226)	Group I (85 cities, 250,000 and over; population 62,520,440)	Group II (207 cities, 100,000 to 249,999; population 30,396,345)	Group III (427 cities, 50,000 to 99,999; population 29,799,314)	Group IV (788 cities, 25,000 to 49,999; population 27,147,744)	Group V (1,644 cities, 10,000 to 24,999; population 26,146,921)	Group VI (7,096 cities, under 10,000; population 20,889,462)	Total city agencies	2019 estimated city population	County[2] (3,000 agencies; population 91,457,371)	Total city and county agencies	2019 estimated total agency population	Suburban areas[3] (7,079 agencies; population 123,692,820)
Total													
Number of employees	569,819	209,882	64,904	61,893	57,795	61,106	114,239	10,247	196,900,226	433,451	13,247	288,357,597	468,532
Average number of employees per 1,000 inhabitants	2.9	3.4	2.1	2.1	2.1	2.3	5.5			4.7			3.8
Northeast													
Number of employees	158,999	67,819	8,052	15,640	18,733	18,713	30,042	2,526	44,387,838				
Average number of employees per 1,000 inhabitants	3.6	5.8	2.9	2.4	2.2	2.2	4.8						
New England													
Number of employees	33,586	2,922	4,020	6,216	7,322	7,054	6,052	781	12,741,851				
Average number of employees per 1,000 inhabitants	2.6	4.2	2.9	2.3	2.3	2.3	3.5						
Middle Atlantic													
Number of employees	125,413	64,897	4,032	9,424	11,411	11,659	23,990	1,745	31,645,987				
Average number of employees per 1,000 inhabitants	4.0	5.9	2.9	2.5	2.2	2.1	5.3						
Midwest													
Number of employees	103,578	34,720	8,237	12,874	12,126	14,394	21,227	2,679	39,233,426				
Average number of employees per 1,000 inhabitants	2.6	3.8	2.0	1.8	1.9	2.1	3.7						
East North Central													
Number of employees	68,219	27,075	4,453	8,186	8,705	8,711	11,089	1,446	24,836,151				
Average number of employees per 1,000 inhabitants	2.7	4.3	2.0	1.9	1.9	2.0	3.5						
West North Central													
Number of employees	35,359	7,645	3,784	4,688	3,421	5,683	10,138	1,233	14,397,275				
Average number of employees per 1,000 inhabitants	2.5	2.8	2.0	1.7	1.9	2.1	3.9						
South													
Number of employees	190,329	55,052	28,746	18,297	18,389	21,229	48,616	3,659	59,614,470				
Average number of employees per 1,000 inhabitants	3.2	2.8	2.5	2.5	2.6	2.9	7.3						
South Atlantic													
Number of employees	88,165	22,582	13,187	10,967	9,166	9,598	22,665	1,582	25,223,887				
Average number of employees per 1,000 inhabitants	3.5	3.4	2.6	2.6	2.7	3.1	8.2						
East South Central													
Number of employees	33,367	6,548	4,931	2,110	4,167	4,335	11,276	852	9,391,674				
Average number of employees per 1,000 inhabitants	3.6	2.8	3.0	2.6	2.7	3.0	6.9						
West South Central													
Number of employees	68,797	25,922	10,628	5,220	5,056	7,296	14,675	1,225	24,998,909				
Average number of employees per 1,000 inhabitants	2.8	2.4	2.1	2.3	2.3	2.7	6.4						
West													
Number of employees	116,913	52,291	19,869	15,082	8,547	6,770	14,354	1,383	53,664,492				
Average number of employees per 1,000 inhabitants	2.2	2.4	1.7	1.7	1.7	2.0	6.5						
Mountain													
Number of employees	41,859	18,575	5,762	4,594	3,171	2,391	7,366	612	17,181,579				
Average number of employees per 1,000 inhabitants	2.4	2.4	2.0	1.9	1.7	2.2	6.6						
Pacific													
Number of employees	75,054	33,716	14,107	10,488	5,376	4,379	6,988	771	36,482,913				
Average number of employees per 1,000 inhabitants	2.1	2.4	1.6	1.6	1.7	1.9	6.3						

1 Full-time law enforcement employees include civilians.   2 The designation county is a combination of both metropolitan and nonmetropolitan counties.   3 Suburban areas include law enforcement agencies in cities with less than 50,000 inhabitants and county law enforcement agencies that are within a Metropolitan Statistical Area. Suburban areas exclude all metropolitan agencies associated with a principal city. The agencies associated with suburban areas also appear in other groups within this table.

Table 71. Full-Time Law Enforcement Officers, by Region, Geographic Division, and Population Group, 2019

(Number, rate per 1,000 inhabitants.)

Region/geographic division	Total (10,247 cities; population 196,900,226)	Group I (85 cities, 250,000 and over; population 62,520,440)	Group II (207 cities, 100,000 to 249,999; population 30,396,345)	Group III (427 cities, 50,000 to 99,999; population 29,799,314)	Group IV (788 cities, 25,000 to 49,999; population 27,147,744)	Group V (1,644 cities, 10,000 to 24,999; population 26,146,921)	Group VI (7,096 cities, under 10,000; population 20,889,462)	Total city agencies	2019 estimated city population	County[1] (3,000 agencies; population 91,457,371)	Total city and county agencies	2019 estimated total agency population	Suburban areas[2] (7,079 agencies; population 123,692,820)
Total													
Number of officers	443,173	160,606	49,987	48,113	46,485	49,861	88,121	10,247	196,900,226	254,022	13,247	288,357,597	307,028
Average number of officers per 1,000 inhabitants	2.3	2.6	1.6	1.6	1.7	1.9	4.2			2.8			2.5
Northeast													
Number of officers	125,176	49,224	6,853	12,975	15,848	16,006	24,270	2,526	44,387,838				
Average number of officers per 1,000 inhabitants	2.8	4.2	2.5	2.0	1.9	1.8	3.9						
New England													
Number of officers	27,416	2,143	3,488	5,210	6,089	5,708	4,778	781	12,741,851				
Average number of officers per 1,000 inhabitants	2.2	3.1	2.5	2.0	1.9	1.9	2.8						
Middle Atlantic													
Number of officers	97,760	47,081	3,365	7,765	9,759	10,298	19,492	1,745	31,645,987				
Average number of officers per 1,000 inhabitants	3.1	4.3	2.5	2.1	1.8	1.8	4.3						
Midwest													
Number of officers	86,159	29,721	6,763	10,395	9,843	11,972	17,465	2,679	39,233,426				
Average number of officers per 1,000 inhabitants	2.2	3.3	1.6	1.5	1.5	1.7	3.0						
East North Central													
Number of officers	57,919	23,850	3,713	6,642	7,108	7,335	9,271	1,446	24,836,151				
Average number of officers per 1,000 inhabitants	2.3	3.8	1.7	1.6	1.6	1.7	2.9						
West North Central													
Number of officers	28,240	5,871	3,050	3,753	2,735	4,637	8,194	1,233	14,397,275				
Average number of officers per 1,000 inhabitants	2.0	2.2	1.6	1.4	1.5	1.7	3.2						
South													
Number of officers	147,357	43,069	22,183	14,216	14,559	16,816	36,514	3,659	59,614,470				
Average number of officers per 1,000 inhabitants	2.5	2.2	1.9	1.9	2.0	2.3	5.5						
South Atlantic													
Number of officers	68,818	17,371	10,275	8,529	7,370	7,712	17,561	1,582	25,223,887				
Average number of officers per 1,000 inhabitants	2.7	2.6	2.0	2.0	2.1	2.5	6.3						
East South Central													
Number of officers	26,143	5,263	3,897	1,730	3,341	3,517	8,395	852	9,391,674				
Average number of officers per 1,000 inhabitants	2.8	2.2	2.4	2.1	2.2	2.5	5.1						
West South Central													
Number of officers	52,396	20,435	8,011	3,957	3,848	5,587	10,558	1,225	24,998,909				
Average number of officers per 1,000 inhabitants	2.1	1.9	1.6	1.7	1.8	2.1	4.6						
West													
Number of officers	84,481	38,592	14,188	10,527	6,235	5,067	9,872	1,383	53,664,492				
Average number of officers per 1,000 inhabitants	1.6	1.7	1.2	1.2	1.2	1.5	4.5						
Mountain													
Number of officers	30,238	13,341	4,272	3,245	2,414	1,843	5,123	612	17,181,579				
Average number of officers per 1,000 inhabitants	1.8	1.7	1.5	1.3	1.3	1.7	4.6						
Pacific													
Number of officers	54,243	25,251	9,916	7,282	3,821	3,224	4,749	771	36,482,913				
Average number of officers per 1,000 inhabitants	1.5	1.8	1.1	1.1	1.2	1.4	4.3						

1 The designation county is a combination of both metropolitan and nonmetropolitan counties.   2 Suburban areas include law enforcement agencies in cities with less than 50,000 inhabitants and county law enforcement agencies that are within a Metropolitan Statistical Area. Suburban areas exclude all metropolitan agencies associated with a principal city. The agencies associated with suburban areas also appear in other groups within this table.

Table 72. Full-Time Law Enforcement Employees,[1] Range in Rate, by Population Group, 2019

(Number, rate per 1,000 inhabitants.)

Rate range	Total cities[2] (8,947 cities; population 196,900,226)	Group I (85 cities, 250,000 and over; population 62,520,440)	Group II (207 cities, 100,000 to 249,999; population 30,396,345)	Group III (427 cities, 50,000 to 99,999; population 29,799,314)	Group IV (788 cities, 25,000 to 49,999; population 27,147,744)	Group V (1,644 cities, 10,000 to 24,999; population 26,146,921)	Group VI (5,796 cities, under 10,000; population 20,889,462)
Total Cities							
Number	8,947	85	207	427	788	1,644	5,796
Percent[3]	100.0	100.0	100.0	100.0	100.0	100.0	100.0
0.1–0.5							
Number	76	0	0	0	1	4	71
Percent	0.8	0.0	0.0	0.0	0.1	0.2	1.2
0.6–1.0							
Number	411	0	1	9	25	49	327
Percent	4.6	0.0	0.5	2.1	3.2	3.0	5.6
1.1–1.5							
Number	1,172	6	51	97	152	204	662
Percent	13.1	7.1	24.6	22.7	19.3	12.4	11.4
1.6–2.0							
Number	1,798	14	57	126	214	412	975
Percent	20.1	16.5	27.5	29.5	27.2	25.1	16.8
2.1–2.5							
Number	1,720	26	51	103	204	385	951
Percent	19.2	30.6	24.6	24.1	25.9	23.4	16.4
2.6–3.0							
Number	1,234	14	22	57	106	311	724
Percent	13.8	16.5	10.6	13.3	13.5	18.9	12.5
3.1–3.5							
Number	747	6	14	16	55	134	522
Percent	8.3	7.1	6.8	3.7	7.0	8.2	9.0
3.6–4.0							
Number	523	6	9	9	21	67	411
Percent	5.8	7.1	4.3	2.1	2.7	4.1	7.1
4.1–4.5							
Number	332	3	1	6	2	39	281
Percent	3.7	3.5	0.5	1.4	0.3	2.4	4.8
4.6–5.0							
Number	229	5	1	1	4	17	201
Percent	2.6	5.9	0.5	0.2	0.5	1.0	3.5
5.1 and over							
Number	705	5	0	3	4	22	671
Percent	7.9	5.9	0.0	0.7	0.5	1.3	11.6

1 Full-time law enforcement employees include civilians.   2 The number of agencies used to compile these figures differs from other tables that include data about law enforcement employees because agencies with no resident population are excluded from this table. Agencies not included in this table are associated with universities and colleges (see Table 79) and other agencies (see Table 81), as well as some state agencies that have concurrent jurisdiction with other local law enforcement.   3 Because of rounding, the percentages may not sum to 100.

Table 73. Full-Time Law Enforcement Officers, Range in Rate, by Population Group, 2019

(Number, rate per 1,000 inhabitants.)

Rate range	Total cities[1] (8,947 cities; population 196,900,226)	Group I (85 cities, 250,000 and over; population 62,520,440)	Group II (207 cities, 100,000 to 249,999; population 30,396,345)	Group III (427 cities, 50,000 to 99,999; population 29,799,314)	Group IV (788 cities, 25,000 to 49,999; population 27,147,744)	Group V (1,644 cities, 10,000 to 24,999; population 26,146,921)	Group VI (5,796 cities, under 10,000; population 20,889,462)
Total Cities							
Number	8,947	85	207	427	788	1,644	5,796
Percent[2]	100.0	100.0	100.0	100.0	100.0	100.0	100.0
0.1–0.5							
Number	89	0	0	1	4	6	78
Percent	1.0	0.0	0.0	0.2	0.5	0.4	1.3
0.6–1.0							
Number	662	4	38	73	78	84	385
Percent	7.4	4.7	18.4	17.1	9.9	5.1	6.6
1.1–1.5							
Number	1,732	20	75	136	240	403	858
Percent	19.4	23.5	36.2	31.9	30.5	24.5	14.8
1.6–2.0							
Number	2,228	27	48	137	266	546	1,204
Percent	24.9	31.8	23.2	32.1	33.8	33.2	20.8
2.1–2.5							
Number	1,599	12	26	52	126	367	1,016
Percent	17.9	14.1	12.6	12.2	16.0	22.3	17.5
2.6–3.0							
Number	956	6	15	16	61	137	721
Percent	10.7	7.1	7.2	3.7	7.7	8.3	12.4
3.1–3.5							
Number	532	6	2	9	7	55	453
Percent	5.9	7.1	1.0	2.1	0.9	3.3	7.8
3.6–4.0							
Number	326	3	2	0	3	32	286
Percent	3.6	3.5	1.0	0.0	0.4	1.9	4.9
4.1–4.5							
Number	234	5	1	2	1	6	219
Percent	2.6	5.9	0.5	0.5	0.1	0.4	3.8
4.6–5.0							
Number	130	1	0	1	0	3	125
Percent	1.5	1.2	0.0	0.2	0.0	0.2	2.2
5.1 and over							
Number	459	1	0	0	2	5	451
Percent	5.1	1.2	0.0	0.0	0.3	0.3	7.8

1 The number of agencies used to compile these figures differs from other tables that include data about law enforcement officers because agencies with no resident population are excluded from this table. Agencies not included in this table are associated with universities and colleges (see Table 79) and other agencies (see Table 81), as well as some state agencies that have concurrent jurisdiction with other local law enforcement.   2 Because of rounding, the percentages may not sum to 100.

Table 74. Full-Time Law Enforcement Employees, by Population Group, Percent Male and Female, 2019

(Number, percent.)

Population group	Total law enforcement employees (number)	Law enforcement employees (percent)		Total officers (number)	Officers (percent)		Civilians (number) Total civilians	Civilians (percent)		Agencies (number)	Population, 2019, estimated
		Male	Female		Male	Female		Male	Female		
Total Agencies	1,003,270	72.8	27.2	697,195	87.2	12.8	306,075	40.1	59.9	13,247	288,357,597
Total Cities	569,819	75.0	25.0	443,173	87.0	13.0	126,646	32.9	67.1	10,247	196,900,226
Group I (250,000 and over)	209,882	71.5	28.5	160,606	82.8	17.2	49,276	34.9	65.1	85	62,520,440
1,000,000 and over (Group I subset)	112,875	70.5	29.5	85,902	81.5	18.5	26,973	35.4	64.6	11	27,806,004
500,000 to 999,999 (Group I subset)	55,379	73.4	26.6	42,605	84.5	15.5	12,774	36.6	63.4	26	18,452,421
250,000 to 499,999 (Group I subset)	41,628	71.9	28.1	32,099	84.0	16.0	9,529	30.9	69.1	48	16,262,015
Group II (100,000 to 249,999)	64,904	73.8	26.2	49,987	87.6	12.4	14,917	27.3	72.7	207	30,396,345
Group III (50,000 to 99,999)	61,893	75.3	24.7	48,113	88.5	11.5	13,780	29.1	70.9	427	29,799,314
Group IV (25,000 to 49,999)	57,795	77.8	22.2	46,485	89.9	10.1	11,310	28.2	71.8	788	27,147,744
Group V (10,000 to 24,999)	61,106	78.8	21.2	49,861	90.6	9.4	11,245	26.5	73.5	1,644	26,146,921
Group VI (under 10,000)	114,239	78.4	21.6	88,121	90.0	10.0	26,118	39.2	60.8	7,096	20,889,462
Metropolitan Counties	310,337	69.4	30.6	182,053	85.9	14.1	128,284	45.9	54.1	1,208	69,763,099
Nonmetropolitan Counties	123,114	71.7	28.3	71,969	92.0	8.0	51,145	43.2	56.8	1,792	21,694,272
Suburban Areas[1]	468,532	72.4	27.6	307,028	87.4	12.6	161,504	43.8	56.2	7,079	123,692,820

1 Suburban areas include law enforcement agencies in cities with less than 50,000 inhabitants and county law enforcement agencies that are within a Metropolitan Statistical Area. Suburban areas exclude all metropolitan agencies associated with a principal city. The agencies associated with suburban areas also appear in other groups within this table.

Table 75. Full-Time Civilian Law Enforcement Employees, by Population Group, 2019

(Number, percent.)

Population group	Civilian employees (percent)	Agencies (number)	Population, 2019, estimated
Total Agencies	30.5	13,247	288,357,597
Total Cities	22.2	10,247	196,900,226
Group I (250,000 and over)	23.5	85	62,520,440
1,000,000 and over (Group I subset)	23.9	11	27,806,004
500,000 to 999,999 (Group I subset)	23.1	26	18,452,421
250,000 to 499,999 (Group I subset)	22.9	48	16,262,015
Group II (100,000 to 249,999)	23.0	207	30,396,345
Group III (50,000 to 99,999)	22.3	427	29,799,314
Group IV (25,000 to 49,999)	19.6	788	27,147,744
Group V (10,000 to 24,999)	18.4	1,644	26,146,921
Group VI (under 10,000)	22.9	7,096	20,889,462
Metropolitan Counties	41.3	1,208	69,763,099
Nonmetropolitan Counties	41.5	1,792	21,694,272
Suburban Areas[1]	34.5	7,079	123,692,820

1 Suburban areas include law enforcement agencies in cities with less than 50,000 inhabitants and county law enforcement agencies that are within a Metropolitan Statistical Area. Suburban areas exclude all metropolitan agencies associated with a principal city. The agencies associated with suburban areas also appear in other groups within this table.

Table 76. Full-Time State Law Enforcement Employees, by Selected State, 2019

(Number.)

State/agency	Law enforcement employees	Officers		Civilians	
		Male	Female	Male	Female
Alabama					
Other state agencies	1,472	835	36	140	461
Alaska					
State Troopers	587	326	20	106	135
Arizona					
Department of Public Safety	1,946	1,072	43	363	468
Arkansas					
State Patrol	966	499	24	135	308
Other state agencies	49	30	2	10	7
California					
Highway Patrol	10,529	6,780	450	1,421	1,878
Other state agencies	1,418	1,105	192	49	72
Colorado					
State Police	1,155	725	57	145	228
Other state agencies	436	73	12	127	224
Connecticut					
State Police	1,081	787	77	86	131
Other state agencies	95	75	5	9	6
Delaware					
State Police	967	639	94	85	149
Other state agencies	750	243	34	139	334
Florida					
Highway Patrol	2,351	1,700	179	145	327
Other state agencies	4,978	2,278	353	885	1,462
Georgia					
Department of Public Safety	1,481	1,082	30	168	201
Other state agencies	1,199	387	102	192	518
Idaho					
State Police	525	275	16	67	167
Other state agencies	31	23	5	0	3
Illinois					
State Police	2,982	1,535	168	609	670
Other state agencies	262	123	9	93	37
Indiana					
State Police	1,679	1,157	59	180	283
Iowa					
Department of Public Safety	829	512	35	129	153
Kansas					
Highway Patrol	782	467	19	119	177
Other state agencies	670	330	33	106	201
Kentucky					
State Police	1,825	999	22	363	441
Other state agencies	166	149	9	1	7
Louisiana[1]					
Other state agencies	3	2	0	0	1
Maine					
State Police	253	213	22	5	13
Other state agencies	51	27	1	14	9
Maryland					
State Police	2,161	1,358	109	348	346
Other state agencies	1,557	953	141	193	270
Massachusetts					
State Police	2,729	2,054	119	223	333
Other state agencies	261	223	29	4	5
Michigan					
State Police	3,027	1,775	177	445	630
Other state agencies	272	225	21	7	19
Minnesota					
State Patrol	681	493	54	52	82
Other state agencies	719	245	41	181	252
Mississippi[1]					
Other state agencies	106	79	13	2	12

Table 76. Full-Time State Law Enforcement Employees, by Selected State, 2019—Continued

(Number.)

State/agency	Law enforcement employees	Officers		Civilians	
		Male	Female	Male	Female
Missouri					
State Highway Patrol	2,334	1,168	61	524	581
Other state agencies	444	383	40	2	19
Montana					
Highway Patrol	288	220	15	12	41
Other state agencies	43	16	2	10	15
Nebraska					
State Patrol	681	401	28	89	163
Nevada					
Highway Patrol	833	646	52	50	85
Other state agencies	137	81	8	16	32
New Hampshire					
State Police	524	330	29	48	117
Other state agencies	32	13	5	4	10
New Jersey					
State Police	4,050	2,699	143	570	638
Other state agencies	7,662	5,473	144	970	1,075
Port Authority of New York and New Jersey[2]	2,316	1,904	254	66	92
New Mexico[1]					
State Police					
New York					
State Police	6,045	4,591	561	322	571
Other state agencies	244	189	30	11	14
North Carolina					
Highway Patrol	2,093	1,549	45	287	212
Other state agencies	1,142	707	142	121	172
North Dakota					
Highway Patrol	180	137	6	11	26
Ohio					
State Highway Patrol	2,584	1,479	152	462	491
Other state agencies	276	245	20	4	7
Oklahoma					
Highway Patrol	1,380	745	16	287	332
Other state agencies	397	128	21	95	153
Oregon					
State Police	1,254	612	56	193	393
Other state agencies	85	55	22	0	8
Pennsylvania					
State Police	6,547	4,144	301	1,088	1,014
Other state agencies	317	209	24	61	23
Rhode Island					
State Police	312	234	27	25	26
Other state agencies	68	46	5	11	6
South Carolina					
Highway Patrol	1,254	917	56	94	187
Other state agencies	470	306	50	56	58
South Dakota					
Highway Patrol	254	164	12	46	32
Other state agencies	178	51	2	43	82
Tennessee					
Department of Safety	1,675	824	48	230	573
Other state agencies	1,263	715	196	125	227
Texas					
Department of Public Safety	9,679	3,838	309	1,712	3,820
Utah					
Highway Patrol	804	557	11	65	171
Other state agencies	165	142	6	3	14
Vermont					
State Police	608	452	65	31	60
Other state agencies	117	89	9	10	9
Virginia					
State Police	2,681	1,817	127	246	491
Other state agencies	887	529	57	138	163

Table 76. Full-Time State Law Enforcement Employees, by Selected State, 2019—Continued

(Number.)

State/agency	Law enforcement employees	Officers		Civilians	
		Male	Female	Male	Female
Washington					
State Patrol	2,245	947	91	586	621
Other state agencies	115	51	16	13	35
West Virginia					
State Patrol	1,013	619	22	130	242
Other state agencies	222	177	1	21	23
Wisconsin					
State Patrol	652	454	40	78	80
Other state agencies	294	226	27	15	26
Wyoming[1]					
Highway Patrol	334	185	7	52	90

Note: Caution should be used when comparing data from one state to that of another. The responsibilities of the various state police, highway patrol, and department of public safety agencies range from full law enforcement duties to only traffic patrol, which can impact both the level of employment for agencies as well as the ratio of sworn officers to civilians employed. Any valid comparison must take these factors and the other identified variables affecting crime into consideration.
1 Police employee data were not received from the State Police/Highway Patrol/Department of Public Safety for the state.   2 Data reported are the number of law enforcement employees for the state of New Jersey.

Table 77. Full-Time Law Enforcement Employees, by State, 2019

(Number.)

State	Total law enforcement employees	Total officers		Total civilians		Total agencies	Population, 2019, estimated
		Male	Female	Male	Female		
Alabama	16,185	9,897	907	1,977	3,404	314	4,193,828
Alaska	1,979	1,154	117	262	446	38	731,268
Arizona	23,087	11,566	1,463	4,676	5,382	118	7,278,717
Arkansas	10,877	6,347	791	1,454	2,285	298	3,011,695
California	121,251	68,914	10,702	15,749	25,886	469	33,821,670
Colorado	18,757	10,692	1,776	2,316	3,973	237	5,668,232
Connecticut	8,717	6,497	781	597	842	104	3,379,999
Delaware	3,407	2,077	289	367	674	54	968,060
District of Columbia	5,019	3,305	923	328	463	3	705,749
Florida	74,949	38,971	7,399	10,837	17,742	333	19,326,640
Georgia	29,313	17,880	3,682	2,364	5,387	346	8,386,578
Hawaii	3,532	2,467	297	246	522	4	1,415,872
Idaho	5,755	2,775	236	1,167	1,577	110	1,785,978
Illinois	39,998	24,465	4,954	5,539	5,040	432	9,597,444
Indiana	11,135	7,280	694	1,380	1,781	109	3,661,018
Iowa	8,384	4,946	464	1,220	1,754	234	3,085,588
Kansas	10,298	6,325	760	1,235	1,978	314	2,751,561
Kentucky	9,585	6,858	494	917	1,316	300	3,733,182
Louisiana	16,413	9,604	2,552	1,492	2,765	167	3,467,544
Maine	2,757	2,114	188	157	298	134	1,343,699
Maryland	20,330	13,465	2,110	1,807	2,948	128	5,886,486
Massachusetts	20,099	14,889	1,460	1,507	2,243	291	6,307,729
Michigan	25,063	15,740	2,328	3,249	3,746	620	9,590,385
Minnesota	15,960	8,981	1,223	2,570	3,186	402	5,633,036
Mississippi	4,439	2,510	296	642	991	66	1,225,448
Missouri	20,569	13,197	1,565	2,284	3,523	498	5,962,975
Montana	3,152	1,810	148	550	644	109	1,065,455
Nebraska	5,349	3,334	421	560	1,034	161	1,913,370
Nevada	7,693	5,020	529	514	1,630	52	2,384,625
New Hampshire	3,713	2,566	277	267	603	177	1,292,466
New Jersey	48,803	34,225	3,487	4,487	6,604	531	8,592,431
New Mexico	2,705	1,555	239	349	562	49	911,159
New York	84,108	52,799	9,548	7,905	13,856	377	18,245,187
North Carolina	34,036	21,003	2,963	4,493	5,577	517	10,481,307
North Dakota	2,442	1,559	210	252	421	106	761,894
Ohio	16,876	11,007	1,501	1,691	2,677	255	5,138,552
Oklahoma	13,517	8,279	877	1,708	2,653	428	3,952,634
Oregon	10,846	5,756	659	1,917	2,514	210	4,198,487
Pennsylvania	30,490	22,928	2,728	1,967	2,867	999	9,463,952
Rhode Island	3,150	2,333	207	239	371	48	1,059,361
South Carolina	15,964	9,929	1,657	1,623	2,755	285	4,864,993
South Dakota	2,980	1,601	150	541	688	131	868,490
Tennessee	28,200	15,902	1,824	4,865	5,609	448	6,820,658
Texas	85,985	45,001	6,759	14,650	19,575	734	25,524,065
Utah	7,614	4,831	389	1,027	1,367	132	3,112,367
Vermont	1,767	1,255	164	111	237	86	623,009
Virginia	24,385	16,743	2,650	1,319	3,673	282	8,534,356
Washington	16,004	9,910	1,119	1,988	2,987	254	7,586,229
West Virginia	4,566	3,493	138	353	582	292	1,781,758
Wisconsin	18,804	11,171	1,765	2,597	3,271	404	5,706,400
Wyoming	2,263	1,246	163	315	539	57	554,011

Table 78. Full-Time Law Enforcement Employees, by Selected State and City, 2019

(Number.)

State/city	Population	Total law enforcement employees	Total officers	Total civilians
ALABAMA				
Abbeville	2,548	14	9	5
Adamsville	4,302	28	15	13
Addison	721	4	4	0
Alabaster	33,620	89	72	17
Albertville	21,611	69	45	24
Alexander City	14,410	67	51	16
Aliceville	2,280	6	5	1
Andalusia	8,699	35	25	10
Anniston	21,391	96	89	7
Arab	8,350	37	27	10
Ardmore	1,450	11	7	4
Argo	4,335	7	6	1
Arley	345	2	2	0
Ashford	2,154	5	4	1
Ashland	1,900	16	11	5
Ashville	2,332	4	4	0
Athens	26,833	56	45	11
Atmore	9,255	36	28	8
Attalla	5,769	28	22	6
Auburn	67,407	150	130	20
Baker Hill	249	4	4	0
Bay Minette	9,427	31	24	7
Bayou La Batre	2,492	18	13	5
Bear Creek	1,038	2	2	0
Berry	1,093	3	3	0
Bessemer	26,402	149	107	42
Birmingham	209,649	1,023	851	172
Boaz	9,680	33	23	10
Brent	4,751	7	7	0
Brighton	2,766	1	1	0
Brilliant	866	1	1	0
Brookside	1,318	8	5	3
Brookwood	1,861	6	6	0
Brundidge	1,923	17	9	8
Calera	14,750	41	32	9
Camden	1,797	10	8	2
Camp Hill	948	5	5	0
Carbon Hill	1,903	9	3	6
Carrollton	950	3	3	0
Cedar Bluff	1,817	5	5	0
Centre	3,517	12	11	1
Centreville	2,623	7	7	0
Chatom	1,185	4	4	0
Cherokee	999	6	6	0
Chickasaw	5,704	23	20	3
Childersburg	4,846	20	18	2
Citronelle	3,887	17	11	6
Clayton	2,839	4	4	0
Clio	1,259	3	3	0
Coaling	1,660	4	4	0
Collinsville	1,959	10	4	6
Columbia	734	2	2	0
Columbiana	4,644	15	11	4
Coosada	1,311	8	5	3
Cordova	1,917	6	4	2
Cottonwood	1,240	3	3	0
Courtland	584	1	1	0
Creola	2,028	31	14	17
Cullman	15,956	71	50	21
Dadeville	3,063	15	14	1
Daphne	27,157	104	69	35
Dauphin Island	1,306	28	12	16
Decatur	54,074	151	139	12
Demopolis	6,639	24	20	4
Dora	1,881	11	7	4
Double Springs	1,024	8	7	1
Douglas	775	5	5	0
Eclectic	1,026	8	7	1
Elba	3,820	23	12	11
Elberta	1,751	11	10	1
Enterprise	28,463	72	54	18
Eufaula	11,758	59	38	21
Eutaw	2,621	10	9	1
Evergreen	3,572	25	19	6
Excel	637	2	2	0
Fairhope	22,932	64	40	24
Falkville	1,244	6	5	1
Fayette	4,292	12	12	0
Florala	1,894	7	7	0
Florence	40,543	132	106	26
Foley	19,419	94	64	30
Fort Deposit	1,149	5	5	0
Frisco City	1,156	2	2	0
Fultondale	9,344	34	27	7

Table 78. Full-Time Law Enforcement Employees, by Selected State and City, 2019—Continued

(Number.)

State/city	Population	Total law enforcement employees	Total officers	Total civilians
Gardendale	14,036	41	31	10
Geneva	4,321	13	9	4
Georgiana	1,601	9	6	3
Glencoe	5,133	10	9	1
Gordo	1,609	4	4	0
Grant	915	2	2	0
Greenville	7,485	30	25	5
Guin	2,251	6	6	0
Gulf Shores	12,739	69	48	21
Guntersville	8,517	47	36	11
Gurley	812	6	6	0
Haleyville	3,927	16	11	5
Hamilton	6,547	15	13	2
Harpersville	1,725	8	8	0
Hartford	2,586	15	11	4
Hartselle	14,442	31	30	1
Hayneville	796	4	3	1
Headland	4,738	20	12	8
Heflin	3,427	12	11	1
Helena	19,870	30	25	5
Hillsboro	512	2	2	0
Hokes Bluff	4,248	9	7	2
Hollywood	955	5	4	1
Homewood	25,428	117	81	36
Hoover	85,670	225	188	37
Hueytown	15,290	44	35	9
Huntsville	199,465	648	442	206
Irondale	12,582	41	34	7
Jacksons Gap	813	3	3	0
Jacksonville	12,453	38	30	8
Jasper	13,393	70	50	20
Kimberly	3,383	7	7	0
Kinsey	2,221	2	2	0
LaFayette	2,926	14	13	1
Lake View	2,520	4	3	1
Lanett	6,208	31	29	2
Leeds	12,086	27	26	1
Leesburg	1,017	3	3	0
Leighton	706	9	9	0
Level Plains	2,016	3	3	0
Lexington	705	4	4	0
Lincoln	6,763	21	19	2
Linden	1,873	6	6	0
Lineville	2,247	11	7	4
Lipscomb	2,142	8	3	5
Livingston	3,354	8	4	4
Louisville	456	3	3	0
Loxley	2,695	21	15	6
Lynn	640	2	1	1
Madison	51,375	111	82	29
Margaret	5,105	2	2	0
Marion	3,203	7	6	1
McIntosh	218	8	8	0
Mentone	369	3	2	1
Midfield	5,031	23	17	6
Midland City	2,371	8	4	4
Millport	976	1	1	0
Millry	500	2	2	0
Mobile	244,775	635	482	153
Monroeville	5,774	33	26	7
Montevallo	6,720	20	16	4
Montgomery	197,315	563	467	96
Moody	13,240	22	21	1
Morris	2,156	6	6	0
Moulton	3,206	11	11	0
Moundville	2,460	10	9	1
Mountain Brook	20,292	74	59	15
Mount Vernon	1,490	5	4	1
Munford	1,360	1	1	0
New Hope	2,912	6	6	0
New Site	754	2	2	0
North Courtland	608	4	4	0
Northport	26,043	67	48	19
Notasulga	814	16	9	7
Oakman	718	1	1	0
Odenville	3,816	9	9	0
Ohatchee	1,151	6	6	0
Oneonta	6,619	21	20	1
Opelika	31,109	99	78	21
Opp	6,403	29	20	9
Orange Beach	6,202	78	53	25
Owens Crossroads	2,082	5	5	0
Oxford	21,131	78	64	14
Parrish	931	3	3	0

Table 78. Full-Time Law Enforcement Employees, by Selected State and City, 2019—Continued

(Number.)

State/city	Population	Total law enforcement employees	Total officers	Total civilians
Pelham	24,033	85	69	16
Pell City	13,936	42	40	2
Phenix City	36,874	94	71	23
Piedmont	4,555	18	13	5
Pine Hill	862	2	2	0
Pisgah	695	1	1	0
Pleasant Grove	10,101	22	17	5
Prattville	35,857	89	81	8
Priceville	3,761	5	5	0
Prichard	21,405	54	36	18
Ragland	1,700	3	3	0
Rainbow City	9,558	45	29	16
Red Bay	3,051	13	9	4
Red Level	476	2	2	0
Reform	1,550	5	5	0
Riverside	2,325	3	3	0
Roanoke	5,914	28	22	6
Robertsdale	6,978	28	17	11
Rogersville	1,228	5	5	0
Samson	1,865	7	7	0
Saraland	14,763	56	43	13
Sardis City	1,797	5	5	0
Satsuma	6,159	18	14	4
Scottsboro	14,360	74	46	28
Sheffield	8,876	36	27	9
Shorter	396	12	5	7
Silverhill	1,040	7	6	1
Skyline	815	2	1	1
Snead	842	13	13	0
Somerville	769	2	2	0
Southside	8,868	19	14	5
Spanish Fort	9,282	26	22	4
Springville	4,290	11	11	0
Steele	1,077	4	4	0
St. Florian	677	5	5	0
Stevenson	1,941	7	5	2
Sumiton	2,335	18	9	9
Summerdale	1,614	12	11	1
Sylacauga	12,108	39	37	2
Talladega	15,201	45	41	4
Tallassee	4,560	8	8	0
Tarrant	6,131	25	19	6
Thomaston	380	1	1	0
Thomasville	3,879	26	21	5
Trafford	624	7	7	0
Triana	634	1	1	0
Trinity	2,449	8	8	0
Troy	19,245	80	60	20
Trussville	22,609	77	65	12
Tuscaloosa	102,518	356	279	77
Tuskegee	8,250	32	20	12
Union Springs	3,421	19	12	7
Uniontown	2,211	7	6	1
Valley	9,168	29	26	3
Vance	1,678	5	5	0
Vernon	1,839	8	8	0
Vestavia Hills	34,538	99	96	3
Wadley	725	4	4	0
Wedowee	794	9	8	1
West Blocton	1,233	2	2	0
White Hall	754	7	6	1
Winfield	4,451	14	13	1
York	2,235	4	4	0
ALASKA				
Anchorage	287,731	574	427	147
Bethel	6,544	25	13	12
Bristol Bay Borough	852	9	4	5
Cordova	2,150	9	3	6
Craig	1,313	9	4	5
Dillingham	2,405	17	7	10
Fairbanks	31,493	44	39	5
Haines	2,441	8	3	5
Homer	5,913	20	11	9
Hoonah	792	8	4	4
Juneau	31,810	81	48	33
Kenai	7,862	24	16	8
Ketchikan	8,316	34	23	11
Klawock	822	4	4	0
Kodiak	5,947	43	18	25
Kotzebue	3,272	13	6	7
Nome	3,899	12	10	2
North Pole	2,111	11	9	2
North Slope Borough	9,801	76	45	31
Palmer	7,490	25	15	10

Table 78. Full-Time Law Enforcement Employees, by Selected State and City, 2019—Continued

(Number.)

State/city	Population	Total law enforcement employees	Total officers	Total civilians
Petersburg	3,181	10	7	3
Sand Point	1,161	6	5	1
Seward	2,732	22	10	12
Sitka	8,512	22	10	12
Skagway	1,159	11	4	7
Soldotna	4,756	17	14	3
St. Paul	498	8	3	5
Unalaska	4,513	21	11	10
Valdez	3,816	12	12	0
Wasilla	10,915	58	24	34
Whittier	203	7	7	0
Wrangell	2,489	12	5	7
ARIZONA				
Apache Junction	42,531	95	61	34
Avondale	87,117	191	134	57
Benson	4,843	21	13	8
Bisbee	5,161	15	11	4
Buckeye	77,904	129	91	38
Bullhead City	40,532	107	68	39
Camp Verde	11,286	35	22	13
Casa Grande	58,366	99	72	27
Chandler	259,881	484	328	156
Chino Valley	12,162	27	22	5
Clarkdale	4,434	11	10	1
Clifton	3,758	13	6	7
Colorado City	4,862	18	10	8
Coolidge	13,138	43	32	11
Cottonwood	12,331	52	29	23
Douglas	15,786	42	30	12
Eagar	4,897	8	6	2
El Mirage	36,185	68	47	21
Eloy	19,758	38	28	10
Flagstaff	75,013	159	110	49
Florence	26,385	37	29	8
Fredonia	1,296	3	3	0
Gilbert	253,619	409	281	128
Glendale	253,951	550	410	140
Globe	7,323	21	18	3
Goodyear	85,305	154	113	41
Hayden	979	6	6	0
Holbrook	5,098	13	11	2
Huachuca City	1,723	7	5	2
Jerome	459	5	5	0
Kearny	2,170	10	5	5
Kingman	30,600	60	45	15
Lake Havasu City	55,413	109	70	39
Mammoth	1,669	4	3	1
Marana	48,816	125	94	31
Maricopa	50,881	91	67	24
Mesa	518,160	1,202	797	405
Miami	1,768	15	8	7
Nogales	20,112	63	46	17
Oro Valley	45,970	126	98	28
Page	7,588	29	19	10
Paradise Valley	14,733	50	34	16
Parker	3,219	14	11	3
Patagonia	877	4	4	0
Payson	15,760	42	25	17
Peoria	174,571	286	201	85
Phoenix	1,688,722	3,919	2,928	991
Pima	2,530	6	6	0
Pinetop-Lakeside	4,452	17	14	3
Prescott	43,781	91	74	17
Prescott Valley	46,700	92	68	24
Quartzsite	3,776	11	8	3
Safford	9,916	25	22	3
Sahuarita	30,928	55	42	13
San Luis	34,192	59	39	20
Scottsdale	260,464	616	385	231
Sedona	10,373	39	24	15
Show Low	11,401	49	31	18
Sierra Vista	44,310	76	59	17
Snowflake-Taylor	10,173	18	12	6
Somerton	16,771	20	13	7
South Tucson	5,704	17	15	2
Springerville	1,984	8	6	2
St. Johns	3,520	9	6	3
Superior	3,175	15	14	1
Surprise	140,962	198	143	55
Tempe	196,499	480	338	142
Thatcher	5,177	12	11	1
Tolleson	7,399	49	31	18
Tombstone	1,289	9	7	2
Tucson	548,374	1,129	901	228

Table 78. Full-Time Law Enforcement Employees, by Selected State and City, 2019—Continued

(Number.)

State/city	Population	Total law enforcement employees	Total officers	Total civilians
Wellton	3,048	7	6	1
Wickenburg	7,054	27	21	6
Willcox	3,507	19	11	8
Williams	3,251	23	13	10
Winslow	9,393	34	24	10
Yuma	98,769	256	153	103
ARKANSAS				
Alexander	3,315	8	8	0
Alma	5,888	21	14	7
Altus	729	2	2	0
Amity	675	1	1	0
Arkadelphia	10,451	29	23	6
Ashdown	4,370	14	12	2
Ash Flat	1,095	4	4	0
Atkins	3,037	9	8	1
Augusta	1,939	7	6	1
Austin	3,973	4	4	0
Bald Knob	2,872	13	8	5
Barling	5,010	11	11	0
Batesville	10,889	25	24	1
Bay	1,805	4	4	0
Bearden	859	1	1	0
Beebe	8,242	21	15	6
Bella Vista	28,931	49	34	15
Benton	37,161	90	68	22
Bentonville	53,434	115	81	34
Berryville	5,547	16	14	2
Bethel Heights	2,810	7	6	1
Black Rock	605	1	1	0
Blytheville	13,468	50	34	16
Bono	2,444	4	4	0
Booneville	3,829	12	8	4
Bradford	732	3	3	0
Brinkley	2,623	18	11	7
Brookland	3,759	6	6	0
Bryant	21,214	54	43	11
Bull Shoals	1,971	4	4	0
Cabot	26,875	54	44	10
Caddo Valley	588	7	4	3
Camden	10,742	40	22	18
Cammack Village	720	4	3	1
Caraway	1,266	3	3	0
Carlisle	2,184	9	5	4
Cave Springs	5,580	7	7	0
Cedarville	1,413	2	2	0
Centerton	16,542	24	22	2
Charleston	2,454	5	5	0
Cherokee Village	4,634	9	8	1
Cherry Valley	583	1	1	0
Clarendon	1,373	4	4	0
Clarksville	9,813	23	19	4
Clinton	2,489	8	7	1
Concord	233	1	1	0
Conway	67,336	172	127	45
Corning	3,093	12	8	4
Cotter	940	2	2	0
Crossett	4,846	27	17	10
Damascus	377	1	1	0
Danville	2,414	7	6	1
Dardanelle	4,555	17	11	6
Decatur	1,813	6	6	0
De Queen	6,593	16	14	2
Dermott	2,517	10	6	4
Des Arc	1,580	6	6	0
DeWitt	3,019	11	7	4
Diamond City	798	1	1	0
Diaz	1,197	3	3	0
Dierks	1,089	4	4	0
Dover	1,434	5	5	0
Dumas	4,084	24	12	12
Dyer	897	2	2	0
Earle	2,201	6	5	1
El Dorado	17,820	67	51	16
Elkins	3,246	8	8	0
England	2,723	11	7	4
Etowah	317	1	1	0
Eudora	1,930	7	5	2
Eureka Springs	2,092	17	12	5
Fairfield Bay	2,202	16	7	9
Farmington	7,387	17	17	0
Fayetteville	88,500	174	126	48
Flippin	1,340	7	7	0
Fordyce	3,745	14	9	5
Forrest City	13,887	40	28	12

Table 78. Full-Time Law Enforcement Employees, by Selected State and City, 2019—Continued

(Number.)

State/city	Population	Total law enforcement employees	Total officers	Total civilians
Fort Smith	88,041	192	151	41
Gassville	2,156	4	4	0
Gentry	3,924	11	9	2
Glenwood	2,095	2	2	0
Gosnell	3,148	7	7	0
Gravette	3,443	12	11	1
Greenbrier	5,660	15	10	5
Green Forest	2,763	13	12	1
Greenland	1,450	4	4	0
Greenwood	9,436	23	21	2
Greers Ferry	851	5	4	1
Gurdon	2,069	5	4	1
Guy	782	2	2	0
Hamburg	2,636	7	6	1
Hampton	1,281	3	3	0
Hardy	761	4	4	0
Harrisburg	2,368	7	5	2
Harrison	13,107	43	32	11
Haskell	4,715	8	8	0
Hazen	1,336	7	6	1
Heber Springs	6,912	26	16	10
Helena-West Helena	10,187	24	13	11
Higginson	684	1	1	0
Highfill	656	3	3	0
Highland	1,100	3	3	0
Hope	9,666	36	25	11
Hot Springs	37,263	137	102	35
Hoxie	2,588	4	4	0
Huntington	616	1	1	0
Jacksonville	28,273	62	52	10
Johnson	3,781	8	8	0
Jonesboro	78,261	174	158	16
Judsonia	1,981	4	3	1
Kensett	1,618	3	3	0
Lake City	2,598	4	4	0
Lakeview	715	2	2	0
Lake Village	2,241	16	10	6
Lamar	1,740	3	3	0
Lavaca	2,440	3	3	0
Leachville	1,714	5	4	1
Lepanto	1,803	7	3	4
Lewisville	1,105	2	2	0
Lincoln	2,500	6	6	0
Little Flock	2,791	7	7	0
Little Rock	198,382	713	581	132
Lonoke	4,261	16	12	4
Lowell	9,723	24	19	5
Luxora	1,016	1	1	0
Madison	685	6	3	3
Magnolia	11,440	25	23	2
Malvern	10,946	23	21	2
Mammoth Spring	942	2	2	0
Mansfield	1,101	4	4	0
Marianna	3,398	20	13	7
Marion	12,344	35	31	4
Marked Tree	2,462	12	8	4
Marmaduke	1,264	4	4	0
Marvell	920	7	4	3
Maumelle	18,223	50	38	12
Mayflower	2,489	9	9	0
McCrory	1,513	6	5	1
McGehee	3,681	27	10	17
McRae	661	1	1	0
Mena	5,508	13	12	1
Mineral Springs	1,148	3	2	1
Monette	1,603	4	4	0
Monticello	9,438	29	21	8
Morrilton	6,631	27	24	3
Mountainburg	608	3	3	0
Mountain Home	12,458	37	29	8
Mountain View	2,850	11	10	1
Mulberry	1,644	4	4	0
Murfreesboro	1,533	3	3	0
Nashville	4,403	17	16	1
Newport	7,485	25	18	7
North Little Rock	66,604	207	175	32
Ola	1,217	4	3	1
Osceola	6,653	35	25	10
Ozark	3,573	13	11	2
Pangburn	580	2	2	0
Paragould	29,245	75	54	21
Paris	3,392	14	9	5
Parkin	991	2	2	0
Pea Ridge	6,230	16	15	1
Perryville	1,454	6	6	0

Table 78. Full-Time Law Enforcement Employees, by Selected State and City, 2019—Continued

(Number.)

State/city	Population	Total law enforcement employees	Total officers	Total civilians
Piggott	3,569	7	7	0
Pine Bluff	41,505	140	118	22
Plainview	581	1	1	0
Plumerville	773	4	3	1
Pocahontas	6,647	16	15	1
Pottsville	3,332	9	7	2
Prairie Grove	6,595	14	14	0
Prescott	2,985	10	9	1
Quitman	711	4	4	0
Ravenden	443	1	1	0
Redfield	1,564	6	5	1
Rogers	69,168	155	111	44
Rose Bud	483	4	3	1
Russellville	29,446	59	53	6
Salem	1,637	4	4	0
Searcy	23,873	70	51	19
Shannon Hills	4,017	6	6	0
Sheridan	4,954	30	15	15
Sherwood	31,435	97	74	23
Siloam Springs	17,235	53	38	15
Springdale	82,358	204	145	59
Stamps	1,444	4	3	1
Star City	2,058	6	5	1
St. Charles	208	1	1	0
Stuttgart	8,589	33	24	9
Sulphur Springs	534	3	3	0
Swifton	727	2	2	0
Texarkana	29,971	90	79	11
Trumann	7,043	22	16	6
Tuckerman	1,671	4	4	0
Tyronza	734	3	2	1
Van Buren	23,800	64	53	11
Vilonia	4,762	9	9	0
Waldron	3,332	10	9	1
Walnut Ridge	5,019	8	8	0
Ward	5,454	12	10	2
Warren	5,634	19	11	8
Weiner	679	1	1	0
West Fork	2,672	7	6	1
West Memphis	24,442	111	89	22
White Hall	5,014	17	15	2
Wilson	819	1	1	0
Wynne	7,812	21	19	2
CALIFORNIA				
Alameda	78,907	108	74	34
Albany	20,083	31	22	9
Alhambra	84,837	118	76	42
Alturas	2,471	8	7	1
Anaheim	353,915	592	418	174
Anderson	10,545	28	20	8
Angels Camp	3,909	8	7	1
Antioch	112,641	149	106	43
Arcadia	58,899	92	66	26
Arcata	18,332	43	29	14
Arroyo Grande	18,188	30	26	4
Arvin	21,811	26	18	8
Atascadero	30,579	39	28	11
Atherton	7,222	26	17	9
Atwater	29,632	34	25	9
Auburn	14,201	28	20	8
Avenal	12,991	18	17	1
Azusa	50,405	89	56	33
Bakersfield	388,080	559	380	179
Baldwin Park	75,862	93	70	23
Banning	31,450	44	26	18
Barstow	24,121	57	39	18
Bear Valley	5,507	6	5	1
Beaumont	50,990	59	43	16
Bell	35,759	40	29	11
Bell Gardens	42,366	69	46	23
Belmont	27,272	42	30	12
Belvedere	2,114	7	7	0
Benicia	28,471	47	28	19
Berkeley	122,788	253	159	94
Beverly Hills	34,211	217	131	86
Bishop	3,731	19	12	7
Blythe	19,889	28	18	10
Brawley	26,379	39	26	13
Brea	44,155	86	56	30
Brentwood	65,483	90	60	30
Brisbane	4,746	17	13	4
Broadmoor	4,446	11	10	1
Buena Park	82,627	131	89	42
Burbank	103,738	215	139	76

Table 78. Full-Time Law Enforcement Employees, by Selected State and City, 2019—Continued

(Number.)

State/city	Population	Total law enforcement employees	Total officers	Total civilians
Burlingame	30,677	57	38	19
Calexico	40,327	.34	20	14
California City	14,319	23	14	9
Calipatria	7,387	5	5	0
Calistoga	5,341	13	8	5
Campbell	42,697	70	44	26
Capitola	10,101	27	20	7
Carlsbad	117,220	182	126	56
Carmel	3,877	22	14	8
Cathedral City	55,346	72	50	22
Central Marin	34,793	46	42	4
Ceres	49,134	68	49	19
Chico	95,826	146	95	51
Chino	93,348	160	109	51
Chowchilla	18,792	27	18	9
Chula Vista	275,230	315	232	83
Citrus Heights	88,496	134	84	50
Claremont	36,681	63	39	24
Clayton	12,356	12	10	2
Clearlake	15,400	37	23	14
Cloverdale	8,910	21	13	8
Clovis	114,170	160	100	60
Coalinga	16,356	22	14	8
Colma	1,512	25	19	6
Colton	55,059	80	52	28
Colusa	5,903	7	6	1
Concord	130,615	200	146	54
Corcoran	21,353	32	19	13
Corning	7,537	21	13	8
Corona	170,875	209	143	66
Coronado	21,115	67	47	20
Costa Mesa	114,047	192	127	65
Cotati	7,641	18	12	6
Covina	47,985	78	52	26
Crescent City	6,716	12	11	1
Culver City	39,252	155	111	44
Cypress	49,085	65	51	14
Daly City	107,748	127	101	26
Davis	69,767	92	57	35
Delano	53,002	72	51	21
Del Rey Oaks	1,674	10	10	0
Desert Hot Springs	29,107	32	23	9
Dinuba	24,685	44	34	10
Dixon	20,775	30	25	5
Dos Palos	5,594	13	9	4
Downey	112,330	161	117	44
East Palo Alto	29,686	42	34	8
El Cajon	103,686	183	120	63
El Centro	44,303	68	44	24
El Cerrito	25,857	45	37	8
Elk Grove	175,492	238	140	98
El Monte	115,830	160	118	42
El Segundo	16,727	79	61	18
Emeryville	12,380	53	39	14
Escalon	7,644	12	11	1
Escondido	153,215	211	154	57
Etna	716	3	3	0
Eureka	26,973	70	47	23
Exeter	10,557	19	17	2
Fairfax	7,569	16	11	5
Fairfield	118,383	183	116	67
Farmersville	10,781	15	14	1
Ferndale	1,363	5	5	0
Firebaugh	8,433	16	11	5
Folsom	79,927	102	74	28
Fontana	215,883	285	188	97
Fort Bragg	7,366	22	15	7
Fortuna	12,317	24	16	8
Foster City	34,624	50	35	15
Fountain Valley	55,858	79	59	20
Fowler	6,904	12	12	0
Fremont	240,887	281	181	100
Fresno	534,285	1,077	806	271
Fullerton	140,194	193	134	59
Galt	26,796	48	33	15
Gardena	59,833	116	89	27
Garden Grove	172,832	239	163	76
Gilroy	60,106	97	64	33
Glendale	202,601	335	231	104
Glendora	52,211	79	50	29
Gonzales	8,408	15	12	3
Grass Valley	12,919	36	29	7
Greenfield	17,809	28	22	6
Gridley	6,618	18	12	6
Grover Beach	13,574	25	17	8

Table 78. Full-Time Law Enforcement Employees, by Selected State and City, 2019—Continued

(Number.)

State/city	Population	Total law enforcement employees	Total officers	Total civilians
Guadalupe	7,696	13	11	2
Gustine	5,896	7	6	1
Hanford	57,232	87	58	29
Hawthorne	87,305	133	88	45
Hayward	161,588	294	180	114
Healdsburg	12,208	25	17	8
Hemet	86,082	128	90	38
Hercules	25,789	27	24	3
Hermosa Beach	19,460	62	32	30
Hillsborough	11,521	34	24	10
Hollister	40,399	40	33	7
Huntington Beach	201,843	303	196	107
Huntington Park	58,181	85	56	29
Huron	7,359	17	13	4
Imperial	18,090	23	19	4
Indio	92,803	108	68	40
Inglewood	109,386	247	192	55
Ione	8,454	9	9	0
Irvine	292,673	325	224	101
Irwindale	1,469	33	27	6
Jackson	4,797	10	9	1
Kensington	5,407	7	7	0
Kerman	15,223	20	17	3
King City	14,170	22	17	5
Kingsburg	12,123	20	17	3
Laguna Beach	23,020	98	54	44
La Habra	62,416	101	69	32
Lakeport	4,959	12	11	1
Lake Shastina	2,566	2	2	0
La Mesa	59,865	92	62	30
La Palma	15,571	27	20	7
La Verne	32,344	55	37	18
Lemoore	26,728	41	33	8
Lincoln	48,625	29	21	8
Lindsay	13,708	18	15	3
Livermore	91,418	144	95	49
Livingston	14,607	30	20	10
Lodi	67,612	105	74	31
Lompoc	42,818	56	37	19
Long Beach	467,974	1,203	817	386
Los Alamitos	11,541	21	17	4
Los Altos	30,716	43	30	13
Los Angeles	4,015,546	12,954	10,002	2,952
Los Banos	40,607	62	36	26
Los Gatos	30,793	60	37	23
Madera	66,250	92	66	26
Mammoth Lakes	8,114	15	12	3
Manhattan Beach	35,583	100	62	38
Manteca	83,523	106	74	32
Marina	22,911	34	27	7
Martinez	38,692	43	32	11
Marysville	12,572	26	18	8
McFarland	15,529	14	8	6
Mendota	11,433	16	14	2
Menlo Park	34,871	71	48	23
Merced	83,854	133	93	40
Mill Valley	14,343	27	21	6
Milpitas	82,344	114	88	26
Modesto	216,542	309	205	104
Monrovia	36,730	74	46	28
Montclair	39,787	64	44	20
Montebello	62,650	97	72	25
Monterey	28,337	65	49	16
Monterey Park	60,424	99	69	30
Moraga	17,908	13	11	2
Morgan Hill	46,118	61	41	20
Morro Bay	10,624	17	15	2
Mountain View	84,599	135	96	39
Mount Shasta	3,274	12	8	4
Murrieta	116,413	138	99	39
Napa	79,526	120	72	48
National City	61,791	124	84	40
Nevada City	3,150	12	10	2
Newark	48,945	75	53	22
Newman	11,844	16	13	3
Newport Beach	85,325	225	142	83
Novato	56,134	77	58	19
Oakdale	23,808	32	22	10
Oakland	434,036	1,023	740	283
Oceanside	177,129	288	203	85
Ontario	183,322	388	283	105
Orange	139,830	216	143	73
Orange Cove	9,635	12	11	1
Orland	7,679	13	11	2
Oroville	19,268	39	21	18

Table 78. Full-Time Law Enforcement Employees, by Selected State and City, 2019—Continued

(Number.)

State/city	Population	Total law enforcement employees	Total officers	Total civilians
Oxnard	211,349	324	230	94
Pacifica	38,938	35	32	3
Pacific Grove	15,605	30	21	9
Palm Springs	48,846	149	101	48
Palo Alto	66,938	137	77	60
Palos Verdes Estates	13,400	32	20	12
Paradise	26,879	19	11	8
Parlier	15,384	22	17	5
Pasadena	141,913	343	222	121
Paso Robles	32,528	50	36	14
Petaluma	62,425	94	63	31
Piedmont	11,307	27	17	10
Pinole	19,439	42	26	16
Pismo Beach	8,285	33	21	12
Pittsburg	73,637	105	82	23
Placentia	51,756	67	43	24
Placerville	11,123	25	18	7
Pleasant Hill	35,125	56	44	12
Pleasanton	84,017	110	77	33
Pomona	152,776	252	147	105
Porterville	60,209	102	65	37
Port Hueneme	22,232	27	19	8
Red Bluff	14,308	40	25	15
Redding	92,009	140	101	39
Redlands	71,941	124	85	39
Redondo Beach	67,473	142	91	51
Redwood City	87,427	111	84	27
Reedley	25,740	43	28	15
Rialto	103,965	134	102	32
Richmond	110,988	227	163	64
Ridgecrest	29,101	49	31	18
Rio Dell	3,392	6	6	0
Rio Vista	9,502	12	10	2
Ripon	16,103	30	21	9
Riverside	333,260	512	366	146
Rocklin	68,554	84	58	26
Rohnert Park	44,131	101	75	26
Roseville	141,744	191	130	61
Ross	2,470	8	8	0
Sacramento	513,934	993	678	315
Salinas	156,943	192	146	46
San Bernardino	216,715	368	244	124
San Bruno	43,297	61	45	16
Sand City	407	11	10	1
San Diego	1,441,737	2,387	1,764	623
San Fernando	24,621	44	31	13
San Francisco	886,007	2,907	2,279	628
San Gabriel	40,422	66	51	15
Sanger	25,443	43	39	4
San Jose	1,040,008	1,607	1,150	457
San Leandro	90,297	129	87	42
San Luis Obispo	47,735	89	61	28
San Marino	13,196	34	26	8
San Mateo	106,020	142	103	39
San Pablo	31,336	82	57	25
San Rafael	58,819	82	60	22
San Ramon	76,387	85	66	19
Santa Ana	333,664	558	340	218
Santa Barbara	91,717	206	132	74
Santa Clara	131,173	222	150	72
Santa Cruz	65,263	122	81	41
Santa Maria	108,414	184	135	49
Santa Monica	91,621	394	219	175
Santa Paula	30,098	45	32	13
Santa Rosa	177,884	243	166	77
Sausalito	7,118	23	17	6
Scotts Valley	11,875	24	17	7
Seal Beach	24,120	53	38	15
Seaside	34,036	45	33	12
Sebastopol	7,815	21	14	7
Selma	24,983	48	36	12
Shafter	20,456	35	26	9
Sierra Madre	10,917	18	15	3
Signal Hill	11,624	44	32	12
Simi Valley	126,025	165	119	46
Soledad	26,015	21	16	5
Sonora	4,867	17	10	7
South Gate	94,445	114	72	42
South Lake Tahoe	22,116	59	38	21
South Pasadena	25,612	51	33	18
South San Francisco	68,251	111	80	31
Stallion Springs	2,648	2	2	0
St. Helena	6,195	16	11	5
Stockton	313,604	664	459	205
Suisun City	29,922	32	20	12

Table 78. Full-Time Law Enforcement Employees, by Selected State and City, 2019—Continued

(Number.)

State/city	Population	Total law enforcement employees	Total officers	Total civilians
Sunnyvale	154,859	292	217	75
Susanville	14,878	19	16	3
Sutter Creek	2,624	4	4	0
Taft	9,413	24	14	10
Tehachapi	12,211	26	17	9
Tiburon	9,135	17	13	4
Torrance	145,183	311	206	105
Tracy	92,895	135	86	49
Truckee	16,611	38	24	14
Tulare	65,134	105	67	38
Tulelake	985	3	3	0
Turlock	74,120	111	75	36
Tustin	80,356	141	90	51
Ukiah	16,197	45	26	19
Union City	75,202	88	71	17
Upland	77,398	106	71	35
Vacaville	101,147	167	110	57
Vallejo	122,657	148	101	47
Ventura	111,596	183	135	48
Vernon	112	55	41	14
Visalia	134,961	219	147	72
Walnut Creek	70,546	121	82	39
Watsonville	54,261	94	75	19
Weed	2,673	14	9	5
West Covina	106,335	141	88	53
Westminster	91,086	120	81	39
Westmorland	2,275	5	5	0
West Sacramento	54,372	96	69	27
Wheatland	3,940	9	8	1
Whittier	86,158	167	118	49
Williams	5,348	13	11	2
Willits	4,937	13	8	5
Winters	7,374	13	11	2
Woodlake	7,682	12	11	1
Woodland	61,176	80	65	15
Yreka	7,527	22	14	8
Yuba City	67,164	88	59	29
COLORADO				
Alamosa	10,086	28	24	4
Arvada	122,312	200	157	43
Aspen	7,461	37	27	10
Ault	1,885	6	5	1
Aurora	380,600	911	688	223
Avon	6,496	19	17	2
Basalt	4,209	10	9	1
Bayfield	2,754	9	8	1
Black Hawk	128	33	21	12
Blue River	937	2	2	0
Boulder	108,519	271	177	94
Breckenridge	5,079	24	20	4
Brighton	42,267	101	75	26
Broomfield	70,798	223	117	106
Brush	5,372	15	12	3
Buena Vista	2,857	9	8	1
Burlington	3,072	8	5	3
Calhan	840	4	4	0
Canon City	16,793	44	34	10
Carbondale	6,941	14	11	3
Castle Rock	67,208	99	71	28
Cedaredge	2,269	7	6	1
Centennial	112,129	179	133	46
Center	2,312	20	5	15
Cherry Hills Village	6,734	29	25	4
Collbran	699	2	2	0
Colorado Springs	479,648	1,028	725	303
Columbine Valley	1,519	5	5	0
Commerce City	60,198	136	110	26
Cortez	8,748	48	29	19
Craig	8,886	26	21	5
Crested Butte	1,708	9	8	1
Cripple Creek	1,271	19	12	7
Dacono	6,074	16	13	3
De Beque	504	4	4	0
Del Norte	1,548	3	2	1
Delta	8,929	22	18	4
Denver	728,941	1,859	1,551	308
Dillon	981	11	10	1
Dinosaur	328	2	2	0
Durango	19,271	63	51	12
Eagle	7,021	10	9	1
Eaton	5,690	12	10	2
Edgewater	5,363	15	15	0
Elizabeth	1,424	10	8	2
Empire	306	1	1	0

Table 78. Full-Time Law Enforcement Employees, by Selected State and City, 2019—Continued

(Number.)

State/city	Population	Total law enforcement employees	Total officers	Total civilians
Englewood	35,273	107	76	31
Erie	26,523	40	34	6
Estes Park	6,406	33	19	14
Evans	21,585	37	33	4
Fairplay	773	4	4	0
Federal Heights	13,021	38	25	13
Firestone	15,558	34	27	7
Florence	3,965	14	13	1
Fort Collins	170,889	317	214	103
Fort Lupton	8,388	22	19	3
Fort Morgan	11,355	29	22	7
Fountain	31,041	59	52	7
Fowler	1,139	3	3	0
Fraser/Winter Park	2,371	11	9	2
Frederick	14,238	25	21	4
Frisco	3,220	13	10	3
Fruita	13,504	18	15	3
Garden City	267	4	4	0
Georgetown	1,095	3	3	0
Glendale	5,289	40	29	11
Glenwood Springs	10,027	31	24	7
Golden	21,522	67	50	17
Granby	2,133	10	8	2
Grand Junction	63,949	193	110	83
Greeley	109,255	209	152	57
Green Mountain Falls	714	1	1	0
Greenwood Village	16,046	78	59	19
Gunnison	6,689	31	16	15
Gypsum	7,467	4	4	0
Haxtun	902	3	3	0
Hayden	1,992	8	6	2
Holyoke	2,204	4	4	0
Hotchkiss	932	4	4	0
Hudson	1,806	5	4	1
Idaho Springs	1,803	12	9	3
Ignacio	892	7	7	0
Johnstown	15,547	24	21	3
Keenesburg	1,242	11	10	1
Kersey	1,679	5	4	1
Kremmling	1,511	5	4	1
Lafayette	29,522	50	41	9
La Junta	6,983	18	12	6
Lakeside	8	5	4	1
Lakewood	158,645	437	311	126
Lamar	7,619	31	16	15
La Salle	2,400	8	8	0
La Veta	812	2	2	0
Leadville	2,785	9	7	2
Limon	1,929	7	6	1
Littleton	48,831	102	78	24
Lochbuie	7,265	12	10	2
Log Lane Village	874	2	2	0
Lone Tree	15,129	63	55	8
Longmont	97,928	227	150	77
Louisville	21,532	36	31	5
Loveland	78,856	161	113	48
Mancos	1,429	4	4	0
Manitou Springs	5,388	15	13	2
Manzanola	417	2	2	0
Mead	4,924	10	8	2
Meeker	2,238	4	4	0
Milliken	7,978	14	11	3
Monte Vista	4,084	16	13	3
Montrose	19,564	56	37	19
Monument	8,298	22	18	4
Morrison	425	10	9	1
Mountain View	541	10	9	1
Mountain Village	1,450	10	7	3
Mount Crested Butte	859	9	8	1
Nederland	1,560	5	4	1
New Castle	5,095	10	9	1
Northglenn	39,420	77	58	19
Oak Creek	975	3	3	0
Olathe	1,824	4	4	0
Ouray	1,011	5	5	0
Pagosa Springs	2,044	8	7	1
Palisade	2,723	11	10	1
Palmer Lake	2,819	2	2	0
Paonia	1,463	4	4	0
Parachute	1,125	6	5	1
Parker	57,050	113	74	39
Platteville	3,922	10	9	1
Pueblo	112,381	269	218	51
Rangely	2,278	9	4	5
Ridgway	1,032	3	3	0

Table 78. Full-Time Law Enforcement Employees, by Selected State and City, 2019—Continued

(Number.)

State/city	Population	Total law enforcement employees	Total officers	Total civilians
Rifle	9,782	25	20	5
Rocky Ford	3,811	13	8	5
Salida	6,061	20	18	2
Sanford	880	1	1	0
Severance	5,362	9	7	2
Sheridan	6,233	35	34	1
Silt	3,215	7	6	1
Silverthorne	4,948	20	16	4
Simla	642	3	3	0
Snowmass Village	2,767	12	9	3
South Fork	348	3	3	0
Springfield	1,369	2	2	0
Steamboat Springs	13,365	38	27	11
Sterling	13,573	29	23	6
Telluride	2,518	13	8	5
Thornton	142,168	319	242	77
Timnath	5,027	9	8	1
Trinidad	8,116	35	21	14
Walsh	513	1	1	0
Westminster	114,392	271	195	76
Wheat Ridge	31,553	101	83	18
Wiggins	1,010	2	2	0
Windsor	30,587	48	41	7
Woodland Park	7,863	26	18	8
Wray	2,331	6	5	1
Yuma	3,452	8	6	2
CONNECTICUT				
Ansonia	18,656	50	43	7
Avon	18,320	41	32	9
Berlin	20,500	54	41	13
Bethel	19,855	51	38	13
Bloomfield	21,406	61	48	13
Branford	28,002	66	53	13
Bridgeport	144,908	411	365	46
Bristol	59,977	142	117	25
Brookfield	17,071	44	34	10
Canton	10,267	21	16	5
Cheshire	29,167	62	48	14
Clinton	12,914	35	27	8
Coventry	12,411	21	16	5
Cromwell	13,894	35	26	9
Danbury	85,167	153	148	5
Darien	21,880	64	51	13
Derby	12,468	36	34	2
East Hampton	12,842	18	16	2
East Hartford	49,842	145	111	34
East Haven	28,635	54	50	4
East Lyme	18,588	32	24	8
Easton	7,519	20	15	5
East Windsor	11,399	34	25	9
Enfield	44,443	115	93	22
Fairfield	62,239	127	106	21
Farmington	25,525	61	46	15
Glastonbury	34,497	74	56	18
Granby	11,386	21	16	5
Greenwich	62,905	182	155	27
Groton	8,967	34	27	7
Groton Long Point	509	5	5	0
Groton Town	29,046	83	65	18
Guilford	22,194	44	37	7
Hamden	60,855	129	102	27
Hartford	122,245	483	447	36
Ledyard	14,698	32	23	9
Madison	18,087	42	30	12
Manchester	57,630	152	112	40
Meriden	59,378	131	120	11
Middlebury	7,750	12	10	2
Middletown	45,963	125	112	13
Milford	54,898	136	112	24
Monroe	19,466	56	43	13
Naugatuck	31,214	67	56	11
New Britain	72,354	166	158	8
New Canaan	20,268	52	46	6
Newington	30,060	65	52	13
New London	26,856	85	69	16
New Milford	26,835	57	45	12
Newtown	27,795	48	45	3
North Branford	14,127	28	23	5
North Haven	23,642	59	50	9
Norwalk	89,440	214	176	38
Norwich	38,964	101	85	16
Old Saybrook	10,069	32	24	8
Orange	13,948	56	45	11
Plainfield	15,145	21	16	5

Table 78. Full-Time Law Enforcement Employees, by Selected State and City, 2019—Continued

(Number.)

State/city	Population	Total law enforcement employees	Total officers	Total civilians
Plainville	17,610	46	38	8
Plymouth	11,573	26	21	5
Portland	9,281	13	12	1
Putnam	9,374	23	15	8
Redding	9,120	22	16	6
Ridgefield	25,050	46	41	5
Rocky Hill	20,199	48	37	11
Seymour	16,505	43	41	2
Shelton	41,287	58	50	8
Simsbury	25,169	49	38	11
Southington	43,886	87	68	19
South Windsor	26,097	55	41	14
Stamford	130,678	285	266	19
Stonington	18,439	51	39	12
Stratford	52,034	108	103	5
Suffield	15,740	26	19	7
Thomaston	7,521	16	13	3
Torrington	33,972	86	76	10
Trumbull	35,772	86	76	10
Vernon	29,318	61	47	14
Wallingford	44,457	98	72	26
Waterbury	107,812	335	293	42
Waterford	18,812	55	49	6
Watertown	21,534	49	40	9
West Hartford	62,875	141	122	19
Weston	10,254	18	17	1
Westport	28,332	70	64	6
Wethersfield	26,009	63	48	15
Willimantic	17,660	49	44	5
Wilton	18,439	42	39	3
Winchester	10,585	27	22	5
Windsor	28,717	64	51	13
Windsor Locks	12,924	36	28	8
Wolcott	16,642	37	26	11
Woodbridge	8,782	31	24	7
DELAWARE				
Bethany Beach	1,244	11	10	1
Blades	1,469	3	3	0
Bridgeville	2,407	7	7	0
Camden	3,507	9	9	0
Cheswold	1,639	5	5	0
Dagsboro	916	4	4	0
Delaware City	1,830	5	4	1
Delmar	1,822	14	13	1
Dewey Beach	394	10	8	2
Dover	38,361	130	99	31
Ellendale	444	1	1	0
Elsmere	5,963	13	12	1
Felton	1,420	4	4	0
Fenwick Island	445	8	7	1
Georgetown	7,558	23	19	4
Greenwood	1,138	4	3	1
Harrington	3,652	14	13	1
Laurel	4,469	20	19	1
Lewes	3,286	14	13	1
Middletown	23,079	42	34	8
Milford	11,592	48	36	12
Millsboro	4,524	18	16	2
Milton	3,017	8	7	1
Newark	33,957	89	71	18
New Castle	5,558	16	15	1
Newport	1,026	7	7	0
Ocean View	2,180	12	11	1
Rehoboth Beach	1,546	29	17	12
Seaford	7,987	33	26	7
Selbyville	2,540	10	9	1
Smyrna	11,768	32	25	7
South Bethany	528	5	5	0
Wilmington	70,624	360	306	54
Wyoming	1,565	3	3	0
DISTRICT OF COLUMBIA				
Washington	705,749	4,524	3,809	715
FLORIDA				
Altamonte Springs	44,582	115	95	20
Apopka	55,072	139	100	39
Arcadia	8,274	23	19	4
Astatula	2,091	7	7	0
Atlantic Beach	13,983	41	28	13
Atlantis	2,126	16	11	5
Auburndale	16,679	43	35	8
Aventura	38,259	126	89	37
Bal Harbour Village	3,086	37	24	13

Table 78. Full-Time Law Enforcement Employees, by Selected State and City, 2019—Continued

(Number.)

State/city	Population	Total law enforcement employees	Total officers	Total civilians
Bartow	20,296	55	37	18
Bay Harbor Islands	6,018	27	21	6
Belleair	4,253	14	12	2
Belle Isle	7,326	21	19	2
Belleview	5,086	17	15	2
Blountstown	2,473	18	12	6
Boca Raton	101,163	304	209	95
Bonifay	2,683	6	6	0
Bowling Green	2,899	7	7	0
Boynton Beach	79,360	184	139	45
Bradenton	58,782	148	116	32
Bradenton Beach	1,292	10	10	0
Bunnell	2,865	14	12	2
Carrabelle	2,488	4	4	0
Casselberry	29,244	60	50	10
Cedar Key	685	4	4	0
Center Hill	1,472	2	2	0
Chattahoochee	3,004	10	10	0
Clearwater	117,458	330	245	85
Clermont	37,818	82	75	7
Clewiston	8,098	22	16	6
Cocoa	18,807	92	64	28
Cocoa Beach	11,806	57	37	20
Coconut Creek	62,471	144	106	38
Cooper City	36,890	70	53	17
Coral Gables	51,530	240	169	71
Coral Springs	134,967	308	218	90
Cottondale	902	3	3	0
Crescent City	1,540	7	6	1
Crestview	25,152	55	38	17
Cross City	1,710	5	5	0
Dade City	7,337	30	23	7
Dania Beach	32,593	81	74	7
Davenport	5,814	15	14	1
Daytona Beach	69,834	293	244	49
Daytona Beach Shores	4,579	41	31	10
Deerfield Beach	81,602	128	120	8
DeFuniak Springs	6,940	25	19	6
DeLand	34,468	79	61	18
Delray Beach	70,509	228	162	66
Doral	64,168	180	136	44
Dunnellon	1,830	8	7	1
Eatonville	2,317	14	12	2
Edgewater	22,926	34	29	5
Edgewood	3,044	16	13	3
El Portal	2,479	9	9	0
Eustis	21,432	53	40	13
Fellsmere	5,830	10	9	1
Fernandina Beach	12,710	41	36	5
Fort Lauderdale	184,765	690	525	165
Fort Myers	85,127	314	225	89
Fort Pierce	46,597	138	113	25
Fort Walton Beach	22,645	61	44	17
Gainesville	135,085	343	253	90
Graceville	2,191	8	7	1
Green Cove Springs	8,505	27	21	6
Groveland	15,667	44	31	13
Gulfport	12,449	35	31	4
Gulf Stream	891	12	12	0
Haines City	25,746	65	52	13
Hallandale Beach	40,297	118	87	31
Havana	1,701	15	10	5
Hialeah	240,688	344	272	72
Hialeah Gardens	24,337	66	48	18
Hillsboro Beach	2,038	19	15	4
Holly Hill	12,403	29	25	4
Holmes Beach	4,355	26	17	9
Homestead	71,757	147	113	34
Howey-in-the-Hills	1,185	6	6	0
Indialantic	2,937	15	10	5
Indian Harbour Beach	8,616	29	21	8
Indian Shores	3,816	14	12	2
Interlachen	1,461	4	4	0
Jacksonville	909,142	3,050	1,731	1,319
Jacksonville Beach	23,974	81	62	19
Jasper	4,057	8	7	1
Jennings	862	3	3	0
Juno Beach	3,709	17	15	2
Jupiter	66,906	145	116	29
Jupiter Inlet Colony	459	4	4	0
Jupiter Island	934	23	18	5
Kenneth City	5,074	14	13	1
Kissimmee	75,544	218	141	77
Lake Alfred	6,123	17	12	5
Lake City	12,141	54	38	16

Table 78. Full-Time Law Enforcement Employees, by Selected State and City, 2019—Continued

(Number.)

State/city	Population	Total law enforcement employees	Total officers	Total civilians
Lake Clarke Shores	3,657	10	9	1
Lake Hamilton	1,472	7	6	1
Lake Helen	2,837	7	6	1
Lakeland	112,237	336	236	100
Lake Mary	17,778	54	45	9
Lake Placid	2,459	10	8	2
Lake Wales	16,901	48	43	5
Largo	85,740	179	139	40
Lauderdale-by-the-Sea	6,745	25	23	2
Lauderdale Lakes	36,784	42	40	2
Lawtey	722	3	3	0
Leesburg	23,527	88	67	21
Lighthouse Point	11,403	38	30	8
Live Oak	6,988	36	17	19
Longboat Key	7,379	22	19	3
Longwood	15,320	48	43	5
Madison	2,769	15	14	1
Maitland	18,222	61	53	8
Manalapan	474	16	14	2
Marco Island	18,124	34	31	3
Margate	59,371	149	114	35
Marianna	7,034	22	17	5
Mascotte	5,977	13	12	1
Medley	896	48	40	8
Melbourne	83,668	215	145	70
Melbourne Beach	3,313	11	10	1
Miami	480,505	1,760	1,298	462
Miami Beach	92,185	491	410	81
Miami Gardens	113,786	265	203	62
Miami Shores	10,572	47	40	7
Miami Springs	14,374	55	44	11
Milton	10,460	24	18	6
Miramar	143,334	300	219	81
Monticello	2,413	13	9	4
Mount Dora	14,491	59	40	19
Naples	22,369	103	71	32
Neptune Beach	7,332	29	20	9
New Port Richey	16,703	60	43	17
New Smyrna Beach	27,743	66	47	19
Niceville	15,947	36	25	11
North Bay Village	8,425	37	30	7
North Lauderdale	44,808	57	52	5
North Miami	63,547	145	111	34
North Miami Beach	46,307	133	98	35
North Palm Beach	13,273	35	30	5
North Port	70,181	148	113	35
Oakland	3,160	15	13	2
Oakland Park	45,857	92	81	11
Ocala	60,932	270	178	92
Ocean Ridge	1,978	22	17	5
Ocoee	49,451	99	85	14
Opa Locka	16,501	49	42	7
Orange City	11,920	29	25	4
Orange Park	8,852	34	26	8
Orlando	292,120	962	745	217
Ormond Beach	44,005	92	71	21
Oviedo	42,684	76	68	8
Palatka	10,450	39	32	7
Palm Bay	115,520	219	156	63
Palm Beach	8,884	92	62	30
Palm Beach Gardens	57,236	178	122	56
Palmetto	13,855	50	35	15
Palm Springs	25,303	59	39	20
Panama City	37,199	119	89	30
Panama City Beach	13,266	87	70	17
Parker	4,616	11	10	1
Parkland	35,244	46	41	5
Pembroke Pines	174,641	332	240	92
Pensacola	52,801	200	148	52
Perry	6,918	23	21	2
Pinellas Park	53,589	126	107	19
Plantation	95,474	262	165	97
Plant City	39,725	87	70	17
Pompano Beach	113,536	252	224	28
Ponce Inlet	3,315	13	11	2
Port Richey	2,894	21	15	6
Port St. Joe	3,579	9	9	0
Port St. Lucie	199,433	300	232	68
Punta Gorda	20,458	52	36	16
Quincy	7,143	34	26	8
Riviera Beach	35,130	161	117	44
Rockledge	28,078	66	50	16
Sanford	60,844	154	131	23
Sanibel	7,525	51	25	26
Sarasota	58,470	235	175	60

Table 78. Full-Time Law Enforcement Employees, by Selected State and City, 2019—Continued

(Number.)

State/city	Population	Total law enforcement employees	Total officers	Total civilians
Satellite Beach	11,219	36	25	11
Sea Ranch Lakes	626	11	7	4
Sebastian	26,232	60	41	19
Sebring	11,008	39	34	5
Sewall's Point	2,244	10	9	1
South Daytona	13,159	34	28	6
South Miami	12,284	56	47	9
Starke	5,402	18	16	2
St. Augustine	14,778	66	53	13
St. Petersburg	267,696	757	552	205
Stuart	16,424	61	43	18
Sunny Isles Beach	22,476	63	51	12
Sunrise	96,919	249	187	62
Surfside	5,829	42	31	11
Tallahassee	195,104	434	369	65
Tamarac	66,799	97	80	17
Tampa	400,501	1,215	936	279
Tavares	17,962	30	27	3
Temple Terrace	26,725	61	46	15
Tequesta	6,195	24	19	5
Titusville	46,866	124	79	45
Treasure Island	6,978	23	19	4
Trenton	2,141	3	2	1
Umatilla	3,852	11	10	1
Valparaiso	5,218	16	11	5
Venice	23,726	63	50	13
Vero Beach	17,503	73	52	21
Village of Pinecrest	19,760	70	43	27
Virginia Gardens	2,460	8	7	1
Wauchula	4,890	16	13	3
Welaka	712	1	1	0
West Melbourne	24,077	55	46	9
West Miami	8,362	23	19	4
Weston	71,946	105	87	18
West Palm Beach	112,798	377	285	92
West Park	15,246	43	39	4
White Springs	766	4	4	0
Wildwood	7,310	37	33	4
Wilton Manors	12,948	47	34	13
Winter Garden	46,750	106	79	27
Winter Haven	44,211	117	87	30
Winter Park	31,494	102	74	28
Winter Springs	37,854	54	41	13
Zephyrhills	15,836	48	33	15
GEORGIA				
Abbeville	2,784	6	5	1
Adairsville	4,953	18	16	2
Alamo	3,348	4	4	0
Alapaha	671	3	1	2
Albany	74,989	185	154	31
Alma	3,438	12	10	2
Alpharetta	67,411	152	108	44
Americus	15,110	44	34	10
Arcade	1,946	4	4	0
Athens-Clarke County	127,246	280	215	65
Atlanta	507,369	2,090	1,600	490
Auburn	7,687	22	17	5
Austell	7,287	29	22	7
Avondale Estates	3,179	13	13	0
Bainbridge	11,986	43	34	9
Ball Ground	2,225	4	4	0
Barnesville	6,714	21	19	2
Bartow	253	2	2	0
Baxley	4,697	10	9	1
Blairsville	621	8	7	1
Blakely	4,573	17	15	2
Bloomingdale	2,732	18	15	3
Blue Ridge	1,458	10	9	1
Blythe	697	3	3	0
Boston	1,314	4	4	0
Bowdon	2,110	10	8	2
Braselton	12,297	20	19	1
Braswell	382	3	1	2
Bremen	6,575	21	19	2
Brookhaven	54,734	83	71	12
Brooklet	1,751	6	5	1
Brunswick	16,493	56	52	4
Buchanan	1,167	12	10	2
Buena Vista	2,054	3	3	0
Byron	5,269	24	19	5
Cairo	9,381	29	26	3
Calhoun	17,069	56	48	8
Camilla	4,893	21	18	3
Canon	837	1	1	0

Table 78. Full-Time Law Enforcement Employees, by Selected State and City, 2019—Continued

(Number.)

State/city	Population	Total law enforcement employees	Total officers	Total civilians
Canton	30,109	55	48	7
Carrollton	26,724	84	70	14
Cartersville	21,322	69	60	9
Cecil	277	3	2	1
Cedartown	10,270	33	29	4
Centerville	7,854	24	19	5
Chatsworth	4,321	19	18	1
Chattahoochee Hills	3,285	11	11	0
Clarkston	12,840	19	16	3
Claxton	2,218	11	10	1
Cleveland	4,042	16	15	1
Cochran	4,851	14	11	3
College Park	15,278	128	89	39
Commerce	6,980	26	20	6
Conyers	16,115	88	65	23
Cordele	10,578	37	27	10
Cornelia	4,554	19	17	2
Covington	14,128	69	58	11
Cumming	6,501	20	18	2
Dallas	13,888	37	27	10
Dalton	33,544	101	89	12
Danielsville	592	2	2	0
Darien	1,891	12	11	1
Dawson	4,049	18	13	5
Decatur	26,612	58	44	14
Dillard	370	4	3	1
Doerun	744	5	4	1
Donalsonville	2,539	14	13	1
Doraville	10,600	58	42	16
Douglas	11,608	41	36	5
Douglasville	34,609	110	92	18
Dublin	15,756	74	60	14
Duluth	29,893	88	69	19
Dunwoody	49,868	78	64	14
Eastman	5,127	14	12	2
Eatonton	6,625	28	20	8
Edison	1,430	6	5	1
Elberton	4,321	23	20	3
Ellijay	1,722	12	11	1
Emerson	1,603	9	8	1
Enigma	1,339	3	3	0
Eton	917	4	4	0
Euharlee	4,372	11	10	1
Fairburn	16,264	52	41	11
Fairmount	743	5	5	0
Fayetteville	18,041	62	53	9
Fitzgerald	8,661	33	28	5
Flowery Branch	8,256	19	17	2
Folkston	4,662	7	7	0
Forest Park	20,273	83	64	19
Forsyth	4,150	14	12	2
Fort Oglethorpe	10,126	30	28	2
Fort Valley	8,866	29	25	4
Franklin	916	8	8	0
Franklin Springs	1,232	3	3	0
Gainesville	42,500	113	98	15
Garden City	8,854	44	36	8
Glennville	5,084	11	9	2
Gordon	1,867	11	6	5
Grantville	3,295	14	13	1
Greensboro	3,365	20	17	3
Greenville	837	7	6	1
Griffin	22,840	83	74	9
Grovetown	14,918	31	24	7
Guyton	2,142	2	1	1
Hahira	3,021	11	9	2
Hampton	8,044	20	18	2
Harlem	3,358	9	7	2
Hartwell	4,447	26	21	5
Helen	555	9	8	1
Hephzibah	3,930	4	4	0
Hiawassee	902	5	5	0
Hinesville	32,871	99	83	16
Hiram	4,173	19	16	3
Hogansville	3,113	19	13	6
Holly Springs	13,458	36	35	1
Homerville	2,348	8	7	1
Jackson	5,086	14	13	1
Jasper	3,975	19	17	2
Jesup	9,779	33	31	2
Johns Creek	85,258	87	78	9
Jonesboro	4,927	36	28	8
Kennesaw	34,641	74	67	7
Kingston	656	2	1	1
LaGrange	30,398	96	79	17

Table 78. Full-Time Law Enforcement Employees, by Selected State and City, 2019—Continued

(Number.)

State/city	Population	Total law enforcement employees	Total officers	Total civilians
Lake City	2,858	19	17	2
Lavonia	2,162	15	14	1
Lawrenceville	30,120	94	69	25
Leslie	369	5	4	1
Lilburn	12,769	36	31	5
Lithonia	2,404	8	7	1
Locust Grove	7,409	28	25	3
Loganville	12,822	31	29	2
Louisville	2,142	6	6	0
Lyons	4,258	17	14	3
Madison	4,177	15	13	2
Manchester	3,958	17	12	5
Marietta	61,324	180	135	45
Marshallville	1,237	4	3	1
McDonough	26,277	54	47	7
McIntyre	602	5	5	0
McRae-Helena	8,352	12	11	1
Metter	3,949	12	11	1
Midville	256	1	1	0
Midway	2,020	6	4	2
Milledgeville	18,655	52	34	18
Milton	40,067	47	38	9
Monroe	13,662	48	44	4
Montezuma	2,969	12	10	2
Morrow	7,636	30	27	3
Moultrie	14,126	37	33	4
Newnan	40,720	104	90	14
Norcross	16,769	59	38	21
Norman Park	966	3	1	2
Ocilla	3,606	14	14	0
Omega	1,222	7	5	2
Oxford	2,337	3	3	0
Palmetto	4,743	15	12	3
Peachtree City	35,929	65	60	5
Pelham	3,474	14	12	2
Pembroke	2,623	9	9	0
Pooler	24,917	67	60	7
Port Wentworth	9,015	36	30	6
Remerton	1,083	9	8	1
Rincon	10,260	15	12	3
Ringgold	3,625	10	10	0
Riverdale	16,950	40	33	7
Rockmart	4,320	22	20	2
Sandersville	5,420	21	17	4
Sandy Springs	110,760	151	134	17
Savannah	240,631	572	493	79
Shiloh	485	1	1	0
Smyrna	57,423	138	86	52
Snellville	20,113	59	47	12
Social Circle	4,592	16	15	1
Sparta	1,209	13	7	6
Springfield	4,260	10	9	1
Statham	2,775	5	4	1
Stone Mountain	6,388	17	16	1
Sylvania	2,427	10	8	2
Sylvester	5,704	20	16	4
Tallapoosa	3,154	11	10	1
Thomasville	18,533	65	59	6
Thunderbolt	2,677	11	9	2
Union City	22,200	70	61	9
Vidalia	10,397	35	24	11
Warm Springs	402	2	2	0
Warner Robins	76,623	151	108	43
Waynesboro	5,387	28	22	6
Winder	17,385	47	39	8
Woodstock	33,470	59	54	5
Wrens	1,942	12	11	1
Wrightsville	3,617	7	6	1
HAWAII				
Honolulu	974,902	2,349	1,864	485
IDAHO				
Aberdeen	1,946	5	5	0
American Falls	4,354	7	5	2
Ashton	1,052	2	2	0
Bellevue	2,441	4	4	0
Blackfoot	11,938	30	27	3
Boise	231,314	385	298	87
Bonners Ferry	2,606	7	7	0
Buhl	4,440	10	9	1
Caldwell	57,940	92	76	16
Chubbuck	15,490	36	22	14
Coeur d'Alene	52,256	112	90	22
Cottonwood	935	1	1	0

Table 78. Full-Time Law Enforcement Employees, by Selected State and City, 2019—Continued

(Number.)

State/city	Population	Total law enforcement employees	Total officers	Total civilians
Emmett	6,950	16	13	3
Filer	2,894	5	5	0
Fruitland	5,472	16	12	4
Garden City	12,033	34	27	7
Gooding	3,457	9	7	2
Grangeville	3,205	4	4	0
Hagerman	883	1	1	0
Hailey	8,575	15	14	1
Heyburn	3,460	8	7	1
Homedale	2,681	6	5	1
Idaho City	468	1	1	0
Idaho Falls	62,088	137	90	47
Jerome	11,921	21	18	3
Kellogg	2,117	9	8	1
Ketchum	2,843	12	11	1
Kimberly	4,052	9	8	1
Lewiston	32,931	68	43	25
McCall	3,541	12	10	2
Meridian	111,196	145	112	33
Middleton	8,395	10	9	1
Montpelier	2,514	6	5	1
Moscow	26,018	45	37	8
Mountain Home	14,476	34	30	4
Nampa	98,208	176	125	51
Orofino	3,115	6	5	1
Osburn	1,549	2	2	0
Parma	2,152	5	5	0
Payette	7,535	15	13	2
Pinehurst	1,616	2	2	0
Pocatello	56,514	131	89	42
Ponderay	1,145	7	6	1
Post Falls	35,649	74	46	28
Preston	5,533	9	8	1
Priest River	1,868	6	5	1
Rathdrum	8,968	18	15	3
Rexburg	29,109	41	32	9
Rigby	4,225	8	7	1
Rupert	5,791	13	12	1
Salmon	3,141	8	8	0
Sandpoint	8,873	24	20	4
Shelley	4,423	8	8	0
Shoshone	1,514	6	6	0
Soda Springs	3,029	7	7	0
Spirit Lake	2,596	9	7	2
St. Anthony	3,572	6	6	0
Sun Valley	1,482	13	12	1
Twin Falls	50,463	95	75	20
Weiser	5,369	13	10	3
Wendell	2,707	4	4	0
Wilder	1,827	5	5	0
ILLINOIS				
Albany	868	1	1	0
Aledo	3,448	8	7	1
Algonquin	31,016	54	47	7
Alsip	18,830	43	40	3
Altamont	2,278	6	6	0
Alton	26,360	83	61	22
Amboy	2,301	3	3	0
Anna	4,110	7	7	0
Arlington Heights	75,249	133	106	27
Arthur	2,220	4	4	0
Ashland	1,181	1	1	0
Assumption	1,071	2	2	0
Athens	1,913	5	5	0
Auburn	4,664	6	6	0
Aurora	199,784	362	298	64
Aviston	2,128	1	1	0
Barrington Hills	4,205	20	16	4
Bartonville	6,137	15	10	5
Beardstown	5,425	10	9	1
Bedford Park	602	46	36	10
Berkeley	5,056	19	15	4
Berwyn	54,702	166	114	52
Bethalto	9,270	18	13	5
Bethany	1,258	2	2	0
Bloomington	78,107	157	124	33
Blue Island	23,037	42	32	10
Blue Mound	1,073	1	1	0
Bolingbrook	75,394	123	110	13
Bourbonnais	19,588	28	26	2
Bradley	15,205	44	33	11
Braidwood	6,199	16	13	3
Breese	4,498	8	7	1
Bridgeview	16,153	30	30	0

Table 78. Full-Time Law Enforcement Employees, by Selected State and City, 2019—Continued

(Number.)

State/city	Population	Total law enforcement employees	Total officers	Total civilians
Brighton	2,137	4	4	0
Buffalo Grove	40,768	75	62	13
Burbank	28,483	52	44	8
Burr Ridge	10,828	31	27	4
Byron	3,585	7	6	1
Cahokia	13,864	39	31	8
Calumet City	36,128	97	73	24
Cambridge	2,078	1	1	0
Campton Hills	11,202	5	5	0
Carbondale	25,242	81	64	17
Carlinville	5,498	17	12	5
Carol Stream	39,599	92	74	18
Carrollton	2,404	6	6	0
Carthage	2,448	4	4	0
Cary	17,728	25	24	1
Caseyville	4,088	14	13	1
Centreville	4,922	9	8	1
Champaign	88,891	140	117	23
Charleston	19,987	34	31	3
Chatham	12,809	20	14	6
Chenoa	3,143	4	4	0
Cherry Valley	2,877	15	14	1
Chicago	2,707,064	14,015	13,160	855
Chicago Heights	29,471	93	78	15
Chicago Ridge	14,017	35	31	4
Chillicothe	6,071	12	12	0
Cicero	81,270	180	156	24
Coal City	5,340	14	13	1
Coal Valley	3,760	9	8	1
Colfax	1,017	1	1	0
Cortland	4,369	6	6	0
Countryside	5,957	27	24	3
Crest Hill	20,534	32	30	2
Crete	8,096	20	18	2
Crystal Lake	39,944	68	59	9
Dallas City	870	3	3	0
Dana	152	1	1	0
Danville	30,642	64	55	9
Darien	21,935	37	32	5
Decatur	70,710	149	141	8
Deer Creek	661	1	1	0
Deerfield	18,848	54	40	14
DeKalb	42,428	76	61	15
Delavan	1,605	4	4	0
De Soto	1,510	4	3	1
Des Plaines	59,023	117	100	17
Dupo	3,810	8	8	0
Du Quoin	5,705	13	9	4
Dwight	3,962	10	9	1
East Dubuque	1,571	6	6	0
Edwardsville	25,047	60	45	15
Effingham	12,662	38	24	14
Elburn	5,967	8	7	1
Elgin	112,112	243	180	63
Elizabeth	721	1	1	0
Elk Grove Village	32,371	100	86	14
Elmhurst	46,857	85	67	18
Elmwood	2,021	2	2	0
Elmwood Park	24,185	43	36	7
Elwood	2,257	12	11	1
Essex	759	1	1	0
Eureka	5,276	6	6	0
Evanston	74,047	212	157	55
Evergreen Park	19,260	77	58	19
Fairbury	3,602	6	6	0
Fairfield	4,961	14	10	4
Fairmount	602	1	1	0
Farmington	2,236	6	6	0
Fisher	1,966	2	2	0
Flossmoor	9,211	24	19	5
Fox Lake	10,457	29	23	6
Fox River Grove	4,610	8	8	0
Frankfort	19,352	36	32	4
Freeburg	4,240	11	10	1
Freeport	23,721	63	47	16
Fulton	3,330	10	9	1
Galena	3,155	11	10	1
Genoa	5,211	7	6	1
Georgetown	3,205	4	4	0
Gibson City	3,283	8	7	1
Gifford	1,100	1	1	0
Gillespie	3,097	11	8	3
Glencoe	8,887	39	34	5
Glendale Heights	33,878	70	54	16
Glenview	47,581	72	67	5

Table 78. Full-Time Law Enforcement Employees, by Selected State and City, 2019—Continued

(Number.)

State/city	Population	Total law enforcement employees	Total officers	Total civilians
Glenwood	8,767	25	22	3
Goodfield	998	1	1	0
Grafton	632	3	3	0
Granite City	28,315	68	56	12
Greenfield	981	2	2	0
Greenup	1,486	4	4	0
Gurnee	30,493	97	62	35
Hampshire	6,425	10	10	0
Hampton	1,757	4	4	0
Hanover Park	37,699	83	57	26
Hartford	1,344	5	4	1
Harvard	9,092	20	18	2
Harwood Heights	8,388	27	24	3
Hawthorn Woods	8,651	13	12	1
Henry	2,205	5	4	1
Herrin	12,878	27	18	9
Hickory Hills	13,806	34	27	7
Highland	9,836	27	20	7
Highwood	5,250	12	11	1
Hillsboro	5,972	10	10	0
Hinckley	2,033	3	3	0
Hodgkins	1,883	24	22	2
Hoffman Estates	51,105	103	86	17
Homer	1,165	1	1	0
Homewood	18,831	45	40	5
Hoopeston	5,046	20	11	9
Hudson	1,816	3	3	0
Indian Head Park	3,742	8	7	1
Inverness	7,442	14	12	2
Itasca	10,032	25	22	3
Jacksonville	18,667	43	39	4
Jerseyville	8,208	21	15	6
Joliet	148,155	339	270	69
Kankakee	25,872	72	68	4
Kansas	721	1	1	0
Kildeer	4,033	9	8	1
Kingston	1,159	2	2	0
Kirkland	1,715	2	2	0
Ladd	1,199	1	1	0
La Grange	15,424	28	24	4
La Grange Park	13,260	23	21	2
Lake Bluff	5,606	17	15	2
Lake Forest	19,564	40	35	5
Lake in the Hills	28,811	48	40	8
Lakemoor	6,008	15	14	1
Lake Villa	8,625	18	17	1
Lakewood	4,006	9	8	1
Lake Zurich	20,060	50	33	17
Lemont	17,297	27	22	5
Le Roy	3,542	8	8	0
Lincoln	13,584	26	26	0
Lindenhurst	14,296	15	13	2
Litchfield	6,708	15	14	1
Lockport	25,587	45	39	6
Lombard	44,672	74	62	12
Lovington	1,044	2	2	0
Lyons	10,436	14	12	2
Machesney Park	22,594	23	22	1
Mackinaw	1,901	2	2	0
Manhattan	8,121	11	10	1
Maple Park	1,341	1	1	0
Marissa	1,807	3	3	0
Marquette Heights	2,644	5	5	0
Marseilles	4,844	10	9	1
Maryville	8,033	14	13	1
Mason City	2,133	3	3	0
Mattoon	17,629	40	36	4
Mazon	972	2	1	1
McLean	797	1	1	0
Melrose Park	24,863	89	72	17
Metropolis	5,986	19	13	6
Midlothian	14,433	32	29	3
Milan	5,012	16	15	1
Milledgeville	945	2	2	0
Millstadt	3,869	8	8	0
Minier	1,188	2	2	0
Mokena	20,573	34	31	3
Momence	3,089	8	8	0
Monmouth	8,944	31	20	11
Montgomery	19,927	36	32	4
Morris	15,083	29	25	4
Morrison	4,026	7	7	0
Morrisonville	1,003	2	1	1
Morton	16,209	24	22	2
Morton Grove	22,904	57	46	11

Table 78. Full-Time Law Enforcement Employees, by Selected State and City, 2019—Continued

(Number.)

State/city	Population	Total law enforcement employees	Total officers	Total civilians
Mount Carmel	6,988	15	10	5
Mount Morris	2,786	5	4	1
Mount Olive	1,941	5	4	1
Mount Prospect	54,089	102	83	19
Mount Pulaski	1,471	2	2	0
Mount Vernon	14,802	52	40	12
Mount Zion	5,799	12	10	2
Moweaqua	1,715	3	3	0
Mundelein	31,260	74	53	21
Naperville	149,061	251	166	85
New Athens	1,885	4	4	0
New Lenox	27,103	41	36	5
Newton	2,855	7	6	1
Niles	29,104	69	55	14
Nokomis	2,110	5	4	1
Normal	55,013	90	82	8
Northfield	5,418	21	19	2
North Pekin	1,526	7	7	0
Oak Brook	8,096	46	39	7
Oak Lawn	55,361	128	113	15
Oak Park	52,311	137	109	28
Oakwood	1,496	3	3	0
Oblong	1,368	1	1	0
O'Fallon	29,686	66	48	18
Okawville	1,362	4	4	0
Olney	8,800	13	12	1
Oregon	3,471	9	8	1
Orion	1,790	2	2	0
Orland Hills	7,066	10	10	0
Orland Park	58,519	127	99	28
Ottawa	18,047	50	35	15
Palatine	67,984	131	107	24
Palestine	1,272	1	1	0
Palos Hills	17,158	34	31	3
Palos Park	4,768	11	10	1
Paris	8,288	21	15	6
Park City	7,442	13	11	2
Paxton	4,196	7	7	0
Pecatonica	2,081	3	3	0
Pekin	32,033	61	54	7
Peoria	110,955	225	203	22
Peotone	4,135	11	10	1
Peru	9,738	26	24	2
Petersburg	2,214	6	6	0
Pittsfield	4,228	9	9	0
Plainfield	44,691	70	57	13
Pontiac	11,211	20	18	2
Princeton	7,500	18	17	1
Rantoul	12,657	38	31	7
Raymond	941	1	1	0
Richmond	1,921	7	7	0
Ridge Farm	817	1	1	0
Riverdale	13,161	36	30	6
River Forest	10,869	29	27	2
Riverton	3,398	9	9	0
Riverwoods	3,585	7	7	0
Rockdale	1,924	5	5	0
Rockford	145,719	338	298	40
Rock Island	37,517	105	78	27
Rolling Meadows	23,703	56	49	7
Romeoville	39,616	75	62	13
Roscoe	10,492	14	13	1
Rossville	1,223	3	3	0
Round Lake	18,266	29	26	3
Roxana	1,439	7	6	1
Royalton	1,116	3	3	0
Rushville	2,867	5	5	0
Salem	7,053	26	18	8
Sandwich	7,364	20	16	4
San Jose	602	2	2	0
Sauget	164	10	10	0
Savanna	2,767	6	6	0
Schaumburg	73,412	140	109	31
Shorewood	17,606	33	29	4
Silvis	7,538	20	17	3
Skokie	63,082	159	114	45
Smithton	3,836	6	6	0
South Barrington	5,047	22	19	3
South Beloit	7,636	13	12	1
South Chicago Heights	4,029	10	9	1
South Elgin	23,634	36	32	4
South Holland	21,438	45	42	3
South Pekin	1,088	2	2	0
South Roxana	1,991	5	5	0
Springfield	114,393	269	241	28

Table 78. Full-Time Law Enforcement Employees, by Selected State and City, 2019—Continued

(Number.)

State/city	Population	Total law enforcement employees	Total officers	Total civilians
Spring Valley	5,156	12	11	1
St. Charles	33,118	64	54	10
Steger	9,301	16	15	1
St. Elmo	1,389	3	3	0
Sterling	14,510	38	29	9
Stockton	1,707	6	5	1
Streamwood	39,529	66	57	9
Sullivan	4,487	11	9	2
Summit	11,205	32	30	2
Swansea	13,432	23	21	2
Thayer	658	2	2	0
Thornton	2,423	12	11	1
Tilton	2,638	4	4	0
Tinley Park	56,119	93	80	13
Tolono	3,447	2	2	0
Trenton	2,593	5	5	0
Tuscola	4,336	8	7	1
Urbana	42,080	72	58	14
Vandalia	6,664	12	12	0
Vernon Hills	26,847	66	43	23
Vienna	1,443	3	3	0
Villa Park	21,651	48	39	9
Virden	3,333	10	6	4
Warren	1,301	4	3	1
Warrensburg	1,124	2	2	0
Warrenville	13,268	39	31	8
Watseka	4,809	12	11	1
Waukegan	86,505	189	146	43
Waverly	1,200	1	1	0
Wayne	2,426	2	2	0
Westchester	16,224	37	33	4
West City	640	11	7	4
West Dundee	8,388	21	19	2
Western Springs	13,460	24	21	3
Westmont	24,642	43	37	6
Westville	2,964	4	4	0
Wheaton	53,160	79	64	15
Wheeling	39,028	91	59	32
Willowbrook	8,486	25	22	3
Willow Springs	5,658	11	10	1
Wilmette	27,289	64	44	20
Winfield	9,758	17	16	1
Winnebago	2,963	6	6	0
Wood River	10,108	26	18	8
Woodstock	25,324	41	37	4
Worth	10,534	28	26	2
Yorkville	20,541	33	30	3
Zion	23,617	48	44	4
INDIANA				
Albion	2,337	6	6	0
Anderson	54,899	122	101	21
Angola	8,715	23	18	5
Auburn	13,464	24	23	1
Bargersville	7,973	13	12	1
Batesville	6,704	18	13	5
Bedford	13,271	42	33	9
Bloomington	85,542	157	97	60
Bluffton	10,134	34	21	13
Bremen	4,472	17	12	5
Brownsburg	27,005	49	43	6
Butler	2,712	8	7	1
Cannelton	1,479	3	3	0
Carmel	95,388	144	119	25
Cedar Lake	12,896	22	19	3
Chesterton	13,929	26	22	4
Clarksville	21,630	60	54	6
Clinton	4,701	10	8	2
Columbia City	9,203	22	21	1
Crawfordsville	16,136	44	39	5
Crown Point	30,341	53	48	5
Cumberland	5,894	16	14	2
Dyer	15,939	34	31	3
East Chicago	27,717	88	82	6
Ellettsville	6,731	12	11	1
Fairmount	2,754	7	6	1
Fort Wayne	269,366	542	480	62
Franklin	25,443	57	52	5
Greenfield	22,800	44	42	2
Greenwood	59,797	69	62	7
Hammond	75,201	244	210	34
Hartford City	5,716	12	10	2
Highland	22,220	46	39	7
Hobart	27,880	78	67	11
Huntingburg	6,133	13	12	1

Table 78. Full-Time Law Enforcement Employees, by Selected State and City, 2019—Continued

(Number.)

State/city	Population	Total law enforcement employees	Total officers	Total civilians
Indianapolis	883,699	2,803	2,121	682
Jasper	15,629	30	22	8
Jeffersonville	47,723	88	84	4
Knox	3,515	8	8	0
Kokomo	57,845	99	81	18
Logansport	17,660	41	40	1
Markle	1,085	5	5	0
Merrillville	34,724	67	60	7
Mooresville	9,747	26	20	6
Munster	22,412	44	40	4
Nappanee	6,853	17	15	2
New Whiteland	6,242	9	8	1
Noblesville	64,567	103	92	11
North Webster	1,164	5	5	0
Plainfield	35,317	64	58	6
Plymouth	9,872	26	24	2
Portage	36,800	74	67	7
Rensselaer	5,820	17	10	7
Roseland	633	13	4	9
Rushville	6,012	16	11	5
Schererville	28,412	62	48	14
Sellersburg	8,949	18	16	2
Shelbyville	19,362	58	43	15
Shirley	862	2	2	0
Silver Lake	924	3	3	0
South Bend	101,944	278	234	44
Speedway	12,202	50	35	15
St. John	18,478	25	22	3
Terre Haute	60,749	140	131	9
Valparaiso	33,980	63	57	6
Walkerton	2,274	10	6	4
Warsaw	15,120	43	36	7
Westfield	43,212	59	55	4
West Lafayette	49,154	66	47	19
Whitestown	9,810	31	30	1
Whiting	4,757	20	18	2
Winchester	4,676	13	12	1
Zionsville	27,630	40	38	2
IOWA				
Ackley	1,495	3	3	0
Adel	5,136	10	9	1
Albia	3,725	7	6	1
Algona	5,413	14	10	4
Altoona	19,441	33	31	2
Ames	68,237	80	57	23
Anamosa	5,502	9	8	1
Ankeny	68,238	72	62	10
Asbury	5,834	5	5	0
Atlantic	6,514	13	12	1
Audubon	1,883	4	4	0
Belle Plaine	2,432	5	5	0
Belmond	2,287	5	5	0
Bettendorf	36,972	51	45	6
Blue Grass	1,704	3	3	0
Boone	12,448	18	17	1
Burlington	24,751	49	44	5
Camanche	4,341	9	9	0
Carlisle	4,334	9	8	1
Carroll	9,775	16	15	1
Carter Lake	3,783	11	10	1
Cedar Falls	41,269	61	60	1
Cedar Rapids	134,007	284	220	64
Centerville	5,459	18	11	7
Charles City	7,334	20	13	7
Cherokee	4,855	9	8	1
Clarinda	5,352	11	10	1
Clarion	2,729	8	7	1
Clear Lake	7,555	20	16	4
Clinton	24,982	52	46	6
Clive	17,305	30	27	3
Colfax	2,066	4	4	0
Coralville	22,035	39	34	5
Council Bluffs	62,427	134	113	21
Creston	7,784	16	12	4
Davenport	102,392	192	169	23
Dayton	782	1	1	0
Decorah	7,529	19	11	8
Denison	8,415	18	13	5
Des Moines	218,384	450	351	99
DeWitt	5,153	11	10	1
Dubuque	57,973	112	105	7
Dyersville	4,245	7	7	0
Eldora	2,608	4	4	0
Eldridge	6,972	10	9	1

Table 78. Full-Time Law Enforcement Employees, by Selected State and City, 2019—Continued

(Number.)

State/city	Population	Total law enforcement employees	Total officers	Total civilians
Emmetsburg	3,691	7	6	1
Estherville	5,609	13	13	0
Evansdale	4,758	9	8	1
Fairfield	10,539	20	13	7
Forest City	4,036	9	8	1
Fort Dodge	23,973	43	40	3
Fort Madison	10,392	21	19	2
Glenwood	5,321	12	10	2
Gowrie	959	1	1	0
Grinnell	9,333	16	14	2
Grundy Center	2,679	5	5	0
Hampton	4,207	8	7	1
Harlan	4,796	9	8	1
Hawarden	2,479	4	4	0
Hiawatha	7,441	14	14	0
Humboldt	4,578	6	6	0
Independence	6,086	12	11	1
Indianola	16,235	22	19	3
Iowa City	77,390	108	85	23
Iowa Falls	5,006	14	10	4
Jefferson	4,123	8	8	0
Johnston	22,708	35	31	4
Keokuk	10,214	25	21	4
Knoxville	7,193	15	14	1
Lansing	941	3	3	0
Le Claire	4,000	8	7	1
Le Mars	10,018	16	14	2
Leon	1,815	3	3	0
Lisbon	2,260	3	3	0
Manchester	4,958	15	10	5
Maquoketa	5,972	18	11	7
Marengo	2,447	3	3	0
Marion	40,612	57	43	14
Marshalltown	27,002	47	42	5
Mason City	26,976	58	52	6
Missouri Valley	2,609	6	6	0
Monticello	3,898	8	7	1
Mount Pleasant	8,749	16	14	2
Mount Vernon	4,449	6	6	0
Muscatine	23,823	41	37	4
Nevada	6,744	12	10	2
New Hampton	3,374	6	6	0
Newton	15,205	28	23	5
North Liberty	20,086	24	22	2
Norwalk	11,871	20	19	1
Oelwein	5,886	14	10	4
Ogden	1,988	2	2	0
Onawa	2,762	5	5	0
Orange City	6,112	7	7	0
Osage	3,538	7	6	1
Osceola	5,224	12	11	1
Oskaloosa	11,415	19	17	2
Ottumwa	24,488	51	41	10
Pella	10,334	24	18	6
Perry	7,421	20	13	7
Pleasant Hill	10,228	22	20	2
Polk City	5,013	7	7	0
Postville	2,065	4	4	0
Prairie City	1,736	3	3	0
Princeton	953	1	1	0
Red Oak	5,287	12	10	2
Rock Valley	3,824	6	6	0
Sac City	2,056	4	4	0
Sergeant Bluff	4,993	9	8	1
Sheldon	5,099	6	6	0
Shenandoah	4,859	13	10	3
Sigourney	2,010	4	3	1
Sioux Center	7,688	7	7	0
Sioux City	82,339	149	126	23
Spencer	11,008	29	20	9
Spirit Lake	5,097	10	9	1
Storm Lake	10,430	23	19	4
Story City	3,362	6	6	0
Tama	2,730	6	6	0
Tipton	3,224	7	6	1
University Heights	1,051	4	4	0
Urbandale	44,541	60	52	8
Van Meter	1,202	2	2	0
Vinton	5,074	9	8	1
Washington	7,315	11	10	1
Waterloo	67,723	130	121	9
Waukee	24,255	29	26	3
Waukon	3,654	4	4	0
Waverly	10,187	16	15	1
Webster City	7,684	15	9	6

Table 78. Full-Time Law Enforcement Employees, by Selected State and City, 2019—Continued

(Number.)

State/city	Population	Total law enforcement employees	Total officers	Total civilians
West Branch	2,439	4	4	0
West Burlington	2,882	7	7	0
West Des Moines	67,978	98	86	12
Williamsburg	3,159	7	7	0
Windsor Heights	4,896	14	13	1
Winterset	5,332	8	8	0
KANSAS				
Abilene	6,235	16	13	3
Alma	773	1	1	0
Altamont	1,024	3	3	0
Andale	995	3	3	0
Andover	13,472	31	24	7
Arkansas City	11,718	30	26	4
Arma	1,427	4	4	0
Atchison	10,509	24	24	0
Attica	556	1	1	0
Atwood	1,204	3	3	0
Augusta	9,334	26	19	7
Baldwin City	4,713	13	11	2
Basehor	6,418	16	14	2
Baxter Springs	3,907	14	11	3
Bel Aire	8,252	11	10	1
Belle Plaine	1,555	6	6	0
Belleville	1,877	5	5	0
Benton	868	2	2	0
Blue Rapids	956	2	2	0
Bonner Springs	7,850	27	24	3
Buhler	1,280	3	3	0
Burlingame	885	1	1	0
Burlington	2,545	9	7	2
Burrton	850	2	2	0
Caldwell	990	3	3	0
Caney	1,966	9	5	4
Canton	693	1	1	0
Carbondale	1,371	3	3	0
Cedar Vale	510	1	1	0
Chanute	9,006	18	16	2
Chapman	1,350	2	2	0
Cheney	2,181	5	5	0
Cherokee	710	1	1	0
Cherryvale	2,127	7	6	1
Claflin	608	1	1	0
Clay Center	3,946	7	6	1
Clearwater	2,550	5	4	1
Coffeyville	9,260	32	24	8
Colby	5,305	14	13	1
Columbus	3,042	10	8	2
Colwich	1,419	3	3	0
Concordia	4,904	13	8	5
Council Grove	2,064	8	7	1
Derby	25,012	53	43	10
Dodge City	27,314	55	40	15
Eastborough	732	8	7	1
Edwardsville	4,505	18	17	1
El Dorado	12,899	26	23	3
Elkhart	1,775	2	2	0
Ellinwood	1,950	5	5	0
Ellis	2,024	5	5	0
Ellsworth	2,983	7	6	1
Emporia	24,747	48	41	7
Erie	1,077	4	3	1
Eudora	6,414	12	12	0
Fairway	3,978	8	8	0
Fort Scott	7,729	22	21	1
Fredonia	2,239	7	6	1
Frontenac	3,406	8	7	1
Galena	2,848	12	11	1
Galva	866	1	1	0
Garden City	26,509	83	57	26
Gardner	22,229	38	33	5
Garnett	3,244	8	8	0
Girard	2,692	7	6	1
Goddard	4,764	14	13	1
Goodland	4,374	10	9	1
Grandview Plaza	1,563	8	7	1
Great Bend	15,069	35	31	4
Halstead	2,018	6	5	1
Haven	1,189	3	3	0
Havensville	157	1	1	0
Hays	20,894	40	35	5
Haysville	11,319	31	24	7
Herington	2,277	8	7	1
Hesston	3,736	8	7	1
Hiawatha	3,119	10	9	1

Table 78. Full-Time Law Enforcement Employees, by Selected State and City, 2019—Continued

(Number.)

State/city	Population	Total law enforcement employees	Total officers	Total civilians
Highland	999	2	2	0
Hill City	1,408	4	4	0
Hoisington	2,486	7	6	1
Holcomb	2,082	3	2	1
Holton	3,239	7	7	0
Holyrood	419	1	1	0
Horton	1,679	9	5	4
Howard	593	1	1	0
Hoxie	1,198	2	2	0
Hugoton	3,777	8	6	2
Hutchinson	40,431	104	68	36
Independence	8,497	28	20	8
Inman	1,327	4	4	0
Iola	5,265	16	15	1
Junction City	21,921	67	47	20
Kansas City	153,601	423	324	99
Kechi	2,006	5	4	1
Kingman	2,874	7	7	0
Kiowa	931	2	2	0
La Cygne	1,117	2	2	0
La Harpe	523	1	1	0
Lake Quivira	942	1	1	0
Lansing	12,051	19	18	1
Larned	3,739	6	6	0
Lawrence	98,505	168	143	25
Leavenworth	36,149	74	54	20
Leawood	35,052	76	55	21
Lebo	889	1	1	0
Lenexa	56,240	135	85	50
Liberal	19,368	51	35	16
Lindsborg	3,269	8	7	1
Little River	518	2	2	0
Louisburg	4,532	12	11	1
Lyndon	1,016	1	1	0
Lyons	3,483	6	5	1
Macksville	530	1	1	0
Maize	4,836	14	13	1
Marion	1,770	5	5	0
Marysville	3,264	9	8	1
McLouth	839	2	2	0
McPherson	13,070	43	35	8
Meade	1,546	4	3	1
Merriam	11,197	34	29	5
Minneapolis	1,920	5	5	0
Mission	9,379	35	31	4
Mission Hills	3,588	3	3	0
Moran	508	1	1	0
Mound City	685	1	1	0
Moundridge	1,864	5	5	0
Mount Hope	798	2	2	0
Mulvane	6,451	21	15	6
Neodesha	2,289	8	7	1
Newton	18,697	39	35	4
North Newton	1,752	4	4	0
Oberlin	1,718	4	4	0
Olathe	141,371	215	187	28
Onaga	689	1	1	0
Osage City	2,807	7	7	0
Osborne	1,274	3	3	0
Oswego	1,682	4	4	0
Ottawa	12,221	32	27	5
Overbrook	1,018	2	2	0
Overland Park	194,983	310	246	64
Oxford	1,000	3	3	0
Paola	5,676	22	16	6
Park City	7,779	17	15	2
Parsons	9,569	27	21	6
Peabody	1,098	3	3	0
Pittsburg	20,168	75	48	27
Plainville	1,829	5	5	0
Pleasanton	1,170	2	2	0
Prairie Village	22,508	56	42	14
Pratt	6,606	23	15	8
Roeland Park	6,761	16	14	2
Rose Hill	3,969	9	8	1
Rossville	1,130	2	2	0
Russell	4,455	9	8	1
Sabetha	2,569	10	6	4
Salina	46,567	107	78	29
Scranton	685	1	1	0
Sedan	1,004	1	1	0
Sedgwick	1,635	1	1	0
Seneca	2,058	4	4	0
Shawnee	66,300	113	93	20
South Hutchinson	2,509	6	6	0

Table 78. Full-Time Law Enforcement Employees, by Selected State and City, 2019—Continued

(Number.)

State/city	Population	Total law enforcement employees	Total officers	Total civilians
Spearville	795	1	1	0
Spring Hill	7,186	13	12	1
Sterling	2,194	5	5	0
St. George	1,046	2	1	1
St. John	1,176	2	2	0
St. Marys	2,636	5	5	0
Tonganoxie	5,591	13	12	1
Topeka	125,655	328	278	50
Troy	969	1	1	0
Udall	709	2	2	0
Ulysses	5,709	11	10	1
Valley Center	7,376	19	17	2
Victoria	1,221	2	2	0
Wamego	4,808	12	8	4
Wellington	7,698	17	15	2
Wellsville	1,795	6	5	1
Westwood	1,674	9	8	1
Wichita	390,080	844	649	195
Wilson	731	1	1	0
Winfield	12,023	28	23	5
Yates Center	1,337	4	4	0
KENTUCKY				
Albany	2,001	7	7	0
Alexandria	9,692	20	16	4
Anchorage	2,443	14	10	4
Ashland	20,222	51	48	3
Auburn	1,376	2	2	0
Augusta	1,135	3	3	0
Bancroft	515	1	1	0
Bardstown	13,239	30	28	2
Beattyville	1,194	6	6	0
Beaver Dam	3,600	5	5	0
Bellefonte	827	4	4	0
Benham	426	1	1	0
Benton	4,461	8	8	0
Berea	16,074	36	33	3
Bloomfield	1,063	1	1	0
Booneville	126	1	1	0
Brandenburg	2,902	5	5	0
Brodhead	1,182	2	2	0
Brownsville	835	3	3	0
Burgin	981	1	1	0
Burkesville	1,459	10	6	4
Burnside	905	6	5	1
Cadiz	2,673	8	7	1
Calvert City	2,492	8	7	1
Campbellsville	11,488	12	11	1
Carlisle	1,954	9	5	4
Carrollton	3,817	16	15	1
Catlettsburg	1,746	8	8	0
Cave City	2,451	9	9	0
Central City	5,726	16	14	2
Clinton	1,249	3	3	0
Cloverport	1,160	1	1	0
Coal Run Village	1,486	4	4	0
Cold Spring	6,509	12	12	0
Columbia	4,645	42	37	5
Covington	40,350	121	110	11
Cumberland	1,936	6	6	0
Cynthiana	6,354	17	15	2
Danville	16,873	36	34	2
Dayton	5,527	14	13	1
Dry Ridge	2,229	2	2	0
Eddyville	2,525	6	6	0
Edgewood	8,749	12	12	0
Edmonton	1,567	7	7	0
Elizabethtown	30,383	75	56	19
Elkton	2,115	6	5	1
Elsmere	8,673	16	16	0
Eminence	2,594	6	6	0
Erlanger	23,116	44	41	3
Eubank	331	1	1	0
Evarts	808	3	3	0
Falmouth	2,089	7	6	1
Flatwoods	7,041	13	13	0
Flemingsburg	2,801	8	8	0
Florence	32,848	67	64	3
Fort Mitchell	8,252	15	15	0
Fort Thomas	16,386	24	23	1
Fort Wright	5,744	14	14	0
Frankfort	27,723	70	56	14
Franklin	9,036	24	23	1
Fulton	2,145	12	11	1
Georgetown	35,106	81	57	24

Table 78. Full-Time Law Enforcement Employees, by Selected State and City, 2019—Continued

(Number.)

State/city	Population	Total law enforcement employees	Total officers	Total civilians
Grayson	3,923	12	11	1
Greensburg	2,087	10	6	4
Greenup	1,107	4	4	0
Greenville	4,224	11	11	0
Guthrie	1,398	5	5	0
Hardinsburg	2,346	5	5	0
Harlan	1,507	13	10	3
Harrodsburg	8,509	19	16	3
Hartford	2,749	5	5	0
Hazard	4,938	25	19	6
Heritage Creek	1,148	11	11	0
Highland Heights	7,114	12	11	1
Hillview	9,235	18	17	1
Hodgenville	3,239	7	7	0
Hopkinsville	30,895	111	77	34
Horse Cave	2,402	7	7	0
Hustonville	369	1	1	0
Independence	28,541	38	36	2
Indian Hills	2,998	7	7	0
Irvine	2,307	5	5	0
Irvington	1,187	4	4	0
Jackson	1,954	13	8	5
Jamestown	1,787	5	5	0
Jeffersontown	28,015	62	51	11
Jenkins	1,930	4	4	0
Junction City	2,315	2	2	0
La Grange	9,080	19	17	2
Lakeside Park-Crestview Hills	6,046	13	12	1
Lancaster	3,862	14	14	0
Lawrenceburg	11,538	23	15	8
Lebanon	5,716	26	17	9
Lebanon Junction	1,973	2	2	0
Leitchfield	6,852	20	19	1
Lewisburg	802	1	1	0
Lexington	326,070	692	602	90
Louisa	2,365	6	6	0
Louisville Metro	675,501	1,446	1,191	255
Loyall	606	1	1	0
Ludlow	4,495	12	11	1
Madisonville	18,711	61	47	14
Marion	2,853	10	5	5
Mayfield	9,851	30	28	2
Maysville	8,750	34	24	10
McKee	785	1	1	0
Middlesboro	9,223	27	24	3
Middletown	7,957	11	10	1
Millersburg	799	1	1	0
Monticello	6,015	10	10	0
Morehead	7,736	29	20	9
Morganfield	3,387	7	7	0
Mount Sterling	7,326	24	22	2
Mount Vernon	2,442	8	8	0
Mount Washington	14,855	24	22	2
Muldraugh	1,000	3	3	0
Murray	19,545	44	37	7
New Haven	894	1	1	0
Newport	14,965	39	36	3
Nicholasville	31,188	76	68	8
Oak Grove	7,359	23	17	6
Olive Hill	1,560	7	7	0
Owingsville	1,566	6	6	0
Paducah	24,832	77	71	6
Paintsville	4,013	10	9	1
Paris	9,879	25	23	2
Park Hills	2,980	7	7	0
Pembroke	893	1	1	0
Pewee Valley	1,576	1	1	0
Pikeville	6,592	30	20	10
Pineville	1,763	7	7	0
Pippa Passes	677	9	1	8
Prestonsburg	3,550	22	15	7
Princeton	6,105	15	14	1
Prospect	4,954	7	6	1
Raceland	2,337	7	7	0
Radcliff	22,998	50	36	14
Ravenna	562	1	1	0
Richmond	36,458	66	57	9
Russell	3,221	13	13	0
Russell Springs	2,632	11	10	1
Russellville	7,068	24	23	1
Sadieville	364	1	1	0
Salyersville	1,712	4	4	0
Science Hill	697	3	3	0
Scottsville	4,520	28	16	12
Shelbyville	16,531	30	29	1

Table 78. Full-Time Law Enforcement Employees, by Selected State and City, 2019—Continued

(Number.)

State/city	Population	Total law enforcement employees	Total officers	Total civilians
Shepherdsville	12,515	39	37	2
Shively	15,845	36	30	6
Simpsonville	2,945	9	9	0
Smiths Grove	803	1	1	0
Somerset	11,519	43	38	5
Southgate	3,962	8	8	0
Springfield	2,965	15	8	7
Stamping Ground	802	2	2	0
Stanford	3,679	14	10	4
Stanton	2,651	9	9	0
St. Matthews	18,275	45	39	6
Taylor Mill	6,810	12	11	1
Taylorsville	1,286	5	5	0
Trenton	375	1	1	0
Uniontown	930	1	1	0
Vanceburg	1,387	6	6	0
Versailles	26,625	35	34	1
Villa Hills	7,465	14	14	0
Vine Grove	6,468	7	7	0
Warsaw	1,699	2	2	0
West Buechel	1,285	8	8	0
West Point	870	3	3	0
Whitesburg	1,845	6	5	1
Wilder	3,074	8	8	0
Williamsburg	5,298	19	18	1
Williamstown	3,946	8	7	1
Wilmore	6,489	9	8	1
Winchester	18,605	46	32	14
Woodlawn Park	978	1	1	0
Worthington	1,505	4	4	0
LOUISIANA				
Abbeville	12,142	31	28	3
Addis	5,747	12	11	1
Alexandria	46,630	170	137	33
Arnaudville	1,054	9	5	4
Baker	13,240	36	27	9
Basile	1,799	9	8	1
Bastrop	10,156	25	25	0
Baton Rouge	220,648	770	616	154
Bernice	1,611	2	2	0
Berwick	4,416	14	13	1
Blanchard	3,147	7	6	1
Bogalusa	11,681	48	29	19
Bossier City	69,044	198	162	36
Breaux Bridge	8,237	21	19	2
Broussard	12,985	36	32	4
Carencro	9,387	31	29	2
Church Point	4,424	17	17	0
Clinton	1,500	6	6	0
Crowley	12,621	51	49	2
Cullen	1,069	1	1	0
Denham Springs	9,713	37	29	8
De Ridder	10,765	30	25	5
Epps	819	2	1	1
Erath	2,059	11	7	4
Eunice	9,939	36	22	14
Farmerville	3,725	13	13	0
Fisher	219	1	1	0
Florien	601	3	3	0
Folsom	873	5	4	1
Franklinton	3,761	23	17	6
French Settlement	1,182	5	5	0
Georgetown	326	4	3	1
Golden Meadow	1,969	7	5	2
Gonzales	10,940	45	40	5
Gramercy	3,307	8	8	0
Greensburg	653	5	5	0
Greenwood	3,141	11	10	1
Gretna	17,729	146	103	43
Hammond	20,887	106	79	27
Harahan	9,298	28	21	7
Haughton	3,372	14	13	1
Houma	32,771	89	73	16
Ida	205	1	1	0
Independence	1,921	9	9	0
Iowa	3,262	18	13	5
Jena	3,370	7	6	1
Jennings	9,886	28	22	6
Kaplan	4,465	21	15	6
Kinder	2,388	15	12	3
Krotz Springs	1,208	6	5	1
Lafayette	126,694	334	280	54
Lake Arthur	2,778	9	9	0
Lake Charles	78,733	174	141	33

Table 78. Full-Time Law Enforcement Employees, by Selected State and City, 2019—Continued

(Number.)

State/city	Population	Total law enforcement employees	Total officers	Total civilians
Lake Providence	3,496	11	6	5
Leesville	5,617	26	18	8
Lutcher	3,192	2	2	0
Mamou	3,151	13	13	0
Mandeville	12,331	46	36	10
Mansfield	4,695	20	14	6
Many	2,704	11	11	0
Marion	741	1	1	0
Minden	11,984	29	28	1
Monroe	47,746	169	130	39
Morgan City	10,749	53	47	6
Natchitoches	17,747	65	52	13
New Orleans	394,498	1,448	1,154	294
Oil City	980	4	4	0
Olla	1,349	3	3	0
Opelousas	16,049	58	45	13
Patterson	5,806	25	25	0
Pineville	14,261	75	67	8
Plaquemine	6,562	28	22	6
Pollock	479	5	4	1
Ponchatoula	7,478	32	26	6
Port Allen	4,940	17	16	1
Port Vincent	751	3	3	0
Rayne	8,088	22	21	1
Ruston	22,148	46	34	12
Scott	8,725	31	29	2
Shreveport	187,556	709	536	173
Sibley	1,144	2	2	0
Springhill	4,792	17	15	2
Sterlington	2,912	3	3	0
St. Gabriel	7,458	22	14	8
Sulphur	20,200	68	47	21
Tallulah	6,701	13	9	4
Thibodaux	14,587	65	53	12
Tickfaw	787	5	5	0
Vidalia	3,871	35	29	6
Walker	6,296	23	19	4
Welsh	3,254	16	15	1
Westlake	4,959	20	17	3
West Monroe	12,350	67	46	21
Westwego	8,415	38	38	0
White Castle	1,711	9	7	2
Winnfield	4,307	16	10	6
Youngsville	15,020	33	28	5
Zachary	18,009	45	42	3
MAINE				
Ashland	1,206	3	3	0
Auburn	23,214	60	53	7
Augusta	18,629	59	46	13
Baileyville	1,442	5	5	0
Bangor	31,872	94	78	16
Bar Harbor	7,682	28	20	8
Bath	8,309	23	19	4
Belfast	6,720	16	15	1
Berwick	7,860	13	12	1
Biddeford	21,545	78	55	23
Boothbay Harbor	2,204	8	7	1
Brewer	9,000	22	20	2
Bridgton	5,388	8	7	1
Brunswick	20,510	46	32	14
Bucksport	4,926	12	8	4
Buxton	8,345	14	7	7
Calais	2,973	8	8	0
Camden	4,823	13	11	2
Cape Elizabeth	9,352	15	14	1
Caribou	7,548	17	16	1
Carrabassett Valley	777	1	1	0
Clinton	3,329	4	4	0
Cumberland	8,295	13	11	2
Damariscotta	2,151	6	5	1
Dexter	3,671	6	6	0
Dixfield	2,465	4	4	0
Dover-Foxcroft	4,033	6	6	0
East Millinocket	2,919	3	3	0
Eastport	1,251	3	3	0
Eliot	6,817	9	8	1
Ellsworth	8,088	19	16	3
Fairfield	6,534	10	10	0
Falmouth	12,378	29	20	9
Farmington	7,603	11	10	1
Fort Fairfield	3,256	5	5	0
Fort Kent	3,816	8	4	4
Freeport	8,593	17	15	2
Fryeburg	3,398	5	5	0

Table 78. Full-Time Law Enforcement Employees, by Selected State and City, 2019—Continued

(Number.)

State/city	Population	Total law enforcement employees	Total officers	Total civilians
Gardiner	5,645	12	12	0
Gorham	17,818	25	23	2
Gouldsboro	1,745	2	2	0
Greenville	1,595	3	3	0
Hallowell	2,371	5	5	0
Hampden	7,352	12	11	1
Holden	3,081	4	4	0
Houlton	5,720	17	12	5
Islesboro	565	1	1	0
Jay	4,586	9	8	1
Kennebunk	11,622	27	24	3
Kennebunkport	3,660	19	14	5
Kittery	9,890	27	21	6
Lewiston	35,865	92	80	12
Limestone	2,200	3	3	0
Lincoln	4,886	9	8	1
Lisbon	8,975	20	14	6
Livermore Falls	3,134	6	6	0
Machias	2,055	3	3	0
Madawaska	3,662	7	6	1
Mechanic Falls	2,973	5	5	0
Mexico	2,605	5	5	0
Milbridge	1,255	2	2	0
Millinocket	4,241	7	7	0
Milo	2,270	3	3	0
Monmouth	4,131	4	4	0
Newport	3,269	6	6	0
North Berwick	4,731	9	8	1
Norway	4,979	9	8	1
Oakland	6,296	11	10	1
Ogunquit	931	12	11	1
Old Orchard Beach	8,946	24	22	2
Old Town	7,413	17	16	1
Orono	10,722	16	15	1
Oxford	4,100	8	7	1
Paris	5,112	8	7	1
Phippsburg	2,259	1	1	0
Pittsfield	3,999	7	6	1
Portland	66,458	207	150	57
Presque Isle	8,918	19	14	5
Rangeley	1,143	3	3	0
Richmond	3,440	4	4	0
Rockland	7,128	19	17	2
Rockport	3,378	6	6	0
Rumford	5,670	13	13	0
Sabattus	5,064	9	8	1
Saco	19,908	46	33	13
Sanford	21,233	44	40	4
Scarborough	20,542	61	40	21
Searsport	2,648	3	3	0
Skowhegan	8,214	16	15	1
South Berwick	7,564	9	8	1
South Portland	25,686	58	52	6
Southwest Harbor	1,795	9	5	4
Thomaston	2,767	2	2	0
Topsham	8,863	16	15	1
Van Buren	1,972	3	3	0
Veazie	1,814	4	4	0
Waldoboro	5,041	9	8	1
Washburn	1,533	2	2	0
Waterville	16,765	37	29	8
Wells	10,670	32	23	9
Westbrook	19,166	43	37	6
Wilton	3,924	6	6	0
Windham	18,627	30	27	3
Winslow	7,598	12	11	1
Winthrop	5,979	12	8	4
Wiscasset	3,697	5	4	1
Yarmouth	8,540	15	14	1
York	13,231	38	27	11
MARYLAND				
Aberdeen	16,194	51	39	12
Annapolis	39,277	148	118	30
Baltimore	597,239	2,940	2,465	475
Baltimore City Sheriff		187	122	65
Bel Air	10,031	39	29	10
Berlin	4,862	16	13	3
Berwyn Heights	3,278	10	9	1
Bladensburg	9,476	35	24	11
Boonsboro	3,596	4	3	1
Bowie	59,093	81	61	20
Brentwood	3,494	5	4	1
Brunswick	6,426	16	16	0
Cambridge	12,264	42	38	4

Table 78. Full-Time Law Enforcement Employees, by Selected State and City, 2019—Continued

(Number.)

State/city	Population	Total law enforcement employees	Total officers	Total civilians
Capitol Heights	4,551	15	13	2
Centreville	4,882	13	13	0
Chestertown	5,027	13	12	1
Cheverly	6,482	12	10	2
Chevy Chase Village	2,073	16	10	6
Colmar Manor	1,468	3	2	1
Cottage City	1,363	4	4	0
Crisfield	2,554	12	9	3
Cumberland	19,321	56	49	7
Delmar	3,248	14	13	1
Denton	4,504	15	14	1
District Heights	6,015	8	7	1
Easton	16,523	51	43	8
Edmonston	1,499	4	3	1
Elkton	15,662	46	40	6
Fairmount Heights	1,533	2	2	0
Federalsburg	2,652	9	8	1
Forest Heights	2,583	8	7	1
Frederick	73,030	189	140	49
Frostburg	8,510	20	17	3
Fruitland	5,346	22	20	2
Glenarden	6,234	19	17	2
Greenbelt	23,417	63	43	20
Greensboro	1,874	4	4	0
Hagerstown	40,258	101	81	20
Hampstead	6,397	10	9	1
Hancock	1,539	3	2	1
Havre de Grace	13,890	44	34	10
Hurlock	2,013	8	7	1
Hyattsville	18,331	53	38	15
Landover Hills	1,656	4	3	1
La Plata	9,538	20	18	2
Laurel	25,814	83	62	21
Luke	61	1	1	0
Manchester	4,858	6	6	0
Morningside	1,296	8	7	1
Mount Airy	9,472	12	10	2
Mount Rainier	8,143	18	16	2
New Carrollton	13,036	29	22	7
North East	3,639	11	10	1
Oakland	1,816	2	2	0
Ocean City	6,905	137	105	32
Ocean Pines	12,264	16	12	4
Oxford	598	3	3	0
Perryville	4,431	14	12	2
Pocomoke City	4,025	24	17	7
Princess Anne	3,549	14	12	2
Ridgely	1,652	5	5	0
Rising Sun	2,799	6	6	0
Riverdale Park	7,258	27	20	7
Rock Hall	1,264	3	3	0
Salisbury	33,132	108	85	23
Seat Pleasant	4,803	24	20	4
Smithsburg	2,967	5	4	1
Snow Hill	2,029	6	6	0
St. Michaels	1,025	10	9	1
Sykesville	3,959	7	6	1
Takoma Park	17,893	46	34	12
Taneytown	6,824	22	12	10
Thurmont	6,824	14	11	3
University Park	2,651	9	8	1
Upper Marlboro	675	3	3	0
Westminster	18,664	55	42	13
MASSACHUSETTS				
Abington	16,448	29	27	2
Acton	23,780	54	43	11
Acushnet	10,533	24	21	3
Agawam	28,736	67	54	13
Amesbury	17,595	37	30	7
Amherst	39,603	64	46	18
Andover	36,547	73	54	19
Aquinnah	328	4	4	0
Arlington	45,614	78	64	14
Ashburnham	6,330	17	12	5
Ashby	3,228	11	6	5
Ashfield	1,734	1	1	0
Ashland	17,742	34	27	7
Attleboro	44,959	86	73	13
Auburn	16,724	47	36	11
Avon	4,504	19	15	4
Ayer	8,192	32	20	12
Barnstable	44,032	132	106	26
Barre	5,573	10	9	1
Becket	1,724	4	4	0

Table 78. Full-Time Law Enforcement Employees, by Selected State and City, 2019—Continued

(Number.)

State/city	Population	Total law enforcement employees	Total officers	Total civilians
Bedford	14,193	37	29	8
Belchertown	15,195	26	20	6
Bellingham	17,143	37	30	7
Berkley	6,799	13	13	0
Berlin	3,241	11	10	1
Bernardston	2,113	3	3	0
Beverly	42,317	69	66	3
Billerica	43,882	70	65	5
Blackstone	9,294	20	16	4
Bolton	5,393	13	12	1
Boston	698,941	2,922	2,143	779
Bourne	19,734	50	41	9
Boxborough	6,540	19	12	7
Boxford	8,352	13	13	0
Boylston	4,694	14	10	4
Braintree	37,145	100	84	16
Brewster	9,725	29	24	5
Brockton	95,287	218	195	23
Brookfield	3,440	5	5	0
Brookline	58,928	158	128	30
Buckland	1,872	2	2	0
Burlington	29,082	71	64	7
Cambridge	119,908	301	267	34
Canton	23,706	44	44	0
Carlisle	5,255	15	10	5
Carver	11,721	22	17	5
Chatham	6,117	27	21	6
Chelmsford	35,218	67	53	14
Chelsea	40,496	115	107	8
Cheshire	3,133	1	1	0
Chicopee	55,293	157	130	27
Clinton	13,964	38	28	10
Cohasset	8,609	20	19	1
Concord	19,253	46	36	10
Dalton	6,546	12	10	2
Danvers	27,664	56	44	12
Dartmouth	34,035	83	68	15
Dedham	25,203	59	56	3
Deerfield	5,032	11	10	1
Dennis	13,738	55	45	10
Dighton	7,935	18	13	5
Douglas	8,946	19	15	4
Dover	6,118	17	16	1
Dracut	31,786	46	41	5
Dudley	11,754	14	13	1
Dunstable	3,405	9	8	1
East Bridgewater	14,472	28	22	6
Eastham	4,823	23	17	6
Easthampton	15,979	34	28	6
East Longmeadow	16,269	29	27	2
Easton	25,079	46	37	9
Edgartown	4,362	21	19	2
Egremont	1,206	4	4	0
Erving	1,771	6	6	0
Essex	3,795	9	8	1
Everett	47,195	139	123	16
Fairhaven	15,996	38	32	6
Fall River	89,066	286	227	59
Falmouth	30,717	58	54	4
Fitchburg	40,621	95	77	18
Foxborough	17,631	39	36	3
Framingham	73,127	143	125	18
Franklin	33,149	54	52	2
Freetown	9,388	24	19	5
Gardner	20,628	46	33	13
Georgetown	8,777	18	13	5
Gill	1,490	2	2	0
Gloucester	30,362	66	60	6
Goshen	1,065	2	2	0
Grafton	18,880	24	20	4
Granby	6,360	15	11	4
Great Barrington	6,822	18	17	1
Greenfield	17,464	46	33	13
Groton	11,388	27	20	7
Groveland	6,846	13	11	2
Hadley	5,358	20	16	4
Halifax	7,874	13	12	1
Hamilton	8,075	18	13	5
Hampden	5,199	16	11	5
Hanson	10,876	25	20	5
Hardwick	3,039	5	5	0
Harwich	12,028	42	35	7
Haverhill	63,935	108	90	18
Hingham	23,960	49	47	2
Holbrook	10,990	22	21	1

Table 78. Full-Time Law Enforcement Employees, by Selected State and City, 2019—Continued

(Number.)

State/city	Population	Total law enforcement employees	Total officers	Total civilians
Holland	2,484	2	2	0
Holliston	14,996	29	23	6
Holyoke	40,178	130	112	18
Hopedale	5,929	16	12	4
Hopkinton	18,585	34	24	10
Hudson	19,910	42	32	10
Hull	10,402	29	27	2
Ipswich	14,095	29	25	4
Kingston	13,758	33	25	8
Lakeville	11,419	22	19	3
Lancaster	8,136	12	11	1
Lanesboro	2,950	6	6	0
Lawrence	80,243	162	141	21
Leicester	11,368	21	20	1
Lenox	4,951	9	9	0
Leominster	41,631	92	75	17
Lexington	33,824	63	46	17
Lincoln	6,798	18	13	5
Littleton	10,334	28	20	8
Longmeadow	15,737	33	27	6
Lowell	111,423	342	244	98
Ludlow	21,395	49	38	11
Lunenburg	11,781	17	16	1
Lynn	94,449	187	168	19
Lynnfield	13,130	26	21	5
Malden	60,746	111	100	11
Mansfield	23,987	48	38	10
Marblehead	20,574	42	31	11
Marion	5,132	15	15	0
Marlborough	39,673	75	66	9
Marshfield	25,794	43	40	3
Mashpee	14,094	44	35	9
Mattapoisett	6,372	20	20	0
Maynard	10,654	27	21	6
Medfield	12,913	20	14	6
Medford	57,484	122	102	20
Medway	13,405	24	23	1
Melrose	28,120	49	48	1
Mendon	6,176	19	14	5
Methuen	50,727	116	96	20
Middleboro	25,183	49	42	7
Middleton	10,113	18	16	2
Millbury	13,837	25	21	4
Millis	8,252	18	16	2
Millville	3,249	7	6	1
Montague	8,298	21	17	4
Nahant	3,511	13	12	1
Natick	36,358	72	54	18
Needham	31,275	56	49	7
New Bedford	94,613	301	243	58
Newton	88,658	194	149	45
Norfolk	11,992	23	21	2
Northampton	28,735	70	63	7
North Andover	31,428	49	37	12
North Attleboro	29,202	63	48	15
Northborough	15,075	29	22	7
Northbridge	16,732	27	20	7
North Reading	15,687	34	31	3
Norton	19,894	35	34	1
Norwell	11,105	25	22	3
Norwood	29,185	72	61	11
Orange	7,643	14	13	1
Orleans	5,742	27	21	6
Oxford	13,973	27	21	6
Palmer	12,258	25	21	4
Paxton	4,944	19	15	4
Peabody	53,104	112	92	20
Pelham	1,322	2	2	0
Pembroke	18,378	34	32	2
Pepperell	12,146	17	16	1
Pittsfield	42,268	110	88	22
Plymouth	60,870	144	128	16
Plympton	2,980	8	8	0
Princeton	3,459	7	6	1
Provincetown	2,939	27	19	8
Quincy	94,113	240	209	31
Randolph	34,385	64	58	6
Raynham	14,322	36	29	7
Reading	25,305	62	45	17
Rehoboth	12,252	33	27	6
Revere	53,654	113	106	7
Rockport	7,280	21	17	4
Salem	43,443	104	94	10
Sandwich	20,016	35	35	0
Saugus	28,378	72	59	13

Table 78. Full-Time Law Enforcement Employees, by Selected State and City, 2019—Continued

(Number.)

State/city	Population	Total law enforcement employees	Total officers	Total civilians
Scituate	18,774	38	35	3
Sharon	18,973	36	31	5
Sherborn	4,334	13	12	1
Somerset	18,036	36	31	5
Somerville	81,668	159	127	32
Southborough	10,140	24	19	5
Southbridge	16,826	45	34	11
Southwick	9,772	23	18	5
Spencer	11,911	23	18	5
Springfield	154,306	552	489	63
Stockbridge	1,898	8	7	1
Stoneham	22,732	45	39	6
Stoughton	28,961	72	60	12
Stow	7,234	15	11	4
Sturbridge	9,611	26	19	7
Sudbury	19,727	41	30	11
Sunderland	3,656	6	5	1
Sutton	9,551	19	14	5
Swampscott	15,296	31	30	1
Swansea	16,681	40	34	6
Taunton	57,028	121	115	6
Templeton	8,109	13	8	5
Tewksbury	31,424	75	62	13
Topsfield	6,644	14	13	1
Townsend	9,546	15	14	1
Truro	1,984	18	13	5
Uxbridge	14,066	23	18	5
Wakefield	27,178	44	43	1
Walpole	25,150	54	43	11
Waltham	62,737	176	144	32
Wareham	22,592	56	45	11
Watertown	36,189	83	70	13
Wayland	13,891	31	24	7
Wellesley	29,651	55	41	14
Wellfleet	2,705	20	15	5
Wenham	5,295	11	10	1
Westborough	19,155	35	33	2
West Brookfield	3,767	6	6	0
Westfield	41,507	94	88	6
Westford	24,403	50	46	4
Westminster	7,902	15	13	2
West Newbury	4,712	15	10	5
Weston	12,138	35	25	10
Westport	15,920	33	30	3
West Springfield	28,628	95	85	10
West Tisbury	2,911	10	9	1
Westwood	16,199	43	33	10
Weymouth	57,776	119	99	20
Whitman	15,134	27	26	1
Wilbraham	14,730	28	27	1
Williamsburg	2,489	1	1	0
Williamstown	8,021	13	12	1
Wilmington	23,915	51	48	3
Winchendon	10,897	20	15	5
Winchester	22,850	46	36	10
Winthrop	18,692	35	34	1
Woburn	40,251	84	80	4
Worcester	184,945	506	456	50
Wrentham	11,989	22	21	1
Yarmouth	23,076	74	60	14
MICHIGAN				
Adrian	20,334	33	31	2
Adrian Township	6,239	2	2	0
Akron	374	1	1	0
Albion	8,462	17	16	1
Allegan	5,038	9	8	1
Allen Park	26,945	45	42	3
Alma	8,866	14	13	1
Almont	2,814	7	7	0
Alpena	9,901	20	18	2
Ann Arbor	122,893	153	124	29
Argentine Township	6,506	4	4	0
Armada	1,730	2	2	0
Auburn Hills	24,393	54	49	5
Au Gres	834	1	1	0
Bad Axe	2,923	8	7	1
Bangor	1,823	5	5	0
Baraga	1,949	2	2	0
Baroda-Lake Township	3,859	4	4	0
Barry Township	3,510	3	3	0
Bath Township	13,131	13	12	1
Battle Creek	60,607	132	111	21
Bay City	32,793	56	51	5
Beaverton	1,176	3	3	0

Table 78. Full-Time Law Enforcement Employees, by Selected State and City, 2019—Continued

(Number.)

State/city	Population	Total law enforcement employees	Total officers	Total civilians
Belding	5,747	8	8	0
Bellaire	1,067	2	2	0
Belleville	3,873	10	8	2
Bellevue	1,291	2	2	0
Benton Harbor	9,801	25	20	5
Benton Township	14,372	26	22	4
Berkley	15,482	35	28	7
Berrien Springs-Oronoko Township	8,940	9	8	1
Beverly Hills	10,429	29	25	4
Big Rapids	10,389	17	17	0
Birch Run	1,462	6	5	1
Birmingham	21,479	43	32	11
Blackman Township	37,002	41	39	2
Blissfield	3,250	6	6	0
Bloomfield Hills	4,027	26	23	3
Bloomfield Township	42,326	86	68	18
Boyne City	3,752	7	6	1
Breckenridge	1,261	1	1	0
Bridgeport Township	9,778	9	8	1
Bridgman	2,224	5	5	0
Brighton	7,684	18	15	3
Bronson	2,308	4	4	0
Brown City	1,240	2	2	0
Brownstown Township	32,083	39	31	8
Buchanan	4,274	10	9	1
Buena Vista Township	8,095	14	13	1
Burton	28,496	38	36	2
Cadillac	10,466	17	15	2
Calumet	691	1	1	0
Cambridge Township	5,657	4	4	0
Canton Township	93,406	131	91	40
Capac	1,822	2	2	0
Carleton	2,356	4	3	1
Caro	3,969	7	7	0
Carrollton Township	5,626	6	6	0
Carson City	1,117	2	2	0
Caseville	731	2	2	0
Caspian-Gaastra	1,165	1	1	0
Cass City	2,268	4	4	0
Cassopolis	1,695	5	5	0
Center Line	8,232	22	18	4
Central Lake	938	1	1	0
Charlevoix	2,498	8	7	1
Charlotte	9,088	15	14	1
Cheboygan	4,695	9	9	0
Chelsea	5,543	14	10	4
Chesterfield Township	46,774	56	42	14
Chikaming Township	3,108	6	5	1
Chocolay Township	5,931	5	4	1
Clare	3,061	8	8	0
Clawson	11,948	18	17	1
Clayton Township	7,110	7	6	1
Clay Township	8,844	23	18	5
Clinton	2,274	4	4	0
Clinton Township	101,308	104	95	9
Clio	2,483	4	4	0
Coldwater	12,098	20	18	2
Coleman	1,188	2	2	0
Coloma Township	6,362	11	8	3
Colon	1,159	3	3	0
Columbia Township	7,359	7	7	0
Constantine	2,105	6	5	1
Corunna	3,337	3	3	0
Covert Township	2,853	7	7	0
Croswell	2,262	6	6	0
Crystal Falls	1,359	2	2	0
Davison	4,874	7	6	1
Davison Township	19,207	21	19	2
Dearborn	93,902	234	187	47
Dearborn Heights	55,368	98	79	19
Decatur	1,731	5	5	0
Denton Township	5,379	4	4	0
Detroit	663,502	3,126	2,517	609
DeWitt	4,790	7	6	1
DeWitt Township	15,613	16	15	1
Dowagiac	5,719	15	14	1
Dryden Township	4,734	4	4	0
Dundee	4,486	3	3	0
Durand	3,825	29	12	17
East Grand Rapids	12,040	29	27	2
East Jordan	2,351	4	4	0
East Lansing	47,913	64	52	12
Eastpointe	32,340	46	42	4
Eaton Rapids	5,216	10	9	1
Eau Claire	599	1	1	0

Table 78. Full-Time Law Enforcement Employees, by Selected State and City, 2019—Continued

(Number.)

State/city	Population	Total law enforcement employees	Total officers	Total civilians
Ecorse	9,601	18	16	2
Elk Rapids	1,618	5	5	0
Emmett Township	11,668	16	14	2
Erie Township	4,342	3	3	0
Escanaba	12,129	46	32	14
Essexville	3,296	4	3	1
Evart	1,865	4	3	1
Fair Haven Township	1,038	1	1	0
Farmington	10,587	24	23	1
Farmington Hills	81,262	138	106	32
Fennville	1,421	1	1	0
Fenton	11,281	22	13	9
Ferndale	20,097	50	42	8
Flat Rock	10,024	18	18	0
Flint	95,212	117	94	23
Flint Township	30,319	51	43	8
Flushing	7,860	9	9	0
Flushing Township	10,174	6	6	0
Forsyth Township	6,197	10	8	2
Fowlerville	2,869	7	6	1
Frankenmuth	5,458	7	7	0
Frankfort	1,289	4	4	0
Franklin	3,268	10	10	0
Fraser	14,578	44	34	10
Fremont	4,103	8	7	1
Fruitport Township	14,346	10	10	0
Gaines Township	6,080	1	1	0
Galesburg	2,082	4	4	0
Garden City	26,420	37	34	3
Garfield Township	838	1	1	0
Gaylord	3,709	10	9	1
Genesee Township	20,410	18	16	2
Gerrish Township	2,922	5	5	0
Gibraltar	4,467	10	9	1
Gladstone	4,699	11	10	1
Gladwin	2,880	5	5	0
Grand Beach	281	2	2	0
Grand Blanc	7,865	18	15	3
Grand Blanc Township	36,523	49	42	7
Grand Haven	11,155	36	33	3
Grand Ledge	7,862	14	14	0
Grand Rapids	201,799	368	299	69
Grandville	16,021	27	25	2
Grant	892	1	1	0
Grayling	1,833	8	8	0
Green Oak Township	19,075	17	15	2
Greenville	8,447	19	17	2
Grosse Ile Township	10,135	24	17	7
Grosse Pointe	5,141	27	22	5
Grosse Pointe Farms	9,108	37	32	5
Grosse Pointe Park	11,041	37	32	5
Grosse Pointe Shores	2,836	17	17	0
Grosse Pointe Woods	15,350	33	27	6
Hamburg Township	21,755	21	18	3
Hampton Township	9,428	9	9	0
Hamtramck	21,633	35	30	5
Hancock	4,533	8	8	0
Harbor Beach	1,584	4	4	0
Harbor Springs	1,208	9	9	0
Harper Woods	13,746	33	30	3
Hart	2,089	5	5	0
Hartford	2,589	5	5	0
Hastings	7,313	17	15	2
Hazel Park	16,478	39	34	5
Hesperia	941	2	2	0
Highland Park	10,703	8	6	2
Hillsdale	8,020	15	13	2
Holland	33,356	66	57	9
Holly	6,185	8	8	0
Home Township	1,373	1	1	0
Hopkins	611	1	1	0
Houghton	8,029	11	10	1
Howell	9,637	20	18	2
Hudson	2,207	2	2	0
Huntington Woods	6,321	18	17	1
Huron Township	16,089	26	20	6
Imlay City	3,575	11	8	3
Inkster	24,268	37	25	12
Ionia	10,907	17	15	2
Iron Mountain	7,320	12	12	0
Iron River	2,816	4	4	0
Ironwood	4,883	10	10	0
Ishpeming	6,426	12	11	1
Ishpeming Township	3,528	1	1	0
Jackson	32,503	56	44	12

Table 78. Full-Time Law Enforcement Employees, by Selected State and City, 2019—Continued

(Number.)

State/city	Population	Total law enforcement employees	Total officers	Total civilians
Jonesville	2,204	3	3	0
Kalamazoo	76,827	262	240	22
Kalamazoo Township	24,613	40	33	7
Kalkaska	2,086	3	3	0
Keego Harbor	3,462	9	9	0
Kentwood	52,274	79	68	11
Kingsford	4,950	19	19	0
Kingston	409	1	1	0
Kinross Township	7,288	2	2	0
Laingsburg	1,281	1	1	0
Lake Angelus	309	1	1	0
Lake Linden	962	1	1	0
Lake Odessa	2,036	4	4	0
Lake Orion	3,177	5	4	1
Lakeview	1,007	2	2	0
L'Anse	1,855	4	4	0
Lansing	118,953	246	200	46
Lansing Township	8,294	15	14	1
Lapeer	8,597	20	19	1
Lathrup Village	4,124	11	10	1
Laurium	1,912	4	4	0
Lawton	1,799	5	5	0
Lennon	482	1	1	0
Leslie	1,909	3	3	0
Lexington	1,099	3	3	0
Lincoln Park	36,336	54	47	7
Lincoln Township	14,615	11	10	1
Linden	3,908	5	5	0
Litchfield	1,333	2	2	0
Livonia	93,644	160	124	36
Lowell	4,198	6	5	1
Ludington	8,144	15	14	1
Luna Pier	1,407	2	2	0
Mackinac Island	468	5	5	0
Mackinaw City	797	7	7	0
Madison Heights	30,081	56	45	11
Madison Township	8,287	5	5	0
Mancelona	1,364	1	1	0
Manistee	6,103	39	17	22
Manistique	2,915	8	8	0
Manton	1,544	1	1	0
Marenisco Township	1,434	1	1	0
Marine City	4,061	5	4	1
Marlette	1,756	4	4	0
Marquette	20,599	39	34	5
Marshall	6,997	14	14	0
Marysville	9,656	16	14	2
Mason	8,483	13	12	1
Mattawan	1,970	7	7	0
Mayville	882	1	1	0
Melvindale	10,264	24	22	2
Memphis	1,184	1	1	0
Mendon	854	2	2	0
Menominee	8,052	17	16	1
Meridian Township	43,790	42	38	4
Metamora Township	4,287	4	4	0
Metro Police Authority of Genesee County	19,931	27	24	3
Michiana	181	3	3	0
Midland	41,791	52	50	2
Milan	6,106	9	9	0
Milford	16,984	21	19	2
Millington	995	2	2	0
Monroe	19,600	43	38	5
Montague	2,359	5	5	0
Montrose Township	7,447	9	8	1
Morenci	2,146	2	2	0
Morrice	894	2	2	0
Mount Morris	2,834	4	4	0
Mount Morris Township	20,274	31	28	3
Mount Pleasant	25,315	34	28	6
Munising	2,177	4	4	0
Muskegon	37,178	76	68	8
Muskegon Heights	10,717	25	22	3
Muskegon Township	17,937	15	14	1
Napoleon Township	6,757	5	5	0
Nashville	1,678	4	4	0
Negaunee	4,544	9	9	0
Newaygo	2,068	7	7	0
New Baltimore	12,444	18	17	1
New Buffalo	1,877	5	5	0
New Era	446	1	1	0
Niles	11,106	26	17	9
Northfield Township	8,788	12	10	2
North Muskegon	3,797	9	8	1

Table 78. Full-Time Law Enforcement Employees, by Selected State and City, 2019—Continued

(Number.)

State/city	Population	Total law enforcement employees	Total officers	Total civilians
Northville	5,971	13	12	1
Northville Township	29,170	45	33	12
Norton Shores	24,702	33	31	2
Norway	2,756	6	6	0
Novi	61,699	93	70	23
Oak Park	29,654	61	49	12
Olivet	1,857	2	2	0
Ontwa Township-Edwardsburg	6,553	7	7	0
Orchard Lake	2,483	9	8	1
Oscoda Township	6,746	12	11	1
Otsego	4,007	7	6	1
Ovid	1,611	2	2	0
Owosso	14,399	18	17	1
Oxford	3,574	5	5	0
Paw Paw	3,370	9	8	1
Pentwater	853	3	3	0
Perry	2,075	4	4	0
Petoskey	5,747	19	19	0
Pigeon	1,123	1	1	0
Pinckney	2,410	6	6	0
Pinconning	1,238	1	1	0
Pittsfield Township	39,417	41	40	1
Plainwell	3,804	9	8	1
Pleasant Ridge	2,465	6	6	0
Plymouth	9,175	17	16	1
Plymouth Township	27,020	43	28	15
Portage	49,583	70	57	13
Port Austin	620	1	1	0
Port Huron	28,783	69	53	16
Portland	3,932	6	6	0
Potterville	2,712	2	2	0
Prairieville Township	3,525	2	2	0
Quincy	1,616	3	3	0
Raisin Township	7,760	5	5	0
Reading	1,042	1	1	0
Redford Township	46,742	68	60	8
Reed City	2,377	4	4	0
Reese	1,364	2	2	0
Richfield Township, Genesee County	8,358	11	9	2
Richfield Township, Roscommon County	3,630	6	5	1
Richland	806	3	3	0
Richland Township, Saginaw County	3,925	3	3	0
Richmond	5,904	11	9	2
River Rouge	7,404	20	18	2
Riverview	12,027	25	24	1
Rochester	13,429	30	22	8
Rockford	6,377	10	9	1
Rockwood	3,165	6	6	0
Rogers City	2,663	6	6	0
Romeo	3,608	11	8	3
Romulus	23,507	51	39	12
Roosevelt Park	3,793	5	5	0
Roseville	47,381	72	69	3
Royal Oak	59,742	111	78	33
Saginaw	47,954	61	53	8
Saginaw Township	39,022	48	43	5
Saline	9,431	18	14	4
Sandusky	2,508	6	5	1
Sault Ste. Marie	13,478	28	24	4
Schoolcraft	1,559	3	3	0
Scottville	1,210	2	2	0
Sebewaing	1,629	2	2	0
Shelby	2,032	2	2	0
Shelby Township	80,806	92	73	19
Shepherd	1,489	2	2	0
Somerset Township	4,541	3	3	0
Southfield	73,335	148	123	25
Southgate	28,979	45	40	5
South Haven	4,326	26	20	6
South Lyon	11,896	16	15	1
South Rockwood	1,670	2	2	0
Sparta	4,391	5	5	0
Spring Arbor Township	8,009	2	2	0
Springport Township	2,148	2	2	0
Stanton	1,435	1	1	0
St. Charles	1,891	2	2	0
St. Clair	5,286	7	7	0
St. Clair Shores	59,365	87	82	5
Sterling Heights	133,377	174	152	22
St. Ignace	2,309	4	4	0
St. Johns	7,938	11	10	1
St. Joseph	8,355	23	22	1
St. Joseph Township	9,738	12	11	1
St. Louis	7,104	8	6	2
Stockbridge	1,257	3	3	0

Table 78. Full-Time Law Enforcement Employees, by Selected State and City, 2019—Continued

(Number.)

State/city	Population	Total law enforcement employees	Total officers	Total civilians
Sturgis	10,779	24	19	5
Sumpter Township	9,407	18	16	2
Sylvan Lake	1,864	5	5	0
Tawas	4,471	5	4	1
Taylor	60,923	90	74	16
Tecumseh	8,382	15	14	1
Thomas Township	11,438	9	8	1
Three Rivers	7,643	16	15	1
Tittabawassee Township	9,863	7	6	1
Traverse City	15,772	31	29	2
Trenton	18,147	35	34	1
Troy	84,688	154	107	47
Tuscarora Township	2,934	9	8	1
Ubly	785	1	1	0
Unadilla Township	3,425	3	3	0
Union City	1,566	5	5	0
Utica	5,195	18	14	4
Van Buren Township	28,294	55	40	15
Vassar	2,534	5	5	0
Vernon	770	1	1	0
Vicksburg	3,490	6	6	0
Walker	25,051	42	38	4
Walled Lake	7,184	8	8	0
Warren	134,653	241	203	38
Waterford Township	73,105	74	58	16
Watersmeet Township	1,359	1	1	0
Watervliet	1,652	3	3	0
Wayland	4,272	7	6	1
Wayne	16,816	22	21	1
West Bloomfield Township	66,067	107	78	29
West Branch	2,048	6	5	1
Westland	81,444	105	81	24
White Cloud	1,395	2	2	0
Whitehall	2,785	8	8	0
White Lake Township	31,556	38	28	10
White Pigeon	1,521	4	4	0
Williamston	3,972	7	6	1
Wixom	14,074	24	21	3
Wolverine Lake	4,825	7	7	0
Woodhaven	12,438	31	30	1
Wyandotte	24,829	46	35	11
Wyoming	76,295	101	87	14
Yale	1,875	3	3	0
Ypsilanti	21,178	33	28	5
Zeeland	5,572	13	12	1
Zilwaukee	1,523	1	1	0
MINNESOTA				
Adrian	1,220	2	2	0
Aitkin	1,985	7	6	1
Akeley	442	1	1	0
Albany	2,752	5	4	1
Albert Lea	17,597	31	28	3
Alexandria	13,914	29	25	4
Annandale	3,415	6	5	1
Anoka	17,591	39	29	10
Appleton	1,322	3	3	0
Apple Valley	54,779	61	53	8
Arlington	2,163	4	4	0
Atwater	1,110	1	1	0
Audubon	527	1	1	0
Austin	25,224	37	34	3
Avon	1,597	4	3	1
Babbitt	1,498	5	5	0
Bagley	1,405	3	3	0
Barnesville	2,608	5	5	0
Battle Lake	938	2	2	0
Baxter	8,401	16	15	1
Bayport	3,834	5	5	0
Becker	4,957	8	7	1
Belgrade/Brooten	1,524	3	3	0
Belle Plaine	7,232	12	10	2
Bemidji	15,550	35	32	3
Benson	3,050	8	7	1
Big Lake	11,236	15	13	2
Blackduck	838	2	2	0
Blaine	66,260	84	67	17
Blooming Prairie	1,956	3	3	0
Bloomington	85,902	151	119	32
Blue Earth	3,113	5	5	0
Bovey	785	2	2	0
Braham	1,791	5	5	0
Brainerd	13,449	31	25	6
Breckenridge	3,175	8	8	0
Breezy Point	2,418	7	6	1

Table 78. Full-Time Law Enforcement Employees, by Selected State and City, 2019—Continued

(Number.)

State/city	Population	Total law enforcement employees	Total officers	Total civilians
Breitung Township	612	2	2	0
Brooklyn Center	31,000	61	49	12
Brooklyn Park	81,211	140	106	34
Brownton	723	1	1	0
Buffalo	16,421	21	17	4
Buffalo Lake	680	2	2	0
Burnsville	61,306	81	71	10
Caledonia	2,718	7	6	1
Callaway	231	1	1	0
Cambridge	9,008	16	15	1
Canby	1,674	3	3	0
Cannon Falls	4,063	10	8	2
Centennial Lakes	11,025	18	16	2
Champlin	25,636	31	26	5
Chaska	27,143	29	23	6
Chisholm	4,875	11	10	1
Clara City	1,282	2	2	0
Clearbrook	520	1	1	0
Cloquet	12,009	23	21	2
Cold Spring/Richmond	5,656	11	10	1
Coleraine	1,973	2	2	0
Columbia Heights	20,632	31	25	6
Coon Rapids	62,652	76	66	10
Corcoran	6,195	10	9	1
Cottage Grove	37,534	48	42	6
Crookston	7,794	18	16	2
Crosby	2,335	7	7	0
Crosslake	2,294	5	5	0
Crystal	23,184	40	34	6
Danube	457	1	1	0
Dawson/Boyd	1,547	3	3	0
Dayton	6,542	9	8	1
Deephaven	3,980	8	7	1
Deer River	933	4	4	0
Detroit Lakes	9,362	19	17	2
Dilworth	4,491	6	5	1
Duluth	85,846	180	148	32
Dundas	1,623	2	2	0
Eagan	66,824	87	72	15
Eagle Lake	3,195	3	3	0
East Grand Forks	8,597	25	23	2
East Range	3,590	8	8	0
Eden Prairie	64,777	91	68	23
Eden Valley	1,035	1	1	0
Edina	53,076	79	55	24
Elko New Market	4,783	5	5	0
Elk River	25,081	42	34	8
Elmore	617	1	1	0
Ely	3,344	8	7	1
Eveleth	3,582	12	11	1
Fairfax	1,127	2	2	0
Fairmont	10,023	20	18	2
Faribault	23,913	41	33	8
Farmington	23,335	27	24	3
Fergus Falls	13,900	29	24	5
Floodwood	523	3	2	1
Foley	2,671	4	4	0
Forest Lake	20,457	28	25	3
Frazee	1,397	3	3	0
Fridley	27,805	49	44	5
Fulda	1,209	2	2	0
Gaylord	2,236	4	4	0
Gilbert	1,788	7	6	1
Glencoe	5,444	9	8	1
Glenwood	2,593	6	5	1
Golden Valley	21,934	41	31	10
Goodhue	1,178	2	2	0
Goodview	4,149	5	4	1
Grand Rapids	11,267	23	20	3
Granite Falls	2,700	7	6	1
Hallock	899	1	1	0
Hastings	22,774	31	27	4
Hawley	2,223	5	5	0
Hector	1,045	2	2	0
Henning	814	2	2	0
Hermantown	9,770	18	15	3
Heron Lake	647	1	1	0
Hibbing	15,895	30	27	3
Hill City	585	1	1	0
Hokah	543	1	1	0
Hopkins	18,735	37	29	8
Houston	963	2	2	0
Howard Lake	2,091	3	3	0
Hutchinson	13,960	36	23	13
International Falls	5,871	12	12	0

Table 78. Full-Time Law Enforcement Employees, by Selected State and City, 2019—Continued

(Number.)

State/city	Population	Total law enforcement employees	Total officers	Total civilians
Inver Grove Heights	35,668	46	41	5
Isanti	5,985	8	7	1
Isle	803	4	4	0
Janesville	2,261	4	4	0
Jordan	6,384	13	11	2
Kasson	6,514	10	9	1
Keewatin	1,008	3	3	0
Kenyon	1,805	3	3	0
Kimball	797	1	1	0
La Crescent	4,981	9	8	1
Lake City	5,140	11	10	1
Lake Crystal	2,496	3	3	0
Lakefield	1,610	3	3	0
Lake Park	801	2	2	0
Lakes Area	9,833	15	13	2
Lake Shore	1,056	2	2	0
Lakeville	67,206	68	58	10
Lamberton	766	1	1	0
Le Center	2,482	3	3	0
Lester Prairie	1,722	3	3	0
Le Sueur	4,016	8	7	1
Lewiston	1,558	2	2	0
Lino Lakes	21,925	30	27	3
Litchfield	6,632	12	11	1
Little Falls	8,669	16	14	2
Long Prairie	3,297	6	6	0
Lonsdale	4,141	8	7	1
Madelia	2,266	4	4	0
Madison Lake	1,198	2	2	0
Mankato	42,955	61	53	8
Maple Grove	73,170	83	68	15
Mapleton	2,203	3	3	0
Maplewood	41,341	58	53	5
Marshall	13,511	25	22	3
Medina	6,852	11	10	1
Melrose	3,642	6	5	1
Menahga	1,326	3	3	0
Mendota Heights	11,373	22	21	1
Milaca	2,909	7	6	1
Minneapolis	431,016	1,041	861	180
Minneota	1,360	1	1	0
Minnesota Lake	640	1	1	0
Minnetonka	54,497	65	57	8
Minnetrista	10,527	17	13	4
Montevideo	5,071	12	11	1
Montgomery	2,995	8	7	1
Moorhead	43,847	73	58	15
Moose Lake	2,821	6	5	1
Morris	5,360	10	8	2
Motley	650	2	2	0
Mounds View	13,307	24	22	2
Mountain Lake	2,047	4	4	0
Nashwauk	947	4	4	0
New Brighton	23,058	36	30	6
New Hope	21,147	43	34	9
New Prague	8,326	12	10	2
New Richland	1,188	2	2	0
New Ulm	13,205	23	21	2
New York Mills	1,228	3	3	0
Nisswa	2,066	6	6	0
North Branch	10,641	13	11	2
Northfield	20,707	29	24	5
North Mankato	13,977	14	13	1
North St. Paul	12,595	18	16	2
Oakdale	28,097	40	33	7
Oak Park Heights	4,972	11	10	1
Olivia	2,328	5	5	0
Onamia	861	3	3	0
Orono	20,349	31	27	4
Ortonville	1,774	4	4	0
Osakis	1,750	3	3	0
Osseo	2,801	7	6	1
Owatonna	25,792	39	35	4
Parkers Prairie	1,002	2	2	0
Park Rapids	4,262	12	11	1
Paynesville	2,510	5	5	0
Pelican Rapids	2,507	5	5	0
Pequot Lakes	2,328	7	6	1
Perham	3,625	7	6	1
Pierz	1,364	2	2	0
Pike Bay	1,681	2	2	0
Pillager	482	1	1	0
Pine River	925	4	4	0
Plainview	3,295	8	7	1
Plymouth	80,616	95	79	16

Table 78. Full-Time Law Enforcement Employees, by Selected State and City, 2019—Continued

(Number.)

State/city	Population	Total law enforcement employees	Total officers	Total civilians
Preston	1,290	3	3	0
Princeton	4,711	14	12	2
Prior Lake	27,362	31	27	4
Proctor	3,038	8	7	1
Ramsey	27,358	29	26	3
Red Wing	16,408	32	28	4
Redwood Falls	4,951	13	11	2
Renville	1,177	3	3	0
Rice	1,389	2	2	0
Richfield	36,100	54	45	9
Robbinsdale	14,555	28	24	4
Rochester	118,267	203	138	65
Rogers	13,417	21	18	3
Roseau	2,665	6	5	1
Rosemount	24,961	29	24	5
Roseville	36,750	58	48	10
Rushford	1,703	3	3	0
Sartell	18,754	23	20	3
Sauk Centre	4,492	8	7	1
Sauk Rapids	14,015	18	17	1
Savage	32,336	44	34	10
Sebeka	674	2	2	0
Shakopee	41,892	60	48	12
Sherburn	1,088	4	4	0
Silver Bay	1,764	5	5	0
Silver Lake	813	1	1	0
Slayton	1,979	5	4	1
Sleepy Eye	3,347	7	7	0
South Lake Minnetonka	12,762	16	14	2
South St. Paul	20,148	35	30	5
Springfield	1,999	5	5	0
Spring Grove	1,264	2	2	0
Spring Lake Park	6,994	14	11	3
St. Anthony	9,172	23	20	3
Staples	2,945	7	6	1
Starbuck	1,255	4	4	0
St. Charles	3,773	7	7	0
St. Cloud	68,311	140	113	27
St. Francis	7,894	15	12	3
Stillwater	19,496	27	22	5
St. James	4,426	8	7	1
St. Joseph	7,227	10	9	1
St. Louis Park	49,535	70	56	14
St. Paul	310,263	832	649	183
St. Paul Park	5,410	9	9	0
St. Peter	12,032	19	14	5
Thief River Falls	8,825	19	17	2
Tracy	2,094	3	3	0
Trimont	699	1	1	0
Truman	1,045	2	2	0
Twin Valley	761	2	2	0
Two Harbors	3,523	9	8	1
Tyler	1,071	2	2	0
Verndale	573	2	2	0
Virginia	8,398	23	23	0
Wabasha	2,471	8	7	1
Wadena	4,097	10	9	1
Waite Park	7,764	21	18	3
Walker	930	3	3	0
Warroad	1,796	6	5	1
Waseca	8,841	19	17	2
Waterville	1,874	4	4	0
Wayzata	6,560	15	13	2
Wells	2,170	5	5	0
Westbrook	706	1	1	0
West Concord	768	1	1	0
West Hennepin	5,670	12	10	2
West St. Paul	19,694	35	31	4
Wheaton	1,295	3	3	0
White Bear Lake	26,176	34	30	4
Willmar	19,684	38	34	4
Windom	4,393	10	9	1
Winnebago	1,341	3	3	0
Winona	26,720	43	39	4
Winsted	2,247	4	4	0
Woodbury	72,527	89	77	12
Worthington	13,329	34	23	11
Wyoming	7,993	11	10	1
Zumbrota	3,477	6	6	0
MISSISSIPPI				
Ackerman	1,443	5	5	0
Amory	6,819	27	20	7
Batesville	7,234	53	41	12
Biloxi	46,185	187	131	56

Table 78. Full-Time Law Enforcement Employees, by Selected State and City, 2019—Continued

(Number.)

State/city	Population	Total law enforcement employees	Total officers	Total civilians
Booneville	8,742	25	20	5
Brandon	24,426	49	36	13
Brookhaven	12,037	46	36	10
Byram	11,672	39	26	13
Clinton	25,167	74	55	19
D'Iberville	14,125	40	37	3
Edwards	991	1	1	0
Florence	4,500	23	18	5
Flowood	9,401	67	51	16
Fulton	4,044	10	10	0
Gautier	18,563	45	34	11
Gulfport	72,383	204	152	52
Hattiesburg	45,971	157	106	51
Hernando	16,613	51	42	9
Horn Lake	27,256	61	47	14
Iuka	2,945	12	9	3
Leakesville	896	1	1	0
Madison	25,862	88	68	20
Magee	4,184	27	17	10
Meridian	36,878	94	74	20
Natchez	14,917	44	36	8
New Albany	8,858	28	26	2
Ocean Springs	17,864	45	35	10
Olive Branch	38,761	91	83	8
Oxford	25,306	100	85	15
Pascagoula	21,610	77	55	22
Pass Christian	6,285	25	20	5
Petal	10,702	31	26	5
Philadelphia	7,135	29	22	7
Ridgeland	24,171	88	59	29
Starkville	25,485	80	58	22
Summit	1,577	8	7	1
Vicksburg	21,928	81	65	16
West Point	10,430	31	27	4
Yazoo City	10,757	21	15	6
MISSOURI				
Adrian	1,599	3	3	0
Advance	1,337	3	3	0
Anderson	2,000	6	6	0
Annapolis	338	1	1	0
Appleton City	1,068	1	1	0
Archie	1,210	4	4	0
Arnold	21,102	61	54	7
Ash Grove	1,447	11	5	6
Ashland	3,975	9	8	1
Aurora	7,455	22	16	6
Ava	2,902	12	7	5
Ballwin	30,158	53	44	9
Battlefield	6,348	9	9	0
Bella Villa	726	5	5	0
Bellefontaine Neighbors	10,416	28	26	2
Bel-Nor	1,398	6	6	0
Bel-Ridge	2,681	15	15	0
Belton	23,657	57	36	21
Berkeley	8,868	31	24	7
Bernie	1,884	9	5	4
Bertrand	745	1	1	0
Bethany	3,065	4	4	0
Billings	1,114	3	3	0
Bloomfield	1,835	5	4	1
Blue Springs	55,415	142	96	46
Bolivar	11,129	26	18	8
Bonne Terre	7,081	11	11	0
Boonville	8,410	28	21	7
Bourbon	1,596	3	3	0
Bowling Green	5,662	12	10	2
Branson	11,688	69	46	23
Branson West	449	8	7	1
Breckenridge Hills	4,590	17	15	2
Brentwood	7,992	27	26	1
Bridgeton	11,608	63	53	10
Brookfield	4,232	10	8	2
Buckner	3,025	8	7	1
Buffalo	3,073	6	5	1
Butler	4,017	15	9	6
Byrnes Mill	3,024	6	6	0
Cabool	2,103	12	8	4
California	4,438	8	7	1
Calverton Park	1,269	8	8	0
Camdenton	4,138	20	17	3
Cameron	9,674	24	16	8
Campbell	1,812	4	4	0
Canalou	301	1	1	0
Canton	2,314	6	5	1

Table 78. Full-Time Law Enforcement Employees, by Selected State and City, 2019—Continued

(Number.)

State/city	Population	Total law enforcement employees	Total officers	Total civilians
Cape Girardeau	40,077	118	82	36
Carl Junction	8,242	15	10	5
Carrollton	3,477	8	7	1
Carterville	1,971	5	5	0
Carthage	14,808	37	28	9
Caruthersville	5,451	19	17	2
Cassville	3,327	12	12	0
Charleston	5,490	19	13	6
Chesterfield	47,663	104	92	12
Chillicothe	9,700	27	19	8
Clarkson Valley	2,614	6	6	0
Clarkton	1,156	2	2	0
Claycomo	1,501	11	11	0
Clayton	16,936	56	48	8
Cleveland	663	2	2	0
Clever	2,787	6	5	1
Clinton	8,939	23	22	1
Cole Camp	1,120	2	2	0
Columbia	125,017	195	158	37
Concordia	2,354	5	5	0
Cottleville	5,849	12	12	0
Country Club Hills	1,265	7	7	0
Country Club Village	2,485	1	1	0
Crestwood	11,845	33	27	6
Creve Coeur	18,829	52	47	5
Crocker	1,016	4	4	0
Crystal City	4,698	22	15	7
Cuba	3,293	16	15	1
Delta	438	1	1	0
Desloge	4,841	12	11	1
De Soto	6,355	24	17	7
Des Peres	8,697	49	41	8
Dexter	7,861	23	18	5
Diamond	923	2	2	0
Dixon	1,421	5	4	1
Doolittle	600	1	1	0
Duenweg	1,378	4	4	0
Duquesne	1,577	9	8	1
Edgar Springs	193	1	1	0
Edina	1,111	2	2	0
Edmundson	830	11	10	1
Eldon	4,649	18	17	1
El Dorado Springs	3,594	10	6	4
Ellisville	9,946	25	24	1
Eminence	578	1	1	0
Eureka	10,834	29	26	3
Excelsior Springs	11,715	34	24	10
Exeter	773	1	1	0
Fair Grove	1,520	6	6	0
Farmington	19,178	38	29	9
Fayette	2,719	7	7	0
Ferrelview	866	1	1	0
Festus	12,098	39	29	10
Flordell Hills	776	5	5	0
Florissant	51,148	120	94	26
Fordland	850	2	2	0
Foristell	589	6	6	0
Forsyth	2,582	7	6	1
Fredericktown	3,999	14	13	1
Frontenac	3,851	21	20	1
Fulton	12,620	32	26	6
Gallatin	1,750	1	1	0
Gideon	967	2	2	0
Gladstone	27,553	61	45	16
Glasgow	1,095	3	3	0
Glendale	5,873	14	11	3
Goodman	1,257	2	2	0
Gower	1,461	1	1	0
Grain Valley	14,464	28	23	5
Grandview	25,022	71	56	15
Greenfield	1,309	3	3	0
Greenwood	5,854	11	11	0
Hamilton	1,694	5	5	0
Hannibal	17,487	48	37	11
Hardin	533	1	1	0
Harrisonville	10,095	31	23	8
Hartville	605	2	2	0
Hayti	2,548	6	6	0
Hazelwood	25,146	76	60	16
Henrietta	354	1	1	0
Herculaneum	4,149	9	8	1
Hermann	2,325	13	7	6
Higginsville	4,588	23	10	13
Highlandville	1,052	1	1	0
Hillsboro	3,231	11	11	0

Table 78. Full-Time Law Enforcement Employees, by Selected State and City, 2019—Continued

(Number.)

State/city	Population	Total law enforcement employees	Total officers	Total civilians
Hillsdale	1,568	9	8	1
Holden	2,220	7	7	0
Hollister	4,608	21	13	8
Holts Summit	4,697	11	10	1
Hornersville	596	1	1	0
Houston	2,091	8	8	0
Howardville	339	2	1	1
Humansville	1,059	1	1	0
Huntsville	1,513	3	3	0
Iberia	749	1	1	0
Independence	116,931	272	199	73
Ironton	1,380	7	7	0
Jackson	15,151	36	29	7
Jasper	969	2	2	0
Jefferson City	42,793	123	88	35
Jonesburg	709	1	1	0
Joplin	50,635	134	100	34
Kansas City	495,964	1,819	1,299	520
Kearney	10,736	18	17	1
Kennett	10,093	27	20	7
Kimberling City	2,286	6	6	0
Kirksville	17,572	33	30	3
Kirkwood	27,785	79	60	19
Knob Noster	2,753	7	6	1
Laddonia	494	1	1	0
Ladue	8,650	32	26	6
La Grange	902	5	5	0
Lake Lotawana	2,126	4	4	0
Lake Ozark	1,832	16	10	6
Lakeshire	1,393	3	3	0
Lake St. Louis	16,444	42	33	9
Lake Tapawingo	720	4	3	1
Lake Winnebago	1,194	5	5	0
Lamar	4,279	15	13	2
Lanagan	410	2	2	0
La Plata	1,312	4	4	0
Lathrop	2,009	5	5	0
Laurie	947	6	6	0
Lawson	2,389	10	9	1
Leadington	613	4	4	0
Leadwood	1,153	4	4	0
Lebanon	14,841	40	28	12
Lee's Summit	99,365	203	145	58
Leeton	547	1	1	0
Lexington	4,514	9	7	2
Liberty	32,109	56	39	17
Licking	3,087	5	5	0
Lincoln	1,191	3	3	0
Linn	1,627	4	4	0
Linn Creek	252	3	3	0
Lone Jack	1,342	9	8	1
Louisiana	3,241	8	5	3
Macon	5,339	14	12	2
Manchester	18,176	37	33	4
Mansfield	1,250	4	4	0
Maplewood	8,108	35	33	2
Marble Hill	1,463	3	3	0
Marceline	2,092	10	10	0
Marionville	2,177	3	3	0
Marshall	12,915	29	24	5
Marshfield	7,566	13	12	1
Maryland Heights	26,964	96	77	19
Maryville	11,643	26	19	7
Matthews	597	3	3	0
Memphis	1,866	3	3	0
Merriam Woods	1,870	3	3	0
Mexico	11,529	28	27	1
Milan	1,796	5	5	0
Miner	943	10	6	4
Moberly	13,559	36	24	12
Moline Acres	2,352	11	10	1
Monett	9,148	23	21	2
Monroe City	2,439	10	9	1
Montgomery City	2,647	6	6	0
Morehouse	865	1	1	0
Moscow Mills	3,298	6	6	0
Mound City	1,025	2	2	0
Mountain Grove	4,681	16	14	2
Mountain View	2,643	9	8	1
Mount Vernon	4,504	11	11	0
Neosho	12,076	28	26	2
Nevada	8,237	25	21	4
Newburg	437	1	1	0
New Franklin	1,072	1	1	0
New Haven	2,071	11	11	0

Table 78. Full-Time Law Enforcement Employees, by Selected State and City, 2019—Continued

(Number.)

State/city	Population	Total law enforcement employees	Total officers	Total civilians
New London	970	2	2	0
New Madrid	2,825	22	14	8
Niangua	426	2	2	0
Nixa	22,235	41	35	6
Noel	1,833	1	1	0
Normandy	7,489	28	27	1
North Kansas City	4,573	50	39	11
Northwoods	4,386	18	17	1
Oak Grove	8,226	15	14	1
Oakland	1,378	79	60	19
Odessa	5,190	10	9	1
O'Fallon	89,611	145	112	33
Olivette	7,842	24	23	1
Oregon	755	1	1	0
Oronogo	2,694	5	5	0
Orrick	799	2	2	0
Osage Beach	4,598	24	20	4
Osceola	900	3	3	0
Overland	15,587	55	44	11
Owensville	2,574	9	8	1
Ozark	20,490	35	32	3
Pacific	7,265	23	18	5
Pagedale	3,293	17	17	0
Palmyra	3,606	9	8	1
Park Hills	8,484	18	17	1
Parkville	7,143	18	17	1
Peculiar	5,417	11	10	1
Perry	694	1	1	0
Perryville	8,466	30	24	6
Pevely	5,917	20	14	6
Piedmont	1,915	6	6	0
Pierce City	1,305	3	3	0
Pilot Grove	758	1	1	0
Pilot Knob	719	2	2	0
Pineville	801	12	12	0
Platte City	5,002	11	11	0
Platte Woods	409	2	2	0
Plattsburg	2,245	5	5	0
Pleasant Hill	8,705	17	13	4
Pleasant Valley	3,073	13	8	5
Polo	532	1	1	0
Poplar Bluff	17,044	57	44	13
Portageville	2,964	15	11	4
Potosi	2,609	11	10	1
Purdy	1,099	2	2	0
Queen City	619	1	1	0
Qulin	456	1	1	0
Raymore	22,121	37	28	9
Raytown	28,932	46	32	14
Republic	16,715	25	21	4
Rich Hill	1,323	1	1	0
Richland	1,757	4	4	0
Richmond	5,615	14	12	2
Richmond Heights	8,550	41	40	1
Riverside	3,522	35	26	9
Riverview	2,836	12	12	0
Rockaway Beach	880	2	1	1
Rock Hill	4,620	12	11	1
Rock Port	1,188	3	3	0
Rogersville	3,888	8	8	0
Rolla	20,482	53	31	22
Salem	4,895	18	13	5
Salisbury	1,520	4	3	1
Sarcoxie	1,321	3	3	0
Savannah	5,212	8	7	1
Scott City	4,493	18	13	5
Sedalia	21,742	57	41	16
Seligman	848	1	1	0
Senath	1,611	2	2	0
Seneca	2,392	6	6	0
Seymour	2,016	7	7	0
Shelbina	1,612	6	5	1
Shrewsbury	6,098	22	20	2
Sikeston	16,079	73	58	15
Smithville	10,503	19	19	0
Southwest City	962	3	3	0
Sparta	1,937	4	4	0
Springfield	169,235	421	347	74
St. Ann	12,670	78	49	29
St. Charles	71,341	149	109	40
St. Clair	4,695	16	14	2
Steele	1,921	5	5	0
Steelville	1,664	7	7	0
Ste. Genevieve	4,445	11	11	0
Stewartsville	739	1	1	0

Table 78. Full-Time Law Enforcement Employees, by Selected State and City, 2019—Continued

(Number.)

State/city	Population	Total law enforcement employees	Total officers	Total civilians
St. James	4,048	13	12	1
St. John	6,354	22	21	1
St. Joseph	75,872	173	130	43
St. Louis	300,521	1,609	1,201	408
Stover	1,073	2	2	0
St. Peters	57,697	120	92	28
Strafford	2,477	6	6	0
St. Robert	6,034	24	16	8
Sugar Creek	3,269	21	16	5
Sullivan	7,111	26	19	7
Summersville	487	2	2	0
Sunrise Beach	500	3	3	0
Sunset Hills	8,480	32	25	7
Sweet Springs	1,414	3	3	0
Tarkio	1,422	4	2	2
Terre du Lac	2,382	6	6	0
Thayer	2,132	10	6	4
Town and Country	11,177	30	29	1
Trenton	5,779	19	12	7
Troy	12,705	25	23	2
Truesdale	870	1	1	0
Union	11,905	27	25	2
University City	34,211	91	68	23
Urbana	411	1	1	0
Van Buren	800	5	5	0
Vandalia	4,072	6	5	1
Velda City	1,373	5	5	0
Verona	606	4	2	2
Versailles	2,450	11	10	1
Vienna	582	2	2	0
Vinita Park	10,979	44	40	4
Walnut Grove	803	1	1	0
Warrensburg	20,435	41	36	5
Warrenton	8,247	24	20	4
Warsaw	2,206	7	7	0
Warson Woods	1,925	6	6	0
Washington	14,064	33	30	3
Waverly	836	2	1	1
Waynesville	5,265	13	12	1
Weatherby Lake	2,079	5	5	0
Webb City	11,999	27	23	4
Webster Groves	22,876	47	45	2
Wellsville	1,144	3	3	0
Wentzville	42,892	93	72	21
Weston	1,829	5	5	0
West Plains	12,284	33	26	7
Wheaton	693	2	2	0
Willard	5,616	10	9	1
Willow Springs	2,103	7	6	1
Winfield	1,492	5	5	0
Winona	1,290	1	1	0
Woodson Terrace	4,043	19	17	2
Wright City	4,052	16	15	1
MONTANA				
Baker	1,928	5	5	0
Belgrade	9,204	20	16	4
Billings	110,198	177	151	26
Boulder	1,278	3	3	0
Bozeman	50,152	72	62	10
Bridger	760	3	3	0
Chinook	1,282	4	4	0
Colstrip	2,271	11	7	4
Columbia Falls	5,695	11	10	1
Columbus	2,069	5	5	0
Cut Bank	3,038	7	7	0
Deer Lodge	2,888	5	5	0
Dillon	4,276	11	10	1
East Helena	2,098	3	3	0
Ennis	1,019	1	1	0
Eureka	1,125	4	4	0
Fairview	884	3	3	0
Fort Benton	1,441	4	4	0
Glasgow	3,334	10	6	4
Glendive	4,964	12	8	4
Great Falls	58,637	129	88	41
Hamilton	4,879	16	14	2
Havre	9,738	24	18	6
Helena	32,806	78	53	25
Hot Springs	570	2	2	0
Kalispell	24,473	48	39	9
Laurel	6,768	19	13	6
Lewistown	5,790	13	13	0
Libby	2,750	6	6	0
Livingston	7,884	22	15	7

Table 78. Full-Time Law Enforcement Employees, by Selected State and City, 2019—Continued

(Number.)

State/city	Population	Total law enforcement employees	Total officers	Total civilians
Manhattan	1,865	4	4	0
Miles City	8,393	18	18	0
Missoula	75,422	133	106	27
Plains	1,116	3	3	0
Polson	5,075	17	16	1
Red Lodge	2,316	7	7	0
Ronan City	2,113	6	6	0
Sidney	6,376	13	12	1
Stevensville	2,051	3	2	1
Thompson Falls	1,403	5	5	0
Troy	936	3	3	0
West Yellowstone	1,396	14	7	7
Whitefish	8,079	18	16	2
Wolf Point	2,761	9	7	2
NEBRASKA				
Albion	1,584	3	3	0
Alliance	8,022	21	15	6
Ashland	2,604	5	4	1
Aurora	4,539	10	9	1
Bayard	1,090	4	4	0
Beatrice	12,227	36	22	14
Bellevue	53,880	106	90	16
Bennington	1,529	1	1	0
Blair	7,836	18	16	2
Boys Town	579	14	14	0
Broken Bow	3,532	8	7	1
Burwell	1,175	2	2	0
Central City	2,868	6	5	1
Chadron	5,446	20	13	7
Columbus	23,406	43	36	7
Cozad	3,757	8	8	0
Crete	7,094	13	12	1
Emerson	796	2	2	0
Falls City	4,130	12	8	4
Fremont	26,523	38	33	5
Gering	8,189	19	17	2
Gordon	1,497	6	4	2
Gothenburg	3,433	6	5	1
Grand Island	51,821	100	83	17
Harvard	963	2	2	0
Hastings	24,778	53	38	15
Holdrege	5,394	17	10	7
Imperial	2,074	4	4	0
Kearney	34,124	70	56	14
Kimball	2,343	6	5	1
Laurel	916	1	1	0
La Vista	17,223	45	39	6
Lexington	10,108	22	20	2
Lincoln	291,128	480	344	136
Madison	2,378	3	3	0
McCook	7,533	20	16	4
Milford	2,095	3	3	0
Minden	2,985	5	5	0
Mitchell	1,633	2	2	0
Morrill	892	2	2	0
Nebraska City	7,273	14	13	1
Neligh	1,503	3	3	0
Norfolk	24,698	56	39	17
North Platte	23,705	65	41	24
Ogallala	4,476	10	9	1
Omaha	470,481	1,020	868	152
O'Neill	3,615	9	8	1
Ord	2,087	4	3	1
Papillion	20,580	48	44	4
Pierce	1,721	3	3	0
Plattsmouth	6,478	17	14	3
Ralston	7,468	15	14	1
Randolph	888	1	1	0
Ravenna	1,369	2	2	0
Schuyler	6,396	10	9	1
Scottsbluff	15,862	37	31	6
Scribner	800	1	1	0
Seward	7,250	13	12	1
Sidney	6,331	15	13	2
South Sioux City	12,771	28	27	1
St. Paul	2,354	4	4	0
Superior	1,812	4	4	0
Tekamah	1,692	4	4	0
Tilden	934	1	1	0
Valentine	2,751	7	6	1
Valley	2,904	6	6	0
Wahoo	4,513	7	7	0
Waterloo	923	4	4	0
Wayne	5,615	13	8	5

Table 78. Full-Time Law Enforcement Employees, by Selected State and City, 2019—Continued

(Number.)

State/city	Population	Total law enforcement employees	Total officers	Total civilians
West Point	3,307	7	6	1
Wymore	1,329	2	2	0
York	7,877	17	14	3
NEVADA				
Boulder City	16,102	52	36	16
Carlin	2,259	8	6	2
Elko	20,601	44	37	7
Fallon	8,478	33	24	9
Las Vegas Metropolitan Police Department	1,666,803	4,562	3,115	1,447
Lovelock	1,806	5	3	2
Mesquite	19,612	53	41	12
Reno	254,349	442	324	118
Sparks	106,010	156	111	45
West Wendover	4,247	23	13	10
Winnemucca	7,800	26	23	3
Yerington	3,185	6	5	1
NEW HAMPSHIRE				
Alexandria	1,620	2	2	0
Allenstown	4,435	12	10	2
Alstead	1,931	2	2	0
Alton	5,339	14	12	2
Amherst	11,344	20	19	1
Antrim	2,702	6	5	1
Ashland	2,053	5	5	0
Atkinson	7,037	9	8	1
Auburn	5,608	11	9	2
Barnstead	4,668	5	5	0
Barrington	9,263	12	11	1
Bartlett	2,809	4	2	2
Bedford	22,887	49	36	13
Belmont	7,293	18	15	3
Bennington	1,512	2	2	0
Berlin	10,230	31	23	8
Bethlehem	2,569	6	6	0
Boscawen	4,095	8	7	1
Bow	8,004	14	13	1
Bradford	1,710	3	3	0
Brentwood	4,730	6	6	0
Bristol	3,057	9	8	1
Brookline	5,461	9	8	1
Campton	3,305	9	7	2
Canaan	3,896	7	6	1
Candia	3,945	7	6	1
Canterbury	2,468	3	3	0
Carroll	740	4	4	0
Center Harbor	1,099	3	3	0
Charlestown	4,998	10	6	4
Chester	5,295	8	7	1
Chesterfield	3,602	7	6	1
Chichester	2,709	5	5	0
Claremont	12,920	30	24	6
Colebrook	2,114	5	5	0
Concord	43,509	93	82	11
Conway	10,287	33	24	9
Danville	4,584	5	5	0
Deerfield	4,562	9	8	1
Deering	1,967	2	2	0
Derry	33,672	67	54	13
Dover	31,950	73	52	21
Dublin	1,538	4	3	1
Dunbarton	2,870	5	5	0
Durham	16,810	24	21	3
East Kingston	2,430	5	5	0
Effingham	1,480	1	1	0
Enfield	4,563	8	7	1
Epping	7,117	16	15	1
Epsom	4,777	6	5	1
Exeter	15,425	33	24	9
Farmington	6,932	15	14	1
Fitzwilliam	2,373	4	3	1
Franconia	1,111	3	3	0
Franklin	8,743	24	16	8
Freedom	1,562	2	2	0
Fremont	4,803	6	5	1
Gilford	7,197	21	16	5
Gilmanton	3,754	4	3	1
Goffstown	18,163	43	28	15
Gorham	2,579	9	5	4
Grantham	2,946	5	4	1
Greenland	4,195	9	8	1
Hampstead	8,662	9	9	0
Hampton	15,616	45	36	9

Table 78. Full-Time Law Enforcement Employees, by Selected State and City, 2019—Continued

(Number.)

State/city	Population	Total law enforcement employees	Total officers	Total civilians
Hampton Falls	2,385	4	4	0
Hancock	1,658	3	3	0
Hanover	11,531	33	19	14
Haverhill	4,568	9	8	1
Henniker	5,009	10	9	1
Hillsborough	5,990	23	15	8
Hinsdale	3,888	7	6	1
Holderness	2,109	6	6	0
Hollis	7,976	18	13	5
Hooksett	14,554	38	28	10
Hopkinton	5,759	7	6	1
Hudson	25,695	62	46	16
Jackson	856	2	2	0
Jaffrey	5,278	12	11	1
Keene	22,999	49	38	11
Kensington	2,118	5	4	1
Kingston	6,362	8	7	1
Laconia	16,534	49	40	9
Lancaster	3,219	8	7	1
Lebanon	13,661	46	33	13
Lee	4,494	9	8	1
Lincoln	1,775	14	9	5
Lisbon	1,583	3	3	0
Litchfield	8,660	15	13	2
Littleton	5,889	14	11	3
Londonderry	26,567	75	60	15
Loudon	5,660	7	6	1
Lyme	1,675	2	2	0
Lyndeborough	1,740	1	1	0
Madison	2,613	4	4	0
Manchester	112,895	279	225	54
Marlborough	2,068	3	3	0
Mason	1,441	2	2	0
Meredith	6,424	17	13	4
Merrimack	26,028	53	41	12
Middleton	1,827	3	3	0
Milford	16,121	32	27	5
Milton	4,652	9	8	1
Mont Vernon	2,603	3	3	0
Moultonborough	4,174	11	10	1
Nashua	89,586	223	167	56
New Boston	5,856	9	8	1
Newbury	2,245	4	4	0
New Castle	982	4	4	0
New Durham	2,704	4	4	0
Newfields	1,735	3	3	0
New Hampton	2,216	7	6	1
Newington	810	11	10	1
New Ipswich	5,408	7	6	1
New London	4,470	14	9	5
Newmarket	9,161	21	14	7
Newport	6,348	17	12	5
Newton	4,972	9	7	2
Northfield	4,940	7	6	1
North Hampton	4,512	13	12	1
Northwood	4,302	7	6	1
Nottingham	5,149	7	6	1
Orford	1,302	1	1	0
Ossipee	4,401	10	9	1
Pelham	14,198	31	24	7
Pembroke	7,240	14	12	2
Peterborough	6,669	13	11	2
Pittsburg	807	1	1	0
Pittsfield	4,142	7	7	0
Plainfield	2,381	2	2	0
Plaistow	7,734	22	15	7
Plymouth	6,755	19	12	7
Portsmouth	21,951	89	66	23
Raymond	10,475	25	17	8
Rindge	6,308	9	8	1
Rochester	31,527	70	55	15
Rollinsford	2,591	5	5	0
Rye	5,464	11	10	1
Salem	29,612	79	63	16
Sanbornton	2,975	6	5	1
Sandown	6,501	7	6	1
Sandwich	1,358	2	2	0
Seabrook	8,880	31	24	7
Somersworth	11,979	33	26	7
South Hampton	829	2	2	0
Springfield	1,342	2	2	0
Strafford	4,205	6	5	1
Stratham	7,479	12	11	1
Sugar Hill	579	2	2	0
Sunapee	3,489	6	5	1

Table 78. Full-Time Law Enforcement Employees, by Selected State and City, 2019—Continued

(Number.)

State/city	Population	Total law enforcement employees	Total officers	Total civilians
Tamworth	3,077	3	3	0
Thornton	2,513	6	5	1
Tilton	3,557	21	16	5
Troy	2,091	2	2	0
Tuftonboro	2,414	4	4	0
Wakefield	5,789	12	11	1
Warner	2,953	4	3	1
Washington	1,104	1	1	0
Waterville Valley	243	7	6	1
Weare	9,111	12	11	1
Webster	1,962	2	2	0
Whitefield	2,201	7	6	1
Wilton	3,768	6	6	0
Winchester	4,192	8	7	1
Windham	14,876	27	20	7
Wolfeboro	6,403	19	13	6
Woodstock	1,369	6	6	0
NEW JERSEY				
Aberdeen Township	18,700	47	40	7
Absecon	8,436	31	25	6
Allendale	6,795	20	15	5
Allenhurst	484	13	9	4
Allentown	1,784	6	5	1
Alpine	1,856	12	12	0
Andover Township	5,870	17	12	5
Asbury Park	15,437	94	90	4
Atlantic City	37,593	224	190	34
Atlantic Highlands	4,308	19	14	5
Audubon	8,601	19	18	1
Avalon	1,236	31	21	10
Avon-by-the-Sea	1,766	12	12	0
Barnegat Township	23,399	51	49	2
Barrington	6,620	16	15	1
Bay Head	976	11	10	1
Bayonne	65,032	247	184	63
Beach Haven	1,191	14	13	1
Beachwood	11,275	22	20	2
Bedminster Township	8,043	18	16	2
Belleville	36,531	110	102	8
Bellmawr	11,294	24	23	1
Belmar	5,562	30	25	5
Belvidere	2,564	7	6	1
Bergenfield	27,432	56	45	11
Berkeley Heights Township	13,592	33	27	6
Berkeley Township	41,738	92	72	20
Berlin	7,510	19	18	1
Berlin Township	5,651	18	17	1
Bernards Township	27,228	42	38	4
Bernardsville	7,670	26	20	6
Beverly	2,476	8	8	0
Blairstown Township	5,703	9	8	1
Bloomfield	50,307	152	125	27
Bloomingdale	8,089	18	17	1
Bogota	8,403	20	15	5
Boonton	8,157	29	23	6
Boonton Township	4,279	13	13	0
Bordentown City	3,786	14	14	0
Bordentown Township	12,018	24	23	1
Bound Brook	10,257	31	26	5
Bradley Beach	4,158	22	18	4
Branchburg Township	14,551	25	23	2
Brick Township	75,592	210	141	69
Bridgeton	24,331	73	61	12
Bridgewater Township	44,610	86	79	7
Brielle	4,683	17	16	1
Brigantine	8,684	44	34	10
Brooklawn	1,899	7	7	0
Burlington City	9,877	37	33	4
Burlington Township	22,516	58	49	9
Butler	7,613	18	16	2
Byram Township	7,875	14	14	0
Caldwell	7,943	23	22	1
Camden County Police Department	73,270	390	350	40
Cape May	3,428	28	23	5
Carlstadt	6,170	31	26	5
Carney's Point Township	7,664	20	19	1
Carteret	23,645	74	64	10
Cedar Grove Township	12,508	31	30	1
Chatham	8,696	25	21	4
Chatham Township	10,219	24	22	2
Cherry Hill Township	70,716	169	139	30
Chesilhurst	1,616	10	9	1
Chesterfield Township	7,474	11	10	1
Chester Township	7,731	24	23	1

Table 78. Full-Time Law Enforcement Employees, by Selected State and City, 2019—Continued

(Number.)

State/city	Population	Total law enforcement employees	Total officers	Total civilians
Cinnaminson Township	16,477	27	27	0
Clark Township	16,022	51	40	11
Clayton	8,709	16	15	1
Clementon	4,919	13	12	1
Cliffside Park	26,115	49	47	2
Clifton	85,021	186	153	33
Clinton	2,679	10	10	0
Clinton Township	12,801	23	22	1
Closter	8,562	21	20	1
Collingswood	13,850	31	27	4
Colts Neck Township	9,846	28	27	1
Cranbury Township	4,013	20	19	1
Cranford Township	24,251	68	54	14
Cresskill	8,761	27	22	5
Deal	719	21	17	4
Delanco Township	4,463	13	12	1
Delaware Township	4,419	8	7	1
Delran Township	16,473	34	30	4
Demarest	4,912	13	13	0
Denville Township	16,590	42	33	9
Deptford Township	30,258	71	65	6
Dover	17,852	43	38	5
Dumont	17,649	40	32	8
Dunellen	7,244	19	19	0
Eastampton Township	5,938	18	17	1
East Brunswick Township	47,857	108	83	25
East Greenwich Township	10,658	21	19	2
East Hanover Township	10,990	38	34	4
East Newark	2,661	7	7	0
East Orange	64,200	267	215	52
East Rutherford	9,831	40	37	3
East Windsor Township	27,343	52	46	6
Eatontown	12,215	49	37	12
Edgewater	12,821	37	31	6
Edgewater Park Township	8,644	15	15	0
Edison Township	100,282	223	173	50
Egg Harbor City	4,085	15	14	1
Egg Harbor Township	42,475	117	86	31
Elizabeth	128,753	411	313	98
Elk Township	4,154	12	11	1
Elmer	1,300	2	2	0
Elmwood Park	20,104	52	47	5
Emerson	7,640	25	22	3
Englewood	28,683	101	77	24
Englewood Cliffs	5,368	22	21	1
Englishtown	1,937	7	7	0
Essex Fells	2,072	13	13	0
Evesham Township	44,999	102	92	10
Ewing Township	36,338	103	83	20
Fairfield Township, Essex County	7,472	46	42	4
Fair Haven	5,784	13	13	0
Fair Lawn	33,064	69	60	9
Fairview	14,285	36	32	4
Fanwood	7,718	18	17	1
Far Hills	909	6	6	0
Flemington	4,590	14	14	0
Florence Township	12,593	31	29	2
Florham Park	11,522	40	34	6
Fort Lee	38,062	113	92	21
Franklin	4,699	17	16	1
Franklin Lakes	11,109	30	23	7
Franklin Township, Gloucester County	16,264	45	41	4
Franklin Township, Hunterdon County	3,560	6	6	0
Franklin Township, Somerset County	66,173	132	111	21
Freehold Borough	11,733	34	30	4
Freehold Township	34,560	70	66	4
Frenchtown	1,348	3	2	1
Galloway Township	35,813	79	59	20
Garfield	31,888	73	63	10
Garwood	4,361	20	16	4
Gibbsboro	2,212	8	8	0
Glassboro	20,082	54	49	5
Glen Ridge	7,574	26	22	4
Glen Rock	11,803	25	23	2
Gloucester City	11,168	34	32	2
Gloucester Township	63,500	162	130	32
Green Brook Township	7,071	24	23	1
Greenwich Township, Gloucester County	4,777	18	17	1
Greenwich Township, Warren County	5,447	12	12	0
Guttenberg	11,289	27	26	1
Hackensack	44,505	120	98	22
Hackettstown	9,431	20	19	1
Haddonfield	11,261	23	21	2
Haddon Heights	7,515	16	15	1
Haddon Township	14,489	27	26	1

Table 78. Full-Time Law Enforcement Employees, by Selected State and City, 2019—Continued

(Number.)

State/city	Population	Total law enforcement employees	Total officers	Total civilians
Haledon	8,277	18	18	0
Hamburg	3,102	10	9	1
Hamilton Township, Atlantic County	25,667	80	56	24
Hamilton Township, Mercer County	87,027	204	170	34
Hammonton	14,003	35	29	6
Hanover Township	14,447	38	31	7
Harding Township	3,805	14	13	1
Hardyston Township	7,760	24	18	6
Harrington Park	4,751	11	11	0
Harrison	18,374	56	43	13
Harrison Township	13,125	24	23	1
Harvey Cedars	339	10	9	1
Hasbrouck Heights	12,049	31	29	2
Haworth	3,420	13	12	1
Hawthorne	18,699	38	32	6
Hazlet Township	19,739	51	45	6
High Bridge	3,427	7	7	0
Highland Park	13,791	36	28	8
Highlands	4,739	17	14	3
Hightstown	5,264	13	12	1
Hillsborough Township	39,813	62	53	9
Hillsdale	10,382	23	19	4
Hillside Township	22,024	79	67	12
Hi-Nella	855	12	12	0
Hoboken	53,641	156	140	16
Ho-Ho-Kus	4,091	20	16	4
Holland Township	5,081	8	7	1
Holmdel Township	16,648	49	42	7
Hopatcong	14,091	32	24	8
Hopewell Township	17,854	38	30	8
Howell Township	52,242	104	88	16
Independence Township	5,420	10	9	1
Irvington	54,034	234	172	62
Island Heights	1,675	7	7	0
Jackson Township	57,380	116	96	20
Jamesburg	5,931	20	16	4
Jefferson Township	20,877	42	34	8
Jersey City	266,508	1,284	1,005	279
Keansburg	9,674	42	33	9
Kearny	41,314	151	113	38
Kenilworth	8,218	31	26	5
Keyport	7,032	22	20	2
Kinnelon	9,984	17	16	1
Lacey Township	29,247	60	46	14
Lakehurst	2,701	14	12	2
Lakewood Township	105,403	182	149	33
Lambertville	3,782	12	10	2
Laurel Springs	1,860	7	7	0
Lavallette	1,846	14	12	2
Lawnside	2,874	8	8	0
Lawrence Township, Mercer County	32,415	62	58	4
Lebanon Township	6,061	11	10	1
Leonia	9,088	22	19	3
Lincoln Park	10,162	30	25	5
Linden	42,592	171	140	31
Lindenwold	17,197	47	44	3
Linwood	6,697	19	18	1
Little Egg Harbor Township	21,508	55	44	11
Little Falls Township	14,513	36	30	6
Little Ferry	10,794	33	28	5
Little Silver	5,793	21	16	5
Livingston Township	29,998	81	71	10
Lodi	24,488	50	47	3
Logan Township	5,854	21	20	1
Long Beach Township	3,060	49	36	13
Long Branch	30,352	110	87	23
Long Hill Township	8,500	25	23	2
Longport	854	13	13	0
Lopatcong Township	8,350	17	16	1
Lower Alloways Creek Township	1,663	11	11	0
Lower Township	21,325	55	49	6
Lumberton Township	12,162	24	22	2
Lyndhurst Township	22,741	56	53	3
Madison	16,533	39	31	8
Magnolia	4,247	12	12	0
Mahwah Township	26,317	62	53	9
Manalapan Township	39,662	59	56	3
Manasquan	5,839	22	16	6
Manchester Township	43,369	93	73	20
Mansfield Township, Burlington County	8,520	16	15	1
Mansfield Township, Warren County	7,347	16	15	1
Mantoloking	252	11	10	1
Mantua Township	14,779	30	28	2
Manville	10,205	27	24	3
Maple Shade Township	18,451	38	34	4

Table 78. Full-Time Law Enforcement Employees, by Selected State and City, 2019—Continued

(Number.)

State/city	Population	Total law enforcement employees	Total officers	Total civilians
Maplewood Township	25,297	77	65	12
Margate City	5,912	36	28	8
Marlboro Township	39,850	115	89	26
Matawan	8,716	23	22	1
Maywood	9,667	29	25	4
Medford Lakes	3,922	12	11	1
Medford Township	23,393	41	37	4
Mendham	4,876	13	12	1
Mendham Township	5,700	16	15	1
Merchantville	3,687	15	14	1
Metuchen	14,423	35	29	6
Middlesex Borough	13,659	34	31	3
Middle Township	18,225	66	53	13
Middletown Township	65,361	125	113	12
Midland Park	7,246	19	18	1
Millburn Township	20,085	61	55	6
Milltown	7,020	19	16	3
Millville	27,528	84	74	10
Monmouth Beach	3,222	10	9	1
Monroe Township, Gloucester County	36,884	66	60	6
Monroe Township, Middlesex County	45,342	80	61	19
Montclair	38,625	124	109	15
Montgomery Township	23,364	40	34	6
Montvale	8,657	27	25	2
Montville Township	21,208	46	40	6
Moonachie	2,736	24	21	3
Moorestown Township	20,307	38	33	5
Morris Plains	5,935	18	16	2
Morristown	19,153	60	56	4
Morris Township	22,080	44	41	3
Mountain Lakes	4,269	14	13	1
Mountainside	6,888	29	23	6
Mount Arlington	5,964	16	15	1
Mount Ephraim	4,567	14	13	1
Mount Holly Township	9,568	28	25	3
Mount Laurel Township	41,109	79	72	7
Mount Olive Township	29,025	59	49	10
Mullica Township	5,897	13	12	1
Neptune City	4,625	20	19	1
Neptune Township	27,549	91	79	12
Netcong	3,151	10	10	0
Newark	281,422	1,533	1,187	346
New Brunswick	55,995	173	150	23
New Hanover Township	8,123	3	3	0
New Milford	16,506	42	36	6
New Providence	13,592	28	26	2
Newton	7,916	30	25	5
North Arlington	15,710	39	32	7
North Bergen Township	61,447	134	116	18
North Brunswick Township	41,706	99	83	16
North Caldwell	6,645	18	14	4
Northfield	8,163	23	22	1
North Haledon	8,379	24	19	5
North Hanover Township	7,476	11	10	1
North Plainfield	21,474	55	47	8
Northvale	4,937	12	12	0
North Wildwood	3,763	35	27	8
Norwood	5,816	17	16	1
Nutley Township	28,384	85	72	13
Oakland	12,992	32	27	5
Oaklyn	3,936	17	16	1
Ocean City	10,962	70	61	9
Ocean Gate	2,025	10	9	1
Oceanport	5,739	15	14	1
Ocean Township, Monmouth County	26,638	75	62	13
Ocean Township, Ocean County	9,134	32	23	9
Ogdensburg	2,247	6	6	0
Old Bridge Township	65,659	121	100	21
Old Tappan	5,944	14	13	1
Oradell	8,181	24	23	1
Orange City	30,558	144	122	22
Palisades Park	20,877	39	34	5
Palmyra	7,134	19	18	1
Paramus	26,460	110	91	19
Park Ridge	8,761	20	19	1
Parsippany-Troy Hills Township	51,907	126	103	23
Passaic	69,639	194	160	34
Paterson	144,866	526	419	107
Paulsboro	5,828	22	20	2
Peapack-Gladstone	2,591	9	8	1
Pemberton Borough	1,321	6	6	0
Pemberton Township	26,966	46	42	4
Pennington	2,516	6	5	1
Pennsauken Township	35,506	80	73	7
Penns Grove	4,746	17	16	1

Table 78. Full-Time Law Enforcement Employees, by Selected State and City, 2019—Continued

(Number.)

State/city	Population	Total law enforcement employees	Total officers	Total civilians
Pennsville Township	12,345	23	21	2
Pequannock Township	15,045	37	32	5
Perth Amboy	51,816	149	119	30
Phillipsburg	14,228	40	39	1
Pine Beach	2,173	7	6	1
Pine Hill	10,419	24	22	2
Pine Valley	12	6	6	0
Piscataway Township	56,783	103	82	21
Pitman	8,709	18	17	1
Plainfield	50,576	142	121	21
Plainsboro Township	22,976	48	36	12
Pleasantville	20,388	71	65	6
Plumsted Township	8,545	15	14	1
Pohatcong Township	3,181	16	15	1
Point Pleasant	18,684	43	33	10
Point Pleasant Beach	4,516	29	23	6
Pompton Lakes	10,953	29	25	4
Princeton	31,610	64	56	8
Prospect Park	5,831	19	18	1
Rahway	30,072	93	76	17
Ramsey	14,978	39	33	6
Randolph Township	25,490	41	35	6
Raritan	7,999	22	21	1
Raritan Township	22,220	34	31	3
Readington Township	15,805	25	23	2
Red Bank	12,016	45	39	6
Ridgefield	11,240	31	29	2
Ridgefield Park	12,983	41	34	7
Ridgewood	25,192	52	47	5
Ringwood	12,165	26	21	5
Riverdale	4,255	22	17	5
River Edge	11,500	28	25	3
Riverside Township	7,806	16	16	0
Riverton	2,675	6	6	0
River Vale Township	10,063	23	22	1
Robbinsville Township	14,635	37	29	8
Rochelle Park Township	5,598	24	20	4
Rockaway	6,325	16	15	1
Rockaway Township	25,756	63	52	11
Roseland	5,826	24	23	1
Roselle	21,903	66	54	12
Roselle Park	13,630	36	34	2
Roxbury Township	22,755	45	42	3
Rumson	6,740	21	17	4
Runnemede	8,262	16	15	1
Rutherford	18,423	42	40	2
Saddle Brook Township	13,897	39	34	5
Saddle River	3,186	24	19	5
Salem	4,702	20	18	2
Sayreville	44,581	100	85	15
Scotch Plains Township	24,383	52	49	3
Sea Bright	1,352	20	11	9
Sea Girt	1,764	13	12	1
Sea Isle City	2,035	30	23	7
Seaside Heights	2,902	28	25	3
Seaside Park	1,538	13	12	1
Secaucus	21,217	88	73	15
Ship Bottom	1,144	12	11	1
Shrewsbury	4,122	20	15	5
Somerdale	5,492	18	17	1
Somers Point	10,224	31	24	7
Somerville	12,198	34	32	2
South Amboy	8,922	33	28	5
South Bound Brook	4,570	13	13	0
South Brunswick Township	46,038	115	83	32
South Hackensack Township	2,465	24	21	3
South Orange Village	16,740	52	45	7
South Plainfield	24,114	73	59	14
South River	15,945	42	32	10
South Toms River	3,780	12	11	1
Sparta Township	18,532	43	31	12
Spotswood	8,276	28	24	4
Springfield Township, Burlington County	3,252	11	10	1
Springfield Township, Union County	17,661	46	42	4
Spring Lake	2,917	13	13	0
Spring Lake Heights	4,538	15	15	0
Stafford Township	27,609	79	55	24
Stanhope	3,281	10	9	1
Stone Harbor	804	19	17	2
Stratford	6,926	15	15	0
Summit	21,980	50	46	4
Surf City	1,193	10	10	0
Teaneck Township	40,533	108	91	17
Tenafly	14,586	40	34	6
Teterboro	68	24	21	3

Table 78. Full-Time Law Enforcement Employees, by Selected State and City, 2019—Continued

(Number.)

State/city	Population	Total law enforcement employees	Total officers	Total civilians
Tewksbury Township	5,765	12	11	1
Tinton Falls	17,506	43	41	2
Toms River Township	93,836	192	163	29
Totowa	10,754	32	28	4
Trenton	83,457	347	279	68
Tuckerton	3,370	13	12	1
Union Beach	5,396	20	16	4
Union City	68,459	210	172	38
Union Township	58,736	181	130	51
Upper Saddle River	8,245	20	16	4
Ventnor City	9,966	46	33	13
Vernon Township	21,912	42	33	9
Verona	13,355	36	30	6
Vineland	59,860	173	146	27
Voorhees Township	29,099	64	55	9
Waldwick	10,240	26	21	5
Wallington	11,568	24	23	1
Wall Township	25,648	84	67	17
Wanaque	11,772	29	24	5
Warren Township	15,772	38	31	7
Washington Township, Bergen County	9,219	25	20	5
Washington Township, Gloucester County	47,126	87	79	8
Washington Township, Morris County	18,296	30	29	1
Washington Township, Warren County	6,391	27	26	1
Watchung	6,054	37	31	6
Waterford Township	10,664	29	28	1
Wayne Township	53,279	145	117	28
Weehawken Township	15,115	72	54	18
Westampton Township	8,666	27	24	3
West Amwell Township	2,727	6	6	0
West Caldwell Township	10,840	29	25	4
West Deptford Township	20,902	46	43	3
Westfield	29,688	74	61	13
West Long Branch	7,889	22	21	1
West Milford Township	26,287	50	43	7
West New York	53,145	125	112	13
West Orange	47,696	108	95	13
Westville	4,128	14	13	1
West Wildwood	553	6	6	0
West Windsor Township	28,026	60	48	12
Westwood	11,129	36	30	6
Wharton	6,417	23	21	2
Wildwood	4,959	54	44	10
Wildwood Crest	3,051	26	23	3
Willingboro Township	31,920	76	67	9
Winfield Township	1,507	10	10	0
Winslow Township	38,390	80	74	6
Woodbridge Township	100,125	272	206	66
Woodbury	9,768	28	26	2
Woodbury Heights	2,949	8	7	1
Woodcliff Lake	5,853	20	19	1
Woodland Park	12,657	34	30	4
Woodlynne	2,901	8	6	2
Wood-Ridge	9,328	28	24	4
Woodstown	3,440	10	9	1
Woolwich Township	13,075	29	27	2
Wyckoff Township	17,030	26	26	0
NEW MEXICO				
Albuquerque	561,920	1,464	908	556
Anthony	9,284	11	9	2
Capitan	1,417	3	3	0
Clayton	2,691	13	7	6
Corrales	8,715	14	11	3
Deming	14,011	39	35	4
Dexter	1,236	6	5	1
Edgewood	6,161	14	10	4
Hatch	1,605	8	7	1
Hobbs	38,835	114	81	33
Las Cruces	103,520	259	187	72
Las Vegas	12,994	47	34	13
Lovington	11,322	34	25	9
Magdalena	873	3	3	0
Milan	3,632	9	7	2
Portales	11,675	33	23	10
Raton	5,939	22	14	8
Ruidoso	7,826	32	22	10
Santa Clara	1,765	4	3	1
San Ysidro	199	2	2	0
Springer	898	2	2	0
Sunland Park	18,103	22	20	2
Taos	5,963	27	22	5
Texico	1,078	2	2	0

Table 78. Full-Time Law Enforcement Employees, by Selected State and City, 2019—Continued

(Number.)

State/city	Population	Total law enforcement employees	Total officers	Total civilians
NEW YORK				
Addison Town and Village	2,471	3	3	0
Akron Village	2,851	2	2	0
Albany	97,221	382	293	89
Albion Village	5,802	13	13	0
Alfred Village	3,988	5	5	0
Altamont Village	1,679	1	1	0
Amherst Town	120,864	180	152	28
Amityville Village	9,430	25	24	1
Amsterdam	17,773	44	40	4
Arcade Village	1,933	5	5	0
Ardsley Village	4,538	19	19	0
Asharoken Village	644	3	3	0
Attica Village	2,411	4	4	0
Auburn	26,307	61	56	5
Avon Village	3,201	5	5	0
Baldwinsville Village	7,931	14	13	1
Ballston Spa Village	5,257	4	4	0
Bath Village	5,446	11	10	1
Beacon	14,510	37	35	2
Bedford Town	17,791	45	40	5
Belmont Village	904	1	1	0
Bethlehem Town	35,275	53	38	15
Binghamton	44,475	144	131	13
Blooming Grove Town	11,816	17	15	2
Bolivar Village	976	1	1	0
Briarcliff Manor Village	8,267	21	21	0
Brighton Town	36,036	44	38	6
Brockport Village	8,241	16	15	1
Bronxville Village	6,459	23	21	2
Buffalo	255,686	908	729	179
Cairo Town	6,413	2	2	0
Cambridge Village	1,794	3	3	0
Camillus Town and Village	24,160	27	24	3
Canajoharie Village	2,136	5	5	0
Canandaigua	10,217	26	24	2
Canisteo Village	2,131	2	2	0
Canton Village	6,407	12	11	1
Carmel Town	34,251	39	32	7
Carthage Village	3,336	3	3	0
Catskill Village	3,797	15	13	2
Cayuga Heights Village	3,666	7	6	1
Cazenovia Village	2,842	6	5	1
Cheektowaga Town	76,821	154	117	37
Chester Town	8,043	15	15	0
Chester Village	4,120	14	13	1
Chittenango Village	4,835	3	2	1
Clarkstown Town	80,599	188	164	24
Clayton Village	1,828	3	3	0
Cobleskill Village	4,329	11	11	0
Coeymans Town	7,297	4	3	1
Cohoes	16,717	35	33	2
Colchester Town	1,965	2	2	0
Colonie Town	79,509	152	118	34
Corning	10,533	24	20	4
Cornwall-on-Hudson Village	2,914	3	3	0
Cornwall Town	9,502	12	9	3
Cortland	18,655	45	42	3
Crawford Town	9,171	12	11	1
Croton-on-Hudson Village	8,131	22	20	2
Cuba Town	3,083	5	5	0
Deerpark Town	7,714	4	4	0
Delhi Village	3,094	5	5	0
Depew Village	15,008	35	29	6
DeWitt Town	25,000	46	43	3
Dobbs Ferry Village	10,990	28	26	2
Dryden Village	2,121	4	4	0
Dunkirk	11,712	37	36	1
East Aurora-Aurora Town	13,785	21	16	5
Eastchester Town	20,073	48	46	2
East Greenbush Town	16,324	33	25	8
East Hampton Town	19,901	89	66	23
East Hampton Village	1,129	29	24	5
East Rochester Village	6,522	9	8	1
Eden Town	7,621	4	3	1
Ellenville Village	3,980	10	10	0
Ellicott Town	5,014	13	13	0
Ellicottville	1,575	4	4	0
Elmira	26,958	82	72	10
Elmira Heights Village	3,819	9	9	0
Elmira Town	5,589	3	3	0
Elmsford Village	5,295	25	22	3
Evans Town	16,118	29	22	7
Fairport Village	5,334	11	10	1
Floral Park Village	15,927	46	34	12

Table 78. Full-Time Law Enforcement Employees, by Selected State and City, 2019—Continued

(Number.)

State/city	Population	Total law enforcement employees	Total officers	Total civilians
Florida Village	2,851	1	1	0
Fort Edward Village	3,253	5	5	0
Fort Plain Village	2,224	3	3	0
Frankfort Town	4,817	3	3	0
Frankfort Village	2,432	4	4	0
Freeport Village	43,064	111	99	12
Fulton City	11,163	36	35	1
Garden City Village	22,514	65	51	14
Gates Town	28,366	35	31	4
Geddes Town	10,038	19	17	2
Geneseo Village	8,158	8	8	0
Geneva	12,708	35	33	2
Glen Cove	27,228	57	52	5
Glens Falls	14,306	32	30	2
Glenville Town	21,634	25	24	1
Gloversville	14,738	38	35	3
Goshen Town	8,798	6	6	0
Goshen Village	5,337	21	18	3
Gouverneur Village	3,660	9	6	3
Granville Village	2,422	5	5	0
Great Neck Estates Village	2,884	17	14	3
Greece Town	95,777	107	99	8
Greenburgh Town	45,040	144	112	32
Greenwood Lake Village	3,074	4	3	1
Guilderland Town	34,133	55	39	16
Hamburg Town	46,445	62	62	0
Hamburg Village	9,725	15	14	1
Hamilton Village	4,081	4	4	0
Harriman Village	2,439	7	7	0
Harrison Town	27,946	78	67	11
Hastings-on-Hudson Village	7,916	19	19	0
Hempstead Village	55,404	139	110	29
Highland Falls Village	3,816	10	7	3
Homer Village	3,100	5	4	1
Hoosick Falls Village	3,359	3	3	0
Horseheads Village	6,390	9	9	0
Hudson	6,076	30	25	5
Hudson Falls Village	7,023	12	12	0
Hunter Town	2,628	3	3	0
Huntington Bay Village	1,434	4	4	0
Hyde Park Town	20,808	18	15	3
Ilion Village	7,685	19	18	1
Inlet Town	302	2	2	0
Irondequoit Town	49,729	59	50	9
Irvington Village	6,506	22	22	0
Ithaca	31,122	72	63	9
Jamestown	29,102	72	62	10
Johnson City Village	14,196	43	38	5
Johnstown	8,198	25	24	1
Kenmore Village	15,025	30	26	4
Kensington Village	1,189	6	6	0
Kent Town	13,235	23	18	5
Kingston	22,844	76	71	5
Lackawanna	17,724	53	46	7
Lake Placid Village	2,369	16	13	3
Lake Success Village	3,153	28	24	4
Lakewood-Busti	7,193	11	10	1
Lancaster Town	37,571	67	52	15
Larchmont Village	6,096	26	24	2
Le Roy Village	4,146	7	7	0
Lewisboro Town	12,582	3	3	0
Lewiston Town and Village	15,763	12	11	1
Liberty Village	4,083	20	18	2
Little Falls	4,642	12	11	1
Liverpool Village	2,202	4	4	0
Lloyd Harbor Village	3,667	14	12	2
Lloyd Town	10,463	13	11	2
Lockport	20,345	51	49	2
Long Beach	33,552	84	66	18
Lowville Village	3,315	6	6	0
Lynbrook Village	19,492	49	49	0
Macedon Town and Village	8,877	7	6	1
Malone Village	5,581	13	13	0
Malverne Village	8,514	24	24	0
Mamaroneck Town	12,088	37	36	1
Mamaroneck Village	19,183	57	50	7
Manlius Town	24,168	42	37	5
Marlborough Town	8,601	9	7	2
Massena Village	10,177	26	20	6
Medina Village	5,631	13	12	1
Menands Village	3,885	14	11	3
Middleport Village	1,745	4	4	0
Middletown	27,801	81	68	13
Mohawk Village	2,533	4	4	0
Monroe Village	8,593	23	19	4

Table 78. Full-Time Law Enforcement Employees, by Selected State and City, 2019—Continued

(Number.)

State/city	Population	Total law enforcement employees	Total officers	Total civilians
Montgomery Town	9,168	17	13	4
Montgomery Village	4,621	4	4	0
Moriah Town	4,557	2	2	0
Mount Pleasant Town	27,044	51	45	6
Mount Vernon	67,619	270	208	62
Newark Village	8,799	17	16	1
New Berlin Town	1,510	1	1	0
Newburgh	28,070	92	80	12
Newburgh Town	31,128	46	35	11
New Castle Town	17,896	39	37	2
New Hartford Town and Village	20,294	23	20	3
New Paltz Town and Village	14,212	23	20	3
New Rochelle	78,936	222	164	58
New Windsor Town	27,971	62	50	12
New York	8,379,043	52,696	36,563	16,133
New York Mills Village	3,217	5	5	0
Niagara Falls	47,900	164	146	18
Niagara Town	7,958	7	6	1
Niskayuna Town	22,407	29	27	2
Nissequogue Village	1,731	1	1	0
North Castle Town	12,248	34	32	2
North Greenbush Town	12,274	20	18	2
Northport Village	7,288	21	17	4
North Syracuse Village	6,637	12	11	1
North Tonawanda	30,228	53	49	4
Norwich	6,581	14	14	0
Ogdensburg	10,484	30	25	5
Ogden Town	20,144	15	12	3
Old Brookville Village	2,202	34	26	8
Old Westbury Village	4,752	30	25	5
Olean	13,499	40	34	6
Oneida	10,864	29	25	4
Oneonta City	13,915	27	22	5
Orangetown Town	37,371	89	82	7
Orchard Park Town	29,599	46	35	11
Ossining Village	24,991	68	60	8
Oswego City	17,239	53	46	7
Owego Village	3,887	3	2	1
Peekskill	24,243	62	53	9
Pelham Manor Village	5,567	27	26	1
Pelham Village	6,911	29	26	3
Penn Yan Village	4,910	13	12	1
Perry Village	3,442	4	4	0
Plattsburgh City	19,367	51	45	6
Pleasantville Village	7,261	23	21	2
Port Chester Village	29,317	64	62	2
Port Dickinson Village	1,527	5	4	1
Port Jervis	8,523	32	31	1
Port Washington	19,396	69	61	8
Potsdam Village	8,917	18	15	3
Poughkeepsie	30,422	116	89	27
Pound Ridge Town	5,159	2	1	1
Quogue Village	1,015	15	14	1
Ramapo Town	94,633	126	105	21
Rensselaer City	9,193	35	28	7
Riverhead Town	33,536	102	87	15
Rochester	205,769	850	738	112
Rockville Centre Village	24,669	64	55	9
Rome	32,019	74	72	2
Rosendale Town	5,826	1	1	0
Rotterdam Town	29,855	45	42	3
Rye	15,756	40	36	4
Rye Brook Village	9,530	26	25	1
Sag Harbor Village	2,298	12	11	1
Salamanca	5,439	15	15	0
Saranac Lake Village	5,221	12	12	0
Saratoga Springs	28,186	86	72	14
Saugerties Town	19,095	27	23	4
Scarsdale Village	17,954	46	41	5
Schenectady	65,504	187	161	26
Schodack Town	11,722	12	11	1
Scotia Village	7,641	13	12	1
Seneca Falls Town	8,632	19	17	2
Shawangunk Town	13,853	4	4	0
Shelter Island Town	2,413	10	9	1
Sherrill	2,991	3	3	0
Sidney Village	3,573	8	8	0
Skaneateles Village	2,464	3	2	1
Solvay Village	6,227	14	13	1
Southampton Town	51,090	139	98	41
Southampton Village	3,326	46	32	14
South Glens Falls Village	3,677	6	6	0
South Nyack Village	3,500	6	6	0
Southold Town	19,915	69	49	20
Spring Valley Village	32,367	64	55	9

Table 78. Full-Time Law Enforcement Employees, by Selected State and City, 2019—Continued
(Number.)

State/city	Population	Total law enforcement employees	Total officers	Total civilians
Stony Point Town	15,413	26	25	1
Suffern Village	11,063	25	21	4
Syracuse	142,438	471	403	68
Tarrytown Village	11,416	35	32	3
Ticonderoga Town	4,790	7	7	0
Tonawanda	14,754	34	28	6
Tonawanda Town	56,717	146	100	46
Troy	49,286	138	128	10
Trumansburg Village	1,757	2	2	0
Tuckahoe Village	6,584	26	23	3
Tupper Lake Village	3,466	8	8	0
Ulster Town	12,625	27	23	4
Utica	59,842	173	162	11
Vernon Village	1,156	1	1	0
Walden Village	6,670	16	13	3
Wallkill Town	29,236	50	49	1
Warsaw Village	3,251	5	5	0
Warwick Town	18,372	38	33	5
Washingtonville Village	5,740	17	15	2
Waterloo Village	4,885	9	8	1
Watertown	25,102	70	67	3
Watervliet	9,954	24	23	1
Waverly Village	4,119	10	9	1
Webb Town	1,790	6	6	0
Webster Town and Village	45,163	38	34	4
Weedsport Village	1,711	1	1	0
Wellsville Village	4,366	12	11	1
Westfield Village	2,981	6	6	0
Westhampton Beach Village	1,811	16	14	2
West Seneca Town	45,399	80	66	14
White Plains	58,259	190	181	9
Woodbury Town	11,006	25	21	4
Woodstock Town	5,781	10	10	0
Yonkers	200,075	681	598	83
Yorktown Town	36,426	68	59	9
NORTH CAROLINA				
Aberdeen	7,892	30	28	2
Ahoskie	4,772	17	15	2
Albemarle	16,134	49	42	7
Andrews	1,839	5	5	0
Angier	5,363	16	16	0
Apex	56,276	108	88	20
Archdale	11,509	32	26	6
Asheboro	25,894	81	73	8
Asheville	93,641	286	232	54
Atlantic Beach	1,506	16	15	1
Ayden	5,128	22	18	4
Badin	1,968	2	2	0
Bailey	560	2	2	0
Bakersville	450	1	1	0
Bald Head Island	182	27	24	3
Banner Elk	1,101	9	8	1
Beaufort	4,417	18	17	1
Beech Mountain	324	13	9	4
Belhaven	1,567	7	6	1
Belmont	12,812	42	35	7
Benson	3,901	15	14	1
Bessemer City	5,552	15	14	1
Bethel	1,610	4	4	0
Beulaville	1,306	4	4	0
Biltmore Forest	1,410	14	11	3
Biscoe	1,724	8	7	1
Black Creek	766	3	3	0
Black Mountain	8,187	24	20	4
Bladenboro	1,627	6	6	0
Blowing Rock	1,316	12	10	2
Boiling Spring Lakes	6,238	12	10	2
Boiling Springs	4,551	10	10	0
Boone	19,893	45	32	13
Boonville	1,152	4	4	0
Brevard	7,928	32	25	7
Bridgeton	441	1	1	0
Broadway	1,290	4	4	0
Bryson City	1,453	6	5	1
Bunn	377	3	2	1
Burgaw	4,176	12	11	1
Burlington	54,108	170	132	38
Burnsville	1,641	8	8	0
Butner	7,847	40	34	6
Candor	815	4	4	0
Canton	4,349	21	16	5
Cape Carteret	2,076	7	7	0
Carolina Beach	6,437	29	26	3
Carrboro	21,542	39	35	4

Table 78. Full-Time Law Enforcement Employees, by Selected State and City, 2019—Continued

(Number.)

State/city	Population	Total law enforcement employees	Total officers	Total civilians
Carthage	2,524	12	11	1
Cary	172,525	227	186	41
Caswell Beach	428	4	4	0
Chadbourn	1,711	9	8	1
Chapel Hill	61,457	96	82	14
Charlotte-Mecklenburg[1]	944,260	2,295	1,823	472
Cherryville	6,062	19	14	5
China Grove	4,220	13	13	0
Chocowinity	794	3	3	0
Claremont	1,407	9	9	0
Clayton	23,842	49	46	3
Cleveland	882	3	3	0
Clinton	8,512	31	27	4
Clyde	1,311	4	4	0
Coats	2,510	7	7	0
Columbus	995	9	8	1
Concord	96,138	201	171	30
Conover	8,426	27	24	3
Conway	729	1	1	0
Cooleemee	969	1	1	0
Cornelius	30,407	78	60	18
Cramerton	4,454	16	16	0
Creedmoor	4,636	19	15	4
Dallas	4,787	15	13	2
Davidson	13,193	22	20	2
Dobson	1,543	8	8	0
Drexel	1,849	5	5	0
Duck	390	13	12	1
Dunn	9,768	44	38	6
Durham	280,282	638	471	167
East Bend	593	2	2	0
East Spencer	1,550	7	7	0
Eden	14,773	47	43	4
Edenton	4,631	47	43	4
Elizabeth City	17,424	66	55	11
Elizabethtown	3,447	16	15	1
Elkin	4,038	21	17	4
Elon	12,214	20	19	1
Emerald Isle	3,706	19	18	1
Enfield	2,288	10	9	1
Erwin	5,148	12	11	1
Fair Bluff	882	3	3	0
Fairmont	2,601	8	7	1
Farmville	4,679	23	18	5
Fayetteville	209,614	560	396	164
Fletcher	8,485	17	16	1
Forest City	7,116	30	28	2
Four Oaks	2,224	8	8	0
Foxfire Village	1,031	3	3	0
Franklin	4,062	18	17	1
Franklinton	2,195	7	7	0
Fremont	1,264	4	4	0
Fuquay-Varina	30,977	57	49	8
Garner	31,137	74	65	9
Garysburg	918	2	2	0
Gaston	1,016	3	3	0
Gastonia	77,716	192	170	22
Gibsonville	7,356	19	18	1
Glen Alpine	1,480	5	5	0
Goldsboro	34,085	114	98	16
Graham	15,185	41	38	3
Granite Falls	4,629	17	13	4
Granite Quarry	2,999	8	8	0
Greensboro	298,025	767	637	130
Greenville	94,193	244	194	50
Grifton	2,658	7	7	0
Hamlet	6,312	19	18	1
Havelock	20,128	37	28	9
Haw River	2,525	9	9	0
Henderson	14,883	57	42	15
Hendersonville	14,234	57	40	17
Hertford	2,109	9	7	2
Hickory	41,040	147	110	37
Highlands	974	14	13	1
High Point	113,307	284	231	53
Hillsborough	7,321	30	28	2
Holden Beach	656	8	8	0
Holly Ridge	2,829	10	9	1
Holly Springs	38,577	74	57	17
Hope Mills	15,878	41	37	4
Hot Springs	578	1	1	0
Hudson	3,704	14	13	1
Huntersville	58,512	101	91	10
Indian Beach	119	5	5	0
Jackson	455	2	2	0

Table 78. Full-Time Law Enforcement Employees, by Selected State and City, 2019—Continued

(Number.)

State/city	Population	Total law enforcement employees	Total officers	Total civilians
Jacksonville	72,300	144	113	31
Jefferson	1,534	5	5	0
Jonesville	2,200	10	9	1
Kannapolis	50,725	101	72	29
Kenansville	855	3	3	0
Kenly	1,574	8	8	0
Kernersville	24,980	86	67	19
Kill Devil Hills	7,268	34	28	6
King	6,878	24	21	3
Kings Mountain	10,965	43	33	10
Kinston	19,886	67	56	11
Kitty Hawk	3,563	18	15	3
Knightdale	18,351	35	32	3
Kure Beach	2,113	13	12	1
Lake Lure	1,150	10	9	1
Lake Royale	2,758	7	7	0
Lake Waccamaw	1,395	4	4	0
Landis	3,133	12	12	0
Laurel Park	2,342	7	7	0
Laurinburg	14,928	43	41	2
Leland	23,360	38	35	3
Lenoir	17,904	68	51	17
Lexington	18,917	66	55	11
Liberty	2,656	11	10	1
Lilesville	485	2	2	0
Lillington	3,658	15	14	1
Lincolnton	11,022	36	32	4
Littleton	589	3	3	0
Locust	3,246	13	13	0
Long View	4,921	14	13	1
Louisburg	3,549	17	16	1
Lowell	3,709	9	9	0
Lumberton	20,754	97	87	10
Madison	2,103	18	18	0
Maggie Valley	1,230	10	9	1
Magnolia	954	2	2	0
Maiden	3,439	19	18	1
Manteo	1,453	7	6	1
Marion	7,837	27	25	2
Marshall	911	3	3	0
Mars Hill	2,054	5	5	0
Marshville	2,748	8	8	0
Matthews	33,372	69	58	11
Maxton	2,359	9	5	4
Mayodan	2,358	14	14	0
Maysville	955	3	3	0
Mebane	16,203	39	35	4
Micro	530	1	1	0
Middlesex	824	5	5	0
Mint Hill	27,776	37	33	4
Misenheimer	692	5	5	0
Mocksville	5,322	21	20	1
Monroe	35,630	99	88	11
Montreat	852	5	5	0
Mooresville	38,967	102	81	21
Morehead City	9,721	43	39	4
Morganton	16,524	97	61	36
Morrisville	28,796	40	38	2
Mount Airy	10,242	46	32	14
Mount Gilead	1,144	7	7	0
Mount Holly	16,475	40	32	8
Mount Olive	4,652	16	15	1
Murfreesboro	3,072	9	8	1
Murphy	1,657	10	9	1
Nags Head	2,963	25	23	2
Nashville	5,523	14	13	1
Navassa	2,217	3	3	0
New Bern	30,187	111	86	25
Newland	684	5	5	0
Newport	4,666	8	8	0
Newton	13,153	40	31	9
Newton Grove	564	3	3	0
Norlina	1,050	5	5	0
North Topsail Beach	738	12	11	1
Northwest	782	2	2	0
North Wilkesboro	4,220	26	25	1
Norwood	2,438	9	9	0
Oakboro	1,899	8	8	0
Oak Island	8,244	25	23	2
Ocean Isle Beach	644	13	12	1
Old Fort	921	4	4	0
Oriental	852	2	2	0
Oxford	8,851	32	30	2
Parkton	414	2	2	0
Pembroke	2,994	17	13	4

Table 78. Full-Time Law Enforcement Employees, by Selected State and City, 2019—Continued

(Number.)

State/city	Population	Total law enforcement employees	Total officers	Total civilians
Pikeville	678	4	4	0
Pilot Mountain	1,416	9	8	1
Pinebluff	1,582	3	3	0
Pinehurst	16,522	30	25	5
Pine Knoll Shores	1,331	8	8	0
Pine Level	2,016	5	5	0
Pinetops	1,240	9	7	2
Pineville	9,088	47	36	11
Pink Hill	507	2	2	0
Pittsboro	4,359	13	13	0
Plymouth	3,400	11	10	1
Polkton	2,880	3	3	0
Princeton	1,402	4	4	0
Raeford	5,001	19	17	2
Raleigh	477,828	646	544	102
Ramseur	1,689	6	6	0
Randleman	4,119	16	16	0
Ranlo	3,661	11	10	1
Red Springs	3,341	13	12	1
Reidsville	13,959	54	49	5
Richlands	1,698	8	8	0
Rich Square	837	1	1	0
River Bend	3,033	6	6	0
Roanoke Rapids	14,354	40	34	6
Robbins	1,215	4	4	0
Robersonville	1,348	7	7	0
Rockingham	8,687	38	36	2
Rockwell	2,151	7	7	0
Rocky Mount	53,827	182	144	38
Rolesville	8,924	21	20	1
Rose Hill	1,623	6	6	0
Rowland	1,002	7	6	1
Roxboro	8,299	35	30	5
Rutherfordton	4,047	15	14	1
Salisbury	33,877	93	79	14
Saluda	690	4	4	0
Sanford	30,135	99	75	24
Scotland Neck	1,852	8	7	1
Seagrove	228	1	1	0
Selma	7,018	23	22	1
Seven Devils	217	6	6	0
Shallotte	4,396	15	14	1
Sharpsburg	2,013	7	6	1
Shelby	20,004	85	72	13
Siler City	8,237	24	18	6
Smithfield	12,882	39	35	4
Snow Hill	1,513	7	7	0
Southern Pines	14,524	48	40	8
Southern Shores	2,940	12	11	1
Southport	3,961	9	9	0
Sparta	1,758	6	6	0
Spencer	3,238	11	11	0
Spindale	4,215	11	11	0
Spring Hope	1,305	7	7	0
Spring Lake	12,069	30	27	3
Spruce Pine	2,138	10	10	0
Stallings	16,173	25	22	3
Stanfield	1,536	5	5	0
Stanley	3,769	11	10	1
Stantonsburg	777	4	4	0
Star	845	4	4	0
Statesville	27,372	93	71	22
Stoneville	1,237	5	5	0
St. Pauls	2,323	16	12	4
Sugar Mountain	197	5	5	0
Sunset Beach	4,002	15	15	0
Surf City	2,487	22	21	1
Swansboro	3,354	14	13	1
Sylva	2,742	12	12	0
Tabor City	4,136	11	10	1
Tarboro	10,765	36	30	6
Taylorsville	2,185	13	13	0
Taylortown	847	4	3	1
Thomasville	26,617	72	66	6
Topsail Beach	435	10	9	1
Trent Woods	4,030	5	5	0
Troutman	2,755	13	13	0
Troy	3,326	10	9	1
Tryon	1,609	9	7	2
Valdese	4,435	12	11	1
Vanceboro	966	3	3	0
Vass	792	4	4	0
Wadesboro	5,228	28	23	5
Wagram	770	1	1	0
Wake Forest	46,145	100	78	22

Table 78. Full-Time Law Enforcement Employees, by Selected State and City, 2019—Continued

(Number.)

State/city	Population	Total law enforcement employees	Total officers	Total civilians
Wallace	3,894	20	16	4
Walnut Creek	863	3	3	0
Warrenton	837	5	4	1
Warsaw	3,115	16	14	2
Washington	9,497	40	31	9
Waxhaw	17,203	28	26	2
Waynesville	10,146	43	33	10
Weaverville	4,013	17	16	1
Weldon	1,472	8	8	0
Wendell	8,096	18	17	1
West Jefferson	1,311	8	8	0
Whispering Pines	3,385	9	8	1
Whitakers	701	2	2	0
White Lake	776	6	6	0
Whiteville	5,338	25	21	4
Wilkesboro	3,491	24	22	2
Williamston	5,217	23	20	3
Wilmington	124,750	336	267	69
Wilson	49,344	131	116	15
Wilson's Mills	2,744	6	6	0
Windsor	3,310	8	8	0
Wingate	4,557	7	7	0
Winston-Salem	248,445	674	518	156
Winterville	9,922	23	22	1
Woodfin	6,634	14	13	1
Woodland	701	1	1	0
Wrightsville Beach	2,550	26	24	2
Yadkinville	2,890	14	13	1
Youngsville	1,365	12	11	1
Zebulon	5,814	22	21	1
NORTH DAKOTA				
Belfield	1,028	3	2	1
Berthold	497	1	1	0
Beulah	3,200	6	5	1
Bismarck	74,705	154	125	29
Bowman	1,604	4	4	0
Burlington	1,233	2	2	0
Carrington	1,980	3	3	0
Cavalier	1,253	3	3	0
Devils Lake	7,294	21	19	2
Dickinson	23,428	59	40	19
Ellendale	1,223	2	2	0
Emerado	456	1	1	0
Fargo	127,423	201	178	23
Fessenden	442	1	1	0
Grafton	4,144	10	9	1
Grand Forks	57,459	105	90	15
Harvey	1,683	4	4	0
Hazen	2,321	4	4	0
Jamestown	15,198	31	27	4
Kenmare	1,010	2	2	0
Killdeer	1,213	5	5	0
Lamoure	898	1	1	0
Lincoln	3,986	5	5	0
Lisbon	2,036	4	4	0
Mandan	23,012	44	37	7
Medora	130	2	2	0
Minot	48,185	109	83	26
Napoleon	763	1	1	0
New Town	2,621	6	5	1
Northwood	904	2	2	0
Oakes	1,694	3	3	0
Powers Lake	279	2	2	0
Ray	866	1	1	0
Rolette	599	1	1	0
Rolla	1,278	4	4	0
Rugby	2,661	5	5	0
Stanley	2,813	5	5	0
Steele	709	1	1	0
Surrey	1,445	4	4	0
Thompson	1,021	1	1	0
Tioga	1,639	7	5	2
Valley City	6,351	16	14	2
Wahpeton	7,752	16	14	2
Watford City	8,488	27	22	5
West Fargo	38,171	76	63	13
Williston	28,966	81	70	11
Wishek	921	2	2	0
OHIO				
Ada	5,509	7	7	0
Addyston	943	1	1	0
American Township	12,050	1	1	0
Amherst	12,166	29	21	8

Table 78. Full-Time Law Enforcement Employees, by Selected State and City, 2019—Continued

(Number.)

State/city	Population	Total law enforcement employees	Total officers	Total civilians
Arcanum	2,006	4	4	0
Archbold	4,320	11	10	1
Ashland	20,410	34	27	7
Aurora	16,319	36	27	9
Barberton	26,015	39	38	1
Bath Township, Summit County	9,659	28	21	7
Bay Village	15,235	27	23	4
Beavercreek	47,672	67	50	17
Beaver Township	6,415	14	10	4
Bedford	12,485	39	34	5
Bellefontaine	13,145	37	30	7
Bellville	1,895	6	6	0
Belpre	6,386	16	11	5
Berea	18,573	31	29	2
Bexley	13,956	37	31	6
Blue Ash	12,307	40	33	7
Bluffton	4,049	9	9	0
Bowling Green	31,719	54	40	14
Brunswick	34,977	51	39	12
Butler Township	7,819	18	17	1
Cambridge	10,318	32	26	6
Canal Fulton	5,450	11	10	1
Canfield	7,199	26	19	7
Canton	70,139	201	167	34
Carlisle	5,457	8	7	1
Catawba Island Township	3,556	5	5	0
Centerville	23,744	55	40	15
Chagrin Falls	3,941	14	13	1
Cheviot	8,269	11	11	0
Chillicothe	21,670	58	47	11
Cincinnati	303,335	1,157	1,024	133
Circleville	14,025	20	13	7
Clayton	13,221	19	18	1
Clearcreek Township	16,070	17	16	1
Cleveland	381,829	1,785	1,560	225
Cleveland Heights	44,098	100	96	4
Clyde	6,147	19	15	4
Colerain Township	59,479	61	53	8
Columbiana	6,209	18	14	4
Copley Township	17,309	22	21	1
Covington	2,694	7	6	1
Cridersville	1,793	4	4	0
Dayton	140,427	426	363	63
Deer Park	5,654	14	10	4
Defiance	16,601	34	30	4
Delaware	40,616	63	56	7
Dublin	49,626	109	68	41
East Cleveland	17,001	42	41	1
Eastlake	18,074	35	24	11
Eaton	8,136	17	16	1
Elida	1,801	2	2	0
Elmore	1,373	5	5	0
Englewood	13,478	27	20	7
Evendale	2,839	22	20	2
Fairfield Township	22,956	25	23	2
Forest Park	18,673	43	36	7
Fort Loramie	1,521	2	2	0
Fort Recovery	1,456	3	3	0
Fostoria	13,230	26	22	4
Frazeysburg	1,309	2	2	0
Genoa	2,284	4	4	0
German Township, Montgomery County	2,897	6	6	0
Glenwillow	932	4	4	0
Grandview Heights	8,581	25	20	5
Greenhills	3,591	11	10	1
Harrison	11,837	25	22	3
Heath	10,933	28	20	8
Hinckley Township	8,076	12	11	1
Hiram	1,128	3	3	0
Holland	1,642	9	9	0
Hubbard Township	5,306	10	9	1
Huber Heights	38,183	74	52	22
Indian Hill	5,897	26	21	5
Ironton	10,576	16	15	1
Kalida	1,586	1	1	0
Kenton	8,198	15	15	0
Kettering	54,974	118	80	38
Kirtland	6,823	14	9	5
Lakewood	49,802	113	94	19
Lancaster	40,622	82	65	17
Lexington	4,666	15	11	4
Liberty Township	11,420	18	18	0
Lockland	3,455	16	15	1
Lordstown	3,248	13	9	4
Lyndhurst	13,407	37	29	8

Table 78. Full-Time Law Enforcement Employees, by Selected State and City, 2019—Continued

(Number.)

State/city	Population	Total law enforcement employees	Total officers	Total civilians
Macedonia	12,028	24	23	1
Madison Township, Franklin County	19,682	18	17	1
Mansfield	46,418	113	77	36
Mariemont	3,473	11	10	1
Mason	33,939	54	50	4
Maumee	13,656	57	43	14
Mayfield Heights	18,519	50	39	11
Miamisburg	19,913	39	37	2
Miami Township, Montgomery County	29,188	44	41	3
Middlefield	2,713	9	9	0
Middletown	48,878	108	67	41
Mifflin Township	2,632	10	10	0
Milan	1,331	3	3	0
Milford	6,880	21	19	2
Milton Township	2,439	4	4	0
Minerva Park	1,334	10	9	1
Mogadore	3,832	8	8	0
Monroe	16,531	42	32	10
Montgomery	10,867	22	20	2
Moraine	6,455	30	22	8
Mount Vernon	16,663	34	31	3
Navarre	1,846	6	6	0
New Albany	11,332	32	23	9
Newark	50,340	75	64	11
New Boston	2,093	13	9	4
New Bremen	2,977	7	7	0
Newcomerstown	3,743	8	5	3
New Franklin	14,162	22	14	8
New London	2,368	5	5	0
New Philadelphia	17,434	26	22	4
Newton Falls	4,481	5	5	0
Newtown	2,666	9	8	1
Niles	18,222	42	36	6
North Ridgeville	34,469	46	39	7
North Royalton	30,177	50	36	14
Northwood	5,445	22	17	5
Norton	12,007	24	23	1
Norwalk	16,903	31	24	7
Oberlin	8,302	22	17	5
Olmsted Falls	8,861	10	10	0
Orrville	8,461	17	16	1
Ottawa	4,317	8	8	0
Oxford Township	2,224	3	3	0
Pandora	1,107	2	2	0
Peninsula	558	3	3	0
Pepper Pike	6,371	17	17	0
Perkins Township	11,687	23	22	1
Perrysburg Township	13,013	31	24	7
Perry Township, Franklin County	3,788	12	11	1
Plain City	4,452	10	9	1
Poland Township	11,859	11	11	0
Port Clinton	5,914	20	15	5
Powell	13,545	21	19	2
Reading	10,995	26	22	4
Reynoldsburg	38,578	79	60	19
Roaming Shores Village	1,451	4	4	0
Rossford	6,575	16	15	1
Russell Township	5,219	11	10	1
Sagamore Hills	10,934	22	21	1
Salem	11,644	23	23	0
Salineville	1,219	2	2	0
Seaman	896	2	2	0
Seven Hills	11,621	17	16	1
Shaker Heights	27,127	78	61	17
Sharonville	13,873	50	39	11
Shawnee Hills	822	6	6	0
Shawnee Township	12,056	20	14	6
Sidney	20,437	47	37	10
Silver Lake	2,498	9	8	1
Solon	22,830	65	47	18
South Charleston	1,613	3	3	0
South Russell	3,767	9	9	0
Springboro	18,975	33	29	4
Springfield	59,128	127	116	11
Springfield Township, Mahoning County	6,415	10	10	0
St. Clairsville	4,991	10	9	1
Steubenville	17,768	43	38	5
St. Henry	2,554	3	3	0
Stow	34,862	50	41	9
Streetsboro	16,561	35	29	6
Sugarcreek	2,220	6	6	0
Sugarcreek Township	8,494	17	15	2
Sylvania	19,046	40	33	7
Sylvania Township	29,754	60	43	17
Tallmadge	17,583	29	25	4

Table 78. Full-Time Law Enforcement Employees, by Selected State and City, 2019—Continued

(Number.)

State/city	Population	Total law enforcement employees	Total officers	Total civilians
Tiffin	17,498	39	29	10
Toledo	273,505	695	637	58
Trenton	13,154	21	16	5
Trotwood	24,435	35	33	2
Troy	26,250	44	41	3
Uhrichsville	5,317	9	9	0
Uniontown	3,353	12	10	2
University Heights	12,852	30	28	2
Upper Sandusky	6,467	17	13	4
Urbana	11,309	19	19	0
Valley View, Cuyahoga County	1,999	20	18	2
Vandalia	15,018	40	30	10
Van Wert	10,662	32	23	9
Wadsworth	24,058	40	31	9
Walton Hills	2,283	15	11	4
Warren	38,012	72	68	4
Washington Court House	14,150	27	22	5
West Liberty	1,787	4	4	0
West Salem	1,475	1	1	0
West Union	3,153	5	4	1
Whitehouse	4,887	11	11	0
Wickliffe	12,758	40	30	10
Wooster	26,615	50	43	7
Wyoming	8,596	22	19	3
Xenia	26,926	68	43	25
Zanesville	25,346	99	59	40
OKLAHOMA				
Achille	541	3	2	1
Ada	17,321	40	36	4
Adair	817	11	9	2
Allen	930	3	2	1
Altus	18,572	50	38	12
Alva	5,022	10	10	0
Amber	467	1	1	0
Anadarko	6,540	19	17	2
Antlers	2,296	11	6	5
Apache	1,399	4	4	0
Arcadia	276	1	1	0
Ardmore	24,830	50	45	5
Arkoma	1,907	4	2	2
Atoka	3,131	15	15	0
Barnsdall	1,143	3	3	0
Bartlesville	36,502	86	63	23
Beaver	1,390	1	1	0
Beggs	1,227	7	3	4
Bennington	366	1	1	0
Bernice	579	2	2	0
Bethany	19,346	38	30	8
Big Cabin	252	4	3	1
Binger	636	1	1	0
Bixby	28,383	44	35	9
Blackwell	6,610	20	14	6
Blanchard	9,028	15	11	4
Boise City	1,077	2	2	0
Bokchito	688	6	5	1
Bokoshe	493	2	2	0
Boley	1,175	2	2	0
Boswell	679	3	2	1
Bristow	4,195	13	9	4
Broken Arrow	110,480	205	152	53
Broken Bow	4,053	17	12	5
Burns Flat	1,920	5	4	1
Cache	2,814	6	5	1
Caddo	1,091	4	4	0
Calera	2,375	11	10	1
Calvin	273	1	1	0
Caney	196	4	3	1
Canton	592	2	2	0
Carnegie	1,651	8	4	4
Carney	656	1	1	0
Cashion	883	1	1	0
Catoosa	6,975	16	15	1
Cement	481	1	1	0
Chandler	3,094	11	7	4
Chattanooga	441	2	1	1
Checotah	3,143	13	10	3
Chelsea	1,902	4	4	0
Cherokee	1,509	3	3	0
Chickasha	16,395	38	27	11
Choctaw	12,812	21	17	4
Chouteau	2,086	10	9	1
Claremore	18,786	47	39	8
Clayton	794	4	4	0
Cleveland	3,136	8	8	0

Table 78. Full-Time Law Enforcement Employees, by Selected State and City, 2019—Continued

(Number.)

State/city	Population	Total law enforcement employees	Total officers	Total civilians
Clinton	9,179	25	17	8
Coalgate	1,779	5	5	0
Colbert	1,250	3	2	1
Colcord	838	4	4	0
Collinsville	7,271	19	12	7
Commerce	2,392	5	5	0
Cordell	2,753	4	4	0
Covington	533	1	1	0
Coweta	10,016	20	14	6
Crescent	1,547	7	5	2
Cushing	7,639	21	15	6
Cyril	1,022	2	2	0
Davenport	816	1	1	0
Davis	2,911	10	8	2
Del City	21,794	45	35	10
Depew	479	1	1	0
Dewar	847	2	2	0
Dewey	3,405	12	10	2
Dibble	871	5	4	1
Dickson	1,251	3	2	1
Disney	307	2	2	0
Drumright	2,816	5	5	0
Duncan	22,296	66	49	17
Durant	18,478	44	39	5
Earlsboro	652	1	1	0
Edmond	94,699	157	122	35
Eldorado	410	1	1	0
Elgin	3,294	5	5	0
Elk City	11,509	40	26	14
Elmore City	706	5	4	1
El Reno	19,830	55	35	20
Enid	49,598	123	95	28
Erick	988	2	2	0
Eufaula	2,907	9	9	0
Fairfax	1,268	3	1	2
Fairland	1,031	2	2	0
Fairview	2,601	8	4	4
Fletcher	1,128	1	1	0
Forest Park	1,075	3	1	2
Fort Cobb	613	1	1	0
Fort Gibson	3,972	13	12	1
Fort Towson	486	1	1	0
Frederick	3,558	9	6	3
Gans	298	1	1	0
Geary	1,276	10	5	5
Glenpool	14,356	31	24	7
Goodwell	1,289	4	4	0
Gore	939	4	3	1
Grandfield	938	1	1	0
Granite	1,968	3	3	0
Grove	7,129	31	21	10
Guthrie	11,597	32	22	10
Guymon	11,247	24	16	8
Haileyville	753	4	4	0
Harrah	6,602	11	10	1
Hartshorne	1,930	5	3	2
Haskell	1,913	6	6	0
Healdton	2,688	4	4	0
Heavener	3,285	14	13	1
Hennessey	2,241	9	5	4
Henryetta	5,517	18	13	5
Hinton	3,228	6	6	0
Hobart	3,403	12	6	6
Holdenville	5,518	10	9	1
Hollis	1,856	9	5	4
Hominy	3,381	9	4	5
Hooker	1,882	3	3	0
Howe	786	3	3	0
Hugo	5,081	22	16	6
Hulbert	584	7	5	2
Hydro	937	4	3	1
Idabel	6,816	25	20	5
Inola	1,820	6	5	1
Jay	2,532	15	9	6
Jenks	24,264	34	25	9
Jennings	357	1	1	0
Jones	3,196	7	7	0
Kansas	802	4	4	0
Kellyville	1,155	2	2	0
Keota	544	1	1	0
Kiefer	2,039	5	5	0
Kingfisher	4,962	15	12	3
Kingston	1,676	7	7	0
Kiowa	668	7	5	2
Konawa	1,211	3	2	1

Table 78. Full-Time Law Enforcement Employees, by Selected State and City, 2019—Continued

(Number.)

State/city	Population	Total law enforcement employees	Total officers	Total civilians
Krebs	1,922	8	6	2
Lahoma	621	1	1	0
Langley	823	3	3	0
Langston	1,842	3	2	1
Laverne	1,374	2	1	1
Lawton	92,256	222	190	32
Lexington	2,152	11	6	5
Lindsay	2,798	16	10	6
Locust Grove	1,401	10	6	4
Lone Grove	5,111	10	7	3
Luther	1,834	4	4	0
Madill	4,056	12	11	1
Mangum	2,735	10	6	4
Mannford	3,210	11	8	3
Marietta	2,771	7	6	1
Marlow	4,398	10	10	0
Maud	1,060	4	4	0
Maysville	1,208	4	3	1
McAlester	17,840	48	45	3
McCurtain	503	2	1	1
McLoud	4,746	11	10	1
Medford	936	3	3	0
Medicine Park	450	2	2	0
Meeker	1,149	5	5	0
Miami	13,078	31	30	1
Midwest City	57,678	126	100	26
Minco	1,641	5	5	0
Moore	62,998	93	87	6
Mooreland	1,176	4	3	1
Morris	1,416	3	3	0
Mounds	1,253	2	2	0
Mountain View	726	2	2	0
Muldrow	3,226	13	8	5
Muskogee	37,174	91	83	8
Mustang	22,630	38	26	12
Nash	194	1	1	0
Newcastle	10,649	21	20	1
Newkirk	2,181	5	4	1
Nichols Hills	3,945	23	16	7
Nicoma Park	2,481	6	6	0
Ninnekah	1,041	4	3	1
Noble	6,922	19	13	6
Norman	125,076	242	179	63
North Enid	932	4	4	0
Nowata	3,598	8	6	2
Oilton	1,012	2	2	0
Okarche	1,351	6	5	1
Okeene	1,142	2	2	0
Okemah	3,168	14	9	5
Oklahoma City	657,890	1,455	1,173	282
Okmulgee	11,702	26	24	2
Olustee	563	1	1	0
Oologah	1,176	5	5	0
Owasso	37,654	79	58	21
Paoli	613	3	2	1
Pauls Valley	6,157	20	15	5
Pawhuska	3,410	15	10	5
Pawnee	2,107	5	5	0
Perkins	2,833	8	8	0
Perry	4,905	20	13	7
Piedmont	8,553	10	9	1
Pocola	4,124	12	8	4
Ponca City	23,876	72	50	22
Pond Creek	822	2	2	0
Porum	702	3	3	0
Poteau	8,961	33	26	7
Prague	2,385	13	8	5
Pryor Creek	9,395	38	29	9
Purcell	6,481	23	20	3
Quinton	980	4	4	0
Ramona	543	2	1	1
Rattan	297	3	3	0
Ringling	966	1	1	0
Roland	3,894	11	8	3
Rush Springs	1,262	5	5	0
Salina	1,396	6	6	0
Sallisaw	8,391	30	22	8
Sand Springs	20,024	43	33	10
Sapulpa	20,888	56	45	11
Savanna	649	8	6	2
Sawyer	311	4	3	1
Sayre	4,476	12	7	5
Seminole	7,134	17	14	3
Shady Point	998	2	2	0
Shattuck	1,280	1	1	0

Table 78. Full-Time Law Enforcement Employees, by Selected State and City, 2019—Continued

(Number.)

State/city	Population	Total law enforcement employees	Total officers	Total civilians
Shawnee	31,627	84	67	17
Skiatook	8,041	19	15	4
Snyder	1,271	2	2	0
South Coffeyville	740	5	5	0
Spencer	3,989	5	3	2
Sperry	1,329	5	5	0
Spiro	2,171	5	4	1
Sportsmen Acres	307	1	1	0
Stigler	2,719	13	9	4
Stillwater	51,008	127	80	47
Stilwell	4,054	20	13	7
Stratford	1,535	6	3	3
Stringtown	397	3	3	0
Stroud	2,713	12	7	5
Sulphur	5,028	12	10	2
Tahlequah	16,861	45	38	7
Talala	278	1	1	0
Talihina	1,086	8	4	4
Tecumseh	6,667	14	13	1
Texhoma	917	2	2	0
Thackerville	488	2	1	1
The Village	9,535	29	23	6
Thomas	1,205	1	1	0
Tipton	762	1	1	0
Tishomingo	3,040	8	7	1
Tonkawa	3,006	12	8	4
Tryon	499	1	1	0
Tulsa	401,700	1,037	842	195
Tupelo	303	2	2	0
Tushka	303	3	3	0
Tuttle	7,553	16	11	5
Tyrone	760	2	1	1
Union City	2,193	11	10	1
Valley Brook	776	6	5	1
Valliant	731	4	4	0
Velma	595	1	1	0
Verden	535	1	1	0
Verdigris	4,603	7	6	1
Vian	1,351	6	6	0
Vici	708	1	1	0
Vinita	5,343	22	15	7
Wagoner	9,154	22	17	5
Walters	2,379	5	4	1
Warner	1,588	4	4	0
Warr Acres	10,331	33	26	7
Washington	664	2	1	1
Watonga	2,837	11	9	2
Watts	310	2	1	1
Waukomis	1,290	2	2	0
Waurika	1,919	3	3	0
Waynoka	913	3	3	0
Weatherford	12,186	37	23	14
Webbers Falls	593	4	4	0
Weleetka	964	8	5	3
Wellston	783	3	3	0
West Siloam Springs	870	11	10	1
Westville	1,543	9	5	4
Wetumka	1,198	3	3	0
Wewoka	3,252	8	7	1
Wilburton	2,560	7	6	1
Wilson	1,697	4	4	0
Wister	1,063	3	3	0
Woodward	12,195	27	23	4
Wright City	733	1	1	0
Wyandotte	330	5	4	1
Wynnewood	2,207	6	5	1
Yale	1,192	7	4	3
Yukon	28,184	67	46	21
OREGON				
Albany	54,993	95	63	32
Amity	1,729	9	2	7
Ashland	21,415	36	29	7
Astoria	10,040	28	16	12
Aumsville	4,241	7	6	1
Baker City	9,750	17	15	2
Bandon	3,139	8	8	0
Beaverton	100,130	183	142	41
Bend	100,588	133	101	32
Black Butte		8	7	1
Boardman	3,425	12	11	1
Brookings	6,480	21	14	7
Burns	2,781	4	4	0
Canby	17,962	29	25	4
Cannon Beach	1,756	10	8	2

Table 78. Full-Time Law Enforcement Employees, by Selected State and City, 2019—Continued

(Number.)

State/city	Population	Total law enforcement employees	Total officers	Total civilians
Carlton	2,206	5	3	2
Central Point	18,753	34	27	7
Coburg	1,156	4	3	1
Columbia City	2,048	8	5	3
Coos Bay	16,471	35	23	12
Coquille	3,933	8	7	1
Corvallis	59,196	96	62	34
Cottage Grove	10,437	30	17	13
Dallas	16,983	24	19	5
Eagle Point	9,530	12	11	1
Enterprise	1,966	4	4	0
Eugene	173,183	306	181	125
Florence	9,183	20	13	7
Forest Grove	25,063	35	29	6
Gearhart	1,612	3	3	0
Gervais	2,783	6	5	1
Gladstone	12,340	18	15	3
Gold Beach	2,298	9	6	3
Grants Pass	38,475	91	57	34
Gresham	110,692	161	130	31
Hermiston	17,780	32	27	5
Hillsboro	110,549	182	134	48
Hood River	7,876	15	14	1
Hubbard	3,598	6	5	1
Independence	10,367	20	15	5
Jacksonville	2,919	6	5	1
John Day	1,654	6	5	1
Junction City	6,292	9	7	2
Keizer	40,109	47	39	8
King City	4,072	8	7	1
Klamath Falls	22,447	41	34	7
La Grande	13,294	31	18	13
Lake Oswego	39,888	65	42	23
Lebanon	17,304	40	28	12
Lincoln City	9,115	35	25	10
Madras	7,028	11	10	1
Malin	821	7	7	0
Manzanita	664	4	4	0
McMinnville	34,935	49	43	6
Medford	83,316	150	104	46
Milton-Freewater	7,051	15	10	5
Milwaukie	21,075	42	37	5
Molalla	9,328	17	15	2
Monmouth	10,630	14	13	1
Mount Angel	3,621	8	6	2
Myrtle Creek	3,508	9	7	2
Myrtle Point	2,556	6	5	1
Newberg-Dundee	27,378	48	35	13
Newport	10,772	29	21	8
North Bend	9,775	31	24	7
North Plains	2,226	3	3	0
Nyssa	3,191	8	7	1
Oakridge	3,351	7	5	2
Ontario	11,044	27	23	4
Oregon City	37,723	54	46	8
Pendleton	16,796	28	24	4
Philomath	4,871	9	8	1
Phoenix	4,627	11	9	2
Pilot Rock	1,510	3	3	0
Portland	662,114	1,157	889	268
Port Orford	1,150	5	5	0
Prineville	10,479	32	19	13
Rainier	2,017	6	5	1
Redmond	31,558	48	39	9
Reedsport	4,123	12	7	5
Rockaway Beach	1,415	3	3	0
Rogue River	2,365	8	5	3
Roseburg	23,447	41	35	6
Salem	175,867	322	183	139
Sandy	11,555	18	15	3
Scappoose	7,592	11	10	1
Seaside	6,833	26	18	8
Sherwood	19,865	25	22	3
Silverton	10,831	19	16	3
Springfield	63,438	95	65	30
Stayton	8,318	11	10	1
St. Helens	13,900	22	19	3
Sunriver		13	12	1
Sutherlin	8,136	18	14	4
Sweet Home	9,931	22	15	7
Talent	6,604	10	8	2
The Dalles	15,752	26	23	3
Tigard	55,621	84	68	16
Tillamook	5,347	11	10	1
Toledo	3,648	13	7	6

Table 78. Full-Time Law Enforcement Employees, by Selected State and City, 2019—Continued

(Number.)

State/city	Population	Total law enforcement employees	Total officers	Total civilians
Tualatin	27,788	47	40	7
Turner	2,151	2	2	0
Umatilla	7,202	11	9	2
Vernonia	2,288	4	3	1
Warrenton	5,772	13	12	1
West Linn	26,962	31	28	3
Winston	5,515	11	9	2
Woodburn	26,338	40	32	8
Yamhill	1,192	8	3	5
PENNSYLVANIA				
Abington Township, Montgomery County	55,476	109	91	18
Adams Township, Butler County	14,330	17	17	0
Adams Township, Cambria County	5,533	12	5	7
Akron	4,033	7	7	0
Albion	1,457	1	1	0
Alburtis	2,658	4	4	0
Aldan	4,149	5	5	0
Aleppo Township	1,867	17	14	3
Aliquippa	8,844	18	17	1
Allegheny Township, Blair County	6,512	8	7	1
Allegheny Township, Westmoreland County	8,053	11	10	1
Allegheny Valley Regional	3,262	2	2	0
Allentown	121,855	236	214	22
Altoona	43,429	67	59	8
Ambler	6,505	14	13	1
Ambridge	6,601	11	11	0
Amity Township	13,243	14	13	1
Annville Township	5,017	10	8	2
Archbald	7,021	18	18	0
Armagh Township	3,794	1	1	0
Arnold	4,826	9	9	0
Ashland	2,670	2	2	0
Ashley	2,715	4	4	0
Aspinwall	2,701	5	5	0
Aston Township	16,699	18	16	2
Athens	3,191	4	4	0
Athens Township	5,077	10	9	1
Avalon	4,539	6	5	1
Avis	1,489	2	2	0
Avoca	2,617	2	2	0
Baden	3,880	3	3	0
Baldwin Borough	19,426	22	21	1
Baldwin Township	1,926	5	5	0
Bally	1,281	2	2	0
Bangor	5,234	11	10	1
Beaver	4,271	11	10	1
Beaver Falls	9,473	19	18	1
Beaver Meadows	838	1	1	0
Bell Acres	1,380	3	3	0
Bellefonte	6,293	13	10	3
Bellevue	8,064	16	13	3
Bellwood	1,741	3	3	0
Ben Avon	1,738	17	14	3
Ben Avon Heights	362	17	14	3
Bensalem Township	60,647	130	100	30
Bentleyville	2,488	1	1	0
Berlin	1,947	2	2	0
Bern Township	7,033	12	12	0
Berwick	9,943	18	16	2
Bethel Park	32,523	44	38	6
Bethel Township, Berks County	4,178	3	3	0
Bethlehem	75,895	161	146	15
Bethlehem Township	24,088	36	35	1
Biglerville	1,220	2	2	0
Birdsboro	5,167	8	7	1
Birmingham Township	4,210	3	3	0
Blairsville	3,224	5	5	0
Blair Township	4,500	5	5	0
Blakely	6,201	6	6	0
Blawnox	1,379	3	3	0
Bloomsburg Town	13,806	23	18	5
Bonneauville	1,838	1	1	0
Boyertown	4,077	8	7	1
Brackenridge	3,140	4	4	0
Braddock Hills	1,813	2	2	0
Bradford	8,220	18	18	0
Bradford Township	4,597	5	5	0
Branch Township	1,735	2	2	0
Brecknock Township, Berks County	4,669	5	5	0
Brentwood	9,291	14	13	1
Briar Creek Township	2,965	4	4	0
Bridgeport	4,582	10	9	1
Bridgeville	4,970	9	8	1

Table 78. Full-Time Law Enforcement Employees, by Selected State and City, 2019—Continued

(Number.)

State/city	Population	Total law enforcement employees	Total officers	Total civilians
Bridgewater	847	2	2	0
Brighton Township	8,260	12	12	0
Bristol	9,583	16	14	2
Bristol Township	53,508	67	58	9
Brockway	2,038	3	2	1
Brookhaven	8,026	9	8	1
Brookville	3,793	7	6	1
Bryn Athyn	1,410	4	4	0
Buckingham Township	20,279	26	24	2
Buffalo Township	7,334	5	5	0
Buffalo Valley Regional	12,741	15	14	1
Bushkill Township	8,624	16	15	1
Butler	12,901	24	23	1
Butler Township, Butler County	16,447	23	21	2
Butler Township, Luzerne County	9,885	12	11	1
Butler Township, Schuylkill County	5,636	5	5	0
Caernarvon Township, Berks County	4,174	8	7	1
California	6,701	7	6	1
Caln Township	14,363	23	22	1
Cambria Township	5,697	3	3	0
Cambridge Springs	2,648	3	3	0
Camp Hill	7,922	13	12	1
Canonsburg	8,789	18	16	2
Canton	1,878	1	1	0
Carbondale	8,387	10	10	0
Carnegie	7,828	14	13	1
Carrolltown	789	6	6	0
Carroll Township, Washington County	5,459	3	3	0
Carroll Valley	3,944	5	4	1
Castle Shannon	8,249	15	14	1
Catasauqua	6,619	10	9	1
Catawissa	1,471	3	3	0
Cecil Township	12,883	21	20	1
Center Township	11,313	20	19	1
Centerville	3,148	2	2	0
Central Berks Regional	13,528	20	19	1
Central Bucks Regional	15,494	29	26	3
Chambersburg	21,131	35	32	3
Charleroi Regional	6,500	9	8	1
Chartiers Township	8,031	13	13	0
Cheltenham Township	37,274	77	69	8
Chester	33,905	96	85	11
Chippewa Township	7,943	8	7	1
Christiana	1,173	9	9	0
Churchill	2,905	8	8	0
Clairton	6,539	12	12	0
Clarion	5,896	9	8	1
Clarks Summit	6,214	5	5	0
Clearfield	5,844	11	7	4
Cleona	2,221	4	4	0
Clifton Heights	6,685	11	10	1
Clymer	1,265	1	1	0
Coaldale	2,138	3	3	0
Coal Township	10,242	12	11	1
Coatesville	13,118	30	26	4
Cochranton	1,077	2	2	0
Colebrookdale District	6,062	11	9	2
Collegeville	5,115	8	8	0
Collier Township	8,346	17	16	1
Collingdale	8,771	9	8	1
Colonial Regional	18,218	25	23	2
Columbia	10,366	21	19	2
Conemaugh Township, Cambria County	1,838	1	1	0
Conemaugh Township, Somerset County	6,831	6	6	0
Conewago Township, Adams County	7,233	10	9	1
Conneaut Lake Regional	3,436	4	3	1
Connellsville	7,276	16	15	1
Conoy Township	3,465	19	17	2
Conshohocken	8,091	21	19	2
Conway	2,070	4	4	0
Conyngham	1,862	3	3	0
Coopersburg	2,531	7	7	0
Coraopolis	5,482	13	9	4
Cornwall	4,383	7	6	1
Corry	6,249	11	10	1
Coudersport	2,406	4	4	0
Covington Township	2,255	3	3	0
Crafton	6,178	10	9	1
Cranberry Township	32,022	34	31	3
Crescent Township	2,553	5	5	0
Cresson	1,556	10	10	0
Cresson Township	2,492	5	5	0
Croyle Township	2,213	1	1	0
Cumberland Township, Adams County	6,265	6	6	0
Cumberland Township, Greene County	6,180	6	6	0

Table 78. Full-Time Law Enforcement Employees, by Selected State and City, 2019—Continued

(Number.)

State/city	Population	Total law enforcement employees	Total officers	Total civilians
Cumru Township	15,496	26	25	1
Curwensville	2,382	4	3	1
Dallas	2,765	4	4	0
Dallas Township	9,354	12	11	1
Dalton	1,191	3	3	0
Danville	4,613	9	7	2
Darby	10,677	18	17	1
Darby Township	9,256	15	14	1
Delmont	2,545	4	4	0
Derry	2,512	1	1	0
Derry Township, Dauphin County	25,273	59	40	19
Dickson City	5,772	8	7	1
Donegal Township	3,243	2	2	0
Donora	4,574	6	6	0
Dormont	8,286	14	13	1
Douglass Township, Berks County	3,616	6	6	0
Douglass Township, Montgomery County	10,636	13	12	1
Downingtown	7,932	19	16	3
Doylestown Township	17,397	23	21	2
Dublin Borough	2,140	3	2	1
DuBois	7,371	14	13	1
Duncansville	1,162	1	1	0
Dunmore	12,996	17	17	0
Dunnstable Township	1,010	2	2	0
Dupont	2,676	2	2	0
Duquesne	5,546	15	15	0
Duryea	4,855	2	2	0
East Bangor	1,699	1	1	0
East Brandywine Township	9,123	17	15	2
East Cocalico Township	10,568	17	17	0
East Coventry Township	6,771	8	7	1
East Earl Township	6,935	8	8	0
Eastern Adams Regional	7,413	6	6	0
Eastern Pike Regional	4,625	11	10	1
East Fallowfield Township	7,588	7	7	0
East Franklin Township	3,849	1	1	0
East Greenville	2,962	3	3	0
East Hempfield Township	24,750	37	33	4
East Lampeter Township	17,072	41	38	3
East Lansdowne	2,662	5	3	2
East Marlborough Township	7,520	1	1	0
East McKeesport	2,617	3	3	0
East Norriton Township	14,059	28	27	1
Easton	27,268	66	61	5
East Pennsboro Township	21,549	23	22	1
East Pikeland Township	7,356	10	10	0
Easttown Township	10,668	13	12	1
East Union Township	1,592	2	2	0
East Vincent Township	7,392	7	7	0
East Whiteland Township	12,646	22	20	2
Ebensburg	3,060	5	5	0
Economy	9,129	13	12	1
Eddystone	2,404	10	9	1
Edgewood	2,999	9	9	0
Edgeworth	1,647	13	4	9
Edinboro	5,460	8	8	0
Edwardsville	4,697	5	5	0
Elder Township	969	2	2	0
Elizabeth	1,966	1	1	0
Elizabethtown	11,440	19	17	2
Elizabeth Township	12,991	12	12	0
Ellwood City	7,342	12	10	2
Emmaus	11,479	22	20	2
Emporium	1,806	2	2	0
Emsworth	2,358	17	14	3
Erie	95,834	193	172	21
Etna	3,324	8	7	1
Evans City-Seven Fields Regional	4,445	3	3	0
Everett	1,719	3	3	0
Exeter	5,584	2	2	0
Exeter Township, Berks County	26,029	31	29	2
Exeter Township, Luzerne County	2,357	1	1	0
Fairview Township, Luzerne County	4,515	7	7	0
Fairview Township, York County	17,664	21	18	3
Falls Township, Bucks County	33,707	58	50	8
Farrell	4,603	14	13	1
Fawn Township	2,304	2	2	0
Ferguson Township	19,734	24	22	2
Ferndale	1,485	1	1	0
Findlay Township	5,981	18	17	1
Fleetwood	4,123	6	6	0
Folcroft	6,615	12	11	1
Ford City	2,770	3	3	0
Forest City	1,741	2	2	0
Forest Hills	6,284	9	9	0

Table 78. Full-Time Law Enforcement Employees, by Selected State and City, 2019—Continued

(Number.)

State/city	Population	Total law enforcement employees	Total officers	Total civilians
Forks Township	15,741	22	21	1
Forty Fort	4,087	5	5	0
Forward Township	3,270	1	1	0
Foster Township, McKean County	4,047	5	5	0
Fox Chapel	5,261	11	11	0
Frackville	3,609	5	5	0
Franconia Township	13,355	11	10	1
Franklin	6,022	23	17	6
Franklin Park	14,910	15	14	1
Franklin Township, Beaver County	3,858	2	2	0
Franklin Township, Carbon County	4,156	4	4	0
Franklin Township, Columbia County	583	5	5	0
Frazer Township	1,122	2	2	0
Freedom Township	3,324	3	3	0
Freeland	3,428	4	4	0
Freemansburg	2,631	3	3	0
Freeport	1,682	2	2	0
Galeton	1,080	1	1	0
Gallitzin	1,759	6	6	0
Geistown	2,257	3	3	0
German Township	4,801	2	2	0
Gettysburg	7,732	12	11	1
Girard	2,927	4	4	0
Glassport	4,318	8	8	0
Glenolden	7,140	11	10	1
Granville Township	4,971	10	8	2
Greene County Regional Police Department	5,250	3	2	1
Greenfield Township, Blair County	3,944	2	2	0
Greensburg	14,108	38	28	10
Green Tree	4,914	11	10	1
Greenville	5,308	9	8	1
Grove City	7,840	12	11	1
Hamburg	4,398	7	6	1
Hampden Township	30,861	27	26	1
Hampton Township	18,218	19	18	1
Hanover	15,707	28	25	3
Hanover Township, Luzerne County	10,842	17	16	1
Harmar Township	3,019	8	7	1
Harmony Township	2,999	5	5	0
Harrisburg	49,195	165	141	24
Harrison Township	10,271	14	13	1
Harveys Lake	2,768	2	2	0
Hastings	1,171	2	2	0
Hatboro	7,446	21	17	4
Hatfield Township	21,151	30	28	2
Haverford Township	49,370	82	70	12
Hegins Township	3,371	2	2	0
Heidelberg	1,211	3	3	0
Heidelberg Township, Berks County	1,749	1	1	0
Hellam Township	8,632	11	9	2
Hellertown	5,852	11	10	1
Hemlock Township	2,229	9	9	0
Hempfield Township, Mercer County	3,596	7	6	1
Hermitage	15,428	33	30	3
Highspire	2,371	15	15	0
Hilltown Township	15,589	20	17	3
Hollidaysburg	5,701	10	8	2
Homer City	1,591	2	2	0
Honesdale	4,248	5	5	0
Honey Brook	1,765	1	1	0
Hooversville	597	1	1	0
Hopewell Township	12,618	16	15	1
Horsham Township	26,580	48	39	9
Houston	1,237	1	1	0
Hughestown	1,375	1	1	0
Hughesville	2,029	3	3	0
Hummelstown	4,879	7	6	1
Huntingdon	6,943	12	12	0
Independence Township, Beaver County	2,342	2	2	0
Indiana	12,974	22	20	2
Indiana Township	7,157	10	10	0
Indian Lake	380	2	2	0
Ingram	3,212	4	4	0
Irwin	3,742	4	4	0
Jackson Township, Butler County	4,145	10	8	2
Jackson Township, Cambria County	4,041	2	2	0
Jackson Township, Luzerne County	4,638	2	2	0
Jeannette	9,069	14	13	1
Jefferson Hills Borough	11,211	21	20	1
Jefferson Township, Mercer County	1,814	2	2	0
Jenkins Township	4,547	4	4	0
Jenkintown	4,431	16	14	2
Jermyn	2,060	2	2	0
Jim Thorpe	4,645	8	7	1

Table 78. Full-Time Law Enforcement Employees, by Selected State and City, 2019—Continued

(Number.)

State/city	Population	Total law enforcement employees	Total officers	Total civilians
Johnsonburg	2,287	3	3	0
Johnstown	20,663	43	38	5
Kane	3,450	3	3	0
Kennedy Township	8,181	10	8	2
Kennett Square	6,213	15	12	3
Kidder Township	1,931	5	5	0
Kilbuck Township	722	17	14	3
Kingston	12,824	21	19	2
Kingston Township	6,882	13	13	0
Kiskiminetas Township	4,474	9	9	0
Kittanning	3,743	8	7	1
Kline Township	1,360	2	1	1
Knox	1,065	2	2	0
Koppel	713	2	2	0
Kulpmont	2,751	1	1	0
Kutztown	5,099	14	12	2
Lake City	2,877	3	3	0
Lancaster Township, Butler County	2,683	4	4	0
Langhorne Borough	1,580	1	1	0
Lansdale	16,759	36	35	1
Lansdowne	10,621	18	15	3
Lansford	3,800	6	6	0
Larksville	4,394	7	7	0
Latrobe	7,831	14	13	1
Laureldale	3,925	5	5	0
Lawrence Park Township	3,755	9	8	1
Lawrence Township, Clearfield County	7,547	9	8	1
Lebanon	25,959	44	41	3
Leechburg	1,989	3	3	0
Leetsdale	1,173	5	5	0
Lehighton	5,309	12	11	1
Lehigh Township, Northampton County	10,488	13	12	1
Lehman Township	3,499	6	6	0
Lewistown	8,135	13	12	1
Liberty Township, Adams County	1,264	1	1	0
Limerick Township	19,180	32	30	2
Lincoln	1,030	2	2	0
Linesville	978	7	7	0
Lititz	9,496	17	15	2
Littlestown	4,507	9	8	1
Lock Haven	9,030	16	14	2
Locust Township	1,394	5	5	0
Logan Township	12,209	18	16	2
Lower Allen Township	19,650	25	22	3
Lower Burrell	11,077	18	17	1
Lower Chichester Township	3,461	5	5	0
Lower Frederick Township	4,888	3	3	0
Lower Gwynedd Township	11,533	19	18	1
Lower Heidelberg Township	6,192	10	9	1
Lower Makefield Township	32,787	42	38	4
Lower Merion Township	59,796	152	135	17
Lower Moreland Township	13,163	34	30	4
Lower Paxton Township	49,795	65	58	7
Lower Pottsgrove Township	12,115	19	17	2
Lower Providence Township	26,980	32	30	2
Lower Salford Township	15,534	21	19	2
Lower Saucon Township	10,867	17	15	2
Lower Southampton Township	19,225	36	32	4
Lower Swatara Township	8,913	14	13	1
Lower Windsor Township	7,604	10	9	1
Luzerne Township	5,896	1	1	0
Macungie	3,182	5	5	0
Mahanoy Township	3,194	1	1	0
Mahoning Township, Carbon County	4,232	6	6	0
Mahoning Township, Lawrence County	2,875	1	1	0
Mahoning Township, Montour County	4,151	8	7	1
Malvern	3,506	8	7	1
Manheim	4,859	18	17	1
Manheim Township	40,486	78	65	13
Manor	3,378	3	3	0
Manor Township, Armstrong County	4,053	3	3	0
Manor Township, Lancaster County	21,059	21	19	2
Mansfield	2,940	5	5	0
Marcus Hook	2,397	5	4	1
Marietta	2,609	19	17	2
Marion Township, Beaver County	872	2	2	0
Marion Township, Berks County	1,952	3	3	0
Marlborough Township	3,397	4	4	0
Marple Township	23,859	34	31	3
Mars	1,616	1	1	0
Martinsburg	1,837	2	2	0
Marysville	2,556	2	2	0
Masontown	3,287	4	4	0
Mayfield	1,695	2	2	0
McAdoo	2,154	4	4	0

Table 78. Full-Time Law Enforcement Employees, by Selected State and City, 2019—Continued

(Number.)

State/city	Population	Total law enforcement employees	Total officers	Total civilians
McCandless	28,281	30	28	2
McDonald Borough	2,058	6	5	1
McKeesport	20,765	48	45	3
McKees Rocks	5,861	9	8	1
McSherrystown	3,091	4	4	0
Meadville	12,642	28	22	6
Mechanicsburg	8,994	16	14	2
Media	5,713	22	14	8
Mercer	1,851	5	5	0
Mercersburg	1,541	2	2	0
Meshoppen	1,422	2	2	0
Middleburg	1,289	4	3	1
Middlesex Township, Butler County	5,608	4	4	0
Middlesex Township, Cumberland County	7,502	14	13	1
Middletown	9,327	13	12	1
Middletown Township	45,013	61	55	6
Midland	2,469	3	3	0
Mifflinburg	3,512	10	9	1
Mifflin County Regional	16,923	15	14	1
Milford	980	2	2	0
Millbourne	1,157	1	1	0
Millcreek Township, Erie County	52,965	81	64	17
Millcreek Township, Lebanon County	5,783	2	2	0
Millersburg	2,544	3	2	1
Millersville	8,416	15	13	2
Millvale	3,578	6	6	0
Milton	6,711	9	8	1
Minersville	4,150	6	6	0
Mohnton	3,043	4	4	0
Monaca	5,427	9	9	0
Monessen	7,225	12	11	1
Monongahela	9,795	7	6	1
Monroeville	27,429	55	44	11
Montgomery	1,509	1	1	0
Montgomery Township	26,317	45	43	2
Montour Township	1,289	3	3	0
Moon Township	25,647	38	31	7
Moore Township	9,415	11	10	1
Morrisville	8,522	13	11	2
Morton	2,663	5	4	1
Moscow	2,061	2	2	0
Mount Carmel	5,537	8	8	0
Mount Carmel Township	2,970	6	6	0
Mount Gretna Borough	208	7	6	1
Mount Holly Springs	2,047	3	3	0
Mount Joy	8,303	13	12	1
Mount Lebanon	32,001	54	45	9
Mount Pleasant	4,213	3	3	0
Mount Pleasant Township	3,529	5	5	0
Mount Union	2,343	4	4	0
Muhlenberg Township	20,392	31	29	2
Muncy	2,420	3	3	0
Muncy Township	1,207	2	2	0
Munhall	11,041	26	24	2
Murrysville	19,655	23	21	2
Nanticoke	10,318	14	13	1
Nanty Glo	2,487	1	1	0
Narberth	4,356	7	6	1
Neshannock Township	9,230	8	8	0
Nesquehoning	3,248	5	5	0
Nether Providence Township	13,747	16	15	1
Neville Township	1,047	17	14	3
Newberry Township	15,885	18	16	2
New Bethlehem	2,701	3	3	0
New Brighton	8,708	9	7	2
New Britain Township	11,444	15	14	1
New Castle	21,624	38	37	1
New Cumberland	7,304	10	9	1
New Florence	648	1	1	0
New Hanover Township	13,314	12	11	1
New Holland	5,485	16	15	1
New Hope	2,527	11	9	2
New Kensington	12,273	22	22	0
Newport Township	5,386	3	3	0
New Sewickley Township	7,175	11	10	1
Newtown	2,239	6	6	0
Newtown Township, Bucks County	22,796	32	28	4
Newtown Township, Delaware County	13,928	20	18	2
Newville	1,350	2	2	0
New Wilmington	2,178	5	5	0
Norristown	34,430	81	68	13
Northampton	9,921	14	12	2
Northampton Township	39,171	49	43	6
North Belle Vernon	1,858	2	2	0

Table 78. Full-Time Law Enforcement Employees, by Selected State and City, 2019—Continued

(Number.)

State/city	Population	Total law enforcement employees	Total officers	Total civilians
North Catasauqua	2,839	5	5	0
North Cornwall Township	7,976	9	9	0
North Coventry Township	8,004	12	11	1
North East, Erie County	4,051	7	7	0
Northeastern Regional	11,938	13	12	1
Northern Berks Regional	13,475	17	16	1
Northern Cambria Borough	3,510	2	2	0
Northern Lancaster County Regional	36,506	26	24	2
Northern Regional	35,875	31	29	2
Northern York County Regional	70,378	55	51	4
North Hopewell Township	2,807	1	1	0
North Huntingdon Township	30,387	34	28	6
North Londonderry Township	8,632	10	9	1
North Middleton Township	11,713	11	10	1
North Strabane Township	14,751	24	23	1
Northumberland	3,605	5	5	0
North Versailles Township	12,034	24	19	5
North Wales	3,270	5	5	0
Northwest Lancaster County Regional	20,480	21	19	2
Norwood	5,881	7	6	1
Oakmont	6,566	7	7	0
O'Hara Township	8,671	17	16	1
Ohio Township	7,067	17	14	3
Ohioville	3,284	2	2	0
Oil City	9,654	22	16	6
Old Forge	7,891	5	5	0
Old Lycoming Township	4,913	9	9	0
Olyphant	5,032	6	6	0
Orangeville Area	1,728	1	1	0
Orwigsburg	2,952	6	6	0
Oxford	5,637	11	10	1
Palmerton	5,334	9	8	1
Palmer Township	21,558	37	35	2
Palmyra	7,609	9	8	1
Parkesburg	3,963	9	8	1
Parkside	2,322	3	3	0
Parks Township	2,554	2	2	0
Patterson Township	4,161	4	4	0
Patton	1,609	2	2	0
Patton Township	16,075	21	19	2
Penbrook	2,977	6	6	0
Penndel	2,140	1	1	0
Penn Hills	40,809	53	50	3
Pennridge Regional	10,977	15	13	2
Penn Township, Butler County	4,887	5	4	1
Penn Township, Westmoreland County	19,308	23	21	2
Penn Township, York County	16,669	25	23	2
Perkasie	8,621	19	17	2
Perryopolis	1,671	2	2	0
Peters Township	22,163	23	21	2
Philadelphia	1,589,014	7,412	6,584	828
Phoenixville	17,019	32	31	1
Pine Creek Township	3,242	2	2	0
Pitcairn	3,173	3	3	0
Pittsburgh	300,548	1,064	1,013	51
Pittston	7,758	9	9	0
Pittston Township	3,384	6	5	1
Plains Township	9,689	19	18	1
Pleasant Hills	8,061	20	18	2
Plum	27,134	30	24	6
Plumstead Township	14,588	18	16	2
Plymouth	5,780	4	4	0
Plymouth Township, Montgomery County	17,704	51	44	7
Pocono Mountain Regional	43,086	48	43	5
Pocono Township	10,949	20	20	0
Point Township	3,598	6	6	0
Polk	775	2	2	0
Portage	2,391	2	2	0
Port Allegany	2,001	3	3	0
Port Carbon	1,772	2	2	0
Port Vue	3,658	2	2	0
Pottstown	22,705	57	46	11
Pottsville	13,463	23	22	1
Pringle	957	21	19	2
Prospect Park	6,480	9	9	0
Pulaski Township, Lawrence County	3,248	2	2	0
Punxsutawney	5,734	9	8	1
Pymatuning Township	3,057	7	6	1
Quakertown	8,793	20	18	2
Quarryville	2,769	4	4	0
Raccoon Township	2,905	4	4	0
Radnor Township	31,796	46	42	4
Ralpho Township	4,214	6	6	0
Rankin	2,033	1	1	0

Table 78. Full-Time Law Enforcement Employees, by Selected State and City, 2019—Continued

(Number.)

State/city	Population	Total law enforcement employees	Total officers	Total civilians
Reading	88,549	176	154	22
Reading Township	5,859	2	2	0
Redstone Township	4,173	3	3	0
Reilly Township	688	2	2	0
Renovo	1,210	1	1	0
Reserve Township	3,221	4	4	0
Reynoldsville	2,648	1	1	0
Rice Township	3,585	6	6	0
Richland Township, Bucks County	13,411	17	15	2
Richland Township, Cambria County	11,865	21	20	1
Ridgway	3,756	7	6	1
Ridley Park	7,046	13	10	3
Ridley Township	31,154	37	32	5
Riverside	1,850	3	3	0
Roaring Brook Township	1,970	2	2	0
Roaring Creek Township	532	5	5	0
Roaring Spring	2,448	3	3	0
Robeson Township	7,491	5	5	0
Robinson Township, Allegheny County	13,711	31	29	2
Rochester Township	2,638	4	4	0
Rockledge	2,533	5	5	0
Ross Township	30,410	46	44	2
Rostraver Township	11,005	17	16	1
Royalton	1,040	5	5	0
Royersford	4,770	9	9	0
Rural Valley	815	1	1	0
Rush Township	3,254	1	1	0
Sadsbury Township, Chester County	4,117	4	4	0
Salem Township, Luzerne County	4,189	7	7	0
Salisbury Township	13,991	21	19	2
Sandy Lake	629	1	1	0
Sandy Township	10,445	11	10	1
Saxonburg	1,445	2	2	0
Saxton	686	3	3	0
Sayre	6,402	13	10	3
Schuylkill Haven	5,100	8	8	0
Schuylkill Township, Chester County	8,655	13	11	2
Scottdale	4,093	6	6	0
Scott Township, Allegheny County	16,456	23	22	1
Scott Township, Columbia County	5,092	6	6	0
Scott Township, Lackawanna County	4,772	4	4	0
Scranton	77,323	161	146	15
Selinsgrove	5,962	7	6	1
Seward	464	1	1	0
Sewickley Heights	803	3	3	0
Shaler Township	27,860	28	26	2
Shamokin	6,938	11	10	1
Shamokin Dam	1,723	3	3	0
Sharon Hill	5,674	10	9	1
Sharpsburg	3,324	6	6	0
Shenandoah	4,755	5	5	0
Shenango Township, Lawrence County	7,182	7	7	0
Shenango Township, Mercer County	3,675	10	10	0
Shillington	5,338	8	7	1
Shinglehouse	1,054	1	1	0
Shippensburg	5,586	10	9	1
Shippingport	190	1	1	0
Shiremanstown	1,621	2	2	0
Silver Lake Township	1,587	1	1	0
Silver Spring Township	18,580	24	23	1
Sinking Spring	4,132	6	5	1
Slate Belt Regional	12,506	24	23	1
Slatington	4,317	5	5	0
Slippery Rock	3,517	4	4	0
Smethport	1,530	2	2	0
Smith Township	4,362	4	4	0
Solebury Township	8,542	16	14	2
Somerset	5,856	7	6	1
Souderton	7,164	6	5	1
South Abington Township	8,960	12	11	1
South Beaver Township	2,648	4	4	0
South Buffalo Township	2,520	2	2	0
South Centre Township	4,169	7	7	0
South Coatesville	1,461	2	2	0
South Connellsville Borough	1,865	1	1	0
Southern Chester County Regional	16,428	19	17	2
Southern Regional York County	11,568	16	14	2
South Fayette Township	15,928	18	17	1
South Fork	842	1	1	0
South Greensburg	1,988	2	2	0
South Heidelberg Township	7,436	10	10	0
South Lebanon Township	10,043	9	8	1
South Londonderry Township	8,679	8	8	0
South Park Township	13,257	16	15	1
South Pymatuning Township	2,526	4	4	0

Table 78. Full-Time Law Enforcement Employees, by Selected State and City, 2019—Continued

(Number.)

State/city	Population	Total law enforcement employees	Total officers	Total civilians
Southwestern Regional	17,870	15	14	1
Southwest Greensburg	2,016	2	2	0
Southwest Regional, Washington County	131	5	2	3
South Whitehall Township	19,994	42	40	2
South Williamsport	6,071	10	9	1
Spring City	3,316	2	2	0
Springdale	3,294	4	4	0
Springettsbury Township	26,888	35	32	3
Springfield Township, Bucks County	5,044	4	4	0
Springfield Township, Delaware County	24,208	37	32	5
Springfield Township, Montgomery County	19,971	30	29	1
Spring Garden Township	13,237	23	20	3
Spring Township, Berks County	27,681	29	28	1
Spring Township, Centre County	7,944	8	7	1
St. Clair Boro	2,821	9	9	0
Steelton	5,945	14	12	2
St. Marys City	12,277	16	15	1
Stoneboro	984	1	1	0
Stonycreek Township	2,583	5	5	0
Stowe Township	6,141	10	9	1
Strasburg	3,005	5	5	0
Stroud Area Regional	35,351	59	52	7
Sugarcreek	4,924	3	3	0
Sugarloaf Township, Luzerne County	3,920	5	5	0
Sugar Notch	960	1	1	0
Summerhill Township	2,260	2	2	0
Summit Hill	2,950	7	5	2
Sunbury	9,352	19	15	4
Susquehanna Regional	8,436	19	17	2
Susquehanna Township	1,841	2	2	0
Susquehanna Township, Dauphin County	25,238	43	41	2
Swarthmore	6,428	9	9	0
Swatara Township	26,643	52	49	3
Sweden Township	817	1	1	0
Swissvale	8,652	15	15	0
Swoyersville	4,942	5	5	0
Sykesville	1,117	1	1	0
Tamaqua	6,657	9	8	1
Tarentum	4,373	8	7	1
Tatamy	1,141	1	1	0
Taylor	5,886	7	7	0
Throop	3,902	7	7	0
Tiadaghton Valley Regional	7,578	11	10	1
Tilden Township	3,616	4	4	0
Tinicum Township, Bucks County	3,956	5	5	0
Tinicum Township, Delaware County	4,097	18	16	2
Tioga	646	1	1	0
Titusville	5,194	9	9	0
Towamencin Township	18,604	28	28	0
Towanda	2,832	7	7	0
Trafford	3,038	5	5	0
Trainer	1,843	4	4	0
Tredyffrin Township	29,523	47	41	6
Tremont	1,665	2	2	0
Troy	1,244	2	2	0
Tullytown	1,919	6	5	1
Tulpehocken Township	3,412	3	3	0
Tunkhannock Township, Wyoming County	6,068	9	8	1
Turtle Creek	5,155	5	5	0
Tyrone	5,160	14	11	3
Union City	3,126	5	4	1
Uniontown	9,774	27	20	7
Union Township, Lawrence County	4,863	7	7	0
Upland	3,303	8	7	1
Upper Allen Township	20,432	24	23	1
Upper Burrell Township	2,220	2	2	0
Upper Chichester Township	16,925	24	23	1
Upper Darby Township	82,708	145	126	19
Upper Dublin Township	26,624	50	40	10
Upper Gwynedd Township	15,891	26	26	0
Upper Macungie Township	25,384	31	29	2
Upper Makefield Township	8,560	17	16	1
Upper Merion Township	31,410	90	71	19
Upper Moreland Township	24,109	42	36	6
Upper Nazareth Township	7,072	9	8	1
Upper Perkiomen	3,876	4	4	0
Upper Pottsgrove Township	5,785	10	9	1
Upper Providence Township, Delaware County	10,437	16	15	1
Upper Providence Township, Montgomery County	24,674	31	29	2
Upper Saucon Township	17,451	22	21	1
Upper Southampton Township	14,987	25	22	3

Table 78. Full-Time Law Enforcement Employees, by Selected State and City, 2019—Continued

(Number.)

State/city	Population	Total law enforcement employees	Total officers	Total civilians
Upper St. Clair Township	19,741	37	30	7
Upper Uwchlan Township	11,653	11	11	0
Upper Yoder Township	5,047	13	13	0
Uwchlan Township	19,011	23	22	1
Valley Township	7,934	6	6	0
Vandergrift	4,873	9	8	1
Vernon Township	5,371	4	4	0
Verona	2,407	4	3	1
Versailles	1,459	2	2	0
Walnutport	2,090	4	4	0
Warminster Township	32,293	48	44	4
Warren	9,054	20	16	4
Warrington Township	24,607	35	32	3
Warwick Township, Bucks County	14,646	18	17	1
Washington Township, Fayette County	3,619	4	4	0
Washington Township, Northampton County	5,259	6	5	1
Washington Township, Westmoreland County	7,062	9	9	0
Washington, Washington County	13,448	33	31	2
Watsontown	2,247	6	6	0
Waverly Township	1,679	4	4	0
Waynesburg	3,996	8	8	0
Weatherly	2,458	4	4	0
Wellsboro	3,236	7	7	0
Wesleyville	3,120	8	7	1
West Brandywine Township	7,508	7	6	1
West Brownsville	962	1	1	0
West Caln Township	9,113	4	4	0
West Carroll Township	1,203	2	2	0
West Chester	20,255	64	47	17
West Conshohocken	1,435	13	12	1
West Cornwall Township	2,058	7	6	1
West Deer Township	11,996	12	11	1
West Earl Township	8,484	6	6	0
Western Berks Regional	4,847	3	3	0
West Fallowfield Township	2,596	2	2	0
Westfield	1,034	2	2	0
West Goshen Township	23,157	36	31	5
West Hazleton	4,463	7	5	2
West Hempfield Township	16,603	23	21	2
West Hills Regional	9,925	12	11	1
West Homestead	1,875	7	6	1
West Lampeter Township	16,039	17	16	1
West Mahanoy Township	2,708	3	3	0
West Manchester Township	18,860	30	27	3
West Manheim Township	8,663	10	9	1
West Mead Township	5,008	4	2	2
West Mifflin	19,628	41	34	7
West Newton	2,478	2	2	0
West Norriton Township	15,650	31	29	2
West Penn Township	4,246	2	2	0
West Pike Run	1,541	1	1	0
West Pittston	4,737	3	3	0
West Pottsgrove Township	3,876	7	7	0
West Reading	4,224	15	13	2
West Sadsbury Township	2,487	4	4	0
West Salem Township	3,369	9	8	1
West Shore Regional	7,732	13	12	1
Westtown-East Goshen Regional	32,366	33	30	3
West View	6,528	13	11	2
West Vincent Township	5,887	7	6	1
West Whiteland Township	18,389	26	24	2
West York	4,581	12	12	0
Whitehall	13,611	25	20	5
Whitehall Township	27,829	51	46	5
White Haven Borough	1,103	3	3	0
Whitemarsh Township	18,213	41	36	5
White Oak	7,456	12	11	1
Whitpain Township	19,294	38	32	6
Wiconisco Township	1,201	1	1	0
Wilkes-Barre	40,722	80	76	4
Wilkes-Barre Township	2,886	13	12	1
Wilkinsburg	15,389	25	23	2
Wilkins Township	6,137	13	12	1
Williamsburg	1,174	2	2	0
Williamsport	28,220	52	48	4
Willistown Township	11,052	20	18	2
Wilson	7,822	15	14	1
Windber	3,825	3	2	1
Womelsdorf	2,899	1	1	0
Woodward Township	2,356	2	2	0
Wyoming	3,011	4	4	0
Wyomissing	10,504	25	23	2
Yardley	2,517	5	5	0

Table 78. Full-Time Law Enforcement Employees, by Selected State and City, 2019—Continued

(Number.)

State/city	Population	Total law enforcement employees	Total officers	Total civilians
Yeadon	11,474	14	13	1
York	44,150	120	105	15
York Area Regional	54,192	50	45	5
Youngsville	1,611	2	2	0
Zelienople	3,614	10	9	1
Zerbe Township	1,761	1	1	0
RHODE ISLAND				
Barrington	16,090	33	26	7
Bristol	22,070	50	40	10
Burrillville	16,859	32	25	7
Central Falls	19,423	42	35	7
Charlestown	7,819	25	20	5
Coventry	34,751	72	57	15
Cranston	81,471	180	149	31
Cumberland	35,206	57	46	11
East Greenwich	13,119	37	30	7
East Providence	47,590	103	86	17
Foster	4,730	13	9	4
Glocester	10,281	20	15	5
Hopkinton	8,110	19	14	5
Jamestown	5,508	19	14	5
Johnston	29,424	79	66	13
Lincoln	21,891	44	36	8
Little Compton	3,488	14	10	4
Middletown	15,934	41	37	4
Narragansett	15,411	53	40	13
Newport	24,584	97	81	16
New Shoreham	1,032	8	4	4
North Kingstown	26,286	62	51	11
North Providence	32,655	81	63	18
North Smithfield	12,568	27	26	1
Pawtucket	72,030	171	137	34
Portsmouth	17,330	38	36	2
Providence	179,762	526	436	90
Richmond	7,701	18	13	5
Scituate	10,707	28	17	11
Smithfield	21,790	54	41	13
South Kingstown	30,656	70	53	17
Tiverton	15,745	41	29	12
Warren	10,419	30	25	5
Warwick	80,749	207	162	45
Westerly	22,475	63	49	14
West Greenwich	6,375	19	13	6
West Warwick	28,847	60	48	12
Woonsocket	41,709	113	100	13
SOUTH CAROLINA				
Abbeville	5,017	22	19	3
Aiken	30,922	144	90	54
Allendale	2,924	6	6	0
Anderson	27,498	120	107	13
Andrews	2,851	7	6	1
Atlantic Beach	440	5	4	1
Bamberg	3,195	11	9	2
Barnwell	4,321	17	15	2
Batesburg-Leesville	5,389	28	22	6
Beaufort	13,485	49	44	5
Belton	4,434	1	1	0
Bennettsville	7,726	33	31	2
Bishopville	2,927	14	12	2
Blacksburg	1,883	9	8	1
Blackville	2,194	7	6	1
Bluffton	24,812	57	51	6
Bonneau	483	2	2	0
Bowman	904	3	3	0
Branchville	952	3	2	1
Briarcliffe Acres	593	1	1	0
Burnettown	2,751	1	1	0
Calhoun Falls	1,912	3	3	0
Camden	7,242	36	32	4
Cameron	396	1	1	0
Campobello	588	9	8	1
Cayce	14,211	76	64	12
Central	5,380	10	9	1
Chapin	1,653	6	6	0
Charleston	138,254	510	403	107
Cheraw	5,589	30	23	7
Chester	5,368	29	19	10
Chesterfield	1,415	6	5	1
Clemson	17,547	43	32	11
Clinton	8,412	27	21	6
Clio	660	4	4	0
Clover	6,575	26	21	5
Columbia	133,790	442	349	93

Table 78. Full-Time Law Enforcement Employees, by Selected State and City, 2019—Continued

(Number.)

State/city	Population	Total law enforcement employees	Total officers	Total civilians
Conway	26,127	58	50	8
Coward	767	1	1	0
Cowpens	2,408	10	8	2
Darlington	5,886	31	28	3
Denmark	2,924	11	10	1
Dillon	6,318	27	26	1
Due West	1,240	5	5	0
Duncan	3,573	19	18	1
Easley	21,390	62	51	11
Edgefield	4,771	11	11	0
Edisto Beach	406	7	7	0
Ehrhardt	481	3	1	2
Elgin	1,612	7	6	1
Elloree	642	3	3	0
Estill	1,855	10	8	2
Eutawville	292	2	2	0
Florence	37,640	106	83	23
Folly Beach	2,657	23	17	6
Forest Acres	10,320	34	27	7
Fort Lawn	879	3	2	1
Fort Mill	21,219	64	54	10
Fountain Inn	10,375	31	25	6
Gaffney	12,528	42	37	5
Gaston	1,692	4	4	0
Georgetown	8,733	41	34	7
Gifford	261	3	2	1
Goose Creek	43,683	95	70	25
Great Falls	1,875	4	4	0
Greenville	69,830	249	202	47
Greenwood	23,427	55	50	5
Greer	32,976	82	59	23
Hampton	2,499	12	12	0
Hanahan	26,941	30	28	2
Hardeeville	7,075	23	21	2
Hartsville	7,524	40	38	2
Hemingway	400	4	3	1
Holly Hill	1,181	6	6	0
Honea Path	3,810	13	13	0
Irmo	12,516	28	25	3
Isle of Palms	4,366	22	16	6
Jackson	1,792	5	4	1
Jamestown	83	5	4	1
Johnsonville	1,494	7	6	1
Johnston	2,353	8	8	0
Jonesville	834	4	4	0
Lake City	6,541	25	21	4
Lake View	755	4	4	0
Landrum	2,658	18	17	1
Lane	452	3	1	2
Latta	1,288	6	6	0
Laurens	8,823	28	23	5
Lexington	22,160	61	58	3
Liberty	3,152	16	12	4
Loris	2,740	15	12	3
Lyman	3,661	13	12	1
Marion	6,373	21	18	3
Mauldin	25,453	57	46	11
McCormick	2,298	6	6	0
Moncks Corner	11,986	32	29	3
Mount Pleasant	92,448	171	148	23
Mullins	4,290	19	18	1
Myrtle Beach	34,860	308	229	79
Newberry	10,333	30	26	4
New Ellenton	2,145	2	2	0
Ninety Six	2,039	6	6	0
North	716	5	5	0
North Augusta	23,875	89	64	25
North Charleston	115,312	413	332	81
North Myrtle Beach	16,942	154	84	70
Norway	308	1	1	0
Pamplico	1,221	3	3	0
Pelion	704	3	2	1
Pickens	3,171	15	15	0
Port Royal	13,368	25	24	1
Quinby	927	1	1	0
Ridgeland	3,807	13	12	1
Ridge Spring	758	1	1	0
Ridgeville	1,750	2	2	0
Rock Hill	75,342	195	149	46
Salley	416	1	1	0
Saluda	3,641	11	10	1
Simpsonville	23,682	53	43	10
Society Hill	533	3	3	0
South Congaree	2,483	7	6	1
Spartanburg	37,754	143	124	19

Table 78. Full-Time Law Enforcement Employees, by Selected State and City, 2019—Continued

(Number.)

State/city	Population	Total law enforcement employees	Total officers	Total civilians
Springdale	2,753	9	9	0
Springfield	486	2	2	0
St. George	2,197	11	10	1
Summerton	939	5	5	0
Sumter	39,546	154	109	45
Surfside Beach	4,553	23	19	4
Swansea	959	4	3	1
Tega Cay	11,322	27	25	2
Travelers Rest	5,339	21	15	6
Trenton	260	1	1	0
Union	7,694	32	29	3
Wagener	838	2	2	0
Walhalla	4,384	14	13	1
Walterboro	5,429	30	28	2
Ware Shoals	2,156	7	7	0
Wellford	2,697	11	9	2
West Columbia	17,986	57	51	6
Westminster	2,570	5	5	0
West Pelzer	948	3	3	0
West Union	325	2	2	0
Whitmire	1,469	4	3	1
Williamston	4,249	18	17	1
Winnsboro	3,165	19	18	1
Woodruff	4,356	12	11	1
Yemassee	954	8	8	0
York	8,294	41	35	6
SOUTH DAKOTA				
Aberdeen	28,870	57	48	9
Alcester	744	2	2	0
Avon	597	1	1	0
Belle Fourche	5,600	13	11	2
Beresford	1,989	4	4	0
Box Elder	10,077	16	14	2
Brandon	10,244	14	13	1
Brookings	24,823	53	37	16
Burke	586	1	1	0
Canton	3,521	6	6	0
Centerville	879	2	2	0
Chamberlain	2,345	6	6	0
Clark	1,056	2	2	0
Deadwood	1,307	18	15	3
Eagle Butte	1,350	1	1	0
Elk Point	1,857	4	4	0
Faith	413	2	2	0
Flandreau	2,323	8	7	1
Freeman	1,290	2	2	0
Gettysburg	1,110	2	2	0
Gregory	1,244	3	3	0
Groton	1,506	4	4	0
Hot Springs	3,485	8	7	1
Huron	13,840	26	25	1
Jefferson	507	2	2	0
Kadoka	714	1	1	0
Lake Norden	506	2	2	0
Lead	2,958	7	6	1
Lennox	2,476	4	4	0
Madison	7,558	14	13	1
Martin	1,071	4	4	0
Menno	622	1	1	0
Milbank	3,131	7	7	0
Miller	1,353	4	4	0
Mitchell	15,733	41	27	14
Mobridge	3,550	14	7	7
Murdo	442	2	2	0
North Sioux City	2,932	8	8	0
Parkston	1,497	2	2	0
Philip	773	2	2	0
Pierre	14,018	41	24	17
Platte	1,263	2	2	0
Rapid City	76,343	168	134	34
Scotland	814	1	1	0
Sioux Falls	185,628	290	255	35
Sisseton	2,423	7	7	0
Spearfish	11,842	31	23	8
Springfield	1,935	2	2	0
Sturgis	6,983	18	15	3
Summerset	2,796	5	4	1
Tea	5,898	7	7	0
Tripp	630	3	3	0
Tyndall	1,036	2	2	0
Vermillion	10,833	21	19	2
Wagner	1,561	4	4	0
Watertown	22,233	52	36	16
Webster	1,746	5	5	0

Table 78. Full-Time Law Enforcement Employees, by Selected State and City, 2019—Continued

(Number.)

State/city	Population	Total law enforcement employees	Total officers	Total civilians
Whitewood	969	3	3	0
Winner	2,843	10	10	0
Yankton	14,730	31	30	1
TENNESSEE				
Adamsville	2,171	7	6	1
Alamo	2,294	3	3	0
Alcoa	10,798	51	43	8
Alexandria	1,006	4	3	1
Algood	4,549	15	15	0
Ardmore	1,229	11	7	4
Ashland City	4,708	17	15	2
Athens	13,879	34	32	2
Atoka	9,510	23	22	1
Baileyton	445	3	3	0
Bartlett	59,610	159	123	36
Baxter	1,514	6	6	0
Bean Station	3,085	7	7	0
Belle Meade	2,879	23	15	8
Bells	2,455	5	5	0
Benton	1,258	7	6	1
Berry Hill	515	18	14	4
Big Sandy	522	1	1	0
Blaine	1,871	3	3	0
Bluff City	1,661	8	8	0
Bolivar	4,888	24	22	2
Bradford	983	4	4	0
Brentwood	43,217	80	63	17
Brighton	2,926	8	8	0
Bristol	26,900	85	67	18
Brownsville	9,336	40	36	4
Bruceton	1,400	5	3	2
Burns	1,456	2	2	0
Calhoun	498	4	3	1
Camden	3,573	20	12	8
Carthage	2,276	12	8	4
Caryville	2,146	6	6	0
Celina	1,453	8	5	3
Centerville	3,564	17	15	2
Chapel Hill	1,532	7	6	1
Charleston	695	3	3	0
Chattanooga	181,848	563	469	94
Church Hill	6,671	11	9	2
Clarksville	159,996	353	289	64
Cleveland	45,453	112	100	12
Clifton	2,665	5	5	0
Clinton	10,062	44	34	10
Collegedale	11,929	20	20	0
Collierville	51,273	127	93	34
Collinwood	939	4	4	0
Columbia	40,001	99	88	11
Cookeville	34,373	93	71	22
Coopertown	4,590	5	4	1
Cornersville	1,271	2	2	0
Covington	8,755	31	30	1
Cowan	1,657	3	3	0
Crossville	11,643	46	43	3
Cumberland City	308	2	2	0
Dandridge	3,168	12	11	1
Dayton	7,408	19	19	0
Decatur	1,646	6	6	0
Decaturville	860	1	1	0
Decherd	2,386	12	11	1
Dickson	15,703	66	59	7
Dover	1,489	3	3	0
Dresden	2,908	9	8	1
Dunlap	5,155	12	12	0
Dyer	2,204	7	6	1
Dyersburg	16,300	65	57	8
Eagleville	714	2	2	0
East Ridge	21,027	49	44	5
Elizabethton	13,409	42	38	4
Elkton	528	2	2	0
Englewood	1,524	7	6	1
Erin	1,287	6	5	1
Erwin	5,826	16	16	0
Estill Springs	2,030	7	7	0
Ethridge	489	4	3	1
Etowah	3,482	12	11	1
Fairview	9,153	22	22	0
Fayetteville	7,047	28	27	1
Franklin	83,517	144	132	12
Friendship	670	1	1	0
Gainesboro	944	4	4	0
Gallatin	41,918	98	84	14

Table 78. Full-Time Law Enforcement Employees, by Selected State and City, 2019—Continued

(Number.)

State/city	Population	Total law enforcement employees	Total officers	Total civilians
Gallaway	644	4	4	0
Gatlinburg	4,163	55	45	10
Germantown	39,127	127	105	22
Gibson	394	4	3	1
Gleason	1,364	5	5	0
Goodlettsville	16,976	57	42	15
Gordonsville	1,239	6	6	0
Grand Junction	266	3	3	0
Graysville	1,564	5	5	0
Greenbrier	6,887	15	14	1
Greeneville	14,881	55	53	2
Greenfield	2,063	6	5	1
Halls	2,079	7	7	0
Harriman	6,121	22	21	1
Henderson	6,314	16	16	0
Hendersonville	58,388	144	128	16
Henry	466	1	1	0
Hohenwald	3,680	14	14	0
Hollow Rock	675	1	1	0
Hornbeak	394	1	1	0
Humboldt	8,165	31	25	6
Huntingdon	3,805	18	14	4
Huntland	839	2	2	0
Jacksboro	1,919	6	5	1
Jackson	66,915	257	217	40
Jamestown	1,960	9	9	0
Jasper	3,361	8	8	0
Jefferson City	8,193	30	28	2
Jellico	2,161	5	4	1
Johnson City	67,197	170	141	29
Jonesborough	5,487	21	16	5
Kenton	1,195	3	3	0
Kimball	1,421	9	9	0
Kingsport	54,218	158	118	40
Kingston	5,809	13	12	1
Kingston Springs	2,750	7	5	2
Knoxville	188,666	490	370	120
Lafayette	5,309	24	16	8
La Follette	6,651	31	22	9
La Vergne	36,227	71	55	16
Lawrenceburg	10,877	39	34	5
Lebanon	36,337	129	101	28
Lenoir City	9,392	27	25	2
Lewisburg	12,245	31	30	1
Lexington	7,723	34	28	6
Livingston	4,014	22	17	5
Lookout Mountain	1,866	20	15	5
Loretto	1,789	5	5	0
Loudon	5,869	17	16	1
Madisonville	4,949	20	17	3
Manchester	11,020	38	34	4
Martin	10,488	40	30	10
Maryville	29,415	64	58	6
Mason	1,549	4	4	0
Maynardville	2,397	4	4	0
McEwen	1,733	5	5	0
McKenzie	5,509	22	17	5
McMinnville	13,696	36	32	4
Medina	4,334	8	8	0
Memphis	650,410	2,635	2,058	577
Metropolitan Nashville Police Department	687,361	1,775	1,412	363
Middleton	637	3	3	0
Milan	7,613	32	25	7
Millersville	6,829	16	15	1
Millington	10,669	44	32	12
Minor Hill	532	2	2	0
Monteagle	1,225	7	6	1
Monterey	2,888	10	9	1
Morristown	30,044	87	82	5
Moscow	559	3	3	0
Mountain City	2,407	9	9	0
Mount Carmel	5,295	7	6	1
Mount Juliet	37,359	77	62	15
Mount Pleasant	4,934	20	14	6
Munford	6,083	18	18	0
Murfreesboro	145,929	300	248	52
Newbern	3,312	12	12	0
New Johnsonville	1,900	5	5	0
New Market	1,372	5	2	3
Newport	6,786	31	27	4
New Tazewell	2,702	10	10	0
Niota	727	4	3	1
Nolensville	9,488	13	12	1
Norris	1,609	5	5	0
Oakland	8,323	19	17	2

Table 78. Full-Time Law Enforcement Employees, by Selected State and City, 2019—Continued

(Number.)

State/city	Population	Total law enforcement employees	Total officers	Total civilians
Oak Ridge	29,084	79	63	16
Obion	1,042	2	2	0
Oliver Springs	3,419	14	10	4
Oneida	3,704	16	11	5
Paris	10,047	37	26	11
Parsons	2,304	8	8	0
Petersburg	564	1	1	0
Pigeon Forge	6,383	74	59	15
Piperton	1,887	8	8	0
Pittman Center	581	4	4	0
Plainview	2,126	2	2	0
Pleasant View	4,686	6	6	0
Portland	12,995	33	29	4
Pulaski	7,628	27	24	3
Puryear	666	1	1	0
Red Bank	11,779	25	23	2
Red Boiling Springs	1,140	5	5	0
Ridgely	1,641	5	5	0
Ripley	7,818	29	23	6
Rockwood	5,439	17	16	1
Rocky Top	1,766	9	6	3
Rogersville	4,277	14	13	1
Rossville	950	7	7	0
Rutherford	1,066	4	3	1
Rutledge	1,352	3	3	0
Savannah	6,941	23	21	2
Scotts Hill	977	3	3	0
Selmer	4,401	17	15	2
Sevierville	16,760	72	56	16
Sharon	911	2	2	0
Shelbyville	22,062	51	41	10
Signal Mountain	8,605	17	15	2
Smithville	4,828	15	14	1
Smyrna	52,225	110	87	23
Soddy-Daisy	13,818	37	30	7
Somerville	3,213	10	9	1
South Carthage	1,386	4	4	0
South Fulton	2,214	8	7	1
South Pittsburg	3,008	9	9	0
Sparta	4,957	17	14	3
Spencer	1,646	2	2	0
Spring City	1,865	10	10	0
Springfield	17,022	42	37	5
Spring Hill	43,303	65	61	4
St. Joseph	814	1	1	0
Surgoinsville	1,772	1	1	0
Sweetwater	5,875	20	19	1
Tazewell	2,273	7	7	0
Tellico Plains	921	6	5	1
Tiptonville	4,286	7	7	0
Townsend	446	4	4	0
Tracy City	1,389	5	5	0
Trenton	4,022	22	16	6
Trezevant	842	2	2	0
Trimble	613	1	1	0
Troy	1,317	5	5	0
Tullahoma	19,468	38	33	5
Tusculum	2,805	2	2	0
Union City	10,340	40	31	9
Vonore	1,539	9	9	0
Wartburg	896	6	6	0
Wartrace	692	2	1	1
Watertown	1,519	4	4	0
Waverly	4,081	14	13	1
Waynesboro	2,307	6	6	0
Westmoreland	2,431	11	10	1
White Bluff	3,659	5	5	0
White House	12,822	25	22	3
White Pine	2,356	11	10	1
Whiteville	4,466	6	6	0
Whitwell	1,723	5	4	1
Winchester	8,733	26	24	2
Woodbury	2,878	10	9	1
TEXAS				
Abernathy	2,713	5	5	0
Abilene	123,665	274	213	61
Addison	16,339	71	60	11
Alamo	19,903	41	34	7
Alamo Heights	8,808	33	21	12
Alice	18,858	41	32	9
Allen	105,961	197	138	59
Alton	18,096	25	20	5
Alvarado	4,468	20	18	2
Alvin	27,159	77	48	29

Table 78. Full-Time Law Enforcement Employees, by Selected State and City, 2019—Continued

(Number.)

State/city	Population	Total law enforcement employees	Total officers	Total civilians
Amarillo	201,036	413	333	80
Andrews	14,133	21	20	1
Angleton	19,660	60	36	24
Anson	2,275	6	5	1
Aransas Pass	8,118	40	27	13
Archer City	1,732	2	2	0
Arcola	2,627	6	6	0
Argyle	4,339	11	9	2
Arlington	402,304	882	680	202
Arp	1,016	8	7	1
Athens	12,807	31	24	7
Atlanta	5,497	17	12	5
Austin	986,062	2,469	1,802	667
Azle	13,691	34	24	10
Baird	1,508	2	2	0
Balch Springs	25,511	60	41	19
Balcones Heights	3,366	24	19	5
Ballinger	3,615	8	6	2
Bangs	1,540	2	2	0
Bastrop	9,714	28	24	4
Bay City	17,501	59	38	21
Baytown	77,707	220	170	50
Beaumont	118,562	318	248	70
Bedford	49,771	129	81	48
Beeville	12,866	28	20	8
Bellaire	19,233	56	41	15
Bellmead	10,817	29	20	9
Bells	1,506	4	4	0
Bellville	4,288	12	11	1
Belton	22,741	48	36	12
Benbrook	23,872	50	41	9
Beverly Hills	1,989	12	6	6
Big Spring	28,278	47	33	14
Blanco	2,040	11	10	1
Blue Mound	2,485	10	6	4
Boerne	18,135	62	41	21
Bogata	1,060	5	5	0
Borger	12,536	30	28	2
Bovina	1,807	2	2	0
Brady	5,288	15	9	6
Brazoria	3,123	12	7	5
Breckenridge	5,453	16	11	5
Bremond	962	3	3	0
Brenham	17,375	38	35	3
Bridge City	7,998	18	13	5
Bridgeport	6,670	23	16	7
Brookshire	5,592	22	17	5
Brookside Village	1,603	4	4	0
Brownfield	9,270	24	19	5
Brownsboro	1,283	4	4	0
Brownsville	184,418	317	234	83
Brownwood	18,646	60	38	22
Bryan	86,632	181	149	32
Bullard	3,722	11	10	1
Burkburnett	11,305	24	17	7
Burleson	48,743	93	67	26
Cactus	3,194	10	7	3
Caddo Mills	1,656	7	7	0
Caldwell	4,433	10	9	1
Cameron	5,530	14	10	4
Canyon	16,312	29	26	3
Carrollton	139,179	207	162	45
Carthage	6,491	21	16	5
Castle Hills	4,515	28	22	6
Castroville	3,144	9	8	1
Cedar Hill	48,866	92	70	22
Celina	13,977	26	25	1
Center	5,271	23	16	7
Chandler	3,142	8	8	0
Chillicothe	668	2	2	0
Cibolo	32,112	42	38	4
Cisco	3,735	13	11	2
Cleburne	30,860	64	49	15
Cleveland	8,284	30	18	12
Clifton	3,454	8	7	1
Clute	11,740	36	24	12
Clyde	3,868	11	10	1
Coleman	4,341	7	7	0
College Station	119,246	204	141	63
Collinsville	1,951	3	3	0
Colorado City	3,831	15	8	7
Combes	3,064	7	7	0
Commerce	9,467	19	14	5
Converse	28,598	53	48	5
Coppell	42,181	68	59	9

Table 78. Full-Time Law Enforcement Employees, by Selected State and City, 2019—Continued

(Number.)

State/city	Population	Total law enforcement employees	Total officers	Total civilians
Copperas Cove	32,693	64	46	18
Corinth	22,090	37	31	6
Corpus Christi	329,320	660	426	234
Corrigan	1,605	15	9	6
Corsicana	23,823	56	42	14
Crane	3,725	15	9	6
Crockett	6,484	18	15	3
Crosbyton	1,602	1	1	0
Crowley	16,027	39	26	13
Crystal City	7,283	16	10	6
Cuero	8,259	16	15	1
Daingerfield	2,360	6	5	1
Dalhart	8,338	16	12	4
Dallas	1,363,295	3,624	3,075	549
Dalworthington Gardens	2,403	16	11	5
Dayton	8,464	31	21	10
Decatur	7,116	34	28	6
Deer Park	34,167	90	63	27
Del Rio	35,947	87	61	26
Denison	25,432	58	44	14
Denton	141,492	224	181	43
Denver City	4,933	16	10	6
Devine	4,931	14	11	3
Diboll	5,228	20	15	5
Dickinson	21,101	46	30	16
Dimmitt	4,146	7	5	2
Donna	16,715	47	35	12
Double Oak	3,073	8	8	0
Driscoll	752	5	3	2
Dumas	14,290	28	23	5
Duncanville	39,430	64	50	14
Early	3,105	11	9	2
Eastland	3,913	13	11	2
Edinburg	100,896	220	160	60
Edna	5,924	10	8	2
El Campo	11,615	43	30	13
Electra	2,696	12	7	5
Elgin	10,475	34	25	9
El Paso	686,793	1,412	1,171	241
Emory	1,353	6	5	1
Falfurrias	4,819	12	10	2
Farmers Branch	41,932	96	72	24
Farwell	1,314	3	3	0
Fate	15,378	19	18	1
Ferris	2,876	17	12	5
Florence	1,288	2	2	0
Floresville	7,970	21	19	2
Flower Mound	79,052	134	89	45
Floydada	2,711	6	6	0
Forney	25,374	43	29	14
Fort Stockton	8,402	30	20	10
Fort Worth	915,237	2,075	1,650	425
Freeport	12,213	46	32	14
Friendswood	40,735	77	58	19
Friona	3,888	9	5	4
Frisco	199,445	299	199	100
Fulshear	13,967	25	23	2
Fulton	1,559	1	1	0
Gainesville	16,688	53	39	14
Galena Park	10,934	22	17	5
Galveston	50,801	193	146	47
Garland	244,277	477	355	122
Garrison	894	2	2	0
Gatesville	12,311	27	18	9
George West	2,586	10	8	2
Gilmer	5,164	19	15	4
Gladewater	6,349	19	14	5
Glenn Heights	13,520	28	20	8
Gorman	1,034	4	2	2
Graham	8,670	22	21	1
Granbury	10,752	44	38	6
Grand Prairie	196,971	422	279	143
Grand Saline	3,171	10	9	1
Grapevine	54,979	150	98	52
Greenville	28,613	75	54	21
Gregory	1,917	5	5	0
Groesbeck	4,302	8	8	0
Groves	15,601	26	22	4
Gun Barrel City	6,273	19	14	5
Hamilton	3,008	10	8	2
Hamlin	1,982	9	5	4
Harker Heights	32,527	56	47	9
Harlingen	65,481	173	133	40
Haskell	3,234	6	5	1
Hawkins	1,331	3	3	0

Table 78. Full-Time Law Enforcement Employees, by Selected State and City, 2019—Continued

(Number.)

State/city	Population	Total law enforcement employees	Total officers	Total civilians
Hawley	616	1	1	0
Hearne	4,510	16	10	6
Heath	9,179	23	22	1
Hedwig Village	2,684	22	16	6
Henderson	13,226	43	33	10
Hewitt	15,019	36	26	10
Hidalgo	14,281	38	29	9
Highland Park	9,251	72	58	14
Highland Village	16,721	42	32	10
Hill Country Village	1,109	14	10	4
Hillsboro	8,476	37	28	9
Hitchcock	8,023	21	15	6
Hollywood Park	3,406	15	14	1
Honey Grove	1,718	4	4	0
Horizon City	20,131	45	26	19
Horseshoe Bay	4,030	20	17	3
Houston	2,355,606	6,337	5,264	1,073
Howe	3,432	6	5	1
Hudson	4,909	4	4	0
Humble	16,157	83	64	19
Huntsville	41,881	67	59	8
Hutto	27,993	52	46	6
Idalou	2,289	4	4	0
Indian Lake	858	2	2	0
Ingleside	10,366	23	16	7
Iowa Colony	2,024	7	7	0
Iowa Park	6,369	17	11	6
Irving	245,423	525	364	161
Italy	1,945	6	5	1
Jacksboro	4,353	10	9	1
Jacksonville	14,969	42	30	12
Jarrell	1,800	7	7	0
Jasper	7,647	29	22	7
Jersey Village	8,006	28	26	2
Jonestown	2,118	9	8	1
Josephine	1,739	4	3	1
Jourdanton	4,537	11	10	1
Katy	19,966	86	66	20
Keene	6,584	13	12	1
Keller	48,387	88	48	40
Kemah	2,056	24	18	6
Kemp	1,219	7	7	0
Kerens	1,532	5	5	0
Kerrville	23,902	62	47	15
Kilgore	15,047	49	36	13
Killeen	151,832	285	235	50
Kingsville	25,401	63	38	25
Kirby	8,841	19	16	3
Knox City	1,110	2	2	0
Kress	684	1	1	0
Lacy-Lakeview	6,720	27	17	10
La Feria	7,341	19	18	1
Lago Vista	7,255	25	18	7
La Grange	4,630	13	12	1
Laguna Vista	3,163	9	9	0
Lake Dallas	8,052	18	15	3
Lake Jackson	27,624	69	49	20
Lakeside	1,614	7	7	0
Lakeview, Harrison County	6,361	14	13	1
Lake Worth	4,993	33	24	9
La Marque	17,088	44	33	11
Lampasas	8,067	32	21	11
Lancaster	39,795	64	58	6
La Porte	35,622	101	77	24
Laredo	264,916	576	498	78
League City	109,401	168	120	48
Leander	61,314	81	61	20
Levelland	13,530	35	24	11
Lewisville	108,000	218	148	70
Liberty	9,471	27	17	10
Lindale	6,338	24	17	7
Littlefield	5,911	20	13	7
Live Oak	16,280	51	37	14
Livingston	5,112	28	21	7
Longview	81,783	214	169	45
Lorena	1,776	10	8	2
Lufkin	35,555	102	77	25
Madisonville	4,776	14	11	3
Magnolia	2,218	16	13	3
Mansfield	72,979	211	111	100
Manvel	12,721	28	22	6
Marble Falls	7,047	36	23	13
Marshall	23,036	56	39	17
Mathis	4,768	14	10	4
McKinney	200,615	277	210	67

Table 78. Full-Time Law Enforcement Employees, by Selected State and City, 2019—Continued

(Number.)

State/city	Population	Total law enforcement employees	Total officers	Total civilians
Meadows Place	4,616	16	15	1
Melissa	11,195	14	14	0
Memorial Villages	12,472	44	31	13
Mercedes	16,882	39	32	7
Merkel	2,623	5	5	0
Mesquite	143,078	311	231	80
Midland	146,806	207	160	47
Midlothian	28,313	90	59	31
Miles	862	1	1	0
Mineola	4,804	19	12	7
Missouri City	75,747	146	104	42
Monahans	7,770	20	14	6
Mont Belvieu	6,647	21	15	6
Morgans Point Resort	4,637	9	9	0
Moulton	910	4	4	0
Mount Pleasant	16,307	46	33	13
Muleshoe	5,029	14	7	7
Murphy	20,962	31	20	11
Mustang Ridge	1,001	5	5	0
Nacogdoches	33,613	86	60	26
Naples	1,302	4	4	0
Nash	3,783	9	9	0
Nassau Bay	4,040	13	12	1
Natalia	1,602	4	4	0
Navasota	7,795	23	18	5
Nederland	17,557	39	23	16
Needville	3,094	7	7	0
New Boston	4,663	20	16	4
Newton	2,346	4	4	0
Nocona	2,975	6	5	1
Northeast	3,404	13	12	1
Northlake	3,341	15	14	1
North Richland Hills	71,816	189	113	76
Oak Ridge North	3,174	16	16	0
Odessa	123,468	197	137	60
O'Donnell	825	1	1	0
Olmos Park	2,478	14	13	1
Olney	3,091	6	5	1
Olton	2,090	2	2	0
Onalaska	2,852	8	8	0
Orange	18,468	58	43	15
Overton	2,510	9	6	3
Palmer	2,079	11	10	1
Palmhurst	2,771	15	11	4
Palm Valley	1,249	5	5	0
Panhandle	2,322	4	4	0
Pantego	2,556	16	11	5
Paris	24,787	82	57	25
Parker	4,951	10	9	1
Pasadena	153,689	369	291	78
Pearland	126,206	227	161	66
Pearsall	10,604	19	15	4
Penitas	4,915	17	15	2
Perryton	8,577	22	13	9
Petersburg	1,133	3	3	0
Pharr	80,896	154	124	30
Pinehurst	2,006	8	6	2
Pittsburg	4,720	13	11	2
Plainview	20,231	38	31	7
Plano	291,611	585	403	182
Pleasanton	10,911	30	24	6
Port Aransas	4,260	29	20	9
Port Arthur	55,084	151	117	34
Port Isabel	5,058	19	15	4
Portland	17,604	47	32	15
Port Lavaca	12,072	23	17	6
Poteet	3,524	11	10	1
Pottsboro	2,488	10	8	2
Prairie View	6,543	11	10	1
Primera	5,103	9	8	1
Princeton	12,569	25	23	2
Prosper	24,814	41	29	12
Queen City	1,450	6	6	0
Quitman	1,855	7	7	0
Ralls	1,814	3	3	0
Rancho Viejo	2,480	8	8	0
Ranger	2,413	6	5	1
Raymondville	10,894	25	16	9
Red Oak	13,429	31	28	3
Reno, Lamar County	3,333	6	5	1
Richardson	123,893	255	168	87
Richmond	12,086	42	30	12
Richwood	4,007	10	10	0
Riesel	1,036	3	3	0
River Oaks	7,738	23	17	6

Table 78. Full-Time Law Enforcement Employees, by Selected State and City, 2019—Continued

(Number.)

State/city	Population	Total law enforcement employees	Total officers	Total civilians
Roanoke	9,563	43	33	10
Robinson	11,945	33	22	11
Robstown	11,347	33	24	9
Rockdale	5,665	11	11	0
Rockport	10,854	31	27	4
Roma	11,527	36	28	8
Rosenberg	38,936	104	80	24
Rowlett	67,604	117	86	31
Royse City	13,539	26	22	4
Rusk	5,582	13	12	1
Sabinal	1,675	5	4	1
Sachse	26,926	45	33	12
Saginaw	24,382	49	38	11
Salado	2,375	5	5	0
San Antonio	1,559,166	3,362	2,297	1,065
San Benito	24,394	46	39	7
San Diego	4,226	6	5	1
San Juan	37,542	60	39	21
San Saba	3,152	5	5	0
Santa Anna	1,032	3	3	0
Santa Fe	13,657	26	20	6
Schertz	42,337	90	59	31
Seabrook	14,611	40	30	10
Seagoville	17,120	32	22	10
Seagraves	2,904	7	5	2
Sealy	6,593	23	21	2
Selma	12,054	32	28	4
Seymour	2,600	7	4	3
Shallowater	2,547	5	5	0
Shavano Park	4,052	19	18	1
Shenandoah	3,077	26	25	1
Sherman	43,002	91	68	23
Slaton	5,877	18	13	5
Snyder	11,161	24	21	3
Sour Lake	1,887	8	7	1
South Houston	17,655	43	30	13
Southlake	33,049	66	60	6
South Padre Island	2,805	37	27	10
Spearman	3,275	4	4	0
Spring Valley	4,414	24	18	6
Stafford	18,380	78	61	17
Stamford	2,898	7	6	1
Stratford	2,103	4	3	1
Sudan	904	2	2	0
Sugar Land	119,944	190	168	22
Sullivan City	4,152	15	9	6
Sulphur Springs	16,220	39	28	11
Sunset Valley	683	14	13	1
Sweetwater	10,467	31	25	6
Taft	2,904	6	6	0
Tahoka	2,624	4	4	0
Tatum	1,394	5	5	0
Taylor	17,405	40	29	11
Temple	77,558	196	157	39
Terrell	18,395	59	40	19
Terrell Hills	5,496	14	14	0
Texarkana	37,401	97	85	12
Texas City	49,659	111	85	26
Three Rivers	1,945	11	10	1
Tioga	1,035	4	4	0
Tomball	11,897	58	42	16
Tool	2,337	10	6	4
Trophy Club	13,031	24	20	4
Tulia	4,644	14	6	8
Tye	1,318	6	5	1
Tyler	106,851	238	193	45
Universal City	21,062	43	32	11
University Park	25,434	56	39	17
Uvalde	16,233	55	40	15
Van	2,713	9	9	0
Van Alstyne	4,437	15	10	5
Venus	3,986	12	12	0
Vernon	10,312	26	19	7
Victoria	67,581	150	112	38
Vidor	10,499	31	24	7
Waco	139,870	334	241	93
Waller	3,611	13	12	1
Watauga	24,685	45	34	11
Waxahachie	37,805	89	69	20
Weatherford	32,656	78	60	18
Webster	11,273	65	48	17
Weimar	2,180	8	7	1
Weslaco	41,729	97	77	20
West Columbia	3,881	17	12	5
West Orange	3,299	11	9	2

Table 78. Full-Time Law Enforcement Employees, by Selected State and City, 2019—Continued

(Number.)

State/city	Population	Total law enforcement employees	Total officers	Total civilians
Westover Hills	685	16	11	5
West University Place	15,818	30	23	7
Westworth	2,720	18	13	5
Wharton	8,627	32	24	8
White Oak	6,345	20	16	4
White Settlement	18,127	45	37	8
Whitney	2,188	7	7	0
Wichita Falls	104,551	282	197	85
Willis	6,587	19	17	2
Wills Point	3,684	11	10	1
Winters	2,448	7	6	1
Wolfforth	5,445	13	12	1
Woodway	9,033	42	30	12
Wylie	52,921	70	62	8
Yoakum	5,962	18	11	7
UTAH				
Alta	383	8	4	4
American Fork/Cedar Hills	43,610	52	44	8
Big Water	506	1	1	0
Blanding	3,738	5	5	0
Bluffdale	15,976	13	13	0
Bountiful	44,280	57	38	19
Brian Head	92	5	5	0
Brigham City	19,592	31	26	5
Cedar City	33,614	44	39	5
Centerville	18,018	23	20	3
Clearfield	32,217	38	30	8
Clinton	22,544	22	19	3
Cottonwood Heights	34,183	47	38	9
Draper	49,112	54	44	10
East Carbon	1,561	4	4	0
Enoch	7,199	8	6	2
Ephraim	7,449	8	7	1
Fairview	1,352	1	1	0
Farmington	25,409	25	21	4
Grantsville	11,942	17	15	2
Gunnison	3,564	6	4	2
Harrisville	6,845	11	10	1
Heber	17,142	28	22	6
Helper	2,077	5	5	0
Herriman	48,948	46	37	9
Hildale	2,928	15	9	6
Hurricane	18,850	31	28	3
Kanab	4,850	8	7	1
Kaysville	32,691	31	28	3
La Verkin	4,442	5	5	0
Layton	78,585	110	78	32
Lehi	68,697	58	52	6
Lindon	11,085	17	15	2
Logan	52,029	83	53	30
Lone Peak	30,273	27	22	5
Mantua	905	1	1	0
Mapleton	10,463	11	8	3
Moab	5,349	25	16	9
Monticello	1,998	3	3	0
Mount Pleasant	3,517	4	4	0
Murray	49,642	88	75	13
Naples	2,113	7	6	1
Nephi	6,207	13	10	3
North Ogden	20,352	21	18	3
North Park	16,411	11	9	2
North Salt Lake	21,501	29	23	6
Ogden	87,875	169	137	32
Orem	98,686	115	85	30
Park City	8,620	38	32	6
Parowan	3,139	5	5	0
Payson	19,981	24	23	1
Perry	5,171	8	7	1
Pleasant Grove	39,066	37	28	9
Pleasant View	11,137	11	10	1
Price	8,174	17	15	2
Provo	117,189	158	109	49
Richfield	7,952	16	15	1
Riverdale	8,821	22	19	3
Riverton	45,153	39	35	4
Roosevelt	7,189	14	12	2
Roy	39,001	45	38	7
Salem	8,760	11	10	1
Salina	2,573	4	4	0
Salt Lake City	202,426	647	503	144
Sandy	97,797	147	109	38
Santa Clara/Ivins	17,346	18	14	4
Santaquin/Genola	14,288	14	13	1
Saratoga Springs	33,647	27	24	3

Table 78. Full-Time Law Enforcement Employees, by Selected State and City, 2019—Continued

(Number.)

State/city	Population	Total law enforcement employees	Total officers	Total civilians
Smithfield	12,107	11	10	1
South Jordan	77,645	65	60	5
South Ogden	17,215	24	21	3
South Salt Lake	25,599	79	64	15
Spanish Fork	40,604	43	39	4
Spring City	1,077	1	1	0
Springdale	620	9	8	1
Springville	33,542	38	28	10
St. George	89,160	160	113	47
Sunset	5,364	8	8	0
Syracuse	31,230	25	23	2
Tooele	35,719	46	38	8
Tremonton	9,038	13	11	2
Washington	29,047	32	28	4
West Bountiful	5,790	11	10	1
West Jordan	117,644	153	117	36
West Valley	137,269	246	203	43
Willard	1,932	2	2	0
Woods Cross	11,531	19	17	2
VERMONT				
Barre	8,551	21	20	1
Barre Town	7,679	8	7	1
Bellows Falls	2,988	8	7	1
Bennington	14,912	33	25	8
Berlin	2,789	11	9	2
Bradford	2,701	2	2	0
Brandon	3,744	8	7	1
Brattleboro	11,401	36	24	12
Brighton	1,184	1	1	0
Bristol	3,883	3	3	0
Burlington	42,958	133	93	40
Canaan	926	1	1	0
Castleton	4,507	4	4	0
Chester	3,018	6	5	1
Colchester	17,548	34	26	8
Dover	1,057	7	6	1
Essex	22,213	31	25	6
Fair Haven	2,554	4	4	0
Hardwick	2,852	8	7	1
Hartford	9,654	28	19	9
Hinesburg	4,601	4	4	0
Killington	757	3	3	0
Ludlow	1,876	11	6	5
Lyndonville	1,160	3	3	0
Manchester	4,242	13	9	4
Middlebury	8,776	17	15	2
Milton	11,064	18	17	1
Montpelier	7,386	27	17	10
Morristown	5,465	11	11	0
Newport	4,216	18	14	4
Northfield	5,990	8	7	1
Norwich	3,307	5	4	1
Pittsford	2,786	1	1	0
Richmond	4,178	5	5	0
Royalton	2,864	1	1	0
Rutland	15,191	51	38	13
Rutland Town	4,096	5	5	0
Shelburne	7,857	16	10	6
South Burlington	19,687	49	40	9
Springfield	8,900	19	13	6
St. Albans	6,800	32	21	11
St. Johnsbury	7,158	16	10	6
Stowe	4,452	12	12	0
Swanton	6,595	7	6	1
Thetford	2,545	3	3	0
Vergennes	2,596	8	8	0
Weathersfield	2,753	2	2	0
Williston	10,026	17	14	3
Wilmington	1,801	7	5	2
Windsor	3,324	11	10	1
Winhall	731	9	8	1
Winooski	7,346	20	16	4
Woodstock	2,925	6	5	1
VIRGINIA				
Abingdon	7,933	27	24	3
Alexandria	162,258	413	322	91
Altavista	3,409	15	14	1
Amherst	2,179	6	6	0
Appalachia	1,544	3	3	0
Ashland	7,916	28	25	3
Bedford	6,588	26	22	4
Berryville	4,363	10	9	1
Big Stone Gap	5,170	13	12	1

Table 78. Full-Time Law Enforcement Employees, by Selected State and City, 2019—Continued

(Number.)

State/city	Population	Total law enforcement employees	Total officers	Total civilians
Blacksburg	44,948	72	62	10
Blackstone	3,360	14	11	3
Bluefield	4,822	20	15	5
Bowling Green	1,187	1	1	0
Bridgewater	6,167	9	9	0
Bristol	16,234	73	52	21
Broadway	3,973	5	5	0
Brookneal	1,098	2	2	0
Buena Vista	6,156	17	16	1
Burkeville	402	1	1	0
Cape Charles	1,002	6	6	0
Cedar Bluff	1,003	3	3	0
Charlottesville	48,453	136	110	26
Chase City	2,212	10	9	1
Chatham	1,433	3	3	0
Chesapeake	243,726	577	388	189
Chilhowie	1,710	6	6	0
Chincoteague	2,872	14	10	4
Christiansburg	22,700	67	62	5
Clarksville	1,170	8	7	1
Clifton Forge	3,465	11	10	1
Clintwood	1,287	2	2	0
Coeburn	1,857	7	6	1
Colonial Beach	3,593	10	9	1
Colonial Heights	17,793	58	54	4
Covington	5,372	26	17	9
Crewe	2,148	7	6	1
Culpeper	18,873	52	45	7
Damascus	787	4	4	0
Danville	40,191	131	120	11
Dayton	1,636	4	4	0
Dublin	2,604	8	7	1
Dumfries	5,265	12	11	1
Elkton	2,900	6	5	1
Emporia	5,000	36	25	11
Exmore	1,368	7	7	0
Fairfax City	24,689	79	60	19
Falls Church	15,008	44	31	13
Farmville	7,830	29	27	2
Franklin	7,899	34	24	10
Fredericksburg	29,641	96	73	23
Front Royal	15,336	52	38	14
Galax	6,320	39	23	16
Gate City	1,857	5	5	0
Glade Spring	1,426	2	2	0
Glasgow	1,111	1	1	0
Gordonsville	1,621	7	7	0
Gretna	1,197	3	3	0
Grottoes	2,860	7	6	1
Grundy	900	6	6	0
Halifax	1,217	5	5	0
Hampton	133,173	377	285	92
Harrisonburg	54,387	127	109	18
Haymarket	1,740	6	6	0
Haysi	472	3	2	1
Herndon	24,693	71	56	15
Hillsville	2,644	12	11	1
Honaker	1,330	4	4	0
Hopewell	22,461	86	66	20
Hurt	1,226	2	2	0
Independence	896	2	2	0
Jonesville	931	3	3	0
Kenbridge	1,180	5	5	0
Kilmarnock	1,410	5	5	0
La Crosse	573	1	1	0
Lawrenceville	993	6	6	0
Lebanon	3,148	15	14	1
Leesburg	55,461	96	80	16
Lexington	7,107	21	18	3
Louisa	1,721	4	4	0
Luray	4,853	13	12	1
Lynchburg	82,512	189	165	24
Manassas	41,850	118	85	33
Manassas Park	17,602	37	30	7
Marion	5,593	19	18	1
Martinsville	12,726	48	43	5
Middleburg	864	7	6	1
Middletown	1,396	4	3	1
Mount Jackson	2,115	6	6	0
Narrows	1,955	5	5	0
New Market	2,256	6	6	0
Newport News	177,319	603	445	158
Norfolk	242,813	783	691	92
Norton	3,940	22	14	8
Occoquan	1,109	1	1	0

Table 78. Full-Time Law Enforcement Employees, by Selected State and City, 2019—Continued

(Number.)

State/city	Population	Total law enforcement employees	Total officers	Total civilians
Onancock	1,210	5	5	0
Onley	500	5	5	0
Orange	5,092	17	15	2
Parksley	810	2	2	0
Pearisburg	2,639	7	7	0
Pembroke	1,085	3	3	0
Pennington Gap	1,716	6	6	0
Petersburg	31,273	112	91	21
Pocahontas	354	1	1	0
Poquoson	12,126	27	26	1
Portsmouth	93,991	274	220	54
Pound	927	4	4	0
Pulaski	8,683	32	28	4
Purcellville	10,346	20	18	2
Radford	18,487	48	35	13
Remington	659	1	1	0
Rich Creek	743	1	1	0
Richlands	5,198	24	19	5
Richmond	230,721	851	734	117
Roanoke	99,752	291	248	43
Rocky Mount	4,744	26	24	2
Rural Retreat	1,453	1	1	0
Salem	25,590	87	65	22
Saltville	1,910	5	5	0
Shenandoah	2,335	5	5	0
Smithfield	8,485	26	22	4
South Boston	7,601	31	29	2
South Hill	4,335	23	21	2
Stanley	1,670	5	5	0
Staunton	24,931	64	48	16
Stephens City	2,069	2	2	0
St. Paul	862	6	6	0
Strasburg	6,686	18	17	1
Suffolk	91,486	233	173	60
Tangier	704	1	1	0
Tappahannock	2,391	9	8	1
Tazewell	4,140	16	15	1
Timberville	2,697	6	6	0
Victoria	1,603	4	4	0
Vienna	16,660	50	40	10
Vinton	8,110	25	23	2
Virginia Beach	449,038	938	760	178
Warrenton	9,977	25	23	2
Warsaw	1,488	4	4	0
Waverly	1,949	14	8	6
Waynesboro	22,711	59	48	11
Weber City	1,204	3	3	0
West Point	3,254	10	9	1
Williamsburg	14,965	43	41	2
Winchester	28,201	86	76	10
Windsor	2,763	7	7	0
Wise	2,926	13	12	1
Woodstock	5,267	19	17	2
Wytheville	7,909	28	25	3
WASHINGTON				
Aberdeen	16,627	51	36	15
Airway Heights	9,545	21	20	1
Algona	3,247	10	8	2
Anacortes	17,483	30	24	6
Arlington	20,043	33	28	5
Asotin	1,299	1	1	0
Auburn	83,468	133	113	20
Bainbridge Island	25,080	29	23	6
Battle Ground	21,375	28	24	4
Bellevue	150,200	221	185	36
Bellingham	91,906	173	117	56
Black Diamond	4,518	11	9	2
Blaine	5,534	16	14	2
Bonney Lake	21,574	37	30	7
Bothell	47,565	97	67	30
Bremerton	41,675	72	59	13
Brewster	2,363	6	5	1
Brier	7,070	8	7	1
Buckley	5,534	12	10	2
Burien	52,388	74	52	22
Burlington	9,219	31	25	6
Camas	24,388	32	28	4
Carnation	2,297	3	2	1
Castle Rock	2,291	5	4	1
Centralia	17,603	37	29	8
Chehalis	7,682	22	17	5
Cheney	12,632	23	17	6
Chewelah	2,673	6	5	1
Clarkston	7,426	16	14	2

Table 78. Full-Time Law Enforcement Employees, by Selected State and City, 2019—Continued

(Number.)

State/city	Population	Total law enforcement employees	Total officers	Total civilians
Cle Elum	2,989	6	6	0
Clyde Hill	3,436	10	9	1
Colfax	2,926	4	4	0
College Place	9,428	17	14	3
Colville	4,845	12	10	2
Connell	5,772	8	7	1
Cosmopolis	1,646	6	5	1
Coulee Dam	1,082	2	2	0
Covington	21,698	25	19	6
Des Moines	32,708	49	38	11
Dupont	9,672	14	10	4
Duvall	8,244	14	13	1
East Wenatchee	14,293	24	21	3
Eatonville	3,061	6	5	1
Edgewood	11,981	12	11	1
Edmonds	43,152	66	51	15
Ellensburg	21,324	32	26	6
Elma	3,323	10	7	3
Enumclaw	11,975	32	19	13
Ephrata	8,253	17	15	2
Everett	112,302	239	199	40
Everson	4,428	7	6	1
Federal Way	98,025	155	128	27
Ferndale	15,007	23	20	3
Fife	10,324	40	30	10
Fircrest	6,852	9	9	0
Forks	3,903	10	4	6
Gig Harbor	10,931	21	19	2
Goldendale	3,508	11	9	2
Grand Coulee	2,079	7	7	0
Grandview	11,179	22	18	4
Granger	3,863	8	8	0
Hoquiam	8,580	26	24	2
Issaquah	40,651	62	36	26
Kalama	2,766	7	6	1
Kelso	12,354	30	26	4
Kenmore	23,430	20	15	5
Kennewick	84,072	118	102	16
Kent	131,003	207	152	55
Kettle Falls	1,636	4	3	1
Kirkland	90,708	147	108	39
Kittitas	1,511	3	3	0
La Center	3,324	9	8	1
Lacey	51,816	65	55	10
Lake Forest Park	13,690	23	20	3
Lake Stevens	34,081	39	32	7
Lakewood	60,916	111	97	14
Langley	1,152	3	3	0
Liberty Lake	11,043	14	13	1
Long Beach	1,441	9	8	1
Longview	38,282	71	59	12
Lynden	15,116	19	15	4
Lynnwood	38,847	101	67	34
Mabton	2,281	3	3	0
Maple Valley	27,705	25	20	5
Marysville	71,081	92	65	27
Mattawa	4,641	6	5	1
McCleary	1,743	4	4	0
Medina	3,337	11	9	2
Mercer Island	26,408	36	31	5
Mill Creek	21,360	29	24	5
Milton	8,381	14	14	0
Monroe	19,630	42	32	10
Montesano	4,033	9	8	1
Morton	1,185	3	3	0
Moses Lake	24,490	46	38	8
Mountlake Terrace	21,617	36	28	8
Mount Vernon	36,274	58	45	13
Moxee	4,151	7	6	1
Mukilteo	21,704	35	29	6
Napavine	1,973	4	3	1
Newcastle	12,015	14	11	3
Newport	2,156	5	4	1
Normandy Park	6,699	10	9	1
Oak Harbor	23,554	38	26	12
Ocean Shores	6,181	10	9	1
Odessa	879	2	2	0
Olympia	53,286	105	72	33
Omak	4,806	12	11	1
Oroville	1,678	4	3	1
Orting	8,629	10	8	2
Othello	8,388	24	17	7
Pacific	7,297	12	11	1
Palouse	1,084	4	2	2
Pasco	76,412	91	82	9

Table 78. Full-Time Law Enforcement Employees, by Selected State and City, 2019—Continued

(Number.)

State/city	Population	Total law enforcement employees	Total officers	Total civilians
Pe Ell	672	1	1	0
Port Angeles	20,207	63	32	31
Port Orchard	14,684	25	22	3
Port Townsend	9,780	19	15	4
Poulsbo	11,154	25	18	7
Prosser	6,388	15	14	1
Pullman	34,585	43	28	15
Puyallup	42,509	90	68	22
Quincy	7,977	30	22	8
Raymond	2,976	6	5	1
Reardan	596	1	1	0
Redmond	69,501	123	84	39
Renton	103,452	157	125	32
Republic	1,071	2	2	0
Richland	58,514	79	62	17
Ridgefield	8,955	12	11	1
Ritzville	1,645	4	4	0
Roy	828	2	2	0
Royal City	2,240	3	3	0
Ruston	855	5	5	0
Sammamish	66,820	37	29	8
SeaTac	29,533	67	49	18
Seattle	763,706	1,960	1,416	544
Sedro Woolley	12,184	19	16	3
Selah	8,110	18	15	3
Sequim	7,599	24	20	4
Shelton	10,432	21	18	3
Shoreline	57,216	69	49	20
Snohomish	10,319	19	17	2
Snoqualmie	14,183	29	25	4
Soap Lake	1,613	5	4	1
South Bend	1,680	6	4	2
Spokane	220,432	412	332	80
Spokane Valley	100,983	132	109	23
Stanwood	7,330	13	11	2
Steilacoom	6,423	11	10	1
Sumas	1,529	7	6	1
Sumner	10,270	23	19	4
Sunnyside	16,839	45	26	19
Tacoma	218,650	400	359	41
Tenino	1,873	5	4	1
Tieton	1,318	2	2	0
Toledo	765	3	2	1
Toppenish	8,886	16	11	5
Tukwila	20,439	94	74	20
Tumwater	24,167	36	28	8
Twisp	964	3	3	0
Union Gap	6,162	20	17	3
University Place	34,085	18	17	1
Vancouver	185,034	265	213	52
Walla Walla	33,047	72	43	29
Wapato	5,045	9	7	2
Warden	2,784	5	3	2
Washougal	16,305	23	20	3
Wenatchee	34,513	50	39	11
Westport	2,080	7	6	1
West Richland	15,343	24	20	4
White Salmon	2,655	7	6	1
Winlock	1,392	1	1	0
Winthrop	457	3	2	1
Woodinville	13,068	21	16	5
Woodland	6,469	12	10	2
Yakima	94,168	171	131	40
Yelm	9,741	17	15	2
Zillah	3,164	9	8	1
WEST VIRGINIA				
Alderson	1,130	4	4	0
Anmoore	739	2	2	0
Ansted	1,321	2	2	0
Athens	896	1	1	0
Barboursville	4,215	24	22	2
Barrackville	1,289	1	1	0
Beckley	16,010	68	52	16
Belington	1,859	3	3	0
Belle	1,128	4	4	0
Benwood	1,268	6	6	0
Berkeley Springs	599	2	2	0
Bethlehem	2,321	5	5	0
Bluefield	9,644	33	27	6
Bradshaw	277	1	1	0
Bramwell	339	2	2	0
Bridgeport	8,751	35	31	4
Buckhannon	5,479	12	11	1
Burnsville	481	1	1	0

Table 78. Full-Time Law Enforcement Employees, by Selected State and City, 2019—Continued

(Number.)

State/city	Population	Total law enforcement employees	Total officers	Total civilians
Cameron	846	2	2	0
Cedar Grove	918	1	1	0
Ceredo	1,299	8	4	4
Chapmanville	1,104	6	6	0
Charleston	46,732	183	159	24
Charles Town	6,171	19	16	3
Chesapeake	1,415	2	2	0
Chester	2,393	6	5	1
Clarksburg	15,349	42	39	3
Clendenin	1,109	5	5	0
Danville	611	2	2	0
Davy	343	1	1	0
Delbarton	498	2	2	0
Dunbar	7,123	14	13	1
Eleanor	1,606	2	2	0
Elkins	7,008	12	11	1
Fairmont	18,372	38	33	5
Fairview	403	1	1	0
Farmington	364	1	1	0
Fayetteville	2,738	13	12	1
Follansbee	2,706	7	7	0
Fort Gay	669	3	3	0
Gary	798	1	1	0
Gassaway	853	1	1	0
Gauley Bridge	554	1	1	0
Gilbert	392	2	2	0
Glasgow	839	1	1	0
Glen Dale	1,375	6	6	0
Glenville	1,454	3	3	0
Grafton	5,025	9	8	1
Grantsville	523	1	1	0
Grant Town	594	1	1	0
Granville	3,105	16	16	0
Hamlin	1,049	3	2	1
Harpers Ferry/Bolivar	1,304	4	3	1
Harrisville	1,699	1	1	0
Hartford City	597	1	1	0
Hinton	2,362	7	6	1
Hundred	264	1	1	0
Huntington	45,675	94	92	2
Hurricane	6,534	21	19	2
Iaeger	246	1	1	0
Kenova	3,010	14	10	4
Kermit	353	1	1	0
Keyser	4,933	15	10	5
Kimball	155	1	1	0
Kingwood	2,939	1	1	0
Lewisburg	3,830	14	12	2
Logan	1,481	11	8	3
Lumberport	839	1	1	0
Mabscott	1,267	2	2	0
Madison	2,720	8	7	1
Man	640	2	2	0
Mannington	2,027	4	4	0
Marmet	1,372	5	5	0
Martinsburg	17,494	57	47	10
Mason	934	5	4	1
Masontown	546	2	1	1
Matewan	428	1	1	0
McMechen	1,722	4	4	0
Milton	2,588	11	10	1
Monongah	1,154	1	1	0
Montgomery	1,516	8	7	1
Moorefield	2,418	10	9	1
Morgantown	31,281	83	71	12
Moundsville	8,323	20	16	4
Mount Hope	1,278	6	5	1
Mullens	1,311	3	3	0
New Cumberland	1,028	2	1	1
New Haven	1,477	3	3	0
New Martinsville	5,114	14	11	3
Nitro	6,406	19	18	1
Nutter Fort	1,522	5	5	0
Oak Hill	8,140	21	17	4
Oceana	1,204	4	4	0
Paden City	2,361	4	3	1
Parkersburg	29,482	80	66	14
Parsons	1,406	1	1	0
Pennsboro	1,023	1	1	0
Petersburg	2,649	1	1	0
Philippi	3,406	6	6	0
Piedmont	796	1	1	0
Pineville	578	3	3	0
Point Pleasant	4,094	8	7	1
Pratt	562	2	2	0

Table 78. Full-Time Law Enforcement Employees, by Selected State and City, 2019—Continued

(Number.)

State/city	Population	Total law enforcement employees	Total officers	Total civilians
Princeton	5,695	24	22	2
Rainelle	1,490	5	4	1
Ranson	5,288	16	15	1
Ravenswood	3,646	11	10	1
Reedsville	611	1	1	0
Rhodell	158	2	1	1
Richwood	1,868	3	3	0
Ridgeley	617	1	1	0
Ripley	3,179	11	10	1
Rivesville	907	1	1	0
Romney	1,702	5	4	1
Ronceverte	1,674	6	6	0
Rupert	895	1	1	0
Salem	1,558	5	4	1
Shepherdstown	1,827	6	5	1
Shinnston	2,108	7	6	1
Sistersville	1,291	3	3	0
Smithers	735	4	3	1
Sophia	1,251	5	5	0
South Charleston	12,094	49	46	3
Spencer	2,063	5	5	0
St. Albans	9,956	26	23	3
Star City	2,003	5	4	1
St. Marys	1,782	5	4	1
Stonewood	1,717	3	3	0
Summersville	3,292	15	14	1
Sutton	1,014	1	1	0
Sylvester	137	1	1	0
Terra Alta	1,507	2	2	0
Triadelphia	749	1	1	0
Vienna	10,157	23	19	4
War	688	2	2	0
Wayne	1,382	1	1	0
Webster Springs	671	5	4	1
Weirton	18,296	42	38	4
Welch	1,645	6	5	1
Wellsburg	2,531	6	5	1
West Logan	361	1	1	0
West Milford	603	2	2	0
Weston	3,887	8	6	2
Westover	4,244	13	12	1
West Union	815	2	1	1
Wheeling	26,562	74	65	9
White Hall	658	5	5	0
White Sulphur Springs	2,395	8	7	1
Whitesville	433	2	2	0
Williamson	2,694	7	6	1
Williamstown	2,879	8	7	1
Winfield	2,378	6	6	0
WISCONSIN				
Adams	1,886	3	3	0
Albany	994	3	3	0
Algoma	3,030	10	5	5
Altoona	7,939	14	13	1
Amery	2,792	6	6	0
Antigo	7,771	17	15	2
Appleton	74,757	137	110	27
Argyle	819	1	1	0
Ashland	7,859	20	18	2
Ashwaubenon	17,311	59	52	7
Athens	1,078	1	1	0
Bangor	1,468	3	3	0
Baraboo	12,151	35	29	6
Barneveld	1,256	1	1	0
Barron	3,306	6	6	0
Bayfield	476	3	3	0
Bayside	4,342	12	12	0
Beaver Dam	16,375	36	32	4
Belleville	2,459	6	5	1
Beloit Town	7,707	14	12	2
Berlin	5,401	13	12	1
Big Bend	1,460	3	3	0
Birchwood	433	2	1	1
Black River Falls	3,454	6	5	1
Blair	1,345	3	3	0
Bloomer	3,499	8	7	1
Bloomfield	6,342	8	8	0
Blue Mounds	1,000	2	1	1
Boscobel	3,129	12	6	6
Boyceville	1,130	2	2	0
Brillion	3,100	8	8	0
Brodhead	3,240	12	8	4
Brookfield	38,879	93	76	17
Brookfield Township	6,281	16	15	1

Table 78. Full-Time Law Enforcement Employees, by Selected State and City, 2019—Continued

(Number.)

State/city	Population	Total law enforcement employees	Total officers	Total civilians
Brown Deer	11,869	34	31	3
Brownsville	573	1	1	0
Burlington	11,057	23	22	1
Butler	1,807	8	7	1
Caledonia	25,123	34	32	2
Campbellsport	1,969	1	1	0
Campbell Township	4,337	5	5	0
Cashton	1,111	1	1	0
Cedarburg	11,548	29	21	8
Chenequa	604	8	8	0
Chetek	2,097	5	4	1
Chilton	3,774	7	7	0
Chippewa Falls	14,237	26	23	3
Cleveland	1,450	3	2	1
Clintonville	4,307	15	11	4
Colby-Abbotsford	4,152	9	8	1
Colfax	1,154	2	2	0
Columbus	5,090	11	9	2
Cornell	1,396	3	3	0
Cottage Grove	7,203	28	13	15
Crandon	1,826	5	4	1
Cross Plains	4,346	7	6	1
Cuba City	2,034	4	4	0
Cudahy	18,164	41	31	10
Cumberland	2,099	6	6	0
Darlington	2,324	5	5	0
Deforest	10,766	22	19	3
Delafield	7,610	18	16	2
Delavan	9,889	28	23	5
Delavan Town	5,339	12	11	1
De Pere	25,163	39	35	4
Dodgeville	4,713	10	10	0
Durand	1,810	4	4	0
Eagle Village	2,112	2	2	0
East Troy	4,327	8	8	0
Eau Claire	69,195	132	96	36
Edgar	1,439	1	1	0
Edgerton	5,646	11	10	1
Eleva	664	1	1	0
Elkhart Lake	1,018	3	3	0
Elkhorn	9,989	16	14	2
Elk Mound	878	1	1	0
Ellsworth	3,306	5	5	0
Elm Grove	6,195	25	17	8
Elroy	1,300	3	3	0
Evansville	5,424	9	8	1
Everest Metropolitan	17,340	30	27	3
Fall Creek	1,308	2	2	0
Fennimore	2,465	5	5	0
Fitchburg	30,854	62	51	11
Fond du Lac	42,954	76	68	8
Fontana	1,729	8	7	1
Fort Atkinson	12,519	28	20	8
Fox Lake	1,445	3	3	0
Fox Point	6,599	16	15	1
Fox Valley Metro	22,190	27	25	2
Franklin	35,875	76	60	16
Frederic	1,086	12	12	0
Galesville	1,571	4	4	0
Geneva Town	5,045	8	7	1
Genoa City	2,992	7	6	1
Germantown	19,983	71	60	11
Gillett	1,295	3	3	0
Gilman	393	2	1	1
Glendale	12,792	48	42	6
Grafton	11,798	26	20	6
Grand Chute	23,450	40	35	5
Grand Rapids	7,405	6	6	0
Grantsburg	1,283	3	3	0
Green Bay	104,992	218	181	37
Greendale	14,057	39	29	10
Greenfield	37,387	79	60	19
Green Lake	961	3	3	0
Hales Corners	7,578	19	17	2
Hartford	15,460	32	28	4
Hartford Township	3,570	3	1	2
Hartland	9,366	19	17	2
Hayward	2,296	14	7	7
Hazel Green	1,225	2	2	0
Highland	833	1	1	0
Hillsboro	1,398	4	2	2
Hobart-Lawrence	15,460	11	10	1
Holmen	10,217	14	13	1
Horicon	3,587	8	7	1
Hortonville	2,805	7	6	1

Table 78. Full-Time Law Enforcement Employees, by Selected State and City, 2019—Continued

(Number.)

State/city	Population	Total law enforcement employees	Total officers	Total civilians
Hudson	14,074	31	28	3
Hurley	1,426	7	6	1
Independence	1,295	3	3	0
Iron Ridge	891	1	1	0
Iron River	1,135	3	3	0
Jackson	7,218	12	11	1
Janesville	64,687	117	104	13
Jefferson	8,042	17	14	3
Juneau	2,639	5	4	1
Kaukauna	16,341	26	25	1
Kenosha	100,255	218	206	12
Kewaskum	4,244	8	8	0
Kewaunee	2,836	6	6	0
Kiel	3,808	8	7	1
Kohler	2,063	8	7	1
Kronenwetter	8,095	9	8	1
La Crosse	51,591	114	94	20
Ladysmith	3,111	8	7	1
La Farge	760	2	1	1
Lake Delton	3,005	24	21	3
Lake Geneva	8,001	32	24	8
Lake Hallie	6,724	10	9	1
Lake Mills	5,949	12	10	2
Lancaster	3,716	7	7	0
Lena	538	2	1	1
Linn Township	2,406	6	6	0
Lodi	3,070	11	5	6
Lomira	2,469	4	3	1
Luxemburg	2,557	1	1	0
Madison	261,270	687	501	186
Manawa	1,286	3	3	0
Manitowoc	32,497	74	64	10
Maple Bluff	1,319	4	3	1
Marathon City	1,500	3	3	0
Marinette	10,569	25	21	4
Marion	1,183	4	4	0
Markesan	1,395	4	4	0
Marshall Village	3,967	10	9	1
Marshfield	18,216	48	41	7
Mauston	4,364	10	9	1
Mayville	4,859	9	8	1
McFarland	8,961	19	17	2
Medford	4,313	10	9	1
Menasha	17,809	38	31	7
Menomonee Falls	37,936	73	58	15
Menomonie	16,573	31	25	6
Mequon	24,548	49	39	10
Merrill	9,017	24	21	3
Middleton	20,072	46	38	8
Milton	5,621	12	11	1
Milwaukee	590,923	2,265	1,850	415
Mineral Point	2,477	6	6	0
Minocqua	4,409	15	10	5
Mishicot	1,382	3	3	0
Mondovi	2,563	4	4	0
Monona	8,106	26	21	5
Monroe	10,537	32	25	7
Montello	1,461	3	2	1
Monticello	1,197	3	3	0
Mosinee	4,072	8	7	1
Mount Horeb	7,481	13	13	0
Mount Pleasant	27,070	62	56	6
Mukwonago	8,144	22	15	7
Muscoda	1,252	3	3	0
Muskego	25,224	48	39	9
Neenah	26,133	50	38	12
Neillsville	2,388	6	5	1
Nekoosa	2,432	7	7	0
New Berlin	39,752	83	69	14
New Glarus	2,187	3	3	0
New Holstein	3,056	7	6	1
New Lisbon	2,513	4	4	0
New London	7,118	18	17	1
New Richmond	9,268	19	18	1
Niagara	1,545	3	3	0
North Fond du Lac	5,098	11	9	2
North Hudson	3,813	4	3	1
Oak Creek	36,679	86	62	24
Oconomowoc	16,980	30	23	7
Oconomowoc Lake	604	7	6	1
Oconomowoc Town	8,741	12	11	1
Oconto	4,517	9	9	0
Oconto Falls	2,793	6	6	0
Omro	3,587	8	7	1
Onalaska	18,825	29	26	3

Table 78. Full-Time Law Enforcement Employees, by Selected State and City, 2019—Continued

(Number.)

State/city	Population	Total law enforcement employees	Total officers	Total civilians
Oregon	10,677	21	18	3
Osceola	2,511	6	5	1
Oshkosh	66,797	113	96	17
Osseo	1,672	4	4	0
Palmyra	1,767	6	6	0
Park Falls	2,212	7	7	0
Pepin	758	1	1	0
Peshtigo	3,333	6	6	0
Pewaukee Village	8,190	18	17	1
Phillips	1,339	5	5	0
Pittsville	829	2	2	0
Plainfield	824	2	1	1
Platteville	12,115	25	18	7
Pleasant Prairie	21,074	45	34	11
Plover	13,164	22	19	3
Plymouth	8,765	15	15	0
Portage	10,452	28	24	4
Port Edwards	1,772	2	2	0
Port Washington	11,908	24	19	5
Poynette	2,499	6	5	1
Prairie du Chien	5,636	13	12	1
Prescott	4,278	11	10	1
Princeton	1,167	4	4	0
Pulaski	3,598	9	8	1
Racine	77,269	229	196	33
Reedsburg	9,554	28	21	7
Rhinelander	7,615	19	17	2
Rice Lake	8,369	18	18	0
Richland Center	4,923	22	10	12
Rio	1,033	2	2	0
Ripon	7,820	18	13	5
Ripon Town	1,374	1	1	0
River Falls	16,069	28	25	3
River Hills	1,579	12	11	1
Rome Town	2,727	6	6	0
Rosendale	1,029	1	1	0
Rothschild	5,266	14	12	2
Sauk Prairie	4,633	16	14	2
Saukville	4,428	24	11	13
Seymour	3,474	6	6	0
Shawano	8,876	22	20	2
Sheboygan	48,035	100	81	19
Sheboygan Falls	7,947	17	15	2
Shiocton	919	2	2	0
Shorewood	13,217	28	24	4
Shorewood Hills	2,079	9	7	2
Shullsburg	1,189	1	1	0
Siren	770	7	3	4
Slinger	5,527	12	11	1
South Milwaukee	20,731	41	35	6
Sparta	9,823	24	22	2
Spencer	1,883	4	4	0
Spooner	2,598	9	7	2
Spring Green	1,644	3	2	1
Stanley	3,710	5	5	0
St. Croix Falls	2,032	11	5	6
Stevens Point	26,095	49	45	4
St. Francis	9,526	22	21	1
Stoughton	13,110	28	22	6
Sturgeon Bay	8,937	23	21	2
Sturtevant	6,645	14	13	1
Summit	4,944	10	10	0
Sun Prairie	34,562	74	53	21
Superior	25,967	65	60	5
Theresa	1,204	2	2	0
Thiensville	3,139	8	7	1
Thorp	1,618	3	3	0
Three Lakes	2,101	4	4	0
Tomah	9,406	22	20	2
Tomahawk	3,130	9	8	1
Town of East Troy	4,064	13	6	7
Town of Madison	6,934	13	12	1
Trempealeau	1,652	3	3	0
Twin Lakes	6,157	17	12	5
Two Rivers	11,027	29	26	3
Verona	13,510	26	24	2
Viroqua	4,412	11	9	2
Walworth	2,837	8	7	1
Washburn	2,039	5	5	0
Waterford Town	6,505	9	8	1
Waterloo	3,350	7	6	1
Watertown	23,596	54	40	14
Waukesha	72,718	159	122	37
Waunakee	14,163	24	22	2
Waupaca	5,874	16	15	1

Table 78. Full-Time Law Enforcement Employees, by Selected State and City, 2019—Continued

(Number.)

State/city	Population	Total law enforcement employees	Total officers	Total civilians
Waupun	11,315	18	17	1
Wausau	38,507	84	76	8
Wautoma	2,118	5	4	1
Wauwatosa	48,562	117	93	24
Webster	616	3	3	0
West Allis	59,302	157	123	34
West Bend	31,638	70	53	17
Westby	2,238	4	4	0
West Milwaukee	4,107	24	19	5
West Salem	5,087	8	7	1
Whitefish Bay	13,816	25	24	1
Whitehall	1,569	4	4	0
Whitewater	14,997	31	22	9
Wild Rose	691	2	2	0
Williams Bay	2,638	17	8	9
Wilton	500	1	1	0
Winneconne	2,506	6	5	1
Wisconsin Dells	3,033	20	15	5
Wisconsin Rapids	17,613	51	47	4
Woodruff	1,962	6	5	1
WYOMING				
Afton	2,017	4	4	0
Casper	57,752	144	97	47
Cheyenne	64,501	126	105	21
Cody	9,865	23	20	3
Diamondville	756	4	4	0
Douglas	6,294	16	13	3
Evanston	11,624	31	26	5
Evansville	2,977	13	11	2
Gillette	31,960	80	53	27
Glenrock	2,544	14	7	7
Green River	11,927	31	25	6
Greybull	1,857	6	5	1
Hanna	766	3	3	0
Jackson	10,534	39	32	7
Kemmerer	2,745	6	6	0
Lander	7,489	19	18	1
Laramie	32,669	75	46	29
Lusk	1,537	6	6	0
Mills	3,975	20	14	6
Moorcroft	1,068	4	3	1
Newcastle	3,386	15	8	7
Pine Bluffs	1,170	3	3	0
Powell	6,310	25	18	7
Rawlins	8,589	27	16	11
Riverton	11,004	41	27	14
Rock Springs	23,092	48	41	7
Saratoga	1,615	8	4	4
Sheridan	17,895	43	27	16
Sundance	1,285	3	3	0
Thermopolis	2,830	13	7	6
Torrington	6,709	25	18	7
Wheatland	3,544	9	8	1
Worland	5,026	12	11	1

1 The employee data presented in this table for Charlotte-Mecklenburg represent only Charlotte-Mecklenburg Police Department and exclude Mecklenburg County Sheriff's Office.

Table 79. Full-Time Law Enforcement Employees, by Selected State and University or College, 2019

(Number.)

State and university/college	Student enrollment[1]	Law enforcement employees	Officers	Civilians
ALABAMA				
Alabama A&M University	6,508	38	17	21
Alabama State University	5,374	31	22	9
Auburn University, Montgomery	6,033	19	11	8
Bevill State Community College	5,537	1	1	0
Bishop State Community College	4,748	9	6	3
Calhoun Community College	15,261	8	7	1
Coastal Alabama Community College	8,415	10	10	0
Jacksonville State University	10,179	23	14	9
Jefferson State Community College	13,608	14	12	2
Lawson State Community College	4,736	7	6	1
Samford University	5,994	16	13	3
Southern Union State Community College	7,132	4	4	0
Troy University	21,809	21	18	3
Tuskegee University	3,347	22	8	14
University of Alabama				
Birmingham	24,943	160	107	53
Huntsville	10,588	29	17	12
Tuscaloosa	42,568	155	88	67
University of Montevallo	2,971	21	10	11
University of North Alabama	8,649	14	12	2
University of South Alabama	17,532	34	27	7
University of West Alabama	6,734	11	8	3
Wallace Community College				
Dothan	6,237	3	3	0
Selma	2,486	4	2	2
ALASKA				
University of Alaska				
Anchorage	24,144	17	11	6
Fairbanks	12,738	12	6	6
ARIZONA				
Arizona State University, Main Campus	127,582	161	85	76
Arizona Western College	11,492	11	6	5
Central Arizona College	8,086	12	10	2
Northern Arizona University	34,803	39	26	13
Pima Community College	33,740	40	25	15
University of Arizona	48,318	109	62	47
Yavapai College	10,116	8	7	1
ARKANSAS				
Arkansas State University				
Beebe	5,423	6	5	1
Jonesboro	19,032	27	21	6
Newport	4,794	3	3	0
Arkansas Tech University	13,487	26	23	3
Henderson State University	3,850	9	9	0
Southern Arkansas University	5,467	9	8	1
Southern Arkansas University Tech	1,976	3	3	0
University of Arkansas				
Fayetteville	30,378	52	34	18
Little Rock	14,429	36	25	11
Medical Sciences	3,106	52	37	15
Monticello	4,302	10	9	1
Pine Bluff	2,872	15	10	5
University of Arkansas Community College at Morrilton	2,513	3	3	0
University of Central Arkansas	12,948	35	25	10
CALIFORNIA				
Allan Hancock College	17,070	16	7	9
California State Polytechnic University				
Pomona	28,093	58	21	37
San Luis Obispo	23,630	26	17	9
California State University				
Bakersfield	12,128	23	14	9
Channel Islands	8,336	25	13	12
Chico	19,754	28	18	10
Dominguez Hills	17,926	28	21	7
East Bay	19,613	20	12	8
Fresno	27,251	37	26	11
Fullerton	47,158	39	25	14
Long Beach	41,221	37	24	13
Los Angeles	30,038	33	18	15
Monterey Bay	8,502	23	14	9
Northridge	44,639	35	21	14
Sacramento	35,173	44	23	21
San Bernardino	22,286	31	18	13
San Jose	39,002	74	29	45
San Marcos	17,042	22	14	8
Stanislaus	11,767	20	12	8
Chaffey College	29,808	15	13	2
College of the Sequoias	15,686	7	6	1
Contra Costa Community College	53,483	33	21	12

Table 79. Full-Time Law Enforcement Employees, by Selected State and University or College, 2019—Continued

(Number.)

State and university/college	Student enrollment[1]	Law enforcement employees	Officers	Civilians
Cuesta College	15,212	11	7	4
El Camino College	33,616	18	10	8
Foothill-De Anza College	61,553	17	11	6
Humboldt State University	9,262	20	12	8
Irvine Valley College	20,065	16	10	6
Marin Community College	8,140	7	5	2
Pasadena Community College	37,252	15	10	5
Riverside Community College	60,699	27	22	5
San Bernardino Community College	28,807	17	9	8
San Diego State University	37,748	52	27	25
San Francisco State University	33,506	46	23	23
San Jose/Evergreen Community College	28,801	17	7	10
Sonoma County Junior College	30,597	21	8	13
Sonoma State University	10,468	15	12	3
State Center Community College District	63,592	25	20	5
University of California				
Berkeley	44,235	104	46	58
Davis	39,783	67	41	26
Irvine	37,170	100	45	55
Los Angeles	46,592	95	57	38
Merced	8,388	28	16	12
Riverside	24,907	40	31	9
San Diego	37,744	78	39	39
San Francisco	3,201	136	48	88
Santa Barbara	26,561	60	41	19
Santa Cruz	20,592	38	21	17
Ventura County Community College District	50,436	16	15	1
West Valley-Mission College	24,612	13	8	5
COLORADO				
Adams State University	4,217	6	5	1
Arapahoe Community College	14,803	12	10	2
Auraria Higher Education Center[2]		41	25	16
Colorado School of Mines	6,994	10	9	1
Colorado State University, Fort Collins	37,676	39	28	11
Fort Lewis College	3,730	9	8	1
Pikes Peak Community College	18,604	19	17	2
Red Rocks Community College	12,042	11	7	4
University of Colorado				
Boulder	39,302	82	41	41
Colorado Springs	16,899	28	17	11
Denver	31,912	57	25	32
University of Northern Colorado	15,825	24	16	8
CONNECTICUT				
Central Connecticut State University	14,006	27	19	8
Eastern Connecticut State University	5,899	20	11	9
Southern Connecticut State University	11,642	30	24	6
University of Connecticut, Storrs, Avery Point, and Hartford[2]		124	94	30
Western Connecticut State University	6,675	20	14	6
Yale University	13,972	109	93	16
DELAWARE				
Delaware State University	4,633	35	13	22
University of Delaware	25,534	85	54	31
FLORIDA				
Florida A&M University	10,986	26	20	6
Florida Atlantic University	37,588	77	43	34
Florida Gulf Coast University	16,878	28	21	7
Florida International University	70,581	94	65	29
Florida SouthWestern State College	22,279	23	11	12
Florida State University				
Panama City[2]		6	5	1
Tallahassee	46,946	94	65	29
New College of Florida	896	20	16	4
Northwest Florida State College	7,962	6	6	0
Pensacola State College	13,734	14	11	3
Santa Fe College	19,571	22	16	6
Tallahassee Community College	16,944	25	12	13
University of Central Florida	78,073	130	83	47
University of Florida	59,603	121	84	37
University of North Florida	19,547	42	31	11
University of South Florida				
St. Petersburg	5,864	21	16	5
Tampa	51,282	76	52	24
University of West Florida	16,374	26	19	7
GEORGIA				
Abraham Baldwin Agricultural College	6,347	13	12	1
Albany State University	10,150	31	18	13
Albany Technical College	4,587	3	3	0
Athens Technical College	6,257	3	2	1
Atlanta Metropolitan State College	3,709	13	7	6

Table 79. Full-Time Law Enforcement Employees, by Selected State and University or College, 2019—Continued

(Number.)

State and university/college	Student enrollment[1]	Law enforcement employees	Officers	Civilians
Atlanta Technical College	6,011	3	2	1
Augusta Technical College	6,445	6	6	0
Augusta University	9,278	54	39	15
Bainbridge State College[2]		7	5	2
Berry College	2,250	16	10	6
Chattahoochee Technical College	14,886	12	10	2
Clark Atlanta University	4,327	44	20	24
Clayton State University	8,525	25	14	11
College of Coastal Georgia	4,498	14	14	0
Dalton State College	6,009	15	12	3
Emory University	15,831	82	54	28
Fort Valley State University	3,044	30	11	19
Georgia College and State University	7,977	22	14	8
Georgia Gwinnett College	15,116	28	23	5
Georgia Institute of Technology	34,108	112	82	30
Georgia Southern University	31,503	56	40	16
Georgia Southwestern State University	3,794	11	11	0
Georgia State University	38,731	269	126	143
Gordon State College	4,696	13	13	0
Gwinnett Technical College	12,129	4	3	1
Mercer University	9,692	30	22	8
Middle Georgia State University	9,182	34	29	5
Piedmont College	3,153	7	4	3
Spelman College	2,171	24	15	9
University of North Georgia	22,256	48	37	11
Valdosta State University	13,418	35	27	8
Wesleyan College	812	5	5	0
West Georgia Technical College	9,627	10	10	0
Young Harris College	1,366	4	4	0
ILLINOIS				
College of DuPage	43,669	22	17	5
Elgin Community College	15,074	18	16	2
Illinois Central College	12,989	19	8	11
Illinois State University	22,948	39	29	10
John Wood Community College	2,838	5	4	1
Joliet Junior College	23,177	25	15	10
Lewis University	7,939	20	8	12
Lincoln Land Community College	11,135	15	13	2
Loyola University of Chicago	19,072	36	36	0
Millikin University	2,236	16	5	11
Northern Illinois University	20,443	81	45	36
Oakton Community College	18,251	15	14	1
Parkland College	12,238	17	13	4
Rend Lake College	4,908	5	5	0
Rock Valley College	10,387	11	10	1
Southern Illinois University, Carbondale	16,271	50	36	14
Southwestern Illinois College	16,187	20	17	3
Triton College	17,777	13	8	5
University of Illinois				
Springfield	5,878	21	14	7
Urbana	52,986	99	64	35
Waubonsee Community College	17,229	8	8	0
Western Illinois University	10,905	26	20	6
INDIANA				
Ball State University	27,369	39	32	7
Indiana University				
East	5,530	13	12	1
Indianapolis	34,699	64	51	13
Kokomo	3,715	4	4	0
South Bend	6,406	14	12	2
Southeast	6,415	13	12	1
Purdue University	45,685	56	39	17
IOWA				
Iowa State University	39,108	51	36	15
University of Iowa	35,876	56	37	19
University of Northern Iowa	14,221	19	16	3
KANSAS				
Butler Community College	12,832	9	9	0
Emporia State University	6,987	7	7	0
Fort Hays State University	17,953	11	10	1
Garden City Community College	3,227	1	1	0
Kansas City Kansas Community College	8,366	18	17	1
Kansas State University	25,450	37	24	13
Pittsburg State University	8,330	14	11	3
University of Kansas				
Main Campus	31,136	66	26	40
Medical Center[2]		139	54	85
Washburn University	7,745	24	18	6
Wichita State University	16,248	42	29	13

Table 79. Full-Time Law Enforcement Employees, by Selected State and University or College, 2019—Continued

(Number.)

State and university/college	Student enrollment[1]	Law enforcement employees	Officers	Civilians
KENTUCKY				
Morehead State University	12,217	19	12	7
Murray State University	11,095	26	16	10
Northern Kentucky University	16,539	21	15	6
University of Kentucky	31,102	174	48	126
Western Kentucky University	24,560	29	21	8
LOUISIANA				
Delgado Community College	20,393	38	28	10
Louisiana State University				
Baton Rouge	33,554	68	50	18
Health Sciences Center, New Orleans	3,172	20	20	0
Health Sciences Center, Shreveport	1,113	55	41	14
Louisiana Tech University	13,893	20	19	1
McNeese State University	8,567	16	10	6
Nicholls State University	7,486	12	8	4
Northwestern State University	13,099	27	21	6
Southeastern Louisiana University	17,714	26	22	4
Southern University and A&M College				
New Orleans	3,111	16	14	2
Shreveport	4,380	8	7	1
University of Louisiana				
Lafayette	19,517	35	32	3
Monroe	10,337	27	26	1
University of New Orleans	9,910	20	19	1
MAINE				
University of Maine				
Farmington	2,477	6	5	1
Orono	12,722	21	13	8
University of Southern Maine	10,213	15	11	4
MARYLAND				
Bowie State University	6,998	27	14	13
Coppin State University	3,357	22	12	10
Frostburg State University	6,122	21	17	4
Hagerstown Community College	5,761	4	4	0
Morgan State University	8,375	55	37	18
Prince George's County Community College	16,868	20	12	8
Salisbury University	9,529	34	19	15
Towson University	25,744	51	37	14
University of Baltimore	6,666	35	15	20
University of Maryland				
Baltimore City	7,495	145	53	92
Baltimore County	15,681	36	25	11
College Park	44,052	123	77	46
Eastern Shore	3,875	17	14	3
MASSACHUSETTS				
Amherst College	1,946	18	13	5
Assumption College	2,728	21	15	6
Babson College	4,079	28	18	10
Becker College	2,290	19	13	6
Bentley University	5,810	36	25	11
Boston College	15,903	79	52	27
Boston University	41,418	64	50	14
Brandeis University	6,330	23	20	3
Bridgewater State University	13,215	27	23	4
Bunker Hill Community College	17,830	18	16	2
Clark University	3,596	15	11	4
College of the Holy Cross	2,922	26	22	4
Dean College	1,595	11	2	9
Emerson College	4,815	19	16	3
Fitchburg State University	11,496	25	20	5
Framingham State University	9,007	18	15	3
Harvard University	40,803	99	76	23
Holyoke Community College	7,113	11	8	3
Massachusetts Bay Community College	7,227	7	7	0
Massachusetts College of Art	2,412	30	10	20
Massachusetts College of Liberal Arts	2,157	16	11	5
Massasoit Community College	10,323	17	16	1
Merrimack College	5,061	20	15	5
Mount Wachusett Community College	5,194	11	10	1
Quinsigamond Community College	10,234	12	10	2
Salem State University	10,556	24	21	3
Springfield College	3,366	38	19	19
Springfield Technical Community College	7,431	15	12	3
University of Massachusetts				
Amherst	35,156	68	52	16
Medical Center, Worcester	1,120	36	29	7
Wellesley College	2,674	18	14	4
Wentworth Institute of Technology	4,763	23	16	7
Western New England University	4,130	26	20	6
Westfield State University	7,598	22	17	5

Table 79. Full-Time Law Enforcement Employees, by Selected State and University or College, 2019—Continued

(Number.)

State and university/college	Student enrollment[1]	Law enforcement employees	Officers	Civilians
Worcester Polytechnic Institute	7,338	25	18	7
Worcester State University	10,276	23	17	6
MICHIGAN				
Central Michigan University	26,971	36	25	11
Delta College	11,644	8	5	3
Eastern Michigan University	23,715	49	38	11
Ferris State University	16,549	17	13	4
Grand Rapids Community College	19,969	17	13	4
Grand Valley State University	28,190	22	18	4
Kalamazoo Valley Community College	12,039	8	6	2
Kellogg Community College	7,236	3	3	0
Kirtland Community College	1,929	1	1	0
Lansing Community College	17,503	15	10	5
Macomb Community College	29,245	26	22	4
Michigan State University	55,423	112	80	32
Michigan Technological University	7,727	15	12	3
Mott Community College	10,504	15	10	5
Northern Michigan University	9,073	24	21	3
Oakland Community College	27,113	23	22	1
Oakland University	22,694	28	21	7
Saginaw Valley State University	9,688	9	8	1
Schoolcraft College	17,002	15	11	4
University of Michigan				
Ann Arbor	47,543	77	61	16
Dearborn	10,905	28	14	14
Flint	9,138	28	18	10
Washtenaw Community College	21,041	6	6	0
Western Michigan University	25,645	39	32	7
MINNESOTA				
University of Minnesota				
Duluth	11,777	14	12	2
Morris	1,778	5	3	2
Twin Cities	64,115	71	54	17
MISSISSIPPI				
Coahoma Community College	2,596	8	7	1
Jackson State University	10,000	60	35	25
Mississippi State University	24,054	53	39	14
University of Mississippi, Oxford	25,416	45	30	15
MISSOURI				
Jefferson College	5,663	8	8	0
Lincoln University	3,096	15	11	4
Metropolitan Community College	24,011	35	28	7
Mineral Area College	4,401	8	7	1
Missouri Southern State University	6,941	8	7	1
Missouri University of Science and Technology	9,466	23	12	11
Missouri Western State University	6,302	11	8	3
Northwest Missouri State University	7,402	14	11	3
Southeast Missouri State University	13,245	19	14	5
St. Charles Community College	9,349	14	12	2
St. Louis Community College, Meramac	28,937	33	28	5
University of Central Missouri	16,665	25	14	11
University of Missouri				
Columbia	34,329	71	48	23
Kansas City	19,485	38	27	11
St. Louis	20,888	27	22	5
Washington University	16,962	63	43	20
MONTANA				
Montana State University	18,722	28	22	6
University of Montana	13,679	23	14	9
NEBRASKA				
Metropolitan Community College, Douglas County	24,779	26	21	5
University of Nebraska				
Kearney	8,041	12	9	3
Lincoln	28,642	62	25	37
NEVADA				
University of Nevada, Reno	24,557	39	29	10
University Police Services	90,603	72	53	19
NEW HAMPSHIRE				
Plymouth State University	5,931	10	10	0
University of New Hampshire	16,859	34	20	14
NEW JERSEY				
Brookdale Community College	18,316	11	10	1
Essex County College	11,840	55	12	43
Kean University	16,577	48	19	29
Middlesex County College	16,876	17	12	5

Table 79. Full-Time Law Enforcement Employees, by Selected State and University or College, 2019—Continued

(Number.)

State and university/college	Student enrollment[1]	Law enforcement employees	Officers	Civilians
Monmouth University	6,936	52	19	33
Montclair State University	24,022	47	38	9
New Jersey Institute of Technology	13,158	76	41	35
Princeton University	8,593	100	32	68
Rowan University	21,305	87	34	53
Rutgers University				
Camden	7,904	71	19	52
New Brunswick	15,220	153	62	91
Newark	55,698	129	62	67
Stevens Institute of Technology	8,015	21	19	2
Stockton University	10,976	42	26	16
The College of New Jersey	8,630	31	16	15
William Paterson University	12,422	43	29	14
NEW MEXICO				
Eastern New Mexico University	7,502	11	10	1
New Mexico Military Institute	450	5	5	0
New Mexico State University	16,383	36	21	15
Western New Mexico University	4,257	7	6	1
NEW YORK				
Ithaca College	7,036	43	24	19
State University of New York Police				
Albany	20,011	61	40	21
Alfred	4,060	17	12	5
Binghamton	18,892	58	39	19
Brockport	9,539	22	16	6
Buffalo	34,183	74	62	12
Buffalo State College	11,048	36	31	5
Canton	4,981	9	8	1
Delhi	4,207	14	12	2
Downstate Medical	2,033	100	20	80
Environmental Science	2,380	12	8	4
Farmingdale	19,903	30	19	11
Fredonia	4,965	14	13	1
Geneseo	6,000	23	16	7
Maritime	1,998	15	9	6
Morrisville	3,741	16	12	4
New Paltz	9,669	28	23	5
Oneonta	7,171	27	17	10
Optometry	413	17	7	10
Oswego	11,159	27	23	4
Plattsburgh	6,558	19	14	5
Polytechnic Institute	3,307	15	11	4
Potsdam	4,365	15	12	3
Purchase	4,789	33	24	9
Stony Brook	30,012	146	63	83
Upstate Medical	1,608	114	19	95
NORTH CAROLINA				
Appalachian State University	20,285	48	29	19
Beaufort County Community College	1,994	4	4	0
Belmont Abbey College	1,721	6	6	0
Davidson College	1,985	10	9	1
Duke University	18,107	163	67	96
East Carolina University	32,477	73	59	14
Elizabeth City State University	1,586	24	13	11
Elon University	7,088	36	19	17
Fayetteville State University	7,662	27	14	13
Meredith College	2,350	16	3	13
Methodist University	2,491	21	9	12
North Carolina Agricultural and Technical State University	13,156	54	23	31
North Carolina Central University	9,134	40	17	23
North Carolina School of the Arts	1,034	21	14	7
North Carolina State University, Raleigh	39,136	67	54	13
Queens University	3,059	14	9	5
Saint Augustine's University	1,040	12	1	11
University of North Carolina				
Asheville	4,397	21	13	8
Chapel Hill	32,180	74	52	22
Charlotte	33,673	60	48	12
Greensboro	22,419	54	35	19
Pembroke	7,405	28	20	8
Wilmington	18,997	61	35	26
Wake Forest University	8,740	51	23	28
Western Carolina University	12,501	25	25	0
Winston-Salem State University	5,881	40	16	24
NORTH DAKOTA				
Bismarck State College	4,948	3	2	1
North Dakota State College of Science	3,657	3	2	1
North Dakota State University	15,065	24	15	9
University of North Dakota	17,646	20	19	1

Table 79. Full-Time Law Enforcement Employees, by Selected State and University or College, 2019—Continued

(Number.)

State and university/college	Student enrollment[1]	Law enforcement employees	Officers	Civilians
OHIO				
Capital University	3,928	16	10	6
Columbus State Community College	46,553	43	24	19
Kent State University	34,023	42	30	12
Lakeland Community College	10,085	16	12	4
Miami University	21,731	37	27	10
Mount St. Joseph University	2,386	10	8	2
Sinclair Community College	31,708	23	17	6
University of Akron	23,217	42	34	8
University of Cincinnati	43,326	149	69	80
University of Toledo	22,945	41	33	8
OKLAHOMA				
Bacone College	1,048	4	4	0
Cameron University	5,750	12	12	0
East Central University	4,491	6	5	1
Eastern Oklahoma State College	1,977	5	5	0
Langston University	2,598	15	11	4
Mid-America Christian University	2,618	5	5	0
Northeastern Oklahoma A&M College	2,663	6	6	0
Northeastern State University, Tahlequah	9,269	17	13	4
Northwestern Oklahoma State University	2,456	4	4	0
Oklahoma City Community College	17,875	27	21	6
Oklahoma City University	3,247	11	7	4
Oklahoma State University				
Main Campus	27,791	47	34	13
Okmulgee	3,290	7	6	1
Tulsa	1,087	8	7	1
Rogers State University	4,612	9	9	0
Seminole State College	2,155	3	3	0
Southeastern Oklahoma State University	5,039	7	6	1
Southwestern Oklahoma State University	6,341	8	7	1
Tulsa Community College	23,778	35	26	9
University of Central Oklahoma	18,751	14	14	0
University of Oklahoma				
Health Sciences Center	3,695	63	40	23
Norman	32,373	67	34	33
OREGON				
Portland State University	35,257	27	12	15
University of Oregon	25,640	33	23	10
PENNSYLVANIA				
Bloomsburg University	10,288	19	13	6
California University	10,077	20	17	3
Clarion University	6,125	15	10	5
Edinboro University	6,573	15	14	1
Indiana University	14,078	29	23	6
Kutztown University	8,997	18	17	1
Lehigh University	7,562	34	26	8
Lock Haven University	4,215	13	10	3
Mansfield University	2,055	12	9	3
Millersville University	9,217	16	14	2
Moravian College	2,739	17	14	3
Pennsylvania State University				
Abington	4,576	9	6	3
Altoona	3,690	9	9	0
Beaver	735	6	6	0
Behrend	4,853	13	9	4
Berks	3,049	9	9	0
Brandywine	1,587	6	6	0
Dubois	672	2	2	0
Fayette	719	2	2	0
Great Valley	516	2	2	0
Greater Allegheny	553	6	6	0
Harrisburg	5,697	11	10	1
Hazleton	868	6	5	1
Lehigh Valley	1,098	2	2	0
Mont Alto	1,038	6	6	0
New Kensington	747	2	2	0
Schuylkill	830	6	6	0
Wilkes-Barre	562	2	2	0
Worthington Scranton	1,131	2	2	0
Shippensburg University	7,345	18	16	2
Slippery Rock University	10,446	15	14	1
University of Pittsburgh				
Bradford	1,478	8	6	2
Greensburg	1,639	10	9	1
Johnstown	2,912	14	11	3
Pittsburgh	31,818	138	79	59
Titusville	326	8	7	1
West Chester University	19,515	47	26	21
Wilkes University	7,299	33	19	14

Table 79. Full-Time Law Enforcement Employees, by Selected State and University or College, 2019—Continued

(Number.)

State and university/college	Student enrollment[1]	Law enforcement employees	Officers	Civilians
RHODE ISLAND				
Brown University	10,694	84	53	31
University of Rhode Island	20,502	36	32	4
SOUTH CAROLINA				
Benedict College	2,291	17	3	14
Bob Jones University	3,383	3	3	0
Clemson University	27,796	52	37	15
Coastal Carolina University	12,015	89	34	55
College of Charleston	13,258	48	33	15
Columbia College	1,880	6	4	2
Denmark Technical College	863	5	1	4
Erskine College	883	4	2	2
Francis Marion University	4,384	15	12	3
Furman University	3,167	21	14	7
Greenville Technical College	15,700	12	7	5
Lander University	3,093	21	13	8
Medical University of South Carolina	3,421	73	55	18
Midlands Technical College	14,571	11	6	5
Orangeburg-Calhoun Technical College	3,324	3	3	0
Presbyterian College	1,327	9	8	1
South Carolina State University	3,205	20	10	10
The Citadel	4,305	20	15	5
Tri-County Technical College	7,784	14	11	3
Trident Technical College	18,207	21	17	4
University of South Carolina				
Aiken	4,281	9	8	1
Beaufort	2,368	11	10	1
Columbia	37,348	111	76	35
Upstate	7,147	16	14	2
Winthrop University	7,009	20	14	6
SOUTH DAKOTA				
South Dakota State University	15,244	17	13	4
TENNESSEE				
Austin Peay State University	12,156	25	14	11
Chattanooga State Community College	10,770	16	9	7
Christian Brothers University	2,522	23	9	14
Cleveland State Community College	3,883	4	3	1
Columbia State Community College	7,703	6	2	4
East Tennessee State University	16,151	25	19	6
Jackson State Community College	6,263	5	4	1
Lincoln Memorial University	5,118	23	5	18
Middle Tennessee State University	25,602	44	35	9
Motlow State Community College	8,014	4	4	0
Nashville State Community College	11,197	25	2	23
Northeast State Community College	7,407	9	8	1
Pellissippi State Community College	15,428	15	13	2
Roane State Community College	7,014	11	10	1
Southwest Tennessee Community College	12,720	24	22	2
Tennessee State University	11,251	63	23	40
Tennessee Technological University	11,451	18	13	5
University of Memphis	24,847	65	39	26
University of Tennessee				
Chattanooga	12,766	32	17	15
Health Science Center	3,355	62	27	35
Knoxville	30,845	94	63	31
Martin	7,837	16	12	4
University of the South	1,984	14	10	4
Vanderbilt University	13,431	242	102	140
Volunteer State Community College	11,419	14	11	3
Walters State Community College	7,471	10	9	1
TEXAS				
Abilene Christian University	5,709	15	14	1
Alamo Colleges District	109,114	105	84	21
Amarillo College	13,075	13	11	2
Austin College	1,250	7	6	1
Baylor University, Waco	18,261	63	38	25
Cisco College	4,630	1	1	0
College of the Mainland	5,619	9	8	1
Dallas County Community College District	160,872	147	125	22
Grayson College	5,542	8	7	1
Hardin-Simmons University	2,483	6	6	0
Houston Community College	82,166	110	73	37
Kilgore College	6,680	8	8	0
Laredo Community College	13,417	23	21	2
Lubbock Christian University	2,217	5	2	3
Midwestern State University	7,088	16	11	5
Paris Junior College	6,529	5	5	0
Rice University	7,362	42	24	18
South Plains College	12,857	7	7	0
Southwestern Baptist Theological Seminary	3,649	19	13	6

Table 79. Full-Time Law Enforcement Employees, by Selected State and University or College, 2019—Continued

(Number.)

State and university/college	Student enrollment[1]	Law enforcement employees	Officers	Civilians
Southwestern University	1,430	9	6	3
St. Thomas University	3,727	13	9	4
Tarleton State University	14,950	17	16	1
Texas A&M International University	8,818	28	19	9
Texas A&M University	7,390	29	20	9
College Station	72,775	157	63	94
Commerce	15,596	32	22	10
Galveston[2]		10	9	1
San Antonio	7,534	20	14	6
Texas Christian University	11,044	56	32	24
Texas Southern University	11,485	82	42	40
Texas State Technical College				
Harlingen[2]		13	10	3
Waco[2]		9	7	2
West Texas[2]		6	6	0
Texas Tech University, Lubbock	39,987	137	63	74
Texas Woman's University	18,773	45	18	27
University of Houston				
Central Campus	51,371	170	61	109
Clearlake	10,502	33	13	20
Downtown Campus	17,188	50	23	27
University of North Texas, Denton	43,730	65	44	21
University of Texas				
Arlington	60,075	103	44	59
Austin	55,097	147	126	21
Dallas	30,572	79	27	52
El Paso	29,598	55	27	28
Health Science Center, San Antonio	3,960	97	34	63
Houston	6,948	326	84	242
Permian Basin	9,651	24	15	9
Rio Grande Valley	33,012	82	47	35
Southwestern Medical School	2,506	143	44	99
Tyler	12,557	35	14	21
West Texas A&M University	11,753	29	17	12
UTAH				
Brigham Young University	39,515	42	27	15
Dixie State University	12,920	7	6	1
Southern Utah University	15,188	7	6	1
University of Utah	38,229	53	39	14
Utah State University				
Eastern[2]		2	2	0
Logan	32,944	24	14	10
Utah Valley University	48,969	19	13	6
Weber State University	35,447	13	10	3
VERMONT				
University of Vermont	15,629	31	19	12
VIRGINIA				
Bridgewater College	1,936	11	5	6
Christopher Newport University	5,227	30	20	10
College of William and Mary	9,805	28	21	7
Eastern Virginia Medical School	1,376	50	20	30
Emory and Henry College	1,302	3	3	0
Ferrum College	1,164	9	9	0
George Mason University	47,049	57	42	15
Germanna Community College	9,077	9	3	6
Hampton University	4,698	28	12	16
James Madison University	24,133	43	34	9
J. Sargeant Reynolds Community College	13,875	19	13	6
Longwood University	5,909	19	17	2
Lord Fairfax Community College	9,112	5	5	0
Norfolk State University	5,855	46	24	22
Northern Virginia Community College	73,657	57	48	9
Old Dominion University	28,297	58	45	13
Radford University	10,296	30	22	8
Richard Bland College	2,882	5	4	1
Thomas Nelson Community College	12,210	10	7	3
University of Mary Washington	5,373	22	18	4
University of Richmond	4,740	34	22	12
University of Virginia	28,244	123	53	70
University of Virginia's College at Wise	3,325	10	9	1
Virginia Commonwealth University	33,636	121	93	28
Virginia Military Institute	1,769	12	11	1
Virginia Polytechnic Institute and State University	36,115	64	45	19
Virginia State University	5,156	35	20	15
Virginia Western Community College	10,130	8	8	0
WASHINGTON				
Central Washington University	17,638	16	14	2
Eastern Washington University	16,208	15	14	1
Evergreen State College	4,587	14	8	6
University of Washington	55,508	74	44	30

Table 79. Full-Time Law Enforcement Employees, by Selected State and University or College, 2019—Continued

(Number.)

State and university/college	Student enrollment[1]	Law enforcement employees	Officers	Civilians
Washington State University				
Pullman	34,356	26	22	4
Vancouver[2]		5	3	2
Western Washington University	17,782	20	13	7
WEST VIRGINIA				
Bluefield State College	1,600	3	3	0
Concord University	2,710	8	5	3
Fairmont State University	4,620	11	9	2
Glenville State College	2,063	5	2	3
Marshall University	16,818	34	31	3
Potomac State College	1,652	7	6	1
Shepherd University	4,700	8	7	1
West Liberty University	2,702	7	7	0
West Virginia State University	4,617	8	6	2
West Virginia University				
Institute of Technology	1,923	5	5	0
Morgantown	31,994	74	57	17
WISCONSIN				
University of Wisconsin				
Eau Claire	11,790	10	10	0
Green Bay	8,534	12	11	1
La Crosse	11,751	16	13	3
Madison	46,827	135	64	71
Milwaukee	28,921	48	35	13
Oshkosh	16,057	15	12	3
Parkside	4,911	13	9	4
Platteville	9,511	11	9	2
River Falls	6,798	7	5	2
Stevens Point	9,144	12	8	4
Stout	10,940	11	9	2
Superior	3,168	6	2	4
Whitewater	14,196	17	15	2
WYOMING				
University of Wyoming	13,963	24	15	9

1 The student enrollment figures provided by the United States Department of Education are for the 2018 school year, the most recent available. The enrollment figures include full-time and part-time students.   2 Student enrollment figures were not available.

Table 80. Full-Time Law Enforcement Employees, by Selected State Metropolitan and Nonmetropolitan Counties, 2019

(Number.)

State/county	Law enforcement employees	Officers	Civilians
ALABAMA			
Metropolitan Counties			
Autauga	43	32	11
Baldwin	319	135	184
Bibb	12	11	1
Blount	48	44	4
Colbert	57	31	26
Etowah	178	67	111
Geneva	25	12	13
Greene	33	13	20
Hale	31	11	20
Henry	19	15	4
Houston	171	72	99
Jefferson	690	530	160
Lauderdale	74	51	23
Lawrence	59	26	33
Lee	170	81	89
Limestone	120	48	72
Lowndes	42	17	25
Madison	339	131	208
Mobile	552	180	372
Montgomery	175	127	48
Morgan	182	55	127
Pickens	35	10	25
Russell	117	39	78
Shelby	221	131	90
St. Clair	108	51	57
Tuscaloosa	204	105	99
Washington	22	10	12
Nonmetropolitan Counties			
Barbour	58	26	32
Bullock	13	6	7
Butler	18	15	3
Clarke	47	14	33
Clay	27	11	16
Cleburne	28	10	18
Coffee	60	29	31
Conecuh	38	11	27
Coosa	23	10	13
Escambia	89	33	56
Jackson	81	35	46
Macon	28	16	12
Marengo	25	10	15
Marion	31	15	16
Marshall	74	38	36
Monroe	51	18	33
Perry	19	7	12
Pike	35	21	14
Randolph	35	16	19
Sumter	25	8	17
Talladega	95	42	53
Tallapoosa	55	23	32
Walker	76	32	44
Wilcox	22	10	12
Winston	29	10	19
ARIZONA			
Metropolitan Counties			
Cochise	180	86	94
Coconino	239	61	178
Maricopa	3,443	670	2,773
Mohave	246	83	163
Pima	1,417	478	939
Pinal	479	207	272
Yavapai	193	120	73
Yuma	331	82	249
Nonmetropolitan Counties			
Apache	72	25	47
Gila	130	51	79
Graham	82	23	59
Greenlee	42	16	26
La Paz	90	38	52
Navajo	135	47	88
Santa Cruz	83	35	48
ARKANSAS			
Metropolitan Counties			
Benton	241	163	78
Cleveland	12	8	4
Craighead	113	40	73
Crawford	78	35	43
Crittenden	144	39	105

Table 80. Full-Time Law Enforcement Employees, by Selected State Metropolitan and Nonmetropolitan Counties, 2019—Continued

(Number.)

State/county	Law enforcement employees	Officers	Civilians
Faulkner	163	50	113
Franklin	25	12	13
Garland	181	54	127
Grant	18	16	2
Jefferson	102	48	54
Lincoln	26	11	15
Little River	34	15	19
Lonoke	69	35	34
Madison	21	19	2
Miller	36	25	11
Perry	24	12	12
Poinsett	44	16	28
Pulaski	534	410	124
Saline	107	57	50
Sebastian	147	45	102
Washington	303	156	147
Nonmetropolitan Counties			
Arkansas	11	11	0
Ashley	22	19	3
Baxter	60	33	27
Boone	56	26	30
Bradley	7	5	2
Calhoun	12	6	6
Carroll	64	20	44
Chicot	8	7	1
Clark	33	17	16
Clay	20	10	10
Cleburne	49	26	23
Columbia	42	22	20
Conway	44	21	23
Cross	40	18	22
Dallas	28	9	19
Desha	8	7	1
Drew	15	14	1
Fulton	18	7	11
Greene	26	23	3
Hempstead	58	25	33
Hot Spring	34	19	15
Howard	24	11	13
Independence	41	37	4
Izard	37	22	15
Jackson	32	14	18
Johnson	35	12	23
Lafayette	27	9	18
Lawrence	37	16	21
Lee	10	5	5
Logan	46	14	32
Marion	22	20	2
Mississippi	94	42	52
Monroe	14	6	8
Montgomery	24	11	13
Nevada	30	6	24
Newton	21	12	9
Ouachita	48	17	31
Phillips	20	14	6
Pike	24	19	5
Polk	29	16	13
Pope	88	35	53
Prairie	31	9	22
Randolph	25	12	13
Scott	28	9	19
Searcy	18	7	11
Sevier	35	30	5
Sharp	26	14	12
St. Francis	42	19	23
Stone	25	12	13
Union	66	30	36
Van Buren	37	21	16
White	104	53	51
Woodruff	11	7	4
Yell	29	16	13
CALIFORNIA			
Metropolitan Counties			
Alameda	1,496	950	546
Butte	252	101	151
Contra Costa	928	612	316
El Dorado	344	154	190
Fresno	1,182	414	768
Imperial	272	187	85
Kern	1,155	779	376
Kings	289	85	204

Table 80. Full-Time Law Enforcement Employees, by Selected State Metropolitan and Nonmetropolitan Counties, 2019—Continued

(Number.)

State/county	Law enforcement employees	Officers	Civilians
Los Angeles	15,930	9,565	6,365
Madera	121	86	35
Marin	298	194	104
Merced	255	122	133
Monterey	430	295	135
Napa	134	100	34
Orange	3,723	1,888	1,835
Placer	534	248	286
Riverside	3,750	1,788	1,962
Sacramento	1,992	1,348	644
San Benito	59	23	36
San Bernardino	3,342	1,927	1,415
San Diego	4,344	2,601	1,743
San Francisco	1,044	857	187
San Joaquin	737	293	444
San Luis Obispo	418	303	115
San Mateo	746	334	412
Santa Barbara	674	477	197
Santa Clara	1,716	1,316	400
Santa Cruz	334	148	186
Shasta	198	138	60
Solano	512	122	390
Sonoma	581	223	358
Stanislaus	706	527	179
Sutter	128	105	23
Tulare	791	563	228
Ventura	1,231	761	470
Yolo	262	84	178
Yuba	163	126	37
Nonmetropolitan Counties			
Alpine	16	13	3
Amador	94	49	45
Calaveras	113	58	55
Colusa	59	40	19
Del Norte	52	21	31
Glenn	73	33	40
Humboldt	245	187	58
Inyo	78	38	40
Lake	122	91	31
Lassen	80	58	22
Mariposa	78	62	16
Mendocino	202	131	71
Modoc	30	20	10
Mono	41	20	21
Nevada	152	59	93
Plumas	66	36	30
Sierra	12	6	6
Siskiyou	103	81	22
Tehama	107	73	34
Trinity	50	36	14
Tuolumne	131	60	71
COLORADO			
Metropolitan Counties			
Adams	583	400	183
Arapahoe	568	243	325
Boulder	396	108	288
Clear Creek	67	25	42
Douglas	522	351	171
Elbert	45	36	9
El Paso	842	525	317
Gilpin	58	35	23
Jefferson	761	532	229
Larimer	408	276	132
Mesa	232	131	101
Park	55	30	25
Teller	75	47	28
Weld	405	129	276
Nonmetropolitan Counties			
Alamosa	46	23	23
Archuleta	39	17	22
Baca	13	5	8
Bent	30	13	17
Chaffee	58	21	37
Cheyenne	10	6	4
Conejos	32	12	20
Costilla	14	8	6
Crowley	15	8	7
Custer	17	11	6
Delta	65	36	29
Dolores	9	5	4

Table 80. Full-Time Law Enforcement Employees, by Selected State Metropolitan and Nonmetropolitan Counties, 2019—Continued

(Number.)

State/county	Law enforcement employees	Officers	Civilians
Eagle	82	46	36
Garfield	128	96	32
Grand	51	24	27
Gunnison	29	14	15
Hinsdale	4	3	1
Huerfano	40	19	21
Jackson	12	5	7
Kiowa	8	5	3
Kit Carson	29	6	23
Lake	21	7	14
La Plata	116	91	25
Las Animas	32	12	20
Lincoln	26	10	16
Logan	45	20	25
Mineral	7	4	3
Moffat	38	18	20
Montezuma	67	27	40
Montrose	86	48	38
Morgan	48	43	5
Otero	23	22	1
Ouray	8	8	0
Phillips	4	4	0
Pitkin	55	22	33
Prowers	29	10	19
Rio Blanco	27	13	14
Rio Grande	43	17	26
Routt	52	23	29
Saguache	17	10	7
San Juan	2	2	0
San Miguel	32	12	20
Sedgwick	3	2	1
Summit	74	53	21
Washington	31	10	21
Yuma	21	7	14
DELAWARE			
Metropolitan Counties			
New Castle County Police Department	463	387	76
FLORIDA			
Metropolitan Counties			
Alachua	378	268	110
Baker	63	44	19
Bay	273	208	65
Brevard	1,282	558	724
Broward	1,329	390	939
Charlotte	448	309	139
Citrus	328	205	123
Clay	579	277	302
Collier	904	570	334
Escambia	655	417	238
Flagler	289	212	77
Gadsden	67	44	23
Gilchrist	66	49	17
Hernando	557	252	305
Highlands	342	147	195
Hillsborough	3,313	1,245	2,068
Indian River	479	190	289
Jefferson	59	26	33
Lake	703	463	240
Lee	1,504	1,030	474
Leon	715	271	444
Levy	151	115	36
Manatee	1,147	753	394
Marion	778	545	233
Martin	387	260	127
Miami-Dade	4,068	2,953	1,115
Nassau	257	140	117
Okaloosa	444	323	121
Orange	2,264	1,581	683
Osceola	637	411	226
Palm Beach	3,623	1,644	1,979
Pinellas	2,385	827	1,558
Polk	1,170	652	518
Santa Rosa	439	220	219
Sarasota	974	414	560
Seminole	1,236	437	799
St. Johns	695	333	362
St. Lucie	741	316	425
Volusia	734	424	310
Wakulla	141	56	85
Walton	534	263	271

Table 80. Full-Time Law Enforcement Employees, by Selected State Metropolitan and Nonmetropolitan Counties, 2019—Continued

(Number.)

State/county	Law enforcement employees	Officers	Civilians
Nonmetropolitan Counties			
Bradford	88	41	47
Calhoun	33	25	8
Columbia	201	153	48
DeSoto	115	56	59
Glades	130	32	98
Gulf	46	32	14
Hamilton	60	19	41
Hardee	105	76	29
Hendry	162	86	76
Jackson	74	49	25
Lafayette	34	13	21
Liberty	32	25	7
Madison	81	64	17
Monroe	508	196	312
Putnam	212	120	92
Taylor	80	55	25
Washington	82	42	40
GEORGIA			
Metropolitan Counties			
Bartow	227	186	41
Bibb	495	408	87
Brooks	45	24	21
Bryan	63	42	21
Burke	120	76	44
Carroll	194	113	81
Catoosa	120	72	48
Chatham County Police Department	144	125	19
Cherokee	358	282	76
Clayton County Police Department	480	347	133
Cobb	737	438	299
Cobb County Police Department	697	628	69
Columbia	338	276	62
Coweta	267	166	101
Dawson	113	71	42
DeKalb	670	462	208
DeKalb County Police Department	946	693	253
Dougherty	234	211	23
Dougherty County Police Department	38	28	10
Douglas	337	298	39
Echols	9	8	1
Effingham	156	80	76
Fayette	201	133	68
Floyd	173	84	89
Floyd County Police Department	81	76	5
Forsyth	441	360	81
Fulton	913	701	212
Fulton County Police Department	77	49	28
Glynn County Police Department	120	114	6
Gwinnett County Police Department	1,007	764	243
Hall	431	293	138
Haralson	77	75	2
Harris	81	79	2
Heard	36	22	14
Henry	313	256	57
Henry County Police Department	259	217	42
Houston	335	133	202
Jasper	44	29	15
Jones	78	39	39
Lamar	62	35	27
Lanier	21	18	3
Long	30	28	2
Madison	95	52	43
Marion	14	6	8
McIntosh	80	52	28
Meriwether	49	27	22
Murray	72	45	27
Newton	290	168	122
Oconee	96	62	34
Paulding	265	226	39
Peach	60	30	30
Pike	51	28	23
Rockdale	270	246	24
Spalding	176	95	81
Walton	206	188	18
Worth	42	27	15
Nonmetropolitan Counties			
Appling	68	29	39
Bacon	29	11	18
Baker	9	8	1
Baldwin	119	59	60

Table 80. Full-Time Law Enforcement Employees, by Selected State Metropolitan and Nonmetropolitan Counties, 2019—Continued

(Number.)

State/county	Law enforcement employees	Officers	Civilians
Banks	64	46	18
Berrien	49	26	23
Bleckley	43	17	26
Candler	29	18	11
Charlton	30	18	12
Chattooga	46	28	18
Clay	7	6	1
Clinch	15	12	3
Coffee	125	55	70
Cook	52	28	24
Crisp	99	59	40
Decatur	63	49	14
Dodge	56	23	33
Dooly	75	37	38
Early	39	18	21
Elbert	62	33	29
Fannin	56	40	16
Franklin	57	36	21
Gilmer	107	61	46
Gordon	122	82	40
Grady	23	19	4
Habersham	87	52	35
Hancock	46	26	20
Hart	32	27	5
Irwin	23	15	8
Jackson	112	98	14
Jefferson	50	47	3
Laurens	108	67	41
Montgomery	21	11	10
Pierce	53	21	32
Screven	22	8	14
Sumter	98	74	24
Taylor	22	11	11
Tift	103	51	52
Towns	38	19	19
Treutlen	20	8	12
Union	46	41	5
Webster	7	7	0
Wilkinson	28	15	13
HAWAII			
Metropolitan Counties			
Maui Police Department	433	334	99
Nonmetropolitan Counties			
Hawaii Police Department	564	434	130
Kauai Police Department	186	132	54
IDAHO			
Metropolitan Counties			
Ada	720	167	553
Bannock	125	42	83
Boise	23	13	10
Bonneville	191	71	120
Butte	14	4	10
Canyon	282	70	212
Franklin	15	10	5
Gem	34	13	21
Jefferson	60	22	38
Jerome	55	22	33
Kootenai	297	97	200
Nez Perce	77	22	55
Owyhee	28	12	16
Power	26	10	16
Twin Falls	118	45	73
Nonmetropolitan Counties			
Adams	24	8	16
Bear Lake	14	8	6
Benewah	28	10	18
Bingham	85	37	48
Blaine	64	50	14
Bonner	99	41	58
Boundary	27	8	19
Camas	6	4	2
Caribou	26	9	17
Cassia	78	33	45
Clark	7	3	4
Clearwater	32	15	17
Custer	17	9	8
Elmore	68	22	46
Fremont	38	21	17
Gooding	34	16	18

Table 80. Full-Time Law Enforcement Employees, by Selected State Metropolitan and Nonmetropolitan Counties, 2019—Continued

(Number.)

State/county	Law enforcement employees	Officers	Civilians
Idaho	38	18	20
Latah	53	29	24
Lemhi	23	7	16
Lewis	16	8	8
Lincoln	12	9	3
Madison	62	23	39
Minidoka	32	21	11
Oneida	14	9	5
Payette	49	18	31
Shoshone	37	15	22
Teton	20	11	9
Valley	41	17	24
Washington	35	14	21
ILLINOIS			
Metropolitan Counties			
Alexander	13	7	6
Bond	23	12	11
Champaign	154	66	88
Cook	5,418	1,849	3,569
DuPage	486	391	95
Fulton	42	20	22
Grundy	45	30	15
Henry	65	22	43
Jackson	86	32	54
Kane	122	87	35
Kankakee	191	49	142
Kendall	118	60	58
Lake	227	162	65
Macon	151	48	103
Macoupin	49	19	30
Madison	167	85	82
Marshall	17	8	9
McHenry	346	98	248
McLean	130	51	79
Mercer	30	12	18
Piatt	36	14	22
Rock Island	154	65	89
Sangamon	204	77	127
Tazewell	60	41	19
Vermilion	97	41	56
Will	596	238	358
Winnebago	331	116	215
Nonmetropolitan Counties			
Brown	8	7	1
Cass	8	7	1
Clay	18	12	6
Coles	29	21	8
Crawford	24	17	7
Cumberland	15	5	10
Douglas	25	12	13
Edgar	6	6	0
Effingham	46	20	26
Fayette	17	11	6
Ford	26	20	6
Franklin	40	16	24
Gallatin	4	4	0
Greene	6	6	0
Hancock	23	11	12
Iroquois	15	13	2
Jasper	15	7	8
Jefferson	61	20	41
Jo Daviess	38	18	20
Livingston	66	30	36
Logan	26	23	3
Mason	22	9	13
McDonough	24	14	10
Montgomery	31	13	18
Perry	21	6	15
Pike	30	13	17
Putnam	13	8	5
Scott	7	3	4
Shelby	28	14	14
Stephenson	38	28	10
Wabash	12	5	7
Wayne	21	9	12
Whiteside	63	20	43
INDIANA			
Metropolitan Counties			
Bartholomew	105	43	62
Brown	44	16	28

Table 80. Full-Time Law Enforcement Employees, by Selected State Metropolitan and Nonmetropolitan Counties, 2019—Continued

(Number.)

State/county	Law enforcement employees	Officers	Civilians
Franklin	11	11	0
Hancock	82	41	41
Howard	148	35	113
Johnson	139	123	16
Lake	441	157	284
La Porte	159	68	91
Madison	101	46	55
Monroe	60	46	14
Porter	75	66	9
Shelby	98	33	65
St. Joseph	284	116	168
Nonmetropolitan Counties			
Clinton	58	20	38
Gibson	46	16	30
Greene	60	20	40
Jackson	74	17	57
Jay	47	13	34
Jennings	20	17	3
Knox	64	28	36
Kosciusko	100	32	68
Montgomery	71	25	46
Noble	74	48	26
Starke	36	13	23
Steuben	53	23	30
Wells	16	16	0
White	45	16	29
IOWA			
Metropolitan Counties			
Benton	35	14	21
Black Hawk	123	74	49
Boone	31	13	18
Bremer	38	13	25
Dallas	72	29	43
Dubuque	91	79	12
Grundy	16	12	4
Guthrie	14	9	5
Harrison	11	10	1
Jasper	47	17	30
Johnson	92	72	20
Jones	27	11	16
Linn	195	129	66
Madison	18	8	10
Mills	27	12	15
Polk	525	157	368
Pottawattamie	201	53	148
Scott	166	49	117
Story	89	32	57
Warren	36	20	16
Washington	45	17	28
Woodbury	113	40	73
Nonmetropolitan Counties			
Adair	13	4	9
Adams	8	8	0
Allamakee	21	10	11
Appanoose	16	8	8
Buchanan	30	13	17
Buena Vista	36	14	22
Butler	18	12	6
Calhoun	12	7	5
Cass	12	9	3
Cedar	39	14	25
Cerro Gordo	73	20	53
Cherokee	21	8	13
Chickasaw	16	10	6
Clarke	22	7	15
Clay	25	11	14
Clayton	29	13	16
Clinton	47	25	22
Crawford	21	11	10
Davis	17	6	11
Decatur	16	6	10
Delaware	21	14	7
Des Moines	26	22	4
Dickinson	20	9	11
Emmet	18	9	9
Fayette	38	12	26
Floyd	19	11	8
Franklin	10	7	3
Fremont	27	10	17
Greene	18	8	10

Table 80. Full-Time Law Enforcement Employees, by Selected State Metropolitan and Nonmetropolitan Counties, 2019—Continued

(Number.)

State/county	Law enforcement employees	Officers	Civilians
Hamilton	31	11	20
Hancock	9	8	1
Hardin	30	11	19
Howard	17	9	8
Humboldt	21	8	13
Ida	16	9	7
Iowa	29	14	15
Jackson	19	10	9
Jefferson	14	12	2
Keokuk	12	6	6
Kossuth	25	10	15
Lee	37	18	19
Louisa	31	11	20
Lucas	13	5	8
Lyon	22	11	11
Mahaska	26	10	16
Marion	38	17	21
Marshall	55	19	36
Mitchell	20	10	10
Monona	18	8	10
Muscatine	81	21	60
O'Brien	28	9	19
Osceola	14	9	5
Page	17	9	8
Palo Alto	17	8	9
Plymouth	34	12	22
Pocahontas	17	7	10
Poweshiek	13	12	1
Ringgold	13	6	7
Sac	22	9	13
Shelby	10	9	1
Sioux	41	14	27
Tama	23	13	10
Taylor	13	8	5
Union	13	6	7
Van Buren	12	6	6
Wapello	44	13	31
Wayne	16	8	8
Webster	36	17	19
Winnebago	8	7	1
Winneshiek	26	11	15
Worth	25	13	12
Wright	25	10	15
KANSAS			
Metropolitan Counties			
Douglas	159	77	82
Geary	105	33	72
Harvey	25	23	2
Jackson	43	22	21
Jefferson	39	23	16
Johnson	635	475	160
Leavenworth	97	62	35
Linn	33	18	15
Miami	61	32	29
Pottawatomie	43	30	13
Riley County Police Department	206	108	98
Sedgwick	516	177	339
Shawnee	182	112	70
Sumner	35	30	5
Wabaunsee	23	10	13
Nonmetropolitan Counties			
Allen	30	12	18
Bourbon	16	13	3
Brown	26	9	17
Chase	10	5	5
Chautauqua	15	6	9
Cherokee	51	24	27
Cheyenne	6	5	1
Clark	10	5	5
Clay	13	7	6
Cloud	9	8	1
Coffey	41	12	29
Cowley	27	24	3
Crawford	36	31	5
Decatur	3	3	0
Dickinson	24	21	3
Edwards	10	6	4
Elk	10	5	5
Ellis	34	17	17
Ellsworth	20	7	13
Ford	35	26	9

Table 80. Full-Time Law Enforcement Employees, by Selected State Metropolitan and Nonmetropolitan Counties, 2019—Continued

(Number.)

State/county	Law enforcement employees	Officers	Civilians
Franklin	45	30	15
Gove	5	4	1
Graham	8	3	5
Grant	15	5	10
Gray	18	11	7
Greeley	8	4	4
Greenwood	22	13	9
Hamilton	6	6	0
Haskell	15	10	5
Jewell	10	5	5
Kearny	16	9	7
Kingman	20	8	12
Labette	20	18	2
Lane	10	5	5
Lincoln	13	8	5
Logan	5	5	0
Lyon	30	25	5
Marion	17	11	6
Marshall	26	11	15
McPherson	22	19	3
Mitchell	9	8	1
Montgomery	39	25	14
Morris	12	8	4
Morton	12	6	6
Nemaha	18	9	9
Neosho	30	16	14
Ness	11	6	5
Norton	9	5	4
Osborne	14	7	7
Ottawa	18	5	13
Pawnee	12	11	1
Phillips	14	9	5
Pratt	17	10	7
Rawlins	4	3	1
Republic	15	9	6
Rice	9	9	0
Rooks	17	6	11
Rush	12	7	5
Russell	11	10	1
Saline	49	38	11
Scott	9	5	4
Seward	37	15	22
Sheridan	4	4	0
Sherman	11	5	6
Smith	6	6	0
Stanton	11	7	4
Trego	6	4	2
Wallace	3	3	0
Washington	8	8	0
Wichita	9	4	5
Woodson	11	7	4
KENTUCKY			
Metropolitan Counties			
Allen	16	14	2
Bourbon	12	11	1
Boyd	46	34	12
Bracken	6	5	1
Bullitt	50	35	15
Butler	10	7	3
Carter	11	7	4
Clark	16	12	4
Daviess	66	35	31
Edmonson	9	6	3
Fayette	89	62	27
Grant	18	16	2
Greenup	17	14	3
Hardin	56	40	16
Henderson	24	19	5
Jefferson	277	223	54
Kenton	43	35	8
Kenton County Police Department	39	37	2
Larue	7	5	2
Meade	18	16	2
Oldham	16	13	3
Oldham County Police Department	41	38	3
Pendleton	9	8	1
Shelby	25	22	3
Spencer	11	5	6
Trigg	10	7	3
Warren	89	50	39

Table 80. Full-Time Law Enforcement Employees, by Selected State Metropolitan and Nonmetropolitan Counties, 2019—Continued

(Number.)

State/county	Law enforcement employees	Officers	Civilians
Nonmetropolitan Counties			
Adair	8	6	2
Anderson	21	19	2
Ballard	11	10	1
Barren	23	18	5
Bath	3	2	1
Boyle	15	14	1
Breathitt	2	2	0
Breckinridge	15	10	5
Caldwell	11	8	3
Calloway	34	25	9
Carlisle	3	2	1
Carroll	7	5	2
Casey	17	10	7
Clay	16	10	6
Crittenden	6	5	1
Cumberland	5	3	2
Estill	5	3	2
Fleming	7	6	1
Floyd	20	10	10
Franklin	36	33	3
Fulton	5	4	1
Garrard	3	2	1
Garrard County Police Department	8	8	0
Graves	20	17	3
Grayson	16	9	7
Green	4	4	0
Harlan	21	18	3
Hart	18	8	10
Hickman	5	3	2
Hopkins	40	32	8
Jackson	9	8	1
Johnson	10	8	2
Knott	5	5	0
Lawrence	13	11	2
Leslie	8	7	1
Letcher	9	5	4
Lewis	8	6	2
Lincoln	11	8	3
Livingston	10	9	1
Logan	26	23	3
Lyon	10	7	3
Madison	34	31	3
Marion	10	7	3
Marshall	42	31	11
Martin	4	1	3
Mason	19	11	8
McCracken	54	49	5
Menifee	5	5	0
Mercer	12	9	3
Metcalfe	5	4	1
Monroe	6	5	1
Montgomery	18	16	2
Morgan	6	5	1
Muhlenberg	19	17	2
Nicholas	3	2	1
Owen	6	5	1
Owsley	4	3	1
Pike	36	23	13
Powell	5	3	2
Pulaski	47	39	8
Robertson	2	1	1
Rockcastle	8	6	2
Rowan	16	14	2
Simpson	18	12	6
Taylor	15	12	3
Todd	8	6	2
Trimble	1	1	0
Washington	14	8	6
Wayne	16	14	2
Webster	16	7	9
Whitley	19	14	5
LOUISIANA			
Metropolitan Counties			
Acadia	104	61	43
Ascension	354	285	69
Assumption	83	59	24
Bossier	414	330	84
Caddo	615	414	201
Calcasieu	869	591	278
Cameron	82	71	11
De Soto	146	101	45

Table 80. Full-Time Law Enforcement Employees, by Selected State Metropolitan and Nonmetropolitan Counties, 2019—Continued

(Number.)

State/county	Law enforcement employees	Officers	Civilians
East Baton Rouge	841	717	124
East Feliciana	53	53	0
Iberia	176	112	64
Iberville	134	77	57
Lafourche	336	228	108
Livingston	304	304	0
Ouachita	392	392	0
Plaquemines	257	257	0
Pointe Coupee	103	57	46
Rapides	474	379	95
St. Charles	411	233	178
St. Helena	47	29	18
St. James	103	59	44
St. John the Baptist	248	225	23
St. Martin	191	146	45
Union	46	28	18
Vermilion	123	100	23
West Baton Rouge	198	63	135
West Feliciana	67	67	0
Nonmetropolitan Counties			
Allen	103	28	75
Beauregard	88	68	20
Bienville	64	40	24
Catahoula	130	22	108
Claiborne	70	31	39
Concordia	293	26	267
East Carroll	46	17	29
Evangeline	46	18	28
Franklin	118	118	0
Jackson	265	41	224
La Salle	47	30	17
Lincoln	77	58	19
Madison	33	23	10
Natchitoches	168	90	78
Red River	70	42	28
Richland	145	115	30
Sabine	89	89	0
St. Landry	204	87	117
St. Mary	145	145	0
Tensas	30	19	11
Vernon	118	64	54
Washington	75	65	10
Webster	150	122	28
West Carroll	17	8	9
Winn	37	37	0
MAINE			
Metropolitan Counties			
Androscoggin	24	22	2
Cumberland	74	62	12
Penobscot	41	36	5
Sagadahoc	21	19	2
York	33	30	3
Nonmetropolitan Counties			
Aroostook	26	19	7
Franklin	20	19	1
Hancock	22	20	2
Kennebec	27	24	3
Knox	22	21	1
Lincoln	25	23	2
Oxford	26	24	2
Piscataquis	10	9	1
Somerset	27	23	4
Waldo	23	21	2
Washington	18	16	2
MARYLAND			
Metropolitan Counties			
Allegany	34	32	2
Anne Arundel	101	78	23
Anne Arundel County Police Department	1,000	773	227
Baltimore County	83	73	10
Baltimore County Police Department	2,102	1,869	233
Calvert	164	138	26
Carroll	273	122	151
Cecil	113	95	18
Charles	429	288	141
Frederick	257	186	71
Harford	389	302	87
Howard	73	54	19
Howard County Police Department	682	476	206

Table 80. Full-Time Law Enforcement Employees, by Selected State Metropolitan and Nonmetropolitan Counties, 2019—Continued

(Number.)

State/county	Law enforcement employees	Officers	Civilians
Montgomery	196	160	36
Montgomery County Police Department	1,970	1,406	564
Prince George's County Police Department	1,790	1,551	239
Queen Anne's	70	62	8
Somerset	29	25	4
St. Mary's	216	145	71
Washington	246	106	140
Wicomico	113	92	21
Worcester	60	52	8
Nonmetropolitan Counties			
Caroline	43	39	4
Dorchester	44	39	5
Garrett	54	39	15
Kent	29	24	5
Talbot	37	34	3
MICHIGAN			
Metropolitan Counties			
Bay	82	35	47
Berrien	153	70	83
Calhoun	179	85	94
Cass	69	32	37
Clinton	61	26	35
Eaton	118	63	55
Genesee	247	113	134
Ingham	156	79	77
Ionia	17	15	2
Jackson	131	52	79
Kalamazoo	211	129	82
Kent	548	207	341
Lapeer	80	49	31
Livingston	135	58	77
Macomb	545	272	273
Midland	70	30	40
Monroe	154	74	80
Montcalm	42	17	25
Muskegon	107	46	61
Oakland	1,089	912	177
Ottawa	239	140	99
Saginaw	116	61	55
Shiawassee	51	21	30
St. Clair	184	84	100
Washtenaw	302	125	177
Wayne	923	632	291
Nonmetropolitan Counties			
Alcona	29	11	18
Alger	18	9	9
Allegan	103	55	48
Alpena	28	13	15
Antrim	51	21	30
Arenac	26	14	12
Baraga	13	6	7
Barry	52	30	22
Benzie	33	15	18
Branch	35	14	21
Charlevoix	30	19	11
Cheboygan	38	22	16
Chippewa	34	16	18
Clare	32	26	6
Crawford	25	15	10
Delta	10	10	0
Dickinson	29	12	17
Emmet	49	27	22
Gladwin	42	16	26
Gogebic	24	16	8
Grand Traverse	124	69	55
Gratiot	42	26	16
Hillsdale	40	22	18
Houghton	28	19	9
Huron	36	20	16
Iosco	22	5	17
Iron	19	10	9
Isabella	48	19	29
Kalkaska	34	16	18
Keweenaw	6	6	0
Lake	36	15	21
Leelanau	21	20	1
Lenawee	106	42	64
Luce	6	5	1
Mackinac	28	12	16
Manistee	37	17	20

Table 80. Full-Time Law Enforcement Employees, by Selected State Metropolitan and Nonmetropolitan Counties, 2019—Continued

(Number.)

State/county	Law enforcement employees	Officers	Civilians
Marquette	64	24	40
Mason	40	20	20
Mecosta	49	20	29
Menominee	15	15	0
Missaukee	26	13	13
Montmorency	13	13	0
Newaygo	63	27	36
Oceana	35	21	14
Ogemaw	34	15	19
Ontonagon	10	6	4
Osceola	42	17	25
Oscoda	17	12	5
Otsego	28	10	18
Presque Isle	13	13	0
Roscommon	41	26	15
Sanilac	57	27	30
Schoolcraft	10	3	7
St. Joseph	60	26	34
Tuscola	44	20	24
Van Buren	110	65	45
Wexford	53	24	29
MINNESOTA			
Metropolitan Counties			
Anoka	272	133	139
Benton	70	25	45
Blue Earth	89	34	55
Carlton	54	25	29
Carver	145	71	74
Chisago	99	44	55
Clay	95	34	61
Dakota	197	83	114
Dodge	38	24	14
Fillmore	31	20	11
Hennepin	830	326	504
Houston	31	13	18
Isanti	62	23	39
Lake	30	17	13
Le Sueur	47	21	26
Mille Lacs	80	36	44
Nicollet	42	16	26
Olmsted	179	72	107
Polk	52	32	20
Ramsey	459	248	211
Scott	140	45	95
Sherburne	295	81	214
Stearns	207	71	136
St. Louis	255	108	147
Wabasha	49	18	31
Washington	249	116	133
Wright	264	146	118
Nonmetropolitan Counties			
Aitkin	50	18	32
Becker	61	22	39
Beltrami	81	28	53
Big Stone	7	5	2
Brown	37	12	25
Cass	74	42	32
Chippewa	20	10	10
Clearwater	20	10	10
Cook	20	12	8
Cottonwood	21	10	11
Crow Wing	124	41	83
Douglas	85	36	49
Faribault	30	14	16
Freeborn	79	26	53
Goodhue	108	41	67
Grant	15	11	4
Hubbard	48	19	29
Itasca	77	33	44
Jackson	27	14	13
Kanabec	53	21	32
Kandiyohi	109	34	75
Kittson	11	6	5
Koochiching	20	10	10
Lac qui Parle	12	7	5
Lake of the Woods	14	7	7
Lincoln	13	7	6
Lyon	53	18	35
Mahnomen	19	13	6
Marshall	24	16	8
Martin	34	14	20

Table 80. Full-Time Law Enforcement Employees, by Selected State Metropolitan and Nonmetropolitan Counties, 2019—Continued

(Number.)

State/county	Law enforcement employees	Officers	Civilians
McLeod	61	25	36
Meeker	49	20	29
Morrison	54	20	34
Mower	77	26	51
Murray	19	12	7
Nobles	36	14	22
Norman	12	7	5
Otter Tail	84	39	45
Pennington	35	10	25
Pine	82	32	50
Pipestone	25	14	11
Pope	14	8	6
Red Lake	11	9	2
Redwood	30	13	17
Renville	37	15	22
Rice	57	31	26
Rock	17	12	5
Roseau	17	9	8
Sibley	29	14	15
Steele	30	24	6
Stevens	15	7	8
Swift	16	9	7
Todd	35	17	18
Traverse	14	6	8
Wadena	22	11	11
Waseca	28	14	14
Watonwan	22	8	14
Wilkin	19	7	12
Winona	63	21	42
Yellow Medicine	26	11	15
MISSISSIPPI			
Metropolitan Counties			
DeSoto	274	134	140
Hancock	146	72	74
Harrison	302	118	184
Hinds	338	80	258
Lamar	53	46	7
Madison	85	81	4
Stone	26	22	4
Tunica	100	45	55
Nonmetropolitan Counties			
Choctaw	14	8	6
Claiborne	29	13	16
George	51	17	34
Greene	22	7	15
Kemper	13	11	2
Lauderdale	127	52	75
Lincoln	52	24	28
Lowndes	108	49	59
Marion	21	15	6
Panola	83	43	40
Pontotoc	40	23	17
Tishomingo	26	12	14
Warren	42	39	3
Washington	50	36	14
MISSOURI			
Metropolitan Counties			
Andrew	17	11	6
Bates	63	19	44
Bollinger	17	12	5
Boone	83	66	17
Buchanan	106	69	37
Caldwell	49	10	39
Callaway	33	30	3
Cape Girardeau	82	46	36
Cass	111	90	21
Christian	93	58	35
Clay	196	132	64
Clinton	22	13	9
Cole	79	49	30
Cooper	10	9	1
Dallas	29	15	14
DeKalb	16	10	6
Franklin	150	137	13
Greene	398	141	257
Howard	8	7	1
Jackson	135	96	39
Jasper	124	79	45
Jefferson	225	155	70
Lafayette	48	31	17

Table 80. Full-Time Law Enforcement Employees, by Selected State Metropolitan and Nonmetropolitan Counties, 2019—Continued

(Number.)

State/county	Law enforcement employees	Officers	Civilians
Lincoln	95	55	40
Osage	18	11	7
Platte	130	99	31
Polk	40	25	15
Ray	33	16	17
St. Charles	49	34	15
St. Charles County Police Department	180	143	37
St. Louis County Police Department	1,231	949	282
Warren	58	36	22
Webster	40	19	21
Nonmetropolitan Counties			
Adair	24	9	15
Atchison	10	5	5
Audrain	43	28	15
Barry	23	21	2
Benton	27	17	10
Butler	43	30	13
Camden	93	54	39
Carroll	9	8	1
Carter	14	8	6
Cedar	38	13	25
Clark	12	5	7
Crawford	41	25	16
Dade	14	9	5
Daviess	7	6	1
Dent	22	17	5
Douglas	13	7	6
Dunklin	24	14	10
Gasconade	16	15	1
Gentry	5	5	0
Grundy	16	6	10
Harrison	11	4	7
Henry	39	25	14
Hickory	13	9	4
Holt	12	6	6
Howell	39	27	12
Iron	16	10	6
Johnson	62	33	29
Knox	2	2	0
Laclede	34	23	11
Lawrence	37	29	8
Lewis	13	7	6
Linn	10	9	1
Livingston	10	10	0
Macon	21	11	10
Madison	10	9	1
Marion	38	16	22
McDonald	29	20	9
Mercer	9	3	6
Miller	24	23	1
Mississippi	27	7	20
Monroe	9	8	1
Montgomery	20	18	2
Morgan	69	37	32
New Madrid	18	16	2
Nodaway	18	15	3
Oregon	10	7	3
Ozark	18	10	8
Pemiscot	49	21	28
Perry	34	22	12
Pettis	28	22	6
Phelps	74	35	39
Pike	23	11	12
Pulaski	40	26	14
Putnam	4	4	0
Ralls	13	12	1
Randolph	40	23	17
Ripley	13	11	2
Saline	26	16	10
Schuyler	9	6	3
Scotland	7	3	4
Shannon	8	3	5
Shelby	8	5	3
St. Clair	66	19	47
Ste. Genevieve	74	47	27
St. Francois	75	61	14
Stoddard	33	16	17
Stone	60	50	10
Sullivan	3	3	0
Taney	59	42	17
Texas	12	12	0
Vernon	46	17	29

Table 80. Full-Time Law Enforcement Employees, by Selected State Metropolitan and Nonmetropolitan Counties, 2019—Continued

(Number.)

State/county	Law enforcement employees	Officers	Civilians
Washington	36	21	15
Wayne	26	9	17
Worth	4	3	1
Wright	14	9	5
MONTANA			
Metropolitan Counties			
Carbon	18	11	7
Cascade	140	39	101
Missoula	72	58	14
Stillwater	20	11	9
Yellowstone	182	56	126
Nonmetropolitan Counties			
Beaverhead	14	8	6
Big Horn	33	17	16
Blaine	13	7	6
Broadwater	25	10	15
Butte-Silver Bow	97	52	45
Carter	5	4	1
Chouteau	22	9	13
Custer	18	7	11
Daniels	6	3	3
Dawson	39	8	31
Deer Lodge	21	21	0
Fallon	5	4	1
Fergus	20	9	11
Flathead	109	56	53
Gallatin	136	55	81
Garfield	4	3	1
Glacier	25	12	13
Golden Valley	2	2	0
Granite	14	7	7
Hill	30	13	17
Jefferson	28	14	14
Judith Basin	6	5	1
Lake	45	23	22
Lewis and Clark	107	48	59
Liberty	6	6	0
Lincoln	40	20	20
Madison	12	11	1
McCone	4	4	0
Meagher	9	4	5
Mineral	12	6	6
Musselshell	7	7	0
Park	25	15	10
Petroleum	2	2	0
Phillips	10	6	4
Pondera	13	7	6
Powder River	8	4	4
Powell	10	5	5
Prairie	4	3	1
Ravalli	74	32	42
Richland	32	10	22
Roosevelt	42	15	27
Rosebud	24	11	13
Sanders	11	11	0
Sheridan	10	8	2
Sweet Grass	13	7	6
Teton	13	10	3
Toole	21	13	8
Treasure	2	2	0
Valley	19	9	10
Wheatland	11	5	6
Wibaux	3	3	0
NEBRASKA			
Metropolitan Counties			
Cass	41	26	15
Dakota	19	17	2
Dixon	14	8	6
Douglas	210	132	78
Hall	40	30	10
Howard	12	5	7
Lancaster	109	89	20
Merrick	16	9	7
Sarpy	220	115	105
Saunders	25	13	12
Seward	18	16	2
Washington	52	31	21
Nonmetropolitan Counties			
Adams	21	18	3

Table 80. Full-Time Law Enforcement Employees, by Selected State Metropolitan and Nonmetropolitan Counties, 2019—Continued

(Number.)

State/county	Law enforcement employees	Officers	Civilians
Antelope	19	5	14
Boone	14	5	9
Box Butte	7	6	1
Brown	8	5	3
Buffalo	47	29	18
Burt	10	5	5
Butler	21	11	10
Cedar	7	7	0
Chase	8	4	4
Cherry	5	4	1
Cheyenne	20	10	10
Clay	11	7	4
Colfax	18	10	8
Cuming	6	5	1
Custer	9	8	1
Dawes	17	7	10
Dawson	66	24	42
Deuel	7	6	1
Dodge	26	23	3
Dundy	8	4	4
Fillmore	14	7	7
Franklin	8	4	4
Frontier	9	5	4
Furnas	12	6	6
Gage	18	15	3
Garden	13	5	8
Garfield	2	2	0
Gosper	6	5	1
Grant	2	2	0
Greeley	3	2	1
Hamilton	22	9	13
Harlan	8	4	4
Hayes	1	1	0
Hitchcock	8	5	3
Holt	8	6	2
Hooker	1	1	0
Jefferson	27	17	10
Johnson	13	7	6
Kearney	11	6	5
Keith	17	9	8
Keya Paha	1	1	0
Kimball	9	4	5
Knox	14	4	10
Lincoln	68	24	44
Logan	1	1	0
Madison	62	33	29
Morrill	14	9	5
Nance	7	6	1
Nemaha	11	11	0
Nuckolls	8	3	5
Otoe	31	16	15
Pawnee	5	4	1
Perkins	7	5	2
Phelps	28	7	21
Platte	65	22	43
Red Willow	21	5	16
Richardson	28	9	19
Rock	7	3	4
Saline	18	18	0
Scotts Bluff	24	17	7
Sheridan	17	7	10
Sherman	6	5	1
Stanton	9	8	1
Thayer	14	8	6
Thurston	14	7	7
Valley	9	4	5
Wayne	6	6	0
Webster	10	6	4
Wheeler	2	2	0
York	23	12	11
NEVADA			
Metropolitan Counties			
Carson City	144	100	44
Storey	29	27	2
Nonmetropolitan Counties			
Churchill	46	38	8
Douglas	124	108	16
Elko	75	62	13
Esmeralda	12	8	4
Humboldt	56	35	21
Lander	31	16	15

Table 80. Full-Time Law Enforcement Employees, by Selected State Metropolitan and Nonmetropolitan Counties, 2019—Continued

(Number.)

State/county	Law enforcement employees	Officers	Civilians
Lyon	117	82	35
Mineral	24	18	6
Nye	147	110	37
Pershing	20	13	7
NEW HAMPSHIRE			
Metropolitan Counties			
Rockingham	46	25	21
Strafford	40	28	12
Nonmetropolitan Counties			
Carroll	27	13	14
Cheshire	22	9	13
Grafton	25	10	15
Merrimack	29	16	13
NEW JERSEY			
Metropolitan Counties			
Atlantic	131	106	25
Bergen	581	496	85
Burlington	88	71	17
Camden	201	171	30
Cape May	163	136	27
Cumberland	63	63	0
Essex	439	367	72
Gloucester	105	95	10
Hudson	409	279	130
Hunterdon	43	38	5
Mercer	191	147	44
Middlesex	233	189	44
Monmouth	612	435	177
Morris	121	91	30
Ocean	278	157	121
Passaic	677	540	137
Salem	224	190	34
Somerset	210	177	33
Sussex	141	119	22
Union	260	213	47
Warren	24	20	4
NEW MEXICO			
Nonmetropolitan Counties			
Colfax	14	12	2
Lincoln	37	25	12
McKinley	43	34	9
San Miguel	11	8	3
Sierra	16	14	2
NEW YORK			
Metropolitan Counties			
Albany	209	146	63
Broome	59	50	9
Chemung	48	43	5
Dutchess	127	105	22
Herkimer	16	6	10
Jefferson	58	44	14
Livingston	75	49	26
Madison	52	40	12
Monroe	330	277	53
Nassau	3,278	2,357	921
Niagara	162	109	53
Oneida	141	102	39
Onondaga	255	212	43
Ontario	128	71	57
Orleans	41	27	14
Putnam	108	87	21
Rensselaer	43	37	6
Schoharie	35	20	15
Suffolk	395	271	124
Suffolk County Police Department	3,052	2,518	534
Tompkins	44	40	4
Ulster	83	60	23
Washington	45	40	5
Wayne	80	72	8
Westchester Public Safety	361	293	68
Yates	30	26	4
Nonmetropolitan Counties			
Cattaraugus	76	50	26
Cayuga	36	29	7
Chautauqua	114	71	43
Chenango	22	22	0
Clinton	39	26	13

Table 80. Full-Time Law Enforcement Employees, by Selected State Metropolitan and Nonmetropolitan Counties, 2019—Continued

(Number.)

State/county	Law enforcement employees	Officers	Civilians
Columbia	75	59	16
Cortland	36	33	3
Delaware	22	18	4
Essex	17	16	1
Franklin	7	5	2
Fulton	32	28	4
Greene	34	32	2
Hamilton	8	7	1
Montgomery	48	27	21
Otsego	22	20	2
Schuyler	21	18	3
Steuben	48	35	13
St. Lawrence	33	31	2
Sullivan	57	57	0
Wyoming	31	31	0
NORTH CAROLINA			
Metropolitan Counties			
Alamance	296	136	160
Alexander	81	41	40
Anson	61	33	28
Brunswick	302	179	123
Buncombe	385	234	151
Burke	125	93	32
Cabarrus	337	202	135
Caldwell	92	83	9
Camden	20	17	3
Catawba	203	144	59
Chatham	138	100	38
Craven	86	79	7
Cumberland	541	281	260
Currituck	98	62	36
Davidson	177	123	54
Davie	96	60	36
Durham	459	190	269
Edgecombe	127	53	74
Forsyth	561	220	341
Franklin	120	84	36
Gaston	216	116	100
Gaston County Police Department	226	128	98
Gates	15	14	1
Granville	114	57	57
Guilford	572	232	340
Harnett	254	155	99
Haywood	126	65	61
Henderson	231	155	76
Hoke	122	69	53
Iredell	258	182	76
Johnston	193	126	67
Jones	28	18	10
Lincoln	175	120	55
Madison	48	19	29
Mecklenburg[1]	1,083	282	801
Nash	132	84	48
New Hanover	547	377	170
Onslow	267	137	130
Orange	152	97	55
Pamlico	49	22	27
Pender	116	70	46
Person	88	51	37
Pitt	307	120	187
Randolph	244	184	60
Rockingham	144	96	48
Rowan	195	124	71
Stokes	78	52	26
Union	311	219	92
Wake	921	368	553
Wayne	135	128	7
Yadkin	76	40	36
Nonmetropolitan Counties			
Alleghany	41	24	17
Ashe	75	32	43
Avery	52	28	24
Beaufort	96	56	40
Bertie	43	26	17
Bladen	97	53	44
Carteret	100	67	33
Caswell	52	36	16
Cherokee	74	31	43
Chowan	28	18	10
Clay	37	17	20
Cleveland	182	98	84

Table 80. Full-Time Law Enforcement Employees, by Selected State Metropolitan and Nonmetropolitan Counties, 2019—Continued

(Number.)

State/county	Law enforcement employees	Officers	Civilians
Columbus	123	83	40
Dare	147	68	79
Duplin	91	62	29
Graham	35	18	17
Greene	30	22	8
Halifax	102	71	31
Hertford	56	24	32
Hyde	15	13	2
Jackson	79	55	24
Lee	84	40	44
Lenoir	106	61	45
Macon	79	57	22
Martin	42	38	4
McDowell	69	50	19
Mitchell	20	19	1
Montgomery	57	31	26
Moore	159	80	79
Northampton	55	31	24
Pasquotank	52	46	6
Perquimans	19	17	2
Polk	60	33	27
Richmond	88	57	31
Robeson	146	131	15
Rutherford	131	75	56
Sampson	134	93	41
Scotland	65	41	24
Stanly	96	53	43
Surry	134	83	51
Swain	48	28	20
Transylvania	84	58	26
Tyrrell	14	12	2
Vance	88	40	48
Warren	49	33	16
Washington	18	17	1
Watauga	82	49	33
Wilkes	136	76	60
Wilson	153	92	61
Yancey	43	23	20
NORTH DAKOTA			
Metropolitan Counties			
Burleigh	136	52	84
Cass	167	110	57
Grand Forks	40	34	6
Morton	44	36	8
Oliver	5	4	1
Nonmetropolitan Counties			
Adams	6	5	1
Barnes	9	8	1
Benson	4	4	0
Billings	6	6	0
Bottineau	21	11	10
Bowman	5	4	1
Burke	7	6	1
Cavalier	12	6	6
Dickey	5	4	1
Divide	7	6	1
Dunn	18	16	2
Eddy	6	5	1
Emmons	6	5	1
Foster	4	3	1
Golden Valley	4	3	1
Grant	5	5	0
Griggs	2	2	0
Hettinger	7	6	1
Kidder	4	3	1
Lamoure	5	4	1
Logan	3	3	0
McHenry	8	8	0
McIntosh	3	3	0
McKenzie	44	29	15
McLean	41	26	15
Mercer	30	16	14
Mountrail	22	9	13
Nelson	6	5	1
Pembina	20	12	8
Pierce	38	4	34
Ramsey	9	8	1
Ransom	7	5	2
Renville	7	6	1
Richland	38	18	20
Rolette	22	8	14

Table 80. Full-Time Law Enforcement Employees, by Selected State Metropolitan and Nonmetropolitan Counties, 2019—Continued

(Number.)

State/county	Law enforcement employees	Officers	Civilians
Sargent	5	4	1
Sheridan	3	3	0
Sioux	1	1	0
Slope	1	1	0
Stark	29	24	5
Steele	3	3	0
Stutsman	15	13	2
Towner	7	6	1
Traill	15	10	5
Walsh	15	10	5
Ward	106	45	61
Wells	5	4	1
Williams	83	38	45
OHIO			
Metropolitan Counties			
Allen	147	65	82
Brown	49	29	20
Carroll	44	27	17
Delaware	230	107	123
Fairfield	150	110	40
Fulton	23	21	2
Geauga	117	49	68
Greene	161	68	93
Licking	229	96	133
Madison	43	29	14
Miami	119	57	62
Morrow	60	33	27
Pickaway	83	39	44
Portage	153	82	71
Richland	134	52	82
Stark	262	128	134
Summit	399	326	73
Union	67	48	19
Warren	193	102	91
Wood	125	56	69
Nonmetropolitan Counties			
Ashland	87	49	38
Ashtabula	79	34	45
Athens	36	31	5
Champaign	30	26	4
Clinton	70	35	35
Fayette	41	23	18
Guernsey	59	28	31
Hancock	97	41	56
Knox	73	49	24
Marion	59	33	26
Mercer	67	30	37
Morgan	17	10	7
Noble	29	12	17
Washington	92	49	43
Wyandot	31	15	16
OKLAHOMA			
Metropolitan Counties			
Canadian	110	67	43
Cleveland	230	68	162
Comanche	41	30	11
Cotton	14	5	9
Creek	77	34	43
Garfield	32	24	8
Grady	34	22	12
Lincoln	35	19	16
Logan	68	38	30
McClain	40	26	14
Oklahoma	591	399	192
Okmulgee	17	15	2
Osage	75	37	38
Pawnee	25	11	14
Rogers	43	38	5
Sequoyah	46	23	23
Tulsa	582	221	361
Wagoner	77	37	40
Nonmetropolitan Counties			
Adair	27	6	21
Alfalfa	12	7	5
Atoka	17	8	9
Beaver	13	7	6
Beckham	41	14	27
Blaine	20	11	9
Bryan	18	15	3

Table 80. Full-Time Law Enforcement Employees, by Selected State Metropolitan and Nonmetropolitan Counties, 2019—Continued

(Number.)

State/county	Law enforcement employees	Officers	Civilians
Caddo	35	15	20
Carter	57	20	37
Cherokee	29	23	6
Choctaw	15	6	9
Cimarron	7	3	4
Coal	14	10	4
Craig	31	16	15
Custer	44	19	25
Delaware	46	19	27
Dewey	16	7	9
Ellis	18	8	10
Garvin	30	20	10
Grant	11	6	5
Greer	6	2	4
Harmon	4	3	1
Harper	7	4	3
Haskell	20	8	12
Hughes	27	13	14
Jackson	39	14	25
Jefferson	13	3	10
Johnston	25	7	18
Kay	26	18	8
Kingfisher	22	11	11
Kiowa	10	4	6
Latimer	16	8	8
Le Flore	21	17	4
Love	22	12	10
Major	19	8	11
Marshall	28	7	21
Mayes	55	27	28
McCurtain	26	22	4
McIntosh	13	12	1
Murray	13	6	7
Muskogee	82	27	55
Noble	21	9	12
Nowata	17	7	10
Okfuskee	20	7	13
Ottawa	26	9	17
Payne	95	40	55
Pittsburg	35	23	12
Pontotoc	18	16	2
Pottawatomie	30	25	5
Pushmataha	16	14	2
Roger Mills	13	8	5
Seminole	33	14	19
Stephens	26	22	4
Texas	30	13	17
Tillman	3	3	0
Washington	59	29	30
Washita	28	6	22
Woods	8	7	1
Woodward	35	12	23
OREGON			
Metropolitan Counties			
Benton	81	67	14
Clackamas	451	206	245
Columbia	57	44	13
Deschutes	253	186	67
Jackson	148	113	35
Josephine	85	63	22
Lane	289	61	228
Linn	179	79	100
Marion	318	94	224
Multnomah	775	131	644
Polk	36	27	9
Washington	595	262	333
Yamhill	85	42	43
Nonmetropolitan Counties			
Baker	43	31	12
Clatsop	75	26	49
Coos	89	60	29
Crook	32	13	19
Curry	38	16	22
Douglas	135	64	71
Gilliam	7	6	1
Grant	18	18	0
Harney	22	17	5
Hood River	47	20	27
Jefferson	43	17	26
Klamath	91	27	64
Lake	21	20	1

Table 80. Full-Time Law Enforcement Employees, by Selected State Metropolitan and Nonmetropolitan Counties, 2019—Continued

(Number.)

State/county	Law enforcement employees	Officers	Civilians
Lincoln	91	30	61
Malheur	63	40	23
Morrow	40	28	12
Sherman	7	6	1
Tillamook	53	45	8
Umatilla	87	25	62
Union	34	16	18
Wallowa	13	5	8
Wasco	31	16	15
Wheeler	5	4	1
PENNSYLVANIA			
Metropolitan Counties			
Adams	18	14	4
Allegheny	196	164	32
Allegheny County Police Department	237	220	17
Beaver	24	20	4
Berks	103	91	12
Blair	27	25	2
Bucks	80	65	15
Butler	31	28	3
Centre	29	25	4
Chester	90	72	18
Erie	48	41	7
Franklin	41	22	19
Lancaster	55	48	7
Lycoming	22	16	6
Mercer	18	14	4
Monroe	50	24	26
Montgomery	125	100	25
Pike	26	22	4
Washington	32	29	3
Westmoreland	63	56	7
Wyoming	6	4	2
York	115	105	10
Nonmetropolitan Counties			
Bedford	11	9	2
Bradford	12	10	2
Clarion	11	8	3
Elk	6	5	1
Greene	15	8	7
Indiana	23	20	3
Jefferson	8	7	1
Juniata	6	5	1
Lawrence	23	18	5
Northumberland	11	9	2
Schuylkill	19	16	3
Snyder	7	7	0
Tioga	10	8	2
Union	8	7	1
Wayne	15	12	3
SOUTH CAROLINA			
Metropolitan Counties			
Aiken	242	132	110
Anderson	313	169	144
Beaufort	309	213	96
Berkeley	184	151	33
Calhoun	40	25	15
Charleston	720	287	433
Chester	102	49	53
Darlington	72	59	13
Dorchester	273	147	126
Fairfield	55	51	4
Florence	254	215	39
Greenville	550	451	99
Horry	81	58	23
Horry County Police Department	287	266	21
Kershaw	77	66	11
Lancaster	140	119	21
Laurens	108	70	38
Lexington	439	292	147
Pickens	179	149	30
Richland	645	536	109
Saluda	62	24	38
Spartanburg	346	317	29
Sumter	201	107	94
York	209	174	35
Nonmetropolitan Counties			
Abbeville	656	333	323
Allendale	14	12	2

Table 80. Full-Time Law Enforcement Employees, by Selected State Metropolitan and Nonmetropolitan Counties, 2019—Continued

(Number.)

State/county	Law enforcement employees	Officers	Civilians
Bamberg	14	13	1
Barnwell	89	34	55
Cherokee	112	60	52
Chesterfield	61	52	9
Georgetown	146	76	70
Greenwood	144	68	76
Hampton	46	30	16
Marion	72	38	34
McCormick	39	18	21
Newberry	103	47	56
Oconee	183	105	78
Orangeburg	123	80	43
Union	49	31	18
Williamsburg	76	35	41
SOUTH DAKOTA			
Metropolitan Counties			
Lincoln	24	20	4
McCook	9	8	1
Meade	50	18	32
Minnehaha	233	95	138
Pennington	421	101	320
Turner	10	8	2
Union	28	18	10
Nonmetropolitan Counties			
Aurora	4	3	1
Beadle	26	5	21
Bennett	4	3	1
Bon Homme	3	3	0
Brookings	25	15	10
Brown	62	20	42
Buffalo	1	1	0
Butte	16	5	11
Campbell	2	2	0
Charles Mix	22	7	15
Clark	3	3	0
Clay	15	8	7
Codington	13	10	3
Corson	4	4	0
Custer	13	12	1
Davison	9	7	2
Day	9	4	5
Deuel	6	5	1
Dewey	3	3	0
Douglas	4	4	0
Edmunds	4	4	0
Fall River	19	7	12
Faulk	17	5	12
Grant	9	5	4
Gregory	5	4	1
Haakon	2	2	0
Hamlin	6	6	0
Hand	4	3	1
Hanson	3	3	0
Harding	3	2	1
Hughes	58	6	52
Hutchinson	3	3	0
Hyde	1	1	0
Jackson	3	2	1
Jerauld	4	4	0
Jones	2	2	0
Kingsbury	6	5	1
Lake	15	8	7
Lawrence	40	17	23
Lyman	5	4	1
Marshall	11	6	5
McPherson	4	4	0
Mellette	4	4	0
Miner	4	3	1
Moody	10	6	4
Oglala Lakota	1	1	0
Perkins	8	7	1
Potter	3	2	1
Roberts	35	6	29
Sanborn	3	3	0
Spink	14	9	5
Stanley	6	5	1
Sully	3	3	0
Tripp	3	2	1
Walworth	13	4	9
Yankton	35	12	23
Ziebach	3	3	0

Table 80. Full-Time Law Enforcement Employees, by Selected State Metropolitan and Nonmetropolitan Counties, 2019—Continued

(Number.)

State/county	Law enforcement employees	Officers	Civilians
TENNESSEE			
Metropolitan Counties			
Anderson	174	64	110
Blount	307	173	134
Bradley	220	110	110
Campbell	87	43	44
Cannon	34	12	22
Carter	134	72	62
Cheatham	90	48	42
Chester	49	16	33
Crockett	39	16	23
Dickson	139	63	76
Fayette	93	45	48
Gibson	81	31	50
Grainger	43	26	17
Hamblen	104	43	61
Hamilton	400	173	227
Hartsville/Trousdale	47	23	24
Hawkins	118	72	46
Jefferson	103	52	51
Knox	1,015	430	585
Loudon	106	57	49
Macon	60	32	28
Madison	282	122	160
Marion	72	34	38
Maury	162	82	80
Montgomery	392	138	254
Morgan	50	25	25
Polk	64	27	37
Roane	79	42	37
Robertson	166	72	94
Rutherford	474	239	235
Sequatchie	49	22	27
Shelby	1,850	638	1,212
Smith	57	28	29
Stewart	55	22	33
Sullivan	318	148	170
Sumner	290	116	174
Tipton	108	63	45
Unicoi	45	26	19
Union	60	35	25
Washington	206	95	111
Williamson	323	198	125
Wilson	266	134	132
Nonmetropolitan Counties			
Bedford	104	52	52
Benton	60	21	39
Bledsoe	41	14	27
Carroll	71	28	43
Claiborne	85	44	41
Clay	24	15	9
Cocke	81	40	41
Coffee	117	47	70
Cumberland	114	57	57
Decatur	31	13	18
DeKalb	51	27	24
Dyer	91	38	53
Fentress	50	21	29
Franklin	77	44	33
Giles	71	38	33
Greene	171	74	97
Grundy	40	18	22
Hancock	48	17	31
Hardeman	70	30	40
Hardin	53	25	28
Haywood	47	19	28
Henderson	68	34	34
Henry	69	35	34
Hickman	50	29	21
Houston	27	10	17
Humphreys	48	23	25
Jackson	48	18	30
Johnson	49	18	31
Lake	21	8	13
Lauderdale	59	20	39
Lawrence	90	49	41
Lewis	34	16	18
Lincoln	85	41	44
Marshall	52	27	25
McMinn	88	41	47
McNairy	38	19	19
Meigs	35	15	20

Table 80. Full-Time Law Enforcement Employees, by Selected State Metropolitan and Nonmetropolitan Counties, 2019—Continued

(Number.)

State/county	Law enforcement employees	Officers	Civilians
Monroe	83	46	37
Moore	31	17	14
Obion	69	34	35
Overton	57	24	33
Perry	29	16	13
Pickett	17	12	5
Putnam	166	81	85
Rhea	57	55	2
Scott	57	30	27
Sevier	212	104	108
Van Buren	23	7	16
Warren	112	56	56
Wayne	50	16	34
Weakley	43	22	21
White	85	39	46
TEXAS			
Metropolitan Counties			
Armstrong	7	3	4
Atascosa	113	44	69
Austin	55	42	13
Bandera	65	29	36
Bastrop	199	79	120
Bexar	1,731	578	1,153
Bowie	45	39	6
Brazoria	335	139	196
Brazos	261	103	158
Burleson	43	18	25
Caldwell	101	34	67
Callahan	15	6	9
Cameron	443	105	338
Clay	26	16	10
Collin	513	153	360
Comal	309	151	158
Crosby	15	6	9
Ector	142	91	51
Ellis	229	83	146
El Paso	991	261	730
Fort Bend	786	551	235
Grayson	182	63	119
Gregg	256	105	151
Guadalupe	223	104	119
Hardin	70	34	36
Harris	4,768	2,274	2,494
Harrison	108	45	63
Hays	359	155	204
Hidalgo	794	282	512
Hudspeth	42	14	28
Hunt	140	48	92
Jefferson	392	104	288
Johnson	125	86	39
Jones	35	9	26
Kaufman	191	77	114
Liberty	95	71	24
Lubbock	494	205	289
Lynn	21	7	14
McLennan	485	140	345
Medina	83	42	41
Montgomery	923	521	402
Nueces	294	47	247
Oldham	12	7	5
Orange	131	61	70
Parker	131	93	38
Potter	202	96	106
Randall	209	91	118
Robertson	35	15	20
Rockwall	124	50	74
Rusk	76	40	36
Smith	382	170	212
Sterling	5	5	0
Tarrant	1,412	372	1,040
Taylor	230	81	149
Tom Green	174	50	124
Travis	1,728	357	1,371
Victoria	205	110	95
Webb	319	148	171
Wichita	187	53	134
Williamson	566	219	347
Wilson	82	36	46
Nonmetropolitan Counties			
Anderson	70	36	34
Angelina	110	47	63

Table 80. Full-Time Law Enforcement Employees, by Selected State Metropolitan and Nonmetropolitan Counties, 2019—Continued

(Number.)

State/county	Law enforcement employees	Officers	Civilians
Aransas	69	23	46
Bailey	27	7	20
Baylor	9	4	5
Bee	69	24	45
Blanco	31	15	16
Borden	4	3	1
Bosque	43	19	24
Brewster	36	19	17
Briscoe	3	3	0
Brooks	37	17	20
Brown	70	32	38
Burnet	147	53	94
Calhoun	64	29	35
Camp	20	9	11
Cass	50	21	29
Castro	23	7	16
Cherokee	77	32	45
Cochran	18	9	9
Coke	6	5	1
Collingsworth	9	9	0
Colorado	53	23	30
Cooke	85	35	50
Cottle	1	1	0
Crane	16	9	7
Dallam	6	5	1
Dawson	21	9	12
Deaf Smith	40	13	27
Delta	22	10	12
DeWitt	52	19	33
Dickens	7	3	4
Dimmit	71	32	39
Donley	10	5	5
Duval	38	20	18
Eastland	30	12	18
Erath	66	24	42
Fannin	30	20	10
Fisher	13	4	9
Floyd	10	7	3
Foard	5	4	1
Franklin	27	27	0
Freestone	36	16	20
Frio	36	17	19
Gaines	39	18	21
Garza	43	9	34
Gillespie	54	34	20
Glasscock	5	4	1
Gonzales	57	21	36
Gray	43	14	29
Hale	64	64	0
Hall	10	4	6
Hansford	13	7	6
Hardeman	12	8	4
Hartley	7	6	1
Haskell	12	3	9
Hemphill	17	8	9
Henderson	164	80	84
Hill	75	34	41
Hockley	28	13	15
Hood	138	50	88
Hopkins	66	28	38
Houston	50	21	29
Howard	61	22	39
Hutchinson	35	14	21
Jack	31	15	16
Jackson	35	15	20
Jasper	24	20	4
Jeff Davis	5	4	1
Karnes	62	31	31
Kent	5	2	3
Kerr	111	48	63
King	2	2	0
Kinney	14	7	7
Lamb	28	10	18
La Salle	129	32	97
Lavaca	34	15	19
Lee	40	14	26
Leon	47	26	21
Limestone	76	20	56
Lipscomb	13	6	7
Madison	31	13	18
Marion	22	11	11
Matagorda	75	39	36
McMullen	13	11	2

Table 80. Full-Time Law Enforcement Employees, by Selected State Metropolitan and Nonmetropolitan Counties, 2019—Continued

(Number.)

State/county	Law enforcement employees	Officers	Civilians
Milam	68	24	44
Mitchell	18	5	13
Montague	32	13	19
Moore	52	20	32
Morris	24	10	14
Motley	2	2	0
Nacogdoches	83	39	44
Navarro	130	56	74
Nolan	43	16	27
Palo Pinto	57	24	33
Panola	61	35	26
Polk	106	47	59
Rains	35	15	20
Reagan	31	15	16
Real	11	5	6
Red River	31	13	18
Refugio	42	17	25
Roberts	6	5	1
Runnels	30	6	24
Sabine	20	10	10
San Augustine	20	10	10
San Jacinto	65	31	34
Schleicher	12	6	6
Scurry	41	7	34
Shelby	37	17	20
Sherman	13	5	8
Starr	109	45	64
Stonewall	9	3	6
Swisher	11	5	6
Terry	33	12	21
Throckmorton	6	2	4
Titus	59	24	35
Trinity	17	13	4
Uvalde	73	32	41
Val Verde	70	46	24
Van Zandt	82	40	42
Walker	72	35	37
Ward	31	14	17
Washington	64	33	31
Wharton	78	44	34
Wheeler	24	10	14
Wilbarger	18	7	11
Willacy	38	16	22
Winkler	25	25	0
Wood	72	32	40
Yoakum	22	10	12
Young	34	12	22
UTAH			
Metropolitan Counties			
Box Elder	79	23	56
Cache	138	45	93
Davis	291	181	110
Juab	29	17	12
Morgan	14	12	2
Salt Lake County Unified Police Department	483	376	107
Tooele	114	28	86
Utah	403	163	240
Washington	167	40	127
Nonmetropolitan Counties			
Beaver	70	22	48
Carbon	48	27	21
Daggett	5	4	1
Duchesne	64	27	37
Emery	40	31	9
Garfield	30	14	16
Iron	79	33	46
Kane	52	21	31
Millard	56	31	25
Piute	4	4	0
Rich	10	4	6
San Juan	32	12	20
Sanpete	64	27	37
Sevier	59	22	37
Summit	105	62	43
Uintah	89	27	62
Wasatch	68	35	33
Wayne	6	5	1
VERMONT			
Metropolitan Counties			
Chittenden	17	15	2

Table 80. Full-Time Law Enforcement Employees, by Selected State Metropolitan and Nonmetropolitan Counties, 2019—Continued

(Number.)

State/county	Law enforcement employees	Officers	Civilians
Franklin	17	16	1
Grand Isle	3	3	0
Nonmetropolitan Counties			
Addison	11	9	2
Bennington	16	13	3
Caledonia	7	6	1
Essex	4	4	0
Lamoille	24	13	11
Orange	8	6	2
Orleans	17	15	2
Rutland	20	15	5
Washington	10	6	4
Windham	19	12	7
Windsor	16	14	2
VIRGINIA			
Metropolitan Counties			
Albemarle County Police Department	184	146	38
Amelia	29	18	11
Amherst	46	40	6
Appomattox	24	22	2
Arlington County Police Department	445	344	101
Augusta	85	74	11
Bedford	93	85	8
Botetourt	124	97	27
Campbell	76	67	9
Charles City	20	13	7
Chesterfield County Police Department	623	515	108
Clarke	30	19	11
Craig	13	8	5
Culpeper	102	88	14
Dinwiddie	44	40	4
Fairfax County Police Department	1,728	1,464	264
Fauquier	171	131	40
Fluvanna	47	34	13
Franklin	105	81	24
Frederick	141	131	10
Giles	37	26	11
Gloucester	96	80	16
Goochland	55	39	16
Greene	39	25	14
Hanover	273	254	19
Henrico County Police Department	826	656	170
Isle of Wight	59	50	9
James City County Police Department	110	104	6
King and Queen	21	13	8
King William	35	21	14
Loudoun	681	558	123
Madison	29	23	6
Mathews	19	11	8
Montgomery	119	112	7
Nelson	28	23	5
New Kent	46	32	14
Powhatan	46	41	5
Prince George County Police Department	76	59	17
Prince William County Police Department	787	648	139
Pulaski	53	51	2
Rappahannock	21	16	5
Roanoke County Police Department	156	142	14
Rockingham	82	65	17
Scott	37	30	7
Southampton	67	53	14
Spotsylvania	253	200	53
Stafford	251	184	67
Sussex	45	42	3
Warren	75	59	16
Washington	93	74	19
York	82	74	8
Nonmetropolitan Counties			
Accomack	64	56	8
Alleghany	71	51	20
Bath	22	15	7
Bland	18	12	6
Brunswick	48	34	14
Buchanan	48	35	13
Buckingham	26	19	7
Caroline	72	50	22
Carroll	43	38	5
Charlotte	40	38	2
Cumberland	22	16	6
Dickenson	37	26	11

Table 80. Full-Time Law Enforcement Employees, by Selected State Metropolitan and Nonmetropolitan Counties, 2019—Continued

(Number.)

State/county	Law enforcement employees	Officers	Civilians
Essex	16	13	3
Floyd	37	27	10
Grayson	34	27	7
Greensville	36	23	13
Halifax	40	36	4
Henry	132	119	13
Highland	13	8	5
King George	54	38	16
Lancaster	41	32	9
Lee	34	34	0
Louisa	63	46	17
Lunenburg	19	13	6
Mecklenburg	52	50	2
Middlesex	27	19	8
Northampton	85	68	17
Northumberland	35	24	11
Nottoway	25	14	11
Orange	43	40	3
Page	71	55	16
Patrick	71	54	17
Pittsylvania	129	111	18
Prince Edward	33	33	0
Richmond	21	13	8
Rockbridge	41	37	4
Russell	52	36	16
Shenandoah	68	62	6
Smyth	51	44	7
Surry	15	14	1
Tazewell	74	50	24
Westmoreland	43	27	16
Wise	69	53	16
Wythe	44	35	9
WASHINGTON			
Metropolitan Counties			
Asotin	31	13	18
Benton	86	73	13
Chelan	74	58	16
Clark	230	141	89
Cowlitz	66	42	24
Douglas	37	31	6
Franklin	81	27	54
King	270	214	56
Kitsap	243	122	121
Pierce	355	290	65
Skagit	136	56	80
Skamania	36	33	3
Snohomish	370	297	73
Spokane	151	125	26
Stevens	60	28	32
Thurston	238	93	145
Walla Walla	35	28	7
Whatcom	191	89	102
Yakima	85	57	28
Nonmetropolitan Counties			
Adams	34	15	19
Clallam	45	37	8
Columbia	9	8	1
Ferry	23	7	16
Garfield	15	8	7
Grant	127	56	71
Grays Harbor	79	62	17
Island	72	39	33
Jefferson	42	22	20
Kittitas	80	33	47
Klickitat	40	21	19
Lewis	109	42	67
Lincoln	28	15	13
Mason	92	48	44
Okanogan	81	30	51
Pacific	43	15	28
Pend Oreille	36	15	21
San Juan	35	20	15
Wahkiakum	20	9	11
Whitman	35	17	18
WEST VIRGINIA			
Metropolitan Counties			
Berkeley	64	57	7
Boone	22	19	3
Brooke	17	17	0
Cabell	49	43	6

Table 80. Full-Time Law Enforcement Employees, by Selected State Metropolitan and Nonmetropolitan Counties, 2019—Continued

(Number.)

State/county	Law enforcement employees	Officers	Civilians
Clay	5	5	0
Fayette	41	34	7
Hampshire	23	18	5
Hancock	35	31	4
Jackson	24	16	8
Jefferson	36	30	6
Kanawha	133	104	29
Lincoln	7	6	1
Marshall	35	32	3
Mineral	19	16	3
Monongalia	45	41	4
Morgan	12	11	1
Ohio	38	36	2
Preston	24	21	3
Putnam	68	42	26
Raleigh	68	53	15
Wayne	25	22	3
Wirt	3	3	0
Wood	61	38	23
Nonmetropolitan Counties			
Barbour	15	7	8
Braxton	11	9	2
Calhoun	6	4	2
Doddridge	10	9	1
Gilmer	6	4	2
Grant	10	10	0
Greenbrier	38	27	11
Hardy	12	11	1
Harrison	57	53	4
Lewis	14	13	1
Logan	22	20	2
Marion	44	29	15
Mason	26	19	7
McDowell	15	13	2
Mercer	41	29	12
Mingo	18	16	2
Monroe	12	9	3
Nicholas	24	21	3
Pendleton	3	3	0
Pleasants	7	6	1
Pocahontas	9	6	3
Randolph	20	14	6
Ritchie	12	8	4
Roane	10	7	3
Summers	8	7	1
Taylor	12	6	6
Tucker	10	8	2
Tyler	13	11	2
Upshur	14	12	2
Webster	6	3	3
Wetzel	19	13	6
Wyoming	18	18	0
WISCONSIN			
Metropolitan Counties			
Brown	468	162	306
Calumet	55	28	27
Chippewa	74	44	30
Columbia	107	43	64
Dane	571	464	107
Douglas	73	31	42
Eau Claire	108	42	66
Fond du Lac	124	59	65
Green	55	41	14
Iowa	38	19	19
Kenosha	333	121	212
Kewaunee	36	31	5
La Crosse	108	40	68
Lincoln	61	29	32
Marathon	184	70	114
Milwaukee	805	330	475
Oconto	71	32	39
Outagamie	183	72	111
Ozaukee	103	78	25
Pierce	50	36	14
Racine	261	159	102
Rock	199	92	107
Sheboygan	189	71	118
St. Croix	84	77	7
Washington	168	76	92
Waukesha	327	166	161
Winnebago	199	140	59

Table 80. Full-Time Law Enforcement Employees, by Selected State Metropolitan and Nonmetropolitan Counties, 2019—Continued

(Number.)

State/county	Law enforcement employees	Officers	Civilians
Nonmetropolitan Counties			
Adams	58	28	30
Ashland	51	24	27
Barron	73	29	44
Bayfield	43	20	23
Buffalo	16	13	3
Burnett	36	18	18
Clark	60	28	32
Crawford	30	23	7
Dodge	157	59	98
Door	49	45	4
Dunn	68	38	30
Florence	21	12	9
Forest	43	22	21
Grant	59	30	29
Green Lake	44	19	25
Iron	23	11	12
Jackson	47	21	26
Jefferson	116	93	23
Juneau	98	42	56
Lafayette	30	28	2
Langlade	45	18	27
Manitowoc	99	62	37
Marinette	77	32	45
Marquette	21	20	1
Menominee	16	9	7
Monroe	56	27	29
Oneida	86	37	49
Pepin	19	8	11
Polk	75	29	46
Portage	107	51	56
Price	25	19	6
Richland	32	17	15
Rusk	31	28	3
Sauk	142	47	95
Sawyer	47	26	21
Shawano	109	38	71
Taylor	44	19	25
Trempealeau	57	27	30
Vernon	51	22	29
Vilas	76	39	37
Walworth	194	82	112
Washburn	35	17	18
Waupaca	111	94	17
Waushara	54	25	29
Wood	71	41	30
WYOMING			
Metropolitan Counties			
Laramie	174	51	123
Natrona	149	109	40
Nonmetropolitan Counties			
Albany	47	44	3
Big Horn	40	15	25
Campbell	151	56	95
Carbon	55	17	38
Converse	44	18	26
Crook	21	14	7
Fremont	93	65	28
Goshen	26	8	18
Hot Springs	13	5	8
Johnson	32	29	3
Lincoln	49	22	27
Niobrara	15	4	11
Park	55	45	10
Platte	37	24	13
Sheridan	58	20	38
Sublette	72	55	17
Sweetwater	86	37	49
Uinta	49	35	14
Washakie	8	7	1
Weston	7	7	0

1 The employee data presented in this table for Mecklenburg represent only Mecklenburg County Sheriff's Office employees and exclude Charlotte-Mecklenburg Police Department employees.

Table 81. Full-Time Law Enforcement Employees, by Selected State and Agency, 2019

(Number.)

State/agency	Law enforcement employees	Officers	Civilians
ALABAMA			
State Agencies			
Alabama Department of Mental Health	3	2	1
Alabama Law Enforcement Agency	1,428	836	592
State Fire Marshal	41	33	8
Tribal Agencies			
Poarch Creek Tribal	55	48	7
Other Agencies			
Huntsville International Airport	20	19	1
Mobile Regional Airport	20	17	3
Norfolk Southern Railway	6	6	0
Trussville Fire Department Fire and Explosion Investigation Unit	2	2	0
ALASKA			
Tribal Agencies			
Metlakatla Tribal	11	7	4
Other Agencies			
Fairbanks International Airport	29	22	7
Ted Stevens Anchorage International Airport	71	58	13
ARIZONA			
Tribal Agencies			
Ak-Chin Tribal	61	13	48
Cocopah Tribal	26	16	10
Colorado River Tribal	30	20	10
Fort McDowell Tribal	29	21	8
Fort Mojave Tribal	38	17	21
Gila River Indian Community	172	129	43
Hopi Resource Enforcement Agency	19	12	7
Hopi Tribal	33	12	21
Hualapai Tribal	17	16	1
Navajo Nation	328	219	109
Pascua Yaqui Tribal	84	29	55
Salt River Tribal	152	118	34
San Carlos Apache	46	27	19
Tonto Apache Tribal	6	6	0
Truxton Canon Agency	7	3	4
White Mountain Apache Tribal	42	23	19
Yavapai-Apache Nation	20	16	4
Yavapai-Prescott Tribal	14	11	3
ARKANSAS			
State Agencies			
Camp Robinson	26	11	15
State Capitol Police	23	21	2
Other Agencies			
Northwest Arkansas Regional Airport	12	8	4
CALIFORNIA			
State Agencies			
Atascadero State Hospital	178	166	12
California State Fair	2	2	0
Coalinga State Hospital	260	230	30
Department of Parks and Recreation, Capital	525	493	32
Fairview Developmental Center	9	7	2
Metropolitan State Hospital	129	121	8
Napa State Hospital	133	121	12
Patton State Hospital	118	101	17
Porterville Developmental Center	64	56	8
Tribal Agencies			
Blue Lake Tribal	2	2	0
Coyote Valley Tribal	5	4	1
Hoopa Valley Tribal	12	6	6
La Jolla Tribal	9	5	4
Los Coyotes Tribal	4	4	0
Sycuan Tribal	20	11	9
Table Mountain Rancheria	23	16	7
Tule River Tribal	29	8	21
Yurok Tribal	13	9	4
Other Agencies			
Baldwin Park Unified School District	11	8	3
Clovis Unified School District	17	16	1
East Bay Regional Park District	85	62	23
Fontana Unified School District	78	17	61
Kern High School District	34	29	5
Port of San Diego Harbor	165	132	33
San Bernardino Unified School District	88	25	63
San Francisco Bay Area Rapid Transit, Contra Costa County	326	216	110

Table 81. Full-Time Law Enforcement Employees, by Selected State and Agency, 2019—Continued

(Number.)

State/agency	Law enforcement employees	Officers	Civilians
Shasta County Marshal	25	19	6
Stockton Unified School District	49	36	13
Twin Rivers Unified School District	22	17	5
COLORADO			
State Agencies			
Colorado Bureau of Investigation	267	47	220
Colorado Mental Health Institute	123	24	99
Division of Gaming Criminal Enforcement and Investigations Section, Golden	46	14	32
Tribal Agencies			
Southern Ute Tribal	39	18	21
Ute Mountain Tribal	10	5	5
Other Agencies			
All Crimes Enforcement Team	4	4	0
Southwest Drug Task Force	7	6	1
CONNECTICUT			
State Agencies			
Department of Motor Vehicles	52	48	4
State Capitol Police	43	32	11
Tribal Agencies			
Mashantucket Pequot Tribal	38	28	10
Mohegan Tribal	37	29	8
Other Agencies			
Metropolitan Transportation Authority	41	41	0
DELAWARE			
State Agencies			
Alcohol and Tobacco Enforcement	18	16	2
Animal Welfare, New Castle County	30	20	10
Attorney General			
Kent County	81	10	71
New Castle County	295	28	267
Sussex County	55	1	54
Environmental Control	11	8	3
Fish and Wildlife	35	28	7
Park Rangers	23	22	1
River and Bay Authority	70	60	10
State Capitol Police	84	66	18
State Fire Marshal	48	18	30
Other Agencies			
Amtrak Police	56	29	27
Wilmington Fire Department	14	9	5
DISTRICT OF COLUMBIA			
Other Agencies			
District of Columbia Fire and Emergency Medical Services, Arson Investigation Unit	16	16	0
Metro Transit Police	479	403	76
FLORIDA			
State Agencies			
Capitol Police	81	58	23
Department of Corrections, Office of the Inspector General, Leon County	148	123	25
Department of Law Enforcement			
Duval County, Jacksonville	128	45	83
Escambia County, Pensacola	95	35	60
Hillsborough County, Tampa	177	60	117
Lee County, Fort Myers	90	38	52
Leon County, Tallahassee	956	110	846
Miami-Dade County, Miami	98	71	27
Orange County, Orlando	189	60	129
Division of Alcoholic Beverages and Tobacco, Leon County	173	101	72
Department of Investigative and Forensic Services, Leon County	289	223	66
Fish and Wildlife Conservation Commission			
Leon County	1,005	820	185
Marion County	341	257	84
Pasco County	1,208	630	578
Tribal Agencies			
Miccosukee Tribal	67	48	19
Seminole Tribal	211	137	74
Other Agencies			
Clay County School Board	48	47	1
Duval County Schools	152	88	64

Table 81. Full-Time Law Enforcement Employees, by Selected State and Agency, 2019—Continued

(Number.)

State/agency	Law enforcement employees	Officers	Civilians
Florida School for the Deaf and Blind	17	9	8
Fort Lauderdale Airport	109	88	21
Jackson County School District	15	15	0
Jacksonville Aviation Authority	52	37	15
Lee County Port Authority	62	41	21
Melbourne International Airport	18	16	2
Miami-Dade County Public Schools	461	363	98
Northwest Florida Beaches International Airport	19	13	6
Palm Beach County School District	348	259	89
Port Everglades	76	54	22
Sarasota County Schools	61	59	2
Sarasota-Manatee Airport Authority	12	12	0
Tampa International Airport	140	76	64
Volusia County Beach Safety	58	52	6
GEORGIA			
State Agencies			
Georgia Bureau of Investigation, Headquarters	800	284	516
Georgia Department of Transportation, Office of Investigations	4	4	0
Georgia Forestry Commission	7	6	1
Georgia Public Safety Training Center	182	62	120
Georgia World Congress	71	29	42
Ports Authority, Savannah	135	104	31
Other Agencies			
Atlanta Public Schools	84	81	3
Bibb County Board of Education	28	22	6
Cherokee County Board of Education	25	21	4
Dougherty County Board of Education	22	21	1
Fayette County Marshal	6	4	2
Forsyth County Fire Investigation Unit	3	3	0
Fulton County Marshal	69	54	15
Fulton County School System	80	78	2
Glynn County School System	27	26	1
Gwinnett County Public Schools	106	96	10
Hall County Marshal	13	13	0
Metropolitan Atlanta Rapid Transit Authority	337	279	58
Paulding County Marshal	10	9	1
Stone Mountain Park	23	20	3
IDAHO			
State Agencies			
Attorney General	31	28	3
Tribal Agencies			
Fort Hall Tribal	28	14	14
Kootenai Tribal	2	2	0
ILLINOIS			
State Agencies			
Secretary of State Police	262	132	130
Other Agencies			
Belt Railway	7	7	0
Capitol Airport Authority	5	5	0
Crystal Lake Park District	1	1	0
Decatur Park District	5	5	0
Fon du Lac Park District	2	2	0
Lake County Forest Preserve	21	19	2
McHenry County Conservation District	12	11	1
Pekin Park District	1	1	0
Springfield Park District	5	4	1
Terminal Railroad Association	6	6	0
Union Pacific Railroad, Cook County	12	12	0
Will County Forest Preserve	12	11	1
INDIANA			
Other Agencies			
Indianapolis International Airport	47	46	1
KANSAS			
State Agencies			
Kansas Alcoholic Beverage Control	37	18	19
Kansas Bureau of Investigation	331	87	244
Kansas Department of Wildlife and Parks	189	187	2
Kansas Lottery Security Division	7	5	2
Kansas Racing Commission, Security Division	71	48	23
Securities Office, Investigation Section	22	6	16
State Fire Marshal	13	12	1
Tribal Agencies			
Iowa Tribal	7	6	1
Kickapoo Tribal	4	4	0
Potawatomi Tribal	21	11	10
Sac and Fox Tribal	4	3	1

Table 81. Full-Time Law Enforcement Employees, by Selected State and Agency, 2019—Continued

(Number.)

State/agency	Law enforcement employees	Officers	Civilians
Other Agencies			
Blue Valley School District	12	11	1
El Dorado School District	2	2	0
Johnson County Park	27	25	2
Metropolitan Topeka Airport Authority	23	18	5
Topeka Fire Department Arson Investigation	4	4	0
Unified School District			
Auburn-Washburn	6	3	3
Bluestem	1	1	0
Goddard	5	5	0
Kansas City	31	28	3
Seaman	4	4	0
KENTUCKY			
State Agencies			
Alcohol Beverage Control			
Enforcement Division	34	32	2
Investigative Division	10	6	4
Department of Agriculture Animal Health			
Enforcement Division	4	4	0
Fish and Wildlife Enforcement	112	110	2
Kentucky Horse Park	6	6	0
Other Agencies			
Barren County Drug Task Force	2	1	1
Clark County School System	9	9	0
Fayette County Schools	59	55	4
FIVCO Area Drug Task Force	4	4	0
Greater Hardin County Narcotics Task Force	2	1	1
Jefferson County School District	25	18	7
Lake Cumberland Area Drug Enforcement Task			
Force	4	3	1
Lexington Bluegrass Airport	7	2	5
Louisville Fire Department Arson Division	11	10	1
Louisville Regional Airport Authority	39	35	4
McCracken County Public Schools	10	10	0
Northern Kentucky Drug Strike Force	15	14	1
South Central Kentucky Drug Task Force	8	7	1
Warren County Drug Task Force	3	2	1
LOUISIANA			
State Agencies			
Tensas Basin Levee District	3	2	1
Tribal Agencies			
Chitimacha Tribal	16	16	0
Tunica-Biloxi Tribal	13	12	1
MAINE			
State Agencies			
Bureau of Capitol Police	13	13	0
Drug Enforcement Agency	3	1	2
State Fire Marshal	35	14	21
Tribal Agencies			
Passamaquoddy Indian Township	8	5	3
Passamaquoddy Pleasant Point Tribal	7	7	0
Penobscot Nation	7	4	3
MARYLAND			
State Agencies			
Comptroller of the Treasury, Field Enforcement			
Division	58	23	35
Department of Public Safety and Correctional			
Services, Internal Investigation Division	88	48	40
General Services			
Annapolis, Anne Arundel County	57	28	29
Baltimore City	178	69	109
Natural Resources Police	302	250	52
Springfield Hospital	6	6	0
State Fire Marshal	70	44	26
Transit Administration	228	170	58
Transportation Authority	570	456	114
Other Agencies			
Maryland-National Capital Park Police			
Montgomery County	113	89	24
Prince George's County	149	125	24
MASSACHUSETTS			
State Agencies			
Massachusetts Bay Transportation Authority,			
Suffolk County	261	252	9
Tribal Agencies			
Wampanoag Tribe of Gay Head	1	1	0

Table 81. Full-Time Law Enforcement Employees, by Selected State and Agency, 2019—Continued

(Number.)

State/agency	Law enforcement employees	Officers	Civilians
Other Agencies			
Beth Israel Deaconess Medical Center	57	14	43
Massachusetts General Hospital	139	68	71
MICHIGAN			
State Agencies			
Department of Natural Resources Law Enforcement Division	272	246	26
Tribal Agencies			
Bay Mills Tribal	10	8	2
Grand Traverse Tribal	12	7	5
Gun Lake Tribal	18	17	1
Hannahville Tribal	11	10	1
Keweenaw Bay Tribal	13	9	4
Lac Vieux Desert Tribal	6	6	0
Little River Band of Ottawa Indians	14	14	0
Little Traverse Bay Bands of Odawa Indians	13	9	4
Nottawaseppi Huron Band of Potawatomi	20	19	1
Pokagon Tribal	51	50	1
Saginaw Chippewa Tribal	36	27	9
Sault Ste. Marie Tribal	25	22	3
Other Agencies			
Bishop International Airport	8	7	1
Capitol Region Airport Authority	16	9	7
Genessee County Parks and Recreation	10	10	0
Gerald R. Ford International Airport	18	17	1
Huron-Clinton Metropolitan Authority			
Hudson Mills Metropark	3	3	0
Kensington Metropark	8	8	0
Lower Huron Metropark	9	9	0
Stony Creek Metropark	11	11	0
Wayne County Airport	138	111	27
MINNESOTA			
State Agencies			
Bureau of Criminal Apprehension	418	75	343
Capitol Security, St. Paul	85	23	62
Department of Natural Resources Enforcement Division	216	188	28
Tribal Agencies			
Fond du Lac Tribal	21	18	3
Leech Lake Band of Ojibwe	47	29	18
Lower Sioux Tribal	9	8	1
Mille Lacs Tribal	28	22	6
Nett Lake Tribal	6	5	1
Red Lake Agency	43	32	11
Upper Sioux Community	4	4	0
White Earth Tribal	29	22	7
Other Agencies			
Metropolitan Transit Commission	154	137	17
Minneapolis-St. Paul International Airport	158	87	71
Three Rivers Park District	12	11	1
MISSISSIPPI			
State Agencies			
State Capitol Police	106	92	14
MISSOURI			
State Agencies			
Capitol Police	34	31	3
Department of Conservation	194	191	3
Department of Revenue, Compliance and Investigation Bureau	17	14	3
Department of Social Services, State Technical Assistance Team	22	15	7
Gaming Commission, Enforcement Division	114	111	3
State Fire Marshal	20	18	2
State Park Rangers	43	43	0
Other Agencies			
Clay County Drug Task Force	4	4	0
Clay County Park Authority	8	7	1
Dunklin R-5 School District	1	1	0
Jackson County Park Rangers	17	15	2
Kansas City International Airport	87	45	42
Lambert-St. Louis International Airport	67	59	8
Logan-Rogersville School District	2	2	0
Springfield-Branson Airport	15	10	5
Springfield-Greene County Park Rangers	5	5	0
Terminal Railroad	6	6	0

Table 81. Full-Time Law Enforcement Employees, by Selected State and Agency, 2019—Continued

(Number.)

State/agency	Law enforcement employees	Officers	Civilians
MONTANA			
State Agencies			
Blackfeet Agency	31	24	7
Crow Agency	17	13	4
Fort Belknap Tribal	14	9	5
Fort Peck Assiniboine and Sioux Tribes	19	16	3
Northern Cheyenne Agency	15	9	6
NEBRASKA			
Tribal Agencies			
Santee Tribal	5	5	0
Winnebago Tribal	7	3	4
NEVADA			
State Agencies			
Capitol Police	21	20	1
Department of Public Safety, Investigative Division	49	30	19
Department of Wildlife, Law Enforcement Division	49	34	15
State Fire Marshal	18	5	13
Tribal Agencies			
Duckwater Tribal	2	2	0
Eastern Nevada Agency	10	7	3
Ely Shoshone Tribal	2	2	0
Fallon Tribal	6	5	1
Las Vegas Paiute Tribal	10	10	0
Lovelock Paiute Tribal	1	1	0
Moapa Tribal	9	9	0
Pyramid Lake Tribal	12	10	2
Reno-Sparks Indian Colony	15	14	1
South Fork Band Tribal	1	1	0
Walker River Tribal	7	7	0
Washoe Tribal	17	14	3
Western Nevada Agency	3	3	0
Western Shoshone Tribal	3	3	0
Other Agencies			
Clark County School District	193	162	31
Las Vegas Fire and Rescue, Arson Bomb Unit	1	1	0
Reno Municipal Court Marshal	14	12	2
Reno Tahoe Airport Authority	25	24	1
Washoe County School District	46	38	8
NEW HAMPSHIRE			
State Agencies			
Liquor Commission	32	18	14
NEW JERSEY			
State Agencies			
Department of Corrections	7,094	5,124	1,970
Department of Human Services	76	72	4
Division of Fish and Wildlife	48	45	3
New Jersey Transit Police	322	260	62
Palisades Interstate Parkway	30	26	4
Port Authority of New York and New Jersey	2,316	2,158	158
State Park Police	92	90	2
Other Agencies			
Park Police			
Morris County	28	27	1
Union County	107	72	35
Prosecutor			
Atlantic County	167	72	95
Bergen County	256	102	154
Burlington County	126	42	84
Camden County	275	181	94
Cape May County	94	43	51
Cumberland County	109	40	69
Essex County	371	249	122
Gloucester County	108	36	72
Hudson County	259	101	158
Hunterdon County	50	24	26
Mercer County	185	64	121
Middlesex County	204	71	133
Monmouth County	281	76	205
Morris County	154	67	87
Ocean County	176	68	108
Passaic County	183	76	107
Salem County	57	21	36
Somerset County	123	52	71
Sussex County	56	36	20
Union County	180	77	103
Warren County	63	22	41

Table 81. Full-Time Law Enforcement Employees, by Selected State and Agency, 2019—Continued

(Number.)

State/agency	Law enforcement employees	Officers	Civilians
NEW MEXICO			
Tribal Agencies			
Acoma Tribal	25	11	14
Isleta Tribal	42	23	19
Jemez Pueblo	12	10	2
Jicarilla Apache Tribal	40	24	16
Laguna Tribal	36	25	11
Mescalero Tribal	19	9	10
Northern Pueblos Agency	11	10	1
Pojoaque Tribal	22	14	8
Ramah Navajo Tribal	17	9	8
Santa Ana Tribal	24	22	2
Santa Clara Pueblo	11	5	6
Southern Pueblos Agency	21	13	8
Taos Pueblo	10	9	1
Tesuque Pueblo	11	6	5
Zia Pueblo	9	8	1
Zuni Tribal	31	19	12
NEW YORK			
State Agencies			
State Park			
Allegany Region	15	12	3
Central Region	19	15	4
Finger Lakes Region	15	12	3
Genesee Region	16	14	2
Long Island Region	62	59	3
New York City Region	22	18	4
Niagara Region	31	30	1
Palisades Region	37	33	4
Taconic Region	13	13	0
Thousand Island Region	14	13	1
Tribal Agencies			
Oneida Indian Nation	40	34	6
St. Regis Tribal	33	27	6
Other Agencies			
New York City Department of Environmental Protection Police, Ashokan Precinct	243	210	33
New York City Metropolitan Transportation Authority	802	733	69
Onondaga County Parks	1	1	0
NORTH CAROLINA			
State Agencies			
Cherry Hospital	15	9	6
Department of Health and Human Resources	7	7	0
Department of Wildlife	220	209	11
Division of Alcohol Law Enforcement	99	91	8
Division of Marine Fisheries	60	51	9
North Carolina Arboretum	4	4	0
North Carolina State Bureau of Investigation	397	239	158
State Capitol Police	85	55	30
State Fairgrounds	7	2	5
State Park Rangers			
Carolina Beach	6	4	2
Carvers Creek	2	2	0
Chimney Rock	7	5	2
Cliffs of the Neuse	3	3	0
Crowders Mountain	12	7	5
Dismal Swamp	3	3	0
Elk Knob	3	3	0
Eno River	9	4	5
Falls Lake Recreation Area	14	12	2
Fort Fisher	5	4	1
Fort Macon	6	5	1
Goose Creek	4	3	1
Gorges	5	4	1
Grandfather Mountain	6	4	2
Hammocks Beach	10	5	5
Hanging Rock	5	5	0
Haw River	2	2	0
Jockey's Ridge	5	5	0
Jones Lake	5	4	1
Jordan Lake State Recreation Area	17	15	2
Kerr Lake	13	10	3
Lake James	4	4	0
Lake Norman	10	3	7
Lake Waccamaw	7	4	3
Lumber River	11	5	6
Mayo River	4	2	2
Merchants Millpond	3	3	0
Morrow Mountain	5	5	0
Mount Mitchell	3	3	0

Table 81. Full-Time Law Enforcement Employees, by Selected State and Agency, 2019—Continued

(Number.)

State/agency	Law enforcement employees	Officers	Civilians
New River-Mount Jefferson	8	8	0
Pettigrew	6	3	3
Pilot Mountain	5	5	0
Raven Rock	5	3	2
Singletary Lake	5	2	3
South Mountains	9	8	1
Stone Mountain	5	5	0
Weymouth Woods/Sandhills Nature Preserve	3	3	0
William B. Umstead	13	7	6
Tribal Agencies			
Cherokee Tribal	83	58	25
Other Agencies			
Asheville Regional Airport	11	9	2
Beaufort County Alcoholic Beverage Control Enforcement	1	1	0
Nash County Alcoholic Beverage Control Enforcement	1	1	0
Piedmont Triad International Airport	39	25	14
Raleigh-Durham International Airport	42	40	2
Triad Municipal Alcoholic Beverage Control Law Enforcement	6	5	1
University of North Carolina Hospitals	116	37	79
WakeMed Campus Police	85	49	36
Wilmington International Airport	5	1	4
NORTH DAKOTA			
Tribal Agencies			
Three Affiliated Tribes	43	34	9
OHIO			
State Agencies			
Ohio Department of Natural Resources	276	265	11
Other Agencies			
Cleveland Metropolitan Park District	94	79	15
Columbus and Franklin County Metropolitan Park District	123	50	73
Hamilton County Park District	34	32	2
Johnny Appleseed Metropolitan Park District	6	6	0
Muskingum Watershed Conservancy District	27	27	0
Preservation Parks of Delaware County	6	6	0
Sandusky County Park District	5	5	0
Wood County Park District	6	6	0
OKLAHOMA			
State Agencies			
Capitol Park Police	65	17	48
State Bureau of Investigation	279	79	200
State Park Rangers	53	53	0
Tribal Agencies			
Absentee Shawnee Tribal	12	11	1
Anadarko Agency	14	9	5
Cherokee Nation	43	35	8
Chickasaw Nation	63	53	10
Choctaw Nation	44	42	2
Citizen Potawatomi Nation	45	29	16
Comanche Nation	35	24	11
Concho Agency	7	7	0
Eastern Shawnee Tribal	17	16	1
Iowa Tribal	15	10	5
Kaw Tribal	7	7	0
Kickapoo Tribal	14	13	1
Miami Agency	5	5	0
Miami Tribal	13	13	0
Muscogee Nation Tribal	57	47	10
Osage Nation	15	14	1
Pawnee Tribal	6	5	1
Ponca Tribal	5	5	0
Quapaw Tribal	18	17	1
Sac and Fox Tribal	11	11	0
Seminole Nation Lighthorse	10	9	1
Tonkawa Tribal	7	5	2
Wyandotte Nation	6	5	1
Other Agencies			
Beggs Public Schools	1	1	0
District 1 Narcotics Task Force	6	6	0
Jenks Public Schools	9	8	1
Lawton Public Schools	15	14	1
Muskogee City Schools	7	5	2
Putnam City Campus	20	12	8
Victory Life	2	1	1

Table 81. Full-Time Law Enforcement Employees, by Selected State and Agency, 2019—Continued

(Number.)

State/agency	Law enforcement employees	Officers	Civilians
OREGON			
State Agencies			
Liquor Commission			
Benton County	3	3	0
Clackamas County	6	6	0
Clatsop County	1	1	0
Columbia County	2	2	0
Coos County	1	1	0
Crook County	2	2	0
Deschutes County	3	2	1
Douglas County	2	2	0
Gilliam County	1	1	0
Harney County	1	1	0
Hood River County	1	1	0
Jackson County	12	11	1
Josephine County	4	4	0
Klamath County	2	2	0
Lake County	1	1	0
Lane County	9	8	1
Lincoln County	1	1	0
Linn County	1	1	0
Marion County	3	2	1
Multnomah County	19	15	4
Polk County	2	2	0
Umatilla County	1	1	0
Wasco County	1	1	0
Washington County	4	4	0
Wheeler County	1	1	0
Yamhill County	1	1	0
Tribal Agencies			
Burns Paiute Tribal	4	3	1
Columbia River Inter-Tribal Fisheries Enforcement	22	14	8
Coos, Lower Umpqua, and Siuslaw Tribal	4	3	1
Coquille Tribal	4	4	0
Grand Ronde Tribal	9	7	2
Umatilla Tribal	27	19	8
Other Agencies			
Hillsboro School District	1	1	0
Port of Portland	72	54	18
PENNSYLVANIA			
State Agencies			
State Capitol Police	103	94	9
State Park Rangers			
Bald Eagle	4	4	0
Beltzville	2	2	0
Ben Rush	5	2	3
Bendigo	1	1	0
Black Moshannon	2	2	0
Blue Knob	2	2	0
Caledonia	1	1	0
Chapman	1	1	0
Codorus	12	4	8
Colonel Denning	5	1	4
Cook Forest	6	6	0
Cowans Gap	2	2	0
Evansburg	3	3	0
Fort Washington	2	2	0
Frances Slocum	2	2	0
French Creek	10	10	0
Gifford Pinchot	3	1	2
Greenwood Furnace	7	2	5
Jacobsburg Environmental Education Center	1	1	0
Jennings Environmental Education Center	6	6	0
Kettle Creek	1	1	0
Keystone	2	2	0
Kings Gap Environmental Education Center	1	1	0
Laurel Hill	5	5	0
Leonard Harrison	2	2	0
Little Buffalo	3	3	0
Little Pine	1	1	0
Lyman Run	2	2	0
Marsh Creek	10	10	0
Moraine	6	6	0
Mount Pisgah	3	1	2
Neshaminy	4	2	2
Nockamixon	1	1	0
Ole Bull	1	1	0
Parker Dam	9	2	7
Pine Grove Furnace	1	1	0
Point	2	2	0
Presque Isle	9	9	0
Pymatuning	8	3	5

Table 81. Full-Time Law Enforcement Employees, by Selected State and Agency, 2019—Continued

(Number.)

State/agency	Law enforcement employees	Officers	Civilians
Raccoon Creek	11	3	8
Raymond B. Winter	4	1	3
Reeds Gap	1	1	0
Ricketts Glen	4	4	0
Ridley Creek	9	4	5
Ryerson Station	4	1	3
Shawnee	1	1	0
Shikellamy	1	1	0
Sinnemahoning	7	1	6
Sizerville	1	1	0
Tuscarora	2	2	0
Tyler	4	2	2
White Clay	9	4	5
Worlds End	7	2	5
Yellow Creek	1	1	0
Other Agencies			
Allegheny County District Attorney, Criminal Investigation Division	36	29	7
Allegheny County Housing Authority	7	6	1
Allegheny County Port Authority	45	39	6
County Detective			
Adams County	2	2	0
Beaver County	7	7	0
Berks County	38	32	6
Bucks County	25	23	2
Butler County	4	4	0
Chester County	26	21	5
Cumberland County	7	5	2
Dauphin County	11	9	2
Erie County	11	9	2
Lackawanna County	13	13	0
Lancaster County	35	33	2
Lawrence County	9	8	1
Lebanon County	6	5	1
Lehigh County	35	33	2
Luzerne County	10	10	0
McKean County	8	2	6
Monroe County	8	7	1
Montgomery County	67	51	16
Pike County	4	4	0
Wayne County	3	3	0
Westmoreland County	60	15	45
Wyoming County	4	4	0
York County	13	11	2
Delaware County District Attorney, Criminal Investigation Division	51	37	14
Delaware County Park	56	55	1
Fort Indiantown Gap	23	16	7
Franklin County Drug Task Force	7	5	2
Lehigh Valley International Airport	10	10	0
Westmoreland County Park	34	33	1
Wyoming Area School District	2	2	0
RHODE ISLAND			
State Agencies			
Department of Environmental Management	39	29	10
Rhode Island State Airport	29	22	7
Tribal Agencies			
Narragansett Tribal	4	4	0
SOUTH CAROLINA			
State Agencies			
Bureau of Protective Services	63	59	4
Department of Mental Health	115	85	30
Department of Public Safety, Illegal Immigration Enforcement Unit	7	6	1
Forestry Commission			
Aiken County	1	1	0
Allendale County	2	1	1
Anderson County	2	1	1
Bamberg County	1	1	0
Berkeley County	1	1	0
Cherokee County	1	1	0
Chesterfield County	2	2	0
Colleton County	1	1	0
Darlington County	1	1	0
Fairfield County	1	1	0
Florence County	1	1	0
Horry County	1	1	0
Kershaw County	2	2	0
Laurens County	1	1	0
Lexington County	3	3	0
Marlboro County	1	1	0

Table 81. Full-Time Law Enforcement Employees, by Selected State and Agency, 2019—Continued

(Number.)

State/agency	Law enforcement employees	Officers	Civilians
Newberry County	1	1	0
Oconee County	1	1	0
Orangeburg County	3	3	0
Pickens County	1	1	0
Richland County	3	3	0
Spartanburg County	1	1	0
Sumter County	2	2	0
Williamsburg County	2	2	0
Hampton County	4	4	0
Horry County	6	6	0
Jasper County	4	4	0
Kershaw County	3	3	0
Lancaster County	2	2	0
Laurens County	4	4	0
Lee County	3	3	0
Lexington County	5	5	0
Marion County	3	3	0
Marlboro County	3	3	0
McCormick County	3	3	0
Newberry County	3	3	0
Oconee County	4	4	0
Orangeburg County	3	3	0
Pickens County	8	8	0
Richland County	49	49	0
Saluda County	4	4	0
Spartanburg County	4	4	0
Sumter County	3	3	0
Union County	3	3	0
Williamsburg County	6	6	0
York County	2	2	0
Santee Cooper	10	9	1
South Carolina School for the Deaf and Blind	1	1	0
State Ports Authority	75	36	39
State Transport Police			
Abbeville County	1	1	0
Allendale County	1	1	0
Anderson County	1	1	0
Barnwell County	1	1	0
Beaufort County	3	3	0
Charleston County	1	1	0
Cherokee County	1	1	0
Chester County	1	1	0
Chesterfield County	2	2	0
Colleton County	3	3	0
Darlington County	1	1	0
Dillon County	1	1	0
Dorchester County	5	4	1
Edgefield County	1	1	0
Florence County	4	3	1
Greenville County	3	3	0
Greenwood County	7	7	0
Hampton County	2	2	0
Horry County	1	1	0
Kershaw County	3	2	1
Lancaster County	1	1	0
Lexington County	13	8	5
Marion County	3	3	0
Newberry County	2	2	0
Oconee County	3	3	0
Orangeburg County	2	1	1
Richland County	26	10	16
Saluda County	3	3	0
Spartanburg County	5	5	0
Sumter County	2	2	0
Williamsburg County	1	1	0
York County	5	5	0
United States Department of Energy Savannah River Plant	54	42	12
Other Agencies			
15th Circuit Drug Enforcement Unit	4	3	1
Charleston County Aviation Authority	49	33	16
Columbia Metropolitan Airport	18	18	0
Greenville Hospital			
Greenville	32	32	0
Laurens	8	8	0
Oconee	4	4	0
Greenville-Spartanburg International Airport	18	17	1
Lexington County Medical Center	52	25	27
SOUTH DAKOTA			
State Agencies			
Division of Criminal Investigation	178	53	125
Tribal Agencies			
Crow Creek Tribal	13	8	5

Table 81. Full-Time Law Enforcement Employees, by Selected State and Agency, 2019—Continued

(Number.)

State/agency	Law enforcement employees	Officers	Civilians
Flandreau Santee Sioux Tribal	3	3	0
Lower Brule Tribal	13	8	5
Rosebud Tribal	41	28	13
TENNESSEE			
State Agencies			
Alcoholic Beverage Commission	80	45	35
Department of Agriculture, Agricultural Crime Unit	6	6	0
Department of Correction, Internal Affairs	93	33	60
State Park Rangers			
Bicentennial Capitol Mall	6	6	0
Big Hill Pond	2	2	0
Big Ridge	4	4	0
Bledsoe Creek	2	2	0
Booker T. Washington	4	4	0
Burgess Falls Natural Area	5	5	0
Cedars of Lebanon	5	5	0
Chickasaw	4	4	0
Cordell Hull Birthplace	2	2	0
Cove Lake	4	4	0
Cumberland Mountain	4	4	0
Cumberland Trail	9	9	0
Cummins Falls	4	4	0
David Crockett	4	4	0
Davy Crockett Birthplace	3	3	0
Dunbar Cave Natural Area	2	2	0
Edgar Evins	4	4	0
Fall Creek Falls	10	10	0
Fort Loudon State Historic Park	4	4	0
Fort Pillow State Historic Park	2	2	0
Frozen Head Natural Area	5	5	0
Harpeth Scenic Rivers	4	4	0
Harrison Bay	4	4	0
Henry Horton	10	8	2
Hiwassee/Ocoee State Scenic Rivers	6	6	0
Indian Mountain	2	2	0
Johnsonville State Historic Park	3	3	0
Long Hunter	5	5	0
Meeman-Shelby Forest	5	5	0
Montgomery Bell	6	6	0
Mousetail Landing	2	2	0
Natchez Trace	5	5	0
Nathan Bedford Forrest	3	3	0
Norris Dam	4	4	0
Old Stone Fort State Archaeological Park	3	3	0
Panther Creek	3	3	0
Paris Landing	5	5	0
Pickett	5	5	0
Pickwick Landing	5	5	0
Pinson Mounds State Archaeological Park	2	2	0
Radnor Lake Natural Area	6	6	0
Red Clay State Historic Park	2	2	0
Reelfoot Lake	4	4	0
Roan Mountain	4	4	0
Rock Island	5	5	0
Rocky Fork	2	2	0
Seven Islands Birding Park	2	2	0
Sgt. Alvin C. York	2	2	0
South Cumberland Recreation Area	9	9	0
Standing Stone	3	3	0
Sycamore Shoals State Historic Park	2	2	0
Tim's Ford	5	5	0
T.O. Fuller	3	3	0
Warrior's Path	5	5	0
TennCare Office of Inspector General	46	19	27
Tennessee Bureau of Investigation	556	360	196
Tennessee Department of Revenue, Special Investigations Unit	43	32	11
Wildlife Resources Agency			
Region 1	45	40	5
Region 2	67	59	8
Region 3	47	44	3
Region 4	55	50	5
Other Agencies			
Chattanooga Housing Authority	5	4	1
Chattanooga Metropolitan Airport	12	10	2
Dickson Parks and Recreation	2	2	0
Drug Task Force			
1st Judicial District	2	1	1
3rd Judicial District	5	5	0
4th Judicial District	1	1	0
8th Judicial District	2	1	1
9th Judicial District	3	2	1
10th Judicial District	4	3	1

Table 81. Full-Time Law Enforcement Employees, by Selected State and Agency, 2019—Continued

(Number.)

State/agency	Law enforcement employees	Officers	Civilians
12th Judicial District	4	4	0
14th Judicial District	1	1	0
17th Judicial District	1	1	0
18th Judicial District	4	3	1
21st Judicial District	3	3	0
22nd Judicial District	1	1	0
23rd Judicial District	9	9	0
24th Judicial District	4	2	2
25th Judicial District	1	1	0
31st Judicial District	2	2	0
Knoxville Metropolitan Airport	46	26	20
Memphis-Shelby County Airport Authority	63	50	13
Metropolitan Nashville Park Police	19	18	1
Nashville International Airport	122	77	45
Tri-Cities Regional Airport	15	14	1
West Tennessee Violent Crime Task Force	6	5	1
TEXAS			
Tribal Agencies			
Ysleta del Sur Pueblo Tribal	15	14	1
Other Agencies			
Amarillo International Airport	13	13	0
Dallas-Fort Worth International Airport	207	191	16
Denton County Water District	16	14	2
Hospital District			
Dallas County	165	102	63
Tarrant County	64	44	20
Independent School District			
Alief	50	44	6
Alvin	44	35	9
Angleton	10	9	1
Aubrey	3	3	0
Bay City	10	9	1
Brownsville	156	57	99
Calhoun County	2	2	0
Conroe	110	83	27
Corpus Christi	64	42	22
Corsicana	15	11	4
East Central	17	15	2
Edinburg	115	86	29
Floresville	7	6	1
Galveston	15	11	4
Hallsville	5	5	0
Houston	244	194	50
Humble	63	45	18
Idalou	1	1	0
Judson	30	29	1
Katy	134	63	71
Klein	72	52	20
Lyford	5	5	0
Midland	15	12	3
Northside	118	98	20
Pasadena	39	31	8
Raymondville	7	6	1
Santa Fe	22	14	8
Santa Rosa	6	3	3
Sealy	4	4	0
Socorro	44	37	7
Taft	3	3	0
United	225	84	141
Port of Brownsville	22	13	9
Port of Houston Authority	50	39	11
UTAH			
State Agencies			
Parks and Recreation	58	57	1
Utah Tax Commission Motor Vehicle Division, Vehicle Investigation Section	34	21	13
Wildlife Resources	73	70	3
Tribal Agencies			
Goshute Tribal	1	1	0
Other Agencies			
Cache-Rich Drug Task Force	5	4	1
Granite School District	32	27	5
Unified Fire Authority Investigations Bureau	5	5	0
Utah County Attorney, Investigations Division	5	5	0
Utah Transit Authority	103	76	27
VERMONT			
State Agencies			
Attorney General	4	4	0
Capitol Police	4	4	0

Table 81. Full-Time Law Enforcement Employees, by Selected State and Agency, 2019—Continued

(Number.)

State/agency	Law enforcement employees	Officers	Civilians
Department of Liquor Control, Division of Enforcement and Licensing	16	14	2
Department of Motor Vehicles	42	29	13
Fish and Wildlife Department, Law Enforcement Division	42	40	2
Secretary of State, Investigations Unit	9	7	2
VIRGINIA			
State Agencies			
Alcoholic Beverage Control Commission	165	99	66
Department of Conservation and Recreation	282	102	180
Department of Game and Inland Fisheries, Enforcement Division	181	163	18
Department of Motor Vehicles	88	74	14
Virginia Marine Resources Commission Law Enforcement Division	80	71	9
Virginia State Capitol	91	77	14
Other Agencies			
Norfolk Airport Authority	44	36	8
Port Authority, Norfolk	56	40	16
Reagan National Airport	221	208	13
Richmond International Airport	39	30	9
WASHINGTON			
State Agencies			
State Gambling Commission, Enforcement Unit	105	59	46
State Insurance Commissioner, Special Investigations Unit	10	8	2
Tribal Agencies			
Chehalis Tribal	35	17	18
Colville Tribal	41	25	16
Jamestown S'Klallam Tribal	42	37	5
Kalispel Tribal	23	21	2
La Push Tribal	4	4	0
Lower Elwha Klallam Tribal	11	8	3
Lummi Tribal	24	21	3
Muckleshoot Tribal	17	15	2
Nisqually Tribal	21	18	3
Nooksack Tribal	8	8	0
Port Gamble S'Klallam Tribal	12	12	0
Puyallup Tribal	55	29	26
Quinault Indian Nation	16	8	8
Sauk-Suiattle Tribal	9	7	2
Shoalwater Bay Tribal	5	5	0
Skokomish Tribal	9	8	1
Snoqualmie Tribal	3	3	0
Spokane Agency	27	14	13
Squaxin Island Tribal	12	11	1
Stillaguamish Tribal	11	11	0
Suquamish Tribal	16	14	2
Swinomish Tribal	20	15	5
Tulalip Tribal	49	33	16
Upper Skagit Tribal	9	9	0
Yakama Nation	58	38	20
Other Agencies			
Port of Seattle	157	115	42
WEST VIRGINIA			
State Agencies			
Capitol Protective Services	47	30	17
Department of Natural Resources			
Barbour County	1	1	0
Berkeley County	1	1	0
Boone County	1	1	0
Braxton County	1	1	0
Brooke County	2	2	0
Cabell County	2	2	0
Calhoun County	2	2	0
Clay County	1	1	0
Doddridge County	2	2	0
Fayette County	2	2	0
Grant County	2	2	0
Greenbrier County	3	3	0
Hampshire County	8	7	1
Hancock County	1	1	0
Hardy County	2	2	0
Harrison County	1	1	0
Jackson County	3	3	0
Jefferson County	1	1	0
Kanawha County	22	16	6
Lewis County	2	2	0
Lincoln County	1	1	0

Table 81. Full-Time Law Enforcement Employees, by Selected State and Agency, 2019—Continued

(Number.)

State/agency	Law enforcement employees	Officers	Civilians
Logan County	1	1	0
Marion County	6	5	1
Marshall County	1	1	0
Mason County	2	2	0
McDowell County	1	1	0
Mercer County	2	2	0
Mineral County	1	1	0
Mingo County	2	2	0
Monongalia County	2	2	0
Monroe County	1	1	0
Morgan County	1	1	0
Nicholas County	3	3	0
Ohio County	1	1	0
Pendleton County	1	1	0
Pleasants County	1	1	0
Pocahontas County	1	1	0
Preston County	3	3	0
Putnam County	2	2	0
Raleigh County	6	5	1
Randolph County	2	2	0
Ritchie County	1	1	0
Roane County	1	1	0
Summers County	3	3	0
Taylor County	1	1	0
Tucker County	1	1	0
Tyler County	1	1	0
Upshur County	5	4	1
Wayne County	1	1	0
Webster County	2	2	0
Wetzel County	1	1	0
Wirt County	1	1	0
Wood County	6	5	1
Wyoming County	3	3	0
State Fire Marshall, Kanawha County	47	31	16
Other Agencies			
Central West Virginia Drug Task Force	2	1	1
Eastern Panhandle Drug and Violent Crime Task Force	22	19	3
Greenbrier County Drug and Violent Crime Task Force	4	3	1
Hancock/Brooke/Weirton Drug Task Force	6	6	0
Harrison County Drug and Violent Crime Task Force	7	7	0
Huntington Drug and Violent Crime Task Force	4	3	1
Kanawha County Parks and Recreation	3	3	0
Logan County Drug and Violent Crime Task Force	4	3	1
Metropolitan Drug Enforcement Network Team	3	3	0
Mon Metro Drug Task Force	9	8	1
Mountain Lakes Drug and Violent Crime Unit	8	7	1
Ohio Valley Drug and Violent Crime Task Force	4	4	0
Parkersburg Narcotics and Violent Crime Task Force	9	8	1
Potomac Highlands Drug and Violent Crime Task Force	2	2	0
Southern Regional Drug and Violent Crime Task Force	9	8	1
Three Rivers Drug and Violent Crime Task Force	2	2	0
WISCONSIN			
State Agencies			
Capitol Police	51	40	11
Department of Natural Resources	243	213	30
Tribal Agencies			
Bad River Tribal	5	4	1
Lac Courte Oreilles Tribal	14	11	3
Menominee Tribal	25	17	8
Oneida Tribal	28	20	8
Red Cliff Tribal	7	6	1
St. Croix Tribal	19	7	12
Stockbridge Munsee Tribal	5	5	0
WYOMING			
Tribal Agencies			
Wind River Agency	22	18	4
PUERTO RICO AND OTHER OUTLYING AREAS			
Puerto Rico	12,766	12,052	714

SECTION VI

HATE CRIMES

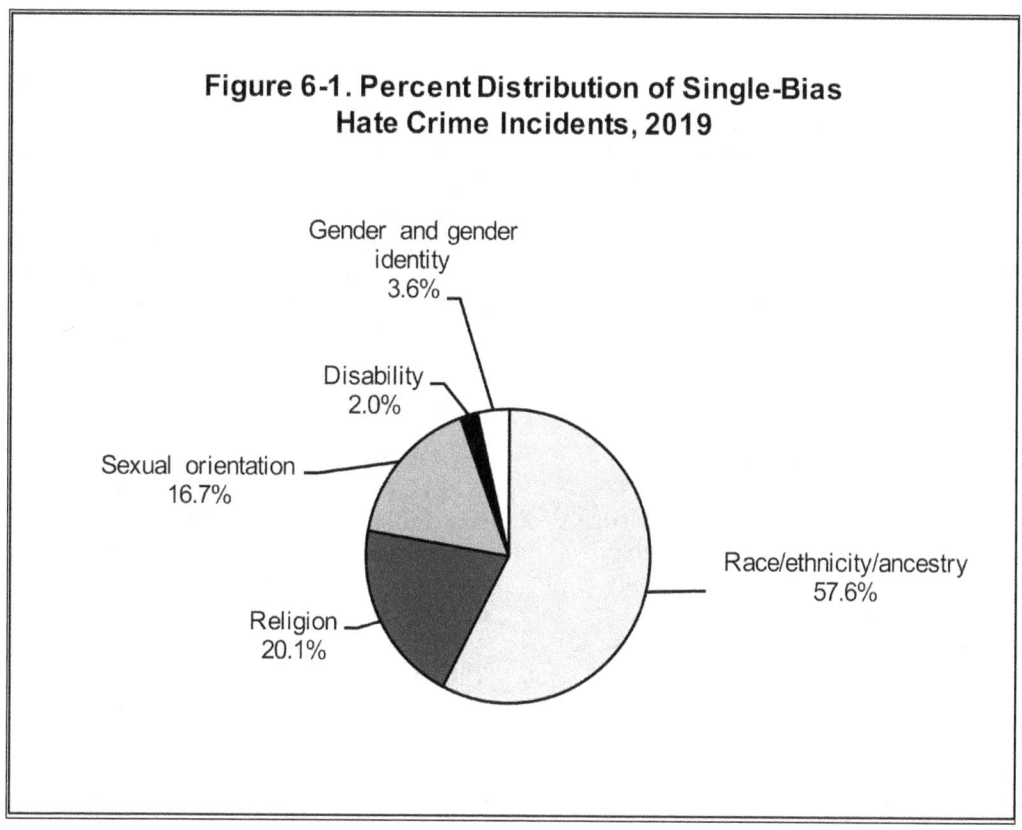

Figure 6-1. Percent Distribution of Single-Bias Hate Crime Incidents, 2019

Gender and gender identity
3.6%

Disability
2.0%

Sexual orientation
16.7%

Religion
20.1%

Race/ethnicity/ancestry
57.6%

The Federal Bureau of Investigation (FBI) began the procedures for implementing, collecting, and managing hate crime data after Congress passed the Hate Crime Statistics Act in 1990. This act required the collection of data "about crimes that manifest evidence of prejudice based on race, religion, sexual orientation, or ethnicity." Beginning in 2013, law enforcement agencies could submit hate crime data in accordance with a number of program modifications. In 1994, the Hate Crime Statistics Act was amended to include bias against persons with disabilities. The Church Arson Prevention Act, which was signed into law in July 1996, removed the sunset clause from the original statute and mandated that the collection of hate crime data become a permanent part of the UCR program. In 2009, Congress further amended the Hate Crime Statistics Act by passing the Matthew Shepard and James Byrd, Jr., Hate Crime Prevention Act. The amendment includes the collection of data for crimes motivated by bias against a particular gender and gender identity, as well as for crimes committed by, and crimes directed against, juveniles. In response to the Shepard/Byrd Act, the FBI modified its data collection so that reporting agencies could indicate whether hate crimes were committed by, or directed against, juveniles.

Definitions

Hate crimes include any crime motivated by bias against race, religion, sexual orientation, ethnicity/national origin, and/or disability. Because motivation is subjective, it is sometimes difficult to know with certainty whether a crime resulted from the offender's bias. Moreover, the presence of bias alone does not necessarily mean that a crime can be considered a hate crime. Only when law enforcement investigation reveals sufficient evidence to lead a reasonable and prudent person to conclude that the offender's actions were motivated, in whole or in part, by his or her bias should an incident be reported as a hate crime.

Data Collection

The UCR (Uniform Crime Reporting) program collects data about both single-bias and multiple-bias hate crimes. A single-bias incident is defined as an incident in which one or more offense types are motivated by the same bias. A multiple-bias incident is defined as an incident in which more than one offense type occurs and at least two offense types are motivated by different biases.

A table enumerating selected places in the United States that did not report hate crimes in 2019 is available at https://ucr.fbi.gov/hate-crime/2019/topic-pages/tables/participation.xls.

Important Note: Rape Data

In 2013, the UCR Program initiated the collection of rape data under a revised definition and removed the term "forcible" from the offense name. The UCR Program now defines rape as follows:

- **Rape (revised definition):** Penetration, no matter how slight, of the vagina or anus with any body part or object, or oral penetration by a sex organ of another person, without the consent of the victim. (This includes the offenses of rape, sodomy, and sexual assault with an object as converted from data submitted via the National Incident-Based Reporting System.)

- **Rape (legacy definition):** The carnal knowledge of a female forcibly and against her will. For tables within this publication that present data for 2018 only or provide a 2-year trend, the rape figures are an aggregate total of the data submitted based on both the legacy and revised UCR definitions. For 5- and 10-year trend tables, the rape figures for the previous year (2014 or 2009) are based on the legacy definition and the 2018 rape figures are an aggregate total based on both the legacy and revised definitions. For this reason, a percent change is not provided.

In 2016, the FBI Director approved the recommendation to discontinue the reporting of rape data using the UCR legacy definition beginning in 2017.

The offenses of fondling, incest, and statutory rape are included in the crimes against persons, *other* category.

CRIMES AGAINST PERSONS, PROPERTY, OR SOCIETY

The UCR program's data collection guidelines stipulate that a hate crime may involve multiple offenses, victims, and offenders within one incident; therefore, the Hate Crime Statistics program is incident-based. According to UCR counting guidelines:

- One offense is counted for each victim in *crimes against persons*

- One offense is counted for each offense type in *crimes against property*

- One offense is counted for each offense type in *crimes against society*

VICTIMS

In the UCR program, the victim of a hate crime may be an individual, a business, an institution, or society as a whole.

OFFENDERS

According to the UCR program, the term *known offender* does not imply that the suspect's identity is known; rather, the term indicates that some aspect of the suspect was identified, thus distinguishing the suspect from an unknown offender. Law enforcement agencies specify the number of offenders, and when possible, the race of the offender or offenders as a group.

RACE/ETHNICITY

The UCR program uses the following racial designations in its Hate Crime Statistics program: White; Black; American Indian or Alaskan Native; Asian; Native Hawaiian or Other Pacific Islander; and Multiple Races, Group. In addition, the UCR program uses the ethnic designations of Hispanic or Latino and Not Hispanic or Latino.

The law enforcement agencies that voluntarily participate in the Hate Crime Statistics program collect details about an offender's bias motivation associated with 11 offense types already being reported to the UCR program: murder and nonnegligent manslaughter, rape, aggravated assault, simple assault, and intimidation (crimes against persons); and robbery, burglary, larceny-theft, motor vehicle theft, arson, and destruction/damage/vandalism (crimes against property). The law enforcement agencies that participate in the UCR program via the National Incident-Based Reporting System (NIBRS) collect data about additional offenses for *crimes against persons* and *crimes against property*. These data appear in the category of other. These agencies also collect hate crime data for the category called *crimes against society*, which includes drug or narcotic offenses, gambling offenses, prostitution offenses, and weapon law violations.

NATIONAL VOLUME AND PERCENT DISTRIBUTION

In 2019, 2,172 law enforcement agencies (out of 15,588 participating agencies) reported 7,314 hate crime incidents involving 8,559 offenses. Of these, 7,103 were single-bias offenses. An analysis of the single-bias incidents revealed that 55.8 percent were racially/ethnically/ancestrally motivated, 21.4 percent were motivated by religious bias, 16.8 percent resulted from sexual orientation bias, 3.8 percent were motivated by gender and gender-identity bias, and 2.2 percent were prompted by a disability bias. (Table 82)

The majority of the 4,784 hate crime offenses that were racially motivated resulted from an anti-Black or African American bias (48.4 percent) followed by an anti-White basis (15.8 percent). Bias against people of more than one race accounted for 3.6 percent of offenses, while anti-Asian bias accounted for 4.3 percent of racially motivated offenses, anti-Arab bias accounted for 2.6 percent of these offenses, anti–Native Hawaiian and Other Pacific Islander accounted for 0.5 percent of these offenses, and anti–American Indian or Alaska Native bias accounted for 2.6 percent of these offenses. Approximately 14.1 percent of crimes were classified as an anti-Hispanic or Latino bias. (Table 82)

Hate crimes motivated by religious bias accounted for 1,650 offenses reported by law enforcement. A breakdown of these offenses revealed 60.3 percent were motivated by anti-Jewish bias, 13.3 percent by anti-Islamic (Muslim) bias, 2.5 percent were anti–multiple religions or groups, 4.0 percent had an anti-Catholic bias, 1.5 percent were anti-Protestant, 2.8 percent were anti–Eastern Orthodox (Russian, Greek, or other), 3.6 percent were anti–other Christian, 0.4 percent were anti-atheism/agnosticism/etc., 0.8 percent were anti-Mormon, 0.4 percent were anti-Hindu, 0.4 percent were anti–Jehovah's Witness, 0.3 percent were anti-Buddhist, 3.0 percent were anti-Sikh, and the remainder, 6.5 percent, of offenses were based on a bias against other religions—those not specified. (Table 82)

In 2019, 1,395 offenses were committed on the basis of sexual orientation bias. Of the offenses based on sexual orientation, 24.5 percent were classified as having an anti–lesbian, gay, bisexual, or transgender (mixed group)

bias; 62.2 percent were classified as having an anti-gay bias; 10.2 percent had an anti-lesbian basis; 1.9 percent had an anti-bisexual bias; and 1.2 percent had an anti-heterosexual bias. (Table 82)

Hate crime offenses committed based on disability totaled 169 offenses. The majority (68.6 percent) were classified as anti-mental disability, with the rest (32.49 percent) classified as anti–physical disability. (Table 82)

Of the 224 gender identity bias offenses reported, 173 (77.2 percent) were anti-transgender and 51 were anti–gender nonconforming. Of the 80 gender bias offenses reported, 62 were anti-female and 18 were anti-male. (Table 82)

CRIMES AGAINST PERSONS

Law enforcement agencies reported 5,512 hate crime offenses against persons in 2019. Approximately 40.0 percent involved intimidation, 36.7 percent involved simple assault, and 21.0 percent involved aggravated assault. There were 51 murders and 30 rapes. (Table 83)

CRIMES AGAINST PROPERTY

In 2019, hate crime offences against property totaled 2,811. Approximately 76.6 percent of offenses involved destruction/damage or vandalism. The remaining 23.4 percent of crimes against property consisted of robbery, burglary, larceny-theft, motor vehicle theft, arson, and other crimes. (Table 83)

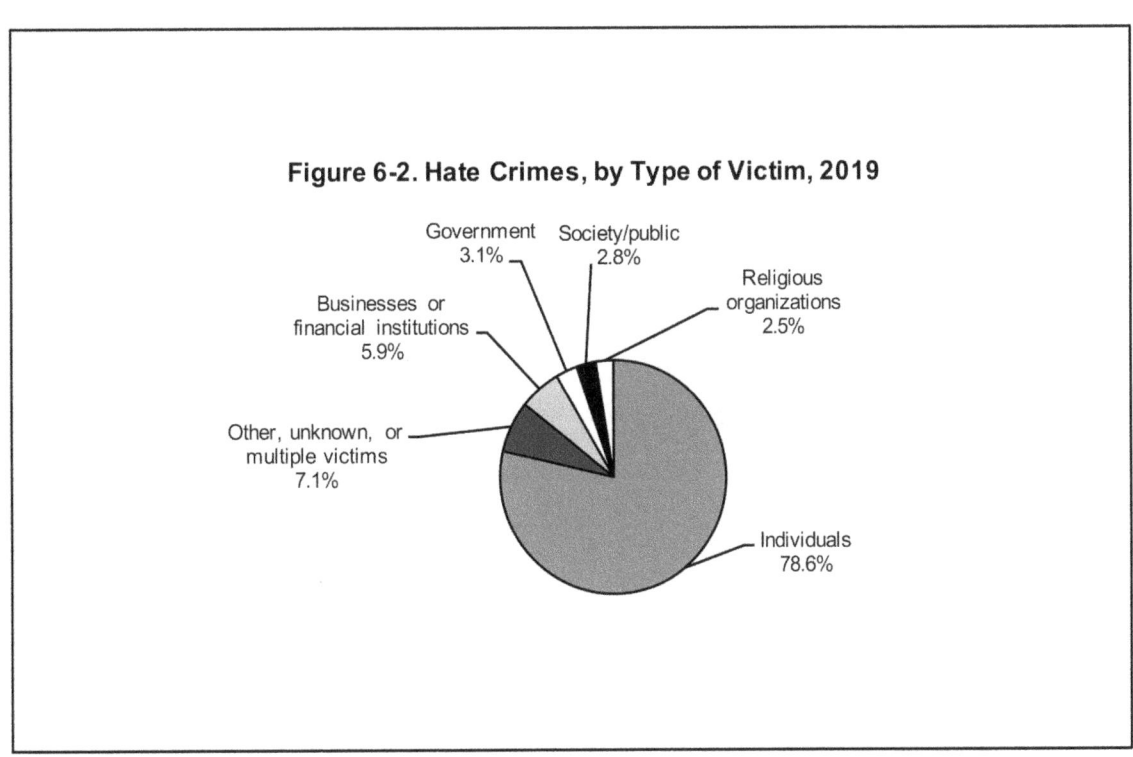

Figure 6-2. Hate Crimes, by Type of Victim, 2019

Table 82. Incidents, Offenses, Victims, and Known Offenders, by Bias Motivation, 2019

(Number.)

Bias motivation	Incidents	Offenses	Victims[1]	Known offenders[2]
Total	7,314	8,559	8,812	6,406
Single-Bias Incidents	7,103	8,302	8,552	6,268
Race/Ethnicity/Ancestry	3,963	4,784	4,930	3,550
Anti-White	666	755	775	645
Anti-Black or African American	1,930	2,314	2,391	1,682
Anti-American Indian or Alaska Native	119	126	135	101
Anti-Asian	158	205	215	153
Anti-Native Hawaiian or Other Pacific Islander	21	25	26	26
Anti-Multiple Races, Group	134	171	173	82
Anti-Arab	95	122	126	86
Anti-Hispanic or Latino	527	676	693	547
Anti-Other Race/Ethnicity/Ancestry	313	390	396	228
Religion	1,521	1,650	1,715	1,012
Anti-Jewish	953	995	1,032	602
Anti-Catholic	64	66	66	42
Anti-Protestant	24	24	24	19
Anti-Islamic (Muslim)	176	219	227	145
Anti-Other Religion	88	108	108	56
Anti-Multiple Religions, Group	37	42	44	26
Anti-Mormon	12	14	15	8
Anti-Jehovah's Witness	7	7	7	7
Anti-Eastern Orthodox (Russian, Greek, Other)	44	47	49	34
Anti-Other Christian	49	60	65	23
Anti-Buddhist	5	5	5	5
Anti-Hindu	7	7	7	4
Anti-Sikh	49	50	60	36
Anti-Atheism/Agnosticism/etc.	6	6	6	5
Sexual Orientation	1,195	1,395	1,429	1,250
Anti-Gay (Male)	746	867	883	828
Anti-Lesbian	115	142	143	107
Anti-Lesbian, Gay, Bisexual, or Transgender (Mixed Group)	291	342	357	279
Anti-Heterosexual	17	17	19	14
Anti-Bisexual	26	27	27	22
Disability	157	169	170	156
Anti-Physical	49	53	53	33
Anti-Mental	108	116	117	123
Gender	69	80	81	67
Anti-Male	17	18	18	17
Anti-Female	52	62	63	50
Gender Identity	198	224	227	233
Anti-Transgender	151	173	175	190
Anti-Gender Non-Conforming	47	51	52	43
Multiple-Bias Incidents[3]	211	257	260	138

1 The term victim may refer to an individual, business/financial institution, government entity, religious organization, or society/public as a whole.   2 The term known offender does not imply the suspect's identity is known; rather, the term indicates some aspect of the suspect was identified, thus distinguishing the suspect from an unknown offender.   3 A multiple-bias incident is an incident in which one or more offense types are motivated by two or more biases.

Table 83. Incidents, Offenses, Victims, and Known Offenders, by Offense Type, 2019

(Number.)

Offense type	Incidents[1]	Offenses	Victims[2]	Known offenders[3]
Total	7,314	8,559	8,812	6,406
Crimes Against Persons	4,526	5,512	5,512	4,857
Murder and nonnegligent manslaughter	18	51	51	19
Rape[4]	30	30	30	36
Aggravated assault	866	1,158	1,158	1,094
Simple assault	1,730	2,023	2,023	2,030
Intimidation	1,849	2,206	2,206	1,640
Human trafficking, commercial sex acts	2	3	3	3
Other[5]	31	41	41	35
Crimes Against Property	2,811	2,811	3,064	1,598
Robbery	125	125	149	227
Burglary	114	114	129	64
Larceny-theft	284	284	297	179
Motor vehicle theft	19	19	19	9
Arson	60	60	78	40
Destruction/damage/vandalism	2,152	2,152	2,316	1,045
Other[5]	57	57	76	34
Crimes Against Society[5]	236	236	236	279

1 The actual number of incidents is 7,314. However, the column figures will not add to the total because incidents may include more than one offense type, and these are counted in each appropriate offense type category.   2 The term victim may refer to an individual, business/financial institution, government entity, religious organization, or society/public as a whole.   3 The term known offender does not imply the suspect's identity is known; rather, the term indicates some aspect of the suspect was identified, thus distinguishing the suspect from an unknown offender. The actual number of known offenders is 6,406. However, the column figures will not add to the total because some offenders are responsible for more than one offense type, and are, therefore, counted more than once in this table.   4 Only the revised Uniform Crime Reporting definition of rape was used for the figures reported in this row.   5 The figures shown include additional offenses collected in the National Incident-Based Reporting System.

Table 84. Offenses, Known Offender's Race and Ethnicity, by Offense Type, 2019

(Number.)

Bias motivation	Total offenses	Known offender's race							Known offender's ethnicity[1]				Unknown offender
		White	Black or African American	American Indian or Alaska Native	Asian	Native Hawaiian or Other Pacific Islander	Group of multiple races	Unknown race	Hispanic or Latino	Not Hispanic or Latino	Group of multiple ethnicities	Unknown ethnicity	
Total	8,559	3,564	1,385	76	57	19	268	784	504	1,862	71	2,775	2,406
Crimes Against Persons	5,512	2,865	1,171	59	40	18	218	342	412	1,531	60	2,209	799
Murder and nonnegligent manslaughter	51	40	5	0	0	0	0	5	0	10	0	34	1
Rape[2]	30	12	13	0	0	0	1	1	2	7	1	15	3
Aggravated assault	1,158	631	295	15	5	7	55	65	135	372	13	418	85
Simple assault	2,023	1,023	505	27	15	7	109	146	171	543	32	831	191
Intimidation	2,206	1,132	343	17	20	4	52	122	99	587	14	887	516
Human trafficking, commercial sex acts	3	3	0	0	0	0	0	0	2	1	0	0	0
Other[3]	41	24	10	0	0	0	1	3	3	11	0	24	3
Crimes Against Property	2,811	532	173	10	13	1	48	441	80	246	8	444	1,593
Robbery	125	26	48	1	2	1	15	12	19	15	2	56	20
Burglary	114	31	6	1	1	0	2	5	5	14	0	24	68
Larceny-theft	284	83	36	2	0	0	4	12	8	27	0	92	147
Motor vehicle theft	19	6	1	0	0	0	0	0	2	2	0	3	12
Arson	60	20	4	0	0	0	1	6	1	17	0	7	29
Destruction/damage/ vandalism	2,152	345	74	6	9	0	26	404	42	166	6	242	1,288
Other[3]	57	21	4	0	1	0	0	2	3	5	0	20	29
Crimes Against Society[3]	236	167	41	7	4	0	2	1	12	85	3	122	14

1 The sum of offenses by the known offender's ethnicity does not equal the sum of offenses by the known offender's race because not all law enforcement agencies that report offender race data also report offender ethnicity data.   2 Only the revised Uniform Crime Reporting definition of rape was used for the figures reported in this row.   3 Includes additional offenses collected in the National Incident-Based Reporting System.

Table 85. Offenses, Offense Type, by Bias Motivation, 2019

(Number.)

Bias motivation	Total offenses	Crimes against persons						
		Murder and nonnegligent manslaughter	Rape[1]	Aggravated assault	Simple assault	Intimidation	Human trafficking, commercial sex acts	Other[2]
Total	8,559	51	30	1,158	2,023	2,206	3	41
Single-Bias Incidents	8,302	51	30	1,139	1,976	2,134	3	41
Race/Ethnicity/Ancestry	4,784	31	12	726	1,225	1,385	0	13
Anti-White	755	0	6	108	240	143	0	3
Anti-Black or African American	2,314	1	2	344	546	797	0	8
Anti-American Indian or Alaska Native	126	0	1	5	26	11	0	1
Anti-Asian	205	4	1	30	78	50	0	0
Anti-Native Hawaiian or Other Pacific Islander	25	0	0	4	4	1	0	0
Anti-Multiple Races, Group	171	3	0	17	27	57	0	0
Anti-Arab	122	0	0	20	36	37	0	0
Anti-Hispanic or Latino	676	1	1	141	195	213	0	0
Anti-Other Race/Ethnicity/Ancestry	390	22	1	57	73	76	0	1
Religion	1,650	12	3	89	159	320	0	9
Anti-Jewish	995	6	1	23	82	164	0	0
Anti-Catholic	66	1	2	1	1	8	0	1
Anti-Protestant	24	0	0	1	1	2	0	0
Anti-Islamic (Muslim)	219	1	0	42	41	92	0	0
Anti-Other Religion	108	1	0	9	8	20	0	6
Anti-Multiple Religions, Group	42	3	0	1	3	8	0	0
Anti-Mormon	14	0	0	3	0	2	0	0
Anti-Jehovah's Witness	7	0	0	2	2	1	0	0
Anti-Eastern Orthodox (Russian, Greek, Other)	47	0	0	2	8	2	0	2
Anti-Other Christian	60	0	0	1	3	20	0	0
Anti-Buddhist	5	0	0	0	1	0	0	0
Anti-Hindu	7	0	0	0	2	0	0	0
Anti-Sikh	50	0	0	4	7	1	0	0
Anti-Atheism/Agnosticism/etc.	6	0	0	0	0	0	0	0
Sexual Orientation	1,395	7	6	246	438	359	1	4
Anti-Gay (Male)	867	2	4	170	292	216	0	3
Anti-Lesbian	142	0	0	33	39	43	0	0
Anti-Lesbian, Gay, Bisexual, or Transgender (Mixed Group)	342	5	1	38	95	92	1	1
Anti-Heterosexual	17	0	0	1	3	3	0	0
Anti-Bisexual	27	0	1	4	9	5	0	0
Disability	169	0	1	20	47	15	2	7
Anti-Physical	53	0	0	4	10	3	2	3
Anti-Mental	116	0	1	16	37	12	0	4
Gender	80	0	3	7	27	18	0	4
Anti-Male	18	0	1	1	8	2	0	0
Anti-Female	62	0	2	6	19	16	0	4
Gender Identity	224	1	5	51	80	37	0	4
Anti-Transgender	173	1	3	48	64	32	0	2
Anti-Gender Non-Conforming	51	0	2	3	16	5	0	2
Multiple-Bias Incidents[3]	257	0	0	19	47	72	0	0

Table 85. Offenses, Offense Type, by Bias Motivation, 2019—Continued

(Number.)

Bias motivation	Crimes against property							Crimes against society[2]
	Robbery	Burglary	Larceny-theft	Motor vehicle theft	Arson	Destruction/ damage/ vandalism	Other[2]	
Total	125	114	284	19	60	2,152	57	236
Single-Bias Incidents	125	109	282	19	55	2,050	57	231
Race/Ethnicity/Ancestry	62	46	149	13	16	901	35	170
Anti-White	16	10	56	4	1	72	15	81
Anti-Black or African American	13	17	19	3	9	516	5	34
Anti-American Indian or Alaska Native	4	5	32	4	1	15	3	18
Anti-Asian	4	3	3	1	2	25	0	4
Anti-Native Hawaiian or Other Pacific Islander	0	0	4	0	0	1	2	9
Anti-Multiple Races, Group	1	0	6	0	0	53	4	3
Anti-Arab	1	1	3	0	0	21	0	3
Anti-Hispanic or Latino	16	4	12	0	1	81	4	7
Anti-Other Race/Ethnicity/Ancestry	7	6	14	1	2	117	2	11
Religion	8	38	57	3	34	877	7	34
Anti-Jewish	2	9	12	0	10	684	0	2
Anti-Catholic	0	5	4	1	5	37	0	0
Anti-Protestant	0	2	6	0	1	10	0	1
Anti-Islamic (Muslim)	2	3	1	0	4	31	2	0
Anti-Other Religion	0	6	7	0	9	38	1	3
Anti-Multiple Religions, Group	1	0	2	0	0	21	0	3
Anti-Mormon	1	0	0	0	0	8	0	0
Anti-Jehovah's Witness	0	0	0	0	0	2	0	0
Anti-Eastern Orthodox (Russian, Greek, Other)	0	5	9	1	0	7	1	10
Anti-Other Christian	0	3	0	0	3	27	1	2
Anti-Buddhist	0	0	2	0	0	2	0	0
Anti-Hindu	0	1	1	0	1	1	0	1
Anti-Sikh	2	4	11	0	1	8	2	10
Anti-Atheism/Agnosticism/etc.	0	0	2	1	0	1	0	2
Sexual Orientation	47	12	25	1	4	233	2	10
Anti-Gay (Male)	33	4	6	1	2	128	1	5
Anti-Lesbian	2	1	5	0	0	18	0	1
Anti-Lesbian, Gay, Bisexual, or Transgender (Mixed Group)	10	4	12	0	2	79	1	1
Anti-Heterosexual	1	2	1	0	0	4	0	2
Anti-Bisexual	1	1	1	0	0	4	0	1
Disability	4	5	37	2	0	12	7	10
Anti-Physical	4	1	14	2	0	5	3	2
Anti-Mental	0	4	23	0	0	7	4	8
Gender	1	3	1	0	1	12	0	3
Anti-Male	1	2	1	0	0	1	0	1
Anti-Female	0	1	0	0	1	11	0	2
Gender Identity	3	5	13	0	0	15	6	4
Anti-Transgender	3	3	5	0	0	9	2	1
Anti-Gender Non-Conforming	0	2	8	0	0	6	4	3
Multiple-Bias Incidents[3]	0	5	2	0	5	102	0	5

1 Only the revised Uniform Crime Reporting definition of rape was used for the figures reported in this column.   2 Includes additional offenses collected in the National Incident-Based Reporting System.   3 A multiple-bias incident is an incident in which one or more offense types are motivated by two or more biases.

Table 86. Offenses, Known Offender's Race, by Bias Motivation, 2019

(Number.)

Bias motivation	Total offenses	White	Black or African American	American Indian or Alaska Native	Asian	Native Hawaiian or Other Pacific Islander	Group of multiple races	Unknown race	Hispanic or Latino	Not Hispanic or Latino	Group of multiple ethnicities	Unknown ethnicity	Unknown offender
									Known offender's ethnicity[1]				
Total	8,496	3,511	1,605	64	95	19	285	718	412	1,847	51	3,065	2,199
Single-Bias Incidents	8,327	3,462	1,536	64	93	19	282	714	402	1,765	49	3,032	2,157
Race/Ethnicity/Ancestry	4,954	2,309	907	46	62	9	185	276	218	1,180	27	1,939	1,160
Anti-White	1,001	252	492	20	6	1	23	36	40	287	12	431	171
Anti-Black or African American	2,325	1,330	115	16	34	3	100	149	106	491	7	918	578
Anti-American Indian or Alaska Native	204	106	27	1	2	0	7	2	8	39	0	97	59
Anti-Asian	171	70	33	0	14	2	4	6	8	42	0	59	42
Anti-Native Hawaiian or Other Pacific Islander	26	8	11	0	0	2	0	0	0	13	0	7	5
Anti-Multiple Races, Group	166	45	8	0	2	0	15	11	2	22	3	42	85
Anti-Arab	100	62	17	0	1	0	1	4	3	29	0	40	15
Anti-Hispanic or Latino	644	322	152	8	2	1	24	47	41	212	1	240	88
Anti-Other Race/Ethnicity/Ancestry	317	114	52	1	1	0	11	21	10	45	4	105	117
Religion	1,550	439	122	6	16	6	30	306	28	193	10	360	625
Anti-Jewish	896	179	41	1	7	0	14	258	7	82	3	143	396
Anti-Catholic	59	26	3	1	1	0	0	5	3	10	0	16	23
Anti-Protestant	38	13	3	0	0	0	2	1	2	3	0	14	19
Anti-Islamic (Muslim)	225	98	32	0	5	0	6	22	7	31	4	88	62
Anti-Other Religion	96	31	12	0	1	5	2	8	2	11	0	33	37
Anti-Multiple Religions, Group	50	12	6	0	0	0	0	3	0	2	0	15	29
Anti-Mormon	9	4	0	0	0	1	0	0	0	1	0	2	4
Anti-Jehovah's Witness	9	3	0	1	0	0	0	0	1	2	0	1	5
Anti-Eastern Orthodox (Russian, Greek, Other)	32	19	4	1	0	0	0	1	1	12	0	12	7
Anti-Other Christian	42	11	5	0	1	0	5	5	2	8	0	8	15
Anti-Buddhist	10	4	3	0	1	0	0	0	0	7	0	1	2
Anti-Hindu	14	8	1	0	0	0	0	3	1	2	0	8	2
Anti-Sikh	64	30	10	2	0	0	1	0	2	21	3	17	21
Anti-Atheism/Agnosticism/etc.	6	1	2	0	0	0	0	0	0	1	0	2	3
Sexual Orientation	1,404	535	380	11	12	4	56	110	130	299	11	531	296
Anti-Gay (Male)	839	307	245	6	6	3	39	83	94	205	9	284	150
Anti-Lesbian	171	80	36	0	2	0	5	7	18	35	1	60	41
Anti-Lesbian, Gay, Bisexual, or Transgender (Mixed Group)	353	128	92	5	4	1	12	19	18	53	1	167	92
Anti-Heterosexual	20	14	1	0	0	0	0	0	0	2	0	12	5
Anti-Bisexual	21	6	6	0	0	0	0	1	0	4	0	8	8
Disability	177	92	37	1	3	0	3	4	8	37	1	92	37
Anti-Physical	67	30	15	0	2	0	1	1	4	9	1	33	18
Anti-Mental	110	62	22	1	1	0	2	3	4	28	0	59	19
Gender	58	30	14	0	0	0	1	0	1	9	0	32	13
Anti-Male	26	13	8	0	0	0	1	0	1	8	0	13	4
Anti-Female	32	17	6	0	0	0	0	0	0	1	0	19	9
Gender Identity	184	57	76	0	0	0	7	18	17	47	0	78	26
Anti-Transgender	157	50	65				7	16	17	36	0	72	19
Anti-Gender Non-Conforming	27	7	11	0	0	0	0	2	0	11	0	6	7
Multiple-Bias Incidents[2]	169	49	69	0	2	0	3	4	10	82	2	33	42

1 The aggregate of offenses by the known offender's ethnicity does not equal the aggregate of offenses by the known offender's race because not all law enforcement agencies that report offender race data also report offender ethnicity data. 2 A multiple-bias incident is an incident in which one or more offense types are motivated by two or more biases.

Table 87. Offenses, Victim Type, by Offense Type, 2019

(Number.)

Offense type	Total offenses	Victim type					
		Individual	Business/ financial institution	Government	Religious organization	Society/public[1]	Other/ unknown/ multiple
Total	8,559	6,731	501	265	216	236	610
Crimes against persons[2]	5,512	5,512	NA	NA	NA	NA	NA
Crimes against property	2,811	1,219	501	265	216	0	610
Robbery	125	109	3	0	0	0	13
Burglary	114	74	20	2	12	0	6
Larceny-theft	284	184	79	5	2	0	14
Motor vehicle theft	19	19	0	0	0	0	0
Arson	60	27	5	0	25	0	3
Destruction/damage/vandalism	2,512	760	385	258	177	0	572
Other[2]	57	46	9	0	0	0	2
Crimes against society[2]	236	NA	NA	NA	NA	289	NA

NA = Not available.
1 The victim type society/public is collected only in the National Incident-Based Reporting System (NIBRS).   2 Includes additional offenses collected in the NIBRS.

Table 88. Victims, Offense Type, by Bias Motivation, 2019

(Number.)

Bias motivation	Total victims[1]	Total number of adult victims[2]	Total number of juvenile victims[2]	Murder and nonnegligent manslaughter	Rape[3]	Aggravated assault	Simple assault	Intimidation	Human trafficking, commercial sex acts	Other[4]
Total	8,812	5,909	719	51	30	1,158	2,023	2,206	3	41
Single-Bias Incidents	8,552	5,770	693	51	30	1,139	1,976	2,134	3	41
Race/Ethnicity/Ancestry	4,930	3,625	435	31	12	726	1,225	1,385	0	13
Anti-White	775	566	41	0	6	108	240	143	0	3
Anti-Black or African American	2,391	1,747	256	1	2	344	546	797	0	8
Anti-American Indian or Alaska Native	135	85	6	0	1	5	26	11	0	1
Anti-Asian	215	172	10	4	1	30	78	50	0	0
Anti-Native Hawaiian or Other Pacific Islander	26	14	3	0	0	4	4	1	0	0
Anti-Multiple Races, Group	173	106	9	3	0	17	27	57	0	0
Anti-Arab	126	93	8	0	0	20	36	37	0	0
Anti-Hispanic or Latino	693	569	75	1	1	141	195	213	0	0
Anti-Other Race/Ethnicity/Ancestry	396	273	27	22	1	57	73	76	0	1
Religion	1,715	699	80	12	3	89	159	320	0	9
Anti-Jewish	1,032	328	33	6	1	23	82	164	0	0
Anti-Catholic	66	19	3	1	2	1	1	8	0	1
Anti-Protestant	24	13	0	0	0	1	1	2	0	0
Anti-Islamic (Muslim)	227	151	30	1	0	42	41	92	0	0
Anti-Other Religion	108	49	2	1	0	9	8	20	0	6
Anti-Multiple Religions, Group	44	16	1	3	0	1	3	8	0	0
Anti-Mormon	15	9	0	0	0	3	0	2	0	0
Anti-Jehovah's Witness	7	5	0	0	0	2	2	1	0	0
Anti-Eastern Orthodox (Russian, Greek, Other)	49	28	6	0	0	2	8	2	0	2
Anti-Other Christian	65	27	2	0	0	1	3	20	0	0
Anti-Buddhist	5	2	0	0	0	0	1	0	0	0
Anti-Hindu	7	4	0	0	0	0	2	0	0	0
Anti-Sikh	60	47	3	0	0	4	7	1	0	0
Anti-Atheism/Agnosticism/etc.	6	1	0	0	0	0	0	0	0	0
Sexual Orientation	1,429	1,106	121	7	6	246	438	359	1	4
Anti-Gay (Male)	883	699	66	2	4	170	292	216	0	3
Anti-Lesbian	143	110	18	0	0	33	39	43	0	0
Anti-Lesbian, Gay, Bisexual, or Transgender (Mixed Group)	357	266	27	5	1	38	95	92	1	1
Anti-Heterosexual	19	11	4	0	0	1	3	3	0	0
Anti-Bisexual	27	20	6	0	1	4	9	5	0	0
Disability	170	115	29	0	1	20	47	15	2	7
Anti-Physical	53	38	8	0	0	4	10	3	2	3
Anti-Mental	117	77	21	0	1	16	37	12	0	4
Gender	81	65	4	0	3	7	27	18	0	4
Anti-Male	18	17	0	0	1	1	8	2	0	0
Anti-Female	63	48	4	0	2	6	19	16	0	4
Gender Identity	227	160	24	1	5	51	80	37	0	4
Anti-Transgender	175	124	20	1	3	48	64	32	0	2
Anti-Gender Non-Conforming	52	36	4	0	2	3	16	5	0	2
Multiple-Bias Incidents[5]	260	139	26	0	0	19	47	72	0	0

Table 88. Victims, Offense Type, by Bias Motivation, 2019—Continued

(Number.)

Bias motivation	Crimes against property							Crimes against society[4]
	Robbery	Burglary	Larceny- theft	Motor vehicle theft	Arson	Destruction/ damage/ vandalism	Other[4]	
Total	149	129	297	19	78	2,316	76	236
Single-Bias Incidents	149	123	294	19	73	2,213	76	231
Race/Ethnicity/Ancestry	75	54	156	13	22	995	53	170
Anti-White	17	13	60	4	3	82	15	81
Anti-Black or African American	17	19	19	3	11	568	22	34
Anti-American Indian or Alaska Native	5	7	34	4	3	16	4	18
Anti-Asian	6	4	3	1	2	32	0	4
Anti-Native Hawaiian or Other Pacific Islander	0	0	4	0	0	2	2	9
Anti-Multiple Races, Group	1	0	7	0	0	54	4	3
Anti-Arab	2	1	3	0	0	24	0	3
Anti-Hispanic or Latino	19	4	12	0	1	95	4	7
Anti-Other Race/Ethnicity/Ancestry	8	6	14	1	2	122	2	11
Religion	11	42	58	3	43	925	7	34
Anti-Jewish	2	9	12	0	19	712	0	2
Anti-Catholic	0	5	4	1	5	37	0	0
Anti-Protestant	0	2	6	0	1	10	0	1
Anti-Islamic (Muslim)	2	4	1	0	4	38	2	0
Anti-Other Religion	0	6	7	0	9	38	1	3
Anti-Multiple Religions, Group	2	0	2	0	0	22	0	3
Anti-Mormon	2	0	0	0	0	8	0	0
Anti-Jehovah's Witness	0	0	0	0	0	2	0	0
Anti-Eastern Orthodox (Russian, Greek, Other)	0	6	9	1	0	8	1	10
Anti-Other Christian	0	5	0	0	3	30	1	2
Anti-Buddhist	0	0	2	0	0	2	0	0
Anti-Hindu	0	1	1	0	1	1	0	1
Anti-Sikh	3	4	12	0	1	16	2	10
Anti-Atheism/Agnosticism/etc.	0	0	2	1	0	1	0	2
Sexual Orientation	53	14	28	1	6	254	2	10
Anti-Gay (Male)	37	6	7	1	2	137	1	5
Anti-Lesbian	2	1	5	0	0	19	0	1
Anti-Lesbian, Gay, Bisexual, or Transgender (Mixed Group)	11	4	13	0	4	90	1	1
Anti-Heterosexual	2	2	2	0	0	4	0	2
Anti-Bisexual	1	1	1	0	0	4	0	1
Disability	4	5	38	2	0	12	7	10
Anti-Physical	4	1	14	2	0	5	3	2
Anti-Mental	0	4	24	0	0	7	4	8
Gender	1	3	1	0	2	12	0	3
Anti-Male	1	2	1	0	0	1	0	1
Anti-Female	0	1	0	0	2	11	0	2
Gender Identity	5	5	13	0	0	15	7	4
Anti-Transgender	5	3	5	0	0	9	2	1
Anti-Gender Non-Conforming	0	2	8	0	0	6	5	3
Multiple-Bias Incidents[5]	0	6	3	0	5	103	0	5

NOTE: The aggregate of adult and juvenile individual victims does not equal the total number of victims because total victims include individuals, businesses/financial institutions, government entities, religious organizations, and society/public as a whole. In addition, the aggregate of adult and juvenile individual victims does not equal the aggregate of victims of crimes against persons because not all law enforcement agencies report the ages of individual victims.
1 The term victim may refer to an individual, business/financial institution, government entity, religious organization, or society/public as a whole.   2 The figures shown are individual victims only.   3 Only the revised Uniform Crime Reporting definition of rape is used for the figures reported in this column.   4 The figures shown include additional offenses collected in the National Incident-Based Reporting System.   5 A multiple-bias incident is an incident in which one or more offense types are motivated by two or more biases.

Table 89. Incidents, Victim Type, by Bias Motivation, 2019

(Number.)

Bias motivation	Total incidents	Victim type					
		Individual	Business/ financial institution	Government	Religious organization	Society/public[1]	Other/unknown/ multiple
Total	7,314	5,524	478	263	208	194	647
Single-Bias Incidents	7,103	5,410	466	240	194	191	602
Race/Ethnicity/Ancestry	3,963	3,269	218	120	12	136	208
Religion	1,521	701	182	103	170	29	336
Sexual Orientation	1,195	1,068	42	14	12	9	50
Disability	157	137	8	1	0	10	1
Gender	69	60	2	1	0	3	3
Gender Identity	198	175	14	1	0	4	4
Multiple-Bias Incidents[2]	211	114	12	23	14	3	45

1 The victim type society/public is collected only in the National Incident-Based Reporting System.   2 A multiple-bias incident is an incident in which one or more offense types are motivated by two or more biases.

Table 90. Known Offenders,[1] by Known Offender's Race, Ethnicity, and Age, 2019

(Number.)

Race/ethnicity/age	Total
Race	6,406
White	3,365
Black or African American	1,532
American Indian or Alaska Native	68
Asian	58
Native Hawaiian or Other Pacific Islander	22
Group of multiple races[2]	425
Unknown race	936
Ethnicity[3]	5,443
Hispanic or Latino	547
Not Hispanic or Latino	1,801
Group of multiple ethnicities[4]	103
Unknown ethnicity	2,992
Age[3]	5,599
Total known offenders 18 and over	4,734
Total known offenders under 18	865

1 The term known offender does not imply the suspect's identity is known; rather, the term indicates some aspect of the suspect was identified, thus distinguishing the suspect from an unknown offender.   2 The term group of multiple races is used to describe a group of offenders of varying races.   3 The total number of known offenders by age and the total number of known offenders by ethnicity do not equal the total number of known offenders by race because not all law enforcement agencies report the age and/or ethnicity of the known offenders.   4 The term group of multiple ethnicities is used to describe a group of offenders of varying ethnicities.

Table 91. Incidents, Bias Motivation, by Location, 2019

(Number.)

Location	Total incidents	Bias motivation						Multiple-bias incidents[1]
		Race/ethnicity/ancestry	Religion	Sexual orientation	Disability	Gender	Gender identity	
Total	7,314	3,963	1,521	1,195	157	69	198	211
Abandoned/condemned structure	11	4	5	0	0	0	0	2
Air/bus/train terminal	113	69	11	23	1	2	1	6
Amusement park	5	2	0	3	0	0	0	0
Arena/stadium/fairgrounds/coliseum	9	3	1	4	0	0	0	1
Auto dealership new/used	6	3	2	0	0	0	1	0
Bank/savings and loan	21	16	3	1	0	0	1	0
Bar/nightclub	124	66	11	41	0	1	2	3
Camp/campground	8	6	2	0	0	0	0	0
Church/synagogue/temple/mosque	322	34	255	19	0	0	0	14
Commercial office building	161	92	28	26	1	1	6	7
Community center	21	8	2	9	0	0	2	0
Construction site	23	14	6	1	1	0	0	1
Convenience store	127	82	16	19	2	1	4	3
Cyberspace	36	21	10	2	0	0	1	2
Daycare facility	4	3	1	0	0	0	0	0
Department/discount store	101	67	14	12	0	2	3	3
Dock/wharf/freight/modal terminal	2	1	1	0	0	0	0	0
Drug store/doctor's office/hospital	94	56	15	8	4	6	4	1
Farm facility	3	2	0	0	0	0	1	0
Field/woods	61	30	19	8	0	0	1	3
Gambling facility/casino/race track	2	1	0	1	0	0	0	0
Government/public building	132	86	24	15	2	1	3	1
Grocery/supermarket	99	65	9	10	7	0	7	1
Highway/road/alley/street/sidewalk	1,329	814	142	268	23	6	50	26
Hotel/motel/etc.	55	33	8	10	1	0	2	1
Industrial site	18	13	2	3	0	0	0	0
Jail/prison/penitentiary/corrections facility	90	64	1	18	1	2	3	1
Lake/waterway/beach	16	9	1	6	0	0	0	0
Liquor store	26	13	7	3	2	0	0	1
Park/playground	196	98	50	26	1	0	3	18
Parking/drop lot/garage	341	245	27	52	4	2	6	5
Rental storage facility	14	10	3	0	0	1	0	0
Residence/home	1,800	1,004	272	336	76	29	51	32
Rest area	4	3	0	1	0	0	0	0
Restaurant	214	138	15	45	3	0	5	8
School/college[2]	50	28	11	9	1	0	1	0
School—college/university	195	93	52	31	2	5	2	10
School—elementary/secondary	458	232	115	47	12	2	9	41
Service/gas station	76	53	9	7	3	0	2	2
Shelter—mission/homeless	32	17	0	10	1	0	3	1
Shopping mall	17	8	0	5	0	0	1	3
Specialty store (TV, fur, etc.)	63	36	15	6	1	0	3	2
Tribal Lands	1	0	0	0	0	0	0	1
Other/unknown	822	311	356	109	7	8	20	11
Multiple locations	12	10	0	1	1	0	0	0

1 A multiple-bias incident is an incident in which one or more offense types are motivated by two or more biases.   2 The location designation School/college has been retained for agencies that have not updated their records management systems to include the new location designations of school—college/university and school—elementary/secondary, which allow for more specificity in reporting.

Table 92. Offenses, Offense Type, by Participating State/Federal, 2019

(Number.)

State	Total offenses	Crimes against persons							Crimes against property							Crimes against society[2]
		Murder and nonnegligent manslaughter	Rape[1]	Aggravated assault	Simple assault	Intimidation	Human trafficking, commercial sex acts	Other[2]	Robbery	Burglary	Larceny-theft	Motor vehicle theft	Arson	Destruction/ damage/ vandalism	Other[2]	
Total	8,559	51	30	1,158	2,023	2,206	3	41	125	114	284	19	60	2,152	57	236
Alabama[3]	0	0	0	0	0	0	0	0	0	0	0	0	0	0	0	0
Alaska	17	0	0	6	6	2	0	0	1	0	0	0	0	2	0	0
Arizona	254	0	0	20	67	110	0	0	0	1	2	0	0	48	2	4
Arkansas	10	0	0	4	0	2	0	0	0	0	2	0	0	2	0	0
California	1,221	1	3	290	272	264	0	0	35	11	5	1	9	330	0	0
Colorado	257	0	1	46	69	70	2	0	2	5	1	0	0	60	0	1
Connecticut	86	0	0	3	22	37	0	0	2	0	1	0	0	18	1	2
Delaware	27	0	0	2	3	12	0	0	0	0	0	0	0	10	0	0
District of Columbia	247	0	0	43	113	45	0	0	11	0	0	0	0	35	0	0
Florida	131	0	1	23	43	20	0	0	0	2	0	0	2	40	0	0
Georgia	123	0	0	11	47	23	0	3	0	3	8	0	1	24	2	1
Hawaii	51	0	0	7	23	16	0	0	2	0	0	0	0	2	0	1
Idaho	38	0	0	4	12	14	0	0	0	1	1	0	0	4	1	1
Illinois	95	0	0	22	39	24	0	0	4	0	0	0	1	5	0	0
Indiana	87	2	0	6	18	36	1	0	0	1	2	0	0	19	1	1
Iowa	13	0	0	2	4	3	0	0	0	0	1	0	0	3	0	0
Kansas	99	0	0	8	15	26	0	2	0	5	9	0	1	22	3	8
Kentucky	179	0	0	9	40	66	0	0	2	7	5	1	3	34	2	10
Louisiana	33	0	0	5	9	5	0	0	0	2	4	1	0	2	0	5
Maine	24	0	0	0	3	17	0	0	0	0	0	0	0	4	0	0
Maryland	18	0	0	0	2	2	0	0	2	0	0	0	0	12	0	0
Massachusetts	441	0	0	54	84	169	0	0	1	2	2	0	3	124	1	1
Michigan	495	0	4	65	135	152	0	6	3	5	24	5	2	64	9	21
Minnesota	123	0	0	17	28	35	0	1	3	0	2	0	2	35	0	0
Mississippi	15	0	0	0	2	2	0	1	1	1	2	1	0	3	1	1
Missouri	106	0	1	27	33	29	0	0	1	0	2	0	1	10	0	2
Montana	35	0	0	10	8	0	0	0	0	0	3	0	0	14	0	0
Nebraska	57	0	0	3	16	9	0	0	0	2	9	0	0	8	0	10
Nevada	53	0	0	13	14	6	0	0	1	0	2	0	2	15	0	0
New Hampshire	17	0	0	0	4	5	0	0	0	0	1	0	0	7	0	0
New Jersey	478	1	0	11	40	152	0	0	4	1	1	0	1	267	0	0
New Mexico	63	1	0	15	22	4	0	1	1	1	2	1	0	12	2	1
New York	618	5	1	35	166	12	0	0	7	3	9	0	1	379	0	0
North Carolina	248	0	1	22	62	91	0	0	3	6	4	0	2	54	0	3
North Dakota	20	0	0	1	6	8	0	0	0	0	0	0	0	5	0	0
Ohio	428	0	4	26	67	107	0	4	9	20	80	7	1	52	8	43
Oklahoma	30	0	0	4	6	8	0	0	0	0	0	0	1	11	0	0
Oregon	205	0	0	30	53	39	0	0	1	1	9	0	4	60	1	7
Pennsylvania	50	0	0	6	6	18	0	0	0	1	0	0	6	13	0	0
Rhode Island	21	0	0	2	6	2	0	0	0	0	0	0	0	11	0	0
South Carolina	82	0	0	10	15	18	0	4	0	4	8	0	0	14	1	8
South Dakota	21	0	0	2	9	3	0	0	0	0	0	0	0	7	0	0
Tennessee	152	0	0	20	37	33	0	0	1	1	1	1	1	19	0	38
Texas	560	22	8	108	127	92	0	4	8	17	45	1	0	84	11	33
Utah	34	0	0	9	4	0	0	7	0	0	4	0	0	7	0	3
Vermont	37	0	0	2	7	1	0	0	0	0	2	0	1	23	0	1
Virginia	185	0	0	12	55	55	0	3	2	0	4	0	0	47	1	6
Washington	664	1	3	82	164	259	0	2	16	6	16	0	1	97	7	10
West Virginia	36	0	0	3	7	8	0	0	1	3	2	0	1	4	1	7
Wisconsin	83	0	3	5	25	15	0	3	1	2	6	0	0	14	2	7
Wyoming	6	0	0	0	2	1	0	0	0	0	1	0	0	2	0	0
Federal																
Federal Bureau of Investigation, Field Offices	180	18	0	53	6	75	0	0	0	0	1	0	14	13	0	0
Pentagon Force Protection Agency	1	0	0	0	0	0	0	0	0	0	0	0	0	1	0	0
United States Army	1	0	0	0	0	0	0	0	0	0	1	0	0	0	0	0
United States Navy Law Enforcement	4	0	0	0	0	4	0	0	0	0	0	0	0	0	0	0

1 Only the revised Uniform Crime Reporting definition of rape was used for the figures shown in this column.   2 The figures shown include additional offenses collected in the National Incident-Based Reporting System.   3 Limited data for 2019 were available for Alabama.

Table 93. Agency Hate Crime Reporting, by Participating State/Territory and Federal, 2019

(Number.)

State	Number of participating agencies	Population covered	Agencies submitting incident reports	Total number of incidents reported
Total	15,588	305,284,239	2,172	7,314
Alabama[1]	2	85,670	0	0
Alaska	33	727,792	5	11
Arizona	92	6,395,924	17	209
Arkansas	278	2,813,597	6	9
California	737	39,502,561	195	1,015
Colorado	221	5,705,335	50	210
Connecticut	102	3,373,874	40	76
Delaware	63	973,764	10	22
District of Columbia	2	705,749	2	222
Florida	638	20,901,840	51	111
Georgia	495	9,290,789	50	102
Hawaii	1	974,902	1	41
Idaho	106	1,782,402	9	24
Illinois	728	12,125,954	23	65
Indiana	214	3,643,904	23	75
Iowa	246	3,135,918	8	10
Kansas	377	2,610,898	53	78
Kentucky	410	4,460,061	67	146
Louisiana	137	3,536,544	11	26
Maine	134	1,344,212	10	19
Maryland	153	6,045,680	9	18
Massachusetts	360	6,772,985	83	388
Michigan	638	9,969,410	188	434
Minnesota	379	5,533,121	35	104
Mississippi	42	882,028	5	14
Missouri	571	6,077,911	28	83
Montana	103	1,055,460	16	32
Nebraska	130	1,813,150	23	46
Nevada	48	3,070,743	5	44
New Hampshire	188	1,313,554	14	16
New Jersey	556	8,638,072	208	472
New Mexico	23	819,112	6	50
New York	558	18,949,575	65	611
North Carolina	332	8,740,258	80	210
North Dakota	109	762,062	12	18
Ohio	551	9,730,885	134	391
Oklahoma	438	3,946,211	22	28
Oregon	204	4,056,079	46	175
Pennsylvania	1,424	12,585,495	15	41
Rhode Island	48	1,058,329	10	17
South Carolina	405	5,081,688	36	68
South Dakota	128	848,738	13	20
Tennessee	465	6,830,634	42	117
Texas	1,059	28,885,669	167	456
Utah	121	3,077,345	14	18
Vermont	89	628,664	17	33
Virginia	415	8,533,624	57	163
Washington	253	7,587,677	77	542
West Virginia	240	1,574,978	18	31
Wisconsin	437	5,810,699	43	74
Wyoming	55	512,713	5	5
Federal[2]				
Federal Bureau of Investigation, Field Offices	45	0	45	118
Pentagon Force Protection Agency	1	0	1	1
United States Air Force, Office of Special Investigations	1	0	0	0
United States Army	1	0	1	1
United States Marine Corps Law Enforcement	1	0	0	0
United States Navy Law Enforcement	1	0	1	4

1 Limited data for 2019 were available for Alabama.   2 Population estimates are not attributed to the federal agencies.

Table 94. Hate Crime Incidents Per Bias Motivation and Quarter, by Selected State and Agency and Federal, 2019

(Number.)

State/agency	Number of incidents per bias motivation						Number of incidents per quarter				Population[1]
	Race/ Ethnicity/ Ancestry	Religion	Sexual orientation	Disability	Gender	Gender Identity	1st quarter	2nd quarter	3rd quarter	4th quarter	
ALASKA											
Total	7	0	4	0	0	0					
Cities	7	0	4	0	0	0					
Anchorage	4	0	2	0	0	0	1	2	3	0	287,731
Fairbanks	1	0	0	0	0	0	0	1	0	0	31,493
Kotzebue	1	0	0	0	0	0	0	0	1	0	3,272
North Pole	1	0	0	0	0	0	0	1	0		2,111
Soldotna	0	0	2	0	0	0	0	0	0	2	4,756
ARIZONA											
Total	143	36	30	3	2	3					
Cities	143	32	30	3	2	3					
Apache Junction	2	1	1	1	0	0	1	3	0	1	42,531
Casa Grande	1	0	0	0	0	0	0	0	1	0	58,366
Coolidge	4	0	0	0	0	0	2	2	0	0	13,138
Flagstaff	0	1	0	0	0	0	1	0	0	0	75,013
Gilbert	0	2	0	0	0	0	1	0	1	0	253,619
Glendale	9	0	0	0	0	0	2	2	4	1	253,951
Mesa	2	0	1	0	0	0	0	0	1	2	518,160
Page	1	0	0	0	0	0	0	1			7,588
Phoenix[2]	111	20	23	0	2	3	31	43	33	44	1,688,722
San Luis	1	0	0	0	0	0	0	0	0	1	34,192
Scottsdale	1	1	1	0	0	0	1	2	0	0	260,464
Somerton	1	0	0	0	0	0	0	0	0	1	16,771
Surprise	2	1	0	0	0	0	0	2	0	1	140,962
Tempe	1	0	0	0	0	0	0	1	0	0	196,499
Tucson	6	6	4	0	0	0	4	5	5	2	548,374
Yuma	1	0	0	2	0	0	1	0	0	2	98,769
Universities and Colleges	0	4	0	0	0	0					
University of Arizona	0	4	0	0	0	0	1	0	1	2	48,318
ARKANSAS											
Total	8	0	1	0	0	0					
Cities	7	0	0	0	0	0					
Benton	1	0	0	0	0	0	0	0	0	1	37,161
Conway	1	0	0	0	0	0	0	0	1	0	67,336
Fort Smith	4	0	0	0	0	0	0	0	2	2	88,041
Searcy	1	0	0	0	0	0	0	0	0	1	23,873
Nonmetropolitan Counties	1	0	1	0	0	0					
Logan	1	0	0	0	0	0	0	0	0	1	
Pope	0	0	1	0	0	0	0	1	0	0	
CALIFORNIA											
Total	524	208	235	10	7	33					
Cities	447	193	212	8	5	30					
Alameda	2	0	0	0	0	0	0	1	0	1	78,907
Antioch	2	1	1	0	0	0	0	2	1	1	112,641
Apple Valley	0	0	2	0	0	0	0	2	0	0	74,051
Arvin	0	1	0	0	0	0	0	1	0	0	21,811
Azusa	2	0	1	0	0	0	0	2	1	0	50,405
Bakersfield	1	0	1	1	0	0	1	0	1	1	388,080
Beaumont	1	0	0	0	0	0	0	0	1	0	50,990
Bell	0	0	1	0	1	0	1	1		0	35,759
Bellflower	1	0	0	0	0	0	0	1	0	0	77,196
Bell Gardens	0	0	1	0	0	0	0	1	0	0	42,366
Belmont	0	0	1	0	0	1	0	0	0	2	27,272
Berkeley	4	2	2	0	0	0	0	2	0	6	122,788
Beverly Hills	1	6	2	0	0	0	2	2	2	3	34,211
Big Bear	1	0	0	0	0	0	0	1	0	0	5,311
Brea	0	1	4	0	0	0	0	4	0	1	44,155
Brentwood	0	4	0	0	0	0	1	0	2	1	65,483
Brisbane	1	0	0	0	0	0	1	0	0	0	4,746
Buena Park	1	0	0	0	0	0	0	1	0	0	82,627
Burbank	7	0	0	0	0	0	2	4	1	0	103,738
Camarillo	1	0	0	0	0	0	0	1	0	0	69,628
Capitola	0	1	0	0	0	0	0	1	0	0	10,101
Carlsbad	5	0	0	0	0	0	0	2	0	3	117,220
Cathedral City	1	0	0	0	0	0	0	0	0	1	55,346
Central Marin	0	1	0	0	0	0	0	0	1	0	34,793
Chico	2	0	0	0	0	0	0	2	0	0	95,826
Chino	2	1	0	0	0	0	0	0	1	2	93,348
Chula Vista	6	2	0	0	1	0	4	1	2	2	275,230
Citrus Heights	1	0	1	0	0	0	0	1	0	1	88,496

Table 94. Hate Crime Incidents Per Bias Motivation and Quarter, by Selected State and Agency and Federal, 2019—Continued

(Number.)

State/agency	Race/ Ethnicity/ Ancestry	Religion	Sexual orientation	Disability	Gender	Gender Identity	1st quarter	2nd quarter	3rd quarter	4th quarter	Population[1]
Claremont	1	0	1	0	0	0	0	0	1	1	36,681
Clearlake	2	1	0	0	0	0	2	0	1	0	15,400
Clovis	1	0	0	0	0	0	0	0	0	1	114,170
Coachella	0	0	1	0	0	0	0	1	0	0	46,485
Compton	1	0	0	0	0	0	1	0	0	0	96,638
Concord	2	0	0	0	0	0	1	0	1	0	130,615
Coronado	0	0	1	0	0	1	0	0	2	0	21,115
Costa Mesa	3	0	0	0	0	0	1	0	2	0	114,047
Cupertino	1	0	0	0	0	0	0	0	0	1	60,357
Cypress	1	0	0	0	0	0	0	0	0	1	49,085
Davis	0	1	0	0	0	0	0	1	0	0	69,767
Delano	2	0	0	0	0	0	1	0	1	0	53,002
Dublin	1	0	0	0	0	0	0	0	1	0	66,072
El Cajon	1	0	0	0	0	0	0	1	0	0	103,686
El Cerrito	1	0	0	0	0	0	0	0	0	1	25,857
Elk Grove	0	1	0	0	0	0	0	0	0	1	175,492
El Monte	3	0	0	0	0	0	2	1	0	0	115,830
El Segundo	1	0	0	0	0	0	0	0	0	1	16,727
Emeryville	1	0	0	0	0	0	0	1	0	0	12,380
Escondido	3	1	0	0	0	0	2	0	0	2	153,215
Eureka	1	0	1	0	0	0	1	1	0	0	26,973
Fairfield	1	0	1	0	0	0	2	0	0	0	118,383
Folsom	0	0	1	0	0	0	0	0	0	1	79,927
Fontana	1	0	0	0	0	0	0	0	1	0	215,883
Fountain Valley	1	0	0	0	0	0	0	1	0	0	55,858
Fremont	2	2	0	0	0	0	0	1	1	2	240,887
Fresno	8	2	2	0	0	2	10	2	2		534,285
Fullerton	1	0	1	0	0	0	1	0	1	0	140,194
Galt	0	0	1	0	0	0	1	0	0	0	26,796
Garden Grove	1	0	1	0	0	1	0	2	0	1	172,832
Greenfield	1	0	0	0	0	0	0	0	1	0	17,809
Hawthorne	2	0	2	0	1	1	0	2	2	2	87,305
Hayward	4	0	0	0	0	0	1	1	1	1	161,588
Huntington Beach	4	3	1	0	0	0	1	1	2	4	201,843
Huntington Park	1	0	1	0	0	0	1	1	0	0	58,181
Imperial	0	1	0	0	0	0	0	0	0	1	18,090
Imperial Beach	2	2	0	0	0	0	1	0	1	2	27,583
Irvine	4	1	2	0	0	0	0	2	4	1	292,673
Laguna Woods	0	1	0	0	0	0	0	0	0	1	16,043
Lake Forest	0	1	0	0	0	0	0	0	1	0	86,691
Lancaster	7	1	1	0	0	0	1	2	5	1	159,335
Lemon Grove	1	0	0	0	0	0	1	0	0	0	27,175
Livermore	1	0	1	0	0	0	1	0	1	0	91,418
Long Beach	18	1	4	0	0	0	6	4	7	6	467,974
Los Angeles[2]	118	81	70	2	0	14	58	77	85	64	4,015,546
Malibu	1	0	0	0	0	0	0	0	1	0	12,794
Marina	1	0	0	0	0	0	0	0	0	1	22,911
Martinez	0	1	1	0	0	0	0	1	1	0	38,692
Marysville	0	1	0	0	0	0	1	0	0	0	12,572
Mission Viejo	0	2	0	0	0	0	1	0	1	0	95,453
Modesto	3	0	0	0	0	0	1	2	0	0	216,542
Montebello	0	1	0	0	0	0	0	1	0	0	62,650
Monterey	0	0	1	0	0	0	0	0	0	1	28,337
Monterey Park	1	0	0	0	0	0	0	0	1	0	60,424
Moreno Valley	1	0	0	0	0	0	1	0	0	0	210,979
National City	1	0	0	0	0	0	0	0	0	1	61,791
Novato	2	0	0	0	0	0	0	0	2	0	56,134
Oakdale	1	0	0	0	0	0	0	0	0	1	23,808
Oakland	5	3	5	0	0	0	2	3	5	3	434,036
Oceanside	3	1	4	0	0	0	1	4	3	0	177,129
Ontario	1	0	0	0	0	0	0	0	1	0	183,322
Orange	3	0	0	0	0	0	0	0	1	2	139,830
Oroville	2	0	0	0	0	0	1	1	0	0	19,268
Oxnard	1	0	0	0	0	0	0	0	1	0	211,349
Pacifica	1	0	0	0	0	0	0	0	1	0	38,938
Palmdale	3	0	0	0	0	0	0	0	2	1	157,138
Palm Springs	4	2	5	0	0	0	3	4	1	3	48,846
Palo Alto[2]	1	2	2	0	0	0	1	0	1	2	66,938
Parlier	0	0	1	0	0	0	0	0	1	0	15,384
Pasadena	2	2	0	0	0	0	0	1	2	1	141,913
Paso Robles	1	0	0	0	0	0	1	0	0	0	32,528
Petaluma	3	0	1	0	0	0	0	1	3	0	62,425
Pico Rivera	0	0	1	0	0	0	0	0	1	0	62,880
Pittsburg	0	1	1	1	0	0	0	1	0	2	73,637
Placentia	0	1	0	0	0	0	1	0	0	0	51,756
Pleasant Hill	1	0	0	0	0	0	0	0	0	1	35,125
Pomona	4	0	1	0	0	0	1	3	1	0	152,776
Poway	1	1	0	0	0	0	0	1	0	1	49,928

Table 94. Hate Crime Incidents Per Bias Motivation and Quarter, by Selected State and Agency and Federal, 2019—Continued

(Number.)

State/agency	Number of incidents per bias motivation						Number of incidents per quarter				Population[1]
	Race/ Ethnicity/ Ancestry	Religion	Sexual orientation	Disability	Gender	Gender Identity	1st quarter	2nd quarter	3rd quarter	4th quarter	
Rancho Cordova	1	0	0	0	0	0	1	0	0	0	75,869
Rancho Cucamonga	1	0	0	0	0	0	1		0	0	179,247
Rancho Santa Margarita	1	0	0	0	1	0	0	0	0	2	48,377
Red Bluff	2	0	0	0	0	0	0	1	1	0	14,308
Redding	1	0	0	0	0	0	1				92,009
Redlands	0	0	2	0	0	0	0	0	2	0	71,941
Redondo Beach	0	1	0	0	0	0	0	0	1	0	67,473
Redwood City	0	0	0	0	0	1	0	0	1	0	87,427
Rialto	1	0	0	0	0	0	0	0	0	1	103,965
Richmond	7	0	2	0	0	0	3	2	0	4	110,988
Ridgecrest	0	0	1	0	0	0	0	0	0	1	29,101
Riverside	10	1	4	0	0	0	8	3	4	0	333,260
Rohnert Park	1	0	0	0	0	0	0	0	1	0	44,131
Rosemead	1	0	0	0	0	0	1	0	0	0	54,489
Roseville	5	0	0	1	0	0	1	3	1	1	141,744
Sacramento	1	1	1	1	0	2	1	0	4	1	513,934
Salinas	0	0	1	0	0	0	0	1	0	0	156,943
San Bernardino	4	0	4	0	0	0	1	0	2	5	216,715
San Bruno	1	0	0	0	0	0	0	0	1	0	43,297
San Clemente	1	2	2	0	0	0	1	0	3	1	65,018
San Diego	8	11	9	1	0	1	9	8	9	4	1,441,737
San Francisco	35	5	22	0	0	2	17	17	24	6	886,007
San Gabriel	2	0	0	0	0	0	0	1	1	0	40,422
San Jose	13	7	10	1	0	2	9	8	7	9	1,040,008
San Leandro	0	0	2	0	0	0	1	1	0	0	90,297
San Luis Obispo	6	2	1	0	0	1	1	2	2	5	47,735
San Marcos	1	1	0	0	0	0	1	0	0	1	98,598
San Mateo	7	0	0	0	0	0	1	0	1	5	106,020
San Rafael	5	0	1	0	0	0	1	1	2	2	58,819
San Ramon	2	0	1	0	0	0	1	1	1	0	76,387
Santa Ana	3	6	2	0	0	0	2	4	3	2	333,664
Santa Clarita	1	1	0	0	0	0	0	1	1	0	218,103
Santa Cruz	1	0	1	0	0	0	1	1	0	0	65,263
Santa Monica	1	2	1	0	0	0	1	0	2	1	91,621
Santa Rosa	2	0	2	0	1	0	2	1	2	0	177,884
Seaside	1	1	0	0	0	0	1	1	0	0	34,036
South El Monte	1	0	1	0	0	0	1	1	0	0	20,852
South Lake Tahoe	0	1	0	0	0	0	0	1	0	0	22,116
Stockton	1	2	1	0	0	0	0	1	1	2	313,604
Sunnyvale	2	4	0	0	0	0	1	2	0	3	154,859
Temecula	1	0	0	0	0	0	0	0	0	1	116,630
Thousand Oaks	0	0	1	0	0	0	0	1	0	0	127,811
Torrance	1	0	1	0	0	0	0	0	2	0	145,183
Tracy	0	1	0	0	0	0	1	0	0	0	92,895
Turlock	1	1	1	0	0	0	2	0	0	1	74,120
Union City	6	0	0	0	0	0	5	1	0	0	75,202
Upland	2	0	0	0	0	0	0	0	0	2	77,398
Vacaville	5	0	0	0	0	0	0	3	0	2	101,147
Ventura	2	1	1	0	0	0	1	1	1	1	111,596
Walnut Creek	2	2	1	0	0	0	1	2	1	1	70,546
West Hollywood	0	1	0	0	0	0	1	0	0	0	37,173
Westminster	2	1	0	0	0	0	2		0	1	91,086
Whittier	0	0	1	0	0	0	0		0	1	86,158
Windsor	1	0	0	0	0	0	1	0	0	0	27,981
Yorba Linda	1	0	1	0	0	0	0	0	2	0	68,225
Yuba City	0	0	0	0	0	1	0	0	1	0	67,164
Yucca Valley	0	0	1	0	0	0	1		0	0	21,858
Universities and Colleges	17	2	1	0	0	0					
California State University											
Chico	1	0	0	0	0	0	0	1	0	0	19,754
East Bay	1	0	0	0	0	0	1	0	0	0	19,613
Northridge	1	0	0	0	0	0	0	0	0	1	44,639
Humboldt State University	7	1	0	0	0	0	1	4	0	3	9,262
San Diego State University	1	0	0	0	0	0	0	1	0	0	37,748
San Francisco State University	1	0	0	0	0	0	0	0	1	0	33,506
University of California											
Davis	4	0	0	0	0	0	0	2	1	1	39,783
Irvine	1	0	0	0	0	0	0	0	0	1	37,170
San Diego	0	1	1	0	0	0	1	1	0	0	37,744
Metropolitan Counties	52	12	17	2	1	3					
Los Angeles	10	1	3	0	1	0	5	5	3	2	
Marin	2	2	0	0	0	0	0	2	2	0	
Merced	1	0	0	0	0	0	1	0	0	0	
Monterey	1	0	0	0	0	0	0	0	1	0	
Napa	1	0	1	0	0	0	0	0	2	0	
Orange	6	1	1	1	0	0	1	4	2	2	
Riverside	3	1	1	0	0	0	2	1	1	1	

Table 94. Hate Crime Incidents Per Bias Motivation and Quarter, by Selected State and Agency and Federal, 2019—Continued

(Number.)

State/agency	Race/ Ethnicity/ Ancestry	Religion	Sexual orientation	Disability	Gender	Gender Identity	1st quarter	2nd quarter	3rd quarter	4th quarter	Population[1]
Sacramento	2	0	0	0	0	2	0	1	1	2	
San Bernardino	0	0	2	0	0	0	2		0	0	
San Diego	12	4	6	1	0	1	6	7	8	3	
San Luis Obispo	0	1	1	0	0	0	0	0	1	1	
San Mateo	3	0	1	0	0	0	0	0	3	1	
Santa Barbara	0	1	0	0	0	0	0	0	1	0	
Santa Clara	4	1	0	0	0	0	1	1	2	1	
Santa Cruz	6	0	1	0	0	0	2	2	1	2	
Tulare	1	0	0	0	0	0	0	0	0	1	
Nonmetropolitan Counties	2	1	2	0	0	0					
Glenn	0	0	1	0	0	0		1	0	0	
Mendocino	1	1	0	0	0	0	1	1	0	0	
Nevada	1	0	0	0	0	0	0	0	1	0	
Tuolumne	0	0	1	0	0	0	0	0	1	0	
Other Agencies	6	0	3	0	1	0					
Los Angeles Transportation Services Bureau	0	0	3	0	1	0	3	0	0	1	
Port of San Diego Harbor	5	0	0	0	0	0	1		3	1	
Santa Clara Transit District	1	0	0	0	0	0	0	1	0	0	
COLORADO											
Total	117	36	47	7	0	5					
Cities	96	30	40	3	0	2					
Aurora	2	0	0	0	0	0	0	1	1	0	380,600
Boulder	4	1	3	0	0	0	2	2	0	4	108,519
Brighton	1	1	0	0	0	0	0	0	0	2	42,267
Broomfield	1	0	0	0	0	0	0	0	1	0	70,798
Canon City	1	1	0	0	0	0	1	1	0	0	16,793
Carbondale	1	0	0	0	0	0	0	0	0	1	6,941
Castle Rock	1	0	0	0	0	0	0	0	0	1	67,208
Centennial	0	2	0	0	0	0	0	1	0	1	112,129
Colorado Springs	6	2	4	0	0	0	1	3	5	3	479,648
Commerce City	2	0	0	0	0	0	1	0	1	0	60,198
Denver	40	15	26	2	0	2	11	39	25	10	728,941
Durango	1	1	0	0	0	0	0	1	0	1	19,271
Edgewater	1	0	0	0	0	0	1	0	0	0	5,363
Englewood	2	0	0	0	0	0	1	1	0	0	35,273
Evans	3	0	0	0	0	0	1	0	2	0	21,585
Fort Collins[2]	4	2	1	0	0	0	2	2	0	2	170,889
Frisco	1	0	0	0	0	0	0	1	0	0	3,220
Glenwood Springs	4	0	0	0	0	0	2	0	1	1	10,027
Grand Junction	2	1	0	0	0	0	1	1	1	0	63,949
Greenwood Village	1	0	1	0	0	0	1	1	0	0	16,046
Hudson	0	0	1	0	0	0	1	0	0	0	1,806
Lone Tree	1	0	0	0	0	0	0	0	1	0	15,129
Longmont	2	0	1	1	0	0	2	1	1	0	97,928
Loveland	1	0	0	0	0	0	1	0	0	0	78,856
Manitou Springs	0	1	0	0	0	0	0	0	1	0	5,388
Parker	2	1	0	0	0	0	2	1	0	0	57,050
Pueblo	1	1	0	0	0	0	1	0	0	1	112,381
Rifle	2	0	0	0	0	0	0	1	1	0	9,782
Silt	1	0	0	0	0	0	1	0	0	0	3,215
Sterling	1	0	0	0	0	0	0	0	1	0	13,573
Thornton[2]	3	1	2	0	0	0	0	2	1	2	142,168
Timnath	1	0	0	0	0	0	0	1	0	0	5,027
Westminster	3	0	1	0	0	0	0	0	3	1	114,392
Universities and Colleges	10	1	1	0	0	0					
Colorado State University, Fort Collins	2	1	0	0	0	0	1	0	1	1	37,676
Fort Lewis College	1	0	0	0	0	0	0	1	0	0	3,730
University of Colorado, Boulder	7	0	0	0	0	0	2	0	3	2	39,302
University of Northern Colorado	0	0	1	0	0	0	0	0	1	0	15,825
Metropolitan Counties	4	4	3	4	0	1					
Adams	1	0	0	1	0	0	1	0	1	0	
Douglas	2	2	0	2	0	0	1	1	2	2	
Jefferson	1	0	0	1	0	0	1	1	0	0	
Larimer	0	1	0	0	0	1	2	0	0	0	
Mesa	0	0	2	0	0	0	0	1	1	0	
Park	0	1	1	0	0	0	0	1	1	0	
Nonmetropolitan Counties	7	1	3	0	0	2					
Bent	0	1	0	0	0	0	0	1	0	0	
Custer	1	0	0	0	0	0	1	0	0	0	
Fremont	1	0	1	0	0	0	0	1	1	0	
Garfield	1	0	0	0	0	2	1	1	1	0	
Huerfano	2	0	1	0	0	0	1	1	1	0	

Table 94. Hate Crime Incidents Per Bias Motivation and Quarter, by Selected State and Agency and Federal, 2019—Continued

(Number.)

State/agency	Number of incidents per bias motivation						Number of incidents per quarter				Population[1]
	Race/ Ethnicity/ Ancestry	Religion	Sexual orientation	Disability	Gender	Gender Identity	1st quarter	2nd quarter	3rd quarter	4th quarter	
San Miguel	1	0	0	0	0	0	0	0	1	0	
Summit	1	0	1	0	0	0	1	0	1	0	
CONNECTICUT											
Total	48	16	11	0	1	0					
Cities	45	12	11	0	1	0					
Bloomfield	0	1	0	0	0	0	0	0	1	0	21,406
Bridgeport	1	1	1	0	0	0	1	2	0	0	144,908
Bristol	1	0	0	0	0	0	1	0	0	0	59,977
Cheshire	0	1	0	0	0	0	0	1	0	0	29,167
Danbury	3	0	0	0	0	0	1	1	1	0	85,167
Derby	1	0	0	0	0	0	0	0	1	0	12,468
East Hartford	1	1	1	0	0	0	0	1	1	1	49,842
East Lyme	1	0	0	0	0	0	0	0	0	1	18,588
Enfield	2	0	0	0	0	0	0	0	1	1	44,443
Farmington	1	0	0	0	0	0	1	0	0	0	25,525
Glastonbury	2	0	1	0	0	0	2	1	0	0	34,497
Madison	1	0	0	0	0	0	0	0	0	1	18,087
Manchester	4	0	1	0	0	0	1	1	2	1	57,630
Middletown	1	0	0	0	0	0	0	0	1	0	45,963
Milford	1	0	1	0	0	0		1	0	1	54,898
New Britain	2	1	0	0	0	0		1	1	1	72,354
New Haven	5	2	2	0	0	0	2	5	1	1	130,494
New London	1	0	0	0	0	0	0	1	0	0	26,856
New Milford	1	0	0	0	0	0	0	1	0	0	26,835
Norwalk	1	0	0	0	0	0	0	0	0	1	89,440
Norwich	0	0	1	0	0	0	0	0	1	0	38,964
Old Saybrook	2	0	0	0	0	0	0	0	2	0	10,069
Orange	1	0	0	0	0	0	0	0	1	0	13,948
Plainville	1	0	0	0	0	0	0	0	1	0	17,610
Plymouth	1	0	0	0	0	0	0	0	0	1	11,573
Ridgefield	1	0	0	0	0	0	0	0	0	1	25,050
Seymour	0	1	0	0	0	0	1	0	0	0	16,505
Stamford	3	3	2	0	0	0	0	1	3	4	130,678
Torrington	1	0	0	0	1	0	1	0	0	1	33,972
Wallingford	1	0	0	0	0	0	1	0	0	0	44,457
West Hartford	1	0	0	0	0	0	1	0	0	0	62,875
West Haven	1	0	0	0	0	0	0	0	1	0	54,794
Westport	0	1	0	0	0	0	0	0	1	0	28,332
Wethersfield	1	0	0	0	0	0	1	0	0	0	26,009
Willimantic	0	0	1	0	0	0	0	1	0	0	17,660
Wilton	1	0	0	0	0	0	1	0	0	0	18,439
Universities and Colleges	2	1	0	0	0	0					
Southern Connecticut State University	1	0	0	0	0	0	0	0	1	0	11,642
University of Connecticut, Storrs, Avery Point, and Hartford[3]	1	0	0	0	0	0	0	0	0	1	
Yale University	0	1	0	0	0	0				1	13,972
State Police Agencies	1	3	0	0	0	0					
Connecticut State Police	1	3	0	0	0	0	0	1	2	1	
DELAWARE											
Total	10	4	7	0	0	1					
Cities	4	2	3	0	0	1					
Bethany Beach	1	0	0	0	0	0	0	0	1	0	1,244
Dover	0	1	2	0	0	0	1	0	1	1	38,361
Milford	2	0	0	0	0	0	0	1	0	1	11,592
Seaford	1	1	0	0	0	0	1	0	1	0	7,987
Wilmington	0	0	1	0	0	1	0	2	0	0	70,624
Universities and Colleges	3	0	2	0	0	0					
Delaware State University	0	0	1	0	0	0	1	0	0	0	4,633
University of Delaware	3	0	1	0	0	0	1	1	1	1	25,534
Metropolitan Counties	1	1	1	0	0	0					
New Castle County Police Department	1	1	1	0	0	0	1	2	0	0	
State Police Agencies	2	1	1	0	0	0					
State Police											
New Castle County	2	1	0	0	0	0	1	0	1	1	
Sussex County	0	0	1	0	0	0	0	0	1	0	
DISTRICT OF COLUMBIA											
Total	119	8	65	1	2	27					
Cities	107	5	60	1	2	27					
Washington	107	5	60	1	2	27	53	57	55	37	705,749

Table 94. Hate Crime Incidents Per Bias Motivation and Quarter, by Selected State and Agency and Federal, 2019—Continued

(Number.)

State/agency	Number of incidents per bias motivation						Number of incidents per quarter				Population[1]
	Race/ Ethnicity/ Ancestry	Religion	Sexual orientation	Disability	Gender	Gender Identity	1st quarter	2nd quarter	3rd quarter	4th quarter	
Other Agencies	12	3	5	0	0	0					
Metro Transit Police	12	3	5	0	0	0	8	3	6	3	
FLORIDA											
Total	48	36	27	0	0	0					
Cities	32	32	19	0	0	0					
Bal Harbour Village	0	1	0	0	0	0	1				3,086
Boca Raton	1	1	0	0	0	0	0	0	1	1	101,163
Cape Coral	1	0	1	0	0	0	0	1	0	1	194,183
Davie	3	0	0	0	0	0	2	1	0	0	108,486
DeLand	1	0	0	0	0	0	1	0	0	0	34,468
Deerfield Beach	0	0	1	0	0	0	0	0	0	1	81,602
Fort Lauderdale	2	0	1	0	0	0	0	3	0	0	184,765
Fort Myers	1	0	0	0	0	0	1	0	0	0	85,127
Gainesville	2	1	1	0	0	0	1	1	1	1	135,085
Jacksonville	4	0	0	0	0	0	0	1	2	1	909,142
Largo	2	0	0	0	0	0	0	0	0	2	85,740
Miami	0	2	0	0	0	0	1	0	1	0	480,505
Miami Beach	0	16	4	0	0	0	8	4	4	4	92,185
Miami Gardens	0	1	0	0	0	0	0	1	0	0	113,786
Miami Shores	0	0	1	0	0	0	0	1	0	0	10,572
Miramar	0	0	2	0	0	0	2	0	0	0	143,334
New Port Richey	1	0	0	0	0	0	0	0	0	1	16,703
North Miami	1	0	0	0	0	0	1	0	0	0	63,547
North Miami Beach	2	1	0	0	0	0		1	1	1	46,307
North Port	1	0	0	0	0	0	1	0	0	0	70,181
Oakland Park	0	0	1	0	0	0	0	0	1	0	45,857
Ocala	1	0	1	0	0	0	0	0	0	2	60,932
Orlando	1	1	2	0	0	0	2	1	0	1	292,120
Palm Bay	0	0	1	0	0	0	0	0	0	1	115,520
Palm Beach Gardens	1	1	0	0	0	0	0	0	2	0	57,236
Pompano Beach	1	0	1	0	0	0	0	0	2	0	113,536
Port St. Lucie	1	1	1	0	0	0		1	1	1	199,433
Royal Palm Beach	1	0	0	0	0	0		1	0	0	40,802
Sarasota	1	0	0	0	0	0	0	0	0	1	58,470
St. Augustine	0	1	0	0	0	0	1	0	0	0	14,778
Sunny Isles Beach	0	0	1	0	0	0	0	1	0	0	22,476
Sunrise	0	1	0	0	0	0	1	0	0	0	96,919
Tampa	0	2	0	0	0	0	1	1	0	0	400,501
Temple Terrace	1	0	0	0	0	0	0	0	0	1	26,725
Titusville	0	1	0	0	0	0	0	0	0	0	46,866
Weston	0	1	0	0	0	0	0	0	0	1	71,946
Winter Garden	2	0	0	0	0	0	0	2	0	0	46,750
Metropolitan Counties	15	4	8	0	0	0					
Alachua	0	0	1	0	0	0	0	0	1	0	
Bay	1	0	0	0	0	0	1	0	0	0	
Lake	2	0	0	0	0	0	2	0	0	0	
Lee	5	0	0	0	0	0	1	0	2	2	
Miami-Dade	0	3	2	0	0	0	1	2	0	2	
Orange	1	1	1	0	0	0	0	2	0	1	
Osceola	1	0	1	0	0	0	1	0	1	0	
Pasco	1	0	1	0	0	0	1	1	0	0	
Santa Rosa	0	0	1	0	0	0	0	0	0	1	
Sarasota	1	0	0	0	0	0	0	0	0	1	
St. Johns	1	0	0	0	0	0	0	0	0	1	
Sumter	1	0	1	0	0	0	2	0	0	0	
Volusia	1	0	0	0	0	0	1	0	0	0	
Other Agencies	1	0	0	0	0	0					
Fort Lauderdale Airport	1	0	0	0	0	0	0	0	1	0	
GEORGIA											
Total	77	9	6	4	3	3					
Cities	48	5	3	1	1	1					
Albany	1	0	0	0	0	0	0	0	1	0	74,989
Atlanta	0	1	0	0	0	0	1	0	0		507,369
Brookhaven	1	0	1	0	0	0	0	0	0	2	54,734
Cartersville	1	0	0	0	0	0	1	0	0	0	21,322
College Park	1	0	0	0	0	0	0	0	0	1	15,278
Columbus	1	1	0	0	0	0	0	1	1		194,356
Douglasville	2	0	0	0	0	0	0	0	0	2	34,609
Dunwoody	3	0	1	0	0	0	2	1	0	1	49,868
Emerson	0	1	0	0	0	0	0	0	1	0	1,603
Fayetteville	0	0	0	0	1	0	0	0	0	1	18,041
Garden City	1	0	0	0	0	0	1	0	0	0	8,854
Glennville	0	0	1	0	0	0	0	0	0	1	5,084

Table 94. Hate Crime Incidents Per Bias Motivation and Quarter, by Selected State and Agency and Federal, 2019—Continued

(Number.)

State/agency	Number of incidents per bias motivation						Number of incidents per quarter				Population[1]
	Race/ Ethnicity/ Ancestry	Religion	Sexual orientation	Disability	Gender	Gender Identity	1st quarter	2nd quarter	3rd quarter	4th quarter	
Griffin	3	0	0	0	0	0	0	0	0	3	22,840
Johns Creek	2	0	0	0	0	0	0	0	0	2	85,258
Kennesaw	3	1	0	0	0	0	0	0	0	4	34,641
Lilburn	1	0	0	0	0	0	0	0	0	1	12,769
Manchester	2	0	0	0	0	0	0	1	1	0	3,958
Marietta	1	0	0	0	0	0	0	0	0	1	61,324
Milledgeville	4	0	0	0	0	0	0	0	0	4	18,655
Monroe	1	0	0	0	0	0	0	0	0	1	13,662
Newnan	1	0	0	0	0	0	0	0	0	1	40,720
Omega	0	0	0	0	0	1				1	1,222
Sandy Springs	4	1	0	1	0	0	0	1	1	4	110,760
Smyrna	2	0	0	0	0	0	0	0	0	2	57,423
Snellville	1	0	0	0	0	0	0	0	0	1	20,113
Sparta	4	0	0	0	0	0	0	0	0	4	1,209
Suwanee	1	0	0	0	0	0	0	1	0	0	21,331
Warner Robins	7	0	0	0	0	0	0	0	0	7	76,623
Universities and Colleges	4	0	0	0	0	0					
Fort Valley State University	4	0	0	0	0	0	0	0	0	4	3,044
Metropolitan Counties	19	3	3	1	1	2					
Cherokee	0	1	0	0	0	0	0	0	0	1	
Cobb County Police Department	11	1	2	0	0	0	3	4	2	5	
Coweta	0	0	1	0	0	0	0	0	1	0	
Douglas	1	0	0	0	0	1	0	0	0	2	
Fayette	1	0	0	0	0	0	0	0	0	1	
Forsyth	2	0	0	0	0	0	0	0	0	2	
Hall	1	0	0	1	0	0	0	1	1	0	
Haralson	1	0	0	0	0	0		0	0	1	
Lee	0	0	0	0	1	0	0	0	1	0	
Murray	0	1	0	0	0	0		0	0	1	
Newton	0	0	0	0	0	1	0	0	1	0	
Paulding	1	0	0	0	0	0	0	0	0	1	
Whitfield	1	0	0	0	0	0	0	0	1		
Nonmetropolitan Counties	4	0	0	1	1	0					
Banks	0	0	0	1	0	0	1	0	0		
Decatur	1	0	0	0	0	0	0	0	0	1	
Fannin	1	0	0	0	0	0	0	0	0	1	
Montgomery	1	0	0	0	0	0		0	1	0	
Pierce	1	0	0	0	1	0	2	0	0	0	
Other Agencies	2	1	0	1	0	0					
Atlanta Public Schools	1	0	0	0	0	0	0	0	0	1	
Fulton County School System	0	1	0	1	0	0	0	0	0	2	
Gwinnett County Public Schools	1	0	0	0	0	0	0	0	1	0	
HAWAII											
Total	30	2	9	0	0	0					
Cities	30	2	9	0	0	0					
Honolulu	30	2	9	0	0	0	15	7	12	7	974,902
IDAHO											
Total	18	1	4	1	0	0					
Cities	12	0	4	0	0	0					
Boise	6	0	2	0	0	0	3	2	1	2	231,314
Chubbuck	1	0	0	0	0	0	1	0	0	0	15,490
Coeur d'Alene	3	0	0	0	0	0	0	0	0	3	52,256
Jerome	1	0	0	0	0	0	1	0	0	0	11,921
Pocatello	0	0	1	0	0	0	0	1	0	0	56,514
Post Falls	1	0	1	0	0	0	1	0	1	0	35,649
Nonmetropolitan Counties	3	0	0	1	0	0					95,386
Bonneville	3	0	0	1	0	0	0	3	0	1	55,304
											49,908
Nonmetropolitan Counties	3	1	0	0	0	0					
Cassia	3	0	0	0	0	0	0	1	2	0	
Idaho	0	1	0	0	0	0	1	0	0	0	
ILLINOIS											
Total	34	9	17	0	0	6					
Cities	30	9	17	0	0	6					
Aurora	0	1	0	0	0	0	0	0	0	1	199,784
Bartonville	0	0	1	0	0	0	1	0	0	0	6,137
Bloomingdale	0	1	0	0	0	0	1	0		0	21,872
Bolingbrook	0	0	2	0	0	0	0	1		1	75,394

Table 94. Hate Crime Incidents Per Bias Motivation and Quarter, by Selected State and Agency and Federal, 2019—Continued

(Number.)

	Number of incidents per bias motivation						Number of incidents per quarter				
State/agency	Race/ Ethnicity/ Ancestry	Religion	Sexual orientation	Disability	Gender	Gender Identity	1st quarter	2nd quarter	3rd quarter	4th quarter	Population[1]
Chicago[2]	18	5	11	0	0	6	13	17	9	0	2,707,064
DeKalb	1	0	0	0	0	0	0	1	0	0	42,428
Elk Grove Village	1	0	0	0	0	0	0	1	0	0	32,371
Fairview Heights	1	0	0	0	0	0	0	0	0	1	16,368
Farmington	1	0	0	0	0	0	0	1	0	0	2,236
Galesburg	0	1	0	0	0	0	1	0	0	0	30,220
Genoa	0	1	0	0	0	0	0	1	0		5,211
Hoopeston	1	0	0	0	0	0	1	0	0	0	5,046
Joliet	0	0	1	0	0	0	1	0	0	0	148,155
Montgomery	1	0	0	0	0	0	0	0	1	0	19,927
Pingree Grove	1	0	0	0	0	0	0	0	1	0	9,765
Pontiac	1	0	0	0	0	0	1	0	0	0	11,211
Rockford	1	0	2	0	0	0	1	1	1	0	145,719
Springfield	1	0	0	0	0	0	0	0	0	1	114,393
Steger	1	0	0	0	0	0	0	1	0	0	9,301
Streamwood	1	0	0	0	0	0	0	0	1	0	39,529
Metropolitan Counties	4	0	0	0	0	0					
Lake	1	0	0	0	0	0	0			1	
Peoria	2	0	0	0	0	0	0	1	1	0	
Sangamon	1	0	0	0	0	0	0	1	0	0	
INDIANA											
Total	47	13	14	0	0	2					
Cities	43	11	10	0	0	2					
Bloomington	1	0	0	0	0	0	1	0	0	0	85,542
Columbus	2	0	1	0	0	0	0	1	0	2	47,991
Evansville	1	0	0	0	0	0		1			117,700
Fort Wayne	1	1	1	0	0	0	1	1	1	0	269,366
Frankfort	1	0	0	0	0	0		1			15,759
Hammond	5	0	1	0	0	0	2	1	3		75,201
Hobart	2	0	0	0	0	0	0	0	1	1	27,880
Indianapolis	13	5	3	0	0	1	5	3	8	6	883,699
Lafayette	6	2	2	0	0	0		4	4	2	72,585
Leavenworth	0	0	1	0	0	0		0		1	232
Linton	1	1	0	0	0	0		0	2		5,185
Plainfield[2]	3	0	1	0	0	0			2	1	35,317
Schererville	0	1	0	0	0	0		1	0	0	28,412
South Bend	4	1	0	0	0	1	2	1	2	1	101,944
Terre Haute	3	0	0	0	0	0	1	0	2	0	60,749
Universities and Colleges	0	1	1	0	0	0					
Butler University	0	0	1	0	0	0	1				5,306
University of Indianapolis[3]	0	1	0	0	0	0			1	0	
Metropolitan Counties	4	1	2	0	0	0					
La Porte	1	0	0	0	0	0	0	0	1	0	
Madison	1	0	0	0	0	0	0	0	0	1	
Porter	0	1	0	0	0	0	0	0	1	0	
St. Joseph	1	0	0	0	0	0	0	0	0	1	
Vigo	1	0	2	0	0	0	0	0	2	1	
State Police Agencies	0	0	1	0	0	0					
State Police, Greene County	0	0	1	0	0	0	0	0	1	0	
IOWA											
Total	6	0	4	0	0	0					
Cities	5	0	4	0	0	0					
Ames	0	0	2	0	0	0	0	1	1	0	68,237
Clive	0	0	1	0	0	0	0	0	0	1	17,305
Davenport	1	0	0	0	0	0	0	0	0	1	102,392
Dubuque	1	0	0	0	0	0	0	0	1	0	57,973
Iowa City	2	0	0	0	0	0	0	2	0	0	77,390
Sioux City	0	0	1	0	0	0	1	0	0	0	82,339
Waterloo	1	0	0	0	0	0	0	0	1	0	67,723
Universities and Colleges	1	0	0	0	0	0					
Iowa State University	1	0	0	0	0	0	0	0	0	1	39,108
Metropolitan Counties	1	1	0	0	0	0					
Dubuque	1	1	0	0	0	0	1	0	1	0	
KANSAS											
Total	38	27	7	3	1	2					
Cities	32	12	5	3	0	2					
Atchison	1	0	0	0	0	0	0	1	0	0	10,509

Table 94. Hate Crime Incidents Per Bias Motivation and Quarter, by Selected State and Agency and Federal, 2019—Continued

(Number.)

	Number of incidents per bias motivation						Number of incidents per quarter				
State/agency	Race/ Ethnicity/ Ancestry	Religion	Sexual orientation	Disability	Gender	Gender Identity	1st quarter	2nd quarter	3rd quarter	4th quarter	Population[1]
Basehor	0	1	0	0	0	0	0	0	0	1	6,418
Bel Aire	0	1	0	0	0	0	1	0	0	0	8,252
Bonner Springs	1	0	0	0	0	0	0	1	0	0	7,850
Cherryvale	0	1	0	0	0	0	0	1	0	0	2,127
Clay Center	0	0	0	1	0	0	0	0	1	0	3,946
Coffeyville	0	1	0	0	0	0	0	0	0	1	9,260
Columbus	1	0	0	0	0	0	0	0	0	1	3,042
Concordia	1	0	1	0	0	0	0	0	0	2	4,904
Dodge City	2	0	0	0	0	0	0	1	0	1	27,314
El Dorado	1	0	0	0	0	0	0	0	1	0	12,899
Garden City	1	0	1	0	0	0	2	0	0	0	26,509
Gardner	1	0	0	0	0	0	0	0	1	0	22,229
Garnett	1	0	0	0	0	0	0	0	0	1	3,244
Goodland	0	1	0	0	0	0	1	0	0	0	4,374
Hays	1	0	0	0	0	0	0	0	1	0	20,894
Haysville	0	1	0	0	0	0	1	0	0	0	11,319
Hiawatha	1	1	0	0	0	0	0	1	1	0	3,119
Hillsboro	1	0	0	1	0	0	2	0	0	0	2,814
Hoisington	1	0	0	0	0	0	0	1	0	0	2,486
Hutchinson	2	0	0	0	0	0	1	0	1	0	40,431
Independence	0	0	1	0	0	0	0	0	1	0	8,497
Larned	1	0	0	0	0	0	0	1	0	0	3,739
Leavenworth	2	0	0	0	0	0	0	0	2	0	36,149
Leawood	0	0	0	1	0	0	1	0	0	0	35,052
Lindsborg	0	1	0	0	0	0	0	1	0	0	3,269
Maize	0	1	0	0	0	0	1	0	0	0	4,836
Paola	1	0	0	0	0	0	0	1	0	0	5,676
Salina	6	0	0	0	0	2	1	6	0	1	46,567
Shawnee	2	0	0	0	0	0	0	1	1	0	66,300
Tonganoxie	1	1	0	0	0	0	1	0	0	1	5,591
Topeka	1	0	0	0	0	0	1	0	0	0	125,655
Valley Center	0	1	0	0	0	0	0	0	1	0	7,376
Wichita	2	0	2	0	0	0	1	0	2	1	390,080
Winfield	0	1	0	0	0	0	0	0	0	1	12,023
Universities and Colleges	2	0	0	0	0	0					
University of Kansas											
Main Campus	1	0	0	0	0	0	1	0	0	0	31,136
Medical Center[3]	1	0	0	0	0	0	1	0	0	0	
Metropolitan Counties	1	6	1	0	1	0					
Doniphan	0	1	0	0	0	0	0	0	1	0	
Jefferson	0	2	0	0	1	0	0	2	1	0	
Johnson	1	0	0	0	0	0	0	1	0	0	
Pottawatomie	0	1	0	0	0	0	0	1	0	0	
Riley County Police Department	0	0	1	0	0	0	0	0	1	0	
Sedgwick	0	2	0	0	0	0	0	2	0	0	
Nonmetropolitan Counties	2	7	1	0	0	0					
Barton	0	1	0	0	0	0	0	1	0	0	
Edwards	0	1	0	0	0	0	1	0	0	0	
Labette	0	3	0	0	0	0	1	1	0	1	
McPherson	0	1	0	0	0	0	1	0	0	0	
Nemaha	0	1	1	0	0	0	0	1	1	0	
Saline	1	0	0	0	0	0	0	0	0	1	
Thomas	1	0	0	0	0	0	0	1	0	0	
State Police Agencies	1	1	0	0	0	0					
Highway Patrol											
Troop B	1	0	0	0	0	0	1	0	0	0	
Troop C	0	1	0	0	0	0	0	1	0	0	
Other Agencies	0	1	0	0	0	0					
Kansas Department of Wildlife and Parks	0	1	0	0	0	0	1	0	0	0	
KENTUCKY											
Total	114	12	19	1	2	4					
Cities	78	7	10	1	1	3					
Ashland	3	0	0	0	0	0	2	1	0	0	20,222
Audubon Park	1	0	0	0	0	0	0	1	0	0	1,504
Berea	2	0	0	0	0	0	1	1	0	0	16,074
Bowling Green	3	0	1	0	0	0	0	2	0	2	69,627
Campbellsville	2	0	0	0	0	0	0	0	1	1	11,488
Covington	8	0	0	0	0	0	6	0	0	2	40,350
Edgewood	1	0	0	0	0	0	0	0	0	1	8,749
Erlanger	1	0	0	0	0	0	1	0	0	0	23,116
Florence	2	0	0	1	0	0	1	1	0	1	32,848
Frankfort	3	0	0	0	0	0	2	0	1	0	27,723
Georgetown	3	0	0	0	0	0	2	1	0	0	35,106

Table 94. Hate Crime Incidents Per Bias Motivation and Quarter, by Selected State and Agency and Federal, 2019—Continued

(Number.)

State/agency	Number of incidents per bias motivation						Number of incidents per quarter				Population[1]
	Race/ Ethnicity/ Ancestry	Religion	Sexual orientation	Disability	Gender	Gender Identity	1st quarter	2nd quarter	3rd quarter	4th quarter	
Glasgow	1	0	0	0	0	0	1	0	0	0	14,475
Hodgenville	1	0	0	0	0	0	1	0	0	0	3,239
Hopkinsville	2	0	0	0	0	0	1	1	0	0	30,895
Jeffersontown	1	0	1	0	0	0	1	1	0	0	28,015
La Grange	1	0	0	0	0	0	1	0	0	0	9,080
Leitchfield	1	0	1	0	0	0	2	0	0	0	6,852
Lexington[2]	15	1	2	0	0	0	4	5	5	3	326,070
Louisville Metro	4	4	2	0	0	1	2	3	2	4	675,501
Mayfield	1	0	0	0	0	0	0	0	1	0	9,851
Maysville	2	0	0	0	0	0	0	2	0	0	8,750
Morehead	1	0	0	0	0	0	0	0	0	1	7,736
Newport	1	0	1	0	0	0	1	0	0	1	14,965
Nicholasville	1	0	0	0	0	0	1	0	0	0	31,188
Owensboro	5	0	0	0	0	0	0	0	4	1	60,107
Paducah	3	2	1	0	0	0	1	2	2	1	24,832
Radcliff	2	0	0	0	0	0	0	0	2	0	22,998
Richmond	1	0	0	0	0	0	1	0	0	0	36,458
Russell Springs	1	0	0	0	0	0	0	1	0	0	2,632
Shively	2	0	0	0	0	0	0	1	1	0	15,845
Simpsonville	0	0	1	0	0	0	1	0	0	0	2,945
Stanton	1	0	0	0	0	0	0	1	0	0	2,651
St. Matthews	0	0	0	0	1	0	0	0	0	1	18,275
Versailles	1	0	0	0	0	1	1	0	0	1	26,625
West Buechel	1	0	0	0	0	0	1	0	0	0	1,285
Winchester	0	0	0	0	0	1	0	1	0	0	18,605
Universities and Colleges	3	0	1	0	0	0					
University of Kentucky	1	0	0	0	0	0	1	0	0	0	31,102
University of Louisville	1	0	1	0	0	0	1	0	0	1	24,828
Western Kentucky University	1	0	0	0	0	0	0	0	0	1	24,560
Metropolitan Counties	9	2	5	0	1	0					
Boone[2]	4	1	3	0	1	0	1	2	3	1	
Bourbon	0	0	1	0	0	0	0	0	1	0	
Campbell County Police Department	1	0	0	0	0	0	0	0	1	0	
Christian	1	0	0	0	0	0	1	0	0	0	
Daviess	1	0	0	0	0	0	0	1	0	0	
Grant	1	0	0	0	0	0	1	0	0	0	
Hardin	1	0	0	0	0	0	0	1	0	0	
Warren	0	1	1	0	0	0	1	0	1	0	
Nonmetropolitan Counties	13	1	2	0	0	0					
Boyle	2	0	0	0	0	0	2	0	0	0	
Franklin	1	0	0	0	0	0	1	0	0	0	
Fulton	0	0	1	0	0	0	0	0	0	1	
Harrison	1	0	0	0	0	0	0	1	0	0	
Hopkins	2	0	0	0	0	0	1	0	0	1	
Knox[2]	1	1	0	0	0	0	0	0	1	1	
Logan	0	0	1	0	0	0	1	0	0	0	
Madison	1	0	0	0	0	0	0	0	0	1	
Marshall	1	0	0	0	0	0	1	0	0	0	
McCracken	2	0	0	0	0	0	0	0	1	1	
Pulaski	1	0	0	0	0	0	1	0	0	0	
Todd	1	0	0	0	0	0	0	0	0	1	
State Police Agencies	6	2	1	0	0	0					
State Police											
Bowling Green	2	0	0	0	0	0	1	0	1	0	
Elizabethtown[2]	2	2	0	0	0	0	0	0	1	2	
Mayfield[2]	1	0	1	0	0	0	0	1	0	0	
Richmond	1	0	0	0	0	0	0	1	0	0	
Other Agencies	5	0	0	0	0	1					
Fayette County Schools	1	0	0	0	0	0	0	1	0	0	
Greater Hardin County Narcotics Task Force	1	0	0	0	0	0	1	0	0	0	
Jefferson County School District	2	0	0	0	0	1	0	1	1	1	
Metcalfe County Schools	1	0	0	0	0	0	0	0	0	1	
LOUISIANA											
Total	9	8	7	2	0	0					
Cities	3	3	4	1	0	0					
Baton Rouge	0	0	1	0	0	0	0	1	0	0	220,648
New Orleans	2	0	3	0	0	0	2	1	1	1	394,498
Thibodaux	1	1	0	1	0	0	0	1	1	1	14,587
West Monroe	0	2	0	0	0	0	1	0	1	0	12,350
Metropolitan Counties	4	4	3	1	0	0					
Ascension	0	1	0	0	0	0	0	0	1	0	
Bossier	1	0	1	1	0	0	1	2	0	0	

Table 94. Hate Crime Incidents Per Bias Motivation and Quarter, by Selected State and Agency and Federal, 2019—Continued

(Number.)

State/agency	Number of incidents per bias motivation						Number of incidents per quarter				Population[1]
	Race/ Ethnicity/ Ancestry	Religion	Sexual orientation	Disability	Gender	Gender Identity	1st quarter	2nd quarter	3rd quarter	4th quarter	
Calcasieu	2	2	2	0	0	0	1	1	2	2	
Lafourche	0	1	0	0	0	0	0	0	1	0	
St. James	1	0	0	0	0	0	0	0	0	1	
Nonmetropolitan Counties	2	1	0	0	0	0					
Evangeline	0	1	0	0	0	0	0	1	0	0	
Madison	2	0	0	0	0	0	2	0	0	0	
MAINE											
Total	10	2	7	0	0	0					
Cities	8	2	7	0	0	0					
Augusta	0	1	1	0	0	0	0	1	0	1	18,629
Biddeford	0	0	1	0	0	0	0	0	1	0	21,545
Lewiston	2	0	0	0	0	0	0	0	0	2	35,865
Portland	4	0	1	0	0	0	1	1	2	1	66,458
Rockland	1	0	0	0	0	0	0	0	1	0	7,128
Saco	1	0	3	0	0	0	1	2	1	0	19,908
Sanford	0	0	1	0	0	0	0	1	0	0	21,233
South Portland	0	1	0	0	0	0	0	0	0	1	25,686
Nonmetropolitan Counties	1	0	0	0	0	0					
Franklin	1	0	0	0	0	0	0	0	0	1	
State Police Agencies	1	0	0	0	0	0					
Maine State Police	1	0	0	0	0	0	1	0	0	0	
MARYLAND											
Total	7	4	7	1	0	0					
Cities	1	0	1	0	0	0					
Takoma Park	0	0	1	0	0	0	0	0	1	0	17,893
Westminster	1	0	0	0	0	0	1	0	0	0	18,664
Universities and Colleges	1	0	0	1	0	0					
University of Maryland											
Baltimore County	0	0	0	1	0	0	1	0	0	0	15,681
College Park	1	0	0	0	0	0	0	0	1	0	44,052
Metropolitan Counties	4	4	6	0	0	0					
Carroll	1	0	0	0	0	0	1	0	0	0	
Harford	1	0	0	0	0	0	0	0	1	0	
Montgomery County Police Department	0	3	1	0	0	0	2	2	0	0	
Prince George's County Police Department[2]	2	1	5	0	0	0	1	0	2	4	
Other Agencies	1	0	0	0	0	0					
Natural Resources Police	1	0	0	0	0	0	1	0	0	0	
MASSACHUSETTS											
Total	213	101	92	1	2	7					
Cities	202	88	86	1	2	7					
Acton	4	2	0	0	0	0	2	1	2	1	23,780
Amherst	0	0	0	0	1	0	0	1	0	0	39,603
Andover	0	2	0	0	0	0	0	0	1	1	36,547
Arlington[2]	3	3	2	0	0	1	1	3	1	2	45,614
Ashburnham	0	0	1	0	0	0	0	1	0	0	6,330
Attleboro	0	0	1	0	0	0	0	1	0	0	44,959
Barnstable[2]	3	3	0	0	0	0	2	0	3	0	44,032
Belmont	1	0	0	0	0	0	0	0	0	1	26,331
Boston[2]	113	26	47	0	1	1	39	57	39	42	698,941
Braintree	1	1	0	0	0	0	0	0	2	0	37,145
Brewster	0	0	1	0	0	0	0	0	1	0	9,725
Brockton	2	0	0	0	0	0	2	0	0	0	95,287
Brookline	4	2	0	0	0	0	1	1	1	3	58,928
Cambridge[2]	9	6	3	0	0	2	4	4	5	5	119,908
Chilmark	1	0	0	0	0	0	0	1	0	0	920
Concord	1	0	0	0	0	0	1	0	0	0	19,253
Danvers[2]	2	2	0	0	0	0	0	1	0	2	27,664
Dracut	1	0	0	0	0	0	0	0	1	0	31,786
Easthampton	0	0	1	0	0	0	0	1	0	0	15,979
Edgartown	1	0	0	0	0	0	0	0	1	0	4,362
Everett	1	0	0	0	0	0	0	0	1	0	47,195
Fall River	0	1	0	0	0	0	1	0	0	1	89,066
Framingham	0	1	0	0	0	0	0	1	0	0	73,127
Gloucester	1	0	0	0	0	0	0	0	1	0	30,362
Greenfield	1	1	1	0	0	0	1	1	1	0	17,464
Hamilton[2]	1	1	0	0	0	0	0	0	1	0	8,075
Haverhill[2]	4	2	1	0	0	0	0	3	2	1	63,935

Table 94. Hate Crime Incidents Per Bias Motivation and Quarter, by Selected State and Agency and Federal, 2019—Continued

(Number.)

State/agency	Number of incidents per bias motivation						Number of incidents per quarter				Population[1]
	Race/ Ethnicity/ Ancestry	Religion	Sexual orientation	Disability	Gender	Gender Identity	1st quarter	2nd quarter	3rd quarter	4th quarter	
Hingham	1	0	0	0	0	0	0	1	0	0	23,960
Hull[2]	1	1	0	0	0	0	0	0	1	0	10,402
Kingston	0	1	0	0	0	0	0	0	1	0	13,758
Leominster	1	0	0	0	0	0	0	0	0	1	41,631
Lynn	2	4	1	0	0	0	0	2	5	0	94,449
Malden	2	1	0	0	0	0	0	1	0	2	60,746
Manchester-by-the-Sea	0	3	0	0	0	0	3	0	0	0	5,423
Medford	1	3	0	0	0	0	0	1	1	2	57,484
Medway	0	1	0	0	0	0	1	0	0	0	13,405
Methuen	0	1	0	0	0	0	0	1	0	0	50,727
Milton	1	0	1	0	0	0	1	1	0	0	27,471
Montague	0	1	0	0	0	0	0	0	0	1	8,298
Natick	1	0	1	0	0	0	1	0	1	0	36,358
Needham	0	1	0	0	0	0	0	1	0	0	31,275
Newburyport	1	0	1	0	0	0	0	2	0	0	18,158
Newton[2]	2	1	2	0	0	1	3	0	0	2	88,658
North Andover	0	1	0	0	0	0	0	1	0	0	31,428
Northampton	1	0	2	0	0	0	0	2	0	1	28,735
Oak Bluffs	2	0	0	0	0	0	1	0	1	0	4,681
Pepperell	0	1	0	0	0	0	0	1	0	0	12,146
Pittsfield	0	0	1	0	0	0	0	0	1	0	42,268
Provincetown	4	0	1	0	0	0	1	2	1	1	2,939
Quincy	3	2	2	0	0	0	2	2	2	1	94,113
Randolph	1	0	0	0	0	0	0	0	0	1	34,385
Revere	1	0	0	0	0	0	0	0	0	1	53,654
Salem[2]	1	3	5	0	0	1	1	4	1	2	43,443
Sharon	0	1	0	0	0	0	0	1	0	0	18,973
Somerville	3	2	0	0	0	0	1	1	1	2	81,668
Spencer	1	1	0	0	0	0	0	0	2	0	11,911
Springfield[2]	7	0	1	1	0	0	1	2	2	3	154,306
Sturbridge	1	0	0	0	0	0	0	1	0	0	9,611
Sunderland[2]	1	1	0	0	0	0	0	0	1	0	3,656
Swampscott	1	1	1	0	0	0	1	0	1	1	15,296
Tewksbury	0	0	1	0	0	0	0	1	0	0	31,424
Tisbury	0	0	1	0	0	0	0	1	0	0	4,116
Waltham	2	0	0	0	0	0	0	1	1	0	62,737
Webster[2]	0	0	1	0	0	1	0	0	1	0	16,925
Wilbraham[2]	1	1	0	0	0	0	0	0	1	0	14,730
Winchester	1	0	2	0	0	0	1	0	0	2	22,850
Winthrop	0	1	0	0	0	0	0	1	0	0	18,692
Worcester	4	2	4	0	0	0	1	5	1	3	184,945
Universities and Colleges	10	13	5	0	0	0					
Boston University	1	0	1	0	0	0	0	0	0	2	41,418
Fitchburg State University	0	0	1	0	0	0	0	0	0	1	11,496
Framingham State University	1	0	0	0	0	0	1		0	0	9,007
Harvard University	2	1	0	0	0	0	0	0	3	0	40,803
Massachusetts College of Liberal Arts	0	1	0	0	0	0	0	1	0	0	2,157
Massasoit Community College	0	1	0	0	0	0	0	1	0	0	10,323
Northeastern University	3	1	0	0	0	0	3	0	0	1	27,795
Salem State University	0	0	1	0	0	0	1	0	0	0	10,556
Smith College	0	1	0	0	0	0	0	0	0	1	3,259
Tufts University, Medford	0	1	1	0	0	0	0	0	1	1	12,492
Westfield State University	1	0	0	0	0	0	0	0	1	0	7,598
Wheaton College	1	6	1	0	0	0	1	0	0	7	1,715
Worcester Polytechnic Institute[2]	1	1	0	0	0	0	0	0	1	0	7,338
Other Agencies	1	0	1	0	0	0					
Massachusetts Bay Transportation Authority											
Middlesex County	0	0	1	0	0	0	1				
Norfolk County	1	0	0	0	0	0	1				
MICHIGAN											
Total	313	51	44	9	15	2					
Cities	208	33	35	9	12	0					
Adrian	2	0	0	0	0	0	0	0	1	1	20,334
Albion	2	0	0	1	0	0	1	1	0	1	8,462
Allen Park	1	0	0	0	0	0	1	0	0	0	26,945
Almont	1	0	0	0	0	0	0	0	0	1	2,814
Ann Arbor	3	0	0	0	0	0	0	0	3	0	122,893
Auburn Hills	1	0	0	0	0	0	0	0	0	1	24,393
Baroda-Lake Township	0	1	0	0	0	0	1	0	0	0	3,859
Bay City	0	1	0	0	0	0	0	1	0	0	32,793
Benton Harbor	0	1	0	0	0	0	0	0	0	1	9,801
Benton Township	1	0	0	0	0	0	0	1	0	0	14,372
Berkley	1	0	0	0	0	0	0	1	0	0	15,482
Bloomfield Township	1	0	0	0	0	0	0	1	0	0	42,326
Bridgeport Township	1	0	0	0	0	0	0	0	0	1	9,778

Table 94. Hate Crime Incidents Per Bias Motivation and Quarter, by Selected State and Agency and Federal, 2019—Continued

(Number.)

State/agency	Number of incidents per bias motivation						Number of incidents per quarter				Population[1]
	Race/ Ethnicity/ Ancestry	Religion	Sexual orientation	Disability	Gender	Gender Identity	1st quarter	2nd quarter	3rd quarter	4th quarter	
Buchanan	0	0	0	1	1	0	0	0	1	1	4,274
Burton	5	0	0	0	0	0	0	1	3	1	28,496
Cadillac	3	0	0	0	0	0	0	2	0	1	10,466
Cambridge Township	1	0	0	0	0	0	0	0	0	1	5,657
Canton Township	4	1	0	0	0	0	2	2	0	1	93,406
Capac	1	0	1	0	0	0	0	0	0	2	1,822
Caro	1	0	0	0	0	0	1	0	0	0	3,969
Carrollton Township	0	0	1	0	0	0	1	0	0	0	5,626
Cassopolis	2	0	0	0	1	0	0	0	3	0	1,695
Clinton Township	1	1	0	0	0	0	0	0	1	1	101,308
Coloma Township	1	0	0	0	0	0	0	1	0	0	6,362
Crystal Falls	4	0	0	0	0	0	1	3	0	0	1,359
Dearborn	1	3	0	0	0	0	2	0	1	1	93,902
Dearborn Heights	2	1	0	0	0	0	0	1	2	0	55,368
Detroit	30	1	18	2	1	0	8	16	16	12	663,502
DeWitt Township	1	0	0	0	0	0	1	0	0	0	15,613
East Grand Rapids	2	0	0	0	0	0	0	2	0	0	12,040
East Lansing	0	2	0	0	0	0	0	2	0	0	47,913
Eastpointe	0	0	1	0	0	0	0	0	0	1	32,340
Ecorse	1	0	0	0	0	0	0	1	0	0	9,601
Escanaba	1	0	0	0	0	0	0	1	0	0	12,129
Farmington	0	2	0	0	0	0	1	1	0	0	10,587
Ferndale	1	0	1	0	0	0	0	2	0	0	20,097
Flint	2	0	0	0	0	0	0	2	0	0	95,212
Flushing	1	0	0	0	0	0	0	1	0	0	7,860
Fowlerville	0	0	0	0	3	0	1	1	0	1	2,869
Frankenmuth	2	0	0	0	0	0	0	1	0	1	5,458
Fraser	2	0	0	0	0	0	1	0	0	1	14,578
Fremont	1	0	0	0	0	0	0	1	0	0	4,103
Garden City	2	0	0	0	0	0	0	0	1	1	26,420
Genesee Township	1	0	0	0	0	0	0	0	1	0	20,410
Grand Blanc Township	1	0	0	0	0	0	0	0	0	1	36,523
Grand Haven	1	2	0	0	0	0	0	2	1	0	11,155
Grand Rapids	5	0	0	0	0	0	0	0	2	3	201,799
Grandville	3	0	0	1	0	0	0	0	2	2	16,021
Grosse Pointe Park	1	0	0	0	0	0	0	0	0	1	11,041
Grosse Pointe Woods	1	0	0	0	0	0	1	0	0	0	15,350
Hartford	1	0	0	0	0	0	0	0	0	1	2,589
Hazel Park	0	1	0	0	0	0	0	0	1	0	16,478
Highland Park	11	0	1	0	4	0	1	10	4	1	10,703
Holly	1	0	0	0	0	0	0	1	0	0	6,185
Huron Township	2	0	0	0	0	0	0	0	2	0	16,089
Imlay City	1	0	0	0	0	0	1	0	0	0	3,575
Inkster	1	0	0	0	0	0	1	0	0	0	24,268
Jackson	0	0	1	0	0	0	0	0	1	0	32,503
Jonesville	0	0	0	1	0	0	0	0	1	0	2,204
Kalamazoo	3	0	0	0	0	0	1	0	2	0	76,827
Lansing	4	0	1	0	0	0	1	1	2	1	118,953
Lincoln Park	1	0	0	0	0	0	0	1	0	0	36,336
Lincoln Township	0	1	0	0	0	0	0	0	0	1	14,615
Livonia	2	0	0	0	0	0	0	0	1	1	93,644
Lowell	1	0	0	0	0	0	0	1	0	0	4,198
Madison Heights	2	1	0	0	0	0	0	2	0	1	30,081
Manistee	0	1	0	0	0	0	0	0	0	1	6,103
Marquette	0	3	0	0	0	0	0	0	1	2	20,599
Melvindale	2	0	0	0	0	0	1	0	0	1	10,264
Menominee	1	0	0	0	0	0	0	0	1	0	8,052
Meridian Township	3	0	0	0	0	0	0	0	1	2	43,790
Metro Police Authority of Genesee County	1	0	0	0	0	0	0	1	0	0	19,931
Midland	2	0	0	0	0	0	1	0	0	1	41,791
Milford	1	0	1	0	0	0	0	1	1	0	16,984
Morenci	1	0	0	0	0	0	1	0	0	0	2,146
Mount Pleasant	1	0	1	0	0	0	0	1	1	0	25,315
Muskegon Heights	0	0	1	0	0	0	0	1	0	0	10,717
Muskegon Township	1	0	0	0	0	0	0	0	1	0	17,937
Newaygo	1	0	0	0	0	0	0	0	0	1	2,068
Northville Township	2	0	0	0	0	0	0	0	0	2	29,170
Norton Shores	1	0	0	0	0	0	0	0	1	0	24,702
Ontwa Township-Edwardsburg	1	0	0	0	0	0	0	1	0	0	6,553
Orion Township	1	0	0	0	0	0	0	0	0	1	36,878
Owosso	0	1	0	0	0	0	1	0	0	0	14,399
Pittsfield Township	1	0	0	0	0	0	2	0	0	0	39,417
Pontiac	1	0	0	0	0	0	0	0	1	0	59,791
Port Huron	1	0	0	0	0	0	0	0	1	0	28,783
Portage	1	0	0	0	0	0	0	0	1	0	49,583
Redford Township	1	0	0	0	0	0	0	0	1	0	46,742
Rochester	0	0	1	0	0	0	0	0	0	1	13,429
Romeo	1	0	0	0	0	0	0	0	1	0	3,608
Romulus	1	0	0	0	0	0	0	0	0	1	23,507

Table 94. Hate Crime Incidents Per Bias Motivation and Quarter, by Selected State and Agency and Federal, 2019—Continued

(Number.)

State/agency	Number of incidents per bias motivation						Number of incidents per quarter				Population[1]
	Race/ Ethnicity/ Ancestry	Religion	Sexual orientation	Disability	Gender	Gender Identity	1st quarter	2nd quarter	3rd quarter	4th quarter	
Roseville	2	0	1	0	0	0	0	1	2	0	47,381
Royal Oak	1	1	0	0	0	0	1	0	0	1	59,742
Saginaw Township	1	0	0	0	0	0	0	0	1	0	39,022
Saline	2	0	0	0	0	0	1	0	1	0	9,431
Shelby Township	1	0	0	0	0	0	1	0	0	0	80,806
South Haven	2	0	1	0	1	0	1	0	3	0	4,326
Southfield	2	1	1	0	0	0	1	1	0	2	73,335
Southgate	1	0	0	0	0	0	0	1	0	0	28,979
St. Johns	0	0	1	0	0	0	0	1	0	0	7,938
St. Joseph	0	0	1	1	0	0	0	0	1	1	8,355
Sterling Heights	2	0	0	0	0	0	0	0	0	2	133,377
Sylvan Lake	2	0	0	0	0	0	0	2	0	0	1,864
Taylor	1	1	0	0	0	0	0	1	1	0	60,923
Tecumseh	2	0	0	0	0	0	2	0	0	0	8,382
Thomas Township	1	0	0	0	0	0	1	0	0	0	11,438
Three Oaks	0	0	0	1	0	0	0	0	1	0	1,549
Tittabawassee Township	1	0	0	0	0	0	0	1	0	0	9,863
Traverse City	2	1	0	0	0	0	0	0	0	3	15,772
Troy	2	0	0	0	0	0	0	0	1	1	84,688
Utica	0	1	0	0	1	0	0	1	1	0	5,195
Van Buren Township	4	0	0	0	0	0	1	1	1	1	28,294
Warren	5	0	1	0	0	0	1	2	2	1	134,653
Waterford Township	3	1	0	0	0	0	1	0	1	2	73,105
West Bloomfield Township	5	2	0	0	0	0	0	2	2	3	66,067
White Lake Township	1	0	0	0	0	0	0	0	1	0	31,556
Wixom	1	0	0	0	0	0	0	0	1	0	14,074
Wyoming	7	0	0	1	0	0	1	2	3	2	76,295
Ypsilanti	2	0	0	0	0	0	0	0	1	1	21,178
Universities and Colleges	7	1	3	0	0	2					
Eastern Michigan University	0	0	1	0	0	1	1	1	0	0	23,715
Oakland University	0	0	0	0	0	1	0	0	1	0	22,694
University of Michigan											
Ann Arbor	6	1	1	0	0	0	2	1	3	2	47,543
Flint	0	0	1	0	0	0	0	0	1	0	9,138
Washtenaw Community College	1	0	0	0	0	0	0	1	0	0	21,041
Metropolitan Counties	30	5	2	0	1	0					
Bay	1	0	0	0	0	0	0	0	1	0	
Berrien	0	2	0	0	0	0	0	0	0	2	
Calhoun	1	0	0	0	0	0	0	0	0	1	
Eaton	3	0	0	0	0	0	1	2	0	0	
Genesee	3	1	0	0	0	0	0	3	0	1	
Ingham	1	0	0	0	0	0	0	0	1	0	
Ionia	6	0	0	0	0	0	1	1	2	2	
Jackson	0	0	1	0	0	0	0	0	1	0	
Kalamazoo	4	0	0	0	0	0	0	1	2	1	
Kent	1	0	0	0	0	0	0	0	0	1	
Lapeer	1	0	0	0	0	0	0	0	0	1	
Livingston	2	0	0	0	0	0	1	0	1	0	
Ottawa	2	1	1	0	0	0	1	2	0	1	
Saginaw	2	0	0	0	1	0	2	0	0	1	
Washtenaw	3	1	0	0	0	0	2	1	0	1	
Nonmetropolitan Counties	17	3	2	0	1	0					
Alcona	1	0	0	0	0	0	0	1	0	0	
Alpena	1	0	0	0	0	0	1	0	0	0	
Baraga	0	1	0	0	0	0	0	0	1	0	
Barry	1	0	1	0	0	0	1	0	0	1	
Benzie	2	0	0	0	0	0	1	0	1	0	
Hillsdale	1	0	0	0	0	0	0	1	0	0	
Isabella	0	0	1	0	0	0	0	0	0	1	
Leelanau	1	0	0	0	0	0	0	0	1	0	
Luce	1	0	0	0	0	0	0	0	1	0	
Mackinac	1	0	0	0	0	0	0	1	0	0	
Mason	2	0	0	0	0	0	0	2	0	0	
Oceana	0	1	0	0	0	0	0	0	1	0	
Ontonagon	0	0	0	0	1	0	0	0	1	0	
Van Buren	3	1	0	0	0	0	0	0	3	1	
Wexford	3	0	0	0	0	0	0	1	1	1	
State Police Agencies	50	9	2	0	1	0					
State Police											
Alger County	0	1	0	0	0	0	0	0	1	0	
Allegan County	1	0	0	0	0	0	0	0	1	0	
Alpena County	4	1	0	0	0	0	0	2	0	3	
Calhoun County	1	0	0	0	0	0	0	1	0	0	
Cass County	1	0	0	0	0	0	0	1	0	0	
Chippewa County	1	0	0	0	0	0	0	0	0	1	

Table 94. Hate Crime Incidents Per Bias Motivation and Quarter, by Selected State and Agency and Federal, 2019—Continued

(Number.)

State/agency	Number of incidents per bias motivation						Number of incidents per quarter				Population[1]
	Race/ Ethnicity/ Ancestry	Religion	Sexual orientation	Disability	Gender	Gender Identity	1st quarter	2nd quarter	3rd quarter	4th quarter	
Grand Traverse County	2	0	0	0	0	0	1	1	0	0	
Gratiot County	1	0	0	0	0	0	0	1	0	0	
Hillsdale County	2	0	0	0	0	0	1	0	1	0	
Houghton County	4	2	0	0	0	0	0	1	3	2	
Ingham County	2	1	0	0	0	0	0	3	0	0	
Ionia County	1	0	0	0	0	0	1	0	0	0	
Iosco County	0	1	0	0	0	0	0	0	0	1	
Jackson County	1	1	0	0	0	0	0	1	1	0	
Kalamazoo County	1	0	0	0	0	0	0	0	1	0	
Kent County	0	1	0	0	0	0	0	0	1	0	
Lapeer County	1	0	0	0	0	0	0	0	1	0	
Livingston County	3	0	0	0	0	0	0	1	1	1	
Mackinac County	1	0	0	0	0	0	1	0	0	0	
Manistee County	1	0	0	0	0	0	0	1	0	0	
Mecosta County	2	0	0	0	0	0	1	0	1	0	
Montcalm County	2	0	0	0	0	0	0	1	1	0	
Muskegon County	1	0	0	0	0	0	0	1	0	0	
Oakland County	3	1	0	0	0	0	0	2	2	0	
Oceana County	2	0	0	0	0	0	1	1	0	0	
Ogemaw County	0	0	1	0	0	0	0	1	0	0	
Ontonagon County	1	0	0	0	0	0	0	0	1	0	
Sanilac County	1	0	0	0	0	0	0	1	0	0	
St. Clair County	1	0	0	0	0	0	0	1	0	0	
St. Joseph County	2	0	0	0	0	0	0	1	0	1	
Washtenaw County	2	0	1	0	1	0	0	2	0	2	
Wayne County	5	0	0	0	0	0	0	1	3	1	
Other Agencies	1	0	0	0	0	0					
Huron-Clinton Metropolitan Authority, Stony Creek Metropark	1	0	0	0	0	0	0	0	1	0	
MINNESOTA											
Total	59	20	17	1	3	4					
Cities	52	17	16	0	1	3					
Alexandria	0	1	0	0	0	0	0	1	0	0	13,914
Coon Rapids	0	0	1	0	0	0	1	0	0	0	62,652
Cottage Grove	1	0	0	0	0	0	1	0			37,534
East Grand Forks	0	0	1	0	0	0	1	0	0	0	8,597
Eden Prairie	2	0	0	0	0	0	0	2			64,777
Edina	0	1	0	0	0	0	1	0			53,076
Fairmont	1	0	0	0	0	0	0	0	0	1	10,023
Faribault	0	1	0	0	0	0	0	1			23,913
Fergus Falls	1	0	0	0	0	0	0	0	0	1	13,900
Hastings	1	0	0	0	0	0	0	1			22,774
Jordan	0	0	1	0	0	0		1			6,384
Mankato	9	1	3	0	0	0	2	0	7	4	42,955
Maple Grove	1	0	0	0	0	0	0	1			73,170
Maplewood	1	0	0	0	0	0	1	0	0	0	41,341
Minneapolis	17	5	6	0	1	3	4	7	16	5	431,016
Minnetonka	1	1	0	0	0	0	1	1			54,497
New Brighton	0	2	0	0	0	0	0	1	0	1	23,058
New Ulm	1	0	0	0	0	0	0	0	1	0	13,205
Plymouth	1	0	0	0	0	0	1	0			80,616
Red Wing	0	0	1	0	0	0	0	1	0	0	16,408
Rochester	3	1	0	0	0	0	1	2	1	0	118,267
Savage	1	0	0	0	0	0	1	0			32,336
St. Louis Park	2	3	0	0	0	0	0	1	3	1	49,535
St. Paul	8	1	2	0	0	0	0	11	1	1	310,263
Wabasha	1	0	0	0	0	0	0	0	1	0	2,471
Waseca	0	0	1	0	0	0	0	0	1	0	8,841
Universities and Colleges	0	2	0	0	2	0					
University of Minnesota, Twin Cities	0	2	0	0	2	0	0	1	2	1	64,115
Metropolitan Counties	4	0	1	1	0	1					
Blue Earth	1	0	0	0	0	0	1	0	0	0	
Carver	2	0	0	0	0	0	0	0	1	1	
Olmsted	0	0	1	0	0	0	0	0	1	0	
Ramsey	1	0	0	1	0	1	0	1	0	2	
Nonmetropolitan Counties	2	1	0	0	0	0					
Hubbard	1	0	0	0	0	0	0	1			
Kandiyohi	1	0	0	0	0	0	0	1			
Lac qui Parle	0	1	0	0	0	0	0	0	0	1	
Other Agencies	1	0	0	0	0	0					
Capitol Security, St. Paul	1	0	0	0	0	0	0	1		0	

Table 94. Hate Crime Incidents Per Bias Motivation and Quarter, by Selected State and Agency and Federal, 2019—Continued

(Number.)

State/agency	Number of incidents per bias motivation						Number of incidents per quarter				Population[1]
	Race/ Ethnicity/ Ancestry	Religion	Sexual orientation	Disability	Gender	Gender Identity	1st quarter	2nd quarter	3rd quarter	4th quarter	
MISSISSIPPI											
Total	6	1	1	6	0	0					
Cities	2	1	1	6	0	0					
Byram	0	0	0	6	0	0	2	0	2	2	11,672
Hernando	0	1	0	0	0	0	0	1	0	0	16,613
Kosciusko	2	0	0	0	0	0	0	0	2	0	6,774
Ridgeland	0	0	1	0	0	0	0	1	0	0	24,171
Nonmetropolitan Counties	4	0	0	0	0	0					
George	4	0	0	0	0	0	0	2	0	2	
MISSOURI											
Total	52	13	16	1	0	1					
Cities	43	9	10	1	0	1					
Belton	1	0	2	0	0	1	0	1	1	2	23,657
Blue Springs	0	1	1	0	0	0	1	0	0	1	55,415
Boonville	1	0	0	0	0	0	0	1	0	0	8,410
Cape Girardeau	0	0	1	0	0	0	0	0	1	0	40,077
Carthage	0	1	0	0	0	0	0	0	0	1	14,808
Fulton	1	0	0	0	0	0	0	0	1	0	12,620
Gladstone	3	0	0	0	0	0	0	1	0	2	27,553
Grain Valley	2	0	0	0	0	0	1	0	1	0	14,464
Independence	3	0	0	0	0	0	0	1	0	2	116,931
Jefferson City	2	0	0	0	0	0	1	0	0	1	42,793
Kansas City	25	6	2	1	0	0	7	3	13	11	495,964
Lawson	0	0	1	0	0	0	0	0	0	1	2,389
Lee's Summit	1	0	0	0	0	0	0	0	1	0	99,365
Springfield	0	0	1	0	0	0	0	0	1	0	169,235
St. Louis	1	1	2	0	0	0	0	2	1	1	300,521
St. Peters	2	0	0	0	0	0	0	1	1	0	57,697
Sunset Hills	1	0	0	0	0	0	0	0	1	0	8,480
Universities and Colleges	2	1	1	0	0	0					
Missouri University of Science and Technology	0	0	1	0	0	0	0	0	1	0	9,466
Missouri Western State University	0	1	0	0	0	0	1	0	0	0	6,302
University of Missouri, Columbia	2	0	0	0	0	0	1	0	1	0	34,329
Metropolitan Counties	3	3	4	0	0	0					
Greene	1	0	0	0	0	0	0	0	0	1	
Howard	0	0	1	0	0	0	0	0	0	1	
St. Charles County Police Department	2	3	1	0	0	0	0	0	3	3	
St. Louis County Police Department	0	0	2	0	0	0	1	1	0	0	
Nonmetropolitan Counties	3	0	1	0	0	0					
Camden	1	0	1	0	0	0	0	1	1	0	
Henry	1	0	0	0	0	0	0	1	0	0	
Johnson	1	0	0	0	0	0	0	0	0	1	
State Police Agencies	1	0	0	0	0	0					
Missouri State Highway Patrol	1	0	0	0	0	0	0	0	1	0	
MONTANA											
Total	16	9	2	1	1	3					
Cities	9	4	2	1	0	3					
Billings	2	1	1	0	0	0	0	0	3	1	110,198
Bozeman	1	0	0	0	0	0	1	0	0	0	50,152
Great Falls	2	1	0	1	0	0	0	0	0	4	58,637
Helena	1	1	0	0	0	0	1	0	0	1	32,806
Kalispell	0	1	0	0	0	2	2	0	0	1	24,473
Livingston	1	0	0	0	0	0	1	0	0	0	7,884
Missoula	1	0	0	0	0	0	0	1	0	0	75,422
Polson	0	0	1	0	0	0	0	0	1	0	5,075
Whitefish	1	0	0	0	0	1	1	1	0	0	8,079
Universities and Colleges	1	1	0	0	1	0					
Montana State University	1	1	0	0	1	0	2	0	0	1	18,722
Metropolitan Counties	2	1	0	0	0	0					
Cascade	1	1	0	0	0	0	1	0	1	0	
Missoula	1	0	0	0	0	0	1	0	0	0	
Nonmetropolitan Counties	4	3	0	0	0	0					
Big Horn	3	0	0	0	0	0	0	2	0	1	
Flathead	0	1	0	0	0	0	0	0	1	0	
Liberty	0	1	0	0	0	0	0	1	0	0	
Ravalli	1	1	0	0	0	0	0	0	1	1	

Table 94. Hate Crime Incidents Per Bias Motivation and Quarter, by Selected State and Agency and Federal, 2019—Continued

(Number.)

State/agency	Number of incidents per bias motivation						Number of incidents per quarter				Population[1]
	Race/ Ethnicity/ Ancestry	Religion	Sexual orientation	Disability	Gender	Gender Identity	1st quarter	2nd quarter	3rd quarter	4th quarter	
NEBRASKA											
Total	38	3	3	2	0	0					
Cities	24	3	3	1	0	0					
Broken Bow	5	0	0	0	0	0	0	0	1	4	3,532
Crete	1	0	0	0	0	0	0	0	0	1	7,094
Fremont	1	0	0	1	0	0	0	0	0	2	26,523
Gordon	1	0	0	0	0	0	0	0	1	0	1,497
Grand Island	1	0	0	0	0	0	0	0	1	0	51,821
Kearney	1	0	0	0	0	0	1	0	0	0	34,124
Lincoln	5	2	2	0	0	0	4	2	3	0	291,128
McCook	1	0	0	0	0	0	0	0	0	1	7,533
Mitchell	1	0	0	0	0	0	0	1	0	0	1,633
Norfolk	1	0	1	0	0	0	0	1	0	1	24,698
North Platte	3	0	0	0	0	0	0	0	3	0	23,705
Omaha	0	1	0	0	0	0	1	0	0	0	470,481
Schuyler	2	0	0	0	0	0	0	0	0	2	6,396
Valentine	1	0	0	0	0	0	0	0	1	0	2,751
Universities and Colleges	3	0	0	0	0	0					
University of Nebraska, Lincoln	3	0	0	0	0	0	0	1	2	0	28,642
Metropolitan Counties	3	0	0	1	0	0					
Douglas	2	0	0	0	0	0	0	1	1	0	
Howard	1	0	0	0	0	0	0	0	1	0	
Sarpy	0	0	0	1	0	0	0	0	0	1	
Nonmetropolitan Counties	8	0	0	0	0	0					
Custer	4	0	0	0	0	0	0	0	0	4	
Hamilton	1	0	0	0	0	0	0	0	0	1	
Jefferson	1	0	0	0	0	0	0	0	0	1	
Keith	1	0	0	0	0	0	0	0	0	1	
Lincoln	1	0	0	0	0	0	0	0	0	1	
NEVADA											
Total	27	10	4	1	0	2					
Cities	22	10	4	1	0	2					
Henderson	2	2	0	0	0	1	1	2	0	2	317,732
Las Vegas Metropolitan Police Department	11	5	4	1	0	1	4	7	8	3	1,666,803
North Las Vegas	6	2	0	0	0	0	2	2	2	2	249,854
Reno	3	1	0	0	0	0	1	0	3	0	254,349
Other Agencies	5	0	0	0	0	0					
Clark County School District	5	0	0	0	0	0	1		1	3	
NEW HAMPSHIRE											
Total	8	5	3	0	0	0					
Cities	7	5	3	0	0	0					
Auburn	0	1	0	0	0	0	0	1	0	0	5,608
Concord	1	1	0	0	0	0	0	1	0	1	43,509
Conway	0	0	1	0	0	0	0	0	1	0	10,287
Hanover	1	0	0	0	0	0	1	0	0	0	11,531
Henniker	1	0	0	0	0	0	1	0	0	0	5,009
Hooksett	1	0	0	0	0	0	0	0	0	1	14,554
Jaffrey	0	1	0	0	0	0	0	1	0		5,278
Keene	1	0	1	0	0	0	1	1	0	0	22,999
Milton	1	0	0	0	0	0	0	0	0	1	4,652
Pelham	0	1	0	0	0	0	0	1	0	0	14,198
Portsmouth	0	0	1	0	0	0	1	0	0	0	21,951
Somersworth	1	0	0	0	0	0	0	1	0	0	11,979
Tilton	0	1	0	0	0	0	0	1	0	0	3,557
Universities and Colleges	1	0	0	0	0	0					
University of New Hampshire	1	0	0	0	0	0	0	0	0	1	16,859
NEW JERSEY											
Total	252	250	65	1	5	8					
Cities	224	228	56	1	5	6					
Aberdeen Township	3	3	0	0	0	0	1	3	0	2	18,700
Barnegat Township	2	0	0	0	0	0	1	0	0	1	23,399
Barrington	0	0	1	0	0	0	0	1	0	0	6,620
Bayonne[2]	2	4	1	0	0	0	0	0	4	0	65,032
Bedminster Township	1	0	0	0	0	0	1	0	0	0	8,043
Berkeley Heights Township[2]	2	1	0	0	0	0	0	0	1	1	13,592
Berkeley Township[2]	2	1	0	0	0	0	1	1	0	0	41,738
Berlin[2]	1	1	0	0	0	0	0	0	1	0	7,510

Table 94. Hate Crime Incidents Per Bias Motivation and Quarter, by Selected State and Agency and Federal, 2019—Continued

(Number.)

State/agency	Number of incidents per bias motivation						Number of incidents per quarter				Population[1]
	Race/ Ethnicity/ Ancestry	Religion	Sexual orientation	Disability	Gender	Gender Identity	1st quarter	2nd quarter	3rd quarter	4th quarter	
Blairstown Township	1	1	0	0	0	0	0	0	0	2	5,703
Bogota	0	0	1	0	0	0	1	0	0	0	8,403
Boonton[2]	1	1	0	0	0	0	0	0	1	0	8,157
Bordentown Township	1	0	0	0	0	0	0	0	1	0	12,018
Brick Township	1	1	0	0	0	0	1	1	0	0	75,592
Bridgeton	3	0	1	0	0	0	3	1	0	0	24,331
Bridgewater Township	1	2	1	0	0	0	0	2	0	2	44,610
Brigantine	1	0	1	0	0	0	0	0	0	2	8,684
Burlington Township	1	0	0	0	0	0	0	0	1	0	22,516
Camden County Police Department	3	0	1	0	0	0	3	0	0	1	73,270
Cape May	1	0	0	0	0	0	1	0	0	0	3,428
Carteret[2]	1	1	0	0	0	0	0	0	0	1	23,645
Chatham Township	0	1	0	0	0	0	0	0	0	1	10,219
Cherry Hill Township[2]	2	2	1	0	0	0	1	1	1	1	70,716
Cinnaminson Township	0	2	0	0	0	0	1	0	0	1	16,477
Clifton	3	1	0	0	0	0	0	2	0	2	85,021
Clinton Township	0	1	0	0	0	0	0	0	0	1	12,801
Collingswood[2]	1	1	0	0	0	0	1	0	0	0	13,850
Colts Neck Township	0	1	0	0	0	0	0	1	0	0	9,846
Cranbury Township	1	0	0	0	0	0	0	1	0	0	4,013
Cranford Township[2]	2	1	0	0	0	0	0	1	0	1	24,251
Dover	1	0	0	0	0	0	1	0	0	0	17,852
Dumont	0	3	0	0	0	0	1	0	2	0	17,649
Dunellen	1	0	0	0	0	0	0	0	1	0	7,244
Eastampton Township	1	0	0	0	0	0	0	1	0	0	5,938
East Brunswick Township	1	2	0	0	0	0	1	1	1	0	47,857
East Windsor Township	0	2	0	0	0	0	0	0	1	1	27,343
Edgewater[2]	1	1	0	0	0	0	0	1	0	0	12,821
Edison Township[2]	2	3	0	1	0	0	1	0	2	2	100,282
Egg Harbor Township	1	1	0	0	0	0	0	1	1	0	42,475
Elizabeth[2]	1	1	1	0	0	0	0	1	1	0	128,753
Elmwood Park[2]	1	1	0	0	0	0	0	0	0	1	20,104
Emerson[2]	1	1	0	0	0	0	0	1	0	0	7,640
Englewood[2]	4	2	0	0	0	0	2	1	1	1	28,683
Evesham Township[2]	1	1	1	0	0	0	0	0	1	1	44,999
Ewing Township	1	1	0	0	0	0	1	0	1	0	36,338
Fair Lawn	0	6	0	0	0	0	0	0	2	4	33,064
Fairview	1	0	0	0	0	0	0	0	0	1	14,285
Fanwood[2]	1	1	0	0	0	0	0	0	1	0	7,718
Florham Park	2	0	0	0	0	0	0	0	1	1	11,522
Franklin	0	1	0	0	0	0	0	0	0	1	4,699
Franklin Township, Gloucester County	1	0	0	0	0	0	0	0	0	1	16,264
Freehold Township	1	0	0	0	0	0	1	0	0	0	34,560
Garfield	1	0	0	0	0	0	0	0	0	1	31,888
Glen Rock	0	5	0	0	0	0	0	2	3	0	11,803
Gloucester City	2	0	0	0	0	0	0	1	1	0	11,168
Hackensack[2]	4	3	0	0	0	0	1	0	3	1	44,505
Haddon Heights	0	0	1	0	0	0	0	0	0	1	7,515
Haddon Township	1	0	0	0	0	0	1	0	0	0	14,489
Hamilton Township, Atlantic County	1	1	0	0	0	0	1	1	0	0	25,667
Hamilton Township, Mercer County[2]	3	1	1	0	0	0	0	0	1	3	87,027
Hardyston Township	0	0	1	0	0	0	0	1	0	0	7,760
Harrison	2	0	0	0	0	0	0	1	1	0	18,374
Harrison Township[2]	1	0	1	0	0	0	0	0	1	0	13,125
Hawthorne	1	0	0	0	0	0	0	0	0	1	18,699
Hazlet Township	0	1	0	0	0	1	0	2	0	0	19,739
Highland Park	1	0	1	0	0	0	0	0	0	2	13,791
Hightstown	0	0	1	0	0	0	0	0	0	1	5,264
Hillsborough Township	0	0	1	0	0	0	0	0	1	0	39,813
Hillsdale[2]	4	2	1	0	0	0	2	1	0	2	10,382
Hoboken[2]	3	2	0	0	0	0	1	1	2	0	53,641
Holmdel Township	3	2	0	0	0	0	3	1	1	0	16,648
Hopewell Township	1	0	0	0	0	0	0	0	0	1	17,854
Howell Township[2]	4	6	1	0	0	0	0	3	1	3	52,242
Jackson Township	0	2	0	0	0	0	0	1	1	0	57,380
Jefferson Township[2]	1	3	0	0	0	0	0	1	0	2	20,877
Jersey City[2]	4	4	1	0	1	0	0	3	2	2	266,508
Keansburg	1	1	0	0	0	0	0	0	0	2	9,674
Lacey Township	0	1	0	0	0	0	0	1	0	0	29,247
Lakewood Township	1	24	0	0	0	0	3	15	3	4	105,403
Lawrence Township, Mercer County[2]	3	1	0	0	0	0	0	1	1	1	32,415
Linden	1	0	0	0	0	0	0	0	1	0	42,592
Lindenwold	1	0	0	0	0	0	0	0	0	1	17,197
Livingston Township[2]	2	2	0	0	0	0	1	2	0	0	29,998
Lodi	1	0	0	0	0	0	1	0	0	0	24,488
Long Beach Township	0	1	0	0	0	0	0	0	1	0	3,060
Long Branch[2]	3	2	3	0	0	1	0	2	2	0	30,352
Lower Township	1	0	0	0	0	0	0	0	1	0	21,325
Madison	1	0	0	0	0	0	1	0	0	0	16,533

Table 94. Hate Crime Incidents Per Bias Motivation and Quarter, by Selected State and Agency and Federal, 2019—Continued

(Number.)

State/agency	Number of incidents per bias motivation						Number of incidents per quarter				Population[1]
	Race/ Ethnicity/ Ancestry	Religion	Sexual orientation	Disability	Gender	Gender Identity	1st quarter	2nd quarter	3rd quarter	4th quarter	
Mahwah Township	1	0	0	0	0	0	0	0	0	1	26,317
Manalapan Township	1	1	0	0	0	0	1	0	1	0	39,662
Manchester Township[2]	6	1	0	0	0	0	2	2	2	0	43,369
Maple Shade Township	1	0	0	0	0	0	0	1	0	0	18,451
Marlboro Township[2]	1	3	2	0	1	0	1	4	0	0	39,850
Maywood	1	0	0	0	0	0	0	0	1	0	9,667
Medford Township	1	0	0	0	0	0	0	0	0	1	23,393
Mendham	0	1	0	0	0	0	0	0	0	1	4,876
Metuchen[2]	1	1	1	0	0	0	0	0	0	1	14,423
Middlesex Borough	1	0	0	0	0	0	1	0	0	0	13,659
Middle Township	1	0	0	0	0	0	1	0	0	0	18,225
Middletown Township[2]	2	0	1	0	0	0	0	0	1	2	65,361
Midland Park	0	1	0	0	0	0	0	0	0	1	7,246
Millville	2	0	0	0	0	0	0	1	0	1	27,528
Montclair[2]	2	4	0	0	0	0	2	0	0	3	38,625
Montvale	0	1	0	0	0	0	1	0	0	0	8,657
Moorestown Township	0	1	0	0	0	0	0	1	0	0	20,307
Morristown	0	1	0	0	0	0	1	0	0	0	19,153
Morris Township	1	0	0	0	0	0	0	0	1	0	22,080
Mountain Lakes	0	1	0	0	0	0	1	0	0	0	4,269
Mountainside	0	1	0	0	0	0	0	0	0	1	6,888
Mount Holly Township	0	0	1	0	0	0	0	0	0	1	9,568
Mount Laurel Township	1	0	0	0	0	0	1	0	0	0	41,109
Mount Olive Township[2]	2	1	1	0	0	0	0	0	2	0	29,025
Neptune Township	1	4	0	0	0	0	1	0	0	4	27,549
Newark[2]	1	1	0	0	0	0	0	0	0	1	281,422
New Brunswick[2]	0	0	1	0	0	1	0	1	0	0	55,995
New Milford	1	0	0	0	0	0	0	0	1	0	16,506
Newton	1	1	0	0	0	0	0	0	0	2	7,916
North Arlington	0	1	0	0	0	0	1	0	0	0	15,710
North Bergen Township[2]	3	1	1	0	1	0	1	1	1	0	61,447
North Caldwell	0	1	0	0	0	0	1	0	0	0	6,645
Norwood	1	0	0	0	0	0	0	0	0	1	5,816
Oakland	1	1	1	0	0	0	0	0	2	1	12,992
Oceanport	1	0	0	0	0	0	1	0	0	0	5,739
Ocean Township, Monmouth County	0	1	0	0	0	0	1	0	0	0	26,638
Old Bridge Township	0	1	0	0	0	0	0	0	1	0	65,659
Oradell[2]	2	0	1	0	0	0	1	0	0	1	8,181
Paramus[2]	1	2	0	0	0	0	0	2	0	0	26,460
Parsippany-Troy Hills Township[2]	3	1	1	0	0	0	1	2	0	1	51,907
Passaic[2]	2	3	1	0	1	0	0	3	3	0	69,639
Paterson	0	1	0	0	0	0	0	0	0	1	144,866
Pequannock Township	0	1	0	0	0	0	1	0	0	0	15,045
Phillipsburg	2	0	0	0	0	0	0	1	1	0	14,228
Piscataway Township	2	1	1	0	0	0	0	4	0	0	56,783
Pitman	1	0	0	0	0	0	0	0	1	0	8,709
Plainfield	1	0	0	0	0	0	0	0	1	0	50,576
Pleasantville	0	1	1	0	0	0	0	2	0	0	20,388
Plumsted Township	0	1	0	0	0	0	0	0	0	1	8,545
Point Pleasant	1	0	0	0	0	0	0	0	0	1	18,684
Princeton	0	0	1	0	0	0	1	0	0	0	31,610
Rahway[2]	1	1	0	0	0	0	0	0	0	1	30,072
Ramsey[2]	1	1	1	0	0	0	0	2	0	0	14,978
Randolph Township	1	2	0	0	0	0	0	1	0	2	25,490
Raritan Township[2]	1	1	0	0	0	0	0	0	0	1	22,220
Ridgefield Park	1	1	1	0	0	0	0	2	1	0	12,983
Ridgewood[2]	3	6	0	0	0	0	3	1	2	1	25,192
Riverdale	0	1	0	0	0	0	0	0	1	0	4,255
River Edge[2]	1	1	1	0	0	0	0	0	0	1	11,500
Riverside Township	1	0	1	0	0	0	1	1	0	0	7,806
Riverton	1	0	0	0	0	0	0	0	0	1	2,675
Rockaway Township[2]	2	4	0	0	0	0	0	2	0	2	25,756
Roselle	0	0	1	0	0	0	0	0	0	1	21,903
Roselle Park	1	0	0	0	0	0	0	1	0	0	13,630
Roxbury Township	0	3	0	0	0	0	1	0	0	2	22,755
Runnemede[2]	1	2	0	0	0	0	1	1	0	0	8,262
Rutherford	1	0	0	0	0	0	1	0	0	0	18,423
Secaucus[2]	1	1	0	0	0	0	1	0	0	0	21,217
South Brunswick Township[2]	1	1	0	0	0	0	0	0	0	1	46,038
South Orange Village	1	1	0	0	0	0	2	0	0	0	16,740
South Plainfield	1	2	0	0	0	0	0	1	2	0	24,114
South River	1	0	0	0	0	0	0	0	1	0	15,945
Sparta Township[2]	1	1	0	0	0	0	0	0	0	1	18,532
Spotswood	0	1	0	0	0	0	0	0	1	0	8,276
Springfield Township, Union County	0	1	0	0	0	0	0	0	0	1	17,661
Stratford	0	0	1	0	0	0	0	1	0	0	6,926
Summit	0	2	0	0	0	0	0	1	0	1	21,980
Teaneck Township[2]	1	4	0	0	0	0	0	3	0	1	40,533
Tenafly	0	1	0	0	0	0	0	1	0	0	14,586

Table 94. Hate Crime Incidents Per Bias Motivation and Quarter, by Selected State and Agency and Federal, 2019—Continued

(Number.)

State/agency	Number of incidents per bias motivation						Number of incidents per quarter				Population[1]
	Race/ Ethnicity/ Ancestry	Religion	Sexual orientation	Disability	Gender	Gender Identity	1st quarter	2nd quarter	3rd quarter	4th quarter	
Tewksbury Township[2]	1	1	0	0	0	0	0	0	1	0	5,765
Tinton Falls	1	1	0	0	0	0	1	1	0	0	17,506
Toms River Township	0	2	0	0	0	0	1	1	0	0	93,836
Trenton[2]	0	1	2	0	0	0	0	0	0	2	83,457
Union City[2]	2	2	0	0	0	0	1	1	0	1	68,459
Union Township	0	2	0	0	0	0	0	2	0	0	58,736
Ventnor City	0	0	1	0	0	0	0	0	0	1	9,966
Verona[2]	1	2	0	0	0	0	1	0	1	0	13,355
Vineland	3	0	0	0	0	1	0	2	1	1	59,860
Voorhees Township	3	5	0	0	0	0	1	0	3	4	29,099
Washington Township, Bergen County	0	0	1	0	0	0	1	0	0	0	9,219
Washington Township, Gloucester County	4	0	0	0	0	0	0	2	1	1	47,126
Wayne Township[2]	3	5	3	0	1	1	0	2	3	2	53,279
Weehawken Township[2]	1	0	2	0	0	0	0	0	0	2	15,115
Westampton Township	1	1	0	0	0	0	0	1	1	0	8,666
West Caldwell Township	1	0	0	0	0	0	0	1	0	0	10,840
Westfield[2]	5	5	0	0	0	0	1	2	1	3	29,688
West Milford Township	1	0	1	0	0	0	0	1	1	0	26,287
Westwood	2	0	0	0	0	0	0	1	0	1	11,129
Wildwood	1	0	0	0	0	0	1	0	0	0	4,959
Willingboro Township[2]	3	1	1	0	0	1	0	0	1	2	31,920
Winslow Township	1	0	0	0	0	0	0	0	0	1	38,390
Woodbridge Township	2	1	0	0	0	0	0	0	2	1	100,125
Woodbury	1	0	0	0	0	0	0	1	0	0	9,768
Woodland Park	1	0	0	0	0	0	0	1	0	0	12,657
Wyckoff Township[2]	1	2	1	0	0	0	0	0	1	1	17,030
Universities and Colleges	13	9	3	0	0	0					
Monmouth University	0	1	0	0	0	0	1	0	0	0	6,936
Montclair State University[2]	1	1	0	0	0	0	1		0	0	24,022
Princeton University[2]	2	2	0	0	0	0	1	0	1	1	8,593
Rutgers University											
Camden[2]	1	1	0	0	0	0	0	1			7,904
Newark	1	1	0	0	0	0	1	0	0	1	15,220
New Brunswick[2]	7	2	3	0	0	0	2	5	1	2	55,698
The College of New Jersey[2]	1	1	0	0	0	0	1	0	0	0	8,630
Metropolitan Counties	4	1	1	0	0	0					
Bergen	1	0	0	0	0	0	0	1	0	0	
Essex[2]	2	1	1	0	0	0	0	2	1	0	
Hudson	1	0	0	0	0	0	0	0	0	1	
State Police Agencies	5	4	4	0	0	2					
New Jersey State Police[2]	5	4	4	0	0	2	1	1	3	4	
Other Agencies	6	8	1	0	0	0					
New Jersey Transit Police[2]	4	3	0	0	0	0	1	3	1	0	
Park Police											
Morris County	1	0	0	0	0	0	0	0	0	1	
Union County	0	1	0	0	0	0	0	0	1	0	
Prosecutor, Cape May County[2]	1	1	1	0	0	0			1		
State Park Police	0	3	0	0	0	0	1	0	2	0	
NEW MEXICO											
Total	30	8	8	1	0	3					
Cities	28	8	8	1	0	3					
Albuquerque	25	7	6	1	0	0	7	9	17	6	561,920
Belen	2	0	0	0	0	0		1	1		7,094
Farmington	0	1	0	0	0	0			1		44,633
Las Cruces	1	0	2	0	0	0	0	0	2	1	103,520
Sunland Park	0	0	0	0	0	3	1	0	1	1	18,103
Metropolitan Counties	2	0	0	0	0	0					
Dona Ana	2	0	0	0	0	0	0	0	1	1	
NEW YORK											
Total	164	357	73	1	0	16					
Cities	125	297	60	1	0	13					
Albany	5	1	3	0	0	0	4	1	3	1	97,221
Amherst Town	0	1	0	0	0	0	0	0	1	0	120,864
Bedford Town	0	1	0	0	0	0	0	0	0	1	17,791
Brighton Town	2	1	0	0	0	0	0	1	1	1	36,036
Buffalo	5	0	0	0	0	0	3	1	1	0	255,686
Canandaigua	0	1	0	0	0	0	0	0	1	0	10,217
Clarkstown Town	0	2	0	0	0	0	1	0	1	0	80,599
Cobleskill Village	0	0	1	0	0	0	0	0	1	0	4,329
Colonie Town	1	0	0	0	0	0	0	1	0	0	79,509

Table 94. Hate Crime Incidents Per Bias Motivation and Quarter, by Selected State and Agency and Federal, 2019—Continued

(Number.)

State/agency	Number of incidents per bias motivation						Number of incidents per quarter				Population[1]
	Race/ Ethnicity/ Ancestry	Religion	Sexual orientation	Disability	Gender	Gender Identity	1st quarter	2nd quarter	3rd quarter	4th quarter	
Cortland	1	1	0	0	0	0	0	0	1	1	18,655
Freeport Village	1	0	0	0	0	0	0	1	0	0	43,064
Geneva	0	3	0	0	0	0	0	0	3	0	12,708
Glen Cove	0	1	0	0	0	0	0	0	0	1	27,228
Greece Town	0	1	0	0	0	0	0	1			95,777
Hastings-on-Hudson Village	0	1	0	0	0	0	0	1	0	0	7,916
Lloyd Harbor Village	0	1	0	0	0	0	0	0	1	0	3,667
Middletown	1	0	0	0	0	0	0	1	0	0	27,801
Mount Vernon	1	1	0	0	0	0	1	1	0	0	67,619
New Castle Town	1	0	0	0	0	0	0	1	0	0	17,896
New York	90	266	53	1	0	13	115	97	94	117	8,379,043
Newburgh	1	0	1	0	0	0	0	1	1	0	28,070
Pelham Village	0	1	0	0	0	0	0	0	1	0	6,911
Port Washington	0	1	0	0	0	0	0	0	1	0	19,396
Poughkeepsie	2	0	0	0	0	0	0	2	0	0	30,422
Poughkeepsie Town	1	0	0	0	0	0	0	0	1	0	38,889
Ramapo Town	0	2	0	0	0	0	0	0	1	1	94,633
Rochester	3	1	1	0	0	0	2	1	1	1	205,769
Rockville Centre Village	0	1	0	0	0	0	0	0	0	1	24,669
Scarsdale Village	0	2	0	0	0	0	0	0	2	0	17,954
Southampton Town	0	3	0	0	0	0	1	0	0	2	51,090
Syracuse	0	1	0	0	0	0	1	0	0	0	142,438
Tonawanda	1	0	0	0	0	0	0	1	0	0	14,754
Utica	2	1	0	0	0	0	1	1	1	0	59,842
White Plains	2	0	0	0	0	0	2	0	0		58,259
Yonkers	4	2	1	0	0	0	3	2	0	2	200,075
Yorktown Town	1	0	0	0	0	0	1	0	0	0	36,426
Universities and Colleges	6	0	0	0	0	0					
State University of New York Police											
Buffalo	1	0	0	0	0	0	0	0	0	1	34,183
New Paltz	1	0	0	0	0	0	0	0	1	0	9,669
Plattsburgh	2	0	0	0	0	0	0	0	1	1	6,558
Stony Brook	2	0	0	0	0	0	1	1	0	0	30,012
Metropolitan Counties	14	27	8	0	0	1					
Dutchess	1	0	4	0	0	0	3	0	1	1	
Madison	0	0	0	0	0	1	0	0	1	0	
Nassau	6	22	1	0	0	0	4	11	8	6	
Suffolk County Police Department	7	4	3	0	0	0	3	6	4	1	
Westchester Public Safety	0	1	0	0	0	0	0	0	0	1	
State Police Agencies	9	18	3	0	0	2					
State Police											
Albany County	0	2	0	0	0	0	0	0	0	2	
Cattaraugus County	1	0	0	0	0	0	0	0	1	0	
Clinton County	0	1	0	0	0	0	0	1	0	0	
Dutchess County	1	0	0	0	0	1	1	0	0	1	
Livingston County	0	1	0	0	0	0	0	0	1	0	
Montgomery County	0	1	0	0	0	0	0	0	1	0	
Niagara County	1	0	0	0	0	0	0	1	0	0	
Onondaga County	0	0	1	0	0	0	0	0	1	0	
Ontario County	1	0	0	0	0	0	1	0	0	0	
Orange County	1	6	0	0	0	0	1	5	1		
Oswego County	0	1	0	0	0	0	0	0	1	0	
Schenectady County	1	0	0	0	0	0	0	1	0	0	
St. Lawrence County	2	0	0	0	0	0	0	0	1	1	
Sullivan County	0	3	0	0	0	0	1	0	2	0	
Tioga County	1	0	0	0	0	0	0	1	0	0	
Ulster County	0	2	0	0	0	1	1	0	1	1	
Wayne County	0	0	1	0	0	0	0	0	1	0	
Westchester County	0	1	1	0	0	0	1	0	1		
Other Agencies	10	15	2	0	0	0					
New York City Department of Environmental Protection Police, Eastview Precinct	1	0	0	0	0	0	1	0	0	0	
New York City Metropolitan Transportation Authority	9	15	2	0	0	0	5	10	7	4	
NORTH CAROLINA											
Total	132	42	30	7	0	0					
Cities	84	31	22	1	0	0					
Aberdeen	0	1	0	0	0	0	0	0	0	1	7,892
Apex	1	0	0	0	0	0	1	0	0	0	56,276
Asheville	3	3	1	0	0	0	2	2	1	2	93,641
Beaufort	3	0	0	0	0	0	1	2	0	0	4,417
Biltmore Forest	0	1	0	0	0	0	1	0	0	0	1,410
Burlington	0	0	1	0	0	0	0	0	1	0	54,108
Canton	1	0	0	0	0	0	1	0	0	0	4,349

Table 94. Hate Crime Incidents Per Bias Motivation and Quarter, by Selected State and Agency and Federal, 2019—Continued

(Number.)

State/agency	Number of incidents per bias motivation						Number of incidents per quarter				Population[1]
	Race/ Ethnicity/ Ancestry	Religion	Sexual orientation	Disability	Gender	Gender Identity	1st quarter	2nd quarter	3rd quarter	4th quarter	
Cary	1	0	0	0	0	0	0	0	0	1	172,525
Chapel Hill	1	0	1	0	0	0	0	1	1	0	61,457
Charlotte-Mecklenburg	10	7	1	0	0	0	2	3	4	9	944,260
Clayton	2	0	0	0	0	0	1	0	1	0	23,842
Cleveland	0	1	0	0	0	0	0	0	0	1	882
Dallas	1	0	0	0	0	0	0	0	1	0	4,787
Dunn	0	1	0	0	0	0	0	1	0	0	9,768
Durham	3	0	0	0	0	0	0	2	1	0	280,282
Elon	1	2	0	0	0	0	1	0	1	1	12,214
Fayetteville	8	1	2	0	0	0	1	3	5	2	209,614
Greensboro	8	1	0	1	0	0	0	4	4	2	298,025
Greenville	3	0	2	0	0	0	1	1	0	3	94,193
Hickory	1	0	2	0	0	0	0	1	2	0	41,040
High Point	2	0	0	0	0	0	1	1	0	0	113,307
Hope Mills	1	0	0	0	0	0	0	1	0	0	15,878
Jacksonville	2	0	0	0	0	0	1	1			72,300
Kernersville	0	0	1	0	0	0	0	0	0	1	24,980
Knightdale	1	0	0	0	0	0	0	1	0	0	18,351
Leland	4	0	0	0	0	0		3	1	0	23,360
Lenoir	1	0	0	0	0	0	0	0	1	0	17,904
Marion	1	0	0	0	0	0	0	0	0	1	7,837
Matthews[2]	0	2	2	0	0	0	0	1	1	1	33,372
Mebane	3	0	0	0	0	0	0	1	0	2	16,203
Mooresville	1	0	0	0	0	0	0	1	0	0	38,967
Morganton	0	1	0	0	0	0	0	1	0	0	16,524
New Bern	0	0	1	0	0	0	0	0	0	1	30,187
Newton	1	0	0	0	0	0	0	0	0	1	13,153
Pineville	0	0	1	0	0	0	1	0	0	0	9,088
Raleigh	7	2	5	0	0	0	4	3	3	4	477,828
Red Springs	0	2	0	0	0	0	0	0	0	2	3,341
Salisbury	1	0	0	0	0	0	1	0	0	0	33,877
Troutman	1	0	0	0	0	0	0	0	0	1	2,755
Wake Forest	2	0	0	0	0	0	0	0	1	1	46,145
Washington	1	0	0	0	0	0	0	0	0	1	9,497
Wilmington	7	6	2	0	0	0	2	3	7	3	124,750
Wilson	1	0	0	0	0	0	1	0	0	0	49,344
Universities and Colleges	1	0	2	0	0	0					
North Carolina State University, Raleigh	0	0	1	0	0	0	1	0	0	0	39,136
University of North Carolina											
Chapel Hill	1	0	0	0	0	0	1	0	0	0	32,180
Greensboro	0	0	1	0	0	0			0	1	22,419
Metropolitan Counties	32	4	6	5	0	0					
Alamance	4	0	0	0	0	0	1	0	1	2	
Buncombe	1	1	2	0	0	0	0	2	1	1	
Burke	3	0	0	0	0	0	1	0	1	1	
Cabarrus	0	1	0	0	0	0	1	0	0	0	
Caldwell	1	0	0	1	0	0	1	0	0	1	
Craven	2	0	1	0	0	0	1	1	0	1	
Cumberland	1	0	1	0	0	0	1	1	0	0	
Currituck	2	0	1	0	0	0	1	1	0	1	
Durham	0	0	1	0	0	0	0	1			
Forsyth	1	0	0	0	0	0			1	0	
Franklin	2	0	0	0	0	0	0	1	1	0	
Granville	1	1	0	0	0	0	1	0	0	1	
New Hanover	1	0	0	0	0	0	0	1	0	0	
Onslow	2	0	0	3	0	0	3	1	0	1	
Pamlico	1	0	0	0	0	0	1	0	0	0	
Person	2	0	0	0	0	0	0	0	0	2	
Pitt	5	0	0	0	0	0	1	3	1	0	
Union	2	1	0	1	0	0	2	1	1	0	
Wake	1	0	0	0	0	0	0	0	0	1	
Nonmetropolitan Counties	12	7	0	1	0	0					
Ashe	0	1	0	0	0	0	0	1	0	0	
Avery	0	2	0	0	0	0	0	1	1	0	
Bertie	0	1	0	0	0	0	1	0			
Carteret	1	0	0	0	0	0	0	1	0	0	
Caswell	4	0	0	0	0	0	0	2	2	0	
Dare	1	0	0	0	0	0	1	0	0	0	
Duplin	0	1	0	0	0	0	0	1			
Jackson	2	0	0	0	0	0	0	1	1		
Macon	1	1	0	0	0	0	1	0	0	1	
McDowell	0	0	0	1	0	0	0	0	0	1	
Moore	1	0	0	0	0	0	0	0	0	1	
Robeson	2	0	0	0	0	0	0	0	1	1	
Watauga	0	1	0	0	0	0	0	0	1	0	

Table 94. Hate Crime Incidents Per Bias Motivation and Quarter, by Selected State and Agency and Federal, 2019—Continued

(Number.)

State/agency	Number of incidents per bias motivation						Number of incidents per quarter				Population[1]
	Race/ Ethnicity/ Ancestry	Religion	Sexual orientation	Disability	Gender	Gender Identity	1st quarter	2nd quarter	3rd quarter	4th quarter	
Other Agencies	3	0	0	0	0	0					
State Capitol Police	1	0	0	0	0	0	1	0	0	0	
WakeMed Campus Police	2	0	0	0	0	0	1	1	0	0	
NORTH DAKOTA											
Total	14	1	3	0	0	0					
Cities	7	1	2	0	0	0					
Bowman	0	0	1	0	0	0	0	0	0	1	1,604
Fargo	1	1	0	0	0	0	0	0	1	1	127,423
Grand Forks	1	0	0	0	0	0	0	0	1	0	57,459
Mandan	2	0	0	0	0	0	1	1	0	0	23,012
Valley City	1	0	0	0	0	0	0	0	1	0	6,351
Williston	2	0	1	0	0	0	0	2	0	1	28,966
Universities and Colleges	1	0	0	0	0	0					
University of North Dakota	1	0	0	0	0	0	0	1	0	0	17,646
Metropolitan Counties	4	0	0	0	0	0					
Burleigh	1	0	0	0	0	0	0	0	1	0	
Grand Forks	3	0	0	0	0	0	1	1	1	0	
Nonmetropolitan Counties	2	0	1	0	0	0					
McLean	1	0	0	0	0	0	0	1	0	0	
Mountrail	1	0	0	0	0	0	0	0	1	0	
Sargent	0	0	1	0	0	0	0	0	1	0	
OHIO											
Total	216	30	60	55	7	23					
Cities	189	23	52	46	7	18					
Akron	1	0	0	2	0	0	2	0	1	0	197,882
Alliance	1	0	0	0	0	0	1	0	0	0	21,536
Archbold	0	0	1	0	0	0	0	0	1	0	4,320
Ashland	0	0	1	0	0	0	0	0	0	1	20,410
Barberton	1	0	0	2	0	0	1	0	2	0	26,015
Bath Township, Summit County	0	0	0	2	0	0	0	2	0	0	9,659
Bay Village	0	0	0	1	0	0	0	0	1	0	15,235
Beachwood	1	0	0	0	0	0	1	0	0	0	11,612
Bexley	0	1	0	0	0	0	0	0	1	0	13,956
Blanchester	1	0	0	0	0	0	1	0	0	0	4,251
Blue Ash	1	0	0	0	0	0	0	0	0	1	12,307
Butler Township	0	0	0	1	0	0	1	0	0	0	7,819
Chillicothe	8	0	0	0	0	0	1	2	3	2	21,670
Cincinnati	24	1	4	3	0	0	6	9	10	7	303,335
Circleville	3	0	0	0	0	0	2	1	0	0	14,025
Cleveland	20	7	7	4	4	3	5	2	10	28	381,829
Colerain Township	2	0	0	0	0	0	0	0	2	0	59,479
Columbiana	0	0	1	0	0	0	0	1	0	0	6,209
Columbus	35	6	12	5	0	8	11	12	26	17	906,120
Copley Township	0	0	1	1	0	0	0	1	1	0	17,309
Dayton	6	0	1	0	0	0	3	2	1	1	140,427
Defiance	1	0	0	0	0	3	0	1	1	2	16,601
Delaware	1	0	1	0	0	0	1	0	1	0	40,616
Delhi Township	1	0	0	0	0	0	1	0	0	0	29,811
East Liverpool	1	0	0	0	0	0	0	1	0	0	10,653
Eaton	0	0	0	0	1	0	0	0	1	0	8,136
Elyria	3	0	1	0	0	0	0	0	2	2	53,806
Englewood	0	0	0	1	0	0	0	0	1	0	13,478
Fairfax	1	0	0	0	0	0	0	0	0	1	1,710
Franklin	1	0	0	0	0	0	1	0	0	0	11,675
Gahanna	3	0	0	0	0	0	1	1	1	0	35,847
Germantown	1	0	0	0	0	0	1	0	0	0	5,500
Grafton	0	0	0	0	1	0	0	1	0	0	5,808
Grandview Heights	0	1	0	0	0	0	0	0	1	0	8,581
Green Township	4	0	0	0	0	0	2	1	0	1	59,273
Greenville	1	0	0	0	0	0	0	1	0	0	12,629
Grove City	0	0	1	0	0	0	1	0	0	0	42,423
Hamilton	3	0	0	0	0	1	2	0	2	0	62,155
Heath	1	0	2	0	0	0	0	1	0	2	10,933
Hilliard	3	0	0	0	0	0	3	0	0	0	37,578
Huber Heights	2	1	0	2	0	0	0	1	3	1	38,183
Hudson	1	0	0	1	0	0	1	1	0	0	22,286
Jackson Township, Stark County	2	0	0	0	0	0	0	1	1	0	40,347
Lancaster	1	0	0	0	0	0	1	0	0	0	40,622
Lebanon	0	0	0	0	0	1	1	0	0	0	20,806
Lithopolis	0	0	1	0	0	0	0	0	1	0	1,777
Lockland	1	0	0	0	0	0	0	0	0	1	3,455
Logan	0	1	0	0	0	0	0	0	0	1	7,039

Table 94. Hate Crime Incidents Per Bias Motivation and Quarter, by Selected State and Agency and Federal, 2019—Continued

(Number.)

State/agency	Number of incidents per bias motivation						Number of incidents per quarter				Population[1]
	Race/ Ethnicity/ Ancestry	Religion	Sexual orientation	Disability	Gender	Gender Identity	1st quarter	2nd quarter	3rd quarter	4th quarter	
Lorain	1	0	0	0	0	0	0	0	1	0	64,022
Louisville	0	0	0	1	0	0	0	1	0	0	9,329
Lyndhurst	0	0	0	1	0	0	0	1	0	0	13,407
Madison Township, Franklin County	0	0	0	3	0	0	1	2	0	0	19,682
Madison Township, Lake County	1	0	0	0	0	0	0	1	0	0	15,646
Mansfield	2	0	1	0	0	0	0	1	1	1	46,418
Mason	1	0	0	0	0	0	0	1	0	0	33,939
Maumee	1	0	0	0	0	0	0	1	0	0	13,656
Mayfield Heights	0	0	1	0	0	0	0	0	0	1	18,519
Mentor-on-the-Lake	1	0	0	1	0	0	1	0	1	0	7,400
Miami Township, Montgomery County	0	0	1	0	0	0	0	0	1	0	29,188
Miamisburg	2	0	0	0	0	0	0	0	1	1	19,913
Middletown	7	1	3	3	0	0	3	3	6	2	48,878
Moraine	2	0	0	0	0	0	1	1	0	0	6,455
Mount Vernon	1	0	0	0	0	0	0	0	1	0	16,663
Napoleon	2	0	0	0	0	0	1	0	1	0	8,188
Nelsonville	1	0	0	0	0	0	0	1	0	0	5,158
New Albany	0	1	0	0	0	0	0	0	1	0	11,332
New Boston	1	0	0	0	0	0	1	0	0	0	2,093
New Franklin	0	0	0	1	0	0	0	0	1	0	14,162
New Knoxville	1	0	0	0	0	0	0	1	0	0	863
New Philadelphia	2	0	0	0	0	0	2	0	0	0	17,434
North Baltimore	1	0	0	0	0	0	0	1	0	0	3,557
North Canton	1	1	0	0	0	0	0	2	0	0	17,251
Norton	0	0	1	0	0	0	0	1	0	0	12,007
Norwood	0	0	0	0	0	1	0	1	0	0	19,922
Orrville	1	0	0	0	0	0	0	0	1	0	8,461
Portsmouth	0	0	2	0	0	0	1	1			20,353
Reading	1	0	0	0	0	0	1	0	0	0	10,995
Riverside	0	0	0	1	0	0	0	0	1	0	25,148
Rocky River	0	0	0	1	0	0	1	0	0	0	20,105
Salem	0	0	0	2	0	0	1	0	1	0	11,644
Shawnee Township	1	0	0	0	0	0	0	0	1	0	12,056
Shelby	0	0	0	1	0	0	1	0	0	0	8,997
Springfield Township, Hamilton County	2	0	0	0	0	0	0	0	2	0	36,696
Streetsboro	0	0	0	1	0	0	0	0	0	1	16,561
Toledo	2	0	2	0	0	0	2	1	0	1	273,505
Trotwood	2	0	0	0	0	1	0	0	2	1	24,435
Upper Arlington	1	1	0	0	0	0	1	1	0	0	35,754
Urbana	1	0	0	1	0	0	0	1	1	0	11,309
Van Wert	1	0	0	0	0	0	0	1	0	0	10,662
Wadsworth	0	0	2	0	0	0	1	0	1	0	24,058
Wapakoneta	1	0	0	0	0	0	0	0	1	0	9,717
Warren	1	0	0	0	0	0	0	0	1	0	38,012
Waverly	0	1	0	0	0	0	0	0	0	1	4,253
Weathersfield	0	0	0	1	0	0	0	1	0	0	8,017
West Carrollton	1	0	0	0	0	0	0	0	0	1	12,886
Whitehall	1	0	0	0	0	0	0	0	0	1	19,121
Wilmington	3	0	0	0	0	0	2	0	0	1	12,391
Wooster	1	0	0	2	0	0	0	1	1	1	26,615
Worthington	1	0	0	0	1	0	1	1	0	0	14,875
Youngstown	1	0	1	0	0	0	0	2	0	0	64,722
Zanesville	3	0	4	1	0	0	0	2	3	3	25,346
Universities and Colleges	2	1	1	0	0	0					
Ohio State University, Columbus	2	1	0	0	0	0	0	0	0	3	64,924
Otterbein University	0	0	1	0	0	0	1	0	0	0	3,258
Metropolitan Counties	13	1	2	0	0	2					
Clermont	0	1	0	0	0	0	0	0	1	0	
Cuyahoga	1	0	0	0	0	0	1	0	0		
Franklin	1	0	0	0	0	0	1	0	0	0	
Geauga	1	0	0	0	0	0	0	0	1	0	
Lawrence	0	0	1	0	0	0	0	1	0	0	
Lorain	0	0	0	0	0	1	0	0	1	0	
Lucas	3	0	0	0	0	0	0	0	1	2	
Medina	1	0	0	0	0	0	0	0	0	1	
Miami	1	0	0	0	0	0	0	1	0	0	
Montgomery	3	0	0	0	0	1	2	1	1	0	
Summit	1	0	1	0	0	0	1	0	1	0	
Union	1	0	0	0	0	0	0	1	0	0	
Nonmetropolitan Counties	11	5	3	8	0	1					
Champaign	1	0	0	2	0	0	1	0	0	2	
Columbiana	0	0	0	4	0	0	0	3	1	1	
Coshocton	1	1	0	0	0	0	0	1	0	1	
Defiance	0	0	1	0	0	0	0	0	1	0	
Hancock	0	1	0	0	0	0	0	0	0	1	
Hardin	0	1	0	1	0	0	2	0	0	0	

Table 94. Hate Crime Incidents Per Bias Motivation and Quarter, by Selected State and Agency and Federal, 2019—Continued

(Number.)

State/agency	Number of incidents per bias motivation						Number of incidents per quarter				Population[1]
	Race/ Ethnicity/ Ancestry	Religion	Sexual orientation	Disability	Gender	Gender Identity	1st quarter	2nd quarter	3rd quarter	4th quarter	
Highland	0	0	1	0	0	0	0	0	1	0	
Knox	2	1	0	0	0	0	1	0	1	1	
Logan	0	0	1	0	0	0	0	1	0	0	
Morgan	1	0	0	0	0	0	1	0	0	0	
Ross	2	0	0	0	0	0	1	0	1	0	
Tuscarawas	1	1	0	0	0	1	0	0	2	1	
Vinton	1	0	0	0	0	0	1	0	0	0	
Washington	0	0	0	1	0	0	0	0	0	1	
Wayne	2	0	0	0	0	0	0	0	2	0	
State Police Agencies	0	0	0	1	0	0					
Ohio State Highway Patrol	0	0	0	1	0	0	0	1	0	0	
Other Agencies	1	0	2	0	0	2					
Cleveland Metropolitan Park District	1	0	0	0	0	0	0	2	0	0	
Greater Cleveland Regional Transit Authority	0	0	0	0	0	1	0	1	0	0	
Ohio Department of Natural Resources	0	0	2	0	0	0	0	1	1	0	
OKLAHOMA											
Total	14	5	8	1	0	0					
Cities	10	3	5	0	0	0					
Chickasha	0	0	1	0	0	0	1	0	0	0	16,395
Collinsville	0	0	1	0	0	0	0	0	0	1	7,271
Cushing	1	0	0	0	0	0	0	1	0	0	7,639
McAlester	0	1	0	0	0	0	0	0	1	0	17,840
Noble	0	1	0	0	0	0	1	0	0	0	6,922
Norman	1	1	0	0	0	0	1	0	1	0	125,076
Oklahoma City	3	0	0	0	0	0	2	0	1	0	657,890
Pawnee	1	0	0	0	0	0	1	0	0	0	2,107
Sallisaw	1	0	0	0	0	0	0	0	1	0	8,391
Sulphur	0	0	1	0	0	0	1	0	0	0	5,028
Tulsa	1	0	2	0	0	0	1	0	2	0	401,700
West Siloam Springs	1	0	0	0	0	0	0	0	1	0	870
Wewoka	1	0	0	0	0	0	1	0	0	0	3,252
Universities and Colleges	0	0	1	0	0	0					
Northeastern Oklahoma A&M College	0	0	1	0	0	0	0	0	0	1	2,663
Metropolitan Counties	2	1	1	0	0	0					
Creek	0	1	0	0	0	0	0	0	1	0	
Logan	2	0	0	0	0	0	0	1	1	0	
Wagoner	0	0	1	0	0	0	0	0	0	1	
Nonmetropolitan Counties	2	1	1	1	0	0					
Craig	0	0	0	1	0	0	0	0	1	0	
Garvin	1	0	0	0	0	0	0	1	0	0	
Major	0	1	0	0	0	0	0	1	0	0	
Roger Mills	1	0	0	0	0	0	0	0	0	1	
Washita	0	0	1	0	0	0	0	1	0	0	
OREGON											
Total	116	29	27	2	2	6					
Cities	96	24	22	2	2	6					
Astoria	1	0	0	0	0	0	0	0	1	0	10,040
Baker City	1	0	0	0	0	0	1	0	0	0	9,750
Beaverton[2]	1	1	1	0	0	0	1	0	0	1	100,130
Bend	4	4	0	0	0	0	2	2	3	1	100,588
Canby	1	0	1	0	0	0	0	0	1	1	17,962
Central Point	1	1	0	0	0	0	1	0	0	1	18,753
Coos Bay	3	0	0	0	0	0	2	0	0	1	16,471
Corvallis	1	0	0	0	0	0	0	1	0	0	59,196
Cottage Grove	0	0	1	0	0	0	0	0	1	0	10,437
Eugene	28	10	2	0	1	1	4	13	13	12	173,183
Forest Grove	1	0	1	0	0	0	0	0	1	1	25,063
Gladstone	2	0	1	0	0	0	0	1	1	1	12,340
Gresham	1	0	0	0	0	0	0	0	1	0	110,692
Hermiston	1	1	0	0	0	0	0	1	0	1	17,780
Hillsboro[2]	5	0	5	0	0	1	3	2	2	2	110,549
Hood River	1	0	0	0	0	0	1	0	0	0	7,876
Klamath Falls	1	0	0	0	0	0	0	0	1	0	22,447
La Grande	0	0	1	0	0	0	1	0	0	0	13,294
Lake Oswego	1	0	0	0	0	0	0	1	0	0	39,888
Madras	1	0	0	0	0	0	0	0	0	1	7,028
McMinnville	1	0	0	0	0	0	0	0	0	1	34,935
Medford	1	0	0	0	0	0	1	0	0	0	83,316
Milwaukie	0	0	1	0	0	0	0	1	0	0	21,075
Myrtle Creek	0	1	0	0	0	0	0	0	0	1	3,508

Table 94. Hate Crime Incidents Per Bias Motivation and Quarter, by Selected State and Agency and Federal, 2019—Continued

(Number.)

State/agency	Number of incidents per bias motivation						Number of incidents per quarter				Population[1]
	Race/ Ethnicity/ Ancestry	Religion	Sexual orientation	Disability	Gender	Gender Identity	1st quarter	2nd quarter	3rd quarter	4th quarter	
North Bend	1	1	1	1	0	0	1	1	1	1	9,775
Ontario	1	0	0	0	0	0	0	0	0	1	11,044
Oregon City	3	0	0	0	0	0	2	0	1	0	37,723
Portland[2]	23	4	5	0	1	3	6	6	10	11	662,114
Redmond	1	0	0	0	0	0	0	0	0	1	31,558
Salem	1	0	0	1	0	1	0	0	0	3	175,867
Sherwood	1	0	0	0	0	0	0	0	0	1	19,865
Springfield	1	0	0	0	0	0	1	0	0	0	63,438
St. Helens	1	0	0	0	0	0	0	0	1	0	13,900
Tigard	3	1	2	0	0	0	1	3	0	2	55,621
Tualatin	2	0	0	0	0	0	0	0	1	1	27,788
West Linn	1	0	0	0	0	0	0	1	0	0	26,962
Universities and Colleges	1	2	0	0	0	0					
Portland State University	1	0	0	0	0	0	0	1	0		35,257
University of Oregon	0	2	0	0	0	0	2	0			25,640
Metropolitan Counties	12	2	2	0	0	0					
Clackamas[2]	9	2	1	0	0	0	2	5	2	2	
Jackson	1	0	0	0	0	0	0	0	1	0	
Washington	2	0	1	0	0	0	0	0	2	1	
Nonmetropolitan Counties	7	1	2	0	0	0					
Coos	6	0	1	0	0	0	4	2	0	1	
Jefferson	1	0	0	0	0	0	0	0	0	1	
Lincoln	0	1	0	0	0	0	0	0	1	0	
Umatilla	0	0	1	0	0	0	1	0	0	0	
State Police Agencies	0	0	1	0	0	0					
State Police, Marion County	0	0	1	0	0	0	1	0	0	0	
PENNSYLVANIA											
Total	28	9	4	0	0	0					
Cities	22	8	4	0	0	0					
East Pennsboro Township	0	1	0	0	0	0	0	1	0		21,549
Forest City	1	0	0	0	0	0		0	1	0	1,741
Hampden Township	1	0	0	0	0	0	0	1	0		30,861
Johnstown	2	0	0	0	0	0		0	2	0	20,663
Kenhorst	2	0	0	0	0	0		0	0	2	2,888
Philadelphia	7	4	1	0	0	0	1	7	2	2	1,589,014
Pittsburgh	5	2	3	0	0	0	0	3	5	2	300,548
Reading	3	0	0	0	0	0		0	3		88,549
Rush Township	1	0	0	0	0	0	0	1			3,254
Westtown-East Goshen Regional	0	1	0	0	0	0		0	1	0	32,366
Universities and Colleges	4	0	0	0	0	0					
Pennsylvania State University, University Park	2	0	0	0	0	0	0	0	2		50,426
Shippensburg University	2	0	0	0	0	0		0	2	0	7,345
State Police Agencies	2	1	0	0	0	0					
Bradford County	0	1	0	0	0	0		0	1	0	
Chester County	1	0	0	0	0	0		0	1		
Venango County	1	0	0	0	0	0		0	1	0	
RHODE ISLAND											
Total	4	5	8	0	0	0					
Cities	4	5	4	0	0	0					
Barrington	1	0	0	0	0	0	0	1	0	0	16,090
Central Falls	0	0	1	0	0	0	0	0	1	0	19,423
Cranston	0	1	0	0	0	0	0	0	0	1	81,471
Cumberland	1	0	0	0	0	0	0	0	1	0	35,206
East Greenwich	0	1	0	0	0	0	0	1	0	0	13,119
East Providence	0	1	0	0	0	0	0	1	0	0	47,590
Johnston	1	0	0	0	0	0	0	0	1	0	29,424
Pawtucket	0	0	2	0	0	0	1	1	0	0	72,030
Providence	1	2	1	0	0	0	1	3	0	0	179,762
Universities and Colleges	0	0	4	0	0	0					
Brown University	0	0	4	0	0	0	1	0	0	3	10,694
SOUTH CAROLINA											
Total	36	20	7	1	3	1					
Cities	20	4	5	1	2	0					
Bluffton	1	1	0	0	0	0	0	1	0	1	24,812
Calhoun Falls	1	0	0	0	0	0	1	0	0	0	1,912
Charleston	1	1	2	0	0	0	2	2	0	0	138,254

Table 94. Hate Crime Incidents Per Bias Motivation and Quarter, by Selected State and Agency and Federal, 2019—Continued

(Number.)

State/agency	Number of incidents per bias motivation						Number of incidents per quarter				Population[1]
	Race/ Ethnicity/ Ancestry	Religion	Sexual orientation	Disability	Gender	Gender Identity	1st quarter	2nd quarter	3rd quarter	4th quarter	
Clio	1	0	0	0	0	0	0	0	1	0	660
Darlington	0	0	1	0	0	0	1	0	0	0	5,886
Florence	2	0	0	0	0	0	1	0	1	0	37,640
Gaffney	1	0	0	0	0	0	0	1	0	0	12,528
Greenville	1	0	1	0	0	0	0	0	1	1	69,830
Hartsville	0	0	0	0	1	0	0	0	0	1	7,524
Inman	1	0	0	0	0	0	0	0	1	0	2,404
Lake View	1	0	0	0	0	0	0	0	1		755
McColl	0	0	0	0	1	0	0	1	0	0	1,981
Myrtle Beach	1	0	0	0	0	0	1	0	0	0	34,860
North Myrtle Beach	1	1	0	0	0	0	0	0	2	0	16,942
Pamplico	1	0	0	0	0	0	1	0	0	0	1,221
Rock Hill	2	0	1	1	0	0	2	0	0	2	75,342
Springdale	1	0	0	0	0	0	0	0	0	1	2,753
St. Matthews	1	0	0	0	0	0	0	1	0	0	1,900
Summerville	1	1	0	0	0	0	1	0	1	0	52,886
Williston	1	0	0	0	0	0	1	0	0	0	2,907
York	1	0	0	0	0	0	1	0	0	0	8,294
Universities and Colleges	1	0	0	0	1	0					
Medical University of South Carolina	1	0	0	0	0	0	0	1	0	0	3,421
The Citadel	0	0	0	0	1	0	0	0	0	1	4,305
Metropolitan Counties	9	13	1	0	0	1					
Beaufort	1	0	0	0	0	1	1	0	0	1	
Berkeley	2	9	0	0	0	0	0	1	1	9	
Charleston	1	1	0	0	0	0	0	0	1	1	
Greenville	1	0	0	0	0	0	0	0	1	0	
Lexington	0	0	1	0	0	0	1	0	0	0	
Pickens	1	0	0	0	0	0	0	0	1	0	
Spartanburg	3	3	0	0	0	0	2	1	1	2	
Nonmetropolitan Counties	6	3	1	0	0	0					
Bamberg	0	2	0	0	0	0	0	0	1	1	
Colleton	2	0	1	0	0	0	0	2	0	1	
Dillon	1	0	0	0	0	0	0	0	1	0	
Greenwood	0	1	0	0	0	0	1	0	0	0	
Marlboro	1	0	0	0	0	0	0	0	1	0	
Orangeburg	2	0	0	0	0	0	0	0	0	2	
SOUTH DAKOTA											
Total	13	3	4	0	0	0					
Cities	9	3	3	0	0	0					
Box Elder	1	0	0	0	0	0	1	0	0	0	10,077
Flandreau	0	1	0	0	0	0	0	0	1	0	2,323
Huron	1	0	0	0	0	0	1	0	0	0	13,840
Martin	1	0	0	0	0	0	0	0	0	1	1,071
Mitchell	0	0	1	0	0	0	0	1	0	0	15,733
Rapid City	1	0	0	0	0	0	0	1	0	0	76,343
Sioux Falls	3	2	2	0	0	0	1	1	2	3	185,628
Tea	1	0	0	0	0	0	0	0	0	1	5,898
Watertown	1	0	0	0	0	0	0	1	0	0	22,233
Metropolitan Counties	1	0	1	0	0	0					
Pennington	1	0	1	0	0	0	1	1	0	0	
Nonmetropolitan Counties	3	0	0	0	0	0					
Brown	1	0	0	0	0	0	0	1	0	0	
Stanley	1	0	0	0	0	0	0	0	1	0	
Walworth	1	0	0	0	0	0	0	0	1	0	
TENNESSEE											
Total	91	12	10	1	2	1					
Cities	38	8	6	1	1	0					
Centerville	1	0	0	0	0	0	0	0	1	0	3,564
Cleveland	7	0	0	0	0	0	2	2	2	1	45,453
Collierville	1	0	0	0	0	0	0	0	0	1	51,273
Cookeville	0	0	0	0	1	0	0	1	0	0	34,373
Covington	1	0	0	1	0	0	0	0	2	0	8,755
Goodlettsville	1	0	0	0	0	0	0	0	0	1	16,976
Greeneville	1	0	0	0	0	0	0	0	1	0	14,881
Kingsport	0	1	1	0	0	0	0	0	0	2	54,218
Knoxville	3	2	2	0	0	0	0	3	1	3	188,666
Lebanon	4	0	0	0	0	0	0	2	1	1	36,337
Livingston	0	1	0	0	0	0	0	1	0	0	4,014
Maryville	1	0	0	0	0	0	0	0	1	0	29,415
Memphis	4	0	1	0	0	0	0	2	1	2	650,410

Table 94. Hate Crime Incidents Per Bias Motivation and Quarter, by Selected State and Agency and Federal, 2019—Continued

(Number.)

State/agency	Race/ Ethnicity/ Ancestry	Religion	Sexual orientation	Disability	Gender	Gender Identity	1st quarter	2nd quarter	3rd quarter	4th quarter	Population[1]
Metropolitan Nashville Police Department	3	2	1	0	0	0	2	2	2	0	687,361
Milan	1	0	0	0	0	0	0	0	0	1	7,613
Morristown	2	0	0	0	0	0	0	0	2	0	30,044
Mountain City	1	0	0	0	0	0	0	1	0	0	2,407
Munford	0	1	0	0	0	0	1	0	0	0	6,083
Murfreesboro	0	0	1	0	0	0	0	1	0	0	145,929
Newbern	1	0	0	0	0	0	0	0	1	0	3,312
Pigeon Forge	2	0	0	0	0	0	0	1	1	0	6,383
Spring Hill	2	0	0	0	0	0	0	1	0	1	43,303
Springfield	1	1	0	0	0	0	0	2	0	0	17,022
White House	1	0	0	0	0	0	1	0	0	0	12,822
Universities and Colleges	0	0	1	0	0	0					
Tennessee Technological University	0	0	1	0	0	0	0	1	0	0	11,451
Metropolitan Counties	17	3	2	0	0	1					
Anderson	0	0	1	0	0	0	0	0	1	0	
Blount	3	1	0	0	0	1	2	0	2	1	
Bradley	2	0	1	0	0	0	0	3	0	0	
Dickson	1	0	0	0	0	0	0	1	0	0	
Knox	3	0	0	0	0	0	0	0	0	3	
Montgomery	1	0	0	0	0	0	1	0	0	0	
Roane	1	0	0	0	0	0	0	1	0	0	
Sullivan	1	2	0	0	0	0	0	0	1	2	
Washington	5	0	0	0	0	0	0	3	1	1	
Nonmetropolitan Counties	5	1	0	0	0	0					
DeKalb	1	0	0	0	0	0	0	1	0	0	
Dyer	0	1	0	0	0	0	0	0	1	0	
Henderson	1	0	0	0	0	0	0	0	0	1	
McMinn	1	0	0	0	0	0	0	1	0	0	
Monroe	1	0	0	0	0	0	0	0	0	1	
Warren	1	0	0	0	0	0	0	0	0	1	
State Police Agencies	30	0	1	0	1	0					
Department of Safety	30	0	1	0	1	0	7	12	10	3	
Other Agencies	1	0	0	0	0	0					
Tennessee Bureau of Investigation	1	0	0	0	0	0	0	0	1	0	
TEXAS											
Total	300	44	71	19	7	18					
Cities	227	33	64	14	5	14					
Abilene	0	0	3	0	0	0	1	2	0	0	123,665
Addison	1	0	0	0	0	0	0	0	0	1	16,339
Alamo	3	1	0	0	0	0	1	0	0	3	19,903
Amarillo	1	0	0	0	0	0	0	1	0	0	201,036
Angleton	1	0	1	0	0	0	1	1	0	0	19,660
Arlington	14	0	2	0	0	0	2	2	8	4	402,304
Austin	5	2	3	0	0	0	3	2	3	2	986,062
Balch Springs	2	0	0	0	0	0	1	0	0	1	25,511
Beaumont	2	0	0	0	0	2	1	0	1	2	118,562
Blue Mound	1	0	0	0	0	0	0	0	0	1	2,485
Boerne	1	0	0	0	0	0	1	0	0	0	18,135
Borger	1	0	0	0	0	0	0	0	0	1	12,536
Brady	1	0	0	0	0	0	1	0	0	0	5,288
Breckenridge	1	0	0	0	0	0	0	1	0	0	5,453
Brenham	2	1	0	0	0	0	1	1	1	0	17,375
Brownwood	1	0	0	0	0	0	0	0	1	0	18,646
Burkburnett	0	1	0	0	0	0	0	0	1	0	11,305
Burleson	2	0	1	0	0	0	0	2	1	0	48,743
Carrollton	1	0	0	0	0	0	0	1			139,179
Cedar Park	2	1	1	1	0	0	1	2	0	2	80,170
Cleburne	1	0	0	0	0	0	0	0	0	1	30,860
College Station	1	0	0	0	0	0	1	0	0	0	119,246
Commerce	4	0	0	0	0	0	2	1	1	0	9,467
Converse	0	0	1	0	0	0	0	0	0	1	28,598
Corpus Christi	1	0	0	0	0	0	0	0	1	0	329,320
Corrigan	1	2	0	0	0	0	0	2	1	0	1,605
Dallas	13	3	13	0	0	1	2	6	10	12	1,363,295
Decatur	1	0	0	1	0	0	1	0	1	0	7,116
Denton	3	1	0	0	1	0	4	1	0	0	141,492
DeSoto	1	1	1	1	0	0	1	1	0	2	54,026
Dickinson	1	0	0	0	0	0	0	0	0	1	21,101
Dumas	2	0	0	0	0	0	0	0	2	0	14,290
Edcouch	18	0	0	0	0	0	11	7			3,378
El Campo	1	0	0	0	0	0	0	0	0	1	11,615
Elgin	3	0	0	0	0	0	0	1	1	1	10,475

Table 94. Hate Crime Incidents Per Bias Motivation and Quarter, by Selected State and Agency and Federal, 2019—Continued

(Number.)

State/agency	Number of incidents per bias motivation						Number of incidents per quarter				Population[1]
	Race/ Ethnicity/ Ancestry	Religion	Sexual orientation	Disability	Gender	Gender Identity	1st quarter	2nd quarter	3rd quarter	4th quarter	
El Paso	3	0	0	0	0	0	1	0	2	0	686,793
Ennis	0	1	0	0	0	1	0	0	1	1	20,096
Fate	0	0	1	0	0	0	0	0	1	0	15,378
Ferris	1	0	0	0	0	0	0	0	0	1	2,876
Floresville	3	0	0	0	0	0	2	0	1	0	7,970
Fort Worth[2]	8	2	5	0	0	0	2	2	5	5	915,237
Frisco	1	1	0	0	0	0	1	0	1	0	199,445
Gainesville	1	0	0	0	0	0	0	0	0	1	16,688
Garland	2	0	0	0	0	0	0	0	1	1	244,277
Gatesville	0	1	0	0	0	0	0	0	0	1	12,311
Georgetown	1	0	0	0	0	0	0	0	1	0	78,332
Giddings	1	0	0	0	0	0	0	0	1	0	5,124
Gladewater	4	0	1	0	0	0	2	1	1	1	6,349
Glenn Heights	1	0	0	0	0	0	0	0	0	1	13,520
Granbury	0	1	0	0	0	0	0	0	0	1	10,752
Grapeland	0	0	0	1	0	0	0	1	0	0	1,421
Greenville	1	0	0	0	0	0	0	0	1	0	28,613
Hamilton	0	1	0	0	0	1	1	0	1	0	3,008
Harker Heights	0	0	0	0	1	0	0	0	0	1	32,527
Harlingen	0	1	1	0	0	0	0	1	1	0	65,481
Henderson	2	0	0	0	0	0	0	1	0	1	13,226
Hillsboro	1	0	0	0	0	0	0	1	0	0	8,476
Hollywood Park	1	0	1	0	0	0	0	1	0	1	3,406
Houston	13	2	9	2	0	3	5	6	9	9	2,355,606
Hurst	0	0	2	0	0	0	0	0	0	2	39,196
Iowa Park	1	0	0	0	0	0	1	0	0	0	6,369
Itasca	1	0	0	0	0	0	0	0	1	0	1,736
Jacksonville	1	0	0	0	0	1	0	2	0	0	14,969
Jarrell	1	0	0	0	0	0	0	1	0	0	1,800
Kennedale	1	0	0	0	0	0	0	0	0	1	8,792
Kingsville	0	0	0	0	1	0	0	0	1	0	25,401
Kyle	0	0	1	0	0	0	0	0	0	1	49,855
Lacy-Lakeview	1	0	0	0	0	0	1	0	0	0	6,720
La Grange	0	1	0	0	0	0	0	0	0	1	4,630
Lake Dallas	0	1	0	0	0	0	0	0	0	1	8,052
Lampasas	2	0	0	0	0	0	0	1	0	1	8,067
La Porte	0	0	1	1	0	0	0	0	0	2	35,622
Laredo	1	0	0	3	1	0	1	0	0	4	264,916
League City	0	0	1	0	0	0	0	0	1	0	109,401
Levelland	1	0	0	0	0	0	1	0	0	0	13,530
Lewisville	1	0	1	0	0	0	0	0	0	2	108,000
Livingston	0	0	1	0	0	0	0	1	0	0	5,112
Longview	2	1	0	0	0	0	1	1	1	0	81,783
Lubbock	1	0	2	0	0	0	0	0	2	1	259,208
Mansfield	1	0	0	0	0	0	0	0	0	1	72,979
Marble Falls	0	0	1	0	0	0	0	1	0	0	7,047
McKinney	2	0	0	0	0	0	0	2	0	0	200,615
Mesquite	3	0	0	0	0	0	2	0	1	0	143,078
Nederland	1	0	0	0	0	0	0	0	0	1	17,557
New Braunfels	5	0	1	0	1	1	0	1	4	3	88,706
North Richland Hills	4	0	0	0	0	0	0	1	1	2	71,816
Odessa[2]	3	0	2	1	0	0	2	0	3	0	123,468
Overton	1	1	0	0	0	0	1	0	0	1	2,510
Palestine	4	0	0	0	0	1	1	3	1	0	18,062
Pasadena	4	0	0	2	0	0	3	1	0	2	153,689
Pearland	1	0	0	0	0	0	0	1	0	0	126,206
Pflugerville	1	0	0	0	0	1	0	1	0	1	66,729
Pleasanton	2	0	0	0	0	0	0	0	0	2	10,911
Port Arthur	2	0	0	0	0	0	0	0	0	2	55,084
Port Isabel	2	0	0	0	0	0	0	1	1	0	5,058
Port Neches	0	0	0	0	0	1	0	0	1	0	12,808
Richardson	0	0	1	0	0	0	0	0	0	1	123,893
Rio Grande City	0	1	0	0	0	0	0	0	1	0	14,607
Rockdale	2	0	0	0	0	0	0	1	1	0	5,665
Rockwall	3	1	0	0	0	0	0	1	1	2	46,096
Roma	1	0	0	0	0	0	0	1	0	0	11,527
Rosenberg	1	1	0	0	0	0	1	0	0	1	38,936
Rowlett	1	0	0	0	0	0	1	0	0	0	67,604
San Antonio	5	0	4	0	0	0	3	3	2	1	1,559,166
San Juan	1	0	1	0	0	0	1	0	0	1	37,542
Santa Fe	0	0	1	0	0	0	0	0	0	1	13,657
Schulenburg	1	0	0	0	0	0	0	1	0	0	2,929
Silsbee	1	0	0	0	0	0	0	1	0	0	6,650
South Padre Island	0	1	0	0	0	0	0	1	0	0	2,805
Spur	2	0	0	0	0	0	0	0	0	2	1,207
Stafford	0	1	0	0	0	0	0	0	0	1	18,380
Sunset Valley	1	0	0	0	0	0	0	1	0	0	683
Sweeny	2	0	0	0	0	0	0	0	1	1	3,745
Sweetwater	1	0	0	0	0	0	0	0	1	0	10,467

Table 94. Hate Crime Incidents Per Bias Motivation and Quarter, by Selected State and Agency and Federal, 2019—Continued

(Number.)

State/agency	Number of incidents per bias motivation						Number of incidents per quarter				Population[1]
	Race/ Ethnicity/ Ancestry	Religion	Sexual orientation	Disability	Gender	Gender Identity	1st quarter	2nd quarter	3rd quarter	4th quarter	
Tahoka	0	0	0	1	0	0	0	0	1	0	2,624
Tool	1	0	0	0	0	0	0	1	0	0	2,337
Tyler	0	0	0	0	0	1	0	0	0	1	106,851
University Park	1	0	0	0	0	0	1	0	0	0	25,434
Vernon	4	0	0	0	0	0	1	0	0	3	10,312
Victoria	1	0	0	0	0	0	0	0	0	1	67,581
Vidor	2	0	0	0	0	0	0	0	1	1	10,499
Waco	4	1	0	0	0	0	2	1	0	2	139,870
Wallis	1	0	0	0	0	0	0	0	0	1	1,322
Wichita Falls	1	0	0	0	0	0	0	0	1	0	104,551
Willow Park	2	0	0	0	0	0	0	0	1	1	5,808
Winters	1	0	0	0	0	0	1	0	0	0	2,448
Universities and Colleges	8	2	1	0	0	0					
Houston Community College	1	0	0	0	0	0	0	0	1	0	82,166
Texas State University, San Marcos	2	0	0	0	0	0	0	0	2	0	42,924
Texas Woman's University	0	0	1	0	0	0	0	0	0	1	18,773
Tyler Junior College	2	0	0	0	0	0	0	0	0	2	15,992
University of Texas											
Austin	2	2	0	0	0	0	0	2	1	1	55,097
Houston	1	0	0	0	0	0	0	0	1	0	6,948
Metropolitan Counties	39	6	4	2	2	1					
Brazoria	1	0	0	0	0	0	0	0	0	1	
Chambers	1	0	0	0	0	0	1	0	0	0	
El Paso	1	0	0	0	0	0	0	0	1	0	
Fort Bend	2	0	0	0	0	0	1	1	0	0	
Galveston	0	0	0	1	0	0	1	0			
Harris	13	2	1	0	2	1	2	5	6	6	
Hudspeth	10	1	0	0	0	0	11	0	0	0	
Johnson	2	0	0	0	0	0	0	1	1	0	
Montgomery	1	1	0	0	0	0	2	0	0	0	
Randall	0	0	1	0	0	0	0	0	0	1	
Tarrant	3	0	0	0	0	0	0	0	1	2	
Travis	2	0	0	0	0	0	0	0	0	2	
Williamson	3	2	2	1	0	0	2	4	1	1	
Nonmetropolitan Counties	15	2	1	1	0	3					
Bailey	0	1	0	0	0	1	0	1	0	1	
Bee	0	0	0	1	0	0	0	0	0	1	
Cherokee	1	0	0	0	0	0	0	0	0	1	
Crockett	1	0	0	0	0	0	0	0	1	0	
Duval	1	0	0	0	0	0	0	1	0	0	
Floyd	1	0	0	0	0	0	0	0	0	1	
Houston	2	1	0	0	0	1	1	1	2	0	
Kerr	1	0	0	0	0	0	1	0	0	0	
Leon	2	0	0	0	0	0	0	0	1	1	
Llano	0	0	0	0	0	1	0	0	0	1	
McCulloch	1	0	0	0	0	0	0	0	1	0	
Nacogdoches	0	0	1	0	0	0	0	0	0	1	
Ward	4	0	0	0	0	0	1	2	1	0	
Washington	1	0	0	0	0	0	0	0	1	0	
Other Agencies	11	1	1	2	0	0					
Dallas-Fort Worth International Airport[2]	1	1	0	0	0	0	0	0	0	1	
Independent School District											
Austin	1	0	0	0	0	0	0	0	1	0	
Bay City	1	0	0	0	0	0	1	0	0	0	
Brazosport	1	0	0	0	0	0	0	1	0	0	
Houston	4	0	0	1	0	0	2	0	1	2	
Hutto	0	0	0	1	0	0	1	0	0	0	
Roma	2	0	0	0	0	0	0	1	1	0	
Spring Branch	1	0	1	0	0	0	1	0	1	0	
UTAH											
Total	12	3	3	0	0	0					
Cities	11	2	3	0	0	0					
Farmington	3	0	0	0	0	0	0	1	1	1	25,409
Kaysville	1	0	0	0	0	0	0	0	1	0	32,691
Layton	1	0	0	0	0	0	0	0	1	0	78,585
Moab	0	0	1	0	0	0	0	0	1	0	5,349
North Salt Lake	1	0	0	0	0	0	0	0	0	1	21,501
Ogden	1	0	0	0	0	0	0	0	0	1	87,875
Roy	0	1	1	0	0	0	0	2	0	0	39,001
Salt Lake City	1	0	0	0	0	0	1	0	0	0	202,426
Sandy	1	0	0	0	0	0	0	1	0	0	97,797
South Jordan	1	0	0	0	0	0	0	0	0	1	77,645
South Ogden	1	0	1	0	0	0	0	0	1	1	17,215
West Valley	0	1	0	0	0	0	0	1	0	0	137,269

Table 94. Hate Crime Incidents Per Bias Motivation and Quarter, by Selected State and Agency and Federal, 2019—Continued

(Number.)

State/agency	Number of incidents per bias motivation						Number of incidents per quarter				Population[1]
	Race/ Ethnicity/ Ancestry	Religion	Sexual orientation	Disability	Gender	Gender Identity	1st quarter	2nd quarter	3rd quarter	4th quarter	
Metropolitan Counties	0	1	0	0	0	0					
Washington	0	1	0	0	0	0	1	0	0	0	
Nonmetropolitan Counties	1	0	0	0	0	0					
Duchesne	1	0	0	0	0	0	0	1	0	0	
VERMONT											
Total	18	4	9	1	0	1					
Cities	15	3	7	0	0	1					
Barre	1	0	0	0	0	0	0	1	0	0	8,551
Bennington	3	1	1	0	0	0	5	0	0	0	14,912
Berlin	1	0	0	0	0	0	0	0	0	1	2,789
Brandon	0	0	1	0	0	0	0	0	0	1	3,744
Brattleboro	0	0	0	0	0	1	0	0	1	0	11,401
Burlington	1	1	1	0	0	0	0	1	1	1	42,958
Hartford	0	0	1	0	0	0	0	0	1	0	9,654
Milton	2	0	1	0	0	0	0	0	2	1	11,064
Montpelier	2	0	0	0	0	0	0	0	1	1	7,386
Newport	1	0	1	0	0	0	0	0	1	1	4,216
Rutland	2	0	1	0	0	0	1	0	2	0	15,191
South Burlington	0	1	0	0	0	0	1	0	0	0	19,687
St. Albans	1	0	0	0	0	0	0	0	1	0	6,800
Windsor	1	0	0	0	0	0	0	0	1	0	3,324
Universities and Colleges	2	1	2	0	0	0					
University of Vermont	2	1	2	0	0	0	0	0	5	0	15,629
State Police Agencies	1	0	0	1	0	0					
State Police											
Middlesex	1	0	0	0	0	0	1	0	0	0	
St. Albans	0	0	0	1	0	0	1	0	0	0	
VIRGINIA											
Total	102	27	27	3	1	3					
Cities	21	6	11	0	0	2					
Alexandria	2	1	2	0	0	0	2	2	0	1	162,258
Charlottesville	2	0	1	0	0	0	1	0	1	1	48,453
Chesapeake	2	0	0	0	0	0	0	1	0	1	243,726
Colonial Beach	0	1	0	0	0	0	0	0	0	1	3,593
Dayton	0	1	0	0	0	0	1	0	0	0	1,636
Glade Spring	0	1	0	0	0	1	0	0	0	2	1,426
Hampton	2	0	0	0	0	0	0	2	0	0	133,173
Harrisonburg	1	0	0	0	0	0	0	1	0	0	54,387
Leesburg	2	1	1	0	0	0	2	1	1	0	55,461
Lynchburg	1	0	0	0	0	0	0	0	0	1	82,512
Newport News	1	0	3	0	0	0	1	0	0	3	177,319
Purcellville	1	0	0	0	0	0	1	0	0	0	10,346
Richlands	1	0	0	0	0	0	0	1	0	0	5,198
Richmond	3	0	2	0	0	0	1	4	0	0	230,721
Roanoke	1	0	0	0	0	0	0	1	0	0	99,752
Suffolk	0	0	1	0	0	0	0	0	0	1	91,486
Vienna	0	0	1	0	0	0	0	0	0	1	16,660
Virginia Beach	1	1	0	0	0	0	1	0	1	0	449,038
Winchester	0	0	0	0	0	1	0	0	0	1	28,201
Woodstock	1	0	0	0	0	0	0	1	0	0	5,267
Universities and Colleges	2	1	4	0	0	0					
Hampton University	0	0	1	0	0	0	1	0	0	0	4,698
James Madison University	0	1	1	0	0	0	1	0	1	0	24,133
Longwood University	1	0	0	0	0	0	0	1	0	0	5,909
University of Mary Washington	1	0	1	0	0	0	0	1	0	1	5,373
University of Virginia	0	0	1	0	0	0	0	1	0	0	28,244
Metropolitan Counties	71	20	10	2	1	1					
Albemarle County Police Department	1	0	0	0	0	0	0	0	0	1	
Amelia	0	0	1	0	0	0	0	0	0	1	
Amherst	2	0	0	0	0	0	0	0	1	1	
Arlington County Police Department	8	4	1	0	0	0	6	6	1	0	
Bedford	1	1	0	0	0	0	0	0	2	0	
Campbell	1	0	0	0	0	0	0	1	0	0	
Chesterfield County Police Department	2	1	0	0	0	0	0	0	2	1	
Dinwiddie	0	2	0	0	0	0	0	1	0	1	
Fairfax County Police Department	27	8	2	0	0	0	9	12	7	9	
Fluvanna	1	0	1	0	0	0	0	0	0	2	
Franklin	2	0	0	0	0	0	1	0	1	0	
Giles	0	0	1	0	0	0	0	0	1	0	
Hanover	1	0	0	0	0	0	1	0	0	0	

Table 94. Hate Crime Incidents Per Bias Motivation and Quarter, by Selected State and Agency and Federal, 2019—Continued

(Number.)

State/agency	Race/Ethnicity/Ancestry	Religion	Sexual orientation	Disability	Gender	Gender Identity	1st quarter	2nd quarter	3rd quarter	4th quarter	Population[1]
Henrico County Police Department	1	0	0	0	0	0	1	0	0	0	
James City County Police Department	1	0	0	0	0	0	0	0	1	0	
Loudoun	12	2	2	1	1	1	9	6	2	2	
Nelson	0	0	1	0	0	0	1	0	0	0	
Prince George County Police Department	2	0	0	0	0	0	0	0	2	0	
Prince William County Police Department	3	1	0	0	0	0	0	2	2	0	
Roanoke County Police Department	0	1	1	0	0	0	0	1	1	0	
Spotsylvania	1	0	0	1	0	0	0	1	1	0	
Stafford	4	0	0	0	0	0	0	0	1	3	
Washington	1	0	0	0	0	0	0	1	0	0	
Nonmetropolitan Counties	5	0	2	0	0	0					
Accomack	1	0	0	0	0	0	0	0	1	0	
Charlotte	2	0	0	0	0	0	0	0	2	0	
Northampton	2	0	0	0	0	0	0	1	0	1	
Page	0	0	1	0	0	0	1	0	0	0	
Pittsylvania	0	0	1	0	0	0	0	1	0	0	
State Police Agencies	3	0	0	1	0	0					
State Police											
Dinwiddie County	1	0	0	0	0	0	0	0	1	0	
Fairfax County	0	0	0	1	0	0	0	1	0	0	
Prince William County	1	0	0	0	0	0	0	1	0	0	
Richmond	1	0	0	0	0	0	0	0	0	1	
WASHINGTON											
Total	331	76	116	8	8	17					
Cities	290	58	109	6	5	17					
Aberdeen	3	0	0	0	0	0	1	0	1	1	16,627
Auburn	1	1	1	1	0	0	0	1	0	3	83,468
Bainbridge Island	0	1	0	0	0	0	0	0	0	1	25,080
Bellevue	5	3	2	0	0	0	1	3	2	4	150,200
Bellingham	5	0	1	0	0	0	1	2	0	3	91,906
Blaine	0	0	1	0	0	0	0	0	1	0	5,534
Bonney Lake	1	0	0	0	0	0	0	0	0	1	21,574
Bothell	2	0	0	0	0	1	1	1	0	1	47,565
Bremerton	1	0	0	0	0	0	0	0	1	0	41,675
Brier	1	2	0	0	0	0	1	1	1	0	7,070
Burien	3	1	2	0	0	0	1	2	2	1	52,388
Chehalis	1	0	0	0	0	0	1	0	0	0	7,682
Covington	2	0	0	0	0	0	1	0	1	0	21,698
Des Moines	3	1	0	0	0	0	1	0	2	1	32,708
Ellensburg	1	0	0	0	0	0	1	0	0	0	21,324
Everett	5	2	1	0	0	0	2	3	0	3	112,302
Federal Way	1	0	0	0	0	0	0	1	0	0	98,025
Index	0	1	0	0	0	0	0	0	1	0	214
Issaquah	1	1	1	0	0	0	1	0	2	0	40,651
Kent	10	4	2	0	0	0	4	6	3	3	131,003
Lake Stevens	1	0	0	0	0	0	1	0	0	0	34,081
Longview	0	0	2	1	0	0	1	0	1	1	38,282
Maple Valley	1	0	0	0	0	0	0	0	0	1	27,705
Marysville	1	0	0	0	0	0	1	0	0	0	71,081
Mercer Island	1	2	0	0	0	0	2	1	0	0	26,408
Monroe	1	0	0	0	0	0	0	1	0	0	19,630
Montesano	1	0	0	0	0	0	1	0	0	0	4,033
Moses Lake	9	0	0	0	0	0	4	4	1	0	24,490
Mount Vernon	3	0	0	0	0	0	0	3	0	0	36,274
Mukilteo	1	1	0	0	0	0	0	1	0	1	21,704
Normandy Park	1	0	0	0	0	0	1	0	0	0	6,699
Oak Harbor	1	0	0	0	0	0	1	0	0	0	23,554
Olympia	1	1	1	0	0	1	4	0	0	0	53,286
Oroville	0	1	0	0	0	0	1	0	0	0	1,678
Port Angeles	1	0	2	0	1	0	3	0	0	1	20,207
Pullman	2	0	1	0	0	0	0	0	1	2	34,585
Puyallup	1	0	0	0	0	0	0	0	0	1	42,509
Redmond	1	0	0	0	0	0	1	0	0	0	69,501
Renton	4	2	1	1	0	0	2	3	3	0	103,452
Richland	0	1	0	0	0	0	0	0	0	1	58,514
Ruston	1	0	0	0	0	0	0	0	1	0	855
Sammamish[2]	2	0	2	0	0	0	2	0	1	0	66,820
SeaTac	3	0	1	0	0	0	1	0	1	2	29,533
Seattle[2]	178	26	80	3	4	13	50	76	98	68	763,706
Shoreline	0	1	1	0	0	0	0	0	2	0	57,216
South Bend	0	0	0	0	0	1	0	0	0	1	1,680
Spokane	4	2	3	0	0	0	2	3	3	1	220,432
Spokane Valley	5	0	2	0	0	0	1	2	2	2	100,983
Steilacoom	2	0	0	0	0	0	0	1	1	0	6,423
Sunnyside	1	0	0	0	0	0	0	0	1	0	16,839

Table 94. Hate Crime Incidents Per Bias Motivation and Quarter, by Selected State and Agency and Federal, 2019—Continued

(Number.)

State/agency	Number of incidents per bias motivation						Number of incidents per quarter				Population[1]
	Race/ Ethnicity/ Ancestry	Religion	Sexual orientation	Disability	Gender	Gender Identity	1st quarter	2nd quarter	3rd quarter	4th quarter	
Tacoma	6	1	0	0	0	0	2	2	1	2	218,650
Tukwila	0	1	0	0	0	0	0	0	0	1	20,439
Vancouver	6	2	2	0	0	1	1	7	2	1	185,034
Walla Walla	1	0	0	0	0	0	0	1	0	0	33,047
West Richland	1	0	0	0	0	0	0	1	0	0	15,343
Yakima	2	0	0	0	0	0	0	0	1	1	94,168
Zillah	1	0	0	0	0	0			1	0	3,164
Universities and Colleges	3	10	0	1	1	0					
Eastern Washington University	1	6	0	0	1	0	0	5	1	2	16,208
Evergreen State College	0	3	0	0	0	0	1	0	1	1	4,587
University of Washington	1	0	0	0	0	0	0	0	1	0	55,508
Western Washington University[2]	1	1	0	1	0	0	1	1	0	0	17,782
Metropolitan Counties	34	7	7	1	2	0					
Chelan	1	1	0	0	0	0	2	0	0	0	
Clark	1	0	1	0	0	0	1	1	0	0	
Cowlitz	0	0	0	1	0	0	0	0	1	0	
King	17	2	4	0	2	0	7	5	10	3	
Kitsap	1	0	0	0	0	0	0	0	1	0	
Pierce	1	1	0	0	0	0	0	1	1	0	
Skagit	2	0	0	0	0	0	0	1	0	1	
Snohomish	3	1	1	0	0	0	0	0	4	1	
Spokane	4	1	0	0	0	0	0	0	2	3	
Stevens	0	0	1	0	0	0	0	0	0	1	
Whatcom	1	1	0	0	0	0	0	0	1	1	
Yakima	3	0	0	0	0	0	0	1	1	1	
Nonmetropolitan Counties	4	0	0	0	0	0					
Clallam	2	0	0	0	0	0	1	0	1	0	
Island	1	0	0	0	0	0	0	0	0	1	
Lewis	1	0	0	0	0	0	0	0	0	1	
Other Agencies	0	1	0	0	0	0					
Port of Seattle	0	1	0	0	0	0	0	0	0	1	
WEST VIRGINIA											
Total	18	6	3	2	1	1					
Cities	8	1	2	1	0	0					
Huntington	2	0	1	0	0	0	1	2	0	0	45,675
Morgantown	2	0	0	0	0	0	1	0	1	0	31,281
Moundsville	1	0	0	0	0	0	0	1	0	0	8,323
St. Albans	0	0	0	1	0	0	1	0	0	0	9,956
Wheeling	3	1	0	0	0	0	2	1	1	0	26,562
White Sulphur Springs	0	0	1	0	0	0	0	1	0	0	2,395
Metropolitan Counties	4	1	0	1	0	0					
Hancock	2	0	0	1	0	0	0	1	1	1	
Kanawha	0	1	0	0	0	0	1	0	0	0	
Monongalia	1	0	0	0	0	0	0	0	0	1	
Putnam	1	0	0	0	0	0	0	0	1	0	
Nonmetropolitan Counties	5	1	0	0	1	0					
Hardy	0	0	0	0	1	0	0	0	0	1	
Lewis	2	1	0	0	0	0	2	1	0	0	
Mason	3	0	0	0	0	0	0	1	1	1	
State Police Agencies	1	3	0	0	0	1					
State Police											
Bridgeport	0	1	0	0	0	0	0	0	0	1	
Hamlin	0	0	0	0	0	1	0	1	0	0	
Morgantown	1	0	0	0	0	0	0	0	0	0	
Wayne	0	2	0	0	0	0	0	1	0	1	
Other Agencies	0	0	1	0	0	0					
Metropolitan Drug Enforcement Network Team	0	0	1	0	0	0	1	0	0	0	
WISCONSIN											
Total	39	18	5	4	2	6					
Cities	29	14	4	4	2	5					
Appleton	2	0	0	2	0	0	0	1	3	0	74,757
Barron	1	0	0	0	0	0	0	0	1	0	3,306
Beloit	0	1	0	0	0	0	0	0	0	1	37,025
Campbell Township	0	1	0	0	0	0	0	1	0	0	4,337
Chippewa Falls	0	0	0	0	1	0	0	1	0	0	14,237
Ellsworth	1	0	0	0	0	0	0	0	1	0	3,306
Fond du Lac	0	2	0	0	0	0	1	1	0	0	42,954

Table 94. Hate Crime Incidents Per Bias Motivation and Quarter, by Selected State and Agency and Federal, 2019—Continued

(Number.)

State/agency	Number of incidents per bias motivation						Number of incidents per quarter				Population[1]
	Race/ Ethnicity/ Ancestry	Religion	Sexual orientation	Disability	Gender	Gender Identity	1st quarter	2nd quarter	3rd quarter	4th quarter	
Green Bay	1	1	0	0	0	0	0	1	1	0	104,992
Hudson	0	0	1	0	0	0	0	0	0	1	14,074
Janesville	2	1	0	1	0	3	1	2	3	1	64,687
Jefferson	1	0	0	0	0	0	0	0	0	1	8,042
Juneau	1	0	0	0	0	0	1	0	0	0	2,639
La Crosse	0	1	0	0	1	0	0	0	1	1	51,591
Lake Delton	1	0	0	0	0	0	0	0	0	1	3,005
Madison	3	1	3	0	0	0	1	0	4	2	261,270
Mayville	2	0	0	0	0	0	0	2	0	0	4,859
Menasha	1	0	0	0	0	0	0	1	0	0	17,809
Milwaukee	2	0	0	0	0	0	0	1	1	0	590,923
Monroe	4	0	0	0	0	0	1	0	3	0	10,537
Neenah	1	0	0	0	0	0	0	0	0	1	26,133
New London	0	1	0	0	0	0	0	0	1	0	7,118
North Fond du Lac	0	0	0	1	0	0	0	0	1	0	5,098
Oshkosh	0	2	0	0	0	0	1	0	0	1	66,797
Platteville	1	0	0	0	0	0	0	0	0	1	12,115
Port Washington	1	0	0	0	0	0	0	0	0	1	11,908
Rice Lake	1	0	0	0	0	2	0	0	3	0	8,369
Ripon	0	1	0	0	0	0	0	0	1	0	7,820
Sheboygan	1	0	0	0	0	0	1	0	0	0	48,035
Town of Madison	1	0	0	0	0	0	0	0	1	0	6,934
Wauwatosa	0	1	0	0	0	0	0	1	0	0	48,562
Winneconne	0	1	0	0	0	0	0	0	1	0	2,506
Wisconsin Rapids	1	0	0	0	0	0	1		0	0	17,613
Metropolitan Counties	4	4	0	0	0	0					
Columbia	0	2	0	0	0	0	1	1	0	0	
Dane	1	0	0	0	0	0	0	0	0	1	
Douglas	1	0	0	0	0	0	0	0	1	0	
Iowa	1	0	0	0	0	0	0	0	1	0	
Outagamie	0	1	0	0	0	0	0	1	0	0	
Rock	1	1	0	0	0	0	1	1	0	0	
Nonmetropolitan Counties	6	0	1	0	0	1					
Dodge	2	0	1	0	0	0	1	0	2	0	
Manitowoc	1	0	0	0	0	0	0	1	0	0	
Monroe	1	0	0	0	0	0	0	0	0	1	
Oneida	1	0	0	0	0	0	0	0	0	1	
Sauk	1	0	0	0	0	1	1	0	1	0	
WYOMING											
Total	4	0	1	0	0	0					
Cities	3	0	1	0	0	0					
Cody	1	0	0	0	0	0	0	1	0	0	9,865
Evanston	1	0	0	0	0	0	0	0	1	0	11,624
Laramie	0	0	1	0	0	0	0	0	1	0	32,669
Sheridan	1	0	0	0	0	0	1	0	0	0	17,895
Universities and Colleges	1	0	0	0	0	0					
University of Wyoming	1	0	0	0	0	0	0	0	1	0	13,963
FEDERAL											
Federal Agencies	63	47	19	0	0	3					
Federal Bureau of Investigation Field Offices											
Albany, NY	1	0	0	0	0	0			1		
Anchorage, AK	1	2	1	0	0	0		2		2	
Atlanta, GA[2]	4	1	0	0	0	0	1	1		2	
Baltimore, MD	2	2	0	0	0	0	1	1	1	1	
Birmingham, AL[2]	0	1	1	0	0	0		1			
Boston, MA	1	2	1	0	0	0	2	2			
Charlotte, NC	1	0	0	0	0	0			1		
Chicago, IL	1	1	0	0	0	0		1		1	
Cincinnati, OH	1	0	0	0	0	0		1			
Cleveland, OH	1	0	0	0	0	0		1			
Columbia, SC	1	0	0	0	0	0			1		
Dallas, TX	1	1	1	0	0	1	1	1	1	1	
Denver, CO	0	1	1	0	0	1		1	1	1	
Detroit, MI	3	1	2	0	0	0		3	2	1	
El Paso, TX	2	4	0	0	0	0		4	1	1	
Houston, TX	1	0	0	0	0	0	1				
Jacksonville, FL	1	0	0	0	0	0		1			
Kansas City, MO	3	0	1	0	0	0	2	1	1		
Las Vegas, NV	0	1	0	0	0	0	1				
Los Angeles, CA	0	1	1	0	0	0		1	1		
Memphis, TN	0	3	0	0	0	0			3		
Miami, FL	1	2	0	0	0	0			2	1	
Milwaukee, WI	1	0	0	0	0	0				1	

Table 94. Hate Crime Incidents Per Bias Motivation and Quarter, by Selected State and Agency and Federal, 2019—Continued

(Number.)

State/agency	Number of incidents per bias motivation						Number of incidents per quarter				Population[1]
	Race/ Ethnicity/ Ancestry	Religion	Sexual orientation	Disability	Gender	Gender Identity	1st quarter	2nd quarter	3rd quarter	4th quarter	
Minneapolis, MN	0	3	0	0	0	0	1		1	1	
Mobile, AL[2]	3	0	1	0	0	0			1	2	
New Haven, CT	0	1	0	0	0	0		1			
New Orleans, LA[2]	4	3	0	0	0	0		3		1	
New York, NY	1	5	0	0	0	0	2		2	2	
Newark, NJ	1	0	0	0	0	0				1	
Norfolk, VA	3	0	0	0	0	0	1			2	
Oklahoma City, OK	1	1	1	0	0	0	1	1	1		
Omaha, NE	2	1	0	0	0	0		3			
Philadelphia, PA	2	0	0	0	0	0		1	1		
Pittsburgh, PA	1	0	0	0	0	0				1	
Portland, OR	1	0	0	0	0	0				1	
Richmond, VA	1	0	0	0	0	0	1				
Sacramento, CA[2]	2	1	1	0	0	0		1	2		
Salt Lake City, UT[2]	4	1	1	0	0	0	2		1	2	
San Antonio, TX	0	1	0	0	0	0		1			
San Diego, CA	0	2	1	0	0	0	1	1		1	
Seattle, WA	0	0	1	0	0	0		1			
Springfield, IL	1	0	0	0	0	0			1		
St. Louis, MO	3	0	2	0	0	0	1	3		1	
Tampa, FL	1	0	0	0	0	1			2		
Washington, DC	1	4	1	0	0	0	1	3	2		
Pentagon Force Protection Agency	0	0	1	0	0	0	1	0	0		
U.S. Navy Law Enforcement	4	0	0	0	0	0	0	0	2	2	
United States Army	0	1	0	0	0	0	0	1	0	0	

1 Population figures are published only for the cities. The figures listed for the universities and colleges are student enrollment and were provided by the United States Department of Education for the 2018 school year, the most recent available. The enrollment figures include full-time and part-time students.   2 The figures shown include one incident reported with more than one bias motivation.   3 Student enrollment figures were not available.

Table 95. Participation Table, Number of Participating Agencies and Population Covered, by Population Group and Federal, 2019

(Number.)

Population group	Number of participating agencies	Population covered
Total	15,588	305,284,239
Group I (cities 250,000 and over)	88	64,003,500
Group II (cities 100,000-249,999)	220	32,129,155
Group III (cities 50,000-99,999)	481	33,572,735
Group IV (cities 25,000-49,999)	872	30,181,113
Group V (cities 10,000-24,999)	1,774	28,305,204
Group VI[1] (cities under 10,000)	7,875	22,762,154
Metropolitan counties[1]	1,924	71,500,130
Nonmetropolitan counties[1]	2,304	22,830,248
Federal[2]	50	

1 The figures shown include universities and colleges, state police agencies, and/or other agencies to which no population is attributed.   2 Population estimates are not attributed to the federal agencies.

APPENDIXES

APPENDIX I. METHODOLOGY

Submitting UCR data to the FBI is a collective effort on the part of city, university/college, county, state, tribal, and federal law enforcement agencies to present a nationwide view of crime. Participating agencies throughout the country voluntarily provide reports on crimes known to the police and on persons arrested. For the most part, agencies submit monthly crime reports, using uniform offense definitions, to a centralized repository within their state. The state UCR Program then forwards the data to the FBI's UCR Program. Agencies in states that do not have a state UCR Program submit their data directly to the FBI. Staff members review the information for accuracy and reasonableness. [The FBI distributes the data presentations, special studies, and other publications compiled from the data to all who are interested in knowing about crime in the nation.] The national UCR Program is housed in the Operational Programs (OP) Branch of the FBI's Criminal Justice Information Services (CJIS) Division. Within the OP Branch, four units (the Crime Statistics Management Unit [CSMU], the CJIS Audit Unit, the Multimedia Productions Group [MPG]), and the CJIS Training and Advisory Process [CTAP] Unit), are involved in the day-to-day administration of the program.

Criteria for State UCR programs

The criteria established for state programs ensure consistency and comparability in the data submitted to the national program, as well as regular and timely reporting. These criteria are:

1. A UCR Program must conform to the FBI UCR Program's submission standards, definitions, specifications, and required deadlines.

2. A UCR Program must establish data integrity procedures and have personnel assigned to assist contributing agencies in quality assurance practices and crime reporting procedures. Data integrity procedures should include crime trend assessments, offense classification verification, and technical specification validation.

3. A UCR Program's submissions must cover more than 50 percent of the law enforcement agencies within its established reporting domain and be willing to cover any and all UCR-contributing agencies that wish to use the UCR Program from within its domain. (An agency wishing to become a UCR Program must be willing to report for all of the agencies within the state.)

4. A UCR Program must furnish the FBI UCR Program with all of the UCR data collected by the law enforcement agencies within its domain.

These requirements do not prohibit the state from gathering other statistical data beyond the national collection.

Data Completeness and Quality

National program staff members contact the state UCR program in connection with crime-reporting matters and, when necessary and approved by the state, they contact individual contributors within the state. To fulfill its responsibilities in connection with the UCR program, the FBI reviews and edits individual agency reports for completeness and quality. Upon request, they conduct training programs within the state on law enforcement record-keeping and crime-reporting procedures. The FBI conducts an audit of each state's UCR data collection procedures once every three years, in accordance with audit standards established by the federal government. Should circumstances develop in which the state program does not comply with the aforementioned requirements, the national program may institute a direct collection of data from law enforcement agencies within the state.

During a review of publication processes, the UCR Program staff analyzed Web statistics from previous editions of *Crime in the United States* (*CIUS*) to determine the tables that users access the most. Based on these criteria, the UCR Program streamlined the 2016 edition by reducing the number of tables from 81 to 29. The publication, however, still presents the major topics (offenses known, clearances, and persons arrested) that readers have come to expect. On June 30, 2017, the UCR Program launched the Crime Data Explorer (CDE), which provides law enforcement and the general public with crime data at the agency, state, and national levels. Offering multiple pathways to reported crime data, the CDE provides data visualizations of high-level trends and incident data with more detailed perspectives through downloads and a system enabling developers to create software applications. Planned enhancements to the CDE include additional tools to create dynamic data presentations, progressing beyond the static data tables of *CIUS* and the National Incident-Based Reporting System (NIBRS).

Beginning January 1, 2017, the UCR Program discontinued collecting rape data via the SRS according to the legacy definition. Therefore, the 2016 editions of *CIUS* and *Hate Crime Statistics* are the final publications which include the legacy definition of rape. Only rape data submitted under the revised definition will be published for 2017 and subsequent years. This change did not affect agencies that submit rape data via NIBRS.

Reporting Procedures

Offenses known and value of property–Law enforcement agencies tabulate the number of Part I offenses reported based on records of all reports of crime received from victims, officers who discover infractions, or other sources, and submit these reports each month to the FBI directly or through their state UCR programs. Part I offenses include murder and nonnegligent manslaughter, forcible rape, robbery, aggravated assault, burglary, larceny-theft, motor vehicle theft, and arson. Each month, law enforcement agencies also submit to the FBI the value of property stolen and recovered in connection with the offenses and detailed information pertaining to criminal homicide.

Unfounded offenses and clearances—When, through investigation, an agency determines that complaints of crimes are unfounded or false, the agency eliminates that offense from its crime tally through an entry on the monthly report. The report also provides the total number of actual Part I offenses, the number of offenses cleared, and the number of clearances that involve only offenders under the age of 18. (Law enforcement can clear crimes in one of two ways: by the arrest of at least one person who is charged and turned over to the court for prosecution or by exceptional means—when some element beyond law enforcement's control precludes the arrest of a known offender.)

Persons arrested—In addition to reporting Part I offenses each month, law enforcement agencies also provide data on the age, sex, and race of persons arrested for Part I and Part II offenses. Part II offenses encompass all crimes, except traffic violations, that are not classified as Part I offenses.

Officers killed or assaulted—Each month, law enforcement agencies also report information to the UCR program regarding law enforcement officers killed or assaulted, and each year they report the number of full-time sworn and civilian law enforcement personnel employed as of October 31.

Hate crimes—At the end of each quarter, law enforcement agencies report summarized data on hate crimes; that is specific offenses that were motivated by an offender's bias against the perceived race, religion, ethnic or national origin, sexual orientation, or physical or mental disability of the victim. Those agencies participating in the UCR program's National Incident-Based Reporting System (NIBRS) submit hate crime data monthly.

Editing Procedures

The UCR program thoroughly examines each report it receives for arithmetical accuracy and for deviations in crime data from month to month and from present to past years that may indicate errors. UCR staff members compare an agency's monthly reports with its previous submissions and with reports from similar agencies to identify any unusual fluctuations in the agency's crime count. Considerable variations in crime levels may indicate modified records procedures, incomplete reporting, or changes in the jurisdiction's geopolitical structure.

Evaluation of trends—Data reliability is a high priority of the FBI, which brings any deviations or arithmetical adjustments to the attention of state UCR programs or the submitting agencies. Typically, FBI staff members study the monthly reports to evaluate periodic trends prepared for individual reporting units. Any significant increase or decrease becomes the subject of a special inquiry. Changes in crime reporting procedures or annexations that affect an agency's jurisdiction can influence the level of reported crime. When this occurs, the FBI excludes the figures for specific crime categories or totals, if necessary, from the trend tabulations.

Training for contributors—In addition to the evaluation of trends, the FBI provides training seminars and instructional materials on crime reporting procedures to assist contributors in complying with UCR standards. Throughout the country, representatives from the national program coordinate with representatives of state programs and law enforcement personnel and hold training sessions to explain the purpose of the program, the rules of uniform classification and scoring, and the methods of assembling the information for reporting. When an individual agency has specific problems with compiling its crime statistics and its remedial efforts are unsuccessful, personnel from the FBI's Criminal Justice Information Services Division may visit the contributor to aid in resolving the problems.

UCR Handbook—The national UCR program publishes the *Uniform Crime Reporting (UCR) Handbook*, which details procedures for classifying and scoring offenses and serves as the contributing agencies' basic resource for preparing reports. The national staff also produces letters to UCR contributors, state program bulletins, and UCR newsletters as needed. These publications provide policy updates and new information, as well as clarification of reporting issues.

The final responsibility for data submissions rests with the individual contributing law enforcement agency. Although the FBI makes every effort through its editing procedures, training practices, and correspondence to ensure the validity of the data it receives, the accuracy of the statistics depends primarily on the adherence of each contributor to the established standards of reporting. Deviations from these established standards that cannot be resolved by the national UCR program may be brought to the attention of the Criminal Justice Information Systems Committees of the International Association of Chiefs of Police and the National Sheriffs' Association.

NIBRS Conversion

Thirty-three state programs are certified to provide their UCR data in the expanded National Incident-Based Reporting System (NIBRS) format. For presentation in this book, the NIBRS data were converted to the historical Summary Reporting System data. The UCR program staff constructed the NIBRS database to allow for such conversion so that UCR's long-running time series could continue.

Crime Trends

By showing fluctuations from year to year, trend statistics offer the data user an added perspective from which to study crime. Percent change tabulations in this publication are computed only for reporting agencies that provided comparable data for the periods under consideration. The FBI excludes from the trend calculations all figures except those received for common months from common agencies. Also excluded are unusual fluctuations of data that the FBI determines are the result of such variables as improved records procedures, annexations, and so on.

Caution to Users

Data users should exercise care in making any direct comparison between data in this publication and those in prior issues of *Crime in the United States*. Because of differing levels of participation from year to year and reporting problems that require the FBI to estimate crime counts for certain contributors, some data may not be comparable. In addition, this publication may contain updates to data provided in prior years' publications.

Offense Estimation

Some tables in this publication contain statistics for the entire United States. Because not all law enforcement agencies provide data for complete reporting periods, the FBI includes estimated crime numbers in these presentations. The FBI estimates data for three areas: Metropolitan Statistical Areas (MSAs), cities outside MSAs, and nonmetropolitan counties; and computes estimates for participating agencies that do not provide 12 months of complete data. For agencies supplying 3 to 11 months of data, the national UCR program estimates for the missing data by following a standard estimation procedure using the data provided by the agency. If an agency has supplied less than 3 months of data, the FBI computes estimates by using the known crime figures of similar areas within a state and assigning the same proportion of crime volumes to nonreporting agencies. The estimation process considers the following: population size covered by the agency; type of jurisdiction; for example, police department versus sheriff's office; and geographic location.

Estimation of State-Level Data

In response to various circumstances, the FBI calculates estimated offense totals for certain states. For example, some states do not provide forcible rape figures in accordance with UCR guidelines. In addition, problems at the state level have, at times, resulted in no useable data. Also, the conversion of the National Incident-Based Reporting System (NIBRS) data to Summary data has contributed to the need for unique estimation procedures.

APPENDIX II. OFFENSE DEFINITIONS

The Uniform Crime Reporting (UCR) program divides offenses into two groups. Contributing agencies submit information on the number of Part I offenses known to law enforcement; those offenses cleared by arrest or exceptional means; and the age, sex, and race of persons arrested for each of these offenses. Contributors provide only arrest data for Part II offenses. These are definitions of offenses set forth by the UCR.

The UCR program collects data on Part I offenses to measure the level and scope of crime occurring throughout the nation. The program's founders chose these offenses because (1) they are serious crimes, (2) they occur with regularity in all areas of the country, and (3) they are likely to be reported to police.

Part I offenses include criminal homicide, forcible rape, robbery, aggravated assault, burglary, larceny-theft, motor vehicle theft, and arson.

Criminal homicide — a.) Murder and nonnegligent manslaughter: the willful (nonnegligent) killing of one human being by another. Deaths caused by negligence, attempts to kill, assaults to kill, suicides, and accidental deaths are excluded. The program classifies justifiable homicides separately and limits the definition to (1) the killing of a felon by a law enforcement officer in the line of duty; or (2) the killing of a felon, during the commission of a felony, by a private citizen. b. Manslaughter by negligence: the killing of another person through gross negligence. Deaths of persons due to their own negligence, accidental deaths not resulting from gross negligence, and traffic fatalities are excluded.

Rape — In 2013, the FBI UCR Program began collecting rape data under a revised definition within the Summary Reporting System. Previously, offense data for forcible rape were collected under the legacy UCR definition: the carnal knowledge of a female forcibly and against her will. Beginning with the 2013 data year, the term "forcible" was removed from the offense title, and the definition was changed. The revised UCR definition of rape is: penetration, no matter how slight, of the vagina or anus with any body part or object, or oral penetration by a sex organ of another person, without the consent of the victim. Attempts or assaults to commit rape are also included in the statistics presented here; however, statutory rape and incest are excluded. In 2016, the FBI director approved the recommendation to discontinue the reporting of rape data using the UCR legacy definition beginning in 2017. However, to maintain the 20-year trend in Table 1, national estimates for rape under the legacy definition are provided along with estimates under the revised definition for 2017. The UCR Program counts one offense for each victim of a rape, attempted rape, or assault with intent to rape, regardless of the victim's age. Non-consensual sexual relations involving a familial member is considered rape, not incest. All other crimes of a sexual nature are considered to be Part II offenses; as such, the UCR Program collects only arrest data for those crimes. The offense of statutory rape, in which no force is used but the female victim is under the age of consent, is included in the arrest total for the sex offenses category.

Robbery — The taking or attempted taking of anything of value from the care, custody, or control of a person or persons by force or threat of force or violence and/or by putting the victim in fear.

Aggravated assault — An unlawful attack by one person upon another for the purpose of inflicting severe or aggravated bodily injury. This type of assault usually is accompanied by the use of a weapon or by means likely to produce death or great bodily harm. Simple assaults are excluded.

Burglary (breaking or entering) — The unlawful entry of a structure to commit a felony or a theft. Attempted forcible entry is included.

Larceny-theft (except motor vehicle theft) — The unlawful taking, carrying, leading, or riding away of property from the possession or constructive possession of another. Examples are thefts of bicycles or automobile parts and accessories, shoplifting, pocket-picking, or the stealing of any property or article that is not taken by force and violence or by fraud. Attempted larcenies are included. Embezzlement, confidence games, forgery, worthless checks, and the like, are excluded.

Motor vehicle theft — The theft or attempted theft of a motor vehicle. A motor vehicle is self-propelled and runs on land surface and not on rails. Motorboats, construction equipment, airplanes, and farming equipment are specifically excluded from this category.

Arson — Any willful or malicious burning or attempt to burn, with or without intent to defraud, a dwelling house, public building, motor vehicle, aircraft, personal property of another, and the like.

The **Part II** offenses for which only arrest data are collected, are:

Other assaults, also known as other assaults (simple) — Assaults and attempted assaults that are not of an aggravated nature and do not result in serious injury to the victim. Included in this category are stalking, intimidation, coercion, and hazing.

Forgery and counterfeiting—The altering, copying, or imitating of something, without authority or right, with the intent to deceive or defraud by passing the copy or thing altered or imitated as that which is original or genuine; or the selling, buying, or possession of an altered, copied, or imitated thing with the intent to deceive or defraud. Attempts are included.

Fraud—The intentional perversion of the truth for the purpose of inducing another person or other entity in reliance upon it to part with something of value or to surrender a legal right. Fraudulent conversion and obtaining of money or property by false pretenses. Confidence games and bad checks, except forgeries and counterfeiting, are included.

Embezzlement—The unlawful misappropriation or misapplication by an offender of money, property, or some other thing of value entrusted to that offender's care, custody, or control.

Stolen property; buying, receiving, possessing—Buying, receiving, possessing, selling, concealing, or transporting any property with the knowledge that it has been unlawfully taken, as by burglary, embezzlement, fraud, larceny, robbery, and the like. Attempts are included.

Vandalism—To willfully or maliciously destroy, injure, disfigure, or deface any public or private property, real or personal, without the consent of the owner or person having custody or control by cutting, tearing, breaking, marking, painting, drawing, covering with filth, or any other such means as may be specified by local law. Attempts are included.

Weapons; carrying, possessing, and the like—The violation of laws or ordinances prohibiting the manufacture, sale, purchase, transportation, possession, concealment, or use of firearms, cutting instruments, explosives, incendiary devices, or other deadly weapons. Attempts are included.

Prostitution and commercialized vice—The unlawful promotion of or participation in sexual activities for profit, including attempts. To solicit customers or transport persons for prostitution purposes; to own, manage, or operate a dwelling or other establishment for the purposes of providing a place where prostitution is performed; or to otherwise assist or promote prostitution.

Sex offenses (except forcible rape, prostitution, and commercialized vice)—Offenses against chastity, common decency, morals, and the like. Incest, indecent exposure, and statutory rape, as well as attempts are included.

Drug abuse violations—The violation of laws prohibiting the production, distribution, and/or use of certain controlled substances. The unlawful cultivation, manufacture, distribution, sale, purchase, use, possession, transportation, or importation of any controlled drug or narcotic substance. Arrests for violations of state and local laws, specifically those relating to the unlawful possession, sale, use, growing, manufacturing, and making of narcotic drugs. The following drug categories are specified: opium or cocaine and their derivatives (morphine, heroin, codeine); marijuana; synthetic narcotics—manufactured narcotics that can cause true addiction (demerol, methadone); and dangerous nonnarcotic drugs (barbiturates, benzedrine).

Gambling—To unlawfully bet or wager money or something else of value; assist, promote, or operate a game of chance for money or some other stake; possess or transmit wagering information; manufacture, sell, purchase, possess, or transport gambling equipment, devices, or goods; or tamper with the outcome of a sporting event or contest to gain a gambling advantage.

Offenses against the family and children—Unlawful nonviolent acts by a family member (or legal guardian) that threaten the physical, mental, or economic well-being or morals of another family member and that are not classifiable as other offenses, such as assault or sex offenses. Attempts are included.

Driving under the influence—Driving or operating a motor vehicle or common carrier while mentally or physically impaired as the result of consuming an alcoholic beverage or using a drug or narcotic.

Liquor laws—The violation of state or local laws or ordinances prohibiting the manufacture, sale, purchase, transportation, possession, or use of alcoholic beverages, not including driving under the influence and drunkenness. Federal violations are excluded.

Drunkenness—To drink alcoholic beverages to the extent that one's mental faculties and physical coordination are substantially impaired. Excludes driving under the influence.

Disorderly conduct—Any behavior that tends to disturb the public peace or decorum, scandalize the community, or shock the public sense of morality.

Vagrancy—The violation of a court order, regulation, ordinance, or law requiring the withdrawal of persons from the streets or other specified areas; prohibiting persons from remaining in an area or place in an idle or aimless manner; or prohibiting persons from going from place to place without visible means of support.

All other offenses—All violations of state or local laws not specifically identified as Part I or Part II offenses, except traffic violations.

Suspicion—Arrested for no specific offense and released without formal charges being placed.

Curfew and loitering laws (persons under 18 years of age)—Violations by juveniles of local curfew or loitering ordinances.

APPENDIX III. GEOGRAPHIC AREA DEFINITIONS

The program collects crime data and supplemental information that make it possible to generate a variety of statistical compilations, including data presented by reporting areas. These statistics enable data users to analyze local crime data in conjunction with those for areas of similar geographic location or population size. The reporting areas that the program uses in its data breakdowns include community types, population groups, and regions and divisions. For community types, the program considers proximity to metropolitan areas using the designations established by the U.S. Office of Management and Budget (OMB). (Generally, sheriffs, county police, and state police report crimes within counties but outside of cities; local police report crimes within city limits.) The number of inhabitants living in a locale (based on the U.S. Census Bureau's figures) determines the population group into which the program places it. For its geographic breakdowns, the program divides the United States into regions and divisions.

Regions and Divisions

The map below illustrates the nine divisions that make up the four regions of the United States. The program uses this widely recognized geographic organization when compiling the nation's crime data. The regions and divisions are as follows:

NORTHEAST

New England—Connecticut, Maine, Massachusetts, New Hampshire, Rhode Island, and Vermont

Middle Atlantic—New York, New Jersey, and Pennsylvania

MIDWEST

East North Central—Illinois, Indiana, Michigan, Ohio, and Wisconsin

West North Central—Iowa, Kansas, Minnesota, Missouri, Nebraska, North Dakota, and South Dakota

SOUTH

South Atlantic—Delaware, District of Columbia, Florida, Georgia, Maryland, North Carolina, South Carolina, Virginia, and West Virginia

East South Central—Alabama, Kentucky, Mississippi, and Tennessee

West South Central—Arkansas, Louisiana, Oklahoma, and Texas

WEST

Mountain—Arizona, Colorado, Idaho, Montana, Nevada, New Mexico, Utah, and Wyoming

Pacific—Alaska, California, Hawaii, Oregon, and Washington

Community Types

To assist data users who wish to analyze and present uniform statistical data about metropolitan areas, the program uses reporting units that represent major population centers. The program compiles data for the following three types of communities:

Metropolitan Statistical Areas (MSAs)—Each MSA contains a principal city or urbanized area with a population of at least 50,000 inhabitants. MSAs include the principal city, the county in which the city is located, and other adjacent counties that have a high degree of economic and social integration with the principal city and county (as defined by the OMB), which is measured through commuting. In the program, counties within an MSA are considered metropolitan counties. In addition, MSAs may cross state boundaries.

Some presentations in this publication refer to Metropolitan Divisions, which are subdivisions of an MSA that consists of a core with "a population of at least 2.5 million persons. A Metropolitan Division consists of one or more main/secondary counties that represent an employment center or centers, plus adjacent counties associated with the main county or counties through commuting ties," (*Federal Register* 65 [249]). Also, some tables reference suburban areas, which are subdivisions of MSAs that exclude the principal cities but include all the remaining cities (those having fewer than 50,000 inhabitants) and the unincorporated areas of the MSAs.

Because the elements that comprise MSAs, particularly the geographic compositions, are subject to change, the program discourages data users from making year-to-year comparisons of MSA data.

Cities Outside MSAs—Ordinarily, cities outside MSAs are incorporated areas. In 2013, cities outside MSAs made up 6.0 percent of the nation's population.

Nonmetropolitan Counties Outside MSAs—Most non-metropolitan counties are composed of unincorporated areas.

Metropolitan and nonmetropolitan community types are further illustrated in the following table:

Metropolitan	Nonmetropolitan
Principal cities (50,000+ inhabitants)	Cities outside metropolitan areas
Suburban cities	
Metropolitan counties	Nonmetropolitan counties

APPENDIX IV. THE NATION'S TWO CRIME MEASURES

The Department of Justice administers two statistical programs to measure the magnitude, nature, and impact of crime in the nation: the Uniform Crime Reporting (UCR) program and the National Crime Victimization Survey (NCVS). Each of these programs produces valuable information about aspects of the nation's crime problem. Because the UCR and NCVS programs are conducted for different purposes, use different methods, and focus on somewhat different aspects of crime, the information they produce together provides a more comprehensive panorama of the nation's crime problem than either could produce alone.

Uniform Crime Reporting (UCR) program

The UCR program, administered by the Federal Bureau of Investigation (FBI), was created in 1929 and collects information on the following crimes reported to law enforcement authorities: murder and nonnegligent manslaughter, forcible rape, robbery, aggravated assault, burglary, larceny-theft, motor vehicle theft, and arson. Law enforcement agencies also report arrest data for 20 additional crime categories.

The UCR program compiles data from monthly law enforcement reports and from individual crime incident records transmitted directly to the FBI or to centralized state agencies that report to the FBI. The program thoroughly examines each report it receives for reasonableness, accuracy, and deviations that may indicate errors. Large variations in crime levels may indicate modified records procedures, incomplete reporting, or changes in a jurisdiction's boundaries. To identify any unusual fluctuations in an agency's crime counts, the program compares monthly reports to previous submissions of the agency and to those for similar agencies.

The FBI annually publishes its findings in a preliminary release in the spring of the following calendar year, followed by a detailed annual report, *Crime in the United States*, issued in the fall. (The printed copy of *Crime in the United States* is now published by Bernan.) In addition to crime counts and trends, this report includes data on crimes cleared, persons arrested (age, sex, and race), law enforcement personnel (including the number of sworn officers killed or assaulted), and the characteristics of homicides (including age, sex, and race of victims and offenders; victim-offender relationships; weapons used; and circumstances surrounding the homicides). Other periodic reports are also available from the UCR program.

The state and local law enforcement agencies participating in the UCR program are continually converting to the more comprehensive and detailed National Incident-Based Reporting System (NIBRS).

The UCR program presents crime counts for the nation as a whole, as well as for regions, states, counties, cities, towns, tribal law enforcement areas, and colleges and universities. This allows for studies among neighboring jurisdictions and among those with similar populations and other common characteristics.

National Crime Victimization Survey

The NCVS, conducted by the Bureau of Justice Statistics (BJS), began in 1973. It provides a detailed picture of crime incidents, victims, and trends. After a substantial period of research, the BJS completed an intensive methodological redesign of the survey in 1993. It conducted this redesign to improve the questions used to uncover crime, update the survey methods, and broaden the scope of crimes measured. The redesigned survey collects detailed information on the frequency and nature of the crimes of rape, sexual assault, personal robbery, aggravated and simple assault, household burglary, theft, and motor vehicle theft. It does not measure homicide or commercial crimes (such as burglaries of stores).

Twice a year, Census Bureau personnel interview household members in a nationally representative sample of approximately 90,000 households (about 160,000 people). Households stay in the sample for 3 years, and new households rotate into the sample on an ongoing basis.

The NCVS collects information on crimes suffered by individuals and households, whether or not those crimes were reported to law enforcement. It estimates the proportion of each crime type reported to law enforcement, and it summarizes the reasons that victims give for reporting or not reporting.

The survey provides information about victims (age, sex, race, ethnicity, marital status, income, and educational level); offenders (sex, race, approximate age, and victim-offender relationship); and crimes (time and place of occurrence, use of weapons, nature of injury, and economic consequences). Questions also cover victims' experiences with the criminal justice system, self-protective measures used by victims, and possible substance abuse by offenders. Supplements are added to the survey periodically to obtain detailed information on specific topics, such as school crime.

The BJS published the first data from the redesigned NCVS in a June 1995 bulletin. The publication of NCVS data includes *Criminal Victimization in the United States*, an annual report that covers the broad range of detailed information collected by the NCVS. The bureau also publishes detailed reports on topics such as crime against women, urban crime, and gun use in crime. The National Archive of Criminal Justice Data at the University of Michigan archives the NCVS data files to help researchers perform independent analyses.

Comparing the UCR program and the NCVS

Because the BJS designed the NCVS to complement the UCR program, the two programs share many similarities. As much as their different collection methods permit, the two measure the same subset of serious crimes with the same definitions. Both programs cover rape, robbery, aggravated assault, burglary, theft, and motor vehicle theft; both define rape, robbery, theft, and motor vehicle theft virtually identically. (Although rape is defined analogously, the UCR program measures the crime against women only, and the NCVS measures it against both sexes.)

There are also significant differences between the two programs. First, the two programs were created to serve different purposes. The UCR program's primary objective is to provide a reliable set of criminal justice statistics for law enforcement administration, operation, and management. The BJS established the NCVS to provide previously unavailable information about crime (including crime not reported to police), victims, and offenders.

Second, the two programs measure an overlapping but nonidentical set of crimes. The NCVS includes crimes both reported and not reported to law enforcement. The NCVS excludes—but the UCR program includes—homicide, arson, commercial crimes, and crimes committed against children under 12 years of age. The UCR program captures crimes reported to law enforcement but collects only arrest data for simple assaults and sexual assaults other than forcible rape.

Third, because of methodology, the NCVS and UCR have different definitions of some crimes. For example, the UCR defines burglary as the unlawful entry or attempted entry of a structure to commit a felony or theft. The NCVS, not wanting to ask victims to ascertain offender motives, defines burglary as the entry or attempted entry of a residence by a person who had no right to be there.

Fourth, for property crimes (burglary, theft, and motor vehicle theft), the two programs calculate crime rates using different bases. The UCR program rates for these crimes are per capita (number of crimes per 100,000 persons), whereas the NCVS rates for these crimes are per household (number of crimes per 1,000 households).

Because the number of households may not grow at the same annual rate as the total population, trend data for rates of property crimes measured by the two programs may not be comparable. In addition, some differences in the data from the two programs may result from sampling variation in the NCVS and from estimating for nonresponsiveness in the UCR program.

The BJS derives the NCVS estimates from interviewing a sample and are, therefore, subject to a margin of error. The bureau uses rigorous statistical methods to calculate confidence intervals around all survey estimates, and describes trend data in the NCVS reports as genuine only if there is at least a 90-percent certainty that the measured changes are not the result of sampling variation. The UCR program bases its data on the actual counts of offenses reported by law enforcement agencies. In some circumstances, the UCR program estimates its data for nonparticipating agencies or those reporting partial data. Apparent discrepancies between statistics from the two programs can usually be accounted for by their definitional and procedural differences, or resolved by comparing NCVS sampling variations (confidence intervals) of crimes said to have been reported to police with UCR program statistics.

For most types of crimes measured by both the UCR program and the NCVS, analysts familiar with the programs can exclude those aspects of crime not common to both from analysis. Resulting long-term trend lines can be brought into close concordance. The impact of such adjustments is most striking for robbery, burglary, and motor vehicle theft, whose definitions most closely coincide.

With robbery, the BJS bases the NCVS victimization rates on only those robberies reported to the police. It is also possible to remove UCR program robberies of commercial establishments, such as gas stations, convenience stores, and banks, from analysis. When users compare the resulting NCVS police-reported robbery rates and the UCR program noncommercial robbery rates, the results reveal closely corresponding long-term trends.

Conclusion

Each program has unique strengths. The UCR program provides a measure of the number of crimes reported to law enforcement agencies throughout the country. The program's Supplementary Homicide Reports provide the most reliable, timely data on the extent and nature of homicides in the nation. The NCVS is the primary source of information on the characteristics of criminal victimization and on the number and types of crimes not reported to law enforcement authorities.

By understanding the strengths and limitations of each program, it is possible to use the UCR program and NCVS to achieve a greater understanding of crime trends and the nature of crime in the United States. For example, changes in police procedures, shifting attitudes towards crime and police, and other societal changes can affect the extent to which people report and law enforcement agencies record crime. NCVS and UCR program data can be used in concert to explore why trends in reported and police-recorded crime may differ.

Appendix V – Calculations by Population, Tables 16, 17, 18, 19 (Section II)

Due to a system upgrade in 2019, the FBI calculates rates for each offense based on the individual offenses and population that were published for each agency in tables 8-11. (Previous to 2019, when agencies were published in tables 8-11, but they had one or two offenses removed from publication due to not meeting UCR publication guidelines, the agency's data was not used to calculate rates for this table.) This table provides the rate per 100,000 inhabitants and the number of offenses known to law enforcement for violent crimes (murder and non-negligent manslaughter, rape, robbery, and aggravated assault) and property crimes (burglary, larceny-theft, and motor vehicle theft) nationally and by city and county groupings for law enforcement agencies submitting 12 months of publishable data for 2019. For the 2019 population estimates used in this table, the FBI computed individual rates of growth from one year to the next for every city/town and county using 2010 decennial population counts and 2011 through 2018 population estimates from the U.S. Census Bureau. Each agency's rates of growth were averaged; that average was then applied and added to its 2018 Census population estimate to derive the agency's 2019 population estimate.

The UCR Program does not have sufficient data to publish arson offenses in this table. Information about arson can be found in Arson Tables 1 and 2. Rape data reported by agencies using the UCR legacy definition are not included in this table.

Group VI city classifications include universities and colleges to which no population is attributed. The nonmetropolitan counties classification includes state police agencies that report aggregately for the entire state. Metropolitan and nonmetropolitan counties include state police to which no population is attributed. Suburban areas include law enforcement agencies in cities with fewer than 50,000 inhabitants and county law enforcement agencies that are within a Metropolitan Statistical Area. Suburban areas exclude all metropolitan agencies associated with a principal city. The agencies associated with suburban areas also appear in other groups within this. The FBI derived the offense rates by first dividing the individual offense counts by the individual populations covered by contributing agencies for which 12 months of publishable data were supplied and then multiplying the resulting figure by 100,000.

Populations Used to Calculate Violent Crime Rates, by Population Group, 2019

	Violent crime total		Murder/nonnegligent manslaughter		Rape		Robbery		Aggravated assault	
	Agency count	Population	Agency count	Population	Agency count	Population	Agency count	Population	Agency count	Population
Total	**12,730**	**279,536,935**	12,721	279,321,521	12,709	279,018,775	12,729	279,424,554	12,728	279,497,051
Total, Cities	**9,195**	**194,512,905**	9,192	194,342,817	9,180	194,253,008	9,194	194,400,524	9,193	194,473,021
GROUP I (250,000 and over)	83	60,188,585	83	60,188,585	83	60,188,585	83	60,188,585	83	60,188,585
Cities with 1,000,000 or over	**10**	**26,216,990**	10	26,216,990	10	26,216,990	10	26,216,990	10	26,216,990
Cities with 500,000 through 999,999	**24**	**17,433,188**	24	17,433,188	24	17,433,188	24	17,433,188	24	17,433,188
Cities with 250,000 through 499,999	**49**	**16,538,407**	49	16,538,407	49	16,538,407	49	16,538,407	49	16,538,407
GROUP II (100,000 to 249,999)	**212**	**30,850,549**	211	30,740,351	211	30,740,351	211	30,740,351	212	30,850,549
GROUP III (50,000 to 99,999)	**458**	**31,931,708**	458	31,931,708	458	31,931,708	458	31,931,708	458	31,931,708
GROUP IV (25,000 to 49,999)	**803**	**27,996,450**	803	27,996,450	803	27,996,450	803	27,996,450	803	27,996,450
GROUP V (10,000 to 24,999)	**1,563**	**25,119,823**	1,563	25,119,823	1,559	25,059,847	1,563	25,119,823	1,561	25,079,939
GROUP VI (under 10,000)	**6,076**	**18,425,790**	6,075	18,416,052	6,066	18,389,166	6,076	18,425,790	6,076	18,425,790
Metropolitan counties	**1,608**	**65,156,789**	1,604	65,134,008	1,604	65,134,008	1,608	65,156,789	1,608	65,156,789
Nonmetropolitan counties	**1,927**	**19,867,241**	1,925	19,844,696	1,925	19,844,696	1,927	19,867,241	1,927	19,867,241
Suburban areas	**6,971**	**118,340,932**	6,967	118,318,151	6,961	118,092,494	6,971	118,340,932	6,970	118,320,268

Populations Used to Calculate Property Crime Rates, by Population Group, 2019

	Property crime total		Burglary		Larceny-theft		Motor vehicle theft	
	Agency count	Population	Agency count	Population	Agency count	Population	Agency count	Population
Total	12,730	279,536,935	12,704	278,387,019	12,720	279,320,446	12,726	278,744,544
Total, Cities	9,195	194,512,905	9,182	193,726,208	9,187	194,354,748	9,191	193,720,514
GROUP I (250,000 and over)	83	60,188,585	82	59,626,665	83	60,188,585	82	59,626,665
Cities with 1,000,000 or over	10	26,216,990	10	26,216,990	10	26,216,990	10	26,216,990
Cities with 500,000 through 999,999	24	17,433,188	23	16,871,268	24	17,433,188	23	16,871,268
Cities with 250,000 through 499,999	49	16,538,407	49	16,538,407	49	16,538,407	49	16,538,407
GROUP II (100,000 to 249,999)	212	30,850,549	211	30,740,351	211	30,740,351	211	30,740,351
GROUP III (50,000 to 99,999)	458	31,931,708	458	31,931,708	457	31,865,408	457	31,865,408
GROUP IV (25,000 to 49,999)	803	27,996,450	798	27,827,090	802	27,971,438	803	27,996,450
GROUP V (10,000 to 24,999)	1,563	25,119,823	1,561	25,1088,221	1,560	25,064,398	1,562	25,1100,993
GROUP VI (under 10,000)	6,076	18,425,790	6,071	18,401,975	6,073	18,414,370	6,075	18,423,524
Metropolitan counties	1,608	65,156,789	1,596	64,083,397	1,607	65,112,211	1,608	65,156,789
Nonmetropolitan counties	1,927	19,867,241	1,926	19,857,414	1,926	19,853,487	1,927	19,867,241
Suburban areas	6,971	118,340,932	6,952	117,846,365	6,965	118,236,886	6,970	118,322,103

INDEX

CPSIA information can be obtained
at www.ICGtesting.com
Printed in the USA
BVHW080037020621
608156BV00004BA/13